Nineteenth-Century Literature Criticism

Guide to Gale Literary Criticism Series

For criticism on	Consult these Gale series
Authors now living or who died after December 31, 1959	*CONTEMPORARY LITERARY CRITICISM (CLC)*
Authors who died between 1900 and 1959	*TWENTIETH-CENTURY LITERARY CRITICISM (TCLC)*
Authors who died between 1800 and 1899	*NINETEENTH-CENTURY LITERATURE CRITICISM (NCLC)*
Authors who died between 1400 and 1799	*LITERATURE CRITICISM FROM 1400 TO 1800 (LC)* *SHAKESPEAREAN CRITICISM (SC)*
Authors who died before 1400	*CLASSICAL AND MEDIEVAL LITERATURE CRITICISM (CMLC)*
Black writers of the past two hundred years	*BLACK LITERATURE CRITICISM (BLC)*
Authors of books for children and young adults	*CHILDREN'S LITERATURE REVIEW (CLR)*
Dramatists	*DRAMA CRITICISM (DC)*
Hispanic writers of the late nineteenth and twentieth centuries	*HISPANIC LITERATURE CRITICISM (HLC)*
Native North American writers and orators of the eighteenth, nineteenth, and twentieth centuries	*NATIVE NORTH AMERICAN LITERATURE (NNAL)*
Poets	*POETRY CRITICISM (PC)*
Short story writers	*SHORT STORY CRITICISM (SSC)*
Major authors from the Renaissance to the present	*WORLD LITERATURE CRITICISM, 1500 TO THE PRESENT (WLC)*

ISSN 0732-1864

Volume 55

Nineteenth-Century Literature Criticism

Criticism of the
Works of Novelists, Poets, Playwrights,
Short Story Writers, Philosophers, and Other
Creative Writers Who Died between 1800
and 1899, from the First Published Critical
Appraisals to Current Evaluations

Denise Kasinec
Mary L. Onorato
Editors

GALE

DETROIT • NEW YORK • TORONTO • LONDON

STAFF

Denise Kasinec and Mary L. Onorato, *Editors*

Susan M. Trosky, *Managing Editor*

Marlene S. Hurst, *Permissions Manager*
Margaret A. Chamberlain, Maria Franklin, Kimberly F. Smilay, *Permissions Specialists*
Diane Cooper, Edna Hedblad, Michele Lonoconus, Maureen Puhl, Susan Salas, Shalice Shah,
Barbara A. Wallace, *Permissions Associates*
Sarah Chesney, Margaret McAvoy-Amato, *Permissions Assistants*

Victoria B. Cariappa, *Research Manager*
Julia C. Daniel, Tamara C. Nott, Michele P. Pica,
Tracie A. Richardson, Cheryl Warnock, *Research Associates*

Mary Beth Trimper, *Production Director*
Deborah L. Milliken, *Production Assistant*

Sherrell Hobbs, *Macintosh Artist*
Randy Bassett, *Image Database Supervisor*
Mikal Ansari, Robert Duncan, *Imaging Specialists*
Pamela A. Hayes, *Photography Coordinator*

∞™
  This book is printed on acid-free paper that meets the minimum requirements of American National Standard for Information Sciences—Permanence Paper for Printed Library Materials, ANSI Z39.48-1984.

Library of Congress Catalog Card Number 84-643008
ISBN 0-8103-7004-2
ISSN 0732-1864
Printed in the United States of America

10 9 8 7 6 5 4 3 2 1

Contents

Preface

Since its inception in 1981, *Nineteenth-Century Literature Criticism* has been a valuable resource for students and librarians seeking critical commentary on writers of this transitional period in world history. Designated an "Outstanding Reference Source" by the American Library Association with the publication of its first volume, *NCLC* has since been purchased by over 6,000 school, public, and university libraries. The series has covered more than 300 authors representing 29 nationalities and over 17,000 titles. No other reference source has surveyed the critical reaction to nineteenth-century authors and literature as thoroughly as *NCLC*.

Scope of the Series

NCLC is designed to introduce students and advanced readers to the authors of the nineteenth century, and to the most significant interpretations of these authors' works. The great poets, novelists, short story writers, playwrights, and philosophers of this period are frequently studied in high school and college literature courses. By organizing and reprinting commentary written on these authors, *NCLC* helps students develop valuable insight into literary history, promotes a better understanding of the texts, and sparks ideas for papers and assignments. Each entry in *NCLC* presents a comprehensive survey of an author's career or an individual work of literature and provides the user with a multiplicity of interpretations and assessments. Such variety allows students to pursue their own interests; furthermore, it fosters an awareness that literature is dynamic and responsive to many different opinions.

Every fourth volume of *NCLC* is devoted to literary topics that cannot be covered under the author approach used in the rest of the series. Such topics include literary movements, prominent themes in nineteenth-century literature, literary reaction to political and historical events, significant eras in literary history, prominent literary anniversaries, and the literatures of cultures that are often overlooked by English-speaking readers.

NCLC continues the survey of criticism of world literature begun by Gale's *Contemporary Literary Criticism (CLC)* and *Twentieth-Century Literary Criticism (TCLC)*, both of which excerpt and reprint commentary on authors of the twentieth century. For additional information about *TCLC, CLC,* and Gale's other criticism series, users should consult the Guide to Gale Literary Criticism Series preceding the title page in this volume.

Coverage

Each volume of *NCLC* is carefully compiled to present:

- criticism of authors, or literary topics, representing a variety of genres and nationalities
- both major and lesser-known writers and literary works of the period
- 5-8 authors or 4-6 topics per volume
- individual entries that survey critical response to an author's work or a topic in literary history, including early criticism to reflect initial reactions, later criticism to represent any rise or decline in reputation, and current retrospective analyses.

Organization

An author entry consists of the following elements: author heading, biographical and critical introduction, list of principal works, excerpts of criticism (each preceded by a bibliographic citation and an annotation), and a bibliography of further reading.

- The **Author Heading** consists of the name under which the author most commonly wrote, followed by birth and death dates. If an author wrote consistently under a pseudonym, the pseudonym will be listed in the author heading and the real name given in parentheses on the first line of the biographical and critical introduction. Also located at the beginning of the introduction to the author entry are any name variations under which an author wrote, including transliterated forms for an author whose language uses a nonroman alphabet.

- The **Biographical and Critical Introduction** outlines the author's life and career, as well as the critical issues surrounding his or her work. References are provided to past volumes of *NCLC* in which further information about the author may be found.

- Most *NCLC* entries include a **Portrait** of the author. Many entries also contain reproductions of materials pertinent to an author's career, including manuscript pages, title pages, dust jackets, letters, and drawings, as well as photographs of important people, places, and events in an author's life.

- The list of **Principal Works** is chronological by date of first publication and identifies the genre of each work. In the case of foreign authors with both foreign-language publications and English translations, the English-language version is given in brackets. Unless otherwise indicated, dramas are dated by first performance, not first publication.

- **Criticism** in each author entry is arranged chronologically to provide a perspective on changes in critical evaluation over the years. All titles of works by the author featured in the entry are printed in boldface type to enable the user to easily locate discussion of particular works. Also for purposes of easier identification, the critic's name and the publication date of the essay are given at the beginning of each piece of criticism. Unsigned criticism is preceded by the title of the journal in which it appeared. Publication information (such as publisher names and book prices) and some parenthetical numerical references (such as page and line references to specific editions of works) have been deleted at the editors' discretion to provide smoother reading of the text.

- A complete **Bibliographic Citation** provides original publication information for each piece of criticism.

- Critical excerpts are prefaced by **Annotations** providing the reader with a summary of the critical intent of the piece. Also included, when appropriate, is information about the critic's reputation, individual approach to literary criticism, and particular expertise in an author's works, as well as information about the relative importance of the critical excerpt. In some cases, the annotations cross-reference excerpts by critics who discuss each other's commentary.

- An annotated list of **Further Reading** appearing at the end of each entry suggests secondary sources on the author. In some cases it includes essays for which the editors could not obtain reprint rights.

Cumulative Indexes

■ Each volume of *NCLC* contains a cumulative **Author Index** listing all authors who have appeared in Gale's Literary Criticism Series, along with cross-references to such biographical series as *Contemporary Authors* and *Dictionary of Literary Biography*. Useful for locating authors within the various series, this index is particularly valuable for those authors who are identified with a certain period but who, because of their death dates, are placed in another, or for those authors whose careers span two periods. For example, Fyodor Dostoevsky is found in *NCLC,* yet Leo Tolstoy, another major nineteenth-century Russian novelist, is found in *TCLC* because he died after 1899.

■ Each *NCLC* volume includes a cumulative **Nationality Index** which lists all authors who have appeared in *NCLC*, arranged alphabetically under their respective nationalities.

■ Each new volume in Gale's Literary Criticism Series includes a cumulative **Topic Index**, which lists all literary topics treated in *NCLC, TCLC, LC 1400-1800*, and the *CLC* Yearbook.

■ Each new volume of *NCLC*, with the exception of the Topics volumes, contains a **Title Index** listing the titles of all literary works discussed in the volume. In response to numerous suggestions from librarians, Gale has also produced a **Special Paperbound Edition** of the *NCLC* title index. This annual cumulation lists all titles discussed in the series since its inception. Additional copies of the index are available on request. Librarians and patrons have welcomed this separate index: it saves shelf space, is easy to use, and is recyclable upon receipt of the following year's cumulation. Titles discussed in the Topics volume entries are not included in the *NCLC* cumulative index.

Citing *Nineteenth-Century Literature Criticism*

When writing papers, students who quote directly from any volume in Gale's Literary Criticism Series may use the following general forms to footnote reprinted criticism. The first example pertains to material drawn from periodicals, the second to material reprinted from books:

[1]T.S. Eliot, "John Donne," *The Nation and Athenaeum*, 33 (9 June 1923), 321-32; excerpted and reprinted in *Literature Criticism from 1400-1800,* Vol. 10, ed. James E. Person, Jr. (Detroit: Gale Research, 1989), pp. 28-9.

[2]Clara G. Stillman, *Samuel Butler: A Mid-Victorian Modern* (Viking Press, 1932); excerpted and reprinted in *Twentieth-Century Literary Criticism,* Vol. 33, ed. Paula Kepos (Detroit: Gale Research, 1989), pp. 43-5.

Suggestions Are Welcome

In response to suggestions, several features have been added to *NCLC* since the series began, including annotations to excerpted criticism, a cumulative index to authors in all Gale literary criticism series, entries devoted to criticism on a single work by a major author, more illustrations, and a title index listing all literary works discussed in the series.

Readers who wish to suggest authors, single works, or topics to appear in future volumes, or who have other suggestions, are cordially invited to write: The Editors, *Nineteenth-Century Literature Criticism,* 835 Penobscot Bldg., 645 Griswold St., Detroit, MI 48226-4094; call toll-free at 1-800-347-GALE; or fax to 1-313-961-6599.

Acknowledgments

The editors wish to thank the copyright holders of the excerpted criticism included in this volume and the permissions managers of many book and magazine publishing companies for assisting us in securing reprint rights. We are also grateful to the staffs of the Detroit Public Library, the Library of Congress, the University of Detroit Mercy Library, Wayne State University Purdy/Kresge Library Complex, and the University of Michigan Libraries for making their resources available to us. Following is a list of the copyright holders who have granted us permission to reprint material in this volume of *NCLC-55*. Every effort has been made to trace copyright, but if omissions have been made, please let us know.

COPYRIGHTED EXCERPTS IN *NCLC,* VOLUME 55, WERE REPRINTED FROM THE FOLLOWING PERIODICALS:

American Literature, v. 33, November, 1961. Copyright © 1961, renewed 1989 Duke University Press, Durham, N.C. Reprinted by permission of the publisher.—*American Literature*, v. 57, December, 1985. Copyright © 1985 Duke University Press, Durham, N.C. Reprinted with permission of the publisher. —*American Review of Canadian Studies*, v. xviii, Autumn, 1988. Reprinted by permission of the publisher.—*Canadian Literature*, n. 81, Summer, 1979 for "Richardson's Indians" by Leslie Monkman. Reprinted by permission of the author.—*Canadian Literature*, n. 128, Spring, 1991 for "Double Entendre: Rebel Angels & Beautiful Losers in John Richardson's *The Monk Knight of St. John*" by Michael Hurley. Reprinted by permission of the author.—*CLA Journal*, v. 29, December, 1985. Copyright, 1985 by The College Language Association. Used by permission of The College Language Association. —*Eighteenth-Century Fiction*, v. 6, July, 1994. Reprinted by permission of the publisher.— *Essays on Canadian Writing*, n. 29, Summer, 1984. © Essays on Canadian Writing Ltd. Reprinted by permission of the publisher. —*Essays on Canadian Writing*, n. 54, Winter, 1994. © 1994 Essays on Canadian Writing Ltd. Reprinted by permission of the publisher.—*Journal of Canadian Studies*, v. 28, Autumn, 1993. Reprinted by permission of the publisher.—*The Journal of Narrative Technique*, v. 19, Spring, 1989. Copyright © 1989 by *The Journal of Narrative Technique*. Reprinted by permission of the publisher.—*The Modern Language Review*, v. 86, January, 1991 for "The Poetics of the Commonplace in *Les Fleurs du Mal*" by Graham Robb. © Modern Humanities Association 1991. Reprinted by permission of the publisher and the author.—*Nineteenth-Century French Studies*, v. 20, Fall-Winter, 1991-92. © 1991-92 by T. H. Goetz. Reprinted by permission of the publisher..—*La Nouvelle Revue Francaise*, 1921. Copyright 1927 by Gallimard. Reprinted by permission.—*Orbis Litterarum*, v. 46, 1991. Reprinted by permission of the publisher.—*Phylon: The Atlanta University Review of Race and Culture*, v. XL, March, 1979. Copyright, 1979, by Atlanta University. Reprinted by permission of *Phylon*.—*Raritan: A Quarterly Review*, v. 6, Fall, 1986. Copyright© 1986 by *Raritan: A Quarterly Review*. Reprinted by permission of the publisher.—*Studies in English Literature, 1500-1900*, v. 23, Summer, 1983 for "Udolpho's Primal Mystery" by Mary Laughlin Fawcett. © William Marsh Rice University. Reprinted by permission of the publisher and the author.—*The University of Windsor Review*, v. 18, Fall-Winter, 1984 for "Mrs. Radcliffe's Landscapes: The Eye and the Fancy" by Charles C. Murrah. Reprinted by permission of the publisher and the author.—*Yale French Studies*, v. 1, Fall-Winter, 1948. Copyright © *Yale French Studies* 1948. Reprinted by permission of the publisher.

COPYRIGHTED EXCERPTS IN *NCLC,* VOLUME 55, WERE REPRINTED FROM THE FOLLOWING BOOKS:

Baker, Houston A., Jr. From *Long Black Song: Essays in Black American Literature and Culture*. The University Press of Virginia, 1972. Copyright © 1972 by the Rector and Visitors of the University of Virginia. Reprinted by permission of the publisher.—Canby, Henry Seidel. From *Classic Americans: A Study of Eminent American Writers from Irving to Whitman*. Russell & Russell, Inc., 1959. Copyright 1939, 1958 by Henry Seidel Canby. Reprinted by permission of Russell & Russell, Inc., a division of Simon & Schuster, Inc.—Chard, Chloe. From an introduction to *The Romance of the Forest*, by Ann Radcliffe. Edited by Chloe Chard. Oxford University Press, 1986. Introduction,

PHOTOGRAPHS AND ILLUSTRATIONS APPEARING IN *NCLC*, VOLUME 55, WERE RECEIVED FROM THE FOLLOWING SOURCES:

Poe, Edgar Allan: —*Southern Literary Messenger*, edited by Poe, photograph of the front cover of the December, 1835 issue.

Richardson, John: —Drawing of Richardson by Frederick Locke. From **The Canadian Don Quixote**, by David R. Beasley.—From **Richardson's War of 1812**, by Richardson, edited by Alexander Clark Casselman, Historical Publishing Co.: Fort Amherstburg (ruins of the north embankment), photograph; letter from Richardson to his uncle; map of Detroit River. — *Wacousta; or, The Prophecy*, by Richardson, cover illustration, Dewitt, 1875. From **The Canadian Don Quixote**, by David R. Beasley.

Les fleurs du mal

Charles Baudelaire

The following entry presents criticism on Baudelaire's *Les fleurs du mal* (1868; *The Flowers of Evil*). For discussions of Baudelaire's complete career see *NCLC,* Volumes 6 and 29.

INTRODUCTION

Although Baudelaire is viewed as one of the world's greatest lyric poets, his importance in literary history rests almost entirely on one book, a volume of poems entitled *Les fleurs du mal* (*The Flowers of Evil*). The book was a critical and popular failure during his lifetime, primarily because people were so shocked by its content—depictions of sexual perversion, moral corruption, and mental and physical illness. Yet this volume introduced themes and a species of self-contemplation that profoundly shaped the literature that followed it, particularly the poetry of the twentieth century. For many critics, *The Flowers of Evil* began the transition from High Romanticism to what we think of as modern poetry. T.S. Eliot considered this volume not only the beginning of modernism but also its crowning achievement; he called *The Flowers of Evil* "the greatest example of modern poetry in any language."

Biographical Information

Baudelaire began writing the poems that would appear in *The Flowers of Evil* while living a life of self-conscious dissipation in Paris. Supported by an inheritance, he aspired to be what he called a dandy. Baudelaire described dandyism as "a cult of the self" and a "new kind of aristocracy" which valued elegance and, above all, distinction. Elegance and distinction involved sexual license as well as other freedoms. The poet frequented Parisian brothels, contracting a venereal disease, and experimented with opium and hashish, documenting his drug usage in poems such as "Poème du haschisch" ("Hashish Poem"). But a dandy was an aesthete above all, and Baudelaire wrote a number of critical pieces during this period. He was one of the first to recognize the talent of composers such as Richard Wagner and painters such as Edouard Manet. In 1846 he became acquainted with the works of the American writer Edgar Allan Poe, whose critical writings stressed technical perfection and the creation of absolute beauty. In the estimation of Paul Valéry and other critics, this experience completed Baudelaire's poetic development. Other important influences on Baudelaire were the French writers Théophile Gautier, to whom *The Flowers of Evil* is dedicated, and Victor Hugo.

Baudelaire published the first edition of *The Flowers of Evil* in 1857. The detailed eroticism in some of the poems and the poet's frank depictions of lesbianism scandalized Paris. Reviewers called him a "sick poet," and even friends such as the critic Charles Sainte-Beuve withheld their approval. Proofs of the book were seized, and six of the offending poems were removed. Baudelaire and his publisher were prosecuted and convicted of offenses against religion and public morality. The six censored poems were published later that same year in Belgium as *Les épaves,* but the ban on the suppressed poems was not lifted in France until 1949. Baudelaire published a second edition of *The Flowers of Evil* in 1861. He was working on additional poetry for a third edition when he died, following a stroke, on August 31, 1867. This edition was published in 1868.

Major Themes

The Flowers of Evil is organized in six sections, which group the poems by themes—"Spleen and Ideal," "Parisian Scenes," "Wine," "Flowers of Evil," "Revolt," and "Death." In his journal, Baudelaire once wrote: "There are in every man at all times two simultaneous impulses — one toward God, the other toward Satan." This contest between two impulses underlies many of the themes in *The Flowers of Evil.* To some critics, this contest is a classic Christian struggle between good and evil. To others, the poet's fascination with sin and redemption is more closely related to his perception of a conflict between the ideal and the actual. For Baudelaire, the goal of art was to find redemption through beauty from the unpleasant aspects of human existence. Many critics believe the struggles that underlie *The Flowers of Evil* have less to do with religion than with the triumphs and defeats of the creative process.

Baudelaire's moral, psychological, and spiritual conflicts are particularly evident in the three cycles of love poems included in *The Flowers of Evil.* He wrote poetry for three different mistresses, traditionally identified as Apollonie Sabatier ("White Venus"), Jeanne Duval ("Black Venus"), and Marie Daubrun ("Green Venus"). Sabatier is treated reverently, in almost celestial terms, in poems that contrast with darker pieces about the other women. The latter works are more sexually explicit, and they contain elements of sadism. Collectively, the love poems provide an important and, to some, frightening commentary on Baudelaire's conflicting feelings about women, whom he appears to have alternately worshiped and loathed. Camille Paglia argues that Baudelaire demonstrates an aversion to women's sexuality—particularly their fertility—which is related to his devotion to art.

Critical Reception

During the nineteenth century, *The Flowers of Evil* was appreciated by only a small number of readers. But it was a select and highly influential group that understood Baudelaire's poetry. This thin volume shaped a generation of European literary figures who would in turn shape modern literature. Baudelaire influenced French poets such as Stéphane Mallarmé and Arthur Rimbaud and French novelists such as Marcel Proust. In England, his admirers included Oscar Wilde, Algernon Swinburne, and William Butler Yeats. It was only in the twentieth century that Baudelaire received wide critical acclaim. This was mostly due to the writings of Paul Valéry, who emphasized that the influence of *The Flowers of Evil* transcended political and linguistic boundaries: "French poetry at length passes beyond our frontiers. It is read throughout the world; it takes its place as the characteristic poetry of modernity."

CRITICISM

Marcel Proust (essay date 1921)

SOURCE: "Apropos of Baudelaire," in *Baudelaire: A Collection of Critical Essays*, edited by Henri Peyre, Prentice-Hall, Inc., 1962, pp. 110-131.

[*In the following excerpt, originally published in June, 1921, as a letter to the literary journal* La Nouvelle Revue Française, *Proust surveys some of the poetic achievements of* Les Fleurs du mal.]

I doubt that a poem equalling Hugo's "Booz endormi" could be found in **Les Fleurs du mal,** that sublime but sardonic book, in which piety sneers, in which debauchery makes the sign of the cross, in which Satan is entrusted with the task of teaching the most profound theology. . . .

No one has written on the poor with more genuine tenderness than Baudelaire, that "dandy," did. The praise of wine might not be approved by the tenants of a good antialcoholic hygiene.

À ton fils je rendrai la force et la vigueur
Et serai pour ce frêle athlète de la vie

L'huile qui raffermit les membres du lutteur.

[To your son I shall restore strength and pink cheeks
And to the frail athlete of life I shall be
The oil to give new vigor to wrestlers' muscles.]
(Baudelaire, **"L'Âme du vin"**)

The poet might retort that the wine is speaking there, not he. In any case, the poem is divine. How admirable the style is ("tombe et caveaux"). What human cordiality, what a sketch of the vineyard! The poet often recaptures that popular vein. The sublime lines on public concerts are well known:

ces concerts, riches de cuivre,
Dont les soldats parfois inondent nos jardins,
Et qui, par ces soirs d'or où l'on se sent révivre
Versent quelque héroïsme au coeur des citadins.

[Those concerts, rich in brass,
With which soldiers at times flood our parks,
And that, on those golden evenings which revive us,
Pour some heroism into the hearts of town dwellers.]
(Baudelaire, **"Les Petites Vieilles"**)

It may seem impossible to go beyond that. Yet Baudelaire was able to heighten that impression still further; he endowed it with a mystical significance in the unexpected finale in which the strange bliss of the elect closes a sinister piece on the "Damnés":

Le son de la trompette est si délicieux,
Dans ces soirs solennels de célestes vendanges,
Qu'il s'infiltre comme une extase dans tous ceux
Dont elle chante les louanges.

[The sound of the trumpet holds such delights,
On those solemn evenings of celestial grape gathering,
That it invades like an ecstatic philter all those
Whose praises it celebrates.]
(Baudelaire, **"L'Imprévu"**)

It may well be surmised that here, to the impressions of the Parisian loiterer that he was, was added the memory of the passionate admirer of Wagner. Even if the young musicians of today were right, which I refuse to believe, in negating Wagner's genius, such lines would prove that it hardly matters whether judgments offered by a writer on the works in another medium are objectively correct or not; the writer's admiration, even if unfounded, inspires him with useful reveries. I for one, who admire Wagner highly, well remember that, in my childhood, at the Lamoureux concerts, the enthusiasm which should be reserved for genuine masterpieces such as *Tristan* or *Die Meistersinger* was indiscriminately "aroused" by insipid pieces like the song to the star or Elizabeth's prayer in *Tannhäuser*. I may err in my musical taste. . . . But the college boys around me who endlessly and noisily applauded shouted their admiration like madmen or like politicians. No doubt as they came home, there sparkled before their eyes a starry night which the poor song could not have conjured up if, instead of being signed Wagner, then at the peak of his fame with the young, it had bore the unexciting name of Gounod. . . .

Baudelaire is incomparable in his relatively shorter poems, such as **"La Pipe."** Longer poems, even **"Le Voyage,"** open splendidly:

> Pour l'enfant, amoureux de cartes et
>   d'estampes
> L'univers est égal à son vaste appétit.
> Ah! que le monde est grand à la clarté des
>   lampes!
> Aux yeux du souvenir que le monde est petit!

> [To the child, in love with maps and prints,
> The universe equals his vast appetite.
> Ah! how wide is the world by lamplight
>   imagined!
> How small it is when seen with memory's
>   eyes!]
>
> (Baudelaire, **"Le Voyage"**)

But then they seem to need the support of rhetoric. This one, like many another long poem by Baudelaire, such as **"Andromaque, je pense à vous"** (**"Le Cygne"**), almost falls flat. It ends with the line:

> Au fond de l'Inconnu pour trouver du
>   nouveau,

> [Into the deep unknown to find something
>   new,]
>
> (Id., Ibid.)

and **"Le Cygne"** with:

> Aux captifs, aux vaincus, à bien d'autres
>   encor.

> [To the captive, to the vanquished, to many
>   others still.]
>
> (Baudelaire, **"Le Cygne"**)

Such simple endings may well be calculated. Yet one

senses that something has been cut short, the breath may have been short.

Still no poet more surely possessed the gift of renewing a poem in its very middle. At times it is by an abrupt change of tone as in the Satanic piece already quoted which begins "Harpagon qui veillait son père, agonisant" and ends with "Le son de la trompette est si délicieux. . . . " An even more striking example, admirably rendered by Gabriel Fauré in one of his melodies, is the poem opening

> Bientôt nous plongerons dans les froides
>   ténèbres.

> [Soon we shall plunge into the cold darkness.]
>
> (Baudelaire, **"Chant d'automne"**)

All of a sudden, with no transition, it continues on another tone with lines which, in the poem itself, are naturally sung:

> J'aime de vos longs yeux la lumière verdâtre.

> [I love the greenish light of your eyes.]
>
> (Id., Ibid.)

At other times the piece is interrupted by a precise action. At the very moment when Baudelaire exclaims: "My heart is a palace . . ." suddenly and without its being stated, he is overtaken with desire; the woman forces him to renewed enjoyment; the poet, at once intoxicated by the delights thus offered and thinking of the morrow's weariness, exclaims:

> Un parfum nage autour de votre gorge nue! . . .
> O Beauté, dur fléau des âmes, tu le peux!
> Avec tes yeux de feu, brillants comme des
>   fêtes,
> Calcine ces lambeaux qu'ont épargnés les
>   bêtes!

> [A fragrance swims around your bare throat! . . .
> O Beauty, harsh courage of souls, it is your
>   will!
> With your fiery eyes, sparkling like beasts,
> Burn to ashes these shreds spared by wild
>   beasts!]
>
> (**"Causerie"**)

There are to be sure a few long poems which, exceptionally, are to the very end controlled unfalteringly, such as **"Les Petites Vieilles,"** dedicated, probably because of that achievement, to Victor Hugo. But that very beautiful poem leaves, like some others, an impression of cruelty which is painful. It is in principle possible to understand suffering and not be kind; but I doubt that Baudelaire meant purposely to be cruel when he blended irony with pity in his portrayal of those old women. He was anxious not to let his pity appear; it was enough for him to extract the "character" of such a sight, so that some stanzas emerge with an atrocious and wicked beauty:

> Ou dansent sans vouloir danser, pauvres
>   sonnettes. . . .
> Je goûte à votre insu des plaisirs clandestins.
>
> [Or they dance without wanting to, poor
>   doorbells. . . .
> I relish, without your knowing it, clandestine
>   pleasures.]
>
> ("Les Petites Vieilles")

My conjecture would mainly be that Baudelaire's line was so vigorous, so firm and beautiful that it lured the poet to overstep some bounds without realizing it. He wrote on those unfortunate little old women the firmest lines anywhere in French without thinking of softening his language so as not to lash those dying creatures any more than Beethoven, when composing his Symphony with choirs, understood that the notes he was writing were not always made for human throats, were not audible to human ears, and would always sound as if not sung right. The very strangeness which, to me, renders Beethoven's last quartets so enrapturing makes it impossible for certain persons to listen to them, unless they are transposed for piano; these persons are certainly not deaf to the divine mystery of these quartets, yet they set their teeth on edge. It is up to us to extract whatever sorrow inhabits those little old women,

> Débris d'humanité pour l'éternité mûrs.
>
> [O wrecks of humankind ripe for eternity.]
>   (Id., Ibid.)

The poet, rather than express that sorrow, tortures us with it. He leaves us with a gallery of extraordinary caricatures of old women, comparable to Leonardo's caricatures, portraits of unequalled greatness and devoid of pity:

> Celle-là, droite encor, fière et sentant la règle,
> Humait avidement le chant vif et guerrier;
> Son oeil parfois s'ouvrait comme l'oeil d'un
>   vieil aigle;
> Son front de marbre avait l'air fait pour le
>   laurier!
>
> [That one, still very straight, proud and like a
>   ruler stiff,
> Avidly sniffed the lively and warlike song;
> Her eye at times opened like that of an aged
>   eagle;
> Her marble brow seemed made to be crowned
>   by laurel.]
>
>   (Id., Ibid.)

That poem, **"Les Petites Vielles,"** is among those in which Baudelaire shows his knowledge of antiquity. It is equally noticeable in **"Le Voyage,"** in which the story of Electra is mentioned as it might have been by Racine in one of his prefaces. The difference is that, in seventeenth century prefaces, the authors resort to those allusions in order to answer a charge. We cannot help smiling when we are shown the whole of antiquity testifying, in the preface to Racine's *Phèdre,* that the author "composed no tragedy in which virtue was more conspicuously put forward than in that one; the slightest faults are severely punished. The thought of crime inspires as much horror as crime itself; the weaknesses of love are treated as true weaknesses; and vice everywhere is depicted in colors which cause its hideousness to be hated." Racine, that skillful pleader, regrets at once that he does not have Aristotle and Socrates as his judges, for they would recognize that his theater is a school in which virtue is no less well taught than in the philosophers' schools. It may be that Baudelaire is more sincere when, in the opening poem addressed to the reader, he addresses him as

> Hypocrite lecteur, mon semblable,—mon frère!
>
> [Hyprocrite reader, my fellow-being—my
>   brother!]
>   ("To the Reader")

To one who keeps in mind the difference between the two ages, nothing appears so Baudelairian as *Phèdre,* nothing is worthier of Racine or even of Malherbe than **Les Fleurs du mal**. Even the difference between the two ages and their styles did not keep Baudelaire from writing like the classical French writers:

> Car c'est encor, seigneur, le meilleur
>   tèmoignage
> Que nous puissions donner de notre dignité . . .
>
> [For it is still, O Lord, the best testimonial
> Which we may give of our dignity. . . .]
>
>   ("Les Phares")

> O Seigneur, donnez-moi la force et le courage. . . .
>
> [O Lord, bestow upon me the strength and the
>   courage. . . .]
>
>   ("Un Voyage à Cythère")

> Ses bras vaincus jetés comme de vaines
>   armes,
> Tout servait, tout parait sa fragile beauté.
>
> [Her defeated arms thrown like vain weapons,
> Everything served and adorned her frail
>   beauty.]
>
>   ("Femmes damneés")

Those last lines, it is remembered, describe a woman whom another woman has just exhausted with her caresses. But would Racine resort to a different language if he protrayed Junie facing Nero? When Baudelaire is inspired by Horace, again in one of the poems which take place between two women, he does better than his model. Instead of "dimidium animae meae," which one is bound to imagine he must then have had in mind, he will write "mon tout et ma moitié." Incidentally, it must be admitted that when Victor Hugo wanted to quote from the ancients, he did so with the all-powerful freedom, the masterly imprint of genius: such is the case in the wonderful piece which ends with

> Ni l'importunité des sinistres oiseaux

> [Nor the importune and sinister birds]
>> (Victor Hugo)

almost literally "importunique volucres."

I am using very truthfully the phrase "Baudelaire's classicism," with scrupulous eagerness not to betray what the poet intended or prove overingenious. For I cannot help finding overingenious, and outside the Baudelairian truth, the contention of a friend of mine that

> Sois sage, ô ma douleur, et tiens-toi plus
>   tranquille.

> [Be good, O my Sorrow, and hold yourself
>   more still.]
>> (Baudelaire, **"Recueillement"**)

is nothing but the

> Pleurez, pleurez, mes yeux, et fondez-vous en
>   eau,

> [Weep, weep, O my eyes, and melt into
>   water,]
>> (Corneille, *Le Cid*)

from Corneille's *Le Cid*. The lines of the Infanta in the same play on the "respect de sa naissance" might appear to be a fitter parallel, although such parallels remain very exterior. The poet's hortatory address to his own sorrow has not much in common with a Cornelian apostrophe. Rather it is the restrained, quivering language of someone who shivers for having cried too much.

The feelings we just described—for suffering, death, and humble fraternity—rank Baudelaire as the man who wrote best on the humble people and on the beyond, if Victor Hugo is the poet who wrote most abundantly on them. Hugo's capitals, his dialogues with God, his thundering brass cannot match what poor Baudelaire found in the suffering intimacy of his body and of his heart. Baudelaire's inspiration owes nothing to Hugo. The one of the two poets who might have been the sculptor of a Gothic cathedral is not Hugo with his fake medievalism, but Baudelaire, the impure devout, the kneeling, grimacing accursèd casuist. Yet if their strains on death and on the poor are thus unequal and if the string of Baudelaire's lyre is more tense and vibrating, I should not submit that Baudelaire towers above Hugo in the delineation of love. To the lines in **"Femmes damnées,"**

> Et cette gratitude infinie et sublime
> Qui sort de la paupière ainsi qu'un long
>   soupir,

> [And that infinite and sublime gratitude
> Which the eyelid heaves like a long sigh,]

I prefer Hugo's lines:

> Elle me regarda de ce regard suprême
> Qui reste à la beauté quand nous en
>   triomphons.

> [She looked at me with that supreme gaze
> Which remains in beauty even while
>   vanquished.]
>> (Victor Hugo, "Elle était déchaussée,"
>> *Contemplations* I, xxi)

Love, besides, is very different in the two poets. Baudelaire's inspiration was in truth drawn from no other poet. His world cuts off strange sections in time, letting only a few notable days appear. That explains the frequent phrases such as "if some evening," and others. As to Baudelaire's furniture, let it serve as a lesson to our elegant ladies of the last twenty years, who would not consent in their "mansions" to the slightest lapse of taste. They strove hard to reach an imaginary purity of style; let them reflect that our poet could be the greatest and the most artistic of writers, yet painted only beds with folding curtains, halls similar to hothouses (**"Une Martyre"**), beds impregnated with light fragrance, couches as deep as tombs, shelves with flowers, lamps which burnt only for a while, so that only the embers in the fireplace threw any light. That Baudelairian world is fitfully visited and enchanted by a fragrant breath from afar, either through reminiscences (as in **"La Chevelure"**) or directly, through those porticoes which often recur in Baudelaire, "ouverts sur des cieux inconnus" (**"La Mort"**) or

> Que les soleils marins teignaient de mille feux.

> [Which ocean suns dyed with a thousand
>   fires.]
>> (Baudelaire, **"La Vie antérieure"**)

I said that Baudelairian love differs widely from love according to Hugo. It has its peculiarities and, where it is not secretive, it appears to hold especially dear in woman—the hair, the feet, and the knees:

> O toison moutonnant jusque sur l'encolure. . . .
> Cheveux bleus, pavillons de ténèbres tendus.
>
> [O fleece down to the neck pressing its
>   waves . . .
> Blue hair, tents out of darkness woven.]
>   (Id., **"La chevelure"**)

> Et tes pieds s'endormaient dans mes mains
>   fraternelles. . . .
>
> [And your feet in my fraternal hands were
>   lulled to sleep:]
>   (Id., **"Le Balcon"**)

> Et depuis tes pieds frais jusqu'à tes noires
>   tresses
> [j'aurais] Déroulé le trésor des profondes
>   caresses.
>
> [And from your cool feet up to your black
>   tresses,
> [I would have] Unrolled the treasure of deep
>   caresses.]
>   (Id., **"Une Nuit que j'étais."**)

Of course between the feet and the hair, there is the whole of the body. Baudelaire must have cherished the knees, from his repeated allusions to them in his poetry:

> Ah! laissez-moi, le front posé sur vos genoux. . . .
>
> [Ah! Allow me, my forehead laid on your lap. . . .]
>   (Id., **"Chant d'Automne"**)

> Dit celle dont jadis nous baisions les genoux
>
> [Says she whose knees we used to kiss]
>   (Id., **"Le Voyage"**)

Still that manner of unrolling the treasure of deep caresses is rather special. And love according to Baudelaire must be touched upon, if we leave out what he chose not to say, what he occasionally and at the most hinted at. When *Les Fleurs du mal* appeared, Sainte-Beuve naïvely wrote that those poems, once gathered together, produced an altogether different impression. That impression which seems a favorable one to the critic of the *Lundis* was grandiose and terrifying for any one who, like men of my own age, had known the volume only in its expurgated edition. We well knew, of course, that Baudelaire had composed **"Femmes damnées"** and we had read those poems. Several other poets had thus had their own secret publication. Who has not read two volumes by Verlaine, as poor as **"Femmes damnées"** is beautiful, entitled *Hommes, Femmes?* Schoolboys pass on to each other works of sheer pornography which they believe to be by Alfred de Musset. I have never thought of finding out whether the attribution is in any way founded. Not so with **"Femmes damnées."** When we open a Baudelaire volume which reproduces the original edition faithfully, those who are not aware of it are amazed to see that the most licentious, the rawest of the pieces on Lesbian loves are to be read there; in his genial innocence, the great poet had granted as much importance to the piece on Delphine and Hippolyte in his volume as to **"Le Voyage"** itself. I would not go so far as to subscribe absolutely to the judgment which I heard Anatole France utter, that the long poem on **"Femmes damnées"** was the most beautiful that Baudelaire had written. There are sublime lines in it, but beside those, others are irritating such as

> Laisse du vieux Platon se froncer l'oeil
>   austère.
>
> [Let old Plato's austere eye frown]
>   (Id., **"Lesbos"**)

André Chénier said that after three thousand years Homer was still young. But how much younger Plato is! Baudelaire's line on him is that of an ignorant schoolboy, and all the more surprising as Baudelaire had a philosophical turn of mind, and was fond of making a Platonic distinction between form and the matter invested by form:

> Alors, ô ma beauté, dites à la vermine
>   Qui vous mangera de baisers
> Que j'ai gardé la forme et l'essence divine
>   De mes amours décomposés!
>
> [Then, O my beauty, whisper to the worms
>   Which with kisses will eat you,
> That I have retained the form and the divine
>   essence
>   Of my decomposed loves!]
>   (Id., **"Une Charogne"**)

Or else

> Réponds, cadavre impur . . .
> Ton époux court le monde et ta forme
>   immortelle
>
> [Answer, impure corpse . . .
> Your husband runs free and your immortal
>   shape. . . .]
>   (Id., **"Une Martyre"**)

Unfortunately, as soon as the reader has had the time to drown his rancor in the lines which follow, which rank among the finest ever written, the poetical form adopted by Baudelaire will, after five more lines, bring again

> Laisse du vieux Platon se froncer l'oeil
>   austère.

The same five line stanza produces the loveliest effects in **"Le Balcon":**

> Les soirs illuminés par l'ardeur du charbon.

> [Evenings illuminated by the glowing embers.]
>   (Id., **"Le Balcon."**)

To that line I even prefer these from **"Les Bijoux":**

> Et la lampe s'étant résignée à mourir,
> Comme le foyer seul illuminait la chambre,
> Chaque fois qu'il poussait un flamboyant
>   soupir,
> Il inondait de sang cette peau couleur
>   d'ambre.

> [And the lamp having resigned itself to die,
> As the fireplace alone illuminated the room,
> Whenever it heaved a flamboyant sigh,
> It flooded with blood that amber-colored skin.]
>   (Id., **"Les Bijoux"**)

But in some of the poems which were condemned, the same repetition becomes useless and wearying. When the first line said already

> Pour savoir si la mer est indulgente et bonne,

> [In order to know if the sea is merciful and
>   kind]
>   (Id., **"Lesbos"**)

why again repeat in the fifth,

> Pour savoir si la mer est indulgente et bonne?

It remains nevertheless true that those stately condemned poems, added to the others, produce a wholly different effect. They are restored to their position among the greatest in the book, like those crystal, haughty waves which majestically rise after the evenings of storm and which broaden the boundless vision of the sea with their alternating crests. One's emotion is still heightened when one learns that those poems were there, not just like any of the others, but that, to Baudelaire, they were the chief pieces in the book; so much so that he first intended to entitle the whole volume, not **Les fleurs du mal,** but *Les Lesbiennes.* The title finally chosen, now inseparable from literary

history, was not found by Baudelaire, but offered to him by his friend Babou. It is more apt. It extends to other themes than Lesbians but it does not exclude them, for they are essential to Baudelaire's aesthetic and moral conception of the flowers of evil.

How did Baudelaire come to take such a special interest in Lesbians that he wished to adopt that title for his splendid volume of verse? When Vigny, angry at woman, explained her by the mysteries of the breast nursing the infant,

> Il rêvera toujours à la chaleur du sein,

> [Forever he will dream of the warm bosom,]
>   (Vigny, "La Colère de Samson")

by the physiological peculiarity of woman,

> La femme, enfant malade et douze fois impur,

> [Woman, that sickly child and twelve times
>   impure,]
>   (Id., Ibid.)

by her psychology also

> Toujours ce compagnon dont le coeur n'est
>   pas sûr,

> [Always that companion whose heart is never
>   sure.]
>   (Id., Ibid.)

It is understandable that, in his disappointed and jealous love, he should have written:

> La Femme aura Gomorrhe et l'Homme aura
>   Sodome.

At least, he opposes them to each other as unreconcilable enemies:

> Et se jetant de loin un regard irrité
> Les deux sexes mourront chacun de leur côté.

> [And casting from afar a mutual and wrathful
>   glance,
> The two sexes will die, apart from each
>   other.]
>   (Id., Ibid.)

Not so in Baudelaire:

> Car Lesbos entre tous m'a choisi sur la terre
> Pour chanter le secret de ses vierges en fleurs
> Et je fus dès l'enfance admis au noir mystère.

> [For Lesbos of all men on this earth elected me

to sing the secret of its virgins in bloom
And from childhood on I was admitted to its
    dark mystery.]

                                    (Baudelaire, **"Lesbos"**)

That "liaison" between Sodom and Gomorrah which, in the parts of my novel recently published, I have entrusted to a coarse individual, Charles Morel (it is on such brutes that such a role usually devolves), it seems that Baudelaire, in a strange privilege, assigned to himself. Why did he thus assume it, how did the poet fill it? It would be fascinating to know. What is understandable in my Charles Morel remains shrouded in the deepest mystery for the author of *Les Fleurs du mal.*

P. M. Pasinetti (essay date 1948)

SOURCE: "The 'Jeanne Duval' Poems in *Les Fleurs de mal,*" in *Yale French Studies,* Vol. 1, No. 2, Fall-Winter, 1948, pp. 86-93.

[*In this essay, Pasinetti analyzes the relationship between Baudelaire's sense of poetic craft and his portrayal of a woman believed to have been Jeanne Duval.*]

When we take poems XX-XXXV (first ed.) of the *Fleurs du mal* as the Jeanne Duval group, as is often done, we do not claim an interest in biographical study. On the contrary, when we accept Baudelaire's own ordering of the book and we isolate an area in it, our assumption is that that ordering did not occur at the documentary level (as a man would order his journal for purposes of record) but at the level where the poet has already invented himself into character. He is the "speaker of the poem," and knows it. Such "invention" is possibly implicit in the very definition of literature; it seems to have been, at any rate, very much Baudelaire's way of looking at it. It is his way of looking at other writers, as would appear for instance in *Salon de 1846:* "Et vous, ô Honoré de Balzac, vous le plus héroïque, le plus singulier, le plus romantique et le plus poétique parmi tous les personnages que vous avez tirés de votre sein!"

Our other obvious assumption—that a study of imagery is a good way to start coming to grips with poems—could also be temptingly justified on Baudelaire's own premises. The imagery, the sensory material would often yield easily to identification with "l'enveloppe amusante, titillante, apéritive, du divin gâteau." ("**Le Peintre de la vie moderne,**" in *L'Art romantique*) ["the entertaining, titillating, appetizing wrapping of the divine cake." ("**The Painter of Modern Life,**" in *L'Art romantique*)]. Even more (in the same passage and elsewhere) imagery seems to be felt by Baudelaire as the "body" of

poetry, the medium toward the continuously elusive revelation of the "divine essence." The images are, so to speak, the objects of the cult. And the importance of this situation could not be too strongly emphasized. Some of this poetry, as I shall try to suggest, is not only based on it; it is about it.

The images used to describe the "bizarre déité" are almost as recurrent as Homeric epithets. Baudelaire's well known craftsmanship seems to invest the very manner in which he handles his materials, the stones, the animals he has so persistently in mind (so that if we reread, e.g., *Fusées* XVII, we are on familiar ground). Intuitive as they may be in origin, in their application they recall the jeweller's poised and well-calculated craft; I use this trite simile to suggest also that they make the poem as single stones the jewel; they are applied with an eye to the whole piece. *Les Bijoux,* which opened the group in the first edition, exemplifies as well as anything this tendency to organize things around a central vision, and suggests, as we shall have occasion to repeat, the poet's preference for the kind of thing which can "faire tableau." The details of the description, subordinate to that inclusive pattern, are from the very start the rather familiar ones. Roughly speaking we have, on one side, the "monde rayonnant de métal et de pierre" ["radiating world of metal and of stone"], a world which is glittering but cold and hard. On the other hand, we have hints of another pattern, the invitation to voyage toward regions of voluptuous calm, typically based on sea allusion: "mon amour profond et doux comme la mer" ["my love profound and sweet like the sea"]. And, of course, animal imagery ("tigre dompté"). And above all, the general tone which is, as we suggested, remarkably one of "composition." The visual angle, the contemplative posture of the speaker, and the feeling of structural firmness which Baudelaire always gives, serve perfectly the manner of presentation of the central figure: moving in charming metamorphoses, she is making a show of herself, or is used as a show: "D'un air vague et rêveur elle essayait des poses." ["With a vague and dreamy air she tried on poses."] Action is, here and elsewhere, described: but action already shaped into posture, bent, so to speak, on itself as potential remembrance. The treatment of action in the light of memory is typical: we suspect already that acts achieve their highest significance only in the ritual of commemoration. The pattern of *Le Balcon,* to mention one, comes to mind ("Tu te rappelleras. . . . " "Je sais l'art d'évoquer. . . .").

It is also clear at once that the image of the mulatto girl has a function which transcends the love story, and that it does so in all its precious details: a halo of special significance is around each of them. And they are so concrete and so individually appropriate that abstract paraphrase becomes particularly inept. We have

in the poems, of course, themes of attraction and repulsion, soft warm and gelid detachment, longing and
ennui, pain and voluptuousness, but since these do
not exist as polarized abstractions (each pair being
part of the same, indivisible impulse) they can only
be expressed through imagery, whose function they
justify: the conciliating function in coping with complexities. Typical is the conciliation of immediate and
distant; the near and tangible mainly serves to excite
longing. The central vision, the dark woman, is the
tangible, Parisian symbol of "là-bas." The possible
illustrations of this pattern are only too abundant; the
slow motions of the calm blue seas provide the underlying rhythm, and in the darkness of closed eyes
and exotic perfume the poet sees "se dérouler des
rivages heureux" in the monotonous sunlight (*Parfum exotique*.) There is a punctual, almost pedestrian
appropriateness in the imagery used to express the
longing toward exotic lands: the woman's hair, in the
famous baroque piece, is the "forêt aromatique"; the
speaker's desires "partent en caravane" and "la bête
implacable et cruelle" of poem XXIV importantly
suggests the oriental God, to be appeased by precious though always insufficient offerings (cf. also
La Chevelure, last stanza.) The idol is unappeased,
unattainable, also frigid; the mineral imagery of *Les
Bijoux* occurs again and again (cf. second part of
Sonnet XXVII).

The pattern of contemplation established at the start
is further stylized in a certain use of animal images. *Le Chat* is pretty, and rather predictable. The
use of the serpent, I feel, shows more complexity.
It is introduced in the sonnet "Avec tes vêtements . . ."
by the slow, dance-like motion of the woman; and
the image is reworked in a special poem, the following *Serpent qui danse*. The serpent is exotic
and secret, it partakes of the "nature étrange et
symbolique / Où l'ange inviolé se mêle au sphinx
antique"; in its immediately descriptive function,
the image is elaborated upon to the point of establishing connections between the serpent's skin and
the woman's "vêtements ondoyants et nacrés"; and
much of the usual imagery connoting cold and
unattainable indifference is adopted (the eyes are
"bijoux froids" etc.)

We cannot help observing, however, the subtle and
precise qualification that the place of the serpent in the
picture implies; it is not so much the idol, to which
appeasing gifts are vainly offered, as the object, the
instrument of the magic performance:

> Comme ces longs serpents que les jongleurs
> sacrés
> Au bout de leurs bâtons agitent en cadence.
>
> [Like those long snakes which sacred
> jugglers

At the end of their sticks rythmically swing.]
("**Avec tes vêtements**")

Also, in the second "serpent" poem, the sea imagery is
relevant. Until then it had been more typically used to
imply a dream of unattainable warmth, longing toward
"île paresseuse," or annihilations, dark "gouffre" (even
her hair was "ce noir océan"). Here it serves as a vision of activity, in a rhythm of unusual vivacity:

> Comme un navire qui s'éveille
>   Au vent du matin,
> Mon âme rêveuse appareille
>   Pour un ciel lointain.
>
> [Like a vessel that awakes
>   At the morning breeze,
> My dreamy soul sets sail
>   Towards a distant sky.]
> ("**Le Serpent qui danse**")

It is "lointain" to be sure, but it does sound different
from the sky we imagine over the

>   . . . rivages heureux
> Qu'éblouissent les feux d'un soleil monotone
>
>   [. . . fortunate
>   shores
> Dazzled by the fires of a monotonous
>   sunlight]

of *Parfum exotique* or from the "immensités bleues"
of poem XXIV. The image of the "navire" in the
morning creates quite a perceptible difference; and
it is tempting to think what the word "navire"
was liable to evoke in Baudelaire's mind. In the
splendid passage in *Fusées* XXII his vision of the
"navire" is given as the very type of the poetic
image.

I am not trying to force this series of poems into a too
well formulated scheme. It seems clear, however, that
at this more or less central point of the group, the
quality of the vision changes. At least, there is shift in
emphasis. In particular I would describe this as an
increased awareness of the fact that the speaker's contemplation is an image of the poetic act. And I would
suggest that consequently the vision of the woman and
of the poet bent toward her in long monologue is more
and more characteristically placed in a light of recollection: recollection being Baudelaire's typical mode
of the artistic evocation.

In the *Bijoux,* by way of example, we had already
noticed how the composition tended to "faire tableau";
now the "tableau" is placed more evidently at what
Wordsworth would call "a distance that was fit"; and
the even more important thing is that memory becomes

not only the method but also the theme of the poetry. In Baudelaire, and we have here the support of some of his most famous passages of criticism, recollection can be said to constitute the proper form of the imaginative vision.

The important stanzas 7 and 8 of *Une Charogne* are a case in point. The moment has been preceded by a gradual shifting from images of death and decomposition to images where the dead body is seen more and more as an inchoate, anonymous mass, suggesting, rather than the dead, the blind, the unnamed, the prenatal. Finally "tout cela" in the crucial passage acquires a rhythmic movement which several types of visual and auditive images contribute to suggest, and "enflé d'un souffle" achieves no less than the meaning of a parable of artistic creation from memory:

> Les formes s'effaçaient et n'étaient plus qu'un
>   rêve,
>   Une ébauche lente á venir,
> Sur la toile oubliée, et que l'artiste achève
>   Seulement par le souvenir.

> [The shapes became blurred and were then but
>   a dream,
>   A sketch slow to come off,
> Forgotten on the canvas, and completed only
>   In the artist's memory.]
>   ("Une Charogne")

The lines 2 and 4 should begin indented, as here printed.

In other words we have, here and elsewhere, the pattern of past event and present evocation, the ritual of recollection which equates the stylizing, purifying and, indeed, commemorative function of art.

Le Vampire in this respect is a sort of ironic counterpart to what seems to me the basic theme of *Une Charogne* and of much that follows it. It adopts some of the same imagery ("comme aux vermines une charogne"). In the last stanza of the poem, the identification of the speaker with the "vermine qui vous mangera de baisers" of *Une Charogne* is, if we keep that vision in mind, as we cannot help doing, rather more than a hint.

The theme of recollection through art or, more generally, that of artistic creation, can naturally be seen in imagery of light and darkness: the imagery with which birth and nonlife are associated in the subconscious patrimony of all people. Roughly speaking, art would be seen as the process of rescuing the image from chaotic darkness and oblivion: its illumination and ordering into beauty and remembrance. *Les Ténèbres* (first sonnet of *Un Fantôme*) is the

nearest thing to a close adherence to that scheme. The speaker is in unfathomable depths of despair and darkness; and the analogy with a chaotic state from which creative power is painfully absent is supported by a comparison with the predicament of an artist. The art is painting, as in *Une Charogne,* as in some of the titles of the final poems of this cycle (*Le Cadre, Le Portrait*) and as in some of the most impressive pieces of Baudelaire's criticism (where, through his notations on painting, we are accustomed to read, as though on a palimpsest, his ideas on poetry.)

> Je suis comme un peintre qu'un Dieu moqueur
> Condamne à peindre, hélas, sur les ténèbres. . . .

> [I am like a painter whom a mocking God
> Condemns to paint, alas! on shades of night. . . .]
>   ("Un Fantôme")

Finally the memory appears, made of grace and splendor, recognizable "á sa rêveuse allure orientale," and the exclamatory conclusion is: "C'est Elle! Noire et pourtant lumineuse."

This suggests, also, the ambiguous complexity of the light-darkness pattern. Appropriately, there is continuous exchange between the two states. Some of the light imagery (temperate, warm light to be sure) throughout these poems has suggested, rather than a burst of creativity, nostalgia toward the inarticulate calm of the lazy islands. There is such a thing as annihilation and peace. And, on the other hand, if darkness indicates chaos, there is the luminous attractiveness of that chaos, the ambivalence toward the "gouffre," the fascination of unrescued darkness, which "la belle tènébreuse" herself, as a matter of fact, has often been there to symbolize.

What makes the "gouffre" of *De Profundis* really horrible, then, is the awareness of it. So that in the last stanza of that sonnet the poet envies

>   . . . le sort des plus vils
>   animaux
> Qui peuvent se plonger dans un sommeil
>   stupide.
>   [. . . the fate of the
>   vilest beasts
> Which can plunge into a stupid sleep.]
>   ("De Profundis clamavi")

Now, the complexity of Jeanne's image is also in the fact that she exemplifies the capability of such a "sommeil stupide." That makes her irritatingly enviable and contemptible. Contemptible, because if on the biographical level this simply means Jeanne Duval talking to Banville about Monsieur Baudelaire, "ses meubles, ses collections, ses manies," in the final poem of the section it makes her the "être maudit, á qui, de l'abîme profond / Jusq'au plus haut du ciel, rien, hors moi, ne répond!" Damned; unrescued; the poet is her only hope of rescue. The final line is possibly the most detached and glorious vision of the series; there for a moment a kind of total liberation in the image seems achieved:

> Statue aux yeux de jais, grand ange au front
>   d'airain!
>
> [Statue with jet-black eyes, great bronze-
>   browed angel!]
>
> ("**Je te donne ces vers**")

It is the supreme moment of a development long prepared, more intensely so in the last contemplations. These are sonnets. With his sense for the "forme juste" Baudelaire chose this, with its possibilities of epigraphic finality. There is here a sort of recapitulation of the known motifs: jewels, metals, "nudité," animal gracefulness, the theme of memory, a metaphorical sea-voyage in the splendid opening:

> Je te donne ces vers afin que si mon nom
> Aborde heureusement aux époques
>   lointaines. . . .
>
> [I give you these verses so that my name,
> If it happily should land on distant ages. . . .]
>
> ("**Je te donne ces vers**")

And, as we have observed, the commemorative function of poetry, its ability to rescue from Time ("noir assassin" etc.) is openly suggested.

I do not wish to stress the unity of this group and force it into a too well classified pattern; but I feel it is legitimate to say that from the early suggestions of the "tableau" pattern, through, for instance, the serpent image (where the woman is seen as the object on the magician's baton) to this concluding part, there is an overall movement toward some sort of revelation: expressed abstractly, this would be the revelation of the poet's true position before the woman, his superiority and, in a sense, his deeper curse. As artist, he is the magician ("Je sais l'art d'ávoquer . . ."), the owner of the secret language. This is *his* counterpart to the "bizarre déité," to the "sorcière," to her mysteries which in the last analysis are of his own creation, because she is not aware of them. So that the relationship becomes one of reciprocal secret, the poet's painful advantage being that he is aware of the predicament, renouncing as he does the animal's dumb inarticulateness. That there are underlying religious analogies, Baudelaire's imagery often implies. When we started these notes by calling the images the object of the cult, his passage on prayer (*Fusées* XVII: "Le chapelet est

un médium, un véhicule" [The beads are a medium, a vehicle"], etc.) was in our mind.

It is a terrible cult, because the "idea behind," the supreme beauty, the divine essence, is bound never to be expressed; but then, on the other hand, if it were achieved, the spoken word would be appeased in utter and still contemplation. (The "ciel lointain," the "calme" etc., inasmuch as they are objective correlatives of that revelation of peace, can exist on the page because they cannot be reached; and art springs characteristically from longing and regret, the two recurrent types of the visionary attitude.) All that the poet can do, then, is to perform again and again the act of desire, the prayer; and perform it well. Baudelaire's preoccupation with the craft of poetry, and also the very recurrence, the very monotony of his images, acquire in this light their full moral and ritualistic meaning.

Jean Prévost (essay date 1953)

SOURCE: "Baudelairean Themes: Death, Evil, and Love," in *Baudelaire: A Collection of Critical Essays*, edited by Henri Peyre, Prentice-Hall, Inc., 1962, pp. 170-77.

[*In this essay, Prévost discusses a number of the themes that dominate* Les Fleurs du mal, *including death, evil, and the transforming power of erotic passion.*]

Baudelaire certainly does not have the extreme variety of subjects, of themes, and of tones found in Victor Hugo. But his poetical themes are broader and more numerous than those of Lamartine, for example. The *Fleurs du mal* offers horizons of an amplitude seldom equalled in any other single volume. There would have been scant, if any, gain in the book's being two or three times larger; if Baudelaire, for sheer mass, equalled Hugo, he would be hardly tolerable. Under the variety of topics, an extreme suppleness of form, a distinctive unity of tone and of feeling is perceptible, with the same tension and the same will. Baudelaire's contemporaries did not fail to notice it, when they mockingly compared him to Boileau, and Sainte-Beauve, unjust as he was in his estimate of the poet's greatness, nevertheless saw his deliberate attempt to transform and transpose. Different as Baudelaire may be from Pascal, aesthetic impressions akin to those produced by the *Pensées* are frequently experienced by those who reread the *Fleurs du mal*. Each of them in his own realm probes our feelings and our thoughts with a very acute knife, cutting narrow and deep furrows into the quick. Both are anatomists rather than contemplators of life; in a few words, they reach straight to the bone, and strip it of all flesh.

Listing the themes of Baudelaire's poetry would not be enough. First and foremost one must ask how the poet *wants* to transform that theme, and to which others he wishes to marry it. A survey of the simple themes, or of those which seem simple at first, could be made fast enough. Again like Pascal, and like all those who load their thought and their looks with passion, Baudelaire feels, sees, understands through antitheses. The most important picture of Baudelairean themes can only be had through contrasting touches.

Naturally it happens that the poet receives or undergoes dreams which he has not organized; even if he has perhaps provoked them through hashish or laudanum, he has not organized their visions. Let us consider the poem **"Rêve parisien"**: nothing appears clearer or simpler, provided we do not look for sources too high or too far, in the clouds or in regions beyond the spirit, of what the poet actually found in a precise craftsmanship and in the resources of his art. That weird vision owes little or nothing to De Quincey, E. A. Poe, Novalis, or Gautier, whose vision was distorted (in the case of the first two through intoxication). Baudelaire is clearcut, even when he describes what is vague.

In **"Rêve parisien,"** the poet sees nothing but his hotelroom. But the perspectives are distorted: the tables, the door, the shelves, the plinths, the plaster moldings on the ceiling, the mantelpiece become prestigious structures. To a vague and magnifying perception, all that shines becomes metal if it is very small, a sheet of water if it is larger. Thus the mirror on the wall can be in turn huge polished glass and a waterfall rushing down from the sky; a few bottles around a wash basin are enough to suggest a colonnade around a garden pond; the little vault of the fireplace, above a metal plate which vaguely shines, becomes an arch or a tunnel above an ocean. The lines on the ruled paper are turned into rivers which come down from the sky; the small fragment of sky which can be seen from the window is projected afar, into the infinite, and instead of standing upright, appears to stretch horizontally; it is a boundless sea, weirdly contained on its sides. And if nothing vegetal appears in that vision, it is because the poet does not have the slightest bunch of flowers in his room; he is honest and refuses to alter anything in that perception so simply and vastly distorted.

It must be distorted a second time, or rather it must be given a shape at last, and pass from a false perception into a work of art. Then only, along with the customary rhymes which associate the images ("crise" and "cristallise," "fééries" and "pierreries," "diamant" and "firmament"), images will appear which have been borrowed from Baudelaire's predecessors, in poetry, or perhaps in painting and engraving. For every sight which he contemplates or interprets, the poet is prepared by all the images he has seen, all the words he has heard.

"La Chambre double," one of the prose poems, with similar simplicity describes another aspect, a humbler one, of the reveries provoked by intoxication. This time, the phial of laudanum is mentioned; it interposes only a happy mist between reality and the poet's eye; it makes the shape of the furniture and the setting more harmonious; its sole task of hallucination, a very modest one, is to spread a veil of muslin between the windows and the bed. The loved woman is dreamt; she is scarcely believed to be present; even the dream seems to wonder about its own presence. The vision as a whole does not create objects, but merely transposes values and invests every commonplace object with an appearance of beauty.

The same "moral message" emerges from **"Rêve parisien"** and **"La Chambre double"**—that which is also proposed by Thomas De Quincey's confessions. The dream which has been voluntarily caused by the dreamer and to which he submits must be followed by a desolate awakening, a bleak and frozen return to earth. . . . But if Baudelaire knew, underwent passively, and recorded the dreams caused by artificial paradises, his dreams are vastly different. These, more vaporous and subtle than the others, are impervious to change and are not followed by that forlorn awakening; they emerge at the mind's highest peak of lucidity.

The Theme of Death

The idea of death, on which the *Fleurs du mal* ends, remains more real and more religious than that of God for the poet. Even in that idea, which might appear to be monolithic and without any diverse hues, similar to the mat black of painters, he finds contrasts. He consents to rest in **"La Fin de la journée,"** but seems to have doubts about doing so in **"Le Squelette laboureur"**; with exaltation, he affirms survival in **"La Mort des amants"**; he denies it in **"Le Mort joyeux,"** which sounds like a challenge to fear and to faith. The vague hope of a glorious blossoming transfigures the end of **"Bénédiction"** and of **"La Mort des artistes"**; but **"Le Rêve d'un curieux"** tells us that even our thirst for the beyond must be frustrated.

The man for whom nature was monotonous and narrow, and who saw the world through a few artists rather than in its original nudity, vaguely expected from death something which no longer would look like what was known, which would not be our shadow or our reflection on things, but a novel sensation. **"Le Voyage"** thus truly deserves to be the final poem of the book, the one in which the stages of the poet's life are, one after the other, most clearly marked: memoirs, in a word, but at the same time the memoirs of all of us. Once again, this time all encompassed in one poem, the world as he has seen it unrolls before our eyes; life, like the sea, wearies us with its monotonous and dazzling brightness. Let us close our eyes, first to rest them, then to implore wildly for newness, "du nouveau." Spiritual flame has extinguished the sumptuous spectacle of nature, and the sun is now only an inner one:

> Si le ciel et la mer sont noirs comme de
>   l'encre,
> Nos coeurs que tu connais sont remplis de
>   rayons!
>
> [If the sky and the sea are black like ink,
> Our hearts which you well knew are filled
>   with bright rays!]

That enchanted and disappointed review of human things sacrifices everything to a last hope, the only one which life cannot take away. The world, so lovely in its images, has shrunk and wilted; love is a stain which obstinately lingers; the lightness of departures, full of fresh hopes when one set out at the dawn of one's life, appears madness to him whose dreams have regularly foundered on rocky reefs. Even the splendor of the Orient, not unlike the grey sadness of our cities, fails to conceal the powerless human misery. The only folly which comes up to our mad expectations is that of opium. One hope alone will restore to the poet the cheerful joy of his earlier departure; in the midst of the vain tumult of old temptations, it will blow like an offshore breeze, the only chance of freshness; death is the only certitude left to man, and the poet attempts to make it the only hope.

The Triumph of Evil

Along with poems in which Baudelaire yearns for the good or for nothingness, there are some in which complacency in plunging into evil is triumphant. His conscientious examinations now appeal to God, now to the Devil. So exacting, so perfect in playing his part is the latter, that he ceases to be the enemy and becomes the object of a desolate cult.

In **"L'Horreur sympathique,"** the misery of the unhappy libertine is relieved by his pride. There, as in **"Le Rebelle,"** the soul agrees to persist in its evil incarnation. The damned one in **"Le Rebelle"** is content with saying: "I do not want." The libertine in **"Horreur sympathique"** refuses to moan; he wants neither the brightness nor the certainty promised to the elect by faith; on the contrary, he is "avide de l'obscur et de l'incertain." What matters it to him if he is expelled from Paradise? At last, he will confess his pride and his taste for Inferno. The two poems are close to

each other: the taste for Inferno is but a fierce taste for freedom; in spite of all hopes, in spite of all the rewards promised to docile submission, I want to choose what appeals to me, "to prefer myself to my happiness."

"L'Irrémédiable" shows another voluptuous aspect of evil, another pride: no longer that of independence, but of lucidity. Yes, I have seen myself, I have gazed clearsightedly at all the evil that is in me, and here I am, God of myself, fully aware of my good and of my evil. In its first part, the poem is a series of comparisons, borrowed from Vigny's "Eloa," Poe, and De Quincey. These comparisons which all bring the reader back to the poet recall the pieces entitled **"Spleen,"** in which the soul, melting in melancholy images of the world, seems to surrender. But the Devil appears, and the poet's admiration for that character who "always does well all that he does" gives a clearer outline to despair. Thus the second half of the poem is introduced, in which the mournful joy of lucidity will give itself free play:

> Soulagement et gloire uniques,
>   La conscience dans le Mal!
> [Unique relief and glory—
>   Conscience in Evil.]

Examination of conscience does not necessarily constitute an exercise toward virtue for Baudelaire. A particular examination impels to energy and hard work; a general examination leads to despair, and to the acceptance of that despair. The Socratic "Know thyself," basis of all virtues, here becomes awareness of and consent to evil; the monastic meditation which leads to good resolutions is utilized against laziness, but it accepts and it exalts the vast realm of sins. We do not have to judge it from the point of view of a moralist, but from the of a lover of poetry. Bound as it was to the constant quest for new and adequate translation into words, it made the poet more acutely aware of his own particular being. It led him to borrow the language of religion for very secular descriptions, to merge into one the two desires to know himself and to judge himself. When he observes man, he starts with himself; lyricism and lucidity are thus married.

The Love Poems Addressed to Madame Sabatier

It appears that once at least Baudelaire experienced romantic passion of the kind which transfigures the loved one into an angelic creature. Most of the poems sent to "La Présidente," as she was called by her friends, or written for her, seem like the rites of acult. The poet occasionally offered the same fervor to Berthe or to Marie, "the child, the sister," but then without pretending to lower himself before them. Does he find in this experience the great "romantic love," and are not those poems as beautiful as the great love elegies by Musset, Lamartine, or Hugo, closely allied to them in their inspiration?

For the romantics, passion is an exchange. The words and the feelings of the loved woman appear to occupy the first place there. She is almost like Dante's Beatrice or Petrarch's Laura, the inspirer, she to whom the poet owes his genius. The inspirer is aware of her role and of her mission, so that her beauty seems but a paltry thing compared to the loftiness of her mind or the impulses of her heart.

Not so with Baudelaire. "La Présidente," for him, is not a living goddess but a nearly mute idol. He calls her Angel, but praises chiefly the merits of a filly in her: splendid eye, beauty, blooming and contagious health. Curiously enough, the confessions in the *Journals* and the other love poems in *Les Fleurs du mal* evince an enduring taste, first instinctive and then reasoned, for the thin, much painted, rather sad-looking type of woman. Does he offer his adoration to this healthy and plump woman precisely because she is not "his type," because he can sympathize with that healthy and overflowing vigor without feeling any desire for it? Doubtless this woman, whom he had long known, a good partner at smoking and hashish parties, the mistress of several of his friends, held little mystery for him at the time when he decided to make her his idol. Biography allows us to see in that "love" only a poetical raw material, a pretext for sonnets; the written work confirms it. From his idol, he received only one confidence, out of which he made the stanzas of **"Confession."** He succeeded there in hiding the extreme banality of the avowal under the description of a Paris night and a simple and faultless rhythm. We owe it to his genius to imagine that, by himself, he would have treated the same theme more profoundly. Elsewhere, she is not supposed to speak ("Taisez-vous, ignorante! âme toujours ravie!"), but at times the demon in her speaks, at times the phantom of the idol; in other words, to the woman herself, the poet prefers the image of her which he makes or unmakes at will.

Poet that he was, he sought two things in Madame Sabatier whom he treated as a work of art rather than as a real being. As early as 1853, in one of the first poems which he sends to her, he shows it ingenuously. First, her refreshing and salutary atmosphere, the contagion of health and cheerfulness which might impart tone and vigor to him. He does not wish to possess her; he wants rather, at times, to share in her robustness and her easy-going gaiety; he wants to believe in the contagion of physical good as the ancients did:

> David, mourant, aurait demandé la santé
> Aux émanations de ton corps enchanté. . . .

> [David on his death bed would have implored
>   health
> From the emanations of your enchanted
>   body. . . .]

But chiefly he asks from her a continuous surprise, an ever-renewed opportunity for contrasts with himself. Obsessed with himself and his own problems, in her he finds his perfect opposite. It may be a chance to forget himself; more often still, an opportunity for comparing and opposing himself to her. That series of methodically developed contrasts is the theme of **"Reversibilité."** The beloved hardly appears; only her vaguest virtues are celebrated; she is the motionless wall against which the foam of her worshipper's contrary passions, the tide of his impure suffering, beats. The last stanza devotes three lines to her. There the real woman appears as if she were a sum of abstractions, a being of reason, an Angel, whose prayers the poet implores in concluding.

In most of the sonnets which come later, Baudelaire does not even ask the loved woman to participate in her own cult. She does not even need to understand herself, to wonder what kind of beauty she represents for the poet. Baudelaire celebrates her eyes; he has taken them as his guides; thanks to them, for a moment he ceases to be demoniacal or Christian. He allows himself to surrender to a love of simple and superficial gaiety, to admiration for the most natural and blossoming beauty. In a word, under a softer and more refined shape, with a suave quality which his elder and master did not have, he seems to profess the aesthetic and pagan religion of Théophile Gautier; he instills into it a mysticism without content, made solely of remote intentions and of purified images. Nothing designates the loved one in particular. These chants of adoration could be equally addressed to all women whose eyes are normal: for example

> Ils marchent devant moi, ces yeux pleins de
>   lumière

> [They walk in front of me, those eyes filled
>   with light]

in **"Le Flambeau vivant,"** or the similar lines in **"L'Aube spirituelle."** According to the poet's own declaration, **"Harmonie du soir"** is a flower from the same bouquet of laudatory hymns: one may wonder whether it celebrates a living creature. A Spaniard, more accustomed than a Frenchman to a poetry of dolorous filial tenderness, might suppose that the poem is addressed to a mother rather than a mistress. The "Présidente" is more exactly depicted in **"Allégorie,"** if it is she who is designated in that poem, as evidence leads us to believe. There Baudelaire magnifies his model, but does not idealize it.

Upon receiving her copy of **Les Fleurs du mal** and rereading the poems which the poet had said were devoted to her, Mme. Sabatier never wondered why, in that volume of verse, she was more vague and indistinct, less real than Jeanne Duval. She apparently did not ask: "But have these pretty lines anything in common with me? Can I see and recognize myself there?" She did not wonder, because she was one of those women who assume a modest air when the name of *beauty* is merely uttered in their presence. She did not understand that she served Baudelaire only as an embodiment of the ideal, and that, in such an ideal, the poet had put nothing of himself: he had only put the very opposite of himself.

Martin Turnell (essay date 1953)

SOURCE: "The Interpretation of the *Fleurs du Mal*," in *Baudelaire: A Study of His Poetry,* New Directions Books, 1953, pp. 175-99.

[*In the following excerpt, Turnell argues that Baudelaire uses the imagery of urban crowds to escape the solitude of the poetic process.*]

I have already suggested that the **'Tableaux Parisiens'** are not incidental glimpses of the city, but an attempt by the poet to re-establish contact with the world of common experience, to escape from the self. The attempt naturally fails, but it produces some of his finest and most original poetry.

The chapter contains eighteen poems. They record a 'circular tour' of the city lasting twenty-four hours, and three of them—*Le Soleil, Le Crépuscule du soir,* and *Le Crépuscule du matin*—mark the changes from morning to night, from night to dawn.

The first poem is a panorama of the city. The poet imagines himself in the traditional garret and adopts, ironically, the pastoral tone:

> Je veux, pour composer chastement mes
>   églogues,
> Coucher auprès du ciel, comme des
>   astrologues,
> Et, voisin des clochers, écouter en rêvant
> Leurs hymnes solennels emportés par le vent.

He looks down across

> Les tuyaux, les clochers, ces mâts de la cité,

but decides to shut out the world and write. The storms may thunder outside, but he will not care:

> Car je serai plongé dans cette volupté
> D'évoquer le Printemps avec ma volonté,

> De tirer un soleil de mon coeur, et de faire
> De mes pensers brûlants une tiède atmosphère.

i think we can take it that the seventeen poems which follow are in fact the vision that he sets to work to 'evoke' in the fastness of his garret, but his picture of Paris turns out to be very different from the one that he suggests in these lines. It will be an autumn and not a spring landscape, nor will it be sunlight—we note the recurrence of the image—that he draws from his 'heart'.

Le Soleil—originally the second poem of **'Spleen et Idéal'**—describes his aims very neatly:

> Je vais m'exercer seul à ma fantasque escrime,
> Flairant dans tous les coins les hasards de la
>   rime,
> Trébuchant sur les mots comme sur les pavés,
> Heurtant parfois des vers depuis longtemps
>   rêvés.

He goes on to compare the sun and the poet:

>   il descend dans les villes,
> Il ennoblit le sort des choses les plus viles,
> Et s'introduit en roi, sans bruit et sans valets,
> Dans tous les hôpitaux et dans tous les palais.

It is, indeed, the relation between 'words' and 'paving-stones', 'dream' and 'reality' which gives the **'Tableaux'** their special fascination. The poet imagines himself leaving his attic, going down into the city and recording his impressions of it, finding his way into palaces, poor-houses, and hospitals, and transforming what he sees into something unique. For he has succeeded better than any other modern poet in conveying the atmosphere of the great city—the mists rising over the Seine at dawn, the sun beating remorselessly down on the dry dusty pavements at noon, and the winter fogs blotting out the city at dusk; the sinister procession of beggars, murderers, drunkards, prostitutes, and rag-pickers slinking through the twilight. His verse catches the sounds as well as the sights. We hear the bugle in the barracks at dawn, the rattle of the traffic in the 'rue assourdissante', the medley of sounds as night-life begins:

>   les cuisines siffler,
> Les théâtres glapir, les orchestres ronfler . . .

the music of a military band:

>   ces concèrts, riches de cuivre,
> Dont les soldats parfois inondent nos jardins . . .

or the haunting melody of a street song:

> Que des noeuds mal attachés
> Dévoilent pour nos péchés

Tes deux beaux seins, radieux
   Comme des yeux;

Que pour te déshabiller
Tes bras se fassent prier
Et chassent à coups mutins
   Les doigts lutins . . .

Tu compterais dans tes lits
Plus de baisers que de lis
Et rangerais sous tes lois
   Plus d'un Valois! . . .

Tu vas lorgnant en dessous
Des bijoux de vingt-neuf sous
Dont je ne puis, oh! pardon!
   Te faire don.

A une Mendiante rousse is based on a combination of two traditional metres, and the use of the word *lois* is a charming archaism. The careful blending of tradition and innovation that we find in the poem is a good indication of Baudelaire's approach to his material and of the way in which he achieves his effects in this part of his work.

> 'Impressionism,' writes Arnold Hauser, 'is an urban art, and not only because it discovers the landscape quality of the city and brings painting back from the country to the town, but because it sees the world through the eyes of the townsman and reacts to external impressions with the overstrained nerves of modern technical man. It is an urban style, because it describes the changeability, the nervous rhythm, the sudden sharp but always ephemeral impressions of the city.'

This passage throws considerable light on the **'Tableaux Parisiens'**. It seems to me to be misleading to suggest, as Vivier does [in *The Social History of Art*, 1952], that the poems are in some way 'objective'. Baudelaire's pictures are traditional in the sense that they are carefully composed and contain a pronounced formal element which we shall not find in Laforgue's much more impressionistic pictures of Paris life; but his main concern is to give a personal 'impression' and not a realistic study of the city and its inhabitants. Nor can it be denied that he brings out to the full 'the overstrained nerves of modern technical man . . . the changeability, the nervous rhythm, the sudden sharp but always ephemeral impressions of the city'. The poems are highly stylized, their imagery a mixture of exact observation and impressionism of the kind that we find in:

Le long du vieux faubourg, où pendent aux
   masures
Les persiennes, abri des secrètes luxures . . .

La Prostitution s'allume dans les rues;
Comme une fourmilière elle ouvre ses issues;

Partout elle se fraye un occulte chemin,
Ainsi que l'ennemi qui tente un coup de main;
Elle remue au sein de la cité de fange . . .

In these lines there is not simply a mixture of exact observation and impression; the impression takes the form of comment or criticism such as we find in 'secrètes luxures', 'Comme une fourmilière' and 'cité de fange'.

When he writes:

Fourmillante cité, cité pleine de rêves,
Où le spectre en plein jour raccroche le
   passant!

we see that the city of swarming multitudes is also the city of dreams where the apparition clutches us by the arm in broad daylight. 'Tout pour moi devient allégorie', he said in **Le Cygne**. 'Rêve', 'cauchemar', 'mythe', and 'allégorie' are among the words to which Baudelaire has given a special resonance and they are key-words for an appreciation of the **'Tableaux Parisiens'**. For these 'pictures' have the sharpness and the intensity of a dream. The dream is a *dédoublement* which enables us to contemplate life simultaneously under two aspects, giving us the sensation of the dream world with its strange shapes continually breaking in on the 'real' world. 'Il aime le mot charmant appliqué aux choses équivoques', said Laforgue. He did so because the use of this and similar words enabled him to render perfectly 'the ecstasy of life and the horror of life':

Dans les plis sinueux des vieilles capitales,
Où tout, même l'horreur, tourne aux
   enchantements,
Je guette, obéissant à mes humeurs fatales,
Des êtres singuliers, décrépits et *charmants.*
Aurais-je, sans mourir, contemplé le huitième,
Sosie inexorable, *ironique* et fatal . . .

I have said sufficient to give some idea of 'the landscape quality of the city', but we can only grasp the significance of the landscape when it is provided with figures, and this leads to a consideration of the general meaning of the chapter. The centre of the **'Tableaux Parisiens'** is a group of four poems which follows *A ne Mendiante rousse*. The theme of all four is exile. *Le Cygne,* which forms the prologue, deals both with the general idea of exile and with the poet's personal sense of exile. The three remaining poems—*Les Sept vieillards, Les Petites vieilles,* and *Les Aveugles*—are concerned with specific examples of those modern exiles and outcasts, old men, old women, and the blind.

Le Cygne begins with an example of exile taken from classical times, with the image of the widowed Andromache weeping beside the river:

Andromaque, je pense à vous! Ce petit fleuve,
Pauvre et triste miroir où jadis resplendit
L'immense majesté de vos douleurs de veuve,
Ce Simoïs menteur qui par vos pleurs grandit,

A fécondé soudain ma mémoire fertile,
Comme je traversais le nouveau Carrousel.
Le vieux Paris n'est plus (la forme d'une ville
Change plus vite, hélas! que le coeur d'un
    mortel);

Je ne vois qu'en esprit tout ce camp de
    baraques,
Ces tas de chapiteaux ébauchés et de fûts,
Les herbes, les gros blocs verdis par l'eau des
    flaques,
Et, brillant aux carreaux, le bric-à-brac confus.

It seems probable that the memory of Andromache—'memory' is a crucial word in this poem—was recalled by the sight of the 'classical' buildings in the centre of Paris. When the poem was first published it had an epigraph from the Third Book of Virgil's *Æneid:* 'Falsi Simonentis ad undam'. For Baudelaire evokes the image of Andromache at the time when she was an exile in Pyrrhus's capital and had made a river there 'in imitation of the river Simois of Troy to remind her of her native land'.

The image of Andromache stirs the poet's personal memories. In the last two lines of the second verse the 'classical' tone, which was admirably suited to the opening of the poem, changes to a more colloquial tone; but though the reference to the changing face of Paris seems almost an aside, we shall find that the contrast between change and the unchanging is one of the central themes of the poem. The poet remembers the swan that he himself had seen many years before when passing through the same part of Paris:

Là s'étalait jadis une ménagerie;
Là je vis, un matin, à l'heure où sous les
    cieux
Froids et clairs le Travail s'éveille, où la
    voirie
Pousse un sombre ouragan dans l'air
    silencieux,

Un cygne qui s'était évadé de sa cage,
Et, de ses pieds palmés frottant le pavé sec,
Sur le sol raboteux traînait son blanc
    plumage.
Près d'un ruisseau sans eau la bête ouvrant le
    bec

Baignait nerveusement ses ailes dans la
    poudre,
Et disait, le coeur plein de son beau lac natal:

'Eau, quand donc pleuvras-tu? quand tonneras-
    tu, foudre?'
Je vois ce malheureux, mythe étrange et fatal,

Vers le ciel quelquefois, comme l'homme d'Ovide,
Vers le ciel ironique et cruellement bleu,
Sur son cou convulsif tendant sa tête avide,
Comme s'il adressait des reproches à Dieu!

I shall discuss Baudelaire's syntax in some detail later on and need only remark here on the effectiveness with which he builds up the confused and sordid background and delays the appearance of the swan, who is the object of 'je vis' in line 2, until the beginning of the next verse. What are mainly interesting, however, are the similarities and contrasts between the images of Andromache and the swan. The word 'mythe' applies to both of them. Andromache belongs to a classical myth, the swan to a new myth which the poet is creating. He is a 'symbol' in the same sense as Baudelaire's albatross, but in this poem the symbol is worked out with consummate skill.

Andromache has been taken from her native land and brought as a captive to Pyrrhus's capital where she stands weeping beside an imitation river. The swan, too, has been taken from his 'beau lac natal' and imprisoned in a 'ménagerie' where he becomes like the weeping Andromache a spectacle for strangers to gaze on. He escaped from his cage, but it was an escape into a fresh 'exile', and he remains an incongruous figure with his white plumage set against the dim background of the city amid the clatter of the refuse bins. The skies, which are 'froids et clairs', remind him tantalizingly of his native lake as the false river reminds Andromache of the real river in her native land. Her tears swell the imitation river, but they cannot make it anything but 'ce petit fleuve'. The swan is deprived of water altogether. The sight of him scratching the dry stones, and dipping his wings into the dust near the 'ruisseau sans eau', appears to be an ironical allusion to 'ce Simoïs menteur' because the swan is lamenting beside a stream which is a caricature of the 'beau lac natal' in the same way that Andromache's river is a caricature of the real Simois.

An American critic [Joseph D. Bennett, in *Baudelaire: A Criticism,* 1946] suggests that there is a parallel between these verses and the fifth section of *The Waste Land.* Baudelaire certainly uses absence of water as a symbol not merely of frustration, but of *stagnation,* in the same way that Mr. Eliot does in *What the Thunder Said* and *Gerontion.* This explains the appeal:

'Eau, quand donc pleuvras-tu? quand tonneras-
    tu, foudre?'

It is an appeal for water to provide him with another, lake, but it is more than that. It is an appeal for a convulsion of nature which will bring water that is literally and metaphorically life-giving to a stagnant civilization.

I have said that the description of the changing face of Paris in the second verse is one of the main themes of the poem. Andromache is a symbol of the unchanging sense of exile which remains in the human heart in spite of the changes that take place in the 'form' of life. 'Le coeur d'un mortel', therefore, stands for something permanent, for something that belongs to the human condition; 'la forme d'une ville' stands for the impermanent, the transitory. In other words, the changes in the face of Paris mark the change from the classical to the modern symbols of exile. The futile, ineffectual movements of the swan scratching 'feverishly', bathing his wings 'nervously', and darting his neck 'convulsively' are contrasted with

> L'immense majesté de vos douleurs de veuve.

Andromache's grief is classical, restrained, majestic. The swan is the symbol of the unrest of the modern exile—the unrest which torments the poet himself.

This brings us to the end of the first part of the poem. The opening verse of the second part reintroduces the theme of the changing face of Paris and the unchanging 'melancholy' of the human heart:

> Paris change! mais rien dans ma mélancolie
> N'a bougé! palais neufs, échafaudages, blocs,
> Vieux faubourgs, tout pour moi devient
> 　　allégorie,
> Et mes chers souvenirs sont plus lourds que
> 　　des rocs.

The sight of the new 'palaces', the scaffolding, and the blocks of stone in the midst of the 'vieux faubourgs' brings home to us the confusion and the shapeless indifference of the modern city. The rocks to which he compares his memories are another symbol of sterility and frustration.

The images of the swan and Andromache reappear and are women together:

> Aussi devant ce Louvre une image
> 　　m'opprime:
> Je pense á mon grand cygne, avec ses gestes
> 　　fous,
> Comme les exilés, ridicule et sublime,
> Et rongé d'un désir sans trêve! et puis á vous,
>
> Andromaque, des bras d'un grand époux
> 　　tombée,
> Vil bétail, sous la main du superbe Pyrrhus,
> Auprès d'un tombeau vide en extase courbée;
> Veuve d'Hector, hélas! et femme d'Hélénus!

The comparison between the classical and the modern exile is maintained, but the sequence of the images is reversed which has the effect of stressing the peculiar position of the modern exile with his frayed nerves and his 'gestes fous'. 'Rongé d'un désir sans trêve' seems to refer to the longing to find a way home. It leads back to the spectacle of Andromache. The words vil bétail' introduce a fresh motif. Andromache is an exile and a captive, but 'vil bétail' turns her into a chattel, a commodity to be bought and sold as the swan was bought and sold and put into a cage. She is bent 'in ecstasy' over an empty tomb—the tomb that she had built beside the imitation Simois in honour of the dead Hector—which apparently stands for the impossibility of any return. 'Ridicule et sublime' seems to identify the poet unmistakably with the swan and recalls that other poem of exile—*L'Albatros*—where we leave the poet

> *Exilé* sur le sol au milieu des huées
> Ses ailes de géant l'empêchent de marcher.

In the last three verses we have a brief glimpse of other exiles and outcasts: the consumptive negress lost in the jostling throng of the modern city, the orphans, the weepers, the shipwrecked mariners. There are continual references back to the two main images. The negress thinking longingly of the coconut trees of her native Africa is Andromache longing for the Simois of her native Troy; the weepers are Andromache weeping into the imitation Simois; the orphans 'séchant comme des fleurs' the swan beside the dried-up stream; and the shipwrecked sailors remind us that the sea, though so often a symbol of liberation, is the greatest barrier between the exile and home.

In the closing verses the poet's own role undergoes a change. We find that he has taken the place of the mourning Andromache, as he stands watching the anonymous procession of the lesser exiles which passes rapidly across the stage and fades away in the 'bien d'autres encor' of the last line. His tone changes to a tone of lamentation and each type of exile is introduced by the words, 'Je pense à . . .' It strikes a note of despair in

> Je pense . .
> A quiconque a perdu ce qui ne se retrouve
> Jamais, jamais!

In the final moving verse he identifies himself with exiles everywhere:

> Ainsi dans la forêt où mon esprit s'exile
> Un vieux Souvenir sonne à plein souffle du
> 　　cor!
> Je pense aux matelots oubliés dans une île,
> Aux captifs, aux vaincus! . . . à bien d'autres
> 　　encor!

'Souvenir' recalls the 'mémoire fertile' of the second verse, and the poem reminds us even more strongly than **La Chevelure** of the close connection between Baudelaire's memory and Proust's *mémoire involontaire*. The sight of an object in the external world sets the machinery in motion, stirring 'forgotten' memories. Emotions buried in the depths of the unconscious float to the surface of the conscious mind, attach themselves to *visual* images, and crystallize in a fresh experience. The whole poem, in fact, is a reverie constructed out of memories, and the word 'Souvenir' completes the familiar 'circle'.

The 'symphonic' construction of this superb poem has been highly praised. It is probable that music did suggest the method of introducing the main images, but the source does not perhaps greatly matter. What does matter is that Baudelaire is using with complete mastery one of the most important and influential *poetic* devices of the century. The recurring image, which was later used with extreme brilliance by Laforgue in his *Derniers vers,* has added enormously to the subtlety and complexity of modern poetry. It was the outcome of that other discovery—the 'analogical' method or the method of 'emotional equivalences'. For once the poet used an image to symbolize an emotion instead of describing emotion or using the image as a mere illustration, he found himself in possession of a sort of poetic shorthand. When this is extended to the recurring image, themes and emotions can be made to weave in and out of one another, sometimes blending and sometimes clashing, in a way that gives the pattern of the poem its new complexity, and is particularly effective in the dream atmosphere of this poem. In **Le Cygne** it does not stop at the main images. It is applied to individual words so that they reinforce and add to the cohesion not merely of the main images, but of the whole poem. When we look back we find that there is in fact a series of words or subsidiary images suggesting fecudity, water, drought, and nervousness—'grandit', 'féconde', 'fertile', 'eau', 'ruisseau', 'sec', 'séchant', 'nerveusement', 'convulsif', 'fous'—which elaborate and prolong the principal themes. Baudelaire 'works' these words so that they all become symbols of frustration in a manner that looks forward to Mallarmé. Andromache's tears 'swell' the river, but it is an imitation river which stands for her frustration at being exiled from Troy. The recollection of her 'fertilizes' the poet's memory, but it leads to the other great image of frustration—the swan and the dried-up stream. The image of drought leads, finally, by way of the 'orphelins séchant comme des fleurs', to the sea which cuts the shipwrecked sailors off from their homes.

The poem possesses an impressive variety of tone which ranges not only from the grand manner to the colloquial style, but includes the ironic-heroic tone in which the swan is described:

Comme s'il adressait des reproches á Dieu!

and the sorrowful tone of the close with its repeated 'Je pense'.

We find a similar variety in the continually changing décors seen through the poet's unchanging 'melancholy'. The scene moves to and fro between the classical landscape of Greece and the rubble of Louis-Philippe's Paris, passes on to a fleeting glimpse of an exotic Africa and the islands lost in the middle of the ocean. The figures sometimes harmonize with their background and sometimes clash with it. Andromache is in harmony with hers; the swan clashes with his, but one of the most vivid moments in the poem is the silhouette of the shattered negress caught, as it were, between 'les cocotiers absents de la superbe Afrique' and 'la muraille immense du brouillard'.

The editors of the critical edition point out that we are not prevented from seeking a symbolical interpretation of **Les Sept vieillards** and suggest, tentatively, that this number may be allusion to the seven deadly sins. Their observation is equally applicable to **Les Petites vieilles** and **Les Aveugles**. The symbolism of all three poems appears to be twofold. The old men, the old women, and the blind are, as we know, specific examples of the modern exile and they proceed logically from the exiles described in the closing verses of **Le Cygne**. I think that the seven old men, who are described significantly as 'ces sept monstres hideux', stand for the seven deadly sins and that there is a parallel between them and the seven kinds of animal and reptile mentioned in **Au Lecteur**. I suspect that there is a further parallel between the allegorical figure of 'Ennui' in that poem and the eighth old man. For the poet is so appalled at the idea that 'the eighth' may appear that he turns tail, goes back to his lodging, and shuts himself in. The introduction of names from classical legend in **Les Petites vieilles** suggests another contrast between classical and modern times in the manner of Andromache and the swan, while the spectacle of the blind men in **Les Aveugles** turning their sightless eyes to heaven is probably an allusion to contemporary unbelief—the exiles have no faith to sustain them—and to the poet's own religious doubts.

Although the poet had gone down into the city in the hope of re-establishing contact with other people he remains imprisoned in his own loneliness, an exile among exiles. The sense of distance between himself and the other exiles—the sympathetic desire to enter into their lives and the impossibility of doing so—is accentuated by his irony. He proceeds to give an account of their plight in a tone in which pity and irony are blended and which gives the poems their distinctive quality.

Whether or not the seven old men represent the seven deadly sins, they are essentially sinister figures. The poet treats them as examples of the exile who has turned sour, and in order to convey the impression that they make on him he uses the words 'méchanceté', 'fiel', 'hostile', 'infâme', 'infernal', 'sinistre'. The poem begins with a general description of the frightening impression caused by the apparition which suddenly clutches the arm of the pedestrian in broad daylight. This creates a tense, uneasy atmosphere which prepares us for the entry of the procession, and the 'spectre' in line 2 looks forward to 'ces spectres baroques' in the eighth verse. The scene is set and the poet goes on to give an account of a personal experience:

> Un matin, cependant que dans la triste rue
> Les maisons, dont la brume allongeait la
>   hauteur,
> Simulaient les deux quais d'une rivière accrue,
> Et que, décor semblable à l'âme de l'acteur,
>
> Un brouillard sale et jaune inondait tout
>   l'espace,
> Je suivais, roidissant mes nerfs comme un
>   héros
> Et discutant avec mon âme déjà lasse,
> Le faubourg secoué par les lourds tombereaux.

There is a deliberate lowering of the tension in these two verses. The poet puts the 'spectre' out of his mind, fixes our attention on the physical details of the scene—the street, the houses, the fog, and the vibration of the dust-carts. The sight of the changing shapes of the houses introduces the element of distortion which is of capital importance in this and the poems that follow. For the *physical* distortion, or the illusion of physical distortion, caused by the fog is the prelude to the *psychological* distortion which belongs to the machinery of the nightmare. In spite of the emphasis on physical details, the atmosphere remains equivocal. We are not sure—the poet does not mean us to feel sure—whether we are awake and a supernatural apparition is about to arrive or whether we are in the middle of a 'bad dream'. The fourth line seems to me to be obscure. The word 'décor' must mean stage scenery—theatres always suggest a mixture of tawdriness and glamour in Baudelaire's poetry—but it is not certain whether the poet is speaking of the way in which the actor's life is divided between the real world and the world of illusion, or whether he himself is for the time being an actor whose mood reflects the confused foggy scene. I think that logically 'l'âme de l'acteur' must mean actors in general, though Baudelaire was probably conscious of the two possible interpretations. In any case 'actor' looks forward to 'a hero' which is clearly an ironical reference to the poet. He is about to relate the 'part' that he played in the comedy of the old men, but we shall see from the close of the poem that his conduct turns out to be very unheroic.

The procession is introduced in the next verse:

> Tout à coup, un vieillard dont les guenilles
>   jaunes
> Imitaient la couleur de ce ciel pluvieux,
> Et dont l'aspect aurait fait pleuvoir les
>   aumônes,
> Sans la méchanceté qui luisait dans ses yeux,
> M'apparut.

His appearance is a careful blending of the matter of fact and the sinister. The comparison between the colour of his rags and the colour of the rainy skies marks a very adroit transition from physical to psychological distortion, and we ramain uncertain whether we are sleeping or waking. 'Imitaient' is the crucial word. It refers back to 'simulaient' and reinforces the image of the actor and of the poet himself suspended between the real world and the world of make-believe. The poem goes on:

> On eût dit sa prunelle trempée
> Dans le fiel; son regard aiguisait les frimas,
> Et sa barbe á longs poils, roide comme une
>   épée,
> Se projetait, pareille à celle de Judas.
> Il n'était pas voûté, mais cassé, son échine
> Faisant avec sa jambe un parfait angle droit,
> Si bien que son bâton, parachevant sa mine,
> Lui donnait la tournure et le pas maladroit
>
> D'un quadrupède infirme ou d'un juif à trois
>   pattes.
> Dans la neige et la boue il allait s'empêtrant,
> Comme s'il écrasait des morts sous ses
>   savates,
> Hostile à l'univers plutôt qu'indifférent.
>
> Son pareil le suivait: barbe, oeil, dos, bâton,
>   loques,
> Nul trait ne distinguait, du même enfer venu,
> Ce jumeau centenaire, et ces spectres baroques
> Marchaient du même pas vers un but inconnu.
>
> A quel complot infâme étais-je donc en butte,
> Ou quel méchant hasard ainsi m'humiliait?
> Car je comptai sept fois, de minute en minute,
> Ce sinistre vieillard qui se multipliait!

The sober, prosaic tone is brilliantly successful in maintaining our doubts about the nature of the old men and in preventing the scene from becoming sensational or melodramatic. The sense of distortion is produced by the contrast between the inhuman geometrical images and the images of the shattered human beings:

> Il n'était pas voûté, mais *cassé,* son échine

> Faisant avec sa jambe *un parfait angle
>   droit* . . .
>
>   son bâton, parachevant sa mine,
> Lui donnait la tournure et le pas maladroit
>
> D'un quadrupède *infirme* ou d'un juif á trois
>   pattes.

The impression is heightened by words and images with intangible or disturbing associations. The old man's beard,

>   roide comme une épée,
> Se projetait, pareille á *celle de Judas.*

He is 'hostile', 'sinistre'; his fellows are 'spectres baroques'. The impression is completed by the inexplicable sight of seven identical old men coming relentlessly forward as though the image of the first were 'multiplied', making the poet wonder whether he is seeing double. He appeals to the reader for sympathy:

> Que celui-là qui rit de mon inquiétude,
> Et qui n'est pas saisi d'un frisson fraternel,
> Songe bien que malgré tant de décrépitude
> Ces sept monstres hideux avaient l'air éternel!

The poem is moving towards its climax. 'Monstres hideux' is stronger than any of the previous expressions that he has used of the old men and is a sign of fear. There is a contrast between 'décrépitude' and 'éternel', between their battered appearance and the violence of its impact on the poet. The word 'éternel' also looks back to 'simulaient' and 'imitaient'. The poet is really beginning to believe that he is faced with a supernatural apparition. The impression is driven home in the next verse by the words 'sosie inexorable, ironique et fatal'. For the last three verses describe the poet very unheroically 'going to pieces':

> Exaspéré comme un ivrogne qui voit
>   double,
> Je rentrai, je fermai ma porte, épouvanté,
> Malade et morfondu, l'esprit fiévreux et
>   trouble,
> Blessé par le mystère et par l'absurdité!

The words 'épouvanté', 'malade', 'fiévreux', and 'trouble' reflect the poet's growing panic. They are helped by the jerky movement of the versification and the double caesura in lines 1 and 2 which isolates the word 'épouvanté':

> Exaspéré—comme un ivrogne—qui voit
>   double,
> Je rentrai,—je fermai ma porte,—épouvanté.

Although the poet has left the scene, the impression of horror not only remains; it becomes more intense and he thinks that he must be 'ill'. 'Ivrogne' like 'malade' refers to a psychological impression; 'porte' to the physical action of banging the door in the vain attempt to blot out the spectacle. His doubts about the nature of the apparition also remain:

> Blessé par le mystère et par l'absurdité!

It is horrible, mysterious, but also absurd. 'Mystère' refers back to 'Les mystères partout coulent commes des sèves' in the first verse; 'l'absurdité' to the images drawn from acting in verses 2 and 3 and to 'ironique et fatal' in verse 12. The final verse beginning

> Vainement ma raison voulait prendre la barre,

describes a state of complete nervous collapse.

Baudelaire displays more sympathy for the old women in *Les Petites vieilles;* but though they are not intrinsically evil like the old men, they too have been turned by their environment into 'monsters' who are repugnant to the poet:

> Ces monstres disloqués furent jadis des
>   femmes,
> Éponine ou Laïs! Monstres brisés, bossus
> Ou tordus, aimons-les! ce sont encor des
>   âmes.
> Sous des jupons troués et sous de froids
>   tissus
>
> Ils rampent, flagellés par les bises iniques,
> Frémissant au fracas roulant des omnibus,
> Et serrant sur leur flanc, ainsi que des
>   reliques,
> Un petit sac brodé de fleurs ou de rébus;
>
> Ils trottent, tout pareils à des marionnettes;
> Se traînent, comme font les animaux blessés,
> Ou dansent, sans vouloir danser, pauvres
>   sonnettes
> Où se pend un Démon sans pitié! Tout
>   cassés . . .

The distortion provides a comment on the civilization which had produced such creatures. Baudelaire was specially concerned with the destructive nature of contemporary life, and the accent falls on the words 'brisés', 'bossus', 'tordus', 'disloqués', 'cassés'. The drama is not so much described as enacted. We hear the snap of breaking bone in 'brisés' and 'cassés', and the queer shuffling tread of the down-and-outs in 'disloqués'. Civilization has reduced these exiles to mindless, inhuman robots moving jerkily across the stage 'towards an unknown goal'.

Baudelaire's use of theological terms is not always free from ambiguity, but words like 'âme', 'ange', 'péché', and 'mal' are often used in a strictly orthodox sense. When he says:

>   . . . aimons-les! ce sont encor des âmes,

or in another poem:

>   Dans la brute assoupie un ange se réveille,

'âme' and 'ange' represent positive values. It was Baudelaire's consciousness of the worth of the individual soul which was being destroyed that makes his view of the modern world a tragic one, and the tragedy is heightened by the ironical 'Eponine ou Laïs!' Yet the total effect of the three poems is one of macabre comedy which is peculiarly Baudelaire's own. It is apparent in the assumed naïveté of:

>   —Avez-vous observé que maints cercueils de
>   vieilles
>   Sont presque aussi petits que celui d'un
>   enfant?

A few lines later he enlarges on the idea:

>   Il me semble toujours que cet être fragile
>   S'en va tout doucement vers un nouveau
>   berceau;
>
>   A moins que, méditant sur la géométrie,
>   Je ne cherche, á l'aspect de ces membres
>   discords,
>   Combien de fois il faut que l'ouvrier varie
>   La forme de la boîte où l'on met tous ces
>   corps.

In *Les Aveugles* the irony becomes still more cruel:

>   Contemple-les, mon âme, ils sont vraiment
>   affreux!
>   Pareils aux mannequins; vaguement ridicules;
>   Terribles, singuliers comme des somnambules;
>   Dardant on ne sait où leurs globes ténébreux.

Baudelaire was sometimes decidedly slapdash in his use of adjectives, but in these poems almost every adjective—even the most commonplace—fits its noun exactly and conveys the impression that he is trying to render. The blind are pitiful, but their mechanical gestures irritate the poet. The mixture of pity and irritation is expressed in the colloquial phrase, 'ils sont vraiment affreux', and by the combination of 'ridicules', 'terribles', 'singuliers'. 'Pareils aux mannequins' significantly recalls 'tout pareils à des marionnettes' in *Les Petites vieilles*. It is reinforced by the wicked 'comme des somnambules' and 'leurs globes ténébreux'. In the next verse:

>   Leurs yeux, d'où la divine étincelle est partie,
>   Comme s'ils regardaient au loin, restent levés
>   Au ciel; on ne les voit jamais vers les pavés
>   Pencher rêveusement leur tête appesantie

the effect depends on a mingling of the mock-heroic— 'la divine étincelle'—exact observation:

>   Leurs yeux . . .
>   Comme s'ils regardaient au loin, restent levés
>   Au ciel . . .

and assumed surprise. But the final shot is the studied casualness of the question in the last line:

>   Je dis: Que cherchent-ils au Ciel, tous ces
>   aveugles?

What is most striking in all these poems is the absence of any sense of community. It is a world of stagnation and confusion, a world of 'memories', 'dreams', 'shadows', and 'ghosts'. The inhabitants are completely rootless. They stumble blindly through the mud and fog and confusion of the 'ant-like' modern city:

>   Traversant de Paris le *fourmillant* tableau.
>
>   Telles vous cheminez, stoïques et sans
>   plaintes,
>   A travers le *chaos* des vivantes cités.

The poet has completed his daylight tour of the city and goes on to explore its night-life. *Le Crépuscule du soir* describes nightfall. The restaurants are full; the theatres open; the man who has worked well looks back with satisfaction on his day; the exhausted workman—'l'ouvrier courbé'—goes home to bed. But it is not this that interests the poet most. For Baudelaire night is primarily the time of sin and crime when thieves and prostitutes emerge from their lairs. A stealthy, furtive note is apparent in the play of the hissing c's and s's and the liquid l's of the opening lines, giving the impression of whispered confidences:

>   Voici le soir charmant, ami du criminel;
>   Il vient comme un complice, à pas de loup; le
>   ciel
>   Se ferme lentement comme une grande alcôve,
>   Et l'homme impatient se change en bête fauve.

He employs the same device to give us a glimpse of the criminals in action:

>   Les tables d'hôte, dont le jeu fait les délices,
>   S'emplissent de catins et d'escrocs, leurs
>   complices,
>   Et les voleurs, qui n'ont ni trêve ni merci,
>   Vont bientôt commencer leur travail, eux
>   aussi,

Et forcer document les portes et les caisses
Pour vivre quelques jours et vêtir leurs
    maîtresses.

He pauses for a moment to reflect on the condition of
the sick and dying in the hospitals:

C'est l'heure où les douleurs des malades
    s'aigrissent!
La sombre Nuit les prend à la gorge; ils
    finissent
Leur destinée et vont vers le gouffre
    commun . . .

But here the hissing sibilants are a sign of life slipping
away.

Le Jeu and **Danse macabre** are both pictures of night-
life. The subject is inevitably a temptation rather than
an opportunity for Baudelaire, but *Le Jeu* contains some
effective vignettes of the gamblers. These are the age-
ing courtesans:

Autour des verts tapis des visages sans lèvre,
Des lèvres sans couleur, des mâchoires sans
    dent,
Et des doigts convulsés d'une infernale
    fièvre,
Fouillant la poche vide ou le sein palpitant . . .

The 'doigts convulsés' and the 'sein palpitant' convey, a little melodramatically no doubt, the feverish
futile passion of the players and the poet feels himself

Enviant de ces gens la passion tenace,
De ces vieilles putains la funèbre gaieté . . .

In the same poem he comments:

Voilà le noir tableau qu'en un rêve nocturne
Je vis se dérouler sous mon oeil clairvoyant.

These poems are followed by a group of five pieces
containing personal memories and reflexions. He has
described prostitution in the city. In **L'Amour du
mensonge,** which is thought by Crépet and Blin to
have been addressed to Marie Daubrun, he describes a
personal relationship with a courtesan. The theme is
similar to that of *Semper eadem.* In the middle of his
tour the poet is overcome by the horror of his situation. He knows that there is no way out, but he is
prepared to try make-believe again and expresses it in
the splendid final verse:

Mais ne suffit-il pas que tu sois l'apparence,
Pour réjouir un coeur qui fuit la vérité?
Qu'importe ta bêtise ou ton indifférence?
Masque ou décor, salut! J'adore ta beauté.

'Je n'ai pas oublié, voisine de la ville' and **'La servante au grand coeur dont vous étiez jalouse'** are
both addressed to his mother and recall, nostalgically,
his childhood days with her. The desire to escape is
also the subject of **Brumes et pluies** with its lovely
opening:

O fins d'automne, hivers, printemps trempés
    de boue,
Endormeuses saisons! je vous aime et vous
    loue . . .

This time the choice seems to lie between insensibility
and the prospect of lulling himself by a chance encounter:

par un soir sans lune, deux à deux,
D'endormir la douleur sur un lit hasardeux.

Rêve parisien, the final poem of this group, is an
outstanding success. He is back in his attic and the
poem purports to describe a real dream as compared with the 'rêveries' and 'allégories' of the
earlier poems in the chapter. Superficially, it may
sound like a prophetic vision of the future, but what
Baudelaire is really doing is to give expression by
a highly original use of language, which was to
have a decisive influence on the Rimbaud of the
Illuminations, to his sense of being trapped in a
hostile universe:

. . . peintre fier de mon génie,
Je savourais dans mon tableau
L'enivrante monotonie
Du métal, du marbre et de l'eau.
Babel d'escaliers et d'arcades,
C'était un palais infini,
Plein de bassins et de cascades
Tombant dans l'or mat ou bruni;

Et des cataractes pesantes,
Comme des rideaux de cristal,
Se suspendaient, éblouissantes,
A des murailles de métal.

The natural propensity of water is to flow, but in this
world it loses its natural properties and is suspended,
motionless, 'comme des rideaux de cristal'.

We know that Baudelaire detested nature—wild, untamed nature—and that one of his aims was to banish
what he calls contemptuously 'le végétal irrégulier';
but in doing so he starved his own senses of the scents,
sounds, and colours for which they craved. The laconic, sober style of this poem describes wonderfully the
desolation of a soundless world:

Nul astre d'ailleurs, nuls vestiges
De soleil, même au bas du ciel,

Pour illuminer ces prodiges,
Qui brillaient d'un feu personnel!

Et sur ces mouvantes merveilles
Planait (terrible nouveauté!
Tout pour l'oeil, rien pour les oreilles!)
Un silence d'éternité.

The poem expresses an element of capital importance in Baudelaire's experience and it cannot be treated in isolation. We have seen that in the first chapter he came to feel that he was the prisoner of his own mood and tried to break out of the *emotional* circle. ***Rêve parisien*** is really the answer to this attempt. For the prison is a twofold one. He escapes from himself simply to find that he has become a prisoner in an inhuman world which can only drive him back into the self from which he has escaped with the realization that all the exits are blocked and that there is no way out. For this reason ***Rêve parisien*** is the reply to ***L'Héautontimorouménos*** and ***L'Irrémédiable.*** When we look at the last two verses of part one of the second of these poems:

Un navire pris dans le pôle,
Comme en un piège de cristal,
Cherchant par quel détroit fatal
Il est tombé dans cette geôle;

—Emblèmes nets, tableau parfait
D'une fortune irrémédiable,
Qui donne à penser que le Diable
Fait toujours bien ce qu'il fait!

we cannot fail to be struck by the similarity of the imagery and that of ***Rêve parisien,*** particularly the 'piège de cristal', the 'rideaux de cristal', and the 'geôle'.

The final poem marks the end of the journey and the awakening from dreams:

La diane chantait dans les cours des casernes,
Et le vent du matin soufflait sur les lanternes.

C'etait l'heure où l'essaim des rêves
    malfaisants
Tord sur leurs oreillers les bruns adolescents;
Où, comme un oeil sanglant qui palpite et qui
    bouge,
La lampe sur le jour fait une tache rouge;
Où l'âme, sous le poids du corps revêche et
    lourd,
Imite les combats de la lampe et du jour.
Comme un visage en pleurs que les brises
    essuient,
L'air est plein du frisson des choses qui
    s'enfuient,
Et l'homme est las d'écrire et la femme
    d'aimer.

Les maisons çà et là commençaient à fumer.
Les femmes de plaisir, la paupière livide,
Bouche ouverte, dormaient de leur sommeil
    stupide;
Les pauvresses, traînant leurs seins maigres et
    froids,
Soufflaient sur leurs tisons et soufflaient sur
    leurs doigts.
C'était l'heure où parmi le froid et la lésine
S'aggravent les douleurs des femmes en
    gésine;
Comme un sanglot coupé par un sang écumeux
Le chant du coq au loin déchirait l'air brumeux;
Une mer de brouillards baignait les édifices,
Et les agonisants dans le fond des hospices
Poussaient leur dernier râle en hoquets inégaux.
Les débauchés rentraient, brisés par leurs
    travaux.
L'aurore grelottante en robe rose et verte
S'avançait lentement sur la Seine déserte,
Et le sombre Paris, en se frottant les yeux,
Empoignait ses outils, vieillard laborieux.

Although **Le Crépuscule du matin** is an early work, it is a brilliant performance which is greatly superior to its companion piece and a superb illustration of the skill with which Baudelaire uses his verbs. It is a panorama of the ravages of the night which began in **Le Crépuscule du soir.** We see the tormented adolescents tossing on their beds, the weary poet—this seems a backward glance at **Paysage**—throwing down his pen, women exhausted by love, prostitutes sprawling in their dens, the poor in their hovels trying to light the fire, the dying in the hospitals, and debauchees, ironically, 'brisés par leurs travaux'. The verbs give the poem its movement and life, but the cumulative effect depends very largely on the alternation of sound and visual images. There are two main sounds—the bugle which is answered from afar by the strident crowing of the cock presented in one masterly line:

Le chant du coq au loin déchirait l'air brumeux.

They are thrown into relief by the undertones: the sighing of the breeze in one of Baudelaire's loveliest couplets:

Comme un visage en pleurs que les brises
    essuient,
L'air est plein du frisson des choses qui
    s'enfuient.

It is followed by the snores of the sleeping prostitutes, the sound of the poor blowing on their fires and their frozen fingers—repeating the image of the wind 'blowing' on the lamps—and the 'hoquets inégaux' of the death-rattle in the hospitals.

The moment between sleeping and waking is caught by the sound of the bugle blending into the trembling of the street lamp. The movement of the fading light battling with the growing day reflects the flickering consciousness of the 'bruns adolescents':

> Où l'âme, sous le poids du corps revêche et
>   lourd,
> *Imite* les combats de la lampe et du jour.

The movement of the lamp melts into the smoke drifting from the chimneys. At this point there is a pause. We are given a *static* picture of the sleeping prostitutes which is contrasted with the uneasy sleep of the adolescents. Movement begins again with the women going about their houses. The 'douleurs des femmes en gésine' is emphasized by 'un sanglot coupé par un sang écumeux'. The smoke from the chimneys disappears into the fog which leads naturally to the choking of the dying whom we saw in the first **Crépuscule** and whose agonies look back to

> Tord sur leurs oreillers les bruns adolescents,

and forward to

> Les débauchés rentraient, brisés par leurs travaux.

The final image is a careful piece of stylization. The disorders of the night are over; the city is going back to work. 'L'ouvrier courbé qui regagne son lit' of **Le Crépuscule du soir,** who has spent a restful night, shoulders his tools and sets out. The 'vieillard laborieux' stands for honest toil—the sound element in a corrupt civilization—in contrast to the 'travaux' of the prosperous debauchees.

Alison Fairlie (essay date 1960)

SOURCE: "The Art of Suggestion," in *Baudelaire: Les Fleurs du Mal,* Edward Arnold Ltd., 1960, pp. 22-32.

[*In the following excerpt, Fairlie demonstrates how Baudelaire's careful choice of words shapes the overall effects of his poetry.*]

'Manier savamment une langue', said Baudelaire, 'c'est pratiquer une espèce de sorcellerie évocatoire' [*Oeuvres completes*, 1954, p. 1035]. It is only by the most acute and exact sense of the exciting possibilities of words, their associations, their sounds, and the ways of combining them, that the poet can create ideas, feelings or sensations. 'Il n'y a pas de hasard dans l'art . . . L'imagination est la plus scientifique des facultés' (621). Far from thinking of poetry as a matter of vague divine inspiration separated from man's other activities, he compares it not only to music and to mathematics for the fascination of its controlled patterns, but also to cooking and cosmetics for its capacity to produce the most subtle effects from the most exact gradation of ingredients:

> La poésie se rattache aux arts de la peinture, de la cuisine et du cosmétique par la possibilité d'exprimer toute sensation de suavité ou d'amertume, de béatitude ou d'horreur, par l'accouplement de tel substantif avec tel adjectif, analogue ou contraire (1383).

The art of suggestion lies sometimes in choosing and setting together words that have rich and multiple associations. This is seen most clearly in the opening line of **La Chevelure:**

> O toison, moutonnant jusque sur l'encolure . . .

The poem evokes the analogy between the waves of his mistress's thick hair, the waves of the sea and his own dreams. From the start, hair and sea come together without transition in 'toison moutonnant'. But by putting these words side by side and leading on to 'encolure' Baudelaire has given several senses at once. 'Moutonnant' normally describes the sea breaking into white-capped waves and has lost its associations with 'mouton'. 'Encolure' can be the shoulder of a human being or the neckline of a dress, but it is also used of the curving neck and withers of a horse. By setting together 'toison', a thick fleece, 'moutonnant' and 'encolure', Baudelaire both intensifies the physical sensation of the luxuriance of the thick hair and the powerful curve of neck and shoulder, and at the same time suggests the associations of a world of rich, primitive animal beauty, to be echoed later in the poem. 'Toison' perhaps also calls up the 'toison d'or'—Jason's pursuit of the golden fleece and so voyages over far seas in search of a magic dream. Even the connecting-words in this line add fully to sense and sound: not simply 'sur' or 'jusqu'à' but 'jusque sur', right down over; this both forms a refrain of *u* sounds leading up to the lovely 'encolure' and emphasises the richness of the flowing waves of hair.

But there is another kind of suggestiveness which is almost the opposite of this rich multiplicity. One of the central problems of art based not on description but on suggestion (Sainte-Beuve saw this in an interesting passage in the *Pensées de Joseph Delorme, XV*) is how to hold the balance between the specific and the general, between the precise and the undefined. Baudelaire sees beauty as 'quelque chose d'un peu vague, laissant carrière à la conjecture' (1195). Suggestion is smothered by over-exact description which leaves no place for the 'lacune complétée par l'imagination de l'auditeur' (1049). Yet if only the most general and undefined words are used, there will be nothing to stimulate or enrich the reader's imagination, which will remain vague and inert.

It is surprising to discover how often Baudelaire uses the most general adjectives: 'charmant', 'étrange', 'vague', 'heureux', 'singulier'. Often their position in the line or in relation to the noun they qualify makes the reader's mind pause over them and call up associations, while set among them are more specific and concrete suggestions. *La Chevelure* might be compared with *Parfum exotique;* their theme is the same, but where *La Chevelure* gives the rich sensuous elaboration, culminating in the 'senteurs confondues De l'huile de coco, du musc et du goudron', *Parfum exotique* moves slowly and dreamily through 'rivages heureux' 'charmants climats', 'arbres singuliers', with just the slight touch of the specific in the scent of the green tamarind trees.

Some of Baudelaire's finest lines fuse fiercely physical and deliberately prosaic images with undefined and abstract terms that suggest infinite prolongations of feeling, and form part of an echoing incantation. In:

> Quand le ciel bas et lourd pèse comme un
>   couvercle
> Sur l'esprit gèmissant en proie aux longs
>   ennuis . . . (146)

he moves from the precise, concrete and familiar image, with its hard consonants forcing home the compression, into the prolonged uncertainty of 'en proie aux longs ennuis'. In the lines:

> Et les vagues terreurs de ces affreuses nuits
> Qui compriment le coeur comme un papier
>   qu'on froisse (118)

the terrors are utterly undefined; the stressing and lengthening of 'vagues' and 'affreuses' through the mute *e* make the line stretch into suggestive distance; then we move into the startling image from the physical world with the heart being crushed and crumpled like a rejected sheet of paper; the sounds of 'compriment' and 'froisse' give a sharp sense of pressure and rustling, and uncertainty contracts into terror.

Constantly Baudelaire fuses abstract and concrete worlds as words from the one are strangely but aptly fitted to the other:

> Mon âme rêveuse appareille . . . (104)
> Mon esprit subtil que le roulis caresse . . .
>   (101)

He fuses also very different tones; the conversational with the eloquent, the dignified with the intimate. *Le Cygne* is one of the finest examples. It moves smoothly and reflectively from the ringing lines that call up the lovely hieratical gestures of the ancient world where Andromache weeps in exile by the river Simois to the anecdote of modern city life, the swan in the dust and

rubble among scavengers' carts at dawn and the wretched negress exiled in fog and mud. Andromache from the distant past is made part of an intimate, bare and familiar present in the direct personal simplicity of the opening: 'Andromaque, je pense à vous!', while the swan and the negress of the everyday world are given the dignity of agelong symbols of suffering, revolt and longing:

> Comme les exilés, ridicule et sublime,
> Et rongé d'un desir sans trève . . .

Most suggestive of all is the end. It has been pointed out that Baudelaire might have chosen to close with a resounding climax as the Parnassians do:

> Auprès d'un tombeau vide en extase courbée;
> Veuve d'Hector, hélas, et femme d'Hélénus!

Instead, he has moved away gradually from plastic and defined description through the curtain of mist and the echo of the distant horn, to give in the simplest words the widest and least defined sense of loss:

> A quiconque a perdu ce qui ne se retrouve
> Jamais, jamais! . . .

and then to fade deliberately and penetratingly into the distance of anonymous and forgotten sorrows:

> Je pense aux matelots oubliés dans une île,
> Aux captifs, aux vaincus! . . . à bien d'autres
>   encor!

Set in Baudelaire's rich evocations of delight or terror there constantly come lines of this piercing simplicity, the strength and bareness of the words brought out by their placing in the rhythm of the single line: in *Le Balcon:*

> Nous avons dit souvent d'impérissables
>   choses . . .

in *Femmes Damnées:*

> Et cependant je sens ma bouche aller vers
>   toi . . .

in *Le Voyage:*

> Nous nous sommes souvent ennuyés, comme
>   ici . . .

Perhaps only Racine can also give this particular suggestiveness, moving from rich dignity or violence into the sudden stab of the nakedly simple line.

Recueillement (243) gives an impression of extreme simplicity; it shows the delicacy and variety in Baudelaire's art of suggestion at its finest. Valéry has point-ed out that there are in this exquisite sonnet three lines dangerously near to the declamatory and the trite (be-ginning 'Pendant que des mortels . . .') with their awkward inversion, obvious adjectives and perhaps banal image. But in their place in the poem these lines make a burst of angry crudity between the moments of perfect tranquillity at beginning and end; they serve their purpose as a moment of contrast, and the sheer movement of the whole passes without damage across them. In the rest of the poem two very different kinds of suggestion are quietly interwoven; the familiar and intimate in the consolation offered to grief by the ev-eryday, soft, coaxing, repeated words of the child's world ('Sois sage, . . . tiens-toi plus tranquille, . . . donne-moi la main, viens par ici'); and the dignified and majestic in the half-allegorical figures who pass like shadows peopling the background of loneliness— le Soir, le Plaisir, les Années, le Soleil, le Regret, la Nuit. The sonnet evokes vast dimensions of time and space—the dimness round the town, the seething mul-titudes, the dead years of the past, the depths of the waters, the setting sun on the horizon, the slow trailing approach of night—and against these far-stretching suggestions it sets the sense of closeness and peace. Without perfect balance, the personifications could have become lofty abstractions, the childhood allusions mere sentimentality or triviality: here the solemn and the intimate have been perfectly fused. There is quiet ten-derness in the gently-moving first line and a breathless waiting in the bare words and split phrasing of the second; then comes the broadening of rhythm and background as evening falls over all mankind. Through the long subordinate clause on the crude clangour of the city the lines move quickly back to pick up again the utterly personal note in tiny phrases giving the withdrawal and the breath of relief:

> Ma douleur, donne-moi la main, viens par ici
> Loin d'eux.

Then again the vision broadens and imagination touch-es alive the friendly phantoms. There is no rich elab-oration; simply the slight detail that transforms abstract allegory into a new meaning as the dead years in dress-es of the past bend closer from high balconies, while from the depths of the waters regret slowly rises, purified and smiling, and the setting sun becomes a vagrant falling peacefully asleep under the arch of a bridge. Depth, space, air, fire and water, the elements and the architecture of a wide-stretching world are caught together in hieratical gesture and familiar inti-macy, till the child grief sees consolation and rest in terms of the familiar things of the city: lovely women on lofty balconies or an old beggar peacefully huddled asleep. In the last two lines the slow and stately evo-cation of the advance of night

> Et, comme un long linceul traînant à l'Orient,

moves into the whisper, the pause, the endearment, the hesitation, and the final flood of relief, again in the simple words of the child's world:

> Entends, ma chère, entends la douce Nuit qui
> marche.

The use of sensations to call up feelings and ideas is obviously central to Baudelaire's art of suggestion. But he is specially original in evoking sensations less eas-ily definable than those usually classified as visual, auditory, olfactory and so on: sensations related to basic muscular or nervous tensions and fundamental rhythms in the human being, which are only half-realised and rarely analysed in conscious experience, and reach obsessive force in dream and nightmare. Through them Baudelaire expresses still more strongly the basic strug-gle between delight and terror, aspiration and impo-tence.

At one extreme there is the sense of stifling: the chok-ing lungs wheeze as they draw in the vitiated city air:

> Et, quand nous respirons, la Mort dans nos
> poumons
> Descend, fleuve invisible, avec de sourdes
> plaintes (81);

or the feeling of claustrophobia and contraction as the whole world presses in crushingly:

> Quand le ciel bas et lourd pèse comme un
> couvercle . . . (146).

The opposite is the feeling of expansion, of breathing and moving freely and joyously:

> La poitrine en avant et les poumons gonflés
> Comme de la toile,
> J'escalade le dos des flots amoncelés (141).

This is pushed to the pitch of ecstatic dream in *Eléva-tion* with its rapturous soaring movement as the weight-less body floats effortlessly through outer ether, bathed in coolness, purity and liquid light.

The terror of the seeping away of man's vital sub-stance is a deeply-rooted nightmare experience. Some of Baudelaire's strongest impressions are those of sap-ping, eating away, undermining, corroding and cor-rupting, seen at their most intense in *l'Amour et le Crâne* where a grimly charming Cupid blows frail soap-bubbles from the substance of the brain, or in *La Fontaine de Sang* with its endless oozing of blood. In this set of images the world shifts into an insinuating and loathly shapelessness.

But the flux and mobility of things that have no fixed shape can be the emblem of just the opposite. Baudelaire is fascinated by the vast stretches of sea and clouds, shapeless and never still, for they suggest the countless possibilities and patterns which the imagination can form from these fluid elements, and so become the symbol not of decomposition but of creation.

The fascination of fluidity is matched by an equally strong delight in the suggestion of structure. Often Baudelaire transforms the real world by suddenly presenting the most human or the most abstract subject as a set of geometrical shapes. By doing this, he can both play on the instinctive excitement in the discovery of mathematical patterns and relationships, and achieve a particular kind of momentary aesthetic detachment in poems where intense feeling might otherwise become raw, exaggerated or sentimental. When he writes of the skeleton dressed for the ball, the grim reflections on human flesh in its *danse macabre* are both balanced and intensified by his sense of the complex and beautiful structure of the human framework in itself: 'L'élégance sans nom de l'humaine armature . . .' In **Les Sept Vieillards** the seven old men are transformed into sinister diagrams; the spine making a right angle with the legs, another with the stick, and the stiff beard adding another angle. But it is specially in **Les Petites Vieilles** that the poet deliberately cuts across pathos and grandeur as, 'méditant sur la géometrie', he works out the mathematical problem of how to shape coffins to these distorted bodies. Then, from the moment of detachment, he moves back, through analogies of shape, to a tender sense of the likenesses between old age and childhood.

Baudelaire is particularly fascinated by geometrical shapes in movement. The masts and rigging of sailing ships as they sway on the sea excite him because of

> la multiplication successive et la génération de toutes
> les courbes et figures imaginaires opérées dans
> l'espace par les éléments réels de l'objet; (1201)

they become a symbol of possibility and of creative pattern.

Probably the sensation which gives most rich and varied effects in Baudelaire's poetry is that of rocking or swaying. It may be the symbol of delight and creative dreams:

> Et mon esprit subtil que le roulis caresse
> Saura te retrouver, ô féconde paresse!
> Infinis bercements du loisir embaumé! . . .
>
> (101)

or of indolence and evil:

> Sur l'oreiller du mal c'est Satan Trismégiste
> Qui berce longuement notre esprit enchanté;
>
> (81)

it reaches the ecstatic and dream-like in the 'Valse mélancolique et langoureux vertige' of **Harmonie du Soir,** and becomes the wild tossing of nightmare at the end of **Les Sept Vieillards**.

Baudelaire's variations on a sense impression may best be seen in **Le Serpent qui danse**. The centre of the poem is the sensation of sway; sway which cannot be pinned down and defined but is a vacillation between two opposing states. This sensation is an essential part of the meaning, which sways back and forward between the supple indolent beauty and the hard coldness of the woman, between the ecstasy and the bitterness of the lover.

The rhythm gives a swaying movement of a particularly strange kind, for it combines the eight-syllabled line not with the familiar six-syllabled one, but with the odd line of five syllables, always seeming to fall short of what we expect and so suggesting an irregular and haunting fascination.

The tiniest details contribute to the impression of swaying, and the poem works in a deliberate crescendo. First Baudelaire evokes impressions of iridescence and fluidity; her skin shimmers like shot silk, calling up the sway between light and shade and the wavering materials as she moves. The scent of her hair sets his dreams sailing on a rocking sea, and suggests both beauty and bitterness by its 'âcres parfums'. Her eyes shimmer with the contradictory suggestions of gold and iron, treasure and harshness. She has the cold, supple attraction of the serpent swaying on the end of a rod; from the tiny shimmer of the start the images have taken on a broader and broader movement, and now the associations of sway with a lazy and fascinating animal beauty reach their climax in the slow dignity of

> Sous le fardeau de ta paresse
>   Ta tête d'enfant
> Se balance avec la mollesse
>   D'un jeune éléphant . . .

The end of the poem shows how rapidly and subtly Baudelaire moves from one image to another through unexpressed sensuous analogies. As he kisses the woman, 'l'eau de ta bouche' becomes a bitter magic wine, then turns without transition to a liquid sky in which is strewn a burst of stars. Behind the shift in images lies the unexpressed analogy: the stars strew the firmament like tiny bubbles rising and sparkling in wine, and both the sparkle of wine and the burst of stars are like the sudden surge of physical pleasure at the touch of her mouth.

To seize the unexpressed details that link images in this way often adds to the sharpness of their impact. This is particularly so in the terrifying poem **L'Horloge,** with its theme of time sucking away strength. Baudelaire is looking at the hand of a clock; it first suggests a pointed finger threatening. He shifts without transition to the darts of pain quivering in the target of the human heart; the pointed clock-hand has called up the shape of the dart. Then comes the horrible whispering voice of the ticking seconds; tiny and insect-like, it combines with the dart-shapes to suggest the job of a loathsome mosquito, sucking the life-blood through its sharp proboscis. The associations with draining away then lead on to the image of the sand-glass, its tiny relentless particles trickling time away as pitilessly as the tick of the seconds or the pricking and sucking of the minute insect that drains the life-blood.

Baudelaire's notes for a Preface to the *Fleurs du Mal* saw versification as vital among the means of suggestion (1383). It is impossible here to analyse in detail his views on how it is intimately connected both with what is most abstract and what is most sensuous in man's experience, or to do more than indicate in the barest way the suppleness with which he uses the traditional verse forms that are his steady rhythmical groundwork. A catalogue of different forms is useless unless the reader can feel how each detail of sound enhances the sense. This is not a dry technical question, nor music for the sake of music; always sound and pattern are part of the essential meaning.

Some of the best-known poems create an obsession through the use of refrain with its incantatory echo, whether lulling and lovely or with the beat of implacable despair. Litanesque rhythms and repetitions, with all their associations of dignity and ritual, intensify the compulsive force and strangeness of feelings often very far from the orthodoxly religious.

The alexandrine is naturally the most frequent line; Baudelaire gives it particular richness or lightness through subtle, not over-obvious alliteration, assonance, onomatopoeia and especially the placing of the mute *e*, but he leaves its basic rhythm strong, clear, dignified and serious; his sentences may be complex and flow with firm construction over several lines, but it is only rarely that there is *enjambement* for conversational tone (parts of *Le Cygne*) or dislocation of the main regular beat (the displacement of the caesura to underline the desperation of sacrilege in 'Criant à Dieu dans sa furibonde agonie,' in *Le Voyage*).

The eight-syllable line, with its lapidary effect, can give a particular concentration to the tone of worship (*A la très-chère; Tout entière*) or to biting despair and hatred (*Le Vampire, L'Irrémédiable*). Alexandrines interwoven with shorter lines are used in many ways to suggest fluctuating and indefinable sensations (*Le Poison, L'Irréparable, La Musique*); often the fall from the alexandrine into the shorter line can intensify the feeling of disillusion or bitterness. And from the mingling of different shorter lines Baudelaire creates some

of his finest poems. We have seen the evocative metre of *Le Serpent qui danse;* but the poem that comes particularly to mind is *L'Invitation au Voyage,* where an even more haunting effect comes from the use of the odd number of syllables, this time in lines of five and seven, with the recurring movement from anticipation into peace as the short line is resolved into the longer:

> Mon enfant, ma soeur,
> Songe à la douceur
> D'aller là-bas vivre ensemble . . .

Neither rhymes nor rhythms, alliterations nor assonances call attention blatantly to any startling novelty. Baudelaire saw verse as appealing to 'cet amour contradictoire et mystérieux de l'esprit humain pour la surprise et la symétrie'. He does not dislocate traditional forms but works his own variations within them. Always it is the combined effect of sound and sense, of music and meaning that counts, in opening lines that slowly unfold long vistas:

> Je suis comme le roi d'un pays pluvieux . . .
> (146)

in echoing refrains:

> Mais le vert paradis des amours enfantines . . .
> (137)

in heavy assonances with all the weight of weariness:

> *Tant* l'écheveau du *temps lentement* se dévide
> (107)

or in biting lines that stand out in bare simplicity:

> De n'avoir pas connu ce que pleurent les
> morts (109).

In his notes for a preface, Baudelaire is deliberately uncompromising in his conviction that great poetry depends on unremitting effort and that every detail has behind it 'les retouches, les variantes, les épreuves barbouillées' (1382). The reader who is interested in the stages of creating a poem might set side by side the first and the final version of *La Mort des Artistes,* a poem on this very subject, to see how the poet changes images that are vague and lofty, and expression verging on the flat and trite, to find a new way of conveying repeated and subtle effort, combined with self-mockery, in the sharpest and most suggestive terms.

But to see how the slightest detail counts, one need only look at two tiny alterations in one stanza of *Un Voyage à Cythère* (188). It now reads:

> Ridicule pendu, tes douleurs sont les miennes!
> Je sentis, à l'aspect de tes membres flottants,

Comme un vomissement, remonter vers mes
  dents
Le long fleuve de fiel des douleurs anciennes.

Originally Baudelaire had written:

Pauvre pendu muet, tes douleurs sont les
  miennes.

'Pauvre' was too near to sentimental self-pity, and
'muet' was unnecessary; with 'ridicule', in the place of
strength before the noun, Baudelaire calls up what is
grotesque, out of place and loathsome in the spectacle,
and still applies it as an emblem to himself, intensify-
ing the struggle between disgust and pity for suffering.
The last line originally read:

Le long fleuve de fiel de mes douleurs
  anciennes.

The change is minute, but in the first reading
'an/ciennes' made only two syllables; by changing
'de mes' into 'des' Baudelaire has been able both to
make the grief more general and through the lengthened
'an/ci/ennes' to suggest ancient and prolonged suffering.

Camille Paglia (essay date 1990)

SOURCE: "Gautier, Baudelaire, and Huysmans," in
*Sexual Personae: Art and Decadence from Nefertiti to
Emily Dickinson,* Yale University Press, 1990, pp. 421-
30.

[*In the following excerpt, Paglia analyzes the role of
sexuality in general and women in particular in* Les
Fleurs du Mal.]

Baudelaire's *Flowers of Evil* (1857) is dedicated to his
"master," Gautier. Baudelaire translated Poe and hailed
him as his second self. Poe's spiritual father was the
Coleridge of the mystery poems. Thus Coleridge, coming through Poe to Baudelaire, daemonizes Gautier,
with his Byronic breeziness. Baudelaire's new Decadent tone is haughty and hieratic. His poems are ritualistic confrontations with the horror of sex and nature,
which he analyzes with Sade's cutting rhetoric. The
chthonian is his epic theme.

Baudelaire grants mother nature neither Rousseau's
benevolence nor Sade's vitality. Poe's Coleridgean
nature is hostile but still sublime, a vast swirling seascape. But Baudelaire is a city poet for whom there
are no more adventures. He adopts Cleopatra's Late
Romantic fatigue. Baudelaire makes ennui hip, an
avant-garde pose. Ennui certifies the sophisticate's
excess of experience: one has seen and done everything. Unlike Poe, Baudelaire invents no secondary

male personae for himself. His subject is the self as
artificial enclave, like the citadel of Poe's *Masque of
the Red Death,* which nature secretly enters and disorders. Baudelaire is the first poet of mental and
physical disease.

For Baudelaire, sex is limitation, not liberation. Desire, normally a spur to masculine action, makes the
male passive toward his mother-born body. He is betrayed by the body, delivered into female hands through
sexual weakness. Nature's power is wielded by pitiless
vampires, the most numerous personae of Baudelaire's
poetry. As in Poe, woman is always superior. Poe likes
to dream of domestic bliss with a mother-bride. But
Baudelaire's women are rigid and uncompanionable.
In his one maternal scene, **"The Giantess,"** he lives
with a primeval titaness at "her terrible games." He
climbs her "enormous knees" and, "like a quiet hamlet," sleeps "in the shadow of her breasts." The female
body is curvy geography, as in the Venus of Willen-
dorf. Sexual connection is patently out of the question,
for the male is no bigger than a trained flea. The play-
ful, sunny tone, uncharacteristic for Baudelaire's erot-
ica, is possible because the scene is archaic rather than
modern—like Salisbury Plain, which prompted Wordsworth to make a similar sexual exception for his pre-
historic warrior.

Baudelaire's women are intimidating. The "impure
woman" is a "blind and deaf machine, fertile in cruelties," "drinker of the blood of the world." Beauty is
"a sphinx" against whose stone breast every man
bruises himself; she has a "heart of snow" and never
weeps or laughs. She is a "monster enormous, frightful." The sphinx Jeanne Duval, Baudelaire's obsession, is like "the bleak sand and blue sky of deserts,
insensible to human suffering." She is nothing but
"gold, steel, light and diamonds." With "the cold
majesty of the sterile woman," she shines "like a
useless star." Duval has a "beautiful body polished
like copper." She is a glistening serpent with eyes
like "two cold jewels in which gold mingles with iron."
She is a "beast implacable and cruel"; her cold cat
gaze "cuts and splits like a dart." She is an "inhuman
Amazon," a "great angel of the bronze brow," a
"charming poniard" leaping from its sheath. Marie
Daubrun, another of the poet's favorites, is a ship
with jutting prow. Her breasts are shields "armed with
rose points." Her mascular arms, like those of infant
Hercules, are "the solid rivals of glossy boa constric-
tors," made to squeeze her lover and imprint him on
her heart. The apocalyptic whore of **"The Metamorphoses of the Vampire"** brazenly boasts, "I replace,
for him who sees me nude and without veils, the moon,
the sun, the sky and the stars!" Sucking the marrow
from her victim's bones, she turns into a bag of pus
and a rattling skeleton screeching in his bed. The
vampire is ever-changing mother nature, whose embrace is rape and ecstasy, death and decay.

Baudelaire's daemonic females renounce Rousseau's tenderness. They have a Sadean sterility, divorcing the chthonian from fecundity. They are inorganic monoliths of steel and stone, their only living associations feline or reptilian. Their mineral hardness comes from their barren habitat, an urban wasteland of "metal, marble, and water" petrifying the flesh (**"Parisian Dream"**). Like Blake's Harlot, they are city-goddesses of polluted terrain. Gautier says of Baudelaire's mythic women, "To none can a name be given. They are types rather than persons." Impersonality always masculinizes a woman. Baudelaire's female personae are hermaphroditic because of their blank indifference to the human. Sterility and emotional torpidity in a heavy-breasted woman constitute my category of androgyne as virago. Baudelaire's viragos resemble Michelangelo's in the Mannerist Medici Chapel, a parallel the poet notes (**"The Ideal"**). Baudelaire is uninterested in boy-girls or transvestites. His androgynes must be voluptuously female in body contour. In women he seeks only hierarchic assertion. They have no other use for him, since they are stripped of their sexual and procreative functions.

What of the male who inhabits this woman-ravaged universe? We meet him in **"A Voyage to Cythera,"** for me one of the poems of the century. A ship is in full sail. The poet's heart flies joyfully round the rigging like a bird in the cloudless sky. Suddenly a black stony island appears—Cythera, once-happy birthplace of Venus. On a three-branched gallows hangs the poet's image, a corpse ravaged by birds, who peck out the eyes and eat the genitals. A prowling pack of wolves wait for the leavings. Cythera is the world of sexual experience, into which the poet presses toward a horrifying revelation. Structurally, the poem echoes Poe's *Masque of the Red Death,* with its climactic phantom in a bloody burial shroud. Baudelaire represents Decadent closure in entirely perceptual terms. The poem opens in space and fresh, free motion, then shuts down to a solitary image, the poet's double, upon whom the eye obsessively fixes. Nature dwindles to the contracted self.

"A Voyage to Cythera" moves from innocence to experience and from High to Late Romanticism. Its first illusion is about nature, which seems benign. The poet, misled by Rousseau, thinks of green myrtle and blooming flowers. But nature's reality is Sadean, red in tooth and claw. Odysseus, tied to the mast, sees piles of moldering skeletons littering the island of the Sirens. Baudelaire's lustful priestess, wandering a temple grove, belongs to the pagan era, which integrated sex with religion. Christianity, on the other hand, afflicts humanity with chronic guilt. The gallows is the crucifix, desolating the sexual world. It is also the tree of nature, a black cypress against the sky. Man is crucified upon his own body. Nature is a Decadent tree loaded with rotten fruit, a

"ripe" corpse bursting its skin and dribbling foul matter.

Baudelaire's double is an androgyne, the male heroine, a Romantic martyr. The passive male is attacked by drill-beaked birds, lacerating sexual desires. Venus' doves turn Harpy. The victim is castrated and his body reshaped in parodic femaleness: his eyes are holes, and his belly spills out its bowels. Like Poe's Morella, he gives birth to a lesser version of himself at the moment of death. The rotten sausage of his hanging intestines mocks his vanished genitals. Vital organs are ransacked because the human body is a house divided against itself, undone by physical needs. Nature coerces man into sexual activity, then punishes him with syphilis, venereal because the gift of Venus. "To make a voyage to Cythera" was French slang for sexual intercourse. Baudelaire, inspired by Nerval, may be sardonically revising Watteau's exuberant painting, *Embarkation for Cythera* (1717). He says in another poem, "I am the wound and the knife!" He is simultaneously female masochist and male sadist, in agonizing psychic coitus, a Decadent self-abuse. In **"A Voyage to Cythera,"** the overexpanded High Romantic self is firmly dealt with by a public ritual of Late Romantic enslavement.

The passivity of all humanity toward rapacious nature is brilliantly dramatized in **"A Carcass."** Strolling one summer morning, the poet and his beloved stumble on an animal carcass: "Legs in the air, like a lewd woman,/Burning and oozing poisons," it opens its putrid belly to the sky. "The sun was shining on that rottenness,/In order to cook it to a turn,/And to render a hundredfold to great Nature / All that she had joined together." The carcass "bloomed like a flower," its perfume an overpowering stench. Flies buzz, and maggots rise and fall like a sparkling wave. The carcass gives out "a strange music," like water and wind or grain in the winnower's basket. Its form is dreamily wavering and dissolving. A hungry female dog skulks, furious at the interruption. The poet tenderly informs his beloved, "You will be like that filth, that horrible infection, star of my eyes!" When she mildews among the bones, vermin like his "decomposed loves" will devour her with kisses. Decadent romance, sweet and sour.

"A Voyage to Cythera" is a portrait of the artist as ritual victim where the poet confronts his physically degenerated double, as Dorian Gray is to do with his corroded portrait. In **"A Carcass,"** Baudelaire forces his beloved to confront her own double, a putrefying animal carcass, which omnipotent nature exploits to feed her microbes, parasites, and beasts. The poem is a kind of *déjeuner sur l'herbe*: nature is dining at home! The animal's gender and identity and even its integrity as an object are receding. It is being reduced to primary materials, much as Sade's victims are rent and abraded into subhuman particles. The teeming maggots are a prophetic vision of inanimate nature-process or matter in molecular wave-motion. Baudelaire's "strange music" is also heard in Melville's *Moby-Dick,* where a tropical grove hums like the loom of vegetable nature.

Nature's dichotomy of sunniness and cannibalism is mirrored in the poem's polished classic form and gross content, beauty and repulsiveness joined. Baudelaire ironically brings love poetry's exalted endearments to bear upon nature's brute physicality, to which they are hopelessly unsuited. **"A Carcass"** is in the *carpe diem* tradition: Renaissance poems also dwell on the future death and decay of a too-virginal beloved. But note Baudelaire's Late Romantic innovation: he no longer uses mortality as an argument to extort sexual favors, for the Decadence always swerves from sexual experience. Intercourse is far from his thoughts. In fact, if there is any eroticism in the poem—and he ostentatiously introduces it by comparing the carcass to a spread-eagled whore—it arises from his imagining the female body undergoing future Decadent disintegration. In Decadent beauty, I said, part triumphs over whole. In **"A Carcass,"** embryogeny is reversed. Death, forcing the beloved to imitate the animal's deconstruction, will make her surrender gender, identity, and coherence. It is this primitive spectacle of degeneration that arouses the poet—an a priori necrophilia. The proud beloved will be raped by dominatrix mother nature, the jealous fanged bitch waiting in the shadows.

So woman in Baudelaire is unsexed by being a vampire, a corpse, or, as we shall now see, a lesbian. The first title of **Flowers of Evil,** advertised by the publisher in 1846, was **The Lesbians.** Martin Turnell says [in *Baudelaire,* 1954], "Baudelaire's interest in Lesbianism is something of a mystery and no one has yet accounted satisfactorily for the prominence given to it in his poetry." Proust, according to Gide, thought the theme proved Baudelaire's homosexuality. I doubt this, for Baudelaire rarely savors male beauty. The solution to the mystery is my principle of sexual metathesis, an artistic sex-change.

Most lavish of the lesbian poems is **"Damned Women: Delphine and Hippolyte."** In a dim curtained chamber, young Hippolyte lies weeping on perfumed cushions. Delphine, like a tigress, gloats at her feet. Their first sex together has just occurred. Women's kisses, says Delphine, are light and delicate, while men are heavy-hooved oxen, making ruts in women's bodies with their wagons or "lacerating plowshares." Yokels and lummoxes! Hippolyte appreciates Delphine's erotic tutelage (like Sade's Eugénie with Madame de Saint-Ange) but feels anxious and dyspeptic, as if she has eaten too rich a night meal. Black phantoms rush at her, leading her along roads closed by "a bloody horizon." Have they sinned? "But I feel my mouth

move toward you," the magnetism of Romantic compulsion. Shaking her mane of hair, Delphine goes into a snit and curses the stupid "useless dreamer" who first mixed morality with love. Hippolyte, drained, longs for annihilation in Delphine's bosom. The poet's doleful voice suddenly intervenes: "Descend, descend, lamentable victims, descend the road of eternal hell!" The lesbians will burn forever in their insatiable passion. They will wander the desert as scorched exiles of cities of the plain, fleeing the infinity in their souls.

Baudelaire owes this long, impressive poem to Balzac. Delphine and Hippolyte are the Marquise de San-Real and Paquita Valdes, and we are in the boudoir of *The Girl with the Golden Eyes.* The psychodrama is identical: a fiery sexual aggressor imprisons a fragile innocent in an opulent, claustrophobic retreat. Balzac never nears the moment of lesbian union, which only appears once removed in De Marsay's transvestite rendezvous. In "Delphine and Hippolyte," however, we ourselves are so close to the characters *post coitum* that our invisible presence inflames the already oppressive atmosphere. The palpable voyeurism of poet and reader comes from Gautier's *Mademoiselle de Maupin.* Hippolyte's "bloody horizon," opening her sexually but sealing up earthly space, is from Gautier's *A Night with Cleopatra.* Baudelaire recasts the sexual realm in entirely female terms. Woman is self-entombed in a perverse cell of sexual solipsism. Delphine repeats Maupin's aesthetic judgments: women are erotically refined, while men are clumsy brutes.

Lesbianism is a breach in procreative nature, which Baudelaire is always eager to insult. The lesbian is therefore another sterile woman, like his metallic city-vampires. Baudelaire thinks homosexuality, as an unnatural practice, can never be fully satisfied. It is a noble pursuit of "the impossible" that attracts Gautier. In a shorter poem also called **"Damned Women,"** Baudelaire hails lesbians, of "unquenched thirsts," as "Virgins, demons, monsters, martyrs, / Great spirits contemptuous of reality, / Seekers of the infinite." Lesbians are great because they defy society, religion, and nature. Baudelaire's celebration of lesbianism must not be mistaken for sexual libertarianism. He would not picket for gay rights. Walter Benjamin remarks, "To him, social ostracism was inseparable from the heroic nature of this passion." Hence the huge metaphysical background of the climax of **"Delphine and Hippolyte."** The poem cinematically opens the boudoir's languid, upholstered intimacy into a vast wasteland, the moral geography of lesbianism. Like Dante, Baudelaire sees the damned buffeted by winds and flames of desire.

In this poem a sex act is destiny, just as it is fraternal identity in *The Girl with the Golden Eyes.* Baudelaire's two women have Greek names and may even be citizens of Lesbos, but the poem's world-view is Christian. Hippolyte is overcome by guilt, and Delphine denounces Jesus (the "useless dreamer") for worsening the "insoluble problem" of sex. Christianity may be the antagonist, but it is also Christianity that gives lesbianism its moral or rather immoral stature. Baudelaire says, "The supreme voluptuous delight of love lies in the certainty of doing *evil*." Like Sade, he needs the fixities of organized religion to give his outrages an ethical significance and therefore erotic charge. He constantly seeks, as Colin Wilson notes, the gratuitous violation of taboo. The original shock of **"Delphine and Hippolyte"** is largely lost to our more tolerant time. Today, nothing sexual can appear quite so evil, unless amplified by violence. Sexuality, by winning the war with religion, has been diminished in scale.

"Delphine and Hippolyte" is highly unusual for Baudelaire in having an entirely feminine woman, victim of lesbian seduction. Who is Hippolyte? I say she is Baudelaire himself, who has, by the same daring warp of imaginative gender we saw in Coleridge's *Christabel,* identified himself with the passive partner of a lesbian couple. Baudelaire, as always, is hierarchically subordinate to his ferocious vampire. I found images elsewhere in Coleridge confirming his projection into his heroine's trauma. There is a parallel between **"Delphine and Hippolyte"** and **"A Voyage to Cythera."** Hippolyte, like the poet's hanged double, is attacked by swooping black creatures, phantoms in one poem and crows in the other. Baudelaire gives Jeanne Duval, "bizarre deity," the name of a notorious Roman lesbian: "I am not able, libertine Megaera, to break your courage and keep you at bay, to become Proserpine in the hell of your bed!" (**"Sed non satiata"**). Baudelaire regrets he cannot do in real life what he elegantly achieves in **"Delphine and Hippolyte"**: to turn himself into a woman to seize the attention of a lesbian dominatrix. If he is the maiden Persephone, Duval is the raptor Pluto, god of the underworld, here a whore's rank crowded bed. In the shorter **"Damned Women,"** the obsessed lesbians are the poet's "poor sisters." Elsewhere he calls the "hypocrite reader" his "double" and "brother." So Baudelaire's lesbian sisters are also his doubles. The title *The Lesbians* was self-characterizing. Orpheus' head, torn off by Maenads, floated to Lesbos from Thrace: Orphic, woman-persecuted Baudelaire is a lesbian both as poet and sexual persona. The premiere lesbian poet was an androgyne: Baudelaire, echoing Horace, calls her "the male Sappho, the lover and the poet" (**"Lesbos"**). She is male not only because she desires women like a man but because she is "*le* poète."

Baudelaire's lesbian poems are complex psychic mechanisms. First, the lesbian aggressor usurps the male privilege of defloration. Second, the poet's gender change intensifies the erotic passivity of his usual subjection to women. Third, women sexually occu-

pied with each other automatically suspend masculine obligation. Man enjoys sexual amnesty from humiliating fears of impotence. Fourth, a lesbian's erotic life is a locked room which man cannot penetrate. Thus lesbianism preserves the mystery of the Great Mother for a poet who finds nature's processes otiose. By becoming a lesbian, the poet wins momentary right of entry into a sexual heart of darkness. Fifth, lesbian self-sterilization thwarts the relentless fertility of nature, for Baudelaire just a mass of "sanctified vegetables" that cannot move him. Hence the increasing frequency of lesbianism, which the poet eagerly records, signals nature's degeneration or apocalyptic decadence.

The sex poems of *Flowers of Evil* caused a scandal, and the book's proofs were seized. Baudelaire and his publisher were tried and fined. Six poems, declared an "offense against morality and decency," were condemned and censored, an official ban not revoked until 1949. These included **"Delphine and Hippolyte," "Lesbos,"** and **"The Metamorphoses of the Vampire."** **"Delphine and Hippolyte"** had diverse progeny during the next decade. Courbet's *The Sleepers* (1866) is surely indebted to Baudelaire and Balzac. Two women, blonde and brunette, lie nude and sensuously intertwined, broken pearls and hair comb cast about the mussed bed as erotic evidence of haste and tumult. The background is a heavy drape of dark blue velvet, ominous cloud of a Baudelairean night sky. Two poetic redramatizations of **"Delphine and Hippolyte"**: Swinburne's *Anactoria* in *Poems and Ballads* (1866) and Verlaine's *The Girlfriends: Scenes of Sapphic Love* (1867). The self-projections of both these poets were demonstrably masochistic. Proust's theory that Baudelaire's lesbian themes prove homosexuality would better fit the openly homosexual Verlaine. Proust, like everyone else, overlooks lesbianism's symbolic meaning in nineteenth-century nature-theory. He has in fact transferred to Baudelaire his own homosexual use of sexual metathesis in *Remembrance of Things Past*: the secret transformation of bewitching Alfred Agostinelli into the lesbian Albertine is a virtuoso act of Late Romantic imagination. Albertine, a mysterious prisoner of love descending from the girl with the golden eyes, did not slip into her new gender without arousing the skepticism of knowledgeable Parisians.

Baudelaire's prose contains a theory of the ideal male persona. *The Painter of Modern Life* (1863) makes the dandy the epitome of personal style. Baudelaire is partly drawing on Barbey d'Aurevilly's essay on dandyism (1845), which descends from Castiglione. Baudelaire calls dandyism a Romantic "cult of the self" arising from "the burning need" to create "a personal originality." High Romantic politics were populist and democratic, but Late Romantic ones are reactionary. Dandyism is "a new kind of aristocracy," a "haughty and exclusive" sect resisting "the rising tide of democracy, which invades and levels everything." Late Romanticism is arrogantly elitist, a point that must be remembered for Oscar Wilde, whose political views have been sentimentalized by modern admirers. Baudelaire loathes the new mass culture, which he identifies with mediocrity. He equally rejects reformers and do-gooders. Gautier says [in *Art and Criticism*], "Baudelaire abhorred philanthropists, progressists, utilitarians, humanitarians, utopists." In other words, Baudelaire condemned Rousseauism in all its forms. Today, Rousseauism has so triumphed that the arts and the avant-garde are synonymous with liberalism, an error reinforced by literature teachers, with their humanist bias. I follow the Decadents in trying to drive Rousseauist benevolence out of discourse on art and nature. The Decadents satirized the liberal faith in progress with sizzling prophecies of catastrophe and cultural collapse.

Baudelaire's dandy is an Apollonian androgyne, drawing a sharp line between himself and reality. The dandy, with "aristocratic superiority of mind," aims for "*distinction* above all things." Distinction is aboveness and apartness. The dandy's vocation is elegance, incarnating the Platonic "idea of beauty" in his own person. He is an artificial personality. The self, sculpted by imperious Apollonian contour, has become an object or objet d'art. In Late Romanticism, the expansive High Romantic self, ecstatically open to nature like Shelley with the West Wind, undergoes hieratic sequestration. Baudelaire was the first artist to live as an aesthete, putting into practice what Poe only imagined. Sartre says [in *Baudelaire,* trans. M. Turnell, 1950] Baudelaire turned the English dandy's virile athleticism into "feminine coquettishness." But Barbey already calls dandies "the Androgynes of History," belonging to "an indecisive intellectual sex," combining grace with power. There was nothing athletic in the languid Baudelaire, who had, says Gautier, a neck of "feminine elegance and whiteness." Gautier calls him a cat, that favorite animal of aesthetes and Decadents. The cat too is a dandy, cold, elegant, and narcissistic, importing hierarchic Egyptian style into modern life.

In Greek and Renaissance art, the Apollonian androgyne represented social order and public values. But Baudelaire's Apollonian dandy represents art divorced from society. No laws are recognized except aesthetic ones. Late Romantic personality is debilitated by its own absolutism. After Baudelaire's generation comes a sexual persona I call the depraved Decadent aesthete, like the court hermaphrodite repellent for its narrow egotism. Baudelaire's languor, the fatigue of one cut off from nature, remains with the aesthete to the fin de siècle. We see it in Wilde's Lord Henry Wotton, with his opium-tainted cigarettes. But Wotton, robustly English, is immune to the occupational

disease of the depraved aesthete, a neurasthenic sickliness covered by ghastly cosmetics. Examples are Huysmans' Des Esseintes, Mann's Aschenbach, and Proust's Charlus. In real life there were the Satanist Aleister Crowley and Count Robert de Montesquiou, model for Des Esseintes and Charlus. In our century, an international class of aging male homosexual conforms to this type, with epicene manners and aesthetic pretensions. The voice is waspish, the figure thin and fluttery; the pallid, puffy face seems boneless, like that of Miss Havisham, Dickens' rouged crone. Homosexual fashion has passed the type by in America, but he still flourishes in Latin countries. The dilettante aesthete is a decayed Apollonian androgyne.

Another chapter of *The Painter of Modern Life* considers the female persona, for whom Baudelaire espouses extremism in cosmetics. In an inimitably French locution, he scornfully dismisses the idea that rouge should be used sparingly to enhance nature: "Who would dare to assign to art the sterile function of imitating Nature?" Rousseau and Wordsworth shrink into their foxhole. Cosmetics are pure artifice, meant to hide nature's insulting blemishes and to create "an abstract unity in the color and texture of the skin." The face is a mask, a canvas on which to paint. Cosmetics must seem unnatural, theatrical. Woman is "an idol," obliged to appear "magical and supernatural." All fashion is "a sublime deformation of nature." Actress Stéphane Audran in *Les Biches* is for me the most stunning exemplar of Baudelairean cosmetics. As usual, Baudelaire makes woman into an *objet de culte* with a hard, metallic surface. To emphasize woman's surface is to deny her internal space, her murky womb-world. The heavily rouged woman—in the nineteenth century a whore (*Gone with the Wind*'s hot-pink Belle Watling)—is another symbol of Baudelairean sterility.

Elsewhere Baudelaire says: "Woman is the opposite of the dandy. Therefore she must inspire horror. . . . Woman is *natural,* that is to say abominable." Why horror?—an oddly intense word in the context of the dandy. The answer is that the mineral flesh of Baudelaire's vampires restricts and confines nature's chthonian liquidity. Woman is the dandy's opposite because she lacks spiritual contour and inhabits the procreative realm of fluids where objects dissolve. All art, as a cult of the autonomous object, is a flight from liquidity. The Decadent swerve from sexual experience is identical with the Decadent creation of a world of glittering art objects. Both are responses to the horror of the female liquid realm. The Baudelairean woman is mentally and physically impenetrable. The hideous bag of pus of **"Metamorphoses of the Vampire"** hardens to stone, into which the poet cannot be sucked. Baudelaire's pagan poems seal up female internality, the maw of rapacious nature.

William Chapman Sharpe (essay date 1990)

SOURCE: "Poet as *Passant:* Baudelaire's 'Holy Prostitution,'" in *Unreal Cities: Urban Figuration in Wordsworth, Baudelaire, Whitman, Eliot, and Williams,* Johns Hopkins University Press, 1990, pp. 39-56.

[*In the following chapter from a longer work, Sharpe examines how the "Parisian Sketches" section of* Les Fleurs du Mal *transforms the urban experience into a metaphor for the poetic process.*]

Although Blake and Wordsworth begin the poetic exploration of the apocalyptic modern metropolis, the unreal city of the nineteenth century finds its laureate in Baudelaire. Baudelaire's poetry is revolutionary because it insists on the motley splendor of the entire city and all its inhabitants, no matter how bizarre, perverse, or degraded. Baudelaire dedicates himself to creating a new, comprehensive urban aesthetic that can take in "tous les hôpitaux et . . . tous les palais." Previously, only Blake had consistently seen the city as a vast, interlocking system of social forces that possessed both a moral and a symbolic dimension burning luminously behind the details of mundane urban existence. Yet if Blake revealed how "mind-forg'd manacles" shackle the lives of representative citizens (the Sweeper, the Soldier, the Harlot), Baudelaire managed to particularize the archetypal urban situation of the wandering poet into something more personal, more intensely threatening, and at the same time more typical of the city as we know it today. The element which he brought to the fore—or which he could not repress—was the crowd. Combining Wordsworth's sense of imperiled consciousness at Bartholomew Fair with Blake's visionary understanding of the city as an imaginative structure, Baudelaire elevates the poet's disorienting encounter with the stranger in the crowd to a primal moment of modern literature.

In 1846, as a young art critic, Baudelaire had declared that the "heroism of modern life" consisted to a large degree in "the spectacle of elegant life and of the thousands of floating existences which circulate in the underworld of a great city." If we would only look about us, he insisted, we would discover that "Parisian life is rich in poetic and wondrous subjects. The marvelous envelops us and saturates us like the atmosphere, but we do not see it." This insight sparked Baudelaire's lifelong effort to transform the artistic potential of the city into poetic reality, an effort which culminated in his creation of the *Tableaux parisiens* section of the 1861 edition of *Les Fleurs du mal*. The poems assembled there announced the poet's determination to fling himself into urban experience, and to record unflinchingly the sublime terrors and pleasures known only to the man of the crowd.

With the exception of **"Le Soleil"** and **"A une mendiante rousse,"** which had appeared in the 1857 edition, Baudelaire wrote an entirely new set of poems for the first half of *Tableaux parisiens*. From **"Paysage"** to **"Le Squelette laboureur,"** they are largely poems in which the encounter of the poet with strangers in the street plays a central role. In particular, the series made up of **"Les Sept Vieillards,"** **"Les Petites Vieilles,"** **"Les Aveugles,"** and **"A une passante"** constitutes the climax of Baudelaire's confrontation with the disintegratory forces of urban life. In the ever-moving crowd, the poet who would objectify others is himself made the object of attention; seeking to fix the passer-by or *passant(e)* with his gaze, he becomes the *passant* whom they assail.

As the poet's sense of identity crumbles, the landscape of the *Tableaux parisiens* inexorably enfolds him in the unreality of its hallucinatory scenes. Paris becomes a phantasmal site where city, street, and text begin to merge, where in the sudden meeting with the unknown Other, heaven and hell, sexuality and textuality combine in the figure of the passing woman. For Baudelaire "holy prostitution" becomes an image of his art and of the sexual ecstasy of merging with the crowd. Attempting to embrace rather than flee the charms of the Babylonian Harlot, the poet pursues, "across the chaos of living cities," the mobile image of unfulfilled desire. He seeks to possess in poetry that which the deafening street promises, frustrates, and snatches away.

CITY FULL OF DREAMS

The title *Tableaux parisiens* suggests that the poet aims to step back and arrest the incessant motion of the city, to capture its special qualities in a series of sketches which, like a painter's canvas or *tableaux vivants,* will artistically freeze the life of Paris. Baudelaire does in fact begin *Tableaux parisiens* with an effort to take imaginative control of the urban tumult. By avoiding direct contact with the city streets where unsettling encounters take place, the ironically entitled **"Paysage"** asserts the poet's ability to depict the contours of the town with impunity. The poet, dreamily gazing from his attic window over the smoky roofs of Paris, paints an urban landscape whose remoteness from him is among its chief attractions:

> Les deux mains au menton, du haut de ma
>   mansarde,
> Je verrai l'atelier qui chante et qui bavarde;
> Les tuyaux, les clochers, ces mâts de la cité,
> Et les grands ciels qui font rêver d'éternité.

> [Chin in hands, from the height of my mansard window I will see the workshop full of singing and chatter, the chimneys, the clock towers, those masts

of the city, and the great skies that make one dream of eternity.]

Here, the poet says, he will be insulated from the riot ("**L'Emeute**") of the city below, which will vainly beat, like rain, at his window.

The future tense identifies this as a landscape of desire, born of the need to escape or remake the disorder of the actual city. But although the poet speaks of "composing eclogues" in his garret, **"Paysage"** rejects the Wordsworthian belief in the countryside as the source of true happiness, moving instead directly from the distant city to a psychologically induced pastoral vision. In the concluding lines, the poet closes himself in his room during winter and there creates "le Printemps avec ma volonté" ["Springtime with my willpower"]. As he converts his burning thoughts into balmy weather ("de faire / De mes pensers brûlants une tiède atmosphère"), he enjoys an inner life that mocks and transcends the outside world with its natural seasons. The imagined city is preferable to the "real" one. As Baudelaire remarks in the *Salon de 1846,* "The first business of an artist is to substitute man for nature, and to protest against her" ([*Oeuvres Complètes,* ed. Claude Pichois, 1975-76], II: 473).

In **"Paysage"** the poet can order urban experience through imaginative and physical detachment, but it is the strategy of an earlier era, belonging to the original *tableau de Paris* and useless at close quarters in the turbulence of the crowd. As the second poem of *Tableaux parisiens,* **"Le Soleil,"** shows, creating the poetry of the modern city is a struggle to be fought in the streets, not with out-moded eclogues, but with stones from the thoroughfares themselves. Blake's "London" turns on the metaphor of walking as marking or writing; in **"Le Soleil"** Baudelaire makes the correspondence literal. When he passes through shabby neighborhoods, he says,

> Je vais m'exercer seul à ma fantasque escrime,
> Flairant dans tous les coins les hasards de la
>   rime,
> Trébuchant sur les mots comme sur les pavés,
> Heurtant parfois des vers depuis longtemps
>   rêvés.
>
> [I go practicing my bizarre fencing alone, scenting chance rhymes in every corner, stumbling over words like paving stones, striking sometimes long-dreamt-of verses.]

To pace the city, **"Le Soleil"** shows, is to become an active—and embattled—sign maker. As the semiologist Michel de Certeau observes, "The act of walking is to the urban system what the act of speaking . . . is to language." The poet's walking becomes a form of writing, forcibly hewing text out of the raw materials

of the city, "Heurtant parfois des vers depuis longtemps rêvés." Tracing a history and inscribing a self upon the streets, walls, and random passers-by, the poet produces a discourse of desire, quest, and loss which records only his passage, never his present position. Thus Baudelaire depicts the writer as practicing a "fantasque escrime," pugnaciously endeavoring to distill eloquence from uproar and living words from silent stones. Here is the portrait of the artist as street-fighting man, Baudelaire's revolutionary poetry recalling his action on the barricades in 1848.

With its vision of the city as a combat zone, **"Le Soleil"** undercuts the tranquillity of **"Paysage."** Yet the poem ends on a note of harmony when the sun, "like a poet," descends on the city, ennobling even the vilest things and "s'introduit en roi, sans bruit et sans valets, / Dans tous les hôpitaux et dans tous les palais" ["he enters like a king, without commotion or attendants, all the hospitals and all the palaces"]. "Sans bruit" suggests that a balance has momentarily been struck between artistic struggle and urban chaos, as sun and poet reach into the utmost corners of the city, illuminating and transforming it, transcending the uproar of the streets.

"Le Cygne" seems designed to unsettle this equilibrium, as the poet's encounters in the city become progressively more disturbing. If the poet was able to fence Paris to a draw in **"Le Soleil,"** in **"Le Cygne"** the city is too quick for him:

> Le vieux Paris n'est plus (la forme d'une ville
> Change plus vite, hélas! que le coeur d'un
>   mortel).
>
> [Old Paris is no more (the shape of a city changes faster, alas! than the heart of mortal man).]

The primary image of this displacement is a swan that the poet once saw bathing in the dust among the rubble and "bric-à-brac confus" caused by Haussmann's massive reconstruction of Paris. Like the swan who yearns in vain for "son beau lac natal" ["his beautiful native lake"], the poet must learn to make the best of his estrangement, not only from the city of his youth, but also from the grand poetic themes of the past. Henceforth the jumble of the city itself—"palais neufs, échafaudages, blocs, / Vieux faubourgs" ["new palaces, scaffoldings, blocks of stone, old neighborhoods"]—will become his materials and his texts, the visible signs of his longing, since "tout pour moi devient allégorie" ["everything becomes allegory for me"].

As in **"Le Soleil,"** the physical city and the poetry about it have become almost interchangeable. But here the Cain-like wandering poet, oppressed by images of old Paris, the swan, and other exiles ranging from

Andromache to a homesick African woman, can effect no miraculous transformation of his environment or his melancholic alienation from it. The "allégorie" remains one of original, irrecoverable loss, and the poet can only roam vanished streets, marking that loss through his own mixture of urban memory and desire. In **"Le Cygne"** modern Paris seems less real than the emotion its barren streets represent; it becomes a textual referent which defines by negation the more durable city hidden in "le coeur d'un mortel."

In bringing to the fore the pervasive themes of urban exile and poetic alienation, **"Le Cygne"** prepares the reader for the more abrupt shocks of **"Les Sept Vieillards."** The sense of dislocation that has been building gradually in the opening poems of *Tableaux parisiens* culminates in **"Les Sept Vieillards"** near the point of death or insanity. Struggling along between the tall banks of apartment houses, in a river of fog surging with mystery, the weary poet finds himself suddenly overwhelmed by the spectacle of a "cortège infernal": seven malicious, hideous old men parade past him, each the double of the last. Unnerving the poet both in its hallucinatory quality and in its apparently hellish origin, the experience calls into question the substantiality of the urban world around him:

> Fourmillante cité, cité pleine de rêves,
> Où le spectre en plein jour raccroche le
>   passant!
> Les mystères partout coulent comme des
>   sèves
> Dans les canaux étroits du colosse puissant.

> [Teeming city, city full of dreams, where in broad daylight the specter accosts the passer-by! Mysteries flow everywhere like sap in the narrow veins of the powerful colossus.]

Even before the old men appear, aesthetic detachment and physical laws are suspended by the city of dreams. As ghosts grab hold of flesh and blood in broad daylight, the boundary between the real and the preternatural vanishes, and the poet who would watch and objectify the passing spectacle as an uninvolved *flâneur* becomes himself the "passant." By collapsing the distance between bemused, remote observer and picturesque, depersonalized urban "type," Baudelaire subverts a central tenet of the *tableau de Paris:* "You must not confuse the *flâneur [l'homme qui se promène]* with the passerby [*passant*]." When, near the end of the poem, the speaker asks that the (male) reader share a "frisson fraternel" with him because of his frightening experience, one crucial function of the poem becomes clear: it transforms the reader too into a *passant,* spectrally accosting him as the specter does the poet. This move, which makes the poet and reader as vulnerable to the gaze of the Other as the Other has

been to them, animates Baudelaire's poetics of encounter in the *Tableaux parisiens*.

The verb that Baudelaire uses to describe the action of the city's specters, *raccrocher,* is the slang term for how the prostitute "hooks" or solicits her customer. The wandering poet thus ensnared casts us back to the Harlot and the midnight walks of Blake and Wordsworth. That the figure of the prostitute should be tinged with ghostliness or death is already implicit in the fatal attractions of the Whore of Babylon, though Baudelaire will deepen the connection between woman and death in "A une passante." And elsewhere in his work Baudelaire explicitly associates prostitution and art: "Qu'est-ce que l'art? Prostitution" (I: 649). Thus **"Les Sept Vieillards"** not only replicates the experience undergone by the poet in the city; it also acts as prostitute to the reader's *passant,* attempting to seduce as it reveals itself to the eye. Instead of seeking to break out of harlotry's bonds, as do Blake and Wordsworth, Baudelaire interweaves them with the lines of his city poetry. Even here, when the woman is not named, her spectral mark is present. Yet if brushes with death in the guise of the feminine Other appear to underlie such writing, they also, like Wordsworth's blind beggar, provide continual reminders of "another world" against which to evaluate the experiences of Parisian Babylon.

For like Wordsworth's London, the city of **"Les Sept Vieillards"** is unreal. As T. S. Eliot, who found in this poem the source of his phrase "unreal city," wrote of Baudelaire: "Either because he cannot adjust himself to the actual world he has to reject it in favour of Heaven and Hell, or because he has the perception of Heaven and Hell he rejects the present world: both ways of putting it are tenable." In either case, the infernal city is so immediately apparent to Baudelaire that the ultimate unearthliness of his urban milieu never seems in doubt. Although like Wordsworth and Eliot he views the city in terms of an opposition between New Jerusalem and Babylon, Baudelaire's "cité pleine de rêves" appears most decisively configured around the negative pole of this antithesis. Far more than Wordsworth, Baudelaire contemplates the fallen sexuality of Babylon and the related images of the Internal City, Satan, demons, and hellish torment. Both poets are stopped in their tracks by the vision of strangers, but the authority speaking through these apparitions differs radically: if Heaven admonishes Wordsworth through the person of the beggar, Hell seeks to ensnare Baudelaire, as multiplying demons seem to emerge from hell for the express purpose of humiliating him: "A quel complot infâme étais-je donc en butte?" ["Of what infamous plot was I the victim?"].

The power of sight both conveys this villainy and determines how the *vieillards* are first met by the poet— through their eyes:

Tout à coup, un vieillard dont les guenilles
   jaunes
Imitaient la couleur de ce ciel pluvieux,
Et dont l'aspect aurait fait pleuvoir les
   aumônes,
Sans la méchanceté qui luisait dans ses yeux,

M'apparut.

[All at once, an old man whose yellow rags imitated the color of the rainy sky, and whose air would have provoked showers of alms, except for the wickedness which gleamed in his eyes, appeared to me.]

The beggarly old man possesses not only a wicked look but an eye "steeped in gall" and a gaze that "puts an edge on the frosty air." When his double appears, the nefarious eye recurs as well. Baudelaire emphasizes the most disturbing aspect of the entire incident: the poet is being looked at rather than looking. Caught without the aggressive initiative that his own bold gaze would provide, the poet is defenseless before the piercing glance of the Other.

In "Droit dans les yeux" Roland Barthes comments that because the gaze always searches for something or someone, we are likely to forget just this possibility: "In the verb 'regarder," the frontiers of the active and the passive are uncertain." Thus the poet of **"Les Sept Vieillards"** learns that the scales can be tipped in another's favor. Even more directly than Wordsworth, he undergoes the near-fatal stare that Barthes, citing Lacan, calls the *fascinum,* or evil eye, which arrests movement, causes impotence, and even kills. Lacan does posit the idea of a life-preserving "counter-eye," associated with the phallus, which provides its own "milk" and acts as a fertilizing agent. But the poet's inability to deploy metaphorically any such weapon in **"Les Sept Vieillards"** indicates that the evil eye has already taken effect. His poetic potency has been dried up by the gaze of the *vieillard* who himself strangely bursts with fecundating power.

The unstoppable replication of the old man's image defeats the poet's desire to still the mobility of meaning in his life, city, and text; longing to control, he is controlled, victim of a castration complex prompted by the groundless motion of signification. For to look and to desire is to recognize a wholeness that has been sundered, a lack whose fulfillment is always elsewhere. Lacan writes that "it is in so far as all human desire is based on castration that the eye assumes its virulent, aggressive function," and thus the penetrating, phallic gaze which seeks to dominate discovers its own unlucky "detachment" in the play of objects and emotions beyond its power. This desire to "know," to organize and comprehend the shattering, aleatory events of urban life, is precisely

the ever-frustrated, ever-engaging quest of the *Tableaux parisiens*. What makes **"Les Sept Vieillards"** so remarkable is the degree to which Baudelaire's poetic "I" exposes itself to the chilling, unmanning eye of the Other.

As with Wordsworth, the poet's identity appears endangered by his specular experience. Buffeted by the apparition of proliferating strangers, he seems to lose control of who and where he is: "Vainement ma raison voulait prendre la barre" ["vainly my reason tried to take the helm"]. As phantoms multiply around him they seem to pull the poet deeper into the hallucinatory dreamworld of the metropolis. The reader unavoidably follows, equally unable to distinguish whether these sights are "real," whether he too is the victim of an "infamous plot." Those readers who do not voluntarily respond with a "fraternal shiver" near the end of the poem are threatened with the revelation that there is an "air éternel" to these apparitions; the phantasmal, the poet seems to be saying, may be the most real, the most inescapable. And these phantoms both signal and embody the omnipresence of the crowd.

"The crowd," writes Walter Benjamin, "of whose existence Baudelaire is always aware, has not served as the model for any of his works, but it is imprinted on his creativity as a hidden figure." In **"Les Sept Vieillards"** the "hidden figure" quite literally emerges with a vengeance, for the maliciously reproducing old men constitute their own unruly crowd. They frighteningly externalize the poet's overpopulated consciousness, the masses that, Benjamin contends, have "become so much a part of Baudelaire." They represent not merely the poet's alienation from his surroundings—the intense Otherness that shakes him until he is "Blessé par le mystère et par l'absurdité!"—but also, paradoxically, his inability to separate himself from them.

For the final terror that the poem unfolds is, like Wordsworth's confounding at Bartholomew Fair, the sense that everything will be reduced to a monstrous, all-engulfing sameness: "Et mon âme dansait, dansait, vieille gabarre / Sans mâts, sur une mer monstrueuse et sans bords!" ["And my soul was dancing, dancing, an old lighter without masts, on a monstrous and shoreless sea!"]. As the poem concludes, the poet can find no place to land, no solid ground. Reproducing at will, the seven old men inundate the city with their unnatural, obliterating genesis; they are as dirty yellow as the sea of fog from which they emerge and which has already engulfed the street. Their proliferation casts the poet adrift on a boundless, stormy sea, transforming him into a kind of despairing Noah, without cargo or covenant. Certain that these deranging visions have come from hell ("du même enfer venu"), the poet is indeed "admonished from another world." But for what reason? No explanation is offered, save that the poem's deluged ending has apparently been conditioned by its fluid and spectral opening: "Les mystères partout coulent comme des sèves / Dans les canaux étroits du colosse puissant."

Characteristic of the slippery, unstable nature of poetic experience in the **Tableaux parisiens,** the poem's lines brim with dreams and nightmares, threatening to wash away the "facts" about the "fourmillante cité," even as they present them. As an ordered description of these disorienting events, the poem would seem to represent the poet's attempt to escape the grotesque and deathly uniformity that the self-duplicating old men bring: "Aurais-je, sans mourir, contemplé le huitième?" ["Could I, without dying, have contemplated the eighth?"]. But it also functions like the flooded street in channeling these multiplying terrors to the reader. The endless wonders that Paris offers can undo the poet as well as make him, for to be unable to differentiate impressions, or to fall victim to a paranoia that finds evil design rather than artistic opportunity in random events, may well mean poetic death. In the tempestuous street that is the poem, finding the means to navigate the waves of urban mystery becomes the poet's most pressing task.

In contrast, **"Les Petites Vieilles,"** the companion piece to **"Les Sept Vieillards,"** is often singled out as one of Baudelaire's supreme expressions of human sympathy, suffused by that generous, self-forgetful identification with suffering that marks the most intense city poetry of **Les Fleurs du mal.**" For although **"Les Petites Vieilles"** opens upon a similarly dreamlike landscape, the speaker's active, inquisitive role differs radically from his passive victimization in the previous poem:

> Dans les plis sinueux des vieilles capitales,
> Où tout, même l'horreur, tourne aux
>   enchantements,
> Je guette, obéissant à mes humeurs fatales,
> Des êtres singuliers, décrépits et charmants.

> [In the sinuous folds of ancient capitals, where everything, even horror, turns into enchantment. Following my fatal whims, I look out for certain singular creatures, decrepit and charming.]

Lying in wait for these bent and bizarre little old women, the poet spies their fragile bodies quivering with the din of the traffic ("Frémissant au fracas roulant des omnibus"). They now absorb the physical tremors of the city that had rolled over the poet himself ("Le faubourg secoué par les lourds tombereaux") in **"Les Sept Vieillards."**

But the gender-specific quality of this unusual identification should be noted. Like Wordsworth, Baudelaire

discovers that the penetration of the male gaze works both ways—when turned, or returned, male upon male, it stops the masculine poet in his tracks, like an evil eye; it plunges him into doubt, uncertainty, even madness. Yet in contrast to the "méchancete" that gleams in the eyes of the infernal *vieillards,* he finds that the *petites vieilles* have "divine eyes," which, though they "pierce like a gimlet," are as full of wonder as those of little girls. As he turns his gaze upon the female Other, he recovers his senses and his tongue and throws himself into their lives with abandon: "Mon coeur multiplié jouit de tous vos vices! / Mon âme resplendit de toutes vos vertus!" ["My multiplied heart thrills with all your vices! My spirit is resplendent with all your virtues!"]. The verb "jouir," with its dual meaning of "enjoy" and "have an orgasm," indicates how complete this intermingling is.

The seven spectral old men threaten to overwhelm the poet and his sense of identity by the voracious sameness of their otherness. The old women, however, are only "feeble phantoms" who inspire pity. They reveal to the poet's gaze the reassuring otherness of their sameness, their "familiarity" to him in the root sense. "Ruines! ma famille!" he salutes them. Many bonds of circumstance tie the poet to the old women (they are "blessés," or wounded by urban life, as he is in **"Les Sept Vieillards"**) but the strongest link is clearly genealogical. While the unnerving *vieillards* reproduce like a "disgusting Phoenix," each one "son and father of himself," the *petites vieilles* restore to this cycle the missing figure of woman. They give birth to an order that the poet can understand, one in which all can take their places as father, mother, son, and daughter. Although Baudelaire alludes to the old women as widows and mothers, he finally confesses that he regards them tenderly, paternally: "Tout comme si j'étais votre père, ô merveille!" ["As if I were your father, O wonder!"]. This assures the poet an intimate yet commanding relation to them, confirmed in the poem's last lines:

> Où serez-vous demain, Eves octogénaires,
> Sur qui pèse la griffe effroyable de Dieu?

> [Where will you be tomorrow, octogenarian Eves, upon whom weighs the terrifying claw of God?]

As he poetically creates and paternally watches over the lives of these elderly Eves, the poet acts as God the Father, but in viewing them as archetypal mothers and sharers in urban exile, he is also Cain, their son. The "claw of God" that falls upon them evokes the mark of Cain, even as it signifies the expulsion from Eden and the entrance into mortality stressed by the poem's earlier references to coffins and death. Moreover, the sexual nature of the Fall and the unique circumstances of Eve's birth give the genealogical motif a final twist. As both Edenic Innocent and knowing Temptress, Eve is the mother of all kinds of women, a point Baudelaire reinforces with an allusion to the recurrent duality of whore and virgin: "Mères au coeur saignant, courtisanes ou saintes" ["mothers with a bleeding heart, courtesans or saints"]. But Eve was born of Adam's rib, and is thus partner to her *own* "mother" or "father." In any case, the pervasive awareness of the sexuality of these women implicitly interjects the poet as lover into the family circle where he has already declared himself father and son. "Where will you be tomorrow?" he asks the old women, a final question anticipating that addressed to the vanishing woman of **"A une passante"** (When will I see you . .?"). The marks of death, "éternité," and widowhood weigh heavily upon them all, and into the place of the absent father or husband, the poet insinuates or thrusts himself.

BATHING IN THE CROWD

In the prose poem **"Les Foules,"** the poet claims as his special domain precisely this ability to penetrate the lives of others and blend with them ecstatically:

> Il n'est pas donné à chacun de prendre un bain de multitude. . . . Le poète jouit de cet incomparable privilège, qu'il peut à sa guise être lui-même et autrui. Comme ces âmes errantes qui cherchent un corps, il entre, quand il veut, dans le personnage de chacun. Pour lui seul, tout est vacant.

> (1: 291)

> [Not everyone has the ability to bathe in the multitude. . . . The poet enjoys that incomparable privilege, that he can as he pleases be himself and another. Like those wandering souls that seek a body, he enters, when he wishes, into the character of each one. For him alone, everything is vacant.]

The sexual quality of this casual plunge into the Other animates Baudelaire's various descriptions of "bathing in the crowd," further illuminating the urban encounters of the *Tableaux parisiens*. For in **"Les Foules"** Baudelaire transforms the notion of art as prostitution into a passionate aesthetic of the city street. This poetic practice revels in physical and emotional intimacy, usually established through eye contact with the Other, even as it questions the stability of personal identity in the "fourmillant tableau" of Paris:

> Ce que les hommes nomment amour est bien petit, bien restreint et bien faible, comparé à cette ineffable orgie, à cette sainte prostitution de l'âme qui se donne tout entière, poésie et charité, à l'imprévu qui se montre, à l'inconnu qui passe.

> (1: 291)

> [That which men call love is very small, very narrow, and very weak, compared to that ineffable orgy, to that holy prostitution of the soul which gives itself

entirely, poetry and charity, to the unforeseen which shows itself, to the stranger who passes by.]

Alert to the sexuality of transient urban experience, Baudelaire elevates the fleeting contact with strangers in the crowd to the level not only of an art but also of a religion. It is a "holy prostitution" that he practices, a mingling of Babylon and New Jerusalem that he praises.

This giving of oneself (which anticipates Eliot's "awful daring of a moment's surrender") is a moment both of artistry ("poésie") and generosity ("charité"), as the poet fills with his spirit the empty vessels of those beggarly souls around him. While "charité" might also signify Christian brotherly love, Baudelaire insists that this chance conjunction of encounter and art be consummated in the flesh:

> Le promeneur solitaire et pensif tire une singulière ivresse de cette universelle communion. Celui-là qui épouse facilement la foule connaît des jouissances fiévreuses.

> (1: 291)

> [The solitary and pensive stroller draws a special intoxication from that universal communion. He who easily marries the crowd knows feverish ecstasies.]

The skillful *flâneur* weds the crowd as freely and appropriately as the Lamb marries the Holy City in Revelation, a communion sealed by the sexually charged word "jouissance." As Baudelaire observes in **"Fusées,"** "The pleasure of being in the crowd is a mysterious expression of the bliss [*jouissance*] of multiplying numbers" (1: 649). The suggestion of the biblical injunction to be fruitful and multiply underlines the procreative aim of the poet's immersion in the crowd: knowing others and producing poetry are part of the same "mysterious" activity.

This poetic fecundation occurs primarily through the agency of the glance. "Si de certaines places paraissent lui être fermées," Baudelaire writes of the poet in **"Les Foules,"** "c'est qu' *à ses yeux* elles ne valent pas la peine d'être visitées" ["If certain spots seem closed to him, it is only that *to his eyes* they are not worth the trouble of being visited"] (1: 291; my emphasis). What the poet sees, he enters. In **"Les Petites Vieilles"** the eyes of the old women and of the poet who regards them are mentioned repeatedly; the poet spies on the women with his "oeil inquiet" fixed on their tottering steps. In **"Les Sept Vieillards"** the poet's act of looking at the old men—or rather their gaze at him—actually begets their monstrous regeneration.

Similarly, in other street poems such as **"Les Aveugles," "A une mendiante rousse,"** and **"A une pas-**

sante," the acts of looking and being looked at precipitate the poet's psychological response that forms the substance of the poem. Though the eye can aggressively glance into the hearts of others, its receptive function, its role in internalizing the complex interplay of emotions in the crowd, is equally important. It can even shape the landscape. The Thames of Wordsworth and Blake has been replaced in **"Les Sept Vieillards"** by rivers of fog the same yellow color as the old men's gall-steeped eyes, and in **"Les Petites Vieilles"** by rivers of tears (a motif repeated in **"Le Cygne"**). In this way Baudelaire creates a geography mediated by the eye in order to investigate the city and the crowd within. As he puts it simply in his notebooks, "Moi, c'est tous; Tous, c'est moi. Tourbillon" ["Me, that's everyone; Everyone, that's me. Vortex"] (1: 651).

Assessing the effect of this interpenetration of poet and crowd, Benjamin notes that in the *Tableaux parisiens* the poet deliberately sacrifices his emotional stability in order to fling himself into the path of this ever-renewing assault on the self. Baudelaire's vulnerability—and success—in writing about the city thus derives from his refusal to separate the psychic damage of his encounters from the self that must painfully reexperience them in the process of composition. Benjamin concludes: "Of all the experiences which made his life what it was, Baudelaire singled out his having been jostled by the crowd as the decisive, unique experience." Baudelaire's own metaphors allow us to be more precise about this process: the poet enters the crowd as a prostitute does her marketplace, willingly surrendering himself to the stimulating but demanding shocks, penetrations, and gazes of this "ineffable orgy." Like the prostitute, he himself is the commodity he offers, and it is only by sacrificing his "integrity" and wholeness that he can turn it to his advantage. He sets up a precarious economy of the "I" and eye whose profit depends on laying himself open and giving himself away.

The poet's empathetic efforts to comprehend the lives of others may be a mark of security and maturity, as he himself seems to claim at the end of **"Les Fenêtres"**: "And I go to bed, proud of having lived and suffered in others than myself" (1: 339). But the extremity of his will-to-multiplicity, his eagerness to throw himself into the world of the Other, also suggests vacuity, loneliness, and the need to escape himself. Thwarted desire and a desperate quest for completeness provide the impetus for the immersion, yet the process, by the poet's own account, is blissfully fulfilling. Whatever the motivation, such excursions into the Other—and the recounting of them—function as devices for the assertion of the poet's own authenticity in the midst of multitudes that may otherwise overcome him with repeated shocks, or dissolve him in a sea of anonymity. The fictiveness of this assertion makes no difference to him: as the narrator remarks of the woman whose life

he imagines in **"Les Fenêtres,"** "What does it matter what might be the reality existing outside of me, so long as she has helped me to live, to feel that I am and that which I am?"—"que je suis et ce que je suis" (1: 339). To write the lives of others, then, or to tell the history of encounters with them, is to bring the self into sharper focus against the blurring continuum of the crowd.

The poem that follows **"Les Sept Vieillards"** and **"Les Petites Vieilles"** exemplifies just this struggle. **"Les Aveugles"** transforms the poet's adversarial relation to the crowd into one of profound self-identification, while still posing disturbing questions about his ability to comprehend and exercise poetic control over his apparently helpless subject. His use here of sexuality and the gaze indicate that such scrutiny of others may well be no defense against—and may even be a revelation of—poetic insecurity and lack of insight. For as in the case of Wordsworth and the beggar, the crucial, complicating factor is that of blindness.

BLINDNESS AND BABEL

"Les Aveugles" opens with the poet contemplating the "ridiculous" and "frightful" sight of blind men darting their eyes uselessly about. What particularly disturbs him is that

> Leurs yeux, d'où la divine étincelle est partie,
> Comme s'ils regardaient au loin, restent levés
> Au ciel; on ne les voit jamais vers les pavés
> Pencher rêveusement leur tête appesantie.

> [Their eyes, from which the divine spark has departed, remain lifted to the sky, as if they were looking at it from afar; one never sees them bend their heavy heads dreamily over the pavement.]

Although the blind men's eyes have lost the celestial quality that distinguishes those of the *petites vieilles,* they still look "rêveusement" toward heaven. The poem reaches its climax when the poet exclaims in frustration:

> Vois! je me traîne aussi! mais, plus qu'eux hébété,
> Je dis: Que cherchent-ils au Ciel, tous ces aveugles?

> [Look! I drag myself along too! but, even more dazed than they are, I say: What are they looking for in the sky, all these blind men?]

In his own desire to see (comprehend) and be seen (recognized), he insists that someone look at him dragging through the city as if he were blind, too. It is from this distraught condition of being sighted, yet figuratively even more in the dark than they are, that the poet demands, "Que cherchent-ils au Ciel, tous ces aveugles?"

If Baudelaire's usual sympathy for the exile seems to change to scorn for the blind men, it is because they in their turn parody the poet's own search for meaning. Certainly his difference from them is ironically underscored when he shouts "Vois!" But the admission that he is "plus qu'eux hébété" by the city, although intended to make the blind men appear even more foolish, indicates to the reader the deeper affinity that binds them. The poet may mock the blind for seeking explanations from on high rather than from the reality of the stones beneath their feet, but can these hieroglyphs of the city be read, any more than the poet can fathom the actions of the blind men? Thus Baudelaire, standing ironically behind his speaker, allows the blind searches of **"Les Aveugles"** to mock the poet's ability as urban *flâneur*, voyeur, and seer. A major difference between the encounters with blind men in Wordsworth and Baudelaire lies in the unwillingness of the latter's narrator to admit the resemblance between them.

The metaphoric blindness that refuses to acknowledge this bond may be a function of the city's total dedication to pleasure. The poet characterizes the metropolis as "Eprise du plaisir jusqu'à l'atrocité" ["smitten with pleasure even to atrocity"] and in his original version of this phrase Baudelaire brought out its sexual implications even further: "Cherchant la jouissance avec férocité" ["Ferociously looking for (sexual) ecstasy"] (1: 1022). If the "globes ténébreux" of the *aveugles* baffle the power of the poet's gaze, this poetic impotence or symbolic castration may well be related to the city's cruel and unfulfilling quest for satisfaction. As he wanders the streets looking for his own delights, his own lives to share, the poet's "daze" betrays his bewilderment in an all-too-sensory world, one that blocks the eye's access to the heaven-directed vision of the blind men.

In a characteristic effort to comprehend what the blind men's disability might mean for them, the poet imagines them crossing the city as if traversing "le noir illimité, / Ce frère du silence éternel" ["limitless night, that brother of eternal silence"]. Jumping from blindness to deafness, he then immediately invokes the most deafening thing he knows: "O cité! / . . . autour de nous tu chantes, ris et beugles" ["O City! . . . around us you sing, laugh, and bellow"]. Not seeing the city would be like not hearing the urban uproar, and the poet who questions the efficacy of his sight by comparing himself to the blind men thereby also suggests that the city is too much for his ears. Both senses, he implies, are "hébété," stunned by it. Thus, when he prefaces his final question, "Que cherchent-ils . . . ?" with the inelegant statement, "Je dis," he is saying in effect, "I speak, I announce my power as a poet to

challenge that deafening noise which is analogous to the blindness that I see before me, and that I fear even in myself." For the "eternal silence" that his words temporarily displace can be none other than that of the grave, also a place of "noir illimité." By linking sight and sound, darkness and deafness, to the celestial-infernal axis of urban experience, Baudelaire refigures in the most elemental sensory terms the search for heavenly answers beyond the unreal city. And within this transcendent frame rages the ongoing battle to open a space of light and harmony amid the urban storm.

Like Wordsworth, Baudelaire is shaken by the uproar of the workaday city: there are the earthshaking tremors of traffic in **"Les Sept Vieillards"** and **"Les Petites Vieilles,"** roadworks sounding like a hurricane in **"Le Cygne,"** the bellows and howls of the street in **"Les Aveugles"** and **"A une passante,"** even brass bands in **"Les Petites Vieilles."** The images of urban noise that pervade *Tableaux parisiens* recall the archetype of Babel. But Baudelaire's Parisian bedlam is the medium for expression, unlike London's "babel din" in *The Prelude,* which is destructive of it. In place of the Wordsworthian longing for the silence of midnight streets, Baudelaire professes a Blakean willingness to listen and hear, however unsettling the experience. Yet what he hears are not harlots' curses but the tumultuous siren-song of the seductive, inspiring metropolis.

In the poet's contest against urban chaos and death, the archetypes of Babylon and New Jerusalem, and their emblems of harlot and virgin, provide the metaphors by which he structures his response to the city. Baudelaire exploits what Wordsworth shuns, not only by situating himself in the thick of urban cacophony but also by undermining the oppositions of heaven and hell through a poetic prostitution and a holy matrimony with the crowd. Indeed, Baudelaire's equating of art and prostitution reveals that his thematics of encounter and the striving for poetic form can be understood to meet in another way, in the verbal and bodily "figure" of the woman passing on the street. This dynamic tension between changing city, imaged as a woman, and the poet's desire for control over "her," lies at the heart of *Tableaux parisiens.*

Graham Robb (essay date 1991)

SOURCE: "The Poetics of the Commonplace in *Les Fleurs du Mal,*" in *The Modern Language Review,* Vol. 86, No. 1, January, 1991, pp. 57-65.

[*In the following article, Robb discusses Baudelaire's use of common words and phrases in* Les Fleurs du Mal.]

Much attention has been lavished on the commonplace in recent years, and it would be futile, not to say unoriginal, to attempt another rehabilitation of the cliché as an expressive literary device. Neither would it be particularly profitable, in a short study, to analyse the manner in which a poet such as Baudelaire exploits and renovates literary stereotypes. The very definition of the stereotype poses several problems: when does a certain figure become a cliché? Is the writer aware of its status as a cliché, or is its use associated with a particular intertext? The commonplace under scrutiny here bears only a distant relation to the literary cliché, and provides a more reliable basis for textual analysis. The word will be taken principally to designate a type of figure generally recognized by speakers of a particular language to express a particular truth, whether explicitly, in the form of a saying, or implicitly, in an expression.

In the case of Baudelaire, the use of such figures has been noted and studied primarily in *Le Spleen de Paris.* Baudelaire himself draws attention to this feature of his prose poems, and his exploitation of popular sayings or expressions is often overtly satirical. In some ways, this renders the figure less interesting stylistically; the reader is invited in an obvious manner to make sense of the distorted saying or to consider the philosophical or moral implications of a certain expression. In *Les Fleurs du Mal,* on the other hand, the more discreet presence of these figures creates more curious effects. I hope to show, in fact, that the poetic commonplace may well be counted as one of the *trucs* which make up the 'mechanism' of Baudelaire's verse poetry. Certainly, in *Fusées,* Baudelaire indicates the poetic potential of the *lieu commun* as a figure that is in some way both universally understandable and strangely provocative: 'Profondeur immense de pensée dans les locutions vulgaires, trous creusés par des générations de fourmis'.

This phrase, which is itself aptly reminiscent of a popular saying, of the 'many a mickle makes a muckle' variety, plays on the idea of *usure:* the wearing away and polishing of a phrase can eventually become the digging-out of a whole mine of possible meanings; the triteness of the 'time-honoured' precept hides a capacity to astonish, to *faire rêver.* Furthermore, this figure is apparently distinguishable in some important respect from other elements of figurative language. The obvious difference between a commonplace and an image invented by the poet is that the commonplace already exists as a linguistic unity. The task of the poet who wishes to exploit a commonplace, then, as Baudelaire's *Fusées* suggests, is practically the opposite of the task which faces the inventor of a symbol or an allegory. Instead of beginning with a particular meaning in mind, the starting-point, as for the reader, is a set of signifiers, and the poet's job is to unravel the message or messages they contain, to explore these 'trous creusés par des générations de fourmis'. This is presumably the aspect of the commonplace which Baudelaire, in the *Salon de 1859,* finds *'excitant'* or 'fertile'. Rather than establishing links between two or more elements, thus expressing a subjective unity, the pre-existing commonplace produces a series of associations: hence the emphasis laid by Baudelaire on the multiplicity and objectivity of the figure—'rendez-vous public', or the 'générations de fourmis'. In examining Baudelaire's use of this figure in *Les Fleurs du Mal,* I shall show how this excitement may also be a feeling of unease, and how the digging of the ants is also an undermining, an inverted construction.

Perhaps the most straightforward way in which Baudelaire exploits clichéd or popular expressions is to use them as providers of a theme. *Une charogne,* for example, is based on the vulgar sense of *charogne* as a slut, the 'femme lubrique' of the second stanza. (This might explain why Baudelaire uses the indefinite article in his title.) The analogy developed by the poet between his mistress and the rotting carcass is already implicit in the popular image, though even this small example shows how he explores the less obvious connotations of the expression. The superficial comparison is between a piece of animal meat and a woman considered only as a body, but, as the poem reveals, it also suggests a more 'fertile' connexion between Eros and Death.

Similarly, *A une Madone* derives its theme from the saying, 'dresser un autel à quelqu'un'—to put someone on a pedestal: 'Je veux bâtir pour toi, Madone, ma maîtresse, / Un autel souterrain au fond de ma détresse.' The entire poem is a detailed expansion of an apparently innocent saying, the very banality of which heightens the irony of the poet's eccentric adoration. Although the sadistic climax of the poem appears to be a mocking inversion of the reverence expressed by the original saying, Baudelaire's development of the image reveals its inherent blasphemy.

This is obviously a common poetic device which is technically related to the fable. Certain *Fleurs du Mal* could in fact be considered as peripheral examples of this genre: *Les Hiboux,* or even *Le Voyage.* The poems I shall examine, however, often take as their starting-point or have as their 'intertext' an idiomatic expression, the content of which tends to be psychological rather than moral, implicit rather than explicit. *La Cloche fêlée,* for instance, plays on the slang meaning of *fêlé.* A more interesting example is *Le Vin des amants* which uses the analogy of horseriding to express the feelings of freedom produced by intoxication:

Aujourd'hui l'espace est splendide!
Sans mors, sans éperons, sans bride,
Partons à cheval sur le vin
Pour un ciel féerique et divin!

The adage evoked by this image, and perhaps its origin, is 'bon vin, bon éperon'. Both nouns occur in the first stanza, though (if we assume this transformation to be deliberate) the cliché is cleverly altered (*'sans éperon'*) and its original meaning thereby intensified.

When used as a source of particular images rather than general themes, the device becomes even less obvious, and all the more effective. The visual elements of the popular saying are emphasized, thus concealing the idea it normally expresses. This can be achieved, as in *Le Vin des amants,* by the syntactic separation of the elements to which the idea is habitually attached. In *Spleen I,* for example, the verse, 'L'âme d'un vieux poète erre dans la gouttière', exploits the phrase 'un poète de gouttière', suggesting a starving Bohemian and a mediocre poet, contributing thus to the general sense of dilapidation and sterility. The same effect can also be achieved, as in *A une Madone,* where 'dresser' becomes 'bâtir', by substituting certain words of the original expression: 'Avec ses vêtements ondoyants et nacrés, / Même quand elle marche on croirait qu'elle danse.' The intertext here (admittedly more a literary cliché than a popular saying) is, 'Même quand l'oiseau marche, on sent qu'il a des ailes', and it serves to emphasize the light and graceful step of the woman. In these verses, of course, the idea is explicit even in the modified expression, but an element of (perhaps unconscious) surprise is introduced when, instead of a bird, a snake appears in the following line. A striking example of this can be found in the first quatrain of *Le Mort joyeux:* 'Et dormir dans l'oubli comme un requin dans l'onde'. The adapted cliché is, of course, 'comme un poisson dans l'eau', its similarity to the new image stressed by the fact that the original phrase would also have occupied a hemistich. The transformation of *poisson* into *requin* adds to the idea of comfort in a natural habitat a sense of peril and latent power.

The examples given thus far could be characterized in the following way: first, the visual imagery of the popular expression is developed, and gives rise to, or becomes part of a more complex series of images; the usual meaning of the expression is thereby concealed, but is none the less present as a discreet echo. Secondly, this usual meaning may be affected by an alteration of the expression, and certain connotations, normally unrecognized, become apparent.

Other images, however, which also recall the usual sense of the figure, actually seem to contradict or undermine it ironically. My first example is the third stanza of *Au lecteur;* it opens with a peculiar image which, perhaps because the second hemistich is more immediately interesting, has received little attention: 'Sur l'oreiller du mal c'est Satan Trismégiste / Qui berce longuement notre esprit enchanté.' The image of the pillow, associated with the idea of lulling, and in the context of sin, hypocrisy, and the 'washing' of 'stains', creates an echo of the saying 'Une bonne conscience est un doux oreiller'. Here, however, the perverse implication is that 'Une mauvaise conscience est un doux oreiller', and this clandestine modification of the commonplace adds, presumably, to the 'hypocritical' reader's sense of unease.

In the same poem, another popular saying is employed for its imagery whilst its usual application is slightly altered: 'Nous volons au passage un plaisir clandestin / Que nous pressons bien fort comme une vieille orange.' 'Presser l'orange' (or 'le citron') means to exploit thoroughly and unscrupulously, the best-known use of the phrase being Voltaire's complaint that Frédéric II had 'pressé l'orange' and was preparing to 'jeter l'écorce'. In *Au lecteur,* however, it is unclear who is exploiting whom: even while squeezing the juice from a 'plaisir clandestin', Man is being squeezed by the Devil. Moreover, Baudelaire brilliantly adapts and intensifies the figure simply by adding an adverbial phrase and an adjective: 'bien fort' and 'vieille'.

My third example is taken from the fourth *Spleen* poem: '—Et de longs corbillards, *sans tambours ni musique,* / Défilent lentement dans mon âme;' (my italics). As in *Au lecteur,* it is possible to consider the figure (usually 'sans tambour ni trompette') in its literal sense: a procession may well be expected normally to include drums and music. But the same characteristic ambiguity is also produced. The conventional sense of the phrase would be 'without making any fuss'; in the poem, however, the connotations are different, suggesting the silence of captivity and despair; the idea of discreet efficiency has become that of monotony and dread.

These various adaptations of *locutions vulgaires* are, generally, forms of verbal humour. (In the terms of Baudelaire's essay on laughter, they might indeed be described as 'satanic', the idea of personal superiority springing here from the individual's correction of a time-honoured and apparently universal perception.) Nowhere is this more evident than in the most extraordinary images of *Les Fleurs du Mal,* those images which Laforgue termed 'comparaisons énormes'. Such images frequently imitate the sort of joke which depends on a literal interpretation of a proverbial expression, a form of humour which Baudelaire seems to have practised. In *Spleen II,* the likening of memory to a 'gros meuble à tiroirs encombré de bilans' has a perfectly banal origin in the expression, 'avoir la mémoire encombrée'. As in *Une charogne* or *A une Madone,* this figure, with its 'profoundeur immense de pensée', provides the basis of the whole poem. Similarly, in *Sed non satiata,* the exotic imagery is continued and subtly justified by a verse ('Quand vers toi mes désirs partent en caravane') which, as Claude Pichois indicates, derives from the expression, 'faire ses caravanes' (to lead an adventurous and dissolute life). In *Réversibilité,* Baudelaire plays on the figurative meanings of *comprimé* and *froissé* to create the strange image of 'les vagues terreurs', 'Qui compriment le cœur comme un papier qu'on froisse'. Finally, yet another 'comparaison énorme' which seems almost humorously to imply its own deflation is that of the *gorge-armoire:* 'Ta gorge triomphante est une belle armoire' (*Le Beau navire*). Graham Chesters points out, in his interesting analysis of the metaphor, that it 'has a respectable English equivalent in the dual meaning of the word "chest"'. But it also has a somewhat less respectable equivalent in French in the application of an 'armoire (à glace)' to a sturdily-built person. This gives added resonance to the epithet, 'triomphante', and stresses the masculine attributes of the 'majestueuse enfant': her neck is 'large et rond', her shoulders 'grasses', and her arms 'se joueraient des précoces hercules'.

The effect of this humour is to deflate the conventional image, to reveal its literal absurdity, and then, on this foundation, to create new images which indicate the profound truth of the determining figure. The elements composing these images can be all the more disparate for being anchored in a generally recognized expression, even though this expression may not in every case be present in the reader's conscious mind. If we take into account the other verses quoted thus far, which also demonstrate the poetic potential of the commonplace, we might tentatively define this operation in terms of Jean Cohen's conclusions in *Structure du language poétique* (1966), and see it as a typical activity of the 'mécanisme de fabrication du poétique':

> La poésie . . . ne détruit que pour reconstruire. . . . L'absurdité du poème lui est essentielle, mais elle n'est pas gratuite. Elle est le prix dont il faut payer une clarté d'un autre ordre. Dans et par la figure, le sens est à la fois perdu et retrouvé. Mais de l'opération il ne sort pas intact.

Cohen's statement that the sense does not emerge intact from this operation leads to the more disquieting aspect of this use of popular expressions. In one respect, it is clear in some of the examples cited that the normally-accepted meaning of the figure is changed. In other cases, such as Baudelaire's 'comparaisons énormes', the meaning is apparently intact, though less evident. In view of the image from *Fusées,* it may not be overly pretentious to say that meaning in general, rather than one particular meaning, is somehow disturbed or undermined.

What I have termed the deflation of the determining popular expression consists in treating the expression above all as a linguistic structure. This is particularly apparent in those verses which invert the original order of the metaphor or which separate its constituent elements. At the end of *Remords posthume,* the poet tells his mistress: '—Et le vers rongera ta peau comme un remords.' The personification of remorse implicit in the phrase 'rongé par des remords' is made explicit here by the changed mood of the verb and by the introduction of the worm itself. In *Au lecteur,* the expression 'nourrir des remords' is spread over two verses and, at the same time, disguised by the separation of verb and object: 'Et nous alimentons nos aimables *remords,* / Comme les mendiants *nourrissent* leur vermine' (my italics). A curious example of this, which will be mentioned again later, occurs in *Spleen IV:*

> Quand la terre est changée en un cachot
>   humide,
> Où l'Espérance, comme une chauve-souris,
> S'en va battant les murs de son aile timide
> Et se cognant la tête à *des plafonds pourris;*
>
> Quand la pluie étalant ses immenses traînées
> D'une vaste prison imite les barreaux,
> Et qu'*un peuple muet d'infâmes araignées*
> *Vient tendre ses filets au fond de nos*
>   *cerveaux,* (my italics)

The image of the last two verses quoted seems to verge on the surrealistic: what logical connexion can there be between these spiders spinning webs in the brain and the mental state called *spleen?* The 'infâmes araignées' appear simply to be vague symbols in an impressionistic *état d'âme,* evoking, for example, evil intent and the Fates. And yet, present perhaps on an unconscious level, linking image to theme, is the expression, 'avoir une araignée dans le plafond' (Littré gives: 'Se dit d'un homme bizarre et un peu fou'). The *plafond* has been replaced by the *cerveau* itself, but this other concrete element of the image is introduced in advance in the 'plafonds pourris' of the preceding stanza. Significantly, Corbiére uses the expression in a similar manner in his Baudelairean pastiche, 'La Pipe au poète'. It is tempting to see in such images evidence of certain ruses which give Baudelaire's poetry its sense of an enigma half-perceived, an unspecified truth underlying the text, but one for which an everyday formula exists.

These figures, often identifiable by their structure as much as by their meaning, would provide interesting material for a Freudian reading of Baudelaire, and it is unfortunate that Leo Bersani entirely neglects the subject in his *Baudelaire and Freud* (1977). Images belonging to the collective unconscious, dulled by usage, are transformed and disguised in such a way that they regain their power to appeal to the unconscious. Obviously it is important that this alteration should not be directly concerned with the sense of the expression, but rather with its structure and constituent elements. If the transformation is explicit, the effect is lost, and the irony operates on only one level. (The verse in *Femmes damnées,* 'On ne peut ici-bas contenter qu'un seul maître!', is an example of this, as is the ironic title of 'Un voyage à Cythère': according to Littré, 'faire un voyage à Cythère' means 'se livrer aux plaisirs de l'amour'.) This is a technique familiar nowadays to advertising companies. In Baudelaire's time, the perception underlying this exploitation of popular expressions had not been formulated, and yet the disturbing and 'exciting' implications of psycholinguistics are certainly present in images such as that of the 'infâmes araignées': that our realities are inextricable from the structures of language. The truth that is half-perceived (in this case, madness) is not only expressed *through* language; it depends entirely upon language for its subjective reality, and it is perhaps for this reason that Baudelaire's use of the device seems often to be associated with the evocation of a disturbed state.

One might at this point object, with hindsight, that the use of certain images is deliberately ironic. On one level, it is true that Baudelaire's manipulation of these figures has a parodic quality which resembles Flaubert's use of *idées reçues.* Irony preserves the integrity of the writer who is painfully aware that his language is inevitably a *sociolecte,* imbued with the notions of a society he despises. This is probably true, as I shall show, of a poem like *La Muse vénale.* It seems to be the case also that there is a conscious attempt on the part of the poet to surprise and disturb the reader. There is, of course, a certain pleasure to be derived from denying what are generally held to be self-evident truths. No doubt the distortion of popular expressions in *Au lecteur,* for example, underlines the assertion that social conventions hide unpleasant and complex realities. This can certainly be said of the more eccentric images of *Le Spleen de Paris.* As J. A. Hiddleston indicates, 'They often have a palpably refutable quality until the mind of the reader, fascinated by their explosive force, comes to an understanding of a deeper reality' (*Baudelaire and 'Le Spleen de Paris'*, 1987). . . . Figures in the verse poetry which might be included in this category have a more subtle and muted effect, whilst displaying a skilful misapplication of the familiar expression: the 'vieille orange' of *Au lecteur,* for example, or the phrase 'sans tambours ni musique' in *Spleen.*

These images are in their way as disturbing as those to be found in *Le Spleen de Paris.* The adaptation of a known figure renders the familiar strange and the strangeness of the altered image curiously familiar. The reader's unease is increased by what might be called the discreet irrelevance of the generative figure. But there is evidence of something more than a desire to confuse the *bourgeois.* This dislocation of habitual forms of discourse expresses an insecurity about language and the convention of 'reality': an insecurity hinted at in the image in *Fusées.*

Significantly, the use of popular figures in *Les Fleurs du Mal* frequently coincides, as suggested, with an expression of poetic impotence, of the meaninglessness of life. *La Muse vénale* provides the most flagrant and uncomplicated examples:

> Il te faut, pour gagner ton pain de chaque
>   soir,
> Comme un enfant de chœur, jouer de
>   l'encensoir,
> Chanter des *Te Deum* auxquels tu ne crois
>   guère,
>
> Ou, saltimbanque à jeun, étaler tes appas
> Et ton rire trempé de pleurs qu'on ne voit pas,
> Pour faire épanouir la rate du vulgaire.

The tercets are principally a series of commonplaces: 'gagner ton pain', 'jouer (or 'donner') de l'encensoir', 'faire épanouir la rate'. These verses are thus both a description and a concrete example of the humiliating work of the venal muse as defined in line II with its monotonous sounds: 'Chanter des *Te Deum* auxquels tu ne crois guère'. The phrases 'de chaque soir' and 'Comme un enfant de chœur' highlight the picturesque elements in the clichés, but, being inessential to the general sense, they also appear simply to allow the insertion of the cliché into the alexandrine. These images have retained their original meaning and form; the poetic imagination (or the muse) has failed to transform the commonplace.

Another, more subtle example of a familiar image used in a 'negative' context to undermine any transcendence of physical realities is the opening of *Obsession,* the poem which immediately follows the *Spleen* poems:

> Grands bois, vous m'effrayez comme des
>   cathédrales;
> Vous hurlez comme l'orgue; et dans nos
>   cœurs maudits,
> Chambres d'éternel deuil où vibrent de vieux
>   râles,
> Répondent les échos de vos *De profundis.*

The hemistich 'Vous hurlez comme l'orgue' echoes the expression 'ronfler comme un orgue'. As with the spinning spiders, the two parts of the image are separated, and the effect is more insidious than in *La Muse vénale:* the word 'ronfler' does not appear but is hinted at in the 'Chambres . . . où vibrent de vieux râles'.

Perhaps the richest example of these figures which not only are associated thematically with the failure of the imagination but are themselves examples of this failure is the fourth *Spleen* poem. As Michael Riffaterre has shown, the comparison of Hope to a bat is an inversion of the stereotype, Hope being represented here by a symbol of despair. This image is followed by a popular expression, 'battre les murs' ('to stagger along like a drunkard'), which is enriched by the adverbial phrase, 'de son aile timide'. The mention of the wing serves moreover to recall another expression which evokes incapacity: 'battre de l'aile'. The third stanza opens with the surprising image of teeming rain which 'D'une vaste prison imite les barreaux'; here again, there is a development of a cliché: 'il pleut des cordes' or 'il pleut des hallebardes', both forms of which, when recalled in the light of Baudelaire's alteration, have connotations of confinement and punishment. Two further images have already been considered: the 'infâmes araignées' and 'sans tambours ni musique'. Finally, yet another cliché is developed in the fourth stanza:

> Des cloches tout à coup sautent avec furie
> Et lancent vers le ciel un affreux hurlement,
> Ainsi que des esprits errants et sans patrie
> Qui se mettent à geindre opiniâtrement.

In this case, the interetext is 'errer comme une âme en peine', echoed by 'errants' and the synonym, in this context, of âme: 'esprits'. (The word âme, in fact, occurs in the second line of the following stanza.) In this way, the idea of damnation is given further confirmation. As in **La Muse vénale,** the clichés on which this poem is based suggest stasis and dull repetition, but, like the 'trous creusés par des générations de fourmis', they also express a certain instability, inviting the reader to search for a hidden truth, a truth which sometimes turns out to be a common saying.

The insecurity evoked in these poems through commonplaces is, then, not simply thematic, and the overt satire of the prose poems is certainly absent. The hidden cliché frequently emphasizes the explicit meaning, but, as I have shown, it can also add another element or dimension to the poem. The *profondeur* of these verses constructed on popular sayings might be seen, or sensed by the reader, to be linguistic in nature. Baudelaire's perverse or even comical use of them suggests a world in which 'philosophical' or 'spiritual' realities are, essentially, lexical patterns which may reinforce the supposed truth, but which can just as easily contradict and undermine it. The popular saying, used as a poetic figure, does indeed appear to have particular properties distinct from those of a symbol or an allegory. It is undeniable, on the one hand, that intertextual reminiscences, to quote Alison Fairlie, 'succinctly relate individual insight to a wide range of significance in . . . time and space'. But it is also true to say that, by means of the device I have examined, common perceptions are related (and contrasted) succinctly to individual experience, thus undermining both the validity of these perceptions and the ability of the individual to assert and formulate a truth coherently. The semantic 'depth' and instability introduced into the poem through these *locutions vulgaires* show that language indeed is a form of prison: in the sense not

only that it tends to coagulate into clichés but also, more specifically (as Baudelaire more clearly suggests in **Le Spleen de Paris**), that reality exists or can be perceived only through patterns of language.

As I deduced from Baudelaire's praise of the locution vulgaire, this device is not merely a safeguarding, through irony, of artistic integrity. That this is so is suggested particularly by the fact that many of Baudelaire's most extraordinary images can be understood in terms of popular sayings. The poet, in these cases, is surely not inviting the reader to confess the stupidity of conventional wisdom, but rather to grasp, through the 'respectable' equivalent, the scandalous truth—a wisdom which lies deeper than social conventions, but which is latent in the popular expression.

Moreover, whilst the popular image is used to underline and reinforce a psychic reality, in most cases it is exploited in a way that tends to confuse the levels on which that reality is commonly thought to exist. We see, in **Les Fleurs du Mal** (to recall Jean Cohen's conclusions), both a demolition and a development of the consecrated expression or saying. No doubt any trite formulation of an idea invites contradiction or deflation: one might think of any shaggy-dog story, or, for example, of Eluard and Péret's *152 proverbes mis au goût du jour*. But, with Baudelaire the apologist of *lieux communs*, the cliché is dismantled in order to allow its evocative power to work on the reader's mind. It is developed not only in the sense that its picturesque or philosophical potential is exploited but also in the sense that the structure of the figure is displayed.

Baudelaire, of course, has contributed to dictionaries of quotations and proverbs his share of sayings, many of which have the same 'profondeur de pensée' he perceived in popular expressions. Perhaps, however, he was equally original in his exploitation of existing expressions. By exploring the relations between words in recognized patterns, he shows, with the excitement that is the mark of truly interesting poetry, that the universal contains the exceptional, and that these locutions vulgaires, whilst neatly encapsulating centuries of human experience, do not necessarily bespeak, as might a symbol or a *correspondance,* a comforting whole, but rather the universal presence of 'l' *exception dans l'ordre moral*'.

T. A. Unwin (essay date 1991)

SOURCE: "The 'Pseudo-Narrative' of *Les Fleurs du Mal,* in *Orbis Litterarum,* Vol. 46, No. 6, 1991, pp. 321-39.

[*In the following essay, Unwin argues that* Les Fleurs du Mal *conveys the suggestion of a story, which the critic calls a "pseudo-narrative."*]

'Le seul éloge que je sollicite pour ce livre est qu'on reconnaisse qu'il n'est pas un pur album et qu'il a un commencement et une fin.' Thus wrote Baudelaire to Vigny on sending him the second edition of *Les Fleurs du mal*. Reluctant students of poetry are indeed often relieved to discover that the collection can be approached in terms of its thematic development. This is not only a matter of recurrent images and symbols in the poems (for such unity is apparent in most poets' work.) Nor even is it what is now commonly referred to as the 'architecture' of the anthology, that is to say, the juxtapositions, contrasts and counterpoints created by the arrangement of poems. Rather, there is a progression of what might be identified as 'states of mind,' an outline of the various stages in the poet's spiritual Odyssey, the suggestion almost of a series of events. This being so, it is possible on a certain reading to bypass something of the formal and technical aspect of the poetry, and concentrate on what we shall call the 'pseudo-narrative': that is, the artist's memory of a lost paradise and his mission to recreate it aesthetically; his fall from grace into the misery of 'spleen' and awareness of his own mortality; his conversion of the sights and sounds of city life into the timeless beauty of the poem; the escape into the false paradise of wine; the rude reawakening to the curse of his own condition; and finally revolt and death. It all has the satisfying appearance of a story, conforming—in outline at least—to the Aristotelian pattern of the beginning, middle and end.

Now whereas to read *Les Fleurs du mal* on this level alone would be a distortion, it is important to ask a number of questions about the components and about the limits of the pseudo-narrative structure. What role do the individual poems play in furthering the 'action'? Are some more important than others? Is there a place in such a scheme for the condemned poems, and how do we view those poems which were added to the collection in later editions? How do we explain the fact that the 'story' seems to hold (or to have held) together even without these? Are they in some sense superfluous? If so, what is necessary to the 'plot'?

In fact, were it possible to abolish the existence of a poem, virtually any piece might be removed from *Les Fleurs du mal* without apparent detriment to the pseudo-narrative (though of course the poetic richness of the collection would thereby be depleted.) The dominant themes in the various sequences of poems have a mutually reinforcing effect, and the orchestration of different elements relies on repeated evocations of the central experiences: the poet's fall from grace is, for example, described in different terms in many of the early poems (*Bénédiction, L'Albatros, J'aime le souvenir . . . , La Muse malade* and others). No poem is absolutely indispensable to an understanding of the pseudo-narrative, which is distributed and re-echoed through each and all of them. Such a principle of organi-

sation will be more radically applied in the later *Spleen de Paris,* where the famous letter to Arsène Houssaye makes the point:

> Mon cher ami, je vous envoie un petit ouvrage dont on ne pourrait pas dire, sans injustice, qu'il n'a ni queue ni tête, puisque tout, au contraire, y est à la fois tête et queue, alternativement et réciproquement. Considérez, je vous prie, quelles admirables commodités cette combinaison nous offre à tous, à vous, à moi et au lecteur. Nous pouvons couper où nous voulons, moi ma rêverie, vous le manuscrit, le lecteur sa lecture; car je ne suspends pas la volonté rétive de celui-ci au fil interminable d'une intrigue superflue. Enlevez une vertèbre, et les deux morceaux de cette tortueuse fantaisie se rejoindront sans peine. Hachez-la en nombreux fragments, et vous verrez que chacun peut exister à part.

In the prose poems a decentring aesthetic operates: the locus of the collection is everywhere and yet nowhere in particular. Something of this perpetual displacement seems to be anticipated in *Les Fleurs du mal,* and yet, despite the potential removal or isolation of many of the poems, it clearly does not go as far. There remains an overall movement and progression, as well as the suggestion of key moments in the pseudo-narrative (such as, for example, the first line of *La Destruction* which opens the *Fleurs du mal* section and describes the poet's brutal reawakening.) How, then, is this movement integrated within the overall framework? And where does the pseudo-narrative differ from (and thus help to define) what we conventionally understand as narrative?

Certainly, one obvious and major factor to be borne in mind is that the pseudo-narrative is not presented as a temporal progression, nor does it rely heavily on the use of a past tense. Although we may think of the fall from grace as heralding the decision to recreate the lost paradise through art, or to think of the stirrings of revolt and blasphemy in the penultimate section as incurring the final wish for death, that is a matter of textual order rather than consequential progression. The different dimensions of the poet's spiritual drama co-exist, interlocking with and reflecting each other in this timeless hall of mirrors. And yet, at the same time, we must ask what it is that makes us understand the poems as an implied chronology. The very fact of their having been set out and ordered into a sequence creates a movement which we are obliged to follow (or at least to acknowledge) in the text. Thus while each poem has a paradigmatic function (for its echoes and reverberations can be traced almost at will throughout the collection) it also fulfils a specific role within the textual distribution. It sets out a new stage in the poet's experience, different from the others, unique and (possibly) self-sufficient. Each poem can, therefore, be understood as determined and yet as gratuitous: determined in that it is a contributory element in the overall symbolism of the work, and gratuitous in its very individuality, in its escape from the constrictions placed upon it by the symbolic network within which it operates. Is it, perhaps, this gratuitousness that creates the sense of progression and of movement? Instead of finally merging into the collection by way of analogy, the poem asserts its difference, stands apart as a separate and distinct allegory, and thus suggests the possibility of temporality.

We shall shortly take some examples from the collection and look at them, partly in terms of this double axis (paradigmatic/vertical on the one hand, distributional/horizontal on the other hand). Three poems will serve our purpose: one from the very beginning of the work, *L'Albatros* (II); one from what is numerically about the mid-point of the collection, *Spleen* (LXXVIII); and finally the last poem of all, *Le Voyage* (CXXVI). The concluding poem will naturally raise additional questions as to the nature of the pseudo-narrative: is this conclusion a 'summing up,' a mere repetition, or does it add some new element to the story? To what extent was the ending anticipated—as is frequently the case in true fictional narrative—by earlier 'events'? But this begs the first question, to which we must return. What are the 'events' of this pseudo-narrative, and how do they relate to what we normally understand as events in fictional narrative?

We may assume, for the purposes of the present argument, that the events of conventional narrative are capable of relatively unproblematic definition. A hero falls in love; he is exiled by his mistress's father; he returns in disguise to expose the evil wrongdoer; his mistress's father (the king) has a change of heart; and so on (such a pattern, would, in fact be a good illustration of the 'recognitions' and 'reversals' which, for Aristotle, were central constituents of the tragic plot.) Events can be either physical or moral, or a combination of the two. Some events have a high profile, occupying a key position in the narrative and setting in motion further events which are thus dependent on them (exile and exposure in the scheme given above). Those key events, or 'fonctions cardinales' as Barthes terms them, ultimately shape the whole narrative and give the story its meaning. What, then, of the 'events' of *Les Fleurs du mal?* Is there a hierarchy, or a pattern of central and peripheral events as is usually the case in fictional narrative? Let us turn to *L'Albatros.*

'Souvent, pour s'amuser, les hommes d'équipage / Prennent des albatros . . . '. After the invocation in *Au Lecteur,* and the poet's account of his early years in *Bénédiction* (a poem which encourages us to view his experience as temporal development) we are confronted here with a single image, a close-up of that essential transition from celestial paradise to ugly terrestrial condition. The poet, that graceful and angelic being, is obliged to submit to the humiliation of existence among

men, and the hideous present is contrasted with a beautiful past. Here, in a sense, is the 'event' which dictates all his subsequent actions, for the poet's fall from grace in the manner of an albatros flopping clumsily onto the ship's deck is the precondition of all potential remedies he may seek; it precedes the implicit call of *Correspondances* to search for and express the secret analogies of the universe; and it precedes the much more explicit statement of the poet's mission in *Le Mauvais Moine,* where the second tercet speaks of transforming the ugly here-and-now of reality into an object of timeless aesthetic beauty. The allegory of *L'Albatros* is, indeed, so clear and so simple in outline that it reinforces the singularity or uniqueness of this event. The poet identifies himself with the condition of the albatros, and the final line dispels any possible trace of ambiguity: 'Ses ailes de géant l'empêchent de marcher'. The fall of the albatros has become the fall of the poet, and what appears to be a key event in the pseudo-narrative has taken place.

And yet, is it really an event? In terms of the textual distribution of *Les Fleurs du mal* (at least from the 1861 edition onwards) yes: *L'Albatros* heralds by its very positioning in the collection that descent into darkness and 'spleen' of the later poems in the section. But this implies that the pseudo-narrative into which we have now entered is not truly mimetic in nature. Rather it dramatizes the production of the text itself: for the story is not about the fate of the albatros, which is hereinafter forgotten, but about that of the poet. After his initial identification with the bird, the artist has substituted himself for it, and when in line thirteen he writes 'Le Poète est semblable au prince des nuées', we may ask whether 'prince des nuées' is here a further reference to the albatros or whether it is henceforth to be seen rather as a direct description of the poet himself. Here we come up against the complications raised by the double reference of allegory. The poet's story, which is the real one, is described in terms of another event. Yet on closer examination we discover that even this other event is itself not a single incident, rather it is a series of similar events, as is revealed by the iterative 'Souvent' with which the poem opens. Moreover, to the frequency with which different albatroses are brought down on the decks of different ships corresponds the generality of the poet's situation: it is not only the poet of *Les Fleurs du mal* whose condition is comparable to that of the albatros, but the condition of all poets. What had the appearance of a story turns out to be a parable. The 'event' which the inclusion of *L'Albatros* appears to constitute on the textual level becomes a variation or restatement of what is said in different ways elsewhere in the collection. The allegory, though apparently precise, contains no more than the possibility of a story, and the real issue to which it refers, that of the condition of the poet, is the subject not just of this poem but of virtually all the poems.

It is thus impossible to read the poem without at some point shifting our attention away from its particular position in the text and towards the vertical axis in which is located the paradigm of the artist's fall from grace. The allegorical fall of the albatros can thus only in a limited sense be classified as a single event. The allegory, by figuring as the 'unreal' representation of the 'real' event, invites us to consider the fall of the artist not only in this poem but also in others. After all, if the drama is about the poet's attempt to come to terms with his condition through the writing of poetry, then it follows that the locus of that struggle is as much in other poems as in this one. The fall from grace—though clearly the first 'event' of the pseudo-narrative—is embedded within a series of references to it through many poems. The choice of *L'Albatros* to illustrate the poet's fall from grace was of course arbitrary: this could have been done through virtually any of the early poems, which express the same event in a different way. It is, indeed, significant for our purposes that *L'Albatros* did not even figure in the 1857 edition of *Les Fleurs du mal,* for its addition is in some sense the proof of what in narrative terms might be called its redundancy. Apart from foreshadowing later poems about the artist's fall, *L'Albatros* is also a repetition of what had been stated in the previous poem, *Bénédiction;* there the poet exiled in the world of mortals looks up to that other world which is his true home:

> Vers le Ciel, où son oeil voit un trône splendide,
> Le Poète serein lève ses bras pieux . . .

Although *L'Albatros* appears, then, through its position in the text and the clarity of its reference, to constitute the first turning point in the pseudo-narrative of *Les Fleurs du mal,* it is in another sense no more than a variation on the theme stated in many other poems. Like others it could be excised without significant loss to our understanding of the 'story,' for it overlays and reduplicates the themes stated elsewhere. Its relation to the sequence of poems in which it is found is thus a synecdochal one, for it contains in miniature the whole story of those early poems which include and complement it. Beyond the single image, there is a doubling-up of the overall message, and the pseudo-narrative thus relies heavily on overlay: the event described elsewhere is also described here, and what is described here is also described elsewhere. If we were to look closely at the images contained within the poem (which is not our purpose here, for the network of images in *Les Fleurs du mal* belong more properly to the category of architecture than to that of pseudo-narrative) it would be possible to discover a more or less endless series of points of encounter between it and other poems in the collection. The image of the sky, and the duality implicit in the contrast between the heavens and the earth, are obviously of immense importance, and the

image of ships and journeys is another key element throughout (*La Chevelure, Le Voyage* etc.) Indeed, *L'Albatros* seems in some ways to be such an obvious anticipation of the final poem of the collection (with which, as we remember, it was first published jointly in 1859) that one might even think of it as a form of prolepsis—a moving forward in 'time' and a disguised reference to the final events in the pseudo-narrative.

Yet although *L'Albatros* evokes an 'event' which has no particular temporal location and which is re-evoked in other ways in many of the poems, it none the less turns upon a central issue of the pseudo-narrative. In prose narrative it is not uncommon for one event to be referred to repeatedly and to recur in different forms at various stages, and the fall from grace, exemplified in *L'Albatros,* can be seen in this manner. The difference from prose narrative is, of course, that we do not have a strong hierarchy of events clustering around two or three central turning points: rather, there is the bare structure of a possible story, the parabolic nature of which requires that it be enacted through the writing and composition of the poems themselves. The 'events' of the pseudo-narrative are few and simple, and they do not have strong dramatic charge, but by contrast the evocation of them is far more repetitive than is usually the case in true fictional narrative. This, then, is one reason why it is appropriate to talk of *pseudo*-narrative, for it is clear that the story of *Les Fleurs du mal* exists in outline alone. But let us move on to poem LXVIII, *Spleen*.

What could be said about the function of *L'Albatros* within the distribution of the text can also be applied, with some modifications, to the last of the four poems entitled *Spleen*. The piece corresponds to a particular moment in the pseudo-narrative, in this case one of intense depression, isolation, and a feeling of defeat. This moment itself divides—as is also often the case in true fictional narrative—into the series of sub-events which constitute it. After the stifling evocation of constraint and stagnation in the three opening stanzas, the harsh and violent jangling of the bells appears as the first of these occurrences. Subsequently the poet tells us that in his soul hearses move by in silent procession, that Hope weeps, and that Anguish plants her black flag upon his skull. We shall return shortly to the way these different images are introduced, for there is a metonymic progression which demonstrates their inclusion within the master image anyway. What should be retained for the time being is the concentration of main verbs at the end of the poem, and the suggestion thereby of a miniature series of pseudo-events. As in *L'Albatros* the poet appears to be giving us a sharply focused account of a particular stage of his spiritual journey.

Yet once again the moment of the poem is allegorical, and it is clear that the dark and oppressive sky which produces it is also the reference to such moments generally. The apparently isolated event becomes a variation on the paradigm. The very subject of the poem—that of the helplessness and despair of the poet—invites us to look out beyond the confines of this single account and see how this version of distress repeats, complements or anticipates other statements of it. The descent into 'spleen,' far from being the monopoly of this poem, is also described explicitly in the four poems that precede it (*La Cloche fêlée* and the three other *Spleen* poems). Despite the variations in the pseudo-narrative situation (the poet's soul as a cracked bell, the poet as king of a rainy country and so on) the network of images which runs through the poems is remarkably consistent and closely wrought, and indeed it is quite feasible (in an 'architectural' approach) to read the whole sequence as a homogenous unit: to the cracked bell of *La Cloche fêlée* corresponds the discordant sound of the bells here in 'Quand le ciel bas et lourd . . .'; or to the darkness and rain of 'Pluviôse, irrité . . .' corresponds the rain of 'Je suis comme le roi d'un pays pluvieux', and again the darkness and rain of 'Quand le ciel bas et lourd . . .'. Such cross-references can more or less be pursued at will, but it is not our purpose here to do anything more than acknowledge their existence. What must be emphasized is that the 'event' of depression and despair described in our *Spleen* poem operates within a network of similar, though (importantly) not identical references. What might seem to be an isolated episode in the pseudo-narrative is nested within a series of specular images of itself. There are not only those one-to-one relations between the images of this poem and the images in the poems immediately preceding it. There is also an anticipation of the following poems, and then there is the relation of this whole sequence of poems to the *Spleen et idéal* section generally (for collectively they appear to symbolize it.) And finally, as we proceed through the looking glass from our final *Spleen* poem to the sequence which contains it, and to the section which contains the sequence, we find at each of these separate levels a synecdochal relationship to the collection as a whole. As was the case with *L'Albatros,* the event of the poem is also the event of other poems and of whole sequences of poems, and in a sense it might also be seen as the central event of the whole collection, vastly multiplied through a series of images of itself.

But what occurs *within* the poem is also of interest in this respect, for we find, internally, exactly the same process of synecdochal reduplication as in the overall distribution of poems. We have already mentioned the series of conjoined verbs in the last two stanzas which give the effect of an array [of] sub-events constituting in their collectivity the occasion of the poet's depression. Closer scrutiny of these suggests that they are not separate stages of either a causal or temporal chain, but that they each overlay the others and present a different facet of what is a static and stagnant condition. There is an ironic contrast in the final stanza: on the one hand there is that enumeration of apparently separate pseudo-occurrences, and on the other hand there is the sameness, the inaction and the mental paralysis of which these so-called 'events' are no more than constituent elements. The increasingly dramatic verbs ('défilent', 'pleure', 'plante',) the sharp distinctions between moods and moments, the fragmented rhythms and the vivid personifications, all these stand in inverse proportion to the undifferentiated, unchanging inner state which they describe and—most importantly—of which they are a product. Though having the appearance of pseudo-events, they dissolve into an absence of events and a sense of eternal and dismal unity, for they are dependent upon and included within the master image:

> —Et de longs corbillards, sans tambours ni
>   musique,
> Défilent lentement dans mon âme; l'Espoir,
> Vaincu, pleure, et l'Angoisse atroce,
>   despotique,
> Sur mon crâne incliné plante son drapeau noir.

The violent ending of the poem is simply a restatement of the morbid and menacing condition of depression which has been evoked in similar images throughout. Despite its dramatic appearance it is neither an event nor a conclusion. Rather it is an elaboration.

Where, then, *is* the event? Perhaps we ought to look to the main verb in line thirteen ('Des cloches tout à coup sautent . . .'.) In this, the first of the series of allegorical images which conclude the poem, we might expect to find the nucleus of action around which the rest of the piece is constructed. And yet, whereas that is clearly the case *grammatically,* it is clearly not the case *semantically,* for in the series of subordinate clauses which precede the jangling of the bells we find precisely the cause and the occasion of that event: in other words, the event is a function of the context which the earlier subordinate clauses evoke; it is introduced by and dependent upon them. The violent clamour of bells, like the weeping of Hope or the murdering gesture of Anguish, is no more than a new image of the despair that has already been evoked, and as an independent reference to some pseudo-reality (that is to say, if it were removed from its context and allowed to stand alone) it would have virtually no meaning. It is a further interpretation of the initial theme of the poem from within the poem itself.

Just as the poem as a unit is embedded in and dependent upon the wider context, so, then, are its separate elements themselves constituted through repetition, interdependence and overlay. Far from being the 'singulative' account of events in some supposedly real world, the poem turns out to be a multiple construction of metaphoric and/or metonymic relations, so that the pseudo-narrative becomes a product of poetic construction. The threefold repetition of 'Quand . . .', with its substitution by 'Et que/Et qu'' in lines three and eleven, is already indicative, on the syntactic level, of the careful interlinking and interweaving of subordinate clauses, but a look at lines one and three of the poem would suggest that this interdependence also operates on the level of the images. The simile of the first line, in which the low and heavy sky is compared to a lid ('Quand le ciel bas et lourd pèse comme un couvercle . . .') is re-echoed in the third line by the suggestion that the sky embraces or contains the complete circle of the horizon ('Et que de l'horizon embrassant tout le cercle . . .'). Now in one sense this seems like a normal continuation of the image: the lid-like sky of line one is round, and it contains within it the circular horizon of line three. It is a fitting and powerful symbol of enclosure, reinforced by the strong rhyme of 'couvercle'/'cercle.' But let us look more closely at the image. The lid-like sky, bearing down on and *enclosing* the horizon, must be a larger entity than that horizon which is contained within it: in other words, the two are separate. And yet, is not the horizon of line three precisely the imagined circumference of the lid, i.e. the sky itself? The horizon of the three is thus both a sky within a sky—that is, a separate entity—and the same sky as the other one, since its visible circumference is also that of the first sky. The initial image of the poem, whilst appearing to become more elaborate and more explicit, in fact produces a synecdochal replay of itself.

The effectiveness of Baudelaire's procedure is obvious, for the sense of enclosure within enclosure through the identification of the sky with its circumference/horizon intensifies the feeling that escape is impossible: this is especially the case when the image of the sky which is developed here is compared to the image of it as a vast and open realm in some earlier poems such as *Elévation*. But, more importantly, what we have discovered through this is that the process of repetition and overlay operates not only in the outer relations between different poems, but also in the inner structuring of the poem itself. The 'event' which appears to be described in the sequence of *Spleen* poems, and in this poem in particular, dissolves within the nesting structure of the poem itself, of the poem in relation of other poems, and of the other poems in relation to the collection. And whereas it is clearly possible to view the descent into 'spleen' as a pseudo-event—for the very distribution of the poems encourages us to look at them as a progression or a sequence—that pseudo-event itself ultimately becomes impossible to locate. Precisely as we home in on it, it moves away from us. Thus we see, in *Les Fleurs du mal,* the foreshadowing of that decentring aesthetic which will operate in the later *Spleen de Paris*.

The last poem of the collection, *Le Voyage,* is a fitting evocation of departure and, finally, of imminent death. It is a moving conclusion, appropriately leaving the reader of this pseudo-narrative at the point where its 'hero' (in the allegorical disguise of the traveller of his poem) is about to make his journey into the unknown. The story ends at the point at which many conventional fictional narratives end, when the experiences of a hero's life are behind him and only death lies ahead. Time appears to have moved forward to the narrative present, and the retrospective account of the life and experiences of the artist meets up, in the final lines of the collection, with what in another context Genette terms the 'instance narrative.' This is, of course, a well contrived illusion (first because there *is* no temporal progression in *Les Fleurs du mal,* and second because the situation of the poet vis-à-vis his work, far from being a framing device, is itself the central event). Yet the overall distribution of the poems seems to imply that this final state of mind is at once a product of the earlier pieces (which it sums up) and the ultimate point of the pseudo-narrative trajectory. Indeed, those famous final lines of this famous final poem introduce a new and dramatic note, the impact of the conclusion being sharpened by the revelation of the attitude with which the pseudo-narrator now arms himself for death. For in his frustration and sorrow at the failure of life to live up to his idealistic dreams, he is prepared to gamble away his very existence in the hope that death may bring something new:

> Verse-nous ton poison pour qu'il nous
>   réconforte!
> Nous voulons, tant ce feu nous brûle le
>   cerveau,
> Plonger, au fond du gouffre, Enfer ou Ciel,
>   qu'importe?
> Au fond de l'Inconnu pour trouver du
>   *nouveau!*

This resounding and defiant rallying call has all the appearance of a decision. After his meanderings through the gamut of human emotions the poet/hero is now prepared, at last, to discard everything for that final gesture, that wholehearted acceptance of death. The earlier poems have produced this decision (and indeed—as happens in some fictional narratives—have also given some important pointers towards it) and yet paradoxically the decision has no further need of them, since by its very definition it must assert a severance with the 'past.' How different is the attitude towards death in *Le Voyage* from the attitude towards death in, say, *Le Rêve d'un curieux* which immediately precedes it: for there, the poet was still grappling with the nightmare that death might, after all, be no different from life itself; here, he puts such fears aside and wagers everything on the mere hope of novelty. But we remain aware that, sequentially, the attitude of the last poem is also a necessary outcome of the earlier ones. Like all good conclusions, the final moment of *Les Fleurs du mal* is thus both a summing up of the past, and a new urge towards the future. Janus-like, the writer seems temporally to be glancing in both directions. The past is re-echoed and certain facets of it repeated and concentrated into this final reliving of it, and yet the very repetition begets novelty and difference. The last 'event' of *Les Fleurs du mal* is steeped in this duality.

At the level of symbols and imagery, the re-emergence of the past is obvious in *Le Voyage,* for many of the earlier poems are implicitly evoked throughout it. The child of the first line, 'amoureux de cartes et d'estampes,' recalls that earlier child of *Bénédiction* whose spirit was equally eager to embrace the infinite. The God who is called upon and addressed as 'mon semblable, mon maître' (line 104) reminds us of the reader at the end of *Au Lecteur* who was addressed as 'mon semblable,—mon frère!' The themes of 'ennui', sin and debauchery, referred to in sections IV and V of the poem, remind us of many early pieces and also return us ultimately to *Au Lecteur.* The contrast of the sky and the sea which runs throughout *Le Voyage* (e.g., 'Nous avons vu des astres / Et des flots') is another of the master images of *Les Fleurs du mal,* as is the image of the voyage itself: the mood and theme of the final poem have, in this respect, been prepared long in advance, not only with *L'Albatros,* but also poems such as *Bohémiens en voyage, L'Homme et la mer* and so on. But it is not our purpose here to enter into such contrasts and counterpoints. Rather we should stress that their presence in the final lines of the pseudo-narrative is itself partly the means by which the conclusion is reached, for by returning to and repeating those images and themes which precede it, *Le Voyage* paradoxically asserts not its dependence upon them, but its own difference and its own finality.

More than almost any other poem, then, *Le Voyage* seems to constitute an 'event' precisely by its merging into the associative unity of the text as a whole. Through the series of symbolic and thematic analogies with which it can be linked to the earlier poems, it allows the final unfolding of the pseudo-narrative. This double function is achieved partly by the allegory of the journey itself. On one level the idea of the journey implies a readiness to break away and make a new departure, and this sets the poem apart from the others in the collection: they were about the poet's experiences within life, this is about his journey towards death. On another level, however, precisely the opposite obtains, for the journey symbolizes the poet's trajectory through life itself, as it has been described in the earlier poems; it refers back to them and constitutes the negative account of all the experiences he has already been through. The journey which his imaginary travellers undertake (and which is his own journey) turns out to be the image of the earlier poems, a veiled reference to them, and without stretching the point too far we might even see it as a form of writing about writing. As a 'representation' of reality, *Le Voyage* thus finds itself at two removes from life itself. The apparent 'mimesis' of this journey, the reality of this decision to undertake something new turns out to be no more than the restatement of what has gone before, and the allegory is not about the poet's own journey through life towards death, but rather an image of closure and conclusion which supplies the required note of finality. The event of the final poem, like the events of many earlier ones, is a self-reflexive one which ultimately leads the reader away from the pseudo-reality which is suggested, and back towards the creation of the text itself.

The extent to which *Le Voyage* both leads back to and emerges from the poems which have preceded might also be gauged by looking more closely at the nature of the reflection it provides, within its limited compass, of the overall 'story' of *Les Fleurs du mal.* The journey described here traces the entire movement of the collection, starting out with the idealistic search for ineffable beauty, then proceeding to the discovery that the real world does not correspond to the world of the imagination, and continuing with the descent into 'ennui,' the reaction of revolt, blasphemy and debauchery, and finally the preparation for death itself. Thus the poem which figures as the last of the section *La Mort* finally leads us back—precisely—to that very section which contains it. It is a perfect 'mise en abyme,' a mirror-image within the totality of that very totality which it helps to constitute and to complete. And just as the poem as a whole reflects the collection as a whole, so too the ending of the poem reflects the ending of the collection, so that the structure of synecdochal relations operates on two levels at once. Yet it is in part the duality of synecdochal relations that reveals the essential difference and separateness of this poem, which refers at once to itself as part of the final sequence and, beyond itself, back to the earlier poems in the collection. For at each level, it escapes complete identification with the totality which it helps to constitute. It does not provide a precise mirror-image of *La Mort* since it contains also a return to the sections which had preceded, nor does it simply reflect the collection as a whole since in its final stages it reaches a conclusion which, though anticipated, had not been reached or expressed earlier (not even in the poems of the final section.) The 'event' of the final poem in this pseudo-narrative is therefore both a repetition and a discovery of difference within repetition. Within the overall sequence of poems of *Les Fleurs du mal,* we thus find progression and alteration despite the high degree of symbolic and thematic analogy between poems.

What, then, are the lessons of this approach to *Les Fleurs du mal?* First and foremost we should stress again that it would be foolish, despite the series of 'events' and states of mind which the collection presents, to read the poems *purely and simply* on the level of pseudo-narrative. On such a reading, we are invariably led back to the poetic function and to the architecture of the work, as we realize that the events dissolve under scrutiny and become the allegorical representation of other events elsewhere (which, in their turn, are subject to the same displacement). The key events are, then, everywhere and nowhere: many poems refer to them, but no single poem gives an indispensable account of them. Whereas the overlay function in conventional fictional narrative is limited, and whereas the events themselves link together in hierarchical sequences, here the opposite is true: the actual sequence of events is in the background, and the same nucleus of issues is constantly re-echoed in different ways. Only in a limited sense can we follow the horizontal progression of events through the text, for we are constantly led back to the vertical axis in which the central paradigms are located. Baudelaire's pseudo-narrative is, then, a function of the poetic, and cannot be dissociated from it.

Yet it also seems clear from what we have said that a purely 'architectural' approach to *Les Fleurs du mal* runs the risk of playing down the differences and progressions which are created by analogy and reduplication between poems. In our desire to pursue the symbolic links from one poem to another, we risk seeing the whole collection as a static and unchangeable totality in which every element performs a fixed function of parallel or contrast. But repetition itself begets a difference and instates progression, and an awareness of the pseudo-narrative dimension of *Les Fleurs du mal* helps us to appreciate more fully the flexibility of relations between the poems. The individual poem stands apart, marks out a new stage in the sequence, and what is most interesting is that it does so precisely as it reflects, re-echoes or anticipates other poems. It is of course obvious that no poem can be symbolically determined and controlled by the other poems: but by standing separate it also asserts in some way its own gratuitousness, just as is the case of certain peripeteia in fictional narrative. To argue therefore that any particular poem is absolutely necessary, or that it is an absolute requirement to a given sequence, would be an error. The temptation of the 'architectural' approach to *Les Fleurs du mal* is that of justifying the order and sequence of poems as they stand and as they are given. Indeed, the somewhat less attractive subtext of its more reactionary versions is the prescription that we must only admire this perfect 'edifice' (whose every brick is crucial to the structure) and accept the pronouncements of those interpreters who—by a happy tautology—are able to confirm that this is so. But the concept of pseudo-narrative stops us looking in static terms at the relations between poems, and we are thus more easily able to avoid the absurdity of justifying the existing

order simply *because* it exists. In so far as it repeats a message stated elsewhere the poem is functioning repetitively, and is therefore not essential to the sequence; in so far as it changes that message it is adding a disposable element to the pseudo-narrative, an element as disposable and as potentially gratuitous as are 'new' events in any prose narrative. Together, the poems create the story, but no one poem is essential to the togetherness.

And on the issue of togetherness and separateness, we might ask ourselves a final question. What does the pseudo-narrative of *Les Fleurs du mal* tell us about the functioning of true fictional narrative? Let us recall Baudelaire's famous remark on the art of short-story writing in the essay on Edgar Allen Poe:

> Si la première phrase n'est pas écrite en vue de préparer cette impression finale, l'œuvre est manquée dès le début. Dans la composition tout entière, il ne doit pas se glisser un seul mot qui ne soit une intention, qui ne tende, directement ou indirectement, à parfaire le dessein prémédité.

Baudelaire's precept in fact lays great emphasis on the element of togetherness. Narrative is a gradual elaboration of the initial premise, and the suggestion is that no divergence is permissible from the pre-established trajectory. Certainly, there are narratives like this, and they tend, precisely, to have a poetic quality; but it is often also the case that, in the sequential arrangement of narrative, the original matrix is either surpassed, deformed or progressively deconstructed. The emphasis will then fall on horizontal progression rather than on paradigmatic conformity of the separate episodes. Let us imagine two possible extremes. On the one hand a purely poetic narrative would, in a sense, be pure repetition of the paradigm without any sequence, which would be an impossibility (such an impossibility was once perfectly expressed by Flaubert when he wrote of his vision of a 'livre sur rien'.) On the other hand an example of absolute prose narrative would be equally impossible, for it would involve pure sequence and a complete absence of relations between the episodes (a sort of picaresque novel run crazy: something of this vision is, paradoxically, also suggested in Baudelaire's famous letter to Arsène Houssaye quoted earlier.) Most fictional narratives are in practice situated at a workable point between these limits: whereas the emphasis is on sequence and progression, the separate episodes also become representations of the same paradigms (and indeed these separate representations themselves help to create sequence and progression.) It is to be expected that, in a collection of poems such as *Les Fleurs du mal,* the suggestion of narrative progression will be subservient to—and indeed a result of—the poetic function: and so, as opposed to what happens in fictional narrative, the relations between the different 'episodes' are heavily emphasized, and the sequence is in the

background. And yet, precisely because the poetic function engenders change within repetition, the story moves
on and—in a momentous act of self-reflection—finally
reaches its conclusion.

John Porter Houston (essay date 1991)

SOURCE: "The Two Versions of *Les Fleurs du Mal*
and Ideas of Form," in *The Ladder of High Designs:
Structure and Interpretation to the French Lyric Sequence,* edited by Doranne Fenoaltea and David Lee
Rubin, University Press of Virginia, 1991, pp. 100-37.

[*In the following essay, Houston examines the structural differences between the 1857 and the 1861 versions of* Les Fleurs du Mal.]

In 1857, upon the publication of the first edition, Barbey d'Aurevilly made his well-known reference to the
"architecture secrète" of *Les Fleurs du mal,* and the
phrase is often quoted, although it patently contains
false associations. To begin with the adjective *secrète,*
architecture is the most overt of arts; moreover, it is
one that shows a pronounced fondness for symmetry,
whether exemplified by a Gothic cathedral or a classical temple, the two architectural forms most likely to
have occurred to a reader in Barbey's day. Symmetry,
however, as the *Encyclopédie* had long before put it,
risks being the ruin of other arts, despite its basic role
in architecture. Nevertheless, we should be inclined to
censure those who mindlessly repeat the phrase rather
than Barbey himself, since the criticism of his period
was notoriously lacking in adequate terms to describe
literary forms.

The more common word applied to works of some
complexity was *composition,* a not very old term in
this sense, which supplemented the classical notion of
dispositio, the latter referring to the arrangement of
arguments in an oration. Since speeches were conceived
of as both a logical (or pseudological) and a histrionic
or emotive kind of persuasion, the idea was not difficult to transfer to poems, although classical rhetoric
scarcely explored the arrangement of parts in a manner suitable for treating the range of Greek and Latin
poetry.

Composition tended to bear with it the pedagogical
association of a neat *plan* or outline, and it is obvious
that even at the level of the individual poem, the ordinary notions of rational arrangement, associated in
France with the name of Buffon, could not always apply
to *Les Fleurs du mal.* While **"Une Charogne"** (A
carrion), **"L'Albatros"** (The albatross), and **"Obsession"** (Obsession) might be reduced to the sort of *plan*
in which order and conclusion are readily perceived,
"Le Balcon" (The balcony) or the elliptical **"Causerie"** (Chat) represent patterns that ordinary rhetorical

criteria could have less successfully explained. **"La
Chevelure"** (The hair) occupies perhaps a middle
ground between the traditional logic of development
and a newer associational movement derived, in this
case, from the process of involuntary memory. On the
level of the individual line or sentence, which is what
compositio referred to in Latin, some startling colloca-
tions appear in *Les Fleurs du mal* that also violate the
customary organization of language:

> Fourmillante cité, cité pleine de rêves,
> Où le spectre en plein jour raccroche le
>   passant!

> Swarming city, full of dreams, where the specter in
> broad daylight accosts the passerby!

The poetic *cité* and *raccroche,* a term of street commerce referring especially to hucksters and whores,
demand, by their coexistence in one grammatical unit,
a more elaborate theory of parts and wholes than was
usual.

Baudelaire's remark to the effect that his book, not
being a pure "album," had a beginning and an end,
prudently avoids the question of what separates the
opening and the closing, a matter he would probably
have had as much difficulty conceptualizing as Flaubert would have had in explaining his fictional technique, even though he foresaw the creation of methods
and terminologies for doing so. The critical faculties
of the artist, to use a notion dear to Eliot and Valéry,
tend generally to be more practical and directed to his
own work than theoretical and disinterested. However,
the peculiar balance between creative work and theorizing that Coleridge exemplifies makes his conception
of literary structures, however flawed, worth considering in the study of romantic literature.

The idea of organic form, expounded by the German
romantics, especially August Wilhelm Schlegel, and
developed by Coleridge, offers a relevant historical term
and theory for describing Baudelaire's work, even
though it found no obvious echo in France. Its analogy
between a plant—whole and yet composed of quite
varied elements—and a work of literature served to
account for the diversity of literary forms, a diversity
quite as conspicuous in French romantic literature as
elsewhere. In the weakness of organic theory lies also
its strength: the affirmation of the plant analogy in the
absence of any serious knowledge of biochemistry
betokens the faith the authors of *Faust, La Comédie
humaine,* and *La Légende des siècles* had in the validity of the singular works they put together and that
contemporary critical thought in France was hardly
equipped to deal with.

I shall treat the ramifications of organic theory in regard to appropriate loci in *Les Fleurs du mal,* but I

should like to make clear from the outset that I consider it primarily of historical value and not, as New Criticism did, an adequate account of literary forms in general. Biochemistry is better understood today, and the genetic mutations, cancerous growths, and other peculiar phenomena that are part of organic life suggest that romantic literary theory based on organicism is as fanciful and arbitrary as trying to explain plants in terms of poems (proceeding from the lower and more commonplace to the higher and rarer, in good Aristotelian fashion). I shall return to the insufficiencies of organic theory and suggest an alternative possibility.

Of the many allusions to the "architecture" of *Les Fleurs du mal,* most are, of course, somewhat vague, belletrist affirmations, but I shall refer to the two most elaborate accounts of it, which represent opposing points of view. Albert Feuillerat [in *Studies by Members of the French Department of Yale University,* 1941] maintained that the 1857 edition of the work was superior in structure and power to the 1861 version, while, in a book-length demonstration [*Baudelaire's Tragic Hero* 1961], D. J. Mossop presented the second edition as a continuation and improvement on the first. For him the general sense of the 1861 edition is implicit in the earlier one. Yet another point of view is possible: Antoine Adam, in his richly annotated edition of *Les Fleurs du mal* [1959], rejected subtle attempts to see anything but the most obvious elements of organization in either edition. The methods employed in discussing the work are not very elaborate in regard to theory. Thematic material tends to be considered as if a conventional *plan* or narrative were at stake. Mossop's arguments are more sophisticated than Feuillerat's, but his comparison of the volume to a "tragedy" with an "action" constrains him to a somewhat more linear and logical reading of Baudelaire than adepts of difficult or problematic literary forms may find appropriate. I believe still another approach to the problem has validity: the 1857 and 1861 versions of *Les Fleurs du mal* are essentially different works, with a somewhat different general sense, and each has a structure that is distinctive and reasonably satisfying in its own way. Organicism provides a useful perspective on both Baudelaire's poem cycles and their interrelations.

It is best to start with a brief analysis of how the 1857 *Fleurs du mal* was put together, since some of the problems commentators have found in it persist in the later edition, and several of the notions of structure that will emerge are relevant to the 1861 version. I shall discuss parts of the opening section, **"Spleen et Idéal,"** in some detail, as a certain number of the greatest changes occurred there.

The relation of the **"Au lecteur"** to what follows presents us with a characteristic peculiarity: to speak of what will come to be identified as a "modern" state of mind or vice, Baudelaire uses a series of personifica-

tions culminating in the more fully developed image of Ennui smoking a water pipe. We have here an allusion to an allegorical convention that is usually traced back to Prudentius and in which abstractions are embodied in a more or less human shape. While Baudelaire uses some imagery that seems distinctly of his own day and renews the apostrophe (**"Hypocrite lecteur";** [Hypocrite reader]) by placing it at the end for maximum surprise and dissonance, he nonetheless reminds us that personification allegory had often been the vehicle for an orthodox moralizing, which contrasts sharply with the praise of a dark and sinister female to be found shortly afterwards in **"Les Bijoux"** (The jewels) or **"Je te donne ces vers"** (I give you these verses). Moreover, the antiquated air of the convention seems to represent some sort of significantly paradoxical taste in a volume that also contains the quite new genre of the dramatic monologue, such as we find it in **"Tu mettrais l'univers entier"** (You would put the entire universe) some twenty poems further on.

Allegory and exemplum are scarcely absent from romantic poetry, and the theoretical distinction between allegory (mechanical and bad) and symbolism (organic and good) formulated in Germany and England, if not in France, has been shown to be untenable. At the same time, however, allegory as used, say, in *Les Contemplations* does not seem calculated to make us aware of a contrast between it and more recent modes of writing. Thus Vigny's personification allegory in "Les Destinées" (The destinies) appears, in the aggregate of his later poetry, merely to conform to a certain Miltonic taste hardly surprising in a poet born more than twenty years before Baudelaire. The periodic recurrence of overtly old-fashioned conventions in *Les Fleurs du mal* suggests the generality of meaning that allegory is supposed to have—in opposition to the autobiographical and personal—as well as the self-conscious didacticism, at once serious and ironic in view of the book's frequently unedifying content.

Right at the beginning, we find an example of Baudelaire's peculiar ways of juxtaposing his poems. **"Au lecteur,"** with its vision of Ennui, seems unrelated to **"Bénédiction,"** the first numbered poem, which deals with the poet's ultimate redemption. However, the poet is said to be born into a "monde ennuyé" (bored world), and this tangential connection is one characteristic means of tying together poems that have no linear thematic movement between them. **"Le Soleil"** followed **"Bénédiction"** in 1857 (**"L'Albatros"** had not yet been written):

> Ce père nourricier, ennemi des chloroses,
> Eveille dans les champs les vers comme les
>   roses;

> This foster father, enemy of anemic pallor, awakens in the fields verses [worms] as well as roses.

The double reference to the poet and to nature does introduce a linear grouping with **"Élévation"** (Elevation) ("Le langage des fleurs et des choses muettes": The language of flowers and mute things) and **"Correspondances"** (Correspondences):

> La Nature est un temple où de vivants piliers
> Laissent parfois sortir de confuses paroles.

> Nature is a temple where living pillars sometimes
> allow indistinct words to be uttered.

It is important to notice that the poet is not the only subject, but that nature—for which the sun is sometimes a synecdoche in *Les Fleurs du mal*—is amply evoked. Many commentators practice, instead of a purely esthetic analysis of *Les Fleurs du mal,* what I would call an archaeological investigation of the work. They are anxious to find the presumed date and circumstances of composition of each poem, and, as a result, they like to dismiss some poems as early and unrepresentative of the Baudelaire they have constructed. Such considerations lead almost always to the remark that Baudelaire detested nature, and therefore they ignore its important role in *Les Fleurs du mal.* However, it is the text of the book that generates meaning, not what Baudelaire said elsewhere or at a different time, and clearly the idea of nature is an essential one as we begin reading the 1857 volume.

The sense of nature emerges more fully in **"J'aime le souvenir de ces époques nues"** (I love the memory of these naked eras), where we see that primordial beauty, that of the body, is related to nature, conceived as dominating an earlier period in the history of man:

> J'aime le souvenir de ces époques nues,
> Dont le soleil se plaît à dorer les statues.
> Alors l'homme et la femme en leur agilité
> Jouissaient sans mensonge et sans anxiété
> Et, le ciel amoureux leur caressant l'échine,
> Exerçaient la santé de leur noble machine.

> I love the memory of those naked ages, whose statues
> the sun is fond of gilding. Then, man and woman
> in their nimbleness loved without lies or anxiety,
> and, with the loving sky caressing their spines, made
> use of the health of their noble machine.

Thus, we have, along with poetic beauty and nature, a third notion introduced, that of history, and, in the course of the poem, the idea of the nineteenth century as a late and fallen age:

> Le Poète aujourd'hui, quand il veut concevoir
> Ces native grandeurs, aux lieux où se font
>   voir
> La nudité de l'homme et celle de la femme,

> Sent un froid ténébreux envelopper son âme
> Devant ce noir tableau plein d'épouvantement.

> The Poet today, when he wants to conceive of these natural splendors, in those places where the nakedness of man and of woman are displayed, feels a shadowy cold envelop his soul before this black vision full of terror.

The somewhat neoclassical diction Baudelaire uses here may elude the modern reader unaccustomed to deciphering that particular version of periphrastic style: the *lieux* in question are public baths. One of the numerous paradoxical effects of *Les Fleurs du mal* derives from the way Baudelaire will at one time use decorous circumlocutions, at another introduce terms like *voirie* (in the sense of street sweepers) or *réverbère* (in the sense of street lamp). Other forms of lexical disparateness in **"J'aime le souvenir"** include a reference to the chapped hands and lips of realist fiction (*gerçures*) just after a phrase on women and man that could have come from an eighteenth-century libretto: "les beautés qui le nommaient leur roi" (The beauties who named him their king). Later, figurative infant wraps (*langes,* the banal nursery term) are made of bronze, more poetically designated *airain*. The inelegant familiar locution *comme qui dirait,* "a sort of," and the rare *épouvantement* (terror)—sometimes considered stronger than *épouvante* (fright)—likewise seem to clash. This poem ostensibly in praise of lost natural beauty acquires, through odd juxtapositions of vocabulary, an effect of bemused irony, the generalized kind of irony we find in Flaubert, which does not so much have an object as represent qualified assertion, a submerged skepticism. Polarities in linguistic usage make one aware of at least potential contrary attitudes.

This oscillation between two conceptions of style that his contemporaries tended to find antithetical and mutually exclusive is paralleled by the increasing contrasts between past and present in the first twenty-five or so poems of the 1857 **"Spleen et Idéal."** Good weather and nature seem opposed to the city, which one inhabits in winter and which is also the characteristic background of modern life. This is not an invariable nexus of associations in the text, but one the reader tends to form almost unconsciously. From the city bathhouse we move to the main point of Baudelaire's gradually evolving chain of notions:

> Nous avons, il est vrai, nations corrompues,
> Aux peuples anciens des beautés inconnues:
> Des visages rongés par les chancres du coeur,
> Et comme qui dirait des beautés de langueur;

> We, corrupted nations, have, it is true, beauties
> unknown to ancient races: faces gnawed by chancres
> of the heart, and a sort of beauty of languor.

The historicizing character of romantic thought is so pronounced that it often makes one uncertain as to whether a writer's work is mythopoeic or documentary. When Baudelaire published a few poems in a review in 1851, he spoke of the historical basis of his work, which depicted "les agitations et les mélancolies de la jeunesse moderne" (The agitations and melancholies of modern youth). This pattern of temporal contrasts, represented sometimes in terms of city and country or sun and darkness, is stronger in the 1857 *Fleurs du mal* by virtue of the absence of certain imposing later additions that distract from it. The description of painters in **"Les Phares"** (The lighthouses), which follows **"J'aime le souvenir"** and runs from the exuberant healthiness of Rubens to the dark romanticism of Goya and Delacroix, might be taken as an implicit illustration of the changes in the conception of beauty.

"La Muse malade" (The sick muse) expresses a hope to return to the inspiration of Phoebus and Pan, but **"La Muse vénale"** (The venal muse) sees art as hopelessly debased. **"Le Mauvais moine"** (The bad monk) and **"L'Ennemi"** (The enemy) contemplate the danger of artistic impotence, and **"Le Guignon"** (Bad luck) considers the inaccessibility of beauty. So far Baudelaire has followed a thematic arrangement of poems that could be described as linear. The sequential relations between poems are fairly easy to grasp, so that the movement between the picture of nature and the poet through to his unfortunate modern situation is deftly accomplished. What follows, however, is a group of five poems that do not fit a linear interpretation.

In **"La Vie antérieure"** (The past life), **"Bohémiens en voyage"** (Bohemians traveling), **"L'Homme et la mer"** (The man and the sea), **"Don Juan aux enfers"** (Don Juan in Hell) and **"Châtiment de l'orgueil"** (Punishment and pride), Feuillerat finds Baudelaire's "qualités": love of liberty, independence, and limited pride. Mossop offers a similar explanation and adds the not unexpected archaeological comment that these are early poems that do not fit the "architecture." It is possible, however, especially in the light of later parts of **"Spleen et Idéal,"** to consider that Baudelaire deliberately violated linear movement at times and that cross-references are as important in *Les Fleurs du mal* as the more smoothly sequential kind of order. Don Juan and the blasphemous theologian of **"Châtiment de l'orgueil"** seem related to later allusions to horrible modern beauty and Lady Macbeth; the story of the impious Don Juan, Shakespearean drama, and man's revolt against an orthodox God are quite characteristic preoccupations of the romantics in their search to define the modern. **"La Vie antérieure"** anticipates exotic references; **"L'Homme et la mer"** illustrates a correspondence, and **"Bohémiens en voyage,"** with its mention of Cybele, recalls the poet's rapport with nature. I do not think I am indulging in any interpretive subtleties here; some familiarity with Baudelaire's contemporaries is perhaps by itself enough to suggest these far-from-recondite associations. Above all, I do not wish to imply that there are hidden keys to the patterns of Baudelaire's volume that I alone have uncovered. It seems to me that such strategies of reading are as unwarranted in regard to *Les Fleurs du mal* as are naive psychological speculations that imply that Baudelaire was somehow unique. Both simply betray unfamiliarity with the nineteenth century and its concerns.

Our awareness that a pseudonarrative linearity is frequently abandoned for an arrangement of cross-references increases when, after the superficially miscellaneous poems I have just mentioned, we encounter **"La Beauté"**:

> Je trône dans l'azur comme un sphinx incompris;
> J'unis un coeur de neige à la blancheur des cygnes;
> Je hais le movement qui déplace les lignes,
> Et jamais je ne pleure et jamais je ne ris.

> I sit enthroned in the azure like an uncomprehended Sphinx; I unite a heart of snow to the whiteness of swans; I hate all movement that displaces lines, and never do I weep, never do I laugh.

This poem is sometimes explained as belonging to Baudelaire's art-for-art's-sake period and unrepresentative of his esthetics. However, this vision of a statue is again an evocation of an early form of art and beauty, one that is no longer available to the poet, and Baudelaire then, by contrast, evokes a more modern art in **"L'Idéal"**:

> Ce qu'il faut à ce coeur profond comme un abîme,
> C'est vous, Lady Macbeth, âme puissante au crime,
> Rêve d'Eschyle éclos au climat des autans.

> What this heart, deep as an abyss, needs is you, Lady Macbeth, a soul powerful in crime, an Aeschylean dream born in the climate of boisterous winds.

This is not, however, the modern art of Gavarni's chlorotic girls but modernism in the sense in which Hugo and other romantics dated it from Shakespeare and the supposed split in conscience and dual sensibility that occurred with him. It is as if Baudelaire had changed his example of the modern in order to complicate matters for those who would eventually try to isolate his "critical theory" or his "doctrine" of modern beauty, to use a term once beloved of French academics. There are, as we shall see in regard to the 1861

Fleurs du mal, a few places where Baudelaire makes use of something like unambiguous statements and abstract propositions, but that should not encourage us to extract one simple idea from a range of attitudes.

From **"La Géante"** the primordial earth woman, to **"Les Bijoux,"** which was placed after it in 1857 and was later suppressed by court order, we have yet another reminder of the strong historical theme present in the early part of *Les Fleurs du mal:*

> Du temps que la Nature en sa verve puissante
> Concevait chaque jour des enfants monstrueux,
> J'eusse aimé vivre auprès d'une jeune géante
> Comme aux pieds d'une reine un chat
>   voluptueux.

> In the age when Nature, in her powerful energy, conceived every day monstrous children, I would have liked to live with a young giant, like a sensual cat at the feet of a queen.

and

> Je croyais voir unis par un nouveau dessin
> Les hanches de l'Antiope au buste d'un
>   imberbe,
> Tant sa taille faisait ressortir son bassin.
> Sur ce teint fauve et brun, le fard était
>   superbe!

> I thought I was seeing the hips of the Antiope united, by a new drawing, to the torso of a beardless youth, so much did her waist make her belly stand out. On that wild and brown skin the cosmetic was superb!

The contrast is rich: the beauty of nature, growth, and fecundity are set against a *new* beauty, suggestive of both the sterile sport and the hermaphrodite; outdoors and indoors, light and darkness are evoked. A reader who has never encountered the condemned poems in the 1857 volume can scarcely imagine how much was lost by their excision: **"La Géante,"** perhaps a dull piece in itself, gains immeasurably by the abrupt movement to **"Les Bijoux."**

This last poem and the immediately following ones— those referred to as the "cycle" of Jeanne Duval—are resolutely poems of somber or exotic modern beauty. It is easy to regard the sequence from **"Les Bijoux"** to the envoi **"Je te donne ces vers"** as a coherent group (though one must remember certain poems were not in the 1857 edition); biographers have taught us that they all refer to Jeanne Duval. But what of the readers of 1857, who had no footnotes or introductions to tell them what to think about the origins of the poems? There are three poems on death, which are carefully separated (**"Une Charogne," "Remords posthume"** (Posthumous remorse), and **"Je te donne ces vers"**).

Might not each of them have been seen as the conclusion of a group? Furthermore, Adam remarks that in **"Le Balcon"** and **"Je te donne ces vers,"** for example, which were juxtaposed in 1857, the vision of the woman is very different. In **"Le Balcon":**

> Je sais l'art d'évoquer les minutes heureuses,
> Et revis mon passé blotti dans tes genoux.
> Car à quoi bon chercher tes beautés
>   langoureuses
> Ailleurs qu'en ton cher corps et qu'en ton
>   coeur si doux?

> I know the art of evoking happy minutes, and I relive my past huddled in your lap. For what use is there in seeking your languorous beauties elsewhere than in your dear body and sweet heart?

In the following poem the poet wishes that:

> Ta mémoire, pareille aux fables incertaines,
> Fatigue le lecteur ainsi qu'un tympanon,
> . . . . .
> Etre maudit à qui, de l'abîme profond
> Jusqu'au plus haut du ciel, rien, hors moi, ne
>   répond!

> Your memory, like dubious fables, may tire the reader like a dulcimer . . . accursed being, whom nothing, from the deep abyss to the highest heaven, nothing except me answers.

Although the poems are not necessarily mutually exclusive, the contrast between the lyricism and the sweetness and gentleness of **"Le Balcon"** and the harsh envoi poem suggests the variety of attitudes that biographical information tends to smooth over in its attempt to epitomize the poet's relations with his Black Venus. Biographical criticism has had perhaps its most dismal success with Baudelaire, in that anyone who has read widely in studies of him finds it difficult to ignore distracting attributions of poems to the inspiration of this or that "Venus" and simply to read what Baudelaire wrote.

The foregoing complaint is especially relevant to the sense of subdivisions or changes in **"Spleen et Idéal."** As I have mentioned, Baudelaire's belated muse is much concerned with things past or coming to an end, so that temporary endings or false conclusions recur in **"Spleen et Idéal."** Indeed, the poems that follow the envoi to Jeanne Duval contain no suggestion of beginnings, and our accounts of Mme. Sabatier, to whom they were sent, seem sometimes to get in the way more than anything else. **"Que diras-tu ce soir"** and **"Le Flambeau vivant"** are a sequence related by the image of the torch. They both have an air of antiquated praise, a suggestion of medieval or renaissance poems of celebration:

"Je suis belle, et j'ordonne
Que pour l'amour de moi vous n'aimiez que
    le Beau;
Je suis l'Ange gardien, la Muse et la
    Madone."
Ils marchent devant moi, ces Yeux pleins de
    lumiéres,
Qu'un Ange très savant a sans doute aimantés;
Ils marchent, ces divins frères qui sont mes
    frères,
Secouant dans mes yeux leurs feux diamantés.

"I am beautiful, and I order you, for love of me, to love only what is beautiful; I am the Guardian Angel, the Muse, and the Madonna." They walk before me, those Eyes full of light, which a very learned Angel has surely made magnetic; they walk, those divine brothers who are my brothers, shaking into my eyes their diamond-studded fires.

There followed in 1857 **"A celle qui est trop gaie"** (To one who is too gay), which some commentators want to assign to someone other than Mme. Sabatier. But the problem is not one of deciding what kind of poem Baudelaire should have sent her, but rather its place in **"Spleen et Idéal"**:

Ta tête, ton geste, ton air
Sont beaux comme un beau paysage;
Le rire joue en ton visage
Comme un vent frais dans un clair.

Your head, your movements, your look are beautiful like a beautiful landscape; laughter plays in your face like a fresh breeze in a bright sky.

Clearly this refers back to the initial idea of nature, to which the poet's reaction has now changed:

Quelquefois dans un beau jardin
Où je traînais mon atonie,
J'ai senti, comme une ironie,
Le soleil déchirer mon sein,

Et le printemps et la verdure
Ont tant humilié mon coeur,
Que j'ai puni sur une fleur
L'insolence de la Nature.

Sometimes, in a beautiful garden where I was dragging my listlessness, I felt, like an irony, the sun tear my bosom, and the springtime and the greenery so humiliated my heart that I punished a flower for the insolence of Nature.

The poet then experiences a modern, nocturnal revolt against nature and threatens the woman with a sadistic nighttime assault, much as in the earlier **"Je t'adore à**

l'égal" (I adore you equally), where, in a dramatic shift of style unparalleled in Baudelaire, antiquated adoration gives way to lurid romantic frenzy. In other words, there are analogous movements of tone quite independent of the woman addressed and very much related to Baudelaire's historical contrast between an older mood, beauty, and literary convention and those peculiar to his own time. (All this, of course, was lost with the poem's suppression.)

The violent contrast between **"A celle qui est trop gaie"** and the preceding poems leads to two confessions, that of the poet (**"Réversibilité"**: Reversibility):

Ange plein de gaieté, connaissez-vous
    l'angoisse,
La honte, les remords, les sanglots, les ennuis,
Et les vagues terreurs de ces affreuses nuits
Qui compriment le coeur comme un papier
    qu'on froisse?

Angel full of gaiety, do you know the anguish, the shame, the remorse, the sobs, the troubles, and the vague terrors of those frightful nights that squeeze the heart like a piece of paper being crumpled?

and that of the woman (**"Confession"**), who affirms:

Que bâtir sur les coeurs est une chose sotte;
    Que tout craque, amour et beautê,
Jusqu'à ce que l'Oubli les jette dans sa hotte
    Pour les rendre à l'Eternité!

Building on hearts is a foolish thing to do, everything cracks, love and beauty, until Oblivion throws them into the basket on his back to return them to Eternity!

These two poems seem in a way to resolve the antithesis between **"Le Flambeau vivant"** and **"A celle qui est trop gaie"**; she is not an angel, and he is not a devil. But when we look a bit closer at the style, we notice that while his confession is eloquent in its anguish, hers contains, before the splendid Shakespearean image of Time with a basket at his back, lines that are a bit equivocal in implication:

Pauvre ange, elle chantait, votre note criade:
    "Que rien ici-bas n'est certain,
Et que toujours, avec quelque soin qu'il se
    farde,
    Se trahit l'égoïsme humain;
Que c'est un dur métier que d'être belle
    femme."

Poor angel, your shrill note was singing, "That nothing on this earth is certain and that, with whatever care it may disguise itself, human selfishness always betrays itself; . . . that it is a hard job being a beautiful woman."

This lament is not much superior in freshness to Emma Bovary's language. In fact, one might infer that, while the woman may be a nice enough object, her finest sentiments are trite and sound lifted from something she has read. The sense of cliché is sometimes difficult to establish in regard to French romantic verse because of its closeness in vocabulary to prose. As Louis Maigron demonstrated long ago, those of Baudelaire's contemporaries whose tastes were literary but who were not professional writers often wrote to one another in a kind of pastiche style that quickly depreciated poetic coinage. Baudelaire's shifts of style elsewhere are frequently cunning, his sense of the hackneyed acute, for whatever reason he may use it. I suspect there is enough irony here to qualify the poem's value as a resolution of contraries. Moreover, to prevent too strong an effect of conclusion, Baudelaire returns to imagery suggestive of Dante and Petrarch in **"L'Aube spirituelle"** (Spiritual dawn), which follows.

Still another example of Baudelaire's avoiding a closure satisfying to biographical readings comes in **"Le Flacon"** (The flask), supposed to be the last of the poems addressed to Mme. Sabatier:

Je serai ton cercueil, aimable pestilence!
Le témoin de ta force et de ta virulence,
Cher poison préparé par les anges! Liqueur
Qui me ronge, ô la vie et la mort de mon
    coeur!

I shall be your coffin, aimiable pestilence! The witness of your strength and virulence, dear poison prepared by the angels! Fluid which eats away at me, O life and death of my heart!

Now his love is a poison, which, by the principle of recurrence, recalls more the Jeanne Duval poems than the immediately preceding ones. Commentators consider this poem an envoi to the "cycle of the White Venus," but Baudelaire clearly intended no such break, for the following poem, **"Le Poison,"** directly picks up the idea of a venomous bond between poet and lover:

Tout cela ne vaut pas le poison qui découle
    De tes yeux, de tes yeux verts.

All that is not worth the poison that flows from your eyes, from your green eyes.

The curious method of biographical commentary is to pretend that some rather varied poems make a coherent whole, but at the same time to break up the sequence of **"Spleen et Idéal"** into sections dealing with different women who are supposed to be treated quite differently. Baudelaire's complicated play of recurrence and cross-references is thereby suppressed, and we are left with the "album" he claimed not to have assembled.

What happens from this point on in **"Spleen et Idéal"** is that Baudelaire arranges his poems so that, while there are thematic sequences of two or more poems (notably the **"Spleen"** group), a good deal of contrast and cross-reference obtains. For example, **"Le Poison"** and **"Ciel brouillé"** (Uncertain sky) both depict, in sequence, a dangerous woman, but **"Le Chat,"** which follows, is more reminiscent of the other cat poems than anything else. Next come poems of praise of beauty, **"Le Beau Navire"** and **"L'Invitation au voyage"** (Invitation to a voyage), but they are followed by **"L'Irréparable"** (The irreparable) (anticipating the later **"L'Irrémédiable"** [The irremediable]) and **"Causerie,"** both poems of aging and pain concerning the past. If the bitterness of **"Causerie"** leads somewhat elliptically to **"L'Héautontimorouménos,"** (The Self-executioner) the subsequent **"Franciscae meae laudes"** (My praises for Frances) could not be more contrastive.

The interplay between thematic linearity and cross-reference has bothered those commentators who note it. They show a distinct preference for the former. Thus the "Spleen" group, with which we can associate the preceding **"Cloche Fêlée"** (Cracked bell) and the following **"Brumes et pluies"** (Mists and rains) and **"L'Irrémédiable,"** seems a satisfactory conclusion to **"Spleen et Idéal,"** while the real conclusion, with its very mixed series of poems, does not. However, the mild mood of some of these later poems, such as **"Je n'ai pas oublié, voisine de la ville"** (I have not forgotten, neighbor of the town), **"Tristesses de la lune"** (Sadness of the moon), or **"La Musique,"** serves a perceptible structural function when we consider that Baudelaire, in 1857, placed the section **"Fleurs du mal"** directly after **"Spleen et Idéal."** "Fleurs du mal" is almost uniformly somber, and therefore some lightening of the tone at the end of the preceding section helps to set off, by a fairly vivid contrast, the series on eroticism and death.

Within **"Fleurs du mal"** we encounter one passage that contains the seed of the conclusion to the 1857 volume. In **"Lesbos"** the poet envisages some kind of redemptory value:

Tu tires ton pardon de l'éternel martyre,
Infligé sans relâche aux coeurs ambitieux,
Qu'attire loin de nous le radieux sourire
Entrevu vaguement au bord des autres cieux!

You obtain your pardon from the eternal martyrdom inflicted unrelentingly on ambitious hearts, which the radiant smile, vaguely glimpsed at the edge of the other heavens, draws far away from us!

This notion of pardon stands out in the midst of so much imagery of deathly eroticism and points toward the final poem. Although making synthesizing generalities about sections of *Les Fleurs du mal* is a more delicate and risky matter than it is with even a complicated but structured collection like Hugo's *Les Contemplations,* we can characterize **"Fleurs du mal"** as the lowest point in the depiction of experience in the whole work. There is a kind of analogy in the 1857 *Fleurs du mal* to a harrowing of hell, with a certain feeling of ascent from the depths on the far side of evil. It is a common romantic idea that the nineteenth century was a sort of purgatory on earth, or even a temporary hell. Thus Baudelaire conveys carefully the idea of a fall from an earlier age at the beginning of *Les Fleurs du mal,* and he will complement it with a rising movement at the end. This cyclic pattern, which Northrop Frye would derive ultimately from the Bible, is, of course, characteristic of the romantic imagination to the point of obsessiveness.

"Révolte" (Revolt) which follows **"Fleurs du mal,"** rejects Christianity and its tyrannical God in favor of man; the theme is a familiar romantic one, and it is idle to argue about Baudelaire's religious convictions in regard to it. Again, the text is the source of meaning, not Baudelaire's comments elsewhere. To say, as is done, that the verse belongs to Baudelaire's "socialist" period does not obviate the fact that it serves as an explosion of energy and decision after the often passive submission to destruction in **"Fleurs du mal."** We note that the pattern of fall, revolt, and ascension is the revolutionary variant, widespread in the nineteenth century, of the Christian cyclic myth. **"Le Vin"** (Wine), the penultimate section in 1857, also suggests escape from the wretched conditions of life. Its flaw, according to Feuillerat, who would otherwise defend the cheerful celebration of wine, lies in the somber **"Vin de l'assassin"** (Assassin's wine). However, the poem, with its depiction of a sordid crime, serves to qualify the praise of wine: wine is not the ultimate good but a step by which some of life's horror can be dispelled. Only death will constitute the final release. In this connection, we observe that to see wine in changing perspectives merely recapitulates a typical movement of **"Spleen et Idéal"** by which, as I have pointed out, occurs the juxtaposition, in the 1857 *Fleurs du mal,* of the female figures of **"Le Balcon"** and **"Je te donne ces vers,"** who, if not quite antithetical, bear very different associations.

"La Mort" (Death) in 1857 consisted of only three sonnets. This has been seen as a great weakness in the "architecture" of the volume, too slim a conclusion for so much that precedes. Obviously, Barbey d'Aurevilly, whose impression of an edifice was based on the 1857 volume, was scarcely thinking of any real building when he made his remark. This asymmetrical ending is a tentative, suggestive one rather than a resounding conclusion, for reasons that emerge from the third and final poem. Death is presented as a consolation for lovers and for the poor in the first two sonnets; then comes **"La Mort des artistes"** (Artists' deaths):

> Combien faut-il de fois secouer mes grelots
> Et baiser ton front bas, morne caricature?
> Pour piquer dans le but, de mystique nature,
> Combien, ô mon carquois, perdre de javelots?

> How many times must I shake my bells and kiss your low forehead, gloomy caricature? To hit the target, mystic in nature, how many javelins must I lose, o my quiver?

The historical reference reaffirms itself here: the lines are reminiscent of **"La Muse vénale,"** the depiction of the low estate to which art has fallen in modern times. A particularly apt word is *caricature;* Baudelaire, like his contemporaries, had observed that the romantic period saw an extraordinary flowering of this minor art. Beyond that, there is perhaps a certain ironic awareness of all the senses the word *artist* had acquired in the nineteenth century: aside from the neutral meaning of one who practices an art, such as sculpture; there was the artistic temperament of the pretentious dabbler or affected sensibilities; the artist like Jeanne Duval, who appeared on the stage as an adjust to prostitution; jugglers or other popular entertainers, who were as much artists as Michelangelo; and all the other dubious applications of the word. The trivialization of the noun was almost simultaneous with its acquiring the most grandiose connotations.

Recalling the effect of allegory that Baudelaire explicitly created in **"Au lecteur"** and periodically reinforces with generalizing, third-person references like **"L'Homme et la Mer"** or **"Le Crépuscule du matin"** (Dawn), we should observe that the lovers, the poor, and the artists whose deaths are depicted in the concluding sonnets are neither the same persons nor different ones. A certain deliberate indeterminacy obtains, as in, say, the Seven Ages of Man speech in *As You Like It*: not every Elizabethan was necessarily and successively a soldier and a justice, any more than Baudelaire's modern youth necessarily and universally experienced alienation from God or morbid sexual tastes. The identification of modern youth with the artist, whom we see at the beginning of the work in **"Bénédiction"** and in the final poem, is more suggestive than definitive. We must simply refer to the romantic artist's tendency to see himself as the most perceptive, aware, and therefore historically distinctive member of society, a role earlier artists had claimed less publicly, whatever their private opinions may have been. Moreover, the notion of young men being poets before they settled down to being grocery storekeepers offers merely a parodic image of a common nineteenth-century idea, which no doubt had a kind of validity for romantic culture that it scarcely has today.

A further reference back to the earlier part of *Les Fleurs du mal* occurs in the tercets. Whereas in **"Bénédiction"** the poet will receive after death a crown of light, here the light imagery is qualified:

> Il en est qui n'ont jamais connu leur Idole,
> Et ces sculpteurs damnés et marqués d'un
>   affront,
> Qui vont se martelant la poitrine et le front,
>
> N'ont qu'un espoir, étrange et sombre
>   Capitole!
> C'est que la Mort, planant comme un soleil
>   nouveau,
> Fera s'épanouir les fleurs de leur cerveau!

> There are those who have never known their Idol,
> and those sculptors, damned and marked by insult,
> who go about beating their chests and foreheads,
> have only one hope—strange and dark triumph! It
> is that death, hovering like a new sun, will make
> the flowers of their dream blossom!

Besides the key words of *soleil* and *fleurs,* we find the peculiar locution "strange and dark triumph" (the sense of *Capitole* here), suggestive of the curious role of language in connection with the past in the book. The old expression *monter au Capitole* ("to triumph") is adapted to a new kind of imagery, but we are conscious of the poet's intense awareness of the outmoded high style of neoclassicism, as we are at a number of points in the volume. Baudelaire's sense of the modern seems necessarily to involve reference to past ideals and ways of expression, but they are unlike the primarily parodic allusions to literary tradition we find in Laforgue. Neither the old nor the contemporary suffices in itself, whence the oddly mixed diction characteristic of *Les Fleurs du mal* and exemplified by the romantic-neoclassical "étrange et sombre Capitole."

Light and dark mingle in this redemption that is equivocal, limited, or uncertain. Here we find Baudelaire rejoining other romantics in the groping, hesitant way they envisaged some end of the purgatory of life. There is a certain analogy, for example, with the end of *Les Contemplations,* where Hugo represents the poet as sitting atop a huge volcano and staring into its dark depths that are God: flashes of light periodically illuminate this ambiguous deity, and the sense is that of a hoped-for but by no means absolute salvation. Baudelaire's imagery follows this pattern of conceiving a perhaps partial redemption, one not to be anticipated in traditional terms of glory. Here we see how the design of the 1857 *Fleurs du mal* reflects a modified and historicized version of the myth of primal innocence, fall, and salvation. Most of the volume deals with the earthly purgatory, since that is what is present and certain, but in the beginning and in the end we glimpse origins and a longed-for ultimate release.

If my necessarily partial account of the 1857 *Fleurs du mal* seems full of qualifications and rather less neat than a paraphrase of the *Discours de la méthode,* the reason is that the volume itself was not conceived in terms of "composition" but belongs rather to that group of romantic works for which the notion of organic form is peculiarly appropriate. The ramifications of this theory correspond not only to certain effects we have observed but also to the general circumstances in which Baudelaire put together the two *Fleurs du mal.* While organic form is thought of as an indissoluble whole, it is not necessarily a static one, for, like a plant, the work of art grows. We are moderately well acquainted with this aspect of *Les Fleurs du mal,* since Baudelaire planned a volume of verse for many years before 1857. The titles chosen were first *Les Lesbiennes* (The lesbians) and then *Les Limbes* (Limbo), which clearly has connotations of an ill-defined, uncertain time or place—like the nineteenth century in romantic thought—before *Les Fleurs du mal* was settled on in the mid-1850s. We also know something of the dating of various poems. It is clear that at any given moment in its maturation the book would have been different from what it was to be in 1857, just as the second edition in 1861 is a different book from the first. However, in terms of organic form the work would not necessarily have been imperfect, all stages of growth, as in a plant, having a valid structure. In this sense any notion of the definitive seems to be eliminated, though at the same time the idea of a perfect whole forms a characteristic part of organic thinking. The fact of growth is, in other words, divorced from teleological considerations.

The opposite of the organic conception of form is the classicizing, mechanistic one, which emphasizes *plan* or outline. In organic terms, each work has its own structure, one that is not imposed from the outside like mechanical form or some preconceived "architecture." This means, of course, that such a thing as symmetry may or may not be present, symmetry being merely, in many cases, an automatic rhetorical pattern that does not grow out of the material but is forced onto it. We can see the implications of organic theory for the general shape of the 1857 *Fleurs du mal:* **"Spleen et Idéal"** is long and contains a great variety of poems; **"La Mort"** is extremely short. This is the way Baudelaire's material worked itself out. We may prefer the second edition because it contains more poems and other formal patterns, but this does not invalidate the 1857 one.

Another facet of the theory of organic form is assimilation of diverse and often opposing elements. This is reflected in the heterogeneity or antithetical relations in the movement from poem to poem that we often perceive. If Baudelaire had had a strictly logical conception of his work, he might well have refused to include many early poems, but whatever Baudelaire the man thought at any given moment, Baudelaire the artist had a comprehensive view of his work by which divergent attitudes and styles belonged together, a fact commentators tacitly avoid by labeling this or that poem early, as if it could thereby be ignored. The once-popular notion of Baudelaire as poetic modernist is an excellent example of the blinkered vision and selectivity from which general interpretations of his work have suffered: his taste for stiffly rhetorical forms like the analogy poem (**"L'Albatros"** or **"Bénédiction"**) and various types of allegory was as pronounced as his interest in elliptic movement, submerged themes (the first **"Spleen,"** of which Michael Riffaterre has said that the unstated key notion is "house," in a negative sense), and implicit plot (**"La servante au grand coeur"**: The magnanimous servant). In fact, Baudelaire amused himself in **"Le Cygne"** (The swan) by writing the poem twice: the same material is first presented in a radically free-associative pattern and an irregular relation of verse to syntax, and is then reintroduced in part two, following a neat reverse chronological order that has a greater coincidence of grammatical and prosodic divisions. To my mind the range of poetic structures in *Les Fleurs du mal* constitutes a far more striking example of assimilation than of any thematic diversity.

Finally, the interdependence of all parts, as well as their subordination to the whole, is an important tenet of organic form that is especially relevant to *Les Fleurs du mal*. The principles of recurrence and cross-reference ensure such an interdependence, as does the reconciliation of the antithetical. Such relations are extremely dense in the work, so much so as to make the linearity prized by a commentator like Mossop seem but an intermittent feature of its organization. Again, the mechanistic conception of *plan* cannot deal with this aspect of the volume.

At the same time, we recognize obvious weaknesses in organic theory. Whether, for example, the last twenty-five or so poems in the **"Spleen et Idéal"** of 1857 are truly assimilated into the book might be contested. I have spoken of their fulfilling a certain contrastive function with regard to the somber **"Fleurs du mal"** that follow, but that is scarcely more than a loose relationship, and to speak of interdependence would be absurd. A plant's assimilation of carbon dioxide and soil nutrients through a chemical process has little to do with juxtaposing poems. Naturally, interpretive sophistication must choose its own limits, since organic theory does not set up any at all, and the temptation of wearisome overreading is a serious one.

With antithetical material a similar problem arises. Aside from the fact that all antithetical elements can be seen as logically necessary to one another, the reconciliation of contraries can take peculiar and debatable forms, such as the phrase "étrange et sombre Capitole," by which we might say that dualisms associated with the modern and the old are collapsed at the end of the 1857 *Fleurs du mal*. Yet we can also see this as merely the verbal device of oxymoron, which deconstructs itself without much critical help. Notions like limited or qualified salvation do not, perhaps, designate redemption at all, but merely play with words idly.

Finally, when the great English exponent of organic theory cut the original end off "Frost at Midnight," supposedly to make it a better poem, Coleridge's action was less consonant with his convictions than suggestive of a neoclassical gardener wielding a set of mechanical snippers according to a "plan." Nonetheless, organicism supplied a more supple approach to poems than the traditional idea of composition, and certainly a work of which two distinct versions exist can profit from this perspective.

Of the thirty-five new poems added to the 1861 edition of *Les Fleurs du mal,* some, like **"La Chevelure"** or **"Chant d'automne,"** have certain similarities in imagery or theme to earlier poems; these take their place in the collection without conspicuously altering it, save that they enrich it with their own peculiar beauty. Certain other pieces, however, bring in new material, especially rich in theological implications, and they tend to color the volume in a special way, which makes it a distinctly new work. A first example is **"Hymne à la beauté"** with its query as to the moral status of beauty:

> Viens-tu du ciel profond ou sors-tu de
>   l'abîme,
> O Beauté! ton regard, infernal et divin,
> Verse confusément le bienfait et le crime,
> Et l'on peut pour cela te comparer au vin.
>   . . . . .
> Que tu viennes du ciel ou de l'enfer,
>   qu'importe,
> O Beauté! monstre énorme, effrayant, ingénu!
> Si ton oeil, ton souris, ton pied, m'ouvrent la
>   porte
> D'un infini que j'aime et n'ai jamais connu?

Do you come from the farthest heaven or do you come out of the abyss, o Beauty? Your glance, infernal and divine, pours forth a mixture of blessing and crime, and in that you can be compared to wine. . . . Whether you come from Heaven or Hell, what does it matter, o Beauty! enormous, frightening, ingenuous monster! if your eye, your smile, your foot open for me the door of an infinity that I love and have never known?

The poem has been added at the head of the Jeanne Duval and other love poems. In a sense, it develops a question implied by the juxtaposition of love poems radically different in tone, but, by its explicitness, it invests everything that follows with a clearer sense of the opposition of good and evil. This illustrates the principle of interdependence of parts; what had been a suggestion we now read as an overt theme in the course of **"Spleen et Idéal."**

Moreover, we note that this "theme" takes the form of a proposition of an abstract and general character: "Whether beauty is good or evil makes no difference." It is rather more difficult and risky to devise so broad a statement subsuming poems as they appear in 1857. We might from the 1857 edition derive the idea that neither modern beauty nor the older kind is good or bad, but that involves more interpretation and the difficulty of deciding whether *bad* means "evil" or "unpleasant" or "monotonous" or whatever. However, to see a reasonably clear proposition in **"Hymne à la beauté"** demands no rash leap in ideas or elaborating a suggestion into a relatively fixed category of thought like "evil."

At the same time, we observe that the historical scheme, which is fairly pronounced in the 1857 volume, becomes less clear when the good or evil of modern experience is thrust forward as a dominant question demanding resolution. This new dilemma complicates the earlier antithesis between past and present by focusing on just one of its terms. Not only does the notion of whether modern beauty derives from good or evil distract us from the historical scheme; it also recalls to us that indifference to good and evil, such as is formulated by **"Hymne à la beauté,"** is a well-developed theological concept. The connotations of the sin of acedia include both sloth and ennui, so that the end of **"Au lecteur"** now seems to have a different sense: ennui becomes connected, by the addition of **"Hymne à la beauté,"** to another system of references in *Les Fleurs du mal,* one that acquires great significance because it reaches its culmination in the new ending of the 1861 volume, the final stanzas of **"Le Voyage."**

But before we reach Baudelaire's new concluding poem, still another antithetical relation is elaborated, which is at most only vaguely present in 1857, if at all. We first become aware of it near the end of **"Spleen et Idéal,"** which was radically transformed. A number of poems of a somewhat restrained tone (such as **"Je n'ai pas oublié, voisine de la ville"**) were removed, and Baudelaire added five poems consonant with the **"Spleen"** ones. **"Le Goût du néant"** (The taste for nothing) gives that last word new prominence and thematic status in *Les Fleurs du mal;* coupled with moral indifference ("Que tu viennes du ciel ou de l'enfer, qu'importe": What does it matter whether you come from heaven or hell?) it seems to commentators to mark a new stage in Baudelaire's sensibility and to cast a

particular light on the whole second edition. But equally important is the imagery of nature in the new poems. Lloyd James Austin was the first to point out [in *L'Univers poétique de Baudelaire,* 1956] that in its new form the structure of **"Spleen et Idéal"** has a strong thematic contrast based on the idea of correspondences. While the correspondences at the beginning of the section are traditional ones between the divine and earth, now nature reflects the infernal:

> L'un t'éclaire avec son ardeur,
> L'autre en toi met son deuil, Nature!
> Ce qui dit à l'un: Sépulture!
> Dit à l'autre: Vie et splendeur!
>   (**"Alchimie de la douleur"**)

One illumines you with his ardor, the other places his mourning in you, Nature! What says to one "Tomb," says to the other "Life and glory!" (Alchemy of pain)

> Cieux déchirés comme des grèves,
> En vous se mire mon orgueil,
> Vos vastes nuages en deuil
>
> Sont les corbillards de mes rêves,
> Et vos lueurs sont le reflet
> De l'Enfer où mon coeur se plaît.
>   (**"Horreur sympathique"**)

Skies torn like strands, my pride admires itself in you, your vast mourning clouds are the hearses of my dreams, and your gleams are the reflection of the Hell where my heart is happy. (Sympathetic horror)

Whereas the **"Spleen"** poems had dealt simply with bad weather, here nature is seen in a generalized way as a correspondence of hell, which does not suit the centuries-old function of correspondence as a form of theodicy. **"Obsession"** is even more specific, taking up the images of trees or "vivants piliers" (living pillars) and of the sea (as in **"L'Homme et la Mer"**) and reinterpreting them in a demonic sense. This new idea tends, as do the 1861 additions in general, not only to submerge the historical theme of the 1857 volume but to differentiate strongly its theology from that of the earlier form of the work. Finally, the artist as the natural representative of romantic times becomes a less conspicuous feature than in 1857, where **"Bénédiction"** and the concluding poem both stressed his importance.

With such a massive thematic buildup at the end of the new **"Spleen et Idéal,"** Baudelaire saw fit to begin the next section with poems milder in tone, **"Paysage"** (Landscape) and **"Le Soleil"** (The Sun). They introduce an entirely new grouping, the **"Tableaux parisiens"** (Parisian tableaux) in which earlier and more recent poems intermingle. Baudelaire's critics seem unanimous in their praise of this new section, but their attempts to characterize it have not always been felicitous. Not all of these poems depict Paris, nor are they free from a *je* who participates as well as contemplates. However, this *je* is perceived as being rather different from that of many poems of **"Spleen et Idéal,"** a fact that has encouraged critics to speak of impersonality. Ross Chambers has recently tried to study this *je* more searchingly, as well as to analyze the complex cyclicity of **"Tableaux parisiens,"** which separates it from the preceding and following sections. There is an intricate arrangement of daytime and nighttime poems, poems of the street and poems of enclosed spaces, which revolves on itself. Pieces that are in some respects heterogeneous are thus held together in a subtle structure.

If **"Tableaux parisiens"** pleases everyone, **"Le Vin"** is a much criticized episode. By placing it after **"Tableaux"** in the second edition, Baudelaire evidently modifies its meaning to suggest merely popular scenes rather than a joyous release from man's condition. The following **"Fleurs du mal"** section is unchanged, except for the elimination of the condemned pieces, which include the stanza on pardon and the glimpse of a redemption that I quoted earlier and that fits so well the thematic pattern of the 1857 edition. While the sense of **"Fleurs du mal"** seems relatively stable in its passage from one edition to another, **"Révolte"** in 1861 appears, in this totally new context, to be more highly theologized. The reaction against the Christian God no longer seems to be the affirmation of man's desire for social justice but rather the low point in the veering between God and Satan: "Enfer ou Ciel, qu'importe?" (**"Le Voyage"**: The voyage). A poem like **"Le Possédé"** (The possessed), added to **"Spleen et Idéal"** would appear to confirm this reading. Satanism may seem distastefully puerile, but it enters into the pattern of *Les Fleurs du mal* in order to form a contrast with the new version of **"La Mort."**

The order of the original three sonnets of **"La Mort"** remained unchanged, but Baudelaire added three more poems that move away from the 1857 ending and even nullify it. This is an interesting example of how context or the interdependence of parts can function. Erich Auerbach wrote a commentary on **"La Mort des artistes"**—based on its place in the second edition—in which he finds mockery, bitterness, and nothingness to be the import of the poem and uses the subsequent **"Le Rêve d'un curieux"** (A curious man's dream) as a gloss. In the latter poem:

> J'étais mort sans surprise, et la terrible aurore
> M'enveloppait.—Eh quoi! n'est-ce donc que cela?
> La toile était levée et j'attendais encore.

I had died without any surprise, and the terrible dawn was enveloping me.—Well! Is that all it is? The curtain had gone up and I was still waiting.

Clearly **"La Mort des artistes"** meant nothing of the sort in 1857, but by the principle of the interdependence of parts, one may reread it in another light according to its repositioning in 1861.

The most extraordinary example of growth in the whole second edition is the conclusion to **"Le Voyage,"** a poem that begins by alluding to preceding sections of *Les Fleurs du mal* in a lengthy summary before an entirely new direction is taken in the end:

> O Mort, vieux capitaine, il est temps! levons l'ancre!
> Ce pays nous ennuie, ô Mort! Appareillons!
> Si le ciel et la mer sont noirs comme de l'encre,
> Nos coeurs que tu connais sont remplis de rayons!
>
> Verse-nous ton poison pour qu'il nous réconforte!
> Nous voulons, tant ce feu nous brûle le cerveau,
> Plonger au fond du gouffre, Enfer ou Ciel, qu'importe?
> Au fond de l'Inconnu pour trouver du *nouveau!*

O Death, old captain, it is time! let's lift anchor! This country wearies us, o Death! Let's get under way! If the sky and the sea are black as ink, our hearts, which you know, are filled with light! Pour your poison for us so that it may comfort us! So much does this fire burn our brain, we want to plunge to the depths of the abyss, Hell or Heaven, what does it matter? Plunge to the depths of the unknown to find what is *new!*

The combination of light and darkness persists, but the burden of the poem is quite different from that of **"La Mort des artistes,"** however it is read. As in **"Hymne à la beauté,"** we find an almost abstractly and generally formulated idea: the poet is indifferent to the distinction between good and evil, the verb *ennuie* defining his state of mind. But here the negative notion of acedia impels him to anticipate a state beyond it, and so we have a succinctly dialectic movement, quite unlike anything in the 1857 *Fleurs du mal*. If there is any broad direction of thought in the earlier volume, it exists largely by implication, and one could maintain that the oxymoronic "sombre Capitole" is merely a version of one of those irreconcilable antitheses French romantic literature is rich in and that seem especially to inform Hugo's work. In **"Le Voyage,"** however, Baudelaire steps beyond opposites in a clear logical move, whose formulation offers nothing especially ambiguous. Moreover, the last word, *nouveau,* creates a notable contrast to the liminary **"Au lecteur,"** with its concluding vision of the sameness of ennui. By analogy we see that indifference to good and evil also involves collapsing the antithesis between divine and demonic correspondences, which constitutes the other prominent new feature of the 1861 *Fleurs du mal.*

However, there is perhaps more to the closing lines of **"Le Voyage"** than a logical movement of broad implication, since this structural function does not precisely define their emotive import, which has been variously interpreted. One of the more subtle readings of the poem takes them as an expression of pre-Nietzschean "tragic joy." This gloss implies an entirely new tone at the end of the volume. If indeed we see Baudelaire as conveying a "joyous, though anxious, faith in the future," the ostensible conclusion to *Les Fleurs du mal* is somewhat open-ended, which, moreover, is a characteristic possibility of organic form. The idea of growth implies further potentialities.

Finally, we notice that the *nous* of the last stanzas of **"Le Voyage"** has been defined in the course of the poem as one part of humanity, the "coureurs sans répit" (relentless runners) seeking various kinds of experience. Beauty is not their concern so much as the anguish of being caught by Time with his net, as Baudelaire expresses it, and they are not, by the end of the poem, particularly identified with the present moment. In fact, this psychological portrait replaces the general allegory of modern man of 1857, although the actual use of personifications and allegorical structures (**"A une madone"**: To a madonna; **"Les Sept Vieillards"**: The seven old men) increases somewhat. Thus, the 1861 *Fleurs du mal,* while necessarily more complicated because of its greater number of parts, is actually a more explicit work to the extent that **"Le Voyage"** retrospectively informs it.

Moreover, if we look at all the longer poems Baudelaire added to the second edition, a further aspect of his design becomes apparent. The movement of historical time—the fall from a higher original estate, as in **"J'aime le souvenir . . ."**—is transferred to personal time. This is the internalization of history, which was a dominant feature of European romantic thought and has been most relevantly treated perhaps by Meyer H. Abrams in *Natural Supernaturalism: Tradition and Revolution in Romantic Literature* (New York: Norton, 1971). The time that forms the subject of **"Le Masque"** (The mask), **"Le Goût du néant,"** **"Chant d'automne"** (Autumn song), and **"L'Horloge"** (The clock) is that of the poet's life, as objective history recedes in importance. A most elegant illustration of the process can be found in **"Le Cygne,"** where the sight of Haussmann's urban renewal project, a characteristic expression of modern life and taste, does not

lead to historical reflections but reminds the poet of his and others' private histories and personal fall. **"Les Petites Vieilles"** (The little old women) deals again with personal time in the framework of modern life. Another kind of internalization occurs in **"La Chevelure,"** where paradise is situated in the tropics rather than in primeval days and will be regained through the inner journey of involuntary memory. The mention of childhood at the beginning of **"Le Voyage"** completes this transference of the pattern of world history to psychological and individual history. The particular brilliance of all these poems has the effect of making the previously established references to world history seem secondary or merely complementary in the 1861 *Fleurs du mal.* While this thematic material is certainly present in the first edition of the work, by the principle of the interdependence of parts, it now assumes greater significance.

I have avoided discussing heretofore the notion of unity, which seems to me to be the weakest legacy of romantic organic theory. If we look, for example, in the *Princeton Encyclopedia of Poetry and Poetics,* we find, *sub verb,* a statement characteristic of organicism filtered through New Criticism: "Unity is the most fundamental and comprehensive aesthetic criterion, upon which all others depend." There follows a farrago of quotations, paraphrases, and allusions running from Plato to the present and which can be reduced to the same concept of unity only by total faith in unitary thinking, analogy run wild. Recently the notion of unity has been called a convention of reading [by Jonathan Culler in *A Pursuit of Signs,* 1981], and the fact that some deconstructionist criticism seems to imply a convention of unresolved conflicts tends to confirm to what extent we approach a work of art with certain expectations. There is little intellectual profit in making some leap of faith and affirming the existence of total unity—because it is absurd, if necessary. Actually, the most useful point of view, I think, is to distinguish various conventions of unity on the part of poets as well as on the part of readers, and as we do so, certain loose historical patterns seem to emerge. To take an obvious example, readers have become adept, since New Criticism, at detecting in a work seemingly secondary elements that create what one might call a submerged or half-concealed pattern, which passes for unity: the ambiguity of height and depth, up and down, in some of Hugo's poems is just such a unity, as is the way in which the characters in Racine's *Andromaque* use expressions that separate them, as it were, from their physical and psychological states and attributes ("Comment lui rendre un coeur que vous me retenez?": How can I give her my heart, which you retain?—1. 4. 344) The ultimate absurdity arises when a classicist, distraught at the seeming insufficiency of metaphoric chains in Homer, invents Homeric "fire symbolism" in order that Greek epic not seem too inferior to *The Waste Land.* It is a critically unsophisticated reader who cannot find unity when he puts his mind to it, and years of this practice have made the concept slightly disreputable. Jacques Derrida's strictures on the notion of perfect form, virtually a synonym of *unity,* are relevant: fervently to proclaim the unity of **Les Fleurs du mal** is a bit like declaring that one believes in God.

While French criticism never absorbed organic theory, which could have been of great usefulness to it at times, Mallarmé formulated a notion of structure that, though scarcely elaborated on by most of his commentators, represents an interesting alternative. He defined the work of art in terms of rapports or relations, his most succinct phrase being *"rhythme de rapports"* ("rhythm of relations"). Analogies like the plant one are eliminated, as is any affirmation about unity or the interdependence of parts. The abstractness of Mallarmé's thinking constitutes its virtue, for he was searching for a concept that would embrace various structures with a temporal dimension: literature, music, dialectic thought. With this in mind, we can see, with whatever elaboration we care to indulge in, the patterns that inform **Les Fleurs du mal:** even heterogeneity, which in a sense is the contrary of unity, furnishes us with a richness of relationships, although their definition might elude us. Ultimately, one could probably, given the variety of these relationships, construct some system by which they would all somehow be at least indirectly connected, but I do not think that kind of demonstration is especially useful to write up or to try to memorize. I am reminded of the (to me) appalling suggestion that one proceed through all of Proust separating the metaphors from the metonymies.

The history of **Les Fleurs du mal** as organic form is incomplete, interrupted as it was by the death of Baudelaire—a nice reminder of the peculiar way literature and the life process are intertwined in such theory. There was to have been a third edition, incorporating poems written since 1861, but since Baudelaire did not live to put it together, the actual third edition was the work of two friends, who crammed the book with poems whose inclusion Baudelaire might not have approved. This edition is generally considered so unsatisfactory that at least one commentator [Robert-Benoît Chérix, *Commentaire des "Fleurs du mal,"* 1949] was inspired to invent his own third edition of **Les Fleurs du mal.** Of course, Baudelaire's intentions are not known, and only speculation, such as Feuillerat indulges in, is possible. In any case, none of the poems Baudelaire published after 1861 are so radically different from his preceding work as **"Le Voyage."** We are left, however, with the frustration of having the condemned pieces and a further group of "Nouvelles Fleurs du mal" forever consigned to the appendices of modern editions. Such are the problems implicit in the theory and practice of organic form.

Karen A. Harrington (essay date 1992)

SOURCE: "Fragmentation and Irony in *Les Fleurs du Mal,*" in *Nineteenth-Century French Studies,* Vol. 20, No. 1, Fall-Winter, 1991-92, pp. 177-86.

[*In this essay, Harrington examines the complex sense of self that Baudelaire reveals in* Les Fleurs du Mal.]

Fragmentation commands special significance in **Les Fleurs du Mal** and stresses an often contradictory split occurring at many levels such as the structural opposition between spleen and ideal. Thematic polarities of love and hate, time and space, good and evil, God and Satan abound in Baudelaire's work. Of greater importance, perhaps, is the position of the fragmented self that shapes the core or nucleus upon which other forms of fragmentation acquire meaning. It finds expression in various ways: the self identifies with others, thereby engaging in an interplay of its own absence and presence. The divided self also calls attention to the distancing of the poetic voice from the poem's movement, while at other times a self-conscious split alienates the self from its own identity.

Baudelaire touches upon this concept in **Les Paradis artificiels,** explaining how differentiation between object and subject is abolished as the self voluntarily renounces its own identity in favor of the object or "other." His crucial quotation in **Mon Coeur Mis à Nu,** "de la vaporisation et de la centralisation du *Moi.* Tout est là," is also indicative of the role fragmentation plays. In such poems as **"La Chevelure,"** centralization or concentration of the self is accompanied by its dispersal, its capacity to permeate other objects, or to appropriate characteristics of "others." Dispersal precedes concentration as the self loses and subsequently regains its identity, but it is now infused with the richness of the experience of the other. In this respect, the loss or absence of the self creates a positive extension of the poetic act, a result of the harmonious transference between vaporization and centralization.

At other times, this interaction points to an impasse. In **"Obsession"** vaporization is hinted at with a potential diffusion of the self into ocean waves. However, vaporization and centralization remain polarized because the position of the poetic voice is too anchored in a self-reflective stance to allow such dispersal. In place of unification, fragmentation intensifies the separation between subject and object.

The paradoxically disruptive and harmonious nature of the divided self in Baudelaire's poetry can perhaps be best understood by exploring to what extent the relation between language and the self determines the ambivalence associated with fragmentation. In **De l'Essence du rire** we find a paradigm that conveys how language alludes to divergent and often opposing expressions of fragmentation. Baudelaire refers to both smiling and joy as "le comique significatif" and argues that they are distinguished by their totality and sense of wholeness. To the contrary, laughter, or "le comique absolu," is associated with an irreconcilable split that denotes its ambiguous and irresolute nature.

"Le comique significatif" corresponds to a model in which the self's relation to the poem is framed by a clear and unequivocal notion of unity and closure. Fragmentation of this kind occurs with the partial or total abandonment of narrative control as the poetic persona assumes a chameleon-like stance to identify with "others." Jean Prévost [in *Baudelaire: Essai sur l'inspiration et la création poétiques,* 1953] terms this "le mimétisme de Baudelaire," a quality characteristic of many of the poet's love poems.

"Le Poison" illustrates this affinity, with the self consumed by the woman's presence. She serves as a guide to an illusory world, a means of transcending reality through the act of forgetting. Though dangerously linked to poison, her eyes are the embodiment of "oubli" and become the focal point through which the poetic self strives to revel in the much sought after oblivion. Other forms of possible transcendence (wine and opium) cannot compare to the woman's fascinating powers, which lure the poet to her:

> Tout cela ne vaut pas le poison qui découle
>   De tes yeux, de tes yeux verts,
> Lacs où mon âme tremble et se voit à
>   l'envers . . .
>   Mes songes viennent en foule
> Pour se désaltérer à ces gouffres amers.
>
> Tout cela ne vaut pas le terrible prodige
>   De ta salive qui mord,
> Qui plonge dans l'oubli mon âme sans
>   remords
>   Et, charriant le vertige,
> La roule défaillante aux rives de la mort!

Drawn to her green eyes and bitter saliva, he hopes to surpass the limits of time and space. But her association with a poisonous lake that quenches one's thirst points to her presence as not only enticing but also foreboding. The poet seeks and fears both the poison dwelling within the woman's eyes and the taste of her bitter saliva yet is cognizant of their imminent threat, projected in the "gouffres amers" and "rives de la mort."

This paradoxical influence marks the potential fulfillment of the poet's daydreams, but at the price of death. Though the woman epitomizes the oblivion that the poet is seeking, this ideal world is itself an illusion and, similar to wine and opium, she does not lead him beyond the ephemeral. Yet, chameleon fragmentation or mimetic association nonetheless offers a momentary escape, a temporary means of shutting out the world. Thus, loss of narrative control can be viewed as a desire to orchestrate and make sense of one's world.

When mimetic association is more closely related to sensory perceptions, as in **"Parfum exotique"** and **"L'Invitation au voyage,"** poetic reverie frequently suggests a more favorable outcome. Through a process of synesthetic transfer, the poetic voice relinquishes control to the sensory perceptions, thus showing the self's appropriation by others as a means of experiencing and yielding to the influence of the imagery.

"Parfum exotique" opens with the association between the olfactory sensory perception and the portrayal of a tropical setting, brought about by the woman's presence. As the sensory perceptions increasingly become the focus of the poem, narrative control weakens with the self relegated to the role of participant. In the last two stanzas the sensory perceptions transform the poet's vision into an imaginary setting:

> Guidé par ton odeur vers de charmants
>   climats,
> Je vois un port rempli de voiles et de mâts
> Encor tout fatigués par la vague marine,
>
> Pendant que le parfum des verts tamariniers
> Qui circule dans l'air et m'enfle la narine,
> Se mêle dans mon âme au chant des
>   mariniers.

The woman's presence is soon consumed by her fragrance, transformed into the aroma of green tamarind trees. Circulating in the air, the olfactory sensory perception reveals its expansion as it becomes the subject of the poem. It also claims narrative control by exerting its far-reaching influence over and through the poetic self.

Sensory perceptions efface distinction between self and others, a position that Baudelaire justifies in *Les Paradis artificiels* by illustrating how the effects of various intoxicants lead the self to identify with the object of observation:

> Il arrive quelquefois que la personnalité disparaît et que l'objectivité, qui est le propre des poètes panthéistes, se développe en vous si anormalement, que la contemplation des objets extérieurs vous fait oublier votre propre existence, et que vous vous confondez bientôt avec eux.

In **"Parfum exotique"** the intoxicants are replaced by the woman's presence and the synesthetic associations it produces on the poet, through whom the expansive transformation occurs. The sensory perceptions link the real and the imaginary: the woman's fragrance is an indicator of the poet's real world, but its subsequent dispersal and consumption find expression in the realm of the imaginary ("Je vois un port rempli de voiles et de mâts / Encor tout fatigués par la vague marine"). Mimetic interaction in **"Parfum exotique"** thus prompts a timeless and inspiring movement that counteracts the cold-heartedness of reality.

While other poems show the mimetic stance as an intensification of harsh realities (**"Le Vampire"**), they all call attention to a self-contained world. There is a sense that, however pleasant or unpleasant the poem's outcome, it concludes on a decisive note and that the self's position, though fragmented, is not questioned. Mimetic association accordingly presents a straightforward view of the self in the world and corresponds to the autonomous vision associated with "le comique significatif."

By contrast, the laughter characteristic of "le comique absolu," symbolizes the duality of human nature, of man's fall from grace. In Baudelaire's estimation, "le comique absolu" is superior to "le comique significatif" yet is defined by its own negativity. Many of his poems show the fragmented self mirroring this negativity. Aware of its own duality, the self is unable to reconcile it, thus emphasizing an ambivalent and often self-deprecating position, which is essentially ironic. For Paul de Man [in *Blindness and Insight,* 1971] the pervasive and obstructive influence of irony calls into play the paradoxical split of the self as both participant and detached observer of the poetic act. The mimetic association of the aforementioned poems is replaced by ironic distancing, which differs from the former in terms of how language functions in the poem. The ironic stance highlights the self's failure to appropriate others to its own identity and magnifies the gulf between self and poem. Irony's relation to the divided self also denotes a separation owing primarily to an endless self-reflective questioning, symbolized by its lack of closure. These two perspectives are exposed either through the ironic severance of the self from the poem or through the status of the ironic self-consciousness and correspond roughly to Leo Bersani's distinction [in *Baudelaire and Freud,* 1917] between the self as doomed artist and the prince-dandy figure.

The ironic stance of the doomed artist implicates the self by relegating it to an alien world through various allegoric or metaphoric associations. Bersani alludes to this when discussing Lacanian theory and how the self moves from the Imaginary to the order of the Symbolic: "The self is still an appropriated self, but what is appropriated is language as the other, and not an ideal but alienated *image* of an individual self." Thus appropriation is evidence of alienation in the form of language. Attaining its fullest potential through irony, language underscores distancing by means of dissimulation. As such, alienation of the fragmented self

may be defined by its detachment from the object, thing, or person that it encounters.

Baudelaire's Spleen poems point to the technique of ironic distancing. In **"Pluviôse, irrité contre la ville entière"** the self's involvement in the various images depicted is diminished with its eventual separation from the poem's movement. Michael Riffaterre [in *The Semiotics of Poetry,* 1978] refers to the essence of this movement as a series of structural permutations through which the matrix of the "home" as "hearth" is subsequently transformed "into a code of the moral and physical discomfort a home is supposed to protect us against." The poem thus operates on an interplay of words and their opposite in which "structural permutation . . . converts a mimesis of intimacy into a code negating intimacy and its attendant happiness."

We can apply Riffaterre's insightful remarks to the fragmented self in the poem. The vision it portrays is progressively reduced to a single spot (a deck of cards), which engulfs the presence of the self. Here, fragmentation can be defined as the doubling of the poetic persona through an absent-present structure. Though responsible for the poem's articulation, narrative voice is enunciated only once ("Mon chat"). Its identity is never fully expressed and remains a floating or rather empty construct.

This problematic position occurs with the self stringing together the seemingly unrelated imagery as it is simultaneously being detached from the unfurling of the narrative. A disconcerting rift ensues between the language and the self, a division that transforms the house matrix into its negation while stressing the almost incidental and fortuitous role of the self.

As Riffaterre points out, the deck of cards and other objects as well reflect a scene of intimacy. The reductive world of the Queen of Spades and Jack of Hearts almost assumes magnified proportions, depicting a true metonymic representation of the house system. The fact that the two cards converse grimly about their past loves creates the illusion of a coherent world. Yet, exclusion of the poetic voice from this self-contained universe gives rise to a gap in which language undermines the role of the self. It severs the poetic voice from the narrative, revealing a discord as the interplay of the self's absence and presence assists in refuting the house matrix. But ironic distancing not only joins forces with the house system, it also orients the reader's understanding of the poem's title, **"Spleen,"** laying bare the doomed poetic voice consumed by linguistic alienation.

Similar to Baudelaire's Spleen poem, **"La Béatrice"** paints the poet as doomed artist but at the same time, the ironic stance alludes to a "dédoublement" of the self with the poet adopting the pose of the prince or dandy. Ironic distancing emphasizes the self as a Hamlet-figure, a histrionic artist who is mercilessly berated by impish demons. Their attack aims at the heart of his artistic endeavors and becomes more poignant at the end when the beloved joins in the ridicule. Though overhearing their conversation, the narrator remains isolated from the demons since they do not suspect that he is listening. Even the poem's structure adds to the separation between subject and object: set apart by a direct quotation of the demons' conversation, the second stanza is disconnected from the first and last stanzas, which present the narrator's subjective perspective.

The reference to **"La Béatrice"** calls further attention to the poem's ironic and dual stance. Commenting upon the relation between self-consciousness and critical distancing, Claude Pichois [in an essay in *Genèse de la conscience moderne,* ed. Robert Ellrodt, 1983] stresses that "La Béatrice du poète n'est évidemment pas celle de Dante: elle est mêlée à la 'troupe obscène' des démons et parfois leur fait 'quelque sale caresse' . . . Le génie de Baudelaire est ici d'instaurer cette confrontation entre Shakespeare et Dante." Questioning artistic enterprise, the irony of this confrontation pits a transformed Beatrice against Shakespeare's Hamlet-figure, which leads to the degradation of self. Yet the irony is twofold: owing to his self-awareness, the narrator also surpasses his ill-fated circumstances.

Another expression of the ironic stance, critical self-awareness also helps to frame the problematic nature between language and fragmentation. Approximating Leo Bersani's references to the prince or dandy in Baudelaire's poetry, the ironic voice becomes a metaphor of the self as it appropriates others or objects, all contained within its own consciousness. Appropriation occurs as a result of the poem's irony, which is directed more at the narrator than at his rapport with others. Paul de Man notes that in Baudelaire's "comique absolu," "the ironic subject at once has to ironize its own predicament and observe in turn, with the detachment and disinterestedness that Baudelaire demands of this kind of spectator, the temptation to which it is about to succumb." The dynamics of this critical position disclose irony as a self-reflective process that implicates the poetic persona: he becomes both the observer and victim of the poetic act who paradoxically knows and comprehends his situation but is unable to act upon such knowledge. Baudelaire refers to this as the "supreme" knowledge of the "Wise" ("le Sage"), a self-knowledge that is nonetheless concealed and frozen within the consciousness of the self. The ironic stance sets the stage for knowledge but prevents its materialization. It is, in other words, a reflection of negativity stemming from an entrapping discourse that mirrors an endless spiral.

Critical self-consciousness in **"La Béatrice"** supersedes the Hamlet-figure through a doubling of the self. In the first stanza the narrator sharpens the dagger of his mind against his heart. As Claude Pichois explains [in his notes to the *Oeuvres Complètes,* 1975], "Le poignard de Baudelaire—sans doute l'ironie—n'est destiné qu'a le tuer lui-même." The narrator knows that his awareness is self-incriminating and that he "is lost in that 'gouffre obscur,' one separated from God's grace. He must live on in the darkness of 'an unweeded garden/(grown) to seed'" [in the words of Rosette Lamont, "'The Hamlet-Myth' in Nineteenth-Century France," *Council on National Literatures/ Quarterly World Report,* 1982]. But the poem also hints at the narrator's "superiority," for he triggers irony's dagger. This critical play is more acutely brought to light with the portrayal of the demons as an imaginary construct of the poet's imagination, prompted by his reverie:

> Comme je me plaignais un jour à la nature,
> Et que de ma pensée, en vaguant au hasard,
> J'aiguisais lentement sur mon coeur le
>   poignard,
> Je vis en plein midi descendre sur ma tête
> Un nuage funèbre et gros d'une tempête,
> Qui portait un troupeau de démons vicieux,
> Semblables à des nains cruels et curieux.

An extension of the artistic self, the demons make disparaging remarks that question the poetic act. That the narrator is aware of their presence, however, not only reveals his deprecation but also his superiority in the knowledge of his victimization. Ironic self-consciousness thus transcends the narrator's position as artistic sham through the assimilation of the object (both the demons and the beloved) to the narrative self. As such, the role of "others" in this poem alludes to the narrator as the prince or dandy who is keenly cognizant of his preeminent status but unable to prevent his own denigration as the unfortunate Hamlet-character.

"L'Héautontimorouménos" similarly provides insight into the critical doubling of the narrative self. The ironic voice echoes Icarus' search for the impossible or the absolute as it seeks to establish the primacy of satanic order over divine rule. The opening stanzas show the poet inflicting pain upon the woman to satisfy and relieve his own suffering, thirst, and desires. This also reflects an effort to surpass conventional order and movement. However, it does not occur; instead, the poet's self-consciousness forces him to acknowledge his singularity as he becomes the vampire of his own heart. Treating the self-other relation in Baudelaire's work, Eric Gans writes [in an article in *Stanford French Review,* 1984], "'L'Héautontimorouménos' throws off the Other of the opening lines as a failed attempt at self-doubling which gives way to the intermediary figure of 'L'ironie,' whose doubleness the poet reflects. . . . The

Self is finally revealed as its own double, and in so doing reacquires a new diabolic substantiality." Irony's doubleness as the "vorace Ironie" tracking the self brings to light the destructive appropriation of the other. This awareness removes the critical self from the interplay of the empirical self-other rapport and forces it to acknowledge its own reflection as "la mégère," the shrew. With this recognition, the self becomes both perpetrator and victim, a position that is appropriated within the consciousness of the poetic voice.

In the last stanza this self-consciousness evokes a superiority in self-knowledge as it perceives the absolute ("le rire éternel"), thus bringing to mind the prince-dandy figure. But the poet's failure to smile also condemns him, revealing that he cannot participate in this knowledge. This is reminiscent of Melmoth's satanic laughter in *De l'Essence du rire:* it discerns its superiority but at its own expense, since it is always linked to a fall or self-destruction.

That the ironic voice recognizes its split or fragmentation symbolizes its superiority. Though this realization ultimately occurs as a result of its fall, which the prince or dandy cannot halt, its prominent status brings it to an even higher, more self-conscious level. We are not far from the poem, **"L'Irrémédiable,"** which approaches the irony of ironies with the self revealed as the ultimate consciousness of desire. Both the imagery (others and objects) and the self are merged into one consciousness. Whereas the heart's "tête-à-tête" enjoys a unique role in this poem, it owes the recognition of its knowledge to its downfall. The fragmented consciousness in part one experiences several metaphoric descents, recognizing its imperfect or corrupt state but powerless to reverse its course:

> —Emblèmes nets, tableau parfait
> D'une fortune irrémédiable,
> Qui donne à penser que le Diable
> Fait toujours bien tout ce qu il fait!

Baudelaire places greater emphasis on the notion of awareness in part two. The self's preeminent status, though fragmented, is clearly delineated by various epithets:

> Tête-à-tête sombre et limpide
> Qu'un coeur devenu son miroir!
> Puits de Vérité, clair et noir,
> Où tremble une étoile livide,
>
> Un phare ironique, infernal,
> Flambeau des grâces sataniques,
> Soulagement et gloire uniques, ...

These images prepare the last verse that points to a source of knowledge, "—La conscience dans le Mal!",

ironically acquired at the price of a downfall. But irony probes deeper because this knowledge is locked within the self's own consciousness. All the images in the first part of the poem are ultimately appropriated by a heart that mirrors itself. Irony is further underscored as the narrative voice refers to this consciousness in indefinite terms ("Qu'*un* coeur devenu son miroir"). Accordingly, the heart or consciousness is isolated from the self with fragmentation assuming increasing significance. The self's superiority is discernible but since consciousness mirrors only itself, absolute knowledge remains enclosed in its own self-reflective form. Though **"L'Irrémédiable"** does not surpass the irony of this position, since this would be Baudelaire's description of pure poetry precluding the notion of a fall, it is nonetheless the exemplary testimony of a self-perpetuating and problematic stance in which the quest for knowledge or the absolute is deemed possible but impenetrable.

The irony framing Baudelaire's "comique absolu" inaugurates a critical process that, situated at the level of the narrative self, vigorously depicts a world constantly questioning itself. Though characterized by lack of closure, the ironic temper nevertheless verbalizes the ambiguities strewn in Baudelaire's poetry, ambiguities and paradoxes that could not otherwise be articulated. For it denotes a unique way of perceiving the world as it creates structures potentially rich and continuously varying in meaning while simultaneously challenging their effectiveness. The open-ended nature of irony and its relation to the fragmented self offer a viable perspective to new discoveries to be made about Baudelaire's poetry.

Edward K. Kaplan (essay date 1993)

SOURCE: "Baudelaire and the Vicissitudes of Venus: Ethical Irony in *Fleurs du Mal,*" in *The Shaping of Text: Style, Imagery, and Structure in French Literature,* edited by Emanuel J. Mickel, Jr., Bucknell University Press, 1993, pp. 113-30.

[*In the following essay, Kaplan explores the relationship between ethics and sexuality in* Les Fleurs du Mal.]

Respectful attention to literary context often helps resolve thorny theoretical issues. The "architecture" (or overall thematic structure) of **Les Fleurs du Mal** can be delineated, with some certainty, through analysis of certain sequences (or cycles), and Baudelaire's deliberate revisions of the first (1857) edition provide empirical confirmation. Here, quite briefly, are the changes. The second (1861) edition, which remained definitive, marks a radical shift from a poetics of transcendent Beauty to a poetics of compassion for imperfect, and afflicted, people. Most of the thirty-two added poems embrace the world as it exists.

Baudelaire altered the first and final sections of *Les Fleurs du Mal* the most radically, and introduced a new one, *Tableaux parisiens*. He added poems to the "Beauty Cycle" (nos. 17-21) in the first section, *Spleen et Idéal,* which depict the poet-narrator's conversion from aesthetics to ethics; two of the new pieces, **"Le Masque"** and **"Hymne à la Beauté"** (nos. 20-21), explicitly repudiate idealized females who symbolize the untruth of art, its denial of human mortality. *Tableaux parisiens* reinforces this acceptance of imperfect life by countering the many attacks against idealized young women—understood in terms of "sadism"—as it features the poet's artistic sympathy for older females, only some of them misshapen, "décrépites et charmantes." The mature Baudelaire favors a type of ethical inspiration revealed in **"Les petites vieilles"**: "Je goûte à votre insu des plaisirs clandestins."

Temporality as such assumes positive poetic value. The three poems Baudelaire added at the very end of the 1861 version of *La Mort,* the collection's concluding sequence, ratify its disenchanted realism. Transcendence of death is no longer preferred. **"La fin de la journée,"** **"Le rêve d'un curieux,"** and especially **"Le Voyage"** revise the idealist dreams of the preceding three sonnets—**"La mort des amants," "La mort des pauvres," "La mort des artistes"**—which had closed the original edition. Death becomes the "vieux capitaine" of a grim but hopeful and courageous voyage.

The two penultimate sections—*Fleurs du Mal* and *Révolte*—form a unity that did *not* change drastically. They contain some of the earliest prepublications of *Les Fleurs du Mal* and anticipate the future collection's complex ethical thrust. Taken together, these notorious cycles defy conventional views of moral corruption. The former appears to savor decadent sexual behaviors, whereas the latter attacks moralistic Christianity by claiming to repudiate Christ, the first "Christian" as it were, while promoting Cain, the first murderer, a proxy of proletarian rebellion. These were the poems most forthrightly condemned by the tribunal in 1857, earning the poet a perilous reputation he has never lost.

In both the 1857 and 1861 editions, *Fleurs du Mal* and *Révolte* preserved their structure despite censorship and subsequent displacement, retaining the same relation to each other and essentially the same contents. In 1857, *Fleurs du Mal* (containing twelve poems) was section 2, followed by *Révolte,* comprised of three poems considered blasphemous. But only three of the former section's offending pieces were excised by the authorities: **"Lesbos," "Femmes damnées. Delphine et Hippolyte"** (*A la pâle clarté . . .*), and **"Les Métamorphoses du vampire"** were suppressed, henceforth to be consigned as *Epaves* to the back of subsequent editions, where adolescents and amateurs of "curiosa" have conveniently relished them. Yet all the surviving poems maintain their undeniable poetic power. Questions of morality, inner psychological struggle, and literary meaning preserve the integrity of this apparently "perverse" section.

Ethical Irony

Fleurs du Mal, section 4 of the 1861 edition, because of its title, and its content, provides a hermeneutical key to the entire collection. The male poet identifies with female love and sexuality, and establishes the poet-narrator's ambiguous ethics by providing a model of *ethical irony,* a feigned promotion of crime and perversion meant to engage readers in dialogue. (At the time, the majority simply felt terrorized.) These disturbing poems render the pleasures of "vice" from the perspective of its practitioners, without moralistic complaining.

Baudelaire's masterpiece suffered—and succeeded—because we remain uncertain as to how far the poet as represented in the text leans on either side. He is not didactic, nor is he uncompromisingly rebellious. His lyricism of evil appeals directly to our ambivalence, and we can pleasantly contemplate private impulses we normally repress or at least guard unspoken. It was the author's misfortune that hostile critics ignored his warning, printed in 1857 as a preface to *Révolte,* that these outrageous poems represent "le pastiche des raisonnements de l'ignorance et de la fureur." After his book was confiscated, Baudelaire wrote a memorandum to his lawyer that laments his misplaced trust: "Mon unique tort a été de compter sur l'intelligence universelle, et de ne pas faire une préface où j'aurais posé mes principes littéraires et dégagé la question importante de la Morale." Readers still confused the author with the poet-narrator.

Fleurs du Mal is not objective in the manner of the *style indirect libre* of *Madame Bovary,* to use the most relevant historical parallel, nor is it resolutely perverse. The poems' "immorality" has a Socratic function, to provoke complacent readers by probing our "hypocrisy," which can be analyzed, charitably, as unacknowledged inner conflicts. These poems juxtapose alluring images of vice with the poet's expressed horror at its causes, thus forcing readers to make moral (and hermeneutical) choices. What evidence of the poet's implicit literary "principles" can be adduced?

In the simplest terms, an overall structural symmetry, established before the collection took shape, provides precious clues. The definitive edition of *Les Fleurs du Mal* traces a path from the liminal poem, **"Au lecteur,"** through **"Voyage à Cythère,"** the cornerstone of section 4, *Fleurs du Mal,* ending with the poem added in 1861 as a finale, **"Le Voyage."** It is significant that, in their original prepublication in the *Revue des Deux Mondes* (1 June 1855), **"Un Voyage à**

Cythère" directly follows "**Au lecteur.**" Our analysis of ethical irony is justified by "**Au lecteur,**" which explains quite plainly that corruption is generated by Ennui, pathological apathy and depression ("Aux objets répugnants nous trouvons des appats"); the poet's snide celebration of "la ménagerie infâme de nos vices" challenges his readers' self-evasion. Yet its final lines establish an almost tender complicity between public and poet which the posturing of ethical irony disguises.

Fleurs du Mal, in both the 1857 and 1861 editions, expands the poet's complex dialogue with his "Hypocrite lecteur, mon semblable, mon frère." We can differentiate between his contradictory roles and attitudes. The 1861 version of *Fleurs du Mal* (which precedes *Révolte* and *La Mort*), provides the itinerary's pivotal moment. It consists of a cycle of nine poems (nos. 109-17) unified by examples of male and female sexuality, the search for authentic love with another person, and the limits of the body—of which death is the fundamental example. These poems' particular energy derives from the conflict between the passion for perfection and despair at being unable to reach it. Male and female characters alike endure the frustration of noble desires. All victims mirror the poet's vulnerability to social prejudices and to the fragility of his self-esteem.

Read as a single sequence, *Fleurs du Mal* interprets vice as a normal (though self-destructive) reaction against oppression, both spiritual and physical. Each poem explores variants of the insight that "evil" behavior often derives from desperation. So the word *mal* in the title of both the section and the collection should be interpreted in a nonjudgmental sense as *affliction* (or le *malheur,* to use Simone Weil's term). More precisely, *Fleurs du Mal* locates the poet's anger in his death anxiety, which he projects as horror of female otherness. Idealized women usually appear in his poetry as victims of male hostility and lust. *Fleurs du Mal* will honor female scapegoats, shunned by polite society, as it relentlessly anatomizes the male imagination.

The Despair of Finitude

The antepenultimate section is organized around the old theme of Love and Death; specifically, anxiety about the mortal body (male or female) may lead to vice, which is a form of distorted love (in Dante's terms). The poet of *Fleurs du Mal* is a self-aware man who strives both to love a woman and to write, and the poems mix fear, compassion, and moral polemic while lingering on the erotic charms of violence and female homosexuality. It is a psychological commonplace, but one worth recalling, that people (in this case, men) intimidated by women's independence fear for their own self-mastery. These poems combine the enchant-

ments of "perversity" with an ethical challenge—expressed through irony—to those who condemn certain forms of loving.

Fleurs du Mal can be divided into four hermeneutic entities. The first two develop the dialectic of infinite desire frustrated by finitude: (1) "**La Destruction**" and "**Une martyre**" show that a man's violence is his primitive response to the impossibility of fulfilling his excessive emotional and sensual needs; (2) "**Femmes damnées**" (*Comme un bétail pensif . . .* (with "**Lesbos**" and "**Delphine et Hippolyte,**" censored from the first edition) present homosexuality as a woman's escape from society's hostility to *her* limitless quest for tenderness. The last two groupings portray male death anxiety through images of sexual intercourse: (3) "**Les Deux Bonnes Soeurs,**" "**La Fontaine de sang,**" "**Allégorie,**" "**La Béatrice**" depict frightened, vulnerable men who apprehend women as lethal. (4) The section closes with a long, metacritical poem, "**Un Voyage à Cythère**" followed by an emblematic clausula, "**L'Amour et le crâne**"), suggesting that a poet might overcome despair through literature.

The section is rigorously constructed and opens with a liminal sonnet which defines a table of contents, as does "**Au lecteur,**" which introduces both the 1855 *Revue des Deux Mondes* series and the 1857 and 1861 collections. "**La Destruction**" identifies the Devil, mortality itself, as responsible for humankind's inherent despair: "Je l'avale et le sens qui brûle mon poumon" (v.3). ("**Au lecteur**" establishes these images: "la Mort dans nos poumons / Descend, fleuve invisible," v. 22-24). In "**La Destruction**" the poet's will, no longer passive, is powerful—though it remains ambivalent, uncontrollable, and infinite: "un désir éternel et coupable." The second quatrain applies our self-destructive condition (i.e., mortality blamed on the Devil) to the aesthetic quest: "Parfois il prend, sachant mon grand amour de l'Art, / La forme de la plus séduisante des femmes."

This opening poem states quite clearly that misdirected or blocked religious impulses can provoke sadistic lust. Truth—not Beauty—is the poet's standard. Lust (or its metaphorical equivalent as existential self-assertion) is sophism, "de spécieux prétextes de cafard." (Baudelaire's expression "hypocrite lecteur" updates the traditional meaning of *cafard* as a religious bigot, used in the satires of Rabelais.) The poem's original title, "**La Volupté**" (also published in the *Revue des Deux Mondes* on 1 June 1855, perhaps emulating Sainte-Beuve's 1834 novel, *Volupte*) makes at least two levels of "**La Destruction**" explicit: (1) the joys of evil from the perspective of blindness or indifference; and (2) remorse for straying from the true path. The delights of illicit love are "des philtres infâmes," both magic and degrading.

"**La Destruction**" rather moralistically denounces the confusion of sensual love and art. The two tercets emphasize a traditional Christian judgment of a man addicted to this vicious inspiration. The woman as Devil alienates the man and undermines his drive toward goodness and even his desire to live. The poet unsuccessfully defends his yearning for spiritual companionship, the "regard de Dieu," and ends up "brisé de fatigue, au milieu / Des plaines de l'Ennui"; only apathy and "confusion" emerge from "l'appareil sanglant de la Destruction!" Because this moral outrage is so obvious, alert readers should not succumb to the ethical irony of the following poem.

The poet of "**Une martyre**" contemplates a female victim of male lust, preparing the ground for an analysis of violence against women. An apparently amoral perspective, however, introduces "**Une martyre**," which describes enticingly a naked, decapitated female corpse. The poet's obscene complacency contradicts the title, which prepares us for an allegory of religious sacrifice. The ironic dissonance is reinforced by the subtitle, "Dessin d'un maître inconnu," identifying the poem as a *transposition d'art,* a literary reinterpretation of an already allegorical work. At the same time, the vivid description surpasses art as it plays the delicate notes of implied cruel joys. (This second poem of the section contains exactly sixty lines, as does "**Un Voyage à Cythère**," the section's penultimate piece. That symmetry confirms ethical irony as an element of structure. It also establishes the figurative equivalence between the male and female victims.)

The poem reveals, gradually and quite concretely, the poet's complex sympathy with both man and woman, victim and assassin. This rhetorical process develops in four stages: (1) lines 1 to 28 describe the dead woman's seductive boudoir and her body; (2) lines 29 to 44 speculate on her "amour ténébreux"; (3) lines 45 to 52 evoke the man who killed her; and (4) the concluding lines 53 to 60 draw a surprising lesson: the poet lifts his cynical mask to condemn society's hypocrisy, declaring that the martyr will survive as a "forme immortelle."

The first nine stanzas (vv. 1-28) establish the ethical irony by maintaining a seductive atmosphere. A cinematographic sweep lingers over a sumptuous "chambre tiède où . . . l'air est dangereux et fatal," gradually to focus on "Un cadavre sans tête." Then the curious observer finds the head and examines its ambiguous gaze: "Un regard vague et blanc comme le crépuscule / S'échappe des yeux révulsés." Are they turned upward in terror or in the ecstasy of orgasm? These dead eyes, in either case, are segregated from her titillating body, as if the person were punished for her sexuality (or the thoughts her head contained):

> Sur le lit, le tronc nu sans scrupules étale
> Dans le plus complet abandon

> La secréte splendeur et la beauté fatale
> Dont la nature lui fit don.

> (v. 21-24)

An exquisite detail renders the victim's "coupable joie" all the more fascinating: "un bas rosâtre, orné de coins d'or." A marker of irony—the disjunctive "sans scrupules"—teases the voyeur's (i.e., the reader's) bourgeois prudery.

The next four stanzas (vv. 29-44) redirect the poet's attitude completely and prepare his compassionate intervention. The voyeur's ornate and lascivious description gives way to his (and our) empathy with the person. Suddenly he notices her "maigreur élégante" (v. 37) and, acknowledging her youth, he reflects on the "cadavre impur" who is—objectively—a teenager led astray and murdered. Description gives way to potential dialogue; the object *elle* becomes *tu:*

> Elle est bien jeune encor!—Son âme exaspérée
> Et ses sens par l'ennui mordus
> S'étaient-ils entr'ouverts à la meute altérée
> Des désirs errants et perdus?
> L'homme vindicatif que tu n'as pu, vivante,
> Malgré tant d'amour, assouvir,
> Combla-t-il sur ta chair inerte et complaisante
> L'immensité de son désir?

> (v. 41-48)

The poet questions the meaning of this scene and introduces moral judgments, though he does not "condemn" the crime. He suspects that her self-defeating "désirs errants et perdus" were imposed by pathological depression ("l'ennui"). Her man's vengeful frustration, too, originates in infinite desire, a misdirected religious impulse. He goes so far as to suggest that the assassin's necrophilia (reconfirmed in the next stanza: "a-t-il sur tes dents froides / Collé les suprêmes adieux?") is the negative expression of a drive toward transcendence. The man's murderous lust degrades the young woman's pure intentions. Her pathetic dignity emerges when we realize that she could not satisfy her man "malgré tant d'amour."

Ethical irony enriches the expression *"cadavre impur!"* (v. 49). In reality, the prurient descriptions are meant to entrap *"la foule impure"* (v. 53), readers who will not own to their pornocratic aspirations. The repetition of *impur* condenses these contradictory perspectives and resolves them in the poem's conclusion, set off by its second dash. (The *cadavre*'s intentions seem to be morally pure.) At fault are guardians of public virtue who condemn private behavior without noticing the spiritual anguish at its inception.

The "sadistic" prologue had disguised the young woman's nostalgia for authentic love. Now freed from the irony, she emerges as a "martyre" in her anonymous death: "—Loin du monde railleur, loin de la foule impure, / Loin des magistrats curieux" (v. 53-54). (Baudelaire, by anticipation, appropriately impeaches the "magistrats curieux" who condemned *Les Fleurs du Mal* a scant fortnight after publication.) The poem ends by translating her sin into a sacrifice; the *cadavre impur* becomes redeemed as memory.

Yet the final ironies prevent us from sentimentalizing her too deftly. Her illicit lover becomes her husband through murder, and the bride receives a bitter recompense for her faith, a spurious immortality in the criminal's guilty conscience:

> Ton époux court le monde, et ta forme
>   immortelle
>   Veille près de lui quand il dort;
> Autant que toi sans doute il te sera fidèle,
>   Et constant jusques à la mort.
>
> (v. 57-60)

The poet has thus transfigured her corpse into a poem, as he had at the end of **"Une Charogne"** when he assures his beloved, with an irony, this time, directed against mortality itself, "J'ai gardé la forme et l'essence divine / De mes amours décomposés" (v. 47-48). The corrupted female, victim of man's equally desperate "désir éternel et coupable," becomes vicious through despair. Baudelaire's poem restores her dignity—but without yielding to bourgeois indignation. The marriage of his "martyre" is consecrated—not by the Church—but by her murder and mutilation.

The next poem in the sequence, **"Femmes damnées,"** recapitulates the poet's sympathy for the women represented in the two preceding pieces. His bold identification with women unjustly condemned is reinforced by this single poem about lesbian love that escaped the tribunal. The pleasures of sexual "deviation" in **"Femmes damnées"** challenges the hypocritical, and equally vicious, moral code that automatically dooms them. Its structure repeats the disequilibrium of **"Une martyre"**; it begins lyrically by nourishing our sympathy with these ostracized lovers, and ends, after the ambiguities are played out, by ratifying their spiritual aspirations.

The first part of **"Femmes damnées"** consists of five stanzas (vv. 1-24) that evoke various sorts of love between women, starting with the innocent need for companionship ("cœurs épris de longues confidences . . . l'amour des craintives enfances," v. 5, 7), through the questionable excitement of self-flagellation and hallucination ("Où saint Antoine a vu surgir comme des laves / Les seins nus et pourprés de ses tentations," v. 12). Two stanzas, in fact, seem to relish a pagan perversion of asceticism that diverts feelings of guilt ("O Bacchus, endormeur des remords anciens!" v. 16). (The section's true culmination, **"Voyage à Cythère,"**

will recall and resolve this excruciating guilt.) Here, the poet's depiction of sadomasochistic joys ("L'écume du plaisir [mêlée] aux larmes des tourments," v. 20) challenges our moral tolerance to the limit—unless, of course, we view this fall from childhood intimacy to depravity as an amusing literary rebellion. Baudelaire would seem, in that instance, as in others (e.g., **"A celle qui est trop gaie," "Les Bijoux,"** and **"Les métamorphoses du vampire,"** also censored from the first edition), straightforwardly to advertise the naturalistic ethics of the Marquis de Sade.

"Femmes damnées" unveils its ethical irony only in the two final stanzas. The poet first expresses horror—pity for the suffering of lesbians and fear of their perversity—and then, somewhat sentimentally, he joins their search for perfected love. He first recapitulates the different female types in this poem and the preceding ones (including the two suppressed), in the penultimate stanza. The final stanza retranslates the entire sequence as the poet confesses his fraternal devotion:

> O vierges, ô démons, ô monstres, ô martyres,
> De la réalité grands esprits contempteurs,
> Chercheuses d'infini, dévotes et satyres,
> Tantôt pleines de cris, tantôt pleines de pleurs,
>
> Vous que dans votre enfer mon âme a
>   poursuivies,
> Pauvres sœurs, je vous aime autant que je
>   vous plains,
> Pour vos mornes douleurs, vos soifs
>   inassouvis,
> Et les urnes d'amour dont vos grands cœurs
>   sont pleins!
>
> (v. 21-28)

The poet enters their *enfer* (recalling the double meaning of "femmes damnées") and deplores their anguish. He too repudiates a flat version of reality, and he shares the "mornes douleurs" of their "soifs inassouvis." Without a trace of irony he celebrates their spiritual passion, which physical love can either reinforce or subvert. The sincerity of his assent is reinforced, stylistically, by the final awkwardness (in line 28), which critics assailed without mercy. He loves the "femmes damnées," especially, for "les urnes d'amour dont [leurs] grands cœurs sont pleins!"

This poem, which concludes with high affirmation and simple sincerity, subverts repressive norms in two areas. On a social level, it attacks wardens of the patriarchal family who would be loath to admit that evil does not inhere in this mode of loving. More profoundly, it repudiates conventional thinking that fears the thirst for the infinite, of which the pursuit of endless intimacy is but one poignant example. Baudelaire's irony upsets the self-satisfied who can endure existence only when they can restrict and control it, those who find it more convenient to scorn these female dissidents on principle than to defy life's limits.

Female Messengers of Mortality

The next four poems establish the poet as the central character of *Fleurs du Mal*. After having identified with female victims of desire—their own or a man's—he focuses on his own death anxiety. The reassuring women now metamorphose into instruments of his destruction, as anticipated in the liminal poem of that name. The very obviousness of these "allegories," these self-translating poems, incites us to question the poet-narrator's stated delectation of death. The first two, **"Les Deux Bonnes Soeurs"** and **"La Fontaine de sang,"** develop a fundamental male fantasy, that sex drains the man: "Il me semble parfois que mon sang coule à flots / Ainsi qu'une fontaine aux rythmiques sanglots" (v. 1-2). Even the poetic process (writing rhythmically) becomes a debilitating seminal ejaculation. The two longer pieces that follow, **"Allégorie"** and **"La Béatrice,"** further specify the woman's role as a projection of the male poet's need for nurturance and affection. His fear of death, however, makes all love impossible.

The two opening sonnets reassert the poet's irony. First and foremost, **"Les Deux Bonnes Soeurs"**—Death and Debauchery—are neither "bonnes" nor "aimables." Should we take more literally the narrator's characterization of himself as a "poète sinistre, ennemi des familles / Favori de l'enfer, courtisan mal renté" (v. 6-7)—malevolent but quick to complain that he is badly subsidized? He claims to surrender both to Love ("les myrtes infectes") and to Death ("tes noirs cyprès"). **"La Fontaine de sang"** continues this gloomy theme as it elaborates the nightmare of being drained of blood, the poet's death anxiety, "la terreur qui me mine" (v. 10). The narcotics he takes to escape only magnify his acute self-awareness: "Le vin rend l'oeil plus clair et l'oreille plus fine" and "L'amour n'est pour moi qu'un matelas d'aiguilles" (v. 11, 13). His expression of despair appears to be in earnest. Does the initial irony remain? Is woman only a relentless messenger of mortality?

These essentially misogynistic poems are more than exercises on an old theme. After all, everyone must die, and the intimacy of love and death came to Baudelaire with a distinguished history. An important clue to his barely voiced yearnings is condensed in the poet's pose as an *"ennemi des familles."* Does he claim to reject married life because of the bourgeois complacency it implies? Or is his "hatred" a Socratic mask? Two crucial lines allow us to unpack the pessimistic claim. "Les deux bonnes soeurs"—"Dont le flanc toujours vierge et drapé de guenilles / Sous l'éternel labeur n'a jamais enfanté" (v. 3-4)—are unreachable, not because they have refused sexual intercourse but because they are not mothers. This fleeting reference to childless women points to the poet's estrangement from *l'éternel labeur,* female fertility and nurturance.

A veiled image of a childless woman unifies *Fleurs du Mal* and explains why the poet features the alienation of men and women from each other. He is the victim. Irremediably isolated, he can only share the tenderness of lesbians, including the sadomasochistic sisters. The male poet, too, is *eternally* sterile.

Negative images of women, in **"Allégorie"** and **"La Béatrice,"** complete this cycle of four poems. The first one recalls the sonnet **"La Beauté"** in which a statue-like Muse, indifferent to the poet's passion, represents an abstract Ideal. The strong woman (or rather, the perfect body) of **"Allégorie"** is a "femme belle et de riche encolure, / Qui laisse dans son vin traîner sa chevelure" (v. 1-2), a prostitute or courtesan whose coldness has two basic meanings: (1) she does not share the man's existential anxiety ("Elle rit à la Mort et nargue la Débauche," v. 5)—neutralizing **"Les Deux Bonnes Soeurs"**—which makes her inaccessible to his empathy; (2) she possesses no conscience ("Elle ignore l'Enfer comme le Purgatoire," v. 17), achieving an odd sort of innocence: "Elle regardera la face de la Mort, / Ainsi qu'un nouveau-né,—sans haine et sans remord" (v. 19-20, the final lines).

This logical impasse inserts us deeper into Baudelaire's text. How can a newborn consciously face death—as the image implies? The disjunction "ainsi qu'un nouveau-né" confronts us with a contradiction. The courtesan's absolute self-abandonment to sex ("Elle a dans le plaisir la foi mahométane," v. 10) may suppress the drive toward Destruction that death anxiety can aggravate in both men and women; however, she does so at the price of her sensitivity to others. The image of ultimate innocence (a newborn baby) as ultimate detachment from human finitude (or so-called Islamic fatalism) is ironic, because it requires moral indifference. Besides, would the poet, to alleviate his anguish, want to start anew, at birth? Perhaps he just wants his mother?

The poetic sequence as a whole reinforces an image of the poet as a victim of women. **"Les Deux Bonnes Soeurs"** and **"La Fontaine de sang"** assert that revolt is the only appropriate response to premature or arbitrary death: "Et la bière et l'alcôve en blasphèmes fécondes / [Nous offrent] De terribles plaisirs et d'affreuses douceurs" (v. 9, 11). Debauchery, depicted as the magnificent but frigid courtesan of **"Allégorie,"** represents another perilous denial of death anxiety. The sculptured female reminds the poet—whose trade consists in carving verbal allegories—of his isolation, vulnerability, and emotional sterility: "Tout glisse et tout s'émousse au granit de sa peau" (v. 4). She joins Love, Death, and lesbians on the list of *"vierges infécondes"* (v. 13). Sexually adept, they all shun motherhood and consequently deny the poet the sympathy he seeks from them.

"La Béatrice" completes this cycle of four as it applies images of female indifference to the poet's professional dilemma. The title continues the irony, because this mediator hardly inspires our post–romantic Dante with a vision of cosmic and personal redemption. Jean Prévost's interpretation of the poem as a portrait of the author through the eyes of hostile critics is plausible. Its significance is broader, however, when read within the sequence. **"La Béatrice"** mocks the poet's artistic self-consciousness, which makes his personal life unbearable: "—'Contemplons à loisir cette caricature / Et cette ombre d'Hamlet imitant sa posture.'" (The next poem, **"Un Voyage à Cythère,"** will redeem that *conscience malheureuse*.)

The three stanzas of **"La Béatrice"** systematically parody the idiom of romantic heroism. Lines 1 to 12 evoke a grim landscape ("Dans des terrains cendreux, calcinés, sans verdure"), similar to the wasteland of the prose fable, **"Chacun sa Chimère."** Another tone disturbs the solemn harmony, expressed by inflated, stereotyped images reminiscent of Musset or Chateaubriand's René: "Comme je me plaignais un jour à la nature. . . . J'aiguisais lentement sur mon coeur le poignard." The "démons vicieux" in the second stanza (vv. 13-22) question the poet's authenticity: "'Ce gueux, cet histrion en vacances, ce drôle / Parce qu'il sait jouer artistement son rôle.'"

These lines validate Baudelaire's repeated warnings that some of his offensive poems represent a "pastiche." At the same time, he could not expect his defensive critics to relish his polemics against self-deception. The government, unwilling to distinguish between narrator and author, would soon denounce *Les Fleurs du Mal* as subverting its moral (and literary) authority.

"Béatrice" reveals herself as the familiar courtesan in the third stanza (vv. 23-30): "La reine de mon coeur au regard nonpareil." The poet's elevated style makes all the more bitter the manner in which she humiliates his "orgueil aussi haut que les monts" by joining the "troupe obscène" of demons (or critics). Hyperboles reinforce the irony, but the images of betrayal decisively reinforce the implicit compassion of the preceding poems. The male artist is vulnerable, not only because his ideal cannot be captured but because the person who should incarnate his aspirations (a lover? his mother?) refuses even to understand his devotion. Finally, his defensive pride is crushed by the "sale caresse" (v. 30, the last words) that she lavishes ostentatiously on his enemies.

Sexuality: Locus of Human Finitude

"Un Voyage à Cythère," a cornerstone of Baudelaire's initial sequence (*Revue des Deux Mondes*, 1855), summarizes the section *Fleurs du Mal* and takes its place at a culminating moment in the masterwork of essentially the same name. *Fleurs du Mal* progresses from poems depicting "corrupt" women (with whom the poet touchingly identifies) to women who endanger him. Acting out the man's internal conflicts, women can be either pure (and victimized) or menacing; the treacherous muse's *sale caresse* contradicts the teenaged martyr's "amour ténébreux" (v. 2) and the lesbians' "soifs inassouvis" (v. 27). All these women mirror the poet's struggles to reconcile infinite passion with its inevitable defeat ("—Son âme exaspérée / Et ses sens par l'ennui mordus," v. 41-42). *Fleurs du Mal* fulfills the program of **"Au lecteur,"** which had defined Ennui—pathological depression—as a two-edged remedy for existential pain.

"Un Voyage à Cythère" concludes *Fleurs du Mal* by interpreting sexuality philosophically, as the locus of a lover's confrontation with finitude. Baudelaire placed it at strategic intervals in both versions of the completed collection. Positioned in the 1861 edition at the end of the antepenultimate section (it was no. 88 in the first, when *Fleurs du Mal* was section 2), it recapitulates the struggle to differentiate self-destructive guilt from the plain facts of mortality. The title's ironic resonances would not be lost on contemporary readers: "*faire le voyage à Cythère* est une sorte d'euphémisme qui signifie se livrer aux plaisirs de l'amour" (the nineteenth-century Larousse, s.v. *Cythère;* the expression implies an erotic joke). More tragic than trivial, Baudelaire's grim voyage definitively translates his ethical irony.

In structural terms, **"Un Voyage à Cythère"** prepares the parallel with **"Le Voyage,"** which Baudelaire added in 1861 as the final poem of *Les Fleurs du Mal*. Readers would in any case ponder **"Un Voyage à Cythère"** quite seriously, for it transposes a Watteau painting of that name and recalls Gérard de Nerval's prose piece, *Voyage à Cythère* (published in *L'Artiste*, 30 June, 11 August 1844), about the Ionian island, "l'antique Cythère," devoted to Venus. Baudelaire repudiates (however ambiguously) the ancient pagan cult whose disappearance Nerval laments. The ironic love journey recapitulates those of the entire section.

The prologue juxtaposes boundless aspirations and their eventual disillusion; the "ange enivré d'un soleil radieux" (v. 4) of the poet's free imagination faces "cette île triste et noire" (v. 5). It is another spiritual Odyssey that plays out the traditional Christian antagonism of body and soul: *coeur* appears in lines 1, 9, 15, 56, and 60, whereas *corps* appears in lines 23,

32, 52, and 60. Various birds (vv. 1, 17, 26, 29, and 51) mediate the conflict between the mobile spirit ("Mon coeur, comme un oiseau, voltigeait tout joyeux," v. 1) and carnivorous beasts that represent carnal sins ("Des corbeaux lancinants et des panthères noires / Qui jadis aimaient tant à triturer ma chair," v. 51-52). The island's history is an emblem of the traveler's past.

Ethical irony intensifies our emotional assent to **"Un Voyage à Cythère."** It arouses our prurient curiosity about the legendary island, "Eldorado banal de tous les vieux garçons" while denouncing its corruption. The idealized beginning of the excursion leads to the exclamation: "J'entrevoyais pourtant un objet singulier!" (v. 20). The poet teasingly does not name the "thing," and continues to play on the lost paradise; the preterition awakens erotic fantasies, before the shock:

> Ce n'était pas un temple aux ombres
>   bocagères,
> Où la jeune prêtresse, amoureuse des fleurs,
> Allait, le corps brûlé de secrètes chaleurs,
> Entrebaillant sa robe aux brises passagères;
>
> Mais voilà qu'en rasant la côte d'assez près
> Pour troubler les oiseaux avec nos voiles
>   blanches,
> Nous vîmes que c'était un gibet à trois
>   branches,
> Du ciel se détachant en noir, comme un
>   cyprès.
>
> (vv. 21-28)

The narrative now becomes extremely bitter. The voyager contemplates a nauseating "punishment" for pagan delights as he details the work of the "féroces oiseaux," which eat the hanging corpse: "Chacun plantant, comme un outil, son bec *impur* / Dans tous les coins saignants de cette pourriture" (v. 31-32). The symbolism is quite literal: "ses bourreaux, gorgés de hideuses délices, / L'avaient à coups de bec absolument châtré" (v. 35-36). The poet seems to condemn the criminal's *impure* religion from a moralistic Christian perspective: "En expiation de tes *infâmes* cultes / Et des péchés qui t'ont interdit le tombeau" (v. 43-44). The opening poem, **"La Destruction,"** had anticipated this result of "des philtres *infâmes*" (v. 8) of love worship (all emphases added).

Readers should not be fooled by the narrator's stated indignation. The expression "infâmes cultes" is ironic and cannot be taken moralistically. The poet favors the metaphysical aspirations of paganism, reinforcing his identification with the young female martyr and the persecuted lesbian lovers. The captivating young priestess makes the defiled man's "corps brûlé de secrètes chaleurs" all the more sympathetic. As he meditates on

the male sacrifice, the poet becomes one with all victims of finitude:

> Ridicule pendu, tes douleurs sont les
>   miennes!
> Je sentis, à l'aspect de tes membres flottants,
> Comme un vomissement, remonter vers mes
>   dents
> Le long fleuve de fiel des douleurs anciennes;
>
> Devant toi, pauvre diable au souvenir si cher,
> J'ai senti tous les becs et toutes les
>   mâchoires
> Des corbeaux lancinants et des panthères
>   noires
> Qui jadis aimaient tant à triturer ma chair.
>
> (vv. 45-52)

The oxymoron *"ridicule pendu"* unveils the ethical irony, for there is nothing even remotely laughable about this mutilated corpse. The shocking adjective eliminates any bathos (such as "Pauvres soeurs, je vous aime autant que je vous plains," v. 26), as does the poet's vomiting memories. The lesson is stark. Just as the "martyre" of poem number 110 had been decapitated for her loving, so the "enfant d'un ciel si beau" was robbed of his organs of generation. Acknowledging that the poem is, in part, a recollection (an experience of "jadis," or of Nerval's account), the poet revives his "douleurs *anciennes*." The witness becomes a brother ("mon semblable, mon frère") to this "pauvre diable au souvenir si cher."

This sixty-line poem completes the thematic symmetry of *Fleurs du Mal* because it completes the sixty-line **"Une martyre."** Male and female are equally sacrificed to "love," as the woman's decapitation anticipates the poet's "symbolic" castration. The rigorous structure of **"Un Voyage à Cythère"** confirms the section's overall logic: (1) lines 1 to 19 elaborate the contrast between the island's resplendent past and its grim present; (2) lines 20 to 44 particularize the lesson of love's decadence by describing, in gory detail, a rotted castrated corpse hanging from a gallows; and (3) finally, the poet (vv. 45-60) applies the image to his own sexual guilt. The conclusion revises the poet's anger or displaced aggression. Death now incites him to sublimate his despair though a literary symbolization.

From Anguish to Redemption

The narrative of **"Un Voyage à Cythère"** has ended, but the two final stanzas lift the poet to a higher level of theoretical awareness. The poem's last eight lines translate the section's meaning as they recapitulate—and transcend—the despair of all the poet's proxies. The first concluding stanza—highlighted by a dash—

returns to the poem's beginning and summarizes the thematic contrasts developed in the first fifty-two lines; then the poet introduces diacritical terminology usually reserved for analysis:

> —Le ciel était charmant, la mer était unie;
> Pour moi tout était noir et sanglant désormais,
> Hélas! et j'avais, comme en un suaire épais,
> Le coeur enseveli dans cette allégorie.
>
> Dans ton île, ô Vénus! je n'ai trouvé debout
> Qu'un gibet symbolique où pendait mon
>   image. . . .
> —Ah! Seigneur! donnez-moi la force et le
>   courage
> De contempler mon coeur et mon corps sans
>   dégoût!
>
>   (v. 53-60)

The final stanza imitates the emergence of poetry from anguish. Lines 57 and 58 summarize the adventure while the last two lines, after the ellipse, reject energetically the poet's self-condemnation. Death now reminds him of redemption within reach. The brusque leap between lines 58 and 59 conceals a complicated faith that allows the poet to survive and to hope. He faces his mortal body (and moral responsibility) through empathy with the corpse that becomes an *allegory* of his own experience. His assumption of guilt, as excruciating as it is, redeems his life.

Why does Baudelaire introduce the notions of "symbol" and "allegory"—so familiar to readers of Walter Benjamin and Paul de Man? Our method of interpreting these poems as a sequence helps entangle this delicate, and often confusing theoretical problem. Context, here, provides an answer. The fact that the poet perceives the corpse as an *image* frees him from debilitating anxiety, despite his feeling that his heart is buried, "*comme en un suaire épais.*" He confronts his earthly limits and then addresses God directly. His extraordinary prayer, in the poem's two final lines, without any irony, completes *Fleurs du Mal* and fulfills his poetic art.

A cognitive process seems to liberate the poet from suicidal despair when he perceives his encounter with lethal sex as symbolic. Of course Baudelaire's terminology is quite lax according to today's standards and is more expressive than rigorous; one cannot systematically distinguish between his use of the words "image" and "allegory." The terminology, as such, incites interpretation, however. Richard Stamelman has insightfully described Baudelaire's poetry as a positive construction of grief, "the shroud of allegory."

Whatever our theoretical preference, the ending of **"Un Voyage à Cythère"** definitely conveys meaning. What

may be a cry of despair ("—Ah! Seigneur!") points to a higher design. The poet no longer submits to the irremediable conflict between his body and his spiritual strivings, but looks, with hope, toward their future integration. His past and present no longer inhibit productive desire.

The poet's prayer confirms the very force and courage for which he prays. He actively anticipates the harmony of his "body" and "heart," his inner and outer lives. Does he imply that a compassionate God listens and understands? We can only hypothesize his possible leap into faith. Although we cannot, in all honesty, interpret this allegory definitively, we finish the poem excited by its unresolved, open significance.

Literary Closure

The section *Fleurs du Mal* is now complete because the poet has formed his body-soul conflict into an aesthetic object. **"L'Amour et le crâne"** provides an emblematic clausula that corresponds to **"La Destruction,"** the opening piece. Further proof of Baudelaire's policy of structural unity is the fact that he had changed the subtitle of **"L'Amour et le crâne"** from "D'après une vieille gravure" (see *Revue des Deux Mondes,* 1 June 1855, which it also closed) to vieux cul-de-lampe," a decorative piece at the end of a book chapter. The poem is a verbal icon that depicts Love as "Ce jeu féroce et ridicule" (v. 15), another "ridicule pendu" in the ultimate perspective of Death. With an ethical irony that is cruder, more obvious than in the preceding poems, the poet ratifies his truce with life's normal terrors. Readers, as well, have come to accept them, at least intellectually, as part of the reassuring construct of poetry. Allegories of mortality frame its meaning.

Could that be Baudelaire's point? Beautiful poems about mortality and affliction probe our anxiety and boundless thirsts, whereas our acts of interpretation can foster understanding and communion. The memory of John Porter Houston [noted scholar of French literature (see excerpt above) to whom the volume in which this essay appeared was dedicated] a man of rigorous erudition and passionate scholarship, reminds us, with Baudelaire, that works of art can help us love the world and contemplate death with equanimity.

FURTHER READING

Biography

Carter, A. E. *Charles Baudelaire.* Boston: Twayne Publishers, 1977, 139 p.
    Provides an account of Baudelaire's life and a critical overview of his poetry.

de Jonge, Alex. *Baudelaire, Prince of Clouds: A Biography.* New York: The Paddington Press Limited, 1976, 240 p.

Offers both an account of Baudelaire's life and a critical evaluation of his work. Excerpted in *NCLC*, Volume 29.

Hyslop, Lois Boe. *Charles Baudelaire Revisited.* New York: Twayne Publishers, 1992, 180 p.

Examines the relationship between Baudelaire's life and his poetry.

Criticism

Auerbach, Erich. "The Aesthetic Dignity of 'Les fleurs du mal'." In *Scenes from the Drama of European Literature: Six Essays,* pp. 149-69. New York: Meridian Books, Inc., 1959.

Discusses the influence on Baudelaire of the treatment of sexuality in the European literary tradition, particularly medieval Christian traditions of love. Excerpted in *NCLC*, Volume 6.

Balakian, Anna. "Those Stigmatized Poems of Baudelaire." *The French Review,* Vol. XXXI, No. 4 (February 1958): 273-7.

Considers Baudelaire's banned love poems, focusing on his treatment of lesbianism. Excerpted in *NCLC*, Volume 29.

Barlow, Norman H. *Sainte-Beuve to Baudelaire: A Poetic Legacy.* Durham, NC: Duke University Press, 1964, 226 p.

A scholarly study of Charles Sainte-Beuve's influence on Baudelaire's poetry.

Bataille, George. "A Perfect Silence of the Will." In *Literature and Evil,* translated by Alastair Hamilton, 1973. Reprinted in *Charles Baudelaire,* ed. Harold Bloom, pp. 11-25. New York: Chelsea House Publishing, 1987.

Examines the complexities of Baudelaire's moral positions.

Benjamin, Walter. *Charles Baudelaire: A Lyric Poet in the Era of High Capitalism,* translated by Harry Zohn. London: NLB, 1973, 79 p.

In a detailed explication of *The Flowers of Evil,* Benjamin examines its structure and content but focuses primarily on poetic vocabulary. His study is incorporated in a broad cultural analysis of nineteenth-century France during Baudelaire's lifetime.

Bishop, Lloyd. "The Coexistence of Contraries: Baudelaire's *La Fanfarlo* and *Les Fleurs du mal.*" In *Romantic Irony in French Literature from Diderot to Beckett,* pp. 96-113. Nashville, TN: Vanderbilt University Press, 1989.

Observes that Baudelaire's poetry holds many contradictory positions simultaneously. Bishop argues that this is the primary reason for the wide influence that *The Flowers of Evil* has had on modern poetry.

Blood, Susan. "The Two Baudelaires: Valéry's Canonization of *Les Fleurs du Mal.*" *The Yale Journal of Criticism,* Vol. 6, No. 2 (Fall 1993): 133-55.

Discusses the critical history of *The Flowers of Evil* and examines how the collection first received broad recognition.

Bloom, Harold, ed. *Charles Baudelaire.* New York: Chelsea House Publishers, 1987, 168 p.

Provides a collection of contemporary critical essays on Baudelaire.

Bonnefoy, Yves. "Baudelaire's *Les Fleurs du mal.*" In *The Act and Place of Poetry,* pp. 44-9. Chicago: University of Chicago Press, 1989.

Discusses the relationship between death and language in *The Flowers of Evil.*

Brombert, Victor. "Baudelaire: City Images and the 'Dream of Stone'." *Yale French Studies,* No. 32 (1964): 99-105.

Discusses urban imagery in Baudelaire's poetry.

Burton, Richard D. E. *Baudelaire in 1859: A Study in the Sources of Poetic Creativity.* Cambridge, England: Cambridge University Press, 1988, 213 p.

Analyzes works that Baudelaire wrote in 1859, which the critic isolates as the most important and productive year of the poet's literary career.

Cargo, Robert T., ed. *A Concordance to Baudelaire's "Les Fleurs du Mal."* Chapel Hill: The University of North Carolina Press, 1965, 417 p.

An alphabetical index of principal words in *The Flowers of Evil.*

Chadwick, Charles. "Baudelaire's 'Correspondences'." In *Symbolism,* pp. 8-16. New York: Methuen, 1971.

Discusses Baudelaire's influence on the French Symbolist movement.

Clements, Patricia. *Baudelaire & the English Tradition.* Princeton: Princeton University Press, 1985, 442 p.

Traces the broad and varied influence of Baudelaire on English poets and critics.

Engstrom, Alfred Garvin. "Charles Baudelaire (1821-1867) and the Alchemy of 'Les fleurs du mal'." In *Darkness and Light: Lectures on Baudelaire, Flaubert, Nerval, Huysmans, Racine, and Time and Its Images in Literature,* pp. 11-34. University, MS: Romance Monographs, Inc., 1975.

Provides an overview of the poems in *The Flowers of Evil.* Excerpted in *NCLC*, Volume 29.

Fairlie, Alison. "Some Remarks on Baudelaire's 'Poème du haschisch'." In *The French Mind: Studies in Honour of Gustave Rudler,* edited by Will Moore, Rhoda Sutherland, and Enid Starkie, pp. 291-317. Oxford: Oxford University Press, 1952.

Argues that the thematic progression of Baudelaire's "Poème du haschisch" mirrors the arrangement of the poems in *The Flowers of Evil.*

Fowlie, Wallace. "Charles Baudelaire: The Experience of Religious Heroism." In *Clowns and Angels: Studies in Modern French Literature,* pp. 93-111. New York: Sheed and Ward, Inc., 1943.

Argues that *The Flowers of Evil* reflects Baudelaire's Christian faith. Fowlie states that Baudelaire proves the Roman Catholic dictum that it is "impossible to dispossess oneself of the spirit of Christianity." Excerpted in *NCLC,* Volume 6.

Gautier, Théophile. "Charles Baudelaire." In *The Complete Works of Théophile Gautier,* Vol. XII, edited and translated by F.C. DeSumichrast, pp. 17-126. New York: Bigelow and Smith & Co., 1903.

Examines the aesthetic goals of *The Flowers of Evil.* Gautier also argues that, though the collection's intention and execution are Romantic, Baudelaire is not to be confined to any literary school or movement. Excerpted in *NCLC,* Volume 6.

Johnston, John H. "Baudelaire." In *The Poet and the City: A Study in Urban Perspectives,* pp. 125-52. Athens: University of Georgia Press, 1984.

Argues that the "Parisian Sketches" section of *The Flowers of Evil* represents a central expression of Baudelaire's worldview. Excerpted in *NCLC,* Volume 29.

Leakey, F. W. *Baudelaire and Nature.* Manchester, England: Manchester University Press, 1969, 382 p.

Traces the evolution of Baudelaire's treatment of nature in both his poetry and his criticism.

——. *Baudelaire: Collected Essays, 1953-1988,* edited by Eva Jacobs. Cambridge, England: Cambridge University Press, 1990, 320 p.

Revised versions of many of the critic's principal essays on Baudelaire's work. Some of the essays are in French, with English summaries.

——. In *Baudelaire: Les Fleurs du Mal.* Cambridge, England: Cambridge University Press, 1992.

Surveys some of the most important themes of *The Flowers of Evil*: Baudelaire's examination of himself, his ideas about the poetic process, his conception of morality, and his attitude toward nature.

MacInnes, John W. *The Comical as Textual Practice in* Les Fleurs du Mal. Gainesville: University of Florida Press, 1988, 150 p.

Contends that the duality of Baudelaire's poetry reflects a conflict between two different approaches to writing poetry.

Marder, Elissa. "Flat Death: Snapshots of History." *Diacritics,* Vol. 22, No. 3 (Fall-Winter 1992): 128-44.

Relates Baudelaire's poem "à un passante" to some modern analyses of death and mourning.

Mossop, D. J. *Baudelaire's Tragic Hero: A Study of the Architecture of* Les Fleurs du Mal. London: Oxford University Press, 1961, 254 p.

Searches for the "secret architecture" of *The Flowers of Evil.*

Peyre, Henri. "'Correspondances' and 'Spleen'." In *The Poem Itself,* edited by Stanley Burnshaw, pp. 8-19. New York: Holt, Rinehart and Winston, 1960.

Provides translations and line-by-line analyses of two of Baudelaire's most important poems, 'Correspondences' and 'Spleen'." Excerpted in *NCLC,* Volume 29.

——. *Baudelaire: A Collection of Critical Essays.* Englewood Cliffs, NJ: Prentice-Hall, Inc., 1962, 184 p.

Provides a selection of twentieth-century critical essays on Baudelaire.

——. "Baudelaire as a Love Poet." In *Baudelaire as a Love Poet and Other Essays,* edited by Lois Boe Hyslop, pp. 3-39. University Park: Pennsylvania State University Press, 1969.

Examines the "sensual, the sentimental, and the cerebral" aspects of Baudelaire's love poetry.

Sainte-Beuve, Charles. "Baudelaire." In *Sainte-Beuve: Selected Essays,* translated and edited by Francis Steegmuller and Norbert Guterman, pp. 275-9. London: Methuen and Co., 1963.

This translation of an 1863 article provides the only critical commentary on Baudelaire by Sainte-Beuve that is available in English. Sainte-Beuve seems to have resented Baudelaire's talent. Here, he begrudgingly acknowledges the younger poet's creative abilities.

Sartre, Jean-Paul. *Baudelaire,* translated by Martin Turnell. Norfolk, CT: New Directions, 1950, 192 p.

Examines Baudelaire in relation to the social conditions under which *The Flowers of Evil* was written. Excerpted in *NCLC,* Volume 6.

Sieburth, Richard. "Poetry and Obscenity: Baudelaire and Swinburne." *Comparative Literature,* Vol. 36, No. 4 (Fall 1984): 343-53.

Compares the charges of obscenity leveled in France against *The Flowers of Evil* with the outcry against Swinburne's *Poems and Ballads* in England in 1866.

Valéry, Paul. "The Position of Baudelaire." In *Variety,* translated by William Aspenwall Bradley, pp. 71-100. New York: Harcourt Brace Jovanovich, Inc., 1938.

Recognizes the juxtaposition of Romantic and classical elements in Baudelaire's poetry and argues that *The Flowers of Evil* is the most important work in the history of French literature. Excerpted in *NCLC,* Volume 6.

Wing, Nathaniel. "The Danaide's Vessel: On Reading Baudelaire's Allegories." In *The Limits of Narrative: Essays on Baudelaire, Flaubert, Rimbaud and Mallarmé*, pp. 8-18. Cambridge, England: Cambridge University Press, 1986.

Examines the function of allegory in *The Flowers of Evil*.

Frederick Douglass

1817(?)-1895

(Born Frederick Augustus Washington Bailey) American lecturer, autobiographer, editor, essayist, and novella writer.

For additional information on Douglass's career see *NCLC*, Volume 7.

INTRODUCTION

Douglass is considered one of the most distinguished black writers in nineteenth-century American literature. Born into slavery, he escaped in 1838 and subsequently devoted his considerable rhetorical skills to the abolitionist movement. Expounding the theme of racial equality in stirring, invective-charged orations and newspaper editorials in the 1840s, 1850s, and 1860s, he was recognized by his peers as an outstanding orator and the foremost black abolitionist of his era. Douglass's current reputation as a powerful and effective prose writer is based primarily on his 1845 autobiography, *Narrative of the Life of Frederick Douglass, an American Slave, Written by Himself.* Regarded as one of the most compelling antislavery documents produced by a fugitive slave, the *Narrative* is also valued as an eloquent argument for human rights. As such, it has transcended its immediate historical milieu and is now regarded as a landmark in American autobiography.

Biographical Information

The son of a black slave and an unidentified white man, Douglass was separated from his mother in infancy. Nurtured by his maternal grandmother on the Tuckahoe, Maryland estate of his master, Captain Aaron Anthony, he enjoyed a relatively happy childhood until he was pressed into service on the plantation of Anthony's employer, Colonel Edward Lloyd. There Douglass endured the rigors of slavery. In 1825, he was transferred to the Baltimore household of Hugh Auld, where Douglass earned his first critical insight into the slavery system. Overhearing Auld rebuke his wife for teaching him the rudiments of reading, Douglass deduced that ignorance perpetuated subjugation and decided that teaching himself to read could provide an avenue to freedom. Enlightened by his clandestine efforts at self-education, Douglass grew restive as his desire for freedom increased, and was eventually sent to be disciplined, or "broken," by Edward Covey. When he refused to submit to Covey's beatings and instead challenged him in a violent confron-

tation, Douglass overcame a significant psychological barrier to freedom. In 1838, he realized his long-cherished goal by escaping to New York. Once free, Douglass quickly became a prominent figure in the abolitionist movement. In 1841, he delivered his first public address—an extemporaneous speech at an antislavery meeting in Nantucket, Massachusetts—and was invited by William Lloyd Garrison and other abolitionist leaders to work as a lecturer for the Massachusetts Antislavery Society. By 1845, Douglass's eloquent and cogent oratory had led many to doubt that he was indeed a former slave. He responded by composing a detailed account of his slave life, the *Narrative of the Life of Frederick Douglass*, which was an immediate popular success. Having opened himself to possible capture under the fugitive slave laws, Douglass fled that same year to Great Britain, where he was honored by the great reformers of the day. Returning to the United States in 1847, he received sufficient funds to purchase his freedom and establish *The North Star*, a weekly abolitionist newspaper. During the 1850s and early 1860s, Douglass continued his activities as a journalist, abolitionist speaker, and autobiographer. By the outbreak of the Civil War, he had emerged as a nationally-recognized spokesman for black Americans and, in 1863, advised President Abraham Lincoln on the use and treatment of black soldiers in the Union Army. His later years were chiefly devoted to political and diplomatic assignments, including a consul-generalship to the Republic of Haiti, which he recounts in the 1892 revised edition of his final autobiographical work, the *Life and Times of Frederick Douglass, Written by Himself.* Douglass died at his home in Anacostia Heights, District of Columbia, in 1895.

Major Works

In his speeches on abolition, Douglass frequently drew on his first-hand experience of slavery to evoke pathos in his audience. He is most often noted, however, for his skillful use of scorn and irony in denouncing the slave system and its abettors. One of the stock addresses in his abolitionist repertoire was a "slaveholders sermon" in which he sarcastically mimicked a pro-slavery minister's travesty of the biblical injunction to "do unto others as you would have them do unto you." His most famous speech, an address delivered on July 5th, 1852, in Rochester, New York, commonly referred to as the "Fourth of July Oration," is a heavily ironic reflection on the significance of Independence Day for slaves. The several installments of Douglass's autobiography—which include the *Narrative of the Life of Frederick Douglass, an American Slave* (1845), *My Bondage and My Freedom* (1855), and the *Life and Times of Frederick Douglass* (1881)—depart from the biting tone of his oratory and are often described as balanced and temperate, though still characterized by Douglass's dry, often ironic, wit. While these works are valued by historians as a detailed, credible account of slave life, the *Narrative* is widely acclaimed as an artfully compressed yet extraordinarily expressive story of self-discovery and self-liberation. In it Douglass records his personal reactions to bondage and degradation with straightforward realism and a skillful economy of words. He based his 1853 novella *The Heroic Slave* on the real-life slave revolt aboard the American ship *Creole* in 1841. Douglass's only work of fiction, it celebrates the bravery of Madison Washington, who is portrayed as a lonely and isolated hero.

Critical Reception

Appealing variously to the political, sociological, and aesthetic interests of successive generations of critics, Douglass has maintained his celebrated reputation as an orator and prose writer. Douglass's contemporaries

viewed him primarily as a talented antislavery agitator whose manifest abilities as a speaker and writer refuted the idea of black inferiority. This view persisted until the 1930s, when both Vernon Loggins and J. Saunders Redding called attention to the "intrinsic merit" of Douglass's writing and acknowledged him to be the most important figure in nineteenth-century black American literature. In the 1940s and 1950s, Alain Locke and Benjamin Quarles respectively pointed to the *Life and Times of Frederick Douglass* and the *Narrative* as classic works which symbolize the black role of protest, struggle, and aspiration in American life. Critics in recent years have become far more exacting in their analysis of the specific narrative and rhetorical strategies that Douglass employed in the *Narrative* to establish a distinctly black identity, studying the work's tone, structure, and placement in American literary history. In addition, scholars have since elevated the reputation of the *Narrative*, while noting that the later installments of his autobiography fail to recapture the artistic vitality of their predecessor. Continued study and praise of the autobiographies and Douglass's other works may be taken as an indication of their abiding interest. As G. Thomas Couser has observed, Douglass was a remarkable man who lived in an exceptionally tumultuous period in American history. By recording the drama of his life and times in lucid prose, he provided works which will most likely continue to attract the notice of future generations of American literary critics and historians.

PRINCIPAL WORKS

Narrative of the Life of Frederick Douglass, an American Slave, Written by Himself (autobiography) 1845

Oration, Delivered in Corinthian Hall, Rochester, by Frederick Douglass, July 5th, 1852 (speech) 1852

The Heroic Slave (novella) 1853

The Claims of the Negro Ethnologically Considered (speech) 1854

The Anti-Slavery Movement (speech) 1855

My Bondage and My Freedom (autobiography) 1855

Men of Color, to Arms! (essay) 1863

What the Black Man Wants (speech) 1865

John Brown (speech) 1881

Life and Times of Frederick Douglass, Written by Himself (autobiography) 1881; revised edition, 1892

The Race Problem (speech) 1890

The Life and Writings of Frederick Douglass. 5 vols. (letters, speeches, and essays) 1950-75

The Frederick Douglass Papers. 2 vols. (speeches and debates) 1979-82

CRITICISM

Margaret Fuller (review date 1845)

SOURCE: Review of *Narrative of the Life of Frederick Douglass, an American Slave,* in *Critical Essays on Frederick Douglass,* edited by William L. Andrews, G. K. Hall & Co., 1991, pp. 21-3.

[*Fuller was a prominent American critic and a recognized feminist and transcendentalist. In the following review, originally published in 1845, she praises Douglass's* Narrative, *commenting on the importance of the "just and temperate" observations that it contains.*]

Frederick Douglass has been for some time a prominent member of the Abolition party. He is said to be an excellent speaker—can speak from a thorough personal experience—and has upon the audience, beside, the influence of a strong character and uncommon talents. In the book before us he has put into the story of his life the thoughts, the feelings, and the adventures that have been so affecting through the living voice; nor are they less so from the printed page. He has had the courage to name the persons, times and places, thus exposing himself to obvious danger, and setting the seal on his deep convictions as to the religious need of speaking the whole truth. Considered merely as a narrative, we have never read one more simple, true, coherent, and warm with genuine feeling. It is an excellent piece of writing, and on that score to be prized as a specimen of the powers of the Black Race, which Prejudice persists in disputing. We prize highly all evidence of this kind, and it is becoming more abundant. The Cross of the Legion of Honor has just been conferred in France on Dumas and Soulie, both celebrated in the paths of light and literature. Dumas, whose father was a General in the French Army, is a Mulatto; Soulie, a Quadroon. He went from New Orleans, where, though to the eye a white man, yet as known to have African blood in his veins, he could never have enjoyed the privileges due to a human being. Leaving the Land of Freedom, he found himself free to develop the powers that God had given.

Two wise and candid thinkers,—the Scotchman, Kinment, prematurely lost to this country, of which he was so faithful and generous a student, and the late Dr. Channing,—both thought that the African Race had in them a peculiar element, which, if it could be assimilated with those imported among us from Europe would give to genius a development, and to the energies of character a balance and harmony beyond what has been seen heretofore in the history of the world. Such an element is indicated in their lowest estate by a talent for melody, a ready skill at imitation and adaptation, an almost indestructible elasticity of nature. It is to be remarked in the writings both of Soulie and Dumas, full of faults but glowing with plastic life and fertile in invention. The same torrid energy and saccharine fulness may be felt in the writings of this Douglass, though his life being one of action or resistance, was less favorable to SUCH powers than one of a more joyous flow might have been.

The book is prefaced by two communications—one from Garrison and one from Wendell Phillips. That from the former is in his usual over-emphatic style. His motives and his course have been noble and generous. We look upon him with high respect, but he has indulged in violent invective and denunciation till he has spoiled the temper of his mind. Like a man who has been in the habit of screaming himself hoarse to make the deaf better, he can no longer pitch his voice on a key agreeable to common ears. Mr. Phillips's remarks are equally decided, without this exaggeration in the tone. Douglass himself seems very just and temperate. We feel that his view, even of those who have injured him most, may be relied upon. He knows how to allow for motives and influences. Upon the subject of Religion, he speaks with great force, and not more than our own sympathies can respond to. The inconsistencies of Slaveholding professors of religion cry to Heaven. We are not disposed to detest, or refuse communion with them. Their blindness is but one form of that prevalent fallacy which substitutes a creed for a faith, a ritual for a life. We have seen too much of this system of atonement not to know that those who adopt it often began with good intentions, and are, at any rate, in their mistakes worthy of the deepest pity. But that is no reason why the truth should not be uttered, trumpet-tongued, about the thing. "Bring no more vain oblations": sermons must daily be preached anew on that text. Kings, five hundred years ago, built churches with the spoils of war; Clergymen to-day command Slaves to obey a Gospel which they will not allow them to read, and call themselves Christians amid the curses of their fellow men. The world ought to get on a little faster than that, if there be really any principle of movement in it. The Kingdom of Heaven may not at the beginning have dropped seed larger than a mustard seed, but even from that we had a right to expect a fuller growth than can be believed to exist, when we read such a book as this of Douglass. Unspeakably affecting is the fact that he never saw his mother at all by day light. "I do not recollect of ever seeing my mother by the light of day. She was with me in the night. She would lie down with me, and get me to sleep, but long before I waked she was gone."

The following extract presents a suitable answer to the background argument drawn by the defender of Slavery from the songs of the Slave, and it is also a good specimen of the powers of observation and manly heart of the writer. We wish that every one may read his book and see what a mind might have been stifled in bondage—what a man may be subjected to the insults of spendthrift dandies, or the blows of mercenary brutes, in whom there is no whiteness except of the skin, no humanity except in the outward form, and of whom the Avenger will not fail yet to demand—"where is thy brother?"

Frederick Douglass, writing about women in *The North Star,* **May 26, 1848:**

By nature, she is fitted to occupy a position as elevated and dignified as her self-created master. And though she is often treated by him as his drudge, or a convenient piece of household furniture, 'tis but a striking evidence of his mental imbecility and moral depravity.

Frederick Douglass, collected in Frederick Douglass on Women's Rights, *edited by Philip S. Foner, Greenwood Press, 1976.*

Ephraim Peabody (essay date 1849)

SOURCE: "Narratives of Fugitive Slaves," in *Critical Essays on Frederick Douglass,* edited by William L. Andrews, G. K. Hall & Co., 1991, pp. 24-7.

[*In the following essay, originally published in 1849, Peabody favorably assesses Douglass's* Narrative *as among the most remarkable productions of the age, but observes that the author's mode of speech is prone to "violent and unqualified statements" that could "diminish his power as an advocate of the antislavery cause."*]

America has the mournful honor of adding a new department to the literature of civilization,—the autobiographies of escaped slaves. . . . The subjects of two of these narratives, Frederick Douglass and Josiah Henson, we have known personally, and, apart from the internal evidence of truth which their stories afford, we have every reason to put confidence in them as men of veracity. The authors of the remaining accounts are, for anything we know to the contrary, equally trustworthy. We place these volumes without hesitation among the most remarkable productions of the age,—remarkable as being pictures of slavery by the slave, remarkable as disclosing under a new light the mixed elements of American civilization, and not less remarkable as a vivid exhibition of the force and working of the native love of freedom in the individual mind.

There are those who fear lest the elements of poetry and romance should fade out of the tame and monotonous social life of modern times. There is no danger of it while there are any slaves left to seek for free-

dom, and to tell the story of their efforts to obtain it. There is that in the lives of men who have sufficient force of mind and heart to enable them to struggle up from hopeless bondage to the position of freemen, beside which the ordinary characters of romance are dull and tame. They encounter a whole Iliad of woes, not in plundering and enslaving others, but in recovering for themselves those rights of which they have been deprived from birth. Or if the Iliad should be thought not to present a parallel case, we know not where one who wished to write a modern Odyssey could find a better subject than in the adventures of a fugitive slave. What a combination of qualities and deeds and sufferings most fitted to attract human sympathy in each particular case! . . .

These biographies of fugitive slaves are calculated to exert a very wide influence on public opinion. We have always been familiar with slavery, as seen from the side of the master. These narratives show how it looks as seen from the side of the slave. They contain the *victim's account* of the working of this great institution. When one escapes from the South, and finds an opportunity of speaking and has the power to speak, it is certain that he will have attentive listeners. Not only curiosity, but a sense of justice, predisposes men to hear the testimony given by those who have suffered, and who have had few among their own number to describe their sufferings. The extent of the influence such lives must exert may be judged of, when we learn the immense circulation which has been secured for them. Of Brown's *Narrative* [*Narrative of William W. Brown, a Fugitive Slave. Written by Himself*], first published in 1847, not less than eight thousand copies have been already sold. Douglass's *Life,* first published in 1845, has in this country alone passed through seven editions, and is, we are told, now out of print. They are scattered over the whole of the North, and all theoretical arguments for or against slavery are feeble, compared with these accounts by living men of what they personally endured when under its dominion. . . .

The narrative of Douglass contains the life of a superior man. Since his escape from slavery, he has been employed as an antislavery lecturer, and is now the editor of a newspaper in Rochester, N.Y. He does not belong to the class, always small, of those who bring to light great principles, or who originate new methods of carrying them out. He has, however, the vividness of sensibility and of thought which we are accustomed to associate with a Southern climate. He has a natural and ready eloquence, a delicacy of taste, a quick perception of proprieties, a quick apprehension of ideas, and a felicity of expression, which are possessed by few among the more cultivated, and which are surprising when we consider that it is but a few years since he was a slave. In any popular assembly met for the discussion of subjects with which he has had the opportunity to become familiar, he is man to command and hold attention. He is a natural orator, and his original endowments and the peculiarity of his position have given him a high place among antislavery speakers.

But while our sympathies go strongly with him, and because they go with him, we are disposed to make a criticism on a mode of address in which he sometimes indulges himself, which we believe is likely to diminish, not only his usefulness, but his real influence. We would not detract from his merits, and we can easily excuse in him a severity of judgment and a one-sidedness of view which might be inexcusable in another. We can hardly condemn one who has been a slave for seeing only the evils of slavery, and for thinking lightly of the difficulty of remedying them; but we have wished, when we have heard him speak, or read what he has written, that he might wholly avoid a fault from which a natural magnanimity does something towards saving him, but to which he is nevertheless exposed. His associates at the North have been among those who are apt to mistake violence and extravagance of expression and denunciation for eloquence;—men who, whatever their virtues otherwise, are not in the habit of using discrimination to their judgments of men or of measures which they do not approve. To him they have doubtless been true and faithful friends, and he naturally adopts their style of speech. But it is a mistaken one, if the speaker wishes to sway the judgment of his hearers and to accomplish any practical end. No matter what the vehemence of tone or expression, whenever a public speaker indulges himself in violent and unqualified statements and in sweeping denunciations, he not only makes it apparent that he is deficient in a sound and fair judgment, but what is worse, he creates in his hearers a secret distrust of his real earnestness,—a vague feeling that after all he is thinking more of his speech than of the end for which he professes to make it. When men are profoundly in earnest, they are not apt to be extravagant. The more earnest, the more rigidly true. A merchant, in discussing the politics of the day, about which he knows or cares little, freely indulges in loose, extravagant, and violent declarations. But follow him to his counting-room; let him be making inquiries or giving directions about some enterprise which he really has deeply at heart, and the extravagance is gone. Nothing will answer here but truth, and the exact truth. His earnestness makes him calm. It is seen in the moderated accuracy, as well as in the decision and strength, of his statements. Extravagance and passion and rhetorical flourishes might do when nothing which he greatly valued was at stake; but here is something too serious for trifling. Just so it is in other cases. A flippant, extravagant speaker, especially if he be gifted with the power of sarcasm, will probably be listened to and applauded, but nothing comes of it. They who applaud the most under-

stand very well that this is not the kind of person whose judgment is to be relied on as a guide in action. His words are listened to with much the same sort of interest that is given to the personated passion of the theatre. A few sober words from a calm, wise, discriminating mind are, after all, the ones which are followed. Nothing is less effective, for any practical end, than the "withering and scorching" eloquence with which American speeches seem so to abound. It conciliates no opponent, and though it may light up the momentary passions, it gives no new strength of conviction to the friends of a cause. It is the last kind of eloquence to be cultivated by those who are heartily in earnest in their desire to promote any great reform.

We by no means think that these remarks apply peculiarly to Douglass. We make them, however, because we think that, more often than he is probably aware, he suffers himself to fall into this mode of speech. He has such ability to appeal to the higher and more generous sentiments, and such appeals do so much to win over enemies and to strengthen friends, he has such personal knowledge of slavery, and is so competent to make all he says effective, through candor and a just appreciation of the difficulties that beset the subject of emancipation, and is withal so much of a man, that we regret any mistake of judgment which tends to diminish his power as an advocate of the antislavery cause. . . .

There are many passages in the narrative of Douglass which we should be pleased to quote, but it has been so long published and so widely circulated, that many of our readers have probably seen it. We would only say, in conclusion, that we feel a deep interest in his career. He is one of the living evidences that there is in the colored population of the South no natural incapacity for the enjoyment of freedom; and he occupies a position and possesses abilities which enable him, if he pursues a wise course, to be a most useful laborer in the cause of human rights.

Benjamin Quarles (essay date 1948)

SOURCE: "Trials of an Editor," in *Frederick Douglass,* The Associated Publishers, Inc., 1948, pp. 80-98.

[*Quarles is regarded as a leading Douglass scholar among American historians. In the following essay, he describes Douglass's journalistic exploits as the publisher of an antislavery weekly newspaper in the late 1840s and 1850s.*]

I think the course to be pursued by the colored Press is to say less about race and claims to race recognition, and more about the principles of justice, liberty, and patriotism.

DOUGLASS

Negro journalism was an outgrowth of the Negro's desire for fuller participation in American life. Significantly, the first of the Negro periodicals was entitled *Freedom's Journal,* published in New York in 1827. Douglass' venture into the field, therefore, was not a pioneer undertaking; his periodical was but one of the seventeen newspapers published by Negroes prior to the outbreak of the Civil War. In 1847, when Douglass decided to issue a weekly, there were then in existence four journals edited by Negroes.

Douglass, it will be remembered, returned from England with the determination to start an anti-slavery paper. The English friends to whom he mentioned the plan had raised a fund of $2,175 as a testimonial of their affection. For a few months Douglass had heeded the negative advice of Garrison and Phillips, but toward the close of September 1847, he presented, through the columns of the *Anti-Slavery Bugle,* a prospectus of the new paper. It aimed to become "a terror to evil-doers." Douglass proposed, so ran the preliminary statement, to publish a weekly that would "attack slavery in all its forms and aspects—advocate Universal Emancipation—exalt the standard of public morality—promote the moral and intellectual improvement of the Coloured people—and hasten the day of Freedom to the three millions of our enslaved countrymen."

On December 3, ten weeks after the introductory announcement, the first issue of the paper appeared. Published in the basement of the African Methodist Episcopal Church, it was named *The North Star.* A paper by that title had been published in Danville, Vermont, since 1806. While in England, Douglass must have become acquainted with the Chartist sheet, *The Northern Star.* Doubtless Douglass was familiar with the lines of a song attributed to runaway slaves:

> I kept my eye on the bright north star,
> And thought of liberty.

Douglass was well satisfied with the title. "Of all the stars in this 'brave, old, overhanging sky,' *The North Star* is our choice. To thousands now free in the British dominions it has been the *Star of Freedom.* To millions, now in our boasted land of liberty, it is the *Star of Hope.*" Prospective readers were informed that the subscription rates were $2 a year, always, optimistically ran the notice, in advance.

The editors were Douglass and Martin R. Delany. The latter brought to the joint editorship a journalistic experience acquired on the Pittsburgh *Mystery,* a Negro paper. It was agreed that Douglass was to remain in Rochester and edit, and Delany was to travel and raise subscriptions. William C. Nell, a self-taught Negro follower of Garrison, was listed as publisher. The first issue of the periodical reported the proceedings of the National Convention of Colored Americans, held at

Troy during the first week of October. The other most lengthy inclusion was a long letter to Henry Clay, ostensibly exposing his folly on the subject of colonization.

Despite their disappointment, the Garrisonians mustered up the good grace to say a word of godspeed. The *Standard* and the *Liberator* greeted the newcomer cordially. The latter, in a puff to Douglass, proclaimed that his facility in adapting himself to his new duties "is another proof of his genius and is worthy of especial praise." The paper itself, ran a somewhat oblique compliment, "surpasses that of any other ever published by a colored man." Other former friends in Massachusetts were verbally happy over the new arrival. At the yearly anti-slavery bazaar in Boston, Mrs. Maria W. Chapman hung a subscription list for the *North Star.*

The reaction of the people of Rochester was mixed. Doubtless a few felt like acting on the suggestion of the New York *Herald* that the editor should be exiled to Canada, and his equipment thrown into the lake. Many felt that an abolitionist sheet edited by a Negro was a community disgrace, to be carried with resignation, as a cross. But local hostility was feeble and of short duration. It was weakened by the attitude of the printers' association which welcomed the paper to Rochester. One month after the publication of the paper, the printers and publishers of the city, with only one dissenting member, invited Douglass and Nell to an anniversary celebration of Franklin's birthday. At the gathering the assembled newspapermen greeted the Negroes warmly. In response to a toast of cordial welcome, Douglass adverted to the uniformly kind treatment he had received from the local press and citizenry.

Doubtless the favorable reaction of the printers was an instance of economic motivation. Douglass was expected to attract money to the city, and he did. In his sixteen years in the newspaper business at Rochester, Douglass, according to his own estimate, "paid out to white men in the city little less than $100,000."

Douglass was proud of his printing establishment, which was the first ever owned by a Negro in the United States. His press, types and other printing materials cost between nine and ten hundred dollars, and were, boasted their possessor, "the best that can be obtained in this country." The office, however, was a modest single room. Cases of type occupied the entire wall space, except for Douglass' desk. Douglass' children and a white apprentice set the type and locked the forms. After the edition was printed the young workers folded, single-wrapped and mailed the copies to subscribers and exchanges.

The anti-slavery paper which issued from Rochester from 1847 to 1863 was to an unusual degree the prod-

product of one man's thinking. Aside from its fitful flirtation with the Liberty party, Douglass' publication was his personal organ. The early issues of the *North Star* were published under a joint editorship, but Delany, a man of diverse and multiple interests, spent no time at Rochester. His failure to raise funds for the paper doubtless led to a dissolution of the dual editorship after a six months' trial. After June 1848, the paper was under Douglass' exclusive control. Nell stayed two years longer, but, as a Garrisonian, his position became untenable when Douglass began to espouse the cause of the Liberty party through the columns of the weekly.

The intimate relationship between the editor and his publication is indicated by the name of the journal for the greater part of its existence. In June 1851, the editor changed the name of the weekly to *Frederick Douglass' Paper.* His alleged reason was to distinguish his periodical from others with "stars" in their titles. Doubtless Douglass also believed that sales resistance would weaken to the magic of his name. In 1853 Garrison, then estranged from Douglass, twitted him on the name of his weekly. Perhaps stung by this criticism Douglass considered other titles. He wrote to Gerrit Smith of possible designations. He thought *The Black Man* "good but common"; *The Agitator* was "good but promises too much"; he liked *The Brotherhood,* but "it implied the exclusion of the sisterhood"; *The Jerry Level* he liked best of all. But he never got around to making the change.

Douglass was not a path-maker in journalistic originality. In make-up and typography he modelled his paper after the *Liberator,* the *Bugle,* the Pennsylvania *Freeman* and the *Standard.* Like these abolitionist sheets, the *North Star* and *Frederick Douglass' Paper* consisted of four pages of six columns each. Their content was also standard abolitionist fare. This included presidential messages, which Douglass published because of their intrinsic interest rather than his agreement with their import. Front page position was also given to anti-slavery speeches in Congress; regardless of length Douglass published in full the attacks on slavery by Henry Wilson, Charles Sumner and Gerrit Smith. A voting abolitionist after 1850, Douglass filled hundreds of columns with the endless debates on the nature of the Constitution and the efficacy of political action. Douglass' weekly welcomed sermons by Henry Ward Beecher and Theodore Parker, each of whom could be relied upon to ally Divinity on the proper side of the slavery question.

Douglass carried full accounts of local and state-wide anti-slavery meetings. Reports from abolitionist societies, generally in the form of letters from the corresponding secretaries, consisted of speeches delivered, resolutions adopted and a statement on the size of the audience and its reaction to the anti-slavery message.

Many of the correspondents wrote from a consistently hopeful viewpoint in order to bolster the morale of the faithful. These reports, therefore, were wistfully optimistic except those from Douglass himself, whose pen was realistic rather than sanguine and whose powers of self-deception were small.

As was customary in the abolitionist press, Douglass' weekly lifted and reprinted items from other reformist sheets. However, it had its own regular contributors who sent in reports of happenings in their home towns. Among this all-Negro staff of unpaid local correspondents was J. McCune Smith who each week, under the pseudonym "Communipaw," wrote a breezy, informative letter from New York City. Holder of three degrees from the University of Glasgow, Smith found time for civic affairs despite a large medical practice. William J. Wilson, another local reporter, signed "Ethiope" to his clever, running accounts of the Brooklyn scene. Samuel Ringgold Ward, safe in Canada from the operation of the Fugitive Slave Law, sent letters written in a vigorous prose style. Ward, whose complexion was "considerably darker than that of Othello, in the Dusseldorf Gallery," had been a Congregational pastor and a staunch supporter of the Liberty party. Until he clashed with Douglass, William Wells Brown dispatched well-written communications from his travels on the anti-slavery circuit. Another frequent contributor was William G. Allen, whose marriage to one of his white students at Central College created a local uproar at McGrawville, New York. Prior to his teaching appointment at Central College, Allen had edited the *National Watchman,* a reformist sheet published at Troy, New York, from 1842 to 1847. Other correspondents to Douglass' weekly included Loguen from Syracuse, George T. Downing and Delany.

Without exception, these Negroes wrote well. Douglass set a high standard—even a typographical error was rarely found in his journal. He would tolerate no grammatical gaucheries. Contributors polished their sentences for his paper. Perhaps many of the correspondents paraded their learning too ostensibly. Some of the communications were interlarded with Latin phrases and classical allusions, doubtless in a conscious attempt to refute the charges of scanty book-training and mental inferiority.

Outside of political events and other occurrences which lent themselves to the propaganda of agitation, Douglass' publication carried almost no current news. Strictly speaking, Douglass' periodical was not a newspaper; but for its large size and weekly appearance, it might have been termed a magazine. *Douglass' Monthly,* issued during the twilight of Douglass' journalistic career, in make-up and size was actually a magazine.

Douglass carried verse. Most of the poems sent in were sentimental or eulogistic. Commonplace in imagery and deficient in literary finish, "anti-slavery verse is proof that by indignation alone one cannot storm Parnassus." Aside from the writings of such figures as Whittier and Lowell, abolitionist verse was rhymed prose—verse perhaps, but not poetry. Their composers, of course, did not write for so much a line. Their rewards were a satisfied conscience and a letter from the editor. A typical recipient of such remuneration was Anne P. Adams who "received a beautiful letter yesterday from Frederick thanking her very kindly for her contributions and regretting his inability to render more substantial evidence of his appreciation of her productions."

Occasionally Douglass reprinted portions of *The Bigelow Papers* or some of Whittier's moving anti-slavery verse. Other purely literary material included the serial publication of a standard novel, generally located on page four, as a sort of filler. One subscriber informed the editor that she read everything except *Bleak House* and the advertisements. The latter were pill medicine encomiums and prosaically-worded publication announcements of anti-slavery tracts and tomes. The book reviews ("literary notices") were handled by Julia Griffiths, an Englishwoman, who for many years was Douglass' closest associate and most intimate friend. Miss Griffiths had met Douglass at Newcastle-on-Tyne. In 1848, she had come to Rochester where for a time she resided in the Douglass home. She had a flair for journalism. Douglass' tribute was heartfelt: "Think what editing a paper was to me before Miss Griffiths came!"

Douglass owed much of his literary precision to Miss Griffiths' careful blue-pencilling. She taught him the rules of grammar that he had hitherto observed simply by an inherent sensitiveness to language forms. Editorials from his pen revealed a style that was uniformly virile and sonorous. Douglass had a feeling for words and a gift of vivid phrases. He was indebted to Whittier for his anti-slavery vocabulary; his other literary gifts came from a wide and careful reading in the innumerable sets of books his friends sent him.

It was largely due to Miss Griffiths' efforts that Douglass was able to issue a periodical for sixteen years. A reform paper is beset by chronic financial difficulties. Many of the ante-bellum Negro periodicals disappeared after two or three numbers; others struggled along for two or three years before suspending publication. Douglass' paper survived only by heroic measures.

Due to the generosity of his friends abroad, Douglass began his undertaking debt-free, but he had to depend on his own efforts to meet publication expenses. In 1848, these were $55 a week. Before three issues had been published Douglass was complaining about the discouraging number of cash subscriptions. Douglass had been forced to raise money by giving lectures, he wrote his associate, "in order to keep our heads above

water." Four months later the situation had become critical. The *North Star* of May 5, 1848, printed an urgent appeal for "pecuniary aid." The editor informed his public that the number of subscribers was so small that he had been compelled to mortgage his house, and as a result was "heavily in debt." A year after this initial appeal the paper was still $200 in debt. Nell took charge at the printing office while Douglass went out lecturing and soliciting subscriptions.

The chief difficulty, in Douglass' opinion, was the "very long list of non-paying and the very short list of paying subscribers." Douglass discovered an "amazing disparity between the disposition to read and the disposition to pay." As if to overrun the editor's cup, many of those who paid did not remit in sound currency. Douglass soon learned that out-of-state bills, even when drawn on solvent banks, had to be discounted at a loss of from five to twelve per cent. Douglass warned that he would accept only "New York money," and would "decline to receive" Western and Southern bills.

Douglass found convenient reasons for the paper's limited mailing list. In May 1848, the *North Star* had fewer than thirty subscribers in Massachusetts. To Douglass this was proof that the Garrisonians would not support the paper because its editor would not denounce all abolitionists who were not moral suasionists. On the other hand, the Liberty party people, remembering Douglass' antecedents, regarded the weekly as strongly Garrisonian, and hence withheld their support.

But more grievous to Douglass than the lack of either abolitionist or political support in these early years was the attitude of the colored people. Negroes did not respond as he expected. In May 1848, the *North Star* had five white subscribers to every Negro subscriber, even though many white friends felt that a Negro paper should be supported primarily by Negroes. On the other hand, Negroes, so concluded Douglass, thought that a colored man's paper ought to be supported by white people, and that Negroes "ought to have copies out of compliment." This apparently parasitical point of view held by some Negroes, combined with the indifference of others, provoked a display of Douglass' ire. "Tell them," he wrote editorially, "that a well conducted press in the hands of colored men is essential to the progress and elevation of the colored man, and they will regard you as one merely seeking a living at public expense, 'to get along without work.'"

The editor's indignation prevented him from making objective analysis. With the exception of the *Liberator*, Negroes gave little support to any of the abolitionist sheets. The majority of Negroes were too poor to subscribe to any paper. Then, as now, the Negro reading public believed in spending its money for what seems best and cheapest. Furthermore, odd as it might

Douglass's Rochester, New York, printing establishment, where he typeset his weekly abolitionist paper.

seem to Negro militants, many colored persons prided themselves on their lack of race consciousness and refused to identify themselves with a cause which they regarded as primarily racial. Perhaps less than twenty per cent of the Negroes in the United States were abolitionists. The Negroes in America were not a homogeneous group with common interests. Having no culture peculiar to a black skin, the transplanted Africans had become a congeries of groups with diverse interests that reflected a typically American individualism. Neither Douglass nor any other Negro leader of his day could assume the role of official spokesman for more than a small fraction of a race whose interests and outlooks were as varied and contradictory as the cross-currents of their adopted civilization.

Douglass' journalistic financial strain was eased somewhat by his conversion to the doctrines of political abolitionism. Early in 1851 he and Gerrit Smith decided to unite the *Liberty Party Paper* with the *North Star*. According to their agreement, Douglass was to assume the editorship of the new publication which would then have a subscription list from two sources. Smith promised to take over the debts of the *North Star* and make a monthly donation to the support of

the new party organ. The new arrangement satisfied everyone except John Thomas, retiring editor of the *Liberty Party Paper,* who was demoted from the office to the shop.

The union of the two papers went through as planned. The first issue of the new weekly, now named *Frederick Douglass' Paper,* appeared on June 26, 1851. Essentially it was a continuation of the *North Star* with the addition of sporadic news of Liberty party activities. The immediate effect of the merger was favorable. For two years the paper managed to steer clear of financial shoals, due largely to Smith's generosity. In 1852 he contributed $1200. But after 1853 financial difficulties multiplied. The extremely low fortunes of the Liberty party after 1852 led Smith to decrease his donations. By 1856 the sheet was $1500 in debt and Douglass in desperation proposed to unite it with the *Radical Abolitionist.*

More important in the life of the paper than the temporary aid given by the Liberty party was the endless exertion of Miss Griffiths. With a business perception rare in the cloistered woman of the period, she devoted her time exclusively to the interests of the paper for

DOUGLASS

nearly eight years. Without her effective and energetic management the paper would have been another short-lived abolitionist sheet. More interested in the economics of abolitionism than in its propaganda, she took over the control of the finances of the *North Star* in the summer of 1848. She immediately divorced Douglass' personal finances from those of the paper. Within three years Douglass paid the mortgage on his home and, despite the fluctuating fortunes of the weekly, steadily increased his private savings.

Occasionally an out-of-state organization sent a donation. As a result of an anti-slavery bazaar held during Christmas week of 1848, "The Colored Ladies in Philadelphia" raised $100 for the paper. Another fair for the *North Star* was held in the same city six months later. For the most part, however, projects for financial aid had their origin in Miss Griffiths' resourceful mind. Direct appeal was one method. Late in 1853, she proposed to raise $1,000, in $10 gifts, toward a contingent fund for the paper. To friends of the cause she sent soliciting letters. By January 1854, she was able to report a collection of $420. Among the forty-two donors were Gerrit Smith, Charles Sumner, Horace Greeley, William Jay, Henry Ward Beecher, Salmon P. Chase, Horace Mann, Cassius Clay and the Tappan brothers.

Another money-raising device was the holding of an anti-slavery bazaar or fair. Following Boston precedent, Miss Griffiths organized the women. She became permanent secretary of the Rochester Ladies' Anti-Slavery Society. Conducting the annual anti-slavery bazaar was the chief activity of the group. Friends and well-wishers, particularly in the British Isles, were urged to send dolls, dresses, laces, mats, cushions and crochet work. The most distinctive article for sale at the Rochester fair was *Autographs for Freedom*. Miss Griffiths appropriated this idea from the Boston Female Society which, since 1840, had annually issued *The Liberty Bell,* written cooperatively by "The Friends of Freedom."

Autographs for Freedom was a collection of poems, letters, essays, statements and excerpts from anti-slavery speeches. The authors thus thrown together under a single cover were a motley group—Negro reformers such as Charles Reason, George Vashon, J. McCune Smith and John Mercer Langston; political abolitionists such as Joshua Giddings, William H. Seward and William Jay; preaching abolitionists such as Henry Ward Beecher and Theodore Parker, and strong-minded women such as Antoinette Brown, Jane Swisshelm and Harriet Beecher Stowe. Facsimiles of the authors' signatures, appended to their respective contributions, gave the volume its title. Most of the selections were brief, frequently not more than a page in length.

The contents of *Autographs* were uneven. An occasional piece of fine writing crept in between an uninspired poem and a hackneyed anti-slavery diatribe. William Wells Brown's, "Visit of a Fugitive Slave to the Grave of Wilberforce," in theme and literary finish is among the best pieces of abolitionist *belles-lettres*. George Vashon's "Vincent Ogé," is an ambitious narrative poem of a Haitian leader, written with rich imagery. However, *Autographs* was better known for its artistic typography and clear-cut engravings than for its literary merit. The book sold for $1.25 in plain muslin; $1.50 with gilt edges, and $2.00 with "full gilt sides and edges." Two printings appeared; one in 1853 and the other in 1854.

The proceeds from the joint sales of *Autographs* and needle goods at the bazaar netted between $200 and $300. If sales were poor in Rochester, Miss Griffiths went to Toronto and there disposed of the unsold items. Douglass was deeply grateful to this indefatigable woman. Editorially, late in 1854, he appraised her services: "In referring to those who have assisted us in keeping up the paper during the year, and for the past three years, we are indebted to none more than to that ever active and zealous friend of the slave, Miss Julia Griffiths."

Miss Griffiths' fertility in expedients, however, was unequal to the dwindling support from political and abolitionist sources. After 1855, the paper was a rapidly declining enterprise. In desperation, Miss Griffiths decided to go abroad with the express purpose of appealing for aid. She returned to her native land, armed with letters recommending the cause. Lewis Tappan's letter praised Douglass "as a man deserving entire confidence. . . . His paper is well conducted, beautifully printed, and is an able auxiliary to the cause of emancipation." William Goodell praised Miss Griffiths and voiced his regret that it was necessary "to tax our English friends for help to emancipate our boasted land of liberty." Gerrit Smith also commended Miss Griffiths and hoped that she would find many sympathizers.

In the British Isles, Miss Griffiths received indorsements from many local abolition societies. One of these printed appeals recommended Douglass' paper "as a standing testimony against the calumny uttered respecting the inferiority of the coloured man." After briefly reviewing the reasons for the paper's financial straits, the pamphlet concluded that Douglass' journal "should have a vested capital, the interest of which would bring in a regular income, that would enable it to stand its ground, otherwise it must go down."

Douglass' friends had high hopes from Miss Griffiths' mission. Many Englishmen remembered Douglass; the anti-slavery cause had been kept before the British public by a stream of fugitive slaves and Negro abolitionists bent on exploiting the moral and evangelical sentiments of the English reformers. From its beginning, Douglass' paper had many British subscribers. In 1850, the *North Star* had forty-two subscribers in Glasgow, fourteen in Edinburgh, eight in Falkirk, seven in Belfast, eight in Dublin, and a total of eighteen in Derby, Liverpool and London. From time to time English friends and admirers had sent donations.

Miss Griffiths set herself to the task with typical energy. Due to her persuasion, a few anti-slavery societies made annual donations of $25. In June 1858, Douglass, apparently following her advice, brought out an additional publication, *Douglass' Monthly,* planned mainly for circulation in the British Isles. It is impossible to determine how much Miss Griffiths raised. Undoubtedly Douglass' attack on the Garrisonians weakened her in collecting monies. At any rate, the results were not encouraging; all efforts failed to reduce the outstanding debts. In 1859, Douglass was compelled to bring his weekly out in a reduced size; it looked, wrote May to Webb, "like one of our one-cent papers." The end came in July 1860. Delinquent subscribers were to blame. The weekly expenses of the skeletonized paper had been $45 to $50: "the receipts were nearly zero."

The inglorious exit of Douglass' periodicals does not diminish the importance of their three-fold contribution: to the editor's personal development, to the promotion of racial self-exertion and self-reliance, and to the edification of the white public in the United States and the British Isles. As to Douglass personally, his editorship expanded the scope of his abilities. He acquired the sense of authority that goes with the power to hire and discharge. He grew familiar with the economics of journalism and learned the mysteries of debit and credit. The making of policy-forming decisions stimulated cerebration.

Douglass' newspaper career gave him a broadened insight concerning the peculiar problems of the Negro. For the more than six years prior to starting his paper, Douglass had travelled almost exclusively in company with white abolitionists and had moved in a white milieu. As a Garrisonian his interest in the many-sided Negro problem extended little beyond the abolitionist movement. With the launching of the *North Star,* Douglass became a Negro leader in the totality of his interests and outlooks. His attention reached out to the question of Negro exclusion from "white" churches, to the practice of racial segregation in the public schools, and to an analysis of the whole principle underlying separate accommodations for white and colored. While anti-slavery rather than Negro protest, Douglass' weekly mirrored his concern with all problems growing out of the color line. His outlook after assuming editorship showed a keen awareness of the problems confronting the rank and file of Negroes whose modest abilities were insufficient to bestride even the lower hurdles of color prejudice.

A typical example of his interest in the Negro masses was his editorial advice to "learn trades or starve." Douglass pointed out that white men were taking jobs—porters, stevedores, hodcarriers and brick-makers—formerly held exclusively by Negroes. "Formerly blacks were almost the exclusive coachmen in wealthy families; this is so no longer; white men are now employed and, for aught we see, they fill their servile state with an obsequiousness as profound as that of the blacks." On the unskilled level the answer to this competition was the mastery of some mechanical art: "If the alternative were presented to us of learning a trade or of getting an education, we should learn the trade, for the reason that with the trade we could get the education while with the education we could not get a trade." Douglass praised the gospel of physical labor: "The American Colonization Society tells you to go to Liberia. Mr. Bibb tells you to go to Canada. Others tell you to go to school. We tell you to go to work."

Douglass' periodicals contributed to the development of Negroes other than their editor. Race-conscious Negroes could experience a vicarious pride at the sight of a well-edited Negro sheet. Colored poets, essayists and letter-writers could gratify the American love of seeing one's name in print. College-trained Negroes could give public expression to literary urges which otherwise might have totally escaped posterity. Colored leaders used the columns of the weekly to express their views and denounce detractors of the race. Inevitably many of these contributions from Negro writers were characterized by special pleading. To the charges of Negro inferiority these race champions answered with a counter-propaganda that was often as questionable in logic as the allegations they purported to refute. But their sincerity was unquestioned and their sense of the purposiveness of history was sure. They were confident that they were on the side of right—the side that would triumph ultimately whether the universe were governed by God's moral law, the stars in their courses or the intuitions of nature.

A final influence exerted by Douglass' weekly was its effect on white readers. The white public, particularly that section that did not uncritically accept the slaveholder's contention that the Negro was congenitally inferior, could not fail to receive a favorable impression from the *North Star, Frederick Douglass' Paper,* and *Douglass' Monthly.* Here was a paper that stood comparison with the best-edited weeklies of the antebellum period. Here was a paper free from orthographical mistakes and rhapsodies in bad grammar. Here—and this was the most telling point of all—here was the work of a Negro who had spent twenty years in the prison-house of slavery. To ignore the influence of Douglass' weekly on reformist sentiment in the decade preceding the Civil War is to tell an incomplete story of the abolitionist crusade.

Houston A. Baker, Jr. (essay date 1972)

SOURCE: "Revolution and Reform: Walker, Douglass, and the Road to Freedom," in *Long Black Song: Essays in Black American Literature and Culture,* 1972. Reprint by The University Press of Virginia, 1990, pp. 58-83.

[*In the following excerpt, Baker analyzes the literary techniques of Douglass's* Narrative *by contrasting it, in terms of style and tone, with David Walker's* Appeal.]

During the first half of the nineteenth century, two monuments of the black literary tradition had their birth. One was David Walker's *Appeal,* written in 1829, and the other was Frederick Douglass's *Narrative of the Life of Frederick Douglass, an American Slave, Written by Himself,* which appeared in 1845. Both captured the spirit of their epoch, and both define certain modes, techniques, and conventions that since their time have played significant roles in the literary tradition of which they are a part.

The first half of the nineteenth century was one of the most dynamic stages in American history. It was an age of territorial expansion carrying the United States to the Pacific; new frontiers were opening, and the quest for frontier was an important element in the American world view. The nation participated fully in world trade, and its northern regions entered into the period of growth that was eventually to carry America to the position of the world's leading producer. It was an age in which power was gradually diffusing itself and moving into the hands of the people, and the election of Andrew Jackson in 1828 and again in 1832 is perhaps the best manifestation of this diffusion of political power.

To a certain extent early nineteenth-century America was like early nineteenth-century England, where increasing industrialization brought about shifts in population and power. Like Englishmen, Americans championed the idea of progress, and in an age of expansion and shifting power, they looked toward a bright and glorious future. England and America, moreover, were both characterized by a high degree of evangelical zeal; belief in salvation by faith and grace and in the authority of the gospel found many ardent followers.

Religious zeal, a moral impulse to reform, and utopian visions of the future—these three elements stand out in the history of England and America in the 1830s. In America they found their readiest expression in the abolitionist movement. In England, the same impulses led to the abolition of West Indian slavery in 1833. William Lloyd Garrison, Wendell Phillips, Arthur Tappan, Charles G. Finney, and James Birney are the names most often associated with the American abolitionist movement. Garrison's *Liberator,* founded in 1831, was one of the many weeklies that aroused America's concern for the plight of the slave. Abolitionist newspapers provided a forum for free blacks in America, and until 1870 they were instrumental in focusing attention on essential reforms such as emancipation, free soil, women's rights, pacifism, and temperance.

There were many reform movements in nineteenth-century America, but the abolitionist movement captured the imagination of a broad segment of the populace and seemed to express the spirit of the age. Numerous antislavery societies were established; by 1836 there were at least five hundred abolition societies in the free states, and by 1840 these societies had a membership of at least 150,000 persons. The names on the membership rolls were not simply those of whites. As Benjamin Quarles has pointed out [in *The Negro in the Making of America,* 1968], "black Americans were conspicuously in their ranks from the outset." Lerone Bennett [in *Before the Mayflower,* 1966] also underscores the important role played by blacks in the movement: "In the forties, fugitive slaves moved into the front lines of the antislavery battle. No abolitionist meeting was complete without the presence of a Negro speaker or a Negro exhibit (a fugitive slave)." Henry Highland Garnet, William Wells Brown, Robert Purvis, and Charles Redmond are just a few of the black Americans who made significant contributions.

The zeal of the abolitionists led some to call them fanatics; others called them worse. The debate over their sanity, moreover, has yet to be resolved; Richard O. Curry's *The Abolitionists,* for example, is subtitled, "Reformers or Fanatics?" Allowing for prejudices and vested interests, it might be said that some abolitionists were more "engaged" than others: a distinction might be made between the "immediatists" who said "now" and meant this very moment and the temperate immediatists who endorsed reform rather than violent revolution. In both camps, however, religion was clearly the sanction for action, and "a merciful providence" had a great deal to do with how one proceeded. The polarity between revolution and reform in the abolitionist movement is well illustrated by the works of David Walker and Frederick Douglass. The Protestant ethical base of the abolitionist movement finds expression in the works of both writers. . . .

[Frederick Douglass's *Narrative*] begins, in the manner of so many slave narratives, at the lowest ebb of humanity; the narrator does not know his age or his father's identity. As nearly as he can ascertain, his father was a white man—his master. He thus belongs to the class of the "tragic mulatto," a figure used by abolitionist writers to symbolize the displacement of the black American caught between two worlds as well as the master's miscegenatory desires. He tells us that he was never close to his mother, since he saw her only four or five times before she died. This is not to say that Douglass starts by presenting himself as an oppressively tragic figure; on the contrary, one is immediately impressed by the straightforward, unornamented presentation with which the *Narrative* opens. Douglass simply says: "I was born in Tuckahoe, near Hillsborough, and about twelve miles from Easton, in Talbot County, Maryland." This approach, much like Walker's, is as detailed and realistic an account as one could imagine. From the beginning, however, we receive more than simple narration; we are plunged at once into an agrarian environment with the narrator's dry quip about the slave and the horse who are in the same condition since neither knows his age. The agrarian setting is further established by the enumeration of the seasons of the slave's year: "planting-time," "harvest-time," "cherry-time," "spring-time," and "fall-time."

Douglass's concern with a realistic setting and straightforward narration (as opposed to Walker's flights of rhetoric) results in part from Douglass's almost exclusive attention to the temporal. Walker, who often wrote in prophetic tones of God's revelations, was never averse to moving in divine regions. For Douglass, however, religion was a much more practical affair. He views Christianity as "pure, peaceable, and impartial," as did the evangelical upper middle-class of nineteenth-century England and America. Although in the "Appendix" to the *Narrative* he turns a scorn equal to Walker's on the "slaveholding religion" of America, he very seldom addresses his audience in the tone of the fire-and-brimstone preachers of America's late-eighteenth-century religious revivals. In the *Narrative* he always seems to view religion as a pursuit designed to make men better and more dignified while on earth; the example of Jesus Christ offers him a paradigm for emulation, while for Walker it was a celestial threat to be used against the sinful and the skeptical. Douglass takes "the Christianity of Christ" (in its most incarnate form) as a sanction for his actions, and proceeds on a much more mundane level than his contemporary.

The techniques that we encounter on the first page of Douglass's work, therefore—the stark, visualized narration and the dry, ironic wit, the verisimilitude, and the agrarian setting—continue throughout the *Narrative;* they make the work at once simple and enthralling. Douglass is far removed from the impassioned writer of the *Appeal,* but interestingly enough his work brings home its point just as effectively as Walker's. Perhaps the difference between the two resides in the fact that Douglass was at the beginning of a long and fruitful career when he wrote his *Narrative;* Walker,

on the other hand, was an embittered middle-aged man, screaming, as a last, desperate measure, at the "world's wrong." Douglass, moreover, was born with a different gift of words, an ability to transport audiences, as Bennett has pointed out, "to slave row," by his highly artistic and sophisticated use of language. While Walker tried to bring about changes by explosive words, cascading phrases, and pyrotechnic catalogues, Douglass was content to present a bleak picture in a sparse style; and the economy of his style tends to reinforce the poverty and oppressiveness of the situations which he describes. Here, for example, is his description of a whipping:

> Before he commenced whipping Aunt Hester, he took her into the kitchen, and stripped her from neck to waist, leaving her neck, shoulders, and back, entirely naked. He then told her to cross her hands, calling her at the same time a d—d b—h. After crossing her hands, he tied them with a strong rope, and led her to a stool under a large hook in the joist, put in for the purpose. He made her get upon the stool, and tied her hands to the hook.

The passage continues in this manner, and the details are so specific and the tone so matter-of-fact that we are almost lulled into insensitivity. We awake with a start when we recall what is actually going on, and the impression that Douglass's presentation of human cruelty makes is a lasting one.

The impact of Douglass's straightforward narration is again demonstrated in his account of the murder of a slave for disobedience:

> The first call was given. Demby made no response, but stood his ground. The second and third calls were given with the same result. Mr. Gore then, without consultation or deliberation with any one, not even giving Demby an additional call, raised his musket to his face, taking deadly aim at his standing victim, and in an instant poor Demby was no more. His mangled body sank out of sight, and blood and brains marked the water where he had stood.

Daniel Defoe or Victor Hugo might well have been proud of this description. The only hints of the author's bias are the words *poor* and *victim,* but with the help of these two words in the proper places, Douglass is able to present a scene of almost unimaginable brutality. A final example further reveals Douglass's craftsmanship; he describes his reduction to a state of abject servility at the hands of a slave breaker: "I was broken in body, soul, and spirit. My natural elasticity was crushed, my intellect languished, the disposition to read departed, the cheerful spark that lingered about my eye died; the dark night of slavery closed in upon me; and behold a man transformed into a brute!" A more telling account of the fall into the slough of despond could hardly be given; the passage is not high-flown, it is not allegorical, it is not symbolic; it is a simple account of the effects of slavery.

Douglass was a masterful chronicler of horrors, but to present him solely in this light is to misrepresent his work. The *Narrative* is charged with a subtle, dry, and ironic humor, which provides comic relief and adds to the reader's sense of a detached and objective narrator. Commenting on the increase of mulatto children in the South, Douglass remarks:

> If the lineal descendents of Ham are alone to be scripturally enslaved, it is certain that slavery at the south must soon become unscriptural; for thousands are ushered into the world, annually, who, like myself, owe their existence to white fathers, and those fathers most frequently their own masters.

Of the demise of a particularly cruel overseer, Douglass says: "His death was regarded by the slaves as the result of a merciful providence." Noting the frequent controversies among slaves as to which had the wealthiest master, he comments:

> These quarrels would almost always end in a fight between the parties, and those that whipped were supposed to have gained the point at issue. They seemed to think that the greatness of their masters was transferable to themselves. It was considered as being bad enough to be a slave; but to be a poor man's slave was deemed a disgrace indeed!

Douglass's humor is valuable not simply because it gives us relief from the gruelling details of slavery. It brings us close to the essential humanity of the situation, and more important, it leads us to a balanced realistic point of view, for if it is a humor of detached irony, it is also, like Wordsworth's, one of loving kindness. Douglass does not turn a satirical, objective glance on the follies of mankind; his smile, like that of Richard Wright's protagonist in *Native Son,* is "a faint, wry, bitter smile." While fully aware of the ridiculousness of certain human situations, he also realizes his own involvement in them and their larger implications.

While humor adds a degree of realism to the *Narrative,* it is Douglass's verisimilitude that brings us fully in touch with the experiences of the man behind the work. We are placed directly on the scene by the author's close attention to specific detail. We learn, for example, the exact number of Colonel Lloyd's slaves, horses, and cultivated acres. We become acquainted with the narrator's place of residence in Baltimore in terms of the area, the street, the neighbors, and the treatment accorded the neighbors' slaves. We learn

exactly how wheat was fanned in Douglass's day, how many men it took to do the job, and the assignment of each.

Douglass's skill at characterization and his ability to evoke a particular setting also lend an air of reality to the *Narrative*. Nearly every activity and character we encounter is connected with an agrarian scene. We watch harvesting and the transporting of goods by water; we witness the actions of overseers, Southern preachers, and slave breakers; we see the slave cabins, barns, and stables. There is no hothouse atmosphere in Douglass's work; never is life reduced to the taking of toast and tea. The world of the *Narrative* is a world of action, one in which only the strong and determined survive. Moreover, Douglass is able to populate his world with highly individualized and believable characters—Captain Auld, Mr. Covey, and Mr. Freeland, for example. The narrator's powers of characterization may be seen in his description of Captain Auld:

> His airs, words, and actions, were the airs, words, and actions of born slaveholders, and, being assumed, were awkward enough. He was not even a good imitator. He possessed all the disposition to deceive, but wanted the power. Having no resources within himself, he was compelled to be the copyist of many, and being such, he was forever the victim of inconsistency; and of consequence he was an object of contempt, and was held as such even by his slaves.

Douglass demonstrates in this passage one of his favorite techniques—the use of antithesis.

One can scarcely treat the agragrian settings and characters in Douglass's *Narrative* without some discussion of the animal metaphors that appear in most of the chapters of the *Narrative*. . . . Douglass uses [such a] figure to describe his joy when given the chance to go to Baltimore: "It was almost a sufficient motive, not only to make me take off what would be called by pig-drovers the mange, but the skin itself." Speaking of the anguish that resulted from a grasp of his situation, Douglass comments: "In moments of agony, I envied my fellow-slaves for their stupidity. I have often wished myself a beast. I preferred the condition of the meanest reptile." These images, of course, serve to reinforce Douglass's descriptions of the "soul-killing" effects of slavery; in a word, they make the effects of the three-fifths clause immediate. Slaves, like horses and other wild animals, were "broken." Like Walker, Douglass is aware of American slavery's chattel principle, which equated slaves with livestock, and he is not reluctant to employ animal metaphors to capture the general inhumanity of the system. Moreover, as were the slave narrators of black animal tales, he was surely aware that he and his "loved fellow-slaves" were usually on better terms with the animals than with the owners of the farms and plantations on which they worked.

Douglass's work is a chronicle of the "soul-killing" effect slavery had on both master and the slave. Time and again in the *Narrative* men's hopes for a better life are crushed: humans are whipped and slaughtered like animals; men and women are changed into maniacal and sadistic creatures by power; the strength of mind and body is destroyed by an avaricious and degrading system. Captain Auld, Douglass and his fellow slaves, Mrs. Hugh Auld, Mr. Covey, Anthony Auld—practically every character we encounter in the *Narrative* is rendered less human by the effects of slavery. Douglass's work, however, does not simply describe the degradation occasioned by slavery; it also illustrates how a sense of community, a spirit of revolt and resistance, and a mastery of disguise and deportment—black survival values which we encountered in the folk tradition—assist in the development and ultimate escape of the person who is willing to employ them. We are confronted in the *Narrative* with a record of the early development of one individual, a *Bildungsroman,* which records the growth to manhood of a small slave boy whom we first see in a tow-linen shirt enjoying a relatively work-free life. Then we see a boy at twelve years of age playing the trickster in order to acquire the rudiments of education:

> After that, when I met with any boy who I knew could write, I would tell him I could write as well as he. The next word would be, "I don't believe you. Let me see you try it." I would then make the letters which I had been so fortunate as to learn, and ask him to beat that. In this way I got a good many lessons in writing, which it is quite possible I should never have gotten in any other way.

At sixteen the boy adopts the code of the badman hero and wrestles a fierce slave breaker into submission, vowing after the struggle that "the white man who expected to succeed in whipping, must also succeed in killing me." The nineteen-year-old *man,* with his fellow slaves, makes an abortive attempt for freedom, and the twenty-year-old man finally gains his liberty using the same type of disguise and deportment that we see in "The Watcher Blinded." Douglass does not tell us so in the *Narrative,* but he made his escape to the North by wearing a sailor's uniform and travelling as a free man.

We must admit that at times the author grows maudlin (in describing the plight of his grandmother, for example), and at times he is clearly too rhetorical (the soliloquy by the bay). For the most part, however, he is a candid, witty and thorough narrator, able to play the diverse stops of the human condition with consummate skill. It seems appropriate, therefore, to classify the

Narrative as a consciously literary work, and one of the first order. The black folk background manifests itself in the values that make survival possible in a brutal system, as well as in individual incidents, such as that in which Sandy Jenkins gives Douglass a root for his protection:

> He told me, with great solemnity, I must go back to Covey; but that before I went, I must go with him into another part of the woods, where there was a certain *root,* which, if I would take some of it with me, carrying it *always on my right side,* would render it impossible for Mr. Covey, or any other white man, to whip me.

Douglass, like thousands of his fellow black men, attributes some power to the root even though he knew (at the time he was writing his *Narrative*) that his own strength and spirit of resistance had perhaps more to do with his escaping Covey's intended lashing than anything else. He again employs and helps to define folk tradition when he deals with the songs of his fellow slaves. He notes that the songs had a subliminal or hidden component: "They would sing [the songs] as a chorus, to words which to many would seem unmeaning jargon, but which, nevertheless, were full of meaning to themselves." He goes on to show that they were actually sorrow songs—"Slaves sing most when they are most unhappy"—and adds: "To those songs I trace my first glimmering conception of the dehumanizing character of slavery." What we have, then, is both explication and appreciation of the folk heritage. Finally, Douglass turns a deflating irony on white preachers. Of Reverend Rigby Hopkins, a devout religionist, he says:

> Mr. Hopkins was even worse than Mr. Weeden. His chief boast was his ability to manage slaves. The peculiar feature of his government was that of whipping slaves in advance of deserving it. He always managed to have one or more of his slaves to whip every Monday morning. He did this to alarm their fears, and strike terror into those who escaped.

The hypocrisy and pretension here are similar in some respects to the human failings seen in black preacher tales, though the purpose of the narration in this instance is much more serious.

Although the connection of Douglass's work with the black American folk tradition is clear, his obvious concern for the craft of writing places the *Narrative* in the realm of sophisticated literary autobiography. More specifically, Douglass's work is a spiritual autobiography akin to the writings of such noted white American authors as Cotton Mather, Benjamin Franklin, and Henry Adams. The narrator wishes to set before the reader not only his fully realized spiritual self, but also the hallowed values that made possible such a self.

The *Narrative,* however, can be distinguished from the works of white American spiritual autobiographers because its essential goal is physical freedom. The narrator is not seeking to become one among the divine elect, nor is he attempting to forge a private, moralizing self as a foil to an intensely practical and political age that stressed the virtues of the public man. He seeks to move, by any means necessary, from a cruel physical bondage to freedom. Arna Bontemps [in *Great Slave Narratives,* 1969] is correct, therefore, in designating Douglass's *Narrative* a representative work in a separate American genre—the slave narrative. The unique angle of vision that characterizes Douglass's work is—for obvious reasons—unmatched in the white American autobiographical tradition, and the author's handling of this perspective is among the most accomplished efforts in the tradition of black autobiography. And his achievements in this genre place him in the front ranks of black authors, since the autobiographical mode is one of the most important in the black American literary tradition. The tasks of portraying the unique character of one's group and of selectively recovering the self, which many writers have considered distinct, are one for the black autobiographer. Douglass's narrator not only secures his own liberty, but also becomes something of a mythic figure, taking his place in the same framework that includes the drinking gourd, the underground railroad, and the North Star.

Although an orator himself, Frederick Douglass, unlike David Walker, was not interested in rendering the intonation and diction of oratory into written form. While the latter's work parallels that of the declamatory poets of black America, Douglass is allied with the formalists. William Robinson characterizes the formalist poets (Phillis Wheatley, George M'Clellan, Ann Plato, and Henrietta Cordelia Ray) as those who "reveal formal influences of classical propriety and restraint and conscious control. . . ." Douglass effectively applies sophisticated literary techniques—irony, wit, caricature, understatement, humor; he never lacks the right word or the proper anecdote to emphasize his point; and he relies upon masterful and convincing literary presentation rather than fiery rhetoric. In fact, it is the passages in which he lapses into oratory that detract from the overall effect of his work. The differences in the forms and styles employed by Douglass and Walker bespeak a larger difference, for David Walker was, in essence, a nineteenth-century revolutionary, and Douglass was a reformer. The *Appeal* reflects the values of those who are labelled "fanatics," while the *Narrative of the Life of Frederick Douglass* manifests the values of the Garrisonian abolitionist reformers who were in favor of moral suasion and opposed to any interaction (especially that of a political character) with slaveholders.

Walker's work, addressed to the "coloured people of the world," is an impassioned, ofttimes bitter appeal for revolutionary action. Douglass's is one of the most finished of many slave narratives, which generally were written for abolitionist purposes and principally for white readership. The incentive for this work was provided by reports that many whites in the audiences Douglass addressed under the auspices of the *Massachusetts Anti-Slavery Society* could not believe such polished speeches came from a man who had been a slave. Philip Foner writes [in *Frederick Douglass,* 1969]:

> Douglass was aware that if such reports continued, they would be fatal to his effectiveness as an Abolitionist agent. So he resolved to throw caution to the winds and write the story of his life. During the winter months of 1844-45 he was busily engaged in setting down an account of his slave experiences.

Douglass intended to convince his white readers that he had suffered the dire effects of slavery, presumably hoping that in their moral outrage they would first acknowledge his remarkable achievement and then go forth to protest the abuses of slavery in America. The prime motivating force for his work and his Garrisonian stance help to explain his restrained posture and sophisticated style.

In some ways these same factors distinguish Douglass's work from the poorer slave narratives. In his attempts to persuade and convince, the author was forced to go beyond the format that was later to become standard for the slave chronicle. We are confronted with a host of fully rounded characters in the *Narrative;* we have a number of finely drawn scenes presented one after the other; and while we sense the irony, we also sense the genuine feeling of sincerity in the work. Only a few American narratives have such characteristics, and only one by an African is so distinguished. (The narratives of Solomon Northup and Henry Bibb are on a par with Douglass's; William Wells Brown's, which copies incidents from Douglass's, has little of the force and power of the latter's; and Gustavus Vassa's *The Life of Olaudah Equiano or Gustavus Vassa the African* is the only close parallel written by an African slave.) Douglass provided one of the most popular and enthralling works of literature written in the nineteenth century and, ironically, he intentionally produced it for an audience almost exclusively white.

Audience expectations, if taken alone, are enough to account for the aesthetic differences in the *Narrative* and the *Appeal,* but beyond these differences there are significant ideological ones. Douglass worked within the existing order to obtain his most salient victories: he was editor and publisher of the *North Star, Frederick Douglass's Paper,* and *The New National Era;* he worked throughout much of his life as an abolitionist or reform lecturer; he served as marshal of the United States for the District of Columbia; and he was minister-resident and consulgeneral to the Republic of Haiti. Walker, on the other hand, wrote for two black abolitionist newspapers—*Freedom's Journal* and *Rights of All*—and was a seller of secondhand clothes whose entire life, as far as we know, was devoted to promulgating a violent overthrow of the existing order. He placed copies of his *Appeal* in the pockets of the clothes which he sold to seamen who were likely to make their way to the South, and he devoted his last energies to revising and editing the third edition of the *Appeal,* one of the most revolutionary texts produced in the nineteenth century. Not that Douglass, who helped to desegregate the public schools of Rochester, New York and talked of striking the "first blow," did not take decisive actions. The dichotomy in approach is somewhat like that between the doctrines of the late Martin Luther King and those of Eldridge Cleaver and Bobby Seale. At times Douglass spoke more forcefully than Dr. King ever did; he often mentioned "blows," "bullets," and "the cartridge box," and he was in great sympathy with John Brown's plan to establish a garrison of runaway slaves in the Allegheny Mountains—although shortly before the raid on Harper's Ferry, he refused to join Brown's party.

Given their significant ideological differences, it is not surprising that Douglass's **Narrative** is akin in style and sensibility to Ralph Ellison's *Invisible Man* and James Baldwin's *Go Tell It on the Mountain,* while Walker's *Appeal* is closer to Eldridge Cleaver's *Soul on Ice.* In one of his fine autobiographical moments, Baldwin describes John Grimes's descent into the white world of New York: "These glories were unimaginable—but the city was real. He stood for a moment on the melting snow, distracted, and then began to run down the hill, feeling himself fly as the descent became more rapid, and thinking: 'I can climb back up. If it's wrong, I can always climb back up.'" And in *Invisible Man,* Ellison's autobiographical narrator describes a scene in the chapel of a black Southern college:

> Here upon this stage the black rite of Horatio Alger was performed to God's own acting script, with millionaires come down to portray themselves; not merely acting out the myth of their goodness, and wealth and success and power and benevolence and authority in cardboard masks, but themselves, these virtues concretely. Not the wafer and the wine, but the flesh and the blood, vibrant and alive, and vibrant even when stooped, ancient and withered. (And who, in the face of this, would not believe? Could even doubt?)

The autobiographical impulse is present in the novels of both Baldwin and Ellison, and it is the informing principle of Douglass's work. The uncertainty of Baldwin's John Grimes as he races toward one type of freedom is much like that of Douglass and his friends as they plan their escape in the **Narrative;** and the combination of irony with the amazing force of description in Ellison's passage is reminiscent of the wit and energy that exposes pretenders throughout the **Narrative.** The finish of style, descriptive power, and ease of narration seen in Baldwin and Ellison as they move their protagonists from bondage toward freedom find ready parallel in Douglass's work.

A passage from *Soul On Ice* demonstrates how close the work as a whole is to Walker's *Appeal,* and how far removed both are from the best of Douglass, Baldwin, and Ellison. Speaking of Muhammad Ali, Cleaver writes:

> A racist Black Muslim heavyweight champion is a bitter pill for racist white America to swallow. Swallow it—or throw the whole bit up, and hope that in the convulsions of your guts, America, you can vomit out the poisons of hate which have led you to a dead end in this valley of the shadow of death.

There is a distinct affinity between this address to the country at large, ringing with denunciation and black pride, and any number of passages in Walker's *Appeal.* In essence, the difference between Douglass, Baldwin, and Ellison on one hand and Walker and Cleaver on the other is the difference between the self-conscious, controlled literary artist and the impassioned pamphleteer. This is by no means to say that the latter two never transcend the limits of the pamphleteer, but rather to suggest that denunciation, righteous indignation, and revolutionary appeals are vastly more prevalent in their works than in those of Douglass, Baldwin, and Ellison.

Nevertheless, when all has been said, we must recognize that both Frederick Douglass and David Walker produced works which expressed the spirit of their age but which transcend the limitations and hazards of time—works, in short, that find their counterparts in the writings of our most recent black American authors. The road for both nineteenth-century writers stretched between two alternatives that are consummately set forth in the **Narrative:**

> On the one hand, there stood slavery, a stern reality, glaring frightfully upon us—its robes already crimsoned with the blood of millions, and even now feasting greedily upon our own flesh. On the other hand, away back in the dim distance, under the flickering light of the north star, behind some craggy hill or snow-covered mountain stood a doubtful freedom—half frozen—beckoning us to come and share her hospitality.

Both writers labored along freedom's road, under the dim light of the north star, and though they chose different modes of travel, both achieved their goals, contributing to humanity on the way.

> **An excerpt from Frederick Douglass's speech at a women's rights convention in Worcester, Massachusetts:**
>
> We advocate woman's rights, not because she is an angel, but because she is a woman, having the same wants, and being exposed to the same evils as man.
>
> Whatever is necessary to protect him, is necessary to protect her. Holding these views, and being profoundly desirous that they should universally prevail, we rejoice at every indication of progress in their dissemination.
>
> *Frederick Douglass, speech printed in* Frederick Douglass' Paper, *October 30, 1851, collected in* Frederick Douglass on Women's Rights, *edited by Philip S. Foner, Greenwood Press, 1976.*

James Matlack (essay date 1979)

SOURCE: "The Autobiographies of Frederick Douglass," in *Phylon: The Atlanta University Review of Race and Culture,* Vol. XL, No. 1, first quarter, March, 1979, pp. 15-28.

[*In the following essay, Matlack assesses the symbolic value of Douglass's three autobiographies and notes an overall decline in the literary quality of his later works.*]

The best-known and most influential slave narrative written in America was probably the *Narrative of the Life of Frederick Douglass*. Within four months of its publication in 1845 five thousand copies were sold. Aided by favorable reviews and new editions, both in America and Britain, some thirty thousand had been sold by 1860. The *Narrative* thrust Douglass into the forefront of the anti-slavery movement. Coupled with his extensive speaking tours, it made Douglass the first black American to "command an audience that extended beyond local boundaries or racial ties."

Douglass' *Narrative* is consistently cited as one of the best-written autobiographies among scores of such accounts produced by or in the name of ex-slaves during the 1840s and 1850s. Much of its effectiveness was due to the superior technique with which Douglass told his tale. Lurid reports on the evils of slavery were plentiful. Douglass' *Narrative* was exceptional in the degree of artistic skill and shaping through which it conveyed a similar message. The following essay will examine the symbolic value of Douglass' autobiographical act, especially the relationship between his literary creation and his actual life. Comparisons among the successive versions of his autobiography will clarify

this relationship and demonstrate the literary excellence of the 1845 *Narrative*. The increasing length, loosened form, and declining literary merit of Douglass' autobiographical accounts issued in 1855, 1881, and 1892 became a sad index of the wearying struggles and frustrations of his later life.

The content of Douglass' *Narrative* was essentially the same material which he had presented countless times as a roving Abolitionist spokesman. His success as a stump speaker virtually forced its publication. The pressure to publish mounted on two sides—Douglass' relations with his widespread audiences and his relations with his white fellow-workers. In the first instance, he had to establish his credibility; in the second, his independence.

As with so many aspects of life in America for blacks, their participation in the crusade against slavery was largely controlled by white leaders. Even among the Abolitionists there were strong racial prejudices. Douglass said in the mid-1850s: "Opposing slavery and hating its victims has come to be a very common form of abolitionism." The crucial role of blacks in the anti-slavery struggle was generally acknowledged but it was narrowly defined. Blacks were to tell of their first-hand experience in bondage and, by the very act of successful platform presentation, refute the charge that Negroes suffered inherent mental disabilities. In addition, they were a strong drawing card. John A. Collins, general agent of the Massachusetts Anti-Slavery Society, told William Lloyd Garrison, "The public have itching ears to hear a colored man speak, and particularly a *slave*. Multitudes will flock to hear one of this class." Frederick Douglass met this need superbly. He became the greatest of the ex-slave orators.

The skill of Douglass' platform performance on tour began to raise doubts. He spoke too well. The sophisticated style and learned tone which he rapidly developed seemed out of character. Collins advised him, "People won't believe you ever were a slave, Frederick, if you keep on this way. . . . Better have a little of the plantation speech than not." Since he did not talk, look, or act like a slave (in the eyes of Northern audiences), Douglass was denounced as an imposter. There could be but one effective rejoinder to this Yankee skepticism.

> In a little less than four years, therefore, after becoming a public lecturer, I was induced to write out the leading facts connected with my experience in slavery, giving the names of persons, places, and dates, thus putting it in the power of any who doubted, to ascertain the truth or falsehood of my story.

Douglass proved that he was not a fake. But the validation of his tales of former bondage opened a direct

Douglass's home, "Cedar Hill," in Anacostia, near Washington,
D.C.

threat of recapture. Once having fully identified himself, he lost the anonymity which was essential to a fugitive slave. In his introductory letter to Douglass' *Narrative,* Wendell Phillips exclaimed, "The whole armory of Northern Law has no shield for you. I am free to say that, in your place, I should throw the MS. into the fire."

The irony of Douglass' predicament was compounded by events following publication of the manuscript. Since he was not safe in the United States, Douglass sailed for England. For two years he campaigned against slavery, winning friends for himself and his cause throughout the British Isles. As a result, when Douglass returned home early in 1847, he came back to America a free man. His supporters in Britain had raised funds and paid $710.96 to purchase his emancipation from his legal owner in Maryland, thereby scandalizing many Abolitionists who condemned payment for human flesh on any pretext. The popularity of Douglass' *Narrative* contributed much to the success of this scheme. Thus the document which verified his origins in slavery and

raised the threat of renewed bondage became the means for achieving his permanent freedom.

The second major factor behind the publication of the *Narrative* also involved Douglass' freedom but in a particular and troubling way. It was an attempt to throw off patronizing manipulation by white Abolitionists. The act of putting his life in print must be seen as an assertion of independence from the prescribed routines of his white sponsors. Douglass was grateful to the reformers who helped him to become a prime mover in the anti-slavery cause. He grew restive, however, at the limited role they envisioned for him. Douglass' lack of formal education was an asset consciously exploited by Abolitionists who toured with him. His rough plantation background was a prerequisite to telling the truth about slavery. Hence the uneasiness when he gained in eloquence and range of knowledge as a stump speaker. "Give us the facts," Collins told him. "We will take care of the philosophy." It was boring and demeaning to be kept at the same rudimentary level through countless repetitions. "'Tell your story,

Frederick,' would whisper my reverend friend, Mr. Garrison, as I stepped upon the platform. I could not always follow the injunction, for I was now reading and thinking. New views of the subject were being presented to my mind. It did not entirely satisfy me to narrate wrongs—I felt like denouncing them." Douglass' white sponsors did not want him to analyze present conditions or try to shape future actions. They were to be the interpreters and prophets—in short, the leaders—and he was merely the showcase specimen of a fugitive slave.

In penning his *Narrative,* Douglass broke this cycle. He jettisoned the obsessive preoccupation with his past life and freed himself for more ambitious work. With that material on the record, he could liberate himself from repeating it, and only it, in future speeches. This was a symbolic gesture of near-defiance, an assertion of independence from a certain kind of psychological and role-playing bondage perpetuated by those whites who were most insistently proclaiming the freedom of Negro Americans. It was also a mark of Douglass' strong self-assurance. This trait later led him to start a black newspaper against the advice of all his white allies and to an acrimonious break with Garrison. Throughout his career, Douglass stubbornly insisted upon the right to "speak just the word that seemed to *me* the word to be spoken *by* me."

However resentful of white paternalism, Douglass remained acutely aware of the audience for whom he was writing. The form and style of the *Narrative* were carefully tailored to persuade and, above all, not to offend a white readership. Only the white majority had the numbers and power to make a difference on the issue of slavery. Douglass therefore had to avoid affronts to the values and prejudices of pious white Northerners. The most conspicuous aspect of form in the *Narrative* designed to allay hostile reaction is the "frame" within which the autobiographical account is placed, a frame provided by two letters of introduction and Douglass' own Appendix.

In putting their work before the American public, many black writers have had to appear in company with a white spokesman to vouch for them. Whether it be William Dean Howells praising Paul Laurence Dunbar or Maxwell Geismar giving the initial testimony for Eldridge Cleaver, a well-known white has given suitable assurances to the audience before permitting an Afro-American to address them. In Douglass' case, there are character references from Garrison and Wendell Phillips, both friends and prominent Abolitionist leaders. What they say—highly complimentary throughout—is less significant than the fact that it was judged necessary that both speak before Douglass' narrative could begin. The aura of paternalism is heightened by Garrison's obvious pride in the success of his protegé.

The Appendix of the *Narrative* is a further effort by Douglass to put his life's story in a safe perspective. The Appendix counters the view that Douglass was too critical of religion. Such an impression would gravely damage the effectiveness of his work. A Garrisonian Abolitionist, he was committed to moral suasion as the way to end slavery. His greatest appeal was to the moral pretentions and guilt feelings of churchly whites in the North. Douglass had to cover himself against the charge that he was ungodly or irreverent. Hence his explanation, "What I have said respecting and against religion, I mean strictly to apply to the slave-holding religion of this land, and with no possible reference to Christianity proper." If the reader accepts this separation, then Douglass can be excused such assertations in the main text as: "For of all the slaveholders with whom I have ever met, religious slaveholders are the worst." He was none too cautious, however. He attacked the hypocrisy of "the overwhelming mass of professed Christians in America. . . . They would be shocked at the proposition of fellowshipping a sheep-stealer; and at the same time they hug to their communion a man-stealer, and brand me an infidel, if I find fault with them for it."

In addition to the Appendix, Douglass appeals to the religious sensibilities of his audience throughout the *Narrative*. He shows his knowledge of the Bible, uses scriptural idiom, and gives suitable professions of his own belief and his incredulity at the perversions of ostensible Christians. Douglass' portrayal of himself as a faithful suffering Christian is part of a careful strategy to expose the sham piety of slave masters, best exemplified in the Sunday School episode. Along with other willing blacks, Douglass was being helped to read the New Testament by a young white. After three Sundays, a mob led by prominent white Methodists "came upon us with sticks and other missiles, drove us off, and forbade us to meet again. Thus ended our little Sabbath school in the pious town of St. Michael's." This event is shrewdly chosen to elicit maximum sympathy and outrage from readers who see eager souls denied an opportunity to study God's Word by self-proclaimed Christians.

In the main part of the *Narrative* Douglass conveys an impression of plain, honest testimony about conditions in slavery. He avoids the stylistic and emotional excesses common in the slave narrative genre. Much of the text is given over to careful explanation of the routines of slave life, an informational service to Northern readers which is more devastating for not becoming a tirade. Through calm control and calculated understatement, Douglass firmly establishes his credibility and heightens the impact of the vivid examples of brutality which he presents at strategic points in the narrative.

In order to emphasize the veracity of his account, Douglass consistently shows slaveholders to be devious and dishonest. Amid so much deceit and self-deception, the narrator stands out as one who can tell the truth. Not only do slavers lie to assuage opinion in the North. They also manipulate their own slaves. Douglass tells how the masters keep down "the spirit of insurrection" by encouraging drunken binges on holidays, "a dose of vicious dissipation, artfully labelled with the name of liberty." Ultimately the trickery and hypocrisy of the slavers renders them incapable of honest self-appraisal. They become moral monsters. Covey is the extreme example. "Every thing he possessed in the shape of learning or religion, he made to conform to his disposition to deceive. He seemed to think himself equal to deceiving the Almighty."

The dishonesty of the masters has an ironic counterpart in the dissembling which slaves were forced to employ in their own defense. From the beginning, the idiom and culture of Afro-Americans have been characterized by a spirit of double-entendre. Outward contentment and surface meanings, perennially misread by whites, have often been contradicted by deeper feelings and private symbolism. Slave songs could be used to express pain, despair, and protest. They were safe because whites mistook their often sprightly manner as evidence of happiness among the blacks. They used "words which to many would seem unmeaning jargon, but which, nevertheless, were full of meaning to themselves." Gradually young Douglass came to understand the symbolism of the songs. "Every tone was a testimony against slavery, and a prayer to God for deliverance from chains."

The basis of Douglass' effectiveness and credibility as narrator is his plain style. His writing is firm, lucid, and brisk. Sentences are usually simple in construction. The reader encounters a direct, confident narrative voice, unencumbered by elaborate rhetorical devices. Saunders Redding has praised the "stringent simplicity" of Douglass' prose. "In utter contrast to the tortured style of most of the slave biographies, Douglass' style is calm and modest." Alain Locke paid tribute to Douglass' "pithy prose so different from the polished and often florid periods of his orations." Douglass weakened his presentation when he tried to be fancy or elegant. The plain facts of slavery are more moving than the artificial devices (such as personification) which he occasionally uses.

Several passages lapse totally from Douglass' usual plain style. The most important are his description of his dying grandmother and his apostrophe to the white-sailed boats on Chesapeake Bay. In both cases Douglass resorts to inflated rhetoric and pumped-up sentimentality. The scenes are intended to draw tears, just as in the sob-fiction of the period, but the rhetorical strategy of both passages fails on the modern reader.

That Douglass was seeking favor with an audience highly susceptible to sentimentality can be inferred from Garrison's praise of the *Narrative* for producing "a tearful eye, a heaving breast, an afflicted spirit." Douglass fares poorly when he approximates the panting, pushy prose of his mentor's high style. Among the many "affecting incidents," Garrison picks out the soliloquy on sail-boats as supreme in its "pathos and sublimity." While on hire to the brutish Covey, Douglass stood on the bank of the Chesapeake Bay one day watching the sails pass by toward the sea.

> Those beautiful vessels, robed in purest white, so delightful to the eye of freemen, were to me so many shrouded ghosts, to terrify and torment me with thoughts of my wretched condition. . . . I would pour out my soul's complaint, in my rude way, with an apostrophe to the moving multitude of ships:—

> "You are loosed from your moorings, and are free; I am fast in my chains, and am a slave! You move merrily before the gentle gale, and I sadly before the bloody whip! You are freedom's swift-winged angels, that fly round the world; I am confined in bands of iron! O that I were on one of your gallant decks, and under your protecting wing! Alas! betwixt me and you, the turbid waters roll. . . ."

This is of course strictly a literary performance, one which inadvertently reminds the reader that Douglass composed his account years after the events described.

In the shaping of his account, Douglass plotted the peaks of intense feeling with care. Though the staple of the *Narrative* is calm, detailed exposition, the overall structure of the work resembles popular melodrama. Vivid, artfully staged episodes seek to draw tears, shock, and anger from the reader (*e.g.* a discussion of hypocrisy among Southern Christians is punctuated by a glimpse of a master quoting Scripture while he lashes the naked shoulders of a crippled black girl). Douglass knew he was competing with hosts of slave narratives, real and invented, which catered to a public taste for the sensational. To his credit, he largely refrained from cheap tricks to elicit emotional responses but one must observe that Douglass appealed to the same elements in popular taste.

Autobiography, especially in America, usually describes the making of a man. Douglass' *Narrative* tells such a story in an unusually profound and literal way. The central movement of the book is a process of liberation. There are two essential components in this process—literacy, to gain awareness of his selfhood; and resistance, to assert his manhood. Paradoxically, Douglass had to liberate himself psychologically before he could attempt to become free. He began, however, with nothing.

Most autobiographies open with a birth date and a description of the author's parentage. Douglass can supply neither. His story opens in the limbo of bondage, the anonymity of the slave. Virtually a motherless child, as in the old spiritual, he saw his mother only a few times in the middle of the night. She died when he was seven. Douglass' father was white, but he never knew which among the slavers it might be. Progeny of the oppressers, lacking any roots or identity, how could young Douglass know or say who he was? His very name was given him by a white master. Nor should one underestimate the power of slavery to dehumanize its subjects.

> I have found that, to make a contented slave, it is necessary to make a thoughtless one. It is necessary to darken his moral and mental vision, and, as far as possible, to annihilate the power of reason. . . . He must be made to feel that slavery is right; and he can be brought to that only when he ceases to be a man.

Out of this nothingness, this non-identity, Douglass must forge his own character and sense of himself.

Early in his life Douglass realized that ignorance was a precondition of his bondage. As a bright eight-year-old in Baltimore, he began to learn his A B C's from Mrs. Auld. Her husband put a stop to such dangerous nonsense. "A nigger should know nothing but to obey his master—to do as he is told to do. Learning would spoil the best nigger in the world." He added that if Douglass learned to read, "it would forever unfit him to be a slave." This information awakened young Frederick. "I now understood what had been to me a most perplexing difficulty—to wit, the white man's power to enslave the black man." Henceforth he knew where he must apply himself if he were to be free.

Over the next seven years, slowly and painfully, Douglass learned to read and write. He had to accomplish the task by subterfuge since he was spied upon to prevent just such self-education. He stole bread and traded it for bits of knowledge from white street urchins. He picked up letters of the alphabet from marks on timbers in the shipyard. He practiced his handwriting between the lines of young Thomas Auld's discarded copy books. Douglass was especially keen to learn about any subject which was condemned by the whites. Thus, he gradually came to understand the meaning of "abolitionist" far beyond its dictionary definition. The struggle for literacy, for command over the power of words, was the first stage of his escape from oppression. Without the power of language and the self-affirmation which it opened to him, Douglass might not have been able to survive and to sustain his will to escape.

If literacy and self-awareness represent the crucial first step in Douglass' liberation, then active resistance was the next stage in securing his freedom. The imaginative creation of a self in opposition to slavery was a gesture which prefigured his escape. The turning-point of the *Narrative* comes in his fight with the "nigger-breaker" Covey, a cunning and ruthless master who constantly harassed and beat the blacks on hire to him. "Mr. Covey succeeded in breaking me. I was broken in body, soul, and spirit." This is the nadir of the *Narrative*. Douglass was ready to kill himself. After collapsing from overwork and another beating, he fled to his old master for redress, only to be forced back to Covey's farm. The following morning, Covey grabbed Douglass unawares and tried to tie him up so that he could be whipped.

> I resolved to fight; and, suiting my action to the resolution, I seized Covey hard by the throat; and, as I did so, I rose. . . . My resistance was so entirely unexpected, that Covey seemed taken aback. He trembled like a leaf. This gave me assurance, and I held him uneasy, causing the blood to run where I touched him with the ends of my fingers.

Though a slave could expect severe punishment for violence against his master, Douglass fought Covey to a draw. Despite being mauled, Covey claimed victory and took no reprisal. He had to protect his reputation as a tough overseer of fractious blacks. As indicated by the imagery of ascendency and renewal which surrounds the fight, it was a moment of deliverance for Douglass.

> This battle with Mr. Covey was the turning-point in my career as a slave. It rekindled the few expiring embers of freedom, and revived within me a sense of my own manhood. . . . I now resolved that, however long I might remain a slave in form, the day had passed forever when I could be a slave in fact.

Through resistance, the assertion of an internalized liberation, Douglass ended the psychological power of slavery over his life. Thereafter it was only a matter of time and opportunity until he would strike for true freedom.

The *Narrative* leaves the actual break from bondage a cryptic and mysterious transit from Baltimore to New York in 1838. By giving no details of what otherwise would be the climax of the story, more emphasis is thrown back on the consequences of Douglass' fight with Covey and the mental attitudes required for such a flight. There were powerful reasons for not being more explicit about his means of escape. Douglass did not want to compromise those who had helped him, nor prevent other fugitive slaves from following the same route. He criticized successful escapees for boasting of their runaway techniques, thereby reducing the chances of later fugitives. A further though less compelling factor in withholding the manner of Douglass' flight to the North was its anticlimactic character. It hardly matched the powerful thematic and structural build-up through the rest of the *Narrative*. Douglass himself said that he would have revealed the secret sooner, "had there been anything very heroic or thrilling in the incidents connected with my escape." In 1873 he finally explained how he had ridden North on the railroad out of Baltimore posing as a sailor with "free papers" borrowed from a black seaman who somewhat resembled him.

My Bondage and My Freedom is more than a mere extension of the *Narrative of the Life of Frederick Douglass*. Major changes in style and structure highlight by comparison the merits of the earlier, shorter version of Douglass' autobiography. The account published in 1855 is longer and more informative. It may provide a better historical and social record but it also represents a distinctly poorer literary performance.

The basic format of *My Bondage and My Freedom* is a division of Douglass' story into contrasting halves— his experience prior to escape and his career as an anti-slavery activist in the North. The continuity and cohesiveness, the mounting of symbolism and suspense in the *Narrative* is negated by the broken-backed form adopted in the 1855 version. Douglass is still the spokesman of a great and unresolved issue. The high moral crusade to which he calls the reader still lends a certain force and drive to his narration. But it is diffused and attenuated by an enormously loosened sense of structure and stylistic control. Nothing is taut and crisp. The increased length of *My Bondage and My Freedom* is due not only to new sections covering the decade of Douglass' life since the appearance of his first autobiography. The old material from the *Narrative* is stretched out and padded with anecdotes and verbiage which clog the narrative flow.

The moment one begins to read Douglass' 1855 account, the stylistic contrast is evident. The text is more leisurely and wordy. Its pace lags. The first chapter is slow and rambling. There is no punch to it, no strong closing comparable to the whipping scene which concludes the first chapter in the 1845 version. That traumatic episode appears in the fifth chapter, after fifty pages instead of five. The author's style in *My Bondage and My Freedom* has become flabby. Gone is the terseness so appropriate to describing life under the hardships of bondage. Sentence structure is often complex and sloppy. Puffy rhetoric weakens the impact of the slave scenes. Chummy asides to "my dear reader" further dilute the earlier tone of cold scorn and righteous anger toward slavery and its masters.

One hesitates to differ with so eminent a commentator as Saunders Redding, who has judged Douglass' performance in 1855 superior to that of 1845 and who

finds a "surer" style in the later work, but comparison of the texts makes clear that Douglass wrote with less crispness and discipline in his second autobiography. The following parallel passages illustrate the process of stylistic inflation at work.

Narrative of the Life (1845)

I had not gone far before my little strength failed me. I could go no farther. I fell down, and lay for a considerable time. The blood was yet oozing from the wound on my head. For a time I thought I should bleed to death; and think now that I should have done so, but that the blood so matted my hair as to stop the wound.

My Bondage and My Freedom (1855)

But I had not gone far, before my little strength again failed me, and I laid down. The blood was still oozing from the wound in my head; and, for a time, I suffered more than I can describe. There I was, in the deep woods, sick and emaciated, pursued by a wretch whose character for revolting cruelty beggars all opprobrious speech—bleeding and almost bloodless. I was not without the fear of bleeding to death. The thought of dying in the woods, all alone, and of being torn to pieces by the buzzards, had not yet been rendered tolerable by my many troubles and hardships, and I was glad when the shade of the trees, and the cool evening breeze, combined with my matted hair to stop the flow of blood.

Any style which protests its own inadequacy so insistently, as Douglass does in the second extract, can hardly impress the reader with its sureness and control. The 1855 version takes nearly twice as many words to cover the same ground. The elaborate diction and syntax of the latter passage, coupled with its manipulative appeals to sentiment, are characteristic of Douglass' swelling style in the 1850s. They helped to make him a great orator but they become a liability in simple prose narration.

There are marks of haste in the composition of *My Bondage and My Freedom* which flaw the form of the book. While the section on slave experience is padded and verbose (*e.g.* the fight with Covey loses its sharp decisiveness), the coverage of Douglass' career in the North is choppy and fragmented. One surmises that it was assembled rapidly out of available materials. Portions of letters, speeches, and extracts from the press are incorporated into the text. Episodes are strung together without much continuity. Following the rather brief chapters on his life between 1845 and 1855, eight of Douglass' best public statements from that decade are reprinted. The content is valuable but the form of the autobiography has virtually disintegrated.

Twenty-six years passed before Douglass issued an-other version of his life's story. He rewrote the last sections of *My Bondage and My Freedom* and added much new material to cover the intervening period. Comparative looseness in both style and structure is more apparent than ever in the *Life and Times of Frederick Douglass,* first published in 1881. More than a hundred pages were added to an expanded edition issued in 1892. Two aspects of Douglass' last book are of interest to the discussion of literary merit among his various autobiographies. One is the retrospective, an-ticlimactic cast to the work. The other is the symbolic relationship between its form and the pattern of Doug-lass' whole life.

Douglass' *Life and Times* suffers from being an ex-ample of the fat volume of memoirs that public men so often produce at the end of a busy career. The bulk and weight of the narrative are made heavier by the retrospective and funereal mood which pervades the text. The author is looking back, not forward. There is no last triumph or peak in his life. Instead there is only the inevitable point at which it finally runs out. The great moments of Douglass' story came relatively ear-ly. He recognized this mid-way through *Life and Times*.

> My great and exceeding joy over these stupendous achievements, especially over the abolition of slavery (which had been the deepest desire and the great labor of my life), was slightly tinged with a feeling of sadness.

> I felt that I had reached the end of the noblest and best part of my life.

Most of the rest is anti-climax, however interesting and valuable to the history of black men in America. It may be unfair to Douglass' notable and energetic labors but his account of the post-war decades often becomes a slow-paced farewell address. Most of his old friends (and enemies) are dead. There are profuse tributes and eulogies for his comrades-in-arms from the bright, distant, early years when the struggle against slavery was a dangerous adventure. The tone and thrust of his *Narrative* partake of that early excitement, an-ger, and expectation. Nothing remains to look forward to in *Life and Times*. The battles are over and an old warrior seeks rest.

Reconciliation replaces partisan fervor and moral out-rage as the dominant note in the narrative. The reader encounters an extraordinary scene when the aged Fre-derick Douglass, then United States Marshall for the District of Columbia, goes back after fifty-six years to revisit the plantation where he grew up a slave. He returns at the invitation of his old master, Thomas Auld, with whom he holds a friendly conversation as the ex-slaver lies on his death-bed. No enmity remains. The brutal reality of slavery, so insistent in the opening pages of the book, has faded away, as has the tough, truth-telling prose which makes Douglass' presenta-tion in his *Narrative* so impressive and compelling.

The symbolic parallels between the telling of Douglass' life and the living of it are stronger in *Life and Times* than in previous accounts. The cluttered and fragmen-tary narrative mirrors the crammed schedule and fre-quent travel of his public career. Chunks of speeches, articles, and letters fill the text, specimens of his hand-iwork from the years under review. After such long and difficult efforts to improve the situation of Afro-Americans, Douglass cannot close with a report of wide success. Though emancipated, blacks at the end of the century remained unequal and were losing ground. The country no longer responded to crusades on behalf of Negroes. Whites ignored Douglass, who seemed an anachronism. *Life and Times* did not sell well. Its publishers told Douglass in 1889 that, though they had "pushed and repushed" the book, sales had been poor since "interest in the days of slavery was not as great as we expected." The failure of *Life and Times,* both in its appeal to the public and in its uncertain, faltering form, duplicated the frustration and inconclusiveness of Douglass' struggles in 1880s and 1890s when America broke its promises to the ex-slaves and tried to forget about its racial problems.

In personal terms, Douglass rose in status and fortune through the last years of his life. He received patron-age jobs in return for political services rendered. Inev-itably, in recounting this personal success, an annoy-ing note of self-gratulation spreads through his narra-tion. Much of Douglass' advancement was due to his fierce, unquestioning loyalty to the Republican Party. He insisted that the party was the deck, all else was the sea. Election after election, Douglass took the stump on behalf of the Republicans. He clung to Grant and the Stalwarts despite scandals and independent reform movements. (He wanted a third term for Grant!) Doug-lass backed the grab for Santo Domingo even when his good friend Summer condemned it. In return, Doug-lass was appointed to the President's Commission which visited the island. It is sad to see the brave Abolitionist and bold reformer reduced to a party wheel-horse, and for such a party as the Republicans in the Gilded Age. This devotion to partisan politics gives the latter part of Douglass' *Life and Times* much the same flavor as the memoirs of party leaders like James Blaine or John Sherman. The moral appeal and personal integ-rity so evident during the anti-slavery fight are ob-scured and the author's good character seems dimin-ished.

More damaging than Douglass' political activity is the degree to which he absorbed and expounded the phi-losophy of the triumphant Republican Party. He ech-oed the businessman's laissez-faire ethos all too readi-ly. It was not by accident that Douglass' most popular lecture was called "**Self-Made Men.**" As he noted in *Life and Times,* "I have sometimes been credited with having been the architect of my own fortune, and have pretty generally received the title of 'self-made man.'" In a manner remarkably similar to Booker T. Washington, he argued for self-help and vocational training, seeming to belittle the role of governmental protection for the rights of Afro-Americans. The concluding paragraphs of his 1881 text are a homily on success, stressing the familiar Puritan virtues. "I have urged upon them self-reliance, self-respect, industry, perseverence, and economy." Little wonder that Alain Locke described *Life and Times* as "a sort of Negro edition of Ben Franklin." Douglass' subservience to commercial and Republican ideals was denounced toward the end of his life by young blacks who harked back to the candor and scorn of his early years. As a Harvard graduate student in 1891, W.E.B. DuBois deplored the cowardice of current Negro leadership, including Douglass. He charged that blacks had only a "time-server for our Moses and a temporizer who is afraid to call a lie a lie."

Is Frederick Douglass' life best seen as a darker version of the traditional American success story? Or was DuBois right to criticize the misleading emphasis on personal aggrandizement and material satisfaction which arises from the rags-to-riches myth? The contest over the emblematic value of Douglass' career is central to any interpretation of him. With encouragement from his *Life and Times,* many commentators have chosen to puff Douglass' achievements in rising from humble origins to a high station in public life. Saunders Redding calls the third autobiography "the most American of American life stories. . . . The story develops the dramatic theme from bondage to the council tables of a great nation." Rayford Logan goes further; Douglass became

> . . . advisor to President Lincoln and the diplomatic representative of the United States to Haiti and the Dominican Republic. Hence, this narrative of his life has inspired Negroes and other disadvantaged Americans to believe that, despite the imperfections of American democracy, a self-made man may aspire to greatness.

Here is precisely the danger of such an interpretation. Douglass' life cannot be permitted to serve as just another encomium to the virtue and upward mobility of American society. Harder truths and grimmer lessons are to be seen in it.

There is also a nobler theme, a more universal meaning to the best of Douglass' autobiographical writing. Alain Locke said of his career and character that they "take on more and more the structure and significance of the epical." The success motif lies deep in Douglass' example but it is best embodied in the earliest impulse of his life. Just as his compact escape narrative is far better written than any of its sprawling successors, so the truest epic for Frederick Douglass is not to see him as a black Horatio Alger hero but as a splendid enactment of man's perennial struggle to be free.

Donald B. Gibson (essay date 1985)

SOURCE: "Reconciling Public and Private in Frederick Douglass' *Narrative,*" in *American Literature,* Vol. 57, No. 4, December, 1985, pp. 549-69.

[*In the following essay, Gibson investigates the intersection of Douglass's public and private personas in the* Narrative, *commenting on the qualities of balance and restraint that inform both.*]

By common consent Douglass' *Narrative of the Life of Frederick Douglass, An American Slave* (1845) is recognized as the best among the many slave narratives that appeared with increasing frequency during the years preceding the Civil War. There are many reasons why Douglass' narrative so clearly stands above the others, chief among them being that Douglass possesses talents, sensitivity, and intellectual capacity superior to those belonging to most people. His experience with written and spoken language by the time he wrote the autobiography has something to do with the quality of Douglass' work. Certainly he modified and polished his style as he improved the addresses he delivered to abolitionist gatherings beginning in August 1841. His account is a better one because it is rehearsed, and he has without doubt mulled over its facts and phases, scenes and phrases, during the years prior to its recording. His narrative, however, is not superior simply for aesthetic reasons, because it is more polished than the others; it is better in large measure because Douglass, more than any other author of a slave narrative, is able and committed at once to articulate and mediate between the fact of the existence of slavery in a Christian, democratic society and state and the facts of his life as felt and understood by the person Frederick Douglass.

The result of such commitment in the autobiography is a dual focus: one, public and social, setting forth to correct the moral and political ills arising from the fact of slavery; the other, personal and private, expressing Douglass' own thoughts, feelings, reactions, and emotions. The social (also public, political, and objective) focus is that which presents the first twenty-one years of the life of Frederick Douglass in such manner as to allow it to serve as a weapon in the arsenal of abolitionism. The public perspective is the one traditionally recognized by nineteenth-century commentators such as William Lloyd Garrison and Wendell Phillips, both of whom wrote prefatory material to the *Narrative,* and some earlier twentieth-century scholars such as Vernon Loggins and Benjamin Quarles. Loggins believes that Douglass' "sole purpose in writing his autobiography was to produce antislavery propaganda." Quarles, addressing the question whether Douglass' facts can be trusted, stresses the issue of subjectivity and the expression of personal vision: "Douglass' treatment of slavery in the *Narrative* may be almost as much the revelation of a personality as it is the description of an institution." This speculation is not, however, pursued. Douglass himself has the political perspective in mind when he says in the final paragraph of the autobiography, "From that time [the time of his first major oration] until now, I have been engaged in pleading the cause of my brethren." That the public dimension should call such attention to itself is not surprising since there is not a single sentence, not a single word in the *Narrative* that does not relate to it.

The private dimension of the *Narrative* comprises Douglass' specific and personal responses to and perceptions of his experience. Obviously Douglass is not Everyman—not even Everyblackman. On the contrary Douglass is a unique, unusually intelligent, and talented man, one whose relation to experience could not possibly be identical to anyone else's. Very many slaves were separated from their mothers at an early age, but that happened specifically to Frederick Douglass and its meaning for us is realized (made real) by his articulation of that fact. Throughout his narrative Douglass uses his personal experience of slavery to lend authority to whatever observations or judgments are to be made about the abstraction "slavery." Even when it is not clear whether he actually witnessed an event or heard it told (as in the case of the slaying of his wife's cousin, or the old man who is killed "fishing for oysters") it is fairly obvious that he perceives it as actual, and hence it carries the weight of fact. Nearly all the events of the *Narrative* are presented as having been directly experienced. The private dimension omits, however, some aspects of Douglass' experience, and what is omitted is probably determined by factors such as relevance to the public focus and decorum. We know little, for example, from his narrative about his courtship of Anna Murray beyond the fact of its occurring; we know few of the particulars of his friendships; and we know nothing about his sexuality. We do learn about his psychological and emotional maturation, a most private and personal matter, but only because, as we shall later see, that matter relates closely to the public focus.

In one sense the two perspectives are perpetually at war; in another they work together, one supporting and lending authority and significance to the other. Douglass the rational, anti-slavery partisan and Douglass the man whose historical, social, and psychological pasts cannot be entirely contained within the abstraction "slavery" often vie for control of the narration, because a strategy of Douglass is to present himself as one whose character, intelligence, and manner hardly belong to one who could by any stretch of the imagination be defined as "slave." Douglass' strong, unique, commanding presence, his cool and controlled narration threaten to usurp the narrative. The personality of the narrator seeks a larger role than the public purpose of the book can allow (as when he steps outside the "circle" of slavery to explain the meaning of slave songs). Meanwhile, the public perspective aims to dominate, to suppress all about the narrator except his representative qualities, to play down any suggestion that Douglass is a special case, "a slave among slaves" (as Booker T. Washington significantly titles the first chapter of *Up from Slavery*).

More often than not, however, the two perspectives work together and are, indeed, incapable of separation. The first chapter of the *Narrative* reveals the relation between the perspectives, a relation to be sustained throughout the narration until the end where they are forever melded into one. The *Narrative* begins, "I was born in Tuckahoe, near Hillsborough, and about twelve miles from Easton, in Talbot County, Maryland. I have no accurate knowledge of my age, never having seen any authentic record containing it. By far the larger part of the slaves know as little of their age as horses know theirs, and it is the wish of most masters within my knowledge to keep their slaves thus ignorant. I do not ever remember to have met a slave who could tell of his birthday." The first two sentences are statements of fact specifically about the person Frederick Douglass and thus express the private focus. The third sentence generalizes from the first two, its abstract meaning based upon Douglass' particular experience. As generalization and abstraction it expresses the public focus; its full meaning, however, depends upon its grounding in the facts of Douglass' life preceding it. The fourth sentence is a personal statement emanating from the private perspective, repeating and buttressing the truth of the generalization again by placing it within the confines of his own experience. Here the two perspectives are not at war but rather mutually supportive, for the complete meaning even of the factuality of the first two sentences depends upon their contextual meaning. The passage continues, "A want of information concerning my own [birthday] was a source of unhappiness to me even during childhood. The white children could tell their ages. I could not tell why I ought to be deprived of the same privilege." The passage, expressive of the private focus in that it directly concerns the private, inner feelings of the narrator, implies the public focus, for underlying the statement is the narrator's knowledge that readers will share his belief that one should be able to tell one's age. No proper, just or moral system, the logic runs, deprives humans of the knowledge of the dates of their birth; I am human; therefore. . . . The statement expresses the private perspective; its logic expresses the public. The two are again melded, though logically separable.

The same balancing strategy obtains again when Douglass writes about his separation from his mother, the personal statement of biographical fact balanced by its generalized meaning in the context of slavery.

> My mother and I were separated when I was but an infant—before I knew her as my mother. It is a common custom, in the part of the land from which I ran away, to part children from their mothers at a very early age. Frequently before the child has reached its twelfth month, its mother is taken from it and hired out on some farm a considerable distance off, and the child is placed under the care of an old woman, too old for field labor . . . I never saw my mother, to know her as such, more than four or five times in my life; and each of these times was very short in duration, and at night.

Note that the passage begins with the personal perspective, generalizes about practices during slavery, then returns to a personal vantage point. This practice prevails throughout most of the *Narrative,* its function being two-fold: to sustain balance between the public and private focus; and to ground abstractions about the evils of slavery in the specific, concrete experience of one person, thus rendering the argument more vivid and more convincing than abstract discourse alone could likely make it. The method is analogous to some grand metaphor: the tenor, slavery; the vehicle, the facts of Douglass' life. Thoreau's method in *Walden* is similar in that he constantly moves back and forth between the concrete and the abstract, between the particularities of his own experiences and the wider implications generated therefrom.

Such strategies are not uncommon in slave narratives, the difference being that Douglass is so intensely engaged in the abolitionist cause that he could not for a moment allow his story to give way to adventure for adventure's sake, adventure intended to entertain readers; he could not allow a plot to govern the rendition of his narrative except in the most general way. Douglass moves from slavery to freedom, but his emphasis is far more on the psychological journey than on the physical one. *Narrative of the Life of Frederick Douglass, an American Slave* is an accurate title in that it points to the broad span of his life, most of which was spent in slavery, rather than to the escape itself, which, it becomes clear, is not the central issue. Douglass was himself aware of this emphasis as he makes clear in the final version of the autobiography, *Life and Times.* "The abolition of slavery in my native State and throughout the country, and the lapse of time, render the caution hitherto observed [of not revealing his means of escape] no longer necessary. But even since the abolition of slavery, I have sometimes thought it well enough to baffle curiosity by saying that while

slavery existed there were good reasons for not telling the manner of my escape, and since slavery had ceased to exist there was no reason for telling it." His lack of interest in entertaining or satisfying the curious has a clear and definite effect on the form of the autobiography.

The *Narrative* has only one climax, though it might be expected to have two—one internal, the other external; one in which the narrator undergoes some psychological transformation, the other in which he projects into the world through action the results of his transformation. One of these climaxes expresses the private focus of the narrative (taking place, as it does, within the psyche of the narrator); the other public, an objective, historical event. The true climax of the autobiography is the private, psychological one, explicitly revealing the formation on Douglass' part of a new consciousness, a different awareness and sense of self, and a firm resolve for the future. The other potential climax of the action, the one which should show the glorious passage of the narrator from slavery to freedom, does not occur. In other words the private perspective of the *Narrative* holds sway insofar as the plot is concerned. How can this be if the work is a "weapon in the arsenal of abolitionism"?

Douglass' explanation of why he conceals his mode of escape—that telling how he escaped would increase the danger to others using that means—is quite reasonable. He reveals it in the final version of his autobiography, as noted above, but there in the context of nearly the whole span of Douglass' life (or nearly so) it cannot begin to have the impact and meaning that it would have had in the context of the *Narrative* alone. Its dramatic significance is drastically diminished. That the lapse of time has decreased the sense of its importance is reflected in Douglass' reluctance (even when the information can have no negative effect on anyone) to fill in the details of his actual escape. In any event, if one seeks the central episode of the work, attention is immediately drawn to the psychological center whose character is such that we might well wonder whether Douglass' expressed motives for deemphasizing the external, public center were indeed the only ones. Here it is significant to note that the most frequently anthologized part of the *Narrative* is the section depicting Douglass' struggle with Covey. There are several compelling reasons for believing that Douglass wished—indeed fully intended—to give this episode the intense emphasis that it has. Douglass might have revealed in his account of his fight with Covey the most important thing he had to say about slavery and freedom.

In chapter 10 Douglass declares himself free after the contest with Covey, a contest from which Douglass does not emerge so much victorious as undefeated (a distinction to be developed later). At this point, after Covey has made it clear that the conflict is terminated,

Douglass declares himself free: "It was a glorious resurrection from the tomb of slavery to the heaven of freedom." Since Douglass does not escape until 1838, four years later, his declaration of freedom is meaningful only in its psychological sense, but the narrative emphasis implies, however, that his psychological sense of being free is more meaningful than his actual escape North. The point is that once he is psychologically free the escape itself is a matter of course. The issue is more fully articulated in *Life and Times* where Douglass makes an astounding statement about his condition: "I was no longer a servile coward, trembling under the frown of a brother worm of the dust, but my long-cowed spirit was roused to an attitude of independence. I had reached the point at which I was *not afraid to die.* This spirit made me a freeman in *fact,* though I still remained a slave in *form.* When a slave cannot be flogged he is more than half free" (Douglass' emphases). If Douglass considers himself "more than half free," then is it any wonder that his actual escape would be other than anticlimactic? The same sentiment is expressed in the *Narrative* in less expanded form, "My long-crushed spirit rose, cowardice departed, bold defiance took its place; and I now resolved that however long I might remain a slave in form, the day had passed forever when I could be a slave in fact."

Astoundingly he announces himself a free man in "fact" despite being held in slavery for the next four years. His enslavement is a matter of form. A person is a slave, then, not when his body is held captive but when his psyche is not his own, when his self does not belong to him, when he does not exert resistance against those who would define him. Being a slave "in fact" has to do with one's attitude toward one's condition. Such is suggested in the contemporary narrative of *The Fugitive Blacksmith or Events in the History of James W. C. Pennington* (1849). Pennington, the minister who married Douglass and Anna Murray in 1838, describes his response after he observes his owner give Pennington's father an extremely brutal lashing: "Although it was some time after this event before I took the decisive step, yet in my mind and spirit, I never was a *Slave* after it." In any case, even if the distinction is not peculiar to Douglass, it places a heavy emphasis on the role of psychological disposition in determining one's status as slave or free. We might wonder whether the definition rests upon a public or private criterion. Is one free because one feels free, or is one free because law, custom and circumstance say so? Douglass' *Narrative* raises this question.

His year's sojourn at Covey's finds Douglass in a less than happy situation. For the first time he is a field hand. His daily work is grueling, and he is brutalized beyond measure, working six days a week, from at least sunrise to sundown, and sometimes into the night. He is severely beaten so frequently that his back is never free from acute pain. His psychological condition matches the physical.

> If at any one time of my life more than another I was made to drink the bitterest dregs of slavery, that time was during the first six months of my stay with Mr. Covey. We were worked in all weathers. It was never too hot or too cold; it could never rain, blow, hail, or snow, too hard for us to work in the field. Work, work, work was scarcely more the order of the day than of the night. The longest days were too short for him and the shortest nights too long for him. I was somewhat unmanageable when I first went there, but a few months of this discipline tamed me. Mr. Covey succeeded in breaking me. I was broken in body, soul, and spirit. My natural elasticity was crushed, my intellect languished, the disposition to read departed, the cheerful spark that lingered about my eye died; the dark night of slavery closed in upon me; and behold a man transformed into a brute!

He is clearly at the nadir of his life. Ill, unable to rise from the ground, brutally kicked in the side by Covey, struck on the head with a barrel stave and bleeding from the blow, Douglass has no external recourse, no awareness of an internal one; he must finally face the dreaded Covey alone, lacking even the consolation of religion and scarcely confident that the magical root given him by his fellow slave Sandy will aid him. At this juncture he must either accept Covey's punishment, thereby finally confirming his status as "animal" or "brute," or he must seek to change his status. To seek change, to confront Covey and avert domination is to risk public flogging, maiming, or even death. Covey's wide reputation as a "nigger breaker," coupled with the fact that Douglass is under his control, means that he is not opposing an ordinary owner or overseer; it is as though he faces the archfiend himself, not as a representative slave but as Frederick Douglass, private person.

The idea that Douglass conceives of Covey as the devil and his circumstance as religious and mythological in its dimensions is not as farfetched as it might seem if we note the terms in which he describes Covey.

> He seldom approached the spot where we were at work openly, if he could do it secretly. He always aimed at taking us by surprise. Such was his cunning, that we used to call him, among ourselves, "the snake."

> He would sometimes mount his horse, as if bound to St. Michael's, a distance of seven miles, and in half an hour afterwards you would see him coiled up in the corner of the wood-fence, watching every motion of the slaves.

Mr. Covey's *forte* consisted in his power to deceive. His life was devoted to planning and perpetrating the grossest deceptions. Everything he possessed in the shape of learning or religion, he made conform to his disposition to deceive. He seemed to think himself equal to deceiving the Almighty.

In order that we comprehend the full meaning of his conflict with Covey, Douglass must make it known that his antagonist is not simply *any* overseer who is cruel and unsympathetic to the slaves in his charge. Covey's dimensions are larger; and the larger Covey's dimensions, the better we understand the significance in Douglass' own mind of his feat in coming to terms with him. Undoubtedly Douglass did see Covey as larger than life in that the overseer embodies at once the authority of the whole slave system, of all whites, especially males, and in his character, attitudes, and actions the very worst features of slavery. The outcome of the struggle produced "a glorious resurrection, from the tomb of slavery, to the heaven of freedom." The effect of the struggle with Covey the archfiend is to bring Douglass back from the dead and to propel him into heaven—again suggesting something of the religious and mythological scope of his conception of his circumstances.

Psychologically, Douglass' conflict with Covey is a private and personal trial whose outcome will determine whether Douglass has earned, through exercise of strength and courage, the prerogatives belonging to free, adult, white males in his society. He is, significantly enough, sixteen years old, physically mature, and wavering in his feeling about whether he is child or adult. His sense of his maturational state is associated in his mind with his being or not being a slave: adults are free; children are "bound to someone." The tension is explicit; the poles of his dilemma clearly and openly expressed.

> God, deliver me! Let me be free! Is there any God? Why am I a slave? I will run away. I will not stand it. Get caught or get clear, I'll try it. I had as well die with ague as with fever. I have only one life to lose. I had as well be killed running as die standing. Only think of it; one hundred miles straight north, and I am free! Try it? Yes! God helping me, I will. It cannot be that I shall live and die a slave. I will take to the water. . . . Meanwhile, I will try to bear up under the yoke. I am not the only slave in the world. Why should I fret? I can bear as much as any of them. Besides, I am but a boy, and all boys are bound to someone.

To confront his worst fears, and the sense of his greatest limitations, embodied in the person of Covey, and to emerge whole from that confrontation means to him the achievement of manhood, the right to gover-

nance of his mind and spirit. In his statement prefatory to the encounter he explicitly says so: "You have seen how a man was made a slave; you shall see how a slave was made a man." The terms in which Douglass describes his sense of his new circumstances and situation are those usually associated with the achievement in western culture of adult male status: "My long crushed spirit rose, cowardice departed, bold defiance took its place. . . . I did not hesitate to let it be known of me, that the white man who expected to succeed in whipping, must also succeed in killing me." The voice here is the authoritative voice of the narrator of the *Narrative,* the private voice, the "I," and what that voice says belongs specifically to him, not to any public person or figure or entity. At least that voice belongs *first* to Douglass the person, though reference to broader elements of culture sets that voice in a public context.

It is of significance that Douglass chooses to cast this highly private experience in more public terms. That is, in grounding his experience in western religious and mythological traditions, Douglass transforms that experience to "public" experience insofar as a culture belongs to all who exist in it. The components of culture have reference both to group and individual, public and private experience. Something of this sort of grounding occurs when Douglass makes reference on more than one occasion to Shakespeare's *Hamlet.* The private is objectified, made analogous to some facet of western culture, and rendered, consequently, public.

Douglass knew the play by the time he wrote the *Narrative,* a fact we may infer from his quoting from it in chapter 10. Further, when we look back at the *Narrative,* it is probable that Douglass has Hamlet in mind when he speaks of the wavering he and his friends experience when thinking about whether to attempt escape: "At times we were almost disposed to give up, and try to content ourselves with our wretched lot; at others, we were firm and unbending in our determination to go. Whenever we suggested any plan, there was shrinking—the odds were fearful. Our path was beset with the greatest obstacles; and if we succeeded in gaining the end of it, our right to be free was yet questionable—we were yet liable to be returned to bondage."

Douglass invokes *Hamlet* (and *Genesis*) when he questions the value of knowlege, of rationality, and of life itself. He is fully aware of the connection between *Hamlet* and *Genesis*. He knows that knowledge may be a burden, a curse even, and that a lack of consciousness may have its value.

> I envied my fellow-slaves for their stupidity. I have often wished myself a beast. I preferred the condition of the meanest reptile to my own. Any thing, no matter what, to get rid of thinking! It was this everlasting thinking of my condition that tormented me. There was no getting rid of it.

I often found myself regretting my own existence, and wishing myself dead; and but for the hope of being free, I have no doubt but that I should have killed myself, or done something for which I should have been killed.

Douglass would have had these thoughts and feelings had he not read *Hamlet;* but I would argue that he found in the play correlatives mirroring his own sense of himself and his situation. Surely Hamlet's line, "O, what a rogue and peasant slave am I," would have caught Douglass' eye; he would almost without question see the analogy, as well as the fact that while for Hamlet the thought that he is a slave is metaphorical, for Douglass it is literal. I doubt that Douglass would have written the following lines had he not read the play. They refer to the plot to escape in chapter 10, " . . . we had talked long enough; we were now ready to move; if not now, we never should be; and if we did not intend to move now, we had as well fold our arms, sit down, and acknowledge ourselves fit only to be slaves."

His physical conflict with Covey leading to his proclamation of freedom, and to his setting right his world just as Hamlet set his right, needs be understood in terms of the peculiarity of its conduct. Throughout the course of the combat Douglass is entirely on the defensive. His intention, unlike that of the combatant in an ordinary conflict, is not to destroy, defeat, or even injure his opponent but to prevent Covey's flogging him. This may be inferred from the *Narrative;* it is explicitly clear in *My Bondage and My Freedom* and *Life and Times:* "Every blow of his was parried though I dealt no blows in return. I was strictly on the *defensive,* preventing him from injuring me, rather than trying to injure him." Hence he strikes no blows against Covey; rather he wards them off and attempts to hold his opponent in such a way that Covey cannot strike him. The *Narrative* implies this fact but does not make it explicit as do the later descriptions. Once one understands what the later descriptions say, the implications of the *Narrative* description of the encounter are clear. "I resolved to fight; and, suiting my action to the resolution, I seized Covey hard by the throat; and as I did so, I rose. He held on to me, and I to him. My resistance was so entirely unexpected that Covey seemed taken all aback. He trembled like a leaf. This gave me assurance, and I held him uneasy, causing the blood to run where I touched him with the ends of my fingers." The remarkable thing about his battle is Douglass' extraordinary control. He seizes Covey by the throat but allows himself to squeeze only so hard. When Covey attempts to pick up a stick to hit him, Douglass brings him "by a sudden snatch to the ground"—but "harmlessly," *Bondage and Freedom* tells us. The agon continues for nearly two hours, and Douglass remains in a completely defensive posture during the whole time (except when he kicks Covey's young cousin in the genitals when he attempts to intervene on Covey's behalf), so much in control of his passions as to suppress great hatred, fear, and anger.

Most commentators on the conflict have not understood the real nature of the fight and have interpreted it as though it were an arena boxing match. Such an interpretation distorts the scene itself and skews our perspective on the whole narrative. Douglass' victory is won not because he beats Covey but because he thwarts Covey's intention to beat him. Failure to understand this distinction leads to the reader's misperception of the basic nature of Douglass' character. In his biography of Douglass, Booker T. Washington reports: "Douglass flew at Covey's throat recklessly, hurled his antagonist to the ground, and held him firmly." This report is not substantiated by any of the three accounts of the encounter. Benjamin Quarles, the noted historian, turns fictionist in writing that "one day, steeled by desperation, the goaded youth soundly thrashed Covey." Another even more imaginative commentator describing the battle writes, "Frightened by that time lest he be worsted by his infuriated slave, Covey took the fight out into the cow-yard with Douglass meeting every blow with a better one." Yet another reporter describes what happens in this way: "In the course of the fight, Douglass whipped Covey's cousin Hughes, stimulated two other slaves to disobey orders, and knocked Covey full-length into a pasture of cow dung." Why is the episode so consistently and universally misinterpreted? The answer is clear and simple. Critics have seen only the public focus of a narrative such as Douglass' which requires that the slave defeat the slaveholder, thus obscuring the private perspective.

Seeing both the public and private dimensions of Douglass' experience, one may realize that the conflict between them mirrors a conflict within Douglass himself between the aggressive impulse to strike against the monster and an alternative impulse not to strike at all. The dynamic of the relation may have some connection with Douglass' identification of his situation with Hamlet's in that Douglass also finds it impossible to reconcile thought and action. Douglass' ruminations suggest this connection.

> Thus I used to think, and thus I used to speak myself; goaded almost to madness at one moment, and at the next reconciling myself to my wretched lot.

> I was fast approaching manhood, and year after year had passed, and I was still a slave. These thoughts roused me—I must do something.

> At times we were almost disposed to give up, and try to content ourselves with our wretched lot; at others, we were firm and unbending in our determination to go.

These conflicting feelings reflect the central metaphor of the whole of the *Narrative:* Douglass presses his fingers around Covey's throat, squeezing, but only so hard—squeezing defensively. This typifies Douglass' character and action throughout the *Narrative* from its beginning to its end, as well as the work itself in its style, tone, plot, and mood. A controlled aggression prevails. He watches, during the four years following the conflict, waiting for his opportunity to move. He hovers with care, not faintheartedly but with firm resolve and meticulously modulated self-control. Never directly aggressive, he is sometimes intentionally provocative, and whereas he never initiates physical confrontation with his owners, overseers, or other whites, he stands by his decision to defend himself, to the death if necessary, against physical abuse.

The balance, reflective of an extraordinarily strong will and character, is taxing and delicate. Douglass cannot allow these warring tendencies to split asunder, for he cannot run away before the opportune moment, nor can he restrain himself to such an extent that action is not possible. The nexus between the impulse to strike out against his oppressor, to run away, to be free, and the quality of character which checks that impulse is the source of the control informing the *Narrative* and in turn the source of its style. The style of Douglass' account is objective in the sense that its rhetorical form and its diction blunt the effect of direct, personal expression of emotion. This is not to deny that the *Narrative* is expressive of emotion; rather, the style is such that it tends to create distance between the writer and the reader because of the high formality of the syntax, sentence structure, and diction, and because of the narrator's tendency to understate. The tone is strictly controlled throughout, the events and episodes rendered in such a way as to suggest their factuality. The effect is of disparity between the subject of the narration and the underlying actuality of the experience. Straightforward rendition gives the most horrendous descriptions of physical brutality an understated quality. Note, for example, the relatively objective description of Douglass' first beating by Covey:

> He then went to a large gum tree and with his axe cut three large switches, and after trimming them up neatly with his pocket-knife, he ordered me to take off my clothes. I made him no answer, but stood with my clothes on. He repeated his order. I still made him no answer, nor did I move to strip myself. Upon this he rushed at me with the fierceness of a tiger, tore off my clothes, and lashed me till he had worn out his switches, cutting me so savagely as to leave the marks visible for a long time after. This whipping was the first of a number just like it and for similar offenses.

The omission of reference to his emotional response, to description of the pain, or even to what Douglass was doing or thinking during the beating has the effect

A portrait of Douglass in his later years.

of objectivity and understatement. The reader is thus invited to supply from the resources of his own imagination the missing currents of thought and feeling. This may all be retraced to the antithetical impulses within Douglass projected in his description of his fight with Covey: his fingers are around the tyrant's throat, yet he squeezes only so hard. This control and restraint, standing in opposition to the deep psychological impulses driving him toward maturity and autonomy, and suggestive of the private dimension of Douglass' life and his narrative, reflect a remarkable balance of attitude and emotion, a balance which dictates the style of the *Narrative.*

In form the style is very much influenced by contemporary oratorical practice. One of his earliest readers, *The Columbian Orator,* was his introduction to oratory, and he tells us that he read its contents "over and over again with unabated interest." Of course by the time he wrote the *Narrative* he would have listened to and delivered scores of speeches in the contemporary manner. His writing style is certainly influenced by an oratorical style of speech making. Loggins points out [in *The Negro Author: His Development in America to 1900,* 1931]: "In his autobiographical account as in everything else he wrote, Douglass seems to be speaking from the platform. His genius lay in his passion for meeting an antagonistic public with the spoken word.

All of his writing is in the spirit of spontaneous and racy and stirring oratory." In agreeing with Loggins ("When he wrote his narrative, it was heavily influenced by his training in rhetoric") Frances Foster refutes O'Meally's argument that Douglass' style was significantly influenced by black pulpit oratory. O'Meally, in identifying features which he relates to the rhetoric of the black pulpit tradition, merely sees characteristics which black pulpit rhetoric and traditional speech making rhetoric share. Douglass' description of his life and his articulation of his values suggest that he would not conceivably have addressed an audience in the manner of the black preacher because he had no identification with that tradition.

The syntactical balance of Douglass' style has been noted, and that probably stems from the same source as the balance of Douglass' account of the conditions of slavery. He makes significant distinctions among his various experiences as a slave, telling what was good and bad, painting a picture of variegated colors and hues. He is not attempting to placate an audience lacking entire sympathy with his cause as, Foster tells us, many narrators do. According to Foster [in *Witnessing Slavery: The Development of Ante-bellum Slave Narratives*, 1979], "Their narratives show great efforts to appease without neutralizing their position. It became almost axiomatic that for every two or three bad experiences related, one good experience must be recounted." Douglass is also not attempting to be "fair" since the system of slavery has for him no redeeming qualities. Rather, he expresses his capacity to make judgments about himself, about his circumstances as a slave, about each of his owners and overseers, about the system of slavery itself, and about the environment in which it functions. He clearly distinguishes among all those under whose authority he finds himself, telling in no uncertain terms when he is fed well and when he goes hungry or has insufficient time to eat; when he is treated kindly and when dealt with brutally. He even distinguishes degrees of kindness or ill treatment. In a work devoted to the abolition of slavery, it is remarkable to read: "While at Baltimore I got few whippings, and few slaves could boast of a kinder master and mistress than myself." On a number of occasions Douglass speaks favorably of slave owners: "Master William Hamilton, my master's father-in-law, always gave his slaves enough to eat. I never left there hungry." And again, "The year passed smoothly. . . . I will give Mr. Freeland the credit of being the best master I ever had, *till I became my own master"* (Douglass' emphasis). At one point he compares the lot of the city slave with that of his plantation counterpart.

> A city slave is almost a freeman compared with a slave on a plantation. He is much better fed and clothed, and enjoys privileges altogether unknown to the slave on the plantation. There is a vestige of decency, a sense of shame that does much to curb and check those outbreaks of atrocious cruelty so commonly enacted upon the plantation. He is a desperate slaveholder, who will shock the humanity of his nonslaveholding neighbor with the cries of his lacerated slave. Few are willing to incur the odiom attaching to the reputation of being a cruel master; and above all things, they would not be known as not giving a slave enough to eat.

The quotation begins with a judgment, particularizes the statement in the next sentence, draws an inference from the preceding particularizing sentence, then in the final two sentences supports the inference through particularization. In other words Douglass makes the judgment, tells in what ways the judgment is true, then tells why the initial judgment is true and sound. These other assessments Douglass makes of his circumstances, slave owners, overseers, and the system of slavery itself are an essential element of the *Narrative* in that Douglass asserts through his delivery of judgments that he has the capacity, unacknowledged in slaves, to judge his former owners and the system which allowed him to be held captive. He judges as an equal and by reference to the standards of morality and conduct embodied in Christianity and professedly held in the slaveholding region, and at the same time he asserts his capacity to exercise one of the highest functions of consciousness: the rendering of judicious distinctions, a capacity literally earned through his "victory" over Covey.

Because Douglass is aware of the relation between knowledge and judgment, knowledge and knowing are prominent themes throughout his narrative. Because of Douglass' explicit awareness that knowledge forms the basis of sound judgment, the chief emphasis of the text as a whole falls on knowledge and knowing, for insofar as the text itself constitutes in its entirety a complex judgment on Douglass' part, knowledge is the basis of that judgment. The first chapter of the *Narrative* demonstrates the role of knowledge in the text. Its point is to tell the reader what Douglass *knows*. The first two pages contain at least twenty explicit references to knowledge or knowing. Lines 3, 5, 6, 29, 30, 31, 39, and 43 use the word. "Who could tell" in line 8 means who "knew." "Want of information" in line 10 means "lack of knowledge." "I could not tell" in line 13 means "I did not know." "Ignorant" in line 7 means of course "without knowledge." Learning to read means so much to him because it allows Douglass to expand his knowledge, heighten his consciousness, and therefore be in a position to render judgment. "The more I read, the more I was led to abhor and detest my enslavers. I could regard them in no other light than a band of successful robbers, who had left their homes, and gone to Africa, and stolen us from our homes, and in a strange land reduced us to slavery. I loathed them as being the meanest as well as the most wicked of men."

Viewed from this perspective, the fight with Covey takes on new significance. Covey's discipline, Douglass tells us, has left him "broken in body, soul, and spirit. My natural elasticity was crushed, my intellect languished, the disposition to read departed, the cheerful spark that lingered about my eye died; the dark night of slavery closed in upon me; and behold a man transformed into a brute!" Douglass believes himself transformed into a brute because his "intellect languished" and he no longer desired to read, suggesting that he is no longer able to exercise the higher functions of consciousness, and in his "dream" or "stupor" is in a nonconscious state. The result of the encounter with Covey is to restore Douglass to his former state of consciousness, allowing him once again to exercise its higher functions of reasoning, reflecting, judging. The reference to Covey as snake, a submerged reference (as suggested above) to the myth of the garden of Eden, is apt, for just as the serpent leads Adam and Eve to eat of the fruit of the tree of the knowledge of good and evil, and allows them to be as the gods (to make intellectual distinctions, to reason, to know and to judge), so does Covey make that possible for Douglass. In fairytale and mythology the relation between the hero's transformation and the exercise of the functions of higher consciousness is rarely as clear as in this true-to-life autobiography. Usually the hero wins some symbol representing one aspect or another of the new state—a mate (symbolic of the sexual prerogatives of adulthood) or treasure (symbolizing the adult power and authority stemming from the possession of wealth). In his narrative Douglass' prize is literal and not symbolic at all (except in an extended sense of the meaning of "symbolic"). Douglass literally wins back the capacity to read, to learn, to think, to know, to judge, to articulate. Interestingly enough, though, this process is undergone by one Frederick Douglass, private person. Surely it is not in the interests of abolitionism to suggest or even imply that every slave need experience this particular pattern of psychological development in order to be free. But this apparent paradox may not be paradoxical at all. His point may be that in being free one need not choose to be either a private or a public person: one may alternately be one or the other or both at once. The end of the *Narrative* would suggest this idea.

On the final page of the *Narrative* Douglass describes his feelings prior to his first major anti-slavery speech before a large, white audience. His feelings are not unlike those he experienced much earlier when he was deciding whether to remain a slave or attempt to be free. "It [the decision to speak or not] was a severe cross, and I took it up reluctantly. The truth was, I felt myself a slave, and the idea of speaking to white people weighed me down. I spoke but a few moments, when I felt a degree of freedom, and said what I desired with considerable ease. From that time until now, I have been engaged in pleading the cause of my brethren. . . ." Essentially here he reenacts his struggle with Covey and resolves the tension between the public and private roles: Douglass feels he is a slave, that the truth of his primary identity resides in the abstraction "slave." The "cross" he refers to is the tension between the social definition that he feels a white audience places on him and his own markedly different, private sense of who he is. In conflict with his private sense that he is a slave is an impulse to assume the public role. The private sense and the public sense of his identity merge as he begins to speak and by his very utterance deny the validity of his feeling that he is a slave. Because he has battled Covey successfully, he may speak, for he has earned the right to exercise the functions of higher consciousness. His words, we may well imagine, are carefully chosen in this his first major oration, and his sentences are measured. His restraint is that exercised when he held his fingers around Covey's throat squeezing only so hard. He does not say directly what his first words were, but we as careful readers of his text know them: "I was born in Tuckahoe, near Hillsborough, and about twelve miles from Easton, in Talbot county, Maryland."

John Sekora (essay date 1985)

SOURCE: "Comprehending Slavery: Language and Personal History in Douglass' *Narrative* of 1845," in *CLA Journal,* Vol. 29, No. 2, December, 1985, pp. 157-70.

[*In the following essay, Sekora argues that Douglass's* Narrative *is not simply autobiography, but rather the "first comprehensive, personal history of American slavery."*]

> The author is therefore the more willing—nay, anxious, to lay alongside of such (pro-slavery) arguments the history of his own life and experiences as a slave, that those who read may know what are some of the characteristics of that highly favored institution, which is sought to be preserved and perpetuated.
>
> —Austin Steward

Because it is one of the most important books ever published in America, Frederick Douglass' *Narrative* of 1845 has justly received much attention. That attention has been increasing for a generation at a rate parallel to the growth in interest in autobiography as a literary genre, and the *Narrative* as autobiography has been the subject of several influential studies. Without denying the insights of such studies, I should like to suggest that in 1845 Douglass had no opportunity to write what (since the eighteenth century) we would call autobiography, that the achievement of the *Narrative* lies in another form.

Elsewhere I have argued the uniqueness of the ante-bellum slave narrative as an American literary form, a signal feature of which is the conditions under which it was printed. Briefly put, eighteenth-century narratives like those of Hammon, Gronniosaw, and Equiano were published only when they could be fitted to such familiar patterns as the captivity tale or the tale of religious conversion. In the abolitionist period when slavery was the central issue, once again printers and editors determined the overall shape of the narrative. Lundy, Garrison, Tappan, and Weld sought to expunge a vile institution, not support individualized Afro-American life stories. They had set the language of abolition—its vocabulary as well as social attitudes and philosophical presuppositions—in place by the early 1830s. Former slaves were wanted primarily as lecturers, later as authors, not for their personal identities as men and women, but for their value as eyewitnesses and victims. (It was significant to Douglass that his white associates tended to see slaves as passive victims.)

Against these conditions, one must place current conceptions of autobiography. Traditionalists and poststructuralists seem to agree that autobiography comes into being when recollection engages memory. Recollection engages people, things, events that at first appear fragmented and unrelated. As an essential part of its activity, recollection brings sequence and/or relation to the enormous diversity of individual experience; it emplots the stages of the subject's journey to selfhood. Meaning emerges when events are connected as parts of a coherent and comprehensive whole. Meaning, relation, and wholeness are but three facets of one characteristic: a narrative self that is more a literary creation than a literal, preexisting fact. The self of autobiography comes into being in the act of writing, not before. This said, the contrast with the antebellum narrative is apparent. From Hammon's *Narrative* of 1760 to Harriet Jacobs's *Incidents* in 1861, the explicit purpose of the slave narrative is far different from the creation of a self, and the overarching shape of that story—the facts to be included and the ordering of those facts—is mandated by persons other than the subject. Not black recollection, but white interrogation brings order to the narration. For eighteenth-century narratives the self that emerges is a preexisting form, deriving largely from evangelical Protestantism. For the abolitionist period, the self is a type of the antislavery witness. In each instance the meaning, relation, and wholeness of the story are given before the narrative opens; they are imposed rather than chosen—what Douglass in *My Bondage and My Freedom* (1855) calls "the facts which I felt almost everybody must know."

This approach would seem to resolve some persistent questions about the *Narrative*: why its structure is so similar to earlier (and later) abolitionist narratives, why

Douglass subordinates so much of his emotional and intellectual life to the experience of slavery, why Garrison and Phillips are at such pains to make it appear a collective enterprise. At the same time it raises at least two others: if not autobiography, what kind of book is the *Narrative?* And how does it succeed so thoroughly?

White Americans, it would seem, have long attempted to cloak the raw experience of slavery—in the eighteenth century masking it in the language of triumphal Christianity, for most of the nineteenth century transmuting it into the language of abolition. For the years between 1870 and 1950, even this genteel transmutation was too raw, too threatening. Thus the slave narratives remained the most important and the most neglected body of early American writing. A consequence of that neglect is that we lack a distinctive term for a unique genre. For one example, most critics use the term *slave narrative* to refer to stories of oppression under slavery; yet before 1830 very few of the narratives concerned themselves with the injustices of the institution. Related to captivity tales, Franklinesque success stories, modern autobiographies, and other forms, the slave narrative is essentially different from all. It resembles other forms, but other forms do not resemble it.

In the absence of a distinguishing critical category, we must make do with that phrase used in authors' prefaces and advertisements as synonymous with abolitionist narrative—"personal history of slavery." Douglass was clearly aware in 1845 of the terms for such a history, for he had referred to them in his lectures earlier and wrote about them at length later. Before he became an antislavery agent, he had been questioned frequently concerning his life under slavery; once selected as an agent, he was coached concerning those aspects of slavery most likely to appeal to an ignorant or indifferent Northern audience. He had read the earlier separately published narratives and followed the shorter tales printed in the *Liberator* and other periodicals. He knew, he said, of the abolitionist emphasis upon facts, verifiable facts; upon instances of cruelty, repression, and punishment; upon the depth of Christianity in the owner's household; and so on. Overall, he knew that he was being woven into a network of clergymen, politicians, tradesmen, writers, editors, sponsors, and societies that was transatlantic in scope and resources. On any given day of lecturing, for example, he knew he would be introduced and followed by white speakers who would testify to his candor, character, and authenticity. And he knew he would conclude his address with an appeal to the audience to do as he had done—become absorbed in the abolitionist crusade.

Douglass was thus situated at the intersection of collectivizing forces. On both sides of the political divide, white people were busy defining and hence depersonalizing him. Apologists for slavery were doing their utmost to discredit him as a fraud; Garrison's agents were doing their best to publicize him as a representative fugitive slave. The issue over which they fought was not Douglass the lecturer or Douglass the author. Rather it was a narrower issue of their own defining. Douglass was important insofar as he embodied the experience of slavery. As author he was therefore caught in a genuine dilemma. He was indeed an individual human being with a particular story to tell, but if he were to discover personalizing words for his life, he must do so within the language of abolition. His success in resolving that dilemma, as arresting today as when it was first published, makes the **Narrative** the most comprehensive personal history of slavery in the language.

It embodies comprehension on several levels and in several successive stages, as intellectual apprehension of the many influences of slavery and narrative compassing its equally many forms. In the beginning Douglass as narrator comprehends the world that slaveholders have made, and Douglass as actor comprehends the power of language to transform that world. In his mature years he apprehends the eloquence of silence as well as the liberating power of words. Finally, as at once actor and narrator, he comprehends his own situation in the tradition of the slave narrative. Douglass highlights these levels with a series of gem-like sentences of Enlightenment irony and compression. Two are notable as preliminary illustrations of his modes of comprehension. Recalling his entrance into the Auld household in Baltimore twenty years before, he reports: "Little Thomas was told, there was his Freddy. . . ." In eight short words of indirect quotation, he signals both the effect of chattel slavery upon the Auld family and his intellectual apprehension of his place in the system. The Auld child is "Little Thomas"—an exalted owner of human property; Douglass is diminished in name as well as status—"*his* Freddy." In the kind of Enlightenment balance and compression sought by Hume and Johnson (but not surpassed by them), two adjectives modifying two nouns carry all the weight of significance: analysis enveloped by description. The Aulds address not Douglass but the child. Douglass is deployed as an object—in the sentence, the child's mind, the household, and the system—and so employs himself to convey his awareness of that situation. The burden of the narrative will be to reveal the necessary reversal of that situation. The Aulds are too vacuous and vulnerable, Douglass too penetrating, for it to hold. In what Albert Stone has rightly called the key sentence of the **Narrative,** Douglass again unites balance, reversal, and narrative time to embody what an abolitionist narrative should be: "You have seen how a man was made a slave; you shall see how a slave was made a man." These two sentences suggest the depth of his enterprise. While operating within the abolitionist code, his adroit use of language would give his narrative a greater personal imprint, a wider historical compass, and a surer view of slavery than had ever been presented before.

That code prescribed that the opening portions of a narrative (as of a lecture) be heavily factual, containing if possible verifiable accounts of birth, parentage, and slaveholders. Douglass provided that—and much more. His opening paragraphs indicate a concern for accuracy designed to satisfy even the most hostile or scrupulous hunter of details. No one can do it better, he says in effect. He is then in position to portray the world of slaveholders and their minions, the world into which he was born. His plays upon the names of "Captain" Anthony, Mr. Severe, and Mr. Freeland are instances of his reduction of diverse personalities to their precise roles in an economic system they barely understand. With Austin Gore he provides a more elaborate description and a more powerful form of comprehension:

> Mr. Gore was proud, ambitious, and persevering. He was artful, cruel, and obdurate. He was just the man for such a place, and it was just the place for such a man.

With two trinities of adjectives and another sentence of finely wrought symmetry, the character of this baneful overseer is caught and reduced as if he were an overweening functionary in MoliEere or Ben Jonson. With Gore's employer, Colonel Lloyd, Douglass's irony is at full stretch. In Lloyd's callousness toward men and women and his sensitivity toward horses, he finds an apt sign of his owner's true worth. Because he is so utterly insecure with people, Lloyd's threat is shown to be hollow and his stature petty. When we learn that on his plantation only horses are treated with regard, we understand the social situation he has created and its underlying structure. He and his class are like the petty gods of Greek myth, absurd whichever way they turn.

In comprehending his own and their assistants, Douglass establishes his grasp of a type representing the most powerful families in the South. In a sense he has *defined* the type, as a dramatist does his primary actors. But he does not stop there, as earlier narrators had done. For his interweaving of interpretation with description has all along recognized the economic machinery of which Anthony and Lloyd are but small cogs. Slavery, he shows, wishes to control more than the labor and physical being of slaves—even to their words, their very language. His first owner must be addressed as Captain Anthony: " . . . a title which, I presume, he acquired by sailing a craft on the Chesapeake Bay." Like the many slaveholders who insisted upon being called "General" or "Colonel," Anthony demands that he be known by a self-conferred military title. Slaves alone could entitle masters, this artifice seems to say. Likewise, Colonel Lloyd rode out to

outlying farms—where he wasn't known by sight—
to question field slaves about how kindly their master was. For a candid answer, a slave would be sold
South. Reporting these episodes, Douglass makes
clear that what is being revealed is larger than his
owner's self-deception. Slaveholders, by seeking to
control slave language, sought to exact slave complicity in their own subjugation. Their self-concep-
tions required the right words, the correct words.
With the proper words, a slave could keep his life
intact. With the proper words, a slaveholder could
keep his self-esteem intact. In each case, the owner
compels the slave to authorize the owner's power.
Slavery and the language of slavery are virtually
coextensive.

In comprehending the equation of words and power,
Douglass relates not only the workings of slavery as a
system, but also the advent of his personal history within
it. He describes his initial situation in Chapter II as a
well of ignorance, typified by his insensitivity to the
words of work songs:

> I did not, when a slave, understand the deep meaning
> of those rude and apparently incoherent songs. I
> was myself within the circle; so that I neither saw
> nor heard as those without might see and hear. They
> told a tale of woe which was then altogether beyond
> my feeble comprehension. . . .

This memory and the image of incomprehension spurred
by it testify that for his life, as for the narrative we are
reading, there will be no stop, no comforting return
until his comprehension is complete. In one of the
passages blending past and present at which he is so
adept, he remarks:

> The mere recurrence to those songs, even now,
> affects me; and while I am writing these lines, an
> expression of feeling has already found its way down
> my cheek. To those songs I trace my first glimmering
> conception of the dehumanizing character of slavery.

The next stage in his understanding of the language
of slavery takes Douglass to Baltimore, the Auld
household, and the forbidden seduction of reading.
Auld's diatribe on the danger of language is well
known as the impelling force for Douglass' climbing
the ladder to literacy. Yet it is equally significant as
a further sketch of the effects of slavery upon white
people. Because they do not know what slavery is
doing to them, the Aulds understand far less what it
is doing to him. The exercise of petty power is for
Mrs. Auld as corrupting as the possession of great
wealth has been for Colonel Lloyd. (It is also possible to see in her decline features of those Garrisonians who turned on Douglass.) It is through them
that Douglass gains his penultimate lessons of the
perversions of slavery.

In most abolitionist narratives the quest for freedom
through literacy would conclude here, the story redi-
rected toward plans for escape. With Douglass, however, simple literacy is merely the ground upon which
a complex psychological drama will be played. Although he has learned much from earlier narratives, he
will not provide exactly the same kind of straight-line
narrative found in, say, Moses Roper, James Curry,
Lunceford Lane, or Moses Grandy. His war with slavery through language consists not of a single battle
with clear-cut victory on either side. Rather it is a
sustained series of costly skirmishes, with losses following hard upon gains. As Auld had predicted, Douglass at twelve years of age is beset by discontent. His
fall is occasioned by his hunger for language, for while
his readings "relieved me of one difficulty, they brought
on another even more painful than the one of which I
was relieved." The more he learns of slavery, the farther freedom seems to recede. The condition is temporary since he refuses to be satisfied. The discontent
brought on by language will be relieved by language:
in this instance by a single word—*abolition*—and its
resonance. The pain that is aggravated by language is
also palliated by language. As he came to apprehend
the meaning of abolition, he records, "The light broke
in upon me by degrees."

The predicament recurs at a higher level when he is
broken by Covey's demands of incessant labor: "I was
broken in body, soul, and spirit. . . . [T]he dark night
of slavery closed in upon me. . . ." The language of
abolition he has been learning possessed the power to
inspire longing and to instill despair when that longing
is thwarted. And once again a call in words evokes a
powerful response, in the apostrophe to the ships on
the Chesapeake so well analyzed by Stone [in "Identity
and Art in Frederick Douglass's *Narrative*," *CLA Journal* 17 (1973)]. His predicament is resolved in a form
of blues sermon that raises all doubts and answers all:
"There is a better day coming." Douglass's career has
been an ascent toward freedom through literacy. His
comprehension of the language—first of slavery, then
of abolition—has been the ladder of his climb. Structurally, he himself marks his rise to the top by his
battle with Covey and the pivotal sentence, "You have
seen how a man was made a slave; you shall see how
a slave was made a man." Thematically it is the "protections" he writes for himself and others in 1835 that
signal his position. With the protections he can *write*
his way North, the ultimate verification of his victory
over slavery and a final proof of his comprehension of
language.

Although the contest with Covey has made Chapter X
the most famous portion of the ***Narrative,*** it is the final
chapter that most reveals its distinction as a personal
history. In half the length of the preceding section,
Chapter XI accomplishes three very large tasks of
comprehension. First, he exercises an eloquence of

silence fully as powerful as his brilliance of language. When he forgoes an account of his escape, he relinquishes an element of the narrative that had made it one of the most popular literary forms in America in the 1840s. For example, in Moses Roper before him, William Wells Brown, Henry Box Brown, the Crafts, and John Thompson after him, the escape is an exciting adventure story in itself, uniting ingenuity, suspense, courage, and endurance. It is, in short, precisely the kind of story Northeastern audiences would pay to hear and read. Douglass' decision to withhold that part of his story is an assertion of personal control within a mandated form. Only he can write this section, not Garrison or Phillips; only he knows what is being withheld. Only he can decide the proper time for its release. At the moment of writing he is painfully aware of the short distance (political as well as temporal) that separates past from present. Hence his silence is evoked by a communal regard for fellow slaves still seeking means of escape: he must "not run the hazard of closing the slightest avenue by which a brother slave might clear himself of the chains and fetters of slavery."

Second, what he does choose to include equally bears his personal stamp, the language of a free man. The two sentences in which he dates his escape and destination are models of laconic understatement, conspicuous in their restraint. By this point he has comprehended the art of the oxymoron, as he provides readers with poised anxiety and loud softness—eloquent silence. Also conspicuous is his inclusion of a second document (the first being the protections), the only one not of his own composition. The certificate of marriage to Anna Murray, subscribed by James W. C. Pennington, appears to be Douglass' proof in language of a new existence. Socially, legally, sexually, religiously, he is indeed a man—in the eyes of most Americans, for the first time. It was to this need for documentation that Pennington returned in his narrative, *The Fugitive Blacksmith,* in 1849. In his preface, he wrote:

> Whatever may be the ill or favored condition of the slave in the matter of mere personal treatment, it is the chattel relation that robs him of his manhood, and transfers his ownership in himself to another. . . . It is this that throws his family history into utter confusion, and leaves him without a single record to which he may appeal in vindication of his character, or honor. And has a man no sense of honor because he was born a slave? Has he no need of character?

Douglass has ensured that his new family will be recorded, will from its inception possess a sense of honor.

In his final narrative gesture, Douglass establishes that he comprehends the tradition of the slave story and

Statue of Douglass in Rochester, New York.

attempts to subvert a portion of that tradition. By closing with his address to the Nantucket convention in 1841, Douglass . . . brings the narrative full circle, to the opening sentence of Garrison's Preface. Garrisonians, he explains in *My Bondage and My Freedom,* often sought to limit his scope: "Give us the facts . . . we will take care of the philosophy" (1855 ed.). Here he makes no mention of Garrison and reverses a persistent abolitionist tactic. Garrison and his associates often spoke as if former slaves were minor characters in *their* great antislavery story. Douglass deftly ensures that Phillips and Garrison will, in this narrative, be minor characters in *his* story. He authenticates them.

It is a bold gesture. For on a philosophical level, one might say that the slave narrative as a form is defined paradoxically by a suppression of the personal voice of the slave. Most sponsors regarded the slave by stipulation as primitive and then proceeded to use the narrative to address other white people. Many sponsors condescendingly saw the narratives as essentially a political form for their own use and said that fugitive slaves had no stories until the abolitionists gave them one. Douglass by 1845 is certainly aware of the complex of attitudes surrounding him: "The truth was, I felt myself a slave, and the idea of speaking to white people weighed me down." Humility and restraint are poised in this final paragraph, for it gains dignity by using Enlightenment language when explosive effusion seems called for. Like his audience in Nantucket, his readers acknowledge the effort, the discipline of his control. Slavery is far worse than anything he can say about it. The tension created between the cruelties which he recounts and his manner of recounting them he will use communally, not to win applause, but to go on working. The surplus of tension will be spent in the future and in language; "engaged in pleading the cause of" his "brethren." Whatever his sponsors intend, he will not be distracted. His tension will be active, always on the move, always renewing and being renewed.

The *Narrative,* I would contend, is the first comprehensive, personal history of American slavery. Autobiography would come a decade later, in *My Bondage and My Freedom.* If many readers prefer the earlier volume, the reasons are not far to search. The *Narrative* is as tightly written as a sonnet, the work of years in the pulpit and on the lecture circuit. It comprehends all major aspects of slavery as Douglass knew it in a narrative that is as dramatically compassing as any first-person novel. It is at the same time a personal history of the struggle with and for language—against words that repress, for words that liberate. It is for author and reader alike a personalizing account of a system that would depersonalize everyone. It is the retelling of the most important Christian story, the Crucifixion, in the midst of the most important American civil crisis, the battle over slavery.

In *The Fugitive Blacksmith* Pennington asked if a slave had no need of character. He answered the question in the following way: "Suppose insult, reproach, or slander, should render it necessary for him to appeal to the history of his family in vindication of his character, where does he find that history? He goes to his native state, to his native county, to his native town; but nowhere does he find any record of himself *as a man.*" It is an acute question, one he is eager to raise, I believe, because of Douglass's example. Douglass renewed the conservative form of the slave narrative at a critical time. He gave record of himself as an antislavery man. And the magnitude of that achievement is difficult to overestimate. For in moral terms the slave narrative and its postbellum heirs are the only history of American slavery we have. Outside the narrative, slavery was a wordless, nameless, timeless time. It was time without history and time without imminence. Slaveholders sought to reduce existence to the duration of the psychological present and to mandate their records as the only reliable texts. Whatever the restrictions placed upon them, Douglass and the other narrators changed that forever. To recall one's per-

sonal history is to *renew* it. The *Narrative* is both instrument and inscription of that renewal.

Henry Louis Gates, Jr., on Douglass:

There have been more biographies of Douglass printed than of any other Afro-American, including the great Du Bois. . . . What is curious and somewhat puzzling about this range of over a dozen biographies is that, in the main, they repeat the same facts in pretty much the same order. At first thought, we can say that so many scholars write about Douglass because he was the first Black Representative Man and, along with Du Bois, perhaps one of the only two truly representative men of letters our people are privileged to have had. Yet, if to his biographers Douglass was indeed this Representative Man, then Douglass himself carefully crafted that public image by which he determined he should be recalled. For, above all, Douglass was demonstrably concerned with the representation in written language of his public self, a self Douglass created, manipulated, and transformed, if ever so slightly, through the three fictive selves he posited in his three autobiographies. . . . [To] his death Douglass was concerned with the representation of this public self.

Henry Louis Gates, Jr., in Figures in Black, *Oxford University Press, 1989.*

Eric J. Sundquist (essay date 1986)

SOURCE: "Frederick Douglass: Literacy and Paternalism," in *Critical Essays on Frederick Douglass,* edited by William L. Andrews, G. K. Hall & Co., 1991, pp. 120-32.

[*In the following essay, originally published in 1986, Sundquist examines Douglass's symbolic and rhetorical use of literacy and paternity—and the powers each represents—in* My Bondage and My Freedom.]

The chronological point at which Frederick Douglass's second autobiography, *My Bondage and My Freedom* (1855), surpasses his first, *Narrative of the Life of Frederick Douglass* (1845), reveals an important discrepancy that goes to the heart of his controversial career. The *Narrative* concludes with a brief description of Douglass's first significant public speech in Nantucket on 11 August 1841. "I spoke but a few moments," Douglass writes, "when I felt a degree of freedom, and said what I desired with considerable ease. From that time until now, I have been engaged in pleading the cause of my brethren—with what success, and with what devotion, I leave those acquainted with my labors to decide." In *My Bondage and My Freedom,* on the other hand, Douglass reports, "It was with the utmost difficulty that I could stand erect, or that I could command and articulate two words without hesitating and stammering. I trembled in every limb."

These different recollections of the occasion may both be relatively accurate; but the later version is more significant because it introduces the rest of Douglass's account of his life to date—his successful oratorical career, his widely acclaimed tour of Britain, his founding of the *North Star,* his battle against discrimination in the North, and the event against which his most important achievements must be judged: his break with the radical abolitionist William Lloyd Garrison. "But excited and convulsed as I was," Douglass continues in the second version of his initiation at Nantucket, "the audience, though remarkably quiet before, became as much excited as myself. Mr. Garrison followed me, taking me as his text; and now, whether I had made an eloquent speech or not, his was one never to be forgotten by those who heard it."

To be presented as Garrison's "text" was for Douglass the primary role of his early career: "I was generally introduced as a *'chattel'*—a *'thing'*—a piece of southern *'property'*—the chairman assuring the audience that *it* could speak." Or, "I was a 'graduate from the peculiar institution . . . *with my diploma written on my back!'*" His eventual disgust with being told to look and act like a slave, to keep "a *little* of the plantation" in his speech, is well known, and the writing career that began with the *Narrative* has been rightly seen as an attempt both to refute accusations that his story was not authentic and to seize personal power over it at the same time. In transfiguring the text of his scarred slave's body into the combative written narrative that forced him to flee to England, Douglass took the first step in a lifelong series of autobiographical revisions that would culminate in the *Life and Times of Frederick Douglass* in 1881 and its extended version in 1892. Both the contents and the serial development of his autobiographical writings make evident the subversive lesson young Frederick first learned in reading the alphabet—that literacy is power.

Even if one prefers the fresh, stark text of the *Narrative,* it must be recognized that it too is no simple recitation of Douglass's slave and fugitive life. As Houston Baker has remarked, the *Narrative* itself represents a public version of Douglass's self already molded by white America, for "the voice of the unwritten self, once it is subjected to the linguistic codes, literary conventions, and audience expectations of a literate population, is perhaps never again the authentic voice of black American slavery." Because this is doubly true of *My Bondage and My Freedom,* part of the interest of the revised text lies in the fact that it is written against the grain both of recent historiography on slavery, which has been preoccupied with recovering the lost facts of Afro-American life, and also most recent work on slave narratives as a distinctive Afro-American genre.

Douglass's language in his second autobiography is thoroughly "American," in political as well as in literary terms, as is the versatile language of the self-made man which dominates the later chapters of *Life and Times.* One might argue that *My Bondage and My Freedom* therefore anticipates what some consider the pompous style and accommodating posture of Douglass's mature career. But a preference for the *Narrative* could also be seen as a later version of the condescending instructions Douglass himself despised: "'Let us have the facts,' . . . said Friend George Foster, who always wished to pin me down to my simple narrative. 'Give us the facts,' said [John] Collins, 'we will take care of the philosophy.' ' . . . Tell your story, Frederick,' would whisper my then revered friend, William Lloyd Garrison, as I stepped upon the platform." As Douglass notes, he was by this time "reading and thinking," and it "did not entirely satisfy me to *narrate* wrongs; I felt like *denouncing* them." In its spirit of individualism and rebellion, *My Bondage and My Freedom* "is an American book, for Americans, in the fullest sense of the idea," as the black abolitionist James McCune Smith wrote in a preface that replaced the authenticating introductory letters of Garrison and Wendell Phillips which had opened the *Narrative.* It is precisely in his adopted American language that Douglass rehearses his own "adoption" by America and acquires the power that was to make him the leading black figure in America for nearly half a century. How could it fail to be the disturbing language of that "double-consciousness"—"American" and "Negro"—which W. E. B. DuBois would identify in the Afro-American tradition at the turn of the century: "two souls, two thoughts, two unreconciled strivings; two warring ideals in one dark body, whose dogged strength alone keeps it from being torn asunder."

DuBois's famous description of the black American dilemma is all the more relevant because Douglass's late career and legend have been subject to as much problematic appropriation and counter-claim as Lincoln's. This is no surprise, for the two figures have at times been mythologically fused, and both were exposed to abuse by the collapse of black civil rights in the last decades of the century. For example, Booker T. Washington's 1906 biography of Douglass is praising but overtly conciliatory in tone; whereas DuBois, whatever his doubts about Douglass on other occasions, argues in the Washington chapter of *The Souls of Black Folk* (1903) that Douglass, throughout his life, "bravely stood for the ideals of his early manhood,—ultimate assimilation *through* self-assertion, and on no other terms." Washington's spirit of compromise in the three crucial areas of suffrage, civil rights, and higher education, DuBois goes on to imply, is an utter betrayal of Douglass.

The argument between Washington and DuBois over Douglass, like the more extreme arguments that found Lincoln alternately a white supremacist and a martyred champion of immediate black rights, brings into focus two aspects of the same doubled character. *My Bondage and My Freedom* makes that doubling a powerful and explicit theme. It reconceives rebellion in terms of an embracing ideology of liberation rooted in the rhetoric of the American Revolution. But it would be a mistake to read the Douglass of 1855 as an embarrassing sentimentalist and "white" patriot, an incipient Booker T. Washington; he would better be likened to Madison Washington, the black hero of the revolt aboard the slave ship *Creole* in 1841 and the subject of Douglass's only work of fiction, *The Heroic Slave*.

Quite apart from the content of *The Heroic Slave,* the very fact of its publication, in Julia Griffiths's gift-book, *Autographs for Freedom* (1853), alerts us to its autobiographical implications: the story represents, in effect, Douglass's own "autograph for freedom," his declaration of liberty through acts of increasingly rebellious literacy. Proceeds from the collection were intended to mitigate the financial difficulties of the *North Star,* and Douglass offered *Autographs* free to new subscribers to his paper. His own contribution to the collection placed him in the mainstream of intellectual antislavery. It invites us to identify him with his quasi-fictional rebel-hero, who appears throughout his speeches of the period as a model of black achievement. In *The Heroic Slave,* Douglass invokes the domestic cult surrounding the legend of George Washington but subverts its inherent conservatism by making Madison Washington, the *black* Virginian rebel, articulate his ideal of liberty: "We have done that which you applaud your fathers for doing, and if we are murderers, *so were they*." These same sentiments pervade *My Bondage and My Freedom* and echo Douglass's endorsement of violent slave rebellion. Dramatized in the fictional setting, however, they suggest as well that Douglass's persona in the new autobiography is also part of a rhetorical masquerade, a deliberate augmentation of his power at a new level of literacy. The Douglass who wrote the *Narrative,* had a successful tour of Britain, moved to Rochester and founded his own paper (against the wishes of Phillips and Garrison), endorsed the Constitution, entered on a struggle against the narrow fanaticism of the Massachusetts abolitionists who would make him their puppet, changed the name of the *North Star* to *Frederick Douglass' Paper* after Garrison blacklisted it in response to Douglass's disavowal of Garrisonian positions—this Douglass is the patriotic rebel-slave, the hero of his own fictionalized story based on fact.

The Heroic Slave thus links the two autobiographies, and by implicitly dramatizing his own rebellion portrays Douglass's escape from a new enslavement to the Boston abolitionists' ethnocentric paternalism. Its narrative form, in which a fugitive slave, through the power of his character and his story, converts a white man to antislavery, anticipates the unlikely role in which Douglass—punning on his recent status as chattel, as a *thing*—cast himself first as a speaker and then as a young editor in *My Bondage and My Freedom:* "A slave, brought up in the very depths of ignorance, assuming to instruct the highly civilized people of the north in the principles of liberty, justice, and humanity! The thing looked absurd." By itself, the lecture platform possibly seemed too much like the auction block. The newspaper, like the autobiography or the short story, offered Douglass, as it had Benjamin Franklin, the opportunity to "edit" his own American identity and thus reach a wider audience, white and black. It leads directly into *My Bondage and My Freedom,* defining the public self as a newly revised and more vitally marketed "thing"—a man with property in himself.

In the *Life and Times,* Douglass's longer account of his newspaper career supports Robert Stepto's observation that, when he renamed his paper *Frederick Douglass' Paper* in 1851, Douglass was expressing less his supposed arrogance than his sense of exile and solitude. As he conceived of it, the change is a signal instance of American self-reliance. "I have come to think," he writes in 1881, "that, under the circumstances, it was the best school possible for me," making it "necessary for me to lean upon myself, and not upon the heads of our antislavery church . . . There is nothing like the lash and sting of necessity to make a man work, and my paper furnished the motive power." Like the title of his always popular lecture on **"Self-Made Men,"** this striking metaphorical appropriation of slavery's whip by the work ethic of American success clarifies the doubleness entailed in Douglass's career as a writer and editor. "My feet have been so cracked with frost, that the pen with which I am writing might be laid in the gashes," Douglass writes in a famous passage that appears in all the autobiographies. Not only the voice, but the pen was the key to liberty, no less for black Americans than it had been for the pamphleteers of the Revolutionary period.

During the late 1840s and 1850s, however, Douglass continually chastised free blacks for their comparative lack of interest in abolitionism, and in antislavery papers like his own (eighty percent of his subscribers were white). If blacks were active in the underground railroad or the freeing of fugitive slaves, they were, Douglass argued, unsupportive of freedom's most crucial instruments—public protest and the written word. "They reason thus: Our fathers got along pretty well through the world without learning and without meddling with abolitionism, and we can do the same." But their fathers were not Douglass's father; his father—probably his first master, Aaron Anthony—was almost certainly white. The intricate attitude toward fathers and family in *My Bondage and My Freedom* is directly related to Douglass's growing literacy, his sense of self-reliance, and his imagined role as another Madison Washington. In a typically American gesture, he makes himself his own father. This fictional self is composed at once of the absent father who so absorbs his attention in *My Bondage and My Freedom,* of the black rebel-slave who leads others to freedom and converts a white audience to antislavery, and of the Founding Fathers, whose rhetoric of democratic liberty punctuates Douglass's writing after 1848 and begins fully to flower in the break with Garrison over the proper reading of the Constitution of the United States. The white father-figure who took Douglass as his "text" is replaced by a self-fathered figure combining black and white ideals. The doctrine of self-reliance that will become conspicuous in Douglass's later speeches and autobiography is thus at the center of this creative process insofar as it partakes of the Emersonian impulse to liberate the ego from inherited constraints, to seize and aggrandize the power of domineering ancestors, or their surrogates, in order to fashion one's own paternity.

Because Douglass's act of self-fathering is embedded in the rhetoric and ideals of the Revolutionary fathers, the literacy he says he acquired from reading speeches on the meaning of liberty in *The Columbian Orator,* his first secret textbook, takes on a special tone in *My Bondage and My Freedom.* His characterization of the Irish orator Richard Sheridan's "bold denunciation of slavery and . . . vindication of human rights," as the *Narrative* phrases it, becomes his "powerful denunciation of oppression, and . . . most brilliant vindication of the rights of man." Not the "silver trump of freedom," but "Liberty! the inestimable birthright of every man," now rouses Douglass; and the much extended passage becomes a virtual oration itself, attacking religion as the opiate of the slaves and indulging in rhetoric at once revolutionary and sentimentally gothic: "Knowledge had come; light had penetrated the moral dungeon where I dwelt; and, behold! there lay the bloody whip, for my back, and here was the iron chain; and my good, *kind master,* he was the author of my situation." Modern readers have tended to disparage such language in *My Bondage and My Freedom.* Yet the text reminds us that the revolutionary language of liberation and the abolitionist language of sentiment are virtually synonymous, not just in the best antislavery writing but in many of the era's literary and political treatments of the problem of bondage. Douglass transplants the language of oppression and liberation from the Romantic and Gothic traditions (where it had been a particular spur to Britain's successful antislavery movement), and binds it to the language of American Revolutionary sentiment. In doing so he reimagines the escape from bondage into a world of natural rights as a new confrontation with the paradox of the Founding Fathers' belief that American freedom was compatible with black slavery.

The "author of my situation" in this case is his Baltimore master Hugh Auld, who forbade his wife to continue teaching young Frederick to read. The meaning of Auld's "authority"—his suppression of Douglass's rebellious literate self—is clarified by other revisions Douglass makes in his second version of his life. In teaching Frederick his "A,B,C," "as if I had been her own child," Sophia Auld makes him, as he now recalls it, "master of the alphabet." In his remonstrance Auld predicts not only that a literate slave would quickly become discontent, but that literacy would produce in the slave a dangerous sequence leading him to seize control of his own self: "'If you learn him how to read, he'll want to know how to write; and, this accomplished, he'll be running away with himself.'" This "true philosophy of training a human chattel," Douglass adds in the revised version, was "the first decidedly antislavery lecture to which it had been my lot to listen." Douglass's conception of himself as an object to be stolen, his mastery of the alphabet, Auld's "iron sentences," which stir up his feelings "into a sort of rebellion" and take their place alongside the many references to the "iron rule" of slavery that echo through *My Bondage and My Freedom*—these revisions suggest that Douglass attributes his literacy as much to the "opposition of my master" as to Sophia Auld's initial kindness, and they predict a more vivid struggle that unfolds along paternal, or more accurately, paternalistic, lines. Literacy is linked to the power to enslave and, alternatively, to the power to liberate and hence father oneself. In *My Bondage and My Freedom* Hugh Auld stands emphatically in a sequence of fathers that now includes the abolitionists and the Revolutionary fathers themselves, against all of whom Douglass must work to define himself as though in "opposition to my master."

This autobiographical portrait of the Romantic mind awakened to the Enlightenment language of liberation is duplicated in the scene in *The Heroic Slave* in which Listwell, the white protagonist and soon-to-be antislavery convert, overhears Madison Washington's plaintive soliloquy in the woods:

> A giant's strength, but not a giant's heart was in him. His broad mouth and nose spoke only of good nature and kindness. But his voice, that unfailing index of his soul, though full and melodious, had that in it which could terrify as well as charm. . . . There came another gush from the same full fountain; now bitter, and now sweet. Scathing denunciations of the cruelty and injustice of slavery; heart-touching narrations of his own personal suffering, intermingled with prayers to the God of the oppressed for help and deliverance, were followed by presentations of the dangers and difficulties of escape, and formed the burden of

his eloquent utterances; but his high resolution clung to him,—for he ended each speech by an emphatic declaration of his purpose to be free.

The self-consciousness revealed here, along with the subtle sense of a predominantly sentimental audience, is played upon throughout *My Bondage and My Freedom.* The heroic figure of Madison Washington, like the heroic figure of Frederick Douglass, speaks to an audience open to the double rhetoric of benevolence and liberty, a language both feminine and masculine. In the figure of Madison Washington the hybrid feminine or maternal image of George Washington—inspired by the popular archetype of mothers instructing their children about the nation's father—is joined to the masculine specter of rebellion and terror, the Nat Turner rebel. The double character of sentiment and rebellion that appears in Douglass's short story and in his autobiography, as in other popular antislavery texts like *Uncle Tom's Cabin,* was reflected in different form in the split slave personality—the docile "Sambo" that concealed the rebellious "Nat"—that John Blassingame has identified in accounts of plantation life following the Turner cataclysm in 1831. Douglass's fictional hero and his created autobiographical self combine these two forms of doubleness. In embracing violent slave rebellion Douglass tapped the energy of Romantic liberation and rescued the unfinished task of American freedom, imposing the mask of subversive uprising upon the face of the nation's archetypal father.

. . . . .

The contradictory laws of the southern slaveholding fathers and the northern democratic fathers—agonizingly fused in the Fugitive Slave Law—required of Douglass a complex response that is evident in his treatment of slaveholding paternalism and the problem of his own paternity. The figure of Douglass's lost or unknown father underlies the combined problems of paternalism and self-fathering rebellion that animate Douglass's revised text. The instrument of such self-fathering was language, through which Douglass reshaped his life into the most effective and powerful form in his autobiographies and other public documents. The famous 1848 public letter to Thomas Auld, which first appeared in Garrison's *Liberator* and was then appended to *My Bondage and My Freedom,* falsely charged Auld with a number of brutalities (Douglass later apologized): but Douglass revealed his hand in saying, "I intend to make use of you as a weapon with which to assail the system of slavery—as a means of concentrating public attention on the system, and deepening their horror of trafficking in the souls and bodies of men."

If Douglass seems somewhat less certain about his true paternity in the 1855 text, it is in part because the ambiguity of his origins has itself become a part of his rhetorical strategy: fathers had become a weapon in Douglass's arsenal of literacy. "Genealogical trees do not flourish among slaves," Douglass writes. "A person of some consequence here in the north, sometimes designated *father,* is literally abolished in slave law and practice." The whimsical punning is less overt in a later passage: "I say nothing of *father,* for he is shrouded in a mystery I have never been able to penetrate. Slavery does away with fathers as it does away with families . . . When they *do* exist, they are not the outgrowths of slavery, but are antagonistic to that system." These revisions indicate more than just new uncertainty about his paternity, for his attack on the slaveholder's breeding of new property and on the tragedy of miscegenation and broken families is expanded throughout the volume into a meditation on the corruption of the family by paternalistic power. In the *Narrative,* for example, he had written of the separation of children and mothers, "for what [reason] this separation is done, I do not know, unless it be to hinder the development of the child's affection toward its mother, and to blunt and destroy the natural affection of the mother for the child. This is the inevitable result." But in *My Bondage and My Freedom,* he contends that the practice of separation "is a marked feature of the cruelty and barbarity of the slave system. But it is in harmony with the grand aim of slavery, which, always and everywhere, is to reduce man to a level with the brute. It is a successful method of obliterating from the mind and heart of the slave, all just ideas of the sacredness of *the family,* as an institution." Like the father, the family, its sacred symbolism claimed by North and South alike, takes its place in an ideological conflict that Douglass the public figure can now more accurately judge and use to advantage.

Accordingly, mothers are now carefully juxtaposed to fathers in Douglass's rendering. The extended description of his mother's death in *My Bondage and My Freedom* may reflect his intervening reading of *Uncle Tom's Cabin,* but it does so with full irony: "Scenes of sacred tenderness, around the deathbed, never forgotten, and which often arrest the vicious and confirm the virtuous during life, must be looked for among the free, though they may sometimes occur among the slaves." Because he has "no striking words of hers treasured up," Douglass has to "learn the value of my mother long after her death, and by witnessing the devotion of other mothers to their children." He recollects her image by looking at a picture in *Pritchard's Natural History of Man* (the Egyptian picture of Ramses the Great, which as James McCune Smith notes is markedly European as well). While he learns after her death that his mother could read and thus can attribute his "love of letters . . . *not* to my admitted Anglo-Saxon paternity, but to the native genius of my sable, unprotected, and uncultivated *mother,*" he must still get her teaching from a series of white "mothers"— the kind Lucretia Auld, Sophia Auld, the abolitionist

Julia Griffiths, and now perhaps Harriet Beecher Stowe herself. Douglass deliberately situates his childhood in the domestic tradition of moral instruction, ironically renders it forbidden and subversive, then reconceives of it as part of the antislavery assault on the law of the proslavery fathers. That is to say, Douglass's maternity, whatever priority it takes over his obscure paternity, is nonetheless ambiguous, bordering on the fictional and participating in the literary construction of an ideological family that mediates between Douglass's slaveholding fathers and the flawed tradition of the Revolutionary fathers he sought to redeem.

In his lectures, Douglass often burlesqued the purported paternalism of slavery and held up the slave codes themselves, along with abundant fugitive testimony to the institution's brutality, in counterpoint. He could do so all the more effectively because he saw, as his farewell speech in England had put it, that "the whip, the chain, the gag, the thumb-screw, the bloodhound, the stocks, and all the other bloody paraphernalia of the slave system are indispensably necessary to the relations of master and slave. The slave must be subjected to these, or he ceases to be a slave." Torture or its threat defines the slave's subjection: but for Douglass, as his spiritually liberating fight with the slave breaker Covey suggests, it also comes to define his subjectivity, his liberation from the status of object, of property, of thing. In *My Bondage and My Freedom* the greater attention given to incidents of whipping is therefore not simply a matter of gothic ornamentation, but as in the newly added story of Doctor Isaac Copper, the old slave who teaches slave children the "Our Father" of the Lord's Prayer with whip in hand, demonstrates the infectious power of power, the fact that "everybody, in the South, wants the privilege of whipping somebody else." The whip defines the paternalism of slaveholding and becomes the primary symbol of Douglass's now much more precisely characterized "total institution" of slavery.

One need not accept the much debated thesis that, in its brutal dehumanization of slaves and its power to induce in them an imitative behavioral bondage, the plantation resembled the concentration camp, the prison, or other total institutions, in order to be struck by Douglass's new account of Colonel Lloyd's immense plantation in *My Bondage and My Freedom*. He not only gives a much fuller picture of slave life, but the greater detail and the emphasis on the plantation's self-sufficient, dark seclusion, maintained by diverse labor and trade with Baltimore on Lloyd's own vessels, turn this deceptively abundant, "Eden-like" garden world into a veritable heart of darkness. Both the unusual size of Lloyd's estate and his prominent public place as Maryland's three-time Governor and two-time Senator allow Douglass to expand his own story into an archetype of life under southern slavery's total institution. In this era of reform movements and utopian communal projects, the plantation posed as a pastoral asylum in which state control and paternal coercion in fact imprisoned the slave in a corrupt "family"—one he might belong to by blood but not by law—and fused the theory of chattel slavery with the sexuality of power. The apotheosis of the total institution of slavery lay for Douglass in this "double relation of master and father," as he called it in the *Narrative* before making it the defining figure of *My Bondage and My Freedom*.

Only outside the peculiar institution could Douglass see its totality and its paternalistic power at full play; similarly, only in the 1850s could he see himself as a self-fathered subject, subject now to the equally contradictory paternal institutions of radical antislavery and Revolutionary America. The range of paternal figures whom Douglass contrasts to the master-father figure of the plantation is striking. The new invocations of Nat Turner in *My Bondage and My Freedom* suggest, as do a number of Douglass's speeches, that his new heroes would not simply be white patriots but, like Joseph Cinque and Madison Washington, black patriots as well. In his greatest instance of ironic oratory, the Fourth of July address of 1852, Douglass places himself outside the American dream but within the circle of the post-Revolutionary generation's principal rhetoric: "It is the birthday of your National Independence, and of your political freedom . . . Your fathers have lived, died, and have done their work, and have done much of it well. You live and must die, and you must do your work. You have no right to enjoy a child's share in the labor of your fathers, unless your children are to be blessed by your labors." As George Forgie has argued, the entrapments of perpetual union and perpetual youth induced in the post-Revolutionary generation a paralysis on the issue of slavery that was not broken until Lincoln, a figure equal to the Fathers' heroic stature, embraced and overcame the Fathers at the same time, saving the union and abolishing slavery. As Douglass spoke, however, Lincoln was still following the moderate proslavery course of Henry Clay's Compromise of 1850, as he would for nearly another decade. Douglass, who derided Clay upon his death in 1852 as a man-stealer who did "more than any man in this country to make slavery perpetual," was at that time—perhaps always—a truer son of the Revolutionary generation than Lincoln. While proslavery ideologues like Thomas Dew and James Henry Hammond warned that abolitionist propaganda would tear down the slave "family" and its paternal structure of protection, making slaves *parricides* instead of *patriots*"—as Dew warned after Turner's revolt—Douglass said it could make them both. For the slave in particular, the post-Revolutionary anxiety over the intent of the Founding Fathers could not be separated from personal fatherhood and, more to the point, from the impulse to self-fathering freedom.

The tendency for *My Bondage and My Freedom* to become an oration does not destroy its coherence, for the moments in which oratory is most evident are often those in which Douglass's new paternal ideology is most strongly espoused. The passage on the ethics of stealing now leads to the assertion that if the slave steals, "he takes his own; if he kills his master, he imitates only the heroes of the revolution." In the most dramatic event of Douglass's life story, his fight with the brutal slave-breaker Covey, the tone of the expanded exclamation of freedom is altered by certain phrases—"embers of liberty," "the unjust and cruel aggressions of a tyrant," and "manly independence"—which appeal to international democratic ideals and differentiate the incident from the then widely popular capitulation of Uncle Tom to the murderous whip of Simon Legree. Most strikingly, Douglass accuses the slaveholder of violating "the just and inalienable rights of man" and thereby "silently whetting the knife of vengeance for his own throat. He never lisps a syllable in commendation of the fathers of this republic, nor denounces any attempted oppression of himself, without inviting the knife to his own throat, and asserting the rights of rebellion for his own slaves." Replacing the lost slaveholding father with the rebel-fathers who authorize parricide in the name of freedom, and replacing his lost literate mother with the tradition of antislavery rhetoric, at once fiery and sentimental, *My Bondage and My Freedom* portrays the rebel-patriot Frederick Douglass as a figure who merges the urgency of eloquent personal facts and the heroic text of a national ideal.

. . . . .

Douglass continually declared himself a man, not a thing, a man, not a child. Freedom and the new powers of literacy it offered countered the fear he experienced on his second arrival at Hugh Auld's in Baltimore when he saw how little Tommy Auld, whose copybooks Douglass had imitated in learning to write, had begun to acquire the habits of adult slaveholding, aware of his place and his power: "He could grow, and become a MAN; I could grow, though I could *not* become a man, but must remain, all my life, a minor—a mere boy." It is not surprising that this passage should be added to *My Bondage and My Freedom,* for Douglass's own growth between 1845 and 1855 must have seemed to him a new phase of maturation that left behind the boy orator of Nantucket. Still, Douglass's life would entail a continued fight for the manhood of his race against the paternalism that prevailed in American custom.

The rhetorical form of that fight was predicted in Douglass's response in 1859 to the voters' rejection of a New York state amendment granting blacks nondiscriminatory voting rights, even as they cast ballots in favor of Lincoln's presidency. "We were overshadowed and smothered by the presidential struggle—overlaid by Abraham Lincoln and Hannibal Hamlin," Douglass wrote. "The black baby of Negro Suffrage was thought too ugly to exhibit on so grand an occasion. The Negro was stowed away like some people put out of sight their deformed children when company comes." It was Douglass's fate, of course, to remain overshadowed by Lincoln, despite his frequent criticism of the president for failing to act more resolutely on the issue of black troops, colonization, emancipation, and civil rights. Douglass's struggle to effect the Negro's "full and complete adoption into the national family of America," as he put it in 1863, employed familial rhetoric in the only logical way, in which the Negro "child" confronted the white "father." Whatever his awareness of the doubleness of his own meanings, perhaps Douglass himself could not have said whether such language was a compromise with racism or instead acted ironically to subvert it. Neither Lincoln's open and generous manner on the two occasions he sought Douglass's advice nor Douglass's appointment to prominent positions by later Republican presidents could make that adoption completely meaningful.

Douglass's own ambivalence can best be seen in the terms by which he memorialized Lincoln at the dedication of the Freedman's Lincoln Monument in 1876. The monument, paid for primarily by the contributions of black veterans, was unveiled on 14 April, the anniversary both of Lincoln's assassination and of the emancipation of slaves in the District of Columbia. Grant and his cabinet, the Supreme Court justices, and other dignitaries listened as Douglass declared that "when the foul reproach of ingratitude is hurled at us, and it is attempted to scourge us beyond the range of human brotherhood, we may calmly point to the monument we have this day erected to the memory of Abraham Lincoln." But this moderate and gracious conclusion suspends a more critical tone in the body of the address, a tone in which Douglass seems to be measuring his own relationship with Lincoln. Was Lincoln "tardy, cold, dull, and indifferent," or "swift, zealous, radical, and determined?" Douglass posed a question historians have not yet answered to satisfaction, and a similar one would later be asked about Douglass himself. Douglass no doubt identified with Lincoln the self-made man, who studied his "English Grammar by the uncertain flare and glare of the light made by a pine-knot," the "son of toil himself [who] was linked in brotherly sympathy with the sons of toil in every loyal part of the Republic." But he stood apart from Lincoln even so: "It must be admitted, truth compels me to admit, even here in the presence of the monument we have erected to his memory, Abraham Lincoln was not, in the fullest sense of the word, either our man or our model. In his interests, in his associations, in his habits of thought, and in his prejudices, he was a white man." "You," Douglass said, returning to the divisive rhetoric he had employed in such powerful forms as the Fourth of July address, "You are the children of Abraham Lincoln. We are at best only his step-children; children by adoption, children by forces of circumstance and necessity."

Freedom's step-children, even Lincoln's step-children: Douglass probes the limits of paternalistic rhetoric even as he accepts a familiar role. Conceivably, Lincoln had become a new weapon in Douglass's arsenal; and yet the subversive power of his literacy was in this case circumscribed and contained by the ritual necessities of the occasion. Douglass later confessed that he did not like Thomas Ball's design for the monument, which may itself have inspired his metaphor of the step-child. The statue, in Benjamin Quarles's words, "revealed Lincoln in a standing position, holding in his right hand the Emancipation Proclamation, while his left hand was poised above a slave whom he gazed upon. The slave was represented in a rising position with one knee still on the ground. The shackles on his wrists were broken. At the base of the monument the word 'EMANCIPATION' was carved." What, then, are we to make of the fact that Douglass appended the speech to his third autobiography, the 1881 *Life and Times?* The matter might seem inconsequential were it not that Douglass's appendices reveal an interesting pattern. In his early oratorical mode, the notorious appendix to the *Narrative* attacks the relations between American church and American slavery with vicious irony; the appendices to *My Bondage and My Freedom* consist of extracts from Douglass's public letter to Thomas Auld, the Fourth of July address, and other documents from the phase of Revolutionary fervor in his thought from 1848 through the war; and the Lincoln Monument speech shows Douglass at his most formal and public, ambiguously embracing America's martyred hero even while resisting him, just as Lincoln himself had both embraced and overthrown the Founding Fathers. Lincoln became for Douglass the last father with whom he would have to struggle, conscious all the while of the continued "double consciousness" that defined him, perhaps now more than ever, as both a Negro and an American, two souls—two bloods—at war in one body.

The spirit of "self-reliance, self-respect, industry, perseverance, and economy" that Douglass urges on his black audience at the end of the *Life and Times* has led commentators to dub him a "Negro edition of Ben Franklin" or a "black Horatio Alger." Rightly seen, Douglass's acceptance of the American enterprise of self-making begins at least as early as the *North Star;* and Smith's preface to *My Bondage and My Freedom* praises Douglass's "self-elevation" from the barbarism of slavery and calls him "a Representative American man—a type of his countrymen," bearing "upon his person and upon his soul every thing that is American." Douglass's American odyssey surely reaches a climax when he inserts into the 1881 version of his life a copy of a Rochester newspaper's description of

a commemorative bust of Douglass placed in the University of Rochester. The notice praises Douglass as one who has seized the opportunities the Republic "offers to self-made men," despite his severe trials as a fugitive, and celebrates him as the eloquent redeemer and deliverer of his race. It makes him, one might say, comparable to—justly equal to—Lincoln, his brother, not his step-child. Douglass is now able to look upon himself as a public figure, even a public monument about which public opinion and encomium, no doubt coincidental with his own, can be quoted. Having created a final public self out of the overcome texts of the past, Douglass has become no mere boy but one of the fathers he had worked at such cost to be.

FURTHER READING

Andrews, William L., ed. *Critical Essays on Frederick Douglass.* Boston: G. K. Hall & Co., 1991, 217 p.
    Comprehensive collection of essays on Douglass, including early reviews and modern scholarship from such critics as Margaret Fuller, J. Saunders Redding, Henry Louis Gates, Jr., Houston A. Baker, Jr., and Robert B. Stepto.

Dorsey, Peter A. "Becoming the Other: The Mimesis of Metaphor in Douglass's *My Bondage and My Freedom.*" *PMLA* 111, No. 3 (May 1996): 435-50.
    Examines Douglass's use of rhetoric in his second autobiographical account.

Evans, James H., Jr. "Sin and the Stain of Blackness: The Autobiography of Frederick Douglass." In *Spiritual Empowerment in Afro-American Literature: Frederick Douglass, Rebecca Jackson, Booker T. Washington, Richard Wright, Toni Morrison,* pp. 23-52. Lewiston, N.Y.: The Edwin Mellen Press, 1987.
    Discusses psychological and socio-political aspects of Douglass's *Narrative,* including issues of freedom, self-discovery, and the crisis of identity.

Fishkin, Shelley Fisher, and Carla L. Peterson. "'We Hold These Truths to Be Self-Evident': The Rhetoric of Frederick Douglass's Journalism." In *Frederick Douglass: New Literary and Historical Essays,* edited by Eric J. Sundquist, pp. 189-204. Cambridge, England: Cambridge University Press, 1990.
    Explores the rhetorical strategies of Douglass's social and political writings.

Foner, Philip S., ed. *Frederick Douglass on Women's Rights.* Westport, Conn.: Greenwood Press, 1976, 190 p.
    Selection of Douglass's writings and speeches on women's rights issues.

Franchot, Jenny. "The Punishment of Esther: Frederick Douglass and the Construction of the Feminine." In

Frederick Douglass: New Literary and Historical Essays, edited by Eric J. Sundquist, pp. 141-65. Cambridge, England: Cambridge University Press, 1990.

> Studies Douglass's placement of the victimized feminine at "the emotional center of his critique on slavery."

Gates, Henry Louis, Jr. "Frederick Douglass and the Language of the Self." In *Figures in Black: Words, Signs, and the "Racial" Self,* pp. 98-124. New York: Oxford University Press, 1989.

> Examines Douglass's strategies of public self-representation.

McFeely, William S. *Frederick Douglass.* New York: W. W. Norton & Company, 1991, 465 p.

> Standard modern biography of Douglass.

Meyer, Michael, ed. *Frederick Douglass: The Narrative and Selected Writings.* New York: Random House, Inc., 1984, 391 p.

> Collection of excerpts from Douglass's autobiographies, journalism, and fiction, preceded by a biographical introduction.

Olney, James. "The Founding Fathers—Frederick Douglass and Booker T. Washington." In *Slavery and the Literary Imagination,* pp. 1-24. Baltimore: Johns Hopkins University Press, 1989.

> Explores the relationship between the autobiographies of Douglass and Washington by examining them in their literary, cultural, and historical contexts.

Quarles, Benjamin. "Abolition's Different Drummer: Frederick Douglass." In *The Antislavery Vanguard: New Essays on the Abolitionists,* edited by Martin Duberman, pp. 123-34. Princeton, N.J.: Princeton University Press, 1965.

> Recounts Douglass's contribution to the abolitionist movement.

Ripley, Peter. "The Autobiographical Writings of Frederick Douglass." *Southern Studies* XXIV, No. 1 (Spring 1985): 5-29.

Focuses on the historical background to each of Douglass's three autobiographies.

Rogers, William B. "Frederick Douglass." In *"We Are All Together Now": Frederick Douglass, William Lloyd Garrison, and The Prophetic Tradition,* pp. 87-129. New York: Garland Publishing, Inc., 1995.

> Opening with a brief biography of Douglass's life, discusses his personal values, criticism of slavery, and efforts to bring about constitutional reform on race issues.

Sundquist, Eric J., ed. *Frederick Douglass: New Literary and Historical Essays.* Cambridge: Cambridge University Press, 1990, 295 p.

> Assortment of contemporary critical perspectives on Douglass's writings.

——. "Signs of Power: Nat Turner and Frederick Douglass." In *To Wake the Nations: Race and the Making of American Literature,* pp. 27-134. Cambridge, Mass.: Harvard University Press, 1993.

> Investigates developments in Douglass's thoughts on and literary portrayal of slavery.

Takaki, Ronald T. "Not Afraid to Die: Frederick Douglass and Violence." In *Violence in the Black Imagination: Essays and Documents,* pp. 17-35. New York: G. P. Putnam's Sons, 1972.

> Examination of Douglass's often ambivalent attitude toward the use of violence in achieving black emancipation.

Yarborough, Richard. "Race, Violence, and Manhood: The Masculine Ideal in Frederick Douglass's 'The Heroic Slave.'" In *Frederick Douglass: New Literary and Historical Essays,* edited by Eric J. Sundquist, pp. 166-88. Cambridge University Press, 1990.

> Considers the problems associated with Douglass's incorporation of an Anglo-American ideal of masculinity into his narrative of Afro-American rebellion.

Additional coverage of Douglass's life and career is contained in the following sources published by Gale Research: *Black Literature Criticism; DISCovering Authors;* and *Dictionary of Literary Biography,* **Volume 1:** *The American Renaissance in New England,* **Volume 43:** *American Newspaper Journalists, 1690-1872,* **Volume 50:** *Afro-American Writers before the Harlem Renaissance,* **Volume 79:** *American Magazine Journalists, 1850-1900.*

Edgar Allan Poe

1809-1849

American short story writer, poet, critic, editor, novelist, and essayist.

The following entry presents criticism of Poe's essays. For further information on Poe's complete career, see *NCLC*, Volume 1, and for a detailed discussion of Poe as a short story writer, see *NCLC*, Volume 16.

INTRODUCTION

Though Poe's fame rests primarily on his brilliant short stories, he is also a major figure in the field of literary criticism. His fictional inventiveness is matched by his theoretical innovations, which not only provided a justification for his creation of the genres of science fiction and the detective story, but also attempted to create a tradition of uniquely American literary criticism that would free the American literary world from its colonial dependence on England. Though the rigid standards demanded by Poe in his construction of a worthy national literature alienated many of his contemporaries, he is now recognized as an influential figure in the development of American as well as European literary traditions.

Biographical Information

Born in Boston in 1809 to an English actress, Poe was left an orphan before the age of three. He was brought up by his foster parents, John and Frances Allan, in Richmond, Virginia. His early life was therefore spent as part of the southern gentry. He distinguished himself academically both at school and at the university, but his expectations to live the life of a southern gentleman were compromised by his deteriorating relationship with John Allan, which left him in a financially precarious position. In 1827 Poe left Richmond and went to Boston in an attempt to create an independent life for himself. He enlisted in the army and simultaneously published his first book of poetry, *Tamerlane, and Other Poems*, which did not earn him any literary recognition. After being honorably discharged from the army in 1829, he entered West Point with Allan's consent. But Allan's continued refusal to allow him sufficient funds to maintain himself, combined now with his refusal to allow Poe to resign from the Academy, forced Poe to gain a dismissal by deliberately violating regulations. Left once more to fend for himself, Poe went to New York and then to Baltimore, and tried to become a part of the successful literary circle centered in New England. However, though several of his short stories were published, he was unable to gain either literary recognition or financial security.

In 1835, a year after Allan's death, Poe moved back to Richmond and became the editor of the *Southern Literary Messenger*. This marked the beginning of his career as a literary critic. For the next decade, though he continued to publish short stories and poetry, his chief occupation remained that of a journalist. However, this professional consistency did not ensure financial stability since literary journalism was not a well-paying field. Furthermore, Poe's strong critical opinions frequently generated conflict with magazine proprietors who wanted to retain editorial control over their publications. As a result, he was forced to move from magazine to magazine in search of a better income and more critical freedom. After being dismissed from the *Messenger* in 1837, he worked for *Burton's*

Gentleman's Magazine from 1839 to 1840. He then moved to *Graham's Magazine* (1841-42), and finally to the *Broadway Journal,* where he worked as chief editor until early 1846, when the journal folded. Though he constantly dreamed of launching his own magazine, the closest he came to fulfilling this ambition was to become the proprietor of the *Broadway Journal* for a short time. He could not, however, make the magazine as successful as he wished—his capabilities as an editor were undercut by his limitations as a business manager.

Major Works

Since Poe's critical output is largely in the form of journalistic essays prompted by specific events of literary publication, it is difficult to point to any single work as being central to his literary theory. As a book reviewer, Poe commented upon a wide range of literary works ranging from Longfellow's *Ballads* to Dickens's *Old Curiosity Shop.* At the same time, he also wrote purely theoretical pieces like "The Poetic Principle" and "The Philosophy of Composition." These two kinds of critical writings are closely interrelated, since the general literary principles developed by Poe in his theoretical essays provided the basis for his critical judgments in his book reviews. Poe thus functioned as a working critic who constantly tested his literary principles against the touchstone of actual literary productions.

Three of Poe's central critical tenets are unity, the creation of a total effect, and originality. Poe's concept of unity differs from the traditional Aristotelian idea of dramatic unity in terms of time, space, and action. For Poe, a unified literary work is one in which every detail, with respect to both style and content, directly contributes to the creation of the total effect of the piece. This emphasis on unity leads to a number of corollary literary principles—the rejection of any verbal ornamentation that merely display the writer's virtuosity without adding intrinsically to the total effect, the preference for shorter works like the lyric and the short story over the longer epic or novel, since the latter are too bulky to allow for such tight construction, and the importance of maintaining generic purity. The focus on unity also leads to Poe's characterization of the artistic process as a self-conscious act of almost mechanical construction; his "Philosophy of Composition" is, in fact, a methodical presentation of the steps involved in the construction of his poem "The Raven." According to Poe, only such careful manipulation of literary raw material can ensure the totality of effect that is the trademark of any good piece of literature.

For Poe, the primary aim of any literary work is to create a mood or an atmosphere that allows the reader to experience the "probable but impossible." Such an affective view of literature does not allow any scope for the utilitarian perspective that dominated the American literary scene during most of the nineteenth century. Poe's ideas on this subject are formulated in oppositional terms which often lead to extremist statements like his "heresy of the Didactic," wherein he denounces all literary works whose chief concerns are moral rather than aesthetic. This view should be distinguished, however, from the later ideas of Oscar Wilde and English aestheticism, since Poe did recognize the presence of moral truth at the core of the best literature. In his more mature and balanced criticism Poe is able to reconcile the moral and the affective aspects of literature and praises works wherein the former is carefully woven into the fabric of the overall literary effect.

Poe's attack on didacticism in literature forms a part of his reviews of Longfellow's poetry. These reviews also contain Poe's controversial views on artistic originality and plagiarism. Poe's eagerness to expose alleged cases of literary plagiarism has frequently led to accusations of psychological instability, and numerous Poe scholars have attempted to explain this obsession with reference to his personal life. Poe's extremely complex definition of originality makes it one of his most knotty critical concepts. However, in the context of his avowed desire to create a uniquely American literary tradition and his view of literature as a reflection of the unperceived "Ideal" rather than a mimetic reproduction of the natural world, Poe's concept of originality can be seen as an integral part of his overall theoretical perspective, rather than as evidence of a psychological aberration.

Critical Reception

Contemporary reception of Poe as a literary critic is marked by controversy and ambiguity. While recognized as an astute editor whose perceptive reviews significantly increased the circulation of the *Southern Literary Messenger,* Poe also aroused strongly negative reactions through his harshly critical reviews that frequently included personal remarks and accusations of plagiarism. During his lifetime he achieved a degree of notoriety during the "Longfellow war," when his attacks on the unofficial poet laureate of America generated a tremendous controversy. Certain scholars perceive this conflict in terms of a North-South division and view Poe as the representative of a southern literary tradition fighting against the domination of the New England literary circle. While southern men of letters did eagerly claim Poe as their literary ancestor in the post-bellum period, such sectarian sentiments did not enable any careful analysis of Poe's critical writings. In the twentieth century there have been numerous attempts to re-evaluate Poe's position in the history of literary criticism. Most scholars see him as the American spokesperson for Romanticism and argue that his emphasis on originality and aesthetics, along with his open admiration for Shelley and Keats, clearly places him in the tradition of English Romanticism. Others, focusing on Poe's scientific predilections in *Eureka* and his very rational perception of literary production, view him as a successor to the Enlightenment. While Poe may not fit neatly into any preconceived category of literary criticism, and though scholars continue to debate the value of his theoretical contributions, he remains an important critical figure who has left an undeniable mark on American literary criticism.

*PRINCIPAL WORKS

"Letter to Mr. ———, in 1831." (criticism) 1831
Marginalia. (criticism) 1846
The Philosophy of Composition. (essay) 1846
"The Poetic Principle." (essay) 1848
Eureka: A Prose Poem (essay) 1848
The Literati: Some Honest Opinions about Authorial Merits and Demerits, with Occasional Works of Personality. (criticism) 1850

*This list includes Poe's nonfiction works. For a complete list of Poe's major writings, see *NCLC,* Volume 1.

CRITICISM

John Esten Cooke (essay date 1851-1852?)

SOURCE: "Poe as a Literary Critic," in *Poe as a Literary Critic,* edited by N. Bryllion Fagin, The Johns Hopkins Press, 1946, pp. 1-15.

[*The following essay is a contemporary unpublished critique of Poe as a literary critic which was found and published by Fagin in 1946. The essay condemns Poe as a petty, self-contradictory critic who had no literary standards and who used his book reviews to air his personal likes and dislikes.*]

In the latter part of 1849 the citizens of Richmond, Virginia, saw passing to and fro in the street a notable-looking stranger whose personal appearance at once invited attention. He was a man a little under the medium height, slender, active, graceful in all his movements, and with quiet and scrupulously courteous manner. The face was a singular one. As he passed, you unconsciously turned round to look again at him. The complexion was pale, almost sallow. The brow was broad, rather than high, and edged by short dark hair circling around the temples which were strongly developed. The eyes were dark and piercing; the nose

well shaped; the upper lip disappeared under a heavy black mustache which concealed the entire expression of the mouth. His dress was plain, neat, and in perfectly good taste.

This notable personage was the famous Edgar A. Poe, the author of **"The Raven,"** of a wonderful series of *Tales of the Grotesque and Arabesque* and of some of the fiercest, most savage, and most unfair literary criticism ever published in America. He was then on his last visit to Richmond, where he had commenced his literary career nearly twenty years before as editor of the *Southern Literary Messenger,* and the object of his visit was to deliver his lecture on **"The Poetic Principle,"** which I had the pleasure of hearing. The lecturer stood in a graceful attitude, leaning one hand on a small table beside him, and his wonderfully clear and musical voice speedily brought the audience under its spell. Those who heard this strange voice once, never afterwards forgot it. It was certainly unlike any other that I have ever listened to: and the exquisite, if objectionable "sing-song," as he repeated **"The Raven,"** Hood's "Fair Inez" and other verse, resembled music. It would be impossible indeed to convey any idea of the manner in which he uttered the line from Shelley "I arise from dreams of thee," or of his low and awestruck tones full of nameless horror, when he repeated from his **"Raven"**

> And the silken sad uncertain rustling of each
>   purple curtain
> Filled me, thrilled me with fantastic terrors
>   never felt before!

The lecture ended in the midst of applause, and Poe disappeared soon afterwards, going northward—to fall a victim in Baltimore to disease and die suddenly.

Each chance encounter with remarkable persons is apt to individualize one's views concerning them; and the personnel of a human being generally illustrates his mental and moral character. In the case of Mr. Poe this rule seemed to be reversed. He impressed you as a gentle, kindly and altogether amiable person, and yet—to sum up the truth concerning him in a single phrase—he was none of these. But with his mere personal character and his shifting, unsettled career, this paper has no concern.

Of his literary character however we have a right to speak, and may do so without being charged with malice or unkindness. Every author surrenders his intellectual organization as manifested in his published writings to the scrutiny of the world; and the "critical" writings of Mr. Poe are so much the more fairly amenable to this nomination and dissection, since he was himself a most bitter and unscrupulous critic, sparing nobody, and scattering on all sides the poisoned and flaming arrows of his invective.

In this character—that of the literary critic—Mr. Poe seems not to have attracted proportionate attention. His wonderful genius as a weird poet, and story teller, has dazzled everybody. Of these poems and narratives— **"The Raven," "Lenore," "Annabel Lee," "The Gold Bug," "The Fall of the House of Usher," "Ligeia"** and other strange fictions—there can be but one opinion: that they are the productions of a remarkable mind. They in fact elude description—especially the prose narratives—and are a "new sensation." For a wondrous power of analysis, a weird and strange fancy, and a startling combination of the supernatural and the matter-of-fact, they are probably unsurpassed, if indeed they have been equalled by any other writer in any country. They are *sui generis* and "due to none." The bitterest enemies of the author—and he had some as bitter as ever man had—were and are compelled to recognize in these works the presence of a vast and sombre genius, unclassified and defying classification.

Such a classification is certainly not meant to be attempted here. The object of this brief paper will be to speak of Mr. Poe as a literary critic, in which character he is far more intelligible—and certainly an altogether different personage. In his poems and wild narratives— take as an illustration **"Arthur Gordon Pym"**—he is a sort of Merlin wandering away into the strange world of dreams, and his figure is lost sight of in mists peopled with phantoms, evoked by a wave of his shadowy wand. In his literary criticisms he is Mr. Edgar A. Poe of Philadelphia or New York, a man of flesh and blood, a commonplace editor of commonplace journals, with bitter dislikes, strong admirations; a writer of squibs; ambitious of praise from people far inferior to him; a warm friend sometimes—often a bitter enemy. To those unacquainted with Mr. Poe's writings these charges may seem exaggerated and unkind. Unfortunately they are just, and are stated less strongly than the truth would warrant. It is impossible to read the series of criticisms collected in his works under the title *The Literati,* and fail to see that invective is the author's favorite style. He searches for weak points in every writer, completely discarding, it would seem, the just maxim that true criticism is appreciation; and when the failing is found, the critic pounces upon it with obvious pleasure, enforces it without mercy, and generally winds up his criticism with some stinging jest full of bitterness and contempt for the writer he is reviewing. You read all this with a sort of wonder, asking yourself why Mr. Poe assumed this Ishmael-like character. He was charged with envy indeed—which seems incredible in a man of such genius—and one who knew him well and admired him greatly said that his cheek grew pale at praise of others.

Another explanation is that he fancied a critic should be severe, and we certainly find in his *Literati* a prevailing tone of depreciation, and the severity of a judge reciting the crimes of a prisoner before pronouncing sentence. Take an example or two. Of Mr. William Ellery Channing's poems, he writes—"His book contains about sixty three things which he calls poems, and which he no doubt seriously supposes so to be. They are full of all kinds of mistakes, of which the most important is that of their having been printed at all!" This would seem to be a sufficient annihilation of the unfortunate Mr. Channing, but his critic adds that the poet is of the "Bobby Button School" and that "nobody ever heard of him." Mr. Poe's critical notices abound in similar sneers, in which the writer seems struggling to express his contempt. Often the hostility is conveyed in a phrase, or negligent "fling" at his subject, as where he gravely speaks of "Mr. Thomas Dunn *Brown*"—not even hinting at the fact that he is referring to Mr. Thomas Dunn *English*. Over Mr. Headley's work on the Sacred Mountains of Holy Writ he makes merry, after a grim fashion: representing the author as standing up gravely and solemnly before each famous mountain and *making a speech* about it!

His commendation of certain writers seemed to be arbitrary and to result from personal feeling, like his denunciation. He praised warmly sometimes, but there was no certainty that he would not denounce the same book or author a month afterwards, or commend after assailing. Quoting the criticism of an English writer that Bulwer was "the most accomplished writer of the most accomplished era of English letters," he says "Mr. Ward . . . could never have put to paper in his sober senses anything as absurd as the paragraph quoted above, without stopping at every third word to hold his sides or thrust his pocket handkerchief into his mouth. As a novelist Bulwer is far more than respectable, though *generally* inferior to Scott, Godwin, D'Israeli, Miss Burney, Sue, Dumas, Dickens, the author of *Ellen Wareham* and the author of *Jane Eyre* and several others. From the list of foreign novels I could select a hundred which he could neither have written or conceived. . . . His 'Athens' has all the happy air of an Etonian prize-essay, revamped. His essays leave no doubt on anybody's mind that they are essays indeed. His criticism is really beneath contempt."

This would seem to indicate Mr. Poe's opinion of Lord Lytton with distinctness: but he returns to the subject and writes—"We have long learned to reverence the fine intellect of Bulwer. We take up any production of his pen with a positive certainty that, in reading it, the wildest passions of our nature, the profoundest of our thoughts, the brightest visions of our fancy, and the most ennobling and lofty of our aspirations will, in due time, be enkindled within us. From the brief tale to the most ponderous and labored of his novels all is richly and glowingly intellectual—all is energetic, or astute, or brilliant, or profound. . . . Viewing him as a novelist he is unsurpassed by any writer living or dead. Who is there uniting in one person the imagination, the passion, the humor, the energy, the knowledge of the heart, the artist-like eye, the originality, the fancy, and the learning of Edward Lytton Bulwer? In a vivid wit—in profundity and a Gothic massiveness of thought, in style—in a calm certainty and definiteness of purpose—in industry—and above all in the power of controlling and regulating by volition his illimitable faculties of mind—he is unequalled—he is unapproached."

Was Mr. Poe jesting?

In his desultory career as a magazine writer—in which he often forgot today what he wrote yesterday—Mr. Poe occasionally betrayed some of the secrets of his literary work-shop, and laid bare to the public the heart of his own mystery. In **"How to Write a *Blackwood* Article"** he makes the editor of that magazine say to Miss Psyche Zenobia, the aspiring authoress, "Above all it is necessary that your article have an air of erudition, or at least afford evidence of extensive general reading. I'll put you in the way of accomplishing this point. See here!—by casting your eye down almost any page of any book in the world, you will be able to perceive at once a host of little scraps of either learning or *bel-espirit-ism,* which are the very thing for the spicing of a Blackwood article. You might as well note down a few while I read them to you. I shall make two divisions; first, *Piquant Facts for the Manufacture of Similes;* and second, *Piquant Expressions to be introduced as occasion may require.* . . . You may make a great deal of that little fact. You see, it is not generally known, and looks *recherché.* You must be careful and give the thing with a downright improviso air!"

This advice, satirically attributed to Mr. Blackwood, Mr. Poe gravely followed, as his voluminous notebooks, ***Marginalia*** and other similar collections of scraps indicate. He seems to have carefully gleaned from almost every book which he read, whatever might prove useful to him—in which there was certainly nothing to find fault with—and these facts, quotations, and "little scraps" he afterwards introduced into his writings with the "downright improviso air" which he recommends. His object seems to have been to attain the reputation of a man of vast reading and erudition. An instance is given:

> Now the words of Ezekiel are—*Venathati eth-har Seir lesh immanah ushemamah vehichrati mimmennu over vasal:* literally *Venathati,* and I will give; *eth-har,* the mountain; *Seir,* Seir, etc. I am sustained in the translation of *over vasal* by Gesenius S 5—vol 2—p. 570, *Leo's Trans.* There is something analogous in the Hebrew-Greek phrase at Acts, 9:28 (the Greek passage is quoted). The Latin *versatus est* is precisely paraphrastic."—"He must use a silk cord as they do in Spain with all grandees of the blue blood, the *sangre azula.*"—"*Pour* savoir ce qu'est Dieu," says Belefeld, "il faut être Dieu même."

These extracts are taken from two consecutive pages, and convey the impression that Mr. Poe was familiar with Hebrew, Greek, Latin, Spanish, and French—which is doubtful. He probably enjoyed the grave discussion of the Hebrew passage in Ezekiel, and laughed as he intimated that he was *sustained by Gesenius!* Of this industrious manner in which he used his voluminous notebooks, introducing their contents with the "downright improviso air" of a writer drawing on his memory, only, his works generally contain the evidence.

Nothing pleased this man of genius, busying himself with small things, more than minute criticism and dissection of the style of some eminent writer. He seemed to relish highly this apparent sitting in judgment. The tone of the judge addressing the criminal was pleasant to him. "This passage," he seemed to say, "appears to you, Sir, who read it carelessly, a very fine passage indeed—but let me show you how blundering it is, and how easily I could improve it." An instance is given in which he arraigns Lord Macaulay at the bar. The following paragraph from Macaulay is selected for dissection:

> Government is to Mr. Southey one of the fine arts. He judges of a theory as a public measure, of a religion, a political party, a peace or a war, as men judge of a picture or a statue, by the effect produced on his imagination. A chain of associations is to him what a chain of reasoning is to other men; and what he calls his opinions are in fact merely his tastes.

This passage will probably be regarded as sufficiently clear, vigorously written, and if marked by the mannerism of its great author, still excellent English. Mr. Poe considers it "inaccurate, pleonastic, awkward, unpleasant and faulty"; passes each phrase of the paragraph in review; and declares that it should have been written thus:—

> With Southey governing is a fine art. Of a theory or a public measure—of a creed, a political party, a peace or a war—he judges by the imaginative effect; as only such things as pictures or statues are judged of by other men. What to them a chain of reasoning is, to him is a chain of association; and as to his opinions they are nothing but his tastes.

It is scarcely necessary to say that the original is more vigorous—it is certainly better English. To judge by *the imaginative effect* is an undesirable change of *"the effect produced on his imagination"*;—*and what to them a chain of reasoning is* violates the idiom of the language, and is certainly "awkward and unpleasant":—terms applied by Mr. Poe to the original.

This brief criticism of a critic has not been inspired by malevolence or any desire to detract from Mr. Poe's personal or literary reputation generally. His personal character has been scarcely touched upon; and the absurdest of all absurd things would be to call in question the genius of the man who wrote the **"Raven," "The Gold Bug"** and **"The Murders in the Rue Morgue."** Had Mr. Poe confined himself to poetry and the realm of weird fiction he would have remained an unapproachable master, ruling the domain of Wonderland without a rival. He did not confine himself to this high ground of letters, but descended into the valley to busy himself with the petty spites and rivalries of the hour, as a literary critic. He chose this character of a severe critic and assailed everybody. It is only fair that he should be criticised in turn, as a critic.

John Brooks Moore (essay date 1926)

SOURCE: Introduction to *Selections from Poe's Literary Criticism,* F. S. Crofts & Co., 1926, pp. vii-xix.

[*In the following essay, Moore argues that Poe's main ambition was to be a magazine proprietor. He therefore examines Poe primarily as a journalist who was committed to the growth of the American magazine culture and, through it, the construction of an American literary criticism distinct from the English critical tradition.*]

> As soon as Fate allows I will have a magazine of my own, and will endeavor to kick up a dust.

> —Poe to P. P. Cook, 1839.

I

That Poe was apparently first of all a journalist—neither a poet nor a writer of fiction—cannot well be doubted. Those of his contemporaries who knew him and left some record of their knowledge almost invariably owed their acquaintance with Poe to his journalistic activities of one sort or another. It is safest to say he was *apparently* first a journalist, for some of his biographers and students treat him as though he were primarily lover, or poet, or solitary dreamer. In examining the much-vexed treatments of Poe, it is necessary to proceed with some method. There are about Poe and his works books that may be called possible only, books that may be called probable, books that may be called actual. Woodberry's biography of Poe remains, after all psycho-analytical flurries, the *actual* book about Poe; while the heralded *Edgar Allan Poe* of J. W. Krutch wavers somewhere between the realms of the possible and the probable, for it begins with an hypothesis and concludes with the same hypothesis, the author (not the reader) having acquired astonishing certitude in the course of his book about a highly

undemonstrable proposition. Mr. Krutch looks for clues to Poe's nature in the poems and the tales for the most part. Here, he believes, is the unconscious revelation of the sexual deficiencies or abnormalities that Poe would fain have concealed. Now, Poe's stories and poems do show not merely a lack of, but an aversion to, physical passion, and it is easy to agree with a student who suspects sexual peculiarities in Poe. The whole matter is at best ingenious speculation—never to be susceptible of proof. It would be almost as easy to build an account of Hawthorne—based upon his somber tales and novels—as a specimen of sexual abnormality; it would be easy if we did not know of Hawthorne's entirely wholesome marriage and family-life. One cannot be so ardently sure of Poe's case as Mr. Krutch is.

On the other hand, a study of Poe's reviews and other journalistic work affords plain, unhypothetic indications of his nature and his preoccupations—at least his conscious preoccupations if not his subconscious. In a letter where there seems little reason to believe that Poe could have been striking an attitude—as he was prone to do in his public utterances—he formulates his own "ultimate purpose."

> Holding steadily in view my ultimate purpose,—to found a magazine of my own, or in which at least I might have a proprietary right,—it has been my constant endeavor in the mean time, not so much to establish a reputation great in itself as one of that particular character which should best further my special objects, and draw attention to my exertions as editor of a magazine. . . .

> Setting aside, for the present, my criticisms, poems, and miscellanies (sufficiently numerous), my tales, a great number of which might be termed fantasy pieces, are in number sixty-six. They would make, perhaps, five of the ordinary novel volumes. I have them prepared in every respect for the press; but, alas, I have no money, nor that influence which would enable me to get a publisher—although I seek *no* pecuniary remuneration. My sole immediate object is the furtherance of my ultimate one. I believe that if I could get my tales fairly before the public, and thus have an opportunity of eliciting foreign as well as native opinion respecting them, I should by their means be in a far more advantageous position than at present in regard to the establishment of a magazine. In a word, I believe that the publication of the work would lead forthwith either directly through my own exertion, or indirectly with the aid of a publisher, to the establishment of the journal I hold in view.

Poe did not only formulate his purpose but achieved a large part of it with surprising vigor. He wished to have a journal of his own—that is, to be himself both editor and proprietor, and he proceeded with striking success to edit *The Southern Literary Messenger,* and then *Graham's Magazine,* and then *The Broadway Journal.* He became proprietor as well as editor of *The Broadway Journal* but failed afterward to make it a success, having probably little capacity as a business manager though great capacity as an editor. Poe was a magazine editor. There his effort, his interests, and his success lay. In the foregoing excerpt, it is to be noted that he regards his short stories as the readiest means of gaining a reputation in the world of magazines. He had thought out carefully the requirements of magazine literature and found himself in general sympathy with these requirements. He tells what he has concluded about the matter in a paragraph later published in **Marginalia**.

> The increase, within a few years, of the magazine literature, is by no means to be regarded as indicating what some critics would suppose it to indicate—a downward tendency in American taste or in American letters. It is but a sign of the times—an indication of an era in which men are forced upon the curt, the condensed, the well-digested—in place of the voluminous—in a word, upon journalism in lieu of dissertation. We need now the light artillery rather than the Peacemakers of the intellect. I will not be sure that men at present think more profoundly than half a century ago, but beyond question they think with more rapidity, with more skill, with more tact, with more of method, and less of excrescence in the thought. Besides all this, they have a vast increase in the thinking material. They have more facts, more to think about. For this reason, they are disposed to put the greatest amount of thought in the smallest compass and disperse it with the utmost attainable rapidity. Hence the journalism of the age, hence, in especial, magazines. Too many we cannot have, as a general proposition; but we demand that they have sufficient merit to render them noticeable in the beginning, and that they continue in existence sufficiently long to permit us a fair estimation of their value.

Poe may have been reserved and somewhat lonely because of his peculiar nature but he was certainly in the thick of American letters of his day, not half so much the Dreamer (as a sentimental female biographer will have him) as the extremely busy and unusually effective journalist. Poe is not even that pathetic denationalized figure so dear to readers of his poems, the figure so un-American, the figure somehow crippled by the dreadful America in which it existed. There are no two ways about it;—Poe wanted to be an eminent "magazinist"; he labored diligently among a throng of fellows in the most populous region of North America; he almost realized his ambition of becoming a proprietor-editor.

To be sure, he also suffered poverty, was without intimate friends, continually ruined his most promising opportunities by insane orgies of drunkenness. These things which throw a shadow over his professional successes can hardly be said to prove him un-American or essentially out of harmony with his environment. In fact, if we adopt the view of Poe as a surprisingly successful journalist, whose heart was in his magazine work, and as a man who perceived early, and sympathized heartily with, the American desire for short, swift magazine fiction and verse, then Poe emerges as one of the most American of the writers of his period. And Poe was American not only in his championship of "the curt, the condensed" in literature but equally in his employment of the sensational (thus demonstrating himself an instinctive journalist!) in his articles and disclosures about hypnotism, mesmerism, and secret ciphers.

In another way, unsuspected by readers who do not know Poe's critical reviews, he shows himself a representative American (representative of the minority of the better reviewers). He never loses an opportunity to deride the subservience of American criticism to contemporary English criticism in the English and Scotch reviews or quarterlies. He urges—and himself exemplifies—an independence in literary judgments; he eagerly declares independence. Further, Poe shows in such a review as his of Irving's *Astoria* an ardent interest in the western lands of America very characteristic of the Americans of that day. In one review he hotly debates the question of slavery, naturally concluding with an emotional plea for the preservation of the happy *status quo.* That was to be expected of Poe; but the writing of the articles reveals a journalistic alertness to events, such as readers of **"Annabel Lee"** or **"The Pit and the Pendulum"** are prone to overlook.

There is, finally, a passage in an ironic little article entitled *Secrets of the Magazine Prison-House,* a passage with patent autobiographic reference to remind readers that Poe, experiencing the pinches of a meager profession, yet adhered strongly to it from predilection.

> . . . A young author, struggling with Despair itself in the shape of a ghastly poverty, which has no alleviation—no sympathy from an every-day world, that cannot understand his necessities, and that would pretend not to understand them if it comprehended them ever so well—this young author is politely requested to compose an article, for which he will "be handsomely paid." Enraptured, he neglects perhaps for a month the sole employment which affords him the chance of a livelihood, and having starved through the month (he and his family) completes at length the month of starvation and the article, and despatches the latter (with a broad hint about the former) to the pursy "editor" and the bottle-nosed "proprietor" who has condescended to honor him (the poor devil) with his patronage. A month (starving still), and no reply. Another month—

still none. Two months more—still none. A second letter, modestly hinting that the article may not have reached its destination—still no reply. At the expiration of six additional months, personal application is made at the "editor and proprietor's" office. Call again. The poor devil goes out and does not fail to call again. Still call again;—and call again is the word for three or four months more. His patience exhausted, the article is demanded. No—he can't have it—(the truth is, it was too good to be given up so easily)—"it is in print," and "contributions of this character are never paid for (it is a *rule* we have) under six months after publication. Call in six months after the issue of your affair, and your money is ready for you—for we are business men ourselves—prompt." With this the poor devil is satisfied, and makes up his mind that the "editor and proprietor" is a gentleman, and that of course he (the poor devil) will wait as requested. And it is supposable that he would have waited if he could—but Death in the meantime would not. He dies, and by the good luck of his decease (which came by starvation) the fat "editor and proprietor" is fatter henceforward and for ever to the amount of five and twenty dollars, very cleverly saved, to be spent generously in canvasbacks and champagne.

There are two things which we hope the reader will not do as he runs over this article: first, we hope that he will not believe that we write from any personal experience of our own, for we have only the reports of actual sufferers to depend upon; and second, that he will not make any personal application of our remarks to any Magazine publisher now living, it being well known that they are all as remarkable for their generosity and urbanity, as for their intelligence and appreciation of Genius.

But Poe himself aspired to become an "editor and proprietor"! He wished to be different from the sort he referred to so sarcastically above. Indeed Poe had something of a vision of what he might make of his projected magazine.

In short, I could see no reason why a magazine, if worthy the name, could not be made to circulate among twenty thousand subscribers, embracing the best intellect and education of the land. This was a thought which stimulated my fancy and my ambition. The influence of such a journal would be vast indeed, and I dreamed of honestly employing that influence in the sacred cause of the beautiful, the just, and the true.

In consideration of the way in which magazine work engrossed Poe, it seems somewhat more natural to attribute his literary theories—especially the theory that comparative brevity is essential in fiction or poetry, and his literary practice, which harmonized marvelously with his theory—to journalistic expediency than (as J. W. Krutch prefers) to psychologic and artistic limitations. Nothing proves that Poe, in his attempt at an aesthetic, was only trying to rationalize his own shortcomings. Perhaps he approved of short stories and lyric poems because he was unable to compose long novels and epics; but as a journalist by inclination may he not with great likelihood have preferred the short to the long, have admired it more, have desired more to excel in it?

Whatever the effect of journalistic ideals was upon Poe's creative writing, the quantity and the quality of his magazine work as such—his reviews—both are remarkable. The criticisms and reviews have never been completely collected for issue in volumes, though Harrison's "Virginia" edition is sufficiently full. In this edition, the so-called criticism occupies more space than either the short stories or the poems, for reviewing was Poe's regular business, stories and poems a sort of avocation. Considering the time and place, Poe's reviews are just as extraordinary as his other writings, though the lapse of years has inevitably impaired their current interest more than that of his creative work. The historic importance of his magazine articles is considerable. First, they reveal (what Poe pretended to scorn) the habits of the reviewers of the day; there is fulsome praise of certain very distinguished female poets; there is an exploiting of personality and frequent uncritical diatribe. Then they show, at their best, the turn that Poe himself was trying to give to that absurd type of criticism,—the attempt always to appraise the shortcomings as well as the excellence of a book, the readiness to commend writers even when the public stamp of approval was not upon them. Poe estimates with positiveness the value of a great number (in fact, nearly all) of writers of his day in America. He feels it a duty to expose mediocrity just as much as to discover genius. Consequently, the most interesting approach to the typical writing of the early nineteenth century in America is probably in these articles by Poe on certain literary nonentities.

The only other critical writer of the period with whom Poe can profitably be compared is obviously James Russell Lowell. Lowell's literary essays give very little of the flavor of American writing of the day, for he did not venture much on reviewing of minor contemporaries. Perhaps he did not consider them worth his attention. Whatever the reason, Lowell writes on safe and approved literary subjects almost always. He lacked something of Poe's boldness and energy and originality of literary creed. But Lowell possessed, of course, humor, in which Poe is often deficient, a genuine scholarly acquaintance with great writers such as Poe never had, and an easy elegance of style quite impossible to Poe. Lowell is pleasanter reading, but Poe is—though something of a poseur—both original and dynamic.

Cover of the December, 1835, issue of the Southern Literary Messenger. *By this edition, Poe had assumed editorial duties along with publisher T. W. White.*

II

The selected essays of Poe in this book [*Selections from Poe's Literary Criticism*] are intentionally those upon American writers. Poe wrote many more criticisms and book-reviews of American books and writers than of English or any others, and it is not difficult to represent his methods and theories adequately by selections altogether upon American subjects. . . .

The first division of the book includes Poe's two most successful essays on literary theory—**"The Poetic Principle"** and *The Philosophy of Composition*. The latter, purporting as it does to be an account of the manner in which Poe composed **"The Raven,"** is still a theoretic piece since it clearly expounds his idea of the way in which a poem as such should be composed by a poet as such. The mooted question whether or not Poe wrote as a hoax this recipe for making poems—this question is not of much importance. Hoax or no

hoax, the essay shows the habit of Poe's mind as well as anything he ever wrote.

The next division comprises good examples of Poe's careful critical work, particularly in the essays on Bryant and Longfellow. Poe wrote many times upon both those poets—now enthusiastically, now severely. It is very instructive to one studying Poe's development or evolution as a critic to work through chronologically his various essays upon Bryant, or upon Longfellow, or Bulwer, or Hawthorne, for Poe never tired of returning to the discussion of these authors. Lowell was also the subject of more than one of Poe's reviews. The essay on Channing is grouped with the other three merely because it is a painstaking piece of writing upon a contemporary versifier. Channing was no favorite with Poe, and this essay is one of the masterpieces of destruction for which Poe was almost infamous in the eyes of his world.

The third division contains two examples of Poe's reviews of prose writers. The essay on Hawthorne is notable both for sound observations upon Hawthorne and for Poe's most explicit manifesto regarding the province and technique of the prose tale, in writing which he and Hawthorne were surely adepts. In the criticism of Cooper, Poe makes an interesting classification of novelists and an unusually just estimate of Cooper's virtues and deficiencies.

The three essays from the series known as *The Literati* stand together for no better reason than that they were originally associated in publication. In certain respects, these are the most typical cases of Poe's reviewing here presented. Willis and Halleck were two far more popular writers—or at any rate far better liked—than Poe himself; two writers who represented the American taste in literature in the second quarter of the nineteenth century admirably. Poe, like everyone else, admired them, though he did not so far lose his sense of poetic values as to rank them with Bryant or Longfellow. The essay on Margaret Fuller is worthy of perusal as a case of Poe's tendency to over-eulogize female writers and as his only at all sympathetic treatment of any of the transcendentalist writers of the day.

The set of short pieces from Poe's *Marginalia* (or as one might better call it—Choice Bits Selected from Poe by Poe!) is purposely miscellaneous to show something of Poe's diversity (perhaps superficiality) of interests. Finally, the **"Letter to Mr.——,"** published in 1831 as a foreword to a volume of Poe's poems, is such a characteristic if intemperate outburst of the ideas which continually shaped the later writing of Poe that it deserves inclusion.

There are often several authentic, though very different, texts of a given essay by Poe, for he was nowhere more the artist than in his tireless revision of style—

even of punctuation. He was also accustomed to re-publish in a magazine with which he had lately become connected, such articles from those originally issued in other magazines (somewhat revised) as he thought worthy. An editor can at best try to give the text of an essay as it appeared at a certain date in a certain periodical. There has been some preposterous editing of Poe. For example, two or three of Poe's essays on Longfellow have been jumbled and spliced in curious ways to comprise a single essay on Longfellow too often reprinted thus in popular editions of Poe's works. There is an essay similarly fabricated from three reviews (at widely different dates) on Hawthorne. Poe had materially changed his estimate of Hawthorne as the years passed; so the fabrication is a royal hodge-podge. The essays on Hawthorne and Longfellow in the present collection actually appeared as they here stand at the date assigned. Since Poe was inclined to modify his opinions, even to reverse them, an appended date is necessary and significant.

Edmund Wilson (essay date 1942)

SOURCE: "Poe as a Literary Critic," in *Nation,* Vol. 155, No. 18, October 13, 1942, pp. 452-3.

[*Wilson attempts to rescue Poe's reputation as a literary critic by focusing on the latter's development of general critical principles that explain his specific criticisms of contemporary writers.*]

Poe at the time of his death in 1849, had had the intention of publishing a book on "The Authors of America in Prose and Verse." He had already worked over to a considerable extent the material of his articles and reviews; and the collection of critical writing printed by Griswold after his death is something between a journalistic chronicle like Bernard Shaw's dramatic notices and a selected and concentrated volume like Eliot's "The Sacred Grove."

Poe as a critic has points of resemblance both with Eliot and with Shaw. He deals vigorously and boldly with books as they come into his hands day by day, as Shaw did with the plays of the season, and manages to be brilliant and arresting even about works of no interest; he constantly insists, as Eliot does, on attempting, in the practice of this journalism, to formulate general principles. His literary articles and lectures, in fact, surely constitute the most remarkable body of criticism ever produced in the United States.

Henry James called it "probably the most complete and exquisite specimen of *provincialism* ever prepared for the edification of men." But though Poe had his share of provincialism, as all American writers did in that period, the thing that most strikes us today is his success in holding himself above it. Intellectually he

---

An excerpt from Poe's *Philosophy of Composition* (1846):

I have often thought how interesting a magazine paper might be written by any author who would—that is to say, who could—detail, step by step, the processes by which any one of his compositions attained its ultimate point of completion. Why such a paper has never been given to the world, I am much at a loss to say; but, perhaps, the autorial vanity has had more to do with the omission than any one other cause. Most writers—poets in especial—prefer having it understood that they compose by a species of fine frenzy—an ecstatic intuition; and would positively shudder at letting the public take a peep behind the scenes, at the elaborate and vacillating crudities of thought, at the true purposes seized only at the last moment, at the innumerable glimpses of idea that arrived not at the maturity of full view, at the fully matured fancies discarded in despair as unmanageable, at the cautious selections and rejections, at the painful erasures and interpolations—in a word, at the wheels and pinions, the tackle for scene-shifting, the stepladders and demon-traps—the cock's feathers, the red paint and the black patches, which, in the ninety-nine cases out of the hundred, constitute the properties of the literary *histrio*.

I am aware, on the other hand, that the case is by no means common, in which an author is at all in condition to retrace the steps by which his conclusions have been attained. In general, suggestions, having arisen pell-mell, are pursued and forgotten in a similar manner.

For my own part, I have neither sympathy with the repugnance alluded to, nor, at any time, the least difficulty in recalling to mind the progressive steps of any of my compositions and, since the interest of an analysis, or reconstruction, such as I have considered a *desideratum,* is quite independent of any real or fancied interest in the thing analyzed, it will not be regarded as a breach of decorum on my part to show the *modus operandi* by which some one of my own works was put together. I select **"The Raven"** as most generally known. It is my design to render it manifest that no one point in its composition is referable either to accident or intuition; that the work proceeded, step by step, to its completion with the precision and rigid consequence of a mathematical problem.

Edgar Allan Poe, in Selections from Poe's Literary Criticism, *edited by John Brooks Moore, F. S. Crofts & Co., 1926, p. 199.*

---

stands on higher ground than any other American writer of his time. He is trying to curb the tendency of the Americans to overrate or overpraise their own books, and at the same time he is fighting a rearguard action against the over-inflation of British reputations and the British injustice to American writers; and he has also a third battle: to break down the monopolistic instincts of the New Englanders, who tended to act as a clique and to keep out New Yorkers and Southerners. On one plane Poe grapples realistically with the practical problems of writers in the United States of that time—the copyright situation and the growth of the American magazines, with their influence on literary technique; and on another plane he is able to take in the large developments of Western literature.

With his general interest in method, he has definite ideas about the procedures in a variety of departments of literature—fiction, poetry, satire, travel, criticism. And he can be elevated, ironic, analytical, as the subject in hand requires. His prose is as taut as in his stories, but it has cast off the imagery of his fiction to become simply sharp and precise—our only first-rate classical prose of this period. His mind is a livid but incandescent shaft that is leveled at the successive objects in the American literary landscape like the searchlight on the Albany night boat that picks out the houses along the Hudson; and as there we are induced to stare at even undistinguished places which have been plucked out of the darkness into a spectral intensity of relief, so here we must read even the essays on insignificant figures whose dead features the critic makes radiant even while he is speeding them to oblivion. When we have put the whole picture together, we see it as clearly—to change the figure—as the geography of a landscape on the moon under an unattainably powerful telescope. There is no other such picture in our literature.

But Poe had tweaked the beard of Longfellow and had made people laugh at a Channing, and the lurking rancor of New England seems to have worked against the acceptance of his criticism. There is an anecdote in W. D. Howells's book, *Literary Friends and Acquaintance,* which shows both the attitude of New England and the influence of this attitude on others. Howells had visited Boston for the first time when he was twenty-three, and he had gone to see Emerson in Concord. Poe had been dead ten years.

> After dinner [says Howells] we walked about in [Emerson's] "pleached garden" a little, and then we came again into his library, where I meant to linger only till I could fitly get away. He questioned me about what I had seen of Concord, and whom besides Hawthorne I had met, and when I told him only Thoreau, he asked me if I knew the poems of Mr. William Ellery Channing. I have known them since, and felt their quality, which I have gladly owned a genuine and original poetry; but I answered then truly that I knew them only from Poe's criticisms: cruel and spiteful things which I should be ashamed of enjoying as I once did. "Whose criticisms?" asked Emerson. "Poe's," I said again. "Oh," he cried out, after a moment, as if he had returned from a far search for my meaning, *"you mean the jingle-man."* I do not know why this should have put me to such

confusion, but if I had written the criticisms myself I do not think I could have been more abashed. Perhaps I felt an edge of reproof, of admonition, in a characterization of Poe which the world will hardly agree with; though I do not agree with the world about him, myself, in its admiration. At any rate, it made an end of me for the time, and I remained as if already absent, while Emerson questioned me as to what I had written in the *Atlantic Monthly.*

That Emerson's opinion of Channing was not so very different from Poe's is shown by an entry in his journal for 1855:

> Ellery Channing's poetry has the merit of being genuine, and not the metrical commonplaces of the magazines, but it is painfully incomplete. He has not kept faith with the reader; 'tis shamefully insolent and slovenly. He should have lain awake all night to find the true rhyme for a verse, and he has availed himself of the first one that came; so that it is all a babyish incompleteness.

The prejudice of New England against Poe was supported by the bad reputation that had been given him by Griswold's mendacious memoir. It was not so long ago that it was possible for President Hadley of Yale to explain the refusal of the Hall of Fame to admit Poe among its immortals on the ground that he "wrote like a drunkard and a man who is not accustomed to pay his debts"; and it was only last year that Professor A. H. Quinn showed the lengths to which Griswold had gone by producing the originals of Poe's letters and printing them side by side with Griswold's falsifications.

We have often been told of Poe's criticism that it is spiteful, that it is pretentious, that it is vitiated by Poe's acceptance of the sentimental bad taste of his time. In regard to the first two of these charges it must be admitted that these essays give us unpleasant moments; they do have their queer knots and wrinkles; they are neurotic as all Poe's work is neurotic; and the distortions do here sometimes throw us off as they do not do in the stories, because it is here a question of judgment, whereas in his fiction the distortion itself is the subject of the story. It is true, as Joseph Wood Krutch has said, that there is constantly felt in Poe's criticism the same element of obsessive cruelty that inspires his tales of horror. Yet in his criticism Poe does try to hold this in check—with an occasional effect of inconsistency, in judgment as well as in tone, as when he will begin by telling us that certain passages in some book he is reviewing are among the best things of their kind to be found in contemporary writing, and then go on to pick the poet to pieces slowly, coldly, and at a length of many pages. It is also true that Poe pretends sometimes, or at least sometimes lets us infer, that he has read things he has not read. The psychology of the pretender is always a factor to be reckoned with in Poe.

The child of a fascinating actress who had died when he was two years old, he had been adopted by a Scotch merchant in Richmond, brought up as a Southern gentleman, and then cast off with no job and no money at the end of his first year of college, during which his adoptive father had failed to pay even his necessary expenses, so that he could associate, as he said, "with no students except those who were in a similar situation with myself." Poe had always been in the false situation of not being Allan's son and of knowing that in the society he was bred to his parents had been déclassés; and now he was suddenly deprived of his role of a well-heeled young Southern gentleman with prospects of inheriting a fortune, and found himself a poor man with no backing who had to survive in the American Grub Street. He had the confidence of faith in superior abilities, and the reports of his work at his English school and at the University of Virginia show that he excelled as a student. But his studies had been aborted at the same time as his social career, and a shade of the uncertainty of the "gentleman" was communicated also to the "scholar." Perhaps, also, though Poe's mind was a first-rate one, there was in him a dash of the actor who delights in elaborating a part.

Out of this consciousness of being a pretender, at any rate, with its infliction of a habitual secretiveness, came certainly Poe's love of cryptograms, his interest in inventing and solving crimes, and his indulgence in concocting and exposing hoaxes. If Poe sometimes plays unavowed tricks by cheating the reader a little about what he has written or read, the imposture is still almost as gratuitous, as innocent, and as unimportant as Stendhal's disguises and aliases and his weakness for taking ladies from the provinces through Paris and misinforming them about the public monuments. And with this we must also write off Poe's rather annoying mania of accusing his contemporaries of plagiarism— a harsh name he is in the habit of brandishing to indicate borrowings and echoes of a kind which, whether more or less abject, is usually perfectly harmless. Poe himself was certainly guilty—in his imitation of Chivers, for example—of borrowings equally harmless. But these, too, touched off the pretender.

As for the charge of Poe's acquiescence in the mawkish bad taste of his period, it is deserved to only a slight degree. He more often ran counter to this taste, as when he came down on Fitz-Greene Halleck; and, for the rest, his excessive enthusiasm for poets like Mrs. Osgood is attributable to the same sort of causes as, say, the praises of Bernard Shaw for the plays of Henry Arthur Jones: the writer who is potentially a master sees in the inferior writer a reflection of the kind of thing that he wants to do himself, but the

possibilities of which will hardly be plain to anyone else till the master himself has made them actual.

We must recognize these warpings of Poe's line; but we must not allow them as serious impugnments of the validity of his critical work. His reading *was* wide and great, and his culture was derived from a plane of the world of thought and art which had hardly been visited by Longfellow with his patient persistent transposition of the poetry of many lands and ages into terms of his own insipidity or by Lowell with his awful cosy titles for his collections of literary essays: *My Study Windows* and *Among My Books.* The truth is that literary America has always resented in Poe the very superiority which made him so quickly an international figure.

He may have been a difficult person, though certain people seem to have got on very well with him; but it seems hard to explain the virulence with which Griswold pursued him after his death and the general hostility toward him which has haunted us ever since, except on the ground that he puts us out by making so much of our culture seem second-rate. In our childhood we read **"The Gold Bug"** and **"The Murders in the Rue Morgue,"** and everybody knows **"Annabel Lee"** and **"Ulalume"** and **"The Bells"** and **"The Raven"**; but Poe is not, as he is with the French and as he ought to be with us, a vital part of our intellectual equipment. It is rare that an American writer points out, as Waldo Frank once did, that Poe belongs not with the clever contrivers of fiction like O. Henry and S. S. Van Dine but, in terms of his constricted personality, with the great inquiring and versatile minds like Goethe. So that it is still worth while to insist on his value.

In the darkness of his solitary confinement Poe is still a prince.

T. S. Eliot (essay date 1948)

SOURCE: "From Poe to Valéry," in *To Criticize the Critic,* by T. S. Eliot, Farrar, Straus & Giroux, 1948, pp. 33-4.

[*One of the best-known and most influential poets of the twentieth century, Eliot is equally noted as a literary critic and theorist. In the following excerpt, he argues that Poe's essays on the art of poetry help to rationalize the latter's own poetic technique, but that they cannot be taken as general principles. For Eliot's critique of Poe as a poet and short-story writer, see NCLC 1.*]

Imperfections in **"The Raven"** . . . may serve to explain why *The Philosophy of Composition,* the essay in which Poe professes to reveal his method in composing **"The Raven"**—has not been taken so seriously in England or America as in France. It is difficult for us to read that essay without reflecting, that if Poe plotted out his poem with such calculation, he might have taken a little more pains over it: the result hardly does credit to the method. Therefore we are likely to draw the conclusion that Poe in analysing his poem was practising either a hoax, or a piece of self-deception in setting down the way in which he wanted to think that he had written it. Hence the essay has not been taken so seriously as it deserves.

Poe's other essays in poetic aesthetic deserve consideration also. No poet, when he writes his own *art poétique,* should hope to do much more than explain, rationalize, defend or prepare the way for his own practice: that is, for writing his own kind of poetry. He may think that he is establishing laws for all poetry; but what he has to say that is worth saying has its immediate relation to the way in which he himself writes or wants to write: though it may well be equally valid to his immediate juniors, and extremely helpful to them. We are only safe in finding, in his writing about poetry, principles valid for any poetry, so long as we check what he says by the kind of poetry he writes. Poe has a remarkable passage about the impossibility of writing a long poem— for a long poem, he holds, is at best a series of short poems strung together. What we have to bear in mind is that he himself was incapable of writing a long poem. He could conceive only a poem which was a single simple effect: for him, the whole of a poem had to be in one mood. Yet it is only in a poem of some length that a variety of moods can be expressed; for a variety of moods requires a number of different themes or subjects, related either in themselves or in the mind of the poet. These parts can form a whole which is more than the sum of the parts; a whole such that the pleasure we derive from the reading of any part is enhanced by our grasp of the whole. It follows also that in a long poem some parts may be deliberately planned to be less 'poetic' than others: these passages may show no lustre when extracted, but may be intended to elicit, by contrast, the significance of other parts, and to unite them into a whole more significant than any of the parts. A long poem may gain by the widest possible variations of intensity. But Poe wanted a poem to be of the first intensity throughout: it is questionable whether he could have appreciated the more philosophical passages in Dante's *Purgatorio.* What Poe had said has proved in the past of great comfort to other poets equally incapable of the long poem; and we must recognize that the question of the possibility of writing a long poem is not simply that of the strength and staying power of the individual poet, but may have to do with the conditions of the age in which he find himself. And what Poe has to say on the subject is illuminating, in helping us to understand the point of view of poets for whom the long poem is impossible. . . .

An excerpt from Poe's *Letter to Mr. B—* (1831):

It has been said that a good critique on a poem may be written by one who is no poet himself. This, according to *your* idea and *mine* of poetry, I feel to be false—the less poetical the critic, the less just the critique, and the converse. On this account, and because there are but few B—s in the world, I would be as much ashamed of the world's good opinion as proud of your own. Another than yourself might here observe, "Shakespeare is in possession of the world's good opinion, and yet Shakespeare is the greatest of poets. It appears then that as the world judges correctly, why should you be ashamed of their favourable judgment?" The difficulty lies in the interpretation of the word "judgment" or "opinion." The opinion is the world's, truly, but it may be called theirs as a man would call a book his, having bought it; he did not write the book, but it is his; they did not originate the opinion, but it is theirs. A fool, for example, thinks Shakespeare a great poet—yet the fool has never read Shakespeare. But the fool's neighbour, who is a step higher on the Andes of the mind, whose head (that is to say, his more exalted thought) is too far above the fool to be seen or understood, but whose feet (by which I mean his every-day actions) are sufficiently near to be discerned, and by means of which that superiority is ascertained, which *but* for them would never have been discovered—this neighbour asserts that Shakespeare is a great poet—the fool believes him, and it is henceforward his *opinion.* This neighbour's own opinion has, in like manner, been adopted from one above *him,* and so, ascendingly, to a few gifted individuals who kneel around the summit, beholding, face to face, the master spirit who stands upon the pinnacle.

Edgar Allan Poe, in The Best Known Works of Edgar Allan Poe, *Blue Ribbon Books, 1927.*

Jay B. Hubbell (essay date 1954)

SOURCE: "Edgar Allan Poe," in *The South in American Literature: 1607-1900,* Duke University Press, 1954, pp. 528-50.

[*In the following excerpt, Hubbell examines Poe's career as the book reviewer for the* Southern Literary Messenger.]

Poe published in the *Messenger* tales and poems that won the admiration of Tucker and Philip Pendleton Cooke, but it was only by his book reviews that he attracted wide attention. Where he had served his apprenticeship as a reviewer is not known, but from the outset he was master of a vigorous critical method which owed much to a study of Coleridge and the British quarterlies. He could not prevent White from printing much inferior material in the body of the magazine, but in his reviews he soon made it evident that here at last was an American critic with the equipment and the courage to appraise by nonprovincial standards the work of poetasters and sentimental novelists accustomed to indiscriminate praise. His standards were too high to please his contemporaries, but he was not lacking in the editorial intuition for what would attract attention to the magazine. When he dissected Theodore Fay's pretentious and widely advertised *Norman Leslie,* he must have known that his review would attract attention in New York, for Fay was one of the editors of the *New-York Mirror.* During his connection with the *Messenger,* according to Poe's estimate, the circulation of the magazine rose from seven hundred to over five thousand. It was largely through his work that a struggling Southern monthly had become for the moment the best literary magazine in the United States. White, however, never gave him a free hand in accepting or rejecting manuscripts; and though Poe had probably saved the *Messenger* from early extinction, he was not willing to let it be stated in his columns that Poe was its editor. He finally made up his mind to part with Poe, but the poet's occasional drinking was not the determining factor. White wrote to Beverley Tucker on December 27, 1836: " . . . I am cramped by him in the exercise of my own judgement, as to articles I shall or shall not admit into my work. It is true that I neither have his sagacity, nor his learning—but I do believe I know a handspike from a saw." No, the *Messenger* was his private property, and he would run it to suit himself. He must have been very stupid, however, if he did not know that he could never find another editor of Poe's competence. Poe, for his part, seeing the profits of his labors going into the proprietor's pockets, had begun to dream of founding a magazine of his own. Like many another Southern writer since his time, he believed that he would fare better in one of the Northern cities. It was already obvious that the important literary centers would be found in the North. There perhaps he would find more time, too, for the creative work he wished to do. . . .

Henry Seidel Canby (essay date 1959)

SOURCE: "Edgar Allan Poe," in *Classic Americans: A Study of Eminent American Writers from Irving to Whitman,* Russell & Russell, Inc., 1959, pp. 263-307.

[*In the following essay, Canby argues that Poe's egomania combined with his interest in contemporary scientific thought can help to explain the uneven nature of his critical writings. While Poe was logical when delineating general literary principles, Canby maintains, his self-obsession made his critique of specific authors arbitrary and unreliable.*]

To leave the society of Emerson, Hawthorne, and Thoreau for the Philadelphia, the New York, the Rich-

---

Perry Miller on "The Longfellow War," during which Poe accused Longfellow of plagiarism:

Poe scholars have spent time that could have been better employed getting straight the chronology of the pieces that appeared in the two *Mirrors* and the *Journal,* and the myriad passages in other newspapers, where editors building circulations were avid for scandal. There is reason to suppose that Poe blew it up by writing at least one attack on himself (signed "Outis") in order to get the maximum of publicity; he was entirely capable of such a ruse. There is equal likelihood that Briggs entered the game deliberately, writing against Poe with Poe's connivance so as to excite further retorts. But the seriousness of the controversy began to appear in February when the *Knickerbocker* was out with a review of *The Waif:* "a goodly number of delightful effusions, various in kind, combining fancy, feeling, pure affection, and pictures of natural scenes." Poe's monomania waxed dangerous because he assaulted the one poet who had become in New York, and was becoming to America, the arch symbol of that "universality" which conservatives had to invoke in the name of the conserving values.

Perry Miller, in The Raven and the Whale, *Harcourt, Brace and Company, 1956.*

---

mond, of Poe is to pass from a quiet village of philosophic Greeks to an active, hustling present, from retirement out of space, and often out of time, to the more familiar world that lives in the moment. And to leave these men for Poe is to exchange elevation for intensity, and the study of man for the practice of art. There is not in the range of literature a wider dissimilarity than that which separates everything that Emerson and Thoreau were and could and wished to be, from this man Poe and his work.

The New Englanders were deeply religious—even Hawthorne; to Poe religion—except the religion of beauty—was meaningless. They were either philosophers, or ready with the least excuse to philosophize, and the goals they set themselves in art were philosophic or ethical—an understanding of the spiritual and moral nature was what they essentially sought. Poe's purpose in writing was to amuse, to interest, to impress, and to enlighten, which last is very different from seeking enlightenment. The others, even Hawthorne, and certainly Melville, were "seekers." Poe was a journalist. Poe the neurotic fits best and easiest into the familiar curves of modern living, Poe the writer is nearest to our norm; the New Englanders belonged to a culture so different from our megalopolitan civilization that they might well have come from that star which Poe was always seeking. Professionals in the life of the soul, they often seem amateurs—sometimes of genius—in the craft of writing. An amateur in scholarship and philosophy, and cursed with hot lunacies, Poe nevertheless, as a man of letters, was the true professional. He is more normal—as an artist—than Thoreau or Emerson or Melville.

2

I shall return to this comparison, which is fundamental. Of Poe himself, the most poignant fact is that he was unfortunate. Unfortunate men who are touched with greatness become notorious, whether or not they achieve fame. They make legends for themselves, and legends are made for them that are colored or interpreted differently by each generation that follows. They are no more complex than happier men of genius, but they seem so, because, having contradictions in themselves, they induce contradictions in others. If, as with Poe, the misfortune is congenital, interpretation is confused between the man and his works. One, of course, explains the other, but in Poe's case the variety of contributory circumstances presents so many possible causes for so many extraordinary results that criticism runs this way and that. Every book on Poe has its thesis, and both his art and the man himself are lost in exegesis and argument.

We know, in fact, almost too much about Poe—or rather, too many Poes—for a clear picture of the man and an easy comprehension of his work. There is no mystery left in him except the supreme mystery of neuroticism and no mystery in his work except the mystery of art, and yet it is as a man of mystery that he is constantly presented. Contradictory, extraordinary, perverse, he certainly is, but not mysterious except in so far as the sources of beauty are always mysterious. Few writers have left more abundant evidence of the workings of their minds. Few writers have had the nature of their minds, with the impact of circumstances upon them, so elaborately analyzed and explained.

We know now, thanks especially to Mr. Hervey Allen's summaries, the story of his relations with the Allan family in reasonable completeness, and can understand the frustrations of a boy who expected to combine the arrogant, chivalrous independence of a Southern gentleman with the pursuit of beauty, and found himself penniless and unclassed. We know enough of his adolescence to guess the effect upon his sex life of his foster father's infidelities. And if Mr. Krutch's theory of sexual impotence (whether real or of the brain) with a consequent singularity in his relations with women, still awaits more knowledge of Poe's youth, it is sufficiently substantiated in his later life and work to serve as a handle for criticism. We know well enough now that Poe the drunkard and opium-taker was simply a psychic victim saving himself from a nervous crisis—that he drank as a woodchuck takes to his hole, from

fear, and then irresistibly. We have rid ourselves of the superficial nonsense about artistic temperament and the immorality of genius. We have accepted—to the detriment of clear criticism, which suffers from the overemphasis, and yet very usefully—the modern ideas of complexes, inferiorities, egomanias, in Poe's case easily accounted for. We understand that Poe was a neurotic, and if we do not know what neuroticism is, we know how it works. We are aware not merely that Poe was abnormal, but why, and that knowledge had to be gained before his reputation could be cleared from the moral obsessions of those who discussed it, and his egregious vanities and incredible megalomanias assigned to cause.

But no man can be restored to an approximation of what he was, or his work criticized as a whole and in its relation to the flow of literary history, solely by abnormalities. He eats, he is cared for by the pathetic Mrs. Clemm and her ever-emptying basket, he works for money, he nurses his ambitions, he is gentle, he is irritable, he is ill, he is mean. These familiar traits do not make him the man he is, unless they are all. Nor does the merely skilful in his work explain its genius, where there is genius to be explained. But these normalities of life and literature do constitute the representational elements of the picture. They define it in terms of normal human effort, and, so defining it, explain more than partisans are willing to admit. The design for the composition may depend upon something deeper—and if in Poe that depth is neurotic, in neuroticism may be found a key to his inspiration. Nevertheless, to see Poe not as he wished to be seen, or as the dark forces sometimes compelled him to become, but as he prevailingly was, it is essential to retreat from the psychic ground his recent critics have trod so confidently, and begin again with aspects of his life that may seem trivial to the psychological critic but which to him were all-important. For a first glimpse of Poe it is wisest to consider him as neither drunkard, neurotic, nor erratic genius, but as a hard-working journalist of the third and fourth decades of the American nineteenth century.

3

Intellectually and from the broadest view it was a curiously dual society. The thirties and forties were astir with spiritual and ethical unrest. Free land and freedom from restraint in a society rapidly democratizing were having their inevitable effect upon the tense sectarians who swarmed in America. The convalescence from Calvinism was well under way, and relaxed nerves tingled to every suggestion. Intelligence was keen and aroused, minds untrained, the country at large undisciplined. From New England westward it was all isms, and all but the deep South was speckled with strange cults. Philosophers went transcendental and scientists toyed with phrenology.

Yet in the cities, and especially in Philadelphia and New York, the sophisticated, worldly life of urban Europe was being imitated with an ardor born of a consciousness of provincialism. Philadelphia in 1840 was in its wish psychology much more cosmopolitan and more cultivated than it is today. Journalism was rampantly active and especially literary journalism. From small beginnings, *Graham's* and *Godey's* attained a national circulation. *The Saturday Evening Post,* and especially *The Ladies' Home Journal,* were already present in the imagination, indeed they needed only better transportation, postal privileges, high-speed printing plants, and advertising to be there—more sentimental, more fastidious, more literary, but in the blend of uplift and interest much like what they actually became. Thoreau, printing his "Walden" as much from a sense of duty as from a hope of cash and reputation, was a century away from the American Grub Street where men's inventions were stimulated by expectation of immediate success. Thanks to the pirating of British and Continental books, the native author was heavily handicapped if he wished to publish a volume, but the timely magazine escaped this competition and was an ever widening field, unfailing, if never rich.

It is true that Poe's sole reality was his self, but this self was an ego of extraordinary magnitude and even greater sensitiveness, which demanded recognition. In the journalistic world of commercial writing he was as much at home as in Eblis, and with it and in it his normal thoughts were so deeply engaged that in his waking moments it is as a journalist that he seems most intensely alive. In contrast with the New Englanders, always reluctant to leave their rural Parnassus, he was certainly happiest in the hurly-burly of production and consumption where professional literature is usually made. The contempt for the writing trade that Cooper expressed and Irving felt, was utterly foreign to his mind. He was an insider, and often by necessity, and not always unwillingly, a hack. He planned no more soul revolutions and retreats into nature than does the feature writer today. Instead, his inventiveness tirelessly wrought new methods of plot development, devised poems that would take with elocutionists, discovered journalistic genres like the detective story and the literary personality (which go on and on), perpetrated hoaxes in order to make the front page, guessed at the publicity value of personal attack, and set out directly, not hesitantly like Hawthorne, to amuse, to interest, to harrow, the reader.

He was, as is now well known, an excellent editor, and a study of his methods and results will make it abundantly clear that his editing was much more than a means of getting his own work published. He knew how to plan a magazine, he knew how to get contributions, he knew how to get new subscribers. His lifelong dream of a national magazine, literary in quality, general in interest, was sound, and except for his ner-

vous disabilities, would certainly have been realized. We should have had a *Harper's* a quarter of a century before its time, nor would Poe's periodical have begun, like *Harper's,* in slavish dependence upon overseas. The neurotic upset whatever the inventive and executive faculty got under way, yet there is no question as to Poe's transcendent ability in journalism. Professionally speaking, he was an editor and journalist first and foremost, and the effect of his profession upon his enduring contributions to literature is of the highest critical importance.

He would, I think, have been a journalist under any conditions permitting journalism—most certainly so today. There is no mistaking the steady flow of interest from his college years onward to his death while on a last attempt to launch his own magazine. Poetry with him "was not a purpose but a passion" and the same in less measure might be said of scientific speculation. That poetry (with some dabbling in science perhaps) would have been "the field of my choice," as he says in the Preface to his '45 poems, would doubtless have been true, if Allan had left him the Southern gentleman of independent means that he expected to be. But that he would have kept away from journalism, never satisfied his craving for immediate returns of praise, never used his abundant invention to fool, perplex, terrify, and fascinate the public generally, must be incredible to anyone who follows through what was essentially a career of journalism. If he had got that government job, if he had taken to teaching, sooner or later he would have been back in Grub Street again, seeking for someone to finance his magazine!

No one is born a journalist. It is a profession made by teaching a quick and articulate mind to satisfy the curiosity of the public. Or rather by adapting the work of that mind to the public need, for the mind, the self, can, and in good journalists often does, stand contemptuously aloof. Poe's faculty of expression was perfectly adapted to journalism; indeed it was very largely conditioned by it. His tricks of puffery, his constant plagiarism from his own writing, his insistent bluffing, his powers of lucid exposition, his indefatigable invention (only a journalist could have invented the detective story), his complete freedom from intellectual conscience, his meticulous craftsmanship, are all attributes of the journalist, particularly the free lance journalist. He had the short breath of the journalist, always ending this side of possible weariness. He had the wide and not too discriminating interests of the editorial type of mind. He differed from other literary journalists of eminence in the nineteenth century chiefly in that he had unusual powers of creation, wrote far worse than the average when he wrote badly, had such a sense of form as comes to only one or two in a generation, and was too vain to be able to distinguish with any consistency his fudge and bunkum from the efforts of his genius.

4

It is often assumed that the trash Poe wrote was forced out of him by circumstance. I doubt it. The fudge was essentially Poe's, and Lowell was generous in his estimate of "Three fifths of him genius, and two fifths sheer fudge." The same impulses that led him toward journalism account for much of his trash.

Perhaps two thirds of Poe's work is not worth reprinting at this distance of time, and of this two thirds not more than a half has any value whatsoever except as an instance of successful pioneering, or for its biographical reference. His fudge is of several sorts. There is the sheer hack work of most of his literary portraits, too many of his reviews, and pieces like **"The Elk,"** which read as if they had been written for a school reader. The man had to live—but the pompous assurance of omniscience and omnipotence makes trash of this kind offensive to later generations. Read his "blurb" on Bayard Taylor, or the review of his admired Mrs. Osgood's poems, which descends from eulogy to this: "Regarding the loftier merits, I am forced to speak of her in more measured terms. She has occasional passages of true imagination—but scarcely the glowing, vigorous, and sustained ideality of Mrs. Maria Brooks, or even, in general, the less ethereal elevation of Mrs. Welby"! It was this series of highly personal criticisms, made up equally of fulsome praise and cutting satire that, before **"The Raven,"** was the chief cause of Poe's notoriety. The flings skyward into general principle which have made his later critical reputation were little regarded, and are but moments in his flow of inconsequential writing relieved only by a pungent phrase or a restatement of a "principle" borrowed from himself.

Lamentable failures are all of Poe's humorous stories. Many of them, as Professor James Southall Wilson has shown, are burlesques of fashionable writing that deserved chastisement. But it is questionable whether they are not worse than their originals, and certainly now they are mirthless. It is sad to be devoid of a sense of humor, it is worse to think that you have humor and pity others for its lack, as Poe did, and then to practise as vile a brand as his. The jokes cackle like bad actors, incongruity and exaggeration in their most extreme forms alone appeal to him, and his parodies are as mirthless as a second-rate revue. Those who say that he reflected the humor of his America may have right on their side, but should remember Irving. All humor not of the first class stales with time, but Poe's humor crumbles and dusts. And yet no writer makes his characters more frequently and more extensively laugh in type. He will take three lines for his teehees.

Worst of all is his meretriciousness. The fake erudition with which he daubed his stories and essays, and even his poems, has often been analyzed, and never to Poe's

credit, who was capable even of stealing his notes. Mr. Allen has suggested that much of this second-hand knowledge came from the English reviews, which Poe as a youth could have seen in his foster father's warehouse. Later, of course, in his various editorial offices, a wide variety of current books and magazines were always at hand. He used this borrowed learning as a boy uses all the tags he can remember for an examination paper, in the hope of impressing the reader. The materials were good, the use he makes of them often pertinent, but it is all a show-off, and is felt to be such.

I make a partial exception for science and mathematics, and a complete one for æsthetics. In science and mathematics he had better than an average good training (of which more later), and when he borrowed he really sought the truth. He tried to be honest, and did hard thinking on an insufficient basis of accurate knowledge. In æsthetics he had that native aptitude which is better than training, since it finds what it needs, and here his thinking bore fruit. And yet even in æsthetics his deficiencies are painful. The value of his **"Rationale of Verse,"** with its clear statement of the principle of prevailing time, is seriously marred by his failure to see the accentual nature of English verse. He hits all around the bull's-eye, but never in the center, and winds up his essay by excluding French poetry from excellence altogether because it will not fit a theory that he has made without grasping essential linguistic differences! Or see him in his review of Horne's "Orion" pouring contempt upon those who prefer the great passages on hell in "Paradise Lost" to the extracts he chooses from his favorite of the moment. The fault here is not merely taste, which is always liable to defects in current consideration, but cocksureness and a desire to be emphatic at all costs.

And consider those extraordinary *tours de force,* **"The Domain of Arnheim"** and **"Landor's Cottage."** In the former, Elliston, the incredibly rich proprietor of the Domain, seeks that beauty which results from "a spiritual interference with nature," and which gives a point and an interest to landscape arrangement, and is only one step depressed from the great art of creation possible only to God. With this characteristically interesting theory Poe begins his description. But alas, the approach to the heart of the Domain is through a fervid landscape that mingles the rococo with the baroque; and the palace at the end of the vista, with its semi-Gothic, semi-Saracenic architecture suggests, and perhaps was suggested by (since we find it often repeated in Poe), the architecture that Mrs. Wharton celebrates as Hudson River Bracketed. **"Landor's Cottage"** is better controlled because the simpler—and how much needed!—idea of due proportion in home and garden architecture was less grandiose in principle and could be satisfied with less strain upon Poe's experience. His search in this sketch for a "proportionate strangeness" in environment was an evidence of his inventiveness in a period that had lost its sense of architectural proportion, but though his description of the tulip poplar is justly famous and should be more often read, the artificiality of the cottage and its surroundings tugs at the memory until one finds the crude original in a Currier & Ives print! Poe had the theory, but he lacked both taste and experience to carry it out. The proof is in his **"Philosophy of Furniture"** (and *seriatim* in his works)—its ideal room with two windows of crimson-tinted glass, and a wall paper of crimson with arabesques of silver and large pictures set thereon. One sees such rooms in the steel engravings of the Annuals! Poor fellow, he bluffed magnificently. But his inventive imagination was often like an expensive automobile carrying an ill-dressed, inexperienced provincial.

I do not call **"The Domain"** and **"Landor's Cottage"** fudge, yet in them as in most of his stories of the grotesque and arabesque there is a strong fudgean element. It is the show-off, that same trait which made him want to be a journalist, and as a professional journalist made him use every scrap, tittle, jot, and ounce of whatever he possessed or could lay his hands on. His invention raced ahead and he threw whatever was handy into the too often empty cars behind it. Thus **"The Raven,"** whatever its inception, was undoubtedly tuned up for the show-off of elocution by precisely the methods described in *The Philosophy of Composition.*

In a study published many years ago I traced the relationship between the obviously—and then modern—journalistic methods of Kipling in the short story and the early influence of Bret Harte, himself a writer trained in American journalism; but the relation, felt but not proved, between Harte and Poe, the originator of the American short story, puzzled me. It is quite evident when Poe is thought of, as he should be, as a magazine writer. Not only are his tales shaped and consciously fitted to the necessity of that quick impression that the magazine requires (since its success is conditioned by the existence of a public that is intelligent but too large to be literary) but his critical theory of the short story—still the best expressed—shows how directly his art was squared to the medium for which he wrote. Stories do not *have* to be written as he describes them in his famous review of Hawthorne's tales, unless they are written as the journalist writes for quick consumption by the many. We have already, outside of journalism, reverted to a looser type of story, capable of more character study, a fuller background, and a subtler dialogue. Nor do poems have to be short poems, unless the writer is a lyrist in talent, or a journalist who can find publication only for the brief. Poe's failures—his forced humor, his sham scholarship, his cocksure criticism, and frequent petulance—are due in large measure to the pressure of his profession of journalism upon his vanity, or the reverse, and his great successes also are deeply indebted to the virtuosity of a master journalist. Fudge and the fruits of genius were alike ripened for the magazine markets of Philadelphia and New York.

The amazing statement has often been made that Poe had no roots in American literary history, and derived nothing from the American tradition. It is a rash assertion to make *a priori,* of an American who after his school years in England fluttered like a spectral moth around the great publishing centres of New York and Philadelphia. His critics have been misled by his inner life, which indeed was of a brand different from the neuroticism of the Puritans and had its roots in universal human nature rather than in the local conditions of America. They have too little considered the circumstances of his Southern upbringing that were responsible for so many manifestations of thwarted pride and intolerant arrogance. They have generously overlooked the provincialism of his lesser work, which was entirely American in its character. But most of all they have failed to note that Poe as a professional writer was trained, his ambition shaped, his powers chiefly exercised, in a flourishing period of American journalism, the first magazine era, when the periodical was proving its admirable adaptiveness to the peculiar conditions of American life. To New England he owed nothing, to New York and the Knickerbocker school substantially nothing, but one can exclude him from the American tradition only by assuming that Thoreau or Irving was fully representative of American life, which is nonsense. His terror, as he said, was of the soul, but his technique was simply the best yet developed for that magazine literature which had already become an American specialty.

I propose no singularity in this description of Poe as a journalist, but only a new and juster view of him regarded as an American man of letters and as a master of a peculiar virtuosity. It is never safe to be snobbish in criticism, and to think of Poe in terms of world literature only is to generalize overmuch and to miss some of the flavor of his genius.

5

Poe's virtuosity, true to the aims of journalism, is a technique for catching the attention of the reader. It is not one trick but a handful. When the subject matter was beyond his narrow apprehensions, and few great writers have gone so often outside their powers as Poe (another trait of the journalist), the result is often what seems to us a failure, but in every instance there is some trick of plot that explains his current success. Poe had no humor and hence his rather dreary burlesques, **"The Spectacles,"** and **"The System of Dr. Tarr and Prof. Fether,"** were foredoomed to artistic failure; he had neither pathos nor sentiment, and therefore **"The Oblong Box"** was sure to be banal; and yet in each story there is a clever trick. The introspective Hawthorne would have recorded the themes of these stories in his notebook as: "A man to marry his own great-great-grandmother because of shortsightedness," "A houseful of lunatics to overpower their keepers and run the asylum according to their own ideas," "A coffin containing the body of a beloved wife to be mistaken for the case of a treasured painting—what might happen?" How Hawthornesque these themes are, how surely he would have made memorable if somewhat stuffy allegories of them! Poe's dreams fitted in none of them, and his logic found nothing it could work upon, but he could catch his audience with the trick in the plot.

Yet how brilliantly he succeeded with a trick when that which caught the attention was worthy of it! **"The Purloined Letter"** in its origin is exactly like these trashy stories. The theme, that it is characteristic of the human animal to overlook the obvious, is a tricky one. Dupin, the great original of detectives, is a symbol of logic and observation personified, the Minister D—is just as unreal as Poe's other characters, the background of the story is conventional melodrama. But the trick by which Dupin finds the missing letter lends itself to an exciting logical analysis, and it is for this that one reads **"The Purloined Letter."** There was no room, and no time, for Poe to go wrong. The detective story, of which this is the prototype, is, if you please, all fudge; but it is good fudge, and fudge is what we read it for; not humor, not character, not truth to typical life, but the application of logical principles to a fabricated sensation or mystery. How delightful is **"The Gold Bug"** for the same reasons! The characters are conventions, the darky absurd, but the trick by which the buried treasure is found is absorbing. And Poe's invention, which throws off grotesque nonsense and banalities in other trick stories, here settles down to work.

"The Fall of the House of Usher" is tricky in the same sense, although in Poe's stories of terror other factors enter in that make the journalistic classification only partial. Every one of his famous tales of mental pathology begins with a problem, and concludes with a revelation that is itself a kind of trick. In **"Usher"** it is the intensification of the senses; in **"Berenice,"** the diseased obsession with a physical object, in **"Eleonora,"** the transmigration of souls, in **"The Cask of Amontillado,"** a macabre practical joke, in **"The Black Cat,"** the invulnerability of the feline kind. And each of these revelations is prepared for and released with the utmost care for emphasis in the best journalistic fashion.

And even in his poetry, where other and more important considerations also enter, a technical trickery was responsible at least for his success in catching the at-

tention of his contemporaries. The theme of **"The Raven"** comes from Poe's deepest experience, but its form—so accurately described in *The Philosophy of Composition*—is technical trickery so able that its artificiality now begins to offend.

So does the careful focus of Poe's stories, and the inweaving of word and sentence in a pattern that in every stitch regards the end and all of the tale, and all craftsmanship that secures a single vivid impression from a brief narrative. These technical tricks have grown out of our fashion and liking because they begin to *seem* tricky. Excellently useful in tales of artifice and supremely successful in Poe's best stories, they have nevertheless, and as I have already said, become a mould from which the modern short story has escaped as from a press.

Even Poe's criticism was shaped in its application by the needs of journalism, and his reviewing depends upon a trick that does not always come off. His practice when he was in good form was to set down a generalization (not necessarily or often a fresh one) so contradictory as to startle the reader into attention:

> It is often said, inconsiderately, that very original writers always fail in popularity, that such and such persons are too original to be comprehended by the mass. . . . It is, in fact, the excitable, undisciplined, and child-like popular mind which most keenly feels the original.

> The decline of the drama . . . The drama has *not* declined.

> I hold that a long poem does not exist. I maintain that the phrase, 'a long poem,' is simply a flat contradiction in terms.

> In America, we have refused to encourage satire—not because what we have had touches us too nearly—but because it has been too pointless to touch us at all.

These are headlines demanding attention. Sometimes they are true and brilliant, sometimes brilliant and partly true, but always the extraordinary lucidity of the exposition that follows persuades the reader that Poe is omniscient. The important contributions of Poe to criticism are taken from such introductory generalizations. They exhibit not only the audacity of the journalist who must make his killing quickly, but also his intuitive inventiveness, and indeed the further applications of his principles are seldom quotable, and seldom reliable beyond the second page. In the fields of the short story and in the æsthetics of poetry he was an expert and there his criticism is good to the end, but as a rule the actual discussion of contemporary books in Poe's reviews is distinguished only by an occasional brilliance of definition or attack from such average reviewing of the period as was practiced by, for example, Simms.

But these technical tricks which Poe mastered or invented in order to conquer the magazine rose to virtuosity when the subject matter was right. When the dark realms of his imagination through which his working mind had thrown roads for an almost scientific exploration were to be the scene of a story, his marvelously contrived order of composition could compress into a few thousands of words a speaking symbol of what was to him a cosmogony and an experience combined. When with a logical chain of reason he set out to discover the cause of murder, or the hidden place of treasure, as La Place had worked in pure mathematics or Newton in pursuit of a planet, his art of intense brevity could create suspense and rouse interest to the highest pitch. One has only to compare the ratiocination of **"The Narrative of Arthur Gordon Pym"** with the coiled intensity of the later **"The Murders in the Rue Morgue"** to see what this virtuosity, acquired for journalism, could accomplish.

6

It is high irony that Poe should have invented the detective story, that stand-by for breadwinning of the hack writer, and yet half starved himself. Why did he leave to Conan Doyle the capitalizing of his invention? For the Sherlock Holmes stories—good as they are—owe everything except the wide application of a formula to Poe, and Sherlock himself is only Dupin materialized a little further and fitted with a few more attributes. Essentially Holmes is a figure of romantic disillusion, a superbrain too contemptuous of his environment to play the usual games for success, who is roused only by a kind of misanthropy when his miserable fellow creatures exploit their viciousness too far. He is a solitary, he takes drugs to relieve his boredom, he is an artist, he lives exotically—he is Dupin revived, which is to say a self-dramatization of Poe.

It was certainly no literary scruple or fear of repetition that held back Poe from adding to his handful of great detective stories. He would have sold **"The Gold Bug"** in ten different versions if he could, and have followed up any likely chance of publication if he had seen it. Of course he did use his famous method of ratiocination in many stories—such as **"Pym"**—and the interpreting of observation that is its central principle is woven through nearly all of his poetic tales of terror. But it was only in the detective story that it was realized as a story itself. I suppose that he failed to capitalize because he was too inventive, and, like many inventors, turned from one creation to another as the wind of interest blew. He thought that he could do anything, but he had little time except for the nearest task. When he was not a practicing editor he was for

considerable periods sick from disease, from alcohol, or from opium, or psychically incapacitated with that mental illness which redoubles every physical pain. And the labors of a literary editor are endless. He has to read—endlessly. Poe read as a journalist reads, who knows that everything is grist for his mill and that the mill must be fed; he read like a man who knows that eventually he must write of everything he reads. And when he was his own man his megalomania led him to the immense and futile efforts of such work as *Eureka.* His inner life was always a conflict. Like the Minister D—he was both mathematician and poet. When he was well, his need and his ambition drew him into the endless routine of editing—when he was at home, in a leisure too often enforced by a breakdown, his sick soul and clear logical mind combated for his pen.

7

That Poe was only a journalist, is, of course, a statement too absurd to rest upon. But I wish to make it clear that as a journalist he could be superb, and to emphasize that everything of importance that he wrote, with the exception of a few of his best poems, like **"Israfel,"** was influenced, and often shaped, and frequently made possible in its existing mould, by the technique he acquired for his profession. Yet to account for the form of his work, unless it be in the detective story (which is, in a true sense, pure form) is by no means enough to account for Poe's place in our imagination. No American writer has sent wider circles of interest and influence across the reading world. I have seen a copy of Baudelaire's translation of Poe's stories open upon a firing platform in a trench in France. Much modern poetry and some modern fiction would never have been if Poe had not written. Leave then the journalist, and look at the man of letters, and the man. Not that the two were dissociated. Poe had a duality of character depending upon whether his nerves were in or out of control, but there is no duality here. What he wrote, he wrote with all of himself, and there is morbidity in **"The Murders in the Rue Morgue,"** a pathologic luxury in **"The Gold Bug,"** and sheer journalism in **"The Bells"** and **"Eleonora."**

So far I have considered Poe's way of working rather than the imagination with which he worked. If in so doing I have leant toward disparagement it is for the double reason that analysis of clever artifice is always disillusioning, and that unquestionably Poe's weaknesses even more than his strengths were exploited by the show-off of journalism. It is the result, not the thing itself, that endures in journalism. Thus in this study of Poe's inventiveness under pressure by the crowd I have viewed from one angle only those creations in which Poe transcended journalism while seldom ceasing to be journalistic. Let us turn then to aspects of the man that make for greatness rather than a great technique.

8

The type to which Poe approximates is familiar enough, increasingly familiar as our civilization grows more febrile. But it is, of course, rarely combined with a passion for beauty amounting to genius, and still more rarely with a powerful, logical intellect, completely articulate. Without attempting a scientific description, it may be said that two attributes go far toward defining the peculiar temperament that made Poe's inner life so fruitful for literature, and yet so calamitous for himself.

He was, in the first place, egoistic in the last degree and, like all his favorite characters, sensitive beyond ordinary comparison. This, of course, is a symptom of his neuroticism, but in literature as in life it was a curse. It is not too much to say that for Poe no one really existed except himself. No one except the un-sexed Virginia, his caretaker, Mrs. Clemm, and the few women who touched him in his youth ever entered the realms of his deepest consciousness, and they only as dim shapes projected from the faint stirrings of the human in his otherwise purely intellectual desires. Such egoism is relieved only by triumphant creation. The I must be entirely successful or the anguish that results from the ordinary casualties of living—hopes thwarted, affection unreturned, and all the slings and arrows of outrageous fortune—is rationalized in the familiar symptoms of paranoia and megalomania. Either the man flings back in suspicious anger at a world that will not adjust itself to him, or he rises above it in a diseased, uncertain assurance that he is greater than his enemies. Yet, granted exquisite sensibilities, the spur of fame desired, and the expressiveness of literary genius, and a tragedy common enough in lower orders becomes articulate and noteworthy. Poe's two characters, so often spoken of by his contemporaries—the gentle husband, so dependent upon love and cherishing, and the truculent, unscrupulous fighter, drunk or "mean"—are only two phases of a single temperament. Their exaggerated difference is due to the excessive sensitiveness of the patient. When his ego was soothed or weary, he was a lamb; when it was inflamed or injured, he was a beast in a corner, frenzied, wounded, smeared with blood and with dirt.

No such egoist can by any possibility have real humor, for a sense of proportion in human relationships is denied him. No such egoist can by any possibility comprehend with any real success the types of human nature that other writers interpret and dramatize but in which his interest is mathematical at best. They are figments for his thinking, aliens to his ego. His self-portraits may be of the utmost vividness, but his generalizations upon temperaments that are not essentially like his own will be platitudes or falsities. He knows only himself, and the temperamental qualities of his own ego will strictly limit his achievement.

This is negative criticism, for we do not ask of our men of letters that they shall all be Goethes or Shakespeares—or even Wordsworths and Hawthornes. Positively speaking, Poe's inner life was rich enough for a great literature, and his excessive egoism gave it an excessive importance in his own eyes that he always carried over into his work, and sometimes with impressive success. It was the inner life of a neurotic, by which I mean here no more than that the waves of thought and emotion, which in self-communion or dreams stir in us all, were vehement in him and out of proportion to their external causes, and were often out of control and in violent odds with apparent reality. And Poe's neuroticism was not only intensified by his violent ego, it was also qualified and defined by a passionate love, inherent and congenital, of that wilder beauty than earth supplies, which he believed to be the origin of poetry. He speaks of "readers who, to hearts of maddening fervor, unite, in perfection, the sentiment of the beautiful, that sense which proves and which alone proves, God's existence"—and so writing, wrote of himself.

The permanent possibility of neuroticism is a universal human attribute, and a great neurotic, such as Poe, has an obvious place in important literature. Alcohol and opium in alternation may have increased the fervor, or defined the sensory nature, of his sublimated dreams, but the drugs were the results, not the causes, of his neuroticism. It is not the "wilder beauty" for which they are responsible, but the excess of morbid sensation. That which made other men gross or fantastic could taint, but not create, the Aiden of Poe's imagination.

The subliminal world of Poe's poetical stories and of such poems as **"Dream-Land"** and **"The City in the Sea,"** reached

> By a route obscure and lonely,
> Haunted by ill angels only,
> Where an Eidolon, named Night,
> On a black throne reigns upright, . . .
> Out of Space—out of Time,

owes little that is good to stimulants, but much to neuroticism. It is a region of supersensation where each sensory faculty trembles with expressiveness like the heart-strings of Israfel. That is its geography and its atmosphere. And in such a clime the perfervid and often irrational emotions of the Great Egoist can escape from the repressions of reality in an environment where every tortured suspicion, fear, or hope is realized with an intensity as great as itself. The mind brooding upon its own terrible propensities finds in these spectral regions its most hidden fears stalking. Sadism, incest, claustrophobia, perversion, paranoia, megalomania—these are but names for phases of the inflamed ego, beating against the cage of self-control, but in dream life they are not names, they are things of human attribute, realized in that air electric with vivid sensation. In **"Eleonora," "The Masque of the Red Death," "Ligeia," "Morella," "Usher,"** Poe's neuroticism freed an ego whose morbidity was not so much abnormal as abnormally representative of the darker emotions. By a "wilder" beauty he meant precisely what he himself achieved—a beauty in which every intense emotin of the ego had validity and finds expression. The fears and cravings that the sane man puts down because they disturb or conflict with reality, were to Poe more real than external reality itself, because they were his, and so he made a life for them in a world of supersensation, where, like electrons in the physicist's laboratory, they could become tangible to other men.

9

Many a neurotic has created his own world—and written of it too—but few such worlds are fit for other minds to live in. Poe's dreams were made habitable by his powerful sense of order, and this instinct for form is closely related to his passion for science and the methods of science, which was second only to his love of æsthetic beauty, of which it was, of course, a part. The interest in science that he manifests from his youth up is, like his journalistic ambition, a link, one of the few links, between his inner life and the external world.

The thirties and forties were the romantic age of science in America, an age rich in premonition of all that science could do for a democratic society in a still new continent. Poe was as deeply enthralled by it as Emerson or Thoreau. His deep interest is displayed in the most unexpected places. Fully half of the tricks in his stories are derived from the discoveries—often the commonplaces—of physical science. Astronomy is never long out of reference, and if there is an opportunity to boast of being *au courant* with the latest researches in this science, or others, or a chance to expose error in his slipshod contemporaries, Poe never misses it. It has been assumed that his knowledge was superficial. That is not entirely true. Of all sciences he pretended to know something, and usually his knowledge is a journalist's, and a bluffing journalist's at that. The solemn nonsense of phrenology took him in completely. He made capital out of mesmerism, and was quite unscrupulous in using what he could pick up, from his abundant sources, of this and better defined sciences for his own literary purposes. But the methods of science he did understand, even if its end—the description and measurement of physical phenomena—was far too modest to appeal to him. Of mathematics and astronomy he had knowledge enough to make him, if not a scholar, at least a connoisseur. There was natural science in his reading at the University of Virginia, and social science in his courses. At West Point he studied advanced mathematics and natural philosophy, which must have embraced some astronomy. He stood seventeenth in his class in mathematics in a class of eighty-seven, and West Point, whatever its educational deficiencies, has never numbered mathematics among them.

At first he used his scientific knowledge chiefly in his stories of ratiocination, and in his hoaxes, of which the voyage to the moon is a good example, but steady reference in his criticism shows that he was thinking not only along the lines of his famous sonnet **"To Science,"** in which he realizes ahead of most of his contemporaries the disillusion that might follow upon the scientific revolution, but also speculatively and philosophically upon the relation of science to a possible explanation of the universe. *Eureka,* the book that he expected in his mounting egomania to sweep the country and establish his reputation as a cosmogonist, is the summary of many years of thought. It is, of course, literary science. What interested Poe was never the experiment, but what could be done with the fruits of experiment to further the expansion of the imagination. Yet, unlike his contemporaries, he did not take his premises from metaphysical assumption, if he could possibly avoid it. He sought them, as best he could, in the latest discoveries of physical science. And to these he applied that mixture of intuition and logic which we call mathematics—a science based upon an art.

Eureka was a failure at publication, and has been called an absurdity ever since. To Mr. Krutch it is "only a wild fancy," which illustrates Poe's growing lack of control over his mental processes. Professor Stringham of the University of California contributed to Professor Woodberry's biography of the poet in 1885 an analysis of *Eureka* that not only points out many errors of fact, but ridicules the whole work as an attempt to combine materialism and Transcendentalism in an undigested mass. It is an attempt, one may say parenthetically, that we have been at ever since. He is severe upon Poe's identification of matter and force, upon the nonsense of explaining material phenomena in terms of the will of God, upon the assumption that space is "given," not created. Physics has moved ahead since Professor Stringham's day. We are not so sure now of the finality of the conservation of energy, or the materiality of the atom! And Poe has many successors and will have more in the attempt to call metaphysics to the aid of experiment. A careful reader of *Eureka* today, reasonably familiar with the complexities in which physics has enmeshed itself, must say, not that *Eureka* is the Great Explanation which Poe in his megalomania thought it, but certainly that it is an extraordinary monument of clear and logical thinking raised upon premises many of which are false, and involved, like every cosmogony, in self-contradiction. While futile as either science or philosophy, it does command respect, does involve the kind of thinking and the method of attack that modern scientific philosophers are beginning to employ. It is a return (as Stringham says disparagingly) to the method of the Greeks, and if Poe had more self-confidence than equipment this does not lessen the interest of his *tour de force,* which is probably as valuable for science as is that other *tour de force* of American logical thinking, Jonathan Edwards's "The Freedom of the Will," for psychology.

For *Eureka* is, as Poe specifically said, "a prose poem," a book offered "not in its character of truth-teller, but for the beauty that abounds in its truth." Incidentally it is a model of lucid exposition. The universe, he argues, is composed of atoms that have been radiated outward by a primal creative act of God, from a unified and homogeneous centre to the bounds of an almost infinite sphere. The act ceasing, reaction began, and the universe is now moving back toward its centre. This is the cause of gravity. When the shrinkage is accomplished both attraction and repulsion will cease in homogeneity, and since attraction plus repulsion is the definition of matter, there will be nothing. God himself is now extended in this creative act. And other gods in other universes may likewise be functioning. We and the inanimate are all parts of God. On the final reuniting He will be entire God again and may re-create. God's will, more specifically, is identified with the æther, a spiritual influence that keeps matter in heterogeneity. It is the separative, repulsive function, and heat, light, magnetism, are all due to æther. Matter exists solely to subserve its purposes, and thought and the animate are due to its influence, which is manifest only through heterogeneity. This theory Poe works out with an elaborate apparatus of mathematics, physics, astronomy, and sheer metaphysics, and he attempts to account in detail for the formation of planets in his universe, and the nature of life. His method, like Eddington's, resorts finally to intuition, which he maintains is an indispensable aid to formal logic in the searching of ultimate causes. He erects a theory by purging scientific fact of its inconsistencies, identifying a perfect consistency with truth; and indeed whatever else *Eureka* may be, it is an extraordinary anticipation of the modern criticism of the use of a purely factual science as a philosophy.

Eureka, of course, is a poem, not a Newtonian or Einsteinian hypothesis, and suffers from its attempts to square imagination with the imperfect cosmogonies of science just as "Paradise Lost" suffers from its tie-up with an intractable theology. Done, like his **"Mellonta Tauta,"** as pure fancy it would have been magnificent. But Poe was overweening. It was not enough to be poet, he must be the all-explainer, the scientist too!

And yet in a criticism of Poe, the evidence that *Eureka* affords of a power to bring into lucid order an extraordinary range of knowledge and to carry through a train of logical thinking that a practiced philosopher might envy, is surely important. His inaccuracies and his errors in metaphysics are less significant than the extraordinary force of mind displayed upon the whole. Undoubtedly it is true that the neurotic Poe, always trembling on the brink of insanity, did dramatize the logical faculties, and did erect in himself the fiction of the supreme logician, the superman of ratiocination from whom nothing was hid, to whom by the cold processes of inflexible reason the universe became subject as to God. Nevertheless, however absurd his monomania, he did possess in a high degree the faculty of logical analysis and that of scientific imagination. Far from being a wild fancy, *Eureka* is a startling indication of what Poe, with a different equipment and purposes differently directed, might have been able to accomplish in the realm of constructive thought. It is certain that the shams of current literary criticism were no more transparent to him than the crooked conventionality of average thinking. If he had been interested, like other American intellectuals of his time, in politics, in slavery, in morality, in religion, he would have been as radical in his way as Emerson or Thoreau. But he was not interested. A little rant upon the Abolitionists (in the attempt to score on Lowell), some lucid remarks about the fallacy of progress and the weakness of democracy, and other notes in passing, sum up his criticism in the area where the most serious American writing was being done. Formal religion touched his brooding soul so little that it no more occurred to him to attack it—than it does to most scientists. The Protestantism of his day was simply irrelevant to his quest for a stranger beauty than this planet affords. When he came back to earth from Aiden or Weir, it was to search for the one beauty which this earth contained for him—the beauty of order, form, of laws beautifully coöperating until they were seen as Law, and controlling that physical matter which he believed existed only to subserve the subtle spirit of the universe. La Place, Descartes, Herschel, Newton, Faraday, spoke to him, when Plato, Christ, Kant, Emerson, were negative or meaningless. His hatred of the whole Transcendental school was surely not all due to his jealousy of Boston's prestige in American literature. He felt, I think, that the Transcendentalists were taking short cuts to omniscience, drowning logic in a sea of words, and using intuition not as an aid, but as a substitute for the lovely art of mathematical thought.

Poe the neurotic was also Poe the logician and analyst, and if his sensitive imagination projected lurid worlds of emotion more darkly terrible than the dreams of his fellow romanticists, in less abandoned hours he could subdue his mind to the rigorous processes of the intellect, follow the direction of scientific thinking, or put plan, order, and form into the supersensitive world of his overcharged fancy. Amid "the gorgeous and fantastic draperies, in the solemn carvings of Egypt, in the wild cornices and furniture, in the Bedlam patterns of the carpets of tufted gold," where his hero "a bounden slave in the trammels of opium" pursues his desperate, perverted love, there are laws of human nature, profoundly illustrated by the spectral figures of his plot, which are reasoned as logically as the plot itself. The tossing seas and fiery depths of neuroticism were charted by the same faculty that dared, in *Eureka,* to force consistency upon the universe. Nor is it without interest to note that when the physical and the moral man were on the verge of final shipwreck, and when, as his last letters show, his tragic fortitude was breaking down into self-pity, it was then that his now uncontrollable egomania raised this intellectual faculty to its height of confidence and display. With it he could order everything but himself, and this is natural, since Poe's self was God, and more than the universe.

And indeed the persuasive beauty of Poe's best work is due not to its subject matter—which is valid only when he projects his own morbidity, and then of a nature that has commanded more interest than liking—but to a subtle relationship between idea and form that gives quality to the childish excitements of **"The Gold Bug"** and to the perverted madness of **"Usher"** alike. It is this feeling for the rhythm of a consistent principle which makes the *aperçus* of his criticism invaluable, and his guesses in science at least remarkable.

10

But Poe suffered as do all who live inwardly and seek absolute beauty (even Shelley and certainly Coleridge) from a failure to assimilate the external world. Such men are so unsure in external reality as to be very dependent upon circumstance, and may remain entirely in the abstract and so fail to be artists, or resort uncritically (like Poe's contemporary, Chivers) to images unworthy of their conceptions. In his best stories of ratiocination, Poe escaped entirely from this disaster, thanks, perhaps, to the artificiality of his medium. He arranged his story as the scientist arranges his experiment in the laboratory, and restricting himself to bare incident, uncolored by his own experience, built up the pure form of his chain of reasoning. But even in these stories, and much more when the beauty he sought to capture was of an idea or an emotion rather than of an exercise in logic, he was dependent upon the furniture of an outside world in which he was well read but little experienced. A Rue Morgue could be described, but for Ligeia, Morella, Berenice, and Eleonora, complete habitations had to be created in which, no matter how fantastically, they might live. For his shapes of beauty he needed a *décor*—and thanks to the provincialism of America in the thirties and forties, and to a life that when not spent in dreams or in routine work was lived almost exclusively in books, Poe's prose and much of his poetry is full of descriptive terms that are second-hand to a degree unusual in

genius. This is the cause of the distaste amounting almost to disgust with which even the most appreciative read too much of Poe at a sitting. The stifling luxury, and the parvenu profusion of his backgrounds, are phases of the same taste that makes the plushy eloquence and tawdry erudition of his prose style in description. Since his own room was bare he lived in his reading, and from his reading he borrowed his stage sets, which are like the furnishings of a de luxe hotel apartment, where everything has just come from somewhere else with the price tags still attached.

This bad bookishness, which, much more than his morbidity, is offensive in both the poetry and prose of Poe, was tragically inevitable. The strange beauty he grasped in exquisite form with an imagination that kept its sense of order even when the dreams seemed maddest, was pathetically dependent for expression upon images that had to be drawn from experience. And Poe's experience outside of his own soul was so largely verbal! Words he knew, knew too well, for in his constant playing with their powers of suggestion he became, like his modernist successors, too often uncritical of what they meant. He pillaged words from his abundant reading and used them for effects precisely as the architects of his period reared their "Saracenic-Gothic" piles out of any column, cornice, or parapet that took their fancy. The backgrounds of his stories come from the pictures that his mind made when he read: it is not Rome or Paris but Bulwer and Moore that he remembers when he needs a scene. Even nature—which was already a specialty in America—he could not see directly, with such rare exceptions as the tulip-tree in **"Landor's Cottage,"** but assembled his descriptions from a half-remembered lumber of reading in his head, into which his genius struck fire only when the scene was on the road that leads to the underworld. Sincere for himself alone, and essentially unrelated to the life about him, it was through words only that Poe made his contacts. No wonder then that he helped himself so freely to quotation, reference, description, wherever he found them, and in matters of taste was dependent in everything but pure literature upon what he read in his books. Books were his chief school and almost his entire external experience. The art of securing great effects with his borrowed furnishings was of course his own, and so was the genius by which in his best work they are transmuted into new and intensely original shapes of pure beauty. He had, indeed, the methods and the conscience of a journalist, combined with the intuitive sense for *ultimate* beauty of a great artist. He could be a great poet and a skilful and unscrupulous and pretentious magazinist, both in the same sketch and almost at the same time.

11

Some writers are capable of a comprehensive, an exalted, and an unshakable unity. They approximate culture itself, and apply to whatever passes through the mint of their genius an intellect and an imagination that are always of the first rank and which always function with magnitude and nearly always with success. Goethe was such a writer. Another order of writers also works in a unity of genius or talent. They are single, not myriad, minded, but the singleness if narrow is consistent and intense. They do one thing well, and are content to be one thing. Such a writer was Tennyson, and Hawthorne was another. But still others are comprehensive in their powers and ambitions, willing and wishing to grasp the universe, yet cursed with a tendency to split upon tension, and hence uneven in a high degree. They have the scope of the broad genius, the intensity of the narrow one, but lack the ability of one and the steadiness of both. Such a writer was Poe, who had the pretensions of a Leonardo, but, like Shakespeare's Antony, could not hold his shape, except in a combination of circumstances exactly right for him. As his character split apart under nervous pressure, so did his work. His reach was infinite, his grasp uncertain except in fortunate moments, but then, tight.

In poetry, the condition that permitted success seems to have been an equal balance and happy correspondence between inspiration and technique. When the dark loveliness of the images that haunted Poe's imagination yielded their beauty to sounds and rhythms exquisitely artificial and yet profoundly expressive, then he wrote that "pure poetry" which was so deeply to intrigue the nineteenth century:

> Banners yellow, glorious, golden,
>   On its roof did float and flow
> (This—all this—was in the olden
>   Time long ago),
> And every gentle air that dallied,
>   In that sweet day,
> Along the ramparts plumed and pallid
>   A wingéd odor went away.

Or:

> Resignedly beneath the sky
> The melancholy waters lie.
> So blend the turrets and shadows there
> That all seem pendulous in air,
> While from a proud tower in the town
> Death looks gigantically down.

Or:

> Come, let the burial rite be read—the funeral
>   song be sung:
> An anthem for the queenliest dead that ever
>   died so young,
> A dirge for her the doubly dead in that she
>   died so young.

Or:

> In Heaven a spirit doth dwell
> Whose heart-strings are a lute;
> None sing so wildly well
> As the angel Israfel.

Or:

> And all my days are trances,
>   And all my nightly dreams
> Are where thy gray eye glances
>   And where thy footstep gleams—
> In what ethereal dances,
>   By what eternal streams.

In these poems the tricks (if you wish to call them so) of repetition and alliteration are only the more obvious touches of a structure of sound that rises in intellectual response to the poetic idea.

But in **"The Raven"** and in **"The Bells"** the artificer has overworked his metal, adding ornament when the inspiration was cold.

> On the cushion's velvet lining that the lamp-
>   light gloated o'er,
> But whose velvet violet lining with the lamp-
>   light gloating o'er
>   *She* shall press, ah, nevermore!

and:

> How the danger sinks and swells,—
> By the sinking or the swelling in the anger of
>   the bells,
>   Of the bells,
> Of the bells, bells, bells, bells,
>   Bells, bells, bells—
> In the clamor and the clangor of the bells!

Here the journalist has exploited the poet.

In his prose success was even more arbitrary. His technical skill seldom failed but his taste betrayed him often. The effort in his satirical and humorous pieces is painful. They are shrill. And so with his works of pseudo-knowledge, his imitations of voyages, his personalities in criticism, and his set pieces of description. Like his God in *Eureka,* he was extended over the universe of literary effort, and he could not concentrate power enough upon these crystallizations. He did them with his left hand, which only his long habit of skill guided.

Thus in his stories the whole man functioned only in two sets of circumstances—and those very different. When his oversensitized dreams sprang from deep intuitions of a human tendency magnified by the abnormality of his ego, then his shapes of beauty had meaning for others. When these dreams crystallized about an idea in an order prepared by his logical mind, then his ever ready eloquence of prose flowed into the pattern.

The popular taste has been right, I think, in preferring **"The Fall of the House of Usher"** as the best of these achievements. Here the blending is complete. The neurotic's intuition is dressed in the folds of macabre but intelligible romance. The idea of tendency is dominant, the images of sensitiveness vivid, the symbolism of soul destruction powerful, the relevance to the dark universals of humanity in nervous tension true with that poetic truth which outlasts apparent fact. And the artifice of style and consummate skill of plot elaboration is such as Poe himself described in the lines from *Eureka* quoted above, and is indispensable if this heavy charge of imagination is to be sublimated by a creative act.

> About the whole mansion and domain there hung an atmosphere peculiar to themselves and their immediate vicinity: an atmosphere which had no affinity with the air of heaven, but which had reeked up from the decayed trees, and the gray wall, and the silent tarn: a pestilent and mystic vapor, dull, sluggish, faintly discernible, and leaden-hued. . . . Perhaps the eye of a scrutinizing observer might have discovered a barely perceptible fissure, which, extending from the roof of the building in front, made its way down the wall in a zigzag direction, until it became lost in the sullen waters of the tarn.

These stories were difficult feats of coördination by a brain grappling with nothing less than the secrets of the universe. But Poe was equally fortunate in lesser but equally original exercises of logic and intuition performed in a more mundane air, when the mystic vapors rising from his inner life were for the moment quiescent. In his tales of ratiocination, his constructive faculties worked in paths cleared by logic, following ideas of the pure intellect unclouded by emotion. And freed for the moment of neuroticism, his clear brain had a task the ease of which is reflected in the perfect narrative sequence and simple, lucid style of the best of these stories. **"The Purloined Letter"** as in **"The Fall of the House of Usher"** he was Poe complete, in a self-unity, even though the dominants and recessives of his temperament differed sharply in the two stories. Effort and idea were exactly balanced.

And this was true also in the best of his criticism, where his subject was the nature of beauty or a device of art, like the tale or the short poem, where he was a familiar. Under such circumstances his intuition is keen, his style lucid, his judgment sound. Let opposition thwart him, a jealousy irritate his ego, or the journalistic challenge of the moment set him to making copy, and he shoots off in exhibitionism, or flounders in

pretense, with only a keen sentence here and there for the profit of the reader. But see him on the short story:

> A skilful literary artist has constructed a tale. If wise, he has not fashioned his thoughts to accommodate his incidents; but having conceived, with deliberate care, a certain unique or single *effect* to be wrought out, he then invents such incidents— he then combines such events as may best aid him in establishing this preconceived effect. If his very initial sentence tend not to the outbringing of this effect, then he has failed in his first step. In the whole composition there should be no word written, of which the tendency, direct or indirect, is not to the one pre-established design.

It is true that this description of *the* short story is really the description of *a* kind of short story, although a very effective one, true also that it much more accurately defines Poe's own work than Hawthorne's, to which it was applied. Nevertheless it is one of the classic analyses—or self-analyses—of critical literature.

But even when the nice adjustment between an oversensitive ego and his ambition was complete, some evidence of split, or at least of tension, is nearly always visible in Poe's writing, and to this no exception can be made except for a few poems and perhaps one or two criticisms. It is always present in his stories, usually in style. That his first great literary reputation was made in France is really not at all surprising. It was, paradoxically, easier for the French than for English readers to apprehend his essential genius. They were not thrown off by the meretricious and the impure in his style, because, like Poe himself, but for a different reason, they were concerned only with the beauty of words. Poe's tawdriness and his dependence upon the second-hand were not evident to them, since they got only the sound and the simple meaning of the words, the connotations, as usual, escaping aliens to the tongue. And for those who read in French, which means of course practically all Frenchmen, it is not too much to say that Poe's prose narrative is usually better for them in French than for us in the original. It is refined and purified by a taste better than his own. As for his best poetry, which made, of course, a particular appeal to perfecters of the beautiful in image and sound, like Baudelaire, the beauty of word sounds and the exquisite art of their arrangement is his peculiar triumph, and if such poems as his cannot be translated, they can at least be far better apprehended by alien readers (as with Virgil and Homer) than poetry less dependent upon verbal music. But Poe's poetry needs no defense. At its best it is the best of its kind, and flawless.

12

I have praised Poe as a great journalist. His merits in pure literature are not so easy to rank, and cannot be allowed to rest only upon a happy coincidence of virtuosity with an appropriate subject.

His passion, well rationalized, for beauty as an end in itself, was not original, of course, with him, indeed, as a philosophy was no more than an ardent adaption, from Coleridge and others, of a principle exactly suited to his own cravings. But since he was an American bred and nourished within the confines of an ethical tradition, his convinced æstheticism gave him a freedom such as no other contemporary man of letters of anything like his power enjoyed. Calvinistic Protestantism had left a sense of duty to the moral principle that was as strong in the South as in the North. This obligation, which Emerson sublimated into a religion, which weighed upon Thoreau, and was the irritant of Hawthorne's genius, the trade of Longfellow, and the obsession of Melville, Poe utterly escaped. He not only did not believe in it; he did not even for an instant feel it. Beside him the antimoralists of our own day are in comparison perverted missionaries. Only Keats in England shared his passionate, unqualified devotion to beauty as such and without a question.

And this beauty which he served was a "wilder" beauty than earth knew. He was like the spirit of his **"Al Aaraaf"** who sought another star, and if he too was driven back, he never ceased to renew his wanderings. It is a romanticist's beauty, transcending normal earthly experience, and seeking forms of expression that suggest the unearthly. Whether his neuroticism was the cause or the result of this passion is hard to say. It was probably both, and more specifically it was the psychical circumstance that conditioned his search. The waves of mental and physical distress that dashed through his sensitive spirit, the exaltations and abasements, were transmuted in his self-centered ego into shapes of grandeur and escape which, though out of space, out of time, were the very fabric for a dream world that could be made precise in art. Nor is this a phenomenon of the romantic movement and to be dismissed as such. The instinct to create forms of beauty free from earthly inconsistency and patterned out of desire, is inevitable at certain arcs of the evolutionary curve. Romanticism, and particularly the dominance of a romantic literature, favor it of course, but the great poets all know it. Poe's distinction is not that he gave a new though late intensity to romanticism, but that the concentration of his life within the ego created a geography so lurid and baleful, so utterly determined by factors of diversity in beauty itself, and projected from the fires of his inner consciousness with such immediacy, and yet with such control, that no saner writer has been able to produce, no insane writer able to master, its like.

I say no saner writer, implying a relative insanity in Poe, yet his world of Weir, while murky with the mists of neuroticism and therefore consonant with visions of that irrationality which lurks in the sanest, was nevertheless and profoundly a world of order. For the visions of Poe differ from the visions of irrational dreamers because they have order. They have form because form was implicit in Poe's imagination, and (as I have already said) they invariably mean something in human experience. If that experience is in the dream stories invariably morbid, that is because in the morbid the wall of reality wears thin, and because, for Poe, morbidity was an inevitable accompaniment of emotional excitement.

And this order, which leads him to explore the mathematics of the universe for symbols, is no accidental attribute of beauty. It is a beauty itself, and clearly Poe belongs with those philosophers who find the ultimate reality to be only man's perception, or imposition, of form in chaos. The science that Poe brings to his aid may be inaccurate, the decorations of his pieces may be stale, but the intuitive perception that only by form is beauty realized is more profound than many an æstheticism more consistently practiced than his.

This beauty, wild yet ordered, pressed upon expression with a vehemence in proportion to its unconventionality. And this is the reason why Poe, in variance from all journalistic practice, wrote and rewrote, both poetry and prose, ever trying phrases in new contexts, or rephrasing with new words. In poetry especially he persisted until the intangibles of ethereal beauty are realized not so much in statement as by sound and rhythm and a subtle play of verbal light and shade.

And furthermore, the intensity of Poe's own ego made this ordered world of strange beauty to seem of dominant importance. His contempt for realism he adequately expressed, but the realism he despised was the realism of supposed fact. Reality for him lay only in the perception of order, because only through order did his insulated soul make contact with the universe. Yet if the universe was important, his own soul was even more so. He made his discoveries with the self-assurance of a God who draws back the veil of the probable and commonplace, to show behind it the livid realms where disordered fancy tortures its victims, then declares that these too are a part of the order of the universe. It was the antithesis of that calm reliance in material comfort upheld by science which his generation was so rapidly acquiring. And if Poe is often shrill and exaggerated it may well be because there was only defeat for him in the new philosophy of efficient and strenuous normalism, and because an aggressive egoism was indispensable in a writer who in such an environment was determined to be heard.

13

There was, as I have tried to indicate on earlier pages of this book, a summary quality in the settled civilization of the Atlantic seaboard in the decades before the great cataclysm of the Civil War and the re-creative processes of industrial development and the opening of the West that followed in the later nineteenth century. This static condition was most notable in the South and New England, but it was discoverable in New York and Philadelphia also, although partly obscured by the rush of a new economic life. The chief product of the South was character, and the South was really articulate only in oratory. But New England was both intellectual and articulate. A type of mind was developed there as a fruit of a long ripening that in America, and perhaps in Western civilization, was an end-product. There are no more Emersons. That serene and yet intensely practical orienting of life toward ideal ends, in which energy and contemplation were reconciled, was an effort that has left its impress upon the mental, and indeed upon the political and social, life of every American, but the creative act is finished. A Thoreau is quite as incredible here and now as the English find Gandhi, although his like may reappear in the future. We are not that kind of man any longer. He states our problem, but we turn from his solution, not because it is impossible, but because it seems impossible to us. The will of God that he, like unbroken generations of Protestants before him, tried to interpret is no longer a reality for us, not even in the monistic form in which he saw it. We belong to a different dispensation, if indeed in our momentary sense of power over physical circumstance we are aware of the necessity for any dispensation. Our prophets are as yet unborn.

Emerson and Thoreau and Hawthorne, in their ideals are further away from us than the humorous, worldly elegance of Irving, or even the romantic simplicities of Cooper. Their ideas are burningly alive, but only as stimulants for new thinking. Melville, too, is an extinct species. However modern his sense of the dark recesses of the human spirit, his ideology can be interpreted but not absorbed by a modern. We in our time will never repeat his desperate Transcendentalism, nor let our imaginations expand into shapes of grandeur symbolizing powers of good and evil that we now permit neither to man nor to God. Instead of God's experiment in New England, instead of Penn's woods where the inner light was to guide a civilization, instead of Brook Farms and Harmonys and Shaker villages, and the pioneer theocracy of Deseret, it was our destiny to carry on (first, if not finally) with Ford factories, Chicago, and New York. They were, it proved, the first order of business for the mature American, although not until after the Civil War did we wholeheartedly realize it. The Emersons and the rest were premature in the history of the United States, but not in the history of the human mind, where they have their place and have borne their fruit.

Poe was not premature, nor does he represent the end-product of a civilization. He belongs in any urban, sophisticated culture. Discount his freight of stale romanticism and he slips into modern life like a hand into a glove. Born in and living in Europe, he would have been the same Poe, with an absorption of a sounder, less provincial culture, and a readier market perhaps for his wares, but without the strong stimulus of American journalism that both permitted and commanded him to make his dreams and ratiocinations lucid and impressive for the general reader. Under fortunate conditions he might, indeed, have written far more poetry, with quicker and more adequate recognition, but Poe fortunate would not have been Poe. Indeed, in a like social and economic condition he would have drifted toward the underworld far more quickly. Mrs. Clemm's basket would have been oftener empty. His pride and vanity would have been oftener hurt. In England the great age of romanticism had definitely passed. The Moores and the Bulwers would have been his guides. And in Europe he would have lacked one pitiful success that meant much to his egoism. Abroad he would not have found a naïve community that he could impress with his scientific learning and literary erudition and surprise by cutting criticisms in a press that was accustomed to be ignorant, tolerant, and good-humored in questions of art. Nor would he have found a quick intelligence among the populace that could be flattered by writing which was always lucid yet well over their heads. These successes, which made life tolerable for him, would have been far harder to come at abroad. The cultured there were more cultured than he was, the uncultured were unintelligent.

I am arguing that Poe was not misplaced in America, in spite of his immense detachment from everything American except journalism, nor premature in spite of his seeming discrepancy with later industrialism. For Poe is in the truest sense a prototype of the modern intellectual who himself is both product and antithesis of industrialism.

He has the complete detachment from those questions of welfare and progress for the mass that would make him at home among the intellectuals of what has aptly been called our North Atlantic civilization, and uneasy in the Y.M.C.A. or a Methodist church. He has their devotion to abstract idea, whether called beauty or logic. He has the modern desire for publicity, which is the intellectual's method of living off a crowd that he despises. Most of all, his intense sensitiveness and congenital morbidity gave him, nearly a century ahead of his successors, that power of acute registration of the life of the nerves which is so entirely characteristic of our modern rebels against the mechanizing of industrialism. Poe's morphine was just such an excitant as the roar and racket, the speed and recurrent stimulation, of New York. He was congenitally febrile and we have become so. He is one of us, as we recognize. And the beauty he attains is the fragile beauty of artifice: exquisite, penetrating, unhealthy, perfect in form, unsubstantial in substance, sincere only in its effects, subtle, but profound only in its dependence upon the subconsciousness. It is the beauty of Proust, of Virginia Woolf, of Cabell, of the modern metaphysical poets.

A Poe in the forties of our literary history was as inevitable as an Emerson or a Hawthorne. He was phenomenal only in his pathology, which made his nervosity abnormal in his time, and of course in his genius, which I believe was essentially a genius for form. Regarded as an American he is essentially a journalist, regarded as a poet he is at his best as a lyricist of unearthly beauty, regarded as a man of letters he is the most articulate of neurotics, and at the same time a cool craftsman, intuitive, inventive, and in full control of the logic of related ideas.

Poor fellow, with his worn, humorless face, and the look of one who expects an affront, what a man he might have been if he could have turned those analytic powers of his upon his own inflamed ego, and seen that a feverish life-long show-off was not the way to convince Philadelphia and New York of his genius! But that, as I have tried to say in these pages, would have been not to have been Poe. I am not much impressed by the arguments that poverty, or impotence, or youthful conditioning made Poe what he was. They had their part no doubt, but the thing that made him was that same psychic tension which kept him from ever once heartily laughing. One laugh, and we might have had not our Poe, but Poe fulfilled as the universal mind he sought to be. He could not laugh, and that was his tragedy—if indeed a world-wide reputation for beauty wrested from the macabre and an exquisiteness of rhythm such as English poetry has rarely elsewhere shown, can be called a tragedy at this space of time from his miseries and frustrations!

Emerson R. Marks (essay date 1961)

SOURCE: "Poe as Literary Theorist: A Reappraisal," in *American Literature,* Vol. 33, No. 3, November, 1961, pp. 296-306.

[*Looking back at Poe's critical writings from a mid-twentieth century perspective, Marks finds them a valuable resource despite Poe's occasional extremism in critical opinions. Mark asserts that Poe had sound critical principles with respect to the art of literary creation and the role of criticism.*]

There is a double motive for a fresh assessment of Edgar Poe's criticism. Every generation finds it necessary to reappraise past writers, a kind of periodic stocktaking as appropriate to dead critics as to dead poets. Often this is true because aspects of a man's work are found to answer some current need or to articulate some newly emerged aspiration of the common psyche.

The poetry of Donne and Blake and the criticism of Coleridge come readily to mind in this regard. My present concern, however, is less to argue that Poe's criticism has in fact taken on such renewed utility than to investigate the question of its general value, which I take to be the necessary prior step.

Aside from this, Poe invites reconsideration because of the longstanding uncertainty about his worth as a critic and especially because of the disparity between his reputation in France, where since Baudelaire he has been idolized, and his reputation in the English-speaking world, where frequently he has been at best patronized. With us, today, Poe seems to stand highest for his stories, which still provide material for serious studies like Levin's *The Power of Blackness* as well as for amateur literary psychoanalyses. His poetry is valued almost exclusively for a few lyrics regarded as excellent examples of a very limited kind. Though his criticism perhaps fares better than his poetry, the homage paid it is mainly historical. When, rarely, his doctrines are considered on their intrinsic merits, Poe is generally credited with having propounded a poetic ontology more thoroughly defined by Coleridge a generation earlier and an analytical method destined to be elaborated by the New Critics a century later. Yet even outside of France one finds occasional sharp dissent from this grudging estimate. Writers as respected and different as Saintsbury, Eliot, and Auden have rated his critical writing highly. Edmund Wilson [in "Poe as a Literary Critic," 1942, reprinted above], called it "the most remarkable body of criticism ever produced in the United States."

Though unanimity in such a matter is an idle hope, some reduction of disagreement now seems possible if we pose a broad initial question: In the whole context of what we believe to be the soundest criticism past and present, what features of Poe's method and theory, what specific evaluations, retain validity? The answer would require a book. I propose here only the tentative emphases of such a book, not in every case the familiar ones given in the literary histories, but those which emerge from a survey of the whole range of Poe's critical prose—the essays, the editorials, the reviews, the letters. If, except to biographers and bibliographers, the great bulk of what he wrote is almost worthless, we still have to scrutinize the trash for the clues it supplies to the value and significance of the treasure and as a check on our too ready tendency to see all Poe's ideas as facile restatements of European Romantic prototypes. When this has been done, I think we may fairly conclude that Poe is worth study today—and I mean by today's critics and literary theorists—on several counts.

In the interest of honest perspective, however, it may be well first to review his critical shortcomings. There are several. For all his insight into the importance of unity, Poe was curiously blind to the aesthetic value of a complex whole that resides in a writer's control of a great mass of material. To this failing, rather than to his misreading of Coleridge or to his romantic lyrical bias, I should ascribe his declaration that a long poem is a contradiction in terms, his preference for the tale over the novel, and his impatience with talk of "sustained power." Only a favored few, if any, he believed, were possessed of the "sculptural taste" needed to take in a novel's "totality of beauty." Poe had got hold of a real critical problem here, one that Percy Lubbock was to explore decades later in *The Craft of Fiction.* But what Lubbock regards only as a challenge to our appreciative powers Poe declares flatly to be prohibitive. It is the same, though for additional reasons, with the long poem.

This ban on mere length is a serious theoretical restriction which produced some unfortunate results in critical practice. Poe is seldom at his best in his many reviews of novels. He resorts to long paraphrases of the plot and to fussing pedantically over minutiae of his author's grammar. His uncertainty leads him to rash and crippling generalizations: that a novel differs radically in kind from a short story; that its unity is only the "unity of the writer's individual thought"; most grotesque, that it must contain the author's observations, *in propria persona,* on the incidents of his narrative. To blame a novelist for keeping himself out of his fiction is at best questionable. To praise Defoe for doing the reverse in *Robinson Crusoe,* as Poe does, is not only hopelessly to confuse author and fictive narrator; it is to reduce the novel to a kind of didactic confessional, which by Poe's own best theory is virtually to deny it any status as an art form.

Second, I should place certain ultra-romantic limitations of taste by which he condemns, among other things, English metaphysical poetry (marred by "bathos, baldness, and utter imbecility"), Greek tragedy (crude and primitive), *Pilgrim's Progress* ("ludicrously over-rated"), Molière's plays, and Fielding's novels. His preferences among poems, especially his choices for the highest honors, Shelley's "The Sensitive Plant" and Keats's "Ode to a Nightingale," suggest that in Poe the nineteenth-century tendency to confine poetry to the lyrical reaches an extreme. He wonders whether a dramatic poem is not a "flat contradiction in terms"; in any case neither the dramatic nor, as he warns Lowell, the narrative has anything to do with "true" poetry.

Nearly allied to this lyrical bias of taste is a relative indifference to comedy and satire that seems oddly inconsistent with his own satirical experiments and his literary hoaxes. Poe brushes aside Fielding and Smollett and is scornful of Molière. To the comic in poetic form he is downright hostile. In his view, the element of rhythm renders the ratiocinative, the sarcastic, and

the humorous, though all admissible in prose fiction, foreign to the essence of poetry. Butler's *Hudibras* and Pope's *Essay on Man* he classes among "humorous pieces," not really poetry at all. Yet the comic and the satiric are perhaps only the most noteworthy of many modes of human response to experience which Poe places off limits to the poet. His perverse dictum that the death of a beautiful woman is the most poetical of all subjects may be charitably excused as an apologia for a favorite theme of his own verse. But on any view his conception of the range of subject matter proper to poetic treatment is ludicrously narrow, at times even "precious"; a mountain, he observes in one place, is "more poetical than a pair of stairs."

A fourth weakness, his emphasis on originality, might be forgiven if it were less obtrusive. In some sense, of course, every good writer is original, and Poe might have invoked Dr. Johnson's massive authority for his insistence on this point. Only in Poe's criticism the notion seems both obsessive and shallow, perhaps no more than a conscious elevation to theoretical dignity of his own fertile inventiveness. The morbid suspicions of derivativeness that darken many of his reviews and his strident charges of plagiarism against Longfellow are a high price to pay for whatever truth may lie in his belief that the "desire of the new is an element of the soul. . . . " It is obvious, in any event, that unless the criterion of originality is restricted by far more rigorous qualifications than Poe offers, it must logically negate his deeply held conviction that poetry can be defined, that every poem belongs, in his own favorite phrase, to a species of composition.

Finally, there is a defect of an excellence. Within its limits Poe's condemnation of the didactic heresy, as he formulated it in **"The Poetic Principle,"** is sound. Too often, though, in his practical criticism, he combats this heresy with the opposite heresy, thus providing ammunition for those who would picture him as a mere aesthete, a kind of early American Oscar Wilde. It is one thing—and a good thing—to insist that poetry is poetry and not metrical polemics; it is quite another to argue, as Poe does in a *Graham's* review of Charles Sprague, that "didactic subjects are utterly *beyond,* or rather beneath, the province of true poesy," or that one of Elizabeth Barrett's poems is least meritorious *because* most philosophical. His proper resentment of poetry that has a design on us (as Keats so nicely put it) enables him to make some provocative remarks on the nature and limitations of allegorical verse. But his bald pronouncement that "*all* allegories are contemptible" is of a kind that degrades his prosecution of the didactic heresy to the level of an inquisition.

Given such grave deficiencies, can we justify Edmund Wilson's opinion that Poe's criticism ought to be with us, as with the French, "a vital part of our intellectual equipment"? I think we can, though my reasons for saying so may not in every instance be those Mr. Wilson would adduce. They refer primarily to four fundamental and closely related theoretical issues: the nature of artistic imitation, poetic form, the creative process, and the function of criticism itself.

Important though it is, Poe's exposure of the didactic heresy rests on shiftier theoretical grounds and is less needed today than his clear-sighted and consistent rejection of another fallacy prevalent in his times and destined despite him to be even more widely entertained after his death. It has been variously called the realist fallacy, the confusion of art and life, the fallacy of imitative form. So far as I know, Poe has yet to be given the place rightly due him among those critics and aestheticians—the very best—who have admitted the aesthetic worthlessness of fidelity of representation. "The mere imitation, however accurate," he writes in one of the **Marginalia** pieces, "of what *is*, in Nature, entitles no man to the sacred name of 'Artist'. . . . " Man can, thanks to his innate sense of beauty, delight in the varied sights and sounds of real life, but repeating them orally or in writing does not constitute "poesy."

In 1913 Clive Bell thought it necessary to explain that the "world of Shakespeare's plays is by no means so lifelike as the world of Mr. Galsworthy's, and therefore those who imagine that the artistic problem must always be the achieving of a correspondence between printed words or painted forms and the world as they know it are right in judging the plays of Shakespeare inferior to those of Mr. Galsworthy." Bell's logic is as fine as the irony of his rhetoric, but Edgar Poe anticipated him in both by seventy years when he reasoned that if "truth is the highest aim of either Painting or Poesy, then Jan Steen was a greater artist than Angelo, and Crabbe is a more noble poet than Milton."

The tendency of some to regard this concept as a mere adjunct to an "escapist" view of poetry, irrelevant to literature closely concerned with human problems, can be discredited by Poe's own reasoning. In judging specific works he applied the criterion generally and without distinction of genre. He praises N. P. Willis for achieving a truthfulness in his drama *Tortesa* which is not a mere "Flemish perception of truth." He invokes the principle again in rejecting what he calls the ill-founded charge that Dickens's characters are caricatures: "caricature seldom exists . . . where the correspondent parts are *in keeping*. . . ." Far from being an escapist crotchet, this perception shrewdly confirms Aristotle's injunction to prefer probable impossibilities to improbable possibilities. Aristotelian, too, is his observation in this same review (of *The Old Curiosity Shop*) that a detailed copying from life is precisely what makes a work of art unnatural.

The truth Poe grasped here of course parallels Coleridge's distinction between a copy and a proper mimesis, but he expresses it with an air of such personal conviction and illustrates it so unerringly that it seems to have been his independent discovery. Almost every major critic has left his version of it somewhere on record, Dr. Johnson being a well-known exception. William Hazlitt's unfortunate habit of forgetting or ignoring the principle is usually overlooked; but not by Poe, who exposed its unhappy consequences in an otherwise laudatory review of the English critic's *Characters of Shakespeare's Plays*.

Perhaps the most insidious form of the art-life confusion still prevalent is that a poem communicates to the reader some passion or passions felt by the poet. Recent critics, in understandable reaction against romantic emotionalism in poetic theory, have made much of Eliot's view that "Poetry is not a turning loose of emotion, but an escape from emotion." This aphorism has been helpful. But if we want an elucidation of the nice problem of how natural and aesthetic emotions are both connected and different, we do better to turn from the "classical" Eliot to the romantic Poe: "True passion is prosaic—homely. Any strong mental emotion excites *all* the mental faculties; thus grief the imagination:—but in proportion as the effect is strengthened, the cause surceases. The excited fancy triumphs—the grief is subdued—chastened,—is no longer grief. In this mood we are poetic, and it is clear that a poem now written will be poetic in the exact ratio of its dispassion. A passionate poem is a contradiction in terms." Poe's reviews abound in applications of this idea, by which, for an interesting example, he censures Tennyson's "Locksley Hall."

When we insist today on the distinction between our experience of grief and our experience of an elegy, or between how it feels to be in love and how it feels to read a love lyric, we prefer to appeal to notions like aesthetic distance, artistic objectification, or controlling form, rather than to Poe's quasi-platonic intuition of the soul's thirst for the supernal. Yet it is no more just for this reason to deny him credit for the distinction itself than to reject Coleridge's secondary imagination along with the outmoded faculty psychology behind it. What counts—and it ought to count for a great deal—is that Poe propounded not a mere tenet of one critical school but a principle that can make the difference between good criticism and bad. It defines a condition of all literature, of Balzac's social novels as of Shelley's lyric poems, of *Madame Bovary* as of **"Ulalume."** According to Joseph Joubert, a remarkable Frenchman unknown to Poe, it is the great rule, the first rule, the only rule of art.

In all this Poe was working, like any good critic, toward a definition, a sound conception of literature as a whole and of poetry as one kind. His attack on the didactic heresy is best understood as part of this broad philosophical enterprise. He does not, at his best moments, espouse a purist position, freely conceding that a poem may be didactic if its morality does not obtrude, if it remains "the undercurrent of a poetical thesis." Though his fondness for dogmatic overstatement led him into intemperate denunciations of allegory and philosophical poetry, it is clear that Poe was grappling honestly with the crucial problem of the status of moral and cognitive values in literature. Perhaps only today, when after long debate critics have begun to see this problem as an aspect of mimesis, can we fully estimate the worth of Poe's pioneering efforts.

On the matter of poetic form, Poe's strong preference for the functional over the merely decorative image is especially remarkable as anticipating a principle of twentieth-century poetics. He objected to the essential splitting of form from content characteristic of poetry that presents truth wreathed "in gems and flowers." Longfellow's "Blind Bartimeus" receives his censure because its imagery (which Poe called the "upper current of meaning") depends for its *sole* interest on its explicit relation to the undercurrent of meaning. "What we read upon the surface," he complains, "would be *vox et praeterea nihil* in default of the Moral beneath." His argument should not be mistaken as an earlier version of J. C. Ransom's idea that the imagery in a poem constitutes a *texture* irrelevant to its *structure* of meaning. Poe rather conceived the nexus of idea and image, of metaphor and meaning, to be organic and symbolic, not illustrative and arbitrary. He was clearly ahead of his time in this conception, which has for us a clarity and significance it could not have had for his own or for several generations thereafter. With him of course it remained only an insight whose ontological implications he never explored. But if in our time we "know" so much more about these things, it is also true, to paraphrase T. S. Eliot in another context, that Poe is part of what we know.

Poe's contribution to the third of the three theoretical issues named above, the nature of the creative process, can be dealt with more briefly. One measure of the stature of any critic is his capacity at once to express the best insights of his age and to resist its ephemeral excesses. By period and taste Poe was a romantic, often in the worst sense. But nothing so eloquently illustrates the superior quality of his intellect than his dissent from aspects of the romantic attitude toward art which, from our point of view at least, are dubious. Chief among these is an unfortunate brand of antirationalism in the vulgar romantic notion of how a poem gets written. The romantics' healthy restoration of the intuitive to an honored place in the creative process tended too easily to degenerate into a complete distrust of the rational. By Poe's day prevailing opinion held the two mental operations to be mutually incompatible. In sharp protest against this obscurantism, he as-

serted not only the possibility but the necessity of reconciling genius and artistic skill. He can thus regard the signs of deliberate technique in Bryant's poems as positive merits rather than evidences of imperfect inspiration or meretricious artificialty. Characteristically exaggerating his case, he declares the making of a poem to be a matter of purely ratiocinative calculation. Creation and appreciation depend upon entirely separate mental faculties. We respond to a poem suprarationally, by what he called, taking the term from phrenology, the "faculty of Ideality." But the poem itself, as a means of eliciting that response, is a product of the "organs of Causality and Comparison," that is, of pure intellection. The poet always knows to the smallest detail what he is about, and the wildest "effusion of the Muse" is owing to *Method* for its value.

Though this doctrine is surely as "heretical" as any Poe deprecated, it was a useful corrective to the opposite bias of his time. More important, it motivated his concern with craftsmanship and his respect for conscious artistry. Too much has been made of the deficiencies of **The Philosophy of Composition,** which are after all not so much in what is said there as in what is left out. In our current understanding that a literary work is not something ineffably mysterious before which we can only emit appreciative gasps, that it is instead an object amenable to orderly and rewarding inspection, we are as much the heirs of Poe as of Coleridge or Henry James.

Like Coleridge and James, too, Poe enforced the inevitable corollary having to do with the critical function itself. He taught us to regard criticism as an exacting and respectable discipline, not an unexamined expression of conflicting and groundless opinions on books. He is at least more nearly right than wrong in his assertion that Schelling, the Schlegels, and Goethe do not and cannot differ in their principles from Kames, Johnson, and Blair, but only in their subtler elaboration and application of them. If his faith that the "science" of phrenology would someday eliminate *all* indefiniteness from critical theory is no better than quaint, his scornful rejection of the otiose relativism of *de gustibus,* then as now a seductive escape from hard thinking about the arts, is admirable. While Poe nowhere regards criticism as an autotelic activity divorced from literature, his declaration of its autonomy is among the earliest on record and the clearest: "Criticism is *not* . . . an essay, nor a sermon, nor an oration, nor a chapter in history, nor a philosophical speculation, nor a prose-poem, nor an art novel, nor a dialogue. In fact, it *can* be nothing in the world but—a criticism. . . . Following the highest authority, we would wish . . . to limit literary criticism to comment upon *Art.* A book is written—and it is only *as the book* that we subject it to review." By themselves, these words seem to place their author in the company of Whistler and Wilde. But read in the context of the total corpus of his critical writing, they associate him rather with Matthew Arnold's plea, two decades later, for critical disinterestedness. If in our time we must object that Poe has not here stated the whole truth about the critic's proper business, we ought at least to see that he has stated the first and the most important, the *point de repère* from which to take the bearing of all other claims.

W. H. Auden [in his introduction to *Edgar Allan Poe: Selected Prose and Poetry,* rev. ed., 1950] has expressed his astonishment that Poe, denied by his time and place issues and subjects of real importance, was nonetheless so fine a critic. Pointing to the contrast between Baudelaire's subjects—Delacroix, Constantin Guys, Wagner—and the worthless stuff assigned to Poe for review, Auden suggests that Poe's limitations were "entirely his misfortune, not his fault." This argument is attractive and plausible, but as much beside the point as it is beyond proof. It is by no means certain that Poe's shortcomings would have been substantially less had his opportunities been greater. On the other hand, there is no more reason to be astounded that Poe could extract sound theory from tawdry literary material than that many a novelist has written well and truly from scanty experience of his subject. The fact is that the critic, like Henry James's novelist, need only be one of those on whom nothing is lost. That Poe was such a one some readers in the past have suspected from the grace and precision of his style, reflecting as it does the combination of his sensitivity with that rare order of intelligence which—like his own Dupin's—can infer truth from very slender evidence. But we need no longer rely on so elusive a standard for taking the measure of Poe's achievement. The revolutionary complexities of recent literature have forced upon our criticism a degree of theoretical sophistication that is producing a revaluation of the critical past. In the light of that sophistication and that revaluation, much in Poe that once seemed obscure or perverse becomes clear and compelling.

Killis Campbell (essay date 1962)

SOURCE: "Contemporary Opinion of Poe," in *The Mind of Poe and Other Studies,* Russell & Russell, Inc., 1962, pp. 54-61.

[*Tracing Poe's career through his editorship of various magazines and the opinions of his contemporaries, Campbell concludes that though Poe was condemned by his fellow writers for being unduly severe in his reviews, he was also appreciated for his critical astuteness.*]

[It] was as critic . . . that Poe was best known to his contemporaries in America. By this I do not mean that his book-reviews and other critical papers were felt to exceed in importance his poems or his tales: the con-

sensus of intelligent opinion would have given first place in the matter of actual worth to his tales. Nevertheless, it is clear from the contemporary references to Poe that it was as critic and book-reviewer that he was most widely known to his generation in America: the mention of his name brought to the minds of his fellow-Americans of the thirties and forties of last century the idea, first of all, of book-reviewer and editor, rather than of tale-writer or of poet.

It does not affect the validity of this assertion to add that Poe was chiefly known as a fearless and caustic critic, rather than as a just and discriminating critic. Indeed, we shall find, I think, in the boldness and the occasional severity of his critical notices the secret of much of his contemporary vogue; for then, as now, it was the controversial and the spectacular that most readily caught the public fancy. And Poe's criticisms, though far more just than his contemporaries could have brought themselves to admit, were in no small degree controversial in nature,—or, at best, calculated to arouse controversy,—and were from the beginning more caustic, I imagine, than anything that had preceded them in American letters.

As in the case of his tales, it was during his connection with the *Southern Literary Messenger* (1835-1837) that he first came into prominence as a critic. Where or when he had served his apprenticeship as a book-reviewer, we shall probably never know. There is no tangible evidence that he had published anything in the way of criticism before 1835, save the **"Letter to B—"** in the *Poems* of 1831. But by the end of his first year with the *Messenger* he had won for that magazine a place among the leading American critical journals and had brought about an increase in its list of subscribers but little short of miraculous. His tales contributed in good part, no doubt, to this result, but it was his book-reviews and his scorching editorials that were mainly responsible; and it was these, even more than the tales, that attracted the newspaper critics of the time.

His reputation as critic seems to have undergone some arrest in its development during his connection with *Burton's Gentleman's Magazine* in 1839-1840, owing, as he would have had us believe, to the "milk-and-water" policy of its proprietor. But he won fresh laurels for himself while editor of *Graham's Magazine* (1841-1842), writing now some of the ablest of his critiques and earning for himself the almost uniform commendation of the Philadelphia press. Graham, in announcing his accession to his editorial staff, spoke of him as "a stern, just, and impartial critic" who held "a pen second to none in the country"; Lowell wrote in praise of his critical work as early as 1842; and Dr. J. Evans Snodgrass, a Baltimore editor of ability, declared in 1843 that his book-reviews were "unequalled in this country."

Messenger. We are grieved, and mortified to hear that you cannot again contribute to its pages but your objection in respect to receiving a copy without equivalent is un- tenable — any one of your pieces already published in our Journal being more than an equivalent to a sub- scription _in perpetuo_ This we say as publishers, without any intention to flatter, and having reference merely to the sum usually paid, to writers of far less reputation for articles immeasurably inferior.

In respect to your question touching the Editor of the Messenger, I have to reply that, for the last six months, the Editorial duties have been undertaken by myself. Of course, therefore, I plead guilty to all the criticisms of the Journal during the period mentioned. In addition to what evidence of misconception on the part of your friends you will assuredly find in the January number, I have now only to say that sincere admi- ration of the book reviewed was the predominant feeling in my bosom while penning the review

It would afford me the highest gratification should I find that you acquit me of this "foul charge". I will look with great anxiety for your reply.

Very resp⁵ & truly

N. Eb. 8ᵗ

Edgar A. Poe

A letter Poe wrote on April 12, 1836, in reply to Lydia H. Sigourney, who reacted negatively to one of his reviews in the Messenger.

As critic Poe also came prominently before the public in 1845 and 1846. During most of 1845 he was either assistant editor or editor of the *Broadway Journal,* and in that capacity wrote, each week, critiques of the more important books appearing at that time. In the spring and summer of 1846 he published in *Godey's Lady's Book* his **Literati.** Of his reviews in the *Broadway Journal* some were very able; but in a number of his papers published there, notably the articles attacking Longfellow, and likewise in the **Literati,** he stooped to personalities of various sorts and displayed a spitefulness that cost him the esteem of some of his staunchest admirers and earned for him the disapproval of most of the influential men of the time. Indeed, the unhappy reputation that he made by these papers he found it impossible to live down during the few remaining years allotted to him.

After 1846 he wrote nothing of importance as critic save **"The Poetic Principle,"** itself a revision in part of work earlier done.

In the notices of Poe published during his lifetime the trait in his criticisms that was most dwelt on was his severity. Before the end of the first year on the *Messenger* he had been taken to task by one of the Richmond newspapers for his "regular cutting and slashing"; and he had been attacked earlier in the year by the New York *Mirror,* in a satirical squib in which he figured as "Bulldog, the critick." Burton reproached him in 1839 for the sharpness of his critical notices in the *Gentleman's Magazine.* Dr. Snodgrass described him in 1842 as "provokingly hypercritical at times"; and in a notice of the *Broadway Journal* in April, 1845, he remarked that it "would be more significant to call this the Broad-axe Journal." George D. Prentice violently attacked the poet in 1843 in consequence of his contemptuous references to Carlyle. And Clark, who had been "used up" in the **Literati,** kept up a continual fire at him for a year or more after these papers began to appear. In the *Knickerbocker* of May, 1846, he speaks of Poe as " '*The Literary Snob*' continually obtruding himself upon public notice; to-day, in the gutter, to-morrow in some milliner's magazine; but in all places, and at all times magnificently snobbish and dirty."

Lowell suggested in his sketch in *Graham's* that Poe sometimes mistook "his phial of prussic acid for his ink-stand"; and he rebuked him in his *Fable for Critics* for throwing mudballs at Longfellow. The *Brook Farm Harbinger* in 1845 lamented the fact that Poe had taken to a sort of "blackguard warfare." A contributor to the *Talisman and Odd Fellow's Magazine* in September, 1846, dubbed him "the tomahawk man" and "the Comanche of literature"; and the Philadelphia editor, Du Solle, remarked in 1847, "If Mr. P. had not been gifted with considerable gall, he would have been devoured long ago by the host of enemies his genius has created." In *Holden's Dollar Magazine* for Janu-ary, 1849 (then edited by C. F. Briggs), Poe is ridiculed in the following doggerel lines:

> With tomahawk upraised for deadly blow,
> Behold our literary Mohawk, Poe!
> Sworn tyrant he o'er all who sin in verse—
> His own the standard, damns he all that's worse;
> And surely not for this shall he be blamed—
> For worse than his deserves that it be damned!
>
> Who can so well detect the plagiary's flaw?
> "Set thief to catch thief" is an ancient saw:
> Who can so scourge a fool to shreds and slivers?
> Promoted slaves oft make the best slave drivers!
> Iambic Poe! of tyro bards the terror—
> *Ego* is he—the world his pocket-mirror!

The articles published shortly after Poe's death also made much of his defects as critic. The trait now most stressed was not his causticity, I think, but his disposition to allow his prejudices and personal likes and dislikes to color his critical judgments. Among the first to make this complaint against him was his early friend, John Neal. Griswold declared in his "Memoir" that "his unsupported assertions and opinions were so apt to be influenced by friendship or enmity, by the desire to please or the fear to offend . . . that they should be received in all cases with distrust of their fairness," an opinion which was echoed by Clark in the *Knickerbocker* for October, 1850. Even Graham admitted that Poe's "outcry" against Longfellow was prejudiced and unjust. A contributor to the *North American Review* expressed the opinion that Poe was intensely prejudiced "against all literature emanating from New England." Evert A. Duyckinck, in 1850, publicly lodged the charge of venality against Poe, declaring that he "was, in the very centre of his soul, a literary attorney, and pleaded according to his fee." Mrs. Gove-Nichols, also, in her novel, *Mary Lyndon,* while apologizing for the poet's weaknesses, admitted that he "sometimes sold favorable opinions, that were not opinions, but shams"; and Clark, in the *Knickerbocker,* characterized him sneeringly as a "jaded hack who runs a broken pace for common hire." Others complained of the over-minuteness of his criticisms and, in particular of his fondness for "verbal fault-finding."

Among those who wrote in praise of his work as a critic were Lowell, Horace Greeley, and Richard Henry Stoddard. Lowell in his sketch of Poe in 1845 declared that he was "at once the most discriminating, philosophical, and fearless critic upon imaginative works . . . in America." Greeley, after hearing his lecture on the American poets in February, 1845, praised him, in the columns of the *Tribune,* dwelling upon his candor and his acuteness, and pronouncing him a "critic of genius and established reputation." Stoddard declared in 1853, "No other modern, save Tennyson, [was] so versed in the philosophy of criticism." Willis praised him enthusiastically in the *Mirror* in 1845 and again in the *Home Journal* at the time of his death. . . .

An excerpt from "Longfellow's Ballads" (1842):

We have said that Mr. Longfellow's conception of the *aims* of poesy is erroneous; and that thus, laboring at a disadvantage he does violent wrong to his own high powers; and now the question is, what *are* his ideas of the aims of the muse, as we gather these ideas from the *general* tendency of his poems? It will be at once evident that, imbued with the peculiar spirit of German song (a pure conventionality) he regards the inculcation of a *moral* as essential. Here we find it necessary to repeat that we have reference only to the *general* tendency of his compositions; for there are some magnificent exceptions, where, as if by accident, he has permitted his genius to get the better of his conventional prejudice. But didacticism is the prevalent *tone* of his song. His invention, his imagery, his all, is made subservient to the elucidation of some one or more points (but rarely of more than one) which he looks upon as *truth*. And that this mode of procedure will find stern defenders should never excite surprise, so long as the world is full to overflowing with cant and conventicles. There are men who will scramble on all fours through the muddiest sloughs of vice to pick up a single apple of virtue. There are things called men who, so long as the sun rolls, will greet with snuffing huzzas every figure that takes upon itself the semblance of truth, even though the figure, in itself only a "stuffed Paddy," be as much out of place as a toga on the statue of Washington, or out of season as rabbits in the days of the dog-star.

Edgar Allan Poe, in Selections from Poe's Literary Criticism, *edited by John Brooks Moore, F. S. Crofts & Co., 1926.*

Sidney P. Moss (essay date 1963)

SOURCE: "Culmination of a Campaign," in *Poe's Literary Battles: The Critic in the Context of His Literary Milieu,* Duke University Press, 1963, pp. 132-89.

[*In a detailed analysis of the Poe-Longfellow literary war, Moss argues that Poe's evaluation of Longfellow's literary capabilities, though over-harsh at times, was ultimately accurate and based on carefully worked-out critical principles.*]

. . . I am but defending a set of principles which no honest man need be ashamed of defending, and for whose defence no honest man will consider an apology required.—*Edgar A. Poe*

Poe's encounters with Longfellow have aroused so much emotionalism in Poe and Longfellow partisans that to look at the evidence afresh and with detachment requires the utmost self-discipline. To forestall such emotionalism from prejudicing the evidence, let it be repeated here that our purpose is not so much to defend Poe as a critic but to understand him in that capacity; to consider this "battle" . . . in the context of his critical career and literary milieu; and, finally, to draw judgments from the evidence, whether those judgments happen to be favorable or unfavorable to Poe or, in this instance, to Longfellow. Thus, let it be acknowledged at once that in his notices of the Cambridge poet Poe was blunt and quarrelsome at times; that he made serious errors of judgment on occasion; that he was not unwilling to use Longfellow for sensational purposes to enlarge the subscription lists of the magazines he was serving; that the last of his protracted replies to "Outis" may even betray the first symptoms of a mental disturbance that became obvious in the following year; and, having acknowledged this, let us proceed to as impartial an examination of the available evidence as is possible in the circumstances.

Poe first took critical notice of Longfellow when his prose tale, *Hyperion: A Romance* (1839), came to his attention as reviewer for *Burton's Gentleman's Magazine.* This was Longfellow's second published work, if we regard the three editions of *Outre-Mer* as one and ignore his textbooks.

The thin autobiographical narrative was, in the persona of Paul Flemming, an account of his second European trip—from the death of his first wife following a miscarriage to his frustrated romance with Frances Appleton (Mary Ashburton). Steeped in German Romanticism, Longfellow responded to his wife's death and to Frances Appleton in a pretentiously literary style which he later abandoned. Thus, in *Hyperion,* his dead wife was the bough which had broken under the burden of the unripe fruit, and Frances Appleton is the wraith who haunts his dreams "with her pale, speaking countenance and holy eyes." The literary influences manifest in the work are many, but Jean Paul's is most obvious. But the story, however derivative its manner, was essentially a frame on which to hang all sorts of miscellaneous materials: anecdotes, legends, travel notes, translations of German poems, and even discussions of literary topics, some drawn from his Harvard lectures on German literature.

Poe, who insisted time and again that "totality, or unity, of effect" is a desideratum of a literary work and who repeatedly held that "than the true originality there is no higher literary virtue," was bound to be unhappy with the book:

Were it possible [he wrote] to throw into a bag the lofty thought and manner of the *Pilgrims of the Rhine,* together with the quirks and quibbles and true humour of *Tristram Shandy,* not forgetting a few of the heartier drolleries of Rabelais, and one or two of the Phantasy Pieces of the Lorrainean Callot, the whole, when well shaken up, and thrown out, would be a very tolerable imitation of "Hyperion." This may appear to be commendation, but we do not intend it as such. Works like this of Professor Longfellow are the triumphs of Tom O'Bedlam, and the grief of all true criticism. They are potent in unsettling the popular faith in Art—a faith which, at no day more than the present, needed the support of men of letters. . . . A man of true talent who would demur at the great labour requisite for the stern demands of high art . . . make[s] no scruple of scattering at random a profusion of rich thought in the pages of such farragos [*sic*] as "Hyperion." Here, indeed, there is little trouble— but even that little is most unprofitably lost. . . . We are indignant that he too has been recreant to the good cause.

Such criticism of *Hyperion* was by no means unusual then or now. Longfellow himself observed: "The Boston papers are very savage, and abuse me shockingly. . . ." One such "abusive" review was written by Orestes A. Brownson, editor of the *Boston Quarterly Review,* whose reaction to *Hyperion* was similar to Poe's: "I do not like the book. It is such a journal as a man who reads a great deal makes from the scraps in his table-drawer. . . . You cannot guess why the book was written. . . . " Another "abusive" reviewer confessed in the Boston *Mercantile Journal* of September 27, 1839, that one "book" of the four "books" of *Hyperion* was a dose as large as he could swallow because he found it a "mongrel mixture of descriptions and criticism, travels and bibliography, common-places clad in purple, and follies 'with not a rag to cover them.'" Amusingly enough, Frances Appleton, unhappy at being served up to the public under the persona of Mary Ashburton, remarked privately: "There are really some exquisite things in this book, though it is desultory, objectless, a thing of shreds and patches like the author's mind."

But not all notices of *Hyperion* were unfavorable, for four of Longfellow's friends—Cornelius Conway Felton, Samuel Ward, and the Clark brothers—published their reviews of that work too. For the *Boston Courier* Felton wrote a stinging reply to the *Mercantile Journal* reviewer, which he trenchantly titled, "Hyperion to a Satyr" (a reply that Willis Clark reprinted in his *Philadelphia Gazette*), as well as a seventeen-page defense of *Hyperion* for the *North American Review.* In the *North American,* Felton conceded what was already the fact, that *Hyperion* "must encounter a variety of critical opinions"; yet, he maintained, the book "must not be judged by the principles of classical composition"—that is to say, by the principle of unity, as

Poe and others had judged it. Readers, he said, who were "attuned to sentiments of tenderness," who had an imaginative turn of mind, and who were "sensitively alive to the influence of the beautiful," would come back to the book again and again. Ward devoted twenty pages of the *New York Review* to affirming that the book is a "lay . . . uttered by the scholar with the lips of a minstrel," and "that the appearance of Hyperion is an event in the annals of our scholarship and literary taste." Willis Clark, who pronounced the work great, promised to review it "with liberal extracts, some Saturday" for his *Philadelphia Gazette.* And Lewis Clark, declaring in the *Knickerbocker* that the Romance "is an exquisite production and will be so pronounced by every reader of taste," urged his subscribers to "possess themselves at once of 'Hyperion,' and sit down to a feast of calm philosophy, poetry, and romance."

Encouraged by the reception of *Hyperion*—he oversanguinely remarked that a large edition of the book had been sold in a few weeks—Longfellow created another opportunity to appear on the literary market in that same year. He collected his "Voices of the Night" (eight "Psalms," including "Hymn to the Night," "A Psalm of Life," "The Beleaguered City," and "Midnight Mass for the Dying Year," which had appeared in the *Knickerbocker*), sorted through his "Earlier Poems" (from which he selected seven), gathered twenty-three of his "Translations" (some of which had appeared in *Hyperion* and elsewhere), and made a modest, three-sectioned volume of the whole, which he inappropriately christened *Voices of the Night.*

Unlike *Hyperion,* this work was widely acclaimed by the press. As Longfellow wrote, "Every one praises the book. Even the Boston papers which so abused Hyperion, praise this highly." Before the volume appeared in December, Lewis Clark announced in the *Knickerbocker*:

> *Voices of the Night.*—Professor Longfellow, of Cambridge, has in press, under the above title, a volume of poems, which is to embrace the several beautiful 'Psalms of Life,' that were written for the *Knickerbocker,* together with many of the earlier original poems and translations of the author. We would not so far slander the feeling and good taste of the public, as to suppose that the volume will not meet with a large and rapid sale.

And when the book was published, Clark observed:

> Perhaps it will be considered altogether a work of supererogation, that we should invite the attention of our readers to a volume of poems from the pen of Professor Longfellow, from whom they have heard so often, and never without delight. . . . Most cordially do we commend these 'Voices of the Night' to the imaginations and hearts of our readers.

Felton, too, in the *North American,* extolled the volume, especially the title section, saying that they "are among the most remarkable poetical compositions, which have ever appeared in the United States"—a verdict that Clark, not to be outdone, quoted in his "Editor's Table," adding that "we are especially gratified to find the praise which has been bestowed in these pages upon . . . 'Hyperion,' . . . and . . . 'Voices of the Night,' reechoed in the deliberate verdict of the *North American.*"

Such acclamation by the press was in great measure deserved. Reviewers familiar with the run of American poetry were bound to be impressed by the command of language, the freshness of imagery, and the sureness of technique that characterize most of the Psalms. Felton's opinion, that the Psalms were "among the most remarkable poetical compositions, which have ever appeared in the United States," was perfectly sound at the time. Reviewers like Poe, however, who held that the world, not America, "is the true theatre of the biblical histrio"; who refused to let literary patriotism enter into their judgments; who felt compelled to compare Longfellow's accomplishments with those of Coleridge, Keats, and Shelley rather than with John Brainard's, Fitz-Greene Halleck's, and Mrs. Sigourney's, were bound to be more moderate in their acclaim. Thus, in reviewing *Voices* for *Burton's Gentleman's Magazine,* Poe remarked that when he had first seen "Hymn to the Night" in a newspaper, he had been impressed with the "firm belief that a poet of high genius had at length arisen amongst us." No poem, he remarked, ever opened with a beauty more august and the first five stanzas are nearly perfect. Had Longfellow always written this way, Poe continued, "we should have been tempted to speak of him not only as *our* finest poet, but as one of the noblest poets of all time." His perusal of *Voices* had not modified his conviction that Longfellow had genius; it had, however, altered his opinion as to his "capacity for . . . any enduring reputation." For though Longfellow possesses the "loftiest qualities of the poetical soul. . . . he has nothing of unity"—the same observation, Poe added, that *Hyperion* had induced in him. Even the five stanzas of the "Hymn" alluded to have defects consequent upon lack of unity—defects which he considered symptoms of inability to achieve "that perfection which is the result only of the strictest proportion and adaptation in all the poetical requisites. . . ." Hence, he said, the defects he had pointed out existed not only in the poems but "in the mind of the writer, and thence ineradicable. . . ."

If we can condone Poe's questioning the degree of Longfellow's talents (and neither in this notice nor in subsequent ones did he fall into the easy fatuity of condemning Longfellow's poems contemptuously or of admiring them vacuously), we may not be so willing to condone his questioning Longfellow's honesty in the high-handed way he proceeded to do at the close of this review. Copying Longfellow's "Midnight Mass for the Dying Year" and Tennyson's "The Death of the Old Year," he called attention to a plagiarism "too palpable to be mistaken, and which belongs to the most barbarous class of literary robbery: that class in which, while the words of the wronged author are avoided, his most intangible, and therefore his least defensible and least reclaimable property is purloined." Aside from occasional lapses, Poe admitted, "there is nothing of a visible or palpable nature by which the source of the American poem can be established. But then nearly all that is valuable in the piece of Tennyson is the . . . conception of personifying the Old Year as a dying old man, with the singularly wild and fantastic *manner* in which that conception is carried out. Of this conception and of this manner he is robbed." Needless to say, Poe ruled out all possibility of coincidence, if he considered it at all.

If the puffing lavished on *Hyperion* by the *North American Review,* the *Knickerbocker,* and the *Philadelphia Gazette* had not provided Poe with evidence of logrolling or, to use his expression, the "corrupt nature of our ordinary criticism," and if the phenomenon of *Voices* passing through four printings within the year had not signalized to him that Longfellow was being abetted by the New York and Boston coteries, he must have at least suspected the fact when he ran into an old adversary, Willis Clark, whom he had encountered under similar circumstances in the *Norman Leslie* incident. Most likely in order to stimulate sales of *Burton's Gentleman's Magazine,* Poe called attention to what he deemed Longfellow's plagiarism in *Alexander's Weekly Messenger,* a journal to which he was contributing at the time. In his column for January 29, 1840, he referred to a review in *Burton's* "which shows up Professor Longfellow as a plagiarist of the first water. . . ." The allegation, made so bluntly, reached Longfellow at Cambridge, and he proceeded to deny it to his friend Ward: "My brother told me yesterday that some paragraphs had appeared in some New York paper [*Alexander's* was printed in Philadelphia] saying I stole the idea of the 'Midnight Mass' from Tennyson. Absurd. I did not even know that he had written a piece on this subject." Unfortunately, the evidence does not entirely support Longfellow's statement. "The Fifth Psalm: A Midnight Mass for the Dying Year" first appeared in the *Knickerbocker* in October, 1839. In 1838 Emerson, in correspondence with C. C. Little, who wanted to bring out the first American edition of Tennyson's *Poems* (London, 1833)—the book that contains "The Death of the Old Year"—told that publisher that Longfellow owned a copy. Moreover, Longfellow in a letter to Frances Appleton written sometime in 1837 or 1838 extolled the virtues of Tennyson ("the nicest ear can ask no richer melody:—and the most lively imagination no lovlier [*sic*] picture, nor more true") and even quoted verses and cited page numbers from the very volume containing "The Death of the Old Year." Had

Longfellow been candid, Poe's charge would appear today, as it must have appeared then, decidedly unfair; but Longfellow's denial in the circumstances tends to draw suspicion from the accuser to the accused.

Having written to Ward, Longfellow wrote to Willis Clark as well: "Pray who is it that is attacking me so furiously in Philadelphia. I have never seen the attacks, but occasionally I receive a newspaper with a defense of my writings, from which I learn there has been an attack. I thank you for what you have done for me; and for your good thoughts and good words." Clark, responding to Longfellow's letter, wrote: "You ask me who attacks you here? The only ones I have seen against you, have been in *Burton's*. . . . I have answered *thoroughly,* any attack upon you—and shall continue to do so, whenever they appear." Clark spoke the truth, for he had answered Poe's anonymous articles in *Burton's* and *Alexander's.* On February 4, 1840, he had printed a statement in his *Gazette* designed to acquit Longfellow of plagiarism by convicting Tennyson of stealing from Longfellow, or, failing that, by suggesting that Longfellow, at worst, had only filched from one of his own earlier poems. His defense, based on the error that Tennyson was a Scotsman and on the reduction of Poe's charge to imitation, only evidenced his partiality for Longfellow:

> A neighboring periodical, we hear, has been attempting to prove that Professor Longfellow's sublime and beautiful "Midnight Mass for the Dying Year," has been imitated from a poem by Tennyson. Preposterous! There is nothing more alike in the two pieces than black and white, with the exception of the personification,—and *that* was Longfellow's, long before the Scotch writer thought of 'doing' his poem. Who does not remember that striking simile in one of the Professor's earlier lyrics,
>
> > —where Autumn, like a faint old man, sits down, By the wayside, aweary?"
>
> This same beautiful piece was copied in Edinburgh, from an English periodical where it was *altered,* to suit the scenery of England; and it is fifty times more probable that Tennyson thus got *his* idea, than that Mr. Longfellow should have done more in the "Mass," than repeat a favorite one of his thought. On himself, one of the most strikingly original poets of this country, and the best translator of any nation known to our language, such a charge falls hurtless—and for the reputation of the maker, (acknowledged, we hear, among his friends) should be withdrawn. We ask the Weekly Messenger, who has repeated the charge of *abstraction,* to clip this *caveat,* and give it utterance.

On February 12, his earliest opportunity, Poe did as Clark bade him. He reprinted Clark's caveat in *Alexander's* and added:

> The "neighboring periodical," alluded to in so parliamentary a style, is the "Gentleman's Magazine," and the accuser, whose "reputation" is so entirely a matter of hearsay with Mr. Clark, is a Mr. Poe, one of the editors of that very excellent and very popular journal. . . .
>
> Mr. Poe does not say that Professor Longfellow's poem is "imitated" from Tennyson. He calls it a bare-faced and barbarous plagiarism. . . . In support of this accusation he has printed the poems in question side by side—a proceeding, which, we must acknowledge, has an air of perfect fairness about it. . . . We mention that the critic had done all this, because we understand, from the opening words of the paragraph quoted above, that Mr. Clarke [sic], is only aware, as usual, through hearsay, of what is really written in the "Gentleman's Magazine."
>
> Matters standing thus, the question is altogether one of opinion. Mr. Poe says the Professor stole the poem; so do we; and so does every body but Mr. Clarke. *He* says the Professor did *not* steal the poem. He says, moreover, that Mr. Poe ought to "withdraw" the charge, lest, being persisted in, it may do injury to his own reputation; (Mr. P's) about which he (Mr. C.) is solicitous. Whether Mr. Poe will oblige the editor of the Gazette, remains yet to be seen.

Poe, needless to say, did not oblige the editor of the *Gazette* and the matter lapsed.

All that can be said here is that Poe was still plumping for sales of *Burton's* and that he exercised some restraint by merely reiterating the original accusation. He could easily have strengthened his position by adducing other and far less questionable instances of "plagiarism" in *Voices*—even from the very poem "Autumn" which Clark had cited. Consider the last nine lines of that poem, for example, in respect to ideas, phrases, and even the blank verse of "Thanatopsis":

> O what a glory doth this world put on
> For him who, with a fervent heart, goes forth
> Under the bright and glorious sky, and looks
> On duties well performed, and days well
>   spent!
> For him the wind, ay, and the yellow leaves
> Shall have a voice, and give him eloquent
>   teachings.
> He shall so hear the solemn hymn, that Death
> Has lifted up for all, that he shall go
> To his long resting-place without a tear.

In his original review of *Voices,* however, Poe had said that no author of mature age should desire to have his poetical character estimated by the productions of his mind at immaturity, and "Autumn," like the rest of the "Earlier Poems," was written, as Longfellow had acknowledged, before he was nineteen.

Twice during the next year Poe had occasion to write to Longfellow—the first and last time letters were exchanged between them. As editor now of *Graham's Magazine,* Poe was asked by the proprietor to solicit contributions from Longfellow, who had become, almost overnight on the strength of *Voices,* America's best-selling poet and thus a most desirable contributor. Poe's position was awkward, for however much he had acclaimed Longfellow as a poet, he had not only pointed out his weaknesses but had accused him of plagiarism, and he felt he could anticipate the poet's response. His letter reflects his dilemma:

> Mr Geo: R. Graham, proprietor of "Graham's Magazine", a monthly journal published in this city, and edited by myself, desires me to beg of you the honor of your contribution to its pages. Upon the principle that we seldom obtain what we *very* anxiously covet, I confess that I have but little hope of inducing you to write for us;—and, to say truth, I fear that Mr Graham would have opened the negotiation much better in his own person—for I have no reason to think myself favorably known to you—but the attempt was to be made, and I made it.

Poe added that if Longfellow were interested, he could submit an article every month, whether in poetry or prose, length, subject, and price at his discretion.

> In conclusion—I cannot refrain from availing myself of this, the only opportunity I may ever have, to assure the author of the "Hymn to the Night", of the "Beleaguered City" and of the "Skeleton in Armor", of the fervent admiration with which his genius has inspired me:—and yet I would scarcely hazard a declaration whose import might be so easily misconstrued, and which bears with it, at best, more or less, of niaiserie, were I not convinced that Professor Longfellow, writing and thinking as he does, will be at no loss to feel and appreciate the honest *sincerity* of what I say.

Longfellow replied on May 19, refusing the offer and acknowledging Poe's existence. With nice discretion, he avoided mentioning Poe's recent strictures on his work and, at the same time, managed to return the compliment Poe had paid him:

> I am much obliged to you for your kind expressions of regard, and to Mr. Graham for his very generous offer. . . . But I am so much occupied at present that I could not do it with any satisfaction either to you or to myself. I must therefore respectfully decline his proposition.

> You are mistaken in supposing that you are not "favorably known to me." On the contrary, all that I have read from your pen has inspired me with a high idea of your power; and I think you are destined to stand among the first romance-writers of the country, if such be your aim.

During the next month Poe sought to establish his own journal. Having found Longfellow more agreeable than he had reason to expect, Poe wrote him a second letter in which he discussed his projected magazine and asked again for contributions: "In your former note you spoke of present engagements. The proposed journal will not be commenced until the 1st January 1842." What Longfellow replied, if he replied at all, is not known, but it can hardly be coincidence that, despite his previous objections, he appeared in *Graham's Magazine* for January, 1842, and soon became one of Graham's headliners.

In the meantime Poe, upon request, submitted some of his poems to Rufus Griswold for inclusion in that compiler's anthology, *The Poets and Poetry of America.* Earlier in the month Poe had praised "The Beleaguered City" in his letter to Longfellow; now, he called Griswold's attention to the similarity between the Longfellow poem and his own **"Haunted Palace"** in what was evidently a private attempt to acquit himself in advance of the charge of plagiarism. "The Beleaguered City" was well known, not only to subscribers of the *Knickerbocker,* but to readers of *Voices,* whereas his own poem had led an obscure, not to say fugitive, existence; and he no doubt felt justified in trying to forestall the charge. It would have been embarrassing, to say the least, to one who had so recently accused Longfellow of plagiarizing from Tennyson to be accused, in turn, of plagiarizing from Longfellow. Thus, Poe furnished Griswold with evidence that **"The Haunted Palace"** antedated Longfellow's poem. If he could have conceded the possibility of coincidence, his tone would have been less offensive, but Poe typically saw such likenesses only as evidence of plagiarism:

> I first published the H.P. in Brooks' "Museum", a monthly journal of Baltimore, now dead. Afterwards, I embodied it in a tale called **"The House of Usher"** in *Burton's Magazine.* Here it was, I suppose, that Prof. Longfellow saw it; for, about 6 weeks afterwards, there appeared in the South. Lit. Mess: a poem by him called "The Beleaguered City", which may now be found in his volume [*Voices*]. The identity in title is striking; for by the Haunted Palace I mean to imply a mind haunted by phantoms—a disordered brain—and by the Beleaguered City Prof. L. means just the same. But the whole tournure of the poem is based upon mine, as you will see at once. Its allegorical conduct, the style of its versification & expression—all are mine.

As matters turned out, plagiarism was adduced from this evidence only by Poe and, after Poe's death, by Griswold. Though in full possession of the facts, that compiler twisted the charge so that Poe was made to appear the plagiarist of Longfellow. Moreover, using these very poems as evidence, Griswold commented that Poe's "plagiarisms are scarcely paralleled for their audacity in all literary history." Griswold even assigned this as "the first cause of all that malignant criticism which for so many years he carried on against Long-fellow."

Before he reviewed another Longfellow volume, Poe alluded to the Cambridge poet on four occasions, twice quite cuttingly and twice quite admiringly, an ambiv-alence that was to become characteristic of his attitude toward Longfellow. If he could have explained imita-tion in terms of coincidence, Poe would have been, allowing for his aesthetic reservations, one of Longfel-low's strongest advocates, for he never doubted his genius. But unable, for most of his career, to explain imitation in any terms other than intention, he praised the poet but condemned the "plagiarist." His attitude became quite clear in his review of Wilmer's *Quacks of Helicon*. Confronted with Wilmer's indictment that Longfellow "Steals all he can and butchers what he steals," Poe treated the statement as a half-truth. "Mr. Longfellow *will* steal," he conceded, "but, perhaps, he cannot help it, (for we have heard of such thing,) and then it must not be denied that *nil tetigit quod non ornavit.*" Similarly, Poe in his signed **"Chapter on Autography"** declared that Longfellow was "entitled to the first place among the poets of America," but that he was guilty of imitation—"an imitation sometimes verging upon downright theft." Yet twice in February, 1842, Poe praised Longfellow without qualification. In atomizing a poem by Cornelius Mathews, he remarked that the poem had first appeared in *Arcturus,* a maga-zine co-edited by Mathews, where, insultingly, "it took precedence of some exceedingly beautiful stanzas by Professor Longfellow. . . ." And in another critique he observed that John Brainard has "written poems which may rank with those of any American, with the single exception of Longfellow. . . ."

The publication of Longfellow's second small collec-tion of verse, *Ballads and Other Poems* (1841), which contained four translations and twelve of his own po-ems, including "The Skeleton in Armour," "The Wreck of the Hesperus," "The Village Blacksmith," and "Ex-celsior," consolidated Longfellow's literary position and entitled him to be called—as he has been called—America's first professional poet and her unofficial poet laureate. Of the many reviews celebrating the book, Felton's in the *North American Review* is perhaps most pertinent. Longfellow had become so established and the salability of his works so certain that Felton, in his thirty-page discussion, conceded that Longfellow no longer needed puffs—that the mere announcement of a book bearing his name would suffice to guarantee a best-seller. Nevertheless, not to blink at the fact, Fel-ton continued to review almost every one of Longfel-low's works and almost always in the *North American*:

> Mr. Longfellow's poetry has become so generally known, and, wherever known, is so universally admired, as to need no aid from the journals of literature. . . . It is, therefore, with no expectation of adding to its widespread renown, or of increasing the number of its admirers, that we call our readers' attention to this second volume [of poetry] from Professor Longfellow's pen.

In the din of such universal and generally uncritical acclaim, Poe's two reviews of the *Ballads* may be unique for their reservations. In the first of these re-views, Poe remarked that he had space only "to say a few random words of welcome to these 'Ballads,' by Longfellow, and to tender him, and all such as he, the homage of our earnest love and admiration." Never-theless, the man who had argued early in his career (in his **"Letter to B—"**) that a poem "is opposed to a work of science by having for its *immediate* object pleasure, not truth," and who, at the end of his career (in **"The Poetic Principle"**) charged that the "heresy of *The Didactic*" had "accomplished more in the cor-ruption of our Poetical Literature than all its other enemies combined," felt compelled to qualify his hom-age. Thus, he said that Longfellow's insistence on didactics was preventing him from realizing his full genius—that his conception of the aim of poetry was, in fact, forcing him to utter conventionalities that, by their nature, seemed imitative and reminiscent. In Poe's words:

> Much as we admire the genius of Mr. Longfellow, we are fully sensible of his many errors of affectation and imitation. His artistical skill is great, and his ideality high. But his conception of the aims of poesy *is all wrong;* and this we shall prove at some future date—to our own satisfaction, at least. His didactics are *all out of place*. He has written brilliant poems—by accident; that is to say when permitting his genius to get the better of his conventional habit of thinking. . . . We do not mean to say that a didactic moral may not be well made the *under-current* of a poetical thesis; but that it can never be well put so obtrusively forth, as in the majority of his compositions.

In the following month Poe devoted another review to the *Ballads* to amplify points he had raised here. This second review was no more an attack upon Longfel-low than the first. Rather, it was Poe's effort to release him from the trammels of didacticism. For Longfel-low's error, Poe contended, is that he regards the in-culcation of a moral as essential to his poetry and there-by does violent wrong to his high powers: "His inven-tion, his imagery, his all, is made subservient to the elucidation of some one or more points . . . which he looks upon as *truth*. . . . Now with as deep a reverence for 'the true' as ever inspired the bosom of mortal man, we would limit, in many respects, its modes of inculcation. . . ." Yet he did not wish to be misunderstood. Poetry "is not forbidden to depict—but to reason and preach of virtue." He then said that the true poet is not concerned with truth but with beauty. He recognized that such a rigorous definition would rule out much of what has been considered poetic—*Hudibras* and the *Essay on Man,* for instance—and he cited Keats as the poet "most fully instinct with the principles now developed. . . . Beauty is always his aim."

> We have thus shown our ground of objection to the general *themes* of Professor Longfellow. In common with all who claim the sacred title of poet, he should limit his endeavors to the creation of novel moods of beauty. . . . To what the world terms *prose* may be safely and properly left all else. . . .

> Of the pieces which constitute the present volume, there are not more than one or two thoroughly fulfilling the idea above proposed . . . [for] the aim of instruction . . . has been too obviously substituted for the legitimate aim, *beauty.*

Poe was either uncertain of his position or else overstated his views in an effort to make a strong case against the heresy of the didactic, a "heresy" that, needless to say, was an orthodoxy in its time. In his first review of the *Ballads,* he made a mechanical division between the aesthetic and the moral (Poe used the term *didactic* loosely, sometimes in connection with moral truth, more often in connection with conventional doctrine and obtrusive moral tags), saying that a "didactic moral may . . . be . . . the *under-current* of a poetical thesis. . . ." In the second review, however, he declared that poetry has nothing to do with truth (the "obstinate oils and waters of Poetry and Truth" are irreconcilable)—an assertion he repeated to the very words in **"The Poetic Principle"** when deriding the idea that "the ultimate object of all Poetry is Truth." Yet in both reviews of the *Ballads* and in other contexts, Poe suggested that when the moral becomes aesthetic— when, in other words, the moral, far from being an appendage to a poem, becomes implicit in the poem—"Poetry and Truth" are perfectly reconcilable. In discussing, for example, Ludwig Uhland's "Das Glück von Edenhall," which Longfellow had translated and included in the *Ballads,* Poe remarked that the "pointed moral with which it terminates is so exceedingly natural—so perfectly fluent from the incidents—that we have hardly heart to pronounce it in bad taste." His objection, clearly, is to the explicit statement of a moral that should have been made implicit in the poem. Even in **"The Poetic Principle"** Poe cited among "a few of the simple elements which induce in the Poet himself the true poetical effect. . . . all noble thoughts . . . all holy impulses. . . ." And in his *Marginalia* Poe categorically declared: "I confidently maintain that the *highest* genius is but the loftiest moral nobility."

Though Poe went too far in denying the relation between the moral and aesthetic, we should not lose sight of the significant fact that he was fighting fire with fire and an extreme position with an extreme position. The position he was opposing is that a work of art is never self-justifying: it justifies itself only insofar as it imparts ethical doctrine—a position that even Emerson, for all his brilliance, rigidly adopted in "The Poet." Thus, artistic value is identified with, if not identical to, moral content; therefore, the loftier the moral, the greater the work of art; and, by the same reasoning a work of art that has no ostensible message must be, a priori, seriously deficient. As Poe stated the case more fully in **"The Poetic Principle"**:

> It has been assumed, tacitly and avowedly, directly and indirectly, that the ultimate object of all Poetry is Truth. Every poem, it is said, should inculcate a moral; and by this moral is the poetical merit of the work to be adjudged. We Americans especially have patronised this happy idea; and we Bostonians, very especially, have developed it in full. We have taken it into our heads that to write a poem simply for the poem's sake, and to acknowledge such to have been our design, would be to confess ourselves radically wanting in the true Poetic dignity and force:—but the simple fact is, that, would we but permit ourselves to look into our own souls, we should immediately there discover that under the sun there neither exists nor *can* exist any work more thoroughly dignified—more supremely noble than this very poem—this poem *per se*—this poem which is a poem and nothing more—this poem written solely for the poem's sake.

Whether Poe misrepresented or had failed to synthesize his views, he did not distort Longfellow's, as anyone familiar with the *Voices* and *Ballads* is aware. Earlier, Longfellow had stated the principle implicit in such poems as "The Rainy Day," "A Psalm of Life," "The Village Blacksmith," and "Excelsior," that the "natural tendency of poetry is to give us correct moral impressions, and thereby advance the cause of truth and the improvement of society"—a tendency he reinforced by emasculating the burly Jean Paul Richter and the passionate Heinrich Heine in his "translations, comments, and frequent imitations of these writers. . . ." Thus a poet in whose work "there was always enough easily recognizable middle-class morality . . . to make him seem entirely safe in a country still distrustful of beauty for its own sake," and who adopted principles associated more with Pope and Gray than with Shelley and Keats, was bound to be received with some reservation by a Romantic critic like Poe. The fact that Poe could not dismiss him out of hand is indication enough that Longfellow was a force to reckon with. We can only conjure with the idea of what Longfellow might have accomplished had Poe become his literary conscience, as Edmund Wilson became Scott Fitzgerald's, at least to the extent of urging him to reexamine his poetic principles or of listening to his neighbor Emerson when he said in "The Poet": ". . . it is not metres, but a metre-making argument that makes a poem—a thought so passionate and alive that like the spirit of a plant or an animal it has an architecture of its own. . . ." Yet America, needless to say, was hardly prepared to receive poets who wrote "simply for the poem's sake" or whose poems (to use Emerson's phrase) did not contain "the ground-tone of conventional life," despite the efforts by Poe and others to prepare the ground for their reception. Had Longfellow been tempted to write otherwise—had he used ideas less comfortably familiar, sentiments less aseptically decent, didactics less obtrusive, language less explicit and mellifluous—his poems might in their time have shared the fate of *Leaves of Grass* (Whitman, after all, had listened to Emerson) rather than have enjoyed what was probably the greatest popular success that any poems ever had—and success more than greatness seems to have been Longfellow's concern.

Poe did not review Longfellow's next volume, his *Poems on Slavery* (1842), disqualifying himself, perhaps, on the grounds of his antipathy to abolitionism and his avowed prejudice to didactic poetry. But in 1843 he used a stanza from "A Psalm of Life" as an epigraph to his story, **"The Tell-Tale Heart,"** and in a letter to Lowell he reaffirmed his conviction that "Longfellow has genius. . . ." Yet, however much he admired the poet, he confessed that he did not know "how to understand him at times. I am in doubt whether he should not be termed an arrant plagiarist." He then called Lowell's attention to Longfellow's recent book, *The Spanish Student: A Play in Three Acts* (1843), and mentioned that he had written "quite a long notice of it for Graham's December number. The play," he added, "is a poor composition, with some fine poetical passages."

This notice was never printed in *Graham's* for two reasons. First, Graham would hardly welcome adverse criticism of a work that had originally appeared in his own magazine. Second, both Graham and Griswold (the latter was now editor of *Graham's*) had had trouble with Longfellow and were using their rejection of Poe's adverse review to reconcile their star contributor. The trouble began in 1842 when an artist, Franquinet by name, had painted a portrait of Longfellow while the poet was abroad, which, without Longfellow's approval, was engraved to appear in *Graham's* in May, 1843. When the poet returned from Europe and saw the portrait, he was angry at the thought that Graham and Griswold would allow this "most atrocious libel imaginable; a very vulgar individual, looking very drunk and very cunning," to appear in the magazine and demanded that the painting and the plate be destroyed. Graham, faced with the choice of sacrificing the $405 he had invested or of losing his headliner, decided to concede to Longfellow's demand and

begin all over again "with a portrait—the best you have." But Longfellow had none that satisfied him and insisted that he be given time to have one done. Graham refused to wait and the portrait made its scheduled appearance. The "libel" was atrocious enough to impel Lewis Clark to condemn the portrait in the *Knickerbocker* as a "'*counterfeit* presentment,' sure enough"; to assert that "the artist ought to be indicted"; and to describe Longfellow as a "handsome man with 'soft and flowing hair,' touched with the slightest possible tinge of 'sable silver;' an eye with a liquid, interior look," etc.

Griswold, who relinquished his editorship of *Graham's* in October of that year, wrote Longfellow in an evident attempt to placate him and smeared Poe in the process. Poe, he said,

> has recently written an elaborate review of your "Student" in his customary vein, but if anything a bit more personal and malignant than usual. This was offered to Graham before I left, and has since been *given* to him—so anxious is the poor critic for its appearance; but of course Mr. Graham refused it. I mention the circumstances because it would be very like Poe, since he cannot find a publisher for his "criticism," to attempt to win your friendship with his praise.

Graham also sought to pacify Longfellow by showing a concern for him which he had failed to show before in respect to the portrait:

> I have a savage review of your *Spanish Student* from the pen of Poe, which shall *not* appear in Graham. I do not know what your crime may be in the eye of Poe, but suppose it may be a better, and more widely established reputation. Or if you have wealth—which I suppose you *have*—that is sufficient to settle your damnation so far as Mr Poe may be presumed capable of effecting it. . . .

> I had to suffer $30 [Poe had asked only $20] for the review of you and you shall have it for as many cents when you come along this way, I do not suppose it will ever be redeemed, and I doubt if the writer of it will be.

As he exaggerated the price, Graham seems to have exaggerated the severity of the review. Soon after Poe had submitted the critique to Graham, he had observed that the *Student* as a play was poor but that it contained fine poetical passages. Moreover, his treatment of that play in his article **"The American Drama"** fails to justify Graham's statement. In that article Poe stated the crux of his position, that the "great adversary of Invention is Imitation." One must forget the old models and "consider *de novo* . . . the *capabilities* of the drama—not merely . . . its conventional purposes." In considering Nathaniel Willis's *Tortesa, the*

Usurer, he objected to mere complexity passing for plot. Ideally, he said, a plot "is perfect only inasmuch as we shall find ourselves unable to detach from it or *disarrange* any single incident involved, without *destruction* to the mass. . . ." Practically, a plot may be considered of "high excellence, when no one of its component parts shall be susceptible of *removal* without *detriment* to the whole."

Then he turned to *The Spanish Student,* which had passed through three editions in the first year of its publication and with which Longfellow confessed himself "much disheartened. Neither you [Ward], nor Sumner, nor Ticknor, nor Felton likes it. . . . shall probably throw it into the fire." Poe dissented from the general opinion regarding the play. The few, he asserted, who do not have their opinions formed for them "received the play with a commendation somewhat less *prononcée* . . . than Professor Longfellow might have desired, or may have been taught to expect." He then quoted the "finer passages. . . . by way of justice to the poet" and proceeded to criticize the dramatist. He demonstrated that Longfellow was imitative of the old models: he mistook complexity for plot; his incidents were the stock-in-trade of a "thousand and one comedies"; two-thirds of his material was unnecessary and the arrangement of it was random; moreover, the play echoed the "quaint and stilted tone of the English dramatists":

> In fact throughout *The Spanish Student,* as well as throughout other compositions of its author, there runs a very obvious vein of *imitation.* We are perpetually reminded of something we have seen before . . . and even where the similarity cannot be said to amount to plagiarism, it is still injurious to the poet in the good opinion of him who reads. . . .

> Upon the whole, we regret that Professor Longfellow has written this work, and feel especially vexed that he has committed himself by its republication. Only when regarded as a mere poem, can it be said to have merit of any kind. . . . We are not too sure, indeed, that a "dramatic poem" is not a flat contradiction in terms. At all events a man of true genius, (and such Mr. L. unquestionably is,) has no business with these hybrid and paradoxical compositions. Let a poem be a poem only; let a play be a play and nothing more. As for *The Spanish Student,* its thesis is unoriginal; its incidents are antique; its plot is no plot; its characters have no character; in short, it is little better than a play upon words, to style it "A Play" at all.

That this is harsh criticism cannot be doubted. The only question is whether the harshness is not an inevitable consequence of Poe's aesthetic principles and critical candor. Poe, of course, thought so. When the New York *Evening Gazette* of August 8, 1845, declared this review a "somewhat sweeping condemna-

tion" and added, "but Mr. Longfellow does not seem to please Mr. Poe in anything that he writes," Poe was indignant. In the *Broadway Journal* of August 16, 1845, he replied that he had been grossly misrepresented by the statement that he could find nothing to admire in Longfellow:

> From Mr. L.'s first appearance in the literary world until the present moment, we have been, if not his warmest admirer and most stead-fast defender, at least *one* of his warmest and most steadfast. We even so far committed ourselves . . . as to place him . . . at the very head of American poets. Yet, because we are not so childish as to suppose that every book is thoroughly good or thoroughly bad—because we are not so absurd as to adopt the common practice of wholesale and indiscriminate abuse or commendation—because upon several occasions we have thought proper to *demonstrate* the sins, while displaying the virtues of Professor Longfellow, is it just, or proper, or even courteous on the part of "The Gazette" to accuse us, in round terms, of uncompromising hostility to this poet?

These were Poe's major reviews of Longfellow, and before we turn to less literary, more journalistic, matters, we should assess them briefly. With one conspicuous exception—the shot-in-the-dark accusation that Longfellow had plagiarized his "Midnight Mass" from Tennyson, not to mention the occasional harshness of tone that Poe seems to have considered an earmark of critical candor—nothing in the Poe critiques we have examined seems in any way discreditable. In the first of them, Poe pronounced *Hyperion* imitative and disunified, a judgment that can hardly be questioned. In the second, he said that *Voices* evinced poetic genius but not of the highest order—a declaration that errs, if at all, on the side of indulgence. In the two reviews of the *Ballads,* Poe demonstrated that Longfellow, by warping his art for didactic ends, was abusing his high powers, and he attempted, in the process, to perform a service for him, from which, at least for his present reputation, he might have benefited enormously. In his article on the American drama, Poe again stated what seems sufficiently clear, that *The Spanish Student* as a drama is devoid of merit. And in passing, Poe remarked that Longfellow was entitled to the first place among American poets, but that his tendency to imitate sometimes verged on plagiarism.

Poe did not notice Longfellow again until he had joined the staff of the *Mirror* as assistant editor. In reviewing his *Waif* (1844, dated 1845), a collection of about fifty poems to which Longfellow contributed only the "Proem" ("The day is done and the darkness . . ."), Poe made three significant comments. First, that the "Proem" was the best poem in the collection, despite the fact the anthology contained works by Herrick, Marvell, Shelley, and Browning. Second, that a comparison of "The Death-Bed" by Hood (which also appeared in *The Waif*) and a poem that appeared in Griswold's *Poets and Poetry of America* (which Poe mentioned neither by title nor author) showed that "*somebody is a thief.*" Third:

> We conclude our notice on the "Waif," with the observation that, although full of beauties, it is infected with a *moral taint*—or is this a mere freak of our fancy? We shall be pleased if it be so;—but there *does* appear . . . a very careful avoidance of all American poets who may be supposed especially to interfere with the claims of Mr. Longfellow. These men Mr. Longfellow can continuously *imitate* (*is* that the word?) and yet never even incidentally commend.

If there was any single reason for the animus of this final comment, one can find it in an anonymous article that, upon its appearance in the London *Foreign Quarterly Review,* became a *cause célèbre.* Typical of the English view except in its wholesale condemnation, the article insisted that American poets were either imitators or plagiarists. The major exception was "the most accomplished of the brotherhood, Henry Wadsworth Longfellow. But we have some doubts whether he can be fairly considered an indigenous specimen. His mind was educated in Europe. . . . But America claims him, and is entitled to him. . . . He is unquestionably the first of her poets, the most thoughtful and chaste; the most elaborate and finished." Among the imitators and plagiarists was Poe, a "capital artist after the manner of Tennyson; [who] approaches the spirit of his original more closely than any of them." The article concluded with the statement that almost every American poet was "on a level with the versifiers who fill up the corners of our provincial journals, into which all sorts of platitudes are admitted by the indiscriminate courtesy of the printer."

Poe, of course, considered the charge of imitation ridiculous. Writing to Lowell, who had been completely ignored by the *Foreign Quarterly* reviewer, Poe asked if he had seen the article:

> It has been denied that Dickens wrote it—but, to me, the article affords so strong internal evidence of his hand that I would as soon think of doubting my existence. He tells much truth—although he evinces much ignorance and more spleen. Among other points he accuses myself of "metrical imitation" of Tennyson, citing, by way of instance, passages from poems which were written & published long before Tennyson was heard of:— but I have, at no time, made any poetical pretension.

In answering Poe's letter, Lowell said that the article was written, not by Dickens but by John Forster, Dickens' friend, though Dickens "may have given him hints. Forster is a friend of some of the Longfellow clique

here which perhaps accounts for his putting L. at the top of our Parnassus."

In reaction to this information, Poe apparently felt that Longfellow, inadvertently or otherwise, had been instrumental in enlisting a translantic journal for the purpose of reducing almost every other American poet's claim to an impertinence so that, relatively, his position would be all the more unquestionable. Moreover, as a consequence, he probably began to see himself as the butt of a bad joke. He who had condemned imitation was now charged with that very sin. The man whose imitativeness he had censured was now held up as an original poet, at least by conspicuous default of any statement to the contrary in an article teeming with charges of imitation and plagiarism. And, as if to make the barb penetrate deeper, the poet he was said to imitate was the very poet he had accused Longfellow of plagiarizing. Whatever the validity of these speculations, Poe found the stigma of imitation so intolerable that, to exculpate himself, he footnoted the section "Poems Written in Youth" in the ***Raven*** volume (1845) as follows: "Private reasons—some of which have reference to the sin of plagiarism, and others to the date of Tennyson's first poems—have induced me, after some hesitation, to republish these, the crude compositions of my earliest boyhood . . . the date of which is too remote to be judiciously acknowledged." Thus, to all appearances, the remarks in the *Foreign Quarterly* were still rankling in Poe when he reviewed *The Waif.*

Poe's innuendoes in the *Mirror* drove Hiram Fuller and George Morris, co-editors of that journal, to print a joint disclaimer of them, saying: "For the opinions of the Daily paper, Mr. Willis is alone the gate-keeper, and by himself or by his direction, all its principal articles are written." Poe's allegations, moreover, elicited a letter from a self-acknowledged friend of Longfellow, a Mr. "H.," now known to have been George S. Hillard, one of the members of the "Five of Clubs" at Cambridge, which included Henry R. Cleveland, Charles Sumner, Cornelius C. Felton, and Longfellow. The letter, coming from Boston and dated January 15, was published in the *Evening Mirror* on January 20, and was prefaced by Willis, who also disclaimed responsibility for the *Waif* review: "We are willing to take any position to serve our friends, and if, by chance, we play the antagonist to shew another's 'skill of fence' in his behalf, we trust not to be believed less his friend, after the joust is over. The criticisms on the 'Waif' . . . were written in our office by an able though very critical hand." Willis also made a point of publishing in this and the next issue of the *Evening Mirror* Lowell's high estimate of Poe as a critic that was to appear in the February number of *Graham's Magazine.*

"H.'s" principal concern was "with the sting in the tail of the second communication [the second instalment of Poe's review of *The Waif*], in which Mr. Longfellow is charged with omitting, from discreditable motives, any extracts from American poets, though he continuously imitates some of them. This is no light accusation; and is one against which his friends feel bound to enter their most emphatic protest." "H." maintained that an anthologist has the privilege of selecting any materials he cares to and declared that the charge of discrimination was wholly untrue, especially in this instance, since he had known the compiler for a long time. "If it be asked," he concluded, "why has he not given public demonstration of this kindness of spirit towards his poetical brethren, the answer is obvious. He is a poet himself, and addresses the public in that capacity, and not as a critic. . . . The charge of habitually imitating other American poets touches Mr. Longfellow in his public character as a poet, and not his personal character as a man, and therefore requires no especial reply from his friends."

Directly following "H.'s" letter and under the title, "Post-Notes by the Critic," Poe published his rejoinder:

> I did not dispute Mr. L.'s '*right*' to construct his book as he thought proper. I reserve to myself the right of thinking what I choose of the construction. . . .
>
> As 'the charge of habitually imitating other American poets requires no especial reply'—it shall surely rest undisturbed by any reply of mine. . . .
>
> It seems to me that the whole state of the case may be paralleled thus:
>
> A accosts B, with—"My dear friend, in common with all mankind, and the angels, I regard you as a demi-god. Your equal is not to be found in the country which is proud to claim you as a son. . . . but permit me! there is a very—a *very* little speck of dust on the extreme end of your nose—oblige yourself and your friends by brushing it away." "Sir," replies B, "what you have asserted is wholly untrue. . . . I consider you a malignant critic, and wish to have nothing further to do with you—for know that there *are* spots upon the sun, but my proboscis is a thing without spot!"

Nothing more was heard from "H." nor, apparently, was anything to be heard again from Boston or Cambridge on this score; and though, most likely, Poe would have furnished articles on imitation and plagiarism for the *Mirror,* he might have ignored Longfellow indefinitely. Unfortunately, however, a series of episodes occurred which gave a sensational vogue to Poe's comments and made it imperative for Longfellow's friends to rescue the poet from the notoriety which, for a time, threatened him.

On January 25 the Buffalo *Western Literary Messenger* published a letter from "Pi Kappa Rho," who com-

pared Longfellow's translation of "The Good George Campbell from the German of O.L.B. Wolf[f]" (which had appeared in *Graham's Magazine* in February, 1843) with the ballad, "Bonnie George Campbell" (which had appeared in William Motherwell's collection, *Minstrelsy, Ancient and Modern,* Glasgow, 1828). "Pi Kappa Rho," assuming that Wolff, a professor at the University of Jena, had not translated the Scotch ballad, accused Longfellow of a "gross plagiarism" and of impudence in "supposing that he can, undetected, palm off upon us, in a mutilated state, this . . . beautiful ancient Scottish song, as a translation from the German of O.L.B. Wolf."

The charge, apparently unanswerable, became common editorial fare, which brought Longfellow's integrity into question and began to make Poe's recent allegations appear valid. Among the New York papers that carried the *Messenger* charge were *The Rover,* the *Broadway Journal,* and the *Daily Tribune. The Rover,* also assuming that the Wolff translation did not exist, noted:

> A writer in the Western Literary Messenger has recently detected this gentleman (Longfellow) in one of the most flagrant and unscrupulous pieces of plagiarism that ever occurred in our literature. In a critique upon his "Waif," in the Evening Mirror, a covert allusion was made to a disposition on the part of the "Professor" to thrive upon the hard-earned laurels of others, and the only fault of Willis's [*sic*] article was, that he merely hit the nail's head. . . .

The editor then printed the Scottish poem and Longfellow's alleged plagiarism side by side and concluded, "Singular *coincidence,* eh?"

The *Broadway Journal* observed: "Charges of plagiarism are very frequently made, and often with good reason, against our popular authors. . . . The 'Rover' . . . contains a very grave charge against Longfellow . . . which, if true, would lead us to distrust everything that came from his pen." The *Tribune,* however, cited a "correspondent of the Boston Post" to explain that Longfellow's error was not one of plagiarism but one of inadvertence:

> In a collection of German poems which Mr. Longfellow owned, was a poem called 'Der gute Ritter [*sic*] Campbell;' this poem happened to be a translation and a plagiarism, as it was given for original, from an old English ballad. Longfellow suspecting nothing, translated it, and has hit so exactly upon a good version, that it is almost word for word with the English original. The remarkable thing is, that Longfellow, celebrated for his acquaintance with ballad literature, should have overlooked this lyric, which is printed in Motherwell's collection of ancient and modern Poems—so far have overlooked it, as to translate it out of German.—Homer occasionally nods.

This was scarcely a vindication. Since the source that Longfellow had used remained unspecified, the charge that Wolff plagiarized instead of merely translated is unsupported. A collection by Wolff that contains the poem is, as Poe later pointed out, *Halle der Völker: Sammlung vorzüglicher Volkslieder der bekanntesten Nationen, grösstentheils zum ersten Male metrisch in das Deutsche übertragen* (Frankfurt, 1837), a title that plainly clears Wolff of plagiarism. Aware that this explanation satisfied few of his critics, Longfellow wrote a letter to Graham, dated February 19, 1845, to explain the situation more convincingly. But mysteriously—and it is only one of the mysteries of this affair—the letter was not published in *Graham's* until May, 1845. The source he had used while abroad in the summer of 1842 was not a collection by Wolff at all, but one by Karl Gollmick. That collection, called *Der Sängersaal: Auswahl von Gedichten zum Komponieren* (Darmstadt, 1842), contained the Wolff translation of "Bonnie George Campbell," where it "appeared as an original poem by Wolf. . . ." Fortunately, Longfellow found that the printer had made an error (actually, the error—or liberty taken—had originated with Wolff) and transcribed the Scottish river *Tay* for the German *Tag,* an error that Longfellow had faithfully translated and that, as he put it, is "an unimpeachable witness of the falsity of the charge brought against me."

In the meantime, with Longfellow's honesty impugned and his reputation at stake, a second defender of Longfellow, now identified as Charles Sumner, Longfellow's friend, decided to take issue with Poe's innuendoes regarding *The Waif.* Willis reopened the controversy with these words:

> Longfellow's Waif.—A friend, who is a very fine critic, gave us, not long since, a review of this delightful new book. Perfectly sure that any thing from that source was a treasure for our paper, we looked up from a half-read proof to run our eye hastily over it, and gave it to the printer—not, however, without mentally differing from the writer as to the drift of the last sentence. . . .

> Notwithstanding the haste with which it passed through our attention (for we did not see it in proof) the question of admission was submitted to a principle in our mind; and, in admitting it, we did by Longfellow, as we would have him do by us. It was a literary charge, by a pen that never records an opinion without some supposed good reason, and only injurious to Longfellow, (to our belief) while circulating, un-replied-to, in *conversation-dom.* In the second while we reasoned upon it [we thought] . . . Our critical friend believes this, though we do not. Longfellow is asleep on velvet; it will do him good to rouse him; his friends will come out and fight his battle; the charges (which to *us* would be a comparative pat on the back) will be openly

disproved, and the acquittal of course leaves his fame brighter than before—the injurious whisper, in Conversation-dom, killed in the bargain!

Willis then proceeded to quote part of Charles Sumner's letter, though he did not disclose his correspondent's identity to the public:

> It has been asked, perhaps, why Lowell was neglected in this collection? Might it not as well be asked why Bryant, Dana and Halleck were neglected? The answer is obvious to any one who candidly considers the character of the collection. It professed to be, according to the Proem, from the humbler poets; and it was intended to embrace pieces that were anonymous, or which were not easily accessible to the general reader—the *waifs* and *estrays* of literature. To put anything of Lowell's, for example, into a collection of *waifs,* would be a particular liberty with pieces which are all collected and christened.

Clearly, Longfellow was becoming good "copy," and, as editor of the *Mirror,* Willis had reason to encourage the "controversy." Yet, though Poe's remarks had apparently helped Mirror sales, Willis felt no need to sully his reputation for geniality by seconding Poe's charges nor, on the other hand, any urge to diminish those sales by discounting Poe's charges entirely. Graham, however, concerned with protecting the reputation of his drawing card, asked Willis to make his "disclaimer" stronger, a request with which Willis complied by saying that he "dissented from *all* the disparagement of Longfellow" in his assistant editor's review of *The Waif.*

Graham wrote to Longfellow too: "What has 'broke loose' in Poe? I see he is down on you in New York papers and has written demanding return of Review [of *The Spanish Student*] I mentioned he had written for me. If he sends money or another article I shall be obliged to let him have it. . . ." He added in a postscript: "Mr. Willis made a disclaimer of being an endorser of Poe's views, at my request. I cannot see what Poe says *now,* can hurt you." And Mrs. Longfellow wrote to Samuel Longfellow just prior to Willis's publishing his stronger disclaimer: "If you see the *Mirror,* you know how shabbily Willis tries to excuse Poe's insolence. Have you seen a curious poem by the latter entitled **'The Raven,'** most artistically rhythmical but 'nothing more,' to quote the burden?"

Despite Willis's disavowal of "*all* the disparagement of Longfellow," Poe was allowed to continue his criticism of Longfellow, this time indirectly in an article entitled "Imitation—Plagiarism." Having in mind such articles as that which had appeared in the *Foreign Quarterly,* Poe wrote that the "British reviewers have very frequently accused us of imitation, and the charge is undoubtedly well based." He explained why this was true:

> The want of an international copy-right law renders it impossible for our men of genius to obtain remuneration for their labors. Now since, as a body, men of genius are proverbially poor, the want of the international law represses their efforts altogether. Our sole writers, in consequence, are from the class of *dilettanti;* and although among this class are unquestionably many gifted men, still as a class—as men of wealth and leisure—they are imbued with a spirit of conservatism, which is merely a mood of the imitative spirit.

He then made the observation that the

> sin of plagiarism involves the quintessence of meanness; and this meanness seems in the direct ratio of the amount of *honor* attained by the theft. A pickpocket is content with his plunder; the plagiarist demands that mankind should applaud him, not for plundering, but for the thing plundered.

He added, with an apparent allusion to Longfellow and his defenders:

> When a plagiarism is detected, it generally happens that the public sympathy is with the plagiarist, and his friends proceed to every extreme in the way of exculpation. But how unjust! We should sympathize rather with him upon whom the plagiarism has been committed. Not only is he robbed of his property—of his fame . . . but he is rendered liable by the crime of *the plagiarist to the suspicion of being a plagiarist himself.*

Briggs in his magazine, the *Broadway Journal,* objected to Poe's allegation that James Aldrich—a New York editor and sometime poet—had stolen from Hood. The resemblance between the two poems, Briggs contended, was insufficient to warrant such a conclusion, and he urged, though he was in error, that Aldrich's poem had been written before Hood's. Poe's reply, printed under the title **"Plagiarism"** and introduced by a brief and neutral foreword by Willis, was that there were ten distinct similarities between the two short poems, which he enumerated to support the conclusion that somebody was a thief, and—he added curtly—the "only doubt in our mind is about the sincerity of any one who shall say that somebody is *not.*"

On February 28 Poe mounted the platform of the New York Historical Society to deliver his lecture on American poets. The event was sensationally announced in the *Evening Mirror* as follows:

> Edgar Poe's Lecture.—The decapitation of the criminal who did not know his head was off till it fell into his hand as he was bowing, is a Poe-kerish

similitude, but it conveys an idea of the Damascene slicing of the critical blade of Mr. Poe. On Friday night we are to have his **"Lecture on the Poets of America,"** and those who would witness fine carving will probably be there.

The nature of the lecture can be inferred from the comments it elicited from the editors of the *Daily Tribune,* the *Evening Mirror, The Town,* and the *Democratic Review.* Greeley observed that the lecture embodied "much acute and fearless criticism," but that Poe was often unjust in his censure of American reviewing. Moreover, he objected to Poe's "broad assertion that Longfellow is a plagiarist. Of all critical cant, this hunting after coincidence of ideas, or phrase, often unavoidable, between authors, is the least endurable." Nevertheless, he asked if the lecture might not be repeated. Willis stated that "one of the most readable and saleable of *books* would be a dozen of such Lectures by Mr. Poe, and we give him a publisher's counsel to print them." He mentioned that Poe discussed Bryant, Halleck, Longfellow, Sprague, and Dana and found Longfellow to have more genius than any of the others, but that "his fatal alacrity at imitation made him borrow, when he had better at home." *The Town* reported that the lecture "was worthy of its author—keen, cutting and withering, when it touched on the mountebanks of American literature; and full of faith and hope, when it spoke of the future." John L. O'Sullivan of the *Democratic Review* praised Poe for the

> devoted spirit in which he advocated the claims and urged the responsibilities of literature. The necessity of a just independent criticism was his main topic. He made unmitigated war upon the prevalent Puffery, and dragged several popular idols from their pedestals. . . . There has been a good deal said about this lecture, which should be either repeated or printed. If published with proper revision and some additions, it would render our literature, at the present time, an important service.

Poe's own comment on the lecture is of interest too:

> In a late lecture on the **"Poets and Poetry of America,"** delivered before an audience made up chiefly of editors and their connexions, I took occasion to speak what I know to be the truth, and I endeavoured so to speak it that there should be no chance of misunderstanding what it was I intended to say. I told these gentlemen to their teeth that, with a *very* few noble exceptions, they had been engaged for many years in a system of indiscriminate laudation of American books—a system which, more than any other one thing in the world, had tended to the depression of "American literature" whose elevation it was designed to effect. I said this, and very much more of a similar tendency, with as thorough a distinctness as I could command. Could

I, at the moment, have invented any terms *more* explicit, wherewith to express my contempt of our general editorial course of corruption and puffery, I should have employed them beyond a shadow of a doubt;—and should I think of anything more expressive *hereafter,* I will endeavour either to find or to make an opportunity for its introduction to the public.

And what, for all this, had I to anticipate? In a very few cases, the open, and, in several, the silent approval of the more chivalrous portion of the press;—but in a majority of instances, I should have been weak indeed to look for anything but abuse. To the Willises—the O'Sullivans—the Duyckincks—to the choice and magnanimous few who spoke promptly in my praise, and who have since taken my hand with a more cordial and more impressive grasp than ever—to these I return, of course, my acknowledgements, for that they have rendered me my due. To my villifiers [*sic*] I return also such thanks as they deserve, inasmuch as without what they have done me the honor to say, there would have been much point wanting in the compliments of my friends.

The opportunity Poe promised to find or make was already awaiting him. A pseudonymous correspondent, "Outis," moved by Poe's editorial, if not forensic, attack upon his friend Longfellow, entered the lists on March 1. Asking Willis for fair play and the privilege of having his remarks published in the *Mirror,* he argued that "identities" between poems do not necessarily imply plagiarism, for if plagiarism was the only inference to be drawn from identities, then every author was liable to the charge, since no one could possibly read everything that was published. To clinch his argument, he added:

> Who, for example, would wish to be guilty of the littleness of detracting from the uncommon merit of that remarkable poem of . . . Mr. Poe's . . . entitled **"The Raven,"** by charging *him* with the paltriness of imitation? And yet, some snarling critic, who might envy the reputation he had not the genius to secure for himself, might refer to the frequent, very forcible, but rather quaint repetition . . . as a palpable imitation of . . . *the Ancient Mariner.*

Outis then submitted excerpts from an "anonymous" poem, "The Bird of the Dream," and, comparing it with **"The Raven,"** pointed out eighteen similarities, outnumbering the ten similarities which Poe had noted in comparing the Aldrich and Hood poems. Outis concluded: "Such criticisms only make the *author* of them contemptible, without soiling a plume in the cap of his victim."

Poe did not reply to Outis in the *Mirror*. Though on excellent terms with Willis, he severed connections with him to accept the more promising position of co-editor of the *Broadway Journal.* Briggs, in charge of the *Journal,* recognized in Poe a drawing card ("his name is of some authority"; "Wiley and Putnam are going to publish a new edition of his tales and sketches"; "Everybody has been raven-mad about his last poem, and his lecture"). Moreover, though Briggs regarded the "very ticklish hobby" of detecting plagiarisms unfortunate for Poe's reputation, he felt that such articles, together with the replies they might provoke from journals avid for scandal, would serve as advertisements of the *Journal* and enlarge its subscription list.

Poe, as expected, replied to Outis as soon as he became associated with the weekly *Journal,* for the innuendoes in Outis's letter were as embarrassing to him as his in the review of *The Waif* must have been to Longfellow. Abandoning editorial anonymity, he began by summarizing the history of the controversy, even reprinting the "documents" in the case—his, Briggs's, Willis's, and those of Longfellow's defenders. Then, proceeding to the matter at hand, he said that he admired the chivalry that prompted Outis's reply, but nothing else, and that he especially disliked the "desperation of the effort to make out a case." Poe then questioned whether a critic might make a charge of plagiarism, not from "littleness" or "envy," but from strictly honorable and even charitable motives. To answer his own question, he reasoned that if the possibility of plagiarism is admitted at all, then the chances are that an established author steals from an obscure one. The obscure author is thus falsely accused of plagiarism, which makes the real culprit guilty on two counts: that of the original theft, which would alone deserve exposure, and that of foisting his crime upon the guiltless struggler. He summed up this phase of the argument by saying that because he, for one, wished to convict the guilty to exonerate the innocent, the charge of "carping littleness" was brought against him. He paused here for want of space, but promised to resume the discussion in the next number of the *Journal.*

Poe's remarks began to arouse newspaper and magazine editors, among them J. Hunt, Jr., of the *National Archives:*

> As a critical tattler, we know of none other which seems to give a more condid [*sic*] review of the works of *authors* [than the *Broadway Journal*]. We own, notwithstanding, that we have cherished rather of a sour feeling towards one of the editors—Mr. Poe in times past, for his sarcastic, and what to us then appeared malicious criticism on other's [*sic*] production. All who have read "Graham" for the last two or three years—will corroberate [*sic*] our statement, and there breathes not a man, having any pretensions to authorship, who so flinchingly squirms at the strictures of others, than does Mr. Poe. This may be seen in the No. now before us. . . .

One quarter of the paper is made use of by Mr. Poe, endeavoring to smooth over and give diminutiveness to what a writer for the Mirror, calling himself "Outis," and some of the other papers have said of him, respecting his late lecture . . . and his Plagarisms [sic]. It is a very true remark, that a Joker will rarely ever receive one in return, good naturedly; and this is to a great extent true of Mr. Poe.

But we will 'pass all his imperfections by' and to show that we are not blind to his good qualities, we will say that, as a writer, on general topics, Mr. Poe, undoubtedly, stands on an equal with the best of his class. Among all the reading which we receive, there is no weekly which more claims our attention than does the Broadway Journal. Every article in it shows the scholar, and yet the language is such that a child may read and understand.

On March 17 Poe, without respect for the full truth, answered the editor of the *National Archives,* but the magazine had become defunct in the meantime:

Let me put it to you as to a frank man of honor— Can you suppose it possible that any human being could pursue a strictly impartial course of criticism for 10 years (as I have done in the S.L. Messenger and in Graham's Magazine) without offending irreparably a host of authors and their connexions?— but because these *were* offended, and gave vent at every opportunity to their spleen, would you consider my course an iota the less honorable on that account? Would you consider it just to measure my deserts by the yelpings of my foes, indepently [sic] of your own judgment in the premises, based upon an actual knowledge of what I have done?

You reply—"Certainly not," and, because I feel that this must be your reply, I acknowledge that I am grieved to see any thing (however slight) in your paper that has the appearance of joi[n]ing in with the outcry so very sure to be made by the 'less['] honorable portion of the press under circumstances such as are my own.

Poe then explained his reasons for commenting upon the Outis letter at length: " . . . it demanded an answer & no proper answer could be given in less compass— . . . the subject of imitation, plagiarism, &c is one in which the public has lately taken much interest & is admirably adapted to the character of a literary journal—and . . . I have some important developments to make, which the commonest principles of self-defence demand imperatively at my hands."

As he had promised, Poe resumed his discussion of plagiarism on March 15. He agreed with Outis that identities between poems might exist by coincidence but that the admission of such a possibility would by no means eliminate the possibility of plagiarism, particularly as in the case of the Aldrich and Hood poems when "in the compass of eight short lines" there are "ten or twelve peculiar identities of thought and identities of expression." To demonstrate, as Outis had demonstrated, that in another instance two writers by coincidence had used an identical metaphor did not by any means prove that "Mr. Longfellow is innocent of the imitation with which I have charged him, and that Mr. Aldrich is innocent of the plagiarism with which I have *not* charged him. . . ." He added that he would "continue, if not conclude this subject, in the next *Journal.* . . ."

In his third reply, Poe said that Outis suffered from the misapprehension that one accusation cancels another— that by insinuating that Poe had committed plagiarism, it could be reasoned that Aldrich and Longfellow had not. When he had accused Aldrich or Hood of plagiarism, Poe said, he printed their poems together and in full, but he had not been accorded such treatment by Outis. Instead,

an *anonymous* gentleman rebuts my accusation by telling me that there is a certain similarity between a poem of my own and an *anonymous* poem which he has before *him,* and which he would like to transcribe if it were not too long. He contents himself, therefore, with giving me, from the too long poem, three stanzas which are shown . . . to have been *culled,* to suit his own purposes, from different portions of the poem, but which (again to suit his own purposes) he places before the public in consecutive connexion!

Then, registering a doubt as to the existence of the poem, he examined the eighteen identities that Outis had pointed out, only to discover that the poems failed to tally except on two points.

In considering plagiarism, Poe continued, one must regard, not only the number of coincidences, but the peculiarity of each one; and not only that, but "the antagonistic differences, if any, which surround them— and very especially *the space* over which the coincidences are spread, and the number or paucity of the events, or incidents, from among which the coincidences are selected." He then used the Aldrich and Hood poems again to explain in greater detail why he considered one of them a plagiarism. He summarized this analysis by remarking:

Now the chances that these fifteen coincidences [in his examination he added five to the original ten], so peculiar in character, and all occurring within the compass of eight short lines, on the one part, and sixteen on the other—the chances, I say, that these coincidences are merely accidental, may be estimated, possibly, as about one to one hundred millions. . . .

He concluded by saying that he would endeavor to bring this subject to an end in the next number of the *Journal.*

In his fourth reply to Outis, Poe declared:

> . . . if Outis has his own private reasons for being disgusted with what he terms the "wholesale mangling of victims without rhyme or reason," there is not a man living, of common sense and common honesty, who has not better reason (if possible) to be disgusted with the insufferable cant and shameless misrepresentation practised habitually by just such persons as Outis, with the view of decrying by sheer strength of lungs—of trampling down—of rioting down—of mobbing down any man with a soul that bids him come out from among the general corruption of our public press, and take his stand upon the open ground of rectitude and honor.

> The Outises who practise this species of bullyism are, as a matter of course, anonymous. They are either the "victims without rhyme or reason who have been mangled by wholesale," or they are the relatives, or the relatives *of* the relatives of the "victims without rhyme or reason who have been mangled by wholesale." Their watchwords are "carping littleness," "envious malignity," and "personal abuse." Their low artifices are insinuated calumnies, and indefatigable whispers of regret, from post to pillar, that "Mr. So-and-So, or Mr. This-and-That *will* persist in rendering himself so dreadfully unpopular."

For himself, he said:

> . . . I am but defending a set of principles which no honest man need be ashamed of defending, and for whose defence no honest man will consider an apology required.

He continued:

> . . . not even an Outis can accuse me . . . of having ever descended, in the most condemnatory of my reviews, to that personal abuse which, upon one or two occasions, has indeed been levelled at myself, in the spasmodic endeavours of aggrieved authors to rebut what I have ventured to demonstrate. . . . no man can point to a single *critique,* among the very numerous ones which I have written during the last ten years, which is either wholly fault-finding or wholly in approbation; nor is there an instance to be discovered, among all that I have published, of my having set forth, either in praise or censure, a single opinion upon any critical topic of moment, without attempting, at least, to give it authority by something that wore the semblance of a reason. . . . If, to be brief, in what I have put forth there has been a preponderance of censure over commendation,—is there not to be imagined for this preponderance a more charitable motive than any which the Outises have been magnanimous enough to assign me—is

not this preponderance, in a word, the natural and inevitable tendency of all criticism worth the name in this age of so universal an authorship, that no man in his senses will pretend to deny the vast predominance of good writers over bad?

Poe then objected to Outis's supposing him to make certain charges against Longfellow and then holding him responsible for them. Thus, he proceeded to cite his own charges. First, as he had in 1839, Poe compared the "Midnight Mass" and the "Death of the Old Year" and repeated that this imitation was too palpable to be mistaken and belongs to the most barbarous class of literary piracy. Second (with Longfellow's explanation still unpublished in *Graham's*), he compared Longfellow's translation of "Der gute George Campbell" from Wolff with the original in Motherwell's and commented: "Professor Longfellow defends himself (I learn) from the charge of *imitation* in this case, by the assertion that he *did* translate from Wolff, but that Wolff copied from Motherwell. I am willing to believe almost anything rather than so gross a plagiarism as this seems to be—but there are difficulties which should be cleared up." How did it happen, "in the translation from the Scotch into the German, and again from the German into the English, not only the versification should have been rigidly preserved, but the *rhymes* and *alliteration*?" Why had Longfellow, "with his known intimate acquaintance with 'Motherwell's Minstrelsy,'" failed to recognize at once "so remarkable a poem when he met it in Wolff"? What was the source that Longfellow had used in retranslating from Wolff? It seemed clear to Poe that the Wolff translation must have appeared in a work "plainly acknowledged as a translation, with its original designated," a work whose subtitle Poe footnoted but a copy of which he had been unable to obtain. Third (and Poe seemed driven to his wits' end here), he argued that Longfellow had modeled a scene in his *Spanish Student* upon his own *Politian,* the thirteen coincidences he pointed out textually being "sufficiently noticeable to establish at least the *imitation* beyond all doubt." Finally, he found certain lines in Longfellow coincidental with lines in Bryant, Sidney, Milton, and Henry King. Poe concluded by remarking that he could point out a "score or two" of such imitations, and that, therefore, Longfellow's friends, instead of charging him with carping littleness, should credit him with great moderation for accusing Longfellow only of imitation: "Had I accused him, in loud terms, of manifest and continuous plagiarism, I should but have echoed the sentiment of every man of letters in the land beyond the immediate influence of the Longfellow *coterie*." Further evidence of his moderation, he said, was the fact that he himself had submitted "to accusations of plagiarism for the very sins of this gentleman against myself," but that, despite this, he had set "forth the *merits* of the poet in the strongest light, whenever an opportunity was afforded me." Yet the moment that he ventured "an infinitesimal sentence of dispraise" of Longfellow, he received—under what he claimed was Longfellow's instigation—"ridiculous anonymous letters from his friends" and, in the *Boston Evening Transcript,* "prickings with the needles of Miss Walter's innumerable epigrams, rendered unnecessarily and therefore cruelly painful to my feelings by being first carefully deprived of the point."

There was a postscript to these replies to Outis still to appear, but, in the meantime, the *Aristidean,* a New York monthly newly founded by Thomas Dunn English, Poe's acquaintance from the Philadelphia days, published the harshest indictment of Longfellow ever made. The article affirmed that Longfellow was vastly overrated by the Boston clique. "In no literary circle out of Boston—or, indeed, out of the small coterie of abolitionists, transcendentalists and fanatics in general, which is the Longfellow junto—have we heard a seriously dissenting voice on this point." Outside of this "knot of rogues and madmen," his real virtues are simply a "sufficient scholarship, a fine taste, a keen appreciation of the beautiful, a happy memory, a happier tact at imitation or transmutation, felicity of phrase and some fancy." The anonymous writer, turning to Poe's recent lecture, confessed surprise to hear that Poe had claimed for Longfellow a "pre-eminence over all poets of this country on the score of the 'loftiest poetical quality—imagination.'" He believed that an opinion so crude must have arisen from "want of leisure or inclination to compare the works of the writer in question with the sources from which they were stolen." However, a letter written by "an unfortunate wight who called himself 'Outis,' seems to have stirred up the critic to make the proper examination. . . ." For himself, he felt that, "whatever may be the talents of Professor Longfellow, he is the Great Mogul of the Imitators," and that he had achieved his eminent position by "accident or chicanery."

The minute analysis and the charges of plagiarism that followed indicate that Poe had more than a hand in the article and that he planted the article in the *Aristidean* to gain corroboration of his own judgments—a corroboration so devastating that his statements in the *Broadway Journal* would appear mild by comparison. The writer pointed out that such rhymes as *angel* and *evangel* are inadmissible because identical. He cited a passage from "Hymn to the Night" to demonstrate that Longfellow had such a strong tendency to imitation "that he not unfrequently imitates himself." He argued that "A Psalm of Life" is "chiefly remarkable for its containing one of the most palpable plagiarisms ever perpetrated by an author of equal character. . . . Mr. Poe, in his late *exposé,* has given some very decisive instances of what he too modestly calls *imitations* on the part of Mr. Longfellow from himself (Mr. Poe)." But there are others that can be adduced: Longfellow's "Footsteps of Angels" has lines taken from Poe's **"The Sleeper"**; "The Beleaguered City" is a palpable imitation of Poe's **"Haunted Palace"**. . . . "We do not like to be ill-natured; but when one gentleman's purse is found in another gentleman's pocket, how did it come there?" *The Spanish Student* as a poem "is meritorious at points—as a drama it is one of the most lamentable failures." Longfellow, it is true, acknowledged that it was "taken, *in part,* from the 'Gitanilla' of Cervantes. *In part,* also, it is taken from '*Politian* . . . by Edgar A. Poe' . . . no acknowledgement, however, is made in the latter instance." Longfellow "has stolen . . . much from Mr. Poe. . . . There are other plagiarisms of Mr. Longfellow which we might easily expose, but we have said enough. There can be no reasonable doubt in the mind of any, out of the little clique, to which we at first alluded, that the author of 'Outre Mer,' is not only a servile imitator, but a most insolent literary thief."

Thus, however often Poe had opposed such malicious attacks as this, however often he had inveighed against a reviewer's remaining anonymous, and however often he had objected to "personalities" in critical articles, he resorted to all the arts of literary assassination for his self-justifying purposes. In commenting on this article in the *Broadway Journal,* Poe only remarked: "There is a long review or rather running commentary upon Longfellow's poems [in the *Aristidean*]. It is, perhaps, a little coarse, but we are not disposed to call it unjust; although there are in it some opinions which, by implication, are attributed to ourselves individually, and with which we cannot altogether coincide."

If Poe acted in his own defense against the ire of editors, O'Sullivan of the *Democratic Review* came to his aid voluntarily:

> Mr. Poe has been for some weeks past engaged in a critical discussion in the *Broadway Journal* on the subject of plagiarism. . . . There is no literary question which requires more discrimination, greater nicety of apprehension and occasionally more courage. We appreciate the latter quality in Mr. Poe; it is especially necessary in a country which numbers some thousand poets, and not one, *in the highest sense,* worthy the name among them all. It is something for a man to encounter so formidable an opposition in this day of newspapers and public opinion, when the opportunities for the gratification of a whim or prejudice, to say nothing of malice and disappointed hate, are so ready at hand. Yet it is necessary that a man should respect himself and tell the truth. . . . Of all pursuits in the world we know of none more humiliating, more dastardly, or less comfortable to an honest man than the aimless, shifting, puffing, practice of literature . . . [which imparts] complacency to a certain number of fools, and persecute[s] a certain number of supposed enemies. . . . It is for the interest of literature that every man who writes should show his honesty and not bring letters into contempt. If in doing this he should happen to fall on the other side of harshness

or rudeness . . . let him be pardoned, for it is better both for the cause of truth and virtue that this should be the case than that a man should be always dull and complaisant.

On April 5 Poe concluded his reply to Outis with an effort at dignity, but if he accomplished that effect, it was at the cost of misrepresentation and special pleading. His purpose in replying to Outis at such length, he said, had been "to place fairly and distinctly before the literary public certain principles of criticism for which I have been long contending, and which . . . were in danger of being misunderstood. . . . The thesis of my argument, in general, has been the definition of the grounds on which a charge of plagiarism may be based, and of the species of ratiocination by which it is to be established: that is all." He had not intended to be malevolent or discourteous, whatever one might suspect; and if anyone would take the trouble to read what he had written, he would see that he had made "*no* charge of moral delinquency against either Mr. Longfellow, Mr. Aldrich, or Mr. Hood:—indeed, lest in the heat of argument, I may have uttered any words which may admit of being tortured into such an interpretation, I here fully disclaim them upon the spot."

Poe's sudden reversal of position, not to mention the fact that these remarks were in the form of a postscript, suggests that he had finally found an explanation for imitation other than one of intention—an explanation with which he seemed delighted, for he used it again on several occasions and here for the first time. Thus, he proceeded to acquit Longfellow of "moral delinquency"—that is, of wilful plagiarism—and to explain his unconscious plagiarism—imitation—in these terms:

> the poetic sentiment (even without reference to the poetic power) implies a peculiarly, perhaps abnormally keen appreciation of the beautiful, with a longing for its assimilation, or absorption, into poetic identity. What the poet intensely admires, becomes thus, in very fact, although only partially, a portion of his own intellect. It has a secondary origination within his own soul—an origination altogether apart, although springing from its primary origination from without. The poet is thus possessed by another's thought, and cannot be said to take of it, possession. But, in either view, he thoroughly feels it as *his own*—and this feeling is counteracted only by the sensible presence of its true, palpable origin in the volume from which he has derived it—an origin which, in the long lapse of years it is almost impossible *not* to forget—for in the meantime the thought itself is forgotten. But the frailest association will regenerate it—it springs up with all the vigor of a new birth—its absolute originality is not even a matter of suspicion—and when the poet has written it and printed it, and on its account is charged with plagiarism, there will be no one in the world more entirely astounded than himself. Now

from what I have said it will be evident that the liability to accidents of this character is in the direct ratio of the poetic sentiment—of the susceptibility to the poetic impression; and in fact all literary history demonstrates that, for the most frequent and palpable plagiarisms, we must search the works of the most eminent poets.

Though Poe "exonerated" Longfellow, he raised more questions than he answered. Agreed that the poetic sentiment and the poetic power coexist in the poet. Agreed too that poetic power compels the poet to render his own vision of the beautiful ("primary origination"), which, by definition, is original, and that the poetic sentiment compels the poet, all unawares, to reproduce reproductions of such visions ("secondary origination"), which, again by definition, are unoriginal. Still, crucial problems remain—and Poe, neither here nor elsewhere, solves them, which may account for his dropping the entire "explanation" by 1847. Do the works of the "most eminent poets" (and Poe in the *Marginalia* article means the greatest) really contain "the most frequent and palpable plagiarisms"? Does not greatness imply primary origination, as every Romantic critic thought, including Poe himself? Is plagiarism—a sign of the poetic sentiment—rendered negligible by the poetic power evinced in such "plagiaristic" works as *Hamlet* and *The Waste Land*? And, by the same token, is plagiarism to be censured only when the poetic sentiment, acting independently of the poetic power, produces merely a copy? In his article on James Aldrich in the *Literati* papers, Poe seems to suggest as much when he said that "A Death-Bed" is indefensible because both "in matter and manner it is nearly identical with . . . '*The* Death-Bed,' by Thomas Hood." And in his *Marginalia,* Poe remarked that "Imitators are not, necessarily, unoriginal—except at the exact points of imitation." And what are we to do with the fact of coincidence, which Poe entirely ignored—the kind of coincidence that caused Longfellow to remark, when he chanced upon a simile in Brainard's "Mocking Bird" identical with one in "Excelsior": "Of a truth one cannot strike a spade into the soil of Parnassus, without disturbing the bones of some dead poet."

With this, the "war," precipitated by a single, ill-advised paragraph concluding Poe's *Waif* review, came lamely to a halt, as far as Poe was concerned. True, he would fire Parthian shots at Longfellow from time to time, but he would never review another book of his—neither his *Belfry of Bruges and Other Poems* (1845), nor the *Estray: A Collection of Poems* (1846), nor the new edition of *Outre-Mer* (1846), nor *Evangeline* (1847), nor *Kavanagh: A Tale* (1849). Only in his essay, **"The American Drama,"** when he struck again at the problem of imitation, did he consider Longfellow once more at any length.

Yet, if only to conclude the "war" with a flourish, it seemed necessary to atomize the *North American Review,* which had felt duty-bound to acclaim the literati of Massachusetts and, in particular, to expatiate upon the virtues of almost every Longfellow book, whether in A. P. Peabody's review of *Outre-Mer,* in Felton's reviews of *Hyperion, Voices, Ballads,* and *Poems,* in Francis Bowen's review of *Poets and Poetry of Europe,* or in various unidentified reviews devoted to the Cambridge poet, including one of *The Waif.* Simms, badly treated by the *North American,* furnished the occasion for that attack in his *Southern and Western Magazine,* and an anonymous writer, presumably Thomas Dunn English, possibly with Poe's assistance, did the devoir for the *Broadway Journal.* The writer in the *Journal* called attention to Simms's observations concerning the "parochial review" and quoted passages from Simms's article so that Northerners "may see in what estimation the North American is held at the South." Simms's theme was that the *North American,* in its thirty years of existence, was guilty of the most flagrant literary sectionalism:

> That the *North American Review* has worked religiously for New England, her sons, her institutions, her claims of every sort, there is no . . . question. . . .

> We do not know that the Middle States have fared very much better than those of the South, in the treatment which they have received at the hands of this journal. Their favorite writers are not employed upon its pages, and their publications are noticed slowly and with evident reluctance. When reviewed, it is very certain that the New England critic employs in the case of the New-Yorker, a very different and less indulgent standard of judgment than that which regulates his criticism when one of his own writers is under analysis. . . .

The writer in the *Journal* reaffirmed Simms's charges and added "that the North American is held in as little reverence in Boston as in South Carolina," and that "we have not seen, in the pages of this journal, a single instance where it has shown the slightest solicitude in behalf of any young writer,—always assuming that he is not a sprout of New England. . . ."

Poe's views of Longfellow, though he ceased to express them at any length, were now voiced by others, who had apparently become emboldened by his example. Simms, for instance, remarked:

> Longfellow is an artist . . . in all the respects of verse-making. . . . but it strikes us that it would not be difficult to point to the ear-mark of another in the thoughts contained in every sentence which he ever penned. . . . It is the grace and sweetness of his verse, and that extreme simplicity of the thought

which taxes no intellect to scan—which we read as we run—that constitutes his claims upon the reader.

Another independent critic, Margaret Fuller, wrote:

> We must confess to a coolness toward Mr. Longfellow, in consequence of the exaggerated praises that have been bestowed upon him. When we see a person of moderate powers receive honors which should be reserved for the highest, we feel somewhat like assailing him and taking from him the crown which should be reserved for grander brows. And yet this is perhaps ungenerous. It may be that the management of publishers, the hyperbole of paid or undiscerning reviewers, or some accidental cause which gives a temporary interest to productions beyond what they would permanently command, have raised such an one to a place as much above his wishes as his claims, and which he would rejoice, with honorable modesty, to vacate at the approach of one worthier. We the more readily believe this of Mr. Longfellow, as one so sensible to the beauties of other writers and so largely indebted to them, *must* know his own comparative rank better than his readers have known it for him. . . . Still we must acquit him of being a willing or conscious plagiarist. Some objects in the collection [*Poems*] are his own; as to the rest, he has the merit of appreciation, and a rearrangement, not always judicious, but the result of feeling on his part.

> Such works as Mr. Longfellow's we consider injurious only if allowed to usurp the place of better things. The reason of his being overrated here, is because through his works breathes the air of other lands with whose products the public at large is but little acquainted. . . . Twenty years hence when he stands upon his own merits, he will rank as a writer of elegant, if not always accurate taste, of great imitative power, and occasional felicity in an original way, where his feelings are stirred.

In the meantime, Longfellow's edition of the *Poets and Poetry of Europe* had appeared. Poe merely noticed the volume in passing, reporting that the "translations are from a great variety of sources" and that "the professor receives three thousand dollars for editing the work." Simms, however, was quite harsh, declaring that the anthology had not been a labor of love with its editor:

> He has not expended much of his own time or talent upon it. . . . He has been content to compile it from whatever materials have been most convenient— has helped himself, without scruple, to the riff-raff translations of beginners, who, learning the several languages, have sent their crude exercises to the magazines. Mr. Longfellow's own hands do not sufficiently appear in these translations, and the work might just as well have been executed by a common workman. Now, it is as a translator, that Mr. Longfellow's chief excellence appears . . . and his

own reputation, no less than the public expectation, required that he should have given himself up more thoroughly to this performance.

Though suddenly a target for the independent critics, Longfellow maintained silence, except to explain the mistake he had made in respect to "The Good George Campbell." His friends, however, were hardly silent. Lewis Clark, for instance, replied to Longfellow's assailants, abusing Poe personally, as we have seen in an earlier chapter, and now, in answering Simms's review, he remarked:

> We are sorry to see . . . the Parthian arrows which are aimed at Mr. Longfellow, one of our most popular poets. . . . Of the writings of his detractors and sneering commentators, how much is remembered, or laid up in the heart? Edition after edition of Longfellow's writings, in prose and verse, are demanded by the public; and it is *The Public* who constitute his tribunal. As to the 'riff-raff translations' to which Mr. Longfellow is said to have 'helped himself' in the 'Poets and Poetry of Europe,' it must strike the sensible reader, we think, that valid condemnation of them should proceed from critics conversant with the languages from which they are rendered.

Clark's sentiment that the public constituted the literary tribunal was shared by Longfellow himself, for on December 30, 1845, he wrote in his journal: "The Belfry [of Bruges and Other Poems] is succeeding famously well. . . . This is the best answer to my assailants." And Longfellow was quite aware of his assailants. On December 9, 1845, he noted: "Read a very abusive article upon my poems by Mr. Simms, the novelist. I consider this the most original and inventive of all his fictions." The next day he observed: "In Graham's Magazine for January, received this morning, is a superb poem by Lowell,—'To the Past.' If he goes on in this vein, Poe will soon begin to pound him." The following day he recorded: "Miss Fuller made a furious onslaught upon me in The New York Tribune. It is what might be called 'a bilious attack.'"

In summary, it must be said at once that the "sting in the tail" of Poe's *Waif* review and his need, in consequence, to defend himself against *his* assailants has obscured the real importance of his encounters with Longfellow. He was the first American critic who, in recognizing Longfellow's real gifts, had the hardihood to tell the poet that his poems were sometimes weak, or warped for didactic purposes, or suspiciously imitative—statements which are safe and easy enough to make now, but which to make then was, as we have seen, to risk one's critical reputation, to have one's motives questioned, and to be charged with envy and spite. Longfellow, if he understood the uses of criticism at all, preferred to ignore Poe's strictures, however he may have regarded his praise. For he was not

a poet in the sense that the Romantic critic understood the term. He was, to borrow a phrase from Coleridge, a man of talents and much reading who had acquired poetry as a trade. Weak in inspiration, conventional though cultivated in taste, and full of bookish ideas and sentiments, he was nevertheless possessed by an intense desire for literary reputation, and his poems as well as his career suggest that poetry was all too often a means to that end than an end in itself.

If Poe was harsh in his criticism, he was so because he continually overrated Longfellow's powers (he was only on occasion the genius that Poe from his first notice to his last insisted he was) and pointed out faults in his work that Longfellow did not or perhaps could not correct. Only belatedly—and Poe was dealing with the emergent poet—did he realize that Longfellow was not debasing his talents wilfully; his talents were simply limited. He came to understand at last that Longfellow's imitations, which he had supposed premeditated, were really accidental—that his highly cultivated taste caused him to assimilate ideas, images, and sentiments in other poets' works and, unconsciously at the moment of creation, to adapt them to his own purposes—and he exonerated Longfellow for a tendency he apparently could not help. Even Lewis Clark agreed with this explanation, the evidence became so clear and the charges so persistent. "Much has been said, at sundry times and in diverse places," he wrote, "concerning Longfellow's alleged plagiarisms. . . . There is such a thing . . . as *unconscious* plagiarism." Yet if Poe could forgive Longfellow for his proneness to imitation, he could as a critic scarcely condone the all too apparent fact that his imitations were acclaimed and the poet himself venerated for them. His explanation no more canceled the fact that Longfellow often imitated than the explanation of kleptomania annuls the charge of continual theft.

There were other matters, of course, that complicated the critic's attitude, especially from the time he wrote the *Waif* review until he took his final notice of the poet. He could not help being aware that Longfellow was a favorite of the two magazines which, because of their cliquishness, were the special objects of his detestation—the *Knickerbocker* and *North American Review*. Nor could he help knowing that Longfellow had "a whole legion of active quacks at his control," to use his exaggerated statement—a legion, as it must have seemed to him, that even managed to use the *Foreign Quarterly Review* to extol his virtues and to deny the merits of other American poets. Nor could he help noticing that Longfellow was being accorded critical indemnity by American critics, a fact that hardly needed the attestation provided by the suppression of his *Spanish Student* review and the animosities aroused by his comments upon Longfellow's poems. Nor, finally, could he help realizing that, though Longfellow was creating an audience for poetry the like of which had never been known in America, readers were being conditioned to receive only the kind of poetry written by a Longfellow and, later, devoid of Longfellow's artistry and culture, a James Whitcomb Riley and, still later, an Edgar A. Guest—that second-, third-, and fourth-rate poetry is not a way toward first-rate poetry but a substitute for it.

Longfellow, no doubt, found Poe's strictures disagreeable, but he must have also found that they served to advertise his books. When Fields, for example, was contemplating lawsuits. to blanket derision of *Hiawatha,* Longfellow told his publisher: " . . . don't you think we had better let those critics go on advertising it?" Whatever the case, Longfellow's attitude toward Poe may be summed up by two statements he made about him after his death. The first, made publicly a month after Poe had died, was kinder for the reason that it was almost accurate: "The harshness of his criticism I have never attributed to anything but the irritation of a sensitive nature, chafed by an indefinite sense of wrong." The second, made privately, was reported by William Winter, a young friend of the poet. Longfellow, Winter wrote, had indicated to him that "Poe had grossly abused and maligned him," but that he felt sorry for his "unfortunate and half-crazed adversary." He attributed Poe's remarks "to a deplorable literary jealousy," and concluded: "My works seemed to give him much trouble, first and last; but Mr. Poe is dead and gone, and I am alive and still writing—and that is the end of the matter."

Whatever may be said of Poe's encounters with Longfellow, Poe was on the side of genius and on the side of a free criticism, where he belonged. One can deplore his harshness, his bad taste, his occasional poor judgment, but one cannot condemn his over-all verdict in respect to Longfellow, nor the principles upon which he based that verdict, nor the cause for which he struggled, even at the cost of such statements as those that Winter attributed to Longfellow.

Edd Winfield Parks (essay date 1964)

SOURCE: "Poe on Fiction," in *Edgar Allan Poe as Literary Critic,* University of Georgia Press, 1964, pp. 24-56.

[*Using Poe's reviews of specific texts, Parks reveals their relationship with Poe's general theories concerning originality, unity, and totality of effect in a literary work. Parks argues that it is these general theoretical principles that led to Poe's emphasis on the short story, or "tale," as the ideal creation in prose. For a more general overview of Park's views on Poe, see NCLC 1.*]

By 1831, when he was twenty-two years old, Poe had become very much interested in the writing of short stories. Clearly in those days in Baltimore he had read and analyzed many magazine tales and sketches; he wrote parodies of several of these types that may well be considered as indirect literary criticism. The most obvious example is **"A Tale of Jerusalem,"** since it is a burlesque of part of a trashily sentimental religious novel; the most interesting example is **"Metzengerstein,"** which started as an imitation of the Gothic romances but in the writing gathered such momentum that it became a powerful allegory, with evil leading to its own self-destruction. Five of these stories were published in the *Philadelphia Saturday Courier* in 1832; by 1833, when his story **"Ms. Found in a Bottle"** won the prize offered by the *Baltimore Saturday Visiter,* Poe had written six more and had collected the eleven (later sixteen) into a unified work that he titled **Tales of the Folio Club**. Each tale was to be read aloud by its author, and followed by remarks of the group on each. Poe specifically stated that "These remarks are intended as a burlesque on criticism." Unfortunately, all the critical commentaries have been lost, so that we can only infer that Poe had been studying the English and American magazine criticism as closely as the fiction.

When early in 1835 Poe began reviewing regularly for the *Southern Literary Messenger,* he discovered that he must deal with novels more often than with stories, for the simple reason that novels were more popular and therefore more readily publishable. Although Poe was willing to praise individual works highly, he did not like the form. In particular, he was dubious about the historical romance, since it was not a self-contained work: "The interweaving of fact with fiction is at all times hazardous, and presupposes on the part of general readers that degree of intimate acquaintance with fact which should never be presupposed. In the present instance, the author has failed, so we think, in confining either his truth or his fable within its legitimate individual domain. Nor do we at all wonder at his failure in performing what no novelist whatever has hitherto performed."

His other doubts about the novel as an art-form developed gradually. Yet in what seems to have been his first review of a novel (Robert Montgomery Bird's *Calavar: A Romance of Mexico,* Feb. 1835), he objected to a certain awkwardness in the invention and arrangement of the story, and objected also that the miraculous agencies employed by the author are "too *unnatural* even for romance." In a brief upsurge of national pride, he proclaimed it "an American production, which will not shrink from competition with the very best European works of the same character," and surpassed by only one or two of James Fenimore Cooper's. Yet he qualified his praise carefully. It was a good work "if boldness of design, vigor of thought, copiousness and power of language,—thrilling incident, and graphic and magnificent description, can make a good novel." When he reviewed Bird's sequel, *The Infidel,* however, Poe complained of a lack of unity in the design. The author hurried from delineating one incident of slaughter and violence to another; he left himself insufficient time for characterization.

Both novels are set in Mexico, at the time of the Spanish conquest. It is worth noting that Poe did not cavil at remoteness of scene, either geographically or historically. Many contemporary critics did, but Poe in fact preferred remoteness. Perhaps as a result, Bird set his next novel, *The Hawks of Hawk-Hollow,* in Pennsylvania during the Revolutionary War. Although the author had the advantage of knowing the locale at first hand and worked in some dramatic incidents, Poe thought that he showed less originality than in his Mexican novels. His indebtedness to Scott was embarrassingly evident, yet there was little to remind the reader of *Ivanhoe* or *Kenilworth* or "above all with that most pure, perfect, and radiant gem of fictitious literature the *Bride of Lammermoor."* Although a few characters were well-drawn, most of them were inconsistent and some even contradictory. If by style the reader meant only the prose, then in general it was faultless; if however by style one meant "the prevailing tone and manner which give character and individuality," Dr. Bird had been less fortunate, for the book had been "composed with great inequality of manner—at times forcible and manly—at times sinking into the merest childishness and imbecility." Regretfully, Poe judged that it had "no pretensions to *originality* of manner, or of style."

When he was confronted in 1836 with *Sheppard Lee,* he did not connect it with Bird. After wryly noting that the book is an original and that its "deviations, however indecisive, from the more beaten paths of imitation, look well for our future literary prospects," Poe outlines for the reader the seven different types of metempsychosis that the protagonist undergoes. Although he writes favorably of "some very excellent chapters on abolition" after Lee has become Nigger Tom, Poe shows relatively little interest in the satire on contemporary social and political conditions. But the fictional idea and the form roused him to critical speculation.

Poe objects even to the possibility (accepted by the sister but not fully shared by Lee) that the transmigrations might have occurred only in delirium, brought on by an accident. This was to trifle with the reader. There were two general methods of telling such stories, and the author had selected the poorer one: "He conceives his hero endowed with some idiosyncrasy beyond the common lot of human nature, and thus introduces him to a series of adventure which, under ordinary circumstances, could occur only to a plurality of persons."

But the character partly changes with each transmigration, and there is little attempt to show the influence of varied events "upon a character *unchanging.*" In fact, the narrative would be more effective if it dealt with seven different individuals.

There is a second and better way. That is for the author to avoid a jocular manner and directness of expression, and leave much to the imagination, "as if the author were firmly impressed with the truth, yet astonished at the immensity, of the wonders he relates, and for which, professedly, he neither claims nor anticipates credence. . . . The attention of the author, who does not depend upon explaining away his incredibilities, is directed to giving them the character and the luminousness of truth, and thus are brought about, unwittingly, some of the most vivid creations of human intellect."

Poe had fewer reservations about the work of his friend and mentor, John Pendleton Kennedy, although friendship did not restrain him from some sharp criticism. When he reviewed *Horse-Shoe Robinson* in May, 1835, he began with a tribute to Kennedy's earlier novel: "We have not yet forgotten, nor is it likely we shall very soon forget, the rich simplicity of diction—the manliness of tone—the admirable traits of Virginian manners, and the striking pictures of still life, to be found in *Swallow Barn.*" But that book was too obviously in the manner of Addison and Irving; oddly, disregarding Scott, Cooper, and other historical romancers, Poe thought that *Horse-Shoe Robinson* deserved to be called original. The characterization was excellent, the descriptions of the Revolutionary War accurate and informative, the style at once simple and forcible, yet richly figurative and poetical. But a form that permitted the author to make the romantic hero less important than the titular hero did not fully adhere to the properties of fiction.

Poe uses the review for one bit of criticism on the form of the novel. Too many writers "delay as long as possible the main interest"; Kennedy with good judgment has "begun at the beginning," introducing his prominent characters and line of action immediately. He objected to Kennedy's over-use of the dash. To prove that it was "unnecessary or superfluous" in many instances, Poe quoted a paragraph as Kennedy had punctuated it and then reproduced the same passage without the dashes. He easily proved his point with this effective textual criticism.

In general, Kennedy seemed to have the eye of a painter rather than the eye of a novelist. Poe thought that each of Kennedy's three novels revealed "boldness and force of thought, (disdaining ordinary embellishment, and depending for its effect upon masses rather than details), with a predominant *sense of the picturesque* pervading and giving color to the whole." This was particularly true of *Swallow Barn,* which "is but a rich succession of picturesque still-life pieces."

Poe's strictures on Bird and Kennedy had been mild enough, and the reviews on the whole favorable. Perhaps, as some later writers have suggested, he had been deliberately waiting for a well-publicized book by a prominent author that he could, in his own favorite phrase, "use up," and thus draw attention to himself and to the *Southern Literary Messenger;* more probably, he was irritated by the frenzied advance publicity and the underserved, lavish praise that a bad novel had received. At any rate, Poe in December, 1835, published a merciless critique of Theodore S. Fay's *Norman Leslie,* and from that time on he was embroiled in the savage literary wars of the period. For Fay was an associate editor of the New York *Mirror* and a favorite of the *Knickerbocker* group.

The review may also be considered as one of Poe's earliest efforts to foster an honest American criticism. The first paragraph tends to bear this out: "This is *the* book—*the* book *par excellence*—the book bepuffed, beplastered, and be-*Mirrored.* . . . For the sake of everything puff, puffing and puffable, let us take a peep at its contents." This charge of over-puffing American books Poe was to repeat many times; although somewhat unevenly, he worked continually toward making American literary criticism more balanced and less indiscriminate. Before he proceeded, as usual, to give a lengthy summary of the plot, Poe descended into the personal ridicule that occasionally disfigures his critical work. For some reason, he objected violently to dedications, and he sneers at this one. With more point if he has in mind fiction, he asks what is the point of Prefaces in general, and of Fay's in particular. When Fay explained that, although his story was founded on fact, he had transformed certain characters, particularly that of a young lady, Poe worked in parenthetically and unnecessarily: "oh fi! Mr. Fay— oh, Mr. Fay, fi!" When Fay requested the "indulgence of the solemn and sapient critics," Poe answered with more pertinence that "*we,* at least, are neither solemn nor sapient, and, therefore, do not feel ourselves bound to show him a shadow of mercy."

Poe's summary of the complex and unbelievable plot is reasonably fair, but in his commentary he unerringly picked those items in which Fay had overstrained, and had achieved only a meretricious effect. The husband threatened to leave his wife; she first beseeched him to stay, then in turn threatened him: "It was the first uncoiling of the basilisk within me (good Heavens, a snake in a lady's stomach!). He gazed on me incredulously, and coolly smiled. You remember that smile— I fainted!!!' Alas! Mr. Davy Crockett,—Mr. Davy Crockett, alas! thou art beaten hollow—thou art defunct, and undone! thou hast indeed succeeded in grinning a squirrel from a tree, but it surpassed even thine

extraordinary abilities to smile a lady into a fainting fit."

This "Tale of the Present Times" he roundly pronounced to be "the most inestimable piece of balderdash with which the common sense of the good people of America was ever so openly or so villainously insulted."

Poe's lowest descent into personalities, in his *SLM* reviews, seems uncalled for. Fay had been unduly puffed and praised; he had written a bad novel. William Gilmore Simms belonged to no clique; he had received only a modicum of praise; he had written some powerful if extremely uneven novels, among them *The Partisan.* Poe listed several of these works, although not indicating whether or not he had read any of them, before getting to the dedication. It is a brief and simple inscription of thirty-three words, to a close friend. It is impossible to see what in it could have infuriated Poe. He objected to the brevity and terseness of the dedication, and imagined the author calling on Richard Yeadon to present him with a copy of *The Partisan.* Poe tortured each word to wrench some unpleasant connotation from it and ascribed this feeling to Yeadon, until at the end he has that worthy "kick the author of 'The Yemassee' downstairs." In fact, Yeadon was flattered by the dedication, as any friend might well have been; there was no factual basis for the vicious burlesque. This was Poe at his nastiest, but the tone of the entire review is little better.

After his usual summary, including his customary fling at the woodenness of the romantic hero, Poe noted that some of the characters are excellent, some horrible: the historical ones well-drawn, the fictional ones hardly credible. He objected to Porgy as "an insufferable bore" and as "a backwoods imitation of Sir Somebody Guloseton, the epicure, in one of the Pelham novels." It is not surprising that Poe found nothing humorous in the character of Porgy, but his condemnation of the soldier's mild oaths seems excessive, especially when he lists a considerable number for the benefit of readers, with the excuse that "such attempts to render profanity less despicable by rendering it amusing, should be frowned down indignantly by the public." With more justice Poe objected to Simmis's hasty and slipshod writing, though it hardly merits the statement that Simms's "English is bad—shockingly bad." Indeed, Poe's examples reveal as much about his own idiosyncrasies as about Simms's ignorance—but at least the critic documented his charge with numerous examples.

The author of **"Berenice"** objected, also, to Simms's use of the horrible in realistically describing floggings and murders. He did not object to Simms's manufacturing his own chapter epigraphs: they are "quite as convenient as the extracted mottoes of his contemporaries. All, we think, are abominable."

Poe had found little that was good in *The Partisan,* but at the end of the review he attempted to modify his earlier sweeping judgments. It was "no ordinary work. Its historical details are replete with interest. The concluding scenes are well drawn. Some passages descriptive of swamp scenery are exquisite. Mr. Simms has evidently the eye of a painter. Perhaps, in sober truth, he would succeed better in sketching a landscape than he has done in writing a novel."

In his review of *The Damsel of Darien,* Poe changed his tone entirely. Simms was worthy of being treated with respect; of his earlier works, *Martin Faber* "well deserves a permanent success," and even *The Partisan* was allowed to have "many excellences," along with "very many disfiguring features." *The Damsel* he thought a "much better book; evincing stricter study and care, with a far riper judgment, and a more rigidly disciplined fancy." This story of the dreams, adventures, and explorations of Vasco Nuñez de Balboa had little plot and adhered too closely to historical fact, but it had many "fine episodical pieces interspersed throughout the book." Yet the "most really meritorious" part of the book was the ballad, "Indian Serenade"—a precursor of Poe's later, more generalized statement that "as a poet, indeed, we like him far better than as a novelist."

It is not surprising, in fact, that the works he praised most highly are novelettes rather than novels, concentrating on psychology rather than on action, or that he reserved his highest praise for Simms's short stories in *The Wigwam and the Cabin.* As tales, each was excellent; together they illustrated the border history of the South. "Grayling, or Murder Will Out" was the best: "We have no hesitation in calling it the best ghost-story we have ever read. It is full of the richest and most vigorous imagination—is forcibly conceived—and detailed throughout with a degree of artistic skill which has had no parallel among American storytellers since the epoch of Brockden Brown."

Poe's admiration for James Fenimore Cooper was decidedly limited. True, he solicited contributions for the *Southern Literary Messenger* and the projected *Penn Magazine,* and he was willing (as in the case of Irving, Paulding, Bryant, Halleck, and Catharine M. Sedgwick) to "make reasonable allowance in estimating the absolute merit of our literary pioneers." He divided writers of fiction into two classes: "a popular and widely circulated class read with pleasure but without admiration—in which the author is lost or forgotten; or remembered, if at all, with something very nearly akin to contempt; and then, a class not so popular, nor so widely diffused, in which, at every paragraph, arises a distinctive and highly pleasurable interest, springing from our perception and appreciation of the skill employed, or the genius evinced in the composition. After perusal of the one class, we think solely of the book—after reading the other, chiefly of the author. The former class leads to popularity—the latter to fame. In the former case, the books sometimes live, while the authors usually die; in the latter, even when the works perish, the man survives. Among American writers of the less circulated, but more worthy and artistical fictions, we may mention Mr. Brockden Brown, Mr. John Neal, Mr. Simms, Mr. Hawthorne; at the head of the more popular division we may place Mr. Cooper."

It is difficult to understand on what basis Poe compiled the first list. Hawthorne assuredly belongs on it; John Neal assuredly does not. Brown's Gothicism appealed to Poe's taste, and presumably it was this element in a few of Simms's novels that caused him to be included, although the same criteria that disqualified Cooper would seem also to disqualify Simms. The distinction once made, however, Poe was willing to allow Cooper some positive merits, along with some glaring defects. He defended Cooper's right to attack the bull-headed prejudices of his own countrymen: "Since it is the fashion to decry the author of 'The Prairie' just now, we are astonished at no degree of malignity or scurrility whatever on the part of the little gentlemen who are determined to follow that fashion." Cooper had never been known to fail, either in the forest or on the sea, although sometimes his success has little to do with the values of fiction. In reviewing *Mercedes of Castile,* Poe started off roundly: "As a history, this work is invaluable; as a novel, it is well nigh worthless—in fact, the "worst *novel* ever penned by Mr. Cooper."

In general, characterization was not Cooper's forte. Neither was plot, of which he seemed "altogether regardless or incapable." In a novel, this was not a fatal handicap: "some of the finest narratives in the world— 'Gil Blas' and 'Robinson Crusoe,' for example—have been written without its employment; and 'The Hutted Knoll,' like all the sea and forest novels of Cooper, has been made deeply interesting, although depending upon this peculiar source of interest not at all. Thus the absence of plot can never be critically regarded as a *defect;* although its judicious use, in all cases aiding and in no case injuring other effects, must be regarded as of a very high order of merit." As a substitute, *Wyandotté* has a three-fold interest: the theme of life in the wilderness (Poe notes sarcastically that only an imbecile author can fail with life in the forest or on the ocean); the Robinson-Crusoe-like detail of its management; and the portraiture of the half-civilized Indian, with the setting on the New York frontier at the beginning of the Revolution.

Although he included Catharine M. Sedgwick (in the quite respectable company of Irving, Cooper, Paulding, Bryant, and Halleck) as one whose literary reputation owed much to her being one "of our literary pioneers," Poe thought highly of her novels. In **"Au-**

tography" he noted that her handwriting "points unequivocally to the traits of her literary style—which are strong common sense, and a masculine disdain of mere ornament." Her best and most popular novels were *Hope Leslie* and *The Linwoods;* these placed her "upon a level with the best of our native novelists. Of American *female* writers we must consider her the first"—a judgment which he qualified in **The Literati,** where it is the public rather than Poe that gives her "precedence among our female writers." The prevailing features of *The Linwoods* (which Poe thought the best of her books) were "ease, purity of style, pathos, and verisimilitude. To plot it has little pretension." But he also noted in her work a "very peculiar fault—that of discrepancy between the words and character of the speaker—the fault, indeed, more properly belongs to the depicting of character itself."

Poe felt that several of her feminine contemporaries surpassed her in a single quality, but that in many of the qualities she excelled and in none was particularly deficient. But she was an author of "marked talent" rather than of genius. In attempting to describe the nature of her talent, he makes an interesting comparison: "Miss Sedgwick has now and then been nicknamed 'the Miss Edgeworth of America'; but she has done nothing to bring down upon her the vengeance of so equivocal a title. That she has thoroughly studied and profoundly admired Miss Edgeworth may, indeed, be gleaned from her works—but what woman has not? Of imitation there is not the slightest perceptible taint. In both authors we observe the same tone of thoughtful morality, but here all resemblance ceases. In the Englishwoman there is far more of a certain Scotch prudence, in the American more of warmth, tenderness, sympathy for the weaknesses of her sex. Miss Edgeworth is the more acute, the more inventive and the more rigid. Miss Sedgwick is the more womanly."

Mainly because he honestly admired the novel but in part, perhaps, because he thought the anonymous *George Balcombe* had been written by a close personal friend, Poe in January, 1837, gave it lavish commendation: "George Balcombe thinks, speaks, and acts, as no person, we are convinced, but Judge Beverly Tucker ever precisely thought, spoke, or acted before." Poe gives a lengthy summary of this complex story of a concealed will, and praises especially the trial scene: "Fiction, thus admirably managed, has all the force and essential value of truth." The delineation of characters is excellent, although there is no originality in the characterization: "we mean to say that the merit here is solely that of observation and fidelity. Original characters, so called, can only be critically praised as such, either when presenting qualities known in real life, but never before depicted, (a combination nearly impossible) or when presenting qualities (moral, or physical, or both) which although unknown, or even known to be hypothetical, are so skillfully adapted to

the circumstances which surround them, that our sense of fitness is not offended, and we find ourselves seeking a reason why these things *might not have been,* which we are still satisfied *are not*. The latter species of originality appertains to the loftier region of the *Ideal*."

Here, as elsewhere, Poe make a distinction between style and grammatical correctness. In treating this aspect of *George Balcombe,* he gives one of his clearest statements on the subject: "The general manner is that of a scholar and gentleman in the best sense of both terms—bold, vigorous, and rich—abrupt rather than diffuse—and not over scrupulous in the use of energetic vulgarisms. With the mere English, some occasional and trivial faults may be found." As examples, Poe cites the use of technical terms, of a dangling modifier, and some unclear sentences. He also noted that the book "bears a strong family resemblance to the Caleb Williams of Godwin." But its positive merits far outweighed its defects; it held the interest from beginning to end; it had "invention, vigor, almost audacity of thought"; it had wholeness, with nothing out of place or out of time. As a result, Poe declared that he was "induced to regard it, upon the whole, as *the best* American novel."

Poe had been right about the authorship of *George Balcombe;* he was wrong when he denied that *The Partisan Leader* had been written by Tucker. When he dealt with Tucker in **"Autography,"** Poe somewhat modified his earlier judgment: *George Balcombe* was "one of the best novels . . . although for some reason the book was never a popular favorite. It was perhaps, somewhat too didactic for the general taste." He did not mention *The Partisan Leader,* but noted that he himself had been thought the author of a highly unfavorable article on the *Pickwick Papers* which Tucker had written, whereas Poe had praised Dickens for a high and just distinction.

It was characteristic of Poe that even in reviewing a popular novel which he considered worthless, he nevertheless made discerning comments on structure that applied to all novels. Joseph H. Ingraham appealed "always to the taste of the ultra-romanticists (as a matter, we believed, rather of pecuniary policy than of choice) and thus is obnoxious to the charge of a certain cut-and-thrust, blue-fire, melodramaticism." Although he did not believe that Ingraham "stole" *Lafitte,* he could see little value in this swashbuckling story of the Louisiana pirate except for the historical detail. There were too many items that strained the credulity or dissipated the concentration of the reader. Lafitte fails to recognize and fights with a man whom he has known well. Even worse is the clumsy jumping from one scene to another: "We have, for example, been keeping company with the buccaneers for a few pages—but now they are to make an attack upon some old family mansion. In an instant the buccaneers are dropped for the mansion, and the definite for the indefinite article. In place of *the* robbers proceeding in the course wherein we have been bearing them company, they are suddenly abandoned for *a* house. *A* family mansion is depicted." Somewhat later, the reader is informed that this is the house which the buccaneers were planning to attack. As these quotations indicate, Poe was campaigning against looseness of structure and lack of consistency. At a time when artistry in the novel was not greatly valued, he was advocating a much stricter and more coherent form.

Poe's commentaries on English novelists were confined almost entirely to writers of his own century. At least in part, this was because as a reviewer he was mainly interested in new books. When he reviewed a reprint of Goldsmith's *Vicar of Wakefield,* he wrote at some length about the illustrations, but of the novel only that it was "one of the most admirable fictions in the language." Poe makes it plain that he thought the tale and the romance to be higher forms of art than the more limited novel. *Robinson Crusoe* seemed to him admirable. Defoe's plotless tale succeeded through "the potent magic of verisimilitude."

At least in the period of the *Messenger* reviews, Poe had no doubt that Scott was the greatest writer of prose fiction in the world. In reviewing Henry F. Chorley's *Conti the Discarded: with other Tales and Fancies* (which he praised as showing a noble, interesting purpose, especially in the attempt to introduce into English literature the type of German art novels that personified individual portions of the Fine Arts), he notes that the title story "bears no little resemblance to that purest, and most enthralling of fictions, *The Bride of Lammermuir* [sic]; and we have once before expressed our opinion of this, the master novel of Scott. It is not too much to say that no modern composition, and perhaps no composition whatever, with the single exception of Cervantes' Destruction of Numantia, approaches so nearly to the proper character of the dramas of Aeschylus, as the magic tale of which Ravenswood is the hero. We are not aware of being sustained by any authority in this opinion—yet we do not believe it the less intrinsically correct."

One opinion, which Poe may have considered earlier, appeared in the same issue. After writing that Bulwer as a novelist was "unsurpassed by any writer living or dead," Poe immediately qualified the judgment: "Scott has excelled him in *many* points, and 'The Bride of Lammermuir' is a better book than any individual work by the author of Pelham—'Ivanhoe' is, perhaps, equal to any."

For the merely popular novelists like G. P. R. James, Harrison Ainsworth, Frederick Marryat, and Charles Lever, Poe had only contempt. They wrote as it were to order, being content with mediocre ideas because these would appeal to the public, and putting in those incidents that would insure popularity. So the ideas of Frederick Marryat were the "common property of the mob; his books crowded incident on incident, without any enriching commentary or philosophy; his characters were frequently stolen from those of Dickens. Its English is slovenly, its events improbable. It was meant for popular consumption, and nothing more."

Occasionally a work of "the highest merit" like Dickens's *Old Curiosity Shop* would seem to rival these works in popularity, but then Poe suddenly remembered that *Harry Lorrequer* and *Charles O'Malley* had surpassed it in "what is properly termed popularity." Excellence may not inevitably make a work unpopular, but these novels by Charles Lever go far toward proving that popularity "is evidence of the book's *demerit*" and that undue popularity indicates that "no extensively *popular* book, in the right application of the term, can be a work of high merit, *as regards those particulars of the work that are popular*." Dickens succeeded in "uniting all suffrages," but his appeals were different: "It is his close observation and imitation of nature which have rendered him popular, while his higher qualities, with the ingenuity evinced in addressing the general taste, have secured him the good word of the informed and intellectual."

Although he later cooled markedly in his critical estimate, Poe in 1836 had little doubt that Bulwer was the greatest of English writers of fiction. The doubt extended only to the admission that Scott might be his equal, or even his superior. Poe started his review of *Rienzi* by noting that he had "long learned to reverence the fine intellect of Bulwer. We take up any production of his pen with a positive certainty that, in reading it, the wildest passions of our nature, the most profound of our thoughts, the brightest visions of our fancy, and the most ennobling and lofty of our aspirations will, in due turn, be enkindled within us." Yet he was not without worthy rivals. D'Israeli had a more brilliant, lofty, and delicate imagination; Theodore Hook more of wit and "our own" Paulding more of broad humor. Others might equal or surpass him in one particular, but "who is there uniting in one person the imagination, the passion, the humor, the energy, the knowledge of the heart, the artist-like eye, the originality, the fancy, and the learning of Edward Lytton Bulwer."

Rienzi was his best novel—a judgment from which Poe did not deviate in later comments. But it is considerably more than a novel. In sweep and character of composition it is essentially epic rather than dramatic; it is also, in the truest sense, a History. Poe digresses to note that "we shall often discover in Fiction the essential spirit and vitality of Historic Truth—while

Truth itself, in many a dull and lumbering archive, shall be found guilty of all the inefficiency of Fiction."

It was vastly superior to *The Last Days of Pompeii* because it was richer, more glowing, more vigorous, but also because it dealt with a period more interesting to us. In a favorable review of Lydia Maria Child's romance of Periclean Athens, *Philothea* (1836), Poe wrote that "We have purely human sympathy in the distantly antique; and this little is greatly weakened by the constant necessity of effort in conceiving *appropriateness* in manners, costume, habits, and modes of thought, so widely at variance with those around us." In *Pompeii*, Bulwer transcended this genre through the "stupendousness of its leading event" and the skill with which it was depicted, but his work failed "only in the proportion" that it belonged "to this species."

When in 1841 Poe reviewed *Night and Morning*, with its commonplace yet complex structure, Poe deviated from the book to make one of his most striking and most important definitions:

> The word *plot*, as commonly accepted, conveys but an indefinite meaning. Most persons think of it as a simple *complexity;* and into this error even so fine a critic as Augustus William Schlegel has obviously fallen, when he confounds its idea with that of the mere *intrigue* in which the Spanish dramas of Cervantes and Calderon abound. But the greatest involution of incident will not result in plot; which, properly defined, is *that in which no part can be displaced without ruin to the whole*. It may be described as a building so dependently constructed, that to change the position of a single brick is to overthrow the entire fabric. In this definition and description, we of course refer only to that infinite perfection which the true artist bears ever in mind— that unattainable goal to which his eyes are always directed, but of the possibility of attaining which he still endeavours, if wise, to cheat himself into the belief. The reading world, however, is satisfied with a less rigid construction of the term. It is content to think that plot a good one, in which none of the *leading* incidents can be *removed* without *detriment* to the mass.

Poe was not insisting on the necessity of plot. As he had in dealing with Cooper, and using some of the same examples, he emphasized the point that "A good tale may be written without it. Some of the finest fictions in the world have neglected it altogether. We see nothing of it in 'Gil Blas,' in the 'Pilgrim's Progress,' or in 'Robinson Crusoe.' Thus it is not an essential in story-telling at all; although, well managed, within proper limits, it is a thing to be desired. At best it is but a secondary and rigidly artistical merit, for which no merit of a higher class—no merit founded in nature—should be sacrified."

The real misconception was the belief that a true unity could be achieved in a long work:

> Very little reflection might have sufficed to convince Mr. Bulwer that narratives, even one-fourth as long as the one now lying upon our table, are *essentially* inadapted to that nice and complex adjustment of incident at which he has made this desperate attempt. In the wire-drawn romances which have been so long fashionable (God only knows how or why) the pleasure we derive (if any) is a composite one, and made up of the respective sums of the various pleasurable sentiments experienced in perusal. Without excessive and fatiguing exertion, inconsistent with legitimate interest, the mind cannot comprehend at one time and in one survey the numerous individual items which go to establish the whole. Thus the high ideal sense of the *unique* is sure to be wanting; for, however absolute in itself be the unity of the novel, it must inevitably fail of appreciation. We speak now of that species of unity which is alone worth the attention of the critic—the unity or totality of *effect*.

Mere length in itself had no artistic value. The talk about continuous and sustained effort seemed to Poe "pure twaddle and nothing more." If a Bulwer insisted on writing long romances simply because they were fashionable, if he could not be satisfied with the brief tale which "admits of the highest development of artistical power in alliance with the wildest vigour of the imagination," then he must content himself with a simple narrative form.

Poe added to his earlier distinction between style and language. The chief constituent of a good style is "what artists have agreed to denominate *tone*." Since Bulwer's tone is always correct, he can scarcely be termed a bad stylist. On the other hand, his English is "turgid, involved, and ungrammatical." Poe cites numerous examples of faulty constructions, and the irritating mannerism of beginning many short sentences with *So*. But Bulwer's predominant failing, in point of style, was "an absolute mania of metaphor—metaphor always running into allegory." Pure allegory was an abomination that appealed only to our faculties of comparison, without interesting our reason or our fancy; metaphor, "its softened image, has indisputable force when sparingly and skillfully employed." Bulwer was neither sparing nor skillful: "He is king-coxcomb of figures of speech."

Poe no longer reverenced Bulwer's intellect, or thought him the first of English novelists. Rather, in a thoughtful summing up, he attempted to assay Bulwer's merits and his place:

> With an intellect rather well balanced than lofty, he has not full claim to the title of a man of genius. Urged by the burning desire of doing much, he has certainly done something. Elaborate even to a fault,

he will never write a bad book, and has once or twice been upon the point of concocting a good one. It is the custom to call him a fine writer, but in doing so we should judge him less by an artistical standard of excellence than by comparison with the drivellers who surround him. To Scott he is altogether inferior, except in that mock and tawdry philosophy which the Caledonian had the discretion to avoid, and the courage to condemn. In pathos, humour, and verisimilitude he is unequal to Dickens, surpassing him only in general knowledge and in the sentiment of Art. Of James he is more than the equal at all points. While he could never fall as low as D'Israeli has occasionally fallen, neither himself nor any of those whom we have mentioned have ever risen nearly so high as that very gifted and very extraordinary man.

When he first acclaimed Bulwer, Poe had never heard of Dickens. Four months later (June, 1836) he reviewed *Watkins Tottle, and other Sketches,* by Boz, and claimed that some of them through magazine publication were "old and highly esteemed acquaintances," but of the author he could only say that "we know nothing more than that he is a far more pungent, more witty, and better disciplined writer of sly articles, than nine-tenths of the Magazine writers in Great Britain." These sketches or stories had a great advantage over the usual novel in that each one could be "taken in at one view, by the reader." Poe especially praised "The Black Veil" as an "act of stirring tragedy," and he continued for years to use it as a touchstone of what such a tale should be. His comment on Dickens's method concentrates on the author's absorption in his subject: there are no anecdotes but "we are enveloped in its atmosphere of wretchedness and extortion." Unfortunately, Poe's mind was still so full of irritation with Colonel William Stone's *Ups and Downs* (which he had "used up" in the same issue) that he employed the sketch for a derogatory comparison: "So perfect, and never-to-be-forgotten a picture cannot be brought about by any such trumpery exertion, or still more trumpery talent, as we find employed in the ineffective daubing of Colonel Stone."

By November, when he reviewed *The Posthumous Papers of the Pickwick Club,* he knew that Boz was Charles Dickens, and the new book, he thought, fully sustained his "high opinion of the comic power and of the rich imaginative conception" of the earlier one. But it was in *The Old Curiosity Shop* that Dickens reached the peak of his genius (Poe was dead before *David Copperfield* and later novels were published). The defects in the story were mainly to be traced to the evils of serial publication. The title itself was a misnomer, for the shop had only a collateral interest, and is spoken of merely in the beginning. Characters are introduced who prove to be supererogatory; incidents that at first seemed necessary turn out to be worthless and are never developed. Yet these were insignificant

defects. *The Old Curiosity Shop* embodied "more originality in every point, but in character especially, than any single work within our knowledge." Misguided critics had called some of these persons caricatures, but "the charge is grossly ill-founded. No critical principle is more firmly grounded in reason than that a certain amount of exaggeration is essential in the proper depicting of truth itself. We do not paint an object to be true, but to appear true to the beholder. Were we to copy nature with accuracy, the object copied would seem unnatural." Dicken's characters were not caricatures but creations.

The most noteworthy feature of the book was "its chaste, vigorous, and glowing *imagination*. This is the one charm, all potent, which alone would suffice to compensate for a world more of error than Mr. Dickens ever committed." The pathos in the concluding scenes "is of that best order which is relieved, in great measure by ideality." The only book that approached it in this respect was Fouqué's *Undine*. But Fouqué was dealing with an imaginary character with purely fanciful attributes, and so "cannot command our full sympathies, as can a simple denizen of earth." These qualities made *The Old Curiosity Shop* "very much the best of the works of Mr. Dickens."

In a carefully reasoned estimate, Poe compared Dickens with Bulwer:

> The Art of Mr. Dickens, although elaborate and great, seems only a happy modification of Nature. In this respect he differs remarkably from the author of "Night and Morning." The latter, by excessive care and patient reflection, aided by much rhetorical knowledge and general information, has arrived at the capability of producing books which might be mistaken by ninety-nine readers out of a hundred for the genuine inspiration of genius. The former, by the promptings of the truest genius itself, has been brought to compose, and evidently without effort, works which have effected a long-sought consummation, which have rendered him the idol of the people, while defying and enchanting the critics. Mr. Bulwer, through art, has almost created a genius. Mr. Dickens, through genius, has perfected a standard from which Art itself will derive its essence, its rules.

Poe may not have been the father of the detective story, but he was certainly the first important critic who attempted to set an aesthetic for the *genre*. Characteristically, this was done in a review of Dickens's *Barnaby Rudge*. He listed explicitly two principles, he suggested a third, and in his practice indicated a fourth.

Under no circumstances may the author in his own right mislead the reader: no "undue or inartistical means be employed to conceal the secret of the plot." When a character asserted that the body of poor Mr. Rudge

Poe's headstone in Baltimore, Maryland. He died at Washington College Hospital in early October, 1849.

was found, this was legitimate and "no misdemeanor against Art in stating what was not the fact; since the falsehood is put into the mouth of Solomon Daisy, and given merely as the impression of this individual and the public. The writer has not asserted it in his own person, but ingeniously conveyed an idea (false in itself, yet a belief in which is necessary for the effect of the tale) by the mouth of one of his characters." On the other hand, it is "disingenuous and inartistical" for the author himself to denominate Mrs. Rudge as "the widow," for the author knows that her husband is not dead.

It is imperative that "the secret be well kept." A failure to preserve the secret until the *denouement* "throws all into confusion, so far as regards the *effect* intended. If the mystery leaks out, against the author's will, his purposes are immediately at odds and ends; for he proceeds upon the supposition that certain impressions *do* exist, which do *not* exist, in the mind of his readers." Poe was uncertain how many readers had solved the mystery in *Barnaby Rudge;* he had done so and had published his analysis immediately after the first installment had appeared. He noted the minor errors that he had made, but correctly insisted that they were minor. For one reader at least, the mystery had not been mysterious enough.

For the story to be legitimately mysterious, the author must to a great extent be engaged in concealing character, whereas the novelist usually was engaged in revealing and developing his characters. This may be done through incidents, such as the occasion when the murderer dresses the corpse of the gardener in his own clothes, puts his ring on its finger and his watch in its pocket—thus deluding the other characters. This may also be done through false or mistaken suspicions, so that an innocent man becomes a prime suspect. Yet this concealment of character should not be done directly by the author, but must be achieved indirectly. It is the purpose of the author to "whet curiosity" in the particulars of the story, as a means of disguising the solution.

These inter-related purposes, as Poe demonstrated in his own stories, can be better achieved through the use of a narrator than by the omniscient author. The narrator does not know everything. He may be duped, or conveniently sent away from the scene so that he had only partial information, or may interpret falsely a key bit of evidence. He must not deliberately present false evidence, but as a character in the story he is absolved from omniscience. This justifies his giving a partial or a mistaken picture, provided he believes that it is a true one.

Poe reviewed only a few foreign novels, and those only in translation. Of these, only one seems to need commentary: the romance *Undine* by the Baron de la Motte Fouqué. This German story of a beautiful but soulless water-spirit who loves and marries a man in order to gain a soul seemed to Poe "what we advisedly consider the finest romance in existence." Poe did not like for a story to have an overt or explicit moral; in *Undine,* the allegorical element was as well-handled as "that most indefensible species of writing" ever could be, for beneath the surface of the story "there runs a mystic or under current of meaning, of the simplest and most easily intelligible, yet of the most richly philosophical character." Its unity was absolute: "every minute point of the picture fills and satisfies the eye. Every thing is attended to, and nothing is out of time or out of place."

Undine remained for Poe one of the three great prose romances, worthy to be ranked with Scott's *Bride of Lammermoor* and Dickens's *Old Curiosity Shop.* He indicated less enthusiasm for the novel, but he consistently placed *Robinson Crusoe* and *Gil Blas* as the best in that *genre.* It may be worth noting, however, that two of the romances are short enough that they might easily be read at one sitting.

From the beginning of his critical career, Poe was more interested in the short story (which he usually called the tale and sometimes the article) than he was in the novel or romance. In the long work, unity or totality of effect was impossible for the author to achieve, and impossible for the reader to feel or grasp. He wrote repeatedly that the tale offered the greatest challenge to the imagination and the fairest field to the artist of any form of prose fiction. Yet it is also significant that a very early treatment emphasized the relation of the tale to the magazine.

When Thomas W. White, Editor of the *Southern Literary Messenger,* complained that **"Berenice"** was "far too horrible," Poe admitted that the accusation was justified. But he admitted that only for the individual story, and not for the type:

> . . . what I wish to say relates to the character of your Magazine more than to any articles I may offer, and I beg you to believe that I have no intention of giving you *advice,* being fully confident that, upon consideration, you will agree with me. The history of all Magazines shows plainly that those which have attained celebrity were indebted for it to articles *similar in nature—to* **"Berenice"**—although, I grant you, far superior in style and execution. I say similar in *nature.* You ask me in what does this nature consist? In the ludicrous heightened into the grotesque: the fearful coloured into the horrible: the witty exaggerated into the burlesque: the singular wrought out into the strange and mystical. You may say all this is bad taste. I have my doubts about it.

> Nobody is more aware than I am that simplicity is the cant of the day—but take my word for it no one cares any thing about simplicity in their hearts. Believe me also, in spite of what people say to the contrary, that there is nothing easier in the world than to be extremely simple. But whether the articles of which I speak are, or are not in bad taste is little to the purpose. To be appreciated you must be *read,* and these things are invariably sought after with avidity.

In this significant passage, Poe put the emphasis squarely on the tale's suitability for a magazine. It must first of all gain and hold the attention of readers; if it failed to do that, its virtues were of no practical value.

Poe seems to have thought of Washington Irving as an essayist and historian rather than as a writer of fiction. This may have been caused in part by the books which he reviewed. *The Crayon Miscellany, No. III,* contained a re-telling of "a few striking and picturesque legends" of the conquest of Spain by the Saracens; although they lacked the authenticity of history, they were "partially *facts*"; all Irving had done was "to adorn them in his own magical language." *Astoria* was straightforward history, executed in "a masterly manner." Only in a side-glance in a discussion of the skillfully-constructed story does he grant Irving much merit in this type of writing: "The 'Tales of a Traveller,' by Irving, are graceful and impressive narratives—'The Young Italian' is especially good—but there is not one of the series which can be commended as a whole. In many of them the interest is subdivided and frittered away."

Poe was flattered when Irving praised **"The Fall of the House of Usher"** and **"William Wilson,"** although he seems to have exaggerated somewhat Irving's compliments. There was a pertinent reason for his delight. Since Irving "heads the school of the quietists," his approbation would give Poe a "complete triumph over those little critics who would endeavor to put me down by raising the hue & cry of *exaggeration* in style, of *Germanism* and such twaddle."

Although he confessed that he was not generally of a "merry mood," Poe hailed with delight the anonymously-published *Georgia Scenes,* by A. B. Longstreet. He knew nothing of the author, but thought him "a clever fellow, inbued with a spirit of the *truest* humor, and endowed, moreover, with an exquisitely discriminative and penetrating understanding of *character* in general, and of Southern character in particular. And we do not mean to speak of *human* character exclusively. To be sure, our Georgian is *au fait* here too—he is learned in all things appertaining to the biped without feathers. In regard, especially to that class of Southwestern mammalia who come under the generic appellation of 'savagerous wild cats,' he is a very Theophrastus in duodecimo. But he is not the less at home in other matters.

Of geese and ganders he is the La Bruyere, and of good-for-nothing horses the Rochefoucault." In spite of this high praise and granting to the author sly humor and an "exquisite dramatic talent," Poe considered the work a collection of sketches rather than of tales; he paraphrased approvingly Longstreet's prefatory statement that "they are, generally, nothing more than fanciful combinations of real incidents and characters," and in some instances literally true. Poe thought the book a landmark in American humor, but not in the development of the American short story.

Except for Hawthorne's work, Poe could in fact find few examples to praise. The British, especially Dickens, were vastly superior. Of skillfully-constructed American tales, perhaps the best was Simms's "Murder Will Out," although it had "some glaring defects." Irving had written graceful and impressive narratives; John Neal's work showed vigor of thought and picturesque combination of incident, but his stories rambled too much and invariably broke down "just before coming to an end." Purely from the point of view of construction (and Poe noted that other points might be more important), the tales of N. P. Willis were consistently the best—"with the exception of Mr. Hawthorne."

Of American story-tellers, only Hawthorne had consistently displayed "an Art subservient to genius of a very lofty order." His distinctive trait was "invention, creation, imagination, originality"—words that Poe here uses as synonyms. True, the originality was a trifle marred by Poe's detecting "something which resembles plagiarism—but which *may be* a very flattering coincidence of thought" in Hawthorne's "Howe's Masquerade." In that story and in his own **"William Wilson"** the two conceptions are identical, and many points are similar. Poe did not press the accusation, however, but contented himself with suggesting the possibility. Instead, he ended the review on a note of high praise:

> In the way of objection we have scarcely a word to say of these tales. There is, perhaps, a somewhat too general or prevalent *tone*—a tone of melancholy and mysticism. The subjects are insufficiently varied. There is not so much of *versatility* evinced as we might well be warranted in expecting from the high powers of Mr. Hawthorne. But beyond these trivial exceptions we have really none to make. The style is purity itself. Force abounds. High imagination gleams from every page. Mr. Hawthorne is a man of the truest genius. We only regret that the limits of our Magazine will not permit us to pay him that full tribute of commendation, which, under other circumstances, we should be so eager to pay.

In 1847, Poe sharply although somewhat confusedly revised his earlier opinion as to Hawthorne's originality. He treated "all subjects in a similar tone of dreamy *innuendo,* yet in this walk he evinces extraordinary genius." But his treatment of subject-matter was too monotonously alike for him to be called truly original: "This true or commendable originality, however, implies not the uniform, but the continuous peculiarity—a peculiarity springing from ever-active vigor of fancy—better still if from ever-present force of imagination, giving its own hue, its own character to everything it touches, and, especially, self-impelled to touch everything." By this stringent definition, Hawthorne was not really original; moreover, he owed too much to the manner of the German Tieck. There was a "sameness, or monotone" in Hawthorne's work; this was the "strain of allegory which completely overwhelms the greater number of his subjects, and which in some measure interferes with the direct conduct of absolutely all." Since Poe felt that in defence of allegory "there is scarcely one respectable word to be said," it is hardly surprising that he qualified his praise of Hawthorne. Even so, he makes a useful aesthetic point: "if allegory ever establishes a fact, it is by dint of overturning a fiction. Where the suggested meaning runs through the obvious one in a *very* profound under-current so as never to interfere with the upper one without our own volition, so as never to show itself unless *called* to the surface, there only, for the proper uses of fictitious narrative, is it available at all. Under the best circumstances, it must always interfere with that unity of effect which to the artist, is worth all the allegory in the world."

Poe's dislike of the Transcendentalists may in part have motivated these strictures. He was willing to allow many virtues to the literary artist, but Hawthorne's "spirit of 'metaphor run-mad' is clearly imbibed from the phalanx and phalanstery atmosphere in which he has been so long struggling for breath. He has not half the material for the exclusiveness of authorship that he possesses for its universality. He has the purest style, the finest taste, the most available scholarship, the most delicate humor, the most touching pathos, the most radiant imagination, the most consummate ingenuity; and with these varied good qualities he has done *well* as a mystic. But is there any one of these qualities which would prevent his doing doubly as well in a career of honest, upright, sensible, prehensible and comprehensible things? Let him mend his pen, get a bottle of visible ink, come out from the Old Manse, cut Mr. Alcott, hang (if possible) the editor of 'The Dial,' and throw out to the window to the pigs all his odd numbers of 'The North American Review'."

When one considers that Hawthorne was his only serious or worthy rival in the writing of tales, Poe's criticism in 1842 seems not only just but amazingly generous. There are a few quibbles, beginning with the title, *Twice-Told Tales.* They were really thrice-told, and many of them were properly essays rather than tales. In themselves the essays were excellent, their predominant feature being "*repose.* There is no attempt at effect. All is quiet, thoughtful, subdued. Yet this repose may exist simultaneously with high originality of thought; and Mr. Hawthorne has demonstrated the fact. At every turn we meet with novel combinations; yet these combinations never surpass the limits of the quiet. . . . The Essays of Hawthorne have much of the character of Irving, with more of originality, and less of finish; while, compared with the Spectator, they have a vast superiority at all points."

Yet they were inferior to the tales in polish and interest. It was characteristic of Poe that before reviewing the stories he digressed far enough to give his own idea of what a tale should be. He had no doubt that it afforded "unquestionably the fairest field for the exercise of the loftiest talent, which can be afforded by the domains of mere prose." The best display of literary genius was in the rhymed poem that was long enough to produce an intense and enduring impression but brief enough to be read at one sitting, in not more than an hour. Second only to this was "the short prose narrative, requiring from a half-hour to one or two hours in its perusal." The ordinary novel was objectionable because of its length, which deprived it of "the immense force derivable from *totality*." Since the tale could be read at one sitting and without distraction, the "soul of the reader is at the writer's control." This had its disadvantages. The novelist could wander and digress; he could stop one line of action to "bring up" another one; he could move freely from character to character and from incident to incident. Since unity of effect was impossible, he did not have to be so much concerned with it. But these advantages were gained at the expense of artistry and of totality; they were in fact when considered properly not advantages at all. Genius would not make such sacrifices to expediency.

Poe was the first critic to consider the short story seriously as a literary type and as an independent art form. Unhesitatingly and often, he declared it to be superior to the novel. He wanted to define what it was and what it should be. He desired to develop an aesthetic for a *genre* that, although by no means new, had been unfairly and uncomprehendingly deprecated. It was second only to the lyric poem as a work of art.

This may have been rationalization, as Joseph Wood Krutch and other writers have baldly declared: Poe may have been justifying his own inability to write a sustained work, in prose or verse. It seems more likely that he was, consciously or unconsciously, setting an aesthetic for an appropriate magazine fiction. The story must gain and hold attention in competition with poems, essays, articles, and reviews. It must for this purpose have a complete and rounded plot, yet it must be short enough to be published in one issue. So in 1842 he defined clearly his own ideal of what a story should be, and in 1847 he retained the basic ideas with only slight changes in wording:

A skilful literary artist has constructed a tale. If wise, he has not fashioned his thoughts to accommodate his incidents; but having conceived, with deliberate care, a certain unique or single *effect* to be wrought out, he then invents such incident—he then combines such events as may best aid him in establishing this preconceived effect. If his very initial sentence tend not to the outbringing of this effect, then he has failed in his first step. In the whole composition there should be no word written, of which the tendency, direct or indirect, is not to the one pre-established design. And by such means, with such care and skill, a picture is at length painted which leaves in the mind of him who contemplates it with a kindred art, a sense of the fullest satisfaction. The idea of the tale has been presented unblemished, because undisturbed; and this is an end unattainable by the novel. Undue brevity is just as exceptionable here as in the poem; but undue length is yet more to be avoided.

Here, clearly stated, is Poe's ideal of prose fiction. It does not sound like rationalization; it has the authentic ring, rather, of a carefully-developed theory that had been evolved not only out of Poe's own practice but as an inevitable result of his critical precepts. The critic reviewing Bulwer's *Night and Morning* was not concerned with his own fiction but with the inadequacy of the novel as an art-form; the critic who so generously praised Hawthorne's stories did not need to call attention to his own work. He desired unity or totality of effect, both in the work itself and on the reader. In fiction, this could only be achieved through the tale. He desired also to edit a good, even a great, magazine, and he thought continually about a literature suited for this purpose. It was not by accident that his theory of fiction set an aesthetic for a magazine literature.

Robert D. Jacobs (essay date 1969)

SOURCE: "Toward Standards," in *Poe: Journalist and Critic,* Louisiana State University Press, 1969, pp. 159-90.

[*Jacobs traces the development of Poe's general literary standards through the book reviews that Poe wrote during his last eight months as editor of the* Southern Literary Messenger *in 1836.*]

A professional book reviewer for an American monthly magazine had little opportunity to practice philosophical criticism, for he had to hammer out notices of the subliterary material that piled up on his desk. Poe did attempt to examine this material by literary standards, however. In May of 1836 he reviewed a travel book, *Spain Revisited,* by a Lieutenant Slidell, and revealed his dislike for fulsome dedications and bad grammar. Poe considered himself an expert in matters of syntax and usage; and of all grammarians, he was one of the most prescriptive. The slightest ambiguity of reference or deviation into colloquialism provoked him into rewriting the passage to demonstrate correct English. His reconstructions, however, did not always go unchallenged. The editor of the *Newbern* (North Carolina) *Spectator* deplored the tone of his reviews in general, and his penchant for demolishing dedications and his hypercriticism of grammar in particular. Poe answered the charge at length, not only defending himself as a grammarian but also subjecting his critic to a personal attack: "We are at a loss to know who is the editor of the Spectator, but have a shrewd suspicion that he is the identical gentleman who once sent us from Newbern an unfortunate copy of verses. It seems to us that he wishes to be taken notice of, and we will for the once, oblige him with a few words. . . . If the editor of this little paper does not behave himself we will positively publish his verses."

Poe was feeling his power. He had received letters of praise from Professor Charles Anthon, Mrs. Sigourney (now mollified), and James Kirke Paulding. Even Halleck, whose poems Poe had criticized severely, had complimented the *Messenger* and Poe. Furthermore, Poe's review of Drake and Halleck had been hailed as "one of the finest pieces of criticism ever published in this country." All this praise was quoted or referred to in the July Supplement to the *Messenger,* and if the notices that were published are a fair sampling of opinion, Poe's criticism was already respected, even feared, from Natchez to Boston; and his fiction was drawing almost equal praise. Yet it was disturbing to find a hometown newspaper, the Richmond *Courier and Daily Compiler,* objecting to the gloom of his tales: "Mr. Poe is too fond of the wild—unnatural and horrible! Why will he not permit his fine genius to soar into purer, brighter, and happier regions? Why will he not disenthrall himself from the spells of German enchantment and supernatural imagery? There is room enough for the exercise of the highest powers, upon the multiform relations of human life, without descending into the dark, mysterious, and unutterable creations of licentious fancy."

This had been the opinion of White's first editor, James Heath, and of White himself, and it illustrates a conventional American attitude that Poe found a perpetual source of frustration. Earlier American critics had wanted cheerful, optimistic accounts of the human condition, not morbid analyses of the darker recesses of the human soul. Thus far, however, Poe gave little evidence that such opposition disturbed him. He wrote the kind of tale he wanted to write, and his inclination was reinforced by his knowledge of the success tales of psychological horror had had in British magazines. Accordingly, he was not disposed to heed the warnings of a few moralists in Richmond, Virginia. If his letter to Philip Pendleton Cooke three years later is honest, it was enough for him that the discriminating

few appreciated tales like **"Morella"** and **"Ligeia."** "As for the mob—let them talk on. I should be grieved if I thought they comprehended me here."

Meanwhile there were books to be reviewed, and Poe continued in his self-appointed task of reforming journalistic criticism in America. In May he challenged American provincialism by praising Mrs. Trollope, whose *Domestic Manners of the Americans* had offended the national sensitivity by intimating that those manners left much to be desired. "We have no patience with that atrabilious set of hyper-patriots," wrote Poe, "who find fault with Mrs. Trollope's book of flum-flummery about the good people of the Union." A book should be judged as a book, he asserted, not as a national affront: "That our national soreness of feeling prevented us, in the case of her work on America, from appreciating the real merits of the book, will be rendered evident by the high praise we find no difficulty in bestowing upon her *Paris and the Parisians*— a production, in whatever light we regard it, precisely similar to the one with which we were so irreparably offended." In this vein Poe might appear to us as the champion of literary America, challenging the dragons of stupidity, false pride, and provinciality; but all too often he deviated from the path of principle to gratify a personal pique. He had been lying in wait for Colonel William L. Stone, editor of the New York *Commercial Advertiser,* ever since that gentleman had used his newspaper to reprimand the "Zoilus" of the *Messenger* for the scathing *Norman Leslie* review. In June the victim was at hand, in the form of *Ups and Downs in the Life of a Distressed Gentleman.* No doubt Colonel Stone's book deserved to be "used up" (as Poe was fond of calling his destructive method), but, as usual when he was gratifying a grudge, Poe's review was splenetic rather than critical.

The first two pages of the review prodded what is always a tender spot, the potential market for the book. Poe announced the price, counted the pages, and concluded that purchasers would be bilked, intimating that the book was so worthless that it should be measured by its size only. A single issue of the *Messenger,* Poe claimed, was six times as long as Stone's book and cost less than half as much. Therefore, unless *Ups and Downs* were sixteen times as high in quality as the *Messenger,* Stone was presuming upon the "excessive patience, gullibility, and good nature" of the public. Poe added insult by naming the anonymous author and stating that the book "should have been printed among the quack advertisements in a space corner of his paper."

Poe had very little else to say about *Ups and Downs.* The stinging but amusing satire of his earlier destructive reviews is less marked in this one, which may indicate that the earlier reviews were prompted by a desire to be "wickedly" good humored after the manner of Christopher North. In this case, however, Poe's ire had been aroused, and the review is more vindictive than humorous. Most of the space is given to a plot summary with quotations designed to show the book at its worst. Very sensitive to harsh criticism of his own work, Poe's retaliation to such criticism was often equally ill tempered and made him a target for violent abuse.

Poe's book reviews in the June number, though generally undistinguished, should not be dismissed completely. A brief notice of Dickens' *Watkins Tottle and Other Sketches* proves that Poe was developing his theory of the short tale. A novel, he said, certainly requires a sustained effort, but this effort is merely perseverance and has only a "collateral relation to talent." The short tale, however, must have unity of effect, a quality which is "not easily appreciated or indeed comprehended by an ordinary mind." It is a quality difficult to attain, "even by those who can conceive it."

We have already noticed that Poe did not apply the criterion of a unified effect to the poems of Drake and Halleck, no doubt because he was more interested in being "philosophical" than in analyzing technique. Unity to Poe, insofar as it could be prescribed, was a question of technique, a logical and psychological strategy of adapting means to the proposed end. Because his reductionism was not so stringent for prose as for poetry, he was able to make a more satisfactory application of the principle to the short tale than he ever did to the poem. Poe did not explain here what he meant by unity of effect, but, remembering his use of Schlegel in the review of Mrs. Sigourney, we may assume that he meant total effect, or that correlation of feeling and thought that would be a unified response. If so, and it seems likely, he was demanding an interdependence among the various elements of form which would enable the objective structural unity, the relationship of part to part and part to whole, to be the vehicle of a subjective unity of impression. This interpretation is supported by his analysis of one of Dickens' tales. Poe offered "The Pawnbroker's Shop" as an illustration of the unity of effect, making the claim that each sentence gives a fuller view of the picture the artist is painting. A novel, Poe asserted, does not lend itself to such a technique; it is admired for its "detached passages, without reference to the work as a whole." As usual, Poe seized every opportunity to explain that the novel was not an art form, but in examining the short tale by the principle of unity of impression he elevated it to the traditional status of a fine art.

Poe's analogy between the short tale and a painting is significant, for it explains his concept of unity more clearly than any of his abstract definitions: "the *Pawnbroker's Shop* engages and enchains our attention—we

are enveloped in its atmosphere of wretchedness and extortion—we pause at every sentence, not to dwell upon the sentence, but to obtain a fuller view of the gradually perfecting picture—which is never at any moment any other matter than the *Pawnbroker's Shop*. To the illustration of this one end all the *groupings* and *fillings in* of the painting are rendered subservient—and when our eyes are taken from the canvas, we remember the personages of the sketch not at all as independent existences, but as essentials of the one subject we have witnessed—as a part and portion of the *Pawnbroker's Shop*." If a narrative is regarded as a picture, it is a design extended in space, not a movement in time, and if characters are regarded as static groupings used as elements of a composition, there is little or no dramatic effect. It is the thematic design which is important, and character and setting are equivalent means by which the design is fulfilled. By Poe's theory one should not attempt to write a "character story" or an "action story," because undue emphasis on person or event would cause an imbalance in the composition. An "atmospheric story" would be allowable, however, for a symbolic rendition of scene would be as adequate for thematic purpose as it would be in a painting.

It would be tempting at this point to analyze one of Poe's own tales to see how well he followed his own theory. **"The Fall of the House of Usher,"** published three years later, would be the obvious choice, for an interpretation of scene is just as necessary for apprehending the import of the tale as is the analysis of character. Yet this story has been competently analyzed many times, and it should be enough to say that Poe's theory of unity works in **"Usher,"** but it works at the expense of certain qualities which many of us today have been taught to expect in fiction. Roderick Usher, for instance, is not so much a convincing character as he is the pictorialization of theme. He is a "symbolic" character, according to some interpretations. Since Usher's fears are revealed more by description than by dramatic action, there is little conflict and almost no tension or suspense. The story can be regarded as mechanical—utterly contrived. For such a reason Cleanth Brooks and Robert Penn Warren criticized it harshly in the first edition of their textbook, *Understanding Fiction*. This textbook divides stories into three types—plot, character, and theme—although the authors are careful to emphasize that the quality of a particular story "may depend upon the organic relation existing among these elements." Thus, although Brooks and Warren, like Poe, would not approve of the isolation of any particular element in a story, their categories do permit the emphasis of one element over the other, which is pragmatically sound. Poe, however, a pioneer in the genre, was not *describing* the tale as it has come to be; he was *prescribing* the tale as he thought it ought to be, the ideal form as he conceived it.

"Usher" is a tableau, the illustration of an idea, in which the symbolic significance of scene is just as important as the sequence of events. In fact, it is more important, for temporal movement is relatively subordinate. The collapse and death motif is foreshadowed in the opening description, and significant change or development does not occur. Poe's own term for this type of tale, the "arabesque," is appropriate. This term, used to describe a graphic design, signifies an ordering of space, not a chronological development.

The review of Dickens was the only real effort at criticism Poe was to make for some time. The other reviews in the June issue and all of those in July were perfunctory notices of nonliterary or subliterary material, although among them Poe did insert a tribute to Coleridge in the form of an announcement of the American publication of the Letters, *Conversations, and Recollections of S.T. Coleridge.* Poe wrote:

> . . . with us (we are not ashamed to confess it) the most trivial memorial of Coleridge is a treasure of inestimable price. He was indeed a "myriad-minded man," and ah, how little understood, and how pitifully vilified! How merely nominal was the difference (and this too in his own land) between what he himself calls the "broad, predetermined abuse" of the Edinburgh Review, and the cold and brief compliments with the warm *regrets* of the Quarterly. If there be any one thing more than another which stirs within us a deep spirit of indignation and disgust, it is that damnation with faint praise which so many of the Narcissi of critical literature have had the infinite presumption to breathe against the majesty of Coleridge—of Coleridge—the man to whose gigantic mind the proudest intellects of Europe found it impossible not to succumb.

This was the most unqualified praise that Poe ever gave to the critic whose work helped form his own critical theory and practice. Later he was to rebel consciously against Coleridge's influence and to complain somewhat petulantly about the British critic's "overprofundity" and "metaphysicianism," as did other American critics who professed to be baffled by Coleridge's obscurities. At the moment, however, he was an ardent admirer. If the *Biographia Literaria* were published in America, Poe concluded, the publishers "would be rendering an important service to the cause of psychological science in America, by introducing a work of great scope and power in itself, and well calculated to do away with the generally received impression here entertained of the *mysticism* of the writer."

Mysticism, which in Poe's time could mean almost anything difficult to understand, was no bugaboo to him as yet; but in subsequent years, as he reacted against the New England transcendentalists, he began to display the usual American reverence for common

sense and plain speaking and deprecated the "cloudland of metaphysics." This tendency became pronounced during his second attempt to make a place for himself in New York journalism and must be regarded, at least in part, as his contribution to the journalistic rivalry between New York and Boston. At the moment, however, he was relatively isolated and could speak his mind with no further inhibition than that imposed by his apprehensive employer. Praising Coleridge and damning two British journals would have disturbed White far less than incurring the risk of a lawsuit by abusing Theodore Fay and William L. Stone.

In August, Poe was able to return to literary criticism with a review of *The Book of Gems,* an anthology of British poets from Chaucer to Prior. This review added nothing to Poe's stature as a critic, for he revealed a narrowly contemporaneous taste. At least a third of our affection for the "old" poets, he claimed, is "simple love of the antique." Even when we do feel something like the "proper poetic sentiment" in reading their poems, he continued, the feeling comes in part from the quaint phraseology and grotesque rhythms, which are not the result of artistry but only the accident of time and place. The "old" English muse was without art, Poe declared, even though her devotees, such as John Donne and Abraham Cowley, might have been very learned in their own way. These so-called metaphysical poets were far from metaphysical in the proper sense, because with them ethics or moral truth was the end of the poem, which to Poe was inadmissible. Wordsworth and Coleridge used metaphysical knowledge properly, because with them the end of a poem was quite properly the stimulation of poetic feeling "through channels suggested by mental analysis." Donne and Cowley had failed where Coleridge, in particular, had succeeded brilliantly, because Coleridge knew what poetry was supposed to do and he knew how to accomplish his purpose. In contrast, Cowley and all the metaphysical poets of the seventeenth century were "simple and single-hearted men" who wrote directly from the "soul" with complete "abandon"—i.e., without art.

With the revival of interest in metaphysical poetry in the twentieth century, we may be disposed to dismiss Poe's strictures as incredibly naïve; but to do so would be to betray our own lack of perspective. From the age of Pope to Poe's own time, most critics had been inclined to think of seventeenth-century poetry, with the one exception of Milton, as an artless exhibition of mental gymnastics, "One glaring chaos and wild heap of wit," as Pope had described it. Without attempting to designate specific sources, we may be sure that Poe's attitude, though not the exact terms of his argument, was formed by such works as Dr. Johnson's *Life of Cowley,* Blair's *Lectures,* which denigrate Cowley (using Johnson as authority), and perhaps even Sir Francis Jeffrey's review of John Ford, who, though a dramatist, was contemporary with Cowley and in Jeffrey's opinion displayed the lack of taste characteristic of his period. From reading Kames and Blair, one would conclude that nothing happened in English literature prior to Shakespeare and that between Shakespeare and Dryden the only poet worth mentioning was Milton. *The Book of Gems* was an unusual anthology because it did contain the "early English poets." It was not uncommon to find Milton in an anthology—along with such late eighteenth-century favorites as Young, Beattie, Gray, and Collins.

It is not surprising, then, that Poe considered Donne and Cowley as primitive in respect to art, for to him art began with the recent application of psychological aesthetics. To compare Poe's opinion of seventeenth-century writers with that of Jeffrey is instructive. Poe writes: "To elevate immeasurably all the energies of the mind—but again—so to mingle the greatest possible fire, force, delicacy, and all good things, with the lowest possible bathos, baldness, and utter imbecility, as to render it not a matter of doubt, but of certainty, that the average results of mind in such a school, will be found inferior to those results in one (ceteris paribus) more artificial [i.e., more conscious of art]: Such, we think, is the view of the older English Poetry, in which a very calm examination will bear us out." Next, Jeffrey: "Unaccountable, however, as it is, the fact is certain, that almost all the dramatic writers of this age appear to be alternately inspired, and bereft of understanding; and pass, apparently without being conscious of the change, from the most beautiful displays of genius to the most melancholy examplification of stupidity. . . . there is an inequality and a capricious uncertainty in the taste and judgment of these good old writers, which excites at once our amazement and compassion."

Historically, then, Poe was exhibiting a stock opinion. More to the point of his development as a critic, however, he was basing his concept of artistry upon the artist's grasp of the psychology of response, his knowledge of emotional reactions and effective stimuli. The complexity of tone of the metaphysical poets, the yoking of intellect with emotion, the ironic indirection of the better metaphysical poems, were all lost on Poe, who considered the unity of emotional effect the prime desideratum of a poem. Poe's constriction of the limits of poetry had previously appeared in his review of Drake and Halleck, but this review is an even more obvious demonstration of his reductionism in practice. The only poem of *The Book of Gems* he was able to praise without qualification was Marvell's "Maiden Lamenting for her Fawn," which contained none of the wit that would have offended the sensibilities of Poe's generation. His rhapsody about the poem reveals how completely his taste was that of sentimental romanticism: "How truthful an air of deep lamentation hangs here upon every gentle syllable! It pervades all. It comes

over the half-playful, half-petulant air with which she lingers on the beauties and good qualities of her favorite. . . . The whole thing is redolent with poetry of the *very loftiest order*. It is positively crowded with *nature* and with *pathos*."

Scarcely a line of the poem is analyzed, and Poe's rapturous language seems hardly appropriate for the Zoilus of the *Messenger*. He was much more forceful in analyzing the defects of what he did not like than in demonstrating the quality of the works his taste approved.

The readers of the *Messenger* might have thought that Poe's hatchet had lost its edge if he had not included one harsh condemnation among the generally bland reviews of the August number. Nathaniel Parker Willis, although only three years older than Poe, was already an established writer in America. He was an editor of the New York *Mirror,* the journal that had attempted to "puff" *Norman Leslie* into success. Willis had published three books of poems and three volumes of literary "letters" called *Pencillings by the Way* before Poe reviewed his book of sketches, *Inklings of Adventure.*

Willis was an aesthete, a literary fop about New York whose mannerisms irritated some of the critics who reviewed his work; but Poe, fresh from having announced in his review of Drake and Halleck that a work should be criticized by principle and not by prejudice, denounced the practice of attacking a book on the basis of the author's personality: "We cannot sufficiently express our disgust at that unscrupulous indelicacy which is in the habit of deciding upon the literary merits of this gentleman by a reference to his private character and manners. . . ." Willis probably appreciated this attitude, for he had been subjected to a number of personal attacks, including two by Poe's enemies, Willis Gaylord Clark and Colonel William L. Stone. This in spite of the fact that the *Mirror* had "puffed" Colonel Stone's writings.

Unfortunately for Willis, Poe found sufficient reason to demolish the book without reference to the author's character. The whole narrative was "disfigured and indeed utterly ruined by the grievous sin of affectation." This charge has been examined in a previous chapter in reference to the romantic requirement of sincerity, but it also represented a stylistic fault. Blair had devoted an entire lecture to the definition of simplicity and its opposite, affectation. Simplicity of composition, he explained, was virtually the same thing as unity, for it represented a design distinguished by a relatively small number of parts, as could be illustrated by Greek tragedy and Greek architecture, in contrast to the Gothic modes. Simplicity of style "stands opposed to too much ornament, or pomp of Language," whereas an affected style was overly ornate, or florid. Another way in which simplicity was manifested was in an easy and natural manner of expressing thought, "in such a manner, that every one thinks he could have written in the same way." Affectation, on the other hand, was not simply ornament, but the labored effort to achieve rhetorical effects.

Poe's charge of affectation was properly applied to Willis' style. His striving for effect, his attempts at cleverness, elegance, and wit were the New Yorker's tokens of a sophistication that was unappreciated in the provinces; but Poe judged Willis' frivolity by a stylistic principle considered sound in his day. Furthermore, in terms of unity of effect, Willis' mannerisms were productive of a greater flaw. There was an "utter want of keeping" in the book, for the "absurd fripperies and frivolities" prevented the reader from appreciating his more serious subjects, such as the grandeur of Niagara Falls. The trivial could not be mixed with the sublime, according to the Allisonian principle of the single emotion.

In later years Poe was to make amends to Willis and was even to become his friend. Willis employed Poe to write for the New York *Evening Mirror* in 1844 and defended him from his enemies in 1846 and after his death; but Poe never had a high regard for Willis as a writer. He judged Willis as a man of fancy rather than of imagination. Few would question his verdict.

In September, Poe reviewed a novel which interested him, *Sheppard Lee,* by Robert Montgomery Bird, author of *Calavar* and *The Infidel. Sheppard Lee* was a humorous fantasy, an "original," Poe thought. Much of the book was social satire, but this element Poe ignored in favor of Bird's exploitation of the occult. The chief character experiences metempsychosis, his psyche inhabiting some seven different bodies (of persons who had recently died) in its transmigration. Poe himself had used metempsychosis in his tale **"Morella,"** and he was to use it again in **"Ligeia"** and in **"A Tale of the Ragged Mountains."** Consequently he was intrigued by Bird's strategy in using the occult. Yet Poe was disturbed, as we might expect, by the humor of *Sheppard Lee.* The journey of the soul should be treated seriously, and the author should have made an effort to secure the reader's assent to the supernatural elements. Instead Bird violated the tone of the novel with incongruities until the final page and then ruthlessly disposed of the problem by alleging that the whole thing was only a dream, thus depriving the reader of the emotional effect he had secured through identification with the character. Any use of the supernatural, Poe claimed, should be carefully planned. It should not be a mere structural device for stringing together six separate narratives. If Bird had caused his hero to preserve his identity through each successive existence, and if the events themselves had been contrasted in

their effect upon an unchanging character, the book would have had a legitimate interest.

Such a method would be satisfactory, Poe asserted, but there was a superior stratagem:

> It consists in a variety of points—principally in avoiding, as may easily be done, that *directness* of expression which we have noticed in Sheppard Lee, and thus leaving much to the imagination—in writing as if the author were firmly impressed with the truth, yet astonished at the immensity, of the wonders he relates, and for which, professedly, he neither claims nor anticipates credence—in minuteness of detail, especially upon points which have no immediate bearing upon the general story—this minuteness not being at variance with indirectness of expression—in short, by making use of the infinity of arts which give verisimilitude to a narration—and by leaving the result as a wonder not to be accounted for. It will be found that *bizarreries* thus conducted, are usually far more effective than those otherwise managed. The attention of the author, who does not depend upon explaining away his incredibilities, is directed to giving them the character and the luminousness of truth, and thus are brought about, unwittingly, some of the most vivid creations of human intellect. The reader, too, readily perceives and falls in with the writer's humor, and suffers himself to be borne on thereby. On the other hand what difficulty, or inconvenience, or danger can there be in leaving us uninformed of the important facts that a certain hero *did not* actually discover the elixir vitae, *could not* really make himself invisible, and *was not* either a ghost in good earnest, or a bona fide Wandering Jew?

Poe wins our respect here by constructing a rationale for the supernatural in fiction. Lame endings that revealed the author's subservience to common sense were frequent in popular fiction. The highly respected Washington Irving had provided natural explanations for the supernatural events of some of his tales, as had Charles Brockden Brown and Mrs. Ann Radcliffe before him. No such apology to reason and science is present in Poe's own tales of the supernatural. Morella's soul invades the body of her daughter, but the mystery is unexplained, as is the more startling transformation of the blonde Rowena into the brunette Ligeia. Poe's theory of unity of effect forbade the intrusion of materials that would dispel the illusion which all good fiction creates. He knew that readers give willing assent to the virtual existence which is the "life" of fiction, however incredible that existence may be when measured by ordinary experience.

Concerned, as always, with questions of technique, Poe explained how to secure the reader's acceptance of the occult by using the "arts" of verisimilitude. No longer did he generalize by referring to the power of identification, as he had in his review of *Robinson Crusoe.* Instead, he indicated that the illusion of reality could be achieved by the multiplication of minute details, even though these details were not directly relevant to the plot. **"The Narrative of Arthur Gordon Pym,"** on which he may have been working at this time (the first installment was published in the *Messenger* only four months later) makes use of such details. The technique itself was not new. The "sensation" stories of *Blackwood's,* from which he had learned part of his craft, had given minute details of bizarre experiences and the consequent emotional reactions; but Poe could not be content with a technique unless he could support it in theory.

The achievement of verisimilitude in action and setting, Poe had perceived, was possible through the multiplication of detail. How to achieve it in characterization was a problem he did not examine in this review but to which he addressed himself in a review published four months later. His own tales, however, furnish evidence that he was aware that the reader's assent to the incredible could be achieved, in part, by the plausibility of the narrator. Most of the sensation stories, including Poe's, made use of first-person narrators. If the character telling the story is obviously psychotic, the bizarre experience may be taken as hallucination, and verisimilitude is destroyed. This credibility-destroying device had been used by Irving in *Tales of a Traveller,* in which the "Adventure of the German Student" is narrated by a "nervous gentleman" who claims to have heard it from the student himself in a madhouse! Poe used the gambit in **"The Tell-Tale Heart,"** with its opening sentence that testifies to the madness of the narrator. There is nothing wrong with such a device if the author has no intention of securing verisimilitude on external terms and wishes only to record the experience of a deranged mind. If, however, the purpose is to describe a strange adventure in an incredible setting, the author must in some way vouch for the sanity of the narrator. Poe went to extreme lengths to accomplish this in **"The Narrative of Arthur Gordon Pym,"** even writing a preface in which Pym, the *character,* makes the claim that Poe, the *author,* fictionalized the facts presented straightforwardly by Pym himself; then Poe added a postscript, claiming that Pym and his companion were still alive.

Such tactics are crude and indefensible. More to Poe's credit is his effort to establish Pym's plausibility by distinguishing the character's periods of near insanity from his periods of self-possession. In other words, the reader is informed of the times at which the character is subject to hallucination. In an earlier tale, **"Ms. Found in a Bottle,"** Poe had endeavored to accomplish the same object by making his narrator unimaginative and skeptical. Pym does have imagination, but he insists that he retains his "powers of mind" at a time when his companions have been reduced to "a

species of second childhood." Even when he encounters the wonders of the South Sea region, Pym merely records details instead of trying to explain the marvels. This technique is that of writing "as if the author were firmly impressed with the truth," the requirement Poe had proposed in his review of *Sheppard Lee.*

Poe's devices worked in a way that he did not expect. *Pym* was reviewed as an attempt at a realistic travel story that neglected probability, surely an indication that his clumsier tactics annoyed his reviewer. For all of his theorizing, Poe had no gift for realism and the super-rationality of some of his narrators strikes most readers in a way quite opposite to what was evidently intended. James W. Cox furnishes this explanation: "He [Pym] is not the observer but forever the *actor,* and his experiences come more and more to seem the hallucinations of a madman." To read *Pym* in terms of the Crusoe-like verisimilitude Poe invokes is unrewarding, to say the least. The novel assumes interest only if we interpret it as Patrick Quinn has done, as a symbolic journey of the mind. Surely, however, it deserves better than Mr. Cox's comment that it is something between "a practical joke at the expense of the reader on one hand and a parody of the sensational adventure tale on the other." Poe undoubtedly wrote the novel to sell and exploited relatively crude effects, but in this case his unconscious is better than his conscious art. It may be taken as a crude thriller with a technique which foreshadows that of the modern science fiction adventure, such as A. E. Van Vogt's *The War Against the Rull,* but a search for symbolic meaning in Van Vogt's work yields no return, whereas both Patrick Quinn and Edward Davidson have found the "sensations" of *Pym* richly joined in implication.

In spite of the relatively inoffensive reviews that Poe had written for the July and August numbers of the *Messenger,* there was trouble in the office. On August 5, 1836, White had written to a contributor, William Cowper Scott, proprietor of the New York *Weekly Messenger,* that the next issue of his journal would be delayed because of illness. Again on August 25 he wrote that the November number was not ready because of "sickness among my most material hands," which evidently meant Poe. In September, White himself was ill. An editorial note in the September issue stated that since both editor and publisher had been ill, there would be no notices of new books. In a letter to Sarah J. Hale, dated October 20, Poe admitted that he had been "sadly thrown back by late illness" and would be unable to contribute anything to the *Ladies Magazine,* which she edited in Boston. About this time White was on the verge of discharging Poe and retained him only on the fulfillment of "certain conditions." What these conditions were, we do not know. Perhaps they had to do with Poe's drinking. At any rate, with a slowly dying wife, financial difficulties, and illness of his own, White was evidently finding the vagaries of his brilliant editor too much to bear. Poe did recover from his indisposition in time to prepare the reviews for the October number—a full seventeen pages, though all of them may not have been Poe's—but in November there were further difficulties. White made a trip to New York about the middle of October, but on his return found his wife very low and his office in a state of confusion. If, as seems certain, he had left Poe in charge, Poe had violated the conditions White had imposed.

The November number was not ready for the press. It did not appear until December, and even then there was an apologetic note in the book review section: "A press of business connected with some necessary arrangements for Volume the third, has prevented us from paying, in this Messenger, the usual attention to our Critical Department. We have many books now lying by us which we propose to notice fully in our next. With this number we close Volume the Second."

The charitable conclusion is that Poe could not manage all of the work in White's absence—write the critical notices, handle the correspondence, pass judgment on contributions, prepare the magazine for the press, and read proof. His normal duties, if we can take White's letters to Lucian Minor as evidence of what he expected from his editor, would have been to handle book reviews and notices and furnish from fifteen to twenty pages of original material a month. But White had expected Minor to work only twenty-four to thirty hours a week, and it is likely that Poe did much more than this. Normally he handled much of White's correspondence and read proof. Though he could be overruled by White, he passed judgment on contributions and wrote letters of acceptance and rejection. Probably Poe's work week was far in excess of thirty hours. When we add the time necessary for his own creative work and for the careful analysis he preferred to give the books he reviewed, it is no wonder that occasionally he took refuge in a bottle and got the reputation of having "bad habits." R. M. T. Hunter, a contemporary observer, gave his impression of the situation, and although we cannot always trust a memory of forty years, Hunter's account in 1875 squares with the impression we get from White's letters to his confidants. Hunter wrote,

> Here his [Poe's] habits were bad and as White did not appreciate his literary excellences I had hard work to save him from dismissal before it actually occurred. During a part of the time I was in Richmond, a member of the Legislature, and frequently volunteered to correct the press when pieces were being published with classical quotations. Poe was the only man on White's staff capable of doing this and when occasionally drinking (the habit was not constant) he was incapacitated for work. On such occasions I have done the work more than once to prevent a rupture between his employer and

himself. He was reckless about money and subject to intoxication, but I was not aware of any other bad habit that he had.

Considering the state of affairs in the *Messenger* office during November, it is not surprising that the November number, when it finally appeared in December, contained only four pages of criticism, of which the only point of interest was another expression of Poe's admiration for Dickens in a review of *The Posthumous Papers of the Pickwick Club*—and this review was chiefly quotation. By January, White had made good his threat to discharge Poe, and among the critical notices in the first number of Volume III was the announcement: "Mr. Poe's attention being called in another direction, he will decline, with the present number, the Editorial duties of the Messenger."

This account of Poe's difficulties between August and December of 1836 has been given in order to illustrate the problems he faced being a critic instead of a journalistic book-reviewer. Poe wanted to be a critic, to analyze the books that crossed his desk thoughtfully and at length; but the exigencies of his routine tasks were a formidable obstacle. It is to his credit that during these exasperating months he still managed to write reviews, a few of them good ones. In the October number, among notices of nonliterary publications such as Dr. Haxall's *Dissertation on Diseases of the Abdomen,* Hall's *Latin Grammar,* and S. A. Roszel's *Address Delivered at the Annual Commencement of Dickinson College,* there is a review of a book of short stories, *Peter Snook . . . and Other Strange Tales.* If we remember that collections of tales were not customarily honored with serious reviews during Poe's time, we can see that this review not only reveals the progress of Poe's ideas concerning the short story as a literary form but also indicates his efforts to establish the genre as worthy of criticism. For once he thought he had found a perfect example of the form: "The incidents of this story are forcibly conceived and even in the hands of an ordinary writer would scarcely fail of effect. But in the present instance so unusual a tact is developed in narration, that we are inclined to rank 'Peter Snook' among the few tales which, each in their own way, are absolutely faultless."

Reviewing Dickens' *Watkins Tottle* in June, Poe had compared the short story to a painting. Now he developed the analogy in detail:

> "Peter Snook" is . . . a Flemish *home-piece,* and entitled to the very species of praise which should be awarded to the best of such pieces. The merit lies in the *chiaro 'scuro*—in that blending of light and shadow where nothing is *too distinct,* yet where the idea is fully conveyed—in the absence of all rigid outlines and all miniature painting—in the not undue warmth of the coloring—and in the slight tone of exaggeration prevalent, yet not amounting

to caricature. We will venture to assert that no painter, who deserves to be called so, will read "Peter Snook" without assenting to what we have to say, and without a perfect consciousness that the principal rules of the plastic arts, founded as they are in a true perception of the beautiful, will apply in their fullest force to every species of literary composition.

To anyone familiar with Poe's aesthetic principles the statement above is astonishing. Usually vehement in his opposition to mimetic realism, he compared "Peter Snook" approvingly with a "Flemish home-piece," in spite of the fact that the Flemish school of painters was normally censured in his time for uncritical literalness and a delight in the commonplace. Their work was marked by accuracy and precision of outline, a result of a tradition of miniature painting, yet these are precisely the qualities that Poe denied to the best of the Flemish work. His use of the term chiaroscuro, however, suggests that he was referring not to the distinctive Flemish paintings of the fifteenth century but to the genre painting of the seventeenth century, after the influence of the Italian artist Caravaggio had made itself felt, particularly in the thematic use of light and shadow. That Poe was making an accurate comparison is indicated by his description of "the slight tone of exaggeration prevalent, yet not amounting to caricature." The Flemish genre painters had retained enough of Pieter Bruegel's passion for the details of homely life, invested with a certain amount of humor, to justify Poe's comparison. The author of "Peter Snook," Poe noted, "has some of the happiest peculiarities of Dickens"; then he quoted enough of the tale to show that these peculiarities had to do with a humorous presentation of a London clerk and his financial and amatory misadventures. The story is a "home-piece" in its exaggeration of low life and uses the technique of chiaroscuro to emphasize elements of character.

Obviously Poe did not object to Dickensian realism in a short tale, provided that details were organized into a total design—a composition that would convey a unity of impression. More surprising is the last sentence of his quotation, that "the principal rules of the plastic arts, founded as they are in a true perception of the beautiful, will apply in their fullest force to *every species of literary composition*" (italics mine). After 1831 he customarily denied, along with most other romantic critics, that poetry resembled painting, for painting was a mimetic art and poetry was not. However, when Poe referred to "principal rules," he was thinking in terms of the psychology of effect. The unity of effect was a first principle, to be observed in all arts. As he was to explain in a later review, effects differed according to genre, but the principle was always the same.

Poe continued to describe the short tale as a design or a composition rather than as a narrative characterized by action and drama. The pleasure to be derived from it was similar to the response to a painting—say by a master of the picturesque such as Salvator Rosa—in which the management of light and shadow is thematically significant. Details that call attention to themselves are to be avoided because they get in the way of the apprehension of the design, the idea of the story. We do not know whether at this time Poe had read any of Hawthorne's tales which S. B. Goodrich had published in *The Token,* but, whether he had read them or not, he described with precision what has been accepted as a chief characteristic of Hawthorne's symbolic art—the blending of light and shadow so that object, character, and event are never seen in insulated detail but only in a kind of relatedness that, taken as a whole, intimates the idea. The review of *Peter Snook* reveals that six years before Poe was to review Hawthorne's *Twice-Told Tales* he was prepared to do them justice. Hawthorne was practicing the technique for which Poe was attempting to formulate a theory. Where Poe's theory and Hawthorne's practice came to terms was in the picturesque tradition, which valued natural objects selectively for their picturesque qualities and their capability of being combined into compositions that would create a unified impression. It is not at all surprising that in the few remarks Poe made about painters he showed preference for Claude Lorraine and Salvator Rosa, whose paintings had helped establish the vogue of the picturesque in the eighteenth century. Since the November number of the *Messenger* did not appear until December and even then contained only four pages of perfunctory notices, the last work of any significance that Poe accomplished as editor of the *Messenger* appeared in January, 1837. The first five reviews in this issue are his; the others are by Judge Abel P. Upshur and Beverley Tucker. Of Poe's five reviews, two merit examination.

Poe gave *George Balcombe,* a novel published anonymously by his friend Beverley Tucker, a full measure of attention. Some months later White wrote to Tucker alleging that the "eulogistic review" was written only because Poe suspected that Tucker was the author of the novel. "Poe seldom or ever done [*sic*] what he knew was just to any books," White charged. Since this charge was made in retrospect, after White should have had time to cool off from whatever heat the immediate friction with Poe had caused, it may have been a firm conviction. As has been shown, Poe did write some caustic reviews, flippant in tone, of what White called "some trashy novels." But White went on to say that Poe rarely read through the books that he reviewed, and this accusation is quite unfair in view of the circumstances. Poe's reviews demonstrated that he read very carefully the books that he thought merited attention. Even when he resorted to plot summary instead of analysis, he appears to have read the books concerned, unless he lifted the summaries from other magazines. When Poe did borrow from other reviewers, which he did infrequently, he was more scrupulous than many of his contemporaries in mentioning his sources. Considering his duties at the *Messenger* office, however, and the number of books he had to review, it is unlikely that he was able to read them all. Any professional reviewer is likely to compile a review of an unimportant work from publisher's notices or previous reviews if he has a deadline to meet. Whenever Poe concentrated on peripheral matters such as dedications, footnotes, or slips in grammar (which could be culled by skimming), he was unjust, in White's sense, to the book reviewed. Otherwise White's charges have to be based on the five books that Poe reviewed harshly: *Confessions of a Poet, Paul Ulric, Norman Leslie, Ups and Downs,* and *The Partisan.* Poe himself had stated in September that he had reviewed ninety-four books for the *Messenger* and that in only five reviews had censure been "greatly predominant." In seventy-nine cases he had praised more than he had blamed.

This was Poe's reaction to the charge of "regular cutting and slashing" which had been made by the Richmond *Courier and Daily Compiler* in August of 1836. Poe had answered the editor of the *Compiler* by supplying the facts, as he interpreted them, but from White's letter to Tucker we must assume that White was not convinced by Poe's facts. Either his troubles with Poe had made him incapable of being fair or Poe's reviewing standards were so strange to White that the publisher had no real basis for judgment. Since Poe judged on literary grounds and White on moral, they were obviously at cross-purposes much of the time.

The review of *George Balcombe* was not blatantly eulogistic. Poe did call Tucker's work the "best American novel," an opinion time has not sustained; and he claimed that no other American novelist had succeeded as well as Tucker in creating female characters. This last was only relative praise. The inability to portray women realistically had been characteristic of the best of the novelists of Poe's time—Cooper, Simms, and Bird. Women thought worthy of portrayal in a novel were usually ladies, paper-and-paste specimens of sensibility. Poe quite rightly took exception to "Elizabeth, the shrinking and matronly wife of Balcombe," who rises "suddenly into the heroine in the hour of her husband's peril." As Poe said, "She is an exquisite specimen of her class, but her class is somewhat hackneyed." The character of Mary Scott, who has the chief female role in the novel, was better, but "her nature is barely sketched." Even in the sketch, however, the novelist showed an unusual "creative vigor."

Unless we are aware that the American critics of Poe's time demanded a measure of realism in the portrayal of character, we would be disposed to grant Poe more credit than he deserves for seeing the defects of the female characters in the American novel. Actually, a number of critics had objected to Cooper's females, and the charge made recently by Leslie Fiedler—that American novelists were unable to present "full-fledged, mature women"—was first intimated in the 1830's. This is not to say that the critics of the period would have accepted Fiedler's definition of a mature woman, but they were aware that American novelists were deficient in the characterization of women. The claim that Poe made for Tucker was that no other American novelist had depicted female character "even nearly so well," and this praise, considering the competition, must be regarded as qualified. Other characters in the novel were less effective:

> Napier himself is, as usual with most professed heroes, a mere non-entity. James is sufficiently natural. Major Swann, although only done in outline, gives a fine idea of a decayed Virginia gentleman. Charles, a negro, . . . is drawn roughly, but to the life. Balcombe, frank, ardent, philosophical, chivalrous, sagacious—and, above all, glorying in the exercise of his sagacity—is a conception which might possibly have been entertained, but certainly could not have been executed, by a mind many degrees dissimilar from that of Balcombe himself, as depicted. Of Keizer, a character evidently much dwelt upon, and greatly labored out by the author, we have but one observation to make. It will strike every reader, not at first, but upon reflection, that George Balcombe, in John Keizer's circumstances, would have been precisely John Keizer. We find the same traits modified throughout—yet the *worldly difference* forms a distinction sufficiently marked for the purpose of the novelist. Lastly, Montague, with his low cunning, his arch-hypocrisy, his malignancy, his quibbling superstition, his moral courage and physical pusillanimity, is a character to be met with every day, and to be recognized at a glance. Nothing was ever more minutely, more forcibly, or more thoroughly painted. He is not original of course; nor must we forget that were he so, he would, necessarily, be untrue, in some measure, to nature. But we mean to say that the merit here is solely that of observation and fidelity.

To anyone familiar with Poe's theories of art, it is apparent that the quotation above is a subtle compliment to the author of the novel as a person but by no means a tribute to his ability as a novelist. Three characters are described as types. Two are said to be indistinguishable except for circumstances. Three are said to be natural, but that this represents limited approval is revealed by Poe's last sentence. Originality in characterization displayed the imagination at work, not mere observation. The question that had been occupying Poe's mind for several months was how to achieve verisimilitude in highly imaginative prose fiction. As we have seen, it was to be secured in terms of setting by the multiplication of detail. What about character? The unimaginative, skeptical type who narrated **"Ms. Found in a Bottle"** would have been to Poe's mind a nonentity, a species of Everyman. How, then, could an author win the reader's assent to a tale that presented a character so unusual as to be called an original? Although Poe's solution was irrelevant to the novel under consideration, he proposed it, following his customary practice of using the particular issue at hand as a point of departure to advance his own theory.

> Original characters, so called, can only be critically praised as such, either when presenting qualities known in real life, but never before depicted, (a combination nearly impossible) or when presenting qualities (moral, or physical, or both) which although unknown, or even known to be hypothetical, are so skilfully adapted to the circumstances which surround them, that our sense of fitness is not offended, and we find ourselves seeking a reason why these things *might not have been,* which we are still satisfied *are not.* The latter species of originality appertains to the loftier regions of the *Ideal.*

This "latter species of originality" began to appear in Poe's own tales, particularly in **"The Fall of the House of Usher."** In **"Berenice"** he had made a rudimentary effort to prepare the reader for the unusual character of Egaeus by summarizing his long isolation in the "gloomy, grey, hereditary halls" of his fathers, but few details were given, and Poe himself admitted that **"Berenice"** was not successful. In the character of Roderick Usher, however, Poe presented hypothetical qualities—neurotic sensitivity and fear exaggerated beyond the probable—but created in Usher's house a microcosm in which such a being could be expected to live, "skilfully" adapting Usher's qualities "to the circumstances which surround them." Such a technique, to Poe, was genuinely creative. An original character was "ideal" in the sense that the concept sprang from the mind of the author, instead of being copied from life like the characters of *George Balcombe.* Yet to secure verisimilitude (this quality was required in prose, but not in poetry), an environment must be invented in which the character would *seem* natural. To increase plausibility, Poe made the narrator of **"Usher"** a commonplace Everyman much like the narrator of **"Ms. Found in a Bottle."**

It will be seen by the above that Poe, quite tactfully, was arguing that the author of *George Balcombe* had displayed little imagination. The characters were true to life, but hackneyed. Other aspects of the novel were less objectionable. The style was "bold, vigorous, and rich," and there were few faults of grammar. The *thought of* the novel was not impeccable, but since it was voiced by the main character, the author should not be held responsible. Poe understood quite well that it was possible for a fictional character to be an independent creation, not the author's voice. This does not

mean that he was fully aware of the problem of identifying the "voice" of a novel, which is still a controversial issue. He customarily located the author voice in the commentary that appeared in the nineteenth-century novel as part of the privilege of the omniscient convention; and in a later review he attributed the chief value of a novel to just such comment.

Finally, Poe commended the plot of *George Balcombe,* but since he did not regard an ingenious plot as necessary or even desirable in longer works of fiction, this must not be taken as anything other than a tribute to the author's skill—his "ingenuity and finish in the adaptation of its component parts." Since a novel did not convey a unity of impression, Poe was to say in other reviews, such skill was only a secondary merit and usually went unappreciated.

Except for the unjustified claim that Tucker's was the best American novel, Poe accorded it no more praise than he had Bird's *The Infidel* and far less than he had given Bulwer. He concluded his review by stating that he did not wish to be understood as ranking *George Balcombe* with "the more brilliant fictions of some of the living novelists of Great Britain." White's accusation that Poe deliberately wrote a eulogistic review to gratify Tucker is unfair. Not that Poe never eulogized his friends. He did so more than once. In this particular instance, however, it is unlikely that White would have made the accusation had he not been making excuses to Tucker for his dismissal of an editor Tucker had praised; either this, or he failed to understand Poe's attempt to judge by literary principle. Remembering Poe's ridicule of Simms, White may have mistaken a tactful employment of standards for unqualified praise. . . .

Robert von Hallberg (essay date 1985)

SOURCE: "Edgar Allan Poe, Poet-Critic," in *Nineteenth-Century American Poetry,* edited by A. Robert Lee, Barnes & Noble, 1985, pp. 80-98.

[*In the following essay, Von Hallberg argues that Poe should be studied as a poet-critic instead of an academic critic. As a poet-critic Poe's focus is on constructing principles of literary criticism that can carve out a unique place for American literature, rather than on tracing the general development of literary history in the larger European context.*]

> We are lamentably deficient not only in invention proper, but in that which is, more strictly, *Art.* What American, for instance, in penning a criticism, ever supposes himself called upon to present his readers with more than the exact stipulation of his title—to present them with a criticism and *something beyond?* Who thinks of making his critique a work of art in itself—independently of its critical opinions?

Who indeed? Surely not I, and few of my colleagues aspire even to scholarly elegance. But Poe did write criticism that can be spoken of as not high art, but art all the same. From professors like myself, the world does not want art, but from poets, even when they thump out reviews, something more has come to be expected. Poet-critics, for instance, have certainly been more amusing than professors; sometimes they have even seemed to joke about their own efforts, though I never understood why they wanted to do so. It would be difficult to stipulate all the differences between the criticism produced by scholars and that of poet-critics, yet the distinction between these ways of writing about literature is commonly felt by both sorts of writers. It should be possible to indicate some of the special procedures and objectives of poet-critics. One justification for this effort is that American poet-critics have rather thoroughly shaken up literary opinion in this century; another is that the lessons academic critics might take from poet-critics have special force now that literary criticism is a major academic industry, the most prestigious branch of which is devoted to the study of itself. More particularly, the connection between Poe's criticism and his poetry shows not only how his poems rest on general poetic principles—we always expect that from poet-critics—but, much more interestingly, how impossible it was for him to write the sort of poetry he admired most.

Poe's literary achievement seems especially hyphenated—much more so than that of other poet-critics; his place in American literary history is still a bit anomalous. He remains a popular poet, but as Eliot has remarked [in *To Criticize the Critic,* 1965] he is read largely by the young and untutored. Sophisticated readers, like Eliot, often seem to regard his popularity as an embarrassment. And yet some poets, such as William Carlos Williams and Hart Crane, or Richard Wilbur and Daniel Hoffman, take Poe as a figure who cannot be ignored by later writers. In the history of American fiction, he seems more a pioneer of secondary genres—detective and gothic tales—than the master of a primary one. As a man of letters—poetry, fiction, and criticism—his place is secure, though as a poet he will always seem to many a mere verse-writer. More particularly, Poe can now be said to be along with Emerson one of the two earliest American poet-critics whose work continues to matter to contemporary writers. Since Poe's first literary critical effort in 1835—also the year in which Emerson began to lecture on English literature—an extraordinarily distinguished line of poet-critics has established this particular combination of talents as somehow distinctly American, and perhaps especially modern.

Insofar as Poe stands at the beginning of a line of poet-critics, this is a provisional sort of writing. These critics resist tradition in the name of independence; they attack the centre from the peripheries of the liter-ary culture. By at least 1835, Poe wrote expressly as a Southerner, aiming his judgements against the literary centres established in Boston and New York. Once he himself had made his way to New York, in 1844, he directed his barbs against Boston. However detailed were his criticisms of Emerson for obscurity, and of Longfellow for indolence, he never lost sight of their being established in Boston.

> [Bostonians] may yet open their eyes to certain facts which have long been obvious to all the world except themselves—the facts that there exist other cities than Boston—other men of letters than Professor Longfellow. . . . The fact is, we despise them [Bostonians] and defy them (the transcendental vagabonds!) and they may all go to the devil together.

When he was invited to speak at the Boston Lyceum, he read a piece of juvenilia out of contempt for the taste of his audience (he may even have been drunk at the time), and later did what he could to publicize the gesture. How pointed was his sense of being an outsider can be guessed from the half-truth on the title-page of his first book: *Tamerlane and Other Poems, By a Bostonian*.

Henry James spoke of Poe's criticism in 1879 [in *Hawthorne*] as 'probably the most complete and exquisite specimen of *provincialism* ever prepared for the edification of man.' A half-century later, Eliot said that Poe was 'a critic of the first rank'. Eliot had reason by then to know that the great American poet-critics would seem in retrospect to be mainly proud provincials: they have spoken from Hayley, Idaho; St. Louis, Missouri; Nashville, Tennessee; Gambier, Ohio; and Palo Alto, California. Poet-critics seem always to aim at independence of mind, an intelligence free of the corruptions of the centre. They have been unbeholden to publishers and reviewers and without the need to promote academic careers. One small sign of how they have insisted on their outré status is typified in Poe's unseemly habit of name-calling.

> In itself, the book before us is too purely imbecile to merit an extended critique. . . .

> The book is despicable in every respect. Such are the works which bring daily discredit upon our national literature.

> Your poem is a curiosity, Mr. Jack Downing; your 'Metrical Romance' is not worth a single half sheet of the pasteboard upon which it is printed.

> That any man could, at one and the same time, fancy himself a poet and string together as many

pitiable inanities as we see here, on so truly suggestive a thesis as that of 'A Lady Taking the Veil,' is to our apprehension a miracle of miracles.

But we doubt if the whole world of literature, poetical or prosaic, can afford a picture more utterly disgusting than the following. . . .

Mr. Channing must be hung, that's true.

What can we do but laugh outright at such phrases . . . such an ass as the author of 'Bug-Jargal?'

Robert Lowell said that Eliot had admitted taking particular delight in Poe's severity when it was directed against two of Eliot's own relatives. Poe, altogether deliberately, set an example of impolite, even reckless criticism—'pretentious, spiteful, vulgar', James said. Nearly a century later, Ezra Pound opened *Guide to Kulchur* with this promise:

> . . . I shall make a number of statements which very few men can AFFORD to make, for the simple reason that such taking sides might jeopard their incomes (directly) or their prestige or 'position' in one or other of the professional 'worlds'. Given my freedom, I may be a fool to use it, but I wd. be a cad not to.

One American poet-critic after another has displayed independence by speaking without respect for the makers of reputation, though no one has been more acutely aware of the finer shades of renown than Poe. Built right into this kind of literary criticism is an inclination to locate principles beyond the competition of contemporary interests. The tradition of poet-critics encourages transcendental rather than historicizing criticism. Poe's attempts to speak of Ideality in particular poems is just one particularly clear instance of this practice.

Poe repeatedly expressed contempt for the literary politics of his own moment. As a provincial he did not have access to the institutions that provide recognition, and there can be no question about his ambition to achieve renown. (He was not too discreet to say in print that his criticism, in a year's time, brought the circulation of the *Southern Literary Messenger* from 700 to nearly 5,000.) He criticized his own literary milieu on two principal counts. The first was its apparatus of boldly reciprocal promotion:

> The corrupt nature of our ordinary criticism has become notorious. . . . The intercourse between critic and publisher, as it now almost universally stands, is comprised either in the paying and pocketing of blackmail, as the price of simple forbearance, or in a direct system of petty and contemptible bribery. . . .

Pound and Yvor Winters later made the same point about London and New York literary life: outsiders are especially sensitive to this particular corruption of criticism. But beyond the moral turpitude of his contemporaries, Poe condemned other literary critics for a lack of independent judgement. 'Few American writers', he said, ' . . . have risen by merely their own intrinsic talents, and without the *a priori* aid of foreign opinion and puffery, to any exalted rank in the estimation of our countrymen.'

His thoroughly American response to this state of affairs was to attempt to establish the world of letters as a meritocracy. He made a point of praising demonstrated achievement rather than capability. And he tried to encourage Americans to attend to details in the examination of literary works:

> . . . Our criticism is nevertheless in some danger— some very little danger—of falling into the pit of a most detestable species of cant—the cant of *generality*. The tendency has been given it, in the first instance, by the onward and tumultuous spirit of the age. With the increase of the thinking-material comes the desire, if not the necessity, of abandoning particulars for masses. Yet in our individual case, as a nation, we seem merely to have adopted this bias from the British Quarterly Reviews. . . .

Poe was conscientious about examining details to the point of tedium; he wanted to cite evidence, like a detective, for all that he claimed about the works he examined, especially since he often criticized poets for plagiarism. The editor of the Virginia edition of Poe's collected works could not afford the space to reproduce Poe's extensive quotations. Poe can certainly seem picayune, but his motive was to free American writers from the domination of British litterateurs, and their American imitators, who cared more for their own notions and opinions than for the poems, novels and stories under review.

Like other poet-critics, Poe was extremely explicit. He did not hesitate to formulate definitions of poetry, drama, and the novel—though he suggested, too, that words cannot hem poetry in. His most celebrated critical essay, *The Philosophy of Composition,* sets out to render explicit every detail of artistic production, for in the best poems, he seems to have believed, all details can be articulated to general principles, however humble those principles may look when they are spelled out. 'If the practice fail,' he said, 'it is because the theory is imperfect'. Circumstance, the chance find of an apt word or phrase, counts for nothing.

> It is my design to render it manifest that no one point in its ["**The Raven**"'s] composition is referrible either to accident or intuition—that the work proceeded, step by step, to its completion with

the precision and rigid consequence of a mathematical problem.

In *Eureka* he claimed that what is commonly taken as intuition could certainly be explicated logically—given sufficient perspicacity and patience. He tried always to demystify literary criticism in order to free writers from those who claim to constitute an aristocracy of taste.

The melancholy that comes from this sort of criticism Poe knew all too well; his mind habitually doubles back on itself. On the one hand, he believed, in Enlightenment fashion, that ' . . . the finest quality of Thought is its self-cognizance. On the other, he felt that it is a

> curse of a certain order of mind, that it can never rest satisfied with the consciousness of its ability to do a thing. Still less is it content with doing it. It must both know and show how it was done.

Behind *The Philosophy of Composition* is that accursed sadness of self-consciousness, as though he had always to suspect himself of prefabricated poems, of mannerism. This self-destructiveness, he suggests, is an inevitable burden on poet-critics:

> To see distinctly the machinery—the wheels and pinions—of any work of Art is, unquestionably, of itself, a pleasure, but one which we are able to enjoy only just in proportion as we do *not* enjoy the legitimate effect designed by the artist:—and, in fact, it too often happens that to reflect analytically upon Art, is to reflect after the fashion of mirrors in the temple of Smyrna, which represent the fairest images deformed.

Poet-critics, then, turn against their own kind. Poe indicated that the most appropriate recognition of great artistic achievement is restraint, or even silence, on the part of critics and explainers.

Poe's constant reach for general principles usually makes him seem driven by abstract policies. He strove so to write logically—rather than tastefully—that his observations often sound woodenly consistent and categorical rather than deeply earnest or knowing; one often suspects this methodical critic of irony, especially when one recalls his belief that 'the style of the profound thinker is never closely logical'. His criticism repeatedly turns on a simple distinction between the true and the false, as though he were speaking mainly for effect. His obsession with plagiarism is just this, though in a characteristically doubled sense, because the greatest poets, he said, are those who, so absorbed in their art, are most prone to plagiarism and least damaged by the indictment. Poe's testing of texts for true and false properties can seem crude, mechan-

ical, and not entirely in good faith. He was indeed a categorical critic in the sense that his distinctions aim at these all-or-nothing discriminations. Seldom is he at pains to identify and somehow name a quality. Like a prosecutor, he rather pushes for conviction, which leaves him a dangerous model for other critics. Yet his bluntness has its rationale: for a critic committed, as Poe vigorously and honourably was, to tracking the literary culture, commenting on it monthly, this winnowing of the authentic from the *ersatz* is just the job at hand.

The most notorious of Poe's categorical conclusions is that a 'long poem is a paradox', since 'All high excitements are necessarily transient'. With that observation, a great deal of literary history recedes into darkness: Chaucer, Spenser, Shakespeare, Milton, and Wordsworth appear to have been unfortunately confused. This is Poe's point exactly. Insofar as his claim is valid, English literary history loses hegemony over American poets. Like a lawyer, Poe marshalled rhetoric and logic, more than wisdom or truth, to gain liberty for his own poetic ambition, and that of his countrymen. The history of American poetry through the 1840s, as he certainly knew, did not suggest that American poets were likely to be remembered in the way that British poets were. The best an ambitious young American poet might do in 1830, one might have thought, would have been to strive through imitation and self-education to live up to standards set on another continent.

Poe, however, for obvious reasons, preferred to argue that some recent American short poems excel 'any transatlantic poems. After all, it is chiefly in works of what is absurdly termed "sustained effort" that we fall in any material respect behind our progenitors.' These are the words of a poet whose longest poetic effort, a blank-verse drama entitled *Politian* (1835), he had the good sense not to bother to finish. The charge that American poetry was deficient in works of 'sustained effort' was put forward by critics writing for the quarterly reviews—the *North American Review* and the *Dial*. Poe framed his argument against this charge so as to attack the very idea of a quarterly review as he had three years earlier attacked the idea of a long poem. Journals, he claimed, were better suited than quarterlies to the contemporary American milieu because one sign of the times is that

> men are forced upon the curt, the condensed, the well-digested in place of the voluminous—in a word, upon journalism in lieu of dissertation. We need now the light artillery rather than the peace-makers of the intellect. I will not be sure that men at present think more profoundly than half a century ago, but beyond question they think with more rapidity, with more skill, with more tact, with more of method and less of excrescence in the thought. Besides all this, they have a vast increase in the thinking

material; they have more facts, more to think about. For this reason, they are disposed to put the greatest amount of thought in the smallest compass and disperse it with the utmost attainable rapidity.

Hence short poems and magazines are faithful to the moment, which is no small advantage in the eyes of one who, like many Enlightenment writers, saw progress wherever he looked. 'The day has at length arrived', Poe thought, 'when men demand rationalities in place of conventionalities.' With this 'rationality' about the advantages of short poems, he tried to think his way out of a mediocre literary milieu.

Poe is often taken as an extreme exemplar of American Romanticism. Yvor Winters, William K. Wimsatt, Jr., Cleanth Brooks, and Edmund Wilson all criticize his poetry and criticism in just these terms. From this view, he is interesting only as an illustrative figure, not influential as a poet or critic. If instead, however, one attends especially to his procedures as a poet-critic, he seems much less pure a Romantic; some of his principles and suppositions rather reflect what can be spoken of as Enlightenment notions. One might note, for instance, his frequent efforts to derive critical judgements from firm distinctions of genre and suppositions of decorum. But the most important of Poe's Enlightenment beliefs was simply the notion that his epoch was 'emphatically the thinking age;—indeed it may very well be questioned whether mankind ever substantially thought before.' From this faith in the power of clear, sceptical thought came the belief that a poet or critic can begin with first principles rather than precedents and, by a train of logical propositions, arrive at truths formerly obscured by blind prejudice. Moreover, one's explanations can fully prevail, because poetry, like all the world, is susceptible to clear, sceptical explanation. From the belief that general laws govern the details of literary history, it is but a short step to the notion that a critic's task is less importantly that of closely describing particular literary works than that of discovering and formulating the general laws that determine literary history. Poe's work is the first instance of a still strong tendency in American literary criticism to hold literary theory in higher regard than literary history.

This is another way of saying that however forceful Romanticism was in literary Europe of the 1830s and 1840s, American letters were still bound up with the Enlightenment ideals that brought nationhood to this former colony. Many of Poe's most distinctive literary ideas were, as he understood them, joined to national ideals. He was not an especially political poet-critic, but to overlook his nationalistic views renders his criticism and his poetry a bit peculiar. His poems and some of his criticism do now seem odd; but they are not properly regarded as incoherent, for they followed from a policy. Moreover, his strength as a model for later poet-critics has been sufficiently great that we still labour with some of his procedures without fully recognizing the policy they were once meant to implement. For instance, in order to sidestep the relative weakness of literary tradition in America, Poe argued that the power of the individual talent is supreme; the poet, for Poe and for many of our contemporaries, is above all an ingenious maker, and the lines of a poem are traces of—as we now say—strategies. Nor would Poe countenance the claim that poems cannot be fully understood independent of a context of thought, belief, or shared experience; poems were autotelic for him, as they have seemed to many modern American critics. And more than ever now, American critics give their pragmatic credence, as Poe urged, to details, especially those of stylistic analysis. Poe's reasons for this particular focus were nationalistic. Of course he hoped, as poet-critics always do, to encourage a taste for his own sort of poetry, but he also wanted to establish a distinctly American type of literary criticism—and the record indicates that he succeeded.

What Poe treasured most in terms of style is *range,* not merely of subject matter, but more particularly of tone. Although he returned to the term 'tone' repeatedly, he never claimed anything extraordinary for his sense of its meaning:

> Without pausing to define what a little reflection will enable any reader to define for himself, we may say that the chief constituent of a good style . . . is what artists have agreed to denominate *tone.* The writer who, varying this as occasion may require, well adapts it to the fluctuations of his narrative, accomplishes an important object of style.

There is a special reason why Poe would not bother to say that by tone he meant to refer, as I. A. Richards later did, to the attitude expressed by a writer; to presume a common understanding was just the point, because the measurement of range is made possible only by a prior sense of neoclassical decorum—of which attitudes are fitting to which subjects. One way of assessing a prose writer's command of tonal range is whether he or she can always seem not only various but, in diverse settings, just. The natural or easeful style—that commanded by Addison, as well as Washington Irving and Nathaniel Hawthorne—

> is but the result of writing with the understanding, or with the instinct, that the *tone,* in composition, should be that which, at any given point or upon any given topic, would be the tone of the great mass of humanity.

Fairness and civility, not novelty, are the objectives of this prose style.

Poe praises two sorts of writers very highly. First are those prose writers who give themselves so generously to their subjects that they seem to write naturally, without art—Defoe sets this standard.

> Men do not look upon it [*Robinson Crusoe*] in the light of a literary performance. . . . The powers which have wrought the wonder have been thrown into obscurity by the very stupendousness of the wonder they have wrought! We read, . . . close the book, and are quite satisfied that we could have written as well ourselves. . . . Indeed the author of Crusoe must have possessed, above all other faculties, what has been termed the faculty of *identification*. . . . Defoe is largely indebted to his subject.

Such a writer makes no compromise with the mere appurtenances of imaginative writing—with the bitter consequence, as Poe put it, that 'books thus written are not the books by which men acquire a contemporaneous reputation'.

The second sort of writer he praises is best exemplified by the Irish poet Thomas Moore, whose verse does not deliberately depart from the patterns of ordinary prose usage. Moore's

> is no poetical *style* (such, for example, as the French have—a distinct style for a distinct purpose), but an easy and ordinary prose manner, *ornamented into poetry*. By means of this he is enabled to enter, with ease, into details which would baffle any other versifier of the age, and at which Lamartine would stand aghast. For anything that we see to the contrary, Moore might solve a cubic equation in verse. . . . His facility in this respect is truly admirable, and is, no doubt, the result of long practice after mature deliberation.

The question of poetic style was rather different for Poe than that of prose style. 'The inventive or original mind', he said, 'as frequently displays itself in novelty of *tone* as in novelty of matter'. Prose writers like Addison do not aspire to novelty of attitude; they rather rely upon a consensus about appropriate attitudes. But poets explore surprising feelings, and the tone of poems is often stunningly unsettling. This is not to say that a poet's novelty of tone will be reflected in novel phrasing or syntax. The best poetic style is, like Moore's, that which is simply not constrained by the differences between poetry and prose. Moore's commitment to a plain, clear style allowed a wide range of subject matter; he concedes no subject, no range of experience (not even cubic equations), to essayists. (T. S. Eliot's well-known praise of the Metaphysicals' possession of 'a mechanism of sensibility which could devour any kind of experience' is much the same as Poe's admiration of Moore.) Poe's dream was less to write about the supremely melancholy subject, as he suggests in *The Philosophy of*

Composition, than to be able to write, like Moore, about anything at all.

How eager and fretful Poe was to extend his own range can be sensed in his strenuous explanation of the oddities of the English Metaphysical poets. For understandable reasons, he argues that Donne and Cowley were exceptionally sincere poets:

> They used but little art in composition. Their writings sprang immediately from the soul—and partook intensely of the nature of that soul. It is not difficult to perceive the tendency of this glorious *abandon*. To elevate immeasurably all the energies of mind—but again—so to mingle to greatest possible fire, force, delicacy, and all good things, with the lowest possible bathos, baldness, and utter imbecility, as to render it not a matter of doubt, but of certainty, that the average results of mind in such a school, will be found inferior to those results in one (ceteris paribus) more artificial: Such, we think, is the view of the older English Poetry, in which a very calm examination will bear us out.

The main line of English poetry is 'frank, guileless, and perfectly sincere'. Donne and Cowley are introduced here as the merely apparent exceptions that can nevertheless be accommodated to the general rule. The eclecticism of the Metaphysicals, their dangerously capacious range of tone, is meant to stand as evidence of their ultimate sincerity, for only poets thoroughly engaged by their subjects could skip over obvious incongruities as easily as they did. Poe strains so to resist reading the Metaphysicals ironically, because he has committed his own poetry and criticism to the belief that the best poems always express melancholy; the one kind of humour he would admit as legitimate to poetry was archness—just what one senses in his most ambitious critical pronouncements. His interest in stylistic range was a fascination for what he must have known he thoroughly lacked as a poet.

Sincerity for Poe, as for Victorian critics, was a term of high praise; or rather, since poets are seldom said to be more or less sincere, it is a test of authenticity in poetry. Self-consciousness is the great corrupter of style:

> . . . had the mind of the poet [John G. C. Brainard] been really 'crowded with strange thoughts', and not merely *engaged in an endeavor to think,* he would have entered at once upon the thoughts themselves, without allusion to the state of his brain. His subject [Niagara Falls] would have left him no room for self.

A false poet displays his or her skills in the hope that they will be mistaken for imagination. An acute critic, however, exposes those skills as wilful, predictable moves, mannerisms. The mannered writer is locked into an inflexible way of writing: 'That man is a des-

perate mannerist who cannot vary his style ad infini-
tum . . . '. Mannerism and range, as Poe properly sees
them, are exact contraries. The varieties of prose usage
provide a proper model for verse-writers, a hedge
against mannerism, but the prose manner must, as Poe
said, be *'ornamented into poetry'*.

Poe's way of thinking about poetic style involves this
one central paradox: the best is a plain style, but poetry is distinguished from prose by its ornaments. His
handling of this paradox had enormous impact on his
own verse. Most of the aspects of figurative language
that are commonly associated with ornamentation were
fiercely suppressed by Poe.

> Similes (so much insisted upon by the critics of the
> reign of Queen Anne) are never, in our opinion,
> strictly in good taste, whatever may be said to the
> contrary, and certainly can never be made to accord
> with other high qualities, except when naturally
> arising from the subject in the way of illustration—
> and, when thus arising, they have seldom the merit
> of novelty. To be novel, they must fail in essential
> particulars. The higher minds will avoid their
> frequent use. They form no portion of the ideal, and
> appertain to the fancy alone.

Poe knew well how often similes derive from self-
consciousness and quite wrongly suggest to many readers great imaginative powers; for him, similes always
reflect mere pride of technique. 'An artist', he said,
'will always contrive to weave his illustrations into the
metaphorical form'. Metaphor too, though, must be held
in tight rein. Poe criticized Edward Bulwer severely
for his 'mania of metaphor—metaphor always running
into allegory'. Pure allegory he regarded as an 'antique barbarism' (though one of his own best poems,
'The Haunted Palace', is plainly an allegory), and
personification as ludicrous (though his **'Stanzas [To
F. S. O.]'** are peppered with personifications). Metaphors should be used seldom and always kept from
escalating into allegory or personification. At just those
moments where modern readers have come to expect
metaphor, Poe argues for literal expression: ' . . . *subjects which surpass in grandeur all efforts of the human imagination are well depicted only in the simplest
and least metaphorical language'*.

Even in poetry, Poe thought, the object of style is clarity and simplicity, certainly not impressiveness. 'What
is worth thinking', he said, 'is distinctly thought: what
is distinctly thought, can and should be distinctly expressed, or should not be expressed at all'. Where figurative language is not conducive to clarity, it is indefensible. Even more importantly, where poetic syntax
impedes immediate clarity, it must be condemned:

> Few things have greater tendency than inversion, to
> render verse feeble and ineffective. In most cases
> where a line is spoken of as 'forcible', the force

may be referred to directness of expression. . . . In
short as regards verbal construction, *the more
prosaic* a poetical style is, the better.

The poetic style Poe admired most was one stripped
bare of most, but not quite all, poetic devices. Quaint-
nesses of phrasing were admissible occasionally, as in
poems on fantastic subjects. But most important of all,
an American poet properly ornaments his or her language into poetry through prosodic invention.

Poe placed a great burden on prosody: each foot lands
with a thud. His rhymes and meters are nothing if not
insistent, as though he had not heard of counterpoint
or off-rhyme. As always with Poe, there are general
principles involved here. *'Verse originates'* he claimed,
'in the human enjoyment of equality, fitness'. The more
absolute the rhymes, and emphatically regular the
rhythm, the closer a poet will be to the human origins
of musical language. No purpose was served, as he
reckoned, by concealing prosodic art. The opening lines
of a poem he placed first on a list of his best poems
rhymes 'moon' and 'June'. An earlier poem brought
'pass' and 'alas' together. He is always pushing so
hard: 'trod upon' / 'Parthenon'; 'gala night' / 'bedight'
(P, 325); 'Dian' / 'dry on'; 'linger' / 'sink her'. Even
when the rhymes are not exact, they are emphatic for
the effort behind them. No one reads Poe without
understanding at once why Emerson called him the
jingle man.

Poe presented himself as an American inventor among
prosodists. Blank verse seemed 'hackneyed' to him, as
it has to many later American poets. 'To break the
pentameter', Pound wrote, 'that was the first heave'.
William Carlos Williams's indebtedness to Poe is nicely
indicated by the small fact that Williams took his most
dubious and idiosyncratic prosodic term, the 'variable
foot', from Poe. In *The Philosophy of Composition*,
Poe said that his intention was above all to be original
in the versification of **'The Raven'**.

> The extent to which [originality] . . . has been
> neglected, in versification, is one of the most
> unaccountable things in the world. Admitting that
> there is little possible of variety in mere *rhythm*
> [i.e., in the choice of a normative foot], it is still
> clear that the possible varieties of metre and stanza
> are absolutely infinite—and yet, *for centuries, no
> man, in verse, has ever done, or ever seemed to
> think of doing, an original thing.*

Beyond the question of his own originality was the
matter of American poetry generally: if his countrymen continued to work in blank verse, for instance,
they would have to stand comparison with the masters
of that line (Milton is constantly on Poe's mind, when
he considers his own accomplishment). In order not to
produce a merely colonial literature, American writers

had to concoct forms of their own, however home-made they might appear. Why Poe thought that the need to innovate bore so exclusively on prosody is not surprising:

> That we are not a poetical people has been asserted so often and so roundly, both at home and abroad, that the slander, through mere dint of repetition, has come to be received as truth. Yet nothing can be further removed from it. The mistake is but a portion, or corollary, of the old dogma, that the calculating faculties are at war with the ideal; while, in fact, it may be demonstrated that the two divisions of mental power are never to be found in perfection apart. The *highest* order of the imaginative intellect is always preëminently mathematical; and the converse.

Americans were compelled by necessity, rather than inclined by temperament, to master the calculating faculties, Poe argued; but given that mastery, prosody was the one part of the art of poetry where it could be made to pay off. 'Faultless versification and scrupulous attention to grammar' were the two poetic virtues Poe was constantly trying to inculcate; he would test nearly every poet, tediously, for correctness. American poets needed to be correct in order to develop their own advantage over British poets, but also to avoid the condescension of their one-time colonizers.

With Poe, as with rather few other poets, one can see that his poems suffer from a particular conception of poetry. He believed that poetry is plain, clear language, but ornamented into poetry. The ornamentation of poetic language is something isolable—a rhyme, a repeated phrase—added to the plain sense. Although the poems are not simply a demonstration of his critical notions, his criticism does throw a special kind of light on the poems. In the poems and in the criticism, the same contradictions assert themselves, at the cost of the poems. For all Poe's admiration of stylistic range, Eliot was surely right to say that Poe lacks just this ability to express different sorts of feeling. Poe must have thought that poems like **"The Bells"** and **"The Raven",** as he explains it, express range, but they display a merely mechanical sort of variation of tone: in these poems the semantic sense of one statement varies from stanza to stanza; the obvious irony is that a misunderstanding has occurred. But two people, or a bird and a person, construing words differently is not what is properly meant by range of tone; Poe has simply concocted a mechanism for producing difference, not range.

Poe was indeed capable of writing verse that is properly spoken of as plain in style. However, the plain passages in his verse come not at all where Poe wanted to write well. Here are two passages from *Politian,* separated by only a few pages:

Lalage.   And dost thou speak of love
     To *me,* Politian?—dost thou speak of
     love
     To Lalage?—ah wo—ah wo is me!
     This mockery is most cruel!—most cruel
     indeed!
Politian. Weep not! oh, sob not thus!—thy
     bitter tears
     Will madden me. Oh mourn not, Lalage—

     Be comforted! I know—I know it all,
     And *still* I speak of love.

          . . . . .

     Sweet Lalage, *I love thee—love thee—
     love thee;*
     Thro' good and ill—thro' weal and wo
     I *love thee.*

                                        (P, 272)

Jacinta.   I made a change
     For the better I think—indeed I'm sure
     of it—
     Besides, you know it was impossible
     When such reports have been in
     circulation
     To stay with her now. She'd nothing
     of the lady
     About her—not a tittle! One would
     have thought
     She was a peasant girl, she was so
     humble.
     I *hate* all humble people!—and then
     she talked
     To one with such an air of
     condescension.
     And she had not common sense—of
     that I'm sure
     Or would she, now—I ask you now,
     Jacinta,
     Do you, or do you not suppose your
     mistress
     Had common sense or understanding
     when
     She gave you all these jewels?
                                        (P, 276-77)

Poe's accomplishment cannot be measured by *Politian,* but my point concerns only the obvious difference between these two passages—and the point is best made with unrhymed verse. The first passage is intended to be dramatic: Politian delivers the last two lines quoted on his knees. The writing is poor because the emotions represented are bluntly named, not examined, and those names are simply repeated relentlessly in order to provide emphasis. Poe clearly thought this an important moment in the play. The later passage is less important to the dramatic action, and the writing is far superior. Jacinta, alone on stage, is not posturing as Politian and Lalage do, but rather thinking and talking in verse; the enjambments and the parenthetical syntax keep the lines moving variously toward the larger coherence of the speech. Jacinta reveals the mix of her own feelings by choosing just the right, telling phrases—'tittle' and 'common sense'. In the second passage, Poe seems to have felt less need to write remarkably, for the sake of the action, whereas in the first he is straining—by merely repeating blunt phrases—to elevate his subject. He was not an inept poet—as the second passage demonstrates—but his poems are inept just when he would have them be sublime. When he wrote without thinking about Poetry, he could write plainly, thoughtfully, and sensitively, as some of his slighter efforts, such as '**To—— — ——**' and '**Deep in Earth**' show.

The great caution advanced by Poe's career as poet-critic is against the excesses of provincialism. Certainly being an outsider among men of letters enabled him to write independently, and fiercely, in ways that remain admirable. And yet his sense that he could concoct formal principles with rather little regard for literary precedents just as surely doomed his poems to remain, like Edsels, a species unto themselves. Effective advocacy of a plain style in American poetry had to wait for later poet-critics—Ezra Pound, T. S. Eliot, and Yvor Winters. At the outset of the American line of poet-critics is this extremist who took a purely intentionalist approach to writing, chiefly because the alternative could so easily have meant, in the 1830s and 1840s, subservience to British letters. This sense that the independent writer was free to write anything at all was enormously invigorating; Poe wrote about naval history, travel literature, middle eastern geography. The job of a literary critic was to educate himself and his readers in very broad terms; the work of Pound, Eliot and Charles Olson show that Poe's example has made a difference. However technical poet-critics can be, they continue to see the job of literary criticism in terms that are much broader, just in terms of subject matter, than academic critics ever dare to believe. Yet that very sense of independence is surely responsible for Poe's odd place in literary history—as a kind of tinkerer among poets.

FURTHER READING

Adkins, Nelson F. "'Chapter on American Cribbage': Poe and Plagiarism." *The Papers of the Bibliographical Society of America* XVII (Third Quarter 1948): 169-210.

Discussion of Poe's views on plagiarism with special reference to the "little Longfellow war."

Alterton, Margaret. *Origins of Poe's Critical Theory.* New York: Russell & Russell, Inc., 1965, 191 p.

Examines the influence of Poe's interest in and knowledge of law, scientific problems, and philosophic ideas on the development of his literary theories.

Campbell, Killis. *The Mind of Poe and Other Studies.* New York: Russell & Russell, Inc., 1962, 238 p.

Detailed analysis of Poe as a man of letters in the context of the critical reception by his contemporaries.

Hubbell, Jay B. "Poe and the Southern Literary Tradition." *Texas Studies in Literature and Language* XI, No. 2 (Summer 1960): 151-71.

Evaluates Poe's contribution to the creation of an American literary tradition with specific reference to his status as a southern writer.

Jacobs, Robert D. *Poe: Journalist and Critic.* Baton Rouge: Louisiana State University Press, 1969, 464 p.

A chronological review of Poe's criticism focusing on the development of Poe's literary theories and his practical application of these theories as an editor and book reviewer. A portion is excerpted above.

Moore, John Brooks. *Selections from Poe's Literary Criticism.* New York: F. S. Crofts & Co., 1926, 199 p.

A good selection of Poe's critical writings that represents him as an important figure in the developing journalistic culture of nineteenth-century America.

Moss, Sidney P. *Poe's Literary Battles: The Critic in the Context of His Literary Milieu.* Durham, North Carolina: Duke University Press, 1963, 266 p.

Analysis of Poe as a working critic which examines his preoccupation with editorial concerns in relation to the embattled journalistic milieu of his times. Chapter 5, concerning the literary controversy between Poe and Longfellow, is excerpted above.

Winters, Yvor. *In Defense of Reason.* Denver: Alan Swallow, 1938, 611 p.

Highlights the connection between Poe's critical and literary works, both of which are seen to exemplify Poe's extreme romantic sentimentalism. For an excerpt from this study of Poe, see *NCLC,* Volume 1.

Ann (Ward) Radcliffe

1764-1823

(Born Ann Ward) English novelist, poet, and journalist.

For further information on Radcliffe's works and career, see *Nineteenth-Century Literature Criticism,* Vol. 6.

INTRODUCTION

Considered the most important writer of the English Gothic school, Radcliffe transformed the Gothic novel from a mere vehicle for the depiction of terror into an instrument for exploring the psychology of fear and suspense. Her emphasis on emotion, perception, and the relationship between atmosphere and sensibility helped pave the way for the Romantic movement in England. Radcliffe's best-known novel, *The Mysteries of Udolpho* (1794), ranks as one of the chief exemplars of the Gothic genre.

Biographical Information

Radcliffe was born in London to a lower-middle class family. Afflicted with asthma from childhood, she was reserved and read widely. Though her parents had given her an education that was typical for a young lady of her class in the nineteenth century, they did not encourage her to continue her studies. But as a young woman, Radcliffe associated with the bluestockings Lady Mary Wortley Montague and Hester Lynch Piozzi, who, it is believed, inspired and stimulated her intellectually. In 1787, she married William Radcliffe, later editor of the *English Chronicle,* who recognized her talent and encouraged her to begin writing novels. It was not many years before she became the most popular novelist of her generation in England. But Radcliffe shunned most publicity; sixty years after the novelist's death, Christina Rossetti would attempt to write her biography and would be unable to find enough information about her subject to complete it. In 1817, at the peak of her fame, Radcliffe withdrew entirely from public life. Perhaps, as Sir Walter Scott believed, she stopped writing out of disgust with tawdry and maudlin imitators who were trivializing the Gothic novel. Her own poor health, her husband's illness, and the deaths of both her parents may also have played a role; moreover, her inheritance from her parents made her financially independent, so that she no longer had to write for income. Radcliffe's virtual disappearance triggered rumors of a nervous breakdown and wild stories that she had died in an insane asylum and that her imitators were haunted by her ghost. These rumors, unchecked, eventuated in premature obituaries appearing in various newspapers.

Major Works

Radcliffe's first novel, *The Castles of Athlin and Dunbayne: A Highland Story* (1789), made no impression on readers or reviewers. Though the novel had plenty of the picturesque description and dark atmospherics that would become her trademark, it was Radcliffe's next work, *A Sicilian Romance* (1790), that earned her critical attention and respect. In this novel, the distinctive features of her style ripened: the use of landscape to create a mood of terror, mystery, and suspense; intricacy of plot; a lyrical prose style; and a focus on individual psychology. Critics have noted that Radcliffe's linking of terror and beauty corresponds to Edmund Burke's philosophy of the sublime. Her standard motif of the heroine in distress shows an acquaintance with sentimental novelists such as Charlotte Smith, but her most direct literary precedent can be found in the Gothic writings of Horace Walpole. Perhaps the most distinctive feature of Radcliffe's style is her explained endings. Once she has elaborately set up a mystery, hinting at supernatural agency and piquing the reader's curiosity, Radcliffe invariably resolves her plots in a rational and orderly way, providing reasoned explanations for ostensibly supernatural events. Not all critics have praised this feature of her style, but it is generally agreed that this is one of her major contributions to the English novel. Radcliffe's next two novels, *The Romance of the Forest* (1791) and *The Mysteries of Udolpho,* firmly established her reputation and popularity as England's preeminent Gothic novelist and as a best-selling author in the United States and Europe as well as in England. In 1797, she published *The Italian; or, The Confessional of the Black Penitents,* considered by some to be her best novel. Its principal villain, the monk Schedoni, is often seen as a forerunner of the Byronic hero—brooding, mysterious, and fascinating. Radcliffe's last novel, *Gaston de Blondeville; or, The Court of Henry III. Keeping Festival in Ardenne* (1826), was published posthumously and never enjoyed the success of her earlier novels.

Critical Reception

Early critical response to Radcliffe's novels was mixed. Samuel Taylor Coleridge complained that her explained endings frustrated the reader's expectations; other detractors found her explanations tedious, her style wooden, and her characters flat. Sir Walter Scott, however, called Radcliffe "the first poetess of romantic fiction" for her elaborate natural descriptions, and others praised her brilliant rhetorical style, her examination of the psychology of fear, and her affirmation of the moral order in concluding each novel. Thomas Noon Talfourd argued that Radcliffe's anticlimactic endings were merely in keeping with the canons of the Gothic style, whose conventions, Radcliffe believed, excluded the genuinely supernatural. At the turn of the century, Walter Raleigh helped to enhance critical understanding of Radcliffe by pointing out her influence on the English Romantic movement. Later, Virginia Woolf disputed Talfourd, arguing that Radcliffe was remarkably free from convention.

In the 1940s Wylie Sypher introduced a radically new critical approach to Radcliffe, applying a Marxist analysis to her works and finding in them conflicting bourgeois and anti-bourgeois tendencies. Radcliffe attracted little other critical attention until the late 1950s, when D. P. Varma's overview of her novels excited a fresh curiosity about her works. Some of this new interest, on the part of such critics as Nelson C. Smith and Robert Kiely, focused on the extent and purpose of Radcliffe's preoccupation with the irrational. Feminist studies by such critics as Ellen Moers, Coral Ann Howells, and Patricia Spacks examined the psychology and sociology of Radcliffe's heroines and their specifically female consciousness. There is general agreement now that Radcliffe novels do not strictly adhere to the Gothic conventions. Radcliffe often exceeded or even undermined the conventional limits of the Gothic, either by a kind of moral didacticism that elevates the Gothic by broadening its scope, as Kate Ellis has suggested, or by a satiric use of certain conventions, as argued by D. L. Macdonald. Many critics, like Kim Michasiw and Mary Fawcett, have examined relationships of power between men and women in Radcliffe's novels as well as the prevailing social and political institutions inside and outside the novel, which set the conditions for the characters' actions and for the text itself. Comparisons of Radcliffe's novels with those of other female novelists outside the Gothic tradition, such as Fanny Burney and Jane Austen, have also helped increase critical understanding of Radcliffe's work. Today, Radcliffe is generally regarded as an influential writer and a key figure in the movement that freed the imagination from conventional and rationalistic constraints, helping to usher in English Romanticism.

PRINCIPAL WORKS

The Castles of Athlin and Dunbayne: A Highland Story (novel) 1789

A Sicilian Romance (novel) 1790
The Romance of the Forest (novel) 1791
The Mysteries of Udolpho (novel) 1794
A Journey Made in the Summer of 1794 through Holland and the Western Frontier of Germany (journal) 1795
The Italian; or, The Confessional of the Black Penitents (novel) 1797
The Poems of A. Radcliffe (poetry) 1815
The Novels of Ann Radcliffe. 10 vols. (novels) 1821-24
Gaston de Blondeville; or, The Court of Henry III. Keeping Festival in Ardenne. St. Alban's Abbey: A Metrical Tale, with Some Poetical Pieces (novel and poetry) 1826

CRITICISM

Mary Laughlin Fawcett (essay date 1983)

SOURCE: "*Udolpho*'s Primal Mystery," in *Studies in English Literature, 1500-1900*, Vol. 23, No. 3, Summer, 1983, pp. 481-94.

[*In this essay, Fawcett discusses how symbols used in* The Mysteries of Udolpho *reveal to the reader the world of 1790s England and especially the condition of sexuality, in a way that confirms Blake's verdict that contemporary love is crippled by the struggle between desire and restraint.*]

In Ann Radcliffe's novel, ***The Mysteries of Udolpho,*** a daughter wishes to know the secrets of her father's past and to understand events which occurred twenty years ago, at the time of her own birth, but which her father has, on his deathbed, forbidden her to search out. Curiosity and taboo, desire and restraint—we readers are drawn into a magic circle of deathbeds and birth anxieties. Mrs. Radcliffe hints at a truth, at a scene to be re-animated; Emily St. Aubert, her main character, looks repeatedly at scenes which remind us of obsessional neurotic dreams, dreams which a psychoanalytic patient might have in order to screen the primal scene, the child's vision of the sexual act between the parents, proleptically that act at which the child was engendered. Readers who become involved in Mrs. Radcliffe's fiction are drawn into this search for the primal scene, and many readers have testified to the compelling power of the novel's pursuit-structure. As an early reviewer said of another of Mrs. Radcliffe's novels, it "engages the attention strongly, and interests the feelings very powerfully. Leslie Fiedler [in *Love and Death in the American Novel*, rev. ed, 1966] recognizes that this engagement is essentially sexual:

The primary meaning of the gothic romance, then, lies in its substitution of terror for love as a central theme of fiction. The titillation of sex denied, it offers its readers a vicarious participation in a flirtation with death—approach and retreat, approach and retreat, the fatal orgasm eternally mounting and eternally checked.

We feel that we may be granted a sight of some kind, so we keep reading and Emily keeps looking. This source of narrative interest may speak especially to women, whether of Mrs. Radcliffe's time or our own, because it promises to reveal, through suggestion and imagery, some of the facts of sexual life, and to re-create, through Emily's desire to "see" the place of her own engendering, some of women's psychic states.

Gothic fiction used to be regarded primarily as a symptom of degenerated taste and a longing to escape from everyday reality. Increasingly now, critics are thinking of it as a kind of psychoanalysis. They use the rich material within the narratives to show how the genre of the gothic embodies the unconscious yearnings of characters and readers. As Fiedler says, the terror in such works as *The Castle of Otranto* is not less true than it seems, but more true, since the imagery of such fictions (for example, the maiden fleeing endlessly through a hostile landscape) is the imagery of our dreams and our repressed guilts and fears. Tzvetan Todorov says [in *The Fantastic: A Structural Approach to a Literary Genre*, trans. R. Howard, 1973] that the supernatural in fantastic works of literature (under which rubric the gothic novel falls) provides the reader with a sense of "pan-determinism," just as does the technique of Freudian dream-analysis. These fictions allow writer and reader to sneak subversive themes past both society and their own superegos. Todorov claims that psychoanalysis "has replaced (and thereby made useless) the literature of the fantastic." The aim of psychoanalysis is to make clear the reasons for the symptoms of an individual's disturbance; if a literary work is like a person, the critic may perform such an analysis for it, too.

Beyond such practical psychoanalysis of each work, the critic must also discuss the *truth* of the symbology discovered. That is, we need to look at what the novel is openly and secretly telling us about its world. Emily discovers scenes which match her need; she also discovers, as I hope to show, scenes which body forth the condition of sexuality in the world of the 1790s. A parallel contemporary perspective on this condition can be found in passages from Blake. One can hardly imagine a meeting between Mrs. Radcliffe and Blake, but in 1794 she had published **The Mysteries of Udolpho,** and he had completed *The Book of Thel, The Songs of Innocence and of Experience,* and *The Marriage of Heaven and Hell*. Their ideas seem diametrically opposed. St. Aubert, Emily's father and the moral

arbiter of the novel, declares "All excess is vicious"; Blake answers that "The road of excess leads to the palace of wisdom." Yet the novel oddly but indirectly affirms Blake's verdict that contemporary love is sick, crippled by contention between desire and restraint, both murdered and murderous.

I

When Blake's Thel "saw the couches of the dead," the source of the heart's "restless twists," at the end of *The Book of Thel,* she asked the question which Emily asks throughout the novel: "Why a little curtain of flesh on the bed of our desire?" **The Mysteries of Udolpho** is made up of a repetitive series of revelations, veils (or curtains) pulled aside, and beds, especially death beds, questioned for meaning. The bedroom is the novel's dreamlike center. Whatever chateau or palazzo Emily enters, we readers soon find ourselves in some bedroom, usually dark, with heavy furniture and ancient hangings. Maria Edgeworth gently mocked this focal point in her description of a hotel-room in Bruges: "It was so large and dark that I could scarcely see the low bed in a recess . . . covered with a dark quilt. I am sure Mrs. Radcliffe might have kept her heroine wandering about this room for six good pages." The bed, the recess, and the veil are all here. If Emily goes to the window to look at the view, the scenery often reinforces the sense of sexual duality: she sees mountains on one side and fruited plains on the other, or a rampart walk on the left and sun-illumined hills on the right. A reader of this novel will easily remember, or confuse, ramparts, walls, galleries, turrets, wings, passages, and staircases surrounding the crucial bedroom with its veiled recess. Emily spends nights *not* sleeping, but wondering, in anxious and wakeful anticipation of something as yet unknown. The bed itself is thus a locus of questioning anxiety, as well as a thing to be searched out and seen; it is a powerful central symbol.

When we turn to the human setting, we ask ourselves what Emily can learn about the primal scene and about sexual relations in general by observing married people - people of the age to have, not merely to look towards or back to, sexual experience. We notice immediately that Emily's parents are the only happy couple in a well-populated novel, and that the St. Auberts are *not* seen in their private apartments or anywhere near a bed; they are placed in the countryside, in favorite "retreats," or at their fishing cottage. Neither parent is robust or vital; the wisdom of both is the wisdom of weakness and restraint. Mme. St. Aubert, the only biological mother in a novel filled with abbesses, aunts, mistresses, and stepmothers, dies of a lingering fever by the end of the first chapter. "The progress of this disorder was marked, on the side of Madame St. Aubert, by patient suffering, and subjected wishes." Her father, also, is a figure in retreat, although it takes him longer to succumb. We first see him despondent over the future destruction of trees on his former estate, a destruction which he is helpless to prevent. Later he languishes on Emily's hands during an abortive trip to recover his health, and he dies of the same wasting fever after thinking himself ruined. "St. Aubert lingered till about three o'clock . . . and, thus gradually sinking into death, he expired without a struggle, or a sigh."

The resignation and passivity of this one "happy" couple is strongly contrasted with the conflicts within other married couples. Each time Emily or the reader is admitted, actually or vicariously, into the private apartments of married people, she finds open anger or wasting silence. When Emily's aunt marries the infamous Montoni, the quarrels begin soon after a brief period of disappointment and coolness. Montoni has sexual experience and energy, but he withholds himself from his wife and directs his aggression into his condottiere schemes, sitting up late with his warrior vassals. In bedroom scenes overheard by Emily and by Annette, the maid, he threatens his wife with deprivation unless she signs over her settlements to him. Rather than sign over what is rightfully hers, Mme. Montoni dies, partly of starvation and partly of a fever. Whatever the rights and wrongs of this situation—and a modern reader may feel that Mme. Montoni is not accorded dignity enough in this novel (since she is a stupid woman, she resists him for the wrong reason)—the marriage seems founded on deprivation and fever, and consummated only in her death.

We see another couple, newly married, disintegrate into stifled conflict when the second plot-line introduces the marriage of the Marchioness de Villeroi (Emily's other aunt) and the Marquis. Each of them has an outside attachment. The (good) wife was really, virtuously in love elsewhere, but has given up her lover to marry her father's choice. The (bad) husband has a distempered Italian mistress, whom he has deceived and abandoned and by whom he is in turn deceived into murdering his wife. Through the words of Dorothée, the servant, we "see" them in privacy—the modesty, grace, and humility of the wife and the "gloomy and fretful" jealousy of her husband. We especially "see" the mixture of realization and horror on the face of the Marquis when he hears his wife has been poisoned. If this is, as I think, a vision of sexual knowledge, it is a gnosis of violation. Once again marriage is consummated in death. Mme. Montoni, with her unfeeling pride and stupidity, and the Marchioness, her eyes mildly raised to heaven, present themselves to us much more vividly than Emily's own mother, as two versions of the effect sexual experience has on women. Though neither woman is Emily's mother, both are, during this narrative, paradoxically both newly married *and* old enough to be her mother. The men react in turn with war schemes or settled melancholy, that is, with aggression or passivity.

II

Admitted to the private apartments, then the inner chamber, then the veiled, recessed bed itself, what privileged sight does Emily see? She looks upon a corpse, in fact, upon several corpses. "Within, appeared a pale and emaciated face. She . . . shuddered as she took up the skeleton hand, that lay stretched upon the quilt; then let it drop, and then viewed the face with a long, unsettled gaze." Mme. Montoni is still alive at this time, and she lingers for another chapter, never revealing exactly "what had abandoned her, she to this present deplorable state." After Montoni abandoned her, she caught a raging fever, perhaps a more virulent strain than the one which killed the St. Auberts. Mme. Montoni dies, it seems, of the consequences of female passion, as a warning to the woman who chooses the wrong husband.

This vision of the actual corpse on the bed is anticipated by two other recess-visions and followed by still a third, all with remarkably similar content. When the mysterious Barnardine leads Emily through a portal (into a literally sub-liminal experience) and locks her in a disused torture chamber, Emily imagines the poor wretch who might have starved to death fastened to that chair in that room. She *imagines* deprivation, but she *sees* violation. Drawing aside a bed curtain in order to find a place to sit, she sees

> a corpse, stretched on a kind of low couch . . . the features, deformed by death, were ghastly and horrible, and more than one livid wound appeared in the face. Emily, bending over the body, gazed, for a moment, with an eager, frenzied eye.

Death in the chamber can come in two ways, by starvation (in imagination) and by blows (to the real body); we may be tempted to call these the female and the male possibilities. Emily's "eager" look does not disclose the corpse's identity; she releases the curtain before she can "know" the sight completely. For not very probable reasons, the sight of this corpse must be kept secret; it is seen but not known or told. Emily's personality, while itself changeless, is filling up with more and more sights, and they are discharged less and less often. She becomes, as I hope to indicate later, a kind of romantic nature-lover, almost pure eyeball.

The other recess-vision is held within her even longer; further knowledge of it is withheld from the reader for over three hundred pages. Emily is curious about the "picture" behind the veil; because it is reported to depict Signora Laurentini, the mysterious former owner of Udolpho who left the castle to Montoni after her disappearance twenty years ago (again, at the time of

Emily's birth). Emily and the servants imagine Montoni has had her murdered. Drawn by curiosity, Emily, stands in front of this massive object. The action which follows her "high expectation" of this sight is curiously muted and suppressed: "She paused again, and then, with a timid hand, lifted the veil; but instantly let it fall—perceiving that what it had concealed was no picture." The thing she sees, about which we are not told, is, she thinks, not art but reality, not a representation which would call for her sympathy but an actuality which calls for identification. This object, when it is finally revealed to us, is in fact mid-way between art and reality, and closely akin to the bed-room corpse revelations. Behind the black veil is "a recess of the wall" containing "a human figure of ghastly paleness, stretched at its length . . . the face appeared partly decayed and disfigured by worms." The lifted veil again reveals a bedroom of death, a scene thought to have come from the period of her birth. Actually this is a wax figure, a grisly *memento mori*. The more Emily investigates her origins, the more such mementi she comes upon in the form of progressive, replicated corpses.

One further instance of this primal discovery will suffice to show that the "horrors" spaced throughout the novel seem to replicate themselves, seem, as in a recurring dream or a hall of mirrors, to force Emily to *see* the same thing each time, in each chateau. In the Count's chateau, Emily, accompanied by the garrulous Dorothée, goes into the bedroom of the Marchioness who died twenty years ago. There, her things are set out in Miss Havisham-like clutter and stasis. Dorothée throws the Marchioness's black veil over Emily, who disengages herself from it. They proceed to the bed— the object of their visit, and almost their reverence. There they see the black pall over the bed shake; then "the apparition of a human countenance rose above it." The two run out "as fast as their trembling limbs would bear them." The bed of death, which ought to memorialize the past, now appears still alive, perhaps still copulating, and able to transfer its shakings to their trembling limbs.

Each of these bed-manifestations is finally explained in the style of rationalized gothic. But even the explanations add something to the mystery and complexity of the image itself, since in each case the horrible sight has, for Emily, a profound sexual ambiguity. Emily apparently thinks the hacked corpse of one of Montoni's male soldiers is the body of her aunt. She thinks the "picture" is the body of Signora Laurentini, but it is presumably male since it was made for an early lord of the line. The Marchioness's bed with its rising countenance proves to be the trick of smugglers who, we later hear, are particularly masculine, rough and evil-looking. All of Emily's "mistakes" about the sexual identities of the corpse figures indicate the *real* content of these visions: behind the veil is an image of the generating marriage bed of her parents, of the violence and "death" of the sexual act. The single image is composed of two sexes, the beast with two backs. The contorted, wounded, or gnawed faces are like faces in orgasm.

To complete our primal picture, there are two other recess-visions to consider, this time of living people. Emily "sees" the Marchioness through the reminiscences of the servant Dorothée, who saw her in the oriel the night she died. *Now,* "in this closet . . . a robe and several articles of her dress were scattered . . . as if they had just been thrown off." *Then,* "the tears fell upon her cheeks, while she sung a vesper hymn. . . . She had been at prayers, I fancy, for there was the book open on the table beside her—aye, and there it lies open still!" The past and the present are simultaneously alive in this description; the one evokes the other. This picture of the Marchioness in despair in a recess recalls to us Emily's sight of her father, early in the novel. Through "panes of glass . . . of a closet-door," she has seen the figure of her father looking over some papers "with a look so solemn . . . which was mingled with a certain wild expression, that partook . . . of horror." He considers a picture (of the Marchioness, we learn later), then prays silently: "When he rose, a ghastly paleness was on his countenance." Emily is spying, out of a concern for his health, but also, as the narrator tells us, out of a "mixture of curiosity and tenderness." It is this combination of motives which suggests the unconscious component, her desire to piece out the primal scene.

If, taking liberties with Mrs. Radcliffe's sequence, we conflate these two scenes, we may recapture something of the scene Emily almost "sees" throughout the novel. A woman is ready for sex, *un*veiled before a man, her clothes "scattered." The man's expression partakes of "horror"; "When he rose, a ghastly [ghost-like, deathlike] paleness was on his countenance." The combined scene behind the veil suggests the woman's passion and its continuance, its ever-open posture, together with the man's horror of that too-great need. We may think of Blake's tautological little poem, and how far it is from Mrs. Radcliffe's primal scene:

> What is it men in women do require
> The lineaments of Gratified Desire
> What is it women do in men require
> The lineaments of Gratified Desire.

The "lineaments" of these corpse images complete the picture of sexual wounding, deprivation, and mutual disappointment. In this novel what is dead comes to life again; what is over, starts over again. The plot itself mirrors this sexual discontinuity. As Fiedler says: "the middle of Mrs. Radcliffe's books seem in their compulsive repetitiveness a self-duplicating nightmare from which it is impossible to wake." The central act represented is stymied in a cycle of need and despair—female openness and male horror. Through the texture of the plot, readers may feel implicated in this act, and even part of the cycle.

III

The veiled content of this primal scene, the passionate woman and the exhausted man, illuminates, I think, some aspects of both the novel's characterization and its moral. The novel educates its women readers to the dangers of too-great sexual energy and desire. For example, the women who surround Emily are a gratuitously unpleasant breed; they want too much, and, even worse, are proud of their desires. Mme. Quesnel, an Italian heiress, wishes to "excite" envy by describing "the splendour of the balls, banquets, and processions . . . in honour of the nuptials of the Duke de Joyeuse." The Countess of Villefort, stepmother of Blanche, "could occasionally throw into [her manners] an affectation of spirits, which seemed to triumph over every person." Valancourt, the hero (or "male ingenue"), nearly falls prey to one of these women, a Countess whose "wit prolonged the triumph of [her beauty's] reign." Emily's aunt is the most notable proof that women of some sexual experience become insatiable, almost inhuman. She "expatiated on the splendour of her house, [and] told of the numerous parties she entertained." There is a strong sexual undercurrent in these entertainings and prolongings; these women are voracious and insatiable, and they stare out at us from the novel, replicating the author's demand that we learn to fear our own desires. Emily's aunt "knew nothing of the conduct of a mind, that fears to trust its own powers." And yet, such portraits, heavily drawn as they are, may allow the female reader to recognize something of herself in them.

In the primal scene, the partner of this gaping, insatiable woman is the pale, exhausted man; accordingly, Emily's father articulates the moral burden of the novel. After his two sons die, St. Aubert turns his attention to his remaining child: "While he watched the unfolding of her infant character, with anxious fondness, he endeavoured, with unremitting effort, to counteract those traits in her disposition, which might hereafter lead her from happiness." Thus the father sets himself against the daughter's openness, her "unfolding," her high "degree of susceptibility." He sets himself, in fact, against the distinctive quality of her character. After the death of Mme. St. Aubert, he chastises Emily's grief:

> I have endeavoured to teach you, from your earliest youth, the duty of self-command; . . . as it preserves us in the various and dangerous temptations . . . [and] as it limits the indulgences which are termed virtuous, yet which, extended beyond a certain boundary, are vicious, for their consequence is evil. All excess is vicious.

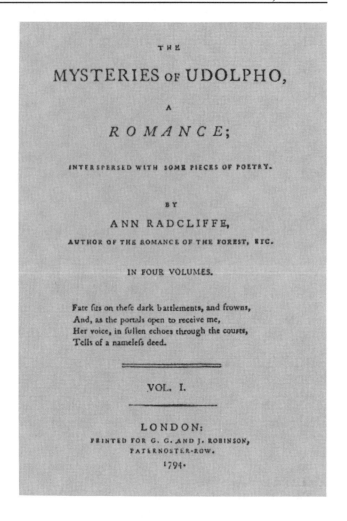

THE

MYSTERIES of UDOLPHO,

A

ROMANCE;

INTERSPERSED WITH SOME PIECES OF POETRY.

BY

A N N   R A D C L I F F E,

AUTHOR OF THE ROMANCE OF THE FOREST, ETC.

IN FOUR VOLUMES.

Fate fits on thefe dark battlements, and frowns,
And, as the portals open to receive me,
Her voice, in fullen echoes through the courts,
Tells of a namelefs deed.

VOL. I.

LONDON:
PRINTED FOR G. G. AND J. ROBINSON,
PATERNOSTER-ROW.
1794.

Title page for Radcliffe's best-known novel.

His "endeavours" already sound weary and exhausted, she is so easily "lead" "beyond" his boundaries. What is true for grief could very well be true for love, since women's sexual response is, strictly speaking, unnecessary to the sexual act. Emily is like Oothoon, "open to joy and to delight," while St. Aubert is like Theotormon, who "sits / Upon the margind ocean conversing with shadows dire" (*Visions of the Daughters of Albion,* plate 6, line 22; plate 8, lines 11-12). In a curious way, St. Aubert would agree with Blake: "You never know what is enough unless you know what is more than enough."

Thus, the novel opposes the restraint of the father to the passion of the daughter. Their differing experiences in nature are evidence of this struggle. Both love nature. Emily's is the new love of landscape, as we can hear in her question to her father:

> But hark! here comes the sweeping sound over the woodtops;—now it dies away. . . . Now the breeze swells again. It is like the voice of some supernatural

being— . . . Ah! what light is yonder? . . . it gleams again, near the root of that large chestnut: look, sir!

Her enthusiasm is not only for the isolated beautiful moment, but for its recurrence, its again-ness. She likes what sweeps and dies away and swells again; the effects she admires in nature have the rhythm of female orgasm. Her father's reaction is to deflate and miniaturize her enthusiasm. He sees a glow-worm where she feels divinity, and he "gaily" invites her to step further and see fairies. On their ill-starred trip for his health, he botanizes over "curious plants," while she wanders "wrapt in high enthusiasm . . . listening in deep silence to the lonely murmur of the woods." The cadence is Wordsworthian. Thus, he implicitly corrects her; by a concentration on the singular and the minute, he desexualizes experience in nature.

Her father's view of nature is fanciful; hers is imaginative. The two stances might almost be said to stand for or anticipate Coleridge's categories of Fancy and Imagination (here, the secondary Imagination). St. Aubert sees fairies; Coleridge says that "the Fancy must receive all its materials ready made from the law of association." Emily "loved . . . still more the mountain's stupendous recesses", her imagination is, in Coleridge's terms, "essentially vital, even as all objects (as objects) are essentially fixed and dead." She eagerly looks out to nature's recesses, just as she looks into the corpse-bed recesses. In looking behind the veil, her mind goes beyond the objects she sees; her imagination, in Coleridge's words, "dissolves, diffuses, dissipates" the actual fixed and dead objects, "in order to recreate" them in the primal scene she discovers. For Coleridge, the Imagination [in the words of Robert D. Hume, "Gothic Versus Romantic," *PMLA* 84 (March 1969)] "struggles to idealize and to unify." As we have seen, Emily's visions of the bed constitute a unity. Further, she does idealize what she sees. Her visions are both "ideal" and "idle" (Mrs. Radcliffe's spelling varies)—*idle* in that her conclusions are mistaken and finally irrelevant to the plot, but *ideal* in that her visions pertain to a conception in her mind. As in a recurring dream, the corpse visions open her mind to its own powers and images; over the real bodies lies the ideal unity of her vision.

IV

Thus we have the paradox of the seeker who looks *out* only to find what is inside herself—in this novel, the fresh, virginal young woman who repeatedly finds wounded and rotting corpses. Emily is especially prone to that "love, so natural to the human mind, of whatever is able to distend its faculties with wonder and astonishment." "Distend" has an unpleasantly full sound here, reminding us of a kind of pregnancy of mind, following a desire to be filled, to take in sights, to have knowledge. The suggestion of multiplicity, of

openness, againness, and repetition is muted but present in this passage, too. The *idle* terror is void, empty, insubstantial, and needs to be filled. The experience which Emily, and to some extent also the reader of this very long novel, undergoes throughout is an opening, a filling, almost a cramming. The narrator explains this human need in more attractive language, when describing why Emily draws the veil to see the "picture" of Laurentini, even though the prospect terrifies her: "But a terror of this nature, as it occupies and expands the mind, and elevates it to high expectation, is purely sublime, and leads us, by a kind of fascination, to seek even the object from which we appear to shrink." The aesthetic has come full circle here, as language used about sublime experience in nature is a prelude to the revelation of the primal corpse-scene. This language could also be applied to a woman's wooing posture in a society which overtly denies her a direct sexual expression: a "high expectation" coming from a "kind of fascination" makes women "seek even the object from which [they must] appear to shrink."

Emily is an aching center, unchanging; she seeks and finds only to seek again. The narrator occasionally interjects explanations, but for the most part remains an absolutely unselfconscious window onto an unselfconscious character. Thus with a peculiar vividness the scenes are conveyed directly into the minds and even the viscera of readers. To end this endless process, the author calls on marriage. Emily's curiosity is superficially satisfied, and she marries the re-validated Valancourt; morality and moralizing triumph over gnosis. But ominously, they marry under banners representing the "exploits of Charlemagne" in subduing the Saracens: "here, were seen the Saracens, with their horrible visors, advancing to battle; and there, were displayed the wild solemnities of incantation, and the necromantic feats . . . before the Emperor." The marriage takes place under the aegis of continuing conflict between reason and restraint (Charlemagne) and magic and desire (the Saracens). The war is not won or lost; it is stopped, in an ending which illustrates the Blakean process of atrophy [in *The Marriage of Heaven and Hell*]:

> Those who restrain desire, do so because theirs is weak enough to be restrained; and the restrainer or reason usurps its place & governs the unwilling.

> And being restrained it by degrees becomes passive till it is only the shadow of desire.

Emily, her sexual gnosis incomplete, retreats into marriage, her desire already, on the last pages, becoming a shadow of itself. In Blake's work, Thel flees backward into the *vales* of Har; Emily returns to "the pleasant shades" of *La Vallée,* her childhood home. Both of these retreats, both shadowy valleys, signify failure of gnosis. But before each young woman retires, she has seen a vision which continues to bear meaning for the reader:

> She saw the couches of the dead, & where the fibrous roots of every heart on earth infixes deep its restless twists: A land of sorrows & of tears where never smile was seen.

Emily's and Thel's twin corpse-visions give out the secrets of sexual love; in this world, sexual relations are wounded or murdered, and female sexual needs *will not* be satisfied. This much the corpse in the veiled recess tell us. On the "couches of the dead," the heart still twists restlessly. Mrs. Radcliffe's imagery of the corpse in the recessed bed, and its implied message, is even stronger than the imagery of the diseased bed which Blake uses in *The Songs of Experience:*

> O Rose thou art sick.
> The invisible worm,
> That flies in the night
> In the howling storm:
>
> Has found out thy bed
> Of crimson joy:
> And his dark secret love
> Does thy life destroy.

Charles C. Murrah (essay date 1984)

SOURCE: "Mrs. Radcliffe's Landscapes: The Eye and the Fancy," in *The University of Windsor Review,* Vol. 18, No. 1, Fall-Winter, 1984, pp. 7-19.

[*In this essay, Murrah discusses how Radcliffe's reflective verbal pictures found in her published* Journey *serve as an introduction to her use of imaginative description of nature in her fiction.*]

Only fifteen years ago, it was still possible to say of Ann Radcliffe that her immense popularity in her own day had not at all survived the early nineteenth century and that only the literary historian or the fancier of fictional oddities continued to appreciate her works. But since that time our contemporary Romantic Movement has so much broadened and diversified its influence that the Gothic novel of the eighteenth century seems to have regained a portion of its former reading public, and the "Great Enchantress" of the English Romantic poets once more receives a certain reverence as the early harbinger of an expanded aesthetic awareness, now associated with the rehabilitation of romance in various modern forms, including science fiction. Since the mid-sixties, all of Mrs. Radcliffe's prose fiction has appeared in new editions or reprints; the yearly output of scholarly and critical articles devoted to her has substantially increased; and the Radcliffean doctoral dissertation has ceased to be a rarity. It is

doubtful, I think, that this recent spate of interest will persist, for, even in its midst, the abler critics of the Gothic Revival have remarked that Mrs. Radcliffe's works do not actually contain, in a fully developed form, those Gothic elements that have recently found most favor in the literary world. Nevertheless, the resurgent enthusiasm might have rewarding results if it redirects critical scrutiny to what the Radcliffe romances do contain and to a more careful reading of them as "documents in the history of the language of literary forms."

I suggest that such a scrutiny should include a careful analysis of Mrs. Radcliffe's descriptions of landscape. Long recognized as a particularly innovative and memorable literary achievement, these descriptive passages embody the most typical attitudes of her special artistic sensibility. They also indicate, in a way that has not been fully recognized, just how and why she failed to adapt that sensibility to the creation of wholly effective works of fiction.

As Raymond Havens has pointed out [in *Modern Language Notes,* 1951] Mrs. Radcliffe's "nature descriptions" exist in three forms: detailed and evocative notes that she jotted down in the unpublished journals of certain English tours, the more reflective and generalized verbal pictures of her published *Journey,* and the characteristically elaborated impressions of scenery that she included in her imaginative works. It will be informative to consider briefly the second of these types, as an introduction to their more important, fictive counterparts.

During the latter half of 1794, Ann Radcliffe and her husband made a sight-seeing tour of Holland, Germany, and the English Lakes. In her detailed journal of this expedition, published the next year, Mrs. Radcliffe describes the travelers' arrival at

> Kendal, white-smoking in the dark vale. As we approached the outlines of its ruinous castle were just distinguishable through the gloom, scattered in masses over the top of a small round hill, on the right. At the entrance of the town, the river Kent dashed in foam down a weir; beyond it, on a green slope, the gothic tower of the church was half hid by a cluster of dark trees; gray fells glimmered in the distance.

Three pages later the Radcliffes pause in reverence before a monument to the "Revolution in 1688," and Mrs. Radcliffe remarks:

> At a time, when the memory of that revolution is reviled, and the praises of liberty itself endeavoured to be suppressed by the artifice of imputing to it the crimes of anarchy, it was impossible to omit any act of veneration to the blessings of this event. Being thus led to ascend the hill, we had a view of the

country over which it presides; a scene simple, great and free as the spirit revered amidst it.

Later, at Ullswater, Mrs. Radcliffe notes the disappearance of former "ruins of monasteries and convents, which though reason rejoices that they no longer exist, the eye may be allowed to regret." She sums up her impressions of Ullswater as follows:

> Severe grandeur and sublimity; all that may give ideas of vast power and astonishing majesty. The effect of Ullswater is, that, awful as its scenery appears, it awakens the mind to expectations still more awful, and, touching all the powers of imagination, inspires that "fine phrensy" descriptive of the poet's eye, which not only bodies forth unreal forms, but imparts to substantial objects a character higher than their own.

The four passages sufficiently illustrate the leading qualities of thought and feeling that enter into Mrs. Radcliffe's descriptions of landscape. In the first passage, describing Kendal, one notes her close relationship to the Picturesque School. Mrs. Radcliffe has "composed a scene" in the manner of Gilpin and other "picturesque" travelers, and one recognizes the influence of the landscape artists—in this case, Salvator Rosa—whose treatment of scenery she had learned to appreciate from actual paintings and engravings, as well as from the nature poets, such as Thomson, whom Salvator, Claude, and other painters had influenced. The cascade in the foreground, the ruinous castle, and the Gothic tower half-hidden in the middle distance, against the background of glimmering gray fells, arrange themselves in a typical picturesque manner that Mrs. Radcliffe used again and again as an aesthetic norm—a point of view from which to observe and describe the external world.

But the same passage reveals another directing force in Mrs. Radcliffe's sensibility: Burke's *Philosophical Enquiry into the Origins of our Ideas of the Sublime and Beautiful*. For, as Samuel H. Monk has shown [in *The Sublime*, 1935], "the two streams of tendency, the purely emotional response to the grand the terrible, and the picturesque appreciation of nature, flow together" in her works. In his widely influential treatise Burke identifies terror as the chief source of the sublime, a passion that may arise from "magnitude in buildings," as well as from a number of more general conditions, such as obscurity, darkness, vastness, and power. Mrs. Radcliffe obviously embodies his theories in the first and last of the passages I have quoted, as she does in countless others throughout her works. By sending the chief characters of her romances on an unceasing quest for sublimity in natural scenery and in architecture, she terrified and delighted the reading public of her time.

The reason why these romances once lost their charm, the reason why they may again interest only the student of literature, as distinct from the common reader, bears a significant relation to an attitude that Mrs. Radcliffe reveals in the second and third passages above, where she favorably contrasts her own England with the past. Here she declares herself a proud daughter of the Enlightenment, the Age of Reason, true to the whiggish principles of the urban, commercial middle class from which she came. In the third passage, she also calls attention to the purely aesthetic quality of her medievalism, for here and throughout her works she similarly derides "superstition" and the barbarism, tyranny, and ignorance of any age or nation deprived of the blessings of Protestantism and British constitutional monarchy.

At the same time, Mrs. Radcliffe yearned for romance, customarily announcing on her title pages that she had chosen it as the genre of her prose fiction. And "the hero of romance," as Northrop Frye reminds us [in *Anatomy of Criticism,* 1957] "moves in a world in which the ordinary laws of nature are slightly suspended: prodigies of courage and endurance, unnatural to us, are natural to him, and enchanted weapons, talking animals, terrifying ogres and witches, and talismans of miraculous power violate no rule of probability once the postulates of romance have been established."

Mrs. Radcliffe could accept some of these conventions. Her heroes and heroines display powers and perfections that one would not expect to encounter in real life, and they triumphantly oppose monsters in human form. But she could not accept the supernatural, and this refusal to exploit the full power of romance, to suspend disbelief for artistic reasons, led to the "difficulties and dilemmas" of which Scott complains in his perceptive estimate of her literary achievement. Granting her the power to titillate us with the possibility of ghosts and to arouse fearful curiosity, he cannot conceal his disappointment in her timidly rationalistic, often trivial explanations of all the mysteries.

Unbeknownst to Scott, Mrs. Radcliffe introduced a real ghost into her last, tedious romance, *Gaston de Blondeville,* but she withheld the manuscript from publication in her lifetime, and the elaborate framework with which she surrounds the actual ghost story casts doubt upon its authenticity. Again, in a dialogue **"On the Supernatural in Poetry,"** which she excised from the manuscript of *Gaston de Blondeville* and also left unpublished at her death, one of the speakers affirms the possibility of supernatural visitations and defends their use in literature, especially in cases where the writer provides them with a suitably mysterious atmosphere. In practice, however, Mrs. Radcliffe never really adhered to this critical theory.

Her half-hearted approach to the tradition of romance helps to account for her unusual concern with the setting of her stories. That is to say, the castles and the landscapes *existed;* she could describe them as inanimate objects, involving the emotions of her characters, without sacrificing the decorum of probability as she understood it.

More significantly, in her glowing descriptions of the beauty and sublimity of nature, Mrs. Radcliffe hoped to achieve an effect not usually associated with romance: she hoped to display the refined good taste of her characters, as enlightened by reason, thereby elevating the tone of her works and imparting moral instruction to her readers, the great end and aim of art in her time. The danger of encouraging an immoral aestheticism did not concern her; she would portray heroic paragons of rationality and taste. And the wise old man, St. Aubert, in *The Mysteries of Udolpho* reassures us that "Virtue and taste are nearly the same, for virtue is little more than active taste, and the most delicate affections of each combine in real love."

In her words, Mrs. Radcliffe tried to "improve" the romance by combining it with the courtesy book or moral apologue. By relying on two approved aesthetic conventions—the sublime and the picturesque—by relating taste to reason and virtue, and by occasionally insinuating religious overtones into her descriptive passages, she sought to establish respectable authority and purpose for ecstasies of appreciation. Freed from their disreputable ancestral connections, her heroes and heroines could function as exemplary, romantic ladies and gentlemen of the eighteenth century. In certain respects, of course, they continue to resemble their forebears: they feel terror during their adventures and melancholy in their more pensive moments; moreover, once rescued from their perils by the ingenuity of comic servants (instead of friendly elves), they relax into traditional, charming attitudes and creative fantasy. But they remain sceptical about the marvelous, and the authorial voice is always didactic.

On the other hand, as I have just suggested, appreciation alone did not satisfy Mrs. Radcliffe in her timid exploration of man's relationship to his natural environment. In the fourth of the passages that I have quoted from her journal, where she speaks of inspiration as well as taste, she reveals her fascination with nature as a stimulus to artistic creativity. After the usual deference to Burke in the opening words, Mrs. Radcliffe expands the idea of sublimity in a manner only hinted at in the *Enquiry*. The great scenes of nature, she says, especially those scenes in which obscurity becomes a source of the sublime, have the special power of awakening the creative fancy, as they did for the great poets of the past. Transformed by rapture, the eye of the refined beholder becomes "the poet's eye, which not only bodies forth unreal forms, but imparts to substan-

tial objects a character higher than their own." Thus the rational romancer cautiously permits at least one supernatural creature to inhabit her landscapes, at the behest of her fictional characters, and that creature is the muse.

In Mrs. Radcliffe's dialogue **"On the Supernatural in Poetry"** this idea receives an even more explicit statement and becomes slightly tinged with pantheism. Invoking the authority of Shakespeare for his own romantic literary theories, W—(Willoughton) asks:

> Where is now the undying spirit . . . that could so exquisitely perceive and feel?—that could inspire itself with the various characters of this world, and create worlds of its own: to which the grand and the beautiful, the gloomy and the sublime of visible Nature, up-called not only corresponding feelings, but passions; which seemed to perceive a soul in everything: and thus in the secret workings of its own characters, and in the combinations of its incidents, kept the elements and local scenery always in unison with them, heightening their effect?

Having cited several examples in Shakespeare, Willoughton ascribes the same power to draw imaginative stimulation from "whatever is graceful, grand, and sublime" to Milton, Gray, Collins, Beattie, and Thomson. In Mrs. Radcliffe's journal she several times suggests that particular scenes inspired famous literary creations. Moreover, *Gaston de Blondeville,* with its background of Kenilworth Castle; her metrical romance, *St. Alban's Abbey;* and a number of her shorter poems all demonstrate her own creative response to the genius of the place.

Since this element in Mrs. Radcliffe's work has received little attention heretofore, it is worthwhile to note just how and where the creative fancy evolves from the landscapes of her prose fiction and to suggest how this idea may have affected her development as a writer.

Even the first of her romances, *The Castles of Athlin and Dunbayne,* boasts a hero whose poetic imagination encourages him to seek inspiration from scenery.

> His warm imagination directed him to poetry, and he followed where she led. He loved to wander among the romantic scenes of the Highlands, where the wild variety of nature inspired him with all the enthusiasm of his favourite art. He delighted in the terrible and in the grand, more than in the softer landscape, and, wrapt in the bright visions of fancy, would often lose himself in awful solitudes.

At one point, under the influence of "the sweet tranquillity of evening," Osbert composes a sonnet about his "visions of fancy;" in it his imagination permits him to observe a distant landscape, where Evening appears, personified, and "fairy echoes" are heard.

On the other hand, at this early stage in her career, Mrs. Radcliffe had by no means fully committed herself to the muse of landscapes, and *The Castles of Athlin and Dunbayne* contains less description of scenery in proportion to its length than any of her other prose works except *Gaston de Blondeville,* in which no character shows the sensitivity of nature that is indicated by the antiquarian, Willoughton (who appears in the introduction to the actual story, as well as in the rejected dialogue).

The proportion of descriptive passages increase in *A Sicilian Romance*. Even the wicked Duke de Luovo, in his pursuit of the fugitive heroine, rests on "the summit of some wild cliffs . . . to view the picturesque imagery of the scene below." The female characters respond more effusively. Madame de Menon, for instance, experiences the full gamut of approved passions in the presence of Nature's "sublime and striking attitudes," ending in creative imagination and deistic piety.

> Fancy caught the thrilling sensation, and at her touch the towering steeps became shaded with unreal blooms; the caves more darkly frowned—the projecting cliffs assumed a more terrific aspect, and the wild overhanging shrubs waved to the gale in deeper murmurs. The scene inspired Madame with reverential awe, and her thoughts involuntarily rose "from Nature up to Nature's God."

Julia, the heroine, demonstrates equal passion and inspiration by composing an ode to Evening, in which "To Fancy's eye fantastic forms appear." In the first part of the romance, she, with her sister, their tutor, and Madame de Menon inhabit the Castle Mazzini on the northern coast of Sicily. "In the fine evenings of summer," they enjoy a most spectacular view from

> a pavilion, which was built on an eminence in the woods belonging to the castle. From this spot the eye had an almost boundless range of sea and land. It commanded the straits of Messina, with the opposite shores of Calabria, and a great extent of the wild and picturesque scenery of Sicily. Mount Aetna, crowned with eternal snows, and shooting from among the clouds, formed a grand and sublime picture in the background of the scene. The city of Palermo was also distinguishable; and Julia, as she gazed on its glittering spires, would endeavour in imagination to depicture its beauties . . . .

Once again, the scene arouses the imagination. But here Mrs. Radcliffe has blundered. By making her setting more specific than the vaguely designated Scottish Highlands of her first work, she betrays her insufficient knowledge of the area that she describes. With the help of a map of Sicily, a good text book on mathematical geography, and a few other details supplied by the writer (which indicate that the castle must be situated near the northeastern tip of the island) one can

calculate that the "eminence" behind the castle would have to rise to a height of at least 8800 feet in order to afford a view of both the shore of Calabria and the towers of Palermo—very inconvenient for climbing in the evening, and higher than any mountain in Sicily except Etna and the peaks immediately adjacent, "in the background of the scene."

Perhaps we should regard this absurdity as mere "carelessness"—imperfect map-reading in the form of correctly observed directions but misjudged distances. Mrs. Radcliffe had never been to Sicily, nor had most of her readers. If inaccuracy in details, of whatever sort, did not concern them, why should it now concern us, or in any way diminish the pleasure that we can still derive from the Radcliffe canon? Frederick Garber, one of Mrs. Radcliffe's modern editors, though acknowledging her partial failure to maintain a consistent tone, nevertheless insists that none of her lapses in realism really matters [in his introduction to *The Italian,* 1968]:

> The basic pleasure in Mrs. Radcliffe's romances comes from a suspension of disbelief that leads to an enjoyment of the world of her fiction in and for itself. Cheerfully anachronistic in the tastes and attitudes she bestows upon her heroines, Mrs. Radcliffe is equally inaccurate in her descriptions of monastic life, the historical surroundings, and, we are told by some critics, even in the landscapes she describes. But this annoys us no more than it would in a fairytale or an opera.

But Ann Radcliffe certainly did not seek the kind of credulous tolerance that Burke identifies with the unrefined reader of the older romances:

> In his favourite author he is not shocked with the continual breaches of probability, the confusion of times, the offences against manners, the trampling upon geography and chronology, and he has never examined the grounds of probability.

Mrs. Radcliffe clearly assumes a different tone, addressing herself to readers of education and taste. By abandoning enchanted lands for Sicily and by substituting well-bred young ladies for fairy princesses, she has justified the reader in a demand for certain minimum standards of mimetic credibility, which she has, at the same time, failed to uphold. And I think that in so doing she allowed her aesthetics to misdirect her art. Determined to provide Julia with a view magnificent enough to produce a romantic fantasy, Mrs. Radcliffe enables her to see "glittering spires" that she could only have imagined. The eye has usurped the domain of the fancy.

In a very real sense, errors of this sort do matter, to those who see them, more than Mrs. Radcliffe's vagueness about the natural environment of remote areas or the manners and mores of former ages, for here she has, at least minimally, belied the very nature of mankind. Characters in fiction whom we are to take seriously as representations of human beings, rather than personifications of abstract qualities, must limit themselves to behaviour that is possible for their species in actual life. Mrs. Radcliffe's attempt to have it both ways gave the special impetus to Jane Austen's superb parody of her gothicism in *Northanger Abbey*.

It is true, nonetheless, that this confusion of eye and fancy has gone almost unnoticed by Ann Radcliffe's multitudinous readers in the English-speaking world. And their error on the side of generosity seems all the more curious in juxtaposition with the keener awareness demonstrated by French critics, from the beginning. In his perceptive article on the influence of Mrs. Radcliffe on Stendhal [in *Stendhal Club*, 1974] Philippe Berthier comes closer than any one I know to the principal line of thought of the present essay. Without assigning to the unwarranted expansiveness of vision of the Radcliffe characters the underlying cause that I have suggested above and will continue to explore, he gives this vision more than ample illustration and characterizes the landscapes eloquently:

> . . . Elles dressent en fait un decor "idéal" qui se soucie moins de reproduire une realité vérifiable sur le terrain que de dressent un cadre propice à la satisfaction de besoins parfaitement subjectifs.

> Rien n'échappe à un regard prospectif et recapitulateur qui, à chaque instant, semble excéder ses pouvoirs pour atteindre à une perspicacité presque cosmique.

The Romance of the Forest, Mrs. Radcliffe's third attempt at prose fiction, contains no blunders of this sort, in spite of the fact that the author has once again increased the proportion of landscape description and chosen as her principal locale a traditional setting of the fairy story. Except for certain lavish and inaccurate botanical details, which also appear in other works, the views of her characters do not actually encompass the impossible, partly because she usually describes them in the "heightened," generalized style that is especially characteristic of her earlier writing.

On the other hand, the principal heroine of *The Romance of the Forest,* Adeline, displays an even more ecstatic response to natural beauty than her predecessors. She several times gives way to the creative impulse, and, during one such interlude, she addresses an ode "To the Visions of Fancy." Furthermore, Mrs. Radcliffe barely saves the secondary heroine, Clara, from merging reality into dream, in the manner of Julia. As she and a group of the other characters sail across the Gulf of Lyons,

> La Luc amused himself at intervals with discoursing, and pointing out the situations of considerable ports on the coast, and the mouths of the rivers that, after wandering through Provence, disembogue themselves into the Mediterranean. The Rhone, however, was the only one of much consequence which he passed. On this object, though it was so distant that fancy, perhaps, rather than sense, beheld it, Clara gazed with peculiar pleasure, for it came from the banks of the Savoy; and the wave which she thought she perceived, had washed the feet of her dear native mountains.

In a sixteenth-century romance, Clara would probably have had an actual vision of her "dear native mountains," with the aid of some magical device, but here she gazes "with peculiar pleasure" upon what she, "perhaps," cannot see, and fancy assumes the role of the magician.

One of the heroines of *The Mysteries of Udolpho,* Mrs. Radcliffe's longest and best known romance, penetrates darkness as easily as Clara annihilates distance, by recourse to the same, unfailing power, her imaginative vision. With irrepressible enthusiasm she continues to enjoy her view of the landscape after night has fallen.

> The windows, which were numerous and large, descended low, and afforded a very extensive, and what Blanche's fancy represented to be a very lovely prospect; and she stood for some time, surveying the grey obscurity, and depicting imaginary woods and mountains, vallies and rivers, on that scene of night. . . .

Mrs. Radcliffe has deepened Burkean "obscurity" into the total darkness of a dream world.

In none of the five romances that came out in her lifetime does Mrs. Radcliffe ever describe a landscape that she herself saw. Even after she had made her picturesque tour, she preferred to work from literary sources, which she embroidered with her own, ever-active fancy. In some cases she has transformed factual accounts of travels into outlandish landscapes that no traveler, however enthusiastic, could ever have beheld. Since *The Mysteries of Udolpho* contains twice the proportion of landscape that we find in any other of Mrs. Radcliffe's romances, it provides abundant material for the study of her methods. Two examples of fanciful description, seldom noted by other critics, will suffice to illustrate her misuse of literary sources.

Having consulted Hester Lynch Piozzi, Pierre Jean Grosley, and possibly Thomas Gray for her account of Emily St. Aubert's crossing of the Alps, Mrs. Radcliffe apparently returned to the first of these sources, the *Observations and Reflections Made in the Course of a Journey Through France, Italy, and Germany,* to garner some details about Turin. Mrs. Piozzi describes the city as "built in form of a star, with a large stone in its centre, on which you are desired to stand and see the streets all branch regularly from it, each street terminating with a beautiful view of the surrounding country . . ." Transformed for Emily this common sight assumes a form that would startle a *torinese*. Mrs. Radcliffe writes: "The general magnificence of that city, with its vistas of churches and palaces, branching from the grand square, each opening to a landscape of the distant Alps or Apennines, was not only such as Emily had never seen in France, but such as she had never imagined." But if this heroine's lust for mountain glory allowed her to see the Apennines from Turin, she must have used her imagination.

Yet another of Emily's visions seems to owe its extravagance to Mrs. Radcliffe's imperfect adaptation of Mrs. Piozzi's *Observations*. Describing the countryside near Pisa, Mrs. Piozzi remarks: "The roadside is indeed hedged with festoons of vines, crawling from olive to olive, which they plant in the ditches of Tuscany as we do willows in Britain: mulberry trees too by the thousand, and some pollarded poplars serve for support to the glorious grapes that will soon be gathered." As the principal heroine of **The Mysteries of Udolpho** descends from the Apennines into "the vale of Arno," Mrs. Radcliffe provides her with an impossibly dilated version of what Mrs. Piozzi observed so accurately:

> At a distance, in the east, Emily discovered Florence, with its towers rising on the brilliant horizon, and its luxuriant plain, spreading to the feet of the Apennines, speckled with gardens and magnificent villas, or coloured with groves of orange and lemon, with vines, corn, and plantations of olives and mulberry; while to the west, the vale opened to the waters of the Mediterranean, so distant, that they were known only by a bluish line, that appeared upon the horizon, and by the light marine vapour, which just stained the aether above.

The daughter of St. Aubert has heeded all too well her father's encouragement to cultivate "that high enthusiasm, which wakes the poet's dream." In fact, both she and Blanche might remind the unsympathetic reader of Thackeray's "Little Billee," who climbs "the maintopgallant mast" to escape being killed and eaten by his shipmates and finds deliverance in an astounding sight:

> "There's land I see:
>
> "There's Jerusalem and Madagascar,
> And North and South Ameri-key.
>
> "There's the British fleet a-riding at anchor,
> With Admiral Napier, K.C.B."

Scott conjectured that Mrs. Radcliffe's actual experience with romantic scenery during her journey down the Rhine may have inspired the detailed description of **The Mysteries of Udolpho,** but C. F. McIntyre has shown that simple chronology makes the influence impossible. On the other hand, it is likely that the tour sharpened Mrs. Radcliffe's vision, turning her away from both generalized and fanciful landscapes to the less heady delights of close and accurate observation. For instance, in her description of the view from Penrith Beacon, she estimates quite accurately the extent of the horizon and we even find an occasional note of disillusionment with the pleasures of the imagination, as in this account of a German city:

> But Nimeguen lost much of its dignity on a nearer approach; for many of the towers which the treachery of fancy had painted at a distance, changed into forms less picturesque; and its situation, which a bold sweep of the Waal had represented to be on a rising peninsula crowning the flood, was found to be only a steep beside it.

Furthermore, towards the end of her journal, Mrs. Radcliffe begins to recognize the essential poverty of her descriptive method—her excessive repetition of borrowed terminology, her weakening of the emotional effect of landscape by the elaboration of details. "It is difficult," she admits

> to spread varied pictures of such scenes before the imagination. A repetition of the same images of rock, wood and water, and the same epithets of grand, vast and sublime, which necessarily occur, must appear tautologous, on paper, though their archetypes in nature, ever varying in outline, or arrangement, exhibit new visions to the eye, and produce new shades of effect on the mind. It is difficult also, where these delightful differences have been experienced, to forbear dwelling on the remembrance, and attempting to sketch the peculiarities which occasioned them.

In the "Memoir" that he wrote to accompany Mrs. Radcliffe's posthumous volumes, T.N. Talfourd quotes several notes that she made in the course of later tours in England. Here she sometimes expresses her sensitive response to landscape and landscape painting in a simple, impressionistic manner that contrasts strikingly with the ornate descriptive style of her published work. Burkean concepts still shape her responses, but she seems more content to observe and record without imaginative elaboration. At the conclusion of one of these notes she admits: "Here the imagination has nothing to do; we have only to preserve the impression of the living picture on the memory, in its own soft colours." Ironically enough, Burke himself would have encouraged Mrs. Radcliffe in a forbearance that she usually found difficult. His *Enquiry* warns the writer that "in reality poetry and rhetoric do not succeed in exact description so well as painting does; their business is to affect rather by sympathy than imitation; to display rather the effect of things on the mind of the speaker, or of others, than to present a clear idea of the things themselves."

Before making her later tours Mrs. Radcliffe had already experimented with certain new descriptive methods in her most competently written romance, *The Italian*. In comparison with *The Mysteries of Udolpho* this work contains a sharply reduced proportion of scenery, perhaps because certain reviewers had complained that Mrs. Radcliffe described too many landscapes. More importantly, her experiences as a traveler benefited Mrs. Radcliffe as a writer. In *The Italian* she never confuses the eye with the fancy, and, by adopting different modes of description she makes certain scenes more vivid and more effective than anything in her earlier fiction. Throughout this romance we notice her attempts—crude attempts, in some cases—to take the landscapes out of their picture frames and give them more fictive relevance.

In describing the Lake of Celano, for instance, Mrs. Radcliffe tries to relate background to character in a new way by contrasting the different reactions of Vivaldi, Ellena, and the servant, Paulo, to the view. Furthermore, a few of the more interesting places, such as the ruins of Paluzzi and the bridge across the chasm in Volume I, becomes so closely related to the events that occur there, at various times, that they remain memorable to the reader, who would have difficulty in recalling any specific scene of sublimity in *The Romance of the Forest*.

In one of the most admired episodes of *The Italian*, the attempt of the evil monk, Schedoni, to murder the heroine, Ellena, in a forlorn mansion on the Adriatic coast, Mrs. Radcliffe demonstrates considerable skill in weaving the description of an approaching storm into the sinister prelude to the actual murder scene. When Ellena encounters Schedoni on the shore, she becomes "alarmed by his manner, and awed by the encreasing gloom, and swelling surge, that broke in thunder on the beach. . . ." Here and elsewhere in the episode Mrs. Radcliffe suggests a symbolic relationship between the storm in external nature and the raging passions in the breast of Schedoni, her most effective villain. Furthermore, she doesn't overelaborate and overtly specify the symbolism; she has managed to avoid the "set piece," in which she so often tried to harmonize nature with the emotions of a heroine in her other stories. For the first time in this romance, Mrs. Radcliffe makes the events take place in her century rather than in a bygone age, though she again chooses a remote locale. Again for the first time, no character in *The Italian* gives vent to the creative impulse by writing verse. But Mrs. Radcliffe has not abandoned her fascination with landscape as a stimulus to the romantic imagination, as she explicitly informs us in this characterization of Ellena and Schedoni:

To the harassed spirits of Ellena the changing scenery was refreshing and she frequently yielded her cares to the influence of majestic nature. Over the gloom of Schedoni, no scenery had, at any moment, power; the shape and paint of external imagery gave neither impression or colour to his fancy. He contemned the sweet illusions, to which other spirits are liable, and which often confer a delight more exquisite, and not less innocent, than any, which deliberative reason can bestow.

By creating her hybrid of romance and courtesy book, which, in *The Italian,* begins to change into a novel, Mrs. Radcliffe tried to satisfy a rather demanding contemporary taste. Having reassured her readers with a certain amount of realism and moral instruction, she then encouraged them to luxuriate in sublimity, picturesque beauty, and creative fantasy. Those who have lost the taste for this ill-sorted accumulation of fictional elements and discover little redeeming artistry in Mrs. Radcliffe's works will not take much pleasure in them. But because her descriptions of landscape helped to stimulate a new sensitivity to natural beauty and because they bear a curious relationship to the fictive structure in which she embedded them, they will always remain interesting to the literary historian and the genre critic. From either point of view it is significant that Mrs. Radcliffe found in nature the ultimate source of the poet's fancy.

Chloe Chard (essay date 1986)

SOURCE: Introduction to *The Romance of the Forest,* by Ann Radcliffe, edited by Chloe Chard, Oxford University Press, 1986, pp. vii-xxiv.

[*In the following essay Chard introduces the general features of this early work of Radcliffe's. In addition to discussing the novel's genre, immediate critical reception, and place in literary history, Chard compares* The Romance of the Forest *to Radcliffe's later work in terms of her use of plot, characterization, and description.*]

Adeline, the heroine of *The Romance of the Forest,* is portrayed, towards the middle of the novel, reading an old and partially illegible manuscript which she has found in a concealed room in a ruined abbey, and which tells a story of imprisonment and suffering within the confines of this same building. As she comes to the words 'Last night! last night! O scene of horror!', her reactions are recounted as follows:

Adeline shuddered. She feared to read the coming sentence, yet curiosity prompted her to proceed. Still she paused: an unaccountable dread came over her. 'Some horrid deed has been done here,' said she; 'the reports of the peasants are true. Murder has been committed.' The idea thrilled her with horror.

In describing the process by which Adeline reads the manuscript, **The Romance of the Forest** underlines the promise of horror and terror on which its own narrative structure is based. Like all works of Gothic fiction, the novel constantly raises the expectation of future horrors, suggesting that dreadful secrets are soon to be revealed, and threatening the eruption of extreme—though often unspecified—forms of violence. The passage just quoted affirms very strongly the power of a narrative of mystery and impending violence to produce such moments of horror and terror: in anticipating imminent confirmation of her suspicion that 'murder has been committed', Adeline is so overcome with horror that she is prevented—for a while—from reading further.

The narrative pattern which the Gothic novel actually follows, however, differs in one very important respect from that which it promises—and which is dramatized in the account of Adeline's reaction to the manuscript. The reader of a work of Gothic fiction, far from being thrown into fits of such overwhelming horror that he or she casts the novel aside unfinished, is constantly urged onwards by that very emotion of 'curiosity' which, in Adeline's case, fails to conquer her fear of what she may discover if she reads further. In order to stimulate this response of curiosity, the moments of climactic horror and terror which the reader is led to anticipate are, in fact, regularly deferred: the dangers which threaten the heroine are continually averted, or displaced by new developments in the narrative. An article by Michel Foucault, 'Language to Infinity' [translated in *Language, Counter-Memory, Practice,* 1977], provides an analysis of this process of deferral, as it operates in French eighteenth-century novels of terror, which is highly relevant to the English Gothic genre as well. In these novels, Foucault argues:

> it is necessary to approach always closer to the moment when language will reveal its absolute power, by giving birth, through each of its feeble words, to terror; but this is the moment in which language inevitably becomes impotent, when its breath is cut short, when it should still itself without even saying that it stops speaking. Language must push back to infinity this limit it bears with itself, and which indicates, at once, its kingdom and its limit.

It might be noted, in considering this analysis of the Gothic narrative, that all Gothic novels, whilst they prevent any full realization of impending threats and dangers, do, on the other hand, eventually reveal the dreadful secrets which, like these threats and dangers, are presented to the reader as potential sources of terror. Instead of producing this promised effect of terror, however, the revelation of such secrets actually dispels the reader's emotions of anticipatory dread. The secrets themselves, moreover, may prove rather less horrific than the novel has originally suggested: as the

contemporary periodical the *Critical Review* remarks, in its assessment of another of Radcliffe's novels, 'curiosity', in the Gothic novel, 'is raised oftener than it is gratified; or rather, it is raised so high that no adequate gratification can be given it'.

The Romance of the Forest, published in 1791, was one of the earlier novels to construct a narrative of mystery, suspense, and ever-impending horror and terror. It was preceded by several other works which are usually regarded as 'Gothic': Horace Walpole's *The Castle of Otranto* (1764), Clara Reeve's *The Old English Baron* (1777), and Ann Radcliffe's own earlier works, **The Castles of Athlin and Dunbayne** (1789) and *A Sicilian Romance* (1790). Many more novels which promised the reader moments of extreme horror and terror, however, were to follow: the Gothic novels which succeeded **The Romance of the Forest** include, for example, Radcliffe's **The Mysteries of Udolpho** (1794) and **The Italian** (1797), Charlotte Smith's *Montalbert* (1795), Matthew Lewis's *The Monk* (1796), Eliza Parsons's *The Mysterious Warning* (1796), Mary Robinson's *Hubert de Sevrac* (1796), Regina Maria Roche's *Clermont* (1798), and Eleanor Sleath's *The Orphan of the Rhine* (1798).

The Romance of the Forest is now less well known than the two novels by Ann Radcliffe which followed it, but it was received by contemporary reviewers with an enthusiasm rather greater than that which greeted either of these later works. The account of **The Mysteries of Udolpho** in the *Critical Review,* for example, includes the comment that 'while we acknowledge the extraordinary powers of Mrs. Radcliffe, some readers will be inclined to doubt whether they have been exerted in the present work with equal effect as in **The Romance of the Forest**'. The review of **The Italian** in this same periodical suggests that **The Romance of the Forest** is superior to both of Radcliffe's later novels. A review of **The Romance of the Forest** itself—also in the *Critical Review*—praises very highly the way in which, as the reader progresses through the narrative, 'the attention is uninterruptedly fixed, till the veil is designedly withdrawn'.

This ability to 'fix the attention'—or, in other words, to maintain the reader's curiosity—is not, however, the only pleasure which the Gothic novel offers. Gothic fiction also provides an extravagant dramatization of various forms of excess and transgression, which are defined as sources of intense fascination precisely by virtue of the expressions of horror and censure which are directed towards them. Instances of the unrestrained indulgence of the passions, and of varieties of transgressive behaviour which are portrayed as the products of this unrestraint, assume a central role both in **The Romance of the Forest** and in every other work of Gothic fiction (including *The Monk,* which, by its different handling of these same themes, provoked contemporary reactions of moral outrage).

Lack of control over the promptings of violent passion is presented, in the Gothic novel, as a failing which is found in all except the most virtuous. Such lack of control assumes a particularly dramatic form in the case of Ambrosio, in *The Monk,* who finds that 'no sooner did opportunity present itself, no sooner did He catch a glimpse of joys to which He was still a Stranger, than Religion's barriers were too feeble to resist the over-whelming torrent of his desires'. Radcliffe's novels, too, however, frequently dwell on the theme of unrestraint. In *The Mysteries of Udolpho,* Signora Laurentini warns the heroine: 'Sister! beware of the first indulgence of the passions; beware of the first! Their course, if not checked then, is rapid—their force is uncontrollable—they lead us we know not whither'. In *The Romance of the Forest,* the ability of 'strong passion' to confuse 'the powers of reason' is emphasized in the account of Madame La Motte's jealousy of the heroine, and a more extreme example of the dangers of indulgence is provided by the description of her husband's similar lack of self-control: La Motte, the reader is told, 'had been led on by passion to dissipation—and from dissipation to vice; but having once touched the borders of infamy, the progressive steps followed each other fast . . .'

In their representation of unrestraint, Gothic novels—like the novels of Sade, which appeared over roughly the same historical period—focus above all on those characters who indulge their passions with particular ruthlessness: the feudal and monastic oppressors, who exercise an almost unlimited power within the confines of the castles, country houses, monasteries, or convents which constitute their primary area of operation (and who enjoy a certain authority even beyond the boundaries of these isolated domains). The characteristic passions of the Gothic oppressor are those of lust and cruelty, and the utter rejection of any form of moderation by the oppressor, in seeking the gratification of these passions, is always emphasized very strongly indeed. *A Sicilian Romance,* for example, describes the two central agents of oppression, a Marquis and his wife, as characters whose lives 'exhibited a boundless indulgence of violent and luxurious passions'. Montoni, the villain of *The Mysteries of Udolpho,* whose castle is perceived by the heroine as a haven for 'vice and violence', is represented as a man 'in whom passions . . . entirely supplied the place of principles', whilst Schedoni, in *The Italian,* is reported by his confessor as declaring that 'I have been through life . . . the slave of my passions, and they have led me into horrible excesses'.

In *The Romance of the Forest,* the most extreme instances both of unrestraint and of oppression are provided by the figure of the Marquis de Montalt, who is consistently characterized by 'the violence and criminality of his passions', and is described, in a fit of anger, 'giving himself up, as usual, to the transports of his passion'. Lesser practitioners of unrestraint are entirely outshone by this more powerful and energetically unprincipled 'votary of vice': La Motte, for example, is depicted in a state of extreme dismay when urged by the Marquis 'to the commission of a deed, from the enormity of which, depraved as he was, he shrunk in horror'.

The Marquis, in his extremity of unrestraint, indulges in the two forms of transgression which Gothic novels—again, like the works of Sade—regularly present as the usual manifestations of lust and cruelty within the feudal family: the crimes of murder and incest. These two crimes are accorded a closely analogous role within the Gothic genre: both are presented as forms of forbidden physical contact, both are portrayed as acts of violence (incest, in Gothic novels, almost always assumes the form of incestuous rape), and both are defined as particularly extreme forms of transgression by the family relationship which exists between the oppressor and the victim (a very large proportion of the murders in Gothic fiction take place within the family).

The close analogy between the two crimes is emphasized particularly strongly in Lewis's *The Monk,* in which one follows the other in swift succession. Ambrosio feels his first presentiment that the heroine, Antonia, is his sister just after he has raped her ('There was something in her look which penetrated him with horror; and though his understanding was still ignorant of it, Conscience pointed out to him the whole extent of his crime'). Very soon afterwards, he kills her. In Radcliffe's novels, the incestuous intentions of the oppressors are never in fact carried out (except between non-blood relations, as when Schedoni, in *The Italian,* rapes his brother's wife, having killed his brother). Both *The Italian* and *The Romance of the Forest,* however, in portraying the threat of incest, construct a very close relation indeed between incest and murder. Schedoni's attempt on the life of the heroine, in *The Italian,* thwarted by his apparent recognition of her as his daughter, is presented as an act which at the same time constitutes a form of incestuous assault: the moment of recognition is situated just as he has gone to Ellena's bedroom and is pulling back her garments: 'Vengeance nerved his arm, and drawing aside the lawn from her bosom, he once more raised it to strike: when, after gazing for an instant, some new cause of horror seemed to seize all his frame.' In *The Romance of the Forest,* the Marquis's unwittingly incestuous designs on the heroine are, when he discovers their close family relationship, swiftly replaced by a plan to murder her.

In its portrayal of murder, incest, and other manifestations of 'vice and violence', the Gothic novel, adopting an imaginative geography of a semi-feudal, Roman Catholic Europe, appropriates from contemporary travel writing an equation between the foreign and the forbidden. (Almost all English Gothic novels have foreign or partially foreign settings; *The Old English Baron,* an early example of the genre, constitutes a rare exception.) The assumption that, in a foreign, Roman Catholic country, all kinds of excessive and transgressive behaviour are to be expected, is found not only in overtly censorious eighteenth-century travel writings such as Samuel Sharp's *Letters from Italy* (1766), but even in works such as Hester Piozzi's *Observations and Reflections Made in the Course of a Journey through France, Italy, and Germany* (1789), in which the traveller proclaims some sympathy with the foreign. Gothic fiction, incorporating this same assumption, implicitly promises the reader the pleasures of a glimpse of the forbidden as soon as it names a foreign setting (as recognized in the ironic allusion, in Jane Austen's *Northanger Abbey* (1818), to the role played in the Gothic genre by 'the Alps and Pyrenees, with their pine forests and their vices').

In its use of the foreign as a setting for the forbidden, *The Romance of the Forest* differs from most Gothic novels in assigning only a marginal role to Roman Catholicism and monasticism; Adeline ecapes with relative ease from the 'cruelty and superstition' of the convent in which she has been educated. There is another feature of its representation of the foreign, however, in which *The Romance of the Forest* exhibits a much sharper divergence from other works of Gothic fiction: the discussion of national character. Many Gothic novels reproduce the portrayal of unrestraint as a quality especially characteristic of southern Europe, of Italy, or even of particular parts of Italy, which is regularly found in eighteenth-century travel writings. (The account of the inhabitants of Naples in Henry Swinburne's *Travels in the Two Sicilies* (1783-5), for example, places a strong emphasis on 'the violence of their passions and the enthusiasm of their character', whilst Piozzi's *Observations and Reflections* indicates an excess of both virtue and vice in southern Europe in the remark that 'in all hot countries . . . flowers and weeds shoot up to enormous growths'.) In *The Mysteries of Udolpho,* as in *A Sicilian Romance* and *The Italian,* violent passions are presented as a well-known attribute of the Italians: Signora Laurentini suffers 'all the delirium of Italian love' for the Marquis de Villeroi, and the heroine lives in terror of the fury of 'Italian revenge'. *The Monk,* though set in Spain rather than Italy, simply shifts the geographical location of excessive passion to this alternative southern setting: at one point, for example, the reader is reminded that 'the climate's heat, 'tis well known, operates with no small influence upon the constitutions of the Spanish Ladies'.

In *The Romance of the Forest,* however, locations which may be defined as unequivocally southern are introduced only at the very end of the novel, in a journey through Piedmont and Nice and along the Mediterranean coast of France, followed by a visit to a town on the borders of France and Spain. Most of the action of the novel takes place in a relatively northern region, somewhere near Lyons, and even when Adeline flees from this area, she spends a large portion of her time in the mountainous country of Savoy.

This use of northern and Alpine settings is not in itself uncommon in Gothic novels: *The Mysterious Warning* and *The Orphan of the Rhine,* for example, are both set, primarily, in Germany, whilst interludes in the Alps play a part in very many works of Gothic fiction. In most cases, however, the traits of character usually attributed to southern Europeans are simply transferred to a northern setting; *The Romance of the Forest* is unusual in constructing its account of the indulgence of the passions to conform with an established national characterization quite distinct from that of the Italians, or of other southern European nations: the established characterization of the French.

The account of the French which is given in Smollett's *Travels through France and Italy* (1766), and which closely resembles that found in other eighteenth-century travel writings, describes them as 'a giddy people, engaged in the most frivolous pursuits', and emphasizes 'their volatility, prattle, and fondness for *bons mots*'. A description of the French national character which is put forward in the course of a conversation in *The Romance of the Forest* lists a series of similar attributes, typifying the French, for example, by 'their sparkling, but sophistical discourse, frivolous occupations, and, withal, their gay animated air'. Such qualities might seem somewhat remote from the violence and unrestraint expected of the Gothic oppressor, but they are all, in fact, exhibited, in the course of the narrative, by the Marquis de Montalt. Not only does the Marquis display a Gallic 'animation' and Gallic powers of 'sophistry', but his excesses, in contrast to those of other Gothic villains, are characterized by an overt and relatively frivolous form of hedonism. Whereas the scenes of 'vice and violence' at which Montoni presides in *The Mysteries of Udolpho* take place within a somewhat comfortless castle, the Marquis de Montalt's château is portrayed as a dwelling in which everything is directed towards the gratification of the senses. (Even Adeline, held a prisoner there, asks as she gazes out onto the garden: 'Is this a charm to lure me to destruction?') The heroine is received, in this château, neither with threats nor with direct violence, but with enticements such as a song 'written with that sort of impotent art, by which some voluptuous poets believe they can at once conceal and recommend the principles of vice', and with such luxuries as 'a collation of fruits, ices and liquors'. (The Marquis is later discovered by Adeline 'flushed with drinking'.)

The prominent role which hedonism and frivolous dissipation assume in *The Romance of the Forest* does not, however—as the preceding account of the novel has made clear—preclude an accompanying fascination with the more grimly violent forms of unrestraint which are usually found in Gothic fiction. A speech by the Marquis, in fact, constructs an apparent continuity between 'French' hedonism and 'Italian' ruthlessness. The speech—a long and 'sophistical' one—begins by attacking the moral constraints which govern human behaviour in 'a civilized country', and praising the spontaneity with which 'the simple, uninformed American follows the impulse of his heart'. It soon becomes clear, however, that the Marquis is not merely advocating a carefree, pleasure-seeking existence, but is referring, in particular, to the lack of 'prejudice' attaching, in other societies, to the crime of murder. (This utilization by the oppressor of a primitivistic questioning of 'civilized' values, in order to justify any course of action which might be prompted by desire or expediency, is another feature which characterizes the portrayal of unrestraint not only in Gothic fiction but also in the novels of Sade.) The impulsiveness of the savage is now equated with 'Italian' indulgence of violent passion (using the Turks as a point of mediation between the primitive and the 'polished'), and 'Italian' murderousness is thereby presented as a natural extension of the more frivolously Gallic form of impulsiveness which the Marquis at first appears to be advocating:

> 'Nature, uncontaminated by false refinement,' resumed the Marquis, 'every where acts alike in the great occurrences of life. The Indian discovers his friend to be perfidious, and he kills him; the wild Asiatic does the same; the Turk, when ambition fires, or revenge provokes, gratifies his passion at the expense of life, and does not call it murder. Even the polished Italian, distracted by jealousy, or tempted by a strong circumstance of advantage, draws his stilletto [*sic*] and accomplishes his purpose.'

One further aspect of the Gothic representation of unrestraint which should be noted here—and which provides yet another point of analogy with the works of Sade—is the use of the figure of a victim, and above all of the victim's body, to dramatize the untrammelled indulgence of lust and cruelty. The victims of Gothic fiction are frequently presented, weak, collapsing, or in chains, as emblems of oppression, and attention is focused particularly sharply on the body of the heroine, who always assumes the role of the main victim of 'vice and violence'. The heroine of *The Romance of the Forest,* like all Gothic heroines, appears throughout the narrative fainting, 'sinking with terror', tottering, trembling, and shuddering; at one point, the reader

learns, 'the palpitations of terror were so strong, that she could with difficulty breathe'. On Adeline's first appearance in the novel, the terror and emotional suffering which mark her role as victim are defined as attributes which serve to display her body to particular advantage for the pleasure of the spectator, since they allow the usual requirements of decorum to be cast aside. The reader is implicitly invited to scrutinize her through the eyes of a male spectator, La Motte, who finds it impossible, as she sinks weeping at his feet, 'to contemplate the beauty and distress of the object before him with indifference'; he is later, the reader is told (without any apparent irony) 'interested . . . more warmly in her favour' by viewing her in another attitude of affliction and disarray: her 'habit of grey camlet', which 'shewed, but did not adorn, her figure', is described as 'thrown open at the bosom, upon which part of her hair had fallen in disorder, while the light veil hastily thrown on, had, in her confusion, been suffered to fall back.'

The heroines of Gothic fiction do not remain in a permanent state of decorative distress, however: their moments of collapse—like those of all other Gothic victims—alternate with moments of revival, when, sustained both by their characteristic virtues of fortitude and patience and by exterior sources of consolation, they recover sufficiently to face the horrors that remain in store for them. When Adeline emerges from a sleepless night in the vaults of the ruined abbey, for example, the reader is told that 'the cheerful beams of the sun played once more upon her sight, and reanimated her spirits'. Another sequence of collapse and revival in *The Romance of the Forest* describes the heroine 'reanimated with hope, and invigorated by a sense of the importance of the business before her', after a period in which, 'sinking under the influence of illness and despair', she 'could scarcely raise her languid head, or speak but in the faintest accents'.

One of the sources of inner sustainment which is named in these narratives of collapse and recovery is the heroine's pleasure in the landscape. When seated on 'some wild eminence' in Savoy, with 'a volume of Shakespear or Milton', Adeline is lulled into 'forgetfulness of grief', whilst the 'sweetly romantic' scenes of nature around the ruined abbey and the abundant fertility of the surroundings of Lyons are invested with similar powers to soothe, console, or distract her.

Descriptions of natural scenery, however, not only play a part in these accounts of the heroine's re-animation; they also assume another important role within the Gothic narrative structure. By delaying any resolution of a threat of impending danger, such descriptions often serve to keep the reader in a state of suspense—as in the episode in *The Romance of the Forest* in which Adeline, waiting to escape from the ruined abbey, and sharply aware of the necessity to leave the building before the Marquis arrives, sits at her window in contemplation of the 'uncommon splendour' of the sunset over the woods and ruins.

Landscape description is of importance, too, within the Gothic novel's mechanisms of self-definition. It is worth discussing these mechanisms in some detail, since an analysis of the literary and intellectual aspirations which are comprehended within them may help to elucidate a number of the characteristic features of the Gothic genre.

Contemporary accounts of Gothic novels often suggest, even when expressing an enthusiasm for these works, that their interest lies almost entirely in the excitement of the narrative; in less favourable commentaries, a strong emphasis is placed on the limitations of the genre. A review of *The Italian* in the *Critical Review,* for example, classifies the Gothic novel, damningly, as a literary form which 'might for a time afford an acceptable variety to persons whose reading is confined to works of fiction', whilst Jane Austen's novel *Emma* assigns to *The Romance of the Forest* the rather undistinguished role of one of the literary works within the scope of the utterly ignorant Harriet Smith. Gothic novels themselves, however, make a vigorous attempt to lay claim to a literary and intellectual status rather more elevated than that which is usually accorded to them. This attempt is evident, above all, in the wide range of references to other areas of writing which Gothic fiction establishes, and in the forms of authority to which it appeals in seeking to provide intellectual authentication for the narrative of horror and terror.

It has already been noted that the Gothic novel, in its portrayal of foreign society and manners, appropriates many of the themes and arguments which are found in eighteenth-century travel writing. In accounts of the landscape, references to travel books become yet more frequent: Gothic fiction derives from travel writing not only a range of general descriptive strategies (such as the strategy of constructing dramatic oppositions between wild and cultivated scenes of nature) but also a large number of precise descriptions of particular spots and of particular varieties of natural scenery. Many of the descriptions of landscape in *The Romance of the Forest,* for example, bear a very close resemblance to passages in works such as Smollett's *Travels through France and Italy,* Bourrit's *Relation of a Journey to the Glaciers, in the Dutchy of Savoy* (1775; translated from the original French edition of 1771) and Gray's letters from France and Savoy, as edited by Mason in *The Poems of Mr. Gray, to which are prefixed Memoirs of his Life and Writings* (1775).

References to travel writing, in Gothic fiction, are not usually proclaimed explicitly as such, but are used to suggest that each Gothic novel is itself the product of a personal experience of travel. The descriptions of the foreign which are found in Gothic fiction are, it is implied, uttered with the authority of the traveller—a form of authority which is derived not only from the traveller's claim to first-hand observation but also from the status of the traveller as a participant, or ex-participant, in the socially and culturally privileged practice of travel on the Grand Tour. (In its flexibility, the Grand Tour regularly included some or all of the regions described in *The Romance of the Forest*.) The success of *The Romance of the Forest* in defining at least some of its landscape descriptions as those of a traveller who has actually visited the spots described is indicated by the remark, in the *Critical Review,* that the accounts of Savoy in this novel 'are often beautiful, and seem to be drawn from personal experience'. (This use of descriptive language, in Gothic fiction, to indicate experience of travel need not, of course, correspond to any actual experience of travel on the part of the author; Ann Radcliffe, in fact, visited neither Savoy nor any of the other regions described in her novels, but only those areas of Europe named in the title of her *Journey made in the Summer of 1794, through Holland and the Western Frontier of Germany, with a return down the Rhine,* published in 1795.)

The self-definition of *The Romance of the Forest* as the product of a personal acquaintance with the regions which the heroine visits is reinforced by a great deal of discussion, towards the end of the novel, of the actual practice of travel: the experiences of two characters making their own versions of the Grand Tour—M. Verneuil and M. Amand—are both recounted, specific sightseeing expeditions (to the glaciers of Savoy and to Roman remains near Nice) are described, and the novel even remarks on the difficulties in finding furnished accommodation which the traveller to Nice encounters. Such allusions to the experiences of the traveller on the Grand Tour are, in fact, found very frequently in almost every work of Gothic fiction: the heroine of *Montalbert,* for example, is rescued from imprisonment in a remote Italian fortress by an Englishman who discovers her by chance whilst purchasing antiquities, 'of little value to them', from the local peasantry.

In its description of various different aspects of foreign countries, the Gothic novel introduces a range of different concepts of horror and terror. These concepts assume a rhetorical continuity with the horror and terror which are constantly promised within the narrative, not only by virtue of the fact that the same terms are used in both contexts, but also by virtue of the role which the horrors of the foreign assume in reinforcing the heroine's sense of dread, and so in encouraging the reader's expectation of future terrors. (Even the horrors of the wild landscape, which are usually described as aesthetically pleasurable, contribute, on occasion, to the heroine's apprehensions.) The horror and terror of the narrative, then, are invested with a certain intellectual authentication, through these apparent affiliations with concepts which form part of the privileged discourse of the traveller.

In descriptions of the foreign landscape, the Gothic genre's preoccupation with horror and terror is endorsed particularly strongly by the strategy of appealing to aesthetic theory—a strategy which also serves, moreover, to proclaim a general familiarity with current intellectual concerns, and to display a responsiveness towards the visual delights of the landscape, of a kind which is frequently exhibited in late eighteenth-century travel writings, and which readily suggests some degree of eyewitness experience of the varieties of scenery described. Gothic novels, in establishing multiple references to the aesthetic principles put forward in such writings as Edmund Burke's *Philosophical Enquiry into the Origin of our Ideas of the Sublime and Beautiful* (1757) and Hugh Blair's *Lectures on Rhetoric and Belles Lettres* (1783), appeal above all to the underlying association which is established in such writings between horror, terror, and the powerful and complex aesthetic effect of sublimity—an effect in which fear and pleasure both play a major part. In *The Romance of the Forest,* for example, the sight of a storm in the Alps is presented both as a source of terror and as a scene of 'dreadful sublimity', and the aesthetic delights which such a spectacle of terror and sublimity may offer are emphasized particularly strongly by a prefatory allusion to the heroine's desire to witness (from a position of safety) 'the tremendous effect of a thunder storm in these regions'.

The Gothic novel's concern with horror and terror is authenticated, too, by another form of reference which the genre establishes: reference to poetry. Epigraphs quoting from the works of Shakespeare, Milton, and a range of eighteenth-century poets (including, for example, Gray, Collins, Beattie, Thomson, and Mason) serve to make it clear that horror, terror, and similar concepts occupy a secure place within the tradition of English poetry, as the Gothic novel defines it. The title page of *The Romance of the Forest,* for example, quotes from *Macbeth* in order to indicate that 'a deed of dreadful note' will soon be recounted, and the epigraph to Chapter 7 cites the same play in its allusion to 'horrible imaginings', whilst two other epigraphs in this same novel quote lines from Collins's 'Ode to Fear'.

The attempt to affiliate the Gothic novel with an English literary tradition, moreover, goes far beyond this emphasis on a common concern with horror and terror. The events and dominant emotions of each chapter—emotions which include not only horror, terror, fear, awe, and dread but also, for example, melancholy and despair, and even joy and hope—are all defined as elements with a literary history of their own by the use of epigraphs, whilst quotations within the text—often short, and encapsulated within a sentence of the narrative, as though spontaneously springing to mind in the course of the narration—are used to suggest that the Gothic novel is composed with constant reference to English poetry. Yet further links with English poetry are established in poems by the novelist and in passages of description: in *The Romance of the Forest,* as in many other Gothic novels, indirect allusions are frequently made, for example, in both these contexts, to Collins's 'Ode to Evening', and to the many other eighteenth-century poems which, themselves referring back to Milton's 'Il Penseroso', dwell on such themes as twilight, obscurity, pensiveness, melancholy, and solemnity. The 'melancholy charm' of the hour 'when Twilight spreads her pensive shade', described in the poem 'To the Nightingale', is emphasized, too, in a large number of the other poems by Radcliffe which are included within the text, and the account of Adeline's state of 'reverie' and 'still melancholy' as she contemplates the French coastline in the obscurity of evening is one of many descriptive passages in the novel which portrays the state of twilight as a source of similar emotional responses.

The Romance of the Forest, then, establishes the same range of reference to other areas of writing as that which is found in the Gothic novels which follow it. It also, however, includes many more allusions to contemporary intellectual concerns than most of these later works. Not only does the novel refer to the themes and arguments of eighteenth-century primitivism, in providing the Marquis with a theoretical defence of his pursuit of vice; it also incorporates a large number of references to Rousseau's *Emile* (1762), and especially to the 'Profession de foi du vicaire savoyard' which forms part of that work, in its account of La Luc, the benevolent Savoyard clergyman who takes Adeline into his family.

The aspirations which such references serve to emphasize are accompanied, however, by a strong element of unease. This unease stems, in part, from an uncertainty as to the kinds of authority which could be invoked within a work of fiction which explicitly proclaimed its female authorship on the title page—one of the tasks which the novel assumes is, in fact, that of negotiating the areas of discourse which might be considered as accessible to women. *The Romance of the Forest,* on the one hand, avoids any overt proclamation of literary or intellectual ambition by situating itself within the genre of romantic fiction. This acceptance of a relatively humble literary status has, on the other hand, the disadvantage that it makes it extremely difficult for the novel to introduce its more ambitious allusions to current intellectual concerns without producing a strong effect of incongruity.

The element of unease in **The Romance of the Forest** is, nevertheless, not entirely unwelcome, since it provides some relief from the unruffled complacency which is displayed, in this novel as in most other works of Gothic fiction, in the discussion of accepted social values and of established forms of authority. The description of the Gothic novel as complacent may sound unnecessarily dismissive; the genre might also be viewed as potentially subversive in its provision of a model for the criticism of oppression, and this view would find support in the use of a highly 'Gothic' setting to dramatize the oppression of women in Mary Wollstonecraft's *The Wrongs of Woman; or, Maria* (published posthumously in 1798). Most Gothic novels, however, far from questioning or attacking established social usages, employ their dramatizations of foreign 'vice and violence' to reaffirm, by contrast, the merits of the familiar values and customs of English society. **The Romance of the Forest,** moreover, is particularly cautious in the forms of authority which it attacks. The portrayal of France under the *ancien régime* in this novel carefully avoids any suggestion that the recent events of the French Revolution might be seen as a response to various forms of injustice: both the French monarch and the French courts are presented as, on the whole, just and benevolent (although accounts of the less politically sensitive areas of Savoy and Nice freely criticize the baneful effects of 'an arbitrary government'). The novel strongly resists the kind of transposition of the theme of oppression to the contemporary political situation which is found in the later Gothic novel *Hubert de Sevrac*. The heroine of this later work boldly ventures to suggest to her father, a French émigré marquis, that in pre-revolutionary days 'we lived amongst such as never felt for those, whose hard fortune placed them in poverty: all our friends, all our associates, were the enemies of the people'.

Rhoda L. Flaxman on Radcliffe as a "word-painter":

Radcliffe was one of the first English novelists to elevate extended, visually oriented landscape description—previously nearly the exclusive province of poetry—to a position of prominence in English fiction. In addition to establishing a new subject (subsequently developed by writers as diverse as Scott, Ruskin, Dickens, Hardy, Lawrence, and Woolf) she was the first to apply a genuinely cinematic technique to these descriptions. Obviously, Radcliffe knew nothing of modern cinematography, but her technique for capturing landscape in language closely resembles [what Alan Spiegel in *Fiction and the Camera Eye* (1976) calls] filmic "visualization through perspective" that combines object and seer.

Rhoda L. Flaxman, in Victorian Word-Painting and Narrative, *UMI Research Press, 1987.*

D. L. Macdonald (essay date 1989)

SOURCE: "Bathos and Repetition: The Uncanny in Radcliffe," in *The Journal of Narrative Technique,* Vol. 19, No. 2, Spring, 1989, pp. 197-204.

[*In this essay, Macdonald uses the critical theories of Tzvetan Todorov that relate to Gothic romance to maintain that Radcliffe, in* The Mysteries of Udolpho, *uses the fantastic satirically and with a didactic purpose.*]

The defining characteristic of the fantastic as a literary genre, according to Tzvetan Todorov, is the hesitation or uncertainty it produces in the reader (and sometimes in the characters) as to the fictional reality of supernatural phenomena [*The Fantastic: A Structural Approach to a Literary Genre,* trans. R. Howard, 1973]. The genre thus defined is extremely small: usually the supernatural events are either explained away, so that the fantastic becomes merely uncanny, or verified, so that it becomes marvelous.

Richard Howard translates Todorov's *étrange* as *uncanny* because Todorov himself invokes Freud's conception of the *unheimlich,* though he notes that "there is not an entire coincidence between Freud's use of the term and [his] own." Indeed, in the lexicographic section of his paper on "The 'Uncanny,'" Freud suggests a number of French equivalents for *unheimlich,* including *inquiétant, sinistre, lugubre,* and *mal à son aise,* but not *étrange*. Much of Freud's paper, moreover, is devoted to considering whether the uncanny might not be equivalent to what Todorov calls the fantastic—whether it depends on the "intellectual uncertainty" the writer creates "by not letting us know . . . whether he is taking us into the real world or into a purely fantastic [or, as Todorov would say, marvelous] one of his own creation," by "keep[ing] us in the dark for a long time about the precise nature of the presuppositions on which the world he writes about is based, or . . . cunningly and ingeniously avoid[ing] any definite information on the point to the last." His conclusion that this almost never happens, so that the uncanny cannot depend on it, is not so far from Todorov's contention that the pure fantastic almost always gives way to the uncanny or the marvelous.

Todorov's distinction between the uncanny and the marvelous corresponds directly to a distinction already drawn in the Romantic period, between the explained and the unexplained supernatural. Ann Radcliffe was considered the foremost exponent of the former Gothic mode, as M. G. Lewis was of the latter.

In Radcliffe's most famous novel, **The Mysteries of Udolpho** (1794), as in almost all her other works, the fantastic events are ultimately all explained away as merely uncanny. They are also comparatively few to begin with. The mysterious music heard in the woods near Chateau-le-Blanc turns out to be the "only amusement" of the demented Sister Agnes Laurentini, whose physician has recommended it "as the only means of soothing her distempered fancy"; its uncanny loveliness is accounted for by her being Italian. The similar music heard at Udolpho, the appearances on the battlements, and the voice which twice interrupts Montoni, all turn out to be produced by the imprisoned Monsieur Du Pont, singing to while away the time, walking on the battlements for fresh air and exercise, and speaking from secret passages to confound his captors. The occurrences in and around the bedroom of the deceased Marchioness de Villeroi at Chateau-le-Blanc—the face in her bed, which frightens Emily and Dorothée when they first enter her room; the apparition on the landing, which terrifies a servant, and the disappearance of Ludovico, who has volunteered to spend a night in the room to prove it is not haunted—turn out to be the work of pirates, who have made the chateau appear to be haunted so that they can store their treasure there without fear of detection.

Some of these explanations do not occur for hundreds of pages after the events they explain, but the events themselves are always undercut on their first occurrence. The story of the music at Chateau-le-Blanc immediately strikes Emily as a "ridiculous superstition", though it soon makes her shrink with "superstitious dread," and, after the death of her father, chills her with "superstitious awe." The music at Udolpho, largely because it reminds her of the earlier music, again inspires "superstitious dread." The apparition on the battlements makes "the terrors of superstition" pervade her mind. The apparition in the bed at Chateau-le-Blanc "affect[s] Emily's imagination with a superstitious awe." These are all the judgements not only of Emily but of the omniscient narrator, who also informs the reader that the disappearance of Ludovico has nothing to do with spirits, except that "the mystery, . . . by exciting awe and curiosity, reduced the mind to a state of sensibility, which rendered it more liable to the influence of superstition in general." A superstition is by definition untrue; by immediately characterizing all these terrors as superstitious, the narrator makes it impossible for the reader (if not for the characters) even to hesitate over the question of the reality of the supernatural. The *fantastic*, in Todorov's sense, is strictly excluded from Radcliffe; it would be more appropriate to employ her own terminology and speak of the *mysterious*: the narrator's repeated assurances that Emily's terrors and confusions are superstitious do still leave something to be explained.

Most of Radcliffe's readers have found that the explanations, when they come, have a bathetic rather than a satisfying effect. In his *Idée sur les romans* (1800), Sade juxtaposed the opposite but equal aesthetic disadvantages of the explained and unexplained supernatural—of the uncanny and the marvelous, in Todorov's terms: once the supernatural has been invoked, it is necessary "either to explain away [développer] all the magic elements, and from then on to be interesting no longer, or never raise the curtain [lever le rideau], and there you are in the most horrible unreality." Radcliffe's problem, of course, is the former: a ghost, however thoroughly called into question, is more interesting (at least, according to the hierarchy of interests the novel takes for granted) than a pirate or a demented nun.

The novel, in fact, foregrounds its own bathetic structure. Just as its mysteries are accompanied by assurances of their speciousness, so its explanations are accompanied by acknowledgements of their bathos. One of the first mysteries of the novel, and one of the most quickly explained, is an apparition in St. Aubert's study after his death; it turns out to be the family dog. No explicit acknowledgement of the bathos seems necessary here. Later, summing up her experiences at Udolpho, Emily smiles ironically and says: "I perceive . . . that all old mansions are haunted; I am lately come from a place of wonders; but unluckily, since I left it, I have heard almost all of them explained." At this point, the mysteries of Chateau-le-Blanc have not yet been explained; when they are,

> Emily could not forbear smiling at this explanation of the deception, which had given her so much superstitious terror, and was surprised, that she could have suffered herself to be thus alarmed, till she considered, that, when the mind has once begun to yield to the weakness of superstition, trifles impress it with the force of conviction.

The bathos is clearly satiric—just as clearly as in *Northanger Abbey*—and the satire reinforces the novel's didacticism. It is "a state of sensibility," the narrator says which renders the mind liable to the influence of superstition, and St. Aubert's deathbed speech to his daughter is above all a warning against "the dangers of sensibility." As David Durant points out, Emily's experiences simply confirm her father's advice—so conclusively, and the household she and Valancourt finally establish reconstitutes her father's household so thoroughly, that the novel is circular. This is one reason why it can be so long: since Emily learns nothing she does not already know from her experiences, there is no reason for them not to repeat themselves over and over—as they do. Since nothing is happening in the novel, there is no reason for it ever to stop. (The other main reason for its length is its extensive use of the rhetoric of the sublime, which intensifies, by contrast, the bathos of the narrative.)

The novel's use of bathos extends beyond the treatment of superstition. Many of the examples of it, moreover, are repeated. On their excursion in the

Pyrenees, St. Aubert and Emily think they are being attacked by banditti; St. Aubert shoots one of them, who turns out to be Valancourt. Over five hundred pages later, back at La Vallée, the unfortunate Valancourt is mistaken for a robber, and shot, again.

Soon after the first shooting of Valancourt, the travelers see approaching what appears to be a band of smugglers, and are apprehensive about the encounter; it is a band of smugglers, but they have already been apprehended by the authorities and are on their way to prison under guard. Later, at Udolpho, Emily is alarmed by the approach of a troop of condottieri, who pass the castle without displaying the least interest in it.

At Udolpho, Emily is terrified by a noise at her door in the middle of the night; it turns out to be only Annette, who has fainted because she thinks she has seen a ghost, which turns out to be Montoni's outlawed friend Orsino. At Chateau-le-Blanc, Emily is terrified again by a noise at her door in the middle of the night; it turns out to be one of the Count's servants, who has fainted because she thinks she has seen a ghost, which turns out to be one of the pirates.

A whole series of bathetic events is associated with Emily's fear of Count Morano. Awakened in the middle of the night in Montoni's palazzo in Venice, Emily is afraid that Montoni is about to force her to marry Morano; in fact, he is only about to take her to Udolpho. She assumes that the purpose of the trip is to allow a secret wedding, and on the morning after her arrival, when Annette asks her to guess who else has shown up at the castle, she immediately guesses that it is Morano, and almost faints; it turns out to be only Ludovico, a character whom neither Emily nor the reader has even met. When Morano finally does show up at Udolpho, and even penetrates into Emily's bedroom at night, Montoni actually intervenes to save his niece. The incident is repeated when Morano tries to have Emily kidnapped by Barnardine the porter.

The whole series is repeated, or mirrored, in the events associated with Emily's belief that Valancourt is also a prisoner at Udolpho. When she hears Du Pont sing the song she once heard in her parents' fishing-house at La Vallée, Emily assumes he must be Valancourt, although she has never heard Valancourt sing and had not met Valancourt when she heard the song in the fishing-house. (It turns out, of course, to have been Du Pont singing in the fishing-house too.) When Annette later hears the singing, she agrees that it must be Valancourt, although she has never heard him sing either. The concurrence of so consistently deluded a character is virtually enough to discredit the belief all by itself: it is the dramatic equivalent of the narrator's warning term *superstitious*. The didactic point of the mirroring seems to be that wishful thinking and fearful thinking are equally doomed to disappointment. (The

two are not so different, since superstition is not only an effect of ignorance, fatigue, and harrassment, but also an expression of "that love, so natural to the human mind, of whatever is able to distend its faculties with wonder and astonishment."

The hesitation that Todorov considers essential to the fantastic is simply, as Christine Brooke-Rose points out [in *A Rhetoric of the Unreal,* 1981], the reader's (or a character's) response to some ambiguity, and the use of ambiguity in the fantastic does not differ significantly from its use in other narrative contexts. Radcliffe's use of the fantastic or mysterious is placed in a larger context not only of bathos, but also of ambiguity. Yet another matching pair of incidents thematizes the reader's response to ambiguity, as Poe does later (though more spectacularly and less bathetically) in "The Fall of the House of Usher." At Udolpho, Annette is telling Emily the story of how Caterina, the caretaker's wife, was frightened by strange noises in the castle, when she herself is so frightened by strange noises that she has to stop. They turn out to be made by Caterina, who has come to fetch Annette for Madame Montoni. In the Marchioness's apartment at Chateau-le-Blanc, Ludovico sits up late reading a ghost story while waiting to disappear. Like his lover Annette, he is repeatedly interrupted by strange noises which mysteriously match the supernatural noises within his story, but which turn out to be natural, and external to the chateau as well as to the story: they are caused by the wind whistling round the chateau and shaking the casements.

Other uses of ambiguity are less trivial. Near the beginning of the novel, Emily and Montoni have a whole conversation, and Emily even writes a postscript to a letter, in which she thinks she is referring to renting La Vallée and he thinks (or pretends to think) she is referring to marrying Morano. The ambiguity arises from the high-minded generalities in which Emily habitually expresses herself. Near the end of the novel, Emily confronts Valancourt with the reports she has heard of his conduct in Paris; or, to be precise, she declines to do so: the reports, "Being such as Emily could not name to the Chevalier, he had no opportunity of refuting them; and, when he confessed himself to be unworthy of her esteem, he little suspected, that he was confirming to her the most dreadful calumnies." The ambiguity in this case arises from the difficulty of speaking about the unspeakable.

The unspeakable is also involved in the two major mysteries of the novel. On his deathbed, St. Aubert asks his daughter to burn some of his papers without examining them; taking them from their hiding-place, however, she absent-mindedly glances over them and reads "a sentence of dreadful import". Even the narrator never says what it is, but it is enough to make Emily wonder (though only momentarily) whether she

Frontispieces for a four-volume 1799 edition of The Mysteries of Udolpho.

should investigate further at the cost of disobeying her father's solemn injunction and breaking her own solemn promise. At Udolpho, Emily is intrigued by the mystery of the picture behind the black veil, which even the loquacious Annette finds almost unspeakable. Emily lifts the veil, finds "that what it had concealed was no picture," and faints. This mystery, unlike that of the dreadful sentence, is cleared up, but not for over four hundred pages. In the meantime, the two unspeakable mysteries are brought together in Emily's memory. In a conversation with Dorothée at Chateau-le-Blanc,

> she remembered the spectacle she had witnessed in a chamber of Udolpho, and, by an odd kind of coincidence, the alarming words, that had accidentally met her eye in the MS. papers, which she had destroyed, in obedience to the command of her father; and she shuddered at the meaning they seemed to impart, almost as much as the horrible appearance, disclosed by the black veil.

These two unspeakable mysteries, unlike the novel's other mysteries, are not even speciously supernatural; nevertheless, they not only dominate but sum up the effects of all the others. The lifting of the veil becomes a symbol of Radcliffe's explanations (Sade accordingly uses the terms *développer* and *lever le rideau*). The reading of the dreadful sentence stands neatly for the reading of the novel itself.

The mystery of the dreadful sentence has something to do with a woman whom Emily's father once loved. By the time she comes to associate it with the mystery of the veil, Emily has begun to suspect that this woman, the Marchioness, may be her mother; or, to be precise, she would have begun to suspect it if the suspicion had not been unspeakable and even unthinkable:

> Her faith in St. Aubert's principles would scarcely allow her to suspect that he had acted dishonourably; and she felt such reluctance to believe herself the daughter of any other, than her, whom she had always considered and loved as a mother, that she would hardly admit such a circumstance to be possible.

(The novel is surprisingly frank about its own repressions.) In short, the sentence is part of what Mary Laughlin Fawcett [in *SEL,* 1983] has called "*Udolpho's* Primal Mystery": not only a sexual secret but the secret of Emily's own conception.

The mystery of the veil is equally primal. When Emily first lifts the veil, she sees (as we eventually learn) a horrible waxwork,

> a human figure of ghastly paleness, stretched at its length, and dressed in the habiliments of the grave. What added to the horror of the spectacle, was, that

the face appeared partly decayed and disfigured by worms, which were visible on the features and hands.

Later, searching for Madame Montoni, she finds herself in a disused torture chamber where "a dark curtain, . . . descending from the ceiling to the floor, was drawn along the whole side of the chamber." It reminds her (as well as the reader) of "the terrible spectacle her daring hand had formerly unveiled," but she draws the curtain anyway, and discovers "a corpse, stretched on a kind of low couch, which was crimsoned with human blood, as was the floor beneath. The features, deformed by death, were ghastly and horrible, and more than one livid wound appeared in the face." She faints again, as she had when she lifted the veil. Later still, she enters the room where her aunt has been imprisoned, draws the bed curtains, and discovers Madame Montoni, pale, emaciated as a skeleton, and on the point of death. Later still, in the bedroom of her other aunt, the Marchioness, she sees the black bedspread "violently agitated," and a face appears above it. Emily and Dorothée flee in terror. In each case Emily has intruded into a forbidden room and drawn a curtain to look at a bed. In one, she sees what she takes for an apparition of the woman whom she so conspicuously declines to suspect is her mother; in another, she really sees Madame Montoni, who really is a substitute for her mother, though a ludicrously inadequate one. The first body is being attacked by phallic worms; the second is soaked with hymeneal blood and gaping with vaginal wounds; the last bed is still disturbed by the violent agitations of copulation.

Leslie Fiedler [in *Love and Death in the American Novel,* 1966] sees the substitution of death for sex as the defining characteristic of the gothic. Todorov sees in the eroticism of the fantastic a progression from promiscuity through perversion to sadism and necrophilia, though he curiously declines to postulate a meaning or theoretical rationale for this progression, contenting himself with an associative empirical presentation. Radcliffe's novel abundantly illustrates the substitution of death for sex, and also provides a meaning for such a substitution: the child stumbling on the primal scene typically mistakes it for a scene of violence (Freud 17: 45 and n.).

Radcliffe's child, however, also makes another mistake, or rather (as one might expect) a whole series of mistakes, which reveals a curious defect in Radcliffe's presentation of the primal scene. With one exception, Emily is always wrong about the gender of the figure in the bed: the waxwork represents the dead body of a Marquis of Udolpho, but she takes it for that of Signora Laurentini; the corpse in the torture chamber is that of a soldier, but she takes it for that of her aunt; the face in the Marchioness's bed is that of a pirate, but she takes it for an apparition of the Marchioness herself. And there is always only one figure in the bed.

Fawcett sees this as an image of sexual union, an androgynous figure, a beast with two backs. To me it looks more like a denial of the reality of the primal scene, parallel to the novel's denial of the reality of the supernatural, and consistent with its generally bathetic method. (Eve Kosofsky Sedgwick, similarly, argues [in *PMLA,* 1981] that the unveiling is always the voiding of an expectation. And Hillis Miller redefines Freud's conception to suggest that the real source of the uncanny is the suspicion that there may not be "any secret at all hidden in the depths.")

Emily never has to learn that women do get into bed with men and that things happen to them there. It is not clear that she learns there is a difference between men and women (Valancourt does not seem to be the man to teach her). In the exceptional case of Madame Montoni, there really is a woman in the bed, and she really is the victim of the violence of her husband, but it is a disembodied, asexual violence: Montoni has been neglecting and starving her, not assaulting her.

The revelation that the Marchioness was St. Aubert's sister rather than his lover has the same effect. Pierre Arnaud sees in it a suggestion of incest. I see an opportunity for Radcliffe to deny that there is a sexual element in the passionate love and sorrow Emily has witnessed in her father—an opportunity, in short, to write a novel of education in which her heroine starts out with nothing to learn, a novel of maturation in which her heroine ends up as innocent, and as infantile, as she began.

The marvelous, Todorov argues, refers the fantastic "to an unknown phenomenon, never seen as yet, still to come—hence to a future"; the uncanny reduces it, as in Radcliffe, "to known facts, to a previous experience, and thereby to the past." This is the conservatism that David Durant sees in Radcliffe's use of bathos. The repetition that is the formal consequence of bathos suggests a more radical conservatism, one that Fiedler hints at in his definition of the Gothic. He sees in Radcliffe's works the "compulsive repetitiveness [of] a self-duplicating nightmare from which it is impossible to wake." The repetition compulsion is a manifestation of "the conservative nature of the instincts," which strive to return to "an *old* state of things, an initial state from which the living entity has at one time or other departed." The origin Emily seeks and finds—over and over again, in all those bedrooms—is not the sexual origin of her own life, but the origin of all life in inanimate matter. To say that the veil conceals nothing is to say that it conceals death; Radcliffe's denial of Eros is an affirmation of Thanatos.

Thus a reading of one novel, an exercise in what Todorov calls interpretation, can supplement what he calls poetics, by suggesting a rationale (for the treatment of eroticism in the fantastic) which his poetics omitted to make explicit; the two activities, as he concedes, are never entirely distinct (Todorov 141). It does so, moreover, by effacing the analogous distinction between what he calls the semantic and syntactical aspects of the fantastic—by finding thematic significance (an affirmation of Thanatos) in a purely formal characteristic like repetition.

Kate Ferguson Ellis (essay date 1989)

SOURCE: "'Kidnapped Romance' in Ann Radcliffe," in *The Contested Castle: Gothic Novels and the Subversion of Domestic Ideology,* University of Illinois Press, 1989, pp. 99-128.

[*In the following excerpt, Ellis suggests that in her Gothic novels Radcliffe elevates the character of romance by using the fanciful conventions of the Gothic tradition as a means of addressing the real problems encountered by a young lady or gentleman entering the world in the eighteenth century.*]

The novels of Ann Radcliffe offer something new to the Gothic tradition still in formation. Working in the domain of romance, which had less prestige even than the novel, she transformed the features of romance on which the novel was thought to improve—its remote, extravagant settings, its reliance on conventions and "fancy" rather than close observation of "nature," its use of coincidence—into instruments of didacticism whose lessons addressed real problems of "entering the world." Her protagonists exist entirely inside parameters of virtue with which "young persons of both sexes" could identify without risk. Yet they respond to difficulties with rationality and, most important, independent initiative, opening the sphere of virtuous endeavour but without appearing to do so. This feat is particularly characteristic of her heroines, who took the lead in expanding the domain of virtue while seeming not to insist that the whole social order must be modified to accommodate it.

This is because they display their rationality and independence within a context in which the thrill of observing "wild" nature—steep precipices, vast forests, sudden thunderstorms and such—can in a moment become terror in the face of the apparently supernatural. Isolated in this setting, Radcliffian heroines can exhibit a hypersensitivity to God's hand working through what seems to be the most intense disorder in nature, thereby exhibiting a quality that became a mark of virtue to a class that did not work outdoors. Then, having established their virtue in this way, they can assert their rationality as a response (though invariably a delayed one) to a supernatural that is "wild nature" in its most extreme form. Thus they could be fiercely rational without really moving outside a definition of femininity that denied this resource to women.

The respectability of Radcliffe's Gothic has to do with the fact that "real contradictions" of eighteenth-century life are so close to the "medieval" surface of her novels. The feudal ties that bind Reeve's and Walpole's characters are supplanted by sixteenth- and seventeenth-century settings, the beginning of the period of early capitalist accumulation that continued through her own time, and one of the lessons to be found throughout Radcliffe's work is the proper attitude to be taken to the very real uncertainties of the marketplace. Her villains see the possibility of capitalism for making money out of money, and chafe at the "slow diligence" that smacks of the old order of agricultural accumulation, with its dependence on nature. This attitude is what brings "death into the world" of the Radcliffian Gothic. Not only Eden as "home" but Pandemonium as "world" have been placed in the embattled realm of eighteenth-century economic life, where the virtues needed to resist the forbidden fruit are precisely those needed to survive there—thrift, prudence, and stoicism.

Exemplary in this respect are Emily St. Aubert and her father in *The Mysteries of Udolpho.* St. Aubert lives in the country, but his relationship to his tenants is not a feudal one: he collects rent and invests it. He gives this money to a M. Motteville, whom he considered worthy of his confidence. Nevertheless "a variety of circumstances have concurred to ruin him," St. Aubert tells his daughter, "and I am ruined with him." Upon hearing this, Emily repeats back her father's wisdom to him. Poverty "cannot deaden our taste for the grand and the beautiful, or deny us the means of indulging it; for the scenes of nature—those sublime spectacles, so infinitely superior to all artificial luxuries! are open to the enjoyment of the poor as well as the rich. Of what, then, are we to complain, so long as we are not in want of necessaries?" This, then, is the value of the exaggerated sensitivity to nature that virtuous Radcliffians display. It indicates an independence from the market without which virtue can turn in a moment into its opposite. Radcliffe's Gothic pastoral uses the city, on the one hand, and art, on the other, to represent those desires which only the marketplace can satisfy, drawing the weak beyond the limits set by nature in a world of agrarian self-sufficiency.

The relationship to money exemplified in Radcliffe's virtuous characters served a didactic function for the reading public of her day, particularly for the women whose leisure time for reading was supported by men whose work took them into the "world" of early industrialization. The message is that nothing desirable is to be found in that world. True happiness is attainable, therefore, only when one is adequately protected from its influence, both mentally and physically. Her villains, male and female, crave the stimulation of meteoric profits and conspicuous consumption. In the country there are not enough people to impress, and they

see its isolation only in terms of its opportunities to recoup their financial and emotional reverses illicitly and unobserved. Caught up in "art" and urban life, Radcliffian villains are unable to appreciate nature transmuted into "scenery," that is, nature emptied of its economic content as producer of food and thus (for agricultural laborers) a place for work as well as (for large landowners) a source of capital.

Radcliffe's ideal is therefore not a retreat from capitalism back into feudal relationships, as it would be for later Gothic revivalists. Her Eden is not a place that included work, as it did for Milton, but a place removed from moneymaking, a haven for self-improving leisure supported by a group of M. Mottevilles of Paris and backed up by the same garrulous but faithful servant class [seen] in Walpole and Clara Reeve, as well as agricultural laborers (recompensed we do not know how) who will bring simple "necessaries" from out of the ground, from off the trees, from the dairy, the kitchen, and the slaughtering place of domestic animals. The household established at the end of a Radcliffian Gothic then becomes a microcosm of the larger societal ideal the novel presents: the home with its (mostly female) defenders, its assailants of both sexes, and its two harmoniously integrated classes, masters and servants. Here are the forms of an earlier ideal, unrealized under feudalism, that become a goal for the future and a place from which to point out the inadequacies of the present.

In her first novel, *The Castles of Athlin and Dunbayne,* Radcliffe announces near the beginning two themes that she will take up repeatedly throughout her immensely successful career. The first is the polarities of innocence and knowledge, youthful sensibility and mature judgment, and the necessity of gaining the second without losing the first. The second, related to it, is the necessity of leaving our first Eden and the danger of so doing. Our prelapsarian state is described as follows:

> When we first enter on the theater of the world, and begin to notice its features, [the] young imagination heightens every scene, and the warm heart expands to all around it. The happy benevolence of our feelings prompts us to believe that every body is good, and excites our wonder why every body is not happy. We are fired with indignation at the recital of injustice, and at the unfeeling vices of which we are told. At a tale of distress our tears flow a full tribute to pity; at a deed of virtue our heart unfolds, our soul aspires, and we feel ourselves the doer.

This capacity for what Mrs. Barbauld calls "virtuous sympathy" represents the zenith of a character's development in a sentimental novel. Radcliffe thus sees "sensibility" in developmental terms, a valuable quality that must be supplemented, as one grows older, by others.

But Radcliffe, like Blake her contemporary and Milton her predecessor, sees beyond such a fugitive and cloistered virtue, one that feels but cannot act. Innocence (even in a female) must sally forth and meet the world of experience. What happens then is the true measure of a character's virtue or villainy. Nor is it possible to avoid this encounter; it is part of growing up. For as we advance in life

> imagination is compelled to relinquish a part of her sweet delirium; we are led reluctantly to truth through the paths of experience; and the objects of our fond attention are viewed with a severer eye. Here an altered scene appears;—frowns where late were smiles; deep shades where late was sunshine; mean passions, or disgusting apathy stain the features of the principal figures. We turn indignant from a prospect so miserable, and court again the sweet illusions of our early days; but ah! they are fled for ever! Constrained, therefore, to behold objects in their more genuine hues, their deformity is by degrees less painful to us. The fine touch of moral susceptibility, by frequent irritation, becomes callous, and too frequently we mingle in the world, till we are added to its votaries.

The world, for Radcliffe, does more than give us a taste for expensive luxuries, thereby making us dependent on money rather than on nature to supply what we think to be our wants. Our moral being "becomes callous," or "hardened," as Ruskin would later put it. Yet Radcliffe would not have accepted Ruskin's assertion, from which he drew the conclusion that a man should guard "the woman from all this," of a world that *always* hardens. We may become its votaries, but we may also develop a Blakean vision of "experience." Such a vision is, in fact, a precondition for entering into the earthly paradise where the happy ending of her novels is situated.

The need to leave behind "the sweet illusions of our happier days" in order to survive is a lesson learned by Julia, the heroine of Radcliffe's second novel, *A Sicilian Romance*. Julia's father, the Marquis of Mazzini, has imprisoned his wife under the east wing of the castle and then told his son and two daughters that their mother was dead. His motive is not direct financial gain, but rather lust for the pleasures of the city and for a woman who shares his jaded tastes. The girls live quietly with their governess, Mme de Menon, who warns them of the dangers of "the world," using her own experience of ill-fated passion as an example. Initially, then, life in the castle is represented as a simple, self-sufficient existence from which men are excluded, the marquis having taken his young son and his mistress to Naples.

But "the world" enters anyway, in the "corporal form" of the marquis, his now-adolescent son, Ferdinand, and Hippolitus, the friend of Ferdinand who, as an "outsid-

er," upsets the peaceful stasis into which the women have settled. Catching sight of him for the first time, "Julia trembled in apprehension, and for a few moments wished the castle was in its former state." But this cannot be, not only because of her own awakened sexuality but also because her father sees in her an opportunity to advance his own fortune by an arranged marriage to the Duke de Luovo, a man much like himself. In no time Julia is plotting flight with Hippolitus, and when her first attempt is foiled, leaving Hippolitus wounded, she tries again without him. This time she succeeds in escaping with her maid, whose lover has stolen a set of keys from another servant. She then wanders, as a Gothic heroine should, until she meets her old governess, who has been so shocked by the behavior of the marquis that she cannot remain under his roof.

Obviously, a higher morality than obedience to one's father or master is at work here. "Believe me," says Ferdinand when his sister consults him about the propriety of her proposed flight, "that a choice which involves the happiness or misery of your whole life, ought to be decided only by yourself." Hippolitus is even more emphatic. "'Fly,' said he, 'from a father who abuses his power, and assert the liberty of choice, which nature assigned to you.'" Hippolitus assumes that a "bond of nature" draws Julia and himself together, and that nature is above the man-made laws of a fallen patriarchal world. If God and nature "bid the same" (as they did before the fall) in the "true home" that Gothic heroines create wherever they go, then they can issue forth, like Milton's waters of creation, and, "with Serpent error wand'ring, [find] thir way." Even when this wandering takes them, as it does Julia and her governess, into a monastery where instead of sanctuary they find a prison, the reader can expect good to be brought out of this evil. A romance plot is superimposed upon the mythological underpinning of a particular culture, and reshapes it.

Once in the monastery, Julia finds that the loyalty of the "Abate" is to her father rather than to her when he makes her entrance into a monastic life a condition of his continued protection. But Ferdinand helps Julia escape, and she runs into a cave where Hippolitus, who has been pursued by bandits, has also taken refuge. Julia finds a doorway in the cave and enters through it an underground dungeon where she is recognized by her mother. Hippolitus is caught by the duke as he defends the entrance to this cave, but he escapes and follows Julia into the castle from below. Ferdinand is imprisoned in the upper part of the castle by his father, but is freed when the marquis has such a violent quarrel with his mistress that she poisons him and then kills herself. These two deaths transform the castle from a multileveled prison into a home, an Eden where sexuality is no longer connected to abuses of power. All the members of the younger generation have a hand in bringing this transformation about, but it is Julia's "courage never to submit or yield," be it to her father, the Church, the duke, or to reverses of fortune, that moves it from one point to the next.

What distinguishes virtuous determination from the Satanic parody of it that we see in Radcliffian villains is that, like Satan, a villain never really wanders in the positive sense of that word. *Wander* is related to the Old English *windan,* meaning "to turn, wind, twist," and comes to mean "to move aimlessly about" with no negative connotations. But being aimless, like being poor, takes on negative connotations in the sixteenth century, and the nonjudgmental use of the word is restricted to "poetic" usage from that time on. So it is important that Julia's wanderings be aimless, even as she is determined not to submit to the abbot, her father, or the man he has chosen for her. As with all Radcliffian heroines, her impetus to flight is to get away from what she does not want, but she does not take the further step of seeking her lover out. The fact that they meet by chance in a cave denotes the hand of Providence sanctioning their union, rather than the unguided human will through which a Gothic villain seeks to control his fortunes.

However, in the two subplots of this novel, each with an unhappy ending, Radcliffe shows passivity to be a greater contributor to female unhappiness than an excess of initiative. In these two stories, virtuous female characters fail to act at a crucial moment and thus experience the fate of sentimental heroines. The first, which doubles the "brother's friend" motif of the main plot, involves Louisa, Julia's mother, and her friend from childhood, Mme de Menon. This virtuous woman and her brother, Orlando, were orphaned and adopted by Louisa's father. Orlando fell in love with Louisa, but "a sentiment of delicacy and generosity kept him silent. He thought, poor as he was, to solicit the hand of Louisa, would be to repay the kindness of the count [her father] with ingratitude." Instead, he went off into the army, and came back for a visit with a friend who became Mme de Menon's husband. They returned to the army, a quarrel ensued between them, and Orlando was killed by his friend, whereupon Louisa, indifferent to the world, married her present husband.

Telling this story to her two charges, the daughters of her unhappily married friend who is now imprisoned in the very castle they find so protective, Mme de Menon says of her husband's return to the army with Orlando: "Had I accompanied him, all might have been well, and the long, long years of affliction which followed had been spared me." But the army is a world of men, and though the presence of women might have changed the course of history, and of this story in particular, Mme de Menon chose to stay with her friend Louisa—both victims of conventions which they let stand unchallenged. For had Louisa dared to speak her love, and thus defy the convention of female silence that, in such situations, denotes virtue, the story might have taken, at that point also, a more fortunate turn.

The other subplot concerns Cornelia, the virtuous daughter who sacrificed herself so that her brother could inherit his father's entire, meager fortune. She was in love with Angelo, but his family was "noble—but poor!" So when her father opposed the match, "he immediately entered into the service of his Neapolitan majesty, and sought in the tumultuous scenes of glory, a refuge from the pangs of disappointed passion." Rebellion of the sort that Hippolitus suggests and Julia carries out is not possible for these two because Cornelia reveres her father, as sentimental heroines often do, even though his behavior is in fact no different from that of Julia's father with respect to his daughter's heart. If only all heroines had villainous fathers, they could all rebel without compromising their virtue, and their real feelings. But "good" Cornelia has remained silent, and so, when a rich suitor comes along, her father, unaware of his daughter's feeling and thus thinking he is doing no harm, gives Cornelia a choice between this suitor and the veil.

Then her brother, who turns out to be Hippolitus, discovers her love for Angelo and persuades his well-meaning father to consent to the marriage. Hardly has this happened, however, when a rumor reaches Cornelia's ears to the effect that Angelo is dead. Believing it, she takes the veil. Then Angelo learns what has happened to his beloved, becomes a monk, and the two lovers pine away in adjacent convents. This subplot points up the complexity that accompanies a woman's barely recognized right to have the final word in "a choice which involves the happiness or misery of [her] whole life." Again, neither one did anything wrong by conventional standards. Yet Cornelia believed immediately the rumor that Angelo was dead, whereas Julia, who saw her lover wounded and carried away before her very eyes the first time she attempted to flee from her father, clings to the hope that he is alive somewhere and finally, quite literally, *runs* into him.

This fidelity of Julia's is in reality a fidelity to herself. It is this that is tested in the course of her journey from castle to monastery to cave and back again to the castle. These tests all involve resistance to coercion at the hands of those who are clearly more powerful than she is. Her triumph, like Osbert's, is the triumph of the weak and inexperienced over the stronger devotees of the world and its power. Like the children of Athlin, the two daughters of the marquis begin in a sham Eden that is untroubled as long as its master keeps his distance. It is when the marquis returns that his children become concerned with the evidence that the castle is fallen, the glimmering light in the east wing that turns out to come from the place where their mother is imprisoned. But with the marquis comes Hippolitus, who awakens in Julia those feelings that signal the end of her innocence by presenting an opportunity (in fact, the necessity, from her perspective) of disobedience.

Julia at least has a prelapsarian childhood, however limited it might have been, before she is cast out into the arena of testing. In Adeline, the heroine of Radcliffe's next novel, *The Romance of the Forest,* the author gives us a heroine who has no such experience to draw on. Thus the object of Adeline's quest is not simply the marriage partner of her choice, but a set of parents from whom she can learn what a domestic space can be. All of the characters in this novel who are not Adeline's age peers function as parents, good or bad, for the heroine. Her release into a home of her own comes only after she has found a set of adequate surrogate parents and learned that her real parents were the unfortunate but blameless victims of the Marquis de Montalt, the villain who is attempting to marry her for her fortune. Thus the novel is about parenting as much as it is about mating, taking up [a theme also found] in Charlotte Smith: what are the requisite qualities that will bring forth the founding members of the triumphant bourgeois order?

The parent figures in the novel can be arranged in three groups: one at the bottom of the moral continuum, one in the middle, and one at the top. The leader of the first group is the Marquis de Montalt, a younger son who bends all his efforts toward gaining the fortune of his brother's wife. This woman died giving birth to Adeline, so the fortune passed to her husband, whom the marquis slowly killed in a dungeon below a deserted abbey he owns. He then placed the orphaned Adeline in a convent until she refused to take the veil, whereupon he placed her with one of his henchmen, who raised her as his daughter. But when the marquis ordered this man to kill Adeline, he could not do it. Instead he brought her to an isolated dwelling where La Motte, in flight from his creditors, had taken refuge. The owner of this fortuitous sanctuary also refused to kill Adeline, and instead forced La Motte to take her with him. These henchmen are not Satanic like the marquis, but they are much too afraid of his power to do more for Adeline than pass on to someone else the responsibility for her safety. (One of them had in fact been paid by the marquis to kill Adeline's father, and had done so.)

La Motte and his wife occupy the middle position of good-bad parents. Their function in the plot is to bring Adeline to the ruined abbey where her real father was murdered by the man she believes to have been her male parent. At a crucial moment La Motte puts Adeline's safety ahead of his own, being a man "whose passions often overcame his reason, and for a time, silenced his conscience." Yet Adeline's presence does have an improving effect on him because, "though the image of virtue, which Nature had impressed upon his

heart, was sometimes obscured by the passing influence of vice, it was never wholly obliterated." He and his wife are the first people who show her love unmixed with greed or guilt. Mme La Motte "loved her as her child, and La Motte himself, though a man little susceptible to tenderness, could not be insensible to her solicitudes." They even have a son who falls in love with her, though unrequitedly.

But all is not harmonious in this found family. La Motte's avarice follows him out of the city and into the forest. In an impulsive moment he robs the marquis, and becomes sullen and withdrawn. Mme La Motte, "being unable to assign any other motive for his conduct, . . . began to attribute it to the influence of illicit passion; and her heart, which now outran her judgement, confirmed the supposition, and roused all the torturing pangs of jealousy." This jealousy proves stronger than her maternal feelings for Adeline, and she in turn withdraws from Adeline, to the distress and bewilderment of the latter. Similarly, La Motte's paternal feeling for her gives way in the presence of his fear of the marquis. So when he finds out that Adeline is planning to flee rather than give in to the demand of the marquis for her hand, La Motte betrays her into the hands of her persecutor. He gets a second chance and allows her to escape, submitting to the consequent arrest and possibility of death. But under pressure both he and his wife are transformed inexplicably, from Adeline's perspective, from being good parents to being bad ones.

People who undergo such sudden shifts cannot provide the domestic models Adeline needs. But having given her her first vision of human goodness, their later behavior tests the strength of Adeline's belief in that goodness. When she hears that La Motte has decided to hand her over to the marquis, and that his wife has not taken her side and given her a warning, she declares: "How had my imagination deceived me! . . . what a picture did it draw of the goodness of the world! And must I then believe that every body is cruel and deceitful? No—let me be still deceived, and still suffer, rather than be condemned to a state of such wretched suspicion." Adeline seems to be trying to "court again the sweet illusions of our early days," but in fact she is moving through a conflict necessary to the birth of adult virtue. Specifically, she refuses to condemn Mme La Motte, attempting instead to grasp the situation of a well-meaning person in a world where evil is no illusion. In this spirit "she now endeavoured to extenuate the conduct of Mme. La Motte, attributing it to a fear of her husband. She dare not oppose his will, she said, else she would warn me of my danger and assist me to escape from it. No—I will never believe her capable of conspiring my ruin. Terror alone keeps her silent." What confirms Adeline's belief to be more than a "sweet illusion" is the fact that she is right about her good-bad mother. Solidarity among women can be broken by men, but this is not sufficient reason to deny its existence altogether.

The ideal family to which her quest for domestic models now takes her is one where the father, named La Luc, functions as father and mother to both a daughter, Clara, and a son, Theodore. The fact that it is La Motte's servant who brings her to her new "father," the husband of his sister, gives Adeline's journey a providential shape, tracing a line from the home of her father's murderer to the place where he was murdered and finally to the home of La Luc, her future father-in-law. Adeline's growing capacity for initiative is shown by the fact that she ends her second captivity in the marquis's castle by jumping out the window. From there she runs into Theodore, who has heard of her plight and left his regiment to rescue her. The terror of her situation sweeps away considerations of "the proprieties," yet there are still obstacles to a matrimonial finale. Adeline does not know who his family is, nor does she know her own origins.

La Luc's credentials as a parent are encapsulated in a short narrative concerning a lute he has given to his daughter, Clara. Overjoyed at her new possession, Clara plays it all day long and neglects her duties, including her duty to care for the poor in the neighborhood. Her aunt (her mother being dead) wants to reprove her, but "La Luc begged she would be silent. Let experience teach her her error, said he; precept seldom brings conviction to young minds." Clara soon perceives the consequences of her neglect, and vows to put her lute aside. But temptation again overcomes her, and she begs her father to take his present back. "The heart of La Luc swelled as she spoke," Radcliffe comments: "'No, Clara,' said he, 'it is unnecessary that I should receive your lute; the sacrifice you would make proves you worthy of my confidence.' . . . 'Dear Sir,' said she, tears of pleasure swelling in her eyes, 'allow me to deserve the praises you bestow, and then I shall indeed be happy.' . . . 'You do already deserve my praises,' said he, 'and I restore your lute as a reward for the conduct which excites them.'" La Luc is following the method articulated by Locke, of internalizing guilt by conferring and withdrawing expressions of affection: "If therefore the father caress and commend [his children] when they do well, and show a cold and neglectful countenance to them upon doing ill, and this accompany'd by a like Carriage of the mother and all others that are about them, it will, in a little Time, make them sensible of the Difference; and this if constantly observ'd, I doubt not but will of itself work more than threats or blows." This substitution of the disciplinary use of affection and its withdrawal in the home, which developed alongside parallel discourses on the prison, the school, the asylum, is the code underlying the formation of [what Ruth Benedict, in *The Chrysanthemum and the Sword*, calls] a "guilt culture." The maternal gaze, here assumed by La Luc since his

children have lost their mother, has the power to constitute its charges as "good" or "bad."

Effective training is the means whereby the child/inmate/pupil registers the power of that gaze and internalizes it. So, for instance, the two children in Mary Wollstonecraft's *Original Stories from Real Life* are taught by Mrs. Mason, who had as one of her rules that "when they offended her, that is, behaved improperly, to treat them civilly, but to avoid those marks of affection which they were particularly delighted to receive." Consequently, she, like La Luc, "was never in a passion, but her quiet, steady displeasure made them feel so little in their own eyes, they wished her to smile that they might become something, for all their consequence seemed to arise from her approbation." We see that Mrs. Mason's strategy has worked when one sister says to the other: "I declare I cannot go to sleep," said Mary, "I am afraid of Mrs. Mason's eyes—would you think, Caroline, that she who looks so good-natured sometimes, could frighten one so?"

However, Adeline needs more than a good surrogate father to complete her mythic progress toward a recovered Eden. La Luc may occupy the highest rung in this novel's ladder of paternity, inasmuch as he extends his benevolence beyond the home, and "the people of his parish looked up to him as a father." But for the formation of an adult self Adeline needs to know the secret of her parentage concealed beneath the ruined abbey to which the La Motte family has magically brought her. She finds a hint one day when she notices in her room in the abbey an arras concealing a door. She enters the passageway behind it, and there discovers a manuscript written by someone who was being slowly tortured. We will learn before the novel ends that this man was her father and that his murderer was the man to whom she was given by the marquis to be brought up. But when Adeline discovers that this man is not her real father, it looks for a while as though the marquis himself may be the missing parent, who abandoned her in the convent on the death of her mother and is now trying to force her to marry him. The threat of incest is the false secret which, like the manifest content of a dream, hides the real one—Adeline's aristocratic parentage and her eligibility to inherit the family fortune.

The importance of wealth that rightly belongs to the heroine, [also an issue in *Emmeline* and *Jane Eyre*,] is a Radcliffian theme that is particularly prominent in ***The Mysteries of Udolpho***. A fortune that fell into female hands would legally become the property of a heroine's husband upon her marriage. But it enables Adeline and Theodore to settle down in the country near La Luc, and frees Theodore from the need to support himself by the male profession of soldiering. The rural endings of the Radcliffian Gothic move away not only from the industrial economy being created by

the bourgeoisie but also from the extremes of the accompanying ideology of separate spheres. This shift,
as I will argue in more detail in discussing the Brontës,
is the trajectory along which the feminine Gothic moves
toward its Lewisite antithesis.

If difficult beginnings were a prerequisite to being a
heroine, then Emily St. Aubert of *The Mysteries of
Udolpho* would be as unqualified as Austen's Catherine
Morland. If anything, her task can be framed in terms of
a situation that is the opposite of Adeline's. Emily's
parents are so overwhelmingly virtuous, so wise in their
precepts toward her, that the question for her is how she
can continue to be worthy, after they die, of the high
expectations they have placed on her. Her father, in
particular, is so anxious to protect her innocence that he
enjoins her, before he dies, not to look at certain of his
papers which would give her disturbing information
about the violent death of her aunt. With respect to the
bourgeois family, the implicit context of Radcliffe's
novels and the object of her didacticism, the problems
of Adeline and Emily represent two sides of a coin.
Either parents refuse to recognize (sometimes even going to the extreme of abandoning) their children, seeing
in them only obstacles to their own advancement, or
else they overwhelm and overprotect them, obstructing
in that way their development toward autonomy.

Just before he dies, St. Aubert gives his daughter the
injunction, coupled with a summing up of all the
knowledge she will need to retain her innocent virtue
and keep out of trouble:

> Above all, my dear Emily, said he, do not indulge
> in the pride of fine feeling, the romantic error of
> amiable minds. Those, who really possess sensibility,
> ought early to be taught that it is a dangerous quality,
> which is continually extracting the excess of misery,
> or delight, from every surrounding circumstance.
> And, since, in our passage through this world,
> painful circumstances occur more frequently than
> pleasing ones, and since our sense of evil is, I fear,
> more acute than our sense of good, we become the
> victims of our feelings, unless we can in some degree
> command them.

St. Aubert's remarks touch directly on the index of
maturity that Emily slowly acquires in the course of this
long novel, an ability to "command" her feelings. The
way of the sentimental heroine represents a danger to
her, a barrier to learning the secret in her past that throws
over her own birth a shadow of mystery. Specifically,
she must learn to command her tendency to respond
with terror and supernatural explanations to unusual
"surrounding circumstances" which prove, upon rational examination, to be *heightened nature* guiding her
wanderings in the direction of the truth she seeks.

St. Aubert thus leaves his daughter "sufficient to
[stand]" but, like Milton's Adam and Eve, free to

fall. But like the God of Genesis, St. Aubert makes
one piece of knowledge off-limits for Emily. It is,
moreover, knowledge that Emily needs if her faith in
the absolute goodness of her parents, and her consequent certainty about her authentic blood tie to them,
is to be a rational faith rather than a blind one. The
"forbidden fruit" is made concrete after Emily's
mother has died and she and her father are about to
set out toward the south for the sake of St. Aubert's
health. That night Emily sees her father sighing deeply over a miniature that is not her mother. The mystery is deepened when St. Aubert commands her to
burn his papers unexamined. Emily attempts to honor
his dying words, though her eye does land, in doing
so, on a few disturbing phrases that rouse her curiosity about the miniature. The truth that he places off-
limits, for the sake of preserving the "sweet illusions"
of Emily's earlier days, is that the woman depicted in
the miniature is his sister, murdered by her husband
for the same reason that the Marquis of Mazzini
imprisoned his spouse: he had a mistress, Signora
Laurentini of Udolpho.

The fact that a scrap of this forbidden knowledge comes
to Emily involuntarily suggests a higher power at work
similar to the one we saw in Osbert's disobedience to
this mother. In this novel one method of that higher
power lies in giving Emily partial knowledge sufficient to create a mystery and then having her wrestle
with, and overcome, the excesses of "fine feeling"
occasioned by its presence. The form that these excesses take in her is terror, an emotion she experiences
for the first time after she has destroyed those disturbing papers: "As she mused she saw the door slowly
open, and a rustling sound in a remote part of the room
startled her. Through the dusk she thought she perceived something move. The subject she had been
considering, and the present tone of her spirits, which
made her imagination respond to every impression of
her senses, gave her a sudden terror of something supernatural. She sat for a moment motionless, and then,
her dissipated reason returning . . ." At first, she thinks
it is simply "one of those unaccountable noises, which
sometimes occur in old houses." "The same sound,
however, returned: and, distinguishing something move
towards her, and in the next instant press beside her
into the chair, she shrieked; but her fleeting senses
were instantly recalled, on perceiving that it was [her
dog] Manchon who sat by her, and who now licked
her hands affectionately." The interval between the
onset of terror and the return of reason is usually more
drawn out than this, and evidence of the good intentions of the "something supernatural" never again take
a form as tangible as licking her hands affectionately.
Nevertheless this scene can stand as a structural model
for a succession of others, each increasingly challenging, that occur between St. Aubert's death and Emily's
apotheosis as a practitioner of her father's precepts
concerning sensibility.

Terror also denotes transgression, as we observed in the case of Smith's heroines. Emily has, in fact, looked at the papers she was supposed to burn unread. By refusing to tell his daughter about her murdered aunt, St. Aubert plants in Emily's mind the very intimation of evil from which he has sought to spare her: a suspicion that the relationship she had with her mother was a false one, and that it is his own infidelity that St. Aubert is trying to conceal, a past that haunts him in the form of the miniature and the papers he wants Emily to burn. It is as if transgression itself is the source of Emily's terror, and the "fine feelings" she must "command" are the trepidations she has about moving beyond the limits of innocence her father has set for her. Error is occasioned, in other words, by a vague sense of guilt, a consciousness of transgression that Smith's heroines—more rebellious but also more righteous—do not experience.

Yet the "wand'ring steps and slow" that lead away from the Eden of her birthplace, though never directed to a particular destination, and over which she has almost no control, do take Emily to the two haunted castles that between them conceal the identity and fate of the woman in the miniature. When father and daughter set out, with no more of a destination than that of going south for St. Aubert's health, they find themselves at the monastery where his sister lies buried. Moreover, they are lodged, just before his death, with a peasant, le Voisin, who gives Emily the first piece of the story her father has withheld from her, namely that the neighboring Chateau-le-Blanc was once owned by the Marquis de Villeroi and is now haunted. Emily experiences the convent itself as "haunted" by strange music, and she turns out to be right. The music is made by the now-mad Laurentini, coconspirator with the Marquis de Villeroi in the murder of Emily's aunt. Some force, which Radcliffe and her Christian readers called providence and Freudians call the return of the repressed, is clearly drawing Emily's father into the presence of the tree he has labeled forbidden knowledge.

In their first wandering steps, Emily and her father are alone, but soon they meet on the road a young man who describes himself as "only a wanderer hero." "I, too, am a wanderer," St. Aubert replies, "but neither my plans nor my pursuits are exactly like yours." Valancourt, the young man, appears to be hunting, but has not had much success. "[N]or do I aim at it," he adds. "I am pleased with the country, and mean to saunter away a few weeks among its scenes. My dogs I take with me more for companionship than for game. This dress, too, gives me an ostensible business, and procures me that respect from the people, which would, perhaps, be refused to a lonely stranger, who had no visible motive for coming among them." Like St. Aubert, Valancourt does not have to provide his own "necessaries." The estates of his family belong to his elder brother but are sufficiently large to make him known in the neighborhood, and to St. Aubert. "Wandering" after the fall, in Radcliffe's Gothic world, denotes an economic position. The aristocracy are too dissipated to appreciate nature as "scenery" in the way that Valancourt is doing. But those who depend on it for food are too predatory: their "aim" is deadly to animals. They are too-visible reminders of God's curse to Adam: "in the sweat of thy face shalt thou eat bread." Only the middle class appreciates nature while positioning itself at a sufficient distance from it.

This unfallen mode of wandering is not the only allusion to the Genesis myth in this early part of the novel. St. Aubert, as we have seen, is a conservative on matters of female innocence. He is also antipathetic to "the city," that symbol of modernity par excellence. The scenes and interests that it offers "distract the mind, deprave the taste, corrupt the heart, and love cannot exist in a heart that has lost the meek dignity of innocence. . . . How then," he asks, "are we to look for love in great cities, where selfishness, dissipation, and insincerity supply the place of tenderness, simplicity, and truth?" Valancourt, who "has never been to Paris," takes the old (in fact, dying) man back to his youth, awakening "a remembrance of all the delightful emotions of his early days, when the sublime charms of nature were first unveiled to him." When he sees Valancourt with his daughter, "they appeared like two lovers who had never strayed beyond these their native mountains, whose situation had secluded them from the frivolities of common life, whose ideas were simple and grand, and who knew no other happiness than in the union of pure and affectionate hearts." This could be a prose portrait of Milton's "blest pair" with St. Aubert urging them to "sleep on . . . and know to know no more."

Yet Valancourt does see Paris before the novel is over. He is parted from Emily after the death of her father, whose will makes his sister, Mme Cheron, Emily's legal guardian. This woman is not impressed with the credentials of Valancourt, a mere second son, and Emily dutifully refuses to see him. Then Mme Cheron is herself the object of a proposal, and Montoni, her new husband, takes the two women to his castle, Udolpho, whereupon Valancourt, in despair, throws himself into the dissipation of Paris life. Once she has escaped from the clutches of Montoni Emily must learn, if she is to forgive her former partner in purity, that love *can* exist in a heart that has lost the meek dignity of innocence. At first, she accords with her father's view of things and refuses to see the contrite Valancourt. But when she discovers that he has used money he won in gambling to rescue an innocent man from jail, she has to reject the idea that actual participation in the life of "great cities" inflicts inevitable and permanent damage. Or, as Milton put it, that

Evil into the mind of God or Man
May come and go, so unapprov'd, and leave
No spot or blame behind:

The reason she can come to this conclusion is that by the time she meets Valancourt again after his fling she herself has spent considerable time in contact with dissipation, not in Paris but as a prisoner in Udolpho. Montoni's interest in her is purely financial: he wants the estates her father left her, extracting a deathbed promise from her never to sell them and to make it an article in her marriage contract "that the chateau should always be hers." To the end of gaining this control he tries to marry her to his friend, Count Morano, who in turn tries to effect her escape with him. Each time the pressure become too much, she thinks of Valancourt and of a marriage in which her fortune will presumably be the primary source of income. Finally she gives in, only to find Montoni unwilling to keep his part of the bargain and leave her alone. Constantly anguished because she cannot lock her bedroom from the inside, she endures a life of terror without losing "her virtue" or mentioning why it is the security of her bedroom about which she is so concerned.

But there comes a point when fortitude becomes foolishness, and when Emily's aunt is killed by Montoni for *her* fortune, and the castle fills up with ladies of questionable virtue, she escapes with a young man, Du Pont, who had fallen in love with her back in the days when she lived innocently in La Vallée with her mother and father. Back then he provided a bit of mystery by carving some verses to her on the wainscot of a nearby fishing hut and appropriating a bracelet of her mother's with her picture on it. Since then he had followed her, and Montoni had imprisoned him thinking he was Valancourt. By revealing himself (in a note) to be the author of the verses, the possessor of the bracelet, and the source of a mysterious serenade that Emily has heard, Du Pont solves an old mystery and also a more recent one concerning the singing, which had let Emily know that someone with sensibilities like hers was in the vicinity of the castle. Finally the threat to her virtue in the castle outweighs the impropriety of traveling alone through the countryside with a strange male her own age. So they *wander* together toward the shore and into a boat that carries them to the very place where St. Aubert and his sister lie buried.

With these two washed up on the shore near the very place where Emily needs to be to complete the puzzle of her birth, thrown into doubt by her father's excessive scrupulousness, Radcliffe now has the problem of having Emily track down this information, and thus give a rational explanation to the mystery surrounding the miniature, without actually seeking the knowledge her father defined as forbidden. In directing Emily's verbal "wanderings" toward the solution to the false

mystery, Radcliffe has her heroine learn a middle way between capitulating to the excesses of "fine feeling" her father warned her about and dismissing the possibilities that terror opens up to her simply because they look strange in the light of common day. She has to become attuned, in other words, to a natural supernaturalism through which the ways of God are revealed to his chosen.

We see Emily struggling with this problem when, after her father's death, her peasant host and informer, le Voisin, drops dark hints to her concerning the former owner of the neighboring Chateau-le-Blanc. She mentions some strange music she has heard, and he tells her he has heard it too. "'You doubtless believe this music to have some connection with the chateau,' said Emily suddenly, 'and are, therefore, superstitious,'" implying, of course, that she is not. But le Voisin's superstitions, disembodied though they are for Emily at this stage, point to a true connection between the convent and the castle that rationally explains the mystery surrounding both spaces. The musician is the murderess, Laurentini, who wanders over the grounds of the convent in a state of guilt-ridden derangement. The clues provided by superstition are thus not present simply as tests for the heroine's sensibility. Their function is to strengthen her command over her imagination and at the same time to alert her to the need to penetrate below the surface of certain phenomena which, when subjected to the probe of reason, provide guidance that is simultaneously "natural" and divine but not, finally, terrifying.

Emily's probing has to be careful, however, not only because of her father's injunction, but also because her inquiry might lead to the discovery of indiscretion, at best, on his part, and the painful knowledge of her illegitimacy—not a subject for a lady to raise in conversation, or even to appear to be interested in. Therefore, when le Voisin responds to her charge of superstition by saying, "It may be so, Ma'amselle, but there are other circumstances, belonging to that chateau, which I remember, and sadly too," Emily bows to a convention to which even Gothic heroines are subject. "Delicacy restrained the curiosity these revived, and she enquired no further."

After her stay at Udolpho, Emily is less restrained, though still conscious of the need to be careful. When she accidentally drops the miniature she had found (and did not burn) with her father's papers, and Dorothée, an old servant, identifies it as her now-dead mistress, Emily suspects that Dorothée may have information about the marchioness that relates to her father's papers. "But with this supposition," Radcliffe notes, "came a scruple, whether she ought to enquire further on a subject, which might prove to be the same, that her father had so carefully endeavoured to conceal." She had a similar scruple when she found the miniature initially, but then assured herself that she need not burn it, that her father had spoken only of "papers."

Yet Radcliffe apparently felt the need to assure her readers that Emily would not have yielded to the impulse of curiosity

> had she been certain that the history of that lady was the subject of those papers, or, that such simple particulars only as it was probable Dorothée could relate were included in her father's command. What was known to her could be no secret to many other persons; and since it appeared very unlikely, that St. Aubert should attempt to conceal what Emily might learn by ordinary means, she at length concluded, that, if the papers had related to the story of the Marchioness, it was not those circumstances of it, which Dorothée could disclose, that he had thought sufficiently important to wish to have concealed. She, therefore, no longer hesitated to make the enquiries, that might lead to the gratification of her curiosity.

This sounds rather like Milton's Eve persuading herself that God could not possibly forbid his children what would make them wise. Dorothée does not, of course, have the whole story. Yet once Emily breaches her vow of silence in this equivocating way, the information she needs flows in. Moreover, she herself generated the evil supposition her father did not want her to have. Clearly the forces guiding Emily toward the identity of the woman in the miniature are working from a concept of innocence that St. Aubert's cloistered virtue did not fully grasp.

The person who leads Emily to the final unfolding of the truth is an abbess of the convent where St. Aubert and his sister are buried. Though the Catholic Church in the Gothic functions mostly as a provider of parodies of family life, there are exceptions, and this convent is one of them. This abbess does not go so far in a Protestant direction as the superior of the Santa della Pieta in **The Italian,** who "conformed to the customs of the Roman Church, without supposing a faith in all of them to be necessary to salvation." But when Emily came to the convent to bury her father, the abbess "suffered [Emily] to weep without interruption, and watched over her with a look of benignity, that might have characterized the countenance of a guardian angel." She calls Emily "my daughter," and introduces her to the other nuns saying, "This is a daughter for whom I have much esteem. Be sisters to her."

These familial appellations are not intended to be taken ironically, as they are when the convent is being used to imprison a heroine. Rather, they suggest that this abbess takes over as Emily's good mother while her relationship to her original one is under a cloud of uncertainty. It is worth noting, therefore, that Radcliffe gives this woman the task of conducting Emily along

that part of her journey that her father on his deathbed had specifically enjoined the abbess (through a messenger) not to let his daughter take. Female wisdom is higher than male wisdom, and in this spirit the abbess tells Emily whose daughter she is. Laurentini, who is known at the convent as Sister Agnes, shows Emily a miniature of the Marchioness de Villeroi that is just like St. Aubert's, and tells Emily that she, Emily, is that unfortunate woman's daughter. But the abbess knows that Laurentini is guilt-ridden and confused by Emily's resemblance to her dead aunt. She therefore reveals to Emily Laurentini's role in the death of the woman she so resembles.

The Mysteries of Udolpho is the most female-centered of Radcliffe's novels. The secrecy that St. Aubert would maintain with respect to the miniature, the fact that Emily sees him contemplating it in such a state of distress, Emily's resemblance to the woman depicted on it, and the rumor that she was secretly in love with, and perhaps even secretly married to, another man before she was forced to accept the marquis, all combine to suggest that St. Aubert was this secret love and that Emily is the child of that union. Like Julia, therefore, but unlike Adeline, Emily is seeking not a lost father but a lost mother. In the abbess she finds a new mother who can give her what her father could not: information that is at the same time about herself and about the effects of unrestrained passion, and that situates her in a world where good can be brought out of evil as well as destroyed by it.

Once Emily incorporates this forbidden knowledge she can forgive Valancourt and accept him as her husband, the step that brings her to the end of her journey. She is able, that is, to transcend her father's belief in the inevitable "hardening" that the capitalist world engenders, with the consequent necessity of protecting women from it. This view of innocence, which constitutes one-half of the central paradox of *Paradise Lost,* had become, by the time Ruskin gave his speech about the true home, enshrined in the ideology of "separate spheres" as the whole nature of woman. Writing in the 1790s, Radcliffe deconstructed this ideology. Her heroines find male protection at best a mixed blessing, at worst an intolerable limitation. By clothing in the romance elements of "accident and superstition" many of the actions that propel her protagonists forward, by having, for instance the mad Agnes/Laurentini tell Emily a mixture of truth and erroneous conjecture that the abbess must then rectify with the whole truth ("Emily, however, thought she perceived something more than madness in the inconsistencies of Agnes"), Radcliffe inscribes the "deep subversive impulse" underlying their journeys, presenting it as part of the natural order, the work of providence.

Finally, **The Mysteries of Udolpho** is woman-centered not only in its mythic dimension, where women are magically guided beyond the limits imposed by men, but in the domain of economics as well. This is true also of *The Romance of the Forest,* where Adeline, to whom "the rich estates of her father were restored" with the discovery of her true parentage, marries a soldier, a mere "son of an ancient family of France, whose decayed fortunes occasioned them to seek a retreat in Switzerland." Indeed not only La Luc *fils* but all the male characters in *The Romance of the Forest* have married women whose incomes are greater than theirs. Both the marquis and La Motte have dissipated the doweries of their wives, though only the marquis has raised his level of villainy from petty to grand by murdering to gain the "superior fortune" that Adeline's mother brought into her marriage to the virtuous Henri. Marrying a wealthy woman is not a crime per se in Radcliffe's world. What matters is not how much wealth you have, but whether or not you want more, and what you do to get it.

In *The Mysteries of Udolpho,* the struggle between good and evil is fought over the estates which passed from St. Aubert to Emily and those which will (and do) go to Emily on the death of her aunt, Mme Cheron. What is notable about the economics of Radcliffe's medieval world is that money and property do not automatically revert to a husband when a woman marries. This appears, in fact, to have been historically accurate for women on the Continent, particularly aristocratic women. By contrast, an eighteenth-century English husband did not have to resort to murder to acquire his wife's estates, since it was a long-established custom, undone by the Married Woman's Property Act of 1837 and subsequent legislation, that they became his on marriage. Sharply contrasting to this we have, in *The Mysteries of Udolpho,* a determination on the part of Emily and her aunt to preserve inheritance in the female line, behind which lies a conviction that without their consent there is nothing Montoni can do to become the legal owner of their property.

But Montoni does go to great lengths. Like the Harlowes in *Clarissa,* he wants to marry Emily to a man from whom he can later extract Emily's estates. Thus he attempts to "sell" Emily to Count Morano, whom he thinks to be a member of the Italian aristocracy. He is actuated "by motives entirely selfish, those of avarice and pride, the last of which would be gratified by an alliance with a Venetian nobleman, the former by Emily's estates in Gascony, which he had stipulated as the price of his favor." If Morano could acquire Emily's property automatically through marriage, we would have to assume that Montoni could have avoided the long process of torture by which he wears Mme Cheron down to the point of her death. But if a woman's consent is necessary, then Montoni's plan involves delegating some of the persuading and forcing to Morano, leaving him to concentrate on Mme Cheron while making sure he gets the fruits of Morano's efforts with Emily.

The need for such machinations suggests considerable economic power on the part of Radcliffian women. Even when Montoni does finally force Emily to sign over her estates to him after the death of her aunt, that document, Du Pont assures her later, will not necessarily be binding in a court of law. The legal system of *Udolpho* protected women to a degree that did not occur in England until half a century after the novel appeared. Before this is proven true, however, Emily sees no possibility of marriage to Valancourt once her property is gone. The question of how she will survive is not even raised. But Montoni dies "in a doubtful and mysterious manner," so Emily inherits not only Udolpho (usurped by Montoni from Laurentini, who wills it to Emily, who in turn gives it away) and the "chateau" of her childhood, La Vallée. She also buys from the relatives who had tried to modernize it the family residence where her father had grown up. These arrangements would be called by anthropologists matrilineal and matrilocal: the husband joins his wife's kin group rather than her joining his.

The Italian is not as female-centered, economically speaking, as *Udolpho* because Vivaldi, its hero, unlike Theodore and Valancourt, is an eldest son of a very wealthy family. His parents therefore do not wish him to marry Ellena, who is beautiful, passive, and poor. The discovery of her true parentage does not bring wealth with it, but merely enables her to marry Vivaldi without crossing class lines. Written in response to Matthew Gregory Lewis's *The Monk,* which claimed inspiration from *The Mysteries of Udolpho,* this last Gothic work of Radcliffe's has more of the features of a realistic novel—credible situations, "mixed" (or as we would now say, "round") characters—and fewer instances of coincidence and other forms of magical guidance that characterize the romance genre.

What makes this an unusual Radcliffian Gothic is that its center of developing consciousness is not the heroine but the villain. Engaged by the Marchesa di Vivaldi to murder her son's sweetheart, Schedoni, her confessor, comes to believe that Ellena is his own daughter by a woman who is now, herself, retired to a convent. He believes this because, at the point at which he is about to murder Ellena, he sees a miniature of himself that Ellena's aunt, Signora Bianchi, had given to her niece. Ellena has been taught that this man is her father, but the truth is that her father is Schedoni's elder brother, whom he has murdered. He also believes he has murdered his wife in a fit of jealousy when in fact this virtuous woman escaped and gave her daughter to her sister.

But why would Bianchi keep a miniature of a man who attempted (and as far as she knows, succeeded in) the murder of her sister? Clearly the miniature has a life of its own, a purpose that will be revealed at the right moment. It is preserved in Bianchi's drawer for some higher destiny, and falls into Ellena's possession precisely so that it can save her from death at the hands of the man it represents. But it saves Schedoni as well as Ellena, making him into a much more complex figure than those almost allegorical figures of evil named Malcolm, Mazzini, de Montalt, and Montoni. For though Schedoni has all the crimes, the flaws, and the birth order that characterize a Radcliffian villain, he too is traveling toward a truth he does not fully know, and it is this journey, rather than those of the virtuous Ellena and Vivaldi, that constitutes for the reader the center of consciousness in the novel. Radcliffe was writing to show her public how *The Monk* ought to have been written, but she is as much, and as little, "of the devil's party" as Milton was.

What makes Schedoni such a complex, appealing villain is that though he is, by reason of his past and his profession, an exile from the circle of domesticity, he is drawn to it, however perversely. His relationship to the marchesa, Vivaldi's mother, certainly stretches the meaning of the word "confessor." She opens up her heart to him on topics she cannot mention to her husband. "My mind is perpetually haunted by a sense of my misfortune," she tells him. "It has no respite; awake or in my dream, this ungrateful son pursues me! The only relief my heart receives is when conversing with you—my only counsellor, my only disinterested friend." We can understand in psychoanalytic and feminist terms the marchesa's feelings of rejection by a son who is in love with another woman, and her obsession with vengeance against the young and beautiful Ellena. What is more subtle is the way Schedoni falls in with her need for a person who can give her the sympathy and attention that neither her husband nor her son is willing to give her.

Schedoni has not yet discovered his own incestuous feelings for the young woman who will later appear to be his daughter. But the marchesa is right in suspecting that, of all the characters in the novel, he is uniquely capable of understanding her pain. Schedoni's own sexuality is caught in the familial net, despite the fact that he has repudiated both by becoming a monk. Yet if we go back to Schedoni's own family we see that he saw himself as an outsider there as well. First, the size of his patrimony as a younger son caused him to suffer "full as much resentment towards [his brother] from system, as he did from passion." It is in his resentment "from system" that Schedoni most resembles the heroic side of Milton's Satan, who objected more to the idea of Christ's elevation than to any consequent change in heavenly arrangements. Secondly, this brother's move to cut off "further aid than was sufficient for [Schedoni's] absolute necessities" pushes the second son's extravagance and reinforces his outsider status.

Finally, the economic aspect of sibling rivalry is augmented, as it is in *The Old English Baron,* by sexual jealousy. "That brother had a wife," Schedoni confesses. "She was beautiful—I loved her; she was virtuous, and I despaired".

Yet even when Schedoni has attained the object of his passion he cannot be happy. Seeing his wife in the mere act of talking to another man throws him into such a rage that he stabs her instead of the man, his intended victim. Schedoni's problem is not that he is contemptuous of, or disbelieving in, domestic happiness in the manner of the eighteenth-century rake. Rather, he is obsessed with it. He "trusted to have equall'd the most High," that is, his older brother, and had hopes he might surpass him in the eyes of the woman they both loved. Unable to accept second place in anything, he sees in the Vivaldi family a substitute for his original domestic relations, one in which he can have power over *their* only son, and therefore be "the most High." Having made himself indispensable to them in their need to control their son's marriage choice, he is willing to go as far as committing murder to secure the preeminence he has won in the eyes of this second family. In return, he looks to them for the advancement in "the world" that his own family did not adequately provide for him.

Yet there is plenty of room for remorse as well as moments when Schedoni becomes "stupidly good," in the manner of Milton's Satan catching sight of Eve before he tempts her. When Schedoni sees Ellena walking near the Adriatic, for instance, her innocent appeal to him for help against his henchman Spaletro brings out a fatherly compassion he had not expected. Ellena has fainted, and

> as he gazed upon her helpless and faded form, he became agitated. He quitted it and traversed the beach in short turns; he came back again, and bent over it—his heart seemed sensible to some touch of pity. At one moment he stepped towards the sea, and taking water in the hollow of his hands, he threw it upon her face; at another, seeming to regret that he had done so, he would stamp with sudden fury upon the shore, and walk abruptly to a distance.... He who had hitherto been insensible to every tender feeling, ... even he could not now look upon the innocent, the wretched Ellena, without yielding to the momentary weakness, as he termed it, of compassion.

We see here, as in the later scene where he comes into Ellena's bedroom and pauses, on the verge of murder, at the sight of the miniature, that Schedoni's tender feelings are most strongly aroused when Ellena is not conscious.

Nevertheless this scene shows that, even before he has seen the miniature, Schedoni has a range of feelings we find in no other Radcliffian villain. Confronted with the "stupid goodness" that gave Milton's Satan momentary pause at the sight of Eve (IX, 465), he girds himself for action as Milton's villain did: "Am I awake! Is one spark of the fire, which has so long smouldered within my bosom, and consumed my peace, alive! Or am I tame and abject as my fortunes? Shall the spirit of my family yield forever to circumstances?" There are no more references to the spirit of the di Bruno family so we do not know directly what it is that Schedoni is referring to. It seems likely, however, that "courage never to submit or yield" was not their response to reverses of fortune, as it was not St. Aubert's, and that such indifference to the perils of early capitalist accumulation is the source of Schedoni's bitterness.

Radcliffe plays up Schedoni's incipient virtue, allowing him to become as genuinely fond of Ellena as a monk in a Gothic novel can be fond of anything good. Unlike Lewis's Ambrosio, against whom she was writing, he is never taken over entirely by evil. He is, rather, the site of a struggle between his old family and his new one, between the di Brunos, who yield forever to circumstances, and the Vivaldis, who are so determined to control their fortune that they will murder a penniless girl. Ellena is the point of connection between these two families, and it is when Schedoni realizes he might have killed his own daughter that "stupid goodness" becomes more than a fleeting deterrent to crime. It becomes the mark of the "outsider," the exile from domestic happiness whose point of view is represented in the masculine or Lewisite Gothic, toward which the feminine Gothic, with its "deep subversive impulse," is developing.

Janet Todd (essay date 1989)

SOURCE: "'The Great Enchantress': Ann Radcliffe," in *The Sign of Angellica: Women, Writing, and Fiction 1660-1800,* Virago Press Limited, 1989, pp. 253-72.

[*In the following excerpt, Todd provides a detailed overview of Radcliffe's novels and discusses the traits that distinguish her from both her eighteenth-century predecessors, such as Samuel Richardson, and her nineteenth-century successors and contemporaries, such as Mary Wollstonecraft.*]

Mrs Radcliffe came into the public consciousness with her third novel, *The Romance of the Forest,* in 1791. This was followed in 1794 by *The Mysteries of Udolpho* and in 1797 by *The Italian.* The three novels span the 1790s, the years of liberal welcome for the early moderate phase of the French Revolution and the later comprehensive reaction in an England now at war. They also surround the publication of the two most notorious works of Wollstonecraft and Hays, and the sensational gothic novel *The Monk* of Matthew Lewis.

Ann Radcliffe was read by those who now form part of the literary heritage of England: Coleridge, Shelley, Keats and Byron, all of whom show her distinctive influence. She was also read by women, servingmen and apprentices. Her popularity was extraordinary. Walter Scott described how the volumes flew from person to person and were sometimes torn from a reader's hand, and she was accepted as 'at the head of a class' according to Mrs Barbauld in her *British Novelists* of 1810. Whatever their considered attitude might have been, many educated women made it clear that the books were a felt presence in their lives. Mrs Piozzi wrote to her daughter in 1794 that she was compared to Radcliffe's Emily in her habit of versifying at odd moments, a comparison also made to flatter the Lichfield poet Anna Seward. When reviewed alone, Radcliffe was considered as a serious historical writer, coupled on the odd occasion with the securely great like Shakespeare.

But, as imitators proliferated and the romantic gothic became firmly associated with women and with pap literature, the carping grew. Along with Jane Austen, E. S. Barrett in *The Heroine* mocked the effect on his ludicrous heroine of the 'inebriating stimulants' of Radcliffe. He also managed to associate her 'extreme of vicious refinement' with the malign destabilising influence of Rousseau. Mrs Radcliffe would not have liked a connection either with inebriation or with revolutionary France. Indeed there is evidence that she would rather have avoided entirely this public discussion of herself and the mode which she so successfully dominated.

Unlike Wollstonecraft and Hays, whose lives became public property, Mrs Radcliffe guarded her privacy. Despite her stature in the women's fictional tradition and in Romantic literature generally, there are remarkably few biographies and Christina Rossetti abandoned the notion of writing her life for lack of material. Indeed in her later years she was so secluded that many contemporaries thought that she had died long before she had or that she was confined in a lunatic asylum, driven mad by her own terrors. It was typical of her extreme value of privacy that she did not write to the newspaper to refute the rumour. The situation was made the more ridiculous and confusing by the weird proliferation of her image, brought about by unscrupulous publishing houses like the Minerva Press. Late into the nineteenth century, books by the far less versatile gothic novelist Mary Anne Radcliffe were still said to be by the author of *The Romance of the Forest,* while the publisher of the polemical *The Female Advocate* by Mary Ann Radcliffe, who had wanted to remain anonymous, also wished to profit from a confusion of names.

The little that is known of Radcliffe concerns mainly her context. She came from lower-middle-class stock, had some connections with Dissenters and some reassuring ties with the gentry. Her husband William was a political journalist with Whig views, a supporter of the early Revolution, but later, once war was declared and the Revolution had entered its violent phase, an upholder of national unity. As they can be gauged from her novels, Ann Radcliffe's own political views responded to the stirring events of the times but did not change with them. Holding to a Whiggish line, she nostalgically valued the sentimental notion of community above individualistic effort and believed with Edmund Burke in the commonsensical English way of slow constitutional reform rather than outright revolution. But she also held the liberal's abhorrence of secretive power, dangerous both to the individual and to the state, whether it was embodied in a person or in an institution like the Catholic Inquisition, and there may be muted references in her novels to the contemporary forms of institutional power in the *ancien régime,* the French revolutionary tribunals, and indeed the repressive war government of England itself.

As an Anglican, Radcliffe opposed religious extremes of all kinds. She disliked Catholic celibacy because it worked against the sense of community and family, on which foundation she placed her values. She accepted divine providence but opposed superstition. In her novels no supernatural explanation is given and the dead do not return to haunt the living, although providence may be working in her plots and many coincidences. Indeed at the end of *The Romance of the Forest* she draws attention to this force, which is not chance but 'a Power whose designs are great and just'.

With such conservative, sentimental values, it is not surprising that Mrs Radcliffe should also also hold to the conventional image of the woman writer, the genteel domestic lady who happens to write and whose writing, in the absence of superior duties—the Radcliffes had no children—could serve as an extension of her domestic social role. Her sign as author was clearly that of the lady, who, like her heroines, fell into verse on many occasions but did not set up primarily for artistry and, while heavily marked by sentimental qualities, entirely avoided the route of individualistic emotion and excess followed by the heroines of Wollstonecraft and Hays. Her obituary by her husband catches the image; it reveals his wife's 'natural repugnance to authorship' although her genius directed her towards it and declares her refusal to 'sink for a moment, the gentlewoman in the novelist'. Unlike Monk Lewis, who dined out on his novel for the rest of his life, she did not desire fame or publicly enjoy success.

Despite her discreet image, Radcliffe was most associated in the popular mind with horror and sensation, a manipulation of menace and terror. Taking the archetypal sentimental story of fatherly male menacing a weak but virtuous female who in the end triumphs over him or neutralises his power, she heightens the elements, obscures and magnifies, making a moody menacing patriarch whose immense shadowy outlines suggest incest, rape and murder. She does so, however, with control. Terror is tamed and her endings see the light switched on in the murky places. Ordinary justice deals with extraordinary guilt.

Consequently the sentimental gothic novel was for Radcliffe and many other women writers a genre suitable for a lady, dealing in the possible but improbable, facing fears in an ultimately decorous because oblique and displaced way. When Matthew Lewis broke through the veil of decorum with his sadistic fantasy, *The Monk,* and made explicit the implicit, not only describing a rape but making the rapist a monk, the victim his sister and blaming male sexual arousal on women, Radcliffe must have felt rather like Lady Echlin contemplating the appalling fate of Clarissa or Clara Reeve coming upon the sexual act in Rousseau's *Héloïse.* She must have considered herself rather more implicated, since Lewis openly claimed to have been inspired by the work of Mrs Radcliffe.

As she aims to use the fearful gothic elements with care, she also aims to use with control the powerful legacy of female sensibility, by this time a potentially dangerous self-indulgent and socially disruptive quality. Unlike so many writers at the end of the decade, she seems not to want to abandon sentimental values altogether, but she clearly does wish to stiffen them. Principle is added to feeling as a guide to action, and fortitude is stressed to combat self-indulgence. Unregulated sensibility creates victims of feeling, sensualists like Laurentini of *The Mysteries of Udolpho* who acts like 'a fiend'. Without regulation sensibility can degenerate into sexuality in an individual and anarchy within a community, but without sensibility at all there can be only selfishness, coldness and cruelty.

In form she seems to have aimed at a judicious mix. The gothic must remain within the sentimental romance or else it can become sensational and horrific like Lewis's *Monk.* But the sentimental must also be contained in the gothic, the obscure, the slightly distanced. In the early *Romance of the Forest* she seems momentarily to have forgotten this in her treatment of the hero when in prison awaiting execution with his father: the scene is so sentimentally realised that it can be halted only by bizarre anticlimax. She does not make a mistake like this in her last two novels.

Because she insists on moral clarity, Radcliffe's gothic romance can become a novel of ideas, harking back to the early novel of sentiment. In *The Romance of the Forest,* for example, the villain puts forward the Hobbesian notion, being revitalised at the time by the Marquis de Sade, that self-preservation is the first law of nature, that the world must be apprehended dialectically and that morality is relative: 'It is the first proof of a superior mind to liberate itself from prejudices of country, or of education,' he insists, echoing the seducers of Delarivier Manley, who also relied on the argument of varying cultures to relieve their victims of their principles. But the sentimentalist knows that all this philosophy ends in the defiling of a woman or of the community she embodies, and their argument has the last word through its expression in conversation and plot.

Holding to the image of the lady writer, then, Radcliffe withdraws from the extremes of sentimental fiction as it had developed in the 1770s and 1780s and as it was being exemplified in the scandalous works of Wollstonecraft and Hays. Her books are launched with a definite and morally reliable storyteller or narrator, who expects to share her values with her readers. As in most earlier female fiction, the narrator does not assume the importance of a main character, as happens in Fielding's novels, since this would suggest for Mrs Radcliffe an unfeminine assumption of authority, but, unlike the characters, this narrator is in control—hence the annoyance of some readers at what seems a wilful refusal to tell all the facts—and any exclamatory writing to the moment in the manner of high sensibility occurs only in interpolated manuscripts. The narrator endorses the heroines but also judges them when inadequate, and the verdicts on lesser characters are absolute. There is none of the conflicting or modifying impressions of Hays and Wollstonecraft, heirs of the epistolary fiction that always had a tendency towards solipsism and relativity.

As in the novel of sentiment, readers are organized in their responses; they are co-opted into the judgements of the narrator and also allowed into the suspense of the characters whose 'thrilling curiosity', paranoia and superstitious terror they are sometimes reproved for sharing too whole-heartedly. The need for control as well as sensitivity is stressed when readers are drawn to follow events as they appear to the protagonists rather than heeding the narrator's admonishments. 'Pleasing dread' is expected for characters and readers, but should not be taken to paralysing excess. The disappointment many male readers, including Hazlitt and Coleridge, felt at the rational explanations and final morals was in a way a proper punishment for too great indulgence in the simple delight of suspense. Only horrors could begin to fulfil the expectations and Mrs Radcliffe unlike Monk Lewis will not provide these; horror, she considers, contracts the soul where terror humbles and opens it. A woman reader might welcome the experience of female powerlessness removed and vulnerability protected by firm narrative, and might dissent from the (still current) male response to Lewis's explicit sexual writing as liberating.

As was suggested by Wollstonecraft and Hays, fiction in the late eighteenth century was often concerned with sensibility as self-expression, with a solipsistic world in which alone the individual feminine sensibility could be pre-eminent. Mrs Radcliffe will have none of this, and readers and characters are taught responsibility through idyllic pictures of sentimental community, through narrative comments and through anecdotes designed for edification. In *The Romance of the Forest* a girl learns that artistic longings must give place to domestic duties for women in an incident that is solely displayed for the improvement of readers. Elsewhere in the same novel they are encouraged to judge what they might indulgently have approved or to be indulgent where they might have mocked: 'If this sensibility was . . . a weakness, it was at least an amiable one, and as such deserves to be reverenced'. In *The Mysteries of Udolpho* readers are taught to temper sensibility with common sense and 'beware of the first indulgence of the passions'. Certainly there is no self-indulgent reference to the author's life—although even Radcliffe could not resist publishing a poem separately under the pseudonym Adeline, the name of the heroine in *The Romance of the Forest*.

Her aim was to harness the sentimental novel once again for serious purpose, to return it to the moral ethical aim of the earlier novel of sentiment while greatly extending its range. With her sure narrative voice and moral purpose, she wanted to pull such fiction out of its self-indulgent morass and ensure its continuing commitment to a conservative vision of harmonious and loving community. At the same time she knew herself to be a writer of romance and a dealer in magic, and she was not prepared to follow the route of the tract-writing Hannah More.

Radcliffe's gothic romances each have similar patterns. In *The Romance of the Forest* the heroine, Adeline, is forced by her captors on the moody La Motte, who is escaping from justice in Paris. The ruin in the forest where they hide belongs to the wicked Marquis Montalt, who first aims to seduce the beautiful Adeline and then to murder her when he discovers in her his dispossessed niece. She is helped in her escape by the hero, Theodore, with whose idyllic family, La Luc, she unknowingly takes refuge in the mountains; it is to this retreat that hero and heroine return once Adeline has been ennobled and enriched by discovery of her birth. In *The Mysteries of Udolpho* the idyllic patriarchal family community of La Vallée begins the novel and it is broken up by the forces of selfishness and materialism when the father of Emily, the heroine, dies. She comes under the guardianship of a rich and trivial aunt, Madame Cheron, whose ill-judged marriage makes the threatening Italian, Montoni, into her uncle. In his enormous and remote castle of Udolpho, parody or reverse of the ideal La Vallée, Emily experiences the terror both of the supernatural and of the natural as she confronts the castle's bloody past and the present possibility of rape and assault. The ending re-establishes the idyllic community of hero and heroine and, as in *The Romance of the Forest,* this is again set in a rural Eden away from aristocratic power.

Perhaps in response to *The Monk,* published nine months before Radcliffe's novel was advertised, her last novel, *The Italian,* is more sombre. Opening with an assassin in an Italian church, it is less about the internal terrors of the mind than about real ones, about human cruelty and material oppression rather than ghostly fears. The heroine, Ellena, is loved by the noble Vivaldi, whose ferocious mother is helped in her persecution of innocence by the mysterious and gloomy monk Schedoni, the most developed of Radcliffe's villains. Idyllic and familial communities are even more threatened than in the earlier novels and the place of imprisonment, the prison of the Inquisition, is made more terrible through its association with religion and state power. The ending resettles the good characters in the social world of emotional personal ties, away from aristocratic cruelty and mercantile greed.

An obvious appeal in all three novels is the gothic interior—castles, monasteries, prisons, dungeons and remote huts—site of the heroine's encounter with the evil guardian. Such places suggest the power of others and yet to the imaginative mind, both of the characters and of the reader, they are strangely ambiguous, in one view oppressive in their force and in another liberating to the mind in their obscurity, rather like the visionary prisons and castles of Piranesi's drawings. They have as comparison the great prison of the Bastille, recently destroyed but still fascinating to a Europe in political turmoil. They are associated with the powerful villains, who are certainly horrific in their potential cruelty but also, in a way, noble beside the other weak and debased men.

In all the Radcliffe endings, as obscure and shifting identity is finally made clear, there is a flight from the shadowy aristocratic edifices, although the legacy of the castle in the shape of the heroine's inheritance is usually accepted when tamed and clarified to benevolent purposes. Despite Adeline's newfound nobility and wealth, she and the more middle-class hero Theodore flee the castles and estates of aristocracy to set up as the new guardians of the rural community with La Luc, aristocrats of sentiment rather than of rank.

This is a nostalgic paternalistic grouping mixing the sentimental visions of Richardsonian service and Rousseauian bonding, in which hierarchy is softened by affection and familial love. Avoiding the potentially disruptive and excessive ties of female friendship, Radcliffe concentrates on the affectionate relationship of husband and wife and of father and daughter, and she socialises the reclusive obsessive tendency of individual sentiment by describing the melancholy moods feeding back into social action, not into exaggerating

self-absorption. La Luc, the exemplary father of Theodore, derives strength for benevolence through his solitary contemplation of his wife's grave.

The benevolent person dominates the community; the philanthropy, described as 'divine', was 'diffused through the whole village, and united the inhabitants in the sweet and firm bonds of social compact', while the happiness of Adeline and Theodore was 'diffused to all who came within the sphere of their influence'. The open community of La Luc contrasts with aristocratic power in the shadowy forest and with the debased society of Nice where arbitrary government has rendered the peasants discontented. It is a sentimental replacement, not by force or forceful revolution but by providential means through the established institutions of the law—even the Inquisition finally delivers justice—or through the activities of individual benevolent men and women. The guardians are not tainted with capitalist competition like city people or with aristocratic privilege, but they have effortlessly the power to do good. The books are full of veils that in the end are understood rather than torn off, suggesting that the 'decent drapery' so appreciated by Burke need not be ripped away but may, if necessary, be slowly removed.

Servants figured both in the gothic extravaganza of Walpole and in the sentimental novel, but it was left to Mrs Radcliffe to raise the tie of master and servant to its affective height. Against the background of middle-class grumbling about uppish domestics and the perennial worry, no doubt exacerbated by the Revolution in France, that servants would form a class antagonistic to the interests of their employers, Radcliffe created a series of comic and devoted retainers, who ministered to the age's desire for an image of selfless service outside the capitalist reality of cash and wages. The most striking of her creations is Paulo in *The Italian*.

Paulo stays with his master when his friends desert him. He tries to cheer him even when it appears that Vivaldi has brought them both to certain death. Indeed he seems to have no life of his own that is not at the service of his master, although it is stressed that he is in fact a lively, gregarious fellow. Given the peculiarly decorous nature of the heroine in *The Italian,* his emotional attachment to Vivaldi very much moves the tie of master and servant into the centre of the stage, and the last section of the novel, which takes Paulo to the dungeons of the Inquisition solely to be with his master and then finds him exulting throughout the town at the final escape, is very much a male love affair excluding any woman. It has all the emotionality of the tableaux of high sensibility:

> 'It is my master! it is my dear master!' cried Paulo, and, sending off a nobleman with each elbow, as he made his way between them, he hugged Vivaldi in his arms, repeating, 'O, my master! my master!' till

joy and affection overcame his voice, and he fell at his master's feet and wept.

The chaste caress of Ellena is no match for this and Paulo with his noisy love dominates the ending with a joy that 'has rendered him delirious'. When asked to name a reward, his only demand is that no money be given to him to make him independent of his master.

Paulo represents a fantasy of service, an exaggeration of the component in the sentimental novel. Thrilled by their tie to their masters—it is more a male than a female image, although there *are* devoted female servants—these unmercenary men become as passionate in their devotion as any lovers. When the tie is between man and maid as in Richardson's *Pamela,* a sado-masochism is latent in the relationship, as Mr B amply shows in the numerous scenes he stages for Pamela to sob at his feet (the Marquis de Sade with his rewritings of Richardson and Rousseau in brutal sexual mode made it difficult for any of his readers to see these exploits as completely innocent again); at the same time there is a threat to the social hierarchy since inappropriate marriage can after all occur, as it does in *Pamela.* When master and servant share the same sex there is less sexual and social threat, and the proper working of the relationship becomes part of the proper working of harmonious community. La Motte alienates his faithful manservant and cannot function as the patriarch of his family and friends.

In its use of obscure interiors and veiled terrors, the world of Radcliffe's novels exemplifies the Burkean sublime. In his *Philosophical Enquiry into the Origin of our Ideas of the Sublime and Beautiful,* Burke had discussed the human fascination with what should repel, for the forbiddingly grand, for the half known and the hidden. Art is not a photographic copy but, in its reference to the sublime, deals with the obscure and the secret. For Radcliffe suspense is in the mind's response to the hidden, in fearful dreams and in faulty perceptions that fashion the supernatural, and in the doubling of character that obscures the proper barrier of inner and outer worlds. Her works show the etiology of illusion and fear, knowing that, as she expressed it, reason may not impose her laws on all the obscurities of the imagination. Terror is sophisticated and it exists in the veil, the curtain or the mist. In *The Mysteries of Udolpho* a black veil becomes a famous symbol of gothic suspense; it conceals the wax image of a corpse from which the heroine flees in unnecessary fear. Readers share the fear—including the most famous reader, Catherine Morland of *Northanger Abbey,* who never seems to get beyond the veil with her reading. Had she done so she would have learned that real fear should be reserved for what is not at all obscure or sublime, the passion of the violent uncontrolled woman with whom the veil and the image are associated.

Fear is an appropriate response in a world where women have property or at least the opportunity of transmitting it, but where they have little power to control it. Mrs Radcliffe does not bring into sharp focus what is so apparent to the modern reader of her books, the financial as well as sexual threat to the heroines, but she does present it. Adeline was to be seduced or raped when she was innocent, but killed when she might be rich; Emily is pursued by Montoni for her money not her body, and even the would-be rapist in *The Mysteries of Udolpho* is a man 'of ruined fortunes' who craves Emily's estates as well as her virginity. Sexual energy turns quickly into capitalist energy, the individualistic enterprising desire of the entrepreneur of sex and money. Where her dying father warns Emily against excessive feeling, her dying aunt talks of the estates in France which, because she has refused to sign them over to her husband, she can leave to her niece.

The villains are uncles. In the sentimental novel the uncle figure, divorced from patriarchal authority but still close kin to the heroine, has often been an influence for good, the giver of sound advice and perhaps the provider of fortune—the experience of Maria in Wollstonecraft's *Wrongs of Woman.* But he could also hark back to Manley and express a threatening desire for the heroine, either directly or through a younger man, often his son. The desire might well be sexual but it is just as likely to be economic as well; usually the uncle has usurped the status and wealth of the heroine's father and the defiling of the daughter becomes a final triumph in a process of wickedness or a horrific act that displaces the economic one not represented. Certainly for Radcliffe the sexual and economic are mingled, but it is not really an equal association; perhaps it might better be said that the economic is sexualised, given the erotic power of sexuality, but that sex itself is played down.

Actual sexual lust appears rather absurd; it tends to motivate the young and uncontrolled. These are no match for the controlled and single-minded older men who crave the always obscurer power of status and money. Despite his wife's fears and despite eroticised descriptions of his encounters with the heroine—he is described as towering over the weeping girl in dishabille—La Motte in *The Romance of the Forest is* not interested in Adeline sexually; Montoni in *The Mysteries of Udolpho* wants Emily's money and arrays her seductively to be bought by others; Schedoni in *The Italian* is concerned with manipulation and control; leaning over to kill Ellena, worrying unnecessarily that her clothes will impede his knife, he is stopped only by a portrait that seems to represent himself. All these men are vigorous and middle-aged; their threat is physical, economic and social but not primarily sexual, although the female fear of violation, rape or incest lends power and vocabulary to their menace, especially for the fearful reader. They do not commit rape and incest, at least not on the body of the heroine, and often they rescue her from sexual assault. Sexuality in Radcliffe suggests lack of self-control and the most obvious feature of her later villains is their icy self-possession.

The exception would seem to be Montalt, the uncle villain of *The Romance of the Forest* who tries to buy Adeline. But even in him the desire is more for the submission of a woman than for sexual pleasure—he would have agreed with Burke's quintessentially masculine statement that 'we submit to what we admire, but we love what submits to us'. Yet he plays a less conspicuous part than the other uncle villains and does not dominate the book as much as the mediocre villain La Motte. After *The Romance of the Forest* Radcliffe does not repeat her overt use of the sexual threat in the uncle villain and her later creations are never motivated by a desire of violation at whatever social and spiritual cost, unlike the wicked Ambrosio of Lewis's *Monk*—nor would she ever have muddied the clear issue of female victimisation by making the victimised woman a seducing devil, as Lewis did.

Ambiguity is not allowed to Radcliffe's heroines and the collusion of heroine and villain which the twentieth-century, psychoanalytical reader insists in finding in the Clarissa myth and in the gothic novel is not the most important feature in the ties of Emily and Ellena with Montoni and Schedoni. Again in Radcliffe there is the spectacle of the female novel pulling away from any founding of villainy on the ultimate fact of rape, perhaps because of the fear that rape as defined in the eighteenth century always might implicate the woman. The threat of rape in Radcliffe is usually embodied in far less terrifying and fascinating men than the uncle villains. Never could a Radcliffe heroine follow Richardson's Pamela into disliking the actions and attitudes of a man but admiring 'his Person'.

But of course it is precisely the unknowable motivation, the brooding sense of menace that does not quite seem contained in the economic motives, that make Radcliffe's villains so fascinating to the reader, caught up in their plots quite as much as the young heroines. When at the end the past is revealed, it is always disappointing, for it is delivered without description of those passions that have etched deep lines on the interesting faces of the villains. Byron's moody heroes in *Childe Harold* and his oriental tales, who descend from Radcliffe's gothic Italians, have usually loved and lost as explanation for their harsh isolation, but they have a similar excess of energy.

The Byronic hero, although influenced by Radcliffe, is not a Radcliffean creation and the distinction between the types is significant. Sympathy may be granted momentarily to a villain in his loneliness or wavering, but Radcliffe will not allow the reader to take the amoral

stance of Byron and find these men the centres of interest. They remain like Milton's Satan evil, not energetically admirable in the manner of Blake's Romantic version. All are ultimately bad and their crimes are real, even if, as in Montoni's case, they may not be as numerous as the imaginative heroine had supposed. All are denied an heroic death that might give them centrality and undermine the re-establishment of the idyllic community which they have menaced. Montalt and Schedoni are simply and banally condemned by the law and they kill themselves; La Motte, only a semi-villain, is tamed into a pensioner of the heroine, and Montoni is killed off as a brigand in one clause of a sentence. The radical notion that villainy can be explained and excused by knowledge of the circumstances and constraints of a life is eschewed in favour of the sentimental idea that there are good and evil; the evil may suddenly and absolutely reform or they may not.

In complete contrast to the villains are the young heroes, whose faces are entirely unlined. Like Radcliffe's other main character types they are taken from the sentimental novel and they function according to type whatever the suspense of the action; as the faithful servant will not prove faithless to the virtuous characters, as the heroine will never lose her virginity, and as the villain may engage the reader but cannot flourish, so the hero may be passive and inept, but the heroine will in the end marry him. As in the earlier sentimental novel he is a refined feminised man, well born but not excessively privileged in his social position. He expresses the sentimental fantasy that unaggressive feminine sentiment can be extended to men. If the villain has an exaggerated menace, the hero has absolutely none—except perhaps the worry that his weakness may lead him into vice—and indeed he is frequently inept in his necessary function of rescuing or saving the heroine. He is often absent during the heroine's ordeals and he is given to moaning and complaining about his own situation as much as pitying hers. Rarely does he encounter the villain directly and there is never the straight battle of romance for the lady. In the end she herself usually takes charge through her superior firmness—or her money and status. In some ways the hero functions as an inferior version of the charming and benevolent heroine, weaker or perhaps less well born and often less perfect.

In Radcliffe's gothic romances there are touches of psychological realism which lure the reader into belief in their world. Whole characters like La Motte in *The Romance of the Forest,* the irascible selfish husband whose moods must be attended to by all his women, and Madame Cheron in *The Mysteries of Udolpho,* the heroine's selfish and trivial aunt who is humanised only in the end by her understanding of the common female predicament, have a realism beyond the schematic needs of romance; in their arbitrary power over the fates of the heroines they must have seemed a pretty convincing threat to young female readers. The heroines too have touches of human complexity; Adeline is too self-pitying, Emily too indulgent of her imaginative susceptibility, and Ellena almost obsessive in her concern for propriety.

Yet there is no real inner life of the kind being investigated by Wollstonecraft and Hays. Terror and anxiety are rendered through fear of doubling images of the self—'There was a glass before her upon the table, and she feared to raise her looks towards it, lest some other face than her own should meet her eyes'—and through dreams recounted in a style that stresses their archetypal nonspecific quality and inevitably brings them close in appearance if not in purpose to the analysed dreams of Freud. Adeline, for example, obsessed with her lack of a conventional loving parent, dreams of herself bleeding and wounded, the situation of the father she will later discover. She dreams again of a dying man, subsequently revealed as her father; like a lover he tries to hold her, but she pulls away from him. Pursuer and pursued are mixed, lover and father, safety and menace. These dreams differ from the simply monitory dreams of, for instance, Fanny Burney, in their use again of the terror of doubled characters, simultaneous existence in and outside the dream, but they are not really allowed psychological import. They function primarily as gothic supernatural without the supernatural being invoked, rather like the phantasmagoria about to become popular in England, which paradoxically made spectres absurd and at the same time 'real' since they were actually to be seen. Radcliffe, famous for explaining the non-natural, does not explain the possible revelations of dreams. But neither does she insist that the truth exists in the unconscious.

As in Sarah Fielding's novel of sentiment, inner drama is often rendered generally and epigrammatically through abstractions: 'Terror was softened into anxiety, and despair into grief.' Or it is given through theatrical soliloquies of the characters that avoid the problem of gradual disclosure. The mind is not clearly individualised, but in the virtuous characters has a generalised, aesthetically pleasing quality. In all it is aptly imaged through the phantasmagoria or magic mirror: 'His mind resembled the glass of a magician, on which the apparitions of long buried events arise, and as they fleet away, point portentously to shapes half hid in the duskiness of futurity.' A kind of fantastic psychology replaces both the supernatural and the earlier mechanistic notion of the mind.

Radcliffe's novels are not really tending to realism of surface and character. She is not trying to recuperate the recent past and display it in all its specificity and detail, as Sir Walter Scott will soon begin to do in his historical novels. Indeed her anachronistic descriptions are closer in effect to the poetic use of the past in the sentimental poets, who, like Gray and Macpherson with Ossian, create an obscure and romantic ancient Britain, still potent in the verse of the 1790s. She is not aiming at 'life' or insisting with a nineteenth-century novelist like George Eliot that what she writes is inevitably the reflection of surface truth. Ultimately for her the novel, although it must powerfully engage the reader, must also be useful in a way the male gothic of Monk Lewis clearly was not. So her characters stop to display feminine propriety, often to the amazement of a modern reader—as when Emily at a moment of extreme danger worries that she is leaving in undress without a hat or when Ellena is concerned about being alone with her fiancé on whose help her life depends.

The heroines of Radcliffean romance are virtue in distress, although passivity alone is not as potent as in earlier sentimental fiction. The beauty of their role is unquestioned and is often expressed in poetry that demands complete assent. In *The Romance of the Forest,* Adeline is introduced with the very sound of feminine sensibility: 'sobs and moanings'. Her first action is worthy of Richardson's Pamela: 'She sunk at his feet, and with supplicating eyes, that streamed with tears, implored him to have pity on her.' She has the spontaneity and authenticity of sensibility; her expressions are artless and simple. 'Mild, persecuted', pale and timid, she is constantly reacting with her body; she goes white, totters, and faints, to the extent that she almost involves the hero in death, since he attacks his commander while trying to support her on one of the many occasions when she is insensible.

The expressive body of sentimental fiction is again clearly the mark of the sincere heroine, but it must also be controlled for it may express more than is proper for the conscious woman. The body may be abducted, stolen and imprisoned, taken out of its own control, but the heroines must not collude in these acts. In uncontrollable situations, unconsciousness or domination, desire may be expressed, but decorum must quickly halt the expression.

As Edmund Burke had noted to Wollstonecraft's irritation and as the Marquis de Sade would exemplify, the affecting pathetic beauty is best calculated to move a man. But, although Radcliffe touches on the sexual attractiveness of the distressed beauty of Adeline and Emily, she refuses to accept this sexuality overtly. She simply will not know and she rejects the escape of irony. In a way she here exemplifies the route of the heroines themselves, who display and yet must efface their own sexuality. 'The languor of sorrow threw a melancholy grace upon her features, that appealed immediately to the heart,' the narrator declares of Adeline, and 'her beauty, touched with the languid delicacy of illness, gained from sentiment what it lost in blood. The negligence of her dress, loosened for the purpose of free respiration, discovered those glowing charms, which her auburn tresses, that fell in profusion over her bosom, shaded, but could not conceal.' Emily had 'the contour of a Madonna with the sensibility of a Magdalen'. It is a watcher's view, for Mrs Radcliffe is always aware of the gaze on and of the woman. Yet she insists, despite these descriptions, so reminiscent of the romances of Haywood or Behn, on the reader's decorous response. (The heroines also avoid sexual involvement and, when Emily watches for Montoni out of the castle window, she is fascinated by his power but inspired less by sexual attraction than by moral amazement, sentimentally disappointed that a fair exterior should clothe inner evil.)

After the publication of *The Monk,* in which the passionate sexual woman *is* the madonna—she has modelled for the picture—and uses the identification to seduce the monk, Radcliffe pulls away from any risqué physical depictions of the heroine. Ellena in *The Italian* is by far the most passive of the three heroines, the most concerned with propriety, the most anxious to refuse sexual allure. Her face is only unveiled for the first time when she stoops to do a kind deed, in complete contrast to the first sensational appearance of Adeline, and, as she faints less, she is less available for scenes of erotic gazing. In addition she divides the book with the hero who is himself often placed in the helpless position of a woman; the possibility of sadistic description is lessened when it is a man who is dominated and tortured.

Because sexual love is the 'selfish passion' and because sensual beauty divorced from sensibility is an economic commodity in these novels, scenes of love between hero and heroine must avoid the erotic. So courtship is conveyed through conversations on 'elegant literature', through appreciation and interpretation in music, and through shared raptures over scenery, in sum through similar sensibility, controlled and refined away from self-indulgence and existing as a kind of surplus in the economic framework of the novel. The quality is essential in both partners, an innate one nurtured by a good home and by nature, and it forms the basis of choice in relationships; if virtue is active sensibility, then such a method of finding a husband is probably preferable to the usual method of following sexual desire. This sensibility opposes both the unprincipled insensibility of the aristocracy and the crude insensibility of the lower orders.

For all their famous fainting, the heroines, unlike Monk Lewis's, are strong and educated, although not in the threatening Wollstonecraftian way. Their accomplishments have a surprising value—in their dungeons and turrets they can strengthen their self-composure by sketching and writing verses—but their first identification is always as lady. Adeline with her facility in poetry never thinks of actually following Priscilla Wakefield's advice into authorship when she lives awkwardly with the impoverished La Mottes. The only earning heroine is Ellena in *The Italian,* who secretly makes money from needlework to support herself and her aunt. She sells her work anonymously to greedy aristocrats who despise her supposed rank. When her noble birth is discovered and her noble marriage assured, no more is made of this accomplishment.

It is as lady that they have most economic value for themselves rather than simply for other people who would use them, and the discovery of noble birth is often an assertion of their intrinsic worth. Adeline who neither works nor hunts to help the community in the forest has a high precise value put on her chastity and beauty; when she is ennobled she acquires economic and social power to such an extent that she can herself determine the time of her marriage.

Yet, for all the generalised moral and social commentary on women that can be squeezed from the heroines, Radcliffe accepts as well their literary nature and she draws attention to the fulfilment of literary expectations in the reader. Undressed distress she knows is a cliché. So Adeline is described as 'like a romance of imagination' and her lamentable situation becomes 'one of those improbable fictions that sometimes are exhibited in a romance'. The habit is taken to an extreme in *The Mysteries of Udolpho,* where Emily is ridiculed by Montoni for playing the heroine. His nakedly pragmatic rhetoric of power easily overtops her sentimental heroic speeches. When Emily urges her fine abstract qualities, her strength of mind and fortitude against oppression, Montoni taunts her, 'You speak like a heroine . . . we shall see if you can suffer like one,' and he later mocks her fearful trembling as ill-becoming her role. Her romantic assumptions that she will be rescued by the hero prove entirely false. The veil that should, romantically, conceal desire and love, as in a bride, conceals a corpse, and a false one at that.

Ann Radcliffe was famous as a creator of fictional scenery or imaginative topography. In this habit she seems to be making a subtle claim for distinction with her genre. She inserted poetry as well as history into her books—a habit for which she was criticised by Leigh Hunt—but more significantly, in her passages of natural description, she edged her prose towards the condition of poetry. In his 1818 lecture on the English novelists Hazlitt depicts her 'describing the indefinable . . . she has all the poetry of romance', while Scott calls her 'the first poetess of romantic fiction' for passages such as this:

> The vessel cut its way through the liquid glass. The water was so transparent that she saw the sun-beams playing at a considerable depth, and fish of various colours glance athwart the current.

Poetic natural description is most associated with the heroines. In this Radcliffe is stressing their sensibility and virtue, both almost seen as products of landscape, but she may also be asserting a kind of female response to the growing Romantic conception of nature and the artist. On the whole, where the male poet sees himself within the sublimity of nature and makes response heroic, the female novelist's stance is more modest, and nature itself remains the sole seat of the sublime. True Romantic poetry with its self-assertion is a mode as inappropriate for the lady writer's image as 'Amazonian' political protest.

The novels liberally quote from sentimental English poetry in which nature is often depicted as an expression of God. In Radcliffe, it is a kind of undoctrinal immanence and spirit, both test of and comfort to the protagonists, working in the world almost in the manner of divine grace. It can provide a code of values and act as 'a talisman' to expel 'all the poison of temporary evils'. Characters reflect nature and their ideas become simple and sublime with the scenes they contemplate. Like the heroines and the gothic edifices, however, nature is also a cultural construction, a mingling of poetry and painting, especially of the dark Salvator Rosa and the idyllic Claude whom Radcliffe so much admired. With the help of poetry and painting nature achieves a pictorial and narrative coherence and the reader progresses through a world that is framed and organised.

The scenery of the novels is operatic and grand, full of contrasts of pinnacles and abysses, flowery rivulets and infinite chasms, representing and inspiring the human mind that perceives it. The contrasts, often clichéd, often wonderfully suggestive, reflect contrasts in the mind as well as in human society and even in gender. Trees are masculine, with their gigantic arms aloft, and Alpine landscape becomes 'beauty sleeping in the lap of horror'. 'Deep valleys, that, winding into obscurity, seemed to invite curiosity to explore the scene below' resemble the veiled elusive heroines and are described in female aesthetic vocabulary as beautiful, sweet, elegant and charming, blushing in the rising sun; mountains are grand and awful guardians of their charms.

The frequent poetic descriptions of nature stop the action and hold suspense. They have no interest in moving the plot along or in explaining and clarifying human action and motive. Mostly landscapes are seen in obscurity through distance or atmospherics of storm, dusk or dawn. The obscurity signifies religious obscurity, as the scenery itself expresses God and as the watcher's reverential response expresses the proper attitude to God. The natural sublime is the nearest people can come to the supernatural on earth; only when contemplating it can they properly imagine what is naturally beyond the world and supernaturally be-

yond everything. In *The Mysteries of Udolpho,* Emily, looking at the landscape, imagines 'vast regions of space, glowing with worlds beyond the reach of human thought'.

Nature, changing but repeating, obscure and revealing, intensifies religious emotion, and ultimately human virtue. Those who are most responsive to landscape are most responsive to God and so most virtuous in inclination:

> The first tender tints of morning now appeared on the verge of the horizon, stealing upon the darkness;—so pure, so fine, so aetherial it seemed as if Heaven was opening to the view. The dark mists were seen to roll off to the west, as the tints of light grew stronger, deepening the obscurity of that part of the hemisphere, and involving the features of the country below; meanwhile, in the east, the hues became more vivid, darting a trembling lustre far around, till a ruddy glow, which fired all that part of the Heavens, announced the rising sun. At first, a small line of inconceivable splendour emerged on the horizon, which, quickly expanding, the sun appeared in all his glory, unveiling the whole face of nature, vivifying every colour of the landscape, and sprinkling the dewy earth with glittering light. The low and gentle responses of birds, awakened by the morning ray, now broke the silence of the hour; the soft warbling rising by degrees till they swelled the chorus of universal gladness. Adeline's heart swelled too with gratitude and adoration.

> The scene before her soothed her mind, and exalted her thoughts to the great Author of Nature; she uttered an involuntary prayer: 'Father of good, who made this glorious scene! I resign myself to thine hands: thou wilt support me under my present sorrows, and protect me from future evil.'

> Thus confiding in the benevolence of God, she wiped the tears from her eyes, while the sweet union of conscience and reflection rewarded her trust; and her mind, losing the feelings which had lately oppressed it, became tranquil and composed.

At other times the effect is less overtly religious and more simply poetic but the movement from outer to inner as the world moves from one state to another is repeated. Although the hero and heroine might discover their kinship in their rapt contemplation of nature, in general the natural passages do not express individual character as much as the sensibility of the novel as a whole. Hence their repetitiveness, their incantatory unspecific effect. Radcliffe was aware of the repetition: 'It is difficult to spread varied pictures of such scenes before the imagination,' she wrote.

> A repetition of the same images of rock, wood and water, and the same epithets of grand, vast and

sublime, which necessarily occur, must appear tautologous, on paper, though their archetypes in nature, ever varying in outline, or arrangement, exhibit new visions to the eye, and produce new shades of effect upon the mind.

Nature and the sentimental poetry of nature, associated with the English poets and with women, function in opposition to sensuality. It is almost nature as real transcendental art against materialistic mundane culture. The luxurious interior of the aristocratic seducer in *The Romance of the Forest* is outside nature, loudly expressing artifice. It is a 'magnificent saloon, splendidly illuminated, and fitted up in the most airy and elegant taste' with silver Etruscan lamps, music and perfumed flowers. It is like a palace of seductive male culture, full of literary references. The heroine warned by nature's darkness and storm is Persephone in this Hades—like the goddess she takes only a single fruit—and she is almost seduced by the display. But soon she understands that sensual art is ranged with masculine vice and should be closed to women. Later she looks from outside through a window and sees the wicked Marquis 'reclining on a sofa, near which stood a table covered with fruit and wine . . . alone and his countenance was flushed with drinking'. The art and artifice simply exaggerate the man's sensual threat; a lady can allow herself to be inebriated only with natural scenery and the 'higher kinds of poetry' that express it.

Yet of course nothing is entirely untinged by its contrast. As the lighted sensuous interiors imply the dark austerity outside, as the landscapes have required light and darkness, obscurity and clarity, as dread has come with desire, so in a way the open valleys of La Luc demand the forests of Montalt or La Vallée the dark castle of Udolpho. The identity so strenuously supported by the heroines is based on the fear of its destruction, the doubling seems to imply dissolution, and enlightenment always suggests a flickering out into night. Consequently a later age, withdrawing from the absolute, sentimental allegorising of Mrs Radcliffe's endings, found, against all her expressed intentions, an ambiguous, subversive, voluptuous quality that linked the novels quite clearly with the excesses of *The Monk* and of the French. It was perhaps such a response that pushed Radcliffe into relative silence for many years after the publication of *The Italian,* fearing that her books like the sentimental body might speak beyond conscious control, that they might escape decorum and suffer misinterpretation, and that sentimental values might not in the end be unpolitical in a political age. She would have been even more horrified by the twentieth century that rescued her gothic fantasies from the oblivion into which they had fallen by making of them dark and explicit images of female claustro-phobia and sexual desire, while it made her genre which, despite Catherine Morland's Midlands experience, she intended as a 'guide to life', into a vehicle for escape and lurid sensationalism.

Patricia Meyer Spacks (book date 1990)

SOURCE: "Fathers and Daughters: Ann Radcliffe," in *Desire and Truth: Functions of Plot in Eighteenth-Century English Novels,* The University of Chicago Press, 1990, pp. 147-74.

[*In the following excerpt, Spacks argues that Radcliffe bases the structure of her fiction on the "moral implications of [Edmund] Burke's theory of the sublime."*]

In Radcliffe's novels . . . literal or metaphoric tensions between fathers and daughters suggest a way to understand the new kind of plot that [Fanny Burney's] *Evelina* introduced. Radcliffe's plots might be called "daughters' plots"—not simply because they originate in a female consciousness, but because they establish internal principles of action by giving due weight to the psychology and morality traditionally associated with daughters as well as to the assumptions of sons.

In an interesting comment on the subversive potential of the Gothic novel, Robert Kiely observes the form's early concentration on domestic disruption.

> The Gothic novel did eventually encourage large-scale social subversion, but, in its earlier forms, the 'natural order' which it disturbed was of a simpler and more fundamental type. The confusion existed not between lawmaker and renegade, but between father and son, brother and sister, lover and mistress. Basic human relationships were thrown into an extreme disorder which was symbolized most commonly in sexual terms—adultery, incest, pederasty.

Kiely's failure to mention daughters and fathers in his loci of "confusion" seems surprising, since symbolic father-daughter incest permeates early Gothic fiction. His general point about the impulse toward social criticism implicit in intimate violations of natural order, however, is illuminating. Radcliffe's exploration of father-daughter relationships extends the radical implications of earlier sentimental novels.

Her male precursors and peers also investigated the subject. In Horace Walpole's *The Castle of Otranto,* for instance, a tyrannical father declares his intention of marrying his daughter's best friend after he divorces his current wife, whose passive compliance with this plan he rightly assumes. Manfred's plots fail, and he accidentally stabs his daughter to death, his dagger striking her where paternal weapons in these novels always seem to land, in her "bosom," thus "effecting both absolute mastery and a type of incestuous violation in a single stroke." He has intended, rather, to kill his daughter's friend Isabella. David Morris comments astutely on the doubling involved in Manfred's relation to the two young women:

> When Manfred in jealous rage stabs the figure he believes to be Isabella, it is not coincidence but the Gothic truth of repetition which substitutes his own daughter, Matilda. Matilda and Isabella—despite their opposite temperaments—are doubles or mirror images, and Manfred's pursuit of Isabella is not simply an expression of unrequited desire but the reenactment of an ancient pattern. What terrifies Isabella as she flees from Manfred through dark, subterranean passages is not the prospect of capture or even rape—however terrible—but sexual violation by the man who, in the repetitions of Walpole's narrative, is the double or dark surrogate of her own absent father.

A more brutal version of comparable events occurs in Matthew Lewis's adolescent fantasy, *The Monk.* As the wicked monk's sexual imaginings accumulate around his innocent girlish victim, she addresses him ever more frequently as "Father"; he combines the authority of all males with the patriarchal authority of the Church. She turns out, after Ambrosio has raped and murdered her (with another stab to the bosom), to be his sister, not literally his daughter (he has also, along the way, strangled his mother to death), but the sexually tinged conflict between paternal power and filial innocence remains central to the Gothic effect.

Neither *The Castle of Otranto* (1764) nor *The Monk* (1796) exemplifies the new "daughters' plot" of the late eighteenth century. Instead, such works recapitulate, with fresh trimmings, the structure of novels by Richardson, Fielding, and early Smollett. Their action derives from struggles of power. Walpole opposes to wicked Manfred two heroic and virtuous male figures: young Theodore, a splendid youth of mysterious birth, like Tom Jones; and a fierce knight eventually identified as the father of Manfred's intended sexual victim. Various versions of male conflict, intensified by supernatural interventions, invigorate the plot. The supernatural, often ludicrously phallic in its manifestations (a sword so big that a hundred men can barely carry it, gigantic human limbs appearing in various parts of the castle), embodies power, a fact implicit in the stress on gigantism. As for the women, they possess no resources beyond obedience and flight. "Perhaps the sacrifice of myself may atone for all," observes Manfred's wife Hippolita—" . . . it boots not what becomes of me." "I must not hear a word against the pleasure of thy father," she warns her daughter, as Matilda tries to tell her of Manfred's plan to marry her to her friend's father, yet another version of faintly disguised incest. The girls from time to time try to run away, and they depend heavily on male help; they serve only as victims, never as embodiments, of power.

The Monk emphasizes its preoccupation with masculine energy even more, playing variations on the Faust legend to give its villain ever greater resources. An apparently enterprising and self-determined woman—another Matilda—seduces the monk at the outset. In the long run, though, she turns out not to be a forceful female at all, but a demon in disguise, doing the bidding of Satan, the novel's ultimate locus of male power. Neither Ambrosio's sister, his principal victim, nor his mother can comprehend or combat evil. They epitomize the helpless.

Ann Radcliffe, shocked by *The Monk,* set out to rewrite it in **The Italian** (1797), which incorporates new versions of many events in Lewis's fiction. It therefore provides a useful test case for my contention that Radcliffe develops a novelistic structure significantly different from that of her important predecessors. Her most obvious modifications of Lewis's model have little apparent bearing on fundamental conceptions of plot. Committed to Burke's conviction that obscurity provides a crucial element in the sublime, she relies heavily on suggestion. Ambrosio (in *The Monk*) rapes and murders his sister; Radcliffe's wicked monk, Schedoni, only *almost* murders the young woman he believes to be his daughter. Lewis dwells on his protagonist's feelings; Radcliffe diffuses emotional interest. And, as literary histories tend to reiterate, she frequently elaborates details of an imagined Italian landscape, her principles of description based on Burke's aesthetic.

What interests me more is how Radcliffe develops covert moral implications of Burke's theory of the sublime into a foundation for fictional structure. Like other late-eighteenth-century aestheticians, Burke interested himself in "our passions in our own breasts" as the basis for understanding sublimity and beauty. Terror and pity, classically defined components of tragic response, particularly concern him. Terror associates itself with the sublime, which "is productive of the strongest emotion which the mind is capable of feeling." Pity seems linked with beauty as "a passion accompanied with pleasure, because [like responses to beauty] it arises from love and social affection." Passion's possibilities, in Burke's view, define themselves by simple opposition, belonging to self-preservation and the sublime or to society and beauty. Mediating between emotions associated with the self and those connected with society is ambition, a "social" passion arising from man's desire to excel his fellows, planted in man by God in order to ensure progress.

Kiely comments astutely on the importance and the fictional possibilities of Burke's dualism.

One finds in Walpole, Radcliffe, Reeve, and Lewis not only Burke's ideas but Burke's problems. Whereas the best romantic poetry achieves, indeed embodies, moments of synthesis, the romantic novel, at best and at worst, is an almost continuous display of divisive tension, paradox, and uncertain focus. The dualism of man's nature—of his taste, his impulses, his ambitions—the deep division in his very way of perceiving reality, seemed an inevitable adjunct to the first romantic stirrings in the young genre.

Ambition, in Burke's system, in its mediating force suggests a possible resolution of division. But as a stereotypically male quality, belonging neither in eighteenth-century fiction nor, apparently, in eighteenth-century society to females (except for *bad* females), ambition does not solve the woman's problem. Radcliffe in her novels found a way to suggest another mode of "progress," based on social feelings, which avoids both the self-abnegation of Hippolita's claim that it boots not what becomes of her and the insane self-assertion of a Manfred, an Ambrosio, or a Schedoni. To convey such a possibility, she devises double plots that imply two different principles of action, two kinds of impetus for fiction. She exploits, in other words, Burke's perception of fundamental division.

The two principles work themselves out on many levels. Not only do individual episodes in Radcliffe's novels embody contrasting moral assumptions, the intricate series of events through which the protagonists of *The Italian* or *The Mysteries of Udolpho* achieve marriage dramatizes opposed systems of value. The crucial sequence in *The Italian* during which Schedoni almost murders his presumed daughter exemplifies Radcliffe's method. Abducted to an isolated, half-ruined house on the seashore, Ellena must sleep in a room with a secret passage opening into it. In the middle of the night, Schedoni steals in, his dagger at the ready. He takes a long time deciding to strike; a highly eroticized scene, with emphasis on the need for denuding the girl, details his hesitations. Sexual innuendo accumulates. "He stooped to examine whether he could turn her robe aside, without waking her." (One might wonder why, exactly, he needs to "turn . . . aside" a robe made of lawn, a particularly fine, sheer fabric.) Again, "as often as he prepared to plunge the poniard in her bosom, a shuddering horror restrained him. . . . Vengeance nerved his arm, and drawing aside the lawn from her bosom, he once more raised it to strike. . . . His respiration was short and laborious, chilly drops stood on his forehead, and all his faculties of mind seemed suspended." The lethal assault the monk has in mind appears essentially sexual in nature.

The assault, however, never takes place. Instead, Ellena wakes up. Schedoni drops the dagger, having noted the miniature she wears around her neck, a representation of himself as a young man: he can now under-stand the young woman as his reflection. Ellena tells him the picture portrays her father. Schedoni then constitutes himself her protector rather than her assassin, but he still proposes to use her in the service of his ambition. If a father exemplifies power, he must concomitantly exemplify danger.

In his person and in his character, Schedoni, a powerful male, represents the human sublime—a concept, in Radcliffe's treatment, permeated with moral ambiguity. The afternoon before the attempted murder, Ellena sees him on the beach, not knowing who he is. "There was something also terrific in the silent stalk of so gigantic a form," the narrator comments; "it announced both power and treachery." Schedoni's physical size, his association with power, and his "terrific" aspect conform to Burkean standards, but the idea of treachery reminds us that human beings, unlike mountains, possess moral natures. Schedoni's actual and potential treachery result from the isolation, the concentration on self, that Burke connects with the sublime and with the masculine. Novelists before Radcliffe had consistently criticized such self-absorption. Radcliffe disapproves too—but she also dramatizes its connection with authentic and inescapable power. From one point of view, Schedoni precipitates all significant events in Radcliffe's novel. He demonstrates the naked operations of power. The novel's title designates him as its center, but he exists partly to raise questions about power as the governing principle of action or of narrative.

Effectively deprived of moral imagination by his concern with what Burke calls "self-preservation," Schedoni can conceive no interests but his own. Yet in discussions with his female co-conspirator, the Marchesa, he repeatedly invokes "justice," which, he argues, requires Ellena's death. Thus he taunts the Marchesa: "though the law of justice demands the death of this girl, yet because the law of the land forbears to enforce it, you, my daughter, even you! though possessed of a man's spirit, and his clear perceptions, would think that virtue bade her live, when it was only fear!" Like Carol Gilligan, he appears to believe women less susceptible than men to justice's claim; in fact *his* perverse version of justice subordinates all to his desires. As he sees it, "Strong minds perceive that justice is the highest of the moral attributes, mercy is only the favourite of weak ones." ("Weak ones" we may take as a periphrasis for women.) Justice is the instrument of power, in the monk's view. Mercy betrays power's absence.

Schedoni employs the phallic dagger in his obsessive efforts to dominate. As plotter, as father, as would-be and as successful murderer (he manages to dispatch a rival monk and has in the past killed his own brother and only accidentally avoided killing his wife), he proves controlled by passion for political, social, psy-

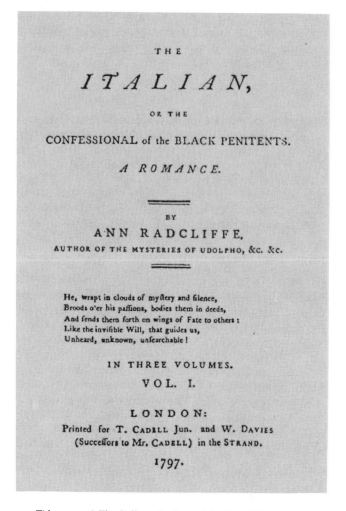

Title page of The Italian, *the last original work by Radcliffe published in her lifetime.*

chological, and financial mastery. In moral terms the sublime comes to only this. Ellena, on the other hand, like her lover, Vivaldi, and her mother, Olivia, governs herself by another system of desire, another structure of value.

The thrust of her psychological and moral orientation, the dimensions of the other system of assumptions shaping the plot, reveal themselves in her reactions to the attempted assassination, its preambles and aftermath. Walking on the shore, in imminent danger of being murdered (although she has avoided full acknowledgement of that possibility), she rejoices "that the fishermen, whose boats she had observed, had escaped the threatening tempest, and were safely sheltered in their little homes, where, as they heard the loud waves break along the coast, they could look with keener pleasure upon the social circle, and the warm comforts around them." This apparent sentimentality reveals Ellena's mode of reflecting on her own condition by displacing her feelings. What troubles her most—since

she represents *beauty,* not *sublimity*—is not her danger but her isolation: "I have no longer a home, a circle to smile welcome upon me! I have no longer even one friend to support, to rescue me!" For her, the idea of a father merges with that of a protector. When Schedoni demands to know the identity of the face in the miniature, Ellena responds, "Alas! he is dead! or I should not now want a protector." Believing herself, subsequently, to have found a father in Schedoni, she obstinately interprets his responses as forms of caretaking. When she finds the dagger under her bed, she decides, implausibly, that someone else has tried to murder her and Schedoni has rescued her. "O! my father, do not deny me the pleasure of shedding these tears of gratitude, do not refuse the thanks, which are due to you! While I slept upon that couch, while a ruffian stole upon my slumber—it was you, yes! can I ever forget that it was my father, who saved me from his poniard!"

That pleasure involved in "shedding . . . tears of gratitude" suggests the shape of Ellena's desire. . . . She yearns for friendship, affiliation, being taken care of, being able to take care. When, in a situation of extreme danger, her lover shows up to rescue her from a nunnery, she repeatedly returns to her friend Olivia (not yet revealed as her mother) for affectionate farewells, apparently valuing friendship more than love or life. At her own wedding, she reflects on a previous aborted attempt at marriage in terms again suggesting that friends and family matter more than erotic love. Vivaldi expresses similar feelings in less extreme terms. In the Inquisition's dungeons, for example, himself in danger, he worries about the situation of other victims, opposing an ethic of compassion to one of justice and denouncing justice's institutional perversions. And he at least momentarily resolves not to claim Ellena for his wife until his family approves—not because of reluctance to defy his parents, but because he wishes not to deprive Ellena of the new family to which she is entitled: he wants his mother and father "willingly [to] admit her in the rank of their child."

In other words, Radcliffe stresses the moral qualities associated with Burke's category of "beauty" through the responses of at least one male character as well as those of the heroine. Yet the notion of sublimity recurs. The sublime of nature, less morally ambiguous than its human equivalent, extends its strength from the physical to the moral realm. Thus Ellena, abducted into the mountains, reflects, "Here, the objects seem to impart somewhat of their own force, their own sublimity, to the soul." Similarly, Vivaldi, on his way to the dungeon, finds inspiration in Roman ruins evoking "a melancholy awe, a sacred enthusiasm, that withdrew him from himself." Moreover, Radcliffe's plot suggests that the human sublime, for all its terrifying aspects, can help to strengthen those committed to softer virtues. Schedoni's manipulations provide a principle of energy; much action derives from the protagonists' efforts to escape or overcome his power and his treachery. In the process, they acquire force. Ellena, at the outset a "good girl," devoted to her elderly aunt, industriously producing needlework as a source of income, turns into a woman with powers of resistance and self-determination. Her integrity displays itself in her refusals: reluctance to marry unless Vivaldi's parents accept her, rejection of nunhood. But she also shows courage and endurance in her repeated ordeals and repeated attempts to escape. Vivaldi, too, who shares her "feminine" concern for other people, learns his own strength and independence by the necessities of resistance.

Inasmuch as the plot of **The Italian** can be defined in these terms—as constituted by the protagonists' resistance of Schedoni—it resembles the plots of previous eighteenth-century novels, although the heroine's development of moral stature from a position of initial passivity perhaps represents something new. (Sophia Western and Clarissa Harlowe of course display moral force—but they clearly possess its potential from the outset.) But the degree to which the plot develops also from the imaginative and emotional capacities of its protagonists—what Radcliffe and her predecessors called "sensibility"—suggests the novelist's fresh direction. The narrator repeatedly calls attention to the deficiencies of a "sublime" consciousness and the resources of one more oriented toward human sympathy. Thus, we learn that Schedoni can interpret other people's responses only by analogy with his own; he therefore makes serious mistakes. As the novel approaches its dénouement, the narrator stipulates, in moralistic terms, the double principle of action.

> It may be worthy of observation, that the virtues of Olivia, exerted in a general cause, had thus led her unconsciously to the happiness of saving her daughter; while the vices of Schedoni had as unconsciously urged him nearly to destroy his niece, and had always been preventing, by the means they prompted him to employ, the success of his constant aim.

Radcliffe's notion of the unconscious is not ours, yet we too might say that the novel opposes two forms of unconscious orientation in working out its action. The principle of sympathy, the ethic associated with "beauty," conflicts with the passions of self-sufficiency, the ethic of "sublimity." On the other hand, only by opposing itself to or identifying itself with the sublime does the beautiful acquire strength.

The Mysteries of Udolpho (1794), Radcliffe's earlier and better-known Gothic romance, marks even more distinctly the ways that "sensibility," the emotional structure associated with the beautiful, can develop into a mode of effectiveness—as, in earlier novels, it typ-

ically had not. Emily St. Aubert, the heroine, suffers pressure from two different father figures. First her literal father, a paternal paragon, concerned about her tendency to imaginative and emotional excess, tries to effect her moral education by a process of deliberate frustration. He wishes to develop in her—he says it repeatedly—"habits of self-command"; words like *strength* and *fortitude* recur as he ponders how to construct her character. He teaches her "to reject the first impulse of her feelings, and to look, with cool examination, upon the disappointments he sometimes threw in her way"; he finds himself "often obliged to witness, with seeming indifference, the tears and struggles which his caution occasioned her." For the best of reasons, this model father frequently behaves like a tyrant.

If such a "good" father throws disappointments in Emily's way with pedagogical intent and watches with *seeming* indifference her tears and struggles, the male authority figure who succeeds him after Emily is orphaned (the requisite state for Gothic heroines) replaces appearance with substance. A mysterious Italian, Montoni, marries Emily's aunt, her guardian. Dark, powerful, courageous, brooding, informed with unimaginable purpose—in short, *sublime*—Montoni supplies a steady series of real, important disappointments for Emily and cares not at all for her tears. He assumes, among other paternal prerogatives, that of disposing of her in marriage for his own advantage. Emily's imperative need to resist him educates her more successfully than her benign true father could have done.

Although Emily often relies on male help, she defies the terrifying Montoni, resists the sexual advances of Count Morano, steadfastly refuses to yield her paternal estate, and keeps her head in desperate situations. A typical Gothic heroine, she, like characters in **The Italian,** identifies with the power of sublime scenery while opposing herself to the moral corruption involved in human sublimity. I want, though, to dwell not on these obvious facts but on the plot's other side, the way that Emily's "sensibility," her need for human attachment, defines itself as strength rather than weakness. It fuels her resistance, generates action, and finally undermines male power.

Emily's aunt, who marries Montoni, proves stupid, snobbish, superficial and misguided; she torments the fatherless girl with unkind suspicions of sexual impropriety. Nonetheless, Emily governs her behavior at Udolpho largely by compassion and sympathy for her aunt, a fellow victim. Undeterred by repeated snubs, she tries steadily to alleviate Mme. Montoni's situation, braving unknown dangers and defying Montoni in repeated efforts to help her aunt. After the aunt finally dies, Emily's concern shifts once more to Valancourt, the man she loves. For his sake she refuses to relinquish her own inheritance until pressed beyond endurance. Safely returned to France, driven to give up Valancourt because of false reports about his Parisian vices, she relies for emotional sustenance and spiritual fortitude on her friends, the text repeatedly emphasizing their importance to her.

Emily's true father thought sensibility enervating, but it fortifies Emily: by considering herself obligated to others, she is empowered to act for herself. Much of what happens in *The Mysteries of Udolpho* happens because of Emily's benevolent concern. Even her commitment to Valancourt involves not merely dependence on him but care for him.

Yet sensibility, that vague term suggesting sensitive responsiveness in its possessor, implies desire. In *The Mysteries of Udolpho,* the figure of Laurentini, destroyed by her passions, emphasizes that fact. Emily indulges sensibility but avoids desire by self-government amounting to repression, and by transforming sexual to altruistic feeling, as "good" women have traditionally done. Clarissa's conversion of sexual to religious devotion exemplifies a comparable transformation.

So far, as my allusion to Clarissa emphasizes, my account of attitudes toward female feeling implicit in Radcliffean Gothic hints that these late-century novels echo assumptions of their novelistic predecessors. The reliance on affiliative impulse to energize plot and to strengthen character (one might contrast the striking passivity of the protagonist in *The Man of Feeling*) constitutes, I have argued, something new, but only indirectly do such attributions of force challenge standard doctrine about the relations of the sexes. But I have so far virtually ignored, in my treatment of Radcliffe, a conspicuous aspect of Gothic novels: their reliance on the supernatural.

As everyone knows, Ann Radcliffe introduces horror only to explain it away. *The Mysteries of Udolpho* provides the most notorious instance: early in the novel, Emily observes behind a black veil something so horrifying that she faints, never revealing to anyone what she has seen. Not until toward the end does the narrator explain that Emily saw a decaying corpse, complete with worms. But the corpse is only a wax image; the mysterious appearances and sounds that generate fear in not one but two castles have originated in relatively unsinister activities of living men.

Ardent imaginations typically prove susceptible to supernatural appearances, and sensibility implies imagination as well as sexuality. I have argued before [in "Ev'ry Woman," *Eighteenth-Century Studies,* 1974] for the covert equivalence between imagination and sexuality in many eighteenth-century treatments of imagination's dangers for women. In Radcliffe's Gothic, imagination generates a dark and relatively unrepressed

version of desire: which brings us back, after a long detour, to the matter of fathers, the question of paternal sublimity. What Emily sees and hears at Udolpho connects itself in her imagination with the character of Montoni, the castle's owner. If she glimpses an apparent corpse, she assumes that Montoni has murdered someone; if she hears inexplicable groans and voices, she believes them to comment on Montoni's immediate wickedness; the eerie figure who flits about the battlements must testify to evil from the past. Only the first of these conclusions ever becomes explicit in the text; the reader's constructions supplement Emily's in the other instances.

That is to say, the reader, male or female, is encouraged, like Emily, to dramatize a conviction of Montoni's badness by associating supernatural possibility with human evil. We need not believe in the actuality of the supernatural; as David Morris points out, "Unlike more subtle shades of feeling or perception, fear is an ancient biological endowment, rooted in human physiology and psychology, as responsive to false alarms or to elaborate fictions as to genuine threats of personal injury." Tzvetan Todorov's notion of "hesitation" is directly relevant. "The fantastic is that hesitation experienced by a person who knows only the laws of nature, confronting an apparently supernatural event," Todorov writes [in *The Fantastic,* tr. R. Howard, 1973]; he adds that "the fantastic . . . implies an integration of the reader into the world of the characters; that world is defined by the reader's own ambiguous perception of the events narrated. . . . *The reader's hesitation* is therefore the first condition of the fantastic."

Radcliffe's version of the fantastic carries insistent moral implication, but morality appears to derive, in the first instance, from feeling. Struggling to interpret ambiguous appearances, the reader may share with Emily a double response to the human sublime connected with such appearances: moral rejection signaled by immediate fear or revulsion, mingled with compelling attraction. The uneasiness linked to supernatural effects helps the reader to identify with the protagonist. "Gothic writers seemed caught between proving the reality of their fantasy and making that fantasy powerful and real," George Haggerty writes [in "Fact and Fancy," *Nineteenth-Century Fiction,* 1985]. He links the latter endeavor with the novelists' "attempt to find a vocabulary for inexpressible private reality." The ostensibly supernatural for Radcliffe supplies an important part of that vocabulary.

The mingled fascination and terror of the supernatural transfer themselves to the male figure who for Emily epitomizes danger. Critics (most cogently, Cynthia Griffin Wolff [in "The Radcliffean Gothic Model," *The Female Gothic,* ed. Juliann E. Fleenor, 1983]) have commented on the attraction and repulsion Gothic heroines feel for powerful villains, and on the sexual components of this emotional pattern. Emily's responses to Montoni and his paternal authority, like Ellena's emotions toward Schedoni in *The Italian,* have an ambivalent aspect. When Count Morano penetrates to her room with the intent of carrying her off and marrying her, Emily announces that she prefers to "remain under the protection of Signor Montoni." Morano, as bemused as the reader may be by this phraseology, given Montoni's brutality, concludes, with outrage, that Emily loves her captor. The narrator encourages us to draw the same conclusion.

Whether or not Emily thrills to Montoni despite her revulsion at his tyranny and injustice, the text urges its reader to identify with or admire Montoni's power while also endorsing Emily's compassionate impulses and her rejection of Montoni's values. The narrator, in other words, invokes in readers a complicated response equivalent to that sensibility overtly characteristic of the heroine: specifically, a symbolic response of daughters to fathers. The reader in effect duplicates a daughter's experience of the sublime.

Thomas Weiskel, in his brilliant [1976] study of the "romantic sublime," suggests the relevance of a Freudian model for the sublime experience. Oedipal competition, in his view, lurks in the background; he finds in the poetry of Collins, for instance, vestiges of "family romance". Radcliffean Gothic embodies a specifically *female* view of the family romance: not the competition of fathers and sons, but the dangerous, ambivalent love of daughters for fathers. Mutual attraction governs the relations of fathers and daughters. The relationship, however, also emphasizes women's exclusion from male power.

Emily experiences in slightly disguised form the fear inspired by the paternal sublime. By embodying the object of fear in the shape of the unnatural, the gruesome, the supernatural, Radcliffe hints at the anger connected with such fear and the possibility of malignant paternal intention as well as the punishment lying in wait for daughters too profoundly attracted to dangerous, beloved fathers. Yet Emily's sensibility also facilitates expression of the impulse to closer attachment with the father (always potentially sexual, as is the danger fathers embody for daughters) by converting it into the more generalized, less dangerous, social impulses that we often label "sentimental" in their presentation.

Both in their sentimentalism and in their efforts to evoke terror, then, such Gothic novels as Radcliffe's invite from the reader reactions appropriate for persons defined as attractive (that is, secondary) rather than powerful when the aesthetic universe is dichotomized into the sublime and the beautiful. Sentimentalism and terror alike, therefore, have profound effects on the plots as well as the emotional atmosphere of Radcliffean

Gothic. Radcliffe's plots can appropriately be described as "daughters' plots" not only because they accord due weight to the daughter's predictable system of values, her stress on attachment, given her exclusion from power. Even more important is the fact that, allowing attachment to triumph, such plots covertly demystify the father's force. The danger of the masculine sublime, embodied in supernatural appearances, is finally illusory, like the imagined danger of the wax corpse. Men's *social* power remains both real and dangerous: Schedoni can have Ellena confined in a convent, Montoni can carry Emily off to his mountain retreat and dictate her marriage. But *phallic* power, the mysterious potency of the dark male figures, derives largely from the imaginations of its potential victims and proves factitious. Although real dangers remain for Gothic heroines, in Radcliffe's plots the most dreaded menaces can be explained away, the ambiguity of what Todorov calls "the fantastic" resolved into the comprehensible and manageable.

So sensibility—that symbolically female value—can win out, obviating separation after abundantly symbolizing the hidden dangers of excessive filial attachment. Sons' plots declare independence: Tom Jones discovers his origins, then, supported by Sophia, in effect succeeds Squire Allworthy as master of Paradise Hall. Ellena, in *The Italian,* on the other hand, attaches herself not only to a husband but to a substitute father (Vivaldi's); Emily and Valancourt replicate the regime of Emily's dead father and in effect apotheosize him, thus insisting on an enduring family bond.

Daughters deal with fathers, these fictions suggest, by indirection and disguise. Radcliffe's plots, through their own indirections, affirm not only that everything turns out all right, but that more was all right all along than appeared to be the case, since phallic power is largely bestowed by the imaginations of others. A wicked father proves not in fact to be a father; a father who appears to have erred has only been misinterpreted; and daughters, as these plots are devised, can prove their fortitude and ingenuity by both resisting and incorporating the sublime, hint at their hidden aggression and their yet more hidden fear, and reaffirm their commitment to the life of the family.

Radcliffe discovers how at once to celebrate and to criticize both the force associated with the sublime and the vulnerable sensibility linked with the beautiful. Her plots explore the relationship of sublimity to beauty (in the wide Burkean sense of those terms) from the vulnerable under side. The double principle of action they dramatize, the notion that affiliative as well as aggressive feeling generates force, and the demystification of purely phallic potency provided a foundation for nineteenth-century English novels by men and women alike. Later novelists found other forms of symbolization than the supernatural to express the darker emotions of the vulnerable, and less ostentatious modes of sublimity than the commanding villains of Radcliffe's fictions. But Radcliffe remains their important precursor.

From Pamela to Evelina, female protagonists in fiction, as we have seen, engage crucially in the activity of interpretation by which they may hope to control stories if not plots. I suggested that Lennox's Arabella approaches heroism in her interpretative fervor, although she finally fails to impose the story she desires on her experience. Pamela and Clarissa achieve control of their stories, though only at the cost of marriage or death; one might claim for them a fuller attainment of Arabella's kind of heroism. Sidney Bidulph and Evelina, on the other hand, heroines of a different sort, appear far from heroic in their attempts to understand their own stories. A depressed sense of possibility governs them. They interpret on the basis of fear rather than desire.

The same could be said, it might seem, about Radcliffe's heroines, who characteristically torment themselves by false "presentiments" of disaster. Yet interpretation as action assumes new importance in Radcliffe's Gothic. Indeed, it becomes in a sense the center of plot—a fact of special interest in relation to the theme of fathers and daughters. "Some deep struggle for control of the springs of being itself seems to be the issue [in Gothic novels]," Judith Wilt writes, [in *Ghosts of the Gothic,* 1980] "some struggle by the parent to unmake or reabsorb the child and thus to stop time, keep power, take back freedom and life where it has inadvertently been given away." One sees such a struggle in the violence by which a father literally murders a daughter, in *The Castle of Otranto,* or in that which makes an apparent father approach such murder, in ***The Italian***. The struggle for control of meaning recapitulates the same contest in subtler terms. If fear appears to form the stories Radcliffe's heroines tell themselves, it sometimes only screens and facilitates desire. And sometimes it uncovers the most sinister dynamics of father-daughter relationships. The Gothic fictions that reveal the ultimate failure of power in the phallus have a more somber aspect; they also show the compromises necessary for daughters in a world controlled by fathers.

Clarissa, I earlier suggested, takes advantage of the gap between ideal and actual. ***The Italian*** works in the space between nightmare and actuality. With much of the same narrative material as her predecessor, M. G. Lewis (*The Monk*), and her successor, Charles Maturin (*Melmoth the Wanderer*), Radcliffe, unlike them, never literalizes the dire possibilities she announces. Such possibilities remain constantly before the reader, however, because they inhabit the characters' imaginations. Ellena's uncertainties about not only what might but what *can* happen generate an atmosphere more disturbing if less horrifying than either Lewis or Maturin can achieve.

Ellena seems remarkably docile for a heroine. Orphaned, as she believes, she has been told of the identity and the deaths of both parents. No mystery about family or life circumstances plagues her; she possesses from the beginning a palpable sense of security.

Yet the narrative immediately announces its concern with questions of interpretation, and such questions will soon become crucial for Ellena. In the frame story, an Englishman shocked to discover that assassins haunt churches is given a manuscript to help him understand what he has seen. The manuscript contains the story of Ellena and Vivaldi; he must figure out its application. The story the Englishman reads (we learn no more about this character or his reactions) opens with the hero's first sight of the heroine:

> The sweetness and fine expression of her voice attracted his attention to her figure, which had a distinguished air of delicacy and grace; but her face was concealed in her veil. So much indeed was he fascinated by her voice, that a most painful curiosity was excited as to her countenance, which he fancied must express all the sensibility of character that the modulation of her tones indicated.

Vivaldi, trying to deduce a woman's nature from her voice, finds possibly moral qualities ("delicacy and grace") in the physical but remains curious about the further moral revelations he imagines in her face. The sequence epitomizes the novel's method. In more momentous matters as well, characters must interpret inadequate and ambiguous appearances. Inevitably, they interpret on the basis of their desire. Their fancies often prove less benign than Vivaldi's.

Ellena's security soon vanishes. Her aunt dies, leaving her alone in the world; Vivaldi's parents bitterly oppose the idea of his marrying her. Mysterious kidnappers abduct Ellena, depositing her in a mountaintop convent where she faces an enforced choice between nunhood and arbitrary marriage. Courageously, she rejects both, though warned of possibly horrible fates as a result. Vivaldi rescues her, but another group of kidnappers wrench her from the altar just before the couple can exchange marriage vows, taking her to the lonely spot where Schedoni shows up to murder her. Yet Ellena is miraculously spared; the nun who earlier befriended her turns out to be her mother; she comes from a better family than she thought, has more money, and proves an appropriate match for Vivaldi, whom, in the final pages, she of course marries.

This partial summary suggests the multiplicity and unpredictability of the novel's events. Beyond the fundamental problem of survival, the heroine confronts the central difficulty of making sense of her experience. She constructs a series of mini-narratives as new happenings refute each successive interpretation. Ellena's ways of "making sense" create fear, the counterpart and equivalent of desire. She imagines herself walled up alive in a convent's dungeon, or separated forever from her beloved Vivaldi, or too weak to travel a few yards. "As they crossed the garden towards the gate, Ellena's anxiety lest Vivaldi should have been compelled to leave it, encreased so much, that she had scarcely power to proceed. 'O if my strength should fail before I reach it!' she said softly to Olivia, 'or if I should reach it too late!'" Olivia points out that the gate is very close, but a few minutes later, "breathless and exhausted, she was once more compelled to stop, and once more in the agony of terror exclaimed—'O, if my strength should fail before I reach it!—O, if I should drop even while it is within my view.'" Such extreme anxiety repeatedly defines Ellena's condition. Although her imaginings rarely correspond to actuality, they convey the truth of a woman's essential limitation and oppression.

Matters finally work out well for Ellena, but not as a result of her independent action. Her capacity for resistance—negative action—protects her, and she undergoes genuine terror without being overcome. But she has no power to make anything happen: only to keep things from happening, or to endure the pain of her experience. Her intense anxiety calls attention to the desperation of dependency. Feeling nightmare ever imminent, Ellena dramatizes the predicament of the powerless.

Ellena's special modes of interpretation, which focus attention on her desire, emerge with particular clarity in the brilliant sequence detailing her situation at Spalatro's lonely seaside house, to which she is abducted. Here interpretation becomes urgent. Ellena, driven by the fear that constitutes the obverse of her desire, decides that the villainous-looking Spalatro wishes to murder her. After she rejects the poisoned milk he provides (one of her more important refusals), he tells her she can walk on the seashore. Ellena watches an approaching storm and thinks "of her own forlorn and friendless situation," perhaps tracked "by the footsteps of the assassin." Her female fantasy of friendlessness, isolation, and persecution, which I considered earlier from another point of view, hardly exaggerates; she errs only in her understanding of the source of danger. Failing to see Spalatro, she congratulates herself on a possibility of escaping, then notes a monk walking along the shore.

> "His, no doubt, are worthy musings!" said Ellena, as she observed him, with mingled hope and surprise. "I may address myself, without fear, to one of his order. It is probably as much his wish, as it is his duty, to succour the unfortunate. Who could

have hoped to find on this sequestered shore so sacred a protector!"

This unique instance of Ellena's hoping when she should fear (still telling the wrong story) emphasizes the degree to which Radcliffe's novel, although it explains away supernatural manifestations, yet deals in the seriously disturbing. Although Ellena will not be murdered, her assumptions and her wishes about the sources of security will be utterly violated. A monk, a "father," functions as symbolic parent; like a literal father, he should help the unfortunate. Ellena trusts in the parental role, *desires* to trust it. But this powerful father seeks her destruction, allied with Vivaldi's comparably powerful mother, who wishes at all costs to prevent her son's marriage. Ellena's experience of parental betrayal exceeds even Clarissa's.

The monk—Schedoni, whom the girl does not know— passes and repasses Ellena, then asks her identity. "I am an unhappy orphan," she replies, her formulation reiterating her concern about parents. Schedoni becomes sufficiently explicit about his enmity to make Ellena faint, but he then foregoes his opportunity to lay her unconscious in the surf and thus eliminate her. But of course Ellena's confrontation with a dangerous father continues, in a scene also considered earlier. Imprisoned once more, left "again to solitude and terror," she awakens to a loud call from Schedoni, who has just dropped the dagger with which he planned to murder her. "Be merciful, O father! be merciful!" she pleads. Schedoni reiterates, "Father!" He demands the identity of the face depicted in the miniature Ellena wears. "This was my father," she finally responds, "pressing it to her lips." "Unhappy child!" Schedoni says at last, "—behold your more unhappy father!" Immediately Ellena's voice softens "into tenderness." In a ludicrous but significant escape into the most conventional of female roles, she asks "with the most soothing accents of compassion, and looks of anxious gentleness, what made him so unhappy, and tried to assuage his sufferings." The problem of interpretation baffles her. She inquires why Schedoni has entered her room at midnight and supplies her own explanation: "Did you come to warn me of danger?" Hastily accepting this hypothesis, Schedoni departs.

The narrator, attributing Ellena's subsequent narrative interpretations to "the ingenuity of hope," calls attention to an important principle of her story making: "The suspicions, however, which she had formerly admitted, respecting his designs, were now impatiently rejected, for she was less anxious to discover truth, than to release herself from horrible suppositions." Ellena cannot face an actuality worse than her worst imaginings. As Schedoni realizes that he too has made up a self-gratifying story, about Ellena's inadequacy as a mate for Vivaldi and about the need to get her out of the way, and that he has thus defeated his own best interests, Ellena tries desperately to construct a new narrative that will allow her to love her father. She could sustain no sense of cosmic order if the universe contained a parent who wished to kill his child. For Ellena and for the reader, Schedoni's character threatens fundamental assumptions of coherence.

Ellena's devoutness, through which she reiterates faith in order, consists in sentiment, registered often in her response to sublime landscapes. A strange instance occurs during her captivity, when she gazes out the window at the mountains.

> Here, . . . looking, as it were, beyond the awful veil which obscures the features of the Deity, and conceals Him from the eyes of his creatures, dwelling as with a present God in the midst of his sublime works; with a mind thus elevated, how insignificant would appear to her the transactions and the sufferings of this world! How poor the boasted power of man, when the fall of a single cliff from these mountains would with ease destroy thousands of his race assembled on the plains below! How would it avail them, that they were accoutred for battle, armed with all the instruments of destruction that human invention ever fashioned? Thus man, the giant who now held her in captivity, would shrink to the diminutiveness of a fairy; and she would experience, that his utmost force was unable to enchain her soul, or compel her to fear him, while he was destitute of virtue.

The worship of God through the mountains somehow leads to the wishful identification of virtue with power. More curious is the location of Ellena's enemy as "man"—at first apparently generic man, but more clearly masculine as the passage continues. The specific location of "man" on the battlefield, armed for destruction, suggests maleness; and the final image of man as a giant, shrinking to a fairy, makes gender more specific. In fact a woman, the abbess, holds Ellena in captivity, and the only clearly identified enemy so far is Vivaldi's mother. Yet the battle of the sexes informs this novel as it does *Clarissa*—and as in *Clarissa,* it is a battle of the opposed values clearly identified by Burke.

Ellena's interpretation of landscape in this instance exemplifies what is at issue in all her interpretations. Her desire to embody "virtue"—meaning especially sympathy, compassion, concern—and to find support for her "feminine" convictions motivates her. I have already argued that such "feminine" ideas of virtue control Radcliffe's plots. Ellena's reaction to what she sees from her window suggests her awareness that these ideas necessarily exist in tension with alternative systems. The sheer energy of her alogical progress from pieties about the Maker and His works to fantasies about virtue's unmanning of power declares hidden anger. It also exemplifies the symbolic as well as lit-

eral force of interpretative acts: the force of embodied feeling. Ellena's vision of warrior turning to fairy betrays her awareness that she is engaged in struggle. The plot of Radcliffe's novel turns on the same struggle.

Although *The Mysteries of Udolpho* does not announce interpretation as its subject so conspicuously as *The Italian* does, it works out yet more intricate relations between interpretation and plot. In a thoughtful examination of the interplay between "reason" and "sensibility" in Radcliffe's novels ["A Constant Vicissitude," *Ariel,* 1979], Gary Kelly has argued that the novelist's fictional structures embody a "typology of emotional states . . . associative in nature," and thus lack "any principle of organization based on moral development or progress."

> All aspects of the novel's formal technique are motivated by the need to create occasions of sensibility or perplexity, but even the description of different kinds of sensibility can be seen as motivated by the need to highlight the perplexities. Here already is the principle of alternation in the overall temporal pattern of the novels, and it is in fact the only strong organizing principle present in any of Radcliffe's fictions. The alternation need not, as in the cruder kinds of Gothic, be between diametrical opposites, but only between differences, and so throughout the novel the heroine merely goes through a variety of emotional states in more or less rapid succession.

Although Kelly considers that Radcliffe's plots lack progressive form, he sees them as inculcating consistent doctrine: reason must control sensibility to create happiness.

Such is the conviction of St. Aubert, father of the heroine in *The Mysteries of Udolpho*. Emily repeatedly proclaims his rightness; she believes herself to have learned, by arduous experience, exactly what Kelly believes her to have learned. But *Udolpho* embodies other kinds of meaning as well: specifically *female* meanings that qualify the official doctrine. Emily faces repeated challenges to interpret ambiguous appearances. The sequence of her interpretations provides the "organizing principle" Kelly misses in an assembly of happenings that, as Kelly rightly observes, seems haphazard and repetitive. But external happenings do not altogether define reality in a novel centered on the interplay between external and internal.

St. Aubert himself early announces the importance of this relationship. "Store [the mind] with ideas," he advises, "teach it the pleasure of thinking; and the temptations of the world without, will be counteracted by the gratifications derived from the world within." Much later in the novel, when Emily is imprisoned at Udolpho, she awakens to thoughts of the various disasters that threaten her, all of which she feels herself helpless to combat. "She rose, and, to relieve her mind from the busy ideas, that tormented it, compelled herself to notice external objects." "Ideas," it seems, may prove tormenting rather than gratifying; "the world without" offers valuable distraction as well as dangerous temptation. Only by paying close attention to actualities of the external world can Emily hope to check her fantasies; conversely, only the interpretative force of imagination enables her to make sense of what she sees.

Formulated in general terms, these notions sound commonplace. But the struggle to find a plausible balance between the claims of inside and outside makes arduous demands on a heroine who, because of her age and her gender, possesses importance in the world only as an object of male love, a pawn for male manipulation. She knows from the beginning the demands of social propriety; she always behaves well. She must learn how properly to interpret her own feelings and how to turn them to her own ends in a social context that declares acceptable only a limited emotional range.

In the course of her career Emily writes a good deal of bad verse. A glance at the developing concerns of this verse may suggest the change in emotional atmosphere that helps to validate the young woman's growth. Indeed, the sequence of verse sketches the structure of the novel's plot, inasmuch as that plot concerns Emily's progress. The girl's earliest poetic effusions, written under the influence of anxiety about her parents' health, display understandable obsession with sickness and grief. Later, she turns to narrative. On her way to Italy with Montoni and her aunt, she composes a sonnet about a young man traveling, like her, in the Alps. Its final couplet reads,

> Desperate, at length the tottering plank he
>   tries,
> His weak steps slide, he shrieks, he sinks—he
>   dies!

This transparent metaphor for her own psychological inadequacy to face the realities of her current situation economically conveys her depressed interpretation of possibilities. Later, leaving Venice by boat, she composes a more elaborate versified story of attempted murder narrowly averted: objectification of her fears and hopes, hope, by this time, only to avoid disaster. Escorted, at Montoni's behest, from Udolpho by a man whom she discovers to be an assassin, she writes a narrative poem in which a pilgrim, stabbed by a concealed "ruffian," breathes a prayer for his murderer as he dies. The poem vividly delineates the temptation to virtuous passivity, the temptation of victimization so prevalent among eighteenth-century fictional females. The goodness of a victim may declare moral superiority to active villains, but it does not rescue him or her

from destruction. Emily might languish for years at Udolpho. Yielding to Montoni does not imply salvation; only by resisting can Emily hope to achieve equanimity.

The last of Emily's narrative poems, allegedly composed on board the ship carrying her back to France and to safety, is her most self-indulgent. Compelled and titillated by images of hopeless, death-implying love, she resembles Sterne's Yorick and Mackenzie's Harley in her insistent pathos. Her highly derivative verses tell of a young sailor parted from his bride, promising her that they will meet again, perishing in a storm as he faintly proclaims, "Farewel, my love!—we ne'er shall meet again!" The bride, predictably, dies too.

> And oft, at midnight, airy strains are heard
> Around the grove, where Ellen's form is laid;
> Nor is the dirge by village-maidens fear'd,
> For lovers' spirits guard the holy shade!

The Collins-like excursion into hints of the benign supernatural implies an alternative to the dark supernatural intimations associated with Montoni and with Udolpho, but this poem too suggests that Emily is heading down the path of sensibility, she and the novelist who has created Emily's verse both content to indulge the fine feelings associated with victimization, separating themselves from the machinations of power.

After returning to France, the young woman turns her talents to lyric. Her lyrics evince no more remarkable literary gifts than do her narrative poems, but a new theme at least dimly informs them. If they speak obsessively of melancholy, they also return consistently to the subject of force. The last two in this series of poems—the final one occurring only six pages before the novel's end—epitomize the emotional ambivalence characteristic of the lyrics. Having just heard that mysterious, troubled Sister Agnes lies at death's door, Emily rests on a cliff looking at the water and composes an "address" called "To the Winds." Evoking the power of the tempest, the first sixteen lines stress the sublime and terrifying aspect of the wind. The final nine lines explicitly reject the terrible:

> Oh! then I deprecate your awful reign!
> The loud lament yet bear not on your breath!
> Bear not the crash of bark far on the main,
> Bear not the cry of men, who cry in vain,
> The crew's dread chorus sinking into death!
> Oh! give not these, ye pow'rs! I ask alone,
> As rapt I climb these dark romantic steeps,
> The elemental war, the billow's moan;
> I ask the still, sweet tear, that listening Fancy
>   weeps!

The "still, sweet tear" relates oddly to the "elemental war" requested in the line immediately preceding. Emily declares herself not to want the winds' destructiveness, to desire only their emotional stimulation. But her sweet tears apparently flow, sympathetically, at the violence of "elemental war." She would preserve the decorum of sensibility, incorporating, somehow, the primitive energies of nature. Similarly, her last lyric address itself "To Melancholy," for several stanzas producing Miltonic sentiments in verse again modeled on Collins. In the next to last stanza, she expresses her desire to be guided to banks laved by Neptune "With measur'd surges, loud and deep," and to hear how "wild the winds of autumn sweep." There she would

> pause at midnight's spectred hour,
> And list the long-resounding gale;
> And catch the fleeting moon-light's pow'r,
> O'er foaming seas and distant sail.

Once more, explicit desire for the wild, noisy, and powerful merges with a wish for gentler forms of self-indulgence.

The "plot" sketched by Emily's series of poems, of movement from passive acceptance of victimization to ambivalent identification with images of force, corresponds to the confused plot of the larger narrative, full of odd duplications and redundancies. At the novel's beginning, Emily exists under the control of a benevolent but autocratic father, concerned to shape her character. Orphaned, she moves into Montoni's sphere of influence. In due time, at an apparently arbitrary moment in the plot, she escapes from Udolpho to France, where she accepts the domination of a new father figure, the Count De Villefort, whose daughter Blanche becomes her close friend. Her true father approved her love for Valancourt, which motivates much of her resistance to Montoni, but the Count, misinformed about the young man's Parisian adventures, urges the cause of another suitor and warns Emily against indulging her love. Convinced that virtue demands her resistance to Valancourt, she sends him away. Once she has had time to hear the warnings against passion delivered by dying Sister Agnes, however, the Count learns of his mistake, invites Valancourt's return, and the two young people can marry at last.

An unsympathetic reading of this sequence might observe Emily's extraordinary docility to moral guidance and Radcliffe's apparent concern to multiply suspense for its own sake. In no obvious sense does character control plot. But if one starts with the notion of plot as a dynamic of desire and seeks the sense in which Emily's desire may be said to drive the plot, matters become rather more interesting. The force of the heroine's *negative* desire—her wish to escape, avoid, reject—plays an important part in shaping the plot. Her

positive desire, both sexual and nonsexual, remains largely obscure to her, and possibly to the reader as well. But it too helps to dictate the direction of plot.

Gary Kelly economically summarizes an interpretation of plot accepted by many commentators.

> The plots . . . are as conventional as the themes and characters, and are all based on the standard romantic plot: cavalier meets damsel, they fall in love, they are separated by circumstances or the machinations of their foes, they overcome or survive separate strings of difficulties, are reunited, and marry.

At one level, this description applies accurately to *Udolpho* and to Radcliffe's other fictions. Yet the possibility of describing the same plot in different terms calls attention to the profound ambiguity of the very notion of plot. A "damsel" lives happily with parents deeply concerned for her moral education. When her mother dies, she travels with her father for the sake of his health. On their trip, they meet a young man, a "cavalier" whom father and daughter both find attractive. Father dies, daughter returns sadly to her home, where the young man finds her and declares his love, to be rebuked by the aunt who has now taken charge of the girl. And so on: the Radcliffean plot can be summarized as a drama of literal and symbolic parents and children.

"The feeling which the new form, the Gothic romance, deals with constantly," Margaret Anne Doody writes [in "Deserts, Ruins, and Troubled Waters," *Genre*, 1977],

> —feelings which sharply set it off from the older sort of romance—are inner rage and unspecified (and unspecifiable) guilt. These passions are essentially related to all sorts of other emotions—fear, anxiety, loneliness—which are unstable, powerful, and unpleasantly associated with helplessness and with some kind of sense of inferiority. . . . Inner rage and overwhelming guilt are, in eighteenth-century circumstances, very feminine emotions—women have to suppress rage because they cannot control things; women feel guilty because they continually fail to live up to expectations.

Guilt and rage contribute to what I have called Emily's negative desire: her intense wish to escape the supervision of fathers—conflicting and often merging with her wish to avoid the burden of independent moral responsibility.

The pattern manifests itself distinctly in the novel's final sequences. Valancourt's misleading guilty hints about his own corruption corroborate the Count's impression of his culpability, so Emily cannot avoid repudiating him. They meet accidentally at the home of an old servant to whom Valancourt has given financial help. The old woman cannot fathom Emily's repudiation of her lover. "Dear! dear!" she says, "to see how gentlefolks can afford to throw away their happiness! Now, if you were poor people, there would be none of this." She reiterates the point several times, calling attention to the moral luxury of Emily's scruples—essentially aristocratic appurtenances, and, as it will turn out, altogether mistaken.

But of course Emily's scruples are not quite her own. The Count has virtually ordered her to reject Valancourt; she behaves as she has been trained to do, submissive to the authority of an older, wiser man. Before accepting his version of reality, she considers the possibility that he may err in his view of Valancourt. Perhaps someone has misrepresented her lover to the Count; perhaps the Count himself is "influenced by some selfish motive, to break her connection with Valancourt." But the hypothesis cannot persuade her; the Count has too good a character to allow such behavior. Nor can Valancourt have been misrepresented, since the Count has "said, that he spoke chiefly from his own observation, and from his son's experience. She must part from Valancourt, therefore, for ever."

Emily allows her belief in the Count's good character to sway her; she does not trust her earlier conviction of Valancourt's rectitude. She accepts the Count's assertion that he possesses trustworthy evidence from his own observation and his son's experience. In both instances, it develops, she is mistaken. Her own feelings would have guided her better than the Count's assertions. Both he and his son have misinterpreted appearances. Until she yields to male authority, Emily herself interprets better than they do.

In her lurid deathbed admonitions, Sister Agnes claims to see in Emily a hidden flaw. "You have passions in your heart,—scorpions; they sleep now—beware how you awaken them!—they will sting you, even unto death!" Employing less decorous terms than his, Agnes here echoes the concerns of Emily's dead father, who never refers to anything so unladylike as passion but who worries a great deal about his daughter's emotional life, imagined as a potential source of disaster. Feeling, he believes, cannot dependably guide a young woman. He urges her to cultivate reason and discipline. Sister Agnes, soon unmasked as Laurentini di Udolpho, embodies the same warning. Her madness and misery result, the text asserts, from passional indulgence. She too should have exercised moral and rational control.

The announced doctrine of *Udolpho* never varies. Yet the plot implies a view rather different from that of the explicit ethical assertions—or, at any rate, it allows dramatically different interpretations. In the story of Laurentini, the possibility of subversive meaning inheres in omissions of commentary. A French aristocrat, Laurentini's "passionate adorer," makes her his mistress instead of his wife because of her sexual looseness. After he marries a compatriot, Laurentini follows him from Italy to France. Thereupon "all the energy, with which he had first loved [her] returned, for his passion had been resisted by prudence, rather than overcome by indifference." Incited by Laurentini, the Marquis murders his wife: "she fell a victim to the jealousy and subtlety of Laurentini and to the guilty weakness of her husband." Both conspirators die remorseful, but only Laurentini's protracted and agonizing years of guilt and intermittent madness are extensively narrated.

Jealousy and subtlety sound worse than guilty weakness. The account of Laurentini, offered in the narrator's voice, emphasizes the culpability of the woman and of the parents who failed to teach her to control her passions; it dwells hardly at all on the man's guilt. Yet the Marquis's passion, not Laurentini's, initiates the connection between them; he administers the poison that kills his wife. A narrative of shared male and female moral failure has been converted into a fable of wicked womanhood.

Similar suppressions mark Emily's story. Her emotions, against which her father warned her from the beginning, in fact provide reliable indices of her actual situation. Like Vivaldi in *The Italian,* she suffers from what Schedoni calls "susceptibility": willingness (although she struggles against it) to accept supernatural explanations and apparent eagerness in ambiguous situations to believe the worst. Her erroneous interpretations cause her suffering. Thus she allows appearances to convince her, mistakenly, of her aunt's death. She believes during most of her stay at Udolpho that a decaying corpse occupies a room down the hall from her. She expects to be murdered by the men Montoni has ordered to escort her from the castle. Consistently wrong about her ways of accounting for facts, she yet penetrates to more profound truths. Her apprehension of Montoni as a destroyer of women, like her perception of something wrong in the history of the Marquis who effectively adopts her, acknowledges emotional actuality. Often she fails to find appropriate correlatives for her anxiety, yet always the anxiety has sufficient cause.

The text treats the female difficulty in discovering emotional correlatives as though it were equivalent to having no adequate cause for feeling—although it also involves the reader in intensities of anxiety comparable to the heroine's. The text warns against emotional self-indulgence and encourages it. And it demonstrates, without ever asserting, the rightness of the emotional "daughter" in opposition to the wrongness of the rational "father." Emily's heart leads her to know Valancourt's integrity, but she yields to the assertedly superior knowledge of an older man. The Marquis's character may, as Emily believes, be too upright to allow him to lie to her, but it does not prevent his being wrong. Despite its elaborate assertions of the need to dominate feeling by reason, *The Mysteries of Udolpho* dramatizes the power of feeling to guide people accurately. It also dramatizes another kind of power: that of authoritative men to enforce their will and their standards on women.

I pointed out earlier that Radcliffe's novels debunk men's phallic but not their social power. These novels in fact insist on the inescapability of social arrangements that grant dominion to men. They do not insist that men prove wrong—make erroneous judgments and interpretations—in exercising that dominion, but they demonstrate precisely this. Not only do Radcliffe's Gothic fantasies assert the "female" values of sensitivity, reconciliation, family; they also show, in contradiction to their announced doctrine, that female assumptions, feminine sensibility, may provide more accurate guidance than does rigorous rationality.

Kari J. Winter on M. G. Lewis and Radcliffe:

M. G. Lewis was heavily influenced by Ann Radcliffe's *The Mysteries of Udolpho* (1794) while writing *The Monk* (1796). According to C. F. McIntyre, Lewis told his mother that reading *The Mysteries of Udolpho* "gave him the inspiration" to finish *The Monk*. In turn, textual evidence shows that Radcliffe was responding to *The Monk* when she wrote *The Italian* (1797). Thus, the three novels "are interconnected in a complex web of influence, disagreement, and rejection" (Punter 62). Both *The Monk* and *The Italian* are set in exotic, Catholic, southern Europe, and both texts represent the exploits of a corrupt monk who is guilty of heinous crimes, including murder and incestuous rape. Ambrosio in *The Monk* kills his mother and rapes and murders his sister. Schedoni in *The Italian* has similar violent intentions: he murders his brother, abducts, forces into marriage, and stabs his sister-in-law, and attempts to murder his daughter while she is sleeping alone at midnight (a situation clearly filled with sexual threat). Lewis gives free rein to Ambrosio's desire to commit violence against women; indeed, he provides Ambrosio with supernatural help to fulfill his fantasies. In contrast, Radcliffe repeatedly circumvents Schedoni's violent endeavors. The striking similarities and subtle divergences in plot, theme, and characterization in these two novels reveal the extent to which Lewis and Radcliffe were deliberately writing in light of and against each other's work.

Kari J. Winter, "Sexual/Textual Politics of Terror," *in* Misogyny in Literature, *edited by Katherine Anne Ackley, Garland Publishing, Inc., 1992.*

Kim Ian Michasiw (essay date 1994)

SOURCE: "Ann Radcliffe and the Terrors of Power," in *Eighteenth-Century Fiction,* Vol. 6, No. 4, July, 1994, pp. 327-46.

[*In the following essay, Michasiw discusses the ways in which individual characters in Radcliffe's novels struggle with other characters and with the political and social institutions that define and determine the limits of power relations. In particular, he focuses on ways in which terror becomes not only an irrational response to illusory horrors in the story, but also a rational response to personal and institutional abuses of power.*]

Late in Ann Radcliffe's last novel, *Gaston de Blondeville,* the narrator pauses to consider the burdens of kingly and other authority:

> Sorrow and remorse . . . alone seemed to occupy the King, who now, with the intention, as he persuaded himself, of preventing further evil, was about to execute an act of injustice and stern cruelty. And thus it is, if kingly power pertain to a weak head, not carefully warned by early instructions against the dangers, which must beset all power, whether public or private, whether in Prince or subject; for, the passions are the helm, whereon designing men seize to steer into action, as they wish. And thus was pity about to be made the instrument of cruelty.

The passage reflects the guiding concerns of the Radcliffe canon: the passions, their influence on action, and power in its public and private manifestations, a concern that has, perhaps, been overlooked. Were the reasons for this oversight accounted, they might suggest much about the institutionalized study of literature's logic and its self-serving disregard of the fates of its ostensible objects. Such an accounting, however, is not the present concern, which takes as given that, despite readerly ignorings or misrecognitions, the novels' and their narrators' obsessings over "power, whether public or private" remain. The urge to domination is the prime characteristic of all Radcliffe's villains; the struggle for even a limited autonomy is the task set each of her heroines; the drive to exert authority over the world outside the self determines the complex structures of her descriptive passages; the need to achieve government of conflicting passions afflicts all her characters.

This complex apprehension of the webs of power manifests itself in Radcliffe's first novel, *The Castles of Athlin and Dunbayne,* when in an inspired moment Baron Malcolm "invents" his creator's aesthetic:

> [Malcolm] was agitated with all the direful passions of hate, revenge, and exulting pride. He racked

imagination for the invention of tortures equal to the force of his feelings; and he at length discovered that the sufferings of suspense are superior to those of the most terrible evils . . . of which the contemplation gradually affords to strong minds the means of endurance.

Here Malcolm achieves power over himself through torturing his imagination only to discover that tormenting the imagination of another is the best revenge. Power is achieved through the mastery of the imaginative faculties, one's own and those of others. Malcolm is, however, fortunate that his is a lonely career of villainy. Unlike Henry III he is free from "designing men" who would seize the helm of his ungoverned passions to steer him into action as they wish. These designing men are of interest not only because they remap the position of the Gothic novelist on political grounds, not only because their actions underscore the difficulty of discerning the public terminations of private failings, and not only because their existence images, if it does not imagine, power without the king. They are of interest primarily because they allow Radcliffe's inscription of a consolatory paranoid fantasy about the personal basis of power, a fantasy which Radcliffe's novels finally decompose.

The troubled relation between the individual's emotional responses and his or her actions in the world is a constant in Radcliffe. In this essay I am principally concerned with these external relations, with the lines of force that are set up between individual characters and between characters and political or social institutions. I begin with a discussion of the terror that seizes the Radcliffean heroine when she enters the world, a terror which proves eventually to be without basis. In this movement Radcliffe's Enlightenment heritage is clear; that heritage, however, becomes a burden when she forces herself to confront terrors that are not irrational, that are entirely logical responses to terrific and uncontrollable power. The last volume of *The Italian* overtly addresses institutional power—that prime political fact of the modern state—a presence before which the novelist's Enlightenment faith breaks down. There she confronts the possibility that, in the words of Horkheimer and Adorno, "the fully enlightened earth radiates disaster triumphant."

Radcliffe's gathering concentration is on relations not between individuals in themselves but between individuals as they are mediated or even produced by social institutions. Moreover, Radcliffe represents the relations between the individual and the social order not in terms of a binary opposition of the individual and society but in terms of a tripartite opposition of the individual, society, and the state. The importance of this third term separates Radcliffe's fiction from the main line of Romantic Gothic. The primary conflict in this form is concisely summarized by Frances Fergu-

son [in *Solitude and the Sublime,* 1992] as being "between the individual perspective on society (which stresses individual agency and experience) and the societal perspective on the individual (the formal claim that an external categorization of an individual can be definitional regardless of the individual's actual experience and action)." *Caleb Williams* typifies this conflict: both Caleb and Falkland struggle to define themselves in the dizzying moiré created by these obliquely opposing perspectives. Typical also, and very much unlike the later Radcliffe, is the dissolution of institutional legal power effected by the process of *Caleb Williams*. The Law becomes a mere instrument in the hands first of Falkland, then of Caleb; its autonomy has severe limits and behind even its apparently autonomous moves are the guiding hands of individuals. This consoling paranoid fantasy is one from which . . . Radcliffe's heroines are weaned. It is one that Pierre Clastres would recognize as an apotropaic delusion engaged to ward off the recognition (or development) of state institutions. So long as there are supermen, so long as power is concentrated in the chief, the state cannot exist. The importance of this fantasy, this individual protest, to Romantic individualism cannot be underestimated—neither can its unsustainability—but long before Beatrice Cenci or Victor Frankenstein, Radcliffe's protagonists and her villains have been obliged to see the fantasy for what it is. So too has their creator, and with a clarity that arrests her writing career.

Each of Radcliffe's three "major" novels begins with a flawless heroine delivered into the hands of the world. The process may be as abrupt as Adeline's kidnapping, or as gradual as Emily's circuitous journey to Udolpho; nonetheless it takes place. The primary experience provoked by the world to which the heroines are exposed is terror, and there is in this terror a distinctive logic, a logic that is epistemological in origin and derives in large part from Radcliffe's idiosyncratic reading of Edmund Burke. Much has been written about Radcliffe and the sublime, most of it assuming that when she writes "sublime" she means it in a Burkean way. Although Radcliffe is much indebted to Burke, when she employs the adjective "sublime" she is using the term as a portion of her affective rhetoric, as a signal to sigh and feel exalted. The moment when the human faculties are overborne—that moment at which Burke's sublime commences—Radcliffe's adjective sublime ceases to be of service. What Radcliffe learned from Burke is not his sublime but her logic of terror. Consider a typical passage from *The Mysteries of Udolpho:*

> It was now the second watch of the night, and about the time when the figure had before appeared. Emily heard the passing steps of the sentinels, on the rampart, as they changed guard; and, when all was again silent, she took her station at the casement. . . .

The moon gave a faint and uncertain light, for heavy vapours surrounded it, and, often rolling over the disk, left the scene below in total darkness. It was in one of these moments of obscurity, that she observed a small and lambent flame, moving at some distance on the terrace. While she gazed, it disappeared, and, the moon again emerging from the lurid and heavy thunder clouds, she turned her attention to the heavens, where the vivid lightnings danced from cloud to cloud, and flashed silently on the woods below. She loved to catch, in the momentary gleam, the gloomy landscape. Sometimes, a cloud opened its light upon a distant mountain, and, while the sudden splendour illuminated all its recesses of rock and wood, the rest of the scene remained in deep shadow; at others, partial features of the castle were revealed by the glimpse—the antient arch leading to the east rampart, the turret above, or the fortifications beyond; and then, perhaps, the whole edifice with all its towers, its dark massy walls and pointed casements would appear, and vanish in an instant.

This is a relatively normal moment in Emily's life at Udolpho; she is not being moved to any particular pitch of terror. What is striking about Emily's watch is the simultaneous privileging of the senses and insistence on their limitations. Despite the constant wakefulness of her eyes and ears, Emily sees but partially and hears only muffled, indistinct sounds. She is condemned to perceive aspects or fragments of the exterior world, a fragmentation threatening to invade the viewer.

Emily is enmeshed in a strange epistemological trap. Her difficulties are rooted in the inadequacy of her senses to her "reasoned" conviction that there is a whole, a pattern. As such her situation appears a surprising parody of the Kantian mathematical sublime. Like Kant's perceiver, Emily is presented with an object which exhausts the apprehensive powers of her senses. She requires the good offices of the rational abstraction, that concept which caps, contains, and controls the infinite. Unfortunately no such abstraction comes to mind; no transcendental signified presents itself to pacify the clamouring incompletion of the shattered signifiers pointing to some focus beyond the frame in which Emily's consciousness is trapped. Instead Emily takes refuge in the manner of Vico's primal giants who, terrified by sudden, disconnected sense data, retreat in terror, start families, create gods. Emily follows their example and the name of her god is male power or, in Italian, Montoni.

That is, in default of a conceptual abstraction, Emily places a designing man. The rational inquiry articulated around Emily's *cri de cœur,* "What can this mean?" short-circuits and yields that peculiar substrate of the sublime that is conspiracy theory, or, in its more exalted phase, the theory of genius. This is a familiar impasse in the late eighteenth century, one perhaps inevitable to those whose Enlightenment is buffered by the

Arminian tradition of Anglican rationalism, and one encountered in the works of Radcliffe's principal mentor in the description of landscape, William Gilpin. Gilpin and the critical tradition from which he derives ground their inquiries into the order of things in an obscure God whose "plans are too immense for our confined optics. . . . [W]e can view only detached parts [and] we must not wonder, if we seldom find in any of them *our confined ideas* of a whole." Anchored by this transcendental term, Gilpin is able to decompose any landscape he encounters, to play enlightenment games of disassembly and reassembly, to create and enshrine a Byzantine codex of self-consciously arbitrary rules governing the use we make of our confined optics and the representations effected by our limited hands.

What is freedom for Gilpin, however, becomes encasement for Emily, who views landscapes as if they were landscape paintings and as if she had somehow fallen, or been thrown, into one. The unremittingly pictorial character of Radcliffe's descriptions serves to emphasize their apparent designedness, a quality Emily attributes to Montoni and which Radcliffe can attribute only to herself. The problem posed here—the basis of Emily's terror and of Radcliffe's crisis in *The Italian*—is one of false analogy. As Gilpin's God is a picturesque designer, so the painter designs the represented scene, and the novelist orders the scene described. The artist is a lesser god, a temporary demiurge, but is so only in the confines of art. In the contrast between the petty artifices practised by humans and the grand designs of Gilpin's God, any artistic pretensions are easily demystified. When the artist is termed godlike, it is with a severe irony. But, and this appears the crucial difficulty, can the assurance with which Gilpin dismisses human endeavours in the face of Nature maintain itself when the object described is a human creation, an institution in the Viconian sense of a re-enactment among the gentiles of the divine institutions delivered by God to the chosen people? Vico's discovery that "this world of nations has been made by men" lurks within the argument from design and haunts the transit from the representation of nature to the representation of the state.

Without the guarantee afforded by an active God and with the recognition of the worldly capacity to design—a recognition enacted on Gilpin's own ground by his land-owning, earth-moving inheritors in the 1790s—what becomes of the enlightening security underwriting Radcliffe's demystifying distance from her benighted heroines? In addition, Radcliffe struggles with the notion of genius, an idea to which Gilpin was happily immune. At Udolpho Emily grafts onto the picturesque aesthetics the concept of an artistic genius capable of imposing an idea of order onto the world. She regards Udolpho and the scenes it presents as a mask stretched over nature by some master artificer. She sees as if enchanted, and all her visions lead her towards Montoni; all the hallucinatory images which are presented are fractures, or fragments pointing to the contorted mind of Udolpho's master. To maintain this mode of understanding, Emily must reject the accidental, the random, the merely fragmentary—possibilities Radcliffe's narrative mode leaves open. At the core of Radcliffe's practice is the gap between her heroine's conviction of their cognitive incapacity, a conviction propped up by their certainty that an order exists, and the narrator's continuing, anti-paranoid registration of the random, the partial. Indicative of this gap is the tendency of Radcliffe's heroines to overrate male power. At those points where the human abuts the natural, someone must be in control, and at Udolpho only Montoni can be that someone. The process of the narrative, however, emphasizes that Montoni is omnipotent only when Emily is in the grip of her assumed nescience. As Mary Poovey points out, whenever Montoni openly attempts to exercise authority over Emily she opposes him successfully. Montoni's power both in Emily's and the reader's mind is generated by a process of mystification. A petty *condottieri* captain becomes a figure imbued with supernal power, a transformation effected almost entirely by Emily and her aunt. Each fresh evidence of their partial vision, of their inability to comprehend, becomes evidence of his knowledge and his control. At Udolpho, male power feeds on female nescience and Radcliffe's terror illumines the parasitic relation.

In this process we observe Radcliffe's domestication of the Enlightenment's counter-theogony. Baron d'Holbach's *Systéme de la Nature* offers a concise statement of this position: "Si l'ignorance de la nature donna la naissance aux dieux, la connaissance de la nature est faite pour les détruire. A mesure que l'homme s'instruit, ses forces et ses ressources augmentent avec ses lumières . . . ses terreurs se dissipent dans la même proportion que son esprit s'éclaire." Humankind invents gods, then forgets they are inventions. Enlightenment reverses this, reminding humankind that it has been terrorized by its own creations. At Udolpho, Emily replays the first portion of the process, creating a godlike Montoni to justify her ignorance and confusion and, as her creation takes on an apparent autonomy, she forgets she is the source of his power. Her female education has primed her to believe both in order and in male genius and has ill fitted her to act in a world in which power has laid claim to the random, the accidental, the obscure. The tie between power, obscurity, and terror that Radcliffe found championed in Burke's *Enquiry* is played out in full in *Udolpho*. So long as Montoni's threats are veiled, so long as the chaotic activity at Udolpho can be attributed to the incomprehensible designs of evil genius, Emily is in thrall. As Burke observes, it is not the actual but the potential exercise of power that prompts subjects to bow to their sovereign's "dread majesty." The crucial

difference is that Burke's sovereigns *are* plenipotent, inheriting their imposing strength from the institutions whose sceptres they bear. Montoni's power is of another order; it is personal, rebellious, dependent on his subjects' self-subjection. Montoni lacks even the institutional backing provided by the title "Father." He is ripe for demystification, a task Radcliffe carries out with remarkable dispatch in the last third of *Udolpho*.

The scattering of myth begins at that moment when Montoni's façade of power crumbles at Emily's appeal to a greater authority. "I am not so ignorant, Signor, of the laws on this subject, as to be misled by the assertion of any person. The law . . . gives me the estates in question, and my own hand shall never betray my right." In this moment, Emily employs her knowledge, asserts herself, and merits the applause of Holbach. She invokes, however, the institution of law, a power greater than any individual and, in doing so, opposes a private pretender to godhead with a true god. She dissipates one superstition but creates another. She discovers that individual tyranny may be counteracted by institutions but, in the act, throws herself at the mercy of those institutions, a mercy on which one depends at one's peril. This movement reverberates through the remainder of Radcliffe's *œuvre* and to its progress we now turn.

The momentary success of Emily's appeal to law exposes, inadvertently perhaps, Montoni's limitations as a villain. The heroine's subjection at Udolpho is but an episode in her progress and, in contrast to Radcliffe's usual practice with villains, Montoni is vanquished long before the novel ends. Not only does he disappear from Emily's life, he vanishes utterly. Hemmed in, then destroyed by machinations as obscure to him as his actions are to Emily, Montoni shrinks to nothing, a dwindling underscored by Radcliffe's final words on his fall: "The celerity and ease, with which this whole transaction was completed, prevented it from attracting curiosity, or even from obtaining a place in any of the published records of that time." Historical process erases such ambitious individuals, leaving no trace even in petty chronicles.

As Montoni vanishes, so too do *Udolpho's* subsidiary terrors. The ghosts are smugglers; the corpse beneath the black veil is a waxwork; Ludovico is kidnapped, not spirited away; the mysterious woman in Emily's father's past is his sister. In all cases, literally or metaphorically, "Had [Emily] dared to look again, her delusion and her fears would have vanished altogether, and she would have perceived . . . that fierce severity, which monkish superstition has sometimes inflicted on mankind." Emily's imaginings are revealed as the last refuge of the nescient, the womb of night in which breed submissions to monstrous hallucinations of personalized male power. A conclusion more in accord with the Enlightenment program of disenchanting the world is difficult to imagine.

Radcliffe's conclusions insist on the ease with which accurate perception and authoritative recreations can illumine the obscure and dispel superstition. She follows her Enlightenment assumptions to their triumphant end. The triumph is, however, too easy, as Montoni's impotence, in part at least, is a function of his social marginality. Montoni is frozen by the threat of law and is crushed by history because he operates without institutional supports. He lacks the reinforcement of family, church, or state; uniquely among Radcliffe's villains, he is neither father, nor priest, nor governor. In *Udolpho,* where terror depends on delusive ascriptions of power, Radcliffe's demystifications are on safe ground. Lurking, though, is the knowledge that not all power relations are based on illusion. The Count de Villefort, to cite a benign example, stands *in loco patris* to Emily after her escape and derives from that role a power over the heroine unmatched by Montoni. And this power is nothing compared to that granted to the Marquis Mazzini, the Marquis de Montalt, and Schedoni by their claims to paternity. In the last two cases these claims are spurious and may be dispelled by further knowledge. But, for Radcliffe, the power of the father is never specious. It derives from the institution of the family and, however weak or criminal the individual father might be, he draws real power from the symbolic Father for whom he stands.

In the process of demystifying certain superstitious adherences, Radcliffe's novels cause others to appear in their places; a superstitious valorization of the family is but one possible consequence of the dissipation of other loyalties. As the law interposes to transform existing power relations between Emily and Montoni, so too can the abstraction of paternity intervene metamorphically in specific parent-child relations. Ellena di Rosalba's wilful blindness to Schedoni's character (and to the dagger he has dropped by her bed) when she believes him to be her father shows this to a degree that can only be read as parody.

Less troubled but as important to the impasse Radcliffe reaches is the recognition that forms of institutional power persist despite enlightenment. Her heroines and heroes are faced with power structures which, though they may depend on societal illusions, are impervious to individual demystification. Radcliffe's committed anti-Roman Catholicism serves well to deflect attention from the general implications of the power made possible by convents, abbeys, and confessionals. But these are as much figures for all institutional power as is the legal system in *Caleb Williams.* From *A Sicilian Romance* to *The Italian,* Radcliffe's landscapes are littered with isolated institutions where arbitrary power flourishes. It is not, however, until *The*

Italian that she confronts directly the limitations of the personalized model of arbitrary power governing Godwin's legal system and her own succession of cloisters.

The crisis confronted by Vivaldi and Schedoni in the chambers of the Inquisition is broached as early as *A Sicilian Romance,* where the Father Abate of St Augustin sets his institutionally granted power against the power of the father. "This man [the Marquis Mazzini] shall tremble . . . who dares defy our power, or question our sacred authority. The Lady Julia is safe. I will protect her from this proud invader of our rights, and teach him at least to venerate the power he cannot conquer." The Father Abate had tremendous power, not only over Julia, but over all who enter his dominion, whatever their own sources of strength. This power cannot be counteracted by any clarity of vision, any effulgence of light. Julia can only be saved by her author's granting her an unlikely escape.

Radcliffe's project is caught between her Enlightenment faith in disenchantment and her recognition of the indomitable reality of what Michel Foucault called, albeit dismissively, power's "terminal forms" [in *The History of Sexuality,* trans R. Hurley, 1980]. This recognition is all the more troubling when the novelist employs such terminal forms as law to dissipate local powers. The law may banish Montoni but what is to banish the law? The real father may unmask pretenders but may not the real father prove a monster? These questions reach the surface of *The Italian,* where the complicity of Radcliffe's characteristic effects with illusory power is consciously juxtaposed with the terror generated by real, institutionalized power. The focal point of this confrontation is the chambers of the Inquisition but the questions are raised earlier, in Ellena's confinement at San Stefano. Typically Ellena spends much of her imprisonment at the window, but the view has changed. Instead of mirroring the situation within, the scenery serves, in exactly the manner of Gilpin's ultimate horizon of design, as consolation.

> Here, gazing upon the stupendous imagery around her, looking, as it were, beyond the awful veil which obscures the features of the Deity, and conceals Him from the eyes of his creatures, dwelling as with a present God in the midst of his sublime works; with a mind thus elevated, how insignificant would appear to her the transactions, and the sufferings of this world! How poor the boasted power of man, when the fall of a single cliff from these mountains would with ease destroy thousands of his race assembled on the plains below! . . . Thus man, the giant who now held her in captivity, would shrink to the diminutiveness of a fairy.

The real danger is the power of the corrupt abbess, a power divorced utterly from the landscape. The scene offers only the consolation of a greater power's capacity to crush humanity, if and when it suits that power's purposes. In light of this form of consolation, the answer to Vivaldi's later question, "Is power then . . . the infallible test of justice?" may well be "yes."

As with her sister heroines, Ellena escapes this captivity before the abbess's powers are indulged, but the text's reorientation is clear. Illusory fears are dispelled not by fuller knowledge but by real fears. The human capacity to terrorize, and the institutions which license this capacity, replace both natural and supernatural sources of terror. The nun Olivia asks, "What are bodily pains in comparison with the subtle, the exquisite tortures of the mind!" a Radcliffean commonplace that echoes more hollowly here than elsewhere in the canon. *The Italian*'s scene of terror is no longer the theatre of the mind; the danger to Ellena in Spalatro's cottage is as clearly defined as that to Vivaldi in the Inquisition. These may not arouse chills but chills are not at issue; the actual threats of power are.

In the cells of the Inquisition, Vivaldi, removed entirely from nature, surrounded by nothing that is not the work of man, hears muffled, distorted sounds similar to those assailing Emily at Udolpho. Here, however, there is no mystery. Vivaldi asks his guard, "Whence come those sounds? . . . They strike at my heart!" The guard responds, "From the place of torture." There is nothing obscure about these threats and dangers. Vivaldi is guilty before he is tried and will confess that guilt with or without the aid of torture. Then he will die. Moreover, although Vivaldi and certain of his inquisitors recognize the injustice, even the unreality of the proceedings, the recognition changes nothing. The institution works by its own logic, devouring its victims and its faithful servants as that logic dictates.

Actual terror transposes Radcliffe's usual methods of generating readerly thrills. In a passage eerily akin to several of Emily's inadequate visions at Udolpho, Vivaldi is led through the subterranean passages of the Inquisition:

> The other man bore a torch, and the passages were so dimly lighted, that the way could scarcely have been found without one. They crossed what seemed to be a burial vault, but the extent and obscurity of the place did not allow it to be ascertained; and, having reached an iron door, they stopped. . . . While they waited, Vivaldi thought he heard, from within, low intermitting sounds, as of persons in their extremity, but, though within, they appeared to come from a distance. His whole heart was chilled, not with fear, for at that moment he did not remember himself, but with horror.

The passage ends with Radcliffe's usual distinction between terror—which is in the self—and horror—which is a response to something entirely without the self. The Inquisition, however, erases the tidy outlines

of this distinction; Vivaldi may forget himself momentarily, but when his self-consciousness returns the horror remains. Shrouded in obscurity as it is, the power of the Inquisition does not depend on sensory or imaginative failure. The more clearly Vivaldi perceives, the worse his situation becomes; the terror inspired in these scenes defies rationalizing dissipation.

Schedoni's experience is more telling still. For the first two-thirds of *The Italian,* the monk proves the most imposing of Radcliffe's villains. By contrast, the voluptuary Montalt enchained by appetite and limited by materialist scepticism appears comic, the rebellious Montoni ineffectual. Schedoni has the support of the church; he has turned Vivaldi's parents to his will; he has seized control of Ellena's life; he has made the mighty Inquisition his tool. In the final third, however, Schedoni's claims to power are negated only to reassert themselves in a new, and surprising, place. The institutions on which his power has depended turn against him. The superstitious religion of the Marchesa di Vivaldi causes the deathbed confession of plots against Ellena. Schedoni's supposed daughter discovers her mother and through her the truth about her fathers, supposed and real. Most damagingly though, the Inquisition he has summoned summons him. Schedoni, having called upon powers beyond his control, becomes their creature.

The downfall of Schedoni is not completely unlike the ends of Radcliffe's earlier villains. The difference lies in the character of the agent of vengeance. In the earlier novels the villain is brought down by constituted authorities which are themselves just. As soon as the French king has sufficient knowledge of Montalt's crimes he moves to punish him; the "commercial senate of Venice," though less just than the king, moves to destroy Montoni as soon as it discerns how it may be done. In both cases the earthly powers lack only the knowledge to act justly. The Inquisition in *The Italian,* on the other hand, serves only its own convenience; the justice of Schedoni's condemnation does nothing to raise the institution's moral stature. The Inquisition remains the chamber of oppression whatever good it may, incidentally, do. Moreover, the presence of the vicar-general, a truly just man, among the Inquisitors serves only to underscore the capacity of the institution to overbear any individual goodness that may inhere among its servants.

The final effect of the Inquisition's charges against Schedoni is to exalt *his* character. As his apparent power is stripped from him, Schedoni reveals a strength without parallel in Radcliffe's earlier villains.

> The emotion betrayed by Schedoni, on the appearance of the last witness, and during the delivery of the evidence, disappeared when his fate became certain; and when the dreadful sentence of

the law was pronounced, it made no visible impression on his mind. From that moment, his firmness or his hardihood never forsook him.

Schedoni is ennobled rather than destroyed by the Inquisition's condemnation; with his worldly powers shorn away he becomes a different sort of sublime object. No longer does he awe through fear; rather he compels admiration through his own fearlessness. The "terrific Schedoni" becomes, in the moments before his death, an avatar of the humanist sublime. That is, in the default of his specious powers, he achieves something approaching superhuman grandeur, as Clarissa Harlowe does, in death. "A humanistic sublime" may be, as Thomas Weiskel argues, "an oxymoron." But this perceptual catachresis is essential to the creation of Romantic subjectivity, the oxymoron in itself serving, as Kenneth Burke suggests, as rhetorical figure for a post-Enlightenment longing for transcendence, for a fusion of opposites impossible in an institutionalized world.

Thus in the death of Schedoni, Radcliffe makes two modernizing turns unique in her canon. First, she locates sublimity in the individual at a moment when the observer is neither deluded nor terrified. Second, she posits for Schedoni an ego, a sovereign self, which exists independent of circumstance. In so doing she creates what a Romantic or post-Romantic age recognizes as a character; in Frederick Garber's words [in his introduction to *The Italian,* 1968], "the only one of her characters who ever really lives." In these turns Radcliffe moves far closer to the Romantic notion of the human subject and she does so in response to her recognition that history was increasingly to be the history of human beings in conflict with the institutions humankind has made. In Schedoni's fall we observe the denial of individual evil and the logical consequent to the demystifying conclusions of the earlier novels. The person who inspires terror does so through the observer's nescience; institutions that terrify do so because they are the true locus of power and the more accurately they are known the more terrifying they become. In an instructional interlude Schedoni tells Vivaldi how Nicola di Zampari can appear in locked cells. "[The Inquisition] . . . has terrible secrets! . . . Know, young man, that almost every cell of every prisoner has a concealed entrance, by which the ministers of death may pass unnoticed to their victims. This Nicola is now one of of those dreadful summoners, and is acquainted with all the secret avenues, that lead to murder." The information banishes the supernatural but does nothing to allay Vivaldi's fear. The Inquisition is understood as an historical reification of Radcliffe's narrative machinery where a demystified supernatural has become the mechanism of the inhuman. In this context Schedoni's individual, domestic evil appears quaintly anachronistic. That Schedoni may contemplate calmly the sentence of such an institution

is possible only because he has set himself above or below its reach. In doing so, he is the precursor of those Romantic egoists whose crimes secure their identities against the institutional powers of the world. In a figure such as Byron's Manfred, the sovereign, self-corrupted ego has become the sole defence against the powers of an inhumanly ordered, bureaucratized world. Schedoni may not have achieved this apogee, but on his deathbed, amongst other sage advice, he directs the way.

In *The Italian,* Radcliffe confronts a contradiction inherent in her project. As daughter to the Enlightenment she is able to oppose individual presumption with institutional constraint. Thus she can demystify the assumption of individual power by the corrupt and, *pari passu,* observe the direct linkage of female subjection to a feminine ideal privileging conduct rather than knowledge. In vindicating institutional checks and balances, however, she is obliged to endorse powers that are not so easily banished. To the degree that her Catholic church is merely what it claims to be, this is not a difficulty, but when it becomes, in *The Italian,* a figure for all state institutions problems begin. There are no obvious "protestant" alternatives to the patriarchal family or to the state, even if that state is not designedly a haven of arbitrary power. The knowledge that liberates Adeline and Emily is seen now as allowing but a limited freedom. Vivaldi achieves that freedom in the cells of the Inquisition and remains a prisoner. The shift from heroine to hero is crucial. Vivaldi may not be an ideal figure after the fashion of Radcliffe's heroines, but neither is he subject to the systematic miseducation of women. He has a degree of social mobility, physical activity, and legal status denied heroines, and he has learned to curb the hot-headed aristocratic excess that has disposed him to superstition. Still he falls prey to the Inquisition. Moreover, if we are not moved by the callow Vivaldi's incarceration, we witness the cunning Schedoni suffering the same fate. More tellingly, perhaps, Schedoni's progress resembles an unhappy version of Radcliffe's narrative strategies. Both summon institutional powers to expedite their plots and in this confess their subservience to those powers.

If, unlike Schedoni, Radcliffe escapes alive, the escape appears to cost her her vocation. Radcliffe's Inquisition marks the terminus of her Enlightenment principles and addresses powers that endure despite knowledge. It exposes also the dependence of the Enlightenment itself on the hypostatization of certain abstractions in institutional form. Hitherto Radcliffe has insulated her fictions from their political implications by means of the Protestant myth of Catholicism. If we replace *The Italian*'s Catholic church with the English legal system, we are not far from *Caleb Williams* and Caleb's hapless, conflicted drive to establish selfhood. For this reason, if for no other, it is of interest that in

Radcliffe's next novel, the withheld *Gaston de Blondeville,* she returns to a medieval Catholic England where no Protestant alternative exists and where religious law is merely a serviceable adjunct to temporal power.

Gaston is a markedly experimental novel departing in many ways from Radcliffe's characteristic manner. In *Gaston* she composes, in the extended frame tale, scenes of contemporary social comedy and creates, in the figure of a monkish chronicler, a sustained characterized narrator. The novel lacks a heroine, features a "real" ghost, and is overtly concerned with political process. In place of a heroine Radcliffe employs a merchant, Hugh Woodreeve, who accuses the king's companion, the eponymous villain, of robbery and murder. This accusation leads to Woodreeve's imprisonment on charges of sorcery, and the remainder of the novel is concerned with the ghostly intercession necessary to keep him from the flames.

The contradiction here—that real sorcery is needed to save Woodreeve from a charge of sorcery trumped up by designing politicians employing superstition to further their ends—is an index to Radcliffe's dilemma. In *Gaston* the enlightened figures are corrupt, and only through superstitions coming to life can the protagonist be saved. The Enlightenment position of Radcliffe's earlier narrators is occupied by rapacious murderers and sycophantic opportunists. In anatomizing such beings, the narrative conducts what we might call, after Peter Sloterdijk, a critique of cynical reason, including the reason that led *The Italian* to its closing impasse. In this "closet" text Radcliffe admits "real" ghosts and presents a temporal power structure riddled to the top with corruption. It is tempting to argue that this is the novel Radcliffe wished to write and could write only without thought of publication. More plausibly *Gaston* can be seen as an experiment, one driven by a desire to find a way not only to criticize but also to provide an alternative to chronicling the independent life of self-perpetuating and anthropophagous institutions. This drive, however, leads only to the proposal of a magical individualism, manifested both in the figure of the enchanting ghost and that of the young Prince Edward "in whose character yet lay hid the virtues which were hereafter to restore the kingdom." In both of these figures Radcliffe anticipates Carlyle's cult of heroes, even if Edward's heroism is military and political and the ghost's is aesthetic. This solution has, I think, limited satisfaction for an heir of the Enlightenment. A fortuitously good king cannot redeem a monarchy that permits so weak a man as Henry III his misguided indulgences of power. The ghostly creative power that allows the murdered Reginald de Folville to avenge himself and to deliver his kinsman Woodreeve may make of him a Shelleyan legislator but the consolation of poetic power in the face of the developing

modern state is limited in ways that Radcliffe's earlier Enlightenment didacticism is not.

The transformation of the narrator marks another self-critical move. The compiling and commenting monk establishes and maintains rigorously a separation between reader and protagonist. The reader cannot simply take the place of the central figure, even in the oscillating, provisional manner invited by the earlier works. The effect is that of an insistent demonstration of the gap between the actual fears of the merchant and the second hand thrills experienced by the reader. This gap is most notable in a night scene in which the merchant is led through the bowels of Kenilworth by the murderous prior. The scene re-enacts, protractedly, Vivaldi's nocturnal marches through the chambers of the Inquisition. Here, however, the merchant's terror is objectified, presented as a response we are not permitted to share. In contrast to Radcliffe's earlier practice, the reader's perceptions are not identical with those of the protagonist. The narrator keeps the reader from Woodreeve's consciousness; the merchant is seen from without. The victim is always "the merchant," or "Woodreeve," or "the wretched prisoner," and the narrator's historical awareness reminds the reader of the protagonist's partial vision. "Had the merchant been aware of this, he might have thought himself safe; yet he might have erred, when thus secure, and found that his worst enemy stood close beside him." In the convolutions of this passage, the merchant is two steps behind narrator and reader, knowing neither that he might think himself safe nor that he would be wrong if he did.

In this scene Radcliffe criticizes her own practice, dilating upon the author's implication in the scenes of terror she represents. Do Gothic thrills serve to insulate the reader from a recognition of the abuses of power? Does Radcliffe's characteristic mode lull us into a sensualized enjoyment of powerlessness? Should not the plight of Woodreeve and, by implication, that of Radcliffe's other virtuous victims be a call to the barricades rather than an occasion for pleasure? These are questions posed by the progress of *Gaston de Blondeville,* and are questions the narrative declines to answer. In the text's generic bifurcation—self-consciously paraded research that asserts the account's actuality colliding with the unapologetic fantasy of the ghost and his miracles—breed some possibilities of response. In describing Woodreeve's journey towards the flames in such material detail and his escape as flamboyant fantasy, *Gaston* points to a separation always present in Radcliffe's novels. The ways of power leading the heroines and heroes into locked chambers are the stuff of documentary realism; the ways of escape are the mere fluff of romance.

Gaston permits, then, a reassessment of the earlier novels and inscribes, perhaps, the author's own reassessment. The impasse to which the author's logic has brought her is hereby revealed. So long as her project was an Enlightenment one, that of banishing superstition and championing knowledge, she remained on safe ground. When, however, she moved to grant the reality of certain forms of power, the faith that buoys the earlier novels deserts her and she is obliged to confront her implication, as *romancière,* in the mystifications she has demolished. Thus the supernatural, banished at the conclusion of the earlier novels, is the means by which Woodreeve is saved. The ghost and the novelist are one. Enlightenment may come eventually but it will do little to change the power the prior and Gaston have over Woodreeve. All it will change is the charge against the merchant. An enlightened England would not burn Woodreeve for sorcery but it might hang him for treason, the modern state being as zealous in its self-protection as the medieval axis of crown and church.

Or worse, it might persecute him for no reason, or no reason accessible to human reason. Even in **Gaston,** Radcliffe guards herself against her latent recognition of the impersonal "nature" of institutional power. Her Inquisitions and courts are not quite Dickens's Court of Chancery or Kafka's Castle; they exist at least in some part as the creations of designing men, as creatures that may devour the hand that feeds, but creatures still. Yet the recognition remains as the conclusion to the author's logic of terror, to her whole method. Radcliffe is left with nowhere to go save into an overt critique of established power repugnant to her conscious politics or into the embrace of the sovereign egoism implicit in her villains. Without a faith, like Walter Scott's, in history as positive progression, the historical novel attempted in **Gaston** holds forth no promise. And without a sense that a separate peace is some sort of gain, the domestic romance cannot allure. Radcliffe's silence is testament both to the author's Enlightenment conviction that fictions were machines with which to think and to her thought's having reached what was to her the unthinkable.

FURTHER READING

Anderson, Howard. "Gothic Heroes." In *The English Hero, 1660 to 1800*, edited by Robert Folkenflik, pp. 205-21. Newark: University of Delaware Press, 1982, 230 p.

  Examines the variety of heroes in Gothic romances, particularly in the works of Radcliffe, Horace Walpole, and Matthew Lewis.

Benedict, Barbara M. "Pictures of Conformity: Sentiment and Structure in Ann Radcliffe's Style." *Philological Quarterly* 68, No. 3 (Summer 1989): 363-77.

  An examination of Radcliffe's style that reveals the relationship between her rationalism and her preoccupation with the emotions and imagination of terror.

Bernstein, Stephen. "Form and Ideology in the Gothic Novel." *Essays in Literature* XVIII, No. 2 (Fall 1991): 151-65.

  A general discussion of the origin and characteristics of the genre that includes discussions of several of Radcliffe's novels.

Bruce, Donald Williams. "Ann Radcliffe and the Extended Imagination." *Contemporary Review* 258, No. 1505 (June 1991): 300-8.

  Briefly reviews the plot, main characters, and style of *The Mysteries of Udolpho* and *The Italian.*

Carter, Margaret L. "The Fantastic-Uncanny in the Novels of Ann Radcliffe." In *Specter or Delusion? The Supernatural in Gothic Fiction*, pp. 23-45. Ann Arbor: UMI Research Press, 1987, 131 p.

  A study of the function of the supernatural in Radcliffe's novels with specific attention to the way in which the fantastic serves the supernatural.

Castle, Terry. "The Spectralization of the 'Other' in *The Mysteries of Udolpho.*" In *The Eighteenth Century: Theory, Politics, English Literature,* edited by Felicity Nussbaum and Laura Brown, pp. 231-53. Methuen, 1987.

  Relates Radcliffe's use of the supernatural to changing attitudes towards death and consciousness in late eighteenth-century Europe.

Delamotte, Eugenia C. "Self-Defense in the Gothic Tradition: Radcliffe, Brockden Brown, Henry James." In *Perils of the Night: A Feminist Study of Nineteenth-Century Gothic,* pp. 29-42. New York: Oxford University Press, 1990, 352 p.

  Examines the function and limitations of "conscious worth"—an acute and perceptible attachment to one's moral integrity—in protecting female protagonists against male aggressors in the works of Radcliffe and other Gothic novelists.

Dobree, Bonamy. Introduction to *The Mysteries of Udolpho*, by Ann Radcliffe, edited by Bonamy Dobree, pp. vii-xvi. London: Oxford University Press, 1966.

  Provides a brief overview of Radcliffe's style throughout her career.

Fitzgerald, Lauren. "Gothic Properties: Radcliffe, Lewis and the Critics." *The Wordsworth Circle* XXIV, No. 3 (Summer 1993): 167-70.

  Examines the literary relationship between Radcliffe and her contemporary Matthew Lewis, author of the Gothic novel *The Monk.*

Flaxman, Rhoda L. "Radcliffe's Dual Modes of Vision." In *Fetter'd or Free?: British Women Novelists, 1670-1815,* edited by Mary Anne Schofield and Cecilia Macheski, pp. 124-33. Athens, Ohio: Ohio University Press, 1986, 441 p.

Argues that through her eplorations of the unknown territory of "cinematic" word-painting, Radcliffe contributed a new subject and technique to the English novel.

——. "Preview: Word-Painting in Radcliffe and Scott." In *Victorian Word-Painting and Narrative: Toward the Blending of Genres,* pp. 9-17. Ann Arbor: UMI Research Press, 1987, 150 p.

Credits Radcliffe with raising detailed visual descriptions of landscape "to a position of prominence in English fiction," thus setting the stage for the "word-painting" of later Romantic and Victorian novelists.

Gamer, Michael. "'The Most Interesting Novel in the English Language:' An Unidentified Addendum to Coleridge's Review of *Udolpho*." *The Wordsworth Circle* XXIV, No. 1 (Winter 1993): 53-4.

Shows how Coleridge's review of Radcliffe's *The Mysteries of Udolpho* reveals the critic's grudging respect for the force of Radcliffe's prose despite his well-known dislike of the Gothic tradition.

Hagstrum, Jean H. "Pictures to the Heart: The Psychological Picturesque in Ann Radcliffe's *The Mysteries of Udolpho*." In *Green Centennial Studies: Essays Presented to Donald Greene in the Centennial Year of the University of Southern California,* edited by Paul J. Korshin and Robert R. Allen, pp. 434-41. Charlottesville: University Press of Virginia, 1984, 489 p.

Suggests that Radcliffe uses detailed descriptions of landscape to evoke the psychological states of her characters.

Holland, Norman N., and Leona F. Sherman. "Gothic Possibilities." In *Gender and Reading: Essays on Readers, Texts, and Contexts,* edited by Elizabeth A. Flynn and Patrocinio P. Schweikart, pp. 215-33. Baltimore: The Johns Hopkins University Press, 1986, 306 p.

The critics examine their individual responses to typical characteristics of the Gothic novel in an effort to determine how the genre has maintained its popularity and why most of its readers are women.

Kadish, Doris Y. "Women and Nature: *The Mysteries of Udolpho* and *Frankenstein*." In *The Literature of Images: Narrative Landscape from* Julie *to* Jane Eyre, pp. 81-106. New Brunswick: Rutgers University Press, 1987, 211 p.

Examines the use by Radcliffe and Mary Wollstonecraft Shelley of "opposing elements in nature" to explore "alternative ways of thinking about women and nature."

Kahane, Claire. "Gothic Mirrors and Feminine Identity." *The Centennial Review* XXIV, No. 1 (Winter 1980): 43-64.

Argues that the exploration of the complex relationship between mothers and daughters is a major characteristic of the Gothic novel and a key reason for its popularity among women readers.

Kostelinck, Charles. "From Picturesque View to Picturesque Vision: William Gilpin and Ann Radcliffe." *Mosaic* 18, No. 3 (Summer 1985): 31-48.

Examines how, in accordance with the eighteenth-century aesthetic theory of the picturesque as articulated by the essayist William Gilpin, Radcliffe uses descriptions of landscape to penetrate the "mental operations" of her characters.

Lewis, Paul. "Fearful Lessons: The Didacticism of the Early Gothic Novel." *CLA Journal: A Quarterly* XXIII, No. 4 (June 1980): 470-84.

Insists on the ultimately rational and morally didactic aspects of the Gothic writings of Radcliffe and Matthew Lewis.

McIntyre, Clara Frances. *Ann Radcliffe in Relation to Her Time.* Yale Studies in English, vol. 62. 1920. Reprint. Hamden, Conn.: Archon Books, 1970, 104 p.

A study of Radcliffe in relation to the political, literary, philosophical, and cultural influences of her time, stressing Radcliffe's contributions to nineteenth-century literature.

Mishra, Vijay. "The Gothic Sublime and Literary History." In *The Gothic Sublime,* pp. 225-57. Albany: State University of New York Press, 1994, 342 p.

In exploring the significance of the Gothic concept of "the sublime" for postmodern literature, the critic examines Radcliffe's treatment of the sublime.

Murray, E. B. *Ann Radcliffe.* New York: Twayne Publishers, 1972. 178 p.

A useful general introduction to Radcliffe's life and works. A full chapter devoted to each of the major novels and a discussion of her influence are included.

Nollen, Elizabeth. "Ann Radcliffe's *A Sicilian Romance*: A New Source for Jane Austen's *Sense and Sensibility*. *English Language Notes* XXII, No. 2 (December 1984): 30-7.

Examines similarities between various characters in both novels and in the two authors' treatments of the "sense and sensibility" theme.

Railo, Eino. *The Haunted Castle: A Study of the Elements of English Romanticism.* London: George Routledge & Sons; New York: E. P. Dutton & Co., 1927, 388 p.

A study of the elements of English Romanticism, especially its Gothic manifestations.

Ross, Deborah. "*The Italian*: A Romance of Manners." In *The Excellence of Falsehood: Romance, Realism, and Women's Contribution to the Novel,* pp. 135-65. Lexington: The University Press of Kentucky, 1991, 249 p.

A study of Radcliffe's *The Italian* in relation to Fanny Burney's *Cecilia*, demonstrating the affinities of Radcliffe's Gothic novel with Burney's romance of manners.

Schmitt, Cannon. "Techniques of Terror, Technologies of Nationality: Ann Radcliffe's *The Italian*." *ELH* 61, No. 4 (1994): 853-76.

Examines Radcliffe's use of the exotically foreign to evoke terror in *The Italian*.

Sedgwick, Eve Kosofsky. "The Character in the Veil: Imagery of the Surface in the Gothic Novel." *PMLA* 96, No. 2 (March 1981): 255-70.

Argues that in Gothic fiction surfaces do not merely disguise deeper meanings but are inscribed with meaning themselves, and discusses the implications of this trait for characterization and figuration in the Gothic novel.

Snyder, William C. "Mother Nature's Other Natures: Landscape in Women's Writing, 1770-1830." *Women's Studies* 21, No. 2 (1992): 143-62.

Included is a brief discussion of the ways in which Radcliffe's descriptions of nature reflect the plight or emotional condition of her heroines, citing *The Italian* as the richest source of this narrative technique.

Spacks, Patricia Meyer. "Female Orders of Narrative: *Clarissa* and *The Italian*. In *Rhetorics of Order/ Ordering Rhetorics in English Neoclassical Literature*, edited by J. Douglas Canfield and J. Paul Hunter, pp. 158-72. Newark: University of Delaware Press, 1989, 200 p.

Argues that for both Radcliffe and Samuel Richardson, Christian belief provided materials for personal narrative orders and some sorts of narrative disorder, and that both authors "explore specifically female possibilities for adapting Christian principles of interpretation."

Spencer, Jane. *The Rise of the Woman Novelist: From Aphra Behn to Jane Austen*. Oxford: Basil Blackwell, 1986, 225 p.

Includes a discussion of the contribution of the female novelist to the Gothic tradition with special emphasis on Radcliffe's work.

Taylor, Michael. "Reluctant Romancers: Self-consciousness and Derogation in Prose Romance." *English Studies in Canada* XVII, No. 1 (March 1991): 80-106.

A brief discussion of *The Mysteries of Udolpho* shows how Radcliffe's Gothic novel is anti-Gothic insofar as she attempts to undermine the romantic sensibility in her readers by implicitly criticizing it in the narrative and through her characters.

Thomas, Donald. "The First Poetess of Romantic Fiction: Ann Radcliffe, 1764-1823." *English* XV, No. 87 (Autumn 1964): 91-5.

Presents Radcliffe's novels as essentially character studies of her persecuted heroines. Other characters are important only in relation to the heroines, who are drawn realistically despite their Gothic environments.

Todd, Janet. "Posture and Imposture: The Gothic Manservant in Ann Radcliffe's *The Italian*." *Women and Literature*, new series 2 (1981): 25-38.

Examines the role of the "perfect servant" in *The Italian* and contrasts this depiction with prevailing late-eighteenth views of the character of servants.

Varma, Devendra P. Introduction to *A Sicilian Romance*, by Ann Radcliffe, pp. vii-xxvi. New York: Arno Press, 1972.

Provides a general survey of Radcliffe's technique in her major novels with a discussion of the contribution of Radcliffe's style to romantic fiction.

Varnado, S. L. *Haunted Presence: The Numinous in Gothic Fiction*. Tuscaloosa: The University of Alabama Press, 1987, 160 p.

Includes a brief discussion of how Radcliffe's use of the sublime serves to partially obscure the supernatural.

Ware, Malcolm. *Sublimity in the Novels of Ann Radcliffe*. Essays and Studies on American Language and Literature, edited by S. B. Liljegren, vol. XXV. Upsala, Sweden: A. B. Lundequistska Bokhandeln, 1963, 62 p.

An application of Edmund Burke's concept of sublimity to Radcliffe's novels, examining Radcliffe's descriptions in her novels as applications of Burke's principles.

Wieten, Alida Alberdina Sibbelina. *Mrs. Radcliffe: Her Relation towards Romanticism*. Amsterdam: H. J. Paris, 1926, 146 p.

Considers Radcliffe "one of [the]first exponents" of Romanticism, primarily because of her response to the natural world.

Williams, Anne. "Ann Radcliffe's Female Plot." *Studies on Voltaire and the Eighteenth Century* 304 (1992): 823-5.

Suggests that Radcliffe's Gothic plot is a retelling of the myth of Psyche and Eros and that it creates a model of feminine heroism based on sympathy and cooperation.

Winter, Kari J. "Sexual/Textual Politics of Terror: Writing and Rewriting the Gothic Genre in the 1790s." In *Misogyny in Literature: An Essay Collection,* edited by Katherine Anne Ackley, pp. 89-103. New York: Garland, 1992, 393 p.

Traces differences in the Gothic writings of male and female authors to differences in the relationships of men and women to the dominant ideology.

Wolstenholme, Susan. "Woman as Gothic Vision (*The Italian*)."
In *Gothic (Re)visions: Writing Women as Readers,* pp. 15-36.
Albany: State University of New York Press, 1993, 201 p.

Argues that Radcliffe claims the Gothic as a female genre "by reclaiming a certain textual space for a woman as reader and writer."

> **Additional coverage of Radcliffe's life and career is contained in the following sources published by Gale Research:** *Dictionary of Literary Biography,* **Volume 39; and** *Nineteenth-Century Literature Criticism,* **Volume 6.**

John Richardson

1796-1852

Canadian novelist, historian, memoirist, autobiographer, travel writer, short story writer, and poet.

INTRODUCTION

Largely ignored during his lifetime by critics and the reading public, Richardson is now regarded as one of Canada's major pre-Confederation novelists. Drawing heavily from the gothic and romantic traditions, Richardson's oeuvre includes several fictional works about the American and Canadian frontier as well as narrative poetry and a history of the War of 1812. His most successful work, the novel *Wacousta* (1832), is a story of revenge and frontier warfare reminiscent of James Fenimore Cooper's Leatherstocking novels. Dennis Duffy has stated: "The century and a half of critical and public attention paid to *Wacousta* has not only confirmed the enduring qualities of the work, but it has made of Richardson's imagination a powerful force to be dealt with when outlining the shape of [Canadian] literary experience."

Biographical Information

Born in Queenston, Ontario, Richardson spent most of his youth in Amherstburg, Ontario, where his father was a medical officer with the British army at Fort Malden. At the age of fifteen, Richardson joined the British army as a gentleman volunteer for service in the War of 1812. Captured after the British defeat at the Battle of Moraviantown in 1813, he spent a year in Kentucky as a prisoner of war. He gained a commission in the British army after his release, then spent a short time in England before being posted to the West Indies. There, he served two years with the Queen's Regiment, returning to Europe in 1818 as a half-pay officer. In 1828, Richardson anonymously published *Tecumseh,* a narrative poem about the death of the Native American chief who formed an alliance with the British in the War of 1812. This sole attempt at poetry was followed by three novels concerning English and French society—*Ecarté* (1829), *Frascati's* (1830), and *Kensington Gardens* (1830). Following the publication and critical and popular success of *Wacousta* in 1832, Richardson returned to active military service in 1835 and fought in the Carlist War in Spain, an experience about which he wrote several memoirs. In 1838, Richardson returned to Canada to cover political events for the London *Times*. His political opinions, however, conflicted with those of the *Times's* editors,

and he was soon released from his contract. Remaining in Canada, Richardson attempted several unsuccessful ventures in newspaper publishing throughout the 1840s, and wrote *The Canadian Brothers* (1840), a sequel to *Wacousta,* and *War of 1812* (1842), a history of the war. Neither work sparked public interest, and Richardson suffered further misfortune in 1845 when his wife died and he lost his commission as superintendent of police on the Welland Canal. He subsequently published two volumes of autobiography, and then left Canada in 1849 for New York City, where he published his last works—*The Monk Knight of St. John* (1850), a story of the Crusades, and three frontier adventure novels. He died in New York City in 1852.

Major Works

Set on the North American frontier, Richardson's major works deal primarily with war and revenge. *Wacousta,* for instance, draws on Chief Pontiac's attacks in 1763 on the English forts at Detroit and Michilimackinac for its historical background; the War of 1812 provides the backdrop for *Tecumseh* and *The Canadian Brothers;* while *Hardscrabble* (1851) and *Wau-Nan-Gee* (1852) center on the 1812 massacre at Fort Dearborn. Combining elements from the gothic and romance genres, *Wacousta* centers on the story of Reginald Morton, also known as Wacousta, who—driven by the desire for revenge against Colonel de Haldimar, the man who betrayed his trust and stole his lover—disavows his European heritage, allies himself with the Native Americans, and seeks to destroy Haldimar and his family. In *The Canadian Brothers,* the sequel to *Wacousta,* the brothers Gerald and Henry—sons of Frederick de Haldimar—are enemies of Desborough, Wacousta's son. Though Richardson is best known for his adventure novels of the North American frontier, he also wrote several works set outside North America. *Ecarté* and *Frascati's,* for instance, depict moral corruption in the gambling halls of Paris, while *The Monk Knight of St. John,* a love story set during the Crusades, ranges from the Holy Land to France.

Critical Reception

With the exception of *Wacousta,* Richardson's novels have been derided by most critics as potboilers. Desmond Pacey, for example, vehemently attacked *The Monk Knight of St. John,* arguing that Richardson's depiction of "sexual aberrations" pushes the novel dangerously close to mere pornography. Indeed, Richardson's interest in sexuality and gothicism, as well as the scenes of voyeurism, cannibalism, and rape that recur in his novels have been noted by commentators. The protagonist of *Westbrook, The Outlaw* (1853), for instance, not only spies on a pair of lovers but later rapes the woman while forcing her lover to watch. Commenting on Richardson's interest in cannibalism and rape, Dennis Duffy has noted that "one, the other, or both occur in every fictional work of Richardson with the exception of *Hardscrabble.*" Another element common to Richardson's works was his tendency to fictionalize incidents from his life. Donald Stephens argues, for instance, that *The Canadian Brothers,* which incorporates Richardson's imprisonment in Kentucky, is "a fictionalized chronicle of actual events, people, and places from Richardson's childhood and adolescence that both revealed the psychology of the author and helped create seminal mythologies about his country." Critical discussions of *Wacousta* have centered on Richardson's examination of revenge, identity, and the dichotomies between civilization and savagery; reason and passion; love and hatred. A number of scholars have also written on the often-made comparisons between Cooper and Richardson. Scholars contend that unlike American frontier stories, which tend to center on a lone protagonist without ancestry, *Wacousta* and *The Canadian Brothers* are dominated by family relationships. In addition, Cooper's depiction of nature is quite distinct from Richardson's:

whereas Cooper provided a balanced view of nature's benevolence and cruelty and praised the virtues of a communion of men in the forest, Richardson persistently emphasized the savage aspects of the wilderness and emphasized the values and order of the military garrison. Although Richardson died penniless and bitter that his countrymen failed to acknowledge him as a man of letters, "a century later," Leslie Monkman has noted, "he . . . is now regarded by many as the major anglophone novelist of pre-Confederation Canada."

PRINCIPAL WORKS

Tecumseh; or, The Warrior of the West: A Poem of Four Cantos with Notes [published anonymously] (poetry) 1828

Ecarté; or, The Salons of Paris (novel) 1829; revised edition, 1851

Frascati's; or, Scenes in Paris (novel) 1830

Kensington Gardens in 1830: A Satirical Trifle (novel) 1830

Wacousta; or, The Prophecy: A Tale of the Canadas (novel) 1832; revised edition, 1851

Journal of the Movements of the British Legion (nonfiction) 1836; enlarged edition published as *Movements of the British Legion with Strictures on the Course of Conduct Pursued by Lieutenant-General Evans* 1837

Personal Memoirs of Major Richardson; As Connected with the Singular Oppression of that Officer While in Spain (memoir) 1838

The Canadian Brothers; or, The Prophecy Fulfilled. A Tale of the Late American War (novel) 1840; revised edition published as *Matilda Montgomerie; or, The Prophecy Fulfilled* 1851

War of 1812; First Series; Containing a Full and Detailed Narrative of the Operations of the Right Division of the Canadian Army (history) 1842; enlarged edition published as *Richardson's War of 1812* [edited by Alexander Clark Casselman] 1902

Correspondence (Submitted to Parliament) between Major Richardson, Late Superintendent of Police on the Welland Canal and the Honorable Dominick Daly, Provincial Secretary (letters) 1846

Eight Years in Canada (autobiography) 1847

The Guards in Canada; or, The Point of Honor (autobiography) 1848

"A Trip to Walpole Island and Port Sarnia" [published anonymously] (travel) 1849; published as *Tecumseh and Richardson; The Story of a Trip to Walpole Island and Port Sarnia* [edited by A. H. U. Colquhoun] 1924

The Monk Knight of St. John: A Tale of the Crusades (novel) 1850

Hardscrabble; or, The Fall of Chicago. A Tale of Indian Warfare (novel) 1851

Wau-Nan-Gee; or, The Massacre at Chicago (novel) 1852

Westbrook, The Outlaw; or, The Avenging Wolf. An American Border Tale (novel) 1853

Major John Richardson's Short Stories (short stories) [edited by David Beasley] 1985

CRITICISM

John Richardson (essay date 1851)

SOURCE: An introduction to *Wacousta; or, The Prophecy: An Indian Tale,* Robert M. De Witt, Publisher, 1851, pp. iii-viii.

[*In the following introduction to the revised edition of his novel, Richardson comments on the sources for* Wacousta *and answers charges of improbability and geographical error.*]

This chapter, written eighteen years subsequent to the original publication of **Wacousta** in London, will be found unavoidably replete with egotism. By none will it be more readily pronounced such than by those who are most open to the charge themselves. Without its exercise, however, the object of this introduction would not be gained.

As the reader may be curious to know on what basis, and in what manner this story (of which I have certainly robbed that first of vigorous American Novelists—the *Last of the Mohicans* Cooper—which tale, albeit I have never read a novel by another author twice, I have absolutely devoured *three* times,) was suggested to me, and on what particular portions of History the story is founded, I am not aware that this introductory Chapter, which I have promised my Publishers, can be better devoted than to the explanation.

It is well known to every man conversant with the earlier History of this country that, shortly subsequent to the cession of the Canadas to England by France, Ponteac the great Head of the Indian race of that period, had formed a federation of the various tribes, threatening extermination to the British posts established along the Western Frontier. These were nine in number, and the following stratagem was resorted to by the artful chief to effect their reduction. Investing one fort with his warriors, so as to cut off all communication with the others, and to leave no hope of succor, his practice was to offer terms of surrender which never were kept in the honorable spirit in which the far more noble and generous Tecumseh always acted with his enemies, and thus in turn, seven of these outposts fell victims to their confidence in his truth. Detroit and Michillimackinac, or Mackinaw as it is now called,

remained, and all the ingenuity of the Chieftain was directed to the possession of these strongholds. The following plan, well worthy of his invention, was at length determined upon. During a temporary truce, and while, Ponteac was holding forth proposals for an ultimate and durable peace, a ball playing was arranged by him to take place simultaneously, on the common or clearing on which rested the forts of Michillimackanac and Detroit. The better to accomplish their object, the guns of the warriors had been cut short and given to their women who were instructed to conceal them under their blankets, and during the game, and seemingly without design, to approach the drawbridge of the fort. This precaution taken, the players were to approach and throw over their ball, permission to regain which they presumed would not be denied. On approaching the drawbridge, they were with fierce yells to make a general rush, and, securing the arms concealed by the women, to massacre the unprepared garrison. The day was fixed—the game commenced, and was proceeded with in the manner previously arranged. The ball was dexterously hurled into the fort, and permission asked to recover it. It was granted. The drawbridge was lowered, and the Indians dashed forward for the accomplishment of their work of blood. How different the result in the two garrisons! At Detroit, Ponteac and his warriors had scarcely crossed the drawbridge when to their astonishment and disappointment, they beheld the guns of the ramparts depressed—the artillerymen with lighted matches at their posts and covering the little garrison, composed of a few companies of the 42d Highlanders, who were also under arms, and so distributed as to take the enemy most at an advantage. Sullenly they withdrew, and without other indication of their purpose than what had been expressed in their manner, and carried off the missing ball. Their design had been discovered and made known by means of significant warnings to the Governor by an Indian woman who owed a debt of gratitude to his family, and was resolved, at all hazards, to save them. On the same day the same artifice was resorted to at Michillimackinac, and with the most complete success. There was no guardian angel there to warn them of danger, and all fell beneath the rifle, the tomahawk, the war-club, and the knife, one or two of the traders—a Mr. Henry among the rest—alone excepted.

It was not long after this event, when the head of the military authorities in the Colony, apprised of the fate of these defeated posts, and made acquainted with the perilous condition of Fort Detroit, which was then reduced to the last extremity, sought an officer who would volunteer the charge of supplies from Albany to Buffalo, and thence across the lake to Detroit, which, if possible, he was to relieve. That volunteer was promptly found in my maternal grandfather, Mr. Erskine, from Strabane, in the North of Ireland, then an officer in the Commissariat Department. The difficulty of the undertaking will be obvious to those who understand the danger attending a journey through the Western wilderness, beset as it was by the warriors of Ponteac, ever on the look out to prevent succor to the garrison, and yet the duty was successfully accomplished. He left Albany with provisions and ammunition sufficient to fill several Schenectady boats—I think seven—and yet conducted his charge with such prudence and foresight, that notwithstanding the vigilance of Ponteac, he finally and after long watching succeeded, under cover of a dark and stormy night, in throwing into the fort the supplies of which the remnant of the gallant "Black-watch," as the 42d was originally named, and a company of whom, while out reconnoitering, had been massacred at a spot in the vicinity of the town, thereafter called the Bloody Run, stood so greatly in need. This important service rendered, Mr. Erskine, in compliance with the instructions he had received, returned to Albany, where he reported the success of the expedition.

The colonial authorities were not regardless of his interests. When the Ponteac confederacy had been dissolved, and quiet and security restored in that remote region, large tracts of land were granted to Mr. Erskine, and other privileges accorded which eventually gave him the command of nearly a hundred thousand dollars—an enormous sum to have been realised at that early period of the country. But it was not destined that he should retain this. The great bulk of his capital was expended on almost the first commercial shipping that ever skimmed the surface of Lakes Huron and Erie. Shortly prior to the Revolution, he was possessed of seven vessels of different tonnage, and the trade in which he had embarked, and of which he was the head, was rapidly increasing his already large fortune, when one of those autumnal hurricanes, which even to this day continue to desolate the waters of the treacherous lake last named, suddenly arose and buried beneath its engulfing waves not less than six of these schooners laden with such riches, chiefly furs, of the West, as then were most an object of barter. Mr. Erskine, who had married the daughter of one of the earliest settlers from France, and of a family well known in history, a lady who had been in Detroit during the siege of the British garrison by Ponteac, now abandoned speculation, and contenting himself with the remnant of his fortune, established himself near the banks of the river, within a short distance of the Bloody Run. Here he continued throughout the Revolution. Early, however, in the present century, he quitted Detroit and repaired to the Canadian shore, where on a property nearly opposite, which he obtained in exchange, and which in honor of his native country he named Strabane—known as such to this day—he passed the autumn of his days. The last time I beheld him, was a day or two subsequent to the affair of the Thames, when General Harrison and Colonel Johnson were temporary inmates of his dwelling.

My father, of a younger branch of the Annadale family, the head of which was attained in the Scottish rebellion of 1745, was an officer of Simcoe's well-known Rangers, in which regiment, and about the same period, the present Lord Hardinge commenced his services in this country. Being quartered at Fort Erie, he met and married at the house of one of the earliest Canadian merchants, a daughter of Mr. Erskine, then on a visit to her sister, and by her had eight children, of whom I am the oldest and only survivor. Having a few years after his marriage been ordered to St. Joseph's, near Michillimackinac, my father thought it expedient to leave me with Mr. Erskine at Detroit, where I received the first rudiments of my education. But here I did not remain long, for it was during the period of the stay of the detachment of Simcoe's Rangers at St. Joseph that Mr. Erskine repaired with his family to the Canadian shore, where on the more elevated and conspicuous part of his grounds which are situated nearly opposite the foot of Hog Island, so repeatedly alluded to in Wacousta, he had caused a flag-staff to be erected, from which each Sabbath day proudly floated the colors under which he had served and never could bring himself to disown. It was at Strabane that the old lady, with whom I was a great favorite, used to enchain my young interest by detailing various facts connected with the siege she so well remembered, and infused into me a longing to grow up to manhood that I might write a book about it. The details of the Ponteac plan for the capture of the two forts were what she most enlarged upon, and although a long lapse of years of absence from the scene, and ten thousand incidents of a higher and more immediate importance might have been supposed to weaken the recollections of so early a period of life, the impression has ever vividly remained. Hence the first appearance of Wacousta in London in 1832, more than a quarter of a century later. The story is founded solely on the artifice of Ponteac to possess himself of these two last British forts. All else is imaginary.

It is not a little curious that I, only a few years subsequent to the narration by old Mrs. Erskine of the daring and cunning feats of Ponteac, and his vain attempt to secure the fort of Detroit, should myself have entered it in arms. But it was so. I had ever hated school with a most bitter hatred, and I gladly availed myself of an offer from General Brock to obtain for me a commission in the king's service. Meanwhile I did duty as a cadet with the gallant 41st regiment, to whom the English edition of Wacousta was inscribed, and was one of the guard of honor who took possession of the fort. The duty of a sentinel over the British colors, which had just been hoisted, was assigned to me, and I certainly felt not a little proud of the distinction.

Five times, within half a century, had the flag of that fortress been changed. First the lily of France, then the red cross of England, and next the stripes and stars of

America had floated over its ramparts; and then again the red cross, and lastly the stars. On my return to this country a few years since, I visited those scenes of stirring excitement in which my boyhood had been passed, but I looked in vain for the ancient fortifications which had given a classical interest to that region. The unsparing hand of utilitarianism had passed over them, destroying almost every vestige of the past. Where had risen the only fortress in America at all worthy to give antiquity to the scene, streets had been laid out and made, and houses had been built, leaving not a trace of its existence, save the well that formerly supplied the closely besieged garrison with water; and this, half imbedded in the herbage of an enclosure of a dwelling house of mean appearance, was rather to be guessed at than seen; while at the opposite extremity of the city, where had been conspicuous for years the Bloody Run, cultivation and improvement had nearly obliterated every trace of the past.

Two objections have been urged against *Wacousta* as a consistent tale—the one as involving an improbability, the other a geographical error. It has been assumed that the startling feat accomplished by that man of deep revenge, who is not alone in his bitter hatred and contempt for the base among those who, like spaniels, crawl and kiss the dust at the instigation of their superiors, and yet arrogate to themselves a claim to be considered gentlemen and men of honor and independence—it has, I repeat, been assumed that the feat attributed to him, in connexion with the flag-staff of the fort, was impossible. No one who has ever seen these erections on the small forts of that day, would pronounce the same criticism. Never very lofty, they were ascended at least one-third of their height by means of small projections nailed to them, for footholds for the artillerymen, frequently compelled to clear the flag lines entangled at the truck; therefore a strong and active man, such as Wacousta is described to have been, might very well have been supposed, in his strong anxiety for revenge and escape with his victim, to have doubled his strength and activity on so important an occasion, rendering that easy of attainment by himself, which an ordinary and unexcited man might deem impossible. I myself have knocked down a gate almost without feeling the resistance, in order to escape the stilettoes of assassins.

The second objection is to the narrowness attributed, in the tale, to the river St. Clair. This was done in the license usually accorded to a writer of fiction, in order to give greater effect to the scene represented as having occurred there and of course in no way intended as a geographical description of the river, nor was it necessary. In the same spirit and for the same purpose, it has been continued.

It will be seen that at the termination of the tragedy enacted at the bridge, by which the Bloody Run was in

Cover of an 1875 edition of Wacousta.

those days crossed, that the wretched wife of the condemned soldier pronounced a curse that could not of course well be fulfilled in the course of the tale. Some few years ago I published in Canada—I might as well have done so in Kamtschatka—the continuation, which was to have been dedicated to the last King of England, but which, after the death of that monarch, was inscribed to Sir John Harvey, whose letter, as making honorable mention of a gallant and beloved brother, I feel it a duty to the memory of the latter to subjoin.

The Prophecy Fulfilled, which, however, has never been seen out of the small country in which it appeared, Detroit perhaps alone excepted, embraces and indeed is intimately connected with the Beauchamp tragedy, which took place at or near Weisiger's Hotel, in Frankfort, Kentucky, where I had been many years before confined as a prisoner of war. While connecting it with the *Prophecy Fulfilled,* and making it subservient to the end I had in view, I had not read, or even heard of the existence of a work of the same character, which had already appeared from the pen of an American author. Indeed, I have reason to believe that the *Prophecy Fulfilled,* although not published until after a lapse of years, was the first written. No similarity of treatment of the subject exists between the two versions, and this, be it remembered, I remark without in the slightest degree impugning the merit of the production of my fellow laborer in the same field.

Alexander Clark Casselman (essay date 1902)

SOURCE: Introduction to *Richardson's War of 1812: With Notes and a Life of the Author,* Historical Publishing Co., 1902, pp. xi-xlv.

[*Casselman was highly regarded for his extensive studies of Richardson's works. In the following excerpt from his authoritative introduction to the* War of 1812, *he provides a detailed and well-documented account of the Canadian author's life and writings.*]

On the Canadian side of the Niagara river, just where its foaming and turbulent waters issue from the narrow, rocky gorge, stands the straggling village of Queenston. The place at the present time is of very little importance except as a terminal port for a magnificent fleet of pleasure vessels that carry tourists and excursion parties to visit the Falls, five or six miles farther up the river. But as the scene of one of the proudest victories of Canadian and British arms during the War of 1812 Queenston has won a fame that is world-wide.

The settlement proper of the country dates from the close of the Revolutionary war, when the disbanded soldiers of Butler's Rangers and other United Empire Loyalists took up grants of land on the banks of the river. At the mouth of the river there soon grew up the town of Niagara (Newark), opposite Fort Niagara, at that time and until 1796 in the hands of the British. The great highway of the trade with Detroit and other western settlements was the Niagara, and as this trade increased the laden vessels from the lakes were taken as far up the river as possible, to shorten the portage around the Falls. This head of navigation was called at first the New Landing, and later Queenstown. Thus favorably situated for trade, the new town prospered and soon became the home of several pioneer merchants, who never dreamed that the stream of commerce could possibly find any other course.

Queenston derived an additional importance, at this early period, from its proximity to the seat of government of the new Province of Upper Canada. The first Lieutenant-Governor of the Province, Colonel John Graves Simcoe, selected Niagara as the capital; and to enforce his authority and protect his person a British Regiment was sent to Canada. This Regiment was recruited in England, Scotland, Nova Scotia and New Brunswick, and was called the Queen's Rangers, from a corps, commanded by Colonel Simcoe, during the war of the Revolution. Among the officers of the new corps who had not held commands in the old one was a young Scotchman named Robert Richardson, the

Assistant Surgeon, a scion of the younger branch of the Annandale family, which had clung to the fortunes of the Pretender. The detachment of the Queen's Rangers, with which Dr. Richardson served, was quartered at Queenston. The young military surgeon became acquainted with the leading merchant of the place, Honorable Robert Hamilton, member of the Legislative Council, who had married Catherine Askin, daughter of Colonel John Askin, a wealthy merchant of Detroit. At his home Dr. Richardson met Miss Madeleine, another daughter of Colonel Askin, then on a visit to her sister. The visits of the handsome young Scotchman were as frequent as his military duties would permit, and the beautiful and accomplished Madeleine encouraged him in his wooing; for we see in the records of St. Mark's church, Niagara, that "Doctor Robert Richardson, bachelor, and Madeleine Askin, spinster," were married by Reverend Robert Addison on January 24th, 1793. In July of this year a part at least of the Queen's Rangers left Queenston for Toronto, and Dr. Richardson accompanied them, leaving his wife with her sister. We learn from a letter written in French by Mrs. Richardson to her stepmother, Mrs. Askin at Detroit, that she is passing a very sad time awaiting news from Toronto, as no boat has arrived from there lately; and that, if she could only know that Mr. Richardson was well, she would be satisfied.

While Mrs. Richardson resided at Queenston their three eldest children were born: Jane, born May 19th, 1794, baptized at Niagara, August 17th; John, born October 4th, 1796, baptized January 5th, 1797; Robert, born September 10th, 1798, baptized December 30th of the same year.

In the fall of 1801 a detachment of the Queen's Rangers was ordered to Fort St. Joseph, a post on the island of the same name, near the head of Lake Huron. Dr. Richardson accompanied this force to the western post, but the prospects of providing suitable accommodation for his wife and young family in this fort were not very promising, so it was arranged that Mrs. Richardson and family should live with her father at Detroit.

In the summer of 1802 the Rangers were disbanded, and the officers and men with their wives and children, were provided with transport if they wished to return to Great Britain. Dr. Richardson remained in Canada, and was appointed surgeon to the Governor and garrison of Fort Amherstburg; and on June 7th, 1807, he was appointed Judge of the District Court of the Western District, an office he held until his death in 1832. Here all his children were reared and educated. His eldest son John was particularly brilliant, and although he hated school he seems to have made considerable progress in Latin, French and Euclid, as well as in the ordinary branches of an English education. Unfortunately this course of instruction was abruptly cut short by the United States declaring war and by the preparations for the invasion of his native province. Much as he may have lost by his lack of schooling, no trace of such loss is perceptible in his writings. And in estimating the formative influences that produced our first novelist of romance, our first delineator of manners and customs, we must look elsewhere.

In that generation such a home and such a family as those of the Richardsons must have been peculiarly stimulating. The father, combining the strictness of the soldier, the kindness of the physician and the sternness of the judge, commanded the love and the respect, not only of his own family, but of the community. Even the redoubtable Simon Girty, the Sampson Gattrie of *The Canadian Brothers,* was awed into decorum at the sight of the judge. The gentler virtues and the gentler graces found their exponent in his mother. Educated at the Convent of Congregation de Notre Dame at Montreal, the foremost institution for young ladies in Canada, Madeleine Richardson, with the national pride of her race, taught her children from their earliest years to speak and write the French language. It has been said that he who knows only one language does not know any. In the learning of two languages young Richardson's mind was broadened, his observation quickened, and a nice perception cultivated—perhaps as only years of training in the class-room could have perfected. His quick eye for natural beauty, his power in vivid description and his marvellous ability in handling the sentence, are an inheritance or an acquisition from his vivacious mother.

Nor was the influence of his grandfather's home less marked. Although a British subject, Colonel Askin had been unable, owing to large mercantile interests, to remove from Detroit to Canada till April, 1802. On the banks of the river Detroit opposite the lower end of Belle Isle, then called Hog Island, there soon rose the modest dwelling named Strabane, after the family seat in Ireland. How greatly this removal influenced young Richardson may be read in his after life. Who can doubt that this devoted British officer would impress on his youthful grandson that to live under that flag which he had served so long was worth the sacrifice of a home and a vast estate? Here it was that Mrs. Askin used to tell the boy those thrilling stories of romance, of Detroit, of Michilimackinac, that enchained his young imagination. None made so deep an impression as the crafty and well-conceived plans of Pontiac, the great chief of the Ottawas, and his persistent efforts to capture Fort Detroit. The events of that historic siege were the most exciting episodes in a life not lacking in exciting incidents. She had been an inmate of the fort, and the lapse of time had not bedimmed one of the startling experiences of this eighteen months. Proofs of the power of this accomplished lady as a story-teller still exist. Her youthful listener even at that early age was enkindled with a desire, not to be realized till he

had passed through thirty years of vicissitudes in two continents, when in 1832 he gave to this world his masterly *Wacousta.*

If the home life was thus wholesome in formative influences, the community also in which he dwelt was rich in a novel and diversified life that presented itself to his daily observation at an age when the sharpest and most lasting impressions are made. No other place on the continent could boast of a floating population so varied in character and race, so rich in well-defined types and civilized and barbarous human nature. At Amherstburg there were the officers and soldiers of the garrison, dressed in brilliant uniforms, moving about with apparently few duties to perform, attracting the boyish fancy and exciting his admiration and his envy. Nor was the British officer wholly unworthy of this adoration. A scion of one of Britain's best families, he obtained promotion oftener by purchase than by proficiency gained from actual service; fully cognizant of his own importance, here he lived in a community that fully acknowledged his superiority.

Next to the soldiers in attractiveness were the Indians that periodically repaired to the town to receive at the hands of the Superintendent of Indian Affairs their customary presents. Many a time young Richardson would wander to the shores of the Detroit to watch the large fleets of canoes in military array, heading for the camping ground of Bois Blanc island; or as the Indians marched to the storekeeper's with a pride and haughty mien that contrasted strangely with the object of their visit, or as they engaged in various games of leaping, wrestling, ball-playing, he would follow and delight in receiving recognition from some chieftain whose acquaintance he had made before. Often, on a visit to the island camp, he would be an interested spectator of their daily habits; it was thus that he acquired that close and accurate knowledge of Indian character and life that he afterwards so successfully used in his literary productions. His delineation of Indian character in *Wacousta* has never been equalled, even by James Fenimore Cooper himself. In *The Canadian Brothers* he gives us a description of the principal Indian chiefs who were allies of the British in the War of 1812, to be found nowhere else.

Besides the soldiers and the Indians, there were those engaged in the fur trade, now fast declining here owing to the march of civilization westward. The French-Canadian and half-breed voyageur had not wholly forsaken the Detroit; and at times was to be seen the trader, just returned from trafficking with the Indians at their homes in the wilds of the interior, and in dress or complexion scarcely distinguishable from the Indians themselves—in some cases not degenerate successors of the *coureurs de bois* of the French period.

It was among such varied surroundings, then, that Richardson must have accumulated almost all the material that he used so effectively in history, poem or novel. The scenes of his boyhood are the favorite setting for his characters; and never after his boyhood had he the opportunity for a lengthened stay in those beloved haunts.

The news of the declaration of war against Great Britain reached Amherstburg, and awoke this frontier garrison from its monotonous routine of regular work. The militia were called out. The marine department became active in fitting out trading schooners and small gunboats for the purpose of defending from invasion the western district. The academic life of John Richardson was brought suddenly to a close. Hull's army had appeared on its march to Detroit, whence as a base it was to invade the land of a contented and happy people, guiltless of wrong to the United States. All the martial spirit of his ancestors was roused in John Richardson, and at the tender age of fifteen he resolved to fight in defence of his native land.

Through the influence of his father, and his grandfather Askin, he was appointed a gentleman volunteer on the strength of the 41st Regiment, a detachment of which was in garrison at Fort Amherstburg. From a District General Order we learn that

> The undermentioned gentlemen are appointed as volunteers in His Majesty's regular forces, from the periods specified opposite their respective names. They will continue to do duty with the 41st Regiment until further orders.
>
> Henry Proctor, Gent., 1st July, 1812
> Alex. Wilkinson,   "   1   "   1812.
> John Richardson,   "   9   "   1812.
>   By Order.   Thomas Evans,
>   Brigade Major.

Richardson fought in every engagement in which the detachment of the 41st took part, until its disastrous defeat at Moraviantown on October 5th, 1813. On this occasion he was taken prisoner, and suffered close imprisonment until released in 1814. The story of these engagements and his experiences during his captivity are fully set forth in his history of the Right Division. With the exception of the official reports of the officers commanding, his account of these engagements, and of the captivity of the prisoners, is the only one that has been written by any of the participators. In his first novel, *Ecarté,* Dormer, one of the characters, and Clifford Delmaine, the hero, meet after years of separation in Paris. Dormer describes his experiences since they were schoolmates. The adventures of Dormer in the army in Canada and his imprisonment coincide closely with the actual events in the part of Richardson's career. In **The Canadian Brothers** one can gather likewise the story of the events in which the Right Division took part, and the story of the imprisonment.

After his return from captivity he was given a lieutenancy in the 2nd Battalion of the 8th (King's) Regiment. In June, 1815, both battalions embarked at Quebec for Ostend, to join the Duke of Wellington's army in Flanders. But Waterloo had been fought and won before they were half way across the Atlantic. As a permanent peace with France seemed to have been made, and as Britain had no need for so large a standing army, several regiments were reduced. Transferring its men fit for duty to the first battalion, the second battalion of the Eighth disbanded on the 24th of December, 1815, and its officers were placed upon half-pay. Within six months Sir Henry Torrens, then Military Secretary, procured Richardson's appointment to his own, the Second or Queen's Regiment; and on the 24th of April, 1816, the regiment embarked at Portsmouth for the West Indies, and landed at Barbadoes on June 5th. How long he remained with the Queen's is not known, but it is probable that he was invalided home after a short term of service in that exceedingly unhealthy climate. He was subsequently transferred to the 92nd Highlanders, and was again placed on half-pay on October 1st, 1818.

For the next ten years Richardson lived the life of a literary man in London with occasional visits to Paris. He wrote sketches of West Indian and Canadian life that appeared in the periodicals of the time, and produced two of his longer works, the poem **Tecumseh** published in 1828(?), and the novel **Ecarté, or the Salons of Paris,** published in 1829.

Tecumseh, Richardson's only effort in poetry consists of four cantos of 188 stanzas of *ottava rima*; in the first canto there are 45 stanzas, in the second 50, in the third 48 and in the fourth 45. No evidence is at hand from which we can judge how this poem was received in literary circles in England. The generation born during the Napoleonic wars would not be enraptured with martial poems: they had experienced too many of the hardships of war. At that time the heroic deeds and statesmanlike achievements of our greatest Indian ally were unknown in Britain, and could appeal to but a limited number of readers. The poem itself is marked by a strict adherence to the conventional stanza form, with which Byron took such liberties in his *Don Juan.* With a few exceptions, there is marked care in the choice of words and in the workmanship. The epic theme follows closely the historical facts and presents many opportunities for effective dramatic treatment. But perhaps the measure chosen was ill-adapted to so stirring a subject. That Richardson was not quite satisfied with his poetic effort is proved by his confining himself to prose in future.

"*Ecarté*," said Captain R. H. Barclay, in a letter to the author, "is assuredly an able and dreadful essay against the most insidious and ruinous of all sorts of dissipation and idleness, gaming, bad enough anywhere, but perhaps in Paris it holds its throne." Paris was then a favorite resort for many young British officers absent on leave; and Richardson, in his visits, appears to have entered fully into the gay life of that metropolis. He had an affair of honor with a French officer of Cuirassiers and probably indulged in play, but it is hardly possible that he lost heavily, got in debt and was given time to contemplate the fickleness of fortune, and form good resolutions for the future in a room in the prison he so accurately describes in *Ecarté*."

This novel was published by Colburn, of London, and was well received in some quarters; but, by a strange circumstance, was doomed in so far as it might possibly bring immediate fame to the author and wealth to the publisher. Jerdan, a leading influential writer on the staff of the *Literary Gazette*, had some disagreement with Colburn, and to be revenged wrote him that he would "cut up" his next book in his review. The next book published by Colburn was *Ecarté*, and Jerdan was as good as his word. This unwarranted criticism, Richardson acknowledges in *Eight Years in Canada*, prevented him from writing many more works.

However, he appears to have been busy with his pen as *Wacousta* appeared in 1832. This story was published in three volumes by T. Cadell, Strand, London, and from the first met with great success. A second edition was published in the same style in 1840. It is considered his best work.

The London *Literary Gazette*, the London *Athenæum*, the London *Satirist*, the *Morning Post*, the London *Atlas* and *Miss Sheridan's Magazine* spoke in very flattering terms of the novel and the author. He was at once recognized as a powerful rival of Cooper, then at the height of his popularity in England and America.

The story is founded upon the designs of Pontiac to possess himself of the fort at Detroit. The principal characters are drawn from the actors in that historic event, and are portrayed with a marked fidelity to historical accuracy. Even Wacousta himself may have been suggested by the career of some real personage. The only feature of the story that it is possible to consider weak may be found in the incident of the capture in the St. Clair river of the schooner, having on board the survivors of the massacre at Fort Michilimackinac. Here, to cause the capture to take place in the river, the author, departing from geographical truth, makes the St. Clair a narrow stream, with the branches of the tall trees meeting in an arch overhead. But even for this he may well plead the licence that is always granted to writers of fiction.

The interview between Pontiac and Governor De Haldimar in the great council hall of the fort is the master-stroke of all Richardson's literary work. For dramatic power and graphic description it has not often been surpassed or even equalled in the language. As a character-sketch, unfolding on the one hand the adroit craft and subtle deceit of Pontiac with all the varied play of motives, and on the other the defiant confidence and intrepid fidelity to principle of the governor, it will compare favorably with those searching analyses of human passions to be found in the works of George Eliot.

Richardson has been accused of imitating Cooper in this novel. How closely one author may follow the style and character of another's productions and still rank as a great writer, will never be very clearly determined. The only ground for such an accusation is that both wrote stories with Indians figuring prominently in the foreground. And it is doubtful that Richardson owes more to Cooper's works than the bare suggestion that a romance dealing with the Canadian Indian would prove both popular and successful. For such a work he possessed peculiar qualifications, in power, in material and in desire. His power had already been revealed in *Ecarté*; his material had been gathered from the experiences of his boyhood and the stirring stories he heard from his grandmother; the desire had been enkindled thirty years before when he heard those stories by the open fireplace at Strabane.

Richardson's characters are never impossible. His Indians have all the virtues and all the vices of the greatest prototypes of the race. He was personally acquainted with Tecumseh. His grandmother had been in the fort when besieged by Pontiac. The original of Captain Erskine is no doubt his grandfather, Colonel John Askin; Lieutenant Johnstone is probably his father's relative. Dr. Richardson belonged to the Annandale family, so did Lieutenant Johnstone; and further to prove the identity, one of Major Richardson's half-brothers was named Johnstone Richardson, plainly showing that Johnstone was a family name. The name of Bombardier Kitson for one of the minor characters is a reminiscence of an officer of that name in the Royal Artillery who fought with the Right Division in the War of 1812. No doubt a careful comparison of the incidents of the novel with the actual events would reveal many other similarities. This is an instance in which we must go to fiction for reliable history.

In 1834 the Spanish Ambassador to Great Britain recruited an army in that country to assist the regent, Christina, to preserve the throne of Spain for her daughter Isabella, against the forces of Don Carlos, who claimed the crown. This force, which consisted of ten regiments of 1,000 men each, was known as the "British Auxiliary Legion," and was under the command of Lieut.-General De Lacy Evans, a veteran officer who

Amherstbury 4th February 1813

My Dear Uncle

You have doubtless heard ere this, of the engagement at the River Raisin on Friday the 22nd ins* however you may probably not have heard the particulars of the business, which are simply these On Monday the 18th we received information that the Americans under the Command of General Winchester after an obstinate resistance, had driven from the River Raisin a detach* of Militia under Major Reynolds, / also a party of Indians / which had been stationed there some time — That they had sustained great loss from the fire of our Indians, and from a 3 pounder which was most ably served by Bombardier Kitson / since dead / of the R. A. —

On Tuesday part of our men moved over the river to Brownstown, consisting of a Detach* R Artill*y with 3–3 pounders and 3–small howitzers — Captain Tallon's Company / 41 Reg* / a few Militia, and the Sailors attached to the Guns — An alarm was given that the enemy were at hand — The Guns were unlimbered, & every thing prepair'd for action, when the alarm was found to be false

On Wednesday the remainder of the army joined us at Brownstown, where / including Regulars, Militia Artillery, Sailors, and Indians / we mustered near 1000 men — We lay the night at Brownstown. Next day The army commenced its march to wards the River Raisin and encamped this night at Rocky River which / you know / is about 12 miles

Excerpt from a letter Richardson wrote to his uncle, February 4th, 1813.

had seen active service in India and the Peninsula, at Washington and New Orleans, and as Quartermaster-General at Waterloo. Richardson was assigned a captaincy in the 2nd Regiment, which sailed from Portsmouth on board the transport Royal Tar, on July 23rd, 1835, and arrived at San Sebastian on the 27th. After a short stay here the Legion marched to Vitoria, where typhus fever carried off about 700 men and 40 officers. The soldierly qualities and executive ability of Richardson were recognized by his being appointed commandant of Vitoria; but on January 30th, 1836, he was stricken down with the prevailing malady. His splendid physique, however, enabled him to combat the disease, and he rose from his bed on the 17th of March. During his illness intrigue and jealousy were at work, and he was displaced on the staff by a relative of the Lieut.-General; and to add to his troubles his regiment and the 5th were broken up, but he was appointed senior captain in the 6th (Scotch Grenadiers). To recuperate, Richardson applied for and received two months' leave of absence to visit England. He left Vitoria in April and proceeded to the coast, but before he had an opportunity to embark for England the Legion marched to the attack of San Sebastian, now occupied by the Carlists. Although on sick leave, Richardson, in his anxiety to be of assistance, volunteered his services on the staff. His offer was refused, and, enfeebled as he was, he led his own company of the 6th Regiment in the battle of the 5th of May.

An account of this battle appears in his memoirs. On the 11th he left Spain for London by way of Paris. While in Spain he kept a journal which he was anxious to publish, as it would in a measure be an answer to the attacks and aspersions made against the character and actions of the Legion by the persons and the press that opposed interference with the internal affairs of a foreign nation.

While in London a *Gazette* appeared which contained a list of the names of officers decorated for their conduct in the action of May 5th. Richardson's name did not appear, and, to add to his disappointment, he was mortified to find in the announcement that a junior officer had been promoted to a majority over his head. In his anger he wrote an addition to the preface of his book, *Movements of the British Legion,* in which he set forth his claims, and in doing so reflected somewhat on the conduct of the other officers. When his wrath had subsided he recalled the irritating paragraphs and substituted others less incisive; but he had already sent a copy of the preface to the Lieut.-General and other officers, which resulted in the appointment of a court of inquiry to investigate and report on the whole affair.

On the 29th of June, just one day before the assembling of this court, his year of service having expired, he tendered his resignation and signified his retirement from the service. He therefore appeared before the commission, not as an officer of the Legion, but as a private citizen, and at the investigation his superior talents, aided by the justice of his cause, enabled him to wring from a hostile court a verdict that exonerated him in every particular. After the announcement of the verdict the Lieut.-General intimated to Richardson that he would like to make reparation for the injury that had been done to him. Consequently it was arranged that his resignation should be withdrawn. On this being done Richardson appeared in general orders as promoted to a vacant majority which was dated May 13th, and at the same time was transferred from the 6th Scotch to the 4th Queen's Own Fusiliers. With this regiment Major Richardson served till the 19th of August, being in command of it at an engagement at the "Heights of Passages" on July 30th, 1836. Soon after, he returned to England.

To Major Richardson's experiences in Spain we owe the existence of three of his works. *Movements of the British Legion,* referred to before, recounts in the form of a journal the operations from their arrival at San Sebastian, July 27th, 1835, till the attack on the same stronghold, May 5th, 1836. The second edition, published in 1837, contains also the narrative to the close of March, 1837. The book in its first edition is a faithful account of the events of the campaign, and is a worthy tribute to the military capacity of Lieutenant-General De Lacy Evans, the commander-in-chief. But the failure of that officer to promote Richardson to a majority to which he was entitled by seniority, led to a bitter personal quarrel with the Lieutenant-General, who does not seem to have been averse to showing a desire for revenge on the Major, who had worsted him before the Court of Inquiry. As De Lacy Evans had estranged his officers, had infringed the rules of service and had secured a reputation for delay and indecision, he was not invulnerable, and Richardson was always a merciless assailant. Accordingly, in the second part of the second edition, the author seldom loses an opportunity of attributing every failure or disaster to the incapacity of the commander. As a fact, only ten of the fifty experienced officers who had originally embarked in the cause chose to remain. It was easy for the officers to withdraw from the service, but with the rank and file it was very different. They had to stay till their term of service expired, and when this time came their pay was in arrears and no passage to England was to be got. Some re-enlisted, others in their desperation joined the Carlists. Their plight was a melancholy one. Neglected by their native country and cast off without pay by the nation they served, the survivors managed to reach Great Britain in a penniless condition, deplorable examples of the neglect usually shown to the private soldier when the nation no longer requires his services.

The affairs of Spain were made the subject of a debate in the British House of Commons on the motion of Sir Henry Hardinge. In this debate the opportunity was seized by O'Connell and some other members to attack Richardson, but his character and conduct were clearly vindicated. His cause was championed by Captain Boldero and Sir Henry Hardinge, the proposer of the motion. It would be exceedingly unfair even to hint that anything but justice could influence a man of the integrity and noble character of Sir Henry Hardinge, but his interest in Richardson in this connection may have arisen from his kindly remembrance of Richardson's father when they served in the same regiment. Sir Henry Hardinge began that military career which shone so brilliantly at Albuera and at Ferozshuhr, as an ensign in the Queen's Rangers in 1798 in Upper Canada, when Dr. Richardson was assistant surgeon of the same corps.

No better example of the appreciation of the subtleties of language can be found than in the volume, ***Movements of the British Legion***. . . . [In] discussing the unhealthy and uncomfortable condition of the hospitals at Vitoria, Richardson had said:

"Things are said to have been better managed in Portugal under Mr. Alcock, who is *second* in rank of the Medical Department here." Mr. Alcock, considering that he had been complimented at the expense of his chief, wrote to the author, asking that the statement be amended or omitted in any future edition. Richardson replied, begging him "to consider it, however, as one of the typographical errors, and that 'said' should be in italics, not 'second.' You cannot fail to observe that this alteration will give a totally distinct reading to the passage." This *amende honorable* has something so genuinely clever about it that it deserves this special notice. It is scarcely paralleled even by Lord Robert Cecil's famous apology to Mr. Gladstone as related by Justin McCarthy.

Richardson's second work on the affairs in Spain entitled ***Personal Memoirs of Major Richardson,*** was published in Montreal in 1838. Events, that will be referred to presently, caused him to come to Canada in that year; hence its appearance in this country. In this volume the injustice that he had suffered is submitted to the public. The documentary evidence adduced clearly shows that he pursued the only course consistent with honor and dignity. As he himself says, . . . :

> By the cold and the calculating—by the selfish and the prudent—I shall no doubt be considered as having adopted a course more chivalrous than wise in the uniform opposition I have shown to the various measures of oppression—so unworthily—so ignobly arrayed against me. By those, however, of high honour—of proud and independent feeling—by those who are incapable of sacrificing the approval of the inward man to mere considerations of personal interests and expediency, I shall be judged in a nobler spirit. *They,* at least, will admit, that in adopting the line of conduct unfolded in the pages of this brief and local memoir, I have studied that which was most befitting an honourable mind. As I have had elsewhere reason to observe, never did a more cruel system of injustice seek to work its slow and sinuous course beneath the mantle of liberalism. Every engine of his power had been put in motion by General Evans, to accomplish the ruin of an officer, who had in no other way offended than by refusing tamely to submit—firstly, to his injustice—secondly, to his oppression, and that the utter overthrow of such officer has not been accomplished, is attributable, not to any forbearance on the part of his persecutor, but to his own innate integrity and right.

His third work was a satire, not issued, however, in book form, but as a serial in *The New Era or Canadian Chronicle,* a paper published by Richardson in Brockville in 1841 and 1842. Theodore Hook in his last volume had transferred his hero, Jack Brag, to the staff of De Lacy Evans in Spain as Acting Assistant Deputy-Deputy Assistant Commissary General. Richardson saw his opportunity and took Hook's hero successfully in hand. Hook was pleased with the continuation of his satire and made an effort to secure a publisher for it. He went to Colburn and to Bently, but they declined to accept it as they considered the delineation of the characters too faithful a reflection of the originals, and the strictures on the Radicals at Westminster too severe.

In 1837 the political affairs of the Canadas caused no little alarm to the British Government of the day. Richardson, eager again to see active service, more particularly in defence of his native land, against those who would have robbed Britain of her fairest colony, embarked at London on the 18th of February, 1838, for Canada, by way of New York. He was accompanied by his wife, a member of a family in Essex, whom he had married about the year 1830. Her family name is not recorded that I have seen, and a diligent inquiry among Richardson's relatives, who knew her, has proved fruitless in the matter. All, however, agree in saying that she was accomplished, talented, and possessed of some literary ability, and that they were devotedly attached to each other.

While waiting in New York for four days Richardson met the Earl of Gosford and Sir Francis Bond Head, who had lately arrived from the Canadas on their way to England. He had a letter of introduction from Lord Glenelg, Colonial Secretary, to Sir Francis, in which was expressed the desire that some official position should be given him in his native province. Sir Francis was so concerned and agitated, probably through fear that violence might be done him by some sympathizers with the rebels in Canada, that after reading the letter he returned it to the Major unsealed, with a request to present it with his compliments to his successor, Sir George Arthur.

On the 29th of March he went by boat to Albany, thence by railroad to Utica, then by coach through Auburn, Geneva, Rochester and Lockport to Lewiston, where he arrived on Wednesday, the 3rd of April. The mingled feelings with which he viewed his native village of Queenston, a spot hallowed with so many recollections, are well described at the close of the second chapter of his *Eight Years in Canada.*

> We reached Lewiston a few miles below the Falls of Niagara about 6 o'clock; and from that point beheld, for the first time since my return to the country and in its most interesting aspect, the Canadian shore. Opposite to Lewiston is the small village of Queenston, and overhanging the latter, the heights on which my early friend and military patron—the warrior beneath whose bright example my young heart had been trained to a love of heroism, and who had procured me my first commission in the service—had perished in the noble but unequal conflict with a foe invading almost from the spot on which I stood. More than five-and-twenty years had gone by, but the memory of the departed Brock lived as vividly in the hearts of a grateful people as it had in the early days of his fall; and in the monument which crowned the height, and which no ruffian hand had yet attempted to desecrate, was evidenced the strong and praiseworthy desire to perpetuate a memory as honored as it was loved. This moment was to me particularly exciting, for it brought with it the stirring reminiscences of the camp, and caused me to revert to many a trying scene in which my younger days had been passed. Since that period I had numbered a good many years, and had experienced in other climes a more than ordinary portion of the vicissitudes of human life; but not one of these had the freshness and warmth of recollection of my earlier services in America, in which (independently of the fact of my having been present at the capture of Detroit, under the gallant soldier whose bones reposed beneath the monument on which my gaze was rivetted, as if through the influence of an irresistible fascination) I had been present in five general engagements, and twelve months a prisoner of war with the enemy before attaining my seventeenth year. These were certainly not 'piping times of peace,' and I must be pardoned the egotism of incidentally alluding to them.

Before leaving London, Richardson had been entrusted with the important duty of furnishing political information to the London *Times.* In availing itself of the services of a writer so singularly competent and eligible as Richardson, the foremost of English dailies showed both enterprise and sagacity. In those times it was well to have source of information on what was

taking place in the Canadas, other than the official despatches of the governors and the news letters appearing in the United States press. Richardson began at once to study the political situation in Upper Canada. His opportunities for obtaining information were excellent. His brother Charles, with whom he lived at Niagara, represented that town in the Legislative Assembly of Upper Canada, and through him Richardson could learn without reserve the state of affairs in the country, and get a description of the events that led up to armed resistance to the Government. He soon began his journey to Quebec to meet Lord Durham on his arrival. While in Toronto he called on and was entertained by Sir George Arthur, and by his own old comrades in arms when Detroit was taken, the Honorable John Beverley Robinson, then Chief Justice, and Colonel S. P. Jarvis, then Superintendent of Indian Affairs. In Montreal he found out the feeling in the province of Lower Canada. His observations in Canada up to this time are embodied in two letters published in the *Times,* one written from Niagara and the other from Montreal, and signed Inquisitor. On his arrival at Quebec he called upon the governor, and was received by him with every mark of respect. He was invited to dine at the Castle of St. Lewis with a brilliant assemblage. Lord Durham made him the special object of his attention, and during the course of a long conversation he unfolded in their entirety all his plans and projects for the government of the colony. Richardson was convinced that these plans were not only the best for the country, but perhaps the only ones that would harmonize the various conflicting interests arrayed in arms against each other. If Richardson was impressed by the honesty and integrity of Lord Durham, and his thorough grasp of the political situation, on the other hand it is merely just to record that he possessed the confidence of that nobleman to the fullest extent.

By birth and training Richardson was personally opposed to the general policy represented by the Melbourne administration. He was the trusted correspondent of a paper that had assailed that administration with a bitterness rarely exhibited by any journal. His salary of £300 and travelling expenses along with his half-pay would have enabled him to live in affluence. Moreover, his work was congenial, and no favor that Lord Durham or any succeeding governor might grant could offer more attractions to a man of Richardson's temperament than his present employment. Accordingly every motive and every prejudice of worldly wisdom would have led an ordinary man into opposition to the governor, but it is very gratifying to know that Richardson viewed the affairs of Canada with notable impartiality, which leaves no doubt of his patriotism and of a marked disregard of any selfish interests. Richardson was convinced that Lord Durham would do for the colony what no other governor had ever attempted in respect to its permanent interests. He realized the wisdom of his policy and grasped the spirit of his plans for the future. Time has already vindicated the action of the governor, and it must in all fairness grant to Richardson credit and honor for the personal sacrifices he made in advocating the cause that has proved so beneficial to British North America. Unfortunately for him the "mighty engine" he was in Canada to represent did not approve his course. The editor did not see fit to publish all his letters, and informed him that his connection with that journal would cease at the termination of his year's engagement. It would seem that a paper that delegates to itself the high position of directing the policy of a great nation should place accuracy of information before every other consideration; that it should have placed more confidence in the opinions of its correspondent than upon its party traditions. The awakening was too sudden for most Englishmen to see clearly. The many reforms that had been gained in England within a half-dozen years were alarming to one party, and the other party [was] not prepared to support their official in his advanced ideas of granting self-government to the colonies. It is therefore too much to expect that a paper like the *Times* could change its colonial policy so quickly. The disavowal of Richardson by the *Times* enlisted the sympathy of Lord Durham, himself suffering from a more cruel desertion. In a letter to Richardson he says:

> It is indeed most disgusting to see such proofs of malignity in those who ought to value truth and fair dealing as the best means of informing the public of which they profess to be the 'best possible instructors.' Your course has been that of a man of honor and integrity, and you can hardly regret the dissolution of a connection which it appears could only have been preserved by the sacrifice on your part of truth and justice—by the *suppressio veri,* if not the *assertio falsi.*

If subsequent events had not clearly proved that the course adopted by Richardson was the proper one, this letter is sufficient exoneration. Lord Durham's policy and his acts while in Canada are fully set forth in chapters III., IV. and V. of Richardson's *Eight Years in Canada.*

On November 2nd, 1838, the day after Lord Durham embarked for England, Richardson left Quebec to join his friends at Niagara. At Kingston he was much impressed by a visit to Von Schoultz, the "patriot" leader recently captured at the Windmill at Prescott. While he was in Toronto the news of the defeat of the brigand invaders at Windsor by Col. Prince was received, and Sir George Arthur employed Richardson to carry the despatches of that event to Sir John Colborne at Montreal, but was anticipated by half an hour by an express from Colonel Dundas at Kingston, to whom also he had carried a despatch of the affair. This duty being performed he joined his wife at Niagara.

On his way to Quebec during the spring of this year (1838), Richardson took the earliest occasion to settle an affair with Colonel Chichester, for which no opportunity offered while at San Sebastian in Spain. It appears that Colonel Chichester seconded a motion to expel Richardson from the San Sebastian club. On learning the truth of the matter Colonel Kirby, the proposer of the motion, apologized to Richardson in England. Richardson now required a similar apology from Colonel Chichester, who granted it. All the documents that were necessary were now in his possession, consequently his *Personal Memoirs* were published this year.

During the winter he made preparations to take up his residence at Amherstburg. On his arrival there he is disappointed in the place. The charms that it possessed in his youth have all departed. No fleet of government vessels now make the little harbor their home. No Indian watchfires add a picturesqueness to the beautiful island opposite the town. No bands of Indians now come there to sit in solemn council or to receive their annual presents. And where in other days a half regiment of regulars and a battery of artillery enlivened the town, now, but a single company remains, to garrison a fort,—but a mere shadow of its former greatness.

Although the town appeared to have every mark of decay, yet Richardson could not hire a vacant house. The quartering of the regulars and militia there in consequence of the rebellion, had increased the population so quickly that all the houses were occupied. He then went to Sandwich, where he made his home in a small brick house "gable end to the street." The house still stands about 100 yards south of St. John's Church, and but for a covering of bright red paint and the addition of a verandah in front, presents the same appearance as 60 years ago. It was pointed out to me last summer by Mr. Thomas McKee, the genial County Clerk of Essex, who remembered Richardson well and had many interesting stories to relate of him. It was in this house that the finishing touches were put upon *The Canadian Brothers,* a sequel to *Wacousta.* Some chapters of this novel had appeared in *The Literary Garland,* a magazine that had been started in December, 1838, in Montreal. One of these contributions was entitled **"Jeremiah Desborough,"** and the other **"The Settler or the Prophecy Fulfilled."**

Having received the encouragement of 250 subscriptions among the military and the people of Canada, Richardson resolved to publish the sequel to *Wacousta* and went to Montreal to see the work through the press. The registration notice of this novel bears the date, January 2nd, 1840. It was published in two volumes in the original edition, and was dedicated to Sir John Harvey, Lieutenant-Governor of New Brunswick. The tale is an historic one and deals with the War of 1812 on the Detroit frontier. In a measure the work is autobiographical and covers the same period as that of his history of the war. General Brock, Colonel Procter, Captain Barclay, Tecumseh, Walk-in-the-Water, Split-Log and Round-head appear in the work under their proper names. Gerald and Henry Grantham, the Canadian Brothers, are Major Richardson and his favorite brother Robert. Simon Girty appears as Sampson Gattrie and the description of this personage in the book is the best ever written. St. Julian is Colonel St. George, Cranstoun is Brevet-Lieutenant-Colonel Short, and Middlemore, Lieutenant Gordon. The other officers all have places in the narrative, but to avoid a multiplicity of characters one personage in the story often represents two or more in the real events. For instance, Gerald Grantham is made to act the parts of Lieutenant Rolette, Lieutenant Irvine and Midshipman Robert Richardson. Some anachronisms occur for which the author prepares us in the preface. Captain Barclay and General Brock meet at Amherstburg before the fall of Detroit and the battle of Queenston Heights is not fought until October, 1813. The story in many respects is not the equal of *Wacousta.* The purely fictitious characters are not so well drawn in *The Canadian Brothers*, while the historical ones are perhaps more faithfully pictured. The weakest part is the attempt to make it a sequel. Jeremiah Desborough, the villain of the novel, is a character without a purpose. He is but an intruder in the insignificant place he has in the tale. When Richardson knows the type of man he is describing, we get a picture that delights us by the boldness and clearness of the delineation of every phase of his character; but when he does not know him the portrayal is a palpable failure. He found out, too late to correct it in the first edition, that the Scotch dialect he makes Cranstoun use is very imperfect. In the second edition, published in New York in 1851, in one volume, under the author's supervision, this imperfection just pointed out does not occur.

After the publication of *The Canadian Brothers,* Richardson made preparations to start for his home in Sandwich. He decided to travel by means of his own equipage, a method affording greater freedom and more ease and convenience. He therefore purchased a sleigh, a team of spirited French-Canadian ponies, and suitable harness and robes, and engaged a servant to care for the ponies at all stopping places. He set out from Montreal during the last days of February. In Cornwall he stayed some days, rehearsing old times with Judge G. S. Jarvis, an old fellow-officer of 8th (King's). His fondness for being entertained by his old friends on the way, and an accident in the early part of the journey, delayed him, and by the time Brockville was reached it was impossible to go farther by sleigh.

While waiting here some days to make the necessary changes to travel by waggon, he was induced to purchase a piece of land, beautifully situated on the high banks of the St. Lawrence, on which were a good house,

a barn and other outbuildings. The journey, which occupied about two months, the greater part of which time was spent in visiting at Kingston, Toronto and London, ended about the last of April.

Preparations were made for the return trip to his "farm" in Brockville. Before the time for starting came round, a grand demonstration was announced, which was to be held at Fort Meigs by the Whigs of Ohio in honor of their candidate for the Presidency of the United States. The place was appropriately chosen, as it was on the Miami that General Harrison won the military renown associated with his name, which contributed not a little to his success at the coming election. Richardson accepted an invitation from his friends at Detroit to be present, and to visit the place where he also had seen some hard fighting against the general whose exploits his party were now commemorating.

The trip to Brockville was begun in the last week in June. The ponies and waggon were again used, and by this picturesque and delightful method he and his wife reached Brockville in the first week in July. For some weeks his time was occupied in superintending the renovation of the house and the improvement of the grounds. But after this work was completed he became somewhat melancholy, a feeling that quite naturally follows when a person who has led a wandering life becomes a fixture in a place.

At this time he appears to have had no settled plans for the future. No event appears to have suggested itself as suitable for weaving into a romantic story. One alluring prospect seems to have taken possession of his very being. He hoped to be appointed to some office, in the gift of the Governor and his Council, which would enable him to live comfortably the rest of his days and to devote his leisure to literary work. He had strong and reasonable claims for such a position upon the government of Canada. His qualifications for many positions in the gift of the government were of the highest order. He was dignified in bearing and a thorough gentleman. He spoke English and French with equal fluency. His military training had specially fitted him to perform the routine duties of a public officer with promptness and attention to detail, necessary acquirements in a public official. He had done not a little for Canada. He fought in her defence at a time when she was most in need of assistance. He was for a year a prisoner of war, and for a part of that period suffered close imprisonment while two governments deliberated whether a certain number of their prisoners should or should not suffer death. When internal dissensions threatened again to make his native country the easy prey of a foreign power, he hastened to her shores to fight once more for British connection, if it were necessary. When he came to Canada in 1838 he represented the most powerful newspaper in the Empire. Through the medium of that paper he endeavored to teach the public of Great Britain that the unity of the Empire depended upon the granting of Responsible Government to the Canadian people. For daring to express these views he was relieved of his position on the paper. As he had not a sufficient income to support himself and his wife it became necessary for him to seek some employment. In this extremity it was quite natural for him to turn, for the aid he required, to those he had served so conscientiously and so faithfully. Lord Durham, cognizant of his devotion to the cause of Responsible Government and of the effort Richardson had made to shield him from the storm about to break about his devoted head, promised to exert himself in his behalf. The early death of that nobleman left him without any hope of reward from that source.

The social conditions of Brockville in 1840 were in marked contrast to the refinement and culture of the large cities of Europe; and it is not difficult for one to believe that Richardson felt himself imprisoned. Of this he says:

> There were moments when the idea of being buried alive, as it were, in this spot, without a possibility, perhaps, of again seeing the beautiful fields and magnificent cities, and mixing in the polished circles of Europe, and of matchless England in particular, came like a blighting cloud upon my thoughts, and filled me with a despondency no effort of my own could shake off.

He, however, felt the necessity of self-exertion. Some of his friends were confident that if a newspaper were started in Brockville, it would prove a profitable investment. He resolved to adopt their advice. His talents and tastes were literary and a periodical seemed to offer the best means of supporting the cause he had so much taken to heart. His judgment in the matter was the more easily influenced in favor of the suggestion because he thought the dawn of a new order of things would quicken the literary activity of the colony.

Type, presses and compositors were necessary for the venture, and to obtain these Richardson went to New York. While transacting the business that brought him to that city he received marked attention from several persons who had been charmed and delighted by reading his works. In him they found a person who could accept their homage with that ease and grace which marked the man whose gentility and decorum had been fashioned in the refined company of Europe.

Hie business having been completed, he started for home, and arrived there on the last day of the year 1840. In the early part of June of the following year the necessary machinery for printing arrived in Brockville, and the first issue of the paper was published. It was named *The New Era or Canadian Chronicle,* a title suggestive of the political change that Lord Sydenham came to Canada to introduce, and which Lord Durham had advised as a solution of the political problem. The paper was a weekly, and the subscription price was four dollars for a year. The leading articles and the other matter were all from the pen of the editor. No paying advertisements or local topics found a place in its columns. His **"Jack Brag in Spain"** and **"Recollections of the West Indies"** were serials that ran through several issues. While the paper was interesting and entertaining, it had not that variety and freshness which would secure and retain a long list of paying subscribers at four dollars a year. Consequently, the editor became involved financially, and the paper was on the verge of suspension. Another brave effort, however, was made to reanimate it by appealing to the patriotism of the Canadian people. Richardson entertained the suggestion of his military comrades in the last war, now in high positions in the country, to write a history of the War of 1812. Although the immediate object was to make money, there was a higher motive that made Richardson eager to undertake the task. The various accounts of that war which had as yet found general circulation in Upper Canada were those contained in United States text-books, which were used almost exclusively in the schools of the province. The whole object of the historians of the United States during the first half of the 19th century seemed to be to create in the minds of their readers a hatred of everything British. A devotion to truth in historical writing, so pretty generally in evidence at the present day among her historians, had not as yet been found acceptable to American readers or profitable to American historians.

Richardson was qualified in a special manner for such an undertaking. He had been an active participator in all the engagements in which the Right Division of the Canadian army had taken part. He had promises of assistance from several of his countrymen who had seen active service in the several campaigns. Sir John Harvey, then Governor of Newfoundland, promised to put at his disposal his personal narrative of the campaigns of 1813 and 1814. His experience in the several capacities of the service from gentleman volunteer to Major in command of a battalion in action, would enable him to comment intelligently on the skirmishes, battles and strategical evolutions of the combatants. The honesty and fairness he had shown in his letters on Lord Durham's administration was a guarantee that his prejudices would not lead him to give any but an impartial treatment of the incidents of the struggle.

The *History of the War* was to be written in Three Series. The first was to contain "A Narrative of the Operations of the Right Division," and was to be published serially in *The New Era.* The first instalment appeared in the first number of the second volume, which was issued on March 2nd, 1842. The paper appeared at intervals that varied from a week to two weeks; and in fourteen numbers, the last of which appeared on July 15th, 1842, the Narrative was completed. Four more numbers were published in which was reprinted his poem *Tecumseh*; the paper ceasing with the 18th number on August 19th, 1842.

The Narrative was set up in wide columns in *The New Era* and by simply dividing the matter into pages, the work could be printed in book form. The history was dedicated to the United Legislature of Canada, to which Richardson applied for financial aid to reimburse him for his expenditure on the First Series and to enable him to complete the work. His petition was introduced and read by Sir Allan MacNab, and approved by the House, only one member dissenting. In consequence £250 was voted by the Assembly and paid to Richardson.

The appeal to the people of Canada to subscribe for *The New Era,* because the history of the War of 1812 was to appear in its columns, was not responded to by any large increase in the circulation. To bring the history generally before the people the author made an effort to get the district councils to recommend it for use in the schools within their boundaries. Johnstown district voted £50 to purchase copies to be used in their schools, but this vote was afterwards rescinded because the council had no power to vote money for that purpose. No other council took any action in the matter. The booksellers of the province with whom it had been placed on sale had disposed of about thirty copies, and in Kingston, the capital of the Province, all that a copy would fetch at auction was seven and one-half pence currency. The poor reception accorded the First Series of the *History of the War* caused the author to postpone the preparation of the other parts; and as the prospect never became more promising during his lifetime the history was not completed. It is of some interest to know that this publication was the third for which a copyright was granted by the old Province of Canada.

The New Era supported in a general way the principle of Responsible Government and the "cabinet" that was administering the government; but Richardson, like many others, became displeased because Sir Charles Bagot, a Conservative, had selected as his advisers persons belonging to both parties and had shown a similar impartiality in his appointments to office. Richardson may have had personal as well as public reasons for his action. However, he resolved to oppose the Ministry and to do so started at Kingston a paper called the *Canadian Loyalist and Spirit of 1812.* The political articles that appeared were very severe upon the members of the Lafontaine-Baldwin Ministry; Mr. Francis Hincks getting more than his share. The appointment to office of "men of more than questionable loyalty—of unmasked traitors and rebels—over the honest and self-sacrificing defender of the rights of the

British Crown" was the "prominent ground on which the political principles of the *Canadian Loyalist* were based." The paper fulfilled its mission. Sir Charles Metcalfe as Governor, maintained that he might appoint officials without consulting his Council; disagreement followed, and all his executive except Mr. Daly resigned. The *Canadian Loyalist* which was started at the beginning of 1843 was discontinued about the middle of the year 1844.

Parliament met next in Montreal on July 1st and during the session Richardson was as active as ever in his support of Sir Charles Metcalfe; and when the House was dissolved both parties made preparations for the coming struggle. In the elections that followed, the Conservatives had a majority. Richardson now expected some reward for the support he had given the party in power. The canals of Canada were being built and a system of police was instituted by the government to prevent disturbances of the peace. The office of Superintendent of Police on the Welland Canal, which was being enlarged, became vacant, and Richardson was appointed to the office by Lord Metcalfe on May 20th, 1845. The pay was only ten shillings a day, but he hoped for something better and entered on his duties with alacrity. To add to the smartness of the force he induced the men to purchase uniforms to be paid for in six equal instalments, he in the meantime advancing the pay for them. The force was disbanded on January 31st, 1846, on seven days' notice, and at that time there was due the Superintendent from the men for equipment £51. At the coming session of Parliament Richardson petitioned the House, complaining of the sudden dismissal of himself and the force, and praying compensation for losses sustained and for clothing for the force. The petition was referred by the House to a select Committee which reported that: An allowance for clothing had been made to the force at Lachine and Beauharnois; that they saw no reason why it should be withheld from the petitioner; that injustice had been done him by the abrupt dismissal; that he and the men be allowed a gratuity; and that he had discharged his responsible duties in a satisfactory and creditable manner. When the question upon the motion, to concur in the report of Committee, was put in the House the motion was negatived. It is very difficult for one at this distance of time to understand how the Legislature could make a distinction between the officials on the Welland Canal and those on the Lachine Canal. One thing is certain, the verdict of the House was not based upon the evidence as it appears in its Journals.

While Superintendent of Police, Richardson suffered the loss of his wife, who died at St. Catharines on the 16th of August, 1845. Her remains were interred in the Butler burial ground, near Niagara, where his eldest sister Jane and other relatives were buried. The inscription on the headstone that he erected to mark her grave is unique. Without indicating the lines or forms of letters the following is the order of the words:

>——Here Reposes, Maria Caroline, the Generous-Hearted, High-Souled, Talented and Deeply-Lamented Wife of Major Richardson, Knight of the Military Order of Saint Ferdinand, First Class, and Superintendent of Police on the Welland Canal during the Administration of Lord Metcalfe. This Matchless Wife and This (illegible) Exceeding Grief of Her Faithfully Attached Husband after a few days' illness at St. Catharines on the 16th August, 1845, at the age of 37 years.

After being relieved of the duties of Superintendent of Police, Richardson prepared for publication *Eight Years in Canada,* an exceedingly well-written description of his career in Canada from 1838 till March, 1847. The administrations of Lord Durham, Lord Sydenham, Sir Charles Bagot and Lord Metcalfe are very fully treated; it is the only contemporary history we have of this transitional period, and in subsequent histories of this epoch he is very freely quoted. Although written after the position he filled had been abolished, and after he had abandoned all hope of receiving any office from the government, it exhibits a fairness one would scarcely expect from a person so unjustly used. Sir Charles Bagot and the Lafontaine-Baldwin ministry are severely handled, while the administration of Lord Metcalfe is eloquently praised. In defending the course of the latter he takes a position beside perhaps the greatest controversial writer of Canada, Reverend Egerton Ryerson.

In 1847 (the book bears the date 1848) Richardson entered for copyright a sequel to his *Eight Years in Canada,* called *The Guards in Canada or the Point of Honor.* In it the story is told of how differences were settled by duels if an apology was not forthcoming. Richardson never allowed an insult tendered him to pass unnoticed. The person offending would apologize if the insult was offered through some misunderstanding, or would meet him. His first duel was in Paris. I have no record of any being fought in England. In Canada he had several affairs: there is living yet in Ontario a person holding an honored and exalted position who, when a mere boy, acted, much against his will, as a second for Major Richardson in a matter, which happily was settled through the seconds by asking mutual apologies from the principals.

The Guards in Canada was the last of Richardson's works published in Canada under his direction. The book was written to vindicate his character for courage in an affair with a resident of Montreal, and incidentally it was a setting in order of his Canadian affairs before taking up his residence in New York, a step he had contemplated for some time.

He did not leave his native province without just cause. He had tried by every honorable means to gain a livelihood among the people he loved best. He squandered his accumulations and all that he had derived from the sale of his best works in the hope that his countrymen would appreciate his efforts. His historical works, thoroughly patriotic in tone and written in a bright vivacious style, were not bought in Canada. In all probability they were as generally read here as any novels or histories of the time. The lack of interest in literature in Canada was general. Education was at a low-water mark, among the great mass of the population, who even as late as the middle of the century felt too keenly the struggle for existence. The intellectual energies of the few, who were educated, were directed into political channels; and the unsettled conditions of our government absorbed all their time, leaving no leisure for those avocations that exercise their benign influence in refining the politics of the Motherland. Even the clergy were drawn into the political whirlpool. The great founder of the educational system of Ontario, Rev. Egerton Ryerson, had been appointed to office only in 1844, and the fruits of his labors were not to be seen for some years. He also was engaged before 1844 in the most remarkable political controversy in the history of Canada.

Richardson's case was not an isolated one by any means. Other writers had started periodicals and magazines, Canadian in sentiment, of an undoubtedly high literary character, and were as hopeful of receiving support as Richardson ever was, but these all were compelled to stop after a few numbers were published. Writers in those days did missionary work and if they did not receive the reward they hoped for, they sow[ed] seed that in some cases fell on good ground. We are beginning to reap the benefit of their self-sacrificing labors and if we are in the morning of a brighter and a more appreciative day, a large share of credit for these hopeful conditions must be attributed to the earlier workers in this unprofitable and unfruitful field.

In New York Richardson was engaged in preparing new editions of his published novels and in writing others. *Hardscrabble or the Fall of Chicago* was published in New York in 1850 or before that year, since it is named on the title page of *Wacousta* published in 1851; but as I have not seen a copy except the one in my library, published in 1888, I cannot give any further information regarding the first edition. The story is much shorter than the author's previous ones and may be considered weak when compared with *Wacousta*. The scene is laid at Fort Dearborn on the Chicago river in the year 1812. In all probability Richardson got the facts for the story from a pamphlet published in 1844, which described the events as seen by an actor in them. Two or three surprises and an affair of love are introduced by means of a slight change in the order of events. The names of the officers at the fort are but transparently disguised in the romance. Captain Heald, Lieut. Helm, Ensign Ronan and Surgeon Von Voorhees, appear as Captain Headley, Lieut. Elmsley, Ensign Ronayne and Surgeon Von Vottenberg in the story. In 1852 a work by Major Richardson entitled *Waunangee or the Massacre of Chicago* was published. I have not been able to see a copy of this work but in all probability it is either the same as *Hardscrabble,* or a sequel to it. The leading Indian character of the historical narrative is Naunongee, who is called Waunangee in the novel; accordingly, the name seems to point to some connection with this romance. As a title *Waunangee* would certainly be both more appropriate and more attractive than *Hardscrabble. Wacousta* and *Ecarté* were revised by the author and published in cheap octavo form, the former by Robert M. De Witt and the latter by Dewitt and Davenport in 1851. In the same year a revised edition of *The Canadian Brothers* appeared under the name *Matilda Montgomerie,* the heroine of the story. It will be readily seen that it would not be politic for the author to issue a story in New York entitled *The Canadian Brothers,* even if the publishers gave their assent. *Matilda Montgomerie* is much improved in the revision. The Scotch dialect, which Richardson himself acknowledges to be so imperfect, he omits in this edition. Sampson Gattrie now appears under his proper name, Simon Girty. But the most marked change from the first edition is the suppression of the several passages in which the author had used all his eloquence to sound the praises of the British in the numerically unequal struggle they had been called upon to maintain. Notable instances are the omission of all reference to Col. Harvey's night attack at Stoney Creek and to the details of the victory at Queenston Heights. It is very interesting to compare the two editions and to notice the passages that are suppressed or modified, evidently to suit the tastes of his new audience.

His other works were *Westbrook, or the Outlaw,* and *The Monk Knight of St. John.* As I have not seen either of these books I cannot give any facts relating to them, except what are gleaned from other bibliographies. *Westbrook* is mentioned by Morgan, but the date of publication is not given. Dr. L. E. Horning, of Victoria University, Toronto, suspects "that this *Westbrook* is only *Wacousta* with another name." I think this scarcely possible. *Wacousta* was the most popular of Richardson's works, and the name had gained a vogue that had a definite cash value to both author and publisher. The names of successful books are not usually changed. If I were to offer any opinion, I should say that the scene is laid in the western peninsula of Upper Canada, and that the tale introduces the exploits of a renegade Canadian named Westbrook, an actual elusive personage who, at the head of some Americans and a few Canadian rebels, went about the district from Long Point to the Talbot Settlement robbing the people and burning homes during the year 1814. It is quite

possible Richardson knew of this marauder's acts, but whether more than the name was suggested by this knowledge, can be settled only by a study of the book itself.

In the *Dictionary of National Biography,* 1850 is given as the date of publication of *The Monk Knight of St. John,* but as I have not a copy of the book I cannot confirm this date. It is a tale of the Crusaders, and those who have read it say that it is a unique story probably suggested by reading Byron and Moore.

These books were all published in cheap form, and consequently the revenue that the author derived must have been comparatively small. It was the day of the cheap novel. About 1840 two New York papers began to reprint in their columns the most popular English novels, which, when finished, were issued in parts at a very low price. No international copyright law protected the British author in the United States. *Wacousta* had been pirated and issued in Philadelphia in 1833. The regular publishers had to issue books in cheap form and at lower prices or go out of business. Richardson arrived in New York when this competition was perhaps the keenest. *Ecarté, Wacousta, Matilda Montgomerie* and *Hardscrabble* appeared in paper-covered 8vo form at 50 cents a volume.

Major Richardson died suddenly on the 12th of May, 1852, at his lodgings No. 113 West Twenty-ninth street, New York. The obituary notice as it appeared in the New York *Journal of Commerce* of May 14th, 1852, is as follows:

> Died—On the 12th inst. Major John Richardson, late of H. B. M. Gordon Highlanders aged 53 (55) years. His friends are invited to attend his funeral, without further invitation, from the Church of the Holy Communion, corner 6th Avenue and 20th Street, this day, at two o'clock, P.M.

His remains were taken outside the city for burial, but diligent inquiry has failed to find his last resting place.

The immediate cause of death was erysipelas; at first the symptoms were not considered alarming, but when medical aid was summoned it came too late. To his many friends the news, besides the shock of suddenness, brought qualms of self-reproach when they learned that Richardson had been living in more straitened circumstances than his appearance or his conversation indicated.

To die in poverty and neglect is no disgrace. Finding no means of livelihood in his native land, he sought a foreign city after his prime of life was past; and if he was unsuccessful in gaining a competence, perhaps the causes arose from the training of his early manhood rather than from circumstances within his control. The camp does not train a man for the mart. He who has entered the army a youth of sixteen, to retire at thirty-nine, seldom, unless in official routine, can adapt himself successfully to the new environment of civilian life. The task of gaining a livelihood by literature in Canada was the harder because he had been accustomed to the cultured circles of London society. It is no reproach to the people of Canada, individually, amid the many difficulties they contended with, that they failed to appreciate and purchase the works of their first novelist. It is a reproach to them collectively, to their government, that Richardson was not given an opportunity of earning enough to enable him to live in simple comfort in his native land. He had no vanity of authorship. On this he says:—"I look upon the art of ingenious writing, not as a merit, but a mere incidental gift, for which one is more indebted to nature than to judicious application." As a man of letters he was publicly honored but once. Yet, because he was not honored more he felt inclined to pity rather than to censure his countrymen. In a careful study of his career, no mean, no dishonorable act will be found. Faithful to his friends, true to his convictions, loyal to his country, he unselfishly served friends and country better than he served himself.

One wish he asked to be respected by future generations of his countrymen, which has not been regarded. He says:

> I cannot deny to myself the gratification of the expression of a hope that should a more refined and cultivated taste ever be introduced into this matter-of-fact country in which I have derived my being, its people will decline to do me the honor of placing my name in the list of their 'Authors.' I certainly have no particular ambition to rank among their future 'men of genius,' or to share any posthumous honor they may be disposed to confer upon them.

Richardson's whole career was a noble and manly struggle. Pugnacious and exclusive in temperament, with but a slight sense of humor, he pursued undeviatingly a course of the strictest integrity. He knew neither tact nor compromise. He fought harder for the political principles he cherished, for the social code he respected, than he did for life itself.

Like the earliest English novelist, Richardson has suffered neglect in his own land. All that Scotland had for her greatest poet was an office worth £70 a year, but her succeeding generations remembered his exquisite productions. Canada could find not even such an office for her first novelist. His own generation refused him a living in his native land; subsequent generations of Canadians know him not. And his works, if obtainable, can be bought only at almost prohibitive prices. Yet three years before Scott died; when Thackeray was a stripling of eighteen; when Dickens had not yet

become a reporter, Richardson was winning, by his first work of the imagination, applause from the English press and a large audience of English readers. In the very year of Scott's death, his masterpiece, **Wacousta** appeared; and the six editions through which it has run bear testimony to its popularity.

Whatever Richardson did he tried to do well. Unlike Cooper, he never trusted to chance to develop the circumstances of his plot; unlike Cooper he tells his story well, and tells it in faultless English. The interest is sustained to the end. There are no carelessnesses, no crudities, no notable mannerisms. Cooper often loses himself in the pathless mazes of his long sentences. Richardson, incisive and logical, builds clause on clause, phrase on phrase, here adding a limiting detail and there a defining circumstance, until you marvel at the accumulated result and you would not have a single word changed. Yet there is no straining after rhetorical effect, no attempt at fine writing. The lucidity of style recalls Macaulay, who at this period was writing his early essays.

A born literary artist, Richardson has drawn with a firm and skilled hand not only the children of his imagination, but the people of his own day. His autobiographical sketches, his historical works, as well as his novels, show us their foibles, their weaknesses, and their merits. His great interest is in men and their achievements; but there are delightful bits of painting from nature. Though a lover of nature, he seldom gives himself up to that revel in the life of nature which is so great a merit of Cooper's work. It is men and women in action that interest him. Only less perhaps did the brute creation claim his attention. His ponies are still a memory among the older people of Windsor and Sandwich. He delights in describing the capture of a young wild deer in the river opposite his grounds in Brockville, which eventually became a great pet. Its antics and actions are not too insignificant to be recorded in one of his most valuable literary productions. But though he took delight in the possession of the ponies and the pet deer, his intimate companions were his dogs. In Sandwich, in Brockville, in Montreal, he was always accompanied by a beautiful specimen of the Newfoundland species named Hector. His grief at the loss of this dog by poison in Brockville was great, and another named after the Trojan hero was his companion in New York till almost the last. At the end of a long and favorable notice of Major Richardson's career in *The New York Journal of Commerce* a few days after his death this pathetic anecdote is told: "A week or two since, he was heard by someone who met him in a bookstore, accompanied as usual by his faithful canine friend, to say, 'Ah, poor Hector, we must part or starve.'" And it is further related that the dog was sold a few days before his master's death to provide him with food.

His notions of life were by no means puritanical. He believed that solace and comfort were to be derived from an after-dinner cigar. In complete accord with the customs of the times among the circle in which he moved in his palmy days, he took his glass of wine, but none abhorred excesses more than he.

If we judge Richardson by the literary success that cheered him even amid his many days of adversity, we can merely wonder that a writer so wholesome in atmosphere, so buoyant in spirit, so notable in our literary development, is now almost completely forgotten. His works, whether we consider their subject-matter, their literary merits, or their position in the growth of the novel, place their gifted author high on that roll we choose to designate as our list of Canadian authors.

These productions of his genius are his sole monument. The bright young Canadian lad who left school to fight his country's battles had to seek in the land he fought against an unknown grave in the teeming solitude of America's greatest city. No votive garland can be laid on that tomb; no admiring young Canadian may visit that shrine.

Ida Burwash (essay date 1912)

SOURCE: "A Young Volunteer of 1812: A Sketch of Major John Richardson, One of the Earliest Canadian Novelists," *Canadian Magazine*, Vol. 34, No. 3, July, 1912, pp. 218-25.

[*In the following essay, Burwash discusses how Richardson used his military experiences as a youth volunteer to compose his history* War of 1812.]

As a century turns with the turning of the year, it recalls a memorable date to Canadians. It recalls at the same time an interesting figure in the person of Major John Richardson, one of the earliest Canadian novelists, and one of the first historians of the war of 1812, whose border strife he shared. To the present generation Richardson's memory is shadowy. His books are little known to-day and difficult of access. Yet a hundred years ago he stood at the centre of a life replete with interest and action. Though in 1812 he was only sixteen, he was known in the small society of Amherstburg, where his father was garrison surgeon, as a lad of promise. Garrison life was just the one to be attractive to a lively boy. The experience of officers and soldiers either as related to himself or as gathered up by him from the conversation of his elders, were of the kind to stimulate ambition. Then close at hand were the Indians bringing suggestion of the woods and wilds so dear to the adventurous nature.

In summer these Indians camped in hundreds on Bois Blanc Island. There Richardson with other lads was a frequent visitor. He was probably as familiar with the habits of the savages as he was with those of the settlers about Amherstburg. He was accustomed, too, to see the chiefs at any time stalking through the settlement on their way for the stores provided by the Government. Nor were fur traders, those equally daring explorers of the wilderness, lacking within the precincts of the fort. Voyageurs and trappers were constantly passing and re-passing the Detroit River on their way to and from the North. For story of adventure then the lad was never at a loss. In his family circle likewise he heard many a tale of pioneer days that must have fired his imagination, for his grandmother had been among those tried and trembling prisoners shut up in Fort Detroit when that fort was besieged by Pontiac.

Apart from local interests, affairs in Canada and abroad had just then reached a heated point. News of Britain's part in the European struggle going on must have been common talk among the little garrison—Napoleon the terrible, an oft-discussed personality. Austerlitz and Jena were then comparatively recent events and the insatiable Emperor having trodden under heel the nations of Western Europe, was in the act of moving on to Russia.

So matters stood at the beginning of 1812. Napoleon master of Europe. England mistress of the seas! And it was at this point and in this year that Napoleon, when stepping beyond his Continental limits to dip his finger in those seas again by stirring up a war between England and America, made his first backward step— that fatal step that opened up the way for his more fatal day of Waterloo. It was the declaration of war in 1812 that shook Alexander of Russia free from his alliance with the despot.

In June, 1812, the news that war had been declared against Great Britain by the United States was received in Canada with mingled feelings. The Canadian frontier was a long one. At the moment there was not a settlement in Upper Canada that could boast a population exceeding a thousand souls. To the Loyalist settlers already worn by thirty years of bitter struggle with the wilderness, war was yet another burden imposed upon them by an enemy still unforgiven.

On the contrary, by young John Richardson it was hailed as "a glorious transition," as a welcome exchange of Cæsar's Commentaries and a stuffy schoolhouse for the King's Regulations, the open field, and soldier's quarters. Boys though they were, he and his young schoolmate Garden managed to get themselves enrolled as "gentlemen volunteers," Richardson in connection with the detachment of the 41st, then part of the garrison at Amherstburg, Garden with the Royal Newfoundland Regiment, a few of whom were also included in that garrison.

The general conditions of the war that followed are too well known to call for repetition. From the beginning to the end of it Canadians, French or English, had but a single purpose. To a man they stood to defend their homes and country irrespective of race or class. They experienced reverses hard to bear. They chafed at times under the leadership of incompetent generals. The names of Proctor and Prevost do not shine in Canadian history. Certain of their officers suffered protracted misery as prisoners of war. Yet, despite all reverses and the far inferior number of her fighting force, at the end of both campaigns, of 1812 and 1813, Canada still held her own. In the following year a peace was arranged between the two Governments. It was one welcomed by both combatants, and one that altogether has proved to be of so satisfactory a nature that it has never since been broken.

Canadians to-day are fully sensible of the benefits of that peace. Yet a glance back at this date to the more intimate conditions of that war-time as described by Richardson, eye-witness of and participant in its events, brings to light many incidents suggestive to a later generation.

Our young volunteer's experience during those years of struggle were confined to the western frontier. Marched from Amherstburg to Queenston and back again to the western border, he took part in every engagement in that region until he was taken prison of war at the surrender of Moraviantown. The succeeding year he spent in hard captivity in Kentucky State.

All through his story of the war, Richardson's interest in our Indian allies is shown. He does not try to hide their barbarous war customs. At the same time he reminds his readers earnestly that every possible means were tried by Colonel St. George of Amherstburg and by Colonel Elliott, Superintendent of Indian affairs, to soften down the fierceness of the savages. As one means high rewards were offered for prisoners taken by the Indians in the hope of saving such unfortunates from torture and death. But the belief of the savage that the spirit of a dead chief would never rest in quiet till an enemy had been offered up as a sacrifice made this attempt of little avail.

One such case of vengeance is described with thrilling brevity. Logan, a young chief and interpreter, almost as much admired by the English as by his own race, was killed in the preliminary skirmish of Brownstown— an occasion on which Tecumseh, with a little band of twenty-four picked braves, defeated Van Horne and turned back his men who were marching with supplies to General Hull at Detroit. In this fray one American prisoner was taken.

When the fighting was over Logan's body was carried into the long low Council Room. Round it his brother warriors ranged themselves in circle solemnly and in silence, placing in the circle with them their one prisoner. After they had remained for some time in absolute stillness, a bowl of food was offered to the prisoner. He seemed to eat of it obediently. "And while occupied in this manner," writes Richardson, "a young warrior, obeying a signal from one of his elders, rose from his seat, and coming round behind the prisoner struck him a blow on his uncovered head and he ceased to live. Not a yell, not a sound, beside that of the crashing tomahawk was heard, not a muscle of an Indian face was moved. The young warrior, replacing his weapon, walked deliberately back and resumed his seat in the circle. The whole party remained a few minutes longer seated, then rose to their feet and silently withdrew, satisfied that they had fulfilled a religious immolation to the ashes of the deceased."

The savage, when fired purely with the lust of blood, committed atrocities too painful for mention. But that association with the whites was gradually having a certain civilizing effect upon the better Indians is shown by the following incident related of Metoss, a noted chief of the Sacs.

During the siege of Fort Miami this chief was in the habit of crossing the river daily to lie in ambush in the woods, ready to pick off any American who dared to leave the fort to carry back water or for other purposes. One such adventurer Metoss even contrived to secure alive and at once conveyed him to his wigwam to be preserved for future vengeance. The day following this capture, the chief's young son, a handsome lad of thirteen, accompanied his father. The pair in hiding were soon detected by means of a telescope within the fort, and a discharge of grape-shot killed the lad almost instantly. Maddened by grief, Metoss carried the body of his son to his canoe and quickly towards his wigwam, with the stern intent of sacrificing the American prisoner then and there. Happily, a Canadian much liked by the Indians, hearing of what had happened, hurried to meet Metoss. Earnestly he entreated him to spare the innocent prisoner, pleading that the surrender of the prisoner instead to the Indian's great father, the King, would please that father very much, whereas the prisoner's death would sorely grieve him.

Metoss, who in his misery had torn off his gay head-dress of battle, listened, speechless. At length he strode silently to his wigwam, where the body of his son had been laid. Cutting at a stroke the thongs that bound his prisoner, he led him out to the White Man with the mournful words—"You tell me that my great father wishes it—take him!" Then no longer able to control his grief, he broke down and sobbed bitterly.

The white men were deeply moved. In their fellow-feeling for the stricken father they buried the young chief the following day with full military honours. Led by Lieutenant Bullock, the funeral party gathered at the wigwam where the boy lay, his little rifle, powder and ball, beside him, while a dozen chiefs of the tribe with bodies painted black danced a solemn war-dance round his remains. So great was the anguish of Metoss he was with difficulty parted from the son whom he had clasped in his arms for a last embrace. But, finally, the soldiers lifting the child, bore him to his grave on the banks of the Miami. As a further mark of the sympathy they added an extra volley to the usual three rounds fired over [a] grave in the soldier's honour.

It was during the campaign of 1813 that the famous Shawnee Chief Tecumseh was slain. His bravery and clever tactics are constantly mentioned by Richardson. But it was not till the night before the fatal battle of Moraviantown that Tecumseh's full power was revealed. The vacillation of General Proctor, followed by his proposal to fall back on the Central Army, with all that can be said for and against it, has often been discussed. To Tecumseh it had but one meaning—rank cowardice!—and in his wrath he did not fail to tell the white man so. Richardson records, word for word, Tecumseh's famous speech at this his last war council. With his young blood aglow, the boy-volunteer listened to those burning clauses of the Indian orator, each one prefaced by its fiery, "Listen!" followed by its array of stern facts and sterner criticism, ending with appeal—"Father! You have got arms and ammunition which our great father sent for his red children. If you have any idea of going away, give them to us, and you may go in welcome. Our lives are in the hands of the Great Spirit. We are determined to defend our lands, and if it is his will, we wish to leave our bones upon them."

Scarcely were the words spoken when a wild scene followed. The chieftains sprang to their feet brandishing their tomahawks, while the vaulted roof of the large Council Room echoed back their fierce yells. Above them, a conspicuous figure in his fringed leather dress, towered Tecumseh, his large waving ostrich plumes of white contrasting strangely with his dark face and piercing black eyes. When quiet was restored Proctor, through his interpreters, finally persuaded his fiery allies to a compromise—to retire with him to the Moravian village about half way between Amherstburg and Niagara.

This decided, orders were given for the dismantling of the border forts. But things were not well managed. The retreat was too dilatory and the fatal engagement of Moraviantown ensued, when closely pressed by a force of 6,000 Americans, the handful of Canadian troops with their 800 allies had no alternative than to surrender.

The loss of Tecumseh in this encounter was as keenly deplored by the whites as by the Indians. Down the receding years his conduct must ever shine the brighter in contrast to the flight of Proctor at the commencement of this action. Richardson recounts simply but graphically the splendid appearance of Tecumseh when, just before the bugle of the advancing enemy was heard, he passed along the line in which the young volunteer was placed, pressing the hand of each officer in turn as he passed and making to each one in Shawnee what proved to be a last farewell. In less than half an hour later in a single attack on Colonel Johnson, the commander of the American Mounted Riflemen, Tecumseh was shot dead upon the spot.

As darkness fell and the news spread that Tecumseh had not only been killed but actually flayed by Johnson's followers, the hearts of the imprisoned soldiers were filled with speechless grief. It is but fair to admit that this brutal conduct of the Americans was equally lamented by their General Harrison, who begged certain of the officers of the 41st to accompany his staff in order if possible to identify the body of the fallen hero.

"Of the deep regret with which his death was regarded," writes Richardson, "no stronger evidence can be given than the fact that there was scarcely an officer of the captured division who, as he reposed his head upon the rude log affording him his only pillow that night, did not wholly lose sight of his unfortunate position in the more lively emotion produced by the untimely fate of the lamented and noble Indian."

Among other intimate details related by this soldier of a century ago are his personal recollections of Queenston Heights, of certain daring feats of individuals, of the Battle of Lake Erie (the one naval encounter witnessed by him), and of his imprisonment in Kentucky.

The story of the battle of Queenston Heights has been told and re-told many times in speech and history. Richardson throws no further light upon the action of the battle. He gives, however, a few sidelights that go to show how far war is from being the thing of glory, bugle strains, and gorgeous uniform which it is so frequently held up to be.

He was daily an observer of Brock's vexation at the incomprehensible action of Prevost in agreeing to an armistice—that calm delay that gave the enemy full time to lay their plans, to cross the river and gain the heights of Queenston for a few hours. He was among those too who shared in the scurry of that chill morning when the alarm was given just before the break of day, and news was spread throughout Fort George that the General, alone, unattended even by his aide, was already on horseback far on his way back along the lonely road to Queenston. He recounts Brock's meeting with Colonel Jarvis on that road in the dim, gray dawn, when though the latter officer was hastening to meet his chief with news of the enemy's movements Brock refused to abate his speed and the messenger as best he could was obliged to turn his own horse, going likewise at full speed, and to catch up with his flying General who, still galloping, listened to his word and shouted back his orders from the saddle without a moment's pause.

No time was lost that morning on Canadian shores. Galloping on in his turn towards Fort George to hurry on Sheaffe and his army according to Brock's orders, Jarvis encountered a second desperate rider, young Macdonnell, the General's aide-de-camp, following at break-neck pace his gallant leader. Neither had a moment to spare. But on passing his brother officer Macdonnell snatched his sword from his hand, shouting out like his General before him a hurried direction to his comrade where to find his own sword on returning to the Fort. The borrowed weapon unfortunately was of short avail.

Richardson of course was not present when that gallant charge of General and aide was made up hill in the face of odds so shortly after. But he conveys to us some idea of the grief and rage striving in the hearts of the advancing soldiers as they marched a little later over the same ground so recently passed by their daring leader and his equally daring aide; every soldier burning to avenge the deaths of the two gallant officers.

The young subaltern, however, had his grim share in the battle of the afternoon, when the reverses of the morning were avenged; when 900 American prisoners were taken and the heights regained for Canada. He was also among the saddened band who looked on while the body of the Hero of Queenston was lifted from its bleak hiding-place; when it was carried forth from the rude house in which it had been hurriedly hidden away under a pile of old blankets, in order to prevent its recognition by the enemy. He was one of those, too, who understood most clearly at what a costly price the Heights of Queenston were regained in the loss to Britain and Canada of that inspiring presence.

Shortly after this battle, the 41st was ordered back to Amherstburg, there to remain in garrison. Not until the 19th of January, 1813, was it once more under marching orders, when the whole force of 500 troops with 800 Indians were ordered out to assist Major Reynolds, who with fifty men and a few Indians had been driven back from Frenchtown by the advance of the American army under Winchester.

The departure of the troops that winter morning made a keen impression on the young soldier, who long remembered the rear of the guns as the troops marched along the ice, the wild yells of the Indians, and the glittering reflection of the rising sun upon the icy cliffs on shore and on the polished arms of the soldiery. Equally keen was his remembrance of the cold of the bivouac at night, before fires kindled on the snow, with only the soldier's coat as covering. The march onward before daylight proved bleaker still but quickly forgotten in the onset of the battle resulting in the capture of Winchester himself and the surrender of his army.

It was during this battle that Lieutenant Irvine, noticing a three pounder gun lying close to the fence behind which the enemy was sheltered, dashed forward under cover of a heavy fire from the Canadian line behind him and seizing the drag rope bore off the gun. For this recklessness he was punished by a shot in the heel that put him out of the contest for some time.

The battle of Lake Erie took place the following autumn on September 9th, 1813. None understood better than the little garrison at Amherstburgh the fatal odds under which Captain Barclay laboured that morning. With heavy hearts they watched him sail from harbour on the lumbering *Detroit*, an unfinished vessel armed chiefly with such guns of any and every size as could be gathered in the neighbourhood. In his wake, the remaining six vessels of his fleet, manned solely by untrained provincial crews, sailed on their doubtful way to meet the nine well-equipped vessels of Perry's squadron. How anxious were the hearts of the watchers on the ramparts needs no telling, as they heard the constant firing and saw the smoke of the guns but could discern nothing of the movements of either side. Later when a change of wind had cleared the clouds away, they saw but too distinctly the wrecked Canadian fleet heavily following the Americans to Sandusky Bay.

Had Barclay's appeal for reinforcements to the Commander of Lake Ontario been listened to Canada might have been spared this fatality. From first to last every Canadian sailor on those ships showed a splendid courage. But courage without training pitted against equal courage with superior skill must submit to the inevitable.

As a further showing of the stern reality behind the glory, we have Richardson's account of the treatment of the prisoner1s of war taken at Moraviantown. Among these were several officers of the 41st.

A dispirited band they left the Moravian village on the morning of October 7th, 1813. Their feelings can be better imagined than described as they passed through Detroit over soil which their regiment had held almost unassisted for the previous fifteen months under great odds as to numbers. Two routes lay open to them; one by way of the Miami, the other the Sandusky route. The few who chose the latter, including Richardson, were sent by a gun-boat across Lake Erie to the harbour where the shattered Canadian fleet still lay. To the disheartened prisoners Barclay's ship was a woeful spectacle—her guns dismantled, her bulwarks broken, her decks covered with wounded soldiers while her Captain suffering terribly from his wounds lay in bed in his cabin, hardly recognisable by his comrades except for his *unchanged spirit.*

From Sandusky began the march to Chilicothe, the place of their detention. As week by week went by a weary march it proved, through cold, unceasing rain with but a filthy hut for shelter, or oftener with halt made in the open without even coats to protect them from the storm. Doggedly they plodded on, unconscious that the day of their misfortune had already been retrieved by the notable success of De Salaberry and his handful of troops at Chateauguay.

For some time after their arrival they were treated fairly. But when news was unexpectedly received that the twenty-three English deserters taken at Queenston had been sent home to England to be tried, the angry Yankees promptly retaliated by ill-treatment of the prisoners in their midst. A number of officers were sent on to the penitentiary at Frankfort, while the few who remained, our volunteer among them, were thrown into the common jail. There, twenty in all, they were crowded into two small rooms, guarded by a sentinel, and placed under control of a low and brutal jailor. The men of the division were kept in a fortified camp on the outskirts of the town.

Some time later, owing to the rumour of a plan being formed for the escape of the officers, their ill-treatment was doubled. Handcuffs were added to the miseries of their confinement, the boy soldier alone being exempt from this precaution. At first in youthful pride he refused any amelioration of his fate, which was not to be shared by his seniors. But as time when on the relief he was able to afford his fellow-prisoners by his freedom made that exemption a boon. With the aid of an old knife he managed to extract the iron nails from the fetters, replacing them by others made of lead which he found in the haversack of one of the officers. Only close observation could have detected the difference in these nails. By this means the fettered officers managed to slip off the irons when unobserved and so to gain relief of circulation and position.

Happily this experience was not extended. About ten days of it had been endured when orders were issued for the removal of all prisoners to Frankfort. They were sent by way of the Ohio under conduct of Lieutenant Harrison. It remains to the credit of this officer that on receiving from the Englishmen the pledge of their parole he at once struck off their handcuffs on his own responsibility. From Cincinnati they crossed on horseback a gloomy hill country. In cold and storm they entered Frankfort, the first sight to greet them being the Penitentiary walls, looming up conspicuous. Here

they found their comrades, thirty in all, confined in two small rooms in the upper story of the prison but accepting the situation calmly.

This further experience was likewise destined to be short. Almost on the heels of their arrival came the news of Napoleon's reverses in Russia. This freeing of England's hands gave a new aspect to American affairs. The quarters of the officers were soon moved to a comfortable hotel though still their guard was retained. Next came freedom on parole and finally permission to such officers as could pay their own means of transport to repair to the Canadian frontier. To those who remained certain kindnesses were shown, especially by Major Madison who having been previously taken prisoner at Quebec now took this opportunity of returning to the British officers the hospitality he had received at the hands of the Quebecers.

At length came the welcome news that all were ordered to the frontier. So intense was the excitement at first, neither officer nor soldier dared express his feeling by word or look. Once fairly started the return march was by comparison a holiday, though it was the end of August when they reached Lake Erie. Here further trial awaited them in that not a boat was forthcoming to carry them across the lake. While awaiting conveyance they were attacked by a violent malaria from which they suffered greatly. Weakened by disease as time went by, the sound of the wolves howling the nights away filled them with forebodings. The thought of dying within sight of home was unendurable.

October had begun before a single craft appeared to take them to Cleveland opposite Long Point. The wretched boat was wrecked the same night in a storm and on the beach once more they shivered the night away in misery. On the following morning, however, their passage was achieved. On October 4th, just one year from the date of their captivity, they stepped upon Canadian soil once more. They were sick, exhausted and penniless. One of the number died from the exposure on the beach. Others never quite recovered from the effects of the disease. But better times were coming. Spring brought to our young volunteer both returning health and promotion. Napoleon at this time escaped from Elba. The war was renewed and the 41st ordered to join the British army in Flanders. To the regret of that faithful regiment Waterloo was fought while it was still upon the sea. There was, however, other work to do. It was not indeed till twenty years had passed and the Peace of Europe was followed by the disbanding of the regiment into which Richardson had exchanged that he turned his attention to letters as a profession.

As an historian he is perhaps unique in that he does not hesitate to state plainly our defeats and sufferings in the war of 1812 equally with our successes. He speaks with equal plainness his contempt of Proctor's cowardice and of Prevost's bungling. He readily expresses his admiration of the enemy in cases where he felt it was deserved, while at the same time he does not fail in scathing criticism of their many injustices, and of their persecution of prisoners of war.

The more complete impressions of this soldier of a century ago are recorded in his history entitled *War of 1812,* in his novel *The Canadian Brothers,* and in his narrative, *Eight Years in Canada.*

Upon the sad circumstances of his death in New York at the age of fifty-four it is not needful here to dwell.

His contemporaries have frequently been held up to shame as lacking in appreciation of his literary efforts. That is a mistaken statement. Circumstances would seem to show that the Canadians who built up Ontario in those early days had a finer, keener appreciation of true literature than have their descendants of our somewhat slipshod generation. That they had neither time nor money to devote to the furthering of native talent was their misfortune not their fault. They did their own good work with single purpose.

Richardson was of their spirit in that he like them faced his tasks unflinchingly. Fearless of consequence, what he had to say, he said frankly, to the best of his ability.

William Renwick Riddell (essay date 1930)

SOURCE: "An Appreciation," in *John Richardson,* The Ryerson Press, 1930, pp. 197-208.

[*In the following excerpt, Riddell argues that Richardson's historical works are superior to his imaginative writings.*]

The status of Major John Richardson as a maker of Canadian literature is perhaps at the present time, not definitely and finally fixed. Very much a mythical figure, he does not belong even to the class of writers, honored but unread; he is not only unread but he is also unknown. It is probable that his great wish, besides his desire for recognition by those whom he so unreservedly served with pen and sword and who always disappointed him, was to be remembered and honored by succeeding generations of his countrymen. It is true that he once cynically wrote:—*"I cannot deny to myself the gratification of the expression of a hope that, should a more refined and cultivated taste ever be introduced into this matter-of-fact country in which I have derived my being, its people will decline to do me the honor of placing my name in the list of their 'Authors.' I certainly have no particular ambition to rank among their future 'men of genius,' or to share*

any posthumous honor they may be disposed to confer upon them." But this was when he was smarting under what he considered undeserved neglect; and it is not to be taken at its face value. He is undoubtedly worthy of a place among our authors.

The secret of Richardson's strength was in the man himself and not in the schools he attended. Little school training did he possess, but the defect was more than made up for in his mother, a capable and cultured woman, and the accomplished society of French ladies among whom she moved. Richardson was able to speak fluently in both French and English, and this assisted in giving to him broad sympathies and grace of thought which was reflected in his cultured and dignified manner. Add to this his wide and varied experience, his frequent travels into out-of-the-way places, interesting society in the cities of two continents, and an insatiable appetite for ever newer quests and crusades and you have the basis for the work to which he set himself so resolutely. Equipped with a good military training, he adopted the career of soldier, which he followed in both Europe and America with great distinction, passing through the rôles of victor, captive, diplomat and trusted despatch rider. This experience prepared him for the historical work he was to excel in.

Many would have taken all this as a matter of course, but Richardson was thrilled to the core by his experiences. His eye was as quick for the ghastly and the brutal as for the subtle beauties of love and nature. The vivacity of his mother warmed his own blood and flung him whole-heartedly into every event. He must live it all. Strong, forceful, dramatic, born with a scent for news and possessed of a prodigious enthusiasm for facts, he developed himself into one of the greatest chroniclers of Canada or of any country. His extraordinary skill in description cannot be too much admired. We have nothing better in our literature. Many sidelights, many historical facts of importance, would for ever have escaped us had it not been for this soldier poet and recorder. *Eight Years in Canada* (1838-1847) is, except the newspaper press, the only contemporary history of this period we possess, but this is rather autobiographical than historical. His *War of 1812,* however, is unique among the contemporary histories of that stirring period in America, and continues to be an inexhaustible historical treasury. The contribution of Major Richardson to the historical literature of Canada has been monumental and of the highest importance.

As a writer of imaginative literature, Richardson will take a somewhat lower place. While he comes first in point of time in Canadian writers of fiction, he can hardly be said to be first in importance; his effect upon subsequent Canadian fiction in particular and English literature in general is as yet, at least, very slight. His poem *Tecumseh,* displays too close and un-original a copying of classic models, and it is too uniformly mediocre and conventional to merit anything more than a mildly favorable comment. The general effect must have been unsatisfactory to Richardson himself as he soon forsook poetry for prose. However, as a dramatic re-creation of historical fact, *Tecumseh* is important. *Ecarté* in the same way is a faithful contemporary portrait of Paris salons, and *Wacousta* contains a valuable, and, for the most part, accurate contemporary record, but neither of them, taken as complete works of art, comes within the charmed circle of great imaginative literature.

One of the finest appreciations of Major John Richardson is to be found in the Introduction to Richardson's *War of 1812,* by Alexander Clark Casselman, a competent authority both in his knowledge of Richardson's works and in his literary taste and skill.

> Like the earliest English novelist, Richardson has suffered neglect in his own land. All that Scotland had for her greatest poet was an office worth £70 a year, but her succeeding generations remembered his exquisite productions. Canada could find not even such an office for her first novelist. His own generation refused him a living in his native land; subsequent generations of Canadians know him not. And his works, if obtainable, can be bought only at almost prohibitive prices. Yet three years before Scott died, when Thackeray was a stripling of eighteen, when Dickens had not yet become a reporter, Richardson was winning, by his first work of the imagination, applause from the English press and a large audience of English readers. In the very year of Scott's death, his master-piece, *Wacousta,* appeared; and the six editions through which it has run bear testimony to its popularity.

> Whatever Richardson did he tried to do well. Unlike Cooper, he never trusted to chance to develop the circumstances of his plot; unlike Cooper he tells his story well, and tells it in faultless English. The interest is sustained to the end. There are no carelessnesses, no crudities, no notable mannerisms. Cooper often loses himself in the pathless mazes of his long sentences. Richardson, incisive and logical, builds clause on clause, phrase on phrase, here adding a limiting detail and there a defining circumstance, until you marvel at the accumulated result and you would not have a single word changed. Yet there is no straining after rhetorical effect, no attempt at fine writing. The lucidity of style recalls Macaulay, who at this period was writing his early essays.

> A born literary artist, Richardson has drawn with a firm and skilled hand not only the children of his imagination, but the people of his own day. His autobiographical sketches, his historical works, as well as his novels, show us their foibles, their weaknesses, and their merits. His great interest is in

men and their achievements; but there are delightful bits of painting from nature. Though a lover of nature, he seldom gives himself up to that revel in the life of nature which is so great a merit of Cooper's work. It is men and women in action that interest him. Only less, perhaps did the brute creation claim his attention. His ponies are still a memory among the older people of Windsor and Sandwich. . . .

> His notions of life were by no means puritanical. He believed that solace and comfort were to be derived from an after-dinner cigar. In complete accord with the customs of the times among the circles in which he moved in his palmy days, he took his glass of wine, but none abhorred excesses more than he.

> If we judge Richardson by the literary success that cheered him even amid his many days of adversity, we can merely wonder that a writer so wholesome in atmosphere, so buoyant in spirit, so notable in our literary development, is now almost completely forgotten. His works, whether we consider their subject-matter, their literary merits, or their position in the growth of the novel, place their gifted author high on that roll we choose to designate as our list of Canadian authors.

> These productions of his genius are his sole monument. The bright young Canadian lad who left school to fight his country's battles had to seek in the land he fought against an unknown grave in the teeming solitude of America's greatest city. No votive garland can be laid on that tomb; no admiring young Canadian may visit that shrine.

With most of this I cordially agree.

Everything Richardson wrote was in vigorous, but dignified and good English. He loves rapid action and chooses his materials with the dramatic possibilities always in view; frequently he tends toward the exciting and melodramatic. Usually the plots of his novels are simple, and, except in *Wacousta,* they have a conventional ending. With Richardson the style was the man; each page was packed with autobiography. He wrote as he experienced, *con amore* and joyously. While he had an eye open for remuneration, and confidently expected no small niche in the Canadian Hall of Literary Fame, still, except at the very last his main reward in writing was the satisfaction it gave himself. In speaking of his literary ability he once wrote: "I look upon the art of ingenious writing, not as a merit, but a mere incidental gift, for which one is more indebted to nature than to judicious application." He loved to employ this gift which neither wars nor intrigues could destroy and poverty and neglect could not impair.

The characterization in his novels is life-like, and a few characters are drawn with extraordinary skill. Exception must however be taken to the Negro dialect of Sambo, the Scotch of the Scottish captain in *The Canadian Brothers,* and the Irish in *Ecarté*—the like of which was never heard from human lips; and indeed even the author himself was not wholly satisfied with it, for he dropped much of it in later works and revisions. The "villain of the play" in *The Canadian Brothers* is wholly artificial and manufactured as a *deus ex machina* for the occasion, while his son is a mere lay figure. Except where straining after effect is most patent, as occasionally in *Wacousta,* we meet human beings who actually live and move and have their being in circumstances quite as real.

Richardson fails in depicting woman; with the exception of Helen Stanley in *Ecarté,* and the wife of Captain Heald in *Hardscrabble* and *Wau-nan-gee,* there is scarcely one that is natural or normal. Matilda Montgomerie is certainly a pure fiction, while Clara de Haldimar, Maria Ronayne and another score or more are "such . . . as never was nor no man ever saw."

The Indian Richardson knew well and he succeeded admirably in depicting him—only once did he fail to apply his own knowledge, and that is when he fills Wau-nan-gee with a pure and romantic love for Maria. The same mistake is made by James Fenimore Cooper in *The Last of the Mohicans,* in his character Uncas, after whom apparently Wau-nan-gee was modelled.

The charge of impurity against *Ecarté* would receive little attention in these days of the sex novel, Freud and psychopathy. In none of his other novels, excepting always the senile and silly *Monk Knight of St. John,* is there anything to shock modesty, if we omit the conduct to each other of the impossible Matilda and the equally impossible Gerald.

The poetry and fiction of Richardson are still worth reading. They are valuable in themselves in that they give the first authentic note of a new literature in Canada, a literature instinct with the life and thought of a new nation even then beginning to take shape, a literature in which extremes meet without impropriety, a literature of expanding life, cosmopolitan sympathies, robust democracy, pioneering idealism and freshness and profusion, prodigal in its richness and lavish in its gifts. They are equally valuable for their lively and sympathetic descriptions of the early formative and transitional times of the Nineteenth Century in Upper Canada and the West, as well as the significant days immediately after the fall of Napoleon in Paris. Others will almost certainly return to Richardson's material and weave out of it fresh Canadian romances. Historians, novelists and poets will turn to Richardson again and again in the days to come, and he will enter more fully into his deserved inheritance of acquaintance and appreciation. Then will it be possible to rewrite this chapter, and to estimate more precisely what effect his pioneering work has had upon the art as well as upon the materials of succeeding generations of Canadian literary craftsmen. Of one thing we are sure; and that is, that time will prove our judgment true and sound when we gave him a first place among the Makers of Canadian Literature.

His real value will be not in his discovery of new poetic forms, or in changing the established traditions of English verse or fiction to suit the new colonial conditions. As Samuel Richardson discovered the novel in England, Major John Richardson showed—and not obscurely or incompletely—where the strength of Canadian poetry, drama and fiction must lie, namely, not in mere imitation and variation of Old World themes, but in fresh and vigorous interpretation of our own life and thought. Only in this way can Canada develop an artistic soul and consciousness, and eventually arrive at that stage of national independence, coordinated and entire, which makes possible a great spiritual contribution in the form of a national literature.

Leslie Monkman (essay date 1979)

SOURCE: "Richardson's Indians," in *Canadian Literature,* No. 81, Summer, 1979, pp. 86-94.

[*In the following essay, Monkman discusses Richardson's portrayal of Native Americans and identifies similar patterns of characterization in the works of James Fenimore Cooper.*]

No writer of nineteenth-century Canada more fully explored the literary potential of the Indian than Major John Richardson. In novels such as *Wacousta* (1832) and *The Canadian Brothers* (1840), Richardson's interest is in the conflict between red man and white man on the Canadian-American frontier. In later formula novels such as *Hardscrabble* (1851) and *Wau-Nan-Gee* (1852), he more directly appeals to the American reading public by shifting his focus to the events preceding the founding of Chicago. Yet Richardson's interest in the Indian was not limited to an exploration of his potential in frontier fiction; *Tecumseh* (1828), a narrative poem paying tribute to the Indian warrior whom he met as a young man, was Richardson's first published volume, and references to the Indian and Indian cultures appear repeatedly in his volumes of history and autobiography. Throughout his work, Richardson affirms his admiration for the red man, and in later works such as **"The North American Indian,"** he writes movingly of his concern for the extinction of the Indian race. Yet he consistently separates red and white cultures into distinct orders and, despite his stated esteem for the Indian, ultimately presents the red man only within the context of savagism.

Richardson's interest in the Indian may have stemmed in part from his own family history; the question of whether or not his maternal grandmother was an Ottawa Indian has not yet been conclusively answered. No such genealogical connection need be assumed, however, in order to explain his interest in the red man; in *Eight Years in Canada* (1847) and "A Trip to Walpole Island and Port Sarnia" (1849), he documents his own first-hand contacts with the Indian, and one of his most treasured memories was of fighting by the side of Tecumseh in the War of 1812. Combined with these personal experiences was his reading of works such as Alexander Henry's *Travels and Adventures in Canada and the Indian Territories* (1809) and his fascination with the novels of James Fenimore Cooper.

In an abridged edition of *Wacousta* published in the New Canadian Library series, Carl Klinck reprints what we are told is Richardson's introduction to the 1851 edition of the novel. However, the first two paragraphs of this introduction in which Richardson explicitly acknowledges Cooper's influence are not included:

> This Chapter, written eighteen years subsequent to the original publication of *Wacousta* in London, will be found unavoidably replete with egotism. By none will it be more readily pronounced such than by those who are most open to the charge themselves. Without its exercise, however, the object of this introduction would not be gained.

> As the reader may be curious to know on what basis, and in what manner this story (of which I have certainly robbed that first of vigorous American novelists—the "Last of the Mohicans" Cooper—which tale, albeit I have never read a novel by another author twice, I have absolutely devoured three times,) was suggested to me, and on what particular portions of History the story is founded, I am not aware that this introductory Chapter, which I have promised my Publishers, can be better devoted than to the explanation.

At the time of the publication of *Wacousta,* three of James Fenimore Cooper's "Leatherstocking Novels" had been published: *The Pioneers* (1823), *The Last of the Mohicans* (1826) and *The Prairie* (1827). But Richardson's interest in the American novelist also encompassed the later novels in the series, *The Pathfinder* (1840) and *The Deerslayer* (1841), as revealed in the enthusiasm expressed in *Eight Years in Canada* (1847) in a description of his thoughts while travelling through upper New York state:

> Never were the characters in Cooper's "Leather Stocking" and the "Pathfinder" more vividly brought before my recollection. This was the sort of scene in which he loved to introduce them, and, I know not how it was, but with what dreamy state of half consciousness which a solitary traveller awakened early from his slumbers, feels in a situation of this kind, when the fancy is fully at work, I looked, at each moment expecting to see a deer or a wild turkey arrested by the crack of a rifle and a hunter, equipped as the charming Indian novelist has painted him, issuing in the pursuit of game.

Despite Richardson's acknowledged familiarity with Cooper's work and his confession to having "robbed" the story of *Wacousta* from the American master, his work rarely indicates the kind of explicit debt declared by Richardson. Yet if he does not owe details of plot structure and character to Cooper, he does share perspectives on Indian culture which have been identified by twentieth-century critics in the American novelist's work.

Paul Wallace, one of several critics who have debated Cooper's role as "Indian novelist," argues that Cooper's principal source, John Heckewelder's *Account of the History, Manners and Customs of the Indian Nations, Who Once Inhabited Pennsylvannia and the Neighbouring States* (1819), provided the novelist with a basic distinction that pervades his work. Wallace contends that the Indian in Cooper's novels is either part of a band of demonic fiends (as embodied in Cooper's "Mingoes") or a member of a tribe of noble savages (Delawares such as Uncas or Chingachgook). This kind of tribal distinction emerges most prominently in a story published in 1850, "The Sunflower. A True Tale of the North-West," and in Richardson's later novels *Wau-Nan-Gee,* and *Hardscrabble.* Thus, in *Wau-Nan-Gee,* the narrator comments on the red villain of the novel, Pee-to-tum:

> It has already been remarked that Pee-to-tum was not a genuine Pottowatomie, but one of that race whose very name is a synonym with treachery and falsehood—a Chippewa. With low, heavy features; a dark scowling brow; coarse, long, dark hair, shading the restless, ever-moving eye that, like that of the serpent, seemed to fascinate where most the cold and slimy animal sought to sting; the broad, coarse nose; the skin partaking more in the Chippewa, of that offensive, rank odor peculiar to the Indian, than any others of the race.

The same Pee-to-tum becomes the rapist of the novel's heroine, and in the face of such grotesque villainy, his heroic counterpart, the Pottowatomie, Wau-Nan-Gee, is almost overwhelmed. Wau-Nan-Gee, a literary descendant of Uncas of *The Last of the Mohicans,* quietly accepts that his love for the white heroine must remain platonic and functions as a diligent and constant agent of virtue throughout the book. His only reward, however, is to be damned as an Indian by the heroine who refuses to make tribal distinctions after her rape by Pee-to-tum.

Although Richardson clearly intends the reader to acknowledge the injustice in the heroine's condemnation of the entire Indian race, her attitude is closely related to the perspective that recurs most frequently in his work. In his discussion of James Fenimore Cooper's treatment of the Indian, Roy Harvey Pearce argues that in the United States, by 1825, the idea of savagism had overwhelmed other perspectives on the Indian, and he identifies this perspective in Cooper's work. Within this context, the Indian's life

> could not be said to be one totally superior or inferior to that of a civilized man. It did not make sense to view his state as one either to be aspired to or to be dismissed with unfeeling contempt; rather it was to be seen as the state of one almost entirely out of contact, for good and for bad, with the life of civilized men.

Within this perspective, one can freely praise a "good Indian," but implicit in this praise is the idea that the Indian is being weighed by a different scale of values than would be used to assess a "good white man." Richardson's shared acceptance of the ideology that Pearce identifies in Cooper's work can be demonstrated through an examination of his two best-known novels and of his poetic tribute to Tecumseh.

In *Wacousta,* the opposition between savage and civilized worlds is initially established in terms of setting through a continuing contrast between North America and Europe. Sir Everard Valletort asserts that he would prefer the life of a barber's apprentice in London to his role as lieutenant in the midst of Canadian "savage scenes." For Valletort, the civilized world of Europe and its extensions in the forts of North America are always preferable to a surrounding wilderness identified with Indians. Richardson's narrator, however, adopts a more neutral stance in contrasting the Indian furnishings of Madeline De Haldimar's apartment at Fort Michilimackinac with European decor and simply notes that "nothing could be more unlike the embellishments of a modern European boudoir." Within the context of savagism and civilization, positive and negative values need not be assigned; instead, the emphasis falls on the existence of two distinct orders.

The separation of these orders in Richardson's perspective provides a key for understanding the transition of "civilized" Sir Reginald Morton into "savage" Wacousta. In the Scottish highlands, Morton meets and falls in love with Clara Beverley in a setting described in the language of conventional pastoral. On a bank, "formed of turf, covered with moss, and interspersed with roses and honey-suckles," Clara sits as "the divinity of the oasis." To Morton, she is a true "child of nature" in what he calls "the Eden of my love." Inevitably, when the innocent Clara is removed from this Edenic setting and exposed to the fallen world of the Scottish army camp, she falls prey (according to Wacousta) to the perfidy of De Haldimar and the world which he inhabits. When the conflict between Morton and De Haldimar resumes in North America, De Haldimar is still resident in an extension of the garrison he inhabited in Scotland. Morton, however, has become Wacousta, an "altered being" who resides in the camp of Pontiac, a setting which Richardson juxtaposes with the European retreat of Clara Beverley's father.

The difficulty of access to both settings is heavily emphasized. Wacousta describes at length his difficulty and athletic feats in crossing the crags and fissures that separated him from Clara's home. Similar difficulties are encountered by Frederick De Haldimar as he is led to Pontiac's camp: "At length they stood on the verge of a dark and precipitous ravine, the abrupt sides of which were studded with underwood so completely interwoven that all passage appeared impracticable." Both settings are frequently identified as oases, a word that does not occur in the novel out of this context: Pontiac's camp is "a sort of oasis of the forest, girt around with a rude belt of underwood," and Clara Beverley's home is "this garden—this paradise—this oasis of the rocks."

Clara Beverley's father creates a retreat from civilization which Richardson presents in the trappings of traditional pastoral. Pontiac's camp, also opposed to the civilized world of army and fort, is not idealized into pastoral but rather emerges within the context of savagism. In this camp, we find not pastoral "children of nature" but female inhabitants

> supporting in their laps the heavy heads of their unconscious helpmates, while they occupied themselves by the firelight in parting the long black matted hair and maintaining a destructive warfare against the pigmy inhabitants of that dark region.

Richardson clearly does not idealize Pontiac's camp into pastoral as he does Clara Beverley's oasis, but neither does he present the savage oasis as an inherently demonic world in simple contrast to that of the Scottish "goddess."

The figure who transforms the savages into a "legion of devils" and "fiend-like bands" is Wacousta. This man, so consumed by his desire for revenge that he crosses the barriers separating civilized and savage orders, becomes a larger than life Satanic figure, exploiting the worst instincts of the savage Indians. During the abortive battle following Pontiac's ruse of the lacrosse game as a means of entering the fort, Wacousta's face is painted black as death and as he stood under the arch of the gateway, with his white turbaned head towering far above those of his companions, this formidable and mysterious enemy might have been likened to the spirit of darkness presiding over his terrible legions.

In his maniacal hatred of the husband and family of the woman he loved, Reginald Morton rejects the world of civilization and becomes not just "a savage both in garb and character" but the chief of demonic savagism.

Pontiac, the historical chief of the Indians, assumes only a secondary role in *Wacousta.* Even the order in which Richardson presents the events of the Detroit attack weakens the dramatic impact of the Ottawa leader's role. The introduction to the novel tells us of the lacrosse ruse; we see its execution and failure; only then does Richardson provide a flashback to the Indian encampment where we hear Pontiac outlining the plan to his warriors. Such a sequence of events does little to focus our attention on Pontiac since his words present "old news." Even in this scene, Wacousta's response is the most significant element; reacting to Pontiac's plan,

> the warrior's swarthy countenance kindled into fierce and rapidly varying expressions. A thousand dark and complicated passions evidently struggled at his heart, and as he dwelt leisurely and emphatically on the sacrifice of human life that must inevitably attend the adoption of the proposed measure his eye grew larger, his chest expanded, nay, his very nostrils appeared to dilate with unfathomably guileful exultation. Captain De Haldimar thought he had never gazed on anything wearing the human shape half so atrociously savage.

Significantly, as soon as Wacousta is killed, Pontiac arranges for peace with the garrison. The malevolent savagism of Wacousta gives way to the benevolent savagism of the young Indian who slays him.

Even Richardson's "good savages" remain decisively separated from the civilized order. The young Amazon, Oucanasta, is saved from drowning by Captain Frederick De Haldimar, and although she falls in love with him, "she knew she was very foolish and that an Indian girl could never be the wife of a handsome chief of the Saganaw." Any possible marriage between Oucanasta and Frederick is unthinkable in the context which the novel establishes; such a union would join two disparate orders, the savage and the civilized.

Richardson's narrator does not simply ascribe negative values to the savage world and positive qualities to the representatives of civilization. Repeatedly he focuses on the duplicity, injustice and treachery of both European civilization and its new world extensions. What

he does insist on is the separation of the two worlds into separate orders and the measure of Wacousta's uniqueness and of his fall lies in his having transcended the barriers separating these orders.

One of the most interesting treatments of this separation between savages and civilized societies in Richardson's work occurs in the sixth chapter of *The Canadian Brothers.* Richardson places in conversation, General Brock, Commodore Barclay and Colonel D'Egville of the British forces in the War of 1812 and an American captive, Major Montgomerie. The chapter begins with dinner host D'Egville apologizing to the American commander for the inclusion of Tecumseh and three other chiefs at the table. To his relief the American ascribes his apparent distraction to other factors. Richardson's narrator maintains an objective stance in regard to this slighting of his Indian hero. After the departure of the Indians at the conclusion of dinner, conversation turns to two major questions: the British use of Indian forces against the Americans and the historical record of the British and the Americans in their treatment of the Indians.

The most surprising element in the treatment of these questions is the cold objectivity of Richardson's narrator. He presents both sides of the conversation, but in fashion uncharacteristic of Richardson's work, the narrator in no way directs the reader's response. Thus, Major Montgomerie argues the following positions either to the assent or polite qualification of his listeners:

> If instances have occurred wherein the sacredness of treaty has been violated, it has only been where the Indians have refused to part with their lands for the proffered consideration and when those lands have been absolutely indispensable to our agricultural purposes.

The factual errors in Montgomerie's argument are simply glossed over and he proceeds to further analysis:

> The uneducated negro is, from infancy and long custom, doomed to slavery, wherefore should the copper coloured Indian be more free? But my argument points not at their subjection. I would merely show that, incapable of benefitting by the advantages of the soil they inherit, they should learn to yield it with a good grace to those who can. Their wants are few, and interminable woods yet remain to them, in which their hunting pursuits may be indulged without a fear of interruption.

The inevitable submission of the individual perceived as savage to civilized man could not be presented more clearly. General Brock points out the swift disappearance of congenial landscapes for the Indian, but finally all concur in the quiet conclusion that the Indians of

North America will disappear, "gone, extirpated, until scarce a vestige of their existence remains."

Discussion of the treatment of the Indian by the United States and Britain leads to the conclusion that both nations have been guilty of treachery and duplicity. None of the participants, however, seems particularly concerned about these reflections on his nation's policy. When Commodore Barclay tries to state Tecumseh's case by cataloguing the injustices suffered by his people, Major Montgomerie grants his points and asserts that they in no way affect his own position which is simply to defend American policy in terms of "civilized" necessity and precedent set by British, French or Spanish governments. Even when General Brock attempts to defend Indian scalpings, the reader's involvement in his arguments is minimized by the awareness that all of this discussion is in some sense pseudo-argument, since each of the participants bears the same assumptions regarding the irreconcilability of civilization and savagism and the inevitable dominance of the former over the latter.

If any Indian could have altered Richardson's sharp distinctions between civilization and savagism, it would have been Tecumseh. Richardson's respect and admiration for the Shawnee chief is reiterated throughout much of his work. In *Eight Years in Canada,* he recalls fighting by the side of Tecumseh in the Battle of Moraviantown and remarks on the imposing physical appearance of the chieftain on that occasion:

> Not an hour before he fell, he had passed along our line in the elegant deer-skin frock, fringed, and ornamented with the stained quills of the porcupine, which he usually wore, and which, on this occasion, surmounted a shirt of snowy whiteness. In addition to this, he wore a plume of white ostrich feathers.

In *The Canadian Brothers,* Richardson returns to his treasured memories of Tecumseh shaking him by the hand before the start of this battle, and in his War of 1812 he reproduces the speech delivered by Tecumseh in which he opposed General Proctor's decision to retreat from Amherstburg and Detroit.

Tecumseh is consistently described in almost adulatory tones. The only successor to Pontiac as a leader capable of uniting a number of diverse Indian tribes, he is also presented by Richardson as Pontiac's superior. In *The Canadian Brothers* Tecumseh is "one of those daring spirits that appear like meteors, few and far between, in the horizon of glory and intelligence, . . . possessed of a genius as splendid in conception, as it was bold in execution." The qualities in Tecumseh's character that are most frequently acknowledged are the pervasiveness of his influence and the authority which he commands among the united tribes. Just as the eye of Pontiac controls the actions of his warriors

in *Wacousta,* Tecumseh in *The Canadian Brothers* supervises the movements of his followers.

Yet in spite of Richardson's obvious admiration for the Ottawa warrior, Tecumseh never emerges as anything other than the best of savages. Thus, he is assigned "a power of analyzing motives which has never been surpassed in savage life"; his death is seen as "the destruction of all that was noble and generous in savage life," and if he possesses some "civilized" virtues, immediate associations link him with the "savage qualities" of Tamburlaine or Genghis Khan.

Even in *Tecumseh or The Warrior of the West,* a narrative poem written "to rescue the name of a hero from oblivion," Tecumseh ultimately emerges as a savage rather than simply as a man. In the opening canto after a description of the victory of the Americans over the British in a naval battle at Amherstburg during the War of 1812, Richardson introduces Tecumseh with all the epithets of the heroic leader: "towering warrior," "godlike form," "monument of strength." Yet as Richardson sets the scene for the land battle at Amherstburg in the final canto, Tecumseh's Indians paint themselves "half white, half black," looking "like wild fiends, raging to devour," and Tecumseh emerges as the embodiment of satanic savagism:

> Amid that scene, like some dark towering fiend,
> With death-black eyes, and hand all spotted o'er,
> The fierce Tecumseh on his tall lance lean'd,
> Fir'd with much spoil, and drunk with human gore.

Despite Richardson's view that Tecumseh represented the hope of his people to sustain some kind of independent sovereignty and that his death marked the end of any hope of aboriginal survival in North America, his admiration for the Indian leader was consistently qualified by a perspective separating savage and civilized orders.

In the first paragraph of Richardson's *War of 1812,* he asserts that "much has been said and written in respect to the Red-men of the forest; but I do not recollect having ever met with a detail sufficiently accurate to convey a just idea of the character of these people." The crucial obstacle to Richardson's answering of this problem lies not in the absence of sufficient detail but rather in basic assumptions regarding savagism and civilization. In **"A Trip to Walpole Island and Port Sarnia,"** Richardson praises the "native dignity and simplicity" of the Indians of this area in contrast to "the loathsome hypocrisy of civilized life." He even asserts:

> If I could always see them as then presented to my observation, I could willingly pass the remainder of my days among them—a son of nature and subject only to nature's laws.

Emphasis must fall on the first word of this comment, for Richardson could dream of a return to primitive bliss, but his way of seeing the red man was insistently dichotomous in its separation of civilized and savage worlds.

An excerpt from *Wacousta* (1851):

It was during the midnight watch, late in September, 1763, that the English garrison of Detroit was thrown into the utmost consternation by the sudden and mysterious introduction of a stranger within its walls. The circumstance at this moment was particularly remarkable; for the period was so fearful and pregnant with events of danger, the fort being assailed on every side by a powerful and vindictive foe, that a caution and vigilance of no common kind were unceasingly exercised by the prudent governor for the safety of those committed to his charge. A long series of hostilities had been pursued by the North American Indians against the subjects of England, within the few years that had succeeded to the final subjection of the Canadas to her victorious arms: and many and sanguinary were the conflicts in which the devoted soldiery were made to succumb to the cunning and numbers of their savage enemies. In those lone regions, both officers and men, in their respective ranks, were, by a communionship of suffering, isolation, and peculiarity of duty, drawn towards each other with feelings of almost fraternal affection: and the fates of those who fell were lamented with sincerity of soul, and avenged, when opportunity offered, with a determination prompted equally by indignation and despair. This sentiment of union, existing even between men and officers of different corps, was, with occasional exceptions, of course doubly strengthened among those who fought under the same colors, and acknowledged the same head; and, as it often happened in Canada, during this interesting period, that a single regiment was distributed into two or three fortresses, each so far removed from the other that communication could with the utmost facility be cut off, the anxiety and uncertainty of these detachments became proportioned to the danger with which they knew themselves to be more immediately beset.

John Richardson, in Wacousta; or The Prophecy, *Robert M. De Witt Publisher, 1851.*

David Beasley (review date 1988)

SOURCE: "Rereading Richardson's *Wacousta*," *American Review of Canadian Studies,* Vol. XVIII, No. 3, Autumn, 1988, pp. 381-86.

[*In the following review of the 1987 edition of* Wacousta *edited by Douglas Cronk, Beasley comments on the publication history of* Wacousta *and suggests Richardson's sources of inspiration for the novel's chief characters.*]

In 1965, while I was researching my biography of Richardson, *The Canadian Don Quixote,* I found a first edition of *Wacousta* in an antiquarian bookstore in New York City for $17.50. It was a rare three volumes at a low price, but Richardson then was unknown. Now he is regarded as one of Canada's greatest writers, and *Wacousta,* his most popular novel, as the keystone to Canadian literature. Douglas Cronk, who edited this reissue of the first English edition, was quite right to choose it for rigorous textual analysis. Not only has he restored maturity to the text of the pirated American edition which flooded North America in the last century, he has returned the vigor and eloquence to Richardson's prose. He discovered that the 1832 English edition, when pirated by the American publisher, Adam Waldie, in 1833, was cut by 15,000 words. Americans of that age were just as apt to reshape a text to suit their image as they are today. American hegemony then was as threatening to British North America as it is today. Mr. Cronk has made a strong case that the American savaging of *Wacousta* in 1833 and its repetition in the many subsequent editions issued in America thenceforth into the twentieth century were willful misrepresentations. In his introduction to this edition, he describes some of the changes prompted by prudery and chauvinism such that "Wacousta was changed from a type of noble outlaw central to the romantic tradition into a sentimental and sensational villain of popular melodrama."

In the case of *Wacousta,* which is a fictional account of Chief Pontiac's siege of Fort Detroit in 1763 and the massacre of the inhabitants of Fort Michillimackinac, the history is common to both the United States and Canada. One can understand, though not forgive, the American publisher editing the text to change its political orientation—and successfully, because its sale in the United States was greater than in England. One also can understand Richardson, who, on returning to Canada after twenty-three years abroad, determined to make the 1832 edition available to his Canadian countrymen. (He complained that the American edition "suppressed certain forcible passages.") Unfortunately this "Canadian" edition sold badly, possibly because of poor distribution.

One, therefore, cannot readily understand Richardson when he consented to write an introduction to the American version published in 1851 by Dewitt and Davenport of New York after he left Canada for the United States. Did Richardson finally endorse the American edition by this action? (Unlike Mr. Cronk, he did not compare it word for word with the 1832 edition and seemed aware only that certain passages were excised.) Mr. Cronk suggests that Richardson was too much in need of money to resist, but this would have been contrary to Richardson's character. I believe he consented to the Americanization of the novel for Americans and to the cuts made to **The Canadian**

Brothers (the sequel to *Wacousta*) which Dewitt and Davenport issued as *Matilda Montgomerie* about the same time. The truth is that he had become exasperated with Canadians, removed to the publishing center of the United States, and devoted his time to writing, among other things, the American National Song. If Americans preferred their version of *Wacousta*, then let them have it, notwithstanding that the English edition was a better book.

My assumption made in *The Canadian Don Quixote* that Richardson had done the cutting for the 1851 edition came from Dewitt and Davenport's claims, such as that made in a notice in the *New York Daily Tribune* for September 28, 1850 informing the public that *Wacousta* was "In Press. . . . This work will be supervised and revised by the author." Possibly after he wrote the introduction to the novel on New Year's Day 1851 and began numbering the chapters at the former second chapter, his publishers paid him without realizing that he was giving them the old Waldie edition. He resented the small lump sum that he was paid as far below the value of the works he was selling them. Certainly they had no concerns about impolite language because they had just published his *The Monk Knight of St. John,* which was widely regarded as a pornographic novel. Moreover, Richardson did cut and change the text of *The Canadian Brothers;* a letter from him to the American critic, Rufus Griswold, at the time, makes it clear that he did the work. Could Richardson have been an early example of a Canadian victim to American commerce? (Could he have been an early harbinger of Canada's fate if the proposed Free Trade Bill, now pending before the Canadian Parliament, is ratified?) Or could he have adopted the aims and attitudes of his new country with enthusiasm?

The importance of the cutting, as Mr. Cronk pointed out with spirit in his M.A. thesis, but unfortunately not in his introduction to this edition, is its misleading of Canadian critics who have badly misrepresented the text in their essays on Canadian literature. Mr. Cronk came also to my conclusion, that *Wacousta* is an attempt at realism, or realistic representation of life, rather than a Gothic tale. But then these critics did not have the first edition available to them—indeed, some of them read a Canadian abridged edition of 1967 (New Canadian Library, No. 58), which edited out one-quarter of the text of the heavily edited Waldie edition.

Thanks to Mr. Cronk and the Centre for Editing Early Canadian Texts, we can now enjoy the original three volumes in one thick paperback volume with explanatory notes and other elucidatory material. They have elevated what had become a book for boys to its true stature of a masterpiece of literature. I want to lament, however, the lack of an introduction which elucidates the story—not the history, which can be found in the

works of Francis Parkman and Robert Rogers—but the authorial background.

First, the impression Mr. Cronk leaves that Richardson's maternal grandmother may not have been Indian must be corrected. There is no doubt that she was Indian. Clarence Burton, the antiquary, suggested that she might have been the slave, Mannette, whom Richardson's grandfather, John Askin, the furtrader, manumitted in 1766; recent articles on Richardson in biographical dictionaries (including my own) which abhor indefiniteness, have seized upon the name. Because her three children by Askin, including Richardson's mother, were born in Arbre Croche, the central Ottawa town, I think she was from the Ottawa tribe and that Mannette, a Panise, may have been *her* slave. The point is that Richardson's Indian heritage gave him sympathy and understanding for the Indian; it helps explain why he was the best delineator of the American Indian in fiction, and provides us with an insight into his fascination for his hero, the Scotsman who became Wacousta, the super-human savage adviser to Pontiac.

Richardson modeled Wacousta upon Colonel John Norton, or Chief Teyoninhokarawen of the Six Nations Indians as he was also called, whom Richardson knew well. Richardson used the name Sir Reginald Morton for Wacousta's English name. Richardson's wife's family through its history in Faversham, Kent was closely associated with the titled Norton family whose Christian names were John and Reginald. Hence, we have Richardson's inspiration for the English side to Wacousta's nature. Richardson's friend, John Norton, a tall, graceful and learned man who spoke European and Indian languages, was born in Scotland of a Scottish mother and Cherokee father. His father was rescued from a ravaged Cherokee town during the American Revolutionary War by an English officer raised in Scotland; he later joined the British Army as a private and was stationed with the 65th Regiment in Niagara. His mother was personal servant to the Commissary-General, Colonel Coffin. John Norton joined the other wing of the Regiment in Ireland as a private and came with it to Canada where he was reunited with his parents. There was a puritanical streak in John Norton which may have caused him to object to his mother's connection with Coffin. Whatever the reason, Coffin discharged him. He went to the Six Nations Indians and then to Detroit where he worked as a trader for John Askin. Joseph Brant, the Chief of the Six Nations, persuaded Norton to adopt Indian ways and trained him to become a Chief. Norton was a skillful and fearsome leader of the Indians in the War of 1812. His father, by the way, deserted the Regiment two years after Norton was discharged and, since he appears not to have been caught and shot, probably returned to the Cherokee country. We have here the ingredients for the Indian side of Sir Reginald Morton's nature and the motivation for his desire for revenge upon the Commander of the Fort, de Haldimar, for stealing away his sweetheart when they were sub-alterns in Scotland.

Could Richardson have imagined a sweetheart in the place of a mother? He adored his own mother, who died when he was a boy (in the novel she is the model for Madeline de Haldimar who is the fiancee of Frederick de Haldimar, son of the Commander), and he was just as shocked as the Askins when his father remarried shortly thereafter. Richardson regarded his father as a stern disciplinarian, like the Commander. In the novel, the formal relationship between Commander de Haldimar and his children was like that between Richardson's father and his children. De Haldimar's eldest son is named Frederick and represents a brave and civilizing force as he frustrates Pontiac's plans. Richardson, also the eldest son, preferred to be called "Frederick" by his friends. But these comparisons are made to reveal sources of inspiration, not to suggest hidden autobiographical meanings.

Richardson also could have seen Colonel Coffin in the role of the short-sighted and suspicious Commander who has Private Frank Halloway, alias Reginald Morton, nephew of Wacousta, shot for dereliction of duty. During the War of 1812 Colonel Coffin, as British General Sheaffe's aide-de-camp, presumed that John Norton and John Brant (Joseph's son) intended to kill the captured American, Winfield Scott, when they approached Scott who was dining with Sheaffe. Coffin held his pistol to Norton's head and called for assistance. The hatred between the two men was extraordinary and might have stemmed from their encounter over Norton's mother. Norton's killing of an Indian in a duel in 1823 for consorting with his young wife and his desertion of his wife and disappearance into the Cherokee country gave Richardson further insight into Wacousta's rejection of the woman and the novel's motive of revenge for a woman's love. Richardson leaves no doubt, however, that his sympathy lies with the fearsome and tormented Wacousta. As for the Commander, Richardson hated his type bitterly: "he was among the number of those (many of whom are indigenous to our soil even at the present day) who look down from a rank obtained, upon that which has just been quitted, with a contempt, and coldness, and consciousness of elevation commensurate only with respect paid to those still above them, and which it belongs only to the little-minded to indulge in."

Other incidents in the novel, such as the warning by a young squaw to the son of the Commander of the Fort about Pontiac's ruse to gain entrance and kill the inhabitants, and the deaths of two officers who set out from Detroit to warn Fort Michillimackinac of Pontiac's intentions, actually took place and are skillfully used by Richardson to create suspense.

The John Norton-Teyoninhokarawen connection helped me to identify the name "Wacousta" as the appellation given to Norton when he traded in the West Virginia and Pennsylvania country as agent for John Askin. That area, known as West Augusta, was called Wagousta. John Richardson, then about five years old and attending school in Detroit while living with his grandparents, heard the tall muscular Scot referred to as the man from Wagousta—which he remembered as "Wacousta." Later, Richardson, a young half-pay lieutenant in the British Army in London, sought Norton's help to secure an active posting. His memorandum to Norton, when the Chief was visiting London in 1815, is in the Ontario Archives. In 1833 after he sent the recently published **Wacousta** to Commodore Robert Barclay under whom his father had served as surgeon to the Royal Navy on Lake Erie in the War of 1812, Richardson suggested that Barclay would know well the person after whom the character of Wacousta was fashioned. (See Richardson's *Eight Years in Canada.*) Barclay guessed that it was Norton but his reply suggested that he was not as familiar with Norton's background as Richardson thought he was. The explanation for this misunderstanding was owing to Richardson confusing the Commodore with Norton's close friend, Robert Barclay of Dorking, Surrey, brewer and farmer. (See *The Journal of Major John Norton 1816*, edited by Carl F. Klinck and James J. Talman. Toronto: Champlain Society, 1970.) One of the major pastimes of the closely knit society of Upper Canada was gossip (as, indeed, it still is). Richardson would have heard references to Norton's friend, Robert Barclay, and assumed this was the famed, one-armed Admiral whom he was featuring in his new novel about the War of 1812, *The Canadian Brothers.* Professor Klinck's assertion that Richardson did not use Norton as a model for Wacousta can only mean that Norton's life story, from his viewpoint, did not seem to form the basis for Wacousta's story. But as I have suggested here, Norton's white-Indian background, his fiery spirit (Teyoninhokarawen was the "War Lord" title given to Norton as adviser to Chief Brant—in this sense, recall that Wacousta was War Lord adviser to Pontiac), and certain incidents in his life furnished Richardson's powerful imagination with the ingredients for the novel. As for the Sir Regional Morton part of the story set in Scotland, there is more to be developed from the history of the Norton-Drayson association in Faversham, Kent. (Drayson is the family name of Richardson's wife.)

The principal achievement of the novel for readers in the nineteenth century was Richardson's masterful portrayal of the Indian character. Critics at first were content to admit that he described Indians better than did James Fenimore Cooper, but by the early twentieth century Richardson's writing talents were considered superior to Cooper's. The difference between them, I think, is the deep look into the soul achieved by Richardson. Evil and goodness clash within the protagonists, appearing as set in the character of de Haldimar versus Wacousta on one level, but reversed at a lower level, and then, lower yet, reversed again. The reader sees into the unfathomable character of man through Richardson's portrayal of Wacousta alias Sir Reginald Morton. The two sides of his nature, European and Indian, form an uneasy peace which could erupt into savage warfare at any moment. Wacousta's volatile nature reflects the conflict between the Europeans in the fort and the Indian nations preparing to massacre them.

This reflection of the story of the novel in the character of the main protagonist, emphasizing one by the other, contributes to its depth of feeling and insight. The Indian whom the European understands only as an unreasoning killer, suddenly, in the character of Wacousta, takes on the reasoning power of the European and becomes formidable. But the passionate desire for revenge of Wacousta for a personal grievance is made to seem petty by contrast to the aims of Pontiac. Pontiac respects the forebearance of de Haldimar when the Commander allows the Chiefs to leave the Fort unharmed after the disclosure of Pontiac's plot. The Indians, motivated by distrust of the English, are prepared to admit that they have been wrong. They are capable of making peace. Wacousta, on the other hand, must destroy his protagonist utterly. In this sense Wacousta could be said to understand his European enemy better than does the Indian. This is because Wacousta, as Reginald Morton, experienced the sly treachery of de Haldimar, who, while pretending to be his friend, stole away the love of his life.

In the same manner, the invading European, pretending to be the friend of the Indian, steals away his land with property claims and legal deeds which are incomprehensible to the Indian nations. Wacousta succeeds in killing de Haldimar's children and brings mortal sorrow to de Haldimar whereas the Indians are persuaded that they were misled about the intentions of the English. Wacousta's European background makes him an implacable opponent because he knows the cold and ruthless cupidity he is confronting, whereas Pontiac has native nobility and is prepared to trust his adversary. De Haldimar seems to symbolize what Richardson saw as the worst in man: the snob who looks down on the ranks from which he has just been elevated, the stickler for rules for their own sake, the coveter of another man's happiness which he secures as his private property—in short, the rising bourgeoisie. Wacousta, the man of great emotion and physical prowess, is a force of nature which, although tragic, is more human.

It is this human side of the Indian which may have attracted an American readership to the novel. Some Americans felt guilty about the forcible removal of the Cherokees from their lands in Georgia by a long march known as the Vale of Tears just prior to the novel's appearance. Americans adapted the novel to the stage immediately, and it replaced *Metamora,* a play about the tragedy of an Indian Chief, in popularity. The character most appreciated in the play, however, was Oucanasta, the Indian girl who loved the son of the Commander and warned him of Pontiac's plot. She was a good Indian. Wacousta, although opposed to the forces of good, won audiences' sympathies because he was given a motivation that could be understood. He was all too human. Poor Wacousta, and, by extension, poor Indians! It would have been quite impossible for the American of that day to have understood the Indian in his own terms as we are able to do today owing to the writings of anthropologists and ethnologists over the past century. Richardson, however, understood, and it is in this unexpurgated first edition just restored to us in which we see the true nature of the Indian through his art.

The savage personality of Wacousta was new in European fiction (where Chateaubriand's Rene and Atala depicted the noble savage), although his romantic origin may be traced back to Milton's Satan, as I did in *The Canadian Don Quixote.* It needed the wilderness setting of America and the combination of the complexity of emotion of the European and the uninhibited emotion of the Indian to create him. Nevertheless, the novel is European in approach largely owing to its romantic associations in the theme of love, but it initiates a characterization and atmosphere that are American. Richardson's sequel, ***The Canadian Brothers,*** continued the American character of his writing which culminated in ***Hardscrabble*** and ***Wau-nan-gee,*** forerunners of the American Western Novel.

Wacousta's importance as literature should be seen in relation to this striving for realism which Richardson stated as his intention in his two earlier novels of Parisian social life. He was one of a new school of English poets and writers who disdained the slick romances and implausible adventure stories which were the order of the day. His novel, ***Ecarté,*** about gambling life, money lenders and debtor's prison in Restoration Paris was attacked by an establishment critic as "unfit for the stews. . . ." (For a quotation of the review by William Jordan in the *Literary Gazette,* see *The Canadian Don Quixote*) ***Wacousta,*** however, brought the Canadian wilderness and savagery convincingly to life and thus reinforced the impressions of the English about America and dumbfounded Richardson's critics. Mr. Cronk reveals that Adam Waldie weakened the verisimilitude of the novel with his editing of the American edition. This may have helped keep Richardson in the shadow of Fenimore Cooper. With this reissue of the original edition Richardson should step into the light as a great artist in his own right.

Michael Hurley (essay date 1991)

SOURCE: "Double Entendre: Rebel Angels & Beautiful Losers in John Richardson's *The Monk Knight of St. John*," *Canadian Literature,* No. 128, Spring, 1991, pp. 107-17.

[*In the essay below, Hurley offers a reappraisal of Richardson's* The Monk Knight of St. John, *focusing on themes of identity, passion, and religion. He also illustrates the novel's parallels with other Gothic and Romantic works.*]

Variously described as lurid, sensational, grotesque, and bizarre, John Richardson's complex and intriguing novel ***The Monk Knight of St. John. A Tale of The Crusades*** (1850) was the *Beautiful Losers* of its day. Response to the work evokes comparison with the reception of novels like Cohen's, Grove's *Settlers of the Marsh,* Symons' *Place d'Armes,* Davies' *The Rebel Angels,* or Engel's *Bear* (at the end of which, we recall, the female narrator who has just reclaimed her body and her sexuality enthusiastically praises Richardson and *Wacousta*). Modern commentary on the black sheep of Richardson's *oeuvre* is still divided. It seems to me that a reappraisal is required, one that sets the novel within a literary context rather than one established exclusively by the particular social or sexual reality inhabited by the critic.

"The St. Simonist objective of equal rights for women," which Richardson unlike many of his contemporaries (male, certainly) subscribed to, is germane to our reading of Richardson's most censured text. Though by no means overcoming the stereotypical literary view of women, *The Monk Knight* vehemently protests the subordinate position of women in the repressive, male-dominated society of the West: "As it is, what are women? Slaves, literally the slaves of men, and regarded principally because they are necessary to their own selfish ends," protests one character. The double standard of a sexist culture is satirized, and the narrator recommends "more liberality on the part of him who arrogantly, but falsely, deems himself the first of creation. . . ." The novel's early readers may have taken offence at such views and how they are woven into a chillingly prophetic vision of an insectoid consumer society devouring its own citizens and growing "arrogant by the humiliating sale of the most petty articles necessary to human existence."

Writing in 1952, Desmond Pacey indignantly attacks both book and author. "Every kind of sexual aberration is displayed," he protests, without "the clinical seriousness . . . which might make it palatable" and "which makes one suspect that Richardson's brain was affected when he wrote the book." Far from convinced of the virulence of Richardson's writing or of any prurient interest, Richardson's biographer David Beasley exonerates the author and lavishly praises the controversial text.

> It dealt with sexual love in a frank manner that, as Richardson must have known, was sacrilegious in his Victorian age. It was not pornographic; on the contrary, it was revolutionary . . . Under the guise of Gothic romance, [it] represented a sexual emancipation that . . . could only be accepted after the 'sexual revolution' of the 1960's.

There is, indeed, much in this strange work which is deliberately grotesque and provocative. Richardson's imagination here is at its most garish but, as critics aver with regard to *Wacousta,* that imagination is by no means undisciplined. One tentative step in the direction of a reappraisal may be taken by citing Frye's distinction between the pornographic and the erotic in *The Secular Scripture:* "The fact that sex and violence emerge whenever they get a chance does mean that sexuality and violence are central to romance." Romance, in particular, he informs both us and "the guardians of taste and learning,"

> is, we say, "sensational": it likes violent stimulus, and the sources of that stimulus soon become clear to the shuddering censor. The central element of romance is a love story, and the exciting adventures are normally a foreplay leading up to sexual union. Hence romance appears to be designed mainly to encourage irregular or excessive sexual activity . . . Most denunciations of popular romance . . . assume that the pornographic and the erotic are the same thing: this overlooks the important principle that it

is the function of pornography to stun and numb the reader, and the function of erotic writing to wake him up.

A *tour de force* of Gothic and Romantic Macabre, when placed beside other works in this genre, **The Monk Knight** can be seen adhering to certain established conventions and flourishing similar shock tactics. Mario Praz's *The Romantic Agony,* a study of Romantic literature under one of its characteristic aspects, that of erotic sensibility, affords a context within which to view Richardson's work. Written around the same time as *Wuthering Heights,* **The Monk Knight** reveals a similar

> Romantic tendency to invent and delight in monsters, the *exaltation du moi,* which has been said to be the secret of the whole Romantic revolt against classical models and restraints; the love of violence in speech and action, the preference for the hideous in character and the abnormal in situation—of all these there are abundant examples in *Wuthering Heights.*

Many elements in **The Monk Knight** recall Richardson's other fiction, in particular **Wacousta.** Mirror and twin themes again branch out into various *doppelganger* formulas, giving rise to an eerie sense of reduplication. There are sacred pledges between friends, psychological metamorphoses, a descent into a cruel night world and the familiar Romantic motif of the demon-lover and vampirism. A Beddoes-like melodramatic tendency shows itself in the creation not of individual but of romantic and stylized characters which expand into psychological archetypes. Dennis Duffy calls our attention to another lament for "a lost emotional and sexual paradise"; "even when he penned a pornographic romance about the Crusades," remarks Duffy, "he displayed an almost Spenserian power to describe erotic, violent encounters within carefully evoked settings that complement the actions and freeze them into a series of tableaux. As in **Wacousta** and **The Canadian Brothers,** there is also a collision of diametrically opposed cultures. Set, like Scott's *The Talisman,* in the eleventh century in the time of the Crusades, the borderlands of Jerusalem separate the antagonistic world of European and Turk, the forces of Christ and the Cross and Mohammed and the Crescent. West and East are fused in a number of doubles and love triangles. The paradigmatic triangle is composed of the dark-skinned Moor, the Monk Knight Abdallah, Alfred the French Baron de Boiscourt and his beautiful wife Ernestina, the Baroness. These larger-than-life figures merge into one another; they belong to the realm of dream (a recurrent word in the last section of the romance) and of myth or legend.

Indeed, we are presented with a story-within-a-story. Wandering the French countryside in 1837, the narrator searches for "an old chateau, connected with which was some wild traditionary tale." He passes the night in the bedroom of the first Baron de Boiscourt perusing a strange manuscript found, not in a copper cylinder, but in a tin case secreted in the leg of the three life-sized statues in the room. The old parchment from the eleventh century tells the history of the three people whose likenesses are to be found in the statutes beside the bed, that "group of three figures—tall as life, beautifully carved, in high relief, and, with clasped hands, grouped round a figure of Cupid, bearing a torch in his right hand." The first words of the scroll offer advice to the reader: "Whoever may condemn, while reading these pages, knows not his own heart. . . . What I have done I repent not of. Be wise also, and make no evil where none exists."

The story of the "mystic triunion" therein related is indebted to Rousseau's *The Confessions* and represents a further development of other such love triangles in Richardson. Beasley even goes so far as to argue that the Baron represents "an idealization of Shelley" while the Monk Knight is "an idealization of the dark and noble warrior about which Byron wrote and with whom he later became identified." As in all romance, the unwieldy plot involving disguise, mystery, surprise, and violence defies easy summary. At the risk of oversimplification and of rending the intricate web of complex interrelationships, some attempt at conveying the basic patterns informing **The Monk Knight** can be made. As in **Wacousta,** there is a central *doppelganger* relationship. The Baron and the Monk Knight are doubles-by-division. The former is a young and impetuous French nobleman; light-hearted and animated, he is a jovial man and even his horse "looks as if a dancing Bacchus were in his veins." "That cold, stern monk" of Herculean build, on the other hand, is older than his companion, calmer and intellectual. He has taken vows of chastity and is engaged in "constant and unflinching war against the flesh." Again, opposition is true friendship; just as Sir Reginald Morton's wild spirit is soothed by the bland amenity of Colonel de Haldimar's manners in **Wacousta,** the Baron's instinctual nature is moderated by the sober Monk's sense of strict duty and religious dedication. At opposite poles of sensuality and asceticism, respectively, they balance each other in an extreme way, and indeed, blend into one another.

Regarding his friend "as something more than human," the Baron declares that "my soul yearns to you, as though you were the first-born of my mother's womb." Out of his love for his "brother," the Baron gets the Monk to promise to wed his beloved wife who has remained in France, should he fall in battle; he overcomes the inhibitions of the chaste Christian ascetic by inflaming his imagination with the glowing ideal of a "superhuman loveliness" as embodied in the "chastely voluptuous" Lady Ernestina. The Baron's imagination also envisions an ideal in which "soul entwines with soul in mystic bonds." His self-sacrificing nature is clarified in the narrator's allusion to the author of *The Confessions* and *The Social Contract*:

> What Rousseau has been since, his noble countryman, de Boiscourt, then was: but more frank, more ardent, more generous, more liberal and self-immolating where the happiness of those he loved required the more than human sacrifice of self. And yet, with him it was no sacrifice to have abstained from the tri-union of hearts it had become [his] chief duty . . . to promote.

When it appears that the Baron has, indeed, perished in the battle to preserve Jerusalem from the Moslems, the Monk Knight decides to journey to France to wed the Baroness. But even before the trip has begun, it is apparent that he has become another of Richardson's "altered" characters. The pious Christian monk who was wont "to impose the most severe self-denial upon his feelings" renounces the monastic life of prudence and propriety. He has undergone a "wondrous change" in the arms of the beautiful "Pagan" Zuleima, "an unblessed heretic and unbeliever." (Zuleima's name conjures up that of Zulietta in *The Confessions* and Zuleika in Byron's "The Bride of Abydos: A Turkish Tale," the latter work also featuring a character called Abdallah.) Revelling for the first time in "all the wildness of reciprocated passion," Mars succumbs to Venus in a Rousseauistic swoon:

> What God-created charms! . . . It was the triumph of nature over art—of truth over falsehood—of a hallowed and divine sentiment, over the cold and abstract conventionalisms of a world which, childlike, forges its own chains, fetters its own limbs, and glories in the display of its own bondage.

The Houri-like Zuleima is one of the wives of Saladin, the Moslem chieftain who is a mirror-reflection of the Baron. She is a catalyst in effecting his transformation from a woman-hating Christian renunciate into a passionate lover and "a renegade from the purity of the Church." Again, opposites run into one another: just as the Baron is now regarded as a saint and a martyr, the Monk Knight seems to assume his friend's impassioned nature. Freed from the mind-forg'd manacles of conventional Christianity, the Monk Knight "rejoiced that God has blessed him by emancipating his mind from bondage." Zuleima and the Monk Knight resemble one another: both are Moors and orphans, the latter as a child compelled by his Christian captors to forsake the Moslem faith. His Moslem identity as "Abdallah," long repressed, is once again in the ascendant.

Abdallah's fiery spirit can no more be contained within orthodox Christian bounds than that of MacLennan's titanic Jerome Martell, another "oddly pure sensualist" involved in an analogous love triangle who

also had been orphaned and brought up by Christians. It is as if Leonard Cohen's Saint Catherine were to shed her Christian identity and become the Mohawk "Kateri" again, a metamorphosis that does, indeed, occur in the mind of the composite figure around which the last section of *Beautiful Losers* revolves. Denying the body and torturing the flesh for the sake of salvation gives way in Abdallah to a recognition—conveyed in similarly heightened language to that in Cohen—of sexual energy as itself a sacrament.

Zuleima and the Monk Knight are complementary personalities. Yet their relationship can no longer be constituted on a sexual basis, each finding in the other the spiritual brother or sister that each has fervently longed for. As the Baroness later states to Zuleima, "you are a part of himself." That forbidden incestuous flavour to their love so dear to Romantics like Byron and Shelley also adds spice to the "mother and son" relationship between Zuleima and Rudolph. The latter, the page of the Baron and now the close friend and more-than-brother of the Monk, is "a beautiful and blooming boy, fair as the Narcissus of old." As in *Wacousta* and *The Canadian Brothers,* the Narcissus archtype structures these incredibly entangled interrelationships which make those in earlier works seem straightforward by comparison. Here, too, the dynamics of the "break-boundary process" (points of reversal where opposites merge, paradoxical inversions of identity) can be seen working themselves out in East-West terms: once across the line dividing Crusader from Mussulman, Rudolph "must . . . transform [himself] from a Christian page into a Saracen" even as the once captive Zuleima was disguised as a Christian page in the Baron's camp. Once again, opposites coincide, and love triangles embody the interface of two worlds.

The eastern woman, in turn, mirrors the French woman whom the Monk Knight is to marry. Zuleima is inclined to "wish I were that woman of the West—she taking my likeness and I transformed to hers." When she and Ernestina finally meet, they respond to each other as sisters; their relationship does not possess the quasi-lesbian aspects characterizing that of Ernestina and her attendant Henrietta. Both Zuleima and Ernestina take the Baron and the Monk Knight as lovers at different times in the story, Zuleima asserting that it was the Baron "who first taught her the value of herself."

Zuleima is a female version of *Wacousta*'s Narcissus-like Sir Reginald Morton/Wacousta. "I created to myself an image," she tells the Monk Knight, "a beau ideal, which I invested with every attribute of excellence, and to which, had it been possible to endow it with vitality, I should have surrendered myself body and soul." "Reality could afford no such joy to her as did the ripe paintings of her own glowing imagination" until she encountered the Baron who "realized her soul's identity." Her brief relationship with "the ideal Christian knight, whom I had invested with superhuman beauty," fulfills her "picture of intensely reciprocated passion," of a fusion of sensuality and spirituality.

Like the Byronic Morton/Wacousta, Zuleima is an impulsive idealist who champions the imagination and the rapture that passion can trigger. To do so is to defy "dogmatic authority" and "the fiat of society and the church." Murder, rape, incest, "blasphemy, and foul slander, were the only crimes she admitted against God; all the others were of human invention." Her pupil, the Monk Knight, learns to redefine the lawful and the criminal; having reclaimed the body and its energies, he realizes that "Nature recoils not from the passion," the "desire . . . which, in fact, is a divine mystery without a name." "Gifted with great but unobtrusive strength of mind, scorning those prejudices which equally influenced the conquerors and the conquered, and had moistened the land with their mutual blood," Zuleima recalls Poe's Ligeia who is similarly endowed with strong intellectual powers and an Eastern voluptuousness.

Zuleima celebrates sexual ecstasy which is "mutually shared"; "mutual" is a recurrent word in the text eliciting a whole series of associations. Zuleima glorifies Allah who

> had bestowed upon them a part of His own
> divinity—delegated to them the
> incomprehensible power to create
> themselves, and by means of such
> transporting joy, as in His great wisdom,
> he hallowed with the mystery of his own
> all-glorious Godhead.

That a female character in the fiction of the 1850's should harbour such notions of "a dionysiac ontology"—Dennis Lee's phrase for a similar philosophy he identifies in *Beautiful Losers*—violated that sense of propriety and decorum that distinguished a large portion of the Victorian readership. It is not surprising that there was no review, no word of the scurrilous text or the perfervid imagination that gave birth to it in the various literary magazines of the day.

Zuleima's Allah, a God of Love for whom sexual passion is not a sin but a sacrament, a means of transcendence, stands in contrast to the perverted conception of God entertained by the sanctimonious and spiritually moribund Crusaders for Christ. "A Juggernaut, at whose bloody shrine whole hecatombs of human victims were to be sacrificed," He is worshipped in fear by those whose creed seems to enjoin the sacrifice of others rather than that "total sacrifice of self" which characterizes the Rousseauistic Baron or that standing

outside the self engendered by ecstasy. In Lee's terminology, a dionysiac ontology is opposed to "the ontology of savage fields"; the former envisions a world of original identity or unified being where "God is alive. Magic is afoot," and "sexual ecstasy and the dislocation of rationality give entry to it."

In *The Monk Knight,* religion when abused becomes a horrible and ghastly perversion, a kind of death force. The narrator no less than Zuleima, whom he regards as an avatar of a future race of superhuman beings to be ushered in by the millennium, is aghast at "that creed which the armed masses of Christendom went forth to propagate with fire and sword." "Those Christian people, who were so anxious, like the churchmen of the present day, to teach what they do so indifferently practice" are distinguished by

> Superstition, under the name of piety—
> fanaticism, under the garb of religion—
> fire, sword, pillage, hatred,
> uncharitableness, revolting lust,
> brutality—all the horrid passions that
> ever lowered man to the condition of the
> brute. . . . What a creed! What a conception
> *they* must have had of the Deity who could
> thus have been propitiated.

This is the God of established Christianity condemned in Callaghan's *Such Is My Beloved,* Cohen's *Beautiful Losers,* MacLennan's *Each Man's Son* and *The Watch That Ends the Night,* Symons' *Place d'Armes,* Wiebe's *The Temptations of Big Bear,* Davies' *Fifth Business,* and in works by other Southern Ontario writers like Gibson and Reaney who protest the Calvinist-Methodist hatred of the body, the instincts, and the natural world.

Thus tutored by the pagan Zuleima and the dionysian Baron, the Monk Knight arrives in Auverge, France, on the wedding anniversary of the Baron and the Baroness. Disguised as an alleged friend of the Baron's, the Monk Gonzalles—"in Palestine we have passed as twins"—he proclaims to Ernestina that the Monk Knight is dead, that the Baron is alive and that "you will think this night, even in your husband's arms, that Gonzales in the semblance of Abdallah will possess you." Discovering the "real" identity of the Monk Knight, she falls madly in love with this "superhuman" being whom she identifies as the Baron's "second self," and they marry. The Baron himself had encouraged her to see the Monk as "the god of her mind's creation." As is the Baron for Zuleima, the "saint-like" Monk Knight with his "Christ-like countenance"—blasphemy of blasphemies!—is for the Baroness that "phantom, which imagination moulded into such life and strength, and beauty, that my sick soul languished for the embodiment." He is at once an erotic and a spiritual ideal.

"No longer the wife of a mortal," the Lady Ernestina lives with the Monk Knight as goddess and god or the prelapsarian Eve and Adam. For them, "passion is . . . not the gross sensuality which priests pronounce it to be, but a divine emanation from the God who created woman . . . the last and most perfect of his creatures." Woman, the body, passion and ecstasy are redeemed from the curse of the church. Here as in Blake, Byron, Shelley and many contemporary Canadian writers, "the priest lays his curse on the fairest joys" and denies that "the nakedness of woman is the work of God" and not the Devil. Ernestina's is "not the cold hackneyed seemingness of the wanton" and "not the dissembling virtue of the cold and prudent wife, which inspires disgust on the one hand, and on the other chills passion in its bud."

While Richardson's "rebel angels" may disregard convention in private, they possess a very Canadian reluctance to openly defy the laws of the land or to overthrow such venerable institutions as marriage. However critical of the church and its self-serving brand of Christianity, they still seek its blessings and prefer to live within a social framework. The major characters are socially conscious: at the head of society in Auverge, "they were not indifferent" to its demands and felt "the necessity for sacrificing something to appearances, in a world made up of appearances and falsehood alone." Like Richardson's Canadian characters, despite the pull of a sometimes fierce and romantic individualism, they accept the compromises of the world and their participation in it. When, through the sheer intensity of their all-absorbing love, the Monk Knight and Ernestina forego the claims of the social dimension of their identity in a world which is all relationship, they court a tragic fate.

In their "transcendant passion," the Baroness and the Monk Knight strive to merge into one another totally. "I would be a part of yourself, identified, infused into the holy father of my child" exclaims Ernestina in a wicked pun, "and because I cannot reach this keen acme of my happiness, that happiness is incomplete." This romantic quest to abrogate the borders between themselves is an ambiguous, double-edged affair. Like Byron's Lara who both soars above and sinks beneath the common man, Richardson's saintly lovers ironically hook twice the darkness when they try to catch twice the romantic glory of love and passion. "The tumult of those heaven-bestowed raptures which blended them into one mystic identity" is also beginning to consume them. "My love for you is destroying me!" wails the titanic Monk Knight. His lineaments as a Manfred or a Fatal Lover who destroys himself and the woman he loves to madness are disclosed in Ernestina's description of him as "the more than man who is slowly killing me with his intensity," a very Cohenesque intensity.

Eventually, the Baron, who has died in battle, attempts to reclaim his wife. Though a bizarre situation, it is one that is repeated in *The Watch That Ends the Night.* In MacLennan's novel, Jerome, who "had returned from the dead," finds his sensuous and angelic wife married to the man whom he has asked to look after her when he is gone: his double, the once celibate George Stewart who at one point feels that Jerome "seemed to be inside me, *to be me* . . ." "'I had hoped to make love to you' he said simply, 'and now you're married to George.'" Like Jerome, the Baron has wished for death but is fated to live, just as Catherine and Ernestina are fated to die.

The Baron is rebuffed by his former friend and his former wife. Ernestina avers that her guiding principle is "constancy" or "fidelity," familiar Richardsonian watchwords. Desperately in love with his better half, he proposes a *menage à trois* or what he terms, appropriately enough, a "double marriage." The couple recoil in shock and dismiss him. With "the seal of our strong friendship . . . broken—the tie . . . snapped asunder," the relationship between the Monk Knight and the Baron now degenerates into that struggle-of-brothers conflict which is prominent throughout Richardson's canon. Banished to the forest, the once noble Baron undergoes one of those "sudden and unaccountable changes in the human mind" which also characterizes tragic figures like Wacousta and Gerald Grantham, the protagonist of *The Canadian Brothers.* Here is that fascination for a "hairspring balance at the very edge of breakdown" that Lee notes again and again in Ondaatje's writing.

The Baron feels betrayed, robbed of his spiritual treasure. Separation from his spiritual likeness or feminine self is intolerable. As in *Wacousta* or Byron's "Manfred," it is the root of a crime of vengeance, wounded pride, and despair. The revengeful Baron succumbs to a cruel viciousness. Like a true Gothic tyrant, he imprisons the lovers in a labyrinthine underground cavern below the chateau. As in *Wacousta* and its sequel, we find descent imagery belonging to the night world of romance as described in Frye's *The Secular Scripture.* These grotesque passages with their strong sado-masochistic colouring suggest the influence of Byron's "The Giaour: A Fragment of a Turkish Tale" and of Poe's tales of horror, especially "Ligeia." Intertextual echoes abound. A parallel scene later in the story involving a grisly live burial complicated by cannibalism is taken almost verbatim from one of the most famous of Gothic novels by an exemplar of the *Schauer-Romantik* or Chamber-of-Horrors School, Maturin's *Melmoth the Wanderer.* Critics have commented on a similar use of a sense of brooding evil and of the details of physical horror to highlight an erotic theme in *Beautiful Losers* and poems like "Lovers" which typify the "decadent" aspects of Cohen's romanticism.

In another sudden reversal "renewing the broken bond of love and friendship," the Baron, the Baroness and the Monk Knight ascend out of "these subterranean tombs," mysteriously reconciled to one another. The Baron and the Baroness remarry. The Monk Knight disappears, only to return again as the Monk Gonzales, having grown darker even as Wacousta grows taller. Since he has become Ernestina's confessor, the expression of his overwhelming love no longer has a physical component. It is at this point when there is a synthesis of opposing attitudes or forces and the three figures are balanced within a larger, integrated psychological entity, that the life-size ebony carving is made that the narrator comes upon centuries later. An essential but elusive equilibrium is momentarily attained; the equally matched opposites are held together in a fruitful rather than a destructive tension. It is a unique moment in Richardson, but only a moment.

The Monk Knight's and Ernestina's excessive passion for identification, though reconstituted on a higher level, has become so intense that it tilts the balance and threatens to destroy them both. In one of the paradoxes of apocalyptic romanticism, the thirst for the infinite that is the source of their vitality also leads to death. Of course, for them at least, death holds no threat but only the assurance of a final complete merging, of "visions of future love and existence" beyond the grave. "The utter surrender as it were, of the identity of each to the other" has passed beyond all human bounds. As with *Wacousta,* Reaney's Donnelly Trilogy, *The Watch That Ends the Night,* and novels by Ondaatje, Kroetsch, and Findley, readers are confronted not only with a paradoxical blurring of identity but also with the problematical status of that natural energy which is embodied in the reckless vitality and violence of disturbingly ambiguous figures. Again, the terms appropriate to Richardson are not those of good and evil but the more ambiguous ones of order and energy.

In this work *à la Beddoes,* in which the forces of life and death interpenetrate and are often surprisingly confused, sex no less than religious teaching is both an instrument of life and death. Lee stresses a similar point in *Beautiful Losers:* "Traditional asceticism and the cult of ecstatic sex are alike in the sinister appetites they release. . . . Opposites coincide." Excess in love as in violence proves as dangerous and destructive as it does in *The Canadian Brothers* with the Canadian garrison officer Gerald Grantham and the American *femme fatale* Matilda Montgomery. They ignore community and seek an intense awareness of self outside the bounds of quotidian reality; their fate suggests that whatever the egotistical assertion achieves, it is an ambiguous triumph. The drive to freedom is also a quest for death: "The raptures they tasted were not of earth. . . . Their depth and fulness had nothing human in them. They would have grown into each other if they could." Abdallah and Ernestina embody the world of violent personal passions, of the exultant self. Like Gina Bixby and Jethroe Chone, Callaghan's criminal saints or saintly outlaws in *Close to the Sun Again,* the Monk Knight and the Baroness are lovers knowing only the law of their own love; the terrible excess of their passion, the terrible beauty in the excess, suggests a dual sense that human beings are both incredibly depraved and incredibly precious.

The further contortions and writhings of the plot of *The Monk Knight* are too complex to faithfully summarize here. Such are a *few* of the instances of overlapping identity. There seems to be no end to the text's "Chinese puzzle-box" scenes and characters which rival those in many Canadian postmodern works. As in *Wacousta* and *The Canadian Brothers,* Richardson's intent seems to be to connect everyone with everyone else. Identity loses its significance as individuation. Defying closure, the entire dream-like cycle appears on the verge of beginning over again in the final chapters. The controversial nature of "such balancing monsters of love" (*Beautiful Losers*) as we find in Cohen, Davies, and Richardson's saints illustrates John Moss's contention in *Sex and Violence in the Canadian Novel* that saintliness in our literature arises from some amazing sources, ones that are often considered strange or perverse.

Donald Stephens (essay date 1992)

SOURCE: An introduction to *The Canadian Brothers; or, The Prophecy Fulfilled. A Tale of the Late American War,* by John Richardson, edited by Donald Stephens, Carleton University Press, 1992, pp. xvii-lxxxii.

[*In the following excerpt, Stephens surveys Richardson's career and discusses the themes, sources, and publication history of* The Canadian Brothers.]

Early in 1840 the publishing firm of A. H. Armour and H. Ramsay of Montreal issued *The Canadian Brothers; Or, The Prophecy Fulfilled. A Tale Of The Late American War.* Printed by John Lovell of Montreal, this two-volume novel was the work of John Richardson (1796-1852), or, as he was described on the titlepage, "Major Richardson, Knight Of The Military Order Of Saint Ferdinand, Author Of *Ecarté, Wacousta,* &c. &c." With its title deliberately echoing that of *Wacousta; Or, The Prophecy: A Tale of the Canadas, The Canadian Brothers* was, in fact, a sequel to this three-volume novel that Thomas Cadell of London and William Blackwood of Edinburgh had first published in 1832. *The Canadian Brothers,* however, was not just a suitably horrific completion to the story of vengeance and hate begun in *Wacousta.* It was also, and more importantly, a fictionalized chronicle of actual events, people, and places from Richardson's child-

A 1901 photograph of the ruins of the north embankment of Fort Amherstburg.

hood and adolescence that both revealed the psychology of the author and helped create seminal mythologies about his country.

John Richardson was born on 4 October 1796 on the Niagara frontier, probably in Queenston, Upper Canada (Ontario), where his mother, Madelaine Askin Richardson, was likely staying with an older sister. His father, Robert Richardson, was a surgeon with the Queen's Rangers stationed at Fort George in nearby Newark (Niagara-on-the-Lake). Richardson spent the early years of his life in Newark, Fort Erie, and York (Toronto). In 1801-02, when his father was stationed at St. Joseph's Island in northern Lake Huron, Richardson went to live in Detroit, Michigan. He stayed with his maternal grandfather, John Askin, the well-known fur trader and merchant, and his wife, the former Marie-Archange Barthe, whom he had married in 1772, probably after the death of the Indian woman who was Madelaine Richardson's mother. In 1802 Richardson accompanied the Askins when they moved across the

Detroit River to live near Sandwich (Windsor) on the Canadian side of the border.

When in the same year Robert Richardson was appointed surgeon to the garrison at Fort Amherstburg (or Malden), Richardson joined his parents, a sister, and two brothers, one of them Robert (b. 1798), in Amherstburg, the village that was developing around the fort and the nearby naval yard. With his connections to the military Richardson obviously followed the life of the garrison with great interest. One also suspects that he made frequent excursions south of Amherstburg along the east bank of the Detroit River to the farms of Matthew Elliott and Simon Girty, both of whom were employed during these years in the British Indian Department. Especially from Matthew Elliott's place, it would have been a short crossing from the mainland to Bois Blanc (Boblo) Island, where the Indian tribes of the northwest who were loyal to the British camped when they came to receive their annual supplies from the Indian Department. Richardson also went to school until June 1812, when the United States declared war on Great Britain.

Recalling these years in his autobiographical memoir, *Eight Years In Canada* (1847), Richardson wrote:

> My . . . boyhood, up to the moment, when at fifteen years of age, I became a soldier, had been passed in a small town (Amherstburg) one of the most remote, while, at the same time, one of the most beautifully situated in Canada. I had always detested school, and the days that were passed in it, were to me days of suffering, such as the boy alone can understand. With the reputation for some little capacity, I had been oftener flogged than the greatest dunce in it, perhaps as much from the caprice of my tutor as from any actual wrong in myself—and this had so seared my heart—given me such a disgust for Virgil, Horace, and Euclid, that I often meditated running away, and certainly should have gratified the very laudable inclination, had I not apprehended a severity from my father—a stern, unbending man, that would have left me no room for exultation at my escape from my tutor. It was therefore a day of rejoicing to me when the commencement of hostilities on the part of the United States, and the unexpected appearance of a large body of their troops, proved the signal of the "break up" of the school, . . . and my exchange of Cæsar's Commentaries for the King's Regulations. . . . The transition was indeed glorious, and in my joy at the change which had been wrought in my position, I felt disposed to bless the Americans for the bold step they had taken.

Richardson served in the War of 1812 from 1812-13. In June 1812 he joined the 41st Regiment, then stationed at Fort Amherstburg, as a gentleman volunteer. He served for the next sixteen months with this regiment, which for most of this time was commanded by Lieutenant-Colonel, later Major-General, Henry Procter. Although Richardson was apparently most proud of his presence at Fort Detroit when it was surrendered to Major-General Isaac Brock in August 1812, in the same month the young volunteer also took part in the action at Brownstown (Gibraltar), Michigan, and at Maguaga (Riverview), Michigan. He also participated in the campaign along the Miami (or Maumee) River in the fall of 1812; the Battle of Frenchtown (Monroe), Michigan, in January 1813; the Battle of the Miami and the siege of Fort Meigs (Perrysburg), Ohio, in the spring of 1813; the second siege of Fort Meigs and the assault on Fort Stephenson (Fremont), Ohio, in the summer of 1813; and, after Commander Robert Heriot Barclay's defeat at the hands of Master-Commandant Oliver Hazard Perry at the Battle of Lake Erie in September 1813, the retreat from Fort Amherstburg northeast along the Thames River in the fall of 1813. On 5 October 1813 at the Battle of the Thames, which took place near Moraviantown, Upper Canada, and where Tecumseh, the well-known Indian chief, was killed, Richardson was captured by the victorious Americans.

Richardson and his fellow prisoners were marched to Detroit. From there he went with one group by boat across Lake Erie to Put-in-Bay, Ohio, where he saw the badly wounded Barclay. They then travelled to Fort Stephenson. After a brief stay there they continued by horseback to Chillicothe, Ohio, a journey of several weeks. From Chillicothe, where Richardson and his fellow prisoners planned an unsuccessful escape, they were sent via Cincinnati to Frankfort, the capital of Kentucky. There they stayed for several months in a hotel owned by Daniel Weisiger. After their release in July 1814 Richardson and his group journeyed by way of Cincinnati to Cleveland, Ohio, from where they crossed Lake Erie to Long Point, Upper Canada, in October 1814. In June 1815, still in the British army, Richardson left for Europe. It was to be twenty-three years before he returned to his native land.

During these years Richardson served as an officer with the British army in the West Indies in 1816-18 and with the British Legion in Spain in 1835-36. Between times, as an officer on half pay, he lived in or near London and, for at least three years in the mid 1820s, in Paris. He married twice. In spite of his previous "disgust for Virgil, Horace, and Euclid," he actively pursued an education in the arts and literature through visits to such institutions as the British Museum and the Louvre and through wide reading, particularly in works of English literature. And he began a new career as a journalist and an author. In addition to *Wacousta,* the works that he had published during these years included **"A Canadian Campaign"** (1826-27); ***Tecumseh; Or, The Warrior Of The West: A Poem, In Four Cantos, With Notes*** (1828); ***Ecarté; Or, The Salons Of Paris*** (1829); ***Kensington Gardens In 1830. A Satirical Trifle*** (1830); ***Frascati's; Or Scenes In Paris*** (1830); ***Journal Of The Movements Of The British Legion*** (1836); and ***Movements Of The British Legion, With Strictures On The Course Of Conduct Pursued By Lieutenant-General Evans*** (1837), the second issue, with additional material, of ***Journal Of The Movements***.

Much about these seven works, all of which were published in London, is conventional. But certain characteristics are especially noteworthy. One is the tendency of Richardson to write about incidents in his own life, even if they are carefully fictionalized. Another is his habit, demonstrated specifically in the two autobiographical narratives about the British Legion in Spain, to return almost obsessively to scenes and events that particularly moved—one might say traumatized—the author. A third is his impulse to go home to North America for his subject matter.

Three of these early works deal specifically with the northwest frontier that Richardson knew so well. Two of these, **"A Canadian Campaign"** and *Tecumseh,* have as their main subject the War of 1812. The third, *Wacousta,* acts as the first half of the story that reaches its conclusion during the War of 1812 in *The Canadian Brothers*. All three, then, form various kinds of pre-texts to this novel.

"A Canadian Campaign, By A British Officer" was serialized in five parts from December 1826 until June 1827 in the *New Monthly Magazine And Literary Journal* published in London by Henry Colburn. In the opening sentence of the first number of this work Richardson explained:

> THIS narrative is intended rather as a private memoir than a relation of the incidents of the war, and professes simply to detail the operations of the right division of the British army in Upper Canada, to which I was myself attached, together with its capture and imprisonment, (in October 1813,) without following in progression the movements of the various other corps.

In fact, in this version of what was eventually to become *War Of 1812. First Series. Containing A Full And Detailed Narrative Of The Operations Of The Right Division, Of The Canadian Army* (1842), Richardson related almost exclusively the events of the War of 1812 in which he was involved.

In describing the events of 1812-13, however, Richardson also included an account of the Battle of Queenston Heights and of the Battle of Lake Erie. Although he did not fight in either, the 41st was one of the regiments at Queenston, and Richardson was stationed in Amherstburg when Barclay and his fleet sailed from that port to engage the Americans. In light of the ending of *The Canadian Brothers,* Richardson's description of the Battle of Queenston Heights after Brock's death seems particularly relevant:

> Filled with grief, and burning to revenge the death of their favourite commander, the men redoubled their exertions in the ascent, and the main body coming up at this moment the action became general. The enemy was soon driven from his position at the point of the bayonet. Those who attempted to escape in the woods were driven back by the Indians and militia, and falling on such of their own lines as yet sustained the shock, threw them into confusion. Little quarter was given in the onset. Driven near the edge of the precipices, with which the heights of Queenston abound, the enemy fought for a moment with all the obstinacy of despair, but, compelled at length to yield to their exasperated foe, their remaining line was entirely broken. Many threw down their arms, and implored the clemency of their victors. Others cast themselves wildly over the precipices, and were dashed in their fall against the rocks, or hung suspended from the bushes which had caught them in their descent, and in parts where no human hand could tender them assistance. Never was victory more complete. Few of the enemy returned to tell the tale of their disaster.

Throughout **"A Canadian Campaign"** Richardson's sympathies with Brock, "who fell a victim to the intrepidity and daring of his character," "the gallant Barclay," and, above all, the "celebrated chieftain Tecumseh" are clear. According to Richardson,

> In any other country, and governing any other men, Tecumseh would have been a hero; at the head of this uncivilized and untractable people he was a savage; but a savage such as Civilization herself might not blush to acknowledge for her child. Constantly opposed to the encroachments of the Americans for a series of years previous to their rupture with England, he had combated their armies on the banks of the Wabash with success, and given their leaders proofs of a skill and judgment in defence of his native soil, which would not have disgraced the earlier stages of military science in Europe.

Richardson's narrative of his imprisonment, which takes up the last two parts of **"A Canadian Campaign,"** is more detailed and in some ways much more of a "private memoir" than the account of his time in Ohio and Kentucky in *War Of 1812*. From the point of view of his later development of the plot of *The Canadian Brothers,* it is also significant. Describing the march from Fort Stephenson to Chillicothe in the fall of 1813, Richardson wrote:

> Our route lay through an inhospitable tract of country, consisting alternately of gloomy forest and extensive savannah, the latter often intersected by streams fed from the distant mountains, and swollen by the unceasing rains. Sometimes a solitary hut, vying in filthiness with the beings by whom it was tenanted, afforded us shelter for the night, but more frequently we found that repose which absolute fatigue and exhaustion ensure to the traveller near the fires we were compelled to kindle in the forest.

When the prisoners-of-war were staying at Weisiger's hotel in Frankfort, they were subjected to the ridicule of the local population:

> Our promenade was the garden, and as some of the officers still retained their uniforms, we were the objects of general attraction to the long-bodied and long-limbed backwoodsmen of Kentucky, assembled daily to behold the "British". . . . Their rude and unceremonious stare generally drew from us boisterous expressions of mirth and ridicule, . . . and on these occasions they would exclaim to each other in evident surprise, and in their usual nasal

drawling tone, "Tarnation seize me if these Britainners don't treat us more as if we were their prisoners than they ours;" "Roar me up a sapling if they arnt mighty saucy;" "By Ch—t I've the swiftest horse, the truest rifle, and the prettiest sister in the whole state of Kentucky, but I'd give 'em all to have one long shot;" and other equally expressive phrases peculiar to themselves. To be gazed at like wild beasts, and to be constantly interrupted in our seclusion, was not altogether desirable, but we were compelled to submit to their impertinent curiosity.

Just before he left Frankfort in July 1814, Richardson was apparently the victim of an assassination attempt. During his stay in the capital he "had been rather intimate in the family of a highly esteemed and much lamented officer, who had fallen in the affair of Frenchtown." At the home of his widow, "Mrs. H——," he had met "Mr. James, a man of vulgar bearing and appearance, and evidently little used to the decorum necessary to be preserved in the society of females." Richardson, who "felt the most decided dislike" for James, avoided him as much as possible. On one occasion, however, he had commented "aloud on the ungentlemanly tenor" of James' "conduct in persisting to smoke a cigar in the drawing-room, to the evident annoyance of the females of the family." James "made no reply," but, "darting a look full of malignant meaning, soon rose from his seat and retired." Returning late one night from a farewell visit to his friends, Richardson had arrived as far as the garden wall of his hotel when

> I perceived a man stationary near the road. . . . The figure proved to be Mr. James, who now placed himself in such a manner as to bar my passage. I endeavoured to avoid him, and demanded the motive of his conduct. This, he said, I should presently know, and swearing a horrid oath, observed, "You have escaped me once, but I'll take good care you don't again." His right hand grasped a stiletto or dirk, which he held behind his back, and with the other he made a sudden movement to seize me by the collar. I felt all the danger of my situation, and found that, unarmed as I was, and opposed to a man whose physical strength exceeded my own, my only chance of safety was in flight.

Richardson later discovered that James had earlier followed him and "a brother-officer" to Lexington, Kentucky. James had at that time "a brace of pistols in his pocket, and . . . the fixed determination to shoot" Richardson "in the crowd, an object which had only been left unaccomplished from the circumstance of" James "having lost sight" of his quarry. Although *The Canadian Brothers* was still several years away when Richardson composed **"A Canadian Campaign,"** the images of the dirty hut, the uncouth Kentuckians, and the violent, sudden attack are the historical seeds from which the novel would grow.

In the preface to **Tecumseh,** Richardson, described on the titlepage as "An English Officer," explained:

> Many of the notes to Tecumseh betray its Author to be that also of the **"Canadian Campaign,"** several passages in both being written nearly in the same words. The fact is, that the Poem was composed five years ago, and before he had thought of compiling the latter narrative.

Why the poem was not published before **"A Canadian Campaign"** is not stated, although it is possible that even then there were few "people interested in the period and scene." Whatever the reason it seems that it was only after the publication of **"A Canadian Campaign"** that Richardson finally decided to complete and to publish his poem about "the high, the noble, the generous, the unfortunate Tecumseh."

Writing to Richardson from London on 18 February 1828, Barclay, who had obviously read a manuscript copy of the poem, commented:

> Its merits, as far as I am able to judge, seem very considerable, and, if the world only knew it, you speak the truth—an ingredient not always to be found even in an epic poem, founded on facts. You have done ample justice to the merits of poor Tecumseh, whose self-devotion to the cause were worthy of a better fate.

Then, apparently replying to a query about its publication, Barclay added, "Had your work been ready some years ago, you might have found many more people interested in the period and scene, but we professional men are so easily scattered over the earth and sea, that it is difficult to catch us on the wing."

Richardson corresponded with Barclay at least once more on the subject of *Tecumseh*. This time he sent Barclay a "Prospectus" and reminded the naval officer that he had visited him on his "couch of pain" after the Battle of Lake Erie. Barclay's response to this reminder was to ask that Richardson include somewhere in his work a compliment to "Commodore Perry's gallantry in action, and generous kindness when it was over." In the concluding paragraph of the preface to *Tecumseh*, dated "*London, May 18th,* 1828," Richardson fulfilled Barclay's request:

> In relation to the naval action which forms a principal incident in the Poem, it may be observed, that if any thing could tend to enhance the glory of Commodore Perry's victory, or to render that gentleman more alive to the importance of his advantages, it must be the generous testimony of his noble, though less successful adversary, whose voice is still loud to proclaim the gallantry of his opponent in action, and his kind and courteous

bearing to a fallen enemy. This high and generous tribute of Captain Barclay lives . . . in the private professions of his esteem,—professions springing from the warm impressions of a noble mind, and which, I am authorised to state, exist not less powerfully now than at that period.

The first canto of **Tecumseh** describes the Battle of Lake Erie and Tecumseh's "despair and harrowing grief" at the British defeat. The second canto deals chiefly with the death of both the son and father of Tecumseh and other fictitious happenings. The last two cantos concentrate on such historical events as the council held in Amherstburg in September 1813 where Tecumseh expressed his anger at Procter's plans to retreat to "the Thames' broad banks," the burning of Amherstburg, and the Battle of the Thames. Tecumseh's death and the subsequent mutilation of his body by the Americans are also described:

> Forth from the copse a hundred foemen
>   spring,
> And pounce like vultures on the bleeding
>   clay;
> Like famish'd blood-hounds to the corse
>   they cling,
> And bear the fallen hero's spoils away:
> The very covering from his nerves they
>   wring,
> And gash his form, and glut them o'er their
>   prey—
> Wild hell-fiends all, and revelling at his death,
> With bursting shrieks and pestilential breath.

The poem ends with a curse on those who left Tecumseh "A lifeless, loathsome mass" and a wish that they may "e'er howl, and creep / As vile through life." Its final stanza is a hope that vengeance may come to these men through members of their own family:

> Then may the presence of some much-lov'd
>   child,
> Some faithful brother, or some hoary sire,
> Recall *his* deeds, who by their arms defil'd,
> Had spar'd their blood in many a battle dire;
> And as the thought occurs, with
>   recollections wild,
> Ere yet the conscience-stricken wretch
>   expire,
> Oh! may he hear his offspring loud proclaim
> That Chieftain's worth, whose glory is his
>   shame!

There is much, then, in **Tecumseh** that foreshadowed the handling of the War of 1812 in **The Canadian Brothers**. The inclusion by name of actual characters, the accounts of historical events, the addition of a fictitious story, the mixture of its imagined incidents with real ones: all these aspects of the poem also appeared

in the novel. With the focus on Tecumseh and his presentation as a tragic hero, furthermore, Richardson began to shape a powerful vision of the War of 1812 and those who fought in it. Finally, the images of death, destruction, disease, and hell, especially in the last canto of **Tecumseh,** looked forward to the bloody darkness of the personal and national myths that were evoked in **The Canadian Brothers** and that made the novel an important chronicle of Canadian history.

Richardson picked up the themes of vengeance and hate and gave them another shape in **Wacousta,** his third early work about the northwest frontier. This time, however, he stepped back in history and took as his subject matter tales that had been told to him by his grandfather Askin and his wife about their experiences in the northwest. Set at Fort Detroit and Fort Michilimackinac (Mackinaw, Michigan) during the Pontiac uprising in the 1760s, **Wacousta** tells the story of Reginald Morton, a Cornishman, whose fiancée, Clara Beverley, had been stolen by his best friend, Charles de Haldimar, when the two, both young officers in the British army, were serving in the highlands of Scotland. Determined to kill De Haldimar and take revenge upon his family for his betrayal, Morton pursues his former colleague throughout the world. In 1763, when **Wacousta** opens, Colonel de Haldimar has just taken over the command of the newly acquired British fort of Detroit, where, Clara having died, he is living with their three children. During the course of the novel Reginald Morton, now disguised as Wacousta, stalks outside the fort and, leagued with Pontiac, plots the destruction of Fort Detroit, Fort Michilimackinac, and the entire De Haldimar family. This last aim is helped when Colonel de Haldimar orders the execution of Reginald Morton, Wacousta's nephew now called Frank Halloway and disguised as a common soldier. Just after Halloway is shot, his wife Ellen utters a curse on Colonel de Haldimar and his family:

> "Inhuman murderer!" she exclaimed, . . . "if there be a God of justice and of truth, he will avenge this devilish deed. Yes, Colonel de Haldimar, a prophetic voice whispers to my soul, that even as I have seen perish before my eyes all I loved on earth, without mercy and without hope, so even shall you witness the destruction of your accursed race. Here—here—here," and she pointed downwards, with singular energy of action, to the corpse of her husband, "here shall their blood flow till every vestige of his own is washed away; and oh, if there be spared one branch of thy detested family, may it only be that they may be reserved for some death too horrible to be conceived!"

By the end of the action of the novel, although Wacousta has been killed, his acts of revenge have made a good part of Ellen Halloway's curse come true. Colonel de Haldimar, his son Charles, and his daughter Clara are all dead. Only Frederick de Haldimar and his fiancée, his cousin Madeline de Haldimar, survive. Ellen Halloway, who lived briefly with Wacousta, has disappeared.

When he took up the story of the De Haldimars again, almost fifty years had passed since the events at Detroit related in *Wacousta*. In *The Canadian Brothers* Richardson sketched the main incidents in the life of the family during this half century. Frederick de Haldimar and his wife Madeline de Haldimar had had four children, two sons and two daughters. Frederick had continued to serve in the British army and had been promoted to the rank of colonel. He had fought in the American Revolution along with his sons, "officers in his own corps," both of whom "had perished in the war." While they were still living in North America, the De Haldimars had also lost a daughter, who "had died young, of a decline." Sometime after the Revolution Colonel de Haldimar's regiment had been "ordered home," and Frederick and Madeline had returned to England. Isabella de Haldimar, their only surviving child, who had in the meantime married Major Grantham, had stayed in North America, where she had given birth to two sons, Gerald and Henry. When Gerald "was in his twelfth year," Mrs. Grantham had died in Amherstburg where the family had settled; her death had been hastened by the shock of learning that "her parents had both perished in a hurricane on their route to the West Indies, whither the regiment of Colonel De Haldimar had been ordered." A short time later Major Grantham had also died; his death was due to a gunshot wound that he had received when he was hunting near his home. Also living in the Amherstburg area was an American settler of unknown origins. Named Jeremiah Desborough, he is revealed during the course of *The Canadian Brothers* to be the son of Wacousta and Ellen Halloway. He is also the father of "Paul, Emilius, Theophilus, Arnoldi" and of Matilda Montgomerie.

Although Desborough is aware of a kind of blood feud between himself and the Granthams, and both Gerald and Henry know that the history of their family is connected with some violent events that happened at Detroit, the conflict between Colonel de Haldimar's descendants and those of Wacousta is worked out in *The Canadian Brothers* chiefly in terms of the War of 1812. When the action of the novel begins, Gerald and Henry are both serving with the British forces on the northwest frontier, Gerald in the navy and Henry in the army, and both are stationed in Amherstburg. Desborough, introduced as one of those Yankee "traitors Canada had so long nourished in her bosom," is first seen attempting to smuggle his son, a member "of the United States Michigan Militia—a prisoner on his parole of honor" across to the United States. According to Henry Grantham, who apprehends the father and the son as they try to escape, Arnoldi is also "a deserter from our service. This fellow . . . is a scoun-

drel, who deserted three years since" from a British regiment serving in Amherstburg. Even Matilda is first introduced as one of the women accompanying the American Army of the Northwest to Fort Detroit. It is the War of 1812, then, as much as Ellen Halloway's curse, that drives the action of *The Canadian Brothers*.

One of the fascinations of the novel is the way in which fact and fiction parallel and intertwine with each other. In *The Canadian Brothers,* for example, Richardson related again the history of the War of 1812 that he had already told in **"A Canadian Campaign."** Richardson's service with the 41st Regiment is the source for many of the settings of the novel, and the details that he provided about the strategies of the military on the northwest frontier are remarkably similar to the official despatches written at the time by the officers planning the war. As in **"A Canadian Campaign,"** the Battle of Queenston Heights and the Battle of Lake Erie are included. Richardson's adventures as a prisoner-of-war in 1813-14 are reflected in such events in the novel as Gerald Grantham's long trek to Frankfort, his stay in Desborough's filthy backwoods hut, and his attempted assassination of Colonel Forrester.

Richardson shaped his plot, however, in a way that involved the fictionalizing of the chronology of the events that introduce and conclude the novel. Barclay arrives in Amherstburg in the summer of 1812, almost a year before he actually came. Tecumseh appears "somewhat earlier than the strict record of facts" would allow. Barclay, Brock, and Tecumseh meet in Amherstburg when in reality the three never assembled together at all. And, creating the "anachronism . . . of too palpable a nature not to be detected at a glance by the reader," Richardson postponed the Battle of Queenston Heights until October 1813. Describing these changes in the preface to *The Canadian Brothers,* Richardson argued that they were "necessary to the action of the story." Certainly they help to enhance the public themes of the novel and to articulate its myths of tragic heroism.

The characters are also a mix of fact and fiction. Barclay, Brock, and Tecumseh each appear as themselves and as the heroes that Richardson believed them to be. Lesser characters in terms of the action of *The Canadian Brothers* such as Procter, Lieutenant-Colonel John Harvey, and the Indian chiefs Splitlog, Roundhead, and Walk-in-the-Water are also named. Other participants in the War of 1812 like William Hull, James Winchester, and William Henry Harrison, the three brigadier-generals who commanded in turn the American Army of the Northwest, also play their historical part in the novel although they are normally identified only by such titles as "the American leader." Still other characters, called by fictitious names, are based on people whom Richardson knew. In a letter dated "Niagara,

Canada, January 15th, 1846" that was published in *Colburn's United Service Magazine* the following March, the author himself identified "the punning Watson" of the 41st as "the "Middlemore" of a work published in this country under the title of the Canadian Brothers." And Sampson Gattrie is a thinly disguised Simon Girty. In *Eight Years In Canada* Richardson actually conflated Simon Girty with Sampson Gattrie when he identified the former as "the "Simon Gattrie" of my Canadian Brothers."

Even the major characters in the Grantham-Desborough plot are drawn at least partly from Richardson's family and friends. Colonel D'Egville, who acts as guardian to the Grantham brothers after their parents have died, resembles in many ways Matthew Elliott. Major Grantham shares personality traits with Richardson's father. The description of Isabella Grantham's death rings so true that there is no doubt that at least in its emotional content it is drawn from the circumstances of Madelaine Richardson's death in Amherstburg in 1811. The relationship between Gerald and Henry reflects feelings that Richardson had for his brother Robert, who served as a midshipman in the War of 1812 and who died in 1819 from wounds received at the Battle of Frenchtown. And Matilda Montgomerie herself may be partly modelled on Mrs. H——. David R. Beasley, Richardson's biographer, identifies her as Elizabeth ("Betsey") Hickman, William Hull's daughter, whose husband, Paschal Hickman, was one of those killed by the Indians after the Battle of Frenchtown. According to Beasley, she was the real reason for James' attempted assassination of Richardson:

> Betsey was not only rich and desirable: she enjoyed a high social standing, which, in spite of three children, made her eligible for remarriage— especially in the mind of a tall and burly Kentuckian named James, who was courting her favour at the time. Richardson, whose background was already known to Betsey through the friendship of her family, the Hulls, with the Askins, was readily received by her. Sensing their attraction to be mutual, he felt bold enough to challenge his rival. . . .

> In his novel *The Canadian Brothers,* the fictional Matilda . . . influenced her young lover to assassinate a man whom she loathed. The theme of assassination was fashioned after a true event in Frankfort, but the insight and sensitivity of the story came largely from Richardson's experience with the mature and strong-willed Betsey.

In 1825 another assassination attempt, this one successful, occurred in Frankfort, Kentucky. In November of that year Jereboam O. Beauchamp (or Beauchampe) stabbed to death Solomon Sharp (or Sharpe), who had been attorney-general of Kentucky from 1820-24. The main motive for the killing was to avenge Sharp's alleged seduction of Beauchamp's wife, the former Ann (or Anna) Cook (or Cooke), who insisted that her husband punish Sharp in this way. Beauchamp was immediately arrested, found guilty of murder, and sentenced to be hanged. Before the sentence could be executed, he and his wife, who was allowed to stay in the jail with him, tried twice to commit suicide. Both survived the first attempt, which was made by taking laudanum. Ann Beauchamp succeeded in stabbing herself mortally in the second attempt, but her husband, who also stabbed himself, lived to be hanged in July 1826. The Beauchamp affair caused a sensation in Kentucky and was reported in newspapers in the United States and Great Britain. *The Confession Of Jereboam O. Beauchamp . . . Written By Himself* was also reprinted several times after it was first published in August 1826.

In February 1828 Richardson, replying in the *New Monthly Magazine* to an article published in the Philadelphia *National Gazette* on 6 August 1827 that criticized some of his statements about Kentucky in **"A Canadian Campaign,"** chastised its author for being "facetious" about his account of James' attempt at assassination:

> Most unfortunately for him, this same Frankfort has been notorious for more than one attempt of the kind. The affair of Beauchamp and Colonel Sharpe is yet fresh in the recollection of the public; and it was the identical hotel of Mr. Weisiger that the foul assassin selected for his temporary abode, on his arrival to execute his diabolical purpose.

Years later, in the concluding paragraph to the new introduction he wrote for the second American edition of **Wacousta** published in 1851, he commented again on "the Beauchamp tragedy." This time he pointed out its connection with **The Canadian Brothers,** although he denied that at the time that he was composing the **Prophecy Fulfilled,** he had read "a work of the same character" by "an American author":

> The **Prophecy Fulfilled** . . . embraces and indeed is intimately connected with the Beauchamp tragedy, which took place at or near Weisiger's Hotel, in Frankfort, Kentucky, where I had been many years before confined as a prisoner of war. While connecting it with the **Prophecy Fulfilled,** and making it subservient to the end I had in view, I had not read, or even heard of the existence of a work of the same character, which had already appeared from the pen of an American author. Indeed, I have reason to believe that the **Prophecy Fulfilled,** although not published until after a lapse of years, was the first written. No similarity of treatment of the subject exists between the two versions, and this, be it remembered, I remark without in the slightest degree impugning the merit

of the production of my fellow laborer in the same field.

This work is probably Thomas Holley Chivers' *Conrad And Eudora; Or The Death Of Alonzo. A Tragedy. In Five Acts. Founded On The Murder Of Sharpe, By Beauchamp, In Kentucky,* which was first published in 1834.

What appears to be an equally significant source of the *Prophecy Fulfilled* is cited in *The Canadian Brothers* itself. During the ball in Amherstburg, Middlemore, reacting to Julia D'Egville's chastisement for his teasing of Raymond, mutters to another officer, "we shall have her next exclaiming, in the words of Monk Lewis' Bleeding Nun, 'Raymond, Raymond, I am thine / 'Raymond, Raymond, thou art mine.'" Middlemore's quotation adds a touch of rather grotesque humour to the scene. But the song itself, which tells a story of ghostly love and lust, is also a fitting introduction to the affair of Gerald Grantham and Matilda Montgomerie. It is in his characterization of Matilda that Richardson's debt to Matthew Lewis' *The Monk: A Romance* (1796) is most clear. Richardson's Matilda, like Lewis', is a woman who lures men to their destruction by her beauty and sexuality. In *The Monk,* for example, the chief character is reminded, "you eagerly yielded to the blandishments of Matilda. Your pride was gratified by her flattery; Your lust only needed an opportunity to break forth; You ran into the snare blindly." The same could be said about Gerald and his response to Matilda Montgomerie. He is warned by others, especially his brother, that Matilda has something evil in her nature. Surrounding Matilda with images of darkness, pestilence, poison, and violence, Richardson appears not only to be using the most Gothic of novels as a model for the fable of Gerald and Matilda, but also to be suggesting the satanic quality of her nature and their relationship.

Gerald's death, however, does not take place at the hands of Matilda or because of her actions. Gerald is killed at the Battle of Queenston Heights by his brother who mistakes him for an American soldier. As in *Tecumseh* the deaths of the chief characters are caused by political events, and the climactic scenes occur during a public battle that is portrayed by Richardson not as a triumph but as a tragedy. At the end of *The Canadian Brothers,* then, the personal and the public combine to provide a vision of a fallen, sinful world where individuals, families, and nations are doomed by ancient actions and old wrongs to murder, fratricide, and war.

Even before the publication of *Wacousta* in December 1832, Richardson had begun planning its sequel. Answering on 24 August 1832 a letter that he had received some time before, Barclay replied to Richardson's description of *The Canadian Brothers:*

In your next, when you say that I may be brought in,—pray do me the favor and justice to exaggerate nothing, whether of difficulty or danger, but in all you say, be as calmly-correct as possible. I am not ashamed of any part of my conduct while on Lake Erie, but hyperbole might tend to make me so.

In the preface to *The Canadian Brothers* Richardson recorded that by midsummer 1833 he had completed enough of his "new work" to have sent to Sir Herbert Taylor, aide-de-camp and secretary of William IV, the chapter (probably Volume One, Chapter Six) "which treats of the policy of employing the Indians in any future war we may have with the United States." He also had received permission from the King, "not usually given for works of fiction," to dedicate his "new work to him." *The Canadian Brothers* was, however, still unfinished when William IV died in June 1837.

In the meantime, Richardson and his second wife, Maria Caroline Drayson, whom he had married in April 1832, had left Farnham Royal, the village in Buckinghamshire where they had been living, for Spain. His duties there with the British Legion in 1835-36 and the quarrels that ensued undoubtedly delayed the completion of *The Canadian Brothers*. This enterprise was further postponed by Richardson's departure for Canada in 1838.

The event that prompted the return of Richardson to the land of his birth was the Rebellion of 1837. In *Eight Years In Canada* he recalled, "as the news, which reached England by every packet, was of a nature to induce the belief that my services might be made available in her [Canada's] defence, I resolved to embark forthwith." Before Richardson and his wife left London in February 1838, there had been "a good deal of delay." When he did depart, moreover, he went not as an officer in the army but as a journalist for the London *Times,* "the proprietors of which" had made Richardson "a most liberal offer" to provide "political information" on the Canadas.

The Richardsons arrived in New York City in March 1838 and travelled from there by way of Rochester to Lewiston, New York, where Richardson "beheld, for the first time since" his "return . . . the Canadian shore." The particular view of Queenston brought back vivid memories of Brock, "the warrior beneath whose bright example" Richardson's "young heart had been trained to a love of heroism," of the "noble but unequal conflict" of the Battle of Queenston Heights, and of his own service in the War of 1812. Richardson entered Canada by way of Niagara and proceeded to Toronto where he began to discover the "state of feverish excitement" that existed as a result of the Rebellion of 1837-38. From there he went to Montreal and Quebec. Richardson continued to live in Lower Canada until the spring of 1839. During this time he not only reported on Canada for the *Times,* although his sympathy with Lord Durham eventually prompted that newspaper not to renew its engagement with him, but he also used the connections that he made as a journalist to explore ways of continuing his career as an author. In May 1838 Richardson proposed to publish by subscription "a revised Canadian Edition" of *Wacousta,* but nothing came of that plan. In the fall of 1838 Armour and Ramsay of Montreal, joined by W. Neilson of Quebec, R. Stanton of Toronto, and J. MacFarlane of Kingston, published *Personal Memoirs Of Major Richardson . . . As Connected With The Singular Oppression Of That Officer While In Spain By Lieutenant General Sir De Lacy Evans*. By February 1839 Richardson was ready to launch another enterprise: that of completing for publication the manuscript of his sequel to *Wacousta.*

In March 1839 the *Literary Garland* published as "Jeremiah Desborough; Or, The Kentuckian: A Chapter From An Unpublished Continuation Of *Wacousta*" what became Volume One, Chapter Seven, of *The Canadian Brothers*. In a note in the same issue the *Literary Garland* explained:

> To the courtesy of the author, we are indebted for a glance over some portions of the MSS. of an unpublished Continuation of *Wacousta.* The high reputation which has already been won by the pen which produced this thrilling tale, will be well sustained on the publication of its sequel; and should it issue from the Canadian press, we shall look upon it as an epoch in our history, well deserving of record in our annals; not that we deem such an event unlikely, for we are certainly justified in the hope, that the press of these colonies will soon teem with works of merit. . . .
>
> The chapter headed "Jeremiah Desborough," which we have obtained permission to extract, will shew that the author's pen has lost none of its vigour since it last commanded the attention of the literary world.

In its April 1839 issue the *Literary Garland* published "A Second Chapter From An Unpublished Continuation Of *Wacousta, Or The Prophecy,* Entitled *The Settler; Or, The Prophecy Fulfilled.*" This became the first chapter of the second volume of *The Canadian Brothers*.

The publication of these excerpts and other notices of the author of *Wacousta* in the Canadian press prompted a letter from Richardson. In this letter, which appeared in the *Quebec Mercury* on 4 May 1839, Richardson thanked "the Press of Canada, for the high encomiums" that the journalists had been "pleased to bestow at various times on his literary productions." He assured them that he would continue to delineate "Canadian subjects," for which they thought that he

was "peculiarly adapted." Finally, he announced that the "ensuing summer" should "be devoted to another Canadian tale, in which will figure characters in no way inferior in villainy to Jeremiah D[es]borough—in short, some of the veriest villains that ever disgraced human nature." Soon after the publication of this letter, Richardson and his wife left for Amherstburg where he intended to rent a house and to complete *The Canadian Brothers*.

In *Eight Years In Canada* Richardson recalled in some detail this return to his boyhood home:

> As I entered the principal street, which ran parallel with the river, a thousand recollections of by-gone days flashed upon my mind. *There* was the spot on which had stood the house (since burnt down) in which my younger days had been nurtured. Close to it had stood the "cage" or prison with which I had so often been threatened while yet in the nursery, and in which the "Simon Gattrie" of my Canadian Brothers . . . had so frequently been made to do penance for his inebriety. *There* was the gate leading to the wharf . . . where my youthful piscatorial prowess had so often been tested; *here* the well-remembered "store" against which I had so often pitched my marbles. . . . But why multiply examples?

During his stay in Amherstburg Richardson attended Christ (Anglican) Church. Here he discovered quite accidentally that the "beautiful willow tree" that he could see through a window of the church marked the grave of his brother Robert. In spite of the ties that bound Richardson to Amherstburg, however, he could not "procure a house" in the village, and he was forced to rent what he called "a den" in Sandwich. There in the summer of 1839 he completed his manuscript of *The Canadian Brothers*.

There is no known record that indicates just how much work Richardson still had to do to prepare his manuscript for publication. Since he had already published two chapters, one from the beginning and the other from the middle of the novel, it is likely that *The Canadian Brothers* was almost finished when its author arrived in Sandwich. Certainly the differences between the version of the two chapters published in the *Literary Garland* and that of the same material in *The Canadian Brothers* are minor. The most important variations occur in the chapter about Jeremiah Desborough. In the periodical he is introduced as "more Kentuckian than Yankee," whereas in *The Canadian Brothers* he is described as "less Kentuckian than Yankee." In both versions, however, he is referred to almost consistently as a "Yankee," so the phrase in the *Literary Garland* may have been an error of composition. The periodical version of the "Desborough" chapter also contains an extra sentence at the end of the paragraph that concerns the benefit to Canada, as a

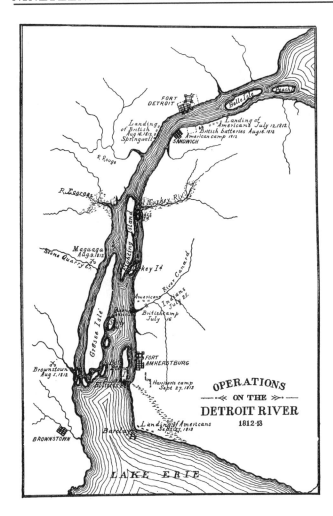

OPERATIONS
ON THE
DETROIT RIVER
1812-13

result of the War of 1812, of getting rid of the American traitors who had been in her midst. To the statement that if Canada were ever to allow these people to move back, she would "merit all the evils which can attach, in a state of warfare, to a people diametrically opposed in their interests, their principles, their habits, and their attachments," which appears in both versions, Richardson added in the periodical, "But we think the cloven foot has been too openly displayed, to afford much chance to the Americans on that score."

In *Eight Years In Canada* Richardson related how during his stay in Sandwich he crossed over to Detroit "to discover the site of the old fort . . . which we had taken possession of in 1812." He was never able, however, to "trace the slightest clue to its situation, not even a ditch remaining to call up a recollection of the past," although his American companions "pointed out what they affirmed (and no doubt correctly enough) to be the spot." To his "American friends" Richardson also showed the apparently completed manuscript of his sequel to *Wacousta,* and they "strongly urged" him "to publish it forthwith":

Having nothing else wherewith to occupy my time, I assented; but aware as I was of the great pecuniary responsibility of the undertaking in a country so indisposed to the encouragement of literature as Canada, where the chief sale of the work was to be looked for, I stipulated for a list of subscribers which should in part guarantee me from loss, even although I did not expect to derive much profit from the publication. This was promised, and in a few days I found about a hundred names appended to a prospectus that had been left at one of the bookstores. The number was quite as great as I could have anticipated in so small a place.

Armed with this success, Richardson decided to pursue the publication of his work.

In August 1839 Richardson sent a letter and his prospectus to each of several newspapers in Canadas. On 20 August the Montreal *Morning Courier* noted that Major Richardson was "engaged in writing a continuation of the highly popular Novel" of *Wacousta* and urged support for "his forth-coming work." On 28 August the Sandwich *Western Herald, And Farmers' Magazine* reprinted part of the *Courier*'s article. The *Montreal Herald* announced on 29 August that it had "received a letter from Major Richardson dated at Amherstburg enclosing some prospectuses of a new work he is about to publish, under the title of *The Brothers, or the Prophecy Fulfilled,* intended to form a continuation of his celebrated" *Wacousta*. "The Major," it explained, was, "in the widest sense of the word, a Canadian author, for he was born in Canada and has devoted himself to delineate the character of the red men of the forest, in which he has been peculiarly successful, as also in rendering historical the truly beautiful and picturesque scenery of Western America." It then quoted three paragraphs from the prospectus:

> *The Brothers, or the Prophecy Fulfilled,* somewhat more voluminous than its predecessor, is, as the title intimates, the fulfilment of the curse pronounced by the maniac, Ellen Halloway, over the mutilated corpse of her husband, on what, at a period not very remote, was still known as the "Bloody Bridge"—a name derived from the cruel massacre, by the Indians, of a portion of British troops then in occupation of the Fort Detroit.

> The scene of the unpublished tale is confined principally to these districts, and during the war of 1812; while the leading characters—American, English, and Indian—are not less known to cis-Atlantic history than to many of the actual residents in this portion of the Western World.

> With those classes of the reading community to whom this notice is addressed, and who, as much from taste as feeling, are likely to entertain a

solicitude for the completion of a story invented with the peculiar power of excitement which attaches to a knowledge of the persons, incidents, and localities professed to be described, it is presumed no objection will exist to a publication which must necessarily, as an original production, be somewhat more expensive than a re-print from one already in type.

Subscription lists, it stated, were available at the "Book Stores of Messrs. Armour & Ramsay, and W. Greig." The article concluded:

we hope that every admirer of Wacousta and all who have any desire to encourage native talent of a very high order will subscribe to "The Brothers." As the publication will depend altogether on the number of subscribers, . . . it is necessary that those who really wish a copy of the work should subscribe without delay.

This item was reprinted in the *Quebec Mercury* on 31 August.

The *Montreal Gazette* also received the prospectus, which it noticed on 5 September 1839:

We have been favoured with the prospectus of a continuation of "Wacousta," which the author, Major RICHARDSON, proposes to publish, under the title of ***The Brothers, or the Prophecy Fulfilled***. The work will be somewhat more voluminous than its predecessor; but we understand that it will be fraught with scenes of the deepest interest, and historically descriptive of real events which occurred in UPPER CANADA. Among the chief characters are General BROCK, Commodore BARCLAY, and TECUMSEH— characters sufficient of themselves to enhance the value of the publication.

The newspaper also stated that subscription lists could be found "in all the booksellers' shops; and we have no doubt that they soon will be filled up."

By late September 1839 Richardson had decided to have his novel published in Montreal. Before he left for that city, however, he sent out more prospectuses. On 23 October 1839, for example, the Kingston *Chronicle & Gazette* published a portion of the prospectus. The newspaper added that it had a subscription list and that the work cost "$3, to be paid on delivery." "It would be desirable," the notice concluded, if "persons intending to subscribe should leave their names as soon as possible," for Major Richardson did "not feel himself warranted" in sending "the work to press" until he had obtained "a certain number of subscribers."

As he made his way to Montreal in late October and early November 1839, Richardson visited newspaper offices on his route to drop off copies of his prospec-

tus and to promote his new work. The *Toronto Patriot,* for example, reported on 1 November 1839 that "Major Richardson" had "just passed through this city, on his way to Montreal, for the purpose of superintending the publication" of his "Historical tale of the War of 1812, in which figures prominently a name that must be dear to the heart of every Anglo-Canadian—that of the gallant and lamented Sir Isaac Brock." The tale would

make its appearance in the course of the month of December, so that we may expect to have our winter evenings amused by a recurrence to scenes and characters which cannot fail to interest the attention of every loyal subject of these Provinces. General Brock, however, although the first is not the only personage of historical reputation introduced in the work.—The gallant Barclay, and the haughty and noble minded Tecumseth, occupy fitting places near the Hero of Queenston Heights.

A subscription list "for the benefit of the public" could be "found at Mr. Stanton's Library, in King Street." The number of copies prepared would be "those actually subscribed for." This notice was reprinted in both the *Cobourg Star* and the Kingston *Chronicle & Gazette* on 6 November. Both newspapers informed their readers that they had subscription lists. A variation of the *Toronto Patriot's* notice, with the information that a "list for the benefit of the public, will be found at the Post Office, Bytown," also appeared in the *Bytown Gazette* on 14 November.

Events moved quickly for Richardson and his novel. On 12 November 1839 the *Montreal Gazette* announced that the author had arrived in Montreal "for the purpose of superintending the publication of ***The Brothers, or the Prophecy Fulfilled.***" It was also "glad to learn that the subscription list to the work, which will be in two volumes, is highly satisfactory and gratifying to the author." A few days later, on 16 November, the *Montreal Gazette* published a correction to its previous notice. The publication of the "continuation of *Wacousta*" would be delayed until January because "the printer" could not "undertake to get it through the press" before then. The title of the novel would be ***The Canadian Brothers.***" Both these notices also appeared in the *Quebec Gazette.* The second notice about the delay and the change of title was published in several newspapers, including the *Montreal Herald* on 16 November, the Kingston *Chronicle & Gazette* on 23 November, and the *Hamilton Gazette* on 16 December 1839.

Even before Richardson arrived in Montreal, he took steps to arrange another matter relevant to the publication of ***The Canadian Brothers,*** that of someone to whom he could dedicate his novel. He chose John Harvey, the hero of the Battle of Stoney Creek, who, knighted in 1824, was in 1839 the lieutenant-governor of New Brunswick. Richardson wrote to Harvey on 2 November to make his request. At the same time he enclosed subscription lists for Harvey to distribute.

On 26 November 1839 the lieutenant-governor replied to Richardson. He accepted the latter's "very flattering proposition to inscribe" the work to him. "I can only say," Harvey wrote, "that, independent of the respect to which the author of so very charming a production as *Waco[u]sta* is entitled, the interesting facts and circumstances so unexpectedly brought to my knowledge and recollection, would ensure a ready acquiesence on my part." He promised to send the subscription lists "to different parts of the province." A notice about *The Canadian Brothers* that mentioned the author's intention of dedicating the work to "His Excellency Major General Sir John Harvey" and that requested those "anxious to obtain a copy of the work" to "leave their names at the Fredericton Reading Room, or at the Royal Gazette Office," appeared in the *Royal Gazette* published in Fredericton on 27 November 1839. An advertisement announcing that the novel was "IN THE PRESS" and would "shortly be Published" was printed in the same newspaper on 4 December. Harvey also put down his "own name for six copies."

On 12 December 1839 the *Montreal Gazette* announced both that *The Canadian Brothers, or the Prophecy Fulfilled* was "making rapid progress through the press" and that the work would be dedicated to Harvey:

> This production which, had it been earlier published, was originally to have been dedicated to His late Majesty, is to be inscribed to His Excellency Sir JOHN HARVEY. To no other officer could a CANADIAN edition of the work be more appropriately offered. Sir JOHN is the only officer of rank, now on the continent of BRITISH NORTH AMERICA, who bore a part in the various military achievements which occurred during the epoch of which it treats, and as the friend and sharer in the glories of the principal character in the tale—the gallant Sir ISAAC BROCK—it cannot but be gratifying to him, to see inscribed to himself a work commemorative of the high character and daring deeds of his noble brother in arms.

This notice was reprinted on 21 December 1839 in the *Montreal Transcript* and on 1 January 1840 in the Fredericton *Royal Gazette*.

In the meantime, Richardson was working on the dedication. On 20 December 1839 he sent Harvey "a rough copy" for his approval. In the accompanying letter Richardson told the lieutenant-governor how important *The Canadian Brothers* would be for Canadian literature:

> I trust I shall not lay myself open to a charge of undue vanity, when I express a belief that the book which I am about to give to the world, will live in this country long after its writer shall have been gathered to his forefathers; nor this from any intrinsic value in the production itself, but because I think I can perceive, through the vista of years, a time when the people of Canada having acquired a higher taste for literature than they now possess, will feel that pride in the first and only author this country has yet produced, which as a matter-of-fact people they do not now entertain.

Because of the national importance of *The Canadian Brothers,* Richardson added that he intended to "distribute circulars" about the work "in almost every town, no matter of how little note, in Canada; and gratifying is it to me, to think that in so doing, I shall at the same time be the means of bringing before the more vivid recollections of its population, the debt of gratitude Canada owes to her most prominent defenders."

During the month of December Richardson also composed his preface. In it, in addition to pointing out the anachronisms made necessary by "the action of the story," he emphasized "the favorable light under which the American character" had "been portrayed." He stated, however, that since "the work was written in England" in the 1830s, this portrayal had nothing to do with "the very strong interest taken" in the publication of *The Canadian Brothers* by "the American public" during the previous summer. The preface concluded with Richardson's "apology for the imperfect Scotch . . . put into the mouth of one of our characters." When he became aware of his error, "the work had been so far printed as not to admit of our remedying it. We are consoled, however, by the reflection that we have given the person in question so much of the national character that he can well afford to lose something in a minor particular."

In January 1840 preparations for the publication of *The Canadian Brothers* continued. On 2 January "Major RICHARDSON, now resident in the City of Montreal," registered in "the Office of the Prothonotary of the Court of King's Bench" for the "District of Montreal" the "Title of a Book, in the following words:—"The Canadian Brothers; or, the Prophecy Fulfilled. A Tale of the late American War, by Major Richardson, Knight of the Military Order of Saint Ferdinand, Author of *Ecarté, Wacousta,* &c. &c. in Two Volumes," the right of which he claims as Author." *The Canadian Brothers* thus "Enregistered, according to the Act of the Provincial Parliament," Richardson had claimed his copyright on it in Canada.

On the same day the *Montreal Gazette* announced that since *The Canadian Brothers* would "very shortly appear," the subscription lists "in both Provinces" should be returned to Montreal "with the least possible delay." It had further to intimate, that as the infant state of literature in the CANADAS, has necessarily, compelled the publication to be one of subscription, it will be but justice to those who have assisted the work with their names, that there should be a difference in the subscribing and selling prices. While the former will, therefore, be that already named, the latter will be increased to the public one-fourth nor from such increase in price will there be any diminution.

The newspaper also requested that the "*Gazette and Mercury* of QUEBEC, the *Sherbrooke Journal*, the *Toronto Patriot*, the *Niagara Chronicle*, and *Sandwich Herald*" publish this notice. It subsequently appeared in several newspapers, including the *Montreal Transcript* on 4 January, the *Quebec Gazette* on 6 January, the *Cobourg Star* and the Kingston *Chronicle & Gazette* on 8 January, the *Toronto Patriot* on 14 January, and the Sandwich *Western Herald* on 25 January 1840.

By mid January copies of the first volume of **The Canadian Brothers** were ready for distribution to the newspapers of the Canadas. On 18 January "*The Canadian Brothers, or the Prophecy Fulfilled. A Tale of the late Americ[a]n War. By Major Richardson, Knight of the Military Order of Saint Ferdinand, Author of Ecarté, Wacousta, etc. etc. In two volumes. Vol. I.* Montreal, Armour & Ramsay, 1840" was listed in the *Montreal Gazette* in its "literature" column. Although its writer wondered if he were "well justified in placing the first volume of Major RICHARDSON's new Tale at the head of this article, as the entire work will not be published before the first of next month," the inclusion of **The Canadian Brothers** allowed him "to notify the subscribers to the work of the rich entertainment which awaits them." The same issue of the newspaper announced that the novel would "be ready for delivery to subscribers on the 1st of February, and to the public generally, on the 5th," that the publishers were "Messrs. ARMOUR & RAMSAY," and that "the several" subscription lists "not yet returned" should "be forwarded" to them.

Over the next two weeks many newspapers reported the receipt of the first volume of **The Canadian Brothers** and the publication date of the second. On 20 January 1840 the *Quebec Gazette* included a brief comment with its notice:

> The present volume, although it belongs to a work of fiction, has much of the historical character.— The author, a native of Upper Canada, and long a resident in that Province, has the advantage of being intimately acquainted with the localities whose scenery he ably describes, as well as the character of the persons who figure in the work; with TECUMSEH and the Western Indians, who are conspicuous personages in the tale, he was personally acquainted.

The events which are chiefly referred to, relate to the period of the war of 1812, the attack of the Americans on the Detroit frontier, and the subsequent military operations in Upper Canada.

The Kingston *Chronicle & Gazette,* which stated on 25 January 1840 that it had received "the first volume" of the novel "this morning," also referred briefly to the nature of the work and promised to "present" its "readers with a specimen of the style of the author" in its next issue. The *Toronto Patriot* on 28 January and the *Bytown Gazette* on 30 January made similar promises of "an early and careful perusal," for which the latter newspaper fully expected to be amply repaid "if we may judge from the talent displayed by the writer in his former works." On 1 February the Sandwich *Western Herald* reprinted the announcement about the novel being ready for delivery to subscribers from the *Montreal Herald* on 18 January. On 8 February the *Detroit Free Press* reproduced the notice that had appeared in the *Toronto Patriot* on 28 January.

By the end of January reviews of the first volume of **The Canadian Brothers** had begun to appear. On 25 January 1840 the *Montreal Herald,* after reprinting passages from the work that described Splitlog, Roundhead, and Tecumseh, expressed sentiments that Richardson probably felt should have been said more often:

> Major Richardson's work is an honour to Canadian literature, and we hope that the patriotic feeling which induced him to publish his novel in Canada instead of in London, as he might easily have done, will, independently of its sterling qualities, be duly appreciated by the public.

The "mode of exhibiting appreciation," it suggested, was "by subscribing to the work." As it had promised, on 29 January the Kingston *Chronicle & Gazette* published the "beautiful description of Amherstburg" and the passage introducing Barclay, Brock, and Tecumseh in the opening chapter of the novel. In its review published on 30 January the *Montreal Transcript* also singled out the "opening scene at Amherstburg" as "one of the happiest specimens of descriptive power that we have for years met with." It chose not to quote any passages "in support of our opinion":

> we might thus forestall the pleasure of the public, while we should nothing advance the interest of the author. The volume we *have* is entitled to public support, on the solid ground of its merits, and therefore we conceive will command it; and while Major Richardson may be justly proud of it, no doubt can exist of the second volume proving its worthy successor; the man who wrote what we have read, could not, if he would, write any thing insipid or derogatory to his established reputation.

In the meantime Lovell was completing the printing of the second volume. It "issued from the press" on 1 February 1840, and copies were immediately sent to the provincial newspapers. The *Montreal Gazette,* for example, announced on 4 February the receipt of its copy of the second volume. Although both volumes were ready for distribution to the subscribers by 6 February, the official publication date of *The Canadian Brothers* was 10 February 1840. On that day, for example, the Montreal *Morning Courier* reported in an advertisement dated "Montreal, Feb. 10, 1840":

> *This Morning, will be Published,*
>
> THE CANADIAN BROTHERS;
>
> AN HISTORICAL TALE OF THE
>
> WAR OF 1812,
>
> *IN TWO VOLUMES.*
>
> BY MAJOR RICHARDSON.
>
> Price 20s.

Although copies of *The Canadian Brothers* were not available for sale in Toronto until late March—they were "delayed by an unavoidable accident"—the *Toronto Patriot* had received a copy of the second volume from "MAJOR RICHARDSON" by the third week of February.

That month the Canadian press began reviewing the complete novel. One of the earliest reviews was included in the February issue of the *Literary Garland,* which the *Montreal Gazette* had received by 6 February. On that day the newspaper commented:

> We are very much pleased with "Our Table" in this number of the *Garland.* It contains a well written and judicious review of Major RICHARDSON's new tale of *The Canadian Brothers,* which cannot fail to recommend the work to the attention of the public, as fraught with interest of a very high character.

The review in "Our Table" was, in fact, one of the longest and most astute assessments that *The Canadian Brothers* received.

The review began with a statement of the *Literary Garland*'s gratification

> at the receipt of this publication, which is, we believe, the first of its class issued from the Canadian Press, and is the "mental-facture" of one who owns his birthplace among us, and who is not, even in the literary world of England, "unknown to fame."

It then pointed out the political value of the novel, especially in view of the proposed union of the Canadas. It

> treats upon subjects which, by analogy, may bear a reference to the present condition of these colonies, inasmuch as, the Imperial and Colonial Governments being engaged upon the maturing of a measure, almost unparalleled for its magnitude and importance, in our Colonial history, with the view of assimilating the different races inhabiting the Canadas, and proportionately advancing their united and individual prosperity, it should be the aim of all to lend assistance towards rendering the measure one of permanent and enduring usefulness. . . . The author of the *Canadian Brothers,* has (unconsciously and indirectly it may be, as the book has been some years written,) contributed the aid of his powerful pen to attain this most desirable end, by exhibiting the readiness with which all classes and creeds flocked round the standard of their common country in an hour of doubt and danger, ready to gage life and limb to maintain the supremacy of Britain, over these fair and extensive colonies.

The Canadian Brothers also presented history in a way that would appeal to the "young student":

> While we deprecate the superficial reading of history to be gleaned from even a connected chain of historical tales, as being a dangerous medium from which to acquire knowledge, we cannot withhold our opinion that the perusal of fictious narratives, founded upon historical truths, which the author, neither in words nor spirit has perverted, will be found to afford much assistance to the young student, as being more free from tedium than the graver details of the formal historian; and, in countries such as these, which are lamentably deficient in works treating upon their past existence, such books must be particularly useful.

The review then outlined the setting of the novel and commented on such characteristics as its plot and dialogue. This section concluded with the observation that "the whole spirit of the work is of the most liberal *caste,* and, withal, bears throughout a thoroughly colonial character." This "character" was further explained:

> Altogether the work deserves well of the Canadas, and the British Provinces in general, for in it is the colonial character vindicated from the aspersions hitherto too frequently cast upon it, as being secondary in sterling worth to that of the parent country—an idea the expression of which was as impolitic as its belief was erroneous and unjust. It is indeed obvious that the materials composing colonial society are of the best producible by the mother country, with occasional exceptions unworthy of remark, for the very fact of a wish to emigrate argues a desire to rise to a more elevated

position, and there is no ingredient in the human composition more deserving of commendation than a just and properly directed ambition.

The review emphasized next the generous nature of Richardson's treatment of "the American social and political character" and contrasted his depiction of the Americans to the way in which "modern tourists" often portrayed the United States. The *Literary Garland* then reprinted a long passage about the capture of Gerald Grantham's boat from Volume Two, Chapter Two, before the review continued with a note on the dedication, the availability of the work from the publishers, and its nature as "two neatly printed duodecimo volumes, from the press of Mr. Lovell, in St. Nicholas Street." The review concluded with the announcement that Major Richardson was still contemplating the publication of "a Canadian edition of **Wacousta,** to enable those who have purchased the **Canadian Brothers,** to complete their sets, as well as to rectify numerous alterations and omissions made in the American reprint of that popular historical novel."

Reviews of **The Canadian Brothers** continued to appear in the newspapers throughout the spring of 1840. On 15 February, for example, the Kingston *Chronicle & Gazette* acknowledged the receipt of "the last volume of the gallant Major's **Canadian Brothers**" and praised the work enthusiastically. After reprinting a passage about the Battle of Queenston Heights from the last chapter, the review concluded:

> The **Canadian Brothers** will, we apprehend, be found very interesting to the general reader; but to all residents in Canada and the Frontier States of the American Republic, it cannot fail to afford a rich treat. . . . We for the present take leave of the accomplished Author, hoping that the success of the present work will be such as to induce him to avail himself of the ample field before him, in a series of Historical Novels on Canadian subjects.

A review in the *Quebec Mercury* on 18 February 1840 was equally laudatory. It was especially interested in the character of Jeremiah Desborough, although it warned that he should not "be considered as a general portrait of the 'settlers' who have come from the United States," and of that of Sampson Gattrie, whom it called "Simon Girty, an Indian interpreter, in the British service." The newspaper, moreover, was so impressed with the faithfulness of the novel's "historical narrative of the events which occurred in the Western District of Upper Canada, on Lake Erie, and on the Niagara Frontier" that it urged the novel's purchase by "every library in these Provinces." This was particularly important because

> Major Richardson has not only clearly stated his facts, but he has mentioned many circumstances,

especially those connected with the division which served under General Procter, that have been suppressed by those writers who have professed to give accounts of the Canadian Campaigns, though they were generally known in the Western and Centre Divisions of the army in the Upper Province.

One selection from this review was reprinted in the Montreal *Morning Courier* on 26 February; another, in the Toronto *Examiner* on 8 April 1840.

In March of that year Richardson used his return journey to Sandwich to create even more interest in **The Canadian Brothers** and to arrange for its wider distribution. On 18 March the Kingston *Chronicle & Gazette* announced that it had been "authorized by Major Richardson, to whom we had named the extensive demand" for the novel "among the farmers and yeomen of the country, to state, that to them the price of the book shall be, as heretofore, the subscription amount—three dollars." Richardson was willing to sell them the book at a cheaper rate because, "the work being in a great degree a national one," its price should "meet the views and means of those who, although in a humble condition of life," had shown "so strong a national (that is to say Canadian) spirit." For "all other persons the book" would be "four dollars—a distinction in price due to those who have supported the publication with their names." On 25 March the *Cobourg Star* noted that it had "been politely presented by the Author with a copy of the new historical novel of Major Richardson." It had marked "some interesting passages for early insertion" in the newspaper. **"Attack on Fort Sandusky"** was published on 15 April; **"Action at Stoney Creek"** and **"Death of General Brock"** appeared on 22 April 1840. On 21 May of the same year the *St. Catharines Journal, And Welland Canal, (Niagara District), General Advertiser* also printed **"Death of General Brock."**

In March 1840 the first reviews of **The Canadian Brothers** were published outside Canada. The New York *Albion* stated on 21 March:

> the book has qualities of a more important nature than those of a pleasing work of fiction; it is a picture, in many respects a faithful one, in all we believe a conscientious one, and assuredly an intelligent one, of the state of affairs in the provinces and on the border about the important period between 1812 and 1815. It is interspersed with many fine local and personal descriptions, discussions of military operations, and, a subject of no little interest—the arguments for and against the propriety of using the Indian aid in warfare. We do not undertake to say that we coincide with this able writer throughout the course of his arguments in this book, but we have no hesitation in saying that they are well entitled to respectful consideration,

and many of them are of so important a nature that they seem to *demand* attention.

The *Colonial Magazine,* the London periodical to which Richardson had sent a copy, noticed **The Canadian Brothers** in its July 1840 issue. It "sincerely" recommended the work as "a faithful portraiture of events which characterized the last war between Great Britain and the United States."

A few other items, as well as these reviews, attest to the interest that **The Canadian Brothers** evoked, especially in the Canadian press. On 11 March 1840 the Montreal *Morning Courier* published "Interesting Mementos of the War of 1812"; one reason for the appearance of this article was the "attention" that Richardson's novel had brought to Sir John Harvey and "the Stoney Creek affair." In the same newspaper on 24 April a correspondent, commenting on the review of **The Canadian Brothers** in the *Quebec Mercury,* pointed out that Richardson had not invented the story of Matilda. Rather he had based it on the Beauchamp affair, which the correspondent then related. He concluded, "Major RICHARDSON has awakened the *memories* of those days:—being awakened, one can scarcely refrain from dropping a tear over the horrible history." When four days later the *Quebec Mercury* reprinted this article, its editor noted:

> We had at the time we wrote the paragraph the *Courier* has quoted from our notice of the **Canadian Brothers,** some vague recollection of the tragical occurrence, the leading particulars of which he has related. But our recollection of it was not sufficiently distinct to enable us to refer to it, in speaking of the picture of the drama by the author of the novel in which he has adhered sufficiently to facts which had occurred in real life to justify the introduction of a character which has been, by many we know, regarded as not a very felicitous invention of the author. We cannot, however, look upon the Beauchamps as objects of sympathy; but our neighbours who deal profusely in that article might possibly have discovered, at the time, some traits in the horrible history to call for compassion upon the criminals.

In spite of these notices of **The Canadian Brothers,** in Richardson's view at least, it was not a publishing success. In **Eight Years In Canada** he stated that, in addition to the one hundred people in the Detroit area who had subscribed for his novel, he had obtained two hundred and fifty names in Canada. Of these subscribers

> —two thirds . . . even went so far as to take their books when published. The other third had been kind enough merely to lend me the encouragement of their names, and nothing, therefore, was more natural when called upon, to decline their copies—

some under the pleas that the volumes, the price of which had been made known to them on subscribing—were too dear; some, that they had been too long delayed in the publication; and not a few, that they did not feel inclined to take them at that moment.

It is likely, then, that at least three hundred and fifty copies were printed, of which perhaps two hundred and fifty were actually purchased. There were also copies printed to be sold by booksellers.

Presumably the remainders of both those prepared for the subscribers and those for booksellers were what Richardson himself was marketing in 1842 in his newspaper the *New Era* when he advertised **Wacousta** and **The Canadian Brothers** for sale as a set. On 26 January in the "Literature" section of the *New Era,* Richardson wrote under the heading *"WACOUSTA AND THE CANADIAN BROTHERS":*

> THESE NATIONAL AND HISTORICAL WORKS, having been got up at great expense and serious inconvenience to the author, without that remuneration from the Canadian public, which as a Canadian writer, he has had a right to expect from the more liberal portion at least of the community, are now to be disposed of, at the reduced price of FIVE dollars for the complete set, containing FIVE VOLUMES, three of which alone, (**Wacousta**) have always been sold in England, for no less than SEVEN dollars. The two sets will be neatly and separately bound, so as to make two books, which as volumes of reference, it cannot but be supposed, will find their way into the library of every Canadian Gentleman, desirous of knowing any thing connected with the early history of his own country.

Along with the two novels, Richardson also offered each subscriber a copy of **Tecumseh** "at halfprice . . . which, it is intended to reprint from the original MSS.—thus completing the series of CANADIAN WORKS." He trusted, Richardson added, that his "contemporaries, who have already afforded the most flattering testimony of the Author's attempt to infuse a spirit of National Literature into his native land," would not be "slow in urging upon the consideration of the public, the reasonableness of his present proposition." To encourage the public further, Richardson appended selections from the reviews of both **Wacousta** and **The Canadian Brothers**. Those of **The Canadian Brothers** were "EXTRACTS FROM THE CANADIAN PRESS." They included passages from the review in each of the *Montreal Herald,* the *Niagara Chronicle,* the *Montreal Gazette,* the *Toronto Commercial Herald,* the *Quebec Mercury,* and the *Sherbrooke Gazette.* In the same section Richardson also printed the "NAMES AND RESIDENCE OF SUBSCRIBERS HITHERTO RECEIVED" This list contained forty-four names.

In the same "Literature" section Richardson announced his intention to serialize in the *New Era* his **Narrative of the Operations of the Right Division of the Army in Upper Canada**. An enlarged and revised version of **"A Canadian Campaign,"** it appeared in the *New Era* from March to July 1842. Richardson then published it immediately in book form as **War Of 1812**. This was the last full-length work that Richardson published in Canada on this war.

The year 1842, in fact, marked the beginning of the series of misfortunes that eventually induced Richardson to leave Canada. They included the failure of three newspapers, one of them the *New Era,* the fiasco of his appointment as Suprintendent of Police on the Welland Canal, and the death of his wife. Richardson's discontent, particularly the unhappiness that he felt at what he considered the neglect by Canadians of one of their first authors, is revealed in **Eight Years In Canada**. In it Richardson contrasted at some length "the custom of the civilized world" of honouring its authors with the lack of recognition that he had received in Canada. Pointing out that "the Canadians are not a reading people," he concluded his remarks:

> As this is the last time I shall ever allude to the humiliating subject, I cannot deny to myself the gratification of the expression of a hope, that should a more refined and cultivated taste ever be introduced into the matter-of-fact country in which I have derived my being, its people will decline to do me the honor of placing my name in the list of their "Authors." I certainly have no particular ambition to rank among their future "men of genius," or to share in any posthumous honor they may be disposed to confer upon them.

With these parting words Richardson closed what had obviously become for him the painful chapter of being a writer in Canada. In the fall of 1849 he left for the United States.

The first work that Richardson sold in his newly adopted country was **Hardscrabble. A Tale Of Chicago,** which ran as a serial in *Sartain's Union Magazine Of Literature And Art* from February to June 1850. While this novel, set on the northwest frontier in 1812, was still appearing in the periodical, Richardson negotiated its publication in volume form with DeWitt and Davenport. A New York firm that had published its first books in 1849, it specialized in issuing cheap paperbacks, frequently of previously published novels. In 1850 and 1851 Richardson made arrangements with DeWitt and Davenport to publish several of his works, including, as well as **Hardscrabble,** which appeared in October 1851, **Wacousta** and **The Canadian Brothers**.

When DeWitt and Davenport published the second American edition of **Wacousta** in the spring of 1851, it had a new introduction written by Richardson and dated "New York City, January 1st, 1851." Otherwise the text of the new edition followed that of the first American edition of the novel published by Adam Waldie in 1833 and altered by his editor at that time to suit the popular American readership that this early enterpreneur sought. The preparation of **The Canadian Brothers** took more time and presented more problems.

In his introduction to DeWitt and Davenport's edition of **Wacousta**, Richardson not only stated that "the Beauchamp tragedy" was a source of the work he called **The Prophecy Fulfilled,** but he also commented that he had published this sequel "Some few years ago . . . in Canada—I might as well have done so in Kamtschatka." In a letter that he wrote to Rufus Griswold probably in June 1851, Richardson reported that he had "arranged" with his "publishers for **Ecarté** and the **Prophecy Fulfilled,** both of which" he had "sold them far below their value." Requesting a loan of "from ten to fifteen dollars," Richardson explained to Griswold that his payment for these works was "delayed until I have made some slight alterations in the last named work," but that these would be done and he would be paid in no "more than a fortnight hence." When the new edition of **The Canadian Brothers** appeared in September 1851, however, it was a much altered version.

Some of the alterations involved changes in such aspects of the text as its punctuation, spelling, capitalization, and, occasionally, word order. Others were attempts to correct obvious errors that had been made when the first edition was typeset but that had not been caught during the course of its proofreading. Still others were due to errors that the new compositors made when they misread the sense of a passage, or when they momentarily forgot the name or the rank of the character who was its subject. In the new edition, too, especially in passages of dialogue, the paragraphs that signified a new speaker were often deleted. Although these changes tended to substitute American for British and Canadian usage, they were not unusual in a new edition, and they did not significantly affect the meaning of the text.

Another group of alterations, however, included additions, changes, and deletions that modified the setting, the characters, the action, and, ultimately, the themes of the novel. Although the change was not made consistently, there was an attempt in the second edition to call the location of much of the action of the story "Malden," its more usual American name, rather than Amherstburg. Descriptions of such natural features of the climate and geography of the area that were denoted in the first edition as "Canadian" were called "American" in the second. Thus the "stern invigorating winter of Canada" became the "stern invigorating winter of beautiful America," "a Canadian sky" "an American sky," and the "Canadian" lakes "American." Although both editions of the novel took place in 1812-13, in the first the war was described as "The war in Canada;" in the second, "The war of 1812."

Similar alterations were made to the characters in the second edition. Sampson Gattrie was consistently called Simon Girty. Passages concerning Gerald and Henry Grantham, especially those that described their parents, including the deathbed scene of Isabella Grantham, were deleted, as were depictions of the character and actions of Barclay, Brock, and Tecumseh. Cranstoun's role as a character was diminished when his speech was either excised or anglicized. Conversations among the other British officers were shortened. One of the passages of dialogue omitted was that which occurred when the officers teased Lieutenant Raymond at the ball in Amherstburg; included in the deletion were the lines from and the reference to *The Monk*. While the role of the British in the novel was made less important, the character traits of the Americans were softened. Jeremiah Desborough, for example, who was repeatedly referred to as a "Yankee" in the first edition, was called in the second a "ruffian," a "culprit," and a "settler," but his "Yankee" origins were mostly deleted. Similarly, phrases in the first edition that suggested that American officers were uncouth or that backwoodsmen were uncivilized were either deleted or changed in the second. The adjectives "half civilized" applied to backwoodsmen in the first edition, for example, became "angry" in the second. Even Cranstoun's comment in the first edition that Matilda had "a bust and hips to warm the bosom of an anchorite" was modified in the second edition by the deletion of "and hips."

The diminution of the role of the British and Canadian characters in the second edition was paralleled by the alterations to the action of the novel. None of the events was totally deleted, but passages describing the British role in a battle were frequently omitted, and occasionally phrases or sentences were added to emphasize the heroism of the Americans. In the description of the Battle of Lake Erie, for example, two long paragraphs were omitted. These discussed Barclay's wound as the possible cause of his defeat; the Indian chiefs who sailed with him in the *Detroit;* the disappointment at Amherstburg at Barclay's misfortunes; and the premonition of Tecumseh of the hopelessness "of retrieving his race from the hated thraldom of American tyranny and American usurpation." A sentence about the American victory at Lake Erie, however, was expanded from "Let it suffice that the Americans triumphed" to "Let it suffice that the Americans faught with determined bravery, and eventually triumphed."

Similar but more dramatic alterations were made in the second edition to the description of the Battle of Queenston Heights, the event that concludes the novel. The final paragraph of *The Canadian Brothers,* for exam-

ple, was significantly shortened, even though a passage about Sambo, the Granthams' black servant, was added. In the second edition this paragraph read:

> Their picked and whitened bones may be seen even to this day, confounded together and shining through the gloom that pervades every part of the abyss, and often may be remarked an aged and decrepit negro, seated on a rock a few feet above them, leaning his elbows upon his knees, and gazing eagerly as if to distinguish the bones of the one from the bones of the other.

In the second edition, furthermore, a final paragraph was added that turned the emphasis from the War of 1812 to the prophecy fulfilled: "AND THUS WAS THE FEARFUL PROPHECY OF ELLEN HALLOWAY, THE MOTHER OF DESBOROUGH BY WACOUSTA FULFILLED!"

In addition to these changes in the setting, characters, and action, there were a number of others in the second edition. What might be considered inappropriately coarse words or phrases were often made more polite. The "doxies" of the Cockneys became "sweethearts," for example. The Latin expressions that Richardson occasionally used were mostly omitted, as were many passages in French. Other sections in French were translated. As a result of all these alterations, the bare bones of the plot remained, but the flesh and blood that gave it life and meaning were torn away. While the subject was still the fulfillment of Ellen Halloway's prophecy during the War of 1812, this war no longer played the crucial role that it did in the first edition. The War of 1812 in the second edition, furthermore, was not predominantly a Canadian war or presented from a Canadian point of view. Rather the emphasis shifted from the public tragedy of war between two closely related nations to the private melodrama of the revenge of a spurned mistress. It is not surprising therefore that in the second edition the dedication to Sir John Harvey and the preface were deleted; the main title of the novel itself was changed from *The Canadian Brothers; Or, The Prophecy Fulfilled* to *Matilda Montgomerie: Or, The Prophecy Fulfilled;* and in this new context the subtitle *A Tale Of The Late American War* took on a new meaning.

Did Richardson make these alterations to *The Canadian Brothers*? He may well have made some, especially since, according to his letter to Griswold, his payment for the copyright of both *Ecarté* and *The Canadian Brothers* depended on "some slight alterations" in the latter. It is impossible now to know what these changes were. They may well have included such relatively minor emendations as correcting compositorial errors in the 1840 edition, calling Simon Girty by his true name, or even substituting "the forty-first regiment" for "the——regiment," although this alteration was not made consistently. Despite Richardson's apology for Cranstoun's Scottish dialect in *The Canadian Brothers,* his changes probably did not include the almost total elimination of Cranstoun as a character in the novel or the deletion of so much of the dialogue of the British officers serving with him. It is hard to believe, moreover, given Richardson's earlier comments about the importance of *The Canadian Brothers* as a Canadian national novel, the consistency of his interest in the Canadian War of 1812, and the enormity of his admiration for Barclay, Brock, and Tecumseh, that Richardson would have willingly altered in such a substantial way the public context of his story. Most importantly, it seems unlikely that Richardson, the skilled and experienced writer who demonstrated in *The Canadian Brothers* such a sense of structural integrity and dramatic unity, would have voluntarily shortened, sanitized, and simplified his novel into the slightly flat, moderately jerky, and mostly melodramatic story that is *Matilda Montgomerie.*

Perhaps the question should focus on the reasons why the alterations were made for the new edition of *The Canadian Brothers* rather than on who actually made them. Then the answer becomes clear. For when Richardson sold *The Canadian Brothers* to DeWitt and Davenport, he placed his novel in the hands of publishers who were marketing their books not only to an American reading public but also to a particular, albeit large and growing, segment of that public. These were the readers who bought cheap paperbacks, who knew only English, who liked sentiment and sensation, who had shown an appetite for the Beauchamp tragedy, and who were totally and patriotically American. For these consumers *The Canadian Brothers* transformed into *Matilda Montgomerie* would almost certainly be a good read. For DeWitt and Davenport, who had already purchased *The Canadian Brothers* for "far below" its "value," *Matilda Montgomerie* was quite definitely the better version and the best commercial venture.

The first announcements of the publication of *Matilda Montgomerie* appeared towards the end of September 1851. In the notice in the *New-York Daily Tribune* on 20 September 1851, for example, the "New Romance by the Author of *Wacousta*" was advertised as a sequel to "that romantic and soul-stirring story":

> All will recollect that in the former the main interest of the story hinges on the curse the unfortunate Ellen Halloway invoked upon the family and descendants of De Haldimar, which the terrible Wacousta was the unpitying instrument in carrying
>
> out.
> In the Sequel the same curse is continued and accomplished, but by a widely different personage— one, the fairest of earth's daughters in form, but, alas, in mind, as cruel and unrelenting as the fierce warrior himself. It might be doubted whether, in

woman's lovely breast, vengeance so dire could find a place; but we all know how dreadful is her revenge when irreparably wronged.

The novel was "well printed on good paper"; its price was "50 Cents." On the same day an advertisement in the *New-York Daily Times* stated that *Matilda Montgomerie* was "READY THIS day."

Advertisements announcing the availability of the novel continued to appear throughout the fall in newspapers published in such places as Auburn, New York, and in Boston, New York City, and Philadelphia. On the last day of September "D. & J. SADLIER & CO.," of "179, Notre Dame Street" in Montreal, advertised in the Montreal *Pilot* that it had "*Matilda Montgomerie,* by Major Richardson" for sale for "2s 6d" at its "CHEAP CASH BOOK STORE." By the next day copies of the novel had arrived in Louisville, Kentucky. "C. HAGAN & CO." included *Matilda Montgomerie* as the first of the "NEW BOOKS" that it had for sale in an advertisement that appeared in the *Louisville Daily Courier,* the *Louisville Daily Democrat,* and the *Louisville Daily Journal* on 1 October 1851.

The novel was also the subject of a few short reviews. On 26 September 1851, for example, the *New-York Daily Tribune* commented that *Matilda Montgomerie* was set during "the late American war. The story is related with great vivacity, and contains passages of considerable vigor." On 11 October 1851 the *Semi-Weekly Courier And New-York Enquirer* reported that the work was "a tale of the late American war and a sequel to Wacousta. This romance is vivid in narration, stirring in incident, clear and bold in portraiture, and is in every respect worthy of its well-known predecessor." In its December 1851 issue *Sartain's Magazine,* announcing the publication of *Matilda Montgomerie,* remarked on each of *Wacousta, Hardscrabble,* and *Matilda Montgomerie.* This novel, it concluded, "with much accurate historical detail, blends the absorbing interest of an exciting romance." Only the *Southern Quarterly Review* published in Charleston, South Carolina, sounded a negative note. Reviewing both *Écarté,* which DeWitt and Davenport also published in 1851, and *Matilda Montgomerie* in its January 1852 issue, the periodical described the latter novel as "one of horrors and loathsome details—inartistically wrought out from complicated materials. The events are borrowed, in part, from the fearful Kentucky tragedy of Beauchampe, though the scene is placed on the Canada frontier, and the events coupled with those of the war of 1812."

This periodical's caveat notwithstanding, *Matilda Montgomerie* proved to be a popular production. After the first impression of the American edition appeared in 1851, there were at least five subsequent impressions issued between 1852 and 1888. Richardson, however, did not live to witness its success. He died, probably of malnutrition, in New York City on 12 May 1852. One of his last public performances was a lecture that he delivered on 20 February of that year. Its subject was "the character and death of Tecumseh."

Despite Richardson's enormous contribution to early Canadian literature, little attention was paid to him in Canada in the latter part of the nineteenth century. With the advent of the twentieth century, however, there developed a curiosity about what the nineteenth had achieved. John Richardson thus began to be recognized as a seminal Canadian author. In 1902 Alexander Clark Casselman prepared an edition of *Richardson's War Of 1812 With Notes And A Life Of The Author* that included a biography of Richardson, a genealogy of the Richardsons and the Askins, and a bibliography of Richardson's works. Archibald MacMurchy's *Handbook of Canadian Literature (English)* in 1906 devoted much space to Richardson as an early Canadian author. In 1914 Thomas Guthrie Marquis in his article "English-Canadian Literature" in *Canada and Its Provinces* discussed Richardson at some length both as an historian and as a novelist. *War Of 1812,* he decided, was in "many ways the most important Canadian history of the War of 1812." Richardson was "a trained writer and soldier, and the events of the war during the years 1812 and 1813 were strongly presented. His characterizations of such men as Brock, Procter and Tecumseh are excellent." Because earlier works of fiction published in Canada "were not true novels and are scarcely worthy of notice in a literary review," Marquis chose Richardson as the writer "entitled to be called the first Canadian novelist" and the publication of *Wacousta* in 1832 as "the true beginning of Canadian fiction." Marquis' admiration for Richardson and his work stopped short of *The Canadian Brothers,* however. The story was "weakly constructed," and Richardson took "unwarranted liberties with historical facts."

In the 1920s, in the enthusiasm for Canadian literature that developed in the wake of post World War One nationalism, John Richardson's name came to the fore again. In his chapter on "John Richardson And The Historical Romance" in *A History of English-Canadian Literature to the Confederation* (1920), Ray Palmer Baker called *The Canadian Brothers* in "many respects . . . the most significant" of Richardson's "romances" and "one of the most significant books of its time." In 1923 the first book-length study about Richardson was published when William Renwick Riddell's *John Richardson* was issued in the Makers of Canadian Literature series. Riddell's study, which covered Richardson's life and works in some detail, had a chapter on *The Canadian Brothers*. In it Riddell discussed the composition and publication of *The Canadian Brothers* and summarized its plot. Much of his attention focussed on *Matilda Montgomerie* and its

differences from the first edition. Riddell pointed out the "many omissions—I have noted over seventy—of more or less length and importance, ranging from three or four pages down to a single sentence" in *Matilda Montgomerie*. Assuming, however, that the text of the new edition was entirely prepared by Richardson, Riddell did not distinguish between the two versions of the novel as in some ways different works. Concluding his remarks in this chapter on *The Canadian Brothers,* he quoted the final sentence from *Matilda Montgomerie* about "THE FEARFUL PROPHECY" being "FULFILLED," and stated, "I may perhaps be permitted to add: 'And no one can fairly say that Fate did not make a complete job of it.'" In "An Appreciation" Riddell criticized various aspects of *The Canadian Brothers,* including "the Negro dialect of Sambo," "the Scotch" of Cranstoun, the artificiality of Desborough as villain, and the "pure fiction" of Matilda Montgomerie as a portrait of a woman. Yet about the "poetry and fiction of Richardson" he concluded, "Of one thing we are sure; and that is, that time will prove our judgment true and sound when we gave him a first place among the Makers of Canadian Literature."

Riddell's prescience has been amply demonstrated in the last half century when John Richardson and his works have been the subjects of many articles and books. Such items as "A Colonial Romantic" (1959-60), Desmond Pacey's articles on Richardson; Carl Ballstadt's collection of reviews and criticism in *Major John Richardson* (1972); William F. E. Morley's *A Bibliographical Study of Major John Richardson* (1973); Beasley's *The Canadian Don Quixote: the life and works of Major John Richardson, Canada's first novelist* (1977) and his biography of Richardson in the *Dictionary of Canadian Biography* (1985); Dennis Duffy's meditation on "Major John Richardson: The Loyalist in Disguise" in his *Gardens, Covenants, Exiles: Loyalism in the Literature of Upper Canada/Ontario* (1982); his "John Richardson (1796-1852)" in *Canadian Writers And Their Works* (1983); and the papers collected in *Recovering Canada's First Novelist* (1984) all demonstrate the interest that Richardson has inspired and the cultural icon that he has become. Much of the criticism about Richardson has focussed on *Wacousta,* however, and the perceptions about this novel, especially if it has been read in a shortened version based on the 1833 American edition, have tended both to distort interpretations of Richardson and to distract attention from his other work.

Consideration has been given to *The Canadian Brothers* nevertheless. A photographic reprint of the first edition of this novel was published in the Literature of Canada series in 1976 with an introduction by Carl F. Klinck. "A Summary of The Canadian Brothers" by Michael Hurley was published the same year in *Halloween 2*. In "Patterns of Significance in the Fiction of John Richardson" (1984) Hurley, discussing "the thematic and structural patterns" of Richardson's "fictional corpus," further developed his ideas about *The Canadian Brothers*. "Richardson's Canadian romances," he commented, "relentlessly assume a tragic trajectory; indeed, our first Canadian brothers recall our first brothers, Cain and Abel." During this time James Reaney, whose dramatization of *Wacousta* was published in 1979, was working on a play based on *The Canadian Brothers*. "*The Canadian Brothers* or The Prophecy Fulfilled," first produced at the University of Calgary in November 1983, was anthologized in *Major Plays Of The Canadian Theatre 1934-1984* (1984).

Perhaps these critics have glimpsed a different view of Richardson and *The Canadian Brothers* because they have not been distracted by *Matilda Montgomerie* and its links with *The Canadian Brothers*. For, unlike *Matilda Montgomerie,* which reads like a conventional nineteenth-century melodrama, *The Canadian Brothers* retains its appeal as a work of historical fiction based on personal experience. It has the melodramatic qualities of *Matilda Montgomerie,* of course, but in *The Canadian Brothers* these characteristics are transformed into the images by means of which Richardson conveyed both his patriotism to Canada as an emerging nation with strong British connections and his appreciation of the Canadian past, especially that associated with the Indians and with the military in Upper Canada in the early years of the nineteenth century.

Yet *The Canadian Brothers* is finally neither a sentimental idyll about the world of one's youth, nor a nostalgic elegy for a prelapsarian world. It is, rather, a sombre tragedy about the fallen one. In this world, in both its private and public manifestations, there is deception, intrigue, mystery, passion, revenge, and violence, for all of which there is neither comfort nor remedy. And in the end there is death—for the descendants of Wacousta and De Haldimar, for Brock and Tecumseh, and for hundreds of others who fought in the War of 1812. Thus, the victory of Queenston Heights becomes in *The Canadian Brothers* the tragedy of the "picked and whitened bones" that shine "through the deep gloom that envelopes every part of the abyss, even to this day." The triumph of *The Canadian Brothers* itself is the unflinching honesty of its documentation of this tragedy that demands to be told about a past that cannot be changed.

Michael Hurley (essay date 1992)

SOURCE: "Border Doubles: Twin Poles of the Canadian Psyche," in *The Borders of Nightmare: The Fiction of John Richardson,* University of Toronto Press, 1992, pp. 69-109.

[*In the following excerpt, Hurley discusses family relationships and the doppelgänger theme in* Wacousta.]

In Canada, the wilderness, symbolized by the north, creates a kind of doppelganger figure who is oneself and yet the opposite of oneself . . . The Canadian recurring themes of self-conflict, of the violating of nature, of individuals uncertain of their social context, of dark, repressed oracular doubles concealed within each of us, are now more communicable outside Canada in the new mood of the world.

NORTHROP FRYE, *Divisions on a Ground*

His own life was no longer a single story but part of a mural, which was a falling together of accomplices.

MICHAEL ONDAATJE, *In the Skin of a Lion*

'Break boundaries'—points of reversal generating a paradoxical blurring, merging, or exchanging of identity—occur between specific characters in *Wacousta* as well as between the larger cultural groupings of regiment and tribe. In the preceding chapter, I sought to show how two cultures, one indigenous, the other immigrant, apparently without any relationship to each other, progressively intertwine and fuse in a curiously complementary fashion. Similarly, the twins, doubles, or doppelgänger figures so prominent in descent imagery participate in the border dialectic of Richardson's works. Here, too, there is opposition in which the opposing forces endlessly turn into one another.

Such doubleness gains in depth and impact from being reflected in the setting and structure of the work and is integral to the exposition of the central themes. Richardson's predilection for doubles and love triangles seems to issue from a psyche fascinated with balancing or undoing one element by another. This tendency plays havoc with conventional notions of identity. Lives reduplicate one another, giving rise to an eerie sense of doubleness, of reflections within reflections. Like the double exposure in a photo, under the intense compressional force of the borderland, characters and situations are superimposed over one another until it becomes hard to distinguish where one leaves off and another begins. Indeed, it soon becomes futile—not to say exasperating—to define identity in terms of separate and neatly isolatable individuals. Identity is communal; the focus is on groups rather than single characters.

Unlike many American frontier romances featuring a lone protagonist devoid of ancestry, *Wacousta* and *The Canadian Brothers* describe a claustrophobic world of uncles, nephews, aunts, cousins, mothers, fathers, daughters, sons, sisters, and brothers. All are caught in a web of family relationships which is so densely interwoven as to be labyrinthine in complexity. Two family trees take root in Richardson's borderland of the Canadian psyche: that of the respectable De Haldimars and that of the outcast Mortons, the former, according to Wacousta, destined to be the bane of the latter. Their branches become inexplicably intertwined to the point where they are indistinguishable; when the Wacousta limb is chopped off, the De Haldimar branch withers and falls to the ground soon thereafter. Moreover, they are set within the tightly knit society of the garrison, itself comprising tense groups who are 'by a communionship of suffering, isolation, and peculiarity of duty, drawn towards each other with feelings of almost fraternal affection.'

The major double, of course, is constituted by the De Haldimar/Wacousta relationship, a relationship examined in depth in this chapter beginning with the section entitled 'The Struggle-of-Brothers Theme.' To borrow a term from separate studies of doppelgängers in literature by Miyoshi and Tymms, this is a 'double-by-division'; it features two characters of opposing yet complementary temperaments who are strangely bonded. In addition, there are also 'doubles-by-duplication' in which one figure is multiplied or mirrored in almost identical form. Here we have two Reginald Mortons. Both adopt pseudonyms, names and naming—as well as 'unnaming'—being of great importance in Richardson's works. ('Wacousta' is the uncle of 'Frank Halloway,' this family connection discovered by the former late in the story.) Besides a common name and lineage, they share similar physical and personality traits and meet the same fate.

Passionate, impetuous, high-spirited, energetic, daring, proudly independent, and defiant, both Reginald Mortons are men of strong feeling unafraid of expressing emotion in a constricted culture within limits and frowns upon such open expression. Tender, generous-hearted, and frank, both are impassioned lovers who risk all for love. Halloway's family rejects him after he, like Wacousta, refuses a marriage of convenience for one of affection. Marrying the woman he loves, Halloway is forced by adverse circumstances to conceal his status as a gentleman by birth and assume a new name and a lower rank. By fateful coincidence, Ellen Halloway becomes the wife of both Mortons. In each case as well, Colonel de Haldimar separates them from the woman they cherish.

Both Mortons form brotherly attachments with De Haldimars. Echoing Sir Reginald Morton's friendship with Ensign de Haldimar, Frank Halloway's best friend is Frederick de Haldimar who closely resembles his father. Such is their affinity that Clara de Haldimar avers that 'Frank Halloway . . . loved my brother as though he had been of the same blood!' Like his uncle in his youth, Halloway is selfless and altruistic: on the Plains of Abraham, he shows himself willing to sacrifice his life to preserve that of his friend, throwing himself in front of Frederick as one of Montcalm's

favourite officers discharges his pistol. Ironically, this 'French' officer turns out to be Wacousta who recognizes the son by his resemblance to the father. Wacousta nearly kills his nephew; Colonel de Haldimar will be the next one to have Halloway shot.

Both Mortons fall victim to De Haldimar. He blackens their honour and their reputation, has them court-martialled on trumped-up charges as traitors, and ensures their exile or execution. What Ellen describes as 'the persecutions of the Morton family' in the Old World continue in the New, prompting her prophetic curse on the race of De Haldimar. A bitter Wacousta laments that his nephew has been rewarded for saving Frederick's life by 'an ignominious death, inflicted, perhaps, for some offense not more dishonouring than those which have thrown me an outcast upon these wilds . . . what but ingratitude of the grossest nature could a Morton expect at the hands of the false family of De Haldimar!' In the sequel, the last of the Mortons, locked in a death embrace with the last of the De Haldimars, perishes in the Niagara border abyss between Canada and the United States during the Battle of Queenston Heights.

Like the defendants themselves, the work's three trials seem to condense into one. Overlapping and paralleling one another, they suggest the cyclic nature of the herd mentality's insatiable appetite for scapegoats. During his second court martial, Wacousta stands on the same spot previously occupied by his nephew. He, too, insists on his status as a gentleman. Both ask for a delay in the proceedings pending Frederick's return, a request initially denied then granted by Governor de Haldimar in each case. Both are accused of conspiring with Ponteac and with François, the Canadian innkeeper; as in modern treatments of Louis Riel, each Morton is branded an outlaw and traitor to be exhibited as an example to native peoples so that 'when they behold your fate, they will take warning from your example; and . . . be more readily brought to obedience.' Both the Reginald Morton within the fort and the one without are killed at the exact centre of the 'Bloody Bridge.' Frank Halloway's declarations that 'Appearances . . . are against me' and 'I am not indeed what I seem to be' echo earlier statements by his uncle and suggest that the work's controlling irony lies in the abyss between appearance and reality.

The merging of the two Mortons is, perhaps, the most obvious example of a pervasive blurring of boundaries between characters in this borderland where identity is never static but always changing and indeterminate. Like De Haldimar and Wacousta, Charles de Haldimar and Sir Everard Valletort are doubles-by-division. 'Nearly of the same age,' 'the one was all gentleness, the other all spirit and vivacity.' Again, a passive and an active figure are bonded in strong friendship. They balance one another even as Wacousta's 'wild spirit was soothed by the bland amenity of his [De Haldimar's] manners.' Unlike that later relationship, 'not a shade of disunion had at any period intervened to interrupt the almost brotherly attachment subsisting between them, and each felt the disposition of the other was the one most assimilated to his own.' Indeed, in yet another important passage from the original 1832 *Wacousta* edited out of subsequent editions, Everard speaks of Charles de Haldimar as one 'whom I loved as though he had been my twin brother.' As in the case with Wacousta and De Haldimar and most doubles, they die within a short time of each other.

Such friendships represent a spirit of selflessness, camaraderie, and community that balances the mean-spirited herd-mind that often dominates garrison life. Recalling Richardson's *Frascati's* and anticipating a similar motif in his *The Monk Knight of St. John,* the bond between the two is further strengthened by Charles's desire that his friend wed his identical sister, his 'counterpart' Clara, 'that dearer half of myself.' (An analogous relationship obtains in Ernest Buckler's *The Mountain and the Valley;* identities merge as the aggressive, energetic Toby and the reflective David are balanced by their common inspiration, the latter's twin sister Anna.) Both brother and sister, in turn, bear an uncanny resemblance to their deceased mother, Clara Beverley, and both are killed by Wacousta at the fatal bridge.

By the end of the story, the identities of Clara, Charles, and Everard have coalesced in bizarre fashion; as Clara suddenly materializes at the opposite side of the bed upon which her dead brother lies in state, Everard is disoriented by the dizzying reflections from this human hall of mirrors: 'Her likeness to her brother, at that moment, was so striking, that, for a second or two, the irrepressible thought passed through the mind of the officer, it was not a living being he gazed upon, but the immaterial spirit of his friend. The whole attitude and appearance of the wretched girl, independently of the fact of her noiseless entrance, tended to favour the delusion. Her features, of an ashy paleness, seemed fixed, even as those of the corpse beneath him.' The permutations of identity are infused with an unsettling gothic light that becomes even more tenebrous during the ensuing vows of love. Declares Everard, 'In you will I love both my friend and the sister he has bequeathed to me.' For Clara, he will be 'both a brother and a husband.'

Like 'The Canadian Brothers,' the De Haldimar brothers also reveal Richardson's obsession with balanced pairs of characters, an obsession to which he, like Kroetsch, will remain faithful throughout his oeuvre. 'Captain de Haldimar had none of the natural weakness and timidity of character which belonged to the gentler and more sensitive Charles. Sanguine and full of enterprise, he is the allegro figure contrasting with the penseroso type his brother represents. While the active Frederick undertakes two heroic quests across vast distances and through the wilderness, his passive brother remains inside the fortress walls. Frederick is Colonel de Haldimar's favourite son; Charles is neglected, even rejected by his father, also named Charles, whose austere and puritanical nature is the opposite of his warm and emotional son's. In an epic informed by the Cain and Abel story, these two brothers, oddly enough, do *not* struggle; in the sequel, however, a similar tension between opposites is more exacerbated in their descendants as they quarrel over a woman (Wacousta's descendant) and one brother—inadvertently—kills the other.

Just as there are two Charles de Haldimars and two Reginald Mortons, so there are two Claras, mother and daughter. Abducting Clara de Haldimar from her father as he had Clara Beverley from hers, Wacousta sometimes confuses the two. Ravishing the former in the Indian oasis which parallels the Highland Eden of the latter, Wacousta—who has just told his other 'bride' Ellen Halloway that she has been the wife of two Reginald Mortons—swears that 'the love I have so long borne the mother [will] be transferred to the child.'

There is a similar commingling of identity among the five major female figures: Oucanasta, Madeline, Ellen, and the two Claras. Clara Beverley's capacity for uninhibited outpouring of affection is shared by Oucanasta, Ellen, and Madeline. The latter, possessing the 'voluptuousness' of 'the Medicean Venus,' shares her aunt's fearless nature and her sexual attractiveness. The portrayal of her impassioned meetings with her fiancé Frederick appears to echo that of the meetings between Morton and Clara Beverley. Madeline de Haldimar and Clara de Haldimar, first cousins, strike admirers at Fort Michillimackinac as a study in contrast, 'Venus and Psyche in the land of the Pottowatomies.'

Passionate and earthy, Oucanasta, the Ottawa woman at home in her forest oasis, is the true New World counterpart of Clara Beverley in her Scottish garden and is, I suggest, the true heroine of the work. Her love for Frederick goes unrequited, however; she is forsaken by the 'civilized' white man much as Keejigo is abandoned by Nairne of the Orkneys in D. C. Scott's *At Gull Lake: August, 1810.* Though fascinated by such liaisons which recall Richardson's own family history, garrison propriety is less offended by Frederick's marriage to his first cousin than to one of another race. Other parallels knit these characters even closer together. Madeline, for instance, bravely throws herself between her doomed father and the attacking Indians at the besieged fort which he commands. Later, she interposes between Frederick and Wacousta aboard the captured schooner; falling at Wacousta's feet, begging for mercy, she is spurned by the warrior even as the supplicating Ellen at the beginning of the story was rebuffed by Colonel de Haldimar and as a wildly distraught Clara de Haldimar at the end pleads at the feet of Wacousta.

Further blurring distinctions between Ellen and Clara de Haldimar are similar physical characteristics: both are delicate, fair-skinned, blue-eyed. Charles remarks that Clara 'had ever treated Ellen Halloway rather as a sister.' Both women are abducted and taken to wife by Wacousta who keeps them in his tent. As Charles is remarkable for his feminine appearance, female characters are sometimes made to look like men, thus blurring sexual identity. Like Clara Beverley who is disguised as a man as she leaves her Eden to cross over the abyss separating it from the garrison world below, Ellen is disguised as a drummerboy as she approaches the bridge over the border abyss dividing European from Indian. So, too, Oucanasta appears in the guise of a male warrior as she leaves the forest to enter Fort Michillimackinac to rescue Madeline.

Not surprisingly, the paradigmatic love triangle constellated by Wacousta, Clara Beverley, and De Haldimar also undergoes eerie multiplication. Shattered in the Old World, we catch reflections from it off a myriad of splinters in the New. Disclosed only towards the end of volume 3 in Wacousta's flashback, like a magnet it draws all the doubles and triangles whose significance may have escaped the reader, or seemed gratuitous, into meaningful patterns. A list which does not pretend to be exhaustive would include the following triangles: Everard—Clara de Haldimar—Charles; Oucanasta—Frederick—Madeline; Frank Halloway—Ellen—Wacousta; Everard—Clara de Haldimar—Wacousta; Clara de Haldimar—Wacousta—Ellen. Wacousta's liaison with François's daughter, Babette, moves us into 'love rectangles,' to borrow a term from Atwood's article on Rider Haggard. As with each double, each triangle is an analogue to, and comment on, the others, tending to suggest by parody, analogy, or correspondence characters and situations not immediately present.

In Richardson's fiction, the ideal triangle emerges out of the dialectic of opposites. An active and a passive male character revolve around an anima-like female who effects or mediates a larger reconciliation or equilibrium between conflicting forces. On a personal and psychological level, this represents a Jungian integration of the personality. On the cultural level, the Apollonian and Dionysian elements are harmonized in a new, dynamic synthesis. Although such themes of reintegration and communion are central to Richardson's art, this 'ideal' is only realized momentarily in *The Monk Knight of St. John,* perhaps because it is set outside the hopelessly schizophrenic nineteenth-century Canadian milieu. Most often, it is as though an original wholeness were split into antithetical fragments which war on each other.

The core triangle in **Wacousta** is homeomorphic to all others. It is traced and retraced with a redundancy characteristic of the borderline which, we recall, McLuhan describes as an area of spiralling repetition, replay, and metamorphosis. One example must suffice to illustrate how **Wacousta**'s proliferating doubles and triangles are deployed by Richardson to recapitulate in miniature the thematic implications of the main plot and to anticipate its further development. The triangle involving Middleton, the Indian 'Venus,' and Baynton portrayed in the chapters on Fort Michillimackinac in volume 2, has complete congruity with that of the Wacousta—Clara Beverley—De Haldimar triangle revealed in volume 3. A variation on this theme, it is set in a comic rather than a tragic key. Chatting idly to Madeline and Clara about his friend Middleton, Captain Baynton remarks that he 'stole cautiously behind him, and saw that he was sketching the head of a tall and rather handsome squaw . . . a Venus, a Juno, a Minerva.' As Middleton goes on duty, Baynton playfully teases him: 'I think I shall go and carry on a flirtation with your Indian Minerva.'

This brief interchange does not draw attention to itself and, indeed, is quickly forgotten in the avalanche of details concerning the Indian attack. It is not until the embedded narrative of Wacousta's flashback many chapters later that the attentive reader begins to see double—or triple. Wacousta tells of being alone in his room sketching a picture of the Highland Clara; he suddenly realizes that De Haldimar has silently entered and is standing looking over his shoulder. Instinctively, 'I asked him, laughingly, what he thought of my Cornish cousin.' De Haldimar feigns indifference; yet, later, when Wacousta—or Morton—is called away on duty, De Haldimar quickly seizes the opportunity and marries the inexperienced Clara. The exactness of the mirror image is blunted by the omission in the edited versions of Charles's fleeting allusion to Baynton and Middleton whom Everard fears may be potential rivals for Clara: 'the musical and sonnetteering Middleton' is an artistic individual like Morton. De Haldimar, who does not appreciate 'the talent of so perfect an artist,' is reflected in the practical, scoffing Baynton with his polished manner.

Spiralling Repetition and Replay

The feeling one has is of entering a haunted world of reflections within reflections, of story within story that is also experienced in the work of Davies, Reaney, Munro, Atwood, Kroetsch, and many Canadian postmodernists. The original situation happens again and again one way or another. One set of relationships is constantly viewed or inflected through another in a kind of infinite regress. I will provisionally call this technique 'amplification by analogy,' a term borrowed from Edward F. Edinger's Jungian inquiry, *Ego and Archetype.* For the most part, the parallels, which tragically evade the awareness of the characters themselves, are casually introduced without any editorializing whatsoever. Richardson leaves it to the reader to make the connection, a considerable act of faith in an audience which has only recently come to appreciate the depth of his artistry.

Despite such a complex web of interrelationships uniting everyone and resonating with ambiguity, the garrison inhabitants themselves perceive things in terms of simplistic, either/or categories, seeing a world of sharp borders and unbridgeable gulfs. The tragic irony of such blinkered vision is nowhere more dramatically underscored than in the network of correspondences between the garrison's major characters—especially those rebuked by Colonel de Haldimar—and Wacousta. Just as the line between Indian and European blurs, so, too, a curious overlapping of identity occurs among the De Haldimar brothers, Everard, Johnstone, and the warrior who seeks to destroy them. As I shall soon suggest, Richardson attempts, not altogether successfully, to create in Frederick de Haldimar a character who balances the Colonel's arid intellectual nature with Wacousta's fiery passions. Tall, handsome, heroic, Frederick shares the latter's adventurousness, daring spirit, and athletic prowess. Ponteac proclaims him a faster runner than the Indians; on one occasion, he even outruns Wacousta.

Both men are passionate lovers. Recalling the language Morton uses to describe his 'cousin' Clara, Frederick's cousin is to him 'a divinity whom he worshipped in the innermost recesses of his being.' Her 'almost superhuman voice' enchants him as Clara's does Morton. 'His brain whirling with very intoxication,' the enraptured Frederick is likewise a lover who obeys 'wild impulse.' Like Wacousta, he also undergoes a series of metamorphoses, disguising himself as a common soldier and a Canadian duck hunter, and at one point he is dressed as an Indian. Like both Mortons, Frederick is ordered arrested by De Haldimar for defying the law. Both men are believed dead on several occasions, although each seems unable to wound or kill the other. Wacousta, however, does kill Donellan who 'was remarkable for the resemblance he bore, in figure, to Captain de Haldimar.' That the first victim of the gigantic Wacousta is Donellan, the tallest and largest grenadier who is also Frederick's mirror-image, suggests the uncanny interdependence of all characters in this radically contracted borderland, down to the least of them.

At first glance, Charles and Wacousta seem to possess little in common. Yet both are men of feeling and sensibility who suffer from broken hearts in a society dominated by those who place value only on the intellect. Each sheds copious tears. Constantly worrying for the safety of his closest friend and Clara, Charles has violent paroxysms of grief which threaten to dis-

lodge his reason; they parallel the fever and madness that plague Wacousta after he loses both Clara and his best friend. Giving vent to his emotion, Charles, like the Mortons and Everard, fears his reputation for courage will be assailed. Like these figures and Ellen, he, too, is intuitive and given to presentiments, making statements which later prove prophetic. (In folklore, meeting one's double foreshadows death or the onset of prophetic power.) Charles is also insulted by De Haldimar and, like Wacousta, impulsively moves to draw his sword to defend his honour. Given such resemblances, it is ironic that he should be the first De Haldimar killed by the Warrior of the Fleur de Lis.

We find other reflections of Wacousta in Johnstone and Clara Beverley's misanthropic father. The latter, also a Jacobite rebel, is an eccentric gentleman heartbroken by the loss of a beloved wife and disgusted with English society. Lieutenant Johnstone is another distorted image of the young Lieutenant Morton. Johnstone is a brave, fiery, and reckless Scot, the motto of his Highland ancestors 'Nunquam non paratus.' (This is the inscription on Richardson's own ring and recalls his Jacobite ancestry.) The head of his family was also branded a traitor by the English. Like Everard and Charles, the impetuous Johnstone is repelled by the obsequious Ensign Delme, a yes-man who recalls Ensign de Haldimar and is, appropriately, the last European shot by Wacousta. Delme insults Johnstone and twists his words, threatening to denounce him as a traitor. Once again, an outspoken, marginalized individual, critical of garrison administration, is associated with treason, his honour challenged in a public manner by a hypocritical representative of law and order.

Sir Everard Valletort also mirrors Sir Reginald Morton in surprising ways. Both are lively and adventurous baronets, heirs to titles. Everard is also somewhat of a romantic idealist out of step with garrison society; the narrator associates him, too, with the power of the imagination and the heart and the quest for ideal beauty. Active and impulsive individuals, each is linked with a more passive and retiring double. Such friendships involve them in love triangles with either Clara or her daughter. Both claim the latter as their bride, and Wacousta sees his own situation reflected in the Everard-Clara relationship. A disoriented Clara confuses the two men herself, imagining that she is in Everard's arms while actually being ravished by Wacousta. Wacousta ties Everard to the Indian flagpole, and later the former is bound to the garrison flagpole; both captives escape carrying Clara, reversing roles of pursuer and pursued. Likewise gifted with a keen eye and ear, Everard, too, is an expert rifleman; his first shot at the beginning of the border romance and his last at the end wound Wacousta.

Like both Mortons, Charles, and Johnstone, Everard begins to manifest many of the outcast stigmata. He is also unjustly accused and publicly humiliated by Colonel de Haldimar. It is Everard's 'undisguised perception' of the man behind the Governor's mask of impartiality that draws down this severity. Again, it is the most frank and astute individuals who are victimized, pushed out of the centre of the garrison world to its borders. It is appropriate that it is Everard, a man appreciative of paradoxes, who alone voices Wacousta's Conradian status as 'one of us': 'That man, savage and even fiendish as he now is, was once possessed of the noblest qualities. . . . Colonel de Haldimar has brought this present affliction upon himself.' Wacousta the wild man is not as primitive as the soldiers imagine, but they haven't known that until this point.

Such is the delirium of doubles, complementary personalities, twins, and modulations of the twin theme characterizing Richardson's border milieu. A product of the author's fascination with dualities and the convergence of opposites, the resultant vertigo is an essential part of the romance's intent: unlike the American frontier of independent loners, the Canadian borderland is a world of uncanny interdependence, a mosaic mesh in which the most disparate and seemingly autonomous groups of people become entangled. Paradoxically, the text confirms both the continuity and discontinuity of this scattered world. Characters seem irresistibly drawn together even when they are bitterly antagonistic. This skillful marshalling of doubles and triangles sustains a great deal of resonant ambiguity; multiplicity, fragmentation, incompleteness, and discontinuity are posited even as their opposites are suggested: unity, completeness, and continuity. It also generates psychic conflict in which anxieties are sharpened to the point of madness. The details of such interpenetrating lives are intricately wrought and attest to a very careful use of echoes—of phrases and images—always setting up parallels and correspondences. Again, this pattern of recurrence, of an unabashed use of coincidence and analogy, emerges out of a very McLuhanesque sense of the borderline as an area 'of maximal interplay and subtle interpenetration.'

Such repetition and duplication is found in a number of Canadian writers, especially in recent years, as our literature has moved in the direction of fantasy. Richardson's proliferating Claras and Reginalds take their place among the doubled Annas, Demeters, and Billys in Robert Kroetsch's *Badlands, The Studhorse Man,* and *Alibi* respectively; the three Maud's in F. P. Grove's *The Master of the Mill;* the array of Georges in George Bowering's *Burning Water;* the nine sisters named Mary in Marian Engel's study of inbred Southwestern Ontario in *The Glassy Sea;* and the numerous Marys in Brian Moore's *I Am Mary Dunne* who have almost as many selves as the protagonist in Alden Nowlan's *Various Persons Named Kevin O'Brien.* As I emphasize throughout this study, a very Richardsonian concern with the overlapping and fusion—and confusion—

of identity, with the very notion of self as isolate, distinct, definable, enclosed, autonomous, is prominent in the work of many modern Canadian authors, with their radical challenges to the humanist notion of the self as coherent, unified, and stable. The twins and other characters who are described as 'Siamesed' in Matt Cohen's Salem novels, no less than the 'characters [who] split, double, multiply, evaporate, condense, disperse, assemble' in Tom Marshall's *Rosemary Goal,* also set in gothic Southern Ontario, suggest the efficacy of Richardson's border model of a radically contracted Canada; 'maybe,' muses the protagonist of the latter work, a novelist fond of stories within stories, 'that's what this town is anyhow. A daisy chain, a sexual commune . . . connections between everyone, the endless interrelationships that make us one people . . . A cast of characters whose lives are all interconnected.'

In two other books structured round an exchange of identity, we discover similar avowals which help place Richardson's modus operandi in a larger context. In Hugh MacLennan's *The Watch That Ends the Night,* the solidly middle-class George Stewart, who finds his double, the dynamic, reckless Jerome Martell 'to be inside me, *to be me,*' declares 'Each one of us is everybody, really.' (Similar realizations are also shared by the protagonist of Chris Scott's postmodernist *Antichthon* and Leonard Cohen's *Beautiful Losers.*) *The Studhorse Man* is one of many Kroetsch tales of a bizarre swapping of identities; it illustrates what this writer, in conversation with Margaret Laurence, asserts as a very Canadian concern: 'the *doppelgänger* thing.' Perched in an insane asylum bathtub, Kroetsch's mirror-gazing narrator recounts the epic story of his roving uncle and adversary into whom he appears to metamorphose; reflecting on 'the act of naming,' the mad historian discourses on 'the fact that we are all, so to speak, one—that each of us is, possibly, everyone else.' Such observations by both madmen and conservative middle-class citizens may help to orient us when confronted by the dizzying prospect of Richardson's fictional world.

The Struggle-of-Brothers Theme

Colonel de Haldimar and Wacousta, like Gerald Grantham and Matilda Montgomery in the sequel, or Abdallah and the Baron in **The Monk Knight of St. John,** are doubles-by-division or by opposition. They are set within the dual cosmology they express—the border world of garrison and wilderness. Here the forces of restraint, repression, and reason present in the imported European culture presided over by Governor de Haldimar are at war with those of spontaneity, passion, and irrationality as expressed in the criminal outcast Wacousta and the North American Indian. In nineteenth-century Canada, the tragedy, as Richardson envisions it, is that no one bridges the psychological and cultural gulf between the two domains.

The De Haldimar-Wacousta relationship, like that of Linton and Heathcliff in Emily Brontë's *Wuthering Heights* (1847), conforms to a recurrent romantic convention which Richardson tailors to reflect the New World border dichotomy of civilization and wilderness. Frye's comments on the struggle-of-brothers motif in *A Study of English Romanticism* illumine all of Richardson's works and echo statements by Chase, Davies, Lee, and McLuhan cited in my earlier discussion of the 'intermingled vision':

> The paradoxical relation of civilized and rude nature, a relation partly antithetical and partly complementary, is often expressed in Romantic fiction and drama by some variant of the struggle-of-brothers theme. This has several Biblical archetypes—Cain and Abel, Esau and Jacob, Ishmael and Isaac—which become important in its development. In the conventional interpretation of the Bible, the figures of the social establishment, Isaac and Jacob, are the accepted ones; with Romanticism, there comes a transfer of sympathy to their exiled brethren. The so-called Byronic hero is often a Romantic version of the natural man, who, like Esau and Ishmael, is an outcast, a solitary much given to communing with untamed nature, and who thus represents the potentially expanding and liberating elements in that nature.

De Haldimar and Wacousta, certainly, are struggling brothers in Frye's sense. So, too, are Manvers and Haverfield in the earlier *Frascati's*. In particular, the fratricide of the first 'Canadian Brothers'—unlike the marriage of American Adams in their forest Edens—ominously recalls the tragic crime of our first brothers. The figures of Cain and Abel may be more relevant to the Canadian experience than that of Adam, as Richardson and later writers suggest. In *The Secular Scripture,* Frye links Cain and Abel with the theme of the demonic double. His further comments on the Byronic hero in his study of romanticism help focus this theme: 'He has great energy, often great powers of leadership, and even his vices are dignified enough to have some aesthetic attraction. He is often aristocratic in birth or behaviour, with a sense that, like Esau, he is the dispossessed rightful heir—here the theme combines with the sense of nostalgia for a vanished aristocracy. When he is evil, there is often the feeling that, as with Byron's Cain, his evil is comprehensible, that he is not wholly evil any more than his evil is a force that society has to reckon with.' For Frye, the greatest of all his incarnations in English literature is Brontë's Heathcliff, an embodiment of the wildness of Yorkshire moors and heath as Wacousta is of Canadian bush and rivers. The hideous Heathcliff, appearing fifteen years after the dark Wacousta, 'has in full the sense of a natural man who eludes all moral categories just as nature itself does, and who cannot be simply condemned or accepted. In contrast, the Jacob-figure, the defender of the establishment, often seems unheroic and spoiled by a soft or decadent civilization.'

The theme of brotherhood or friendship and their betrayal is of paramount importance in all of Richardson's writing, fictional, historical, and autobiographical. It informs his inquires into what constitutes authentic community and his portrayals of North American garrisons. In the flashback in which Wacousta recounts to Clara de Haldimar the history of his family and her own, the betrayed and once very naive outcast blind to the dark side of others bewails the 'intimacy [which] suddenly sprang up between' himself and her father: 'this incongruous friendship—friendship! no, I will not so far sully the sacred name as thus to term the unnatural union that subsisted between us.' 'Fire and ice,' he exclaims, 'are not more opposite than were the elements of which our natures were composed.'

In a key passage, Wacousta, once a romantic idealist, describes his 'partly antithetical and partly complementary' relationship with De Haldimar, the cautious law-and-order figure: 'He, all coldness, prudence, obsequiousness, and forethought. I, all enthusiasm, carelessness, impetuosity, and independence.' Here is the 'original' pattern of opposites in tension. This paradigmatic relationship is boldly stated in order to establish that the ideal bond between 'brothers' implies balance and complementarity. What later appear to be warring opposites are actually two component parts of a complex psychological entity. Their friendship conforms to that outlined by Jean Paul Richter, the coiner of the word 'doppelgänger':

> Jean Paul's characteristic *Doppelgangers* are pairs of friends (in the original sense of 'fellows, two of a pair'), who together form a unit, but individually appear as a 'half,' dependent on the *alter-ego* . . . they are like contrasting, but complementary, sides within one complex nature . . . The divergences seem, in fact, to emphasize the mutual need for completion and support, in the sense of Friedrich Schlegel's definition of intimate friendship: 'A wondrous symmetry of essential characteristics, as if it had been pre-ordained that one should complete the other on every point.' These symmetrical pairs feel as instinctive an impulse towards one another as the urge which impels the Platonic twin-souls to seek out their respective partner and restore the original unity between them.

'Opposition is true friendship,' writes Blake. Wacousta speculates that 'my wild spirit was soothed by the bland amenity of his manners.' Ideally, impulse and intellect, feeling and reason, wild daring and caution, body and head are harmonized, just as, on a larger scale, Indian and European, wilderness and civilization are brought into balance. Such seems to be the case, for a brief moment, only in the Old World. What is dramatized in the New World borderland in peculiarly Canadian terms is a tragic dissociation of sensibility, a separation of thought and feeling, head and heart, which seems to have widened into an unbridgeable gulf. In the Wacousta-De Haldimar struggle, I suggest, Richardson dramatizes what he sees as the conflicting opposites that keep the Canadian psyche in tension, developing them with the fugues and arabesques so dear to the Canadian double vision. One aspect of this vision relevant to Richardson's work is discussed by Robertson Davies in his essay 'The Canada of Myth and Reality.' Davies cites a line from Douglas Le Pan's poem *Coureurs de bois* which encapsulates what he terms the dual nature of the Canadian soul: 'Wild Hamlet with the features of Horatio.' Inside the cautious, prudent Horatio, there lies a dark, fiery brooder. Similarly, in Davies's *The Manticore,* Dunstan Ramsay, the dull Canadian schoolmaster from Southwestern Ontario who is also a vigorous spiritual seeker, avers that 'Mackenzie King rules Canada because he himself is the embodiment of Canada—cold and cautious on the outside, dowdy and pussy in every overt action, but inside a mass of intuition and dark intimations.'

The wild Wacousta's struggle with his staid double is highlighted in his 'Eden' flashback, chapters 7-11, volume 3 of the 1832 edition. Coming as it does towards the end of the romance, revealing the betrayed idealist, the accomplished artist, and man of sensibility behind the shadowy monster, it is literally and figuratively 'the inside story.' It is also the untold story, displaced in the novel's myriad doubles and triangles, and one which the silent Governor de Haldimar would keep the voluble Wacousta from telling. Those qualities which receive the most emphasis as Wacousta tells his story are the aristocratic Morton's 'exiled brethren' qualities: his impassioned communing with the rugged, untamed nature of the Scottish Highlands and the sea, romantic sensibility and intuition, boundless energy and animal boisterousness, athletic prowess and thirst for adventure. Above all, Richardson stresses the young man's aesthetic and mystical strivings and his intense imagination which enshrines the mountain-top maiden Clara Beverley as the embodiment of 'ideal beauty,' 'the being of my fancy's creation.' At the same time, Wacousta himself is presented as a story-teller, a voice, narrating himself into existence and out of the silence in which the tight-lipped Governor has confined him.

'Years of passionate imagining,' exclaims Wacousta to the second Clara, daughter of the woman he loves and the man he hates, had left his vision unrealized. Edited out of most editions is a crucial scene indebted to the Narcissus myth so familiar in Romantic literature and repeated with variations throughout *Wacousta:* 'How often, too, while bending over some dark and threatening precipice, or standing on the utmost verge of some tall projecting cliff, my aching head (aching with the intenseness of its own conceptions) bared to the angry storm, and my eye fixed unshrinkingly on the boiling ocean far beneath my feet, has my whole soul—my every faculty, been bent on that ideal beauty which controlled every sense! Oh, imagination, how tyrannical is thy sway—how exclusive thy power—how insatiable thy thirst.'

Addressing the imagination, Morton/Wacousta proclaims Clara Beverley as its creation: 'no sooner didst thou, with magic wand, conjure up one of thy embodiments, than my heart became a sea of flame, and was consumed in the vastness of its own fires.' The 'master passion' of Reginald Morton is the spiritual or mystical pursuit of an elusive yet consuming vision of the soul's other half. His is a rage for beauty and transcendence as fierce as that of Le Pan's Rusty in *The Deserter,* Cohen's F. in *Beautiful Losers,* or Symon's multiple protagonist in *Combat Journal for Place D'Armes.* By his very nature, he stands in opposition to established society and its official representatives; humourless, practical, unimaginative soldiers preoccupied with the matter-of-fact, utilitarian concerns of a materialistic and puritanical culture, they misunderstand, patronize, ridicule, persecute, and finally forcibly reject him.

It is highly significant that Morton, as representative of 'the imaginative man' devalued and exiled by the garrison, is an artist. Again, this important aspect of his identity is omitted in most editions. Morton speaks of his devotion to painting, an art 'in which I had attained considerable excellence; being enabled, from memory alone, to give a most correct representation of any object that particularly fixed my attention.' Such a 'photographic' memory is not out of place in a romance marked by duplication, water- and mirror-reflection. Given 'the talent of so perfect an artist . . . there could be no question that the painting' of Clara's portrait by Morton 'was exquisite'; 'The likeness was perfect, even to the minutest shading of her costume.' Indeed, she mistakes it for a 'mirror that reflected back her living image.' This portrait is itself 'doubled,' the painter making an exact copy of it.

Like other romantic questers in search of reintegration and wholeness, Morton is alternately restored and torn apart by the 'influencing agency of that Unseen Power' that claims him for its own: 'Why did my evil genius so will it . . . that I should have heard those sounds and seen that face [Clara's]? But for these . . . my life might have been the life—the plodding life—of the multitude; things that are born merely to crawl through existence and die, knowing not at the moment of death why or how they have lived at all. But who may resist the destiny that presides over him from the cradle to the grave?' Mystic and artist, lover and explorer, Morton is odd man out in a regimented garrison society which places little value on individuals following the uncertain inner promptings of an Unseen Power. His reflections appear to be shared, in part, by the narrator: 'It is in solitude, our thoughts, taking their colouring from our feelings, invest themselves with the power of multiplying ideal beauty, until we become in a measure tenants of a world of our own creation, from which we never descend, without loathing and disgust, into the dull and matter-of-fact routine of actual existence. Hence the misery of the imaginative man!—hence his little sympathy with the mass, who, tame and soulless, look upon life and the things of life, not through the refining medium of ideality, but through the grossly magnifying optics of mere sense and materialism.'

The Eden flashback reveals a Morton/Wacousta who represents what D. G. Jones, describing F., the mystic, madman, and terrorist in *Beautiful Losers,* terms 'the two poles of the irrational, the world of the flesh and the world of the spirit.' 'All enthusiasm, carelessness, impetuosity, and independence,' the athletic Morton, unlike the cautious, sedentary De Haldimar, is animated by a 'spirit of adventure,' playfulness and 'wild daring.' An experienced mountain climber, he scales the precipitous crags for the pleasure of overcoming the difficulties they present. Danger, chance, the unpredictable, the tumultuous, the unexpected—everything the garrison worries about and plans against—he delights in encountering. Abjuring the closed-in garrison, he exultingly 'rides' the whirlwind, the vast open spaces of sea and mountain-top, of heights and depths.

Whether in the Highlands or the vast Canadian space, Morton/Wacousta gives himself up to the flux and flow of the cosmos. All is energy, a dynamic interplay of elemental forces as in Gibson's *Perpetual Motion* or the storm-tossed universe of D. C. Scott and Lampman. Morton embraces both the beauty of terror and the beauty of peace. Unlike the static De Haldimar, he is always moving. Moving across continents and oceans, he aligns himself with the fluid realm of wilderness and nomadic Indian, a world constantly in movement; to the garrison soldiers, Wacousta is little more than a blur. His descendants in ***The Canadian Brothers*** are roving American frontiersmen associated with the turbulent border river. His literary progeny also include Reaney's endlessly spinning Donnellys, Callaghan's whirling, changing Peggy Sanderson, Kroetsch's restless Michael Hornyak in *But We Are Exiles,*—a dynamic figure in love with motion, racing crazily across Canada with his reserved Ontario law-student double—and perhaps even Aritha Van Herk's perpetually moving adventuress Arachne Manteia in the parodic, postmodernist *No Fixed Address: An Amorous Journey.*

Wacousta's extremely mobile face—such a contrast to De Haldimar's rigid mask—receives repeated emphasis. 'The constant play of his features betrayed each passing thought with the same rapidity with which it was conceived,' not unlike the strange swift whiteness of Judith West's face, symbolically linking this outcast with the swirling wind blowing across the prairie in Ross's *As For Me and My House.* Associated with the realm of water and the fluctuation of the seasons in the new land, Wacousta can be passionately violent at one moment and tranquil and reflective the next, a paradoxical characteristic he shares with Reaney's Donnellys, Mitchell's Bens, Callaghan's Peggy Sanderson, and Wiebe's Riel. In contrast, the secretive De Haldimar, a stiff 'martial-looking man,' possesses 'stern, haughty, and inflexible features.' A mask concealing his real thoughts, his face denotes his aversion to change, movement, and metamorphosis which disturb De Haldimar as much as they do Ondaatje's Billy and Pat Garrett, because they resist control.

Morton's animal vitality and boisterousness are constantly in evidence throughout the flashback. While the soaring, high-spirited youth is associated here with a stag and an eagle, his Canadian incarnation as Wacousta evokes comparisons with a wide range of animals, ferocious or swift-moving, predatory or hunted: a tiger, a wolf, antelope, deer, and a wounded lion at bay. Dressed in deerskin, Wacousta as wild man is adorned with porcupine quills, wild deer hooves, bird feathers, and a buffalo horn inscribed with pictures of birds, beasts, and fish. Like other impetuous, energetic idealists and passionate outcasts associated with animals and the landscape or seascape, Wacousta symbolizes the life of the body; one thinks of MacLennan's Jerome Martell, Le Pan's Rusty, Cohen's F., Crawford's Max, Reaney's Will Donnelly, Ross's Judith West, and O'Hagan's Tay John. Morton places his confidence in himself—in imaginative vision and love—and in nature and its spontaneous processes rather than in the law, the rules, and regulations of the garrison world which only frustrate and, he feels, unnecessarily limit him.

His is a romantic zest for life, a recklessness and devil-may-care attitude that attends a surrender to one's instincts. In contrast with a society caught up in memories of the past or in anticipating the future, Morton manifests an absorption in the present moment; at times, his is the childlike wonder and awe before nature and the mysteries of a forbidding yet inspiring landscape which characterizes Mitchell's Brian and the Young Ben, Buckler's David, or Grove in *Over Prairie Trails.* 'Obeying, as I ever did, the first impulse of my heart,' the artist-idealist-lover takes delight in and draws strength from the irrational, the devastating, and the savage in nature. At home in 'the raging elements,' he comes to embody their inexhaustible power and variety. Rather than make nature over, he takes it as it is. Morton enters into ecstatic, sensuous communion with the stormy Highlands even as he merges into the more forbidding Canadian environment; in contrast, De Haldimar tries to conquer and consolidate his power over it.

The sailor and mountain climber accepts, even affirms, the violence of an uncontrollable nature. Immersing himself in the destructive element of life, he finds it buoys him up. Morton's energies are rooted in the irrational vitality of nature, not in the rational activity of the intellect, the domain of his prudent friend Ensign de Haldimar. Guided by 'presentiment,' he follows his intuition and the promptings of the unconscious while De Haldimar, going by the rule-book, demonstrates what many observers, discussing our cultural climate, see as an overreliance on the arguing intellect and an insistence that reality be absolutely rational. As a result, Richardson's outcast comes to represent all that is wayward, wanton, mysterious, unpremeditated, overwhelming, illegal, and lusty in life—a Lord of Misrule, a carnivalesque figure of Riot and Dionysian revel.

Wacousta: Poseidon and The Wild Man

> Riding his chariot of horses across the sea, Poseidon, god of the oceans and god of horses, embodies the two age-old symbols of . . . our fluid unconscious. With no predetermined shape of its own, [water] is constantly in movement . . . Poseidon was the most primitive of the gods, the earthshaker, the god of storms and earthquakes, of the sudden devastation of tidal waves—the dangers unleashed when the forces slumbering under the surface of consciousness erupt.

ARIANNA STASSINOPOULOS, *The Gods of Greece*

> Poseidon is also a metaphor for the man or woman who can go deeply into the realm of feeling and emotions, and gain access to what is down there: soul and sorrow, great beauty and monsters of the deep . . . Poseidon's sphere is the realm of emotions, and the man for whom Poseidon is the archetype is directly in touch with his instincts and feelings, which he expresses spontaneously and immediately if he's extroverted, and may harbour within if he's introverted. And he grows up in a culture that prefers boys and men to be unemotional.

JEAN SHINODA BOLEN, *Gods in Everyman*

The struggle between Wacousta and the Governor is a Canadian version of an ancient conflict whose mythological context is the antagonistic yet complementary relationship of the two brothers Poseidon and Zeus who divided the world between themselves (and Hades). Its dimensions are best gauged by an appeal to recent feminist scholarship and commentary by members of the 'mythopoetic' wing of the contemporary men's movement. Both explore the fascinating link between Greek myths—allusions to which abound in Richardson's writings—and the psyche. Jungian analyst Jean Bolen in *Gods in Everyman* (1989) suggests that the pattern of male Greek deities represents differ-

ent qualities in the male psyche; they exist both as archetypes that predispose certain types of behaviour and response and as cultural stereotypes of masculinity. In her chapter on Poseidon, Bolen delineates an archetypal configuration of which *Wacousta* seems a nineteenth-century manifestation.

Poseidon's mythology as she elucidates it encompasses patterns we have been attentive to in Richardson's work and will find greatly elaborated in *The Canadian Brothers*. As in *Wacousta*, the emotionality and spontaneity that the sometimes turbulent, sometimes reflective Poseidon personifies is conveyed through imagery of the powerful, ever-changing moods of the sea which can be both a beautiful and a terrifying realm; like the indistinct border region of wavy curves and circles, the realm of watery depths is another blurred world 'so deep and so dark that clear vision is no longer possible and one can only dimly sense what is there.' Poseidon enjoys a double identity as sea god and as 'husband of the earth' (the meaning of his name), a pre-Olympian consort of the great goddess known for his intense sexuality and fertility. As is the case with Wacousta and De Haldimar, Poseidon contrasts with the impersonal Zeus who submerges feeling to maintain control; Zeus has much to learn from this god, notes Bolen, even as Poseidon might counter a susceptibility to being overwhelmed by rage by developing abilities to plan, reflect, focus, and think objectively. Like Wacousta, Poseidon in his negative or shadow aspect is the ultimate grudge holder; the depths he sinks to in an irrational revenge which drowns all rationality are evident in his relentless ten-year pursuit of a treacherous Odysseus. Like Wacousta, Poseidon reacts emotionally to betrayal, loss, and public humiliation by opening the floodgates to rage and grief. And like Wacousta, Poseidon is father of destructive monsters and savage giants who inherit his own worst nature.

'Poseidon is Zeus's shadow,' states Bolen. This 'lookalike of Zeus' in his positive aspect mediates 'access to emotional depths' which 'is an unappreciated aspect of men's psyches . . . devalued and repressed in patriarchal cultures.' In a section of her study entitled 'Poseidon as Archetype of The Wild Man,' Bolen identifies the rejected god with 'the wild man at the bottom of the pool' in the story of Iron John in *Grimm's Fairy Tales*, the commentary on which forms the basis of poet Robert Bly's *Iron John: A Book about Men* (1990)—perhaps *the* text of the men's movement. As the personification of that vibrant, instinctive masculinity that men must reclaim or be in touch with to be whole, the dishonoured wild man of the forest Bly describes so well is, for Bolen, Poseidon known by another name.

Richardson seems to have been familiar with some variant of this ancient story 'called "Iron John" or "Iron

Hans" . . . first set down by the Grimm brothers around 1820' (Bly). In his non-fictional exposé of the garrison mentality *The Guards in Canada,* Richardson wittily confides to us that such is the apprehension he seems to have inspired in his detractors on one occasion that they, as well as 'the *Militaires,* already felt in anticipation the iron grasp of a Hans of Iceland, a Rob Roy, or a Wacousta himself.' The explicit connection Richardson makes between himself, Wacousta, and Iron Hans is too tantalizing to ignore and invites comment. As the story of Iron John opens, we find out that when travellers or hunters leave the comfortable, familiar surroundings of the king's castle and venture 'beyond the boundaries . . . outside the enclosure' into the strange depths of the nearby wilderness, they never return. One day, a young man risks going into the forest dreamscape alone, and as he passes by a pond, a gigantic hand suddenly reaches up to him from deep down in the water, not unlike that of the spectral Wacousta seizing Frederick at the bottom of the border river abyss. The hand succeeds only in pulling under the dog the man has wisely brought with him. Eventually, with several other companions, he bravely and laboriously buckets out the pond to discover lying at its bottom a huge, wild-looking man covered from head to foot with flowing, rusty-red hair.

This frightening being 'lives in the water, under the water,' comments Bly. Not unlike Poseidon and Wacousta, 'he also lives wholeheartedly on earth; his wildness and hairiness in fact belong to earth and its animals.' The primitive giant is brought back to the castle where the rather security-conscious and judgmental king imprisons him in an iron cage in the sunlight and pronounces him 'Iron John.' Like Wacousta, Iron John or The Wild Man is perceived as dangerous, and labelled as such, especially by those whose goal is to achieve position, keep power, look good, and control emotion. 'Contact with Iron John requires a willingness to descend into the male psyche and accept what's dark down there, including the *nourishing* dark.' What Bly suggests at more length 'is that every modern male has, lying at the bottom of his psyche' under layers of cultural conditioning, just such a 'deep male' being of true strength, exuberance, joyous sexuality, deep feeling, and compassion, one whom Bly is careful to distinguish from the savage or macho male men—and women—already know too well.

Just as Frederick de Haldimar disobeys his father's direct order and journeys into the forest, the king's son sets Iron John free and goes into the dark forest with his unlikely mentor. 'As the boy leaves for the forest, he has to overcome, at least for the moment, his fear of wildness, irrationality, hairiness, intuition, emotion, the body, and nature'—everything De Haldimar's garrison walls out. 'Iron John is not as primitive as the boy imagines,' nor Wacousta as primitive as the soldiers believe, 'but the boy—or the mind—does not

know that yet.' Indeed, the Wild Man is actually a baronial king just as within Wacousta there resides the chivalric Sir Reginald Morton. Before the end of the story, the king's son under Iron John's influence grows into an authentic masculinity issuing in genuine community with other men and women and communion with the earth. Contrary to the conventional wisdom of the king's domesticated enclave no less than the Governor's, he learns from 'the instinctive one' what Morton/Wacousta, the Monk Knight, and his companions the Baron, Zuleima, and Ernestina know, that 'sexual energy is good . . . that animal heat, fierceness, passionate spontaneity is good; and that excess, extravagance, and going with Pan out beyond the castle boundaries is good too.'

Wacousta is a wild man, but he is not the Wild Man Bly delineates far more evocatively than I can suggest here. Though Wacousta the lover, the risk-taker, the instinctive one, the wounded grieving one rings true, Wacousta the killer and rapist is the opposite of Iron John who nurtures and gives life rather than takes it and who enters into equal partnership with the feminine. The Wild Man is not opposed to civilization, but he is not completely contained by it either, notes Bly. Perhaps we see in him that 'good double energy,' a balance of 'both Apollo and Dionysus,' that fascinated but eluded Richardson in his doubles from Wacousta/ De Haldimar to the Monk Knight/the Baron.

Governor de Haldimar: 'Moral Monster' and Establishment Manticore

> The double hook. The total ambiguity that is so essentially Canadian: be it in terms of two solitudes, the bush garden, Jungian opposites, or the raw and the cooked binary structures of Levi-Strauss. Behind the multiplying theories of Canadian literature is always the pattern of equally matched opposites.
>
> ROBERT KROETSCH

Structurally, Wacousta's flashback is juxtaposed to chapter 6, volume 3 of the original 1832 edition. This key chapter, focused exclusively on Colonel de Haldimar, is entirely missing from most editions, transforming the story into the type of black/white melodrama of Manichean opposites favoured by American editors operating out of another literary tradition. As a result, both De Haldimar and Wacousta are thinly rendered as villains, although Richardson has created characters who are an ambiguous mixture of 'positive' and 'negative' traits. Intent on balancing the attractiveness and repulsiveness of these twin figures for the Canadian psyche, Richardson does not resolve the paradoxes and contradictions inherent in the troubled relationship of these equally matched opposites. The original work is characterized by a disturbing ambivalence in the conflict between authority and rebellion—

here linked with the clash of disparate cultures and of modes of being—that we now identify as highly distinctive of our literature. American editors have blurred this issue by creating a totally despicable law-and-order figure consonant with the 'biases' of their own literary tradition. In so doing, they subvert Richardson's intentions by eradicating the ambivalent double response the reader of the original work is obliged to make. They distort the qualified acceptance of the need for boundaries, limits, and some form of societal order, ideally one protective of community and fostering its growth while at the same time allowing for the maximum degree of individual freedom and personal self-realization.

De Haldimar and Wacousta are figured forth as archetypal forces vying for possession of the New World. Together, they explicate the nature of the national psyche as Richardson knew it, the conflicting opposites that keep it in tension. As in Wiebe's *The Temptations of Big Bear* and Scott's *Antichthon,* 'reality' is a double-edged affair in Richardson, and the divergent or multiple perspectives which are generated are part of a system of balances designed to counter the reader's (and author's?) own leanings and prejudices. There is a temptation to side with one or the other at different times in the story, either with De Haldimar, whom Robin Mathews calls 'the perverse expression of law and order,' or with Wacousta, 'the perverse expression of romantic individualism.' To do so is to get caught in defending one extreme without seeing what the author is intent on us seeing: that they are interdependent and, in themselves, tragically incomplete. In this sense, *Wacousta* is a litmus test of the Canadian sensibility.

As often happens, we are pulled both ways at once. The reader's sympathies shift constantly as the text discloses more essential aspects of each figure; their claims on our approval or sanction are alternately supported and undercut. *Wacousta's* balanced appeal to our romantic sympathies and our sober judgment is nowhere more apparent than in the juxtaposition of the outcast's flashback and the chapter reviewing De Haldimar's past. Just as the Eden chapters mitigate Wacousta's ferocity by disclosing his ardent idealism and romantic imagination, chapter 6 of volume 3 establishes the 'survival' value of De Haldimar's prudence and forethought; it shows his previously repressed emotions beginning to thaw his reserve, explains his extremely harsh behaviour towards Halloway, and qualifies his severity, locating the roots of his inhumanity in the tyrannical, patriarchal ideal of order enshrined by the British military institution he so single-mindedly serves. The tragic and inescapable imperfection of the imported garrison social order in the New World is the source of *Wacousta's* endless tragic dilemmas. The most dramatic assimilate themselves to the conflict of group versus individual, of the herd

sacrificing a *pharmakos*. Besides the antagonism between civilization and nature, the romance delineates a parallel opposition of order and violence within the garrison enclave itself. As in Kroetsch, Callaghan, Findley, Reaney, and Davies, the romantic energies of the individual battle with the traditional, unquestioned restraints of the garrison. Both sides, Richardson insists, have their creative and destructive aspects.

What is indicted in Richardson's tale is not so much De Haldimar, however culpable and morally obtuse, but the entire imported military/social system of the British Empire which he represents. His are not just personal defects but cultural ones. As the narrator informs us, 'the stern peculiarities of his character . . . originated in an education purely military.' The zealous empire builder is governed by a strict, unquestioning adherence to a militant ideal that is being transplanted to a New World milieu which resists the imposition of an order foreign to it. It is a vision of imperial order rather than one of freedom that he serves.

Sober, industrious, distrustful of emotion, De Haldimar is a strong-willed, self-righteous exponent—and an unconscious victim—of the old European order and what today would be called the patriarchy. His sensibilities have been irremediably skewed and locked into the fixed posture dictated by the army, and a culture that privileges the head over the heart.

> Without ever having possessed any thing like acute feeling, his heart, as nature had formed it, was moulded to receive the ordinary impressions of humanity; and had he been doomed to move in the sphere of private life, if he had not been distinguished by any remarkable sensibilities, he would not, in all probability, have been conspicuous for any extraordinary cruelties. Sent into the army, however, at an early age, and with a blood not remarkable for its mercurial aptitudes, he had calmly and deliberately imbibed all the starched theories and standard prejudices which a mind by no means naturally gifted was but too well predisposed to receive.

Addiction to Perfection

De Haldimar is an extreme expression of the garrison's either/or mentality, which is a Procrustean bed carving recalcitrant individuals to fit the ideal of a homogenized society. '[H]e was a severe and a haughty man,—one whose military education had been based on the principles of the old school—and to whom the command of a regiment afforded a field for the exercise of an orthodox despotism, that could not be passed over without the immolation of many a victim on its rugged surface.' Both Reginald Mortons may be numbered among such 'victims,' prey to what in *The Studhorse Man* is called 'the eternal violence of law and order.' Both fall foul of what D. G. Jones in *Butterfly on Rock* identifies throughout our literature as an overly exclusive, arid, and militant ideal that would reduce life to a purely rational and mechanical system. And addiction to perfection, as Marion Woodman reminds us in her book of that title, leads to the wasteland. Richardson is our first novelist to inveigh in both fiction and non-fiction against 'the sterile self-destructive character of that ideal,' that 'arrogant and aggressive masculine logos' (Jones) so perceptively assessed by figures associated with the men's movement such as Robert Bly, Robert Moore, James Hillman, Michael Kaufman, and Ray Jones, and feminist writers such as Riane Eisler, Jean Bolen, Charlene Spretnak, and Carol Christ.

Unlike Wacousta who chooses emotion and intuition over practicality and calculation, 'Colonel de Haldimar was not one given to indulge in the mysterious or to believe in the romantic. Everything was plain matter of fact.' A stolid exemplar of the daylight consciousness that Davies and Kroetsch speak of, armed with a sharp, penetrating intellect, the reader first sees this Zeus figure—perhaps symbolically—'bearing a lamp in one hand and a naked sword in the other.' 'A caution and vigilance of no common kind were unceasingly exercised by the prudent governor,' we are told on the first page of the story; De Haldimar's last words urge the officers dutifully to 'pay every attention to the security of the garrison.' Indeed, the opening chapters are choked with the repetition of such garrison watchwords as 'prudence,' 'caution,' 'discipline,' 'vigilance,' and 'precaution.' De Haldimar's first sentence is the now classic opening question of all 'westerns,' one posed by the lawman in baffled pursuit of an elusive outlaw: 'which way did he go?'

De Haldimar opposes to nature and the instinctual side of human beings the world of the mind. Such is his over-emphasis on the intellect and on will-power that he strives to effect what Grove's Edmund Clark, a tyrant likewise motivated by pride and fear, calls an order that represents a dictatorship of mind over matter. As Jones notes in Grove's works, the arid and militant ideal De Haldimar devotes himself to implementing in the New World invariably incurs the destruction of human life and constitutes an assault upon the human spirit. What is gained in security and stability is lost in terms of vital energy and heartfelt passion.

Other establishment or law-and-order figures in Canadian literature have inherited Colonel de Haldimar's perverse, virulent strain of rationality. The cool, detached, intellectual streak that makes him an 'inhuman murderer' renders Mitchell's Mrs Abercrombie 'the town assassin,' Ondaatje's Sheriff Pat Garrett 'a sane assassin' and 'an academic murderer,' and Grove's Edmund Clark 'an almost insane schemer' prepared 'to assume the most absolute power, as a dictator . . .

to maintain law and order' and to 'eliminate' dissenters through 'Police and soldiery . . . machine guns and tanks . . . for the good of the masses themselves.' Although Wacousta seems to be mad, perhaps, as Perry Nodelman notes in an article on Ondaatje's *The Collected Works of Billy the Kid,* 'the real madmen are those who believe that sanity is total control and total lack of emotion.'

Perhaps the most important clue to De Haldimar's ambitious, patriarchal behaviour and the betrayal of his best friend comes right at the beginning of the romance before the full extent of its significance can be gauged. In a work in which so many things are doubled, it is not surprising that there are two curses. '"Ah!" observed Captain Blessington, "this is indeed the greatest curse attached to the profession of a soldier. Even among those who most esteem, and are drawn towards each other as well by fellowship in pleasure as companionship in danger, this vile and debasing principle—this insatiable desire for personal advancement—is certain to intrude itself; since we feel that over the mangled bodies of our dearest friends and companions, we can alone hope to attain preferment and distinction."' If De Haldimar is the victim of Ellen's curse, Wacousta has been the innocent victim of this, 'the greatest curse.' Richardson chooses to emphasize this first curse at length in the opening chapters. He deems it important enough to detract from the surface action of tight suspense and mystery, reiterating it twice. For all the fear of the wilderness, this selfish, divisive desire for personal advancement is the real law of the jungle. Garrison life lived according to this 'debasing principle' is analogous to contemporary business life which for Bly 'allows competitive relationships only, in which the major emotions are anxiety, tension, loneliness, rivalry, and fear . . . Having no soul union with other men can be the most damaging wound of all.'

Here an expression of the Cain and Abel motif, the scramble, for preferment 'over the mangled bodies of our dearest friends' is a particularly fertile theme in Canadian literature; it informs works from Heavysege's *The Advocate* to Richler's *The Apprenticeship of Duddy Kravitz* to Davies's Deptford trilogy. The story opens and closes in an enactment of this curse. Blessington, Charles, and Everard speak out against promotion obtained through the misfortune of others. Delme and Murphy, like the young Ensign de Haldimar, indulge in 'such selfish anticipations.' It is dramatically appropriate, therefore, that Wacousta's first stray shot kills the ambitious Murphy, that 'eternal echo of the opinions of those who look forward to promotion,' while his last shot kills the calculating Ensign Delme, Ensign de Haldimar's mirror-image. Both unfeeling men are shot through the heart, their deaths as symbolic as that of Grove's Edmund Clark, likewise killed by a bullet through the heart whilst defending the mill that now resembles a beleaguered fortress.

Richardson's poignant description of Governor de Haldimar in chapter 6 is a classic portrait of a type now all too familiar to readers of Canadian and feminist writings and the literature of the men's movement. It demands quotation at length.

> As a subaltern, M. de Haldimar had ever been considered a pattern of rigid propriety and decorum of conduct. Not the shadow of military crime had ever been laid to his charge. He was punctual at all parades and drills; kept the company to which he was attached in a perfect hot water of discipline; never missed his distance in marching past, or failed in a military manoeuvre; paid his mess-bill regularly to the hour, nay, minute, of the settling day . . . and, to crown all, he had never asked, consequently never obtained, a day's leave from his regiment . . . With all these qualities, Ensign de Haldimar promised to make an excellent soldier; and, as such, was encouraged by the field-officers of the corps, who unhesitatingly pronounced him a lad of discernment and talent, who would one day rival them in all the glorious privileges of martinetism.

De Haldimar's quest to have and to hold power and position has become his life and has cost him his human features, as Wacousta's quest has cost him his. The Governor resembles an efficient, merciless machine exacting unquestioning obedience and grinding out robot-like conformity—a machine that works incessantly and works at keeping everything under control. Yet despite all his weaknesses, De Haldimar is presented with the same ceasing ambiguity, understanding, and sympathy as is Wacousta. In that very important chapter 6, the narrator maintains that

> Whatever might be the stern peculiarities of his character,—and these had originated in an education purely military,—Colonel de Haldimar was an officer well calculated to the important trust reposed in him; for, combining experience with judgement in all matters relating to the diplomacy of war, and being fully conversant with the character and habits of the enemy opposed to him, he possessed singular aptitude to seize whatever advantages might present themselves. The prudence and caution of his policy have already been made manifest in the two several council scenes with the chiefs.

L. R. Early argues that 'a case can be made for De Haldimar as an exemplar of competence and responsibility.' The Governor is an able administrator and a shrewd organizer. Like the practical business men in *Five Legs,* he knows how to get things done; in both cases, this is part of their Puritan heritage. 'Scrupulously exact in the arrangement of his papers,' the fastidious bureaucrat is efficient, orderly, organized, pragmatic, analytical. Under his prudent supervision, the fledgling British colony does survive and endure, despite hardship and disaster and in the face of what strikes them as cosmic indifference and perhaps hostil-

ity. While his actions often end up sacrificing lives, they also preserve them; as Foucault's works testify, power is an ambivalent force. In some matters, De Haldimar does display a very Canadian genius for compromise. His policy of conciliation with regard to Ponteac and the three tribes he commands receives approbation. When the Indians are trapped inside the fort, De Haldimar cleverly uses the occasion to impress upon them the benevolent intentions of the empire he represents, to declaim against the French and to castigate Wacousta as a treacherous French spy unworthy of associating with a people he only misleads. So impressed is Ponteac by this show of forbearance and good will that he later concludes a peace with the British. Fort Détroit survives, in part then, through De Haldimar's competent deployment of well-disciplined troops who defeat Ponteac's plans to capture it.

Neither De Haldimar nor Wacousta is a one-dimensional character. They may have a symbolic or iconic dimension, but they are also well-defined individuals alive with contradictions. The Governor is as capable of feeling as Wacousta is of systematically formulating a 'feasible and rational plan' to effect Clara Beverley's descent down the mountain. Both men display leadership capabilities, although Wacousta is certainly a more spell-binding orator. At the same time, the excessive severity of De Haldimar's treatment of Halloway, Ellen, Everard, and others proves divisive and increasingly alienates him from his troops; so, too, the extent of Wacousta's revenge estranges Oucanasta and stirs up his nemesis in the person of her brother. Both leaders are capable of change. Chapter 6 reveals a lonely, isolated De Haldimar who is beginning—albeit too late—to moderate his extreme behaviour.

He, too, becomes, in Wacousta's phrase for himself, an 'altered being.'

> Whether it was that he secretly acknowledged the too excessive sternness of his justice in regard to Halloway (who still, in the true acceptation of facts, had been guilty of a crime that entailed the penalty he had paid), or that the apprehensions that arose to his heart in regard to her on whom he yearned with all a father's fondness governed his conduct, certain it is, that, from the hour of the disclosure made by his son, Colonel de Haldimar became an altered man. Without losing any thing of that dignity of manner, which had hitherto been confounded with the most repellent haughtiness of bearing, his demeanour towards his officers became more courteous; and although, as heretofore, he kept himself entirely aloof . . . there was more of conciliation in his manner, and less of austerity in his speech.

This change parallels that mellowing which the ferocious Wacousta undergoes in Clara de Haldimar's company, the captive beauty, in turn, feeling compassion for the savage beast. Growth begins only after the Governor experiences humility, vulnerability—and grief. Grief is the door to feeling in De Haldimar as Bly maintains it is for most men. Charles's death helps free the loving father long buried within the physically and emotionally undemonstrative Governor. The Governor's coldness and cruelty become painfully apparent to him—and to the garrison. The formerly insensitive man of the head 'goes out of his mind with grief' and comes to his senses. Descending from his summit, De Haldimar begins to regain some humanity through 'learning to shudder' (Bly), a phrase Davies also uses to describe a similiar process in David Staunton, his aloof manticore. Explains Bly in a section of *Iron John* entitled 'The Road of Ashes, Descent, and Grief,' 'Gaining the ability to shudder means feeling how frail human beings are, and how awful it is to be a Titan. When one is shuddering, the shudder helps to take away the numbness we spoke of. When a man possesses empathy, it does not mean that he has developed the feminine feeling only; of course he has, and it is good to develop the feminine. But when he learns to shudder, he is developing a part of the masculine emotional body as well.'

As in the fiction of Grove, Davies, Atwood, Laurence, Kroetsch, and Callaghan, it requires a costly irruption of irrational forces to change or moderate the ways of characters like De Haldimar. The Governor appears to be at the very beginning of that painful journey toward the reintegration of undeveloped feelings later undertaken by law-and-order figures like Davies's Justice Staunton or Callaghan's 'Commander' Ira Groome.

Of Shadow Kings, Dark Fathers, and Father-Hungry Sons: Zeus and the Patriarchy

> Zeus is the archetype of the dynastic father . . . Zeus is emotionally distant, does not have an earthy nature, doesn't try to please women, and isn't passionate. Because the Zeus man may focus on achieving power, other aspects of his personality become stunted . . . Zeus's realm was the sky, and the Zeus archetype predisposes a man to live in his head . . . The message that something is wrong needs to get through to the Zeus man.

JEAN BOLEN, *Gods in Everyman*

The sterile and self-destructive character of De Haldimar's ideal of mechanical perfection is tragically manifest in his severe conduct towards members of his own family. Such behaviour forecasts that of Gibson's Robert Fraser in *Perpetual Motion,* Grove's wilful, domineering patriarchs, Hagar Shipley's father in Laurence's *The Stone Angel,* Ostenso's Caleb Gare, Maggie's tyrannical parents in Reaney's *The St. Nicholas Hotel,* Kroetsch's William Dawe in *Badlands,* and

countless others. De Haldimar not only pits his will against the new land but also against anyone who dares question his pronouncements, including his children.

> Much of the despotic military character of Colonel de Haldimar had been communicated to his private life; so much, indeed, that his sons,—both of whom . . . were of natures that belied their origin from so stern a stock,—were kept at nearly as great a distance from him as any other subordinates of his regiment. But although he seldom indulged in manifestations of parental regard towards those whom he looked upon rather as inferiors in military rank, than as beings connected with him by the ties of blood, Colonel de Haldimar was not without the instinctive love for his children which every animal in the creation feels for its offspring.

The father-son bond is treated with great importance in *Wacousta* and *The Canadian Brothers*. The emotionally distant De Haldimar possesses the lineaments of 'The Remote Father' or 'The Darkened Father' whose literary manifestations Bly traces in stories about the Titans Uranus and Cronos through to the contemporary figures of the Emperor and his deadly servant, Darth Vader (whose name is a pun on dark father). Like the suspicious and uneasy Governor, such men tend to compete as rivals even with their own sons. De Haldimar considers his son Charles—a Poseidon 'feeling' type who openly talks about and shares his feelings—embarrassingly inferior and effeminate because he reacts emotionally rather than rationally in a culture that regards such behaviour as negative. Although the father in his dynastic urge has named this son after himself, hoping he will mirror or replicate his ideal of manliness, the gentle, sensitive, and receptive Charles is a 'soft male' (Bly) who recalls the Governor's emotionally expressive wife whom he seems to have singlemindedly pursued only to neglect and let quickly suffocate in his passionless presence.

Charles, in turn, experiences grief due to the remoteness and secretiveness of his workaholic father. Rather than reject his punitive parent outright as an American son might do, the introspective Charles becomes a 'Father-Hungry Son' bent on suppressing his nature and—like 'The Canadian Brothers'—living up to his father's expectations by excelling as a soldier under his command. He also gives himself over to taking care of others at the expense of his own well-being. All such reactions are familiar attempts of emotionally abandoned and shamed sons to 'ascend above their wound,' as Bly would say. Harshly and coldly critical, De Haldimar is unable to give his blessing to his son, who seeks this elsewhere in a male mentor aptly named Blessington. In *Iron John* we read, 'Not receiving any blessing from your father is an injury. Robert Moore said, "If you're a young man and you're not being admired by an older man, you're being hurt."'

As the foregoing quotation from **Wacousta** suggests, in a text that emphasizes relationship and the interconnectedness of all characters, Governor de Haldimar and the culture he tries to establish through force in North America privilege a model of human relationships—whether in personal or professional spheres—based on the principle of ranking and rivalry rather than linking or affiliation. Feminist scholar Riane Eisler in *The Chalice and the Blade* (1987) and *The Partnership Way* (1990) refers to the former as 'dominator model' societies which tend to be authoritarian, hierarchial, competitive, aggressive, frequently patriarchal, and defiantly set apart from nature, and to the latter as 'partnership model' societies which constellate 'feminine' values like egalitarian linking and bonding, non-violence, active caring and nurturance, and connection with the earth. Partnership or 'the power of affiliation'—what Canadian educator Mac Freeman calls 'duetting'—is the hallmark of cultures opposed to dominator modes. It reflects a sense of the interconnectedness of human beings that Richardson surely appreciated and of the interwoven texture of all life which feminist writers like Jean Bolen, Merlin Stone, Charlene Spretnak, Carol Gilligan, Luisah Teish, Starhawk, and Mary Daly discern in goddess cultures. While partnership societies conceptualize the powers governing the universe in the female form of the goddess, dominator ones—of which De Haldimar's garrison is typical—often worship and pattern relationships after a sternly divine Father who wields a thunderbolt or a weapon, devalue the feminine, and equate true masculinity with the power urge, dominance, total control, and rational thinking.

Eisler's historical study of Western civilization helps to clarify some of the male-male and male-female relationships in Richardson's work, throwing light on the Governor's plans to establish a patriarchal dynasty, to rule over the wilderness, his children, and his own instinctual nature. It is a plan shared by his symbolic descendants, the haughty, ambitious, and autocratic empire-builder Abe Spalding in Grove's *Fruits of the Earth,* an Ontarian determined to 'conquer this wilderness,' to force the land to take 'the impress of his mind and will,' and the dogmatic John Elliot senior in *Our Daily Bread,* 'a thinker' 'proud of the preponderance, in him, of brain over impulse' and 'appraising reason above all else.' Interestingly, both men are paired with their opposites. Abe's best friend is the philosophical Nicoll whose words seem the 'utterance of that very landscape itself; as though Nicoll were the true son of the prairie, and he, Abe, a mere interloper.' John Elliot senior is balanced harmoniously with 'his complement,' his wife Martha who 'seemed to do instinctively, action coming from the heart, what he chose to do after mature deliberation, his action being dictated by the brain.'

Like Grove's empire-builders or Atwood's Commander of the Republic of Gilead in *The Handmaid's Tale,*

Governor de Haldimar is a 'Shadow King,' a term coined by psychoanalyst and theologian Robert Moore, author (with Douglas Gilette) of *King, Warrior, Magician, Lover: Rediscovering the Archetypes of the Mature Masculine* (1990). In contrast to the firm but kindly King (or Sacred King) who is powerful and 'uses power to empower,' nurture, validate, and bless others, the Shadow King exercises abusive power over others, and does not foster creativity, facilitate growth or enhance potential. As the shadow part of the father archetype, whether in the individual male psyche or in society at large, he is visible in the Governor's paranoiac suspicion of motives and loyalties and in his capacity to remain unmoved in the face of the suffering of others. It is this very lack of empathy which calls down Ellen's curse on him and his family, thus animating the plot of the epic. In a mythological context, both the King and the Shadow King are manifestations of the Zeus archetype, for Moore, Bly, and Bolen the presiding 'god' of Western culture. Governor de Haldimar possesses positive Zeus energy to some extent; he is not without leadership qualities, an overview perspective, and a capacity for quick, decisive action taken to sustain the community. He also manifests the dark side of this distant, authoritarian, power-seeking sky god who, as Arianna Stassinopoulos puts it, 'becomes in his darkness an enemy of the life-force, locked in his structures and laws, fearing and resisting change and any threat to the status quo.'

Jean Bolen's insightful analysis of the central Olympian god 'who excels . . . at determining boundaries' and of his psychological resonance as an archetype of the male psyche will help draw together my comments on the personality traits of Governor de Haldimar and his symbolic descendants in Canadian literature. 'Like all successful rulers, Zeus was adept at strategy, forming alliances . . . Zeus has the ambition and the ability to establish a realm over which he was the chief god, and the urge to preside over one's own territory is a major drive of this archetype, which shapes men (and women) to be and behave like Zeus . . . He exalts control, reason and will above all other qualities . . . To sit at the summit, with power, authority, and dominion over a chosen realm is the Zeus position . . . The driving force is the urge to extend the boundaries of the kingdom.'

Where the Governor/Zeus establishes, defends, extends borders, Wacousta/Poseidon leaps over them or finds himself unable to recognize or set them. And unlike his counterpart, 'For Zeus, finding a suitable wife is not a matter of heart or soul connection, but a matter of state . . . He went after women with the singleness of purpose that is characteristic of his "eagle" nature. Seeing who he wants, he does whatever is necessary to get close to her . . . Once he has succeeded, his attention most likely again focuses on his work realm.' Bolen's description of Zeus as 'the archetype of the dynastic father' succinctly clarifies the Governor's attitude towards his children: 'His expectation of them is similiar to what he expects of his subordinates: to be obedient and carry out his will. His favourite children replicate his ideal of himself as a fair-minded, superior person who does not let emotions ever get "out of control" . . . He considers showing vulnerability or neediness or being emotional signs of stupidity or weakness.'

Such is the 'god' of the man Richardson depicts as the mythic founder of the Canadas. He is a man whose distant descendants—respectable sons of the patriarchy manning the bastions of Zeus power—are doomed through the curse of the marginalized Ellen to struggle with the offspring of his outlaw double in the sequel to *Wacousta, The Canadian Brothers*.

Dennis Duffy (essay date 1993)

SOURCE: "Present at the Creation: John Richardson and Souwesto," in *Journal of Canadian Studies,* Vol. 28, No. 3, Autumn, 1993, pp. 75-91.

[*In the following essay, Duffy focuses his discussion on Richardson's last novel,* Westbrook the Outlaw, *contending that the novelist led the way in establishing the imaginative tradition of Southwestern Ontario in Canadian literature.*]

"Souwesto" designates one of English Canada's most thickly populated countries of the mind. On the map where Thoreau's true countries never are, Southwestern Ontario covers the peninsula created by Lake Erie, Lake Huron and Georgian Bay. The painterly imagination has dotted it with the views caught in the paintings of Jack Chambers and Greg Curnoe. Hamlets as storied as Hanratty (Munro's *Who Do You Think You Are?*), Biddulph Township (Reaney's *The Donnellys*), and Deptford (Davies's trilogy of that name) flourish there. Though James Reaney is the genius of Souwesto's shore, he credits Curnoe with inventing its name.

In a remarkable paper, Reaney places John Richardson (1796-1852) at the heart of his own Laurentian model of the Canadian literary imagination. No surprise that the poet who dramatized Richardson's two Prophecy novels—*Wacousta* and *The Canadian Brothers*—pays such close attention to an earlier writer. Following Reaney's imaginative mapping, my survey here encompasses nothing beyond a regional outcropping. Lost for better than a century, *Westbrook the Outlaw* can hardly be said to influence the work of Richardson's successors. Yet viewed properly, the wildly plotted, pulp-y fiction in fact foretells many of the preoccupations of the more "serious" literature that will follow. Richardson's last, lost (and perhaps his least) novel seizes instinctively upon material that more closely

resembles folklore than fiction. Through his presence at the creation of Souwesto, Richardson helps to establish a tradition of the transformation of history into legend—with all its attendant implications—in the representation of the region.

Native Others had told their stories earlier, before white settlers came to the territory. Those aboriginal works are not my subject here. With John Richardson begins the imaginative history produced by the Euro-Canadians and their heirs, which concerns me. Almost certainly of mixed blood, Richardson leads the way in the imaginative appropriation of the territory that his immediate, white ancestors grasped in material fact.

The writer's most telling early experiences as a man were set in Souwesto. His military-doctor father belonged to the multinational enclave of the garrison, the Niagara region where John Richardson was born and the Malden (Amherstburg) where he was raised. His mother sprang from the world of the fur trade and the family of John Askin. One of the more prominent traders and land speculators in that vast wilderness region whose capital was Detroit, Askin and his family left their mark upon it. His Askin grandmother told the boy the stories of Pontiac's 1763 uprising that gave the writer the historical framework for *Wacousta,* his best-known fiction. Askin had first married an aboriginal woman according to the custom of the country, and had children by her before marrying Marie Archange Barth. Her daughter Madeleine was the novelist's mother. Unlike the majority of whites who entered into such local arrangements, Askin acknowledged his mixed-blood offspring. They in turn did well by him in seeking to preserve his trading frontier against the encroachment of white, American settlement. John Askin's offspring had fought alongside the confederated Indians at Fallen Timbers in 1794 in their final attempt to hold onto what the victorious Americans called the Old Northwest. An Askin led the Indians who, alongside their British allies, recaptured Michilimackinac from the Americans in 1812. The future novelist, his father, and his brother fought in that Northwest campaign whose conclusion at Moraviantown in 1813 destroyed forever the Indian and trader cause.

John Richardson had been one of the last whites to see the great Tecumseh alive. The gallant, stylish leader wore at his last battle an ostrich plume given to him by one of the novelist's kin. *Wacousta* may have originated at Grandma's knee, but its sequel, *The Canadian Brothers,* sprang from the novelist's own abruptly ended boyhood that included time spent as a prisoner of the Americans. *Westbrook* originated in another kind of American imprisonment, this one voluntary on Richardson's part, one that I will examine later. Souwesto remained with Richardson; toward the end of his life he wrote feelingly of his return to the region and to the towns of his early years. Those times had marked him enough to make Souwesto and its ways the battleground that he chose for his last, desperate struggle to earn his livelihood through writing fiction.

The frontier world that he knew from the inside and whose genetic make-up he bore in his physiognomy determined the shape Richardson's writing took. This is true even of so formulaic a work as **Westbrook**. Two minor details indicate the story's debt to actual experience. In the early 1840s, Richardson passed the night at a squalid inn near Brockville, Ontario. A memorable feature of his accommodation was a rickety partition wall enabling him to peer into the adjoining room. The title character in **Westbrook** takes advantage of a similar arrangement in an inn near Kingston, gazing with perverse delight upon the heroine as she undresses. The second detail is also visual, but perspectival rather than voyeuristic. Andrew Westbrook's log house on the bluffs of the Thames offers its occupant a compelling prospect over a "highly romantic aspect" of the landscape. Richardson's own house in Brockville was set upon a "picturesque and elevated" site. If every congruence between his actual and his imaginary worlds were that specific and simple, then my discussion here would be shorter. His experience—in its rigour a kind of emotional beating of the boundaries—created a mapping more complex than simple one-to-one parallelisms. Exploring one of those sectors—the historical Andrew Westbrook and Richardson's version of him—opens our investigation into the particular contours of his cartography.

Begin by considering the literary market in which **Westbrook** appeared. The politics of culture and publishing explain one arresting, incongruous element in Richardson's choice of characters for a novel set in Upper Canada during 1812. Any census of the colony at that time would have noted as many woolly mammoths as lay members of Roman Catholic monastic orders. Yet this story of a border monster, who outdoes any earlier creature in Richardson's wax museum of frontier horror, also features Anselmo, the Abelard half of the loving couple that includes the voluptuous Emily. She is raped and murdered, and Anselmo killed by Westbrook, though not before the young couple fall in love in a convent and add the ferment of forbidden, runaway passion to the story. Still, what are they doing in Upper Canada?

Imaginative and commercial forces alike generated the doomed affair of near-cleric and quasi-nun. The imaginative drives centred around the 1836 runaway success, Maria Monk's *Awful Disclosures of the Hotel Dieu Nunnery.* Widely known as *The Confessions of Maria Monk,* or simply as "Maria Monk," the work appeared to confirm generations of anti-Catholic suspicions about the sexual practices of Roman Catholic clergy and religious. Protestantism's *Protocols of the*

Elders of Zion, the volume offered the titillation that only the highly moral perusal of obscenity can deliver.

Among the lurid disclosures of "Maria Monk" was the news that the monstrous events that it chronicles—the infant corpses buried in the basement, the secret tunnels connecting convents with monasteries, all the paraphernalia of *grand guignol* Gothic—were happening here, on this continent, in Montreal. American readers, disturbed at the continuing British presence on *their* continent, now found themselves especially threatened. At the root of that alien, royalist, but thankfully Protestant, political melanoma to the north lay the French-speaking, Gothic citadel of Romanism. Even the North was not wholly fortified against Papal aggression.

Richardson's fictional perspective peers beyond the remote outpost of empire that was Upper Canada. His tale of the Great Lakes border discovers the farthest reaches of that Popish power poised like a dagger at the heart of Protestant civilization. Thus Richardson's Paolo and Francesca take as their escape route the lakeshore road leading from Lower to Upper Canada. The voluptuously endowed heroine (Richardson knew of no other kind, whether in literature or life) rivets Westbrook's attention. Westbrook's creator replays a situation that he may well have encountered in actuality. A reader who could swallow the appearance of a loving, upper-class Catholic couple along the Kingston Road would have no difficulty digesting Anselmo's means of earning a livelihood. He is a mathematics tutor. The couple has every reason to flee toward Protestant enlightenment in Upper Canada. There the sciences were honoured, esteemed, and used to build a more progressive world.

In providing these distant, imaginative echoes of Maria Monk, the novelist could well have been writing to order, as may have been the case with other late fiction by him. The commercial roots of the lay brother originate with the New York publishers that the author found—at a price—after his retreat from Canada. His homeland had witnessed his failure as a journalist, novelist, and even as the commander of a detachment of security guards on the Welland Canal. His introduction to his American publishers' new 1851 edition of **Wacousta** spoke of Canada's indifference to his work. As the price of his new allegiance, he had taken his nationalist **The Canadian Brothers** and either gelded it himself or consented to his publisher's excision of its Upper Canadian loyalties. Its new audience was spared what it would never have tolerated: the anti-American remarks that dot the original text. Then he had given his creation a sex change, retitling it **Matilda Montgomerie**.

His accommodation to his publishers' political ideology may well have been followed by a bow to their religious one. New York's Dewitt and Davenport were a well-known dime-novel and reprint house. Its senior partner also enjoyed a certain prominence in nativist (or "Know-Nothing") affairs. Robert Dewitt belonged to the Order of United Americans. In the manner of Tammany Hall, they employed cigar-store Indian designations in their fraternal, anti-Roman gatherings. Richardson worked for a time on the order's journal, *The Sachem.* Dewitt and Davenport had become his bread and butter. He literally starved on the pittance that his writing fetched, but not before he had produced a near-pornographic treatment of medieval Catholicism.

Written a year earlier than *Westbrook,* set far away from the Great Lakes in both space and time, *The Monk Knight of St. John* deals with the Crusades, and the monastic-military order of the Knights of the Hospital of St. John of Jerusalem. It seems rooted in the anti-Catholic crusade of its publishers, seething as it does with sado-masochism. Scott's *Ivanhoe* (1819) showed that Templars made good villains. Yet even Richardson felt uneasy enough about his pandering to anti-Catholic bigotry (did he remember the story-telling grandmother who had recounted to him the material of his best work?) to insert a disclaimer into *Westbrook:* "What occurred in a Catholic convent might as well have taken place in a Protestant, had there been any such establishments attached to them." Though the logic of the statement is elusive, it does indicate some misgivings over the cultural politics of his story-telling.

Much of *Westbrook,* then, is driven by the currents in the metropolitan centres where Richardson worked and where his readers found their fashions. Yet when we consider the details of the historical figure of Andrew Westbrook and the novelist's treatment of him, this truism requires examination.

The subtitle ("An American Border Tale") alerts us to the setting's equivocality. Richardson's character deflates the self-esteem of audiences on either side of the line. Westbrook at first would seem to be the classically democratic, therefore anti-British figure—the fighting blacksmith—that a novelist could present as a token of his new allegiance. He battles the Upper Canadian authorities even as his historical progenitor did. He takes pot shots at retreating British commanders and cheerfully kills a loyal militiaman. He also allies himself with Captain Lee, an American marauder. The historical Westbrook made life unendurable to many in the so-called Talbot Settlement stretching north from Lake Erie. His special hatred for the squirearchical pretensions of Colonel Talbot (whose power cramped Westbrook's own land speculations) led him to bedevil that figure. He came close to wrecking Talbot's life and burning out what is now an entire county. He was also prominent in a sizeable band (250 men) of expa-

triate Upper Canadians who passed the war in raiding Souwesto from the American side. Call him either a bandit or a freedom fighter, depending upon your political allegiance. As the latter, Westbrook appealed to the author's new national audience. Yet Richardson satisfied their longings for the bread of heroism by giving them a stone in the person of this monster.

He gives little more to his former Upper-Canadian compatriots. His process of fictionalization (demonizing) involves plucking Westbrook out of context, disregarding the collective, dissenting forces whose existence had so troubled Isaac Brock. A jagged edge of the early years of Upper Canada is smoothed through the lone, fairy-tale villain's monopolizing of the reader's attention. What is going on?

A rapist, murderer, and incestuous father, Richardson's Westbrook commits a series of crimes outdoing those of the author's earlier creation, Wacousta. Only the cannibalism of Wacousta's son Desborough (*The Canadian Brothers*) can out-Herod Westbrook. An early white settler in Souwesto, the Reverend Edmund Burke wrote in 1795 to a colonial official that an enemy as "terrible" as the Indian "prowls like a wolf in the dark." Richardson got beyond the conventions of racism when he thrust his white monster beyond civility. He is finally slain by a she-wolf who has nurtured the grandson that Westbrook threatens.

Richardson attempts to pacify his United States audience when a bystander thanks God for the fact that Westbrook was not an American. In fact he was. His few years of residence in Upper Canada gave him a factitious Canadian identity, but he settled quite happily in Michigan after the war, enjoying public approbation and emoluments. His military service on behalf of the United States earned him two land grants from a grateful congress.

A novelist more intent on flattering his new readers would have worked this national, collective material into his story, emphasizing Westbrook's communal ties and achievements. A writer more intent on thumbing his nose at his former audience would have emphasized context as well, though of another, pro-American sort. Of course, this would have entailed denaturing his creation. A Westbrook metamorphosed into an American patriot could not have flaunted the monstrous nature that made him imaginatively compelling. Richardson seems intent enough on creating a larger-than-life protagonist to make him risk the alienation of his new-found American audience. His Westbrook may not be an American, yet he is their strongest friend and ally. In order to keep his monster, Richardson has to forgo waving the flag.

Richardson's handling of Westbrook resembles other moments in the legends of Souwesto. A late-Victorian compilation of local lore helps to illuminate a cultural process that I would call the folklorizing of a region: that is, the ascription to it of the power to provide a setting for folk tales and romantic narratives. Literature may come out of this process. But those literary landmarks that I mentioned at the beginning do not engage me here; I am concerned with a less finished literary product.

The narratives that convey my point about folklorization can be found in Marie Caroline Hamlin's *Legends of Le Détroit* (1884). The Detroit compiler's citizenship presents no obstacle to her dealing with borderland Souwesto material. Where the tales display imaginative strength and vitality, they are retellings of the folk tales and legends of the earliest white settlers in the region, who were of course *canadien*. Thus, the reader is regaled with the typical collection of *loups garoux,* yearning village maids, enchanted canoes, and priests in avid pursuit of traces of the devil, that one can encounter in any compilation of Quebec legends. Hamlin's tales may be set in the Detroit region, but they are stories told long ago in Rivière du Loup and Chicoutimi, and before that in Rouen and Quimper. So much for the familiar tales in the volume.

When we reach the new material, however, we find romantic fantasies based on such historical happenings in the War of 1812 as the massacre at River Raisin (Frenchtown) and Hull's surrender of Detroit. Stories like "The Sibyl's Prophecy" and "The Ghost of Montgaugon" are not folklore or legend. They are instead feeble versions of nineteenth-century historical fiction, their distant begetter Sir Walter Scott rather than some oral source. What the collection itself does show is that by the 1880s (and probably well before), the Detroit-Souwesto region had been processed into the material for pseudo legend-making. This was a continent-wide activity, and various regional literary enterprises were well under way by then. William Kirby's *Canadian Idylls* (1894) and *Annals of Niagara* (1896) show a similar process happening at the other end of Lake Erie from Souwesto. In fact, such imaginatively geographical regions as the American south, or the midwest of Willa Cather, indicate that many North American regions acquired a mythic history long before anyone compiled a scientific one. Much of this process we can attribute to such cultural forces as the prevalence of antiquarianism and the invention of tradition, complex undertakings that need not concern us here.

What needs emphasis is that Richardson's creature is an early version of the making of legend out of Souwesto historical material, a process reaching its zenith in Reaney's *The Donnellys* (1975-77). But not all legendary material ends up as legend. Study of a process that failed to happen brings home the cultural politics played out in the work of Richardson.

Consider an incident in the life of the Long Point trader David Ramsay (1740-1810?). We find out about Ramsay largely through depositions against him. Our earliest narrative that is not part of a legal document occurs in Patrick Campbell's *Travels in North America* (1793). Fairness compels me to begin with a version favourable to Ramsay. Campbell considered him "a man of strict veracity, honesty, and integrity," while Joseph Brant thought the trader nothing more than an "unworthy rascal." Perhaps the Mohawk chief knew the story that follows here.

By Feb. 15, 1772 Ramsay had found himself vexed enough at his Indian trading partners to kill and then scalp two of them who had tried—he swore—to murder him. This did not end the Lake Erie businessman's difficulties with his clientele. By the approach of spring he felt forced to kill some more, these from a "wandering" (hunting?) band who continued to threaten him. By that time, he had lost his customary forbearance: "After killing the first Indians, I cut lead, and chewed above thirty balls, and above three pound of Goose shot, for I thought it a pity to shoot an Indian with a smooth ball." His opponents had grown peevish as well. Capturing and binding him, they taunted him with their confidence in the British alliance. They believed with reason that while Sir William Johnson, the crown's great superintendent of Indian affairs, might forgive them for killing Ramsay, he would never forgive Ramsay for killing them. The trader's dexterity—and the aid of a ten-year-old nephew whom he had introduced to the exigencies of commercial travelling—enabled him to unloose himself from his bonds while his captors slept. He then killed a few more. Detained at Niagara and sent to Montreal, he pleaded self-defense eloquently enough to be released eventually. Years later, this case's most surprising feature occurred when the Indians conveyed to Ramsay a four-mile-square tract of land in Upper Canada. "[H]e now lives," Campbell notes with astonishment, "in intimacy and friendship with that very tribe, and the sons and daughters of the very people he had killed."

According to a later historian, everyone in the surrounding countryside knew of these events. Sir William Johnson considered them of sufficient import to write to his London superiors that he considered a fair trial impossible: "the interest which his creditors will make with those who are his Jurors, and the prejudices of the Commonality [*sic*] against Indians, will probably prove the means of his being acquitted . . ." Johnson also raised an even more significant matter. How was trade to continue in light of such consumer dissatisfaction? "I leave Your Lordship to judge how difficult a task it is to calm the passions of incensed Savages and to keep them faithfull [*sic*] to engagements whilst they find themselves exposed to the licentious outrages of our own people against which no remedy is as yet provided." Sir William's account adds that among

Ramsay's victims in his escape from captivity were a woman and an infant, both of whom he had scalped. It was his conveyance of those trophies to Niagara that aroused the suspicions of the commandant there.

Upper Canada's very own Indian-hater! The pathological killer in Melville's *The Confidence-Man* alive and well in Souwesto! Yet when legend is made of Ramsay, it begins when Patrick Campbell credits the man's account of an incident that could have leapt out of any adventure narrative. Ramsay had called out to his unbound nephew in broad Scots, a dialect his captors had not mastered, to fetch him a knife. With this he severed his material ties, and then went on to sever any commercial ones by killing his former customers. The linguistic detail seems legendary, and not from internal evidence alone. Ramsay's relatives retell the incident without any mention of his use of a foreign tongue. All accounts do agree that Ramsay's captors had drunk themselves into insensibility, making them less of a danger to the man who would slay them.

Ramsay's minor incursion into the stuff of legend is offset by his subsequent, ghostly presence in the stories collecting around the life of Souwesto's most celebrated spiritualist, Dr. John Troyer. The white magician of Long Point has been the subject of a play and a children's book. We need not rehearse the Baldoon material here. Ramsay and Troyer link up when the doctor makes his first public entrance as a celebrated diviner. According to the memories of one Simpson McCall, Troyer in 1817 undertook a search for a treasure that Ramsay supposedly buried at Long Point in order to hide it from yet another group of aggrieved clients. Troyer and his son located the iron chest; the doctor's radical Protestant beliefs (he belonged to the Tunker sect) led him to hold an open Bible and a lighted candle in order to ward off evil. Imagine the treasure seekers' surprise when the apparition of a gigantic black dog "rose up beside the chest—grew right up bigger and bigger, until the light went out, and then they took to their boat and went home." McCall was 85 when he told this legend to a travelling scholar interested in these old fireside tales.

What does the Ramsay matter tell us about the legend-making in a region where Richardson's writing fills so early and originating a role? When an Indian-hater with an addiction to murder becomes the stuff of legend, he is transmuted into a character who could have stepped from the pages of Robert Louis Stevenson, with his command of violence and broad Scots, his youthful sidekick, and his reincarnation as a fearsome black dog. He becomes a bogeyman, rather than an extreme exemplar of a social process that in one way or another involved many inhabitants of the territory that the newcomers named Upper Canada. He was a pioneer, a land developer, an entrepreneur, a player in the process of making the country safe for white settlement.

Our own legends—about ourselves as dwellers within a peaceable kingdom—fare better when the Ramsays of our past are linked with the adventures of the benevolent Dr. Troyer. Planter of the first orchard in Norfolk County, a figure willing to work in conjunction with the Ojibway medicine man Bauzi-Geezhig-Waeshikum in his attempts to relieve a family from the attentions of a poltergeist, Troyer is the patriarch transformed into Daddy, whose benign nature makes him a fitting forbear for the likes of us. Figures like Ramsay and Westbrook become Grendels, stalking the marshes as monsters rather than as social misfits whose evil originates in a system that we both inherit and endorse. Such a linkage camouflages any resemblance between our ancestry and the lonesome monsters lurking in the forests to the south. It comfortably defines our own writers in opposition to the American writers who represented those sorts of killers with such aplomb.

Richardson of course remains the master of the Great Lakes monster. When he invented him in the person of Reginald Morton/Wacousta, he forced the reader to endure the bulk of the novel in the company of an ogre before turning Wacousta into a fool for love. Until the narrative-within-a-narrative that forms chapter seven of Volume III, he has been the bloodthirsty military and sexual predator who seemed to have sprung from the dark forest perpetually threatening the fort. Then our author unfolds his story in a way that helps us to know better than that. We absorb the lesson of Wacousta's self-justification: only the skills honed within a high civilization can produce him. The obsessive concentration, the methodical subordination of every aspect of existence to a single goal: these skills of a sophisticated society (especially as evidenced in its military machine), rather than some power-bundle, supply Wacousta with his strength.

That adventurer straddles a pre-settlement border. The son that Richardson gives Wacousta in the sequel, *The Canadian Brothers,* straddles a political one. Desborough shifts back and forth between the lakeside countries, sworn enemy to the Grantham brothers of the novel's title, but restive under the legal restrictions marking life in Upper Canada. His sworn foe is a magistrate, the brothers' father whom he shoots in the back. Like his daughter who corrupts one of the brothers, Desborough too represents a series of abiding Canadian misgivings about the nature of life below the border. Yet no sooner do we rejoice that Richardson has displayed (albeit in hyperbolic fashion) our abiding Canadian righteousness, than he switches countries on us. Now we are faced with Andrew Westbrook. We write him off simply: hackwork churned out by a writer at the end of his tether. A dying man's last attempt to resurrect his old *métier,* marred by the mindless sensationalism of his attempt to recapture a lost public.

Yet if we place the monster Westbrook within his Souwesto context, we discover a greater complexity. When Richardson seeks to conjure up an evil spirit, a black dog of a man, he can turn him only into an example of the Other. He fabricates a bogey-man out of Andrew Westbrook, an historical figure who was nothing more than another traitorous bandit during a time of war. Because Richardson's desperation in the face of his total failure in Upper Canada had driven him elsewhere, he turned Westbrook into someone non-American (un-American he is not!) in order to soothe that new public. Had he produced his novel here, his character would have been clad in the Stars and Stripes. Rather than create a terror like Ramsay writ large, Richardson gives us a creature who wars only on whites. Westbrook brings home the hard times that *we,* and *ours,* have endured at the hands of rapacious men beyond the control of law. In this villainizing of our foes, Richardson becomes the father of us all.

A curiosity in this novel's use of setting alerts us to the nature of the symbolic transformation that I have been describing. One of Richardson's weaknesses as a writer was his inability to describe landscape in any detail or with any sense of drama. He could allude to the romantic grandeur evoked by the placing of figures within a landscape, striving for the kind of figuration Keats admired in Milton when he wrote of that poet's gifts at "stationing." He could never, however, really deliver us that landscape in the manner of a Cooper or Scott. So timid was he about his ability to shape a landscape into whatever image he required that his 1851 introduction to **Wacousta** apologizes for his narrowing of the Detroit River. Whenever the task of describing combat forces him to consider topography, he does so in distant fashion. He narrates, for example, the work of the corps he served in as a soldier of fortune without exhibiting any particular flair in conveying the physical feel of the battlefield. Fond as he was of remarking that certain scenes in his writing were fit subjects for visual reproduction, he went no further than that in presenting detail. So too with his brief combat topographies. Richardson possessed a very strong visual memory, even a discerning eye, but he simply could not exert any descriptive literary power over landscape.

It comes as a pleasant surprise, therefore, when the reader encounters a description, however brief, of the lakeshore marshlands in which so much of the story of Westbrook takes place. Yet the author describes these areas that in his time abounded in game and wildlife as wastelands, mephitic swamps: "one continuous low and foetid extent of unwholesome-looking marsh." Very well, we can applaud his willingness to indulge his powers and create an appropriate setting for a horror story. We can even link this with a personal aside two pages earlier on the dismal prospects that Upper Canada presents to writers. No acute critical insight is necessary to sense some personal symbolism at work in the transformation of marshland into wasteland. In light of our present concern, however, can we sense some other forces at work?

The landscape had to become mythicized in the same hyperbolic manner as his characterization. Nothing less than a monster would do for the figure of Andrew Westbrook, that Grendel who finds no Beowulf, but a real wolf instead. The landscape would in turn become what another Souwesto character—Dunstan Ramsay—terms one of Hell's "visible branch establishments throughout the earth . . ." On the one hand, this turn of the screw seems what we would expect of any popular writer. On the other, does it not create horror shows as a distraction from the actual monstrosities that walk the earth in everyday garb? Far more than Andrew Westbrook, David Ramsay told of something rotten in the history of the region. Ramsay was a very ordinary, disquieting villain whose culture backed him to the hilt, so to speak. He needed no gruesome make-up in order to star in a melodrama. Yet he does not. He becomes instead an off-stage presence, a wicked old dragon of a treasure leaver whose spirit hovers about as a black dog.

We cannot blame Richardson for choosing to fictionalize one figure rather than another, or for choosing to fictionalize the history of his region in the first place. We can observe only that this procedure leaps directly into the folkloric, the legendary, the larger-than-life as an evasion of the stark realities of day-to-day monstrosity governing a region's settlement. The facts of the founding of this new polity lay not in the mists of antiquity, in legends of Romulus and Remus, in the fall of Troy and the dispersion of the Trojans. The fireside stories—as in the case of Richardson's grandmother—concerned historical events. The mists parted to reveal few gods and heroes. They displayed instead folk rather like oneself, involved in activities perfectly comprehensible, understandable even, but disturbing in what they revealed about one's heritage.

Two incidents—one involving a whole community, the other a lone individual—bring home the nature of the world that was passing into legend. Both involve material that no regional romancer thought worthy of "working up" into the stuff of fictional narrative. Both incidents involved on their fringes John Askin, the novelist's grandfather, and show him in a favourable light.

The first we enter through the history of a place name. Tecumseh's confederacy and Richardson's early world ended at Moraviantown. The settlement was also known as Fairfield. It stood at no great distance from the Thamesville, Ontario that Robertson Davies turned into Deptford. It took its name from the "praying Indians" that the Protestant missionaries of the United Brethren

(Moravian) sect had made out of the tribes that they had converted to Christianity and agricultural settlement. These converts had not always been in Upper Canada. Their conversion to full-time agriculturalists and non-violent Christians had first landed them in what was known as Gnadenhütten in Ohio. There they and their German-speaking missionaries established a new community, "Safe Havens." It was to be a hideous misnomer, for in March 1782, 90 of those disarmed Delawares were slaughtered by a western Pennsylvanian militia out to destroy any settlements that they could find. After this notable incident in frontier history, a "trail of tears" followed, in which at least one white person showed himself to be humane. In 1786, John Askin lent his trading vessels *Mackinac* and *Beaver* to the transportation of the Moravian congregation from the Detroit region to the mouth of the Cuyahoga (Cleveland, Ohio). For this and other kindnesses, the Moravian John Heckewelder, the missionary whose accounts gave James Fenimore Cooper his ideas of Indian life and character, called Askin a "good friend" to the praying Indians.

Like Richardson's failure to give a name to the Indian youth who twice saves the romantic lead's life in *Wacousta,* this aspect of Indian-white affairs catches our attention by its absence from his writings. The Pontiac era witnessed in Lancaster, Pennsylvania in December, 1763 a massacre of peaceful and sequestered Indians by a mob calling itself "the Paxton Boys." Who can blame Richardson for failing to include matter of little interest to his audience, material connected only peripherally to his focused narrative set also in the time of Pontiac? We can but notice a void, and speculate about its implications. Only one side in Richardson's fiction seems capable of atrocity. Nowhere does there surface even a hint of the possibility for humanity and reciprocality between the two races, except for (forbidden) erotic yearning or temporary sexual alliance. Not even evil is a matter for exchange between races. Rather, evil stays boundaried within one side. Yet evidence of fellow feeling and human kinship lay all around the author in the history of his region and in the life of his bountiful grandfather who acknowledged his mixed-blood offspring and befriended the dispersed.

The other incident outlining the nature of the new world that was coming to be seems, compared to the fact of massacre and dispersion, minor indeed. It was but one of those potholes on the path of progressive development. Sally Ainse (1728-1823?) had been the second wife of the trader Andrew Montour. Among the sons of this Indian woman was Nicolas Montour, who would play a prominent role in the western fur trade, end up in a Quebec seigneury, and serve as the basis for a character in a significant Quebec historical novel of 1938, *Les engagés du grand portage.* A colourful figure known under a number of names, eventually Sally

Ainse became an Upper Canadian trader. John Askin knew her as a friendly business associate, in one instance forbearing to charge her for a bottle of whisky she had ordered. She is probably the "Sally Hans" mentioned by the Moravian missionary David Zeisberger as a willing donor of land to his charitable enterprise. In 1789, however, she began a search for justice that she never found. A parable of Jesus presents the example of an importunate widow whose unending complaints finally secure a proper verdict from an unjust judge (Luke 18: 1-6). That story came only half true along the Detroit. In a land dispute involving so powerful a local figure as Matthew Elliott, Ainse had the support of such influential people as Joseph Brant. Elliott, however, had something even better: a position on the land-claims board that favoured his suit over hers. No less a figure than Governor John Graves Simcoe saw the justice of her case. He ordered the land restored to her. Nothing happened. Again he ordered it. And nothing happened. Nothing ever did. For years the claim simmered, but nothing ever came of it.

Nothing will come of nothing, cried another old person who was to find himself done in by those whom he knew, but not nearly well enough. Sally Ainse might have been a well-known trader and matriarch, but she was still an Indian, and a "squaw" at that. Governor Simcoe himself could not enforce the law in her favour. When we speak of the monstrous, surely here is an instance of it. But can we really expect a writer to create a character out of a system? Yet in *Wacousta,* Richardson can personify a repressive system in the person of Colonel de Haldimar. Through this, he convinces the reader that something beyond personal pique lies behind the trying behaviour of the Colonel's opponent. No need to seek out the inflated demonizing of Andrew Westbrook in order to find evidence of the monstrous. Richardson and his culture instead chose to seek their monsters amid the haunted fens rather than among the ironfaced potentates of the settlements. This tradition continues throughout the fantasy life we have erected of the early years of Upper Canada, the heritage theme park that gives us our imagery of pioneering. Even when the genius of James Reaney surrounds his Donnellys with the stuff of history—songs, agricultural instruments, judges, schoolhouses, sticks and stones—it cannot resist the flight into apotheosis. The Donnellys live because they come back to haunt a bunch of necking teenagers or furnish the material for a strolling medicine show. The culture will not leave them to history, the author implies, but metamorphoses them into the legendary. Some bit of their richly evoked humanity has been frittered away. This the dramatist seeks to restore, but he will not forgo in the process the spiciness that the legends provide.

Go to the bookshelf and take down the paperback of Alice Munro's *The Progress of Love* (1987). The collection has for its cover illustration a work of Souwesto's finest painter, the late Jack Chambers. *Diego Asleep #2* presents the transformation of the banal into the mysterious and the threatening. The overstuffed, overpriced, blue velvet couch in the centre bears its precious burden of the curled, sleeping child. The meticulously rendered folds of the covering blanket reveal that he has drawn up his legs in a protective, near-fetal position. An unplumped cushion rests at another end of the couch, and an ochre velour garment (a bathrobe?) is strewn carelessly along the top centre of the back of the couch. On the wall behind, centred again, is a print of a masculine version of Michael Snow's iconic *Woman Walking.* In the right foreground stands a dark gray King Kong whose fierceness is modelled in plastic. Slightly behind him rests an open Lego kit. At the opposite diagonal to the Lego, in the manner of Velasquez's *Las Meniñas,* appears the open door to another room. Its vertical off-setting of the couch's horizontality is caught in distant perspective, with a carpeted entrance hallway standing between the room where the boy is sleeping and the alcove where his mother stands, gazing deeply out a barely visible window at something beyond the painting's border.

In the manner of modern life, in the style of Alice Munro's "Fits" (a story that appears in this volume), the scene's banality is simultaneously reassuring and unsettling. The broadloom, the "solid" furniture, the tasteful, trendy painting, and the "educational" Lego kit all bespeak the House Beautiful of Enduring Family Values, of Quality Time redeemed. Yet we dream of monsters, figured forth in the same material in which the rectilinear uniformity of the Lego blocks is cast. Those monsters, as one of the greatest of Spanish painters reminds us, are produced by the "sleep of reason." The doorway to the room where the mother stands is a distance away. She does not look toward the child, but into some vast, unknowable distance, lost in her own dreams. What can she know of those nightmares that could be the psychic force causing the sleeping boy to curl up his legs? We may not have reached the legendary in this painting, but we see here how close to us is the world of terror. The slightest fissure in the surface we inhabit allows that terror to bubble over into our laps. This is not the world of Goya's *Caprichos* and their monstrous dreams. It seems too fragile for that.

In filling Souwesto with monsters and the larger-than-life, Richardson showed himself not only his world's reflector, but one of its shapers as well. His proved a leading role during a period that Reaney describes as "that strange moment when a civilization, having somehow survived its birth pangs and begun to have commercial and physical continuity, decides to put all this into words." Always John Richardson provided the imaginative figuration, deliberate or involuntary, of the world he both inherited and inscribed as his own. He

put it into his own words, and in his own write. Yet neither writer nor audience, as we have seen, always gets it quite right.

Manina Jones (essay date 1994)

SOURCE: "Beyond the Pale: Gender, 'Savagery,' and the Colonial Project in Richardson's *Wacousta,*" in *Essays on Canadian Writing,* No. 54, Winter, 1994, pp. 46-59.

[*In the essay below, Jones discusses themes of assimilation, imperialism, gender, and savagery in* Wacousta.]

> She has perchance wrestled with her engagement, as the aboriginals of a land newly discovered by a crew of adventurous colonists do battle with the garments imposed on them by our considerate civilization;—ultimately to rejoice with excessive dignity in the wearing of a battered cocked-hat and trowsers not extending to the shanks: but she did not break her engagement, sir; and we will anticipate that, moderating a young woman's native wildness, she may, after the manner of my comparison, take a similar pride in her fortune in good season.
>
> —George Meredith

In Reaches of Empire: The English Novel From Edgeworth to Dickens, Suvendrini Perera uses the passage that appears above, taken from a speech in George Meredith's *The Egoist,* to illustrate the displaced inscription of imperial relations in early- and mid-nineteenth-century fictional narratives that do not deal directly with the colonized territories. Perera argues that, as the extract illustrates, the figuring of cultural difference is deeply implicated in the representation of gender in such narratives:

> the culture's negotiations of gender difference supplied both a model and a vocabulary for progressively constituting empire.... Increasingly, the process of managing empire and gender developed as a complex system of exchange and overlap, their interlocking vocabularies and discursive strategies authorizing and reinforcing each other.

Major John Richardson's *Wacousta: Or, The Prophecy: A Tale of the Canadas* is a novel in which the managing of empire and the negotiation of cultural difference are much more obviously figured than in the works on which Perera focuses. Published in 1832, it is based on the events of the 1763 Native uprising against British fortifications at Detroit and Michilimackinac, and, as Michael Hurley implies, its transformation of that historical setting and conflict into the demonic world of Gothic romance has a great deal to tell us about the "identity of an emergent nineteenth-century colonial culture." It is of interest, then, not simply because it is about the struggles for possession of frontier forts but also because it is itself the product of the emergent colonial culture and as such both constructs and constitutes a colonial outpost. Indeed, it is the product of a writer who was, according to T. D. MacLulich, "above all a colonial," whose biography, some would say, is characterized by a series of attempts to mediate between the imperial centre and the colonial periphery. The degree to which *Wacousta*'s representation of gender is implicated in the colonial project is perhaps less obvious, though the quotation from *The Egoist* may help to foreground it. My reading of the novel focuses, in part, on the significance of the kind of cultural cross-dressing that Meredith uses to create an analogy between a woman's resignation to her wifely role and an indigenous culture's submission to colonial rule, though in *Wacousta* attire is almost promiscuously exchanged between Native and European cultures (and even between genders and classes within European culture) with varying degrees of dignity and pride. More specifically, though, I began my thinking about relations between gender and colonialism in the novel with the intriguing figure of Ellen Halloway, who is conspicuously *dis*engaged from her husband and who, because of the "native wildness" that she then manifests (symptomized in part by a change of costume), breaks her "engagement" with the centres of colonial "civilization" and, arguably, with the narrative of the novel itself. The representation of Ellen, whose name—*Ellen*—may be a subtle clue to the importance of the gender dynamic that I want to suggest, may be read as a textual locus where anxieties about the colonial project of administering both the frontiers of empire and the frontiers of gender reveal themselves.

Wacousta concludes with an apparent resolution of both the historical-cultural clash that it proposes between Natives and whites and the related plot of personal revenge that Reginald Morton, also known as Wacousta, takes against the commander of the garrison at Detroit. By the novel's end, the tragic impetus of its plot has ostensibly been reversed. Both the sworn enemies of the central conflict, Colonel De Haldimar, a figure of the perversity of the British empire's old order, and Reginald, a symbol of what Robin Mathews calls the "despotic anarchism" of the New World, have been despatched, and positive alternative alliances have been forged: the marriage of a new generation of colonists, Frederick and Madeline De Haldimar, provides a generically comic ending, and this marital affiliation establishes a new ideal colonial domestic order, incorporating the potential political and cultural reconciliation of British North Americans, *Canadiens,* and Natives, represented by the happy closing triad of the two surviving De Haldimars, François and Babette of the Fleur de lis, and the Ottawa Indians Oucanasta and her brother. The promise held by both the De Haldimar mar-

riage and the new peace with Native people that it seems to inaugurate is particularly stressed in the final paragraph of the novel:

> Time rolled on; and, in the course of years, Oucanasta might be seen associating with and bearing curious presents, the fruits of Indian ingenuity, to the daughters of De Haldimar, now become the colonel of the—regiment; while her brother, the chief, instructed his sons in the athletic and active exercises peculiar to his race.

However, the last line of the novel—"As for poor Ellen Halloway, search had been made for her, but she never was heard of afterwards"—interrupts and undermines the gratifying closing scene by reminding us of the strange disappearance of Ellen, who, even when she is presented in the text, represents, as Robert Lecker puts it, "the most concrete example of structural absence." Margaret E. Turner calls Ellen "the ghost in *Wacousta*" and maintains that she "figures much more largely in her absence than . . . Richardson realized or intended." I want to argue sympathetically that the final note of inconclusiveness, the loophole that Ellen presents to the tidy denouement of the narrative, is significant at several related levels. First, her ghostly persistence at the end of the novel constitutes a generic problem; it is a trace of the Gothic impulse that Richardson's realist formula for rationalizing mysteries seems incapable of eradicating. It also seems to me that Ellen haunts the narrative because she constitutes the site of ideological conflicts central to, and symptomatic of, Richardson's ambivalent colonial discourse, by which the sexual, political, and topographical geography of the New World is mapped either as a cultivated, asexual, feminine commodity or as a wilderness of excessive, sexualized, "savage" energy that remains unassimilated into the colonial economy either of the garrison or of the realist text.

In one sense, colonialism may be seen as an appropriation of foreign cultural/geographic territory that transforms it (in European terms) into a domestic site. White European women had a significant role to play in its processes, in part because they were seen as symbolic preservers of the domestic realm. As Vron Ware observes, they "symbolized the guardians of the race in their reproductive capacity . . . [and]—as long as they were of the right class and breeding—a guarantee that British morals and principles were adhered to in the settler community." They also symbolized the "most valuable property" of white men, property that reinforced the perceived necessity for the regulation of racial relations because it had to be protected from the threatening, indigenous, dark races of the colonies. In *Wacousta,* Ellen's transformation to otherness—her translation from the domestic realm to the wilderness, from European to "savage" husband, habits, and habiliments—is one in which, significantly, threats to racial and gender paradigms are conflated.

The transformation is instigated when Ellen's soldier husband, Frank Halloway, is unjustly convicted of treason and executed on the judgement of a military tribunal headed by Colonel De Haldimar. Ellen illicitly attends the execution by disguising herself as a drummerboy of the grenadiers, initiating a masquerade of gender that threatens the preserves of the male military. Finally revealing herself, she appears, in the throes of her grief, "rather [as] a spectre than a being of earth," and she utters the prophetic curse of the novel's subtitle, a curse that, significantly, contradicts the garrison's rigid system of justice. As Turner describes it, in doing so, Ellen

> steps into Wacousta's camp: like him, she has gone Indian, moving distinctly and dramatically out of the European context and the limits it understands and imposes on behaviour into something unknown and empty—of reason, intelligence, rules, morality. She has also moved out of the frame of discourse in which Richardson and his readers could understand her, and he has her go mad.

Once Ellen leaves the British fort, her Anglo-Saxon features are transfigured: she is described as having maniacal eyes that are still "large, [and] blue," but are now "wild and *unmeaning;* her countenance *vacant*" (emphasis added). Later, after Wacousta's capture, Sir Everard Valletort enquires about the fate of "that unfortunate creature": he asks, "was she brought in?" Captain Blessington replies, significantly, "I understand not. . . . In the confusion and hurry of securing our prisoner, and the apprehension of immediate attack from his warriors, Ellen was entirely overlooked." She has, in effect, sailed off the edge of the prescribed colonial world, becoming unreadable within the rationalist codes of its discourse.

Ellen, of course, does more than step into Wacousta's camp; she literally falls into his arms: "Overcome by the frantic energy with which she had uttered these appalling words [the curse], she sank backwards, and fell, uttering another shriek, into the arms of the warriors of the Fleur de lis." This fall is clearly sexual too. In fact, Ellen is sexualized from the moment of her husband's sentencing, when, in her struggle to detain the colonel physically, her "white and polished bosom . . . burst from its rude but modest confinement, and was now displayed in all the dazzling delicacy of youth and sex" to the mingled voyeuristic pleasure and guilt of the officers of the fort who, if they later overlook her, do not hesitate at this and other points to look her over. On her husband's death, her madness is figured both as a voyeuristic, erotic spectacle and in terms of vampirism or "subtextual necrophilia," other prohibited—and characteristically Gothic—forms of sexual expression:

> Her long fair hair was wild and streaming—her feet, and legs, and arms were naked—and one solitary and scanty garment displayed rather than concealed the symmetry of her delicate person. She flew to the fatal bridge, threw herself on the body of her bleeding husband, and imprinting her warm kisses on his bloody lips, for a moment or two presented the image of one whose reason has fled for ever.

After she takes on Indian dress and becomes Wacousta's "wife," she is seen in further postures of expressive sexuality, "lying prostrate on the form of the warrior; her arms thrown wildly around him, and her lips imprinting kisses on his cheek." With the death of her husband, Ellen becomes surplus in relation to the garrison economy in which women must function asexually within the bourgeois colonial family, an institutional locus of domesticity—like the colony—that is constructed from the energies of male desire and patriarchal power. It is, notably, the De Haldimar family against which the bereaved Ellen's prophecy is directed.

Ellen's madness, corporeality (her maiden name is *Clay*ton), and expressive sexuality—in short, what I want to argue in a moment amounts to her "savagery"—are most obviously opposed to the conventional proto-Victorian angel represented in **Wacousta** by Colonel De Haldimar's daughter Clara, whom her brother Charles describes as "all that is gentle and lovely in woman." The contrast between the two is particularly striking when they are juxtaposed around Wacousta's campfire. Ellen's "dress was entirely Indian, . . . consisting of a machecoti with leggings, mocassins, and a shirt of printed cotton studded with silver brooches,— all of which were of a quality and texture to mark the wearer as the wife of a chief," while Clara wears a blanket "drawn over the top of her head like a veil," yet revealing "an apparel which was strictly European." Later, their opposition in terms of sexual mores is further stressed in a titillating cat fight in which they wrestle for the "naked blade" of a knife and which the virginal Clara ultimately loses when she passes out at the sight of blood. While Ellen participates in the rhetoric of the Gothic novel, in which "hints of Otherness, the potential for disorder, the sexualisation of the world" are made possible, Clara seems "to have wandered into the North American forest directly out of a European novel of sensibility. . . . [She thus links] the sentimental literary tradition with [Richardson's] adaptation of European gothicism." Clara's delicate aristocratic sensibility cannot ultimately survive the colonial experience; she perishes before the conclusion of the novel. Clara's sacrifice might be seen in terms of the "circular route of reciprocal constitution" that Diedre David describes: "native disorder authorizes colonial discipline; colonialism requires [English] woman's sacrifice; and woman's sacrifice symbolically transforms a mythologized native disorder."

Ellen, on the other hand, is portrayed as one of the exotic, threatening figures of Gothic convention. Such figures were conventionally used to demarcate a generic, non-British sensibility. As I have indicated, Ellen's madness, and her violation of gender norms, may be read as analogous to her transgression of racial difference, her movement "beyond the pale" of the European fortress into the space of "savagery." This movement originates from within the literal and discursive construct of the garrison and puts into play its repressed otherness: the two characters who most prominently exhibit the threatening qualities of Indian "savagery" in *Wacousta* are, significantly, both European colonials, a fact that indicates, according to Gerson, how closely Richardson anticipates the critique of colonialism later developed in Joseph Conrad's *Heart of Darkness*. On the other hand, the figuring of racial difference through the transformation of white characters allows Richardson to present the spectacle of resistance to the colonial order and to resolve it in his narrative without coming to terms with the real players in the cultural conflict. Eric Cheyfitz sees such a pattern of transfiguring the domestic and the foreign in terms of one another as a signal gesture of imperialism: "the other is translated into the terms of the self in order to be alienated from those terms. We might say that at the heart of every imperial fiction (the heart of darkness) there is a fiction of translation." Thus, while "savagery" in *Wacousta* is associated with Indians to the point where they seem to be its paradigmatic example, it cannot be read finally as simply inherent to them, particularly because Oucanasta and her brother are, on the contrary, assimilated to the garrison world through the equally objectionable flip side of Indian "savagery," the "civilized" conventions of the noble savage, or even more fittingly, I would argue, simple class servitude along the lines of Robinson Crusoe's man Friday.

One place in the narrative where the doubling of racial and gender codes is conspicuous occurs as Frederick De Haldimar is being guided to the Indian encampment to spy on the chiefs' council by Oucanasta, the faithful Ottawa maiden whose love for Frederick is unrequited. When his military boots prove too noisy to avoid detection, she urges him to take them off, and she proceeds to put her own moccasin on his foot to protect him from the underbrush. However,

> This was too *un-European,*—too much reversing the established order of things, to be borne patiently. As if he had felt the *dignity of his manhood* offended by the proposal, the officer drew his foot hastily back, declaring, as he sprang from the log, he did not care for the thorns, and could not think of depriving a female, who must be much more sensible of pain than himself. (emphasis added)

The prospect of taking on Oucanasta's apparel is simultaneously an affront to Frederick's manhood, his

chivalrous relation to women and his position within European culture.

It is Wacousta who, in the course of his career, is progressively alienated from the European empire's centre, becoming increasingly un-English and un-European: after De Haldimar's betrayal, he is expelled from his English regiment and joins the Scottish forces in the rebellion of 1745, then gives his allegiance to France in the battle of the Plains of Abraham in 1759, where he fights alongside Indian allies, and finally forswears his race altogether to become "a savage both in garb and character" as part of the Pontiac uprisings in 1763. Frederick De Haldimar's reaction to the last transformation draws attention to Wacousta's violation of the European ethos of civility and his consonant resistance to the ideal of imperial domination: De Haldimar tells Wacousta that "There is no country in Europe that would willingly claim you for its subject."

Wacousta's racial conversion is, ironically, but again in keeping with the tradition of the Gothic novel, traceable to an ancient betrayal in the old country. As L. R. Early demonstrates, Richardson also draws on the related conventions of the Jacobean revenge tragedy to structure the narrative and enrich the imagery of *Wacousta.* These literary conventions—the persistence of an old grudge, the revenger whose retribution is more monstrous than the crime it avenges, the corrupt aristocratic milieu, the exotic locale, the sensationalized violence—all play neatly in *Wacousta* into what D. M. R. Bentley documents as a pronounced tendency in eighteenth-century and early nineteenth-century historical writings on the New World to identify a passion for revenge as the central motive for the violent actions of Natives. It is worth noting here that it is precisely the prophecy of revenge that constitutes Ellen's initiation into "savage" society. What happens when these two traditions are superimposed in *Wacousta,* however, is that the motive for Native violence is significantly displaced from the North American social sphere involving legitimate political, cultural, and historical conflicts into the Gothic dynamics of the irrational psyche and of the Old World literary tradition. As Carole Gerson puts it, "Richardson's plots of curses and revenge risk losing sight of the historical issues at hand. While historical events provide a factual anchor as well as local colour and sensational effects, the politically based moral claims of the conflicting parties soon evaporate." Although Richardson the historical novelist is at pains to give documentary background to the Pontiac rebellions early in the first descriptive chapter of the novel, the narrative itself tends to focus on the revenge plot, thereby contradicting Richardson's attempt to set the stage in a realist mode even to the point where the historical rebellions of 1763 are attributed to Wacousta's fictional vendetta:

This mysterious enemy evidently possessed great influence in the councils of the Indians; and while the hot breath of his hatred continued to fan the flame of fierce hostility that had been kindled in the bosom of Ponteac, whose particular friend he appeared to be, there would be no end to the atrocities that must follow.

While the narrator admits that the French may have had something to do with the conflict that the novel describes, he also consistently affirms "the alarming influence exercised" over Pontiac by Wacousta.

This last scenario might be seen as a reversal of a narrative strategy that many readers of Richardson's novel have commented on, a strategy that ties in with what I would call **Wacousta**'s failed aesthetics of rationalization: the narrative repeatedly introduces apparently supernatural or illogical elements and, after much suspenseful delay, reiterates the enigmatic incident but offers a reasonable explanation for it. The apparently motiveless malignity of "the warrior of the Fleur de lis" is, perhaps, the model of this approach: his hatred remains seemingly inexplicable—and even supernaturally evil—until the long, embedded story at the end of the novel provides at least a semirational explanation. Similarly, elements such as Frank Halloway's apparent recognition of Wacousta at the moment of the former's death, the spectral face that rises from the canoe, or (my favourite) the mysterious "killer beaver" that attacks the sailor at Michilimackinac are introduced gothically and recuperated realistically. At several points the language of the narrative even seems to anticipate a later author who was also caught between the rational and the supernatural, Sir Arthur Conan Doyle. When Charles tells Blessington about the secret letters to "Reginald" that he finds in his father's possession, Blessington observes that "there is a mystery in this that baffles all my powers of penetration. Were I in possession of the contents of the letters, I might find some clue to solve the enigma." Reading, or rereading, the signs in the rational manner of Sherlock Holmes is the narrator's key to finding such solutions: he comments, "we hope to bear out our story, by natural explanation and simple deduction." He hopes, in other words, to reconfigure the troubling, unstable world of the Gothic novel in the stable terms of realism, reproducing the empirical reality of colonial ideology. This gesture anticipates a generic variation that Patrick Brantlinger calls the "imperial Gothic," a late nineteenth-century and early twentieth-century combination of the scientific, progressive ideology of imperialism with a contradictory interest in the occult. This form of the Gothic, Brantlinger argues, "expresses a social version of the return of the repressed characteristic of late Victorian and Edwardian fiction" through the revenge of the exotic culture's "destructive magic."

Rational justification of the uncanny is necessary in order to reassert control over a resistant element; it is also necessary in order to establish formal, interpretive, and ideological closure in **Wacousta.** The Gothic element that the novel has invested the most in recuperating is the insubordinate subject of colonialism, the "savage" and/as the undomesticated woman. I indicated at the beginning of this [essay] that Ellen is a pivotal figure of "savagery" who, in effect, unravels the narrative's resolution. The savage figure's threat to the colonial landscape aesthetic—and economy—is indicated elsewhere when a long, picturesque description of the area surrounding the fort at Michilimackinac is visually disrupted. In the description, the narrator scans the landscape, looking favourably on the beauty of Lake Huron because it is the route by which tidings from the imperial centre arrive. However, the narrator's picturesque portrait of the scene is interrupted by the vocabulary of the Gothic:

> Moreover, the light swift bark canoes of the natives often danced joyously on [the lake's] surface; and while the sight was offended at the savage, skulking among the trees of the forest, like some dark spirit moving cautiously in its course of secret destruction, and watching the moment when he might pounce unnoticed on his unprepared victim, it followed, with momentary pleasure and excitement, the activity and skill displayed by the harmless paddler, in the swift and meteor-like race that set the troubled surface of the Huron in a sheet of hissing foam.

The "harmless" Native paddlers are evidently those who know their aesthetic and economic place in the picture; they are aligned with the central water route to Europe, whereas the lurking figures inhabit the narrator's peripheral vision of the wilderness, demonstrating the degree to which the sort of "savagery" that Wacousta embodies accrues to those who inhabit the threatening margins of the colonized historical-aesthetic terrain. That "the sight was offended" by these figures makes the narrator's response a little like Frederick De Haldimar's response to Oucanasta's offer of her moccasin, which upsets "the established order of things." The narrator's visual survey functions not simply as observation but also as a form of regulation of the landscape, one that is troubled by the intrusion of the "savage." The power dynamics of the gaze/narrative observation thus constitute a kind of aesthetic visual/textual attempt to settle the landscape that it oversees.

The disturbance to the narrator's worldview is also interestingly related to norms of feminine beauty during what amounts to an aesthetic debate between officers Baynton and Middleton over whether the latter's sketch of a "handsome squaw" is artistically appropriate. Baynton chides his friend for "his bad taste in devoting his pencil to anything that had a red skin, never combed its hair, and turned its toes in while walking"; using a phrase with Gothic overtones, he pronounces the sketch "an absolute fright." Middleton counters by maintaining that the Indian woman can be assimilated to classical European standards of feminine beauty: she is, he says, "a Venus, a Juno, a Minerva, a beauty of the first water in short." Or at least his aesthetic gaze can constitute her as such, just as the narrator constitutes the vista of Lake Huron and the Natives who paddle it as part of the empire's aesthetic real estate. Possibly, in such instances, the power dynamics of the voyeuristic gaze so obvious elsewhere in the novel are subtly transposed into the context of a colonial desire to dominate aesthetically.

The assimilation of Native features of the colonial terrain to European aesthetic and economic standards is accomplished most obviously by a character who figures prominently in the superficial resolution of the novel and who comes to represent the ideal of British North American womanhood: Madeline De Haldimar. Indeed, just before the conversation about the sketch of the "squaw," Baynton calls Madeline and Clara "Venus and Psyche in the land of the Pottowatamies by all that is magnificent!," and, while Clara's beauty proves too ethereal for the frontier, Madeline's earthier presence seems to suit her for it. In contrast to Clara's "elegant, slight, and somewhat petite form," Madeline is characterized as having a

> less girlish appearance—one that embraced all the full rich contour of the Medicean Venus, and a lazy languor in its movements that harmonised with the speaking outlines of the form, and without which the beauty of the whole would have been at variance and imperfect.

Madeline's standards of beauty, however, turn out to be linked to the material concerns of domestication and settlement. Unlike Ellen, Madeline does not adopt the dress or the habits of the Natives of the region; she does not "go savage." Instead, she displays Native costumes as works of art on the walls of her apartment at Michilimackinac along with other examples of "Indian ingenuity," including a miniature, carved-wood version of the paddlers of the narrator's description of Lake Huron:

> Head-dresses tastefully wrought in the shape of the crowning bays of the ancients, and composed of the gorgeous feathers of the most splendid of the forest birds—bows and quivers handsomely, and even elegantly ornamented with that most tasteful of Indian decorations, the stained quill of the porcupine; war clubs of massive iron wood, their handles covered with stained horsehair and feathers curiously mingled together—machecotis, hunting coats, mocassins, and leggings, all worked in porcupine quill, and fancifully arranged,—these, with many others, had been called into requisition to bedeck and relieve the otherwise rude and naked walls of the apartment.

In short, Madeline turns Native culture (and, notably, the instruments of Native defence and aggression) into an aesthetic commodity, calling them "into requisition" as if she were a military supply officer. Indeed, the interior of her lodgings at the fort is a model of that famous imperialist institution for rationalizing and commodifying the culture(s) of the colonies, the Victorian museum: the room is described as "this wild and museum-like apartment."

Interestingly Wacousta calls his treacherous, energetic escape from the hands of the soldiers "this sample of Indian ingenuity." By the last paragraph of the novel, however, the phrase "the fruits of Indian ingenuity" is innocuously applied to the objects that Oucanasta pays in tribute to Madeline's daughters. As Brantlinger points out, the civilization of "savages" whose claim to the land seemed doubtful because they did not develop it or its resources is often defined in literature from the 1830s onward "in terms of their conversion both to Christianity and to 'productive labor' or 'industry'." In the aesthetic and political economies of *Wacousta,* the account appears to have been settled.

Madeline's apartment also shows signs of the potential for assimilating romantic and realistic aesthetics: the mats that hang on her walls exhibit "both figures that were known to exist in the creation, and those which could have no being save in the imagination of their framers." I have been arguing that a similar impetus toward assimilation informs the narrative of *Wacousta* but that, in effect, the rug is ultimately pulled out from under the novel's realistic resolution because it does not incorporate the "savage" figure of Ellen. Her persistence may suggest a critique of, or a resistance to, both the colonial project and conventionally endorsed gender roles. However, to elaborate Mary Poovey's argument about the persistent appearance of the aggressive, carnal figure of the magdalene, the obverse of the sexless, moral, Victorian angel, I would argue that "savagery" might also be seen as grounding the principle of domestic and colonial government because it makes the enforcement of patriarchal order and rationality both necessary and justified. In *Wacousta,* the colonial garrison and the colonial text are haunted by a "savage" face that is not only the pallid, spectral face of the Gothic novel but also the distorted, troubling reflection of the pale Victorian lady and the pale face of racial cliche. However foreign it may appear, that which lies beyond the pale is the very ground on which the garrison is built.

FURTHER READING

Bibliography

Morley, William F. E. *A Bibliographical Study of Major John Richardson.* Toronto: Bibliographical Society of Canada, 1973, 144 p.

Bibliography of extant editions of Richardson's works, including physical descriptions and locations.

Biography

Beasley, David R. *The Canadian Don Quixote: The Life and Works of Major John Richardson, Canada's First Novelist.* Ontario: The Porcupine's Quill, 1977, 219 p.

  Considered the definitive biography of Richardson.

Darling, Michael. "Major John Richardson: Biographical Facts and Critical Problems." *Essays on Canadian Writing,* No. 9 (Winter 1977-78): 5-11.

  Reviews David R. Beasley's biography of Richardson, *The Canadian Don Quixote.* Darling notes that Beasley's work "confirms the extent to which Richardson drew on his own life and the lives of his relatives and friends for characters and incidents in his novels."

Pacey, Desmond. "A Colonial Romantic: Major John Richardson, Soldier and Novelist, Part I: The Early Years." *Canadian Literature,* No. 2 (Autumn 1959): 20-31.

  Biographical overview of Richardson's life through February 1838, when the novelist returned to Canada from Europe.

——. "A Colonial Romantic: Major John Richardson, Soldier and Novelist, Part II: Return to America." *Canadian Literature,* No. 3 (Winter 1960): 47-56.

  Covers Richardson's life from 1838 to his death in New York City in 1852. Pacey contends that the frustration of Richardson's dreams "was in large part brought about by his own tactless pugnacity."

Criticism

Bentley, D. M. R. Review of *The Borders of Nightmare: The Fiction of John Richardson,* by Michael Hurley, and *The Canadian Brothers; or, The Prophecy Fulfilled,* by John Richardson. *University of Toronto Quarterly* 63, No. 1 (Fall 1993): 211-14.

  Notes that Hurley's study is "concerned with 'images and archetypes' in Richardson's fiction that reflect the 'Canadian sensibility.'"

Carstairs, John Stewart. "Richardson's *War of 1812.*" *The Canadian Magazine* XIX (1902): 72-4.

  Remarks favorably on the 1902 edition of Richardson's history *War of 1812,* edited by Alexander Clark Casselman.

Duffy, Dennis. "Beyond the Last Mohican: John Richardson's Transformation of Cooper in *Wacousta.*" *American Review of Canadian Studies* 22, No. 3 (Autumn 1992): 363-85.

  Considers the similarities and differences between Richardson's novel and James Fenimore Cooper's *The Last of the Mohicans.*

——. *John Richardson and His Works.* Ontario: ECW Press, n. d.

  Brief overview of Richardson's life, works, and critical reception.

——. "John Richardson's Dream World." *Essays on Canadian Writing,* No. 47 (Fall 1992): 1-25.

  Discusses four dreams recounted by Richardson's contemporaries that, Duffy claims, illuminate the subconscious roots of Richardson's frontier fiction.

——. "Major John Richardson: The Loyalist in Disguise." In *Gardens, Covenants, Exiles: Loyalism in the Literature of Upper Canada/Ontario,* pp. 44-54. University of Toronto Press, 1982.

  Examines the dichotomy between liberty and order in Richardson's works.

——. *A Tale of Sad Reality: John Richardson's "Wacousta."* Ontario: ECW Press, 1993, 79 p.

  Detailed analysis of Richardson's novel, focusing on the author's sources and the historical context.

Early, L. R. "Myth and Prejudice in Kirby, Richardson, and Parker." *Canadian Literature,* No. 81 (Summer 1979): 24-36.

  Compares Richardson's *Wacousta* and William Kirby's *The Golden Dog* (1877), arguing that both works draw on Jacobean drama.

Hurley, Michael. *The Borders of Nightmare: The Fiction of John Richardson.* Toronto: University of Toronto Press, 1992, 236 p.

  Centers on psychological and topographical dichotomies in *Wacousta* and *The Canadian Brothers.* Hurley argues that the numerous "doubles, split selves, and love triangles" found in Richardson's works refute conventional concepts of identity and anticipate the fragmented selves found in the works of many postmodern writers. The chapter entitled "Border Doubles" from Hurley's study has been reprinted here in the criticism section of Richardson's entry.

——. "Wacousta as Trickster: 'The Enemy of Boundaries.'" *Journal of Canadian Studies* 26, No. 3 (Autumn 1991): 68-79.

  Compares Wacousta to the Trickster figure from Native North American mythology and argues that various trickster motifs appear in Richardson's novel.

Lecker, Robert A. "Patterns of Deception in *Wacousta.*" *Journal of Canadian Fiction,* No. 19 (1977): 77-85.

  Contends that Richardson's novel is "less concerned with maintaining the pre-established values" of the civilized and the savage than with "locating the qualities and values which define those groups."

MacDonald, Mary Lu. "Canadian Experience?" *Canadian Literature,* No. 141 (Summer 1994): 151-2.

Comments on the critical introduction to a 1994 edition of *The Canadian Brothers; or, The Prophecy Fulfilled, A Tale of the Late American War* and notes the general paucity of material on Richardson's life.

Maclulich, T. D. "The Colonial Major: Richardson and *Wacousta.*" *Essays on Canadian Writing,* No. 29 (Summer, 1984): 66-84.

Points out Richardson's use of the military garrison in *Wacousta* as a model for society and argues that Richardson's career and writings were heavily influenced by his ambivalence toward European society and his sense of inferiority as a colonial.

McGregor, Gaile. "A View from the Fort." In *The Wacousta Syndrome: Explorations in the Canadian Landscape,* pp. 3-25. Toronto: University of Toronto Press, 1985.

Argues that Richardson's *Wacousta,* unlike James Fenimore Cooper's Leatherstocking novels, evokes a "limited view of nature."

Riddell, William Renwick. *John Richardson.* Toronto: The Ryerson Press, 1930, 226 p.

Provides a brief biography of Richardson, plot summaries of his works, and a critical overview titled "An Appreciation," which has been reprinted here in the criticism section of Richardson's entry.

Ross, Catherine Sheldrick. "Lucy & John." *Canadian Literature,* Nos. 138 and 139 (Fall-Winter 1993): 153-5.

Favorably reviews Michael Hurley's *The Borders of Nightmare: The Fiction of John Richardson,* noting that Hurley focuses his analysis on *Wacousta* and *The Canadian Brothers.*

Turner, Margaret E. "Language and Silence in Richardson and Grove." In *Future Indicative: Literary Theory and Canadian Literature,* edited by John Moss, pp. 185-94. University of Ottawa Press, 1987.

Contends that in *Wacousta* Richardson is primarily concerned with "disorder, upheaval, trauma, and violence" and the failure of military structure to "make sense" of the European experience of the New World.

Additional coverage of Richardson's life and career is contained in the following sources published by Gale Research: *Dictionary of Literary Biography,* **Vol. 99:** *Canadian Writers before 1890,* **and** *DISCovering Authors: Canadian Edition.*

Nineteenth-Century Literature Criticism

Cumulative Indexes
Volumes 1-55

How to Use This Index

The main references

Calvino, Italo
1923-1985.....CLC 5, 8, 11, 22, 33, 39,
73; SSC 3

list all author entries in the following Gale Literary Criticism series:

BLC = *Black Literature Criticism*
CLC = *Contemporary Literary Criticism*
CLR = *Children's Literature Review*
CMLC = *Classical and Medieval Literature*
        Criticism
DA = *DISCovering Authors*
DAB = *DISCovering Authors: British*
DAC = *DISCovering Authors: Canadian*
DAM = *DISCovering Authors Modules*
    DRAM: Dramatists module
    MST: Most-studied authors module
    MULT: Multicultural authors module
    NOV: Novelists module
    POET: Poets module
    POP: Popular/genre writers module

DC = *Drama Criticism*
HLC = *Hispanic Literature Criticism*
LC = *Literature Criticism from 1400 to 1800*
NCLC = *Nineteenth-Century Literature Criticism*
PC = *Poetry Criticism*
SSC = *Short Story Criticism*
TCLC = *Twentieth-Century Literary Criticism*
WLC = *World Literature Criticism, 1500 to the*
        Present

The cross-references

See also CANR 23; CA 85-88;
obituary CA 116

list all author entries in the following Gale biographical and literary sources:

AAYA = *Authors & Artists for Young Adults*
AITN = *Authors in the News*
BEST = *Bestsellers*
BW = *Black Writers*
CA = *Contemporary Authors*
CAAS = *Contemporary Authors*
        Autobiography Series
CABS = *Contemporary Authors*
        Bibliographical Series
CANR = *Contemporary Authors New*
        Revision Series
CAP = *Contemporary Authors Permanent*
        Series
CDALB = *Concise Dictionary of American*
Literary Biography
CDBLB = *Concise Dictionary of British*
        Literary Biography

DLB = *Dictionary of Literary Biography*
DLBD = *Dictionary of Literary Biography*
        Documentary Series
DLBY = *Dictionary of Literary Biography Yearbook*
HW = *Hispanic Writers*
JRDA = *Junior DISCovering Authors*
MAICYA = *Major Authors and Illustrators for*
        Children and Young Adults
MTCW = *Major 20th-Century Writers*
NNAL = *Native North American Literature*
SAAS = *Something about the Author Autobiography*
        Series
SATA = *Something about the Author*
YABC = *Yesterday's Authors of Books for Children*

Literary Criticism Series
Cumulative Author Index

Andreae, Johann V(alentin)
1586-1654 .... **LC 32**
See also DLB 164

Andreas-Salome, Lou 1861-1937... **TCLC 56**
See also DLB 66

Andrewes, Lancelot 1555-1626 .... **LC 5**
See also DLB 151

Andrews, Cicily Fairfield
See West, Rebecca

Andrews, Elton V.
See Pohl, Frederik

Andreyev, Leonid (Nikolaevich)
1871-1919 .... **TCLC 3**
See also CA 104

Andric, Ivo 1892-1975 .... **CLC 8**
See also CA 81-84; 57-60; CANR 43;
DLB 147; MTCW

Angelique, Pierre
See Bataille, Georges

Angell, Roger 1920- .... **CLC 26**
See also CA 57-60; CANR 13, 44

Angelou, Maya
1928- .... **CLC 12, 35, 64, 77; BLC; DA;**
DAB; DAC
See also AAYA 7; BW 2; CA 65-68;
CANR 19, 42; DAM MST, MULT,
POET, POP; DLB 38; MTCW; SATA 49

Annensky, Innokenty Fyodorovich
1856-1909 .... **TCLC 14**
See also CA 110

Anon, Charles Robert
See Pessoa, Fernando (Antonio Nogueira)

Anouilh, Jean (Marie Lucien Pierre)
1910-1987 ...... **CLC 1, 3, 8, 13, 40, 50**
See also CA 17-20R; 123; CANR 32;
DAM DRAM; MTCW

Anthony, Florence
See Ai

Anthony, John
See Ciardi, John (Anthony)

Anthony, Peter
See Shaffer, Anthony (Joshua); Shaffer,
Peter (Levin)

Anthony, Piers 1934- .... **CLC 35**
See also AAYA 11; CA 21-24R; CANR 28;
DAM POP; DLB 8; MTCW; SAAS 22;
SATA 84

Antoine, Marc
See Proust, (Valentin-Louis-George-Eugene-)
Marcel

Antoninus, Brother
See Everson, William (Oliver)

Antonioni, Michelangelo 1912- ..... **CLC 20**
See also CA 73-76; CANR 45

Antschel, Paul 1920-1970
See Celan, Paul
See also CA 85-88; CANR 33; MTCW

Anwar, Chairil 1922-1949 .... **TCLC 22**
See also CA 121

Apollinaire, Guillaume .. **TCLC 3, 8, 51; PC 7**
See also Kostrowitzki, Wilhelm Apollinaris
de
See also DAM POET

Appelfeld, Aharon 1932- .... **CLC 23, 47**
See also CA 112; 133

Apple, Max (Isaac) 1941-........ **CLC 9, 33**
See also CA 81-84; CANR 19; DLB 130

Appleman, Philip (Dean) 1926- ..... **CLC 51**
See also CA 13-16R; CAAS 18; CANR 6,
29

Appleton, Lawrence
See Lovecraft, H(oward) P(hillips)

Apteryx
See Eliot, T(homas) S(tearns)

Apuleius, (Lucius Madaurensis)
125(?)-175(?) .... **CMLC 1**

Aquin, Hubert 1929-1977......... **CLC 15**
See also CA 105; DLB 53

Aragon, Louis 1897-1982........ **CLC 3, 22**
See also CA 69-72; 108; CANR 28;
DAM NOV, POET; DLB 72; MTCW

Arany, Janos 1817-1882........ **NCLC 34**

Arbuthnot, John 1667-1735......... **LC 1**
See also DLB 101

Archer, Herbert Winslow
See Mencken, H(enry) L(ouis)

Archer, Jeffrey (Howard) 1940- .... **CLC 28**
See also AAYA 16; BEST 89:3; CA 77-80;
CANR 22; DAM POP; INT CANR-22

Archer, Jules 1915- .... **CLC 12**
See also CA 9-12R; CANR 6; SAAS 5;
SATA 4, 85

Archer, Lee
See Ellison, Harlan (Jay)

Arden, John 1930- .... **CLC 6, 13, 15**
See also CA 13-16R; CAAS 4; CANR 31;
DAM DRAM; DLB 13; MTCW

Arenas, Reinaldo
1943-1990 .... **CLC 41; HLC**
See also CA 124; 128; 133; DAM MULT;
DLB 145; HW

Arendt, Hannah 1906-1975 .... **CLC 66**
See also CA 17-20R; 61-64; CANR 26;
MTCW

Aretino, Pietro 1492-1556 .... **LC 12**

Arghezi, Tudor.................... CLC 80
See also Theodorescu, Ion N.

Arguedas, Jose Maria
1911-1969 .... **CLC 10, 18**
See also CA 89-92; DLB 113; HW

Argueta, Manlio 1936-............ **CLC 31**
See also CA 131; DLB 145; HW

Ariosto, Ludovico 1474-1533........ **LC 6**

Aristides
See Epstein, Joseph

Aristophanes
450B.C.-385B.C........ **CMLC 4; DA;**
DAB; DAC; DC 2
See also DAM DRAM, MST

Arlt, Roberto (Godofredo Christophersen)
1900-1942 .... **TCLC 29; HLC**
See also CA 123; 131; DAM MULT; HW

Armah, Ayi Kwei 1939-.... **CLC 5, 33; BLC**
See also BW 1; CA 61-64; CANR 21;
DAM MULT, POET; DLB 117; MTCW

Armatrading, Joan 1950-......... **CLC 17**
See also CA 114

Arnette, Robert
See Silverberg, Robert

Arnim, Achim von (Ludwig Joachim von
Arnim) 1781-1831 .... **NCLC 5**
See also DLB 90

Arnim, Bettina von 1785-1859.... **NCLC 38**
See also DLB 90

Arnold, Matthew
1822-1888 ..... **NCLC 6, 29; DA; DAB;**
DAC; PC 5; WLC
See also CDBLB 1832-1890; DAM MST,
POET; DLB 32, 57

Arnold, Thomas 1795-1842 ...... **NCLC 18**
See also DLB 55

Arnow, Harriette (Louisa) Simpson
1908-1986 ....**CLC 2, 7, 18**
See also CA 9-12R; 118; CANR 14; DLB 6;
MTCW; SATA 42; SATA-Obit 47

Arp, Hans
See Arp, Jean

Arp, Jean 1887-1966.............. **CLC 5**
See also CA 81-84; 25-28R; CANR 42

Arrabal
See Arrabal, Fernando

Arrabal, Fernando 1932-... **CLC 2, 9, 18, 58**
See also CA 9-12R; CANR 15

Arrick, Fran..................... CLC 30
See also Gaberman, Judie Angell

Artaud, Antonin (Marie Joseph)
1896-1948 ....**TCLC 3, 36**
See also CA 104; 149; DAM DRAM

Arthur, Ruth M(abel) 1905-1979.... **CLC 12**
See also CA 9-12R; 85-88; CANR 4;
SATA 7, 26

Artsybashev, Mikhail (Petrovich)
1878-1927 .... **TCLC 31**

Arundel, Honor (Morfydd)
1919-1973 .... **CLC 17**
See also CA 21-22; 41-44R; CAP 2;
CLR 35; SATA 4; SATA-Obit 24

Asch, Sholem 1880-1957 .... **TCLC 3**
See also CA 105

Ash, Shalom
See Asch, Sholem

Ashbery, John (Lawrence)
1927-...... **CLC 2, 3, 4, 6, 9, 13, 15, 25,**
41, 77
See also CA 5-8R; CANR 9, 37;
DAM POET; DLB 5, 165; DLBY 81;
INT CANR-9; MTCW

Ashdown, Clifford
See Freeman, R(ichard) Austin

Ashe, Gordon
See Creasey, John

Ashton-Warner, Sylvia (Constance)
1908-1984 .... **CLC 19**
See also CA 69-72; 112; CANR 29; MTCW

Asimov, Isaac
1920-1992 ... **CLC 1, 3, 9, 19, 26, 76, 92**
See also AAYA 13; BEST 90:2; CA 1-4R;
137; CANR 2, 19, 36; CLR 12;
DAM POP; DLB 8; DLBY 92;
INT CANR-19; JRDA; MAICYA;
MTCW; SATA 1, 26, 74

Astley, Thea (Beatrice May)
1925-..................... **CLC 41**
See also CA 65-68; CANR 11, 43

Aston, James
See White, T(erence) H(anbury)

Asturias, Miguel Angel
1899-1974 . . . . **CLC 3, 8, 13; HLC**
See also CA 25-28; 49-52; CANR 32;
CAP 2; DAM MULT, NOV; DLB 113;
HW; MTCW

Atares, Carlos Saura
See Saura (Atares), Carlos

Atheling, William
See Pound, Ezra (Weston Loomis)

Atheling, William, Jr.
See Blish, James (Benjamin)

Atherton, Gertrude (Franklin Horn)
1857-1948 . . . . **TCLC 2**
See also CA 104; DLB 9, 78

Atherton, Lucius
See Masters, Edgar Lee

Atkins, Jack
See Harris, Mark

Attaway, William (Alexander)
1911-1986 . . . . **CLC 92; BLC**
See also BW 2; CA 143; DAM MULT;
DLB 76

Atticus
See Fleming, Ian (Lancaster)

Atwood, Margaret (Eleanor)
1939- . . . . . **CLC 2, 3, 4, 8, 13, 15, 25, 44,
84; DA; DAB; DAC; PC 8; SSC 2; WLC**
See also AAYA 12; BEST 89:2; CA 49-52;
CANR 3, 24, 33; DAM MST, NOV,
POET; DLB 53; INT CANR-24; MTCW;
SATA 50

Aubigny, Pierre d'
See Mencken, H(enry) L(ouis)

Aubin, Penelope 1685-1731(?) . . . . **LC 9**
See also DLB 39

Auchincloss, Louis (Stanton)
1917- . . . . . . **CLC 4, 6, 9, 18, 45; SSC 22**
See also CA 1-4R; CANR 6, 29;
DAM NOV; DLB 2; DLBY 80;
INT CANR-29; MTCW

Auden, W(ystan) H(ugh)
1907-1973 . . . . . . **CLC 1, 2, 3, 4, 6, 9, 11,
14, 43; DA; DAB; DAC; PC 1; WLC**
See also CA 9-12R; 45-48; CANR 5;
CDBLB 1914-1945; DAM DRAM, MST,
POET; DLB 10, 20; MTCW

Audiberti, Jacques 1900-1965 . . . . . . **CLC 38**
See also CA 25-28R; DAM DRAM

Audubon, John James
1785-1851 . . . . **NCLC 47**

Auel, Jean M(arie) 1936- . . . . **CLC 31**
See also AAYA 7; BEST 90:4; CA 103;
CANR 21; DAM POP; INT CANR-21

Auerbach, Erich 1892-1957 . . . . **TCLC 43**
See also CA 118

Augier, Emile 1820-1889 . . . . **NCLC 31**

August, John
See De Voto, Bernard (Augustine)

Augustine, St. 354-430 . . . . . . **CMLC 6; DAB**

Aurelius
See Bourne, Randolph S(illiman)

Aurobindo, Sri 1872-1950 . . . . **TCLC 63**

Austen, Jane
1775-1817 . . . . . **NCLC 1, 13, 19, 33, 51;
DA; DAB; DAC; WLC**
See also CDBLB 1789-1832; DAM MST,
NOV; DLB 116

Auster, Paul 1947- . . . . **CLC 47**
See also CA 69-72; CANR 23, 51

Austin, Frank
See Faust, Frederick (Schiller)

Austin, Mary (Hunter)
1868-1934 . . . . **TCLC 25**
See also CA 109; DLB 9, 78

Autran Dourado, Waldomiro
See Dourado, (Waldomiro Freitas) Autran

Averroes 1126-1198 . . . . **CMLC 7**
See also DLB 115

Avicenna 980-1037 . . . . **CMLC 16**
See also DLB 115

Avison, Margaret 1918- . . . . **CLC 2, 4; DAC**
See also CA 17-20R; DAM POET; DLB 53;
MTCW

Axton, David
See Koontz, Dean R(ay)

Ayckbourn, Alan
1939- . . . . **CLC 5, 8, 18, 33, 74; DAB**
See also CA 21-24R; CANR 31;
DAM DRAM; DLB 13; MTCW

Aydy, Catherine
See Tennant, Emma (Christina)

Ayme, Marcel (Andre) 1902-1967 . . . **CLC 11**
See also CA 89-92; CLR 25; DLB 72

Ayrton, Michael 1921-1975 . . . . **CLC 7**
See also CA 5-8R; 61-64; CANR 9, 21

Azorin . . . . **CLC 11**
See also Martinez Ruiz, Jose

Azuela, Mariano
1873-1952 . . . . **TCLC 3; HLC**
See also CA 104; 131; DAM MULT; HW;
MTCW

Baastad, Babbis Friis
See Friis-Baastad, Babbis Ellinor

Bab
See Gilbert, W(illiam) S(chwenck)

Babbis, Eleanor
See Friis-Baastad, Babbis Ellinor

Babel, Isaak (Emmanuilovich)
1894-1941(?) . . . . . . **TCLC 2, 13; SSC 16**
See also CA 104

Babits, Mihaly 1883-1941 . . . . **TCLC 14**
See also CA 114

Babur 1483-1530 . . . . **LC 18**

Bacchelli, Riccardo 1891-1985 . . . . . **CLC 19**
See also CA 29-32R; 117

Bach, Richard (David) 1936- . . . . **CLC 14**
See also AITN 1; BEST 89:2; CA 9-12R;
CANR 18; DAM NOV, POP; MTCW;
SATA 13

Bachman, Richard
See King, Stephen (Edwin)

Bachmann, Ingeborg 1926-1973 . . . . . **CLC 69**
See also CA 93-96; 45-48; DLB 85

Bacon, Francis 1561-1626 . . . . **LC 18, 32**
See also CDBLB Before 1660; DLB 151

Bacon, Roger 1214(?)-1292 . . . . . . **CMLC 14**
See also DLB 115

Bacovia, George . . . . **TCLC 24**
See also Vasiliu, Gheorghe

Badanes, Jerome 1937- . . . . **CLC 59**

Bagehot, Walter 1826-1877 . . . . . **NCLC 10**
See also DLB 55

Bagnold, Enid 1889-1981 . . . . **CLC 25**
See also CA 5-8R; 103; CANR 5, 40;
DAM DRAM; DLB 13, 160; MAICYA;
SATA 1, 25

Bagritsky, Eduard 1895-1934 . . . . . **TCLC 60**

Bagrjana, Elisaveta
See Belcheva, Elisaveta

Bagryana, Elisaveta . . . . **CLC 10**
See also Belcheva, Elisaveta
See also DLB 147

Bailey, Paul 1937- . . . . **CLC 45**
See also CA 21-24R; CANR 16; DLB 14

Baillie, Joanna 1762-1851 . . . . **NCLC 2**
See also DLB 93

Bainbridge, Beryl (Margaret)
1933- . . . . **CLC 4, 5, 8, 10, 14, 18, 22, 62**
See also CA 21-24R; CANR 24;
DAM NOV; DLB 14; MTCW

Baker, Elliott 1922- . . . . **CLC 8**
See also CA 45-48; CANR 2

Baker, Nicholson 1957- . . . . **CLC 61**
See also CA 135; DAM POP

Baker, Ray Stannard 1870-1946 . . . **TCLC 47**
See also CA 118

Baker, Russell (Wayne) 1925- . . . . . . **CLC 31**
See also BEST 89:4; CA 57-60; CANR 11,
41; MTCW

Bakhtin, M.
See Bakhtin, Mikhail Mikhailovich

Bakhtin, M. M.
See Bakhtin, Mikhail Mikhailovich

Bakhtin, Mikhail
See Bakhtin, Mikhail Mikhailovich

Bakhtin, Mikhail Mikhailovich
1895-1975 . . . . **CLC 83**
See also CA 128; 113

Bakshi, Ralph 1938(?)- . . . . **CLC 26**
See also CA 112; 138

Bakunin, Mikhail (Alexandrovich)
1814-1876 . . . . **NCLC 25**

Baldwin, James (Arthur)
1924-1987 . . . . . . **CLC 1, 2, 3, 4, 5, 8, 13,
15, 17, 42, 50, 67, 90; BLC; DA; DAB;
DAC; DC 1; SSC 10; WLC**
See also AAYA 4; BW 1; CA 1-4R; 124;
CABS 1; CANR 3, 24;
CDALB 1941-1968; DAM MST, MULT,
NOV, POP; DLB 2, 7, 33; DLBY 87;
MTCW; SATA 9; SATA-Obit 54

Ballard, J(ames) G(raham)
1930- . . . . **CLC 3, 6, 14, 36; SSC 1**
See also AAYA 3; CA 5-8R; CANR 15, 39;
DAM NOV, POP; DLB 14; MTCW

Balmont, Konstantin (Dmitriyevich)
1867-1943 . . . . **TCLC 11**
See also CA 109

Balzac, Honore de
1799-1850 . . . . **NCLC 5, 35, 53; DA;
DAB; DAC; SSC 5; WLC**
See also DAM MST, NOV; DLB 119

Bambara, Toni Cade
1939-1995 . . . . . . **CLC 19, 88; BLC; DA;
DAC**
See also AAYA 5; BW 2; CA 29-32R; 150;
CANR 24, 49; DAM MST, MULT;
DLB 38; MTCW

Bamdad, A.
See Shamlu, Ahmad

Banat, D. R.
See Bradbury, Ray (Douglas)

Bancroft, Laura
See Baum, L(yman) Frank

Banim, John 1798-1842 . . . . **NCLC 13**
See also DLB 116, 158, 159

Banim, Michael 1796-1874 . . . . . . **NCLC 13**
See also DLB 158, 159

Banks, Iain
See Banks, Iain M(enzies)

Banks, Iain M(enzies) 1954- . . . . **CLC 34**
See also CA 123; 128; INT 128

Banks, Lynne Reid . . . . **CLC 23**
See also Reid Banks, Lynne
See also AAYA 6

Banks, Russell 1940- . . . . **CLC 37, 72**
See also CA 65-68; CAAS 15; CANR 19;
DLB 130

Banville, John 1945- . . . . **CLC 46**
See also CA 117; 128; DLB 14; INT 128

Banville, Theodore (Faullain) de
1832-1891 . . . . **NCLC 9**

Baraka, Amiri
1934- . . . . **CLC 1, 2, 3, 5, 10, 14, 33;
BLC; DA; DAC; DC 6; PC 4**
See also Jones, LeRoi
See also BW 2; CA 21-24R; CABS 3;
CANR 27, 38; CDALB 1941-1968;
DAM MST, MULT, POET, POP;
DLB 5, 7, 16, 38; DLBD 8; MTCW

Barbauld, Anna Laetitia
1743-1825 . . . . **NCLC 50**
See also DLB 107, 109, 142, 158

Barbellion, W. N. P. . . . . **TCLC 24**
See also Cummings, Bruce F(rederick)

Barbera, Jack (Vincent) 1945- . . . . . . **CLC 44**
See also CA 110; CANR 45

Barbey d'Aurevilly, Jules Amedee
1808-1889 . . . . **NCLC 1; SSC 17**
See also DLB 119

Barbusse, Henri 1873-1935 . . . . **TCLC 5**
See also CA 105; DLB 65

Barclay, Bill
See Moorcock, Michael (John)

Barclay, William Ewert
See Moorcock, Michael (John)

Barea, Arturo 1897-1957 . . . . **TCLC 14**
See also CA 111

Barfoot, Joan 1946- . . . . **CLC 18**
See also CA 105

Baring, Maurice 1874-1945 . . . . **TCLC 8**
See also CA 105; DLB 34

Barker, Clive 1952- . . . . **CLC 52**
See also AAYA 10; BEST 90:3; CA 121;
129; DAM POP; INT 129; MTCW

Barker, George Granville
1913-1991 . . . . **CLC 8, 48**
See also CA 9-12R; 135; CANR 7, 38;
DAM POET; DLB 20; MTCW

Barker, Harley Granville
See Granville-Barker, Harley
See also DLB 10

Barker, Howard 1946- . . . . **CLC 37**
See also CA 102; DLB 13

Barker, Pat(ricia) 1943- . . . . **CLC 32, 94**
See also CA 117; 122; CANR 50; INT 122

Barlow, Joel 1754-1812 . . . . **NCLC 23**
See also DLB 37

Barnard, Mary (Ethel) 1909- . . . . . . **CLC 48**
See also CA 21-22; CAP 2

Barnes, Djuna
1892-1982 . . . **CLC 3, 4, 8, 11, 29; SSC 3**
See also CA 9-12R; 107; CANR 16; DLB 4,
9, 45; MTCW

Barnes, Julian 1946- . . . . **CLC 42; DAB**
See also CA 102; CANR 19; DLBY 93

Barnes, Peter 1931- . . . . **CLC 5, 56**
See also CA 65-68; CAAS 12; CANR 33,
34; DLB 13; MTCW

Baroja (y Nessi), Pio
1872-1956 . . . . **TCLC 8; HLC**
See also CA 104

Baron, David
See Pinter, Harold

Baron Corvo
See Rolfe, Frederick (William Serafino
Austin Lewis Mary)

Barondess, Sue K(aufman)
1926-1977 . . . . **CLC 8**
See also Kaufman, Sue
See also CA 1-4R; 69-72; CANR 1

Baron de Teive
See Pessoa, Fernando (Antonio Nogueira)

Barres, Maurice 1862-1923 . . . . **TCLC 47**
See also DLB 123

Barreto, Afonso Henrique de Lima
See Lima Barreto, Afonso Henrique de

Barrett, (Roger) Syd 1946- . . . . **CLC 35**

Barrett, William (Christopher)
1913-1992 . . . . **CLC 27**
See also CA 13-16R; 139; CANR 11;
INT CANR-11

Barrie, J(ames) M(atthew)
1860-1937 . . . . **TCLC 2; DAB**
See also CA 104; 136; CDBLB 1890-1914;
CLR 16; DAM DRAM; DLB 10, 141,
156; MAICYA; YABC 1

Barrington, Michael
See Moorcock, Michael (John)

Barrol, Grady
See Bograd, Larry

Barry, Mike
See Malzberg, Barry N(athaniel)

Barry, Philip 1896-1949 . . . . **TCLC 11**
See also CA 109; DLB 7

Bart, Andre Schwarz
See Schwarz-Bart, Andre

Barth, John (Simmons)
1930- . . . . . . **CLC 1, 2, 3, 5, 7, 9, 10, 14,
27, 51, 89; SSC 10**
See also AITN 1, 2; CA 1-4R; CABS 1;
CANR 5, 23, 49; DAM NOV; DLB 2;
MTCW

Barthelme, Donald
1931-1989 . . . . . . **CLC 1, 2, 3, 5, 6, 8, 13,
23, 46, 59; SSC 2**
See also CA 21-24R; 129; CANR 20;
DAM NOV; DLB 2; DLBY 80, 89;
MTCW; SATA 7; SATA-Obit 62

Barthelme, Frederick 1943- . . . . **CLC 36**
See also CA 114; 122; DLBY 85; INT 122

Barthes, Roland (Gerard)
1915-1980 . . . . **CLC 24, 83**
See also CA 130; 97-100; MTCW

Barzun, Jacques (Martin) 1907- . . . . **CLC 51**
See also CA 61-64; CANR 22

Bashevis, Isaac
See Singer, Isaac Bashevis

Bashkirtseff, Marie 1859-1884 . . . **NCLC 27**

Basho
See Matsuo Basho

Bass, Kingsley B., Jr.
See Bullins, Ed

Bass, Rick 1958- . . . . **CLC 79**
See also CA 126

Bassani, Giorgio 1916- . . . . **CLC 9**
See also CA 65-68; CANR 33; DLB 128;
MTCW

Bastos, Augusto (Antonio) Roa
See Roa Bastos, Augusto (Antonio)

Bataille, Georges 1897-1962 . . . . **CLC 29**
See also CA 101; 89-92

Bates, H(erbert) E(rnest)
1905-1974 . . . . . . **CLC 46; DAB; SSC 10**
See also CA 93-96; 45-48; CANR 34;
DAM POP; DLB 162; MTCW

Bauchart
See Camus, Albert

Baudelaire, Charles
1821-1867 . . . . **NCLC 6, 29, 55; DA;
DAB; DAC; PC 1; SSC 18; WLC**
See also DAM MST, POET

Baudrillard, Jean 1929- . . . . **CLC 60**

Baum, L(yman) Frank 1856-1919 . . . **TCLC 7**
See also CA 108; 133; CLR 15; DLB 22;
JRDA; MAICYA; MTCW; SATA 18

Baum, Louis F.
See Baum, L(yman) Frank

Baumbach, Jonathan 1933- . . . . . . **CLC 6, 23**
See also CA 13-16R; CAAS 5; CANR 12;
DLBY 80; INT CANR-12; MTCW

Bausch, Richard (Carl) 1945- . . . . . . **CLC 51**
See also CA 101; CAAS 14; CANR 43;
DLB 130

Baxter, Charles 1947- . . . . **CLC 45, 78**
See also CA 57-60; CANR 40; DAM POP;
DLB 130

Baxter, George Owen
See Faust, Frederick (Schiller)

Baxter, James K(eir) 1926-1972 .... **CLC 14**
See also CA 77-80

Baxter, John
See Hunt, E(verette) Howard, (Jr.)

Bayer, Sylvia
See Glassco, John

Baynton, Barbara 1857-1929 ..... **TCLC 57**

Beagle, Peter S(oyer) 1939- .... **CLC 7**
See also CA 9-12R; CANR 4, 51;
DLBY 80; INT CANR-4; SATA 60

Bean, Normal
See Burroughs, Edgar Rice

Beard, Charles A(ustin)
1874-1948 .... **TCLC 15**
See also CA 115; DLB 17; SATA 18

Beardsley, Aubrey 1872-1898 ..... **NCLC 6**

Beattie, Ann
1947- .... **CLC 8, 13, 18, 40, 63; SSC 11**
See also BEST 90:2; CA 81-84; DAM NOV,
POP; DLBY 82; MTCW

Beattie, James 1735-1803 .... **NCLC 25**
See also DLB 109

Beauchamp, Kathleen Mansfield 1888-1923
See Mansfield, Katherine
See also CA 104; 134; DA; DAC;
DAM MST

Beaumarchais, Pierre-Augustin Caron de
1732-1799 .... **DC 4**
See also DAM DRAM

Beaumont, Francis
1584(?)-1616 .... **LC 33; DC 6**
See also CDBLB Before 1660; DLB 58, 121

Beauvoir, Simone (Lucie Ernestine Marie
Bertrand) de
1908-1986 .... **CLC 1, 2, 4, 8, 14, 31, 44,**
50, 71; DA; DAB; DAC; WLC
See also CA 9-12R; 118; CANR 28;
DAM MST, NOV; DLB 72; DLBY 86;
MTCW

Becker, Carl 1873-1945 .... **TCLC 63:**
See also DLB 17

Becker, Jurek 1937- .... **CLC 7, 19**
See also CA 85-88; DLB 75

Becker, Walter 1950- .... **CLC 26**

Beckett, Samuel (Barclay)
1906-1989 ...... **CLC 1, 2, 3, 4, 6, 9, 10,**
11, 14, 18, 29, 57, 59, 83; DA; DAB;
DAC; SSC 16; WLC
See also CA 5-8R; 130; CANR 33;
CDBLB 1945-1960; DAM DRAM, MST,
NOV; DLB 13, 15; DLBY 90; MTCW

Beckford, William 1760-1844 .... **NCLC 16**
See also DLB 39

Beckman, Gunnel 1910- .... **CLC 26**
See also CA 33-36R; CANR 15; CLR 25;
MAICYA; SAAS 9; SATA 6

Becque, Henri 1837-1899 .... **NCLC 3**

Beddoes, Thomas Lovell
1803-1849 .... **NCLC 3**
See also DLB 96

Bedford, Donald F.
See Fearing, Kenneth (Flexner)

Beecher, Catharine Esther
1800-1878 .... **NCLC 30**
See also DLB 1

Beecher, John 1904-1980 .... **CLC 6**
See also AITN 1; CA 5-8R; 105; CANR 8

Beer, Johann 1655-1700 .... **LC 5**

Beer, Patricia 1924- .... **CLC 58**
See also CA 61-64; CANR 13, 46; DLB 40

Beerbohm, Henry Maximilian
1872-1956 .... **TCLC 1, 24**
See also CA 104; DLB 34, 100

Beerbohm, Max
See Beerbohm, Henry Maximilian

Beer-Hofmann, Richard
1866-1945 .... **TCLC 60**
See also DLB 81

Begiebing, Robert J(ohn) 1946- .... **CLC 70**
See also CA 122; CANR 40

Behan, Brendan
1923-1964 .... **CLC 1, 8, 11, 15, 79**
See also CA 73-76; CANR 33;
CDBLB 1945-1960; DAM DRAM;
DLB 13; MTCW

Behn, Aphra
1640(?)-1689 ...... **LC 1, 30; DA; DAB;**
DAC; DC 4; PC 13; WLC
See also DAM DRAM, MST, NOV, POET;
DLB 39, 80, 131

Behrman, S(amuel) N(athaniel)
1893-1973 .... **CLC 40**
See also CA 13-16; 45-48; CAP 1; DLB 7,
44

Belasco, David 1853-1931 .... **TCLC 3**
See also CA 104; DLB 7

Belcheva, Elisaveta 1893- .... **CLC 10**
See also Bagryana, Elisaveta

Beldone, Phil "Cheech"
See Ellison, Harlan (Jay)

Beleno
See Azuela, Mariano

Belinski, Vissarion Grigoryevich
1811-1848 .... **NCLC 5**

Belitt, Ben 1911- .... **CLC 22**
See also CA 13-16R; CAAS 4; CANR 7;
DLB 5

Bell, James Madison
1826-1902 .... **TCLC 43; BLC**
See also BW 1; CA 122; 124; DAM MULT;
DLB 50

Bell, Madison (Smartt) 1957- ...... **CLC 41**
See also CA 111; CANR 28

Bell, Marvin (Hartley) 1937- ..... **CLC 8, 31**
See also CA 21-24R; CAAS 14;
DAM POET; DLB 5; MTCW

Bell, W. L. D.
See Mencken, H(enry) L(ouis)

Bellamy, Atwood C.
See Mencken, H(enry) L(ouis)

Bellamy, Edward 1850-1898 ...... **NCLC 4**
See also DLB 12

Bellin, Edward J.
See Kuttner, Henry

Belloc, (Joseph) Hilaire (Pierre)
1870-1953 .... **TCLC 7, 18**
See also CA 106; DAM POET; DLB 19,
100, 141; YABC 1

Belloc, Joseph Peter Rene Hilaire
See Belloc, (Joseph) Hilaire (Pierre)

Belloc, Joseph Pierre Hilaire
See Belloc, (Joseph) Hilaire (Pierre)

Belloc, M. A.
See Lowndes, Marie Adelaide (Belloc)

Bellow, Saul
1915- ...... **CLC 1, 2, 3, 6, 8, 10, 13, 15,**
25, 33, 34, 63, 79; DA; DAB; DAC;
SSC 14; WLC
See also AITN 2; BEST 89:3; CA 5-8R;
CABS 1; CANR 29; CDALB 1941-1968;
DAM MST, NOV, POP; DLB 2, 28;
DLBD 3; DLBY 82; MTCW

Belser, Reimond Karel Maria de
See Ruyslinck, Ward

Bely, Andrey .... **TCLC 7; PC 11**
See also Bugayev, Boris Nikolayevich

Benary, Margot
See Benary-Isbert, Margot

Benary-Isbert, Margot 1889-1979 ... **CLC 12**
See also CA 5-8R; 89-92; CANR 4;
CLR 12; MAICYA; SATA 2;
SATA-Obit 21

Benavente (y Martinez), Jacinto
1866-1954 .... **TCLC 3**
See also CA 106; 131; DAM DRAM,
MULT; HW; MTCW

Benchley, Peter (Bradford)
1940- .... **CLC 4, 8**
See also AAYA 14; AITN 2; CA 17-20R;
CANR 12, 35; DAM NOV, POP;
MTCW; SATA 3

Benchley, Robert (Charles)
1889-1945 .... **TCLC 1, 55**
See also CA 105; DLB 11

Benda, Julien 1867-1956 .... **TCLC 60**
See also CA 120

Benedict, Ruth 1887-1948 .... **TCLC 60**

Benedikt, Michael 1935- .... **CLC 4, 14**
See also CA 13-16R; CANR 7; DLB 5

Benet, Juan 1927- .... **CLC 28**
See also CA 143

Benet, Stephen Vincent
1898-1943 .... **TCLC 7; SSC 10**
See also CA 104; DAM POET; DLB 4, 48,
102; YABC 1

Benet, William Rose 1886-1950 ... **TCLC 28**
See also CA 118; DAM POET; DLB 45

Benford, Gregory (Albert) 1941- .... **CLC 52**
See also CA 69-72; CANR 12, 24, 49;
DLBY 82

Bengtsson, Frans (Gunnar)
1894-1954 .... **TCLC 48**

Benjamin, David
See Slavitt, David R(ytman)

Benjamin, Lois
See Gould, Lois

Benjamin, Walter 1892-1940 ..... **TCLC 39**

Benn, Gottfried 1886-1956 .... **TCLC 3**
See also CA 106; DLB 56

Bennett, Alan 1934- ..... **CLC 45, 77; DAB**
See also CA 103; CANR 35; DAM MST;
MTCW

Bennett, (Enoch) Arnold
1867-1931 . . . . **TCLC 5, 20**
See also CA 106; CDBLB 1890-1914;
DLB 10, 34, 98, 135

Bennett, Elizabeth
See Mitchell, Margaret (Munnerlyn)

Bennett, George Harold 1930-
See Bennett, Hal
See also BW 1; CA 97-100

Bennett, Hal . . . . **CLC 5**
See also Bennett, George Harold
See also DLB 33

Bennett, Jay 1912- . . . . **CLC 35**
See also AAYA 10; CA 69-72; CANR 11,
42; JRDA; SAAS 4; SATA 41, 87;
SATA-Brief 27

Bennett, Louise (Simone)
1919- . . . . **CLC 28; BLC**
See also BW 2; DAM MULT; DLB 117

Benson, E(dward) F(rederic)
1867-1940 . . . . **TCLC 27**
See also CA 114; DLB 135, 153

Benson, Jackson J. 1930- . . . . **CLC 34**
See also CA 25-28R; DLB 111

Benson, Sally 1900-1972 . . . . **CLC 17**
See also CA 19-20; 37-40R; CAP 1;
SATA 1, 35; SATA-Obit 27

Benson, Stella 1892-1933 . . . . **TCLC 17**
See also CA 117; DLB 36, 162

Bentham, Jeremy 1748-1832 . . . . . **NCLC 38**
See also DLB 107, 158

Bentley, E(dmund) C(lerihew)
1875-1956 . . . . **TCLC 12**
See also CA 108; DLB 70

Bentley, Eric (Russell) 1916- . . . . **CLC 24**
See also CA 5-8R; CANR 6; INT CANR-6

Beranger, Pierre Jean de
1780-1857 . . . . **NCLC 34**

Berendt, John (Lawrence) 1939- . . . . **CLC 86**
See also CA 146

Berger, Colonel
See Malraux, (Georges-)Andre

Berger, John (Peter) 1926- . . . . . . **CLC 2, 19**
See also CA 81-84; CANR 51; DLB 14

Berger, Melvin H. 1927- . . . . **CLC 12**
See also CA 5-8R; CANR 4; CLR 32;
SAAS 2; SATA 5

Berger, Thomas (Louis)
1924- . . . . **CLC 3, 5, 8, 11, 18, 38**
See also CA 1-4R; CANR 5, 28, 51;
DAM NOV; DLB 2; DLBY 80;
INT CANR-28; MTCW

Bergman, (Ernst) Ingmar
1918- . . . . **CLC 16, 72**
See also CA 81-84; CANR 33

Bergson, Henri 1859-1941 . . . . **TCLC 32**

Bergstein, Eleanor 1938- . . . . **CLC 4**
See also CA 53-56; CANR 5

Berkoff, Steven 1937- . . . . **CLC 56**
See also CA 104

Bermant, Chaim (Icyk) 1929- . . . . . . **CLC 40**
See also CA 57-60; CANR 6, 31

Bern, Victoria
See Fisher, M(ary) F(rances) K(ennedy)

Bernanos, (Paul Louis) Georges
1888-1948 . . . . **TCLC 3**
See also CA 104; 130; DLB 72

Bernard, April 1956- . . . . **CLC 59**
See also CA 131

Berne, Victoria
See Fisher, M(ary) F(rances) K(ennedy)

Bernhard, Thomas
1931-1989 . . . . **CLC 3, 32, 61**
See also CA 85-88; 127; CANR 32;
DLB 85, 124; MTCW

Berriault, Gina 1926- . . . . **CLC 54**
See also CA 116; 129; DLB 130

Berrigan, Daniel 1921- . . . . **CLC 4**
See also CA 33-36R; CAAS 1; CANR 11,
43; DLB 5

Berrigan, Edmund Joseph Michael, Jr.
1934-1983
See Berrigan, Ted
See also CA 61-64; 110; CANR 14

Berrigan, Ted . . . . **CLC 37**
See also Berrigan, Edmund Joseph Michael,
Jr.
See also DLB 5

Berry, Charles Edward Anderson 1931-
See Berry, Chuck
See also CA 115

Berry, Chuck . . . . **CLC 17**
See also Berry, Charles Edward Anderson

Berry, Jonas
See Ashbery, John (Lawrence)

Berry, Wendell (Erdman)
1934- . . . . **CLC 4, 6, 8, 27, 46**
See also AITN 1; CA 73-76; CANR 50;
DAM POET; DLB 5, 6

Berryman, John
1914-1972 . . . . . . **CLC 1, 2, 3, 4, 6, 8, 10,
13, 25, 62**
See also CA 13-16; 33-36R; CABS 2;
CANR 35; CAP 1; CDALB 1941-1968;
DAM POET; DLB 48; MTCW

Bertolucci, Bernardo 1940- . . . . **CLC 16**
See also CA 106

Bertrand, Aloysius 1807-1841 . . . . **NCLC 31**

Bertran de Born c. 1140-1215 . . . . . **CMLC 5**

Besant, Annie (Wood) 1847-1933 . . . **TCLC 9**
See also CA 105

Bessie, Alvah 1904-1985 . . . . **CLC 23**
See also CA 5-8R; 116; CANR 2; DLB 26

Bethlen, T. D.
See Silverberg, Robert

Beti, Mongo . . . . **CLC 27; BLC**
See also Biyidi, Alexandre
See also DAM MULT

Betjeman, John
1906-1984 . . . **CLC 2, 6, 10, 34, 43; DAB**
See also CA 9-12R; 112; CANR 33;
CDBLB 1945-1960; DAM MST, POET;
DLB 20; DLBY 84; MTCW

Bettelheim, Bruno 1903-1990 . . . . . . **CLC 79**
See also CA 81-84; 131; CANR 23; MTCW

Betti, Ugo 1892-1953 . . . . **TCLC 5**
See also CA 104

Betts, Doris (Waugh) 1932- . . . . **CLC 3, 6, 28**
See also CA 13-16R; CANR 9; DLBY 82;
INT CANR-9

Bevan, Alistair
See Roberts, Keith (John Kingston)

Bialik, Chaim Nachman
1873-1934 . . . . **TCLC 25**

Bickerstaff, Isaac
See Swift, Jonathan

Bidart, Frank 1939- . . . . **CLC 33**
See also CA 140

Bienek, Horst 1930- . . . . **CLC 7, 11**
See also CA 73-76; DLB 75

Bierce, Ambrose (Gwinett)
1842-1914(?) . . . . **TCLC 1, 7, 44; DA;
DAC; SSC 9; WLC**
See also CA 104; 139; CDALB 1865-1917;
DAM MST; DLB 11, 12, 23, 71, 74

Billings, Josh
See Shaw, Henry Wheeler

Billington, (Lady) Rachel (Mary)
1942- . . . . **CLC 43**
See also AITN 2; CA 33-36R; CANR 44

Binyon, T(imothy) J(ohn) 1936- . . . . **CLC 34**
See also CA 111; CANR 28

Bioy Casares, Adolfo
1914- . . . **CLC 4, 8, 13, 88; HLC; SSC 17**
See also CA 29-32R; CANR 19, 43;
DAM MULT; DLB 113; HW; MTCW

Bird, Cordwainer
See Ellison, Harlan (Jay)

Bird, Robert Montgomery
1806-1854 . . . . **NCLC 1**

Birney, (Alfred) Earle
1904- . . . . **CLC 1, 4, 6, 11; DAC**
See also CA 1-4R; CANR 5, 20;
DAM MST, POET; DLB 88; MTCW

Bishop, Elizabeth
1911-1979 . . . . . . **CLC 1, 4, 9, 13, 15, 32;
DA; DAC; PC 3**
See also CA 5-8R; 89-92; CABS 2;
CANR 26; CDALB 1968-1988;
DAM MST, POET; DLB 5; MTCW;
SATA-Obit 24

Bishop, John 1935- . . . . **CLC 10**
See also CA 105

Bissett, Bill 1939- . . . . **CLC 18; PC 14**
See also CA 69-72; CAAS 19; CANR 15;
DLB 53; MTCW

Bitov, Andrei (Georgievich) 1937- . . . **CLC 57**
See also CA 142

Biyidi, Alexandre 1932-
See Beti, Mongo
See also BW 1; CA 114; 124; MTCW

Bjarme, Brynjolf
See Ibsen, Henrik (Johan)

Bjornson, Bjornstjerne (Martinius)
1832-1910 . . . . **TCLC 7, 37**
See also CA 104

Black, Robert
See Holdstock, Robert P.

Blackburn, Paul 1926-1971 . . . . . . **CLC 9, 43**
See also CA 81-84; 33-36R; CANR 34;
DLB 16; DLBY 81

Black Elk 1863-1950 .... **TCLC 33**
See also CA 144; DAM MULT; NNAL

Black Hobart
See Sanders, (James) Ed(ward)

Blacklin, Malcolm
See Chambers, Aidan

Blackmore, R(ichard) D(oddridge)
1825-1900 .... **TCLC 27**
See also CA 120; DLB 18

Blackmur, R(ichard) P(almer)
1904-1965 .... **CLC 2, 24**
See also CA 11-12; 25-28R; CAP 1; DLB 63

Black Tarantula, The
See Acker, Kathy

Blackwood, Algernon (Henry)
1869-1951 .... **TCLC 5**
See also CA 105; 150; DLB 153, 156

Blackwood, Caroline 1931-1996 ... **CLC 6, 9**
See also CA 85-88; 151; CANR 32;
DLB 14; MTCW

Blade, Alexander
See Hamilton, Edmond; Silverberg, Robert

Blaga, Lucian 1895-1961 .... **CLC 75**

Blair, Eric (Arthur) 1903-1950
See Orwell, George
See also CA 104; 132; DA; DAB; DAC;
DAM MST, NOV; MTCW; SATA 29

Blais, Marie-Claire
1939- .... **CLC 2, 4, 6, 13, 22; DAC**
See also CA 21-24R; CAAS 4; CANR 38;
DAM MST; DLB 53; MTCW

Blaise, Clark 1940- .... **CLC 29**
See also AITN 2; CA 53-56; CAAS 3;
CANR 5; DLB 53

Blake, Nicholas
See Day Lewis, C(ecil)
See also DLB 77

Blake, William
1757-1827 .... **NCLC 13, 37, 57; DA;**
DAB; DAC; PC 12; WLC
See also CDBLB 1789-1832; DAM MST,
POET; DLB 93, 163; MAICYA;
SATA 30

Blake, William J(ames) 1894-1969 ... **PC 12**
See also CA 5-8R; 25-28R

Blasco Ibanez, Vicente
1867-1928 .... **TCLC 12**
See also CA 110; 131; DAM NOV; HW;
MTCW

Blatty, William Peter 1928- .... **CLC 2**
See also CA 5-8R; CANR 9; DAM POP

Bleeck, Oliver
See Thomas, Ross (Elmore)

Blessing, Lee 1949- .... **CLC 54**

Blish, James (Benjamin)
1921-1975 .... **CLC 14**
See also CA 1-4R; 57-60; CANR 3; DLB 8;
MTCW; SATA 66

Bliss, Reginald
See Wells, H(erbert) G(eorge)

Blixen, Karen (Christentze Dinesen)
1885-1962
See Dinesen, Isak
See also CA 25-28; CANR 22, 50; CAP 2;
MTCW; SATA 44

Bloch, Robert (Albert) 1917-1994 ... **CLC 33**
See also CA 5-8R; 146; CAAS 20; CANR 5;
DLB 44; INT CANR-5; SATA 12;
SATA-Obit 82

Blok, Alexander (Alexandrovich)
1880-1921 .... **TCLC 5**
See also CA 104

Blom, Jan
See Breytenbach, Breyten

Bloom, Harold 1930- .... **CLC 24**
See also CA 13-16R; CANR 39; DLB 67

Bloomfield, Aurelius
See Bourne, Randolph S(illiman)

Blount, Roy (Alton), Jr. 1941- ..... **CLC 38**
See also CA 53-56; CANR 10, 28;
INT CANR-28; MTCW

Bloy, Leon 1846-1917............ **TCLC 22**
See also CA 121; DLB 123

Blume, Judy (Sussman) 1938-... **CLC 12, 30**
See also AAYA 3; CA 29-32R; CANR 13,
37; CLR 2, 15; DAM NOV, POP;
DLB 52; JRDA; MAICYA; MTCW;
SATA 2, 31, 79

Blunden, Edmund (Charles)
1896-1974 .... **CLC 2, 56**
See also CA 17-18; 45-48; CAP 2; DLB 20,
100, 155; MTCW

Bly, Robert (Elwood)
1926- .... **CLC 1, 2, 5, 10, 15, 38**
See also CA 5-8R; CANR 41; DAM POET;
DLB 5; MTCW

Boas, Franz 1858-1942........... **TCLC 56**
See also CA 115

Bobette
See Simenon, Georges (Jacques Christian)

Boccaccio, Giovanni
1313-1375 .... **CMLC 13; SSC 10**

Bochco, Steven 1943-............. **CLC 35**
See also AAYA 11; CA 124; 138

Bodenheim, Maxwell 1892-1954 ... **TCLC 44**
See also CA 110; DLB 9, 45

Bodker, Cecil 1927- .... **CLC 21**
See also CA 73-76; CANR 13, 44; CLR 23;
MAICYA; SATA 14

Boell, Heinrich (Theodor)
1917-1985 .... **CLC 2, 3, 6, 9, 11, 15, 27,**
32, 72; DA; DAB; DAC; SSC 23; WLC
See also CA 21-24R; 116; CANR 24;
DAM MST, NOV; DLB 69; DLBY 85;
MTCW

Boerne, Alfred
See Doeblin, Alfred

Boethius 480(?)-524(?) .... **CMLC 15**
See also DLB 115

Bogan, Louise
1897-1970 .... **CLC 4, 39, 46, 93; PC 12**
See also CA 73-76; 25-28R; CANR 33;
DAM POET; DLB 45; MTCW

Bogarde, Dirk .... **CLC 19**
See also Van Den Bogarde, Derek Jules
Gaspard Ulric Niven
See also DLB 14

Bogosian, Eric 1953- .... **CLC 45**
See also CA 138

Bograd, Larry 1953-.............. **CLC 35**
See also CA 93-96; SAAS 21; SATA 33

Boiardo, Matteo Maria 1441-1494 .... **LC 6**

Boileau-Despreaux, Nicolas
1636-1711 .... **LC 3**

Bojer, Johan 1872-1959 .... **TCLC 64**

Boland, Eavan (Aisling) 1944-... **CLC 40, 67**
See also CA 143; DAM POET; DLB 40

Bolt, Lee
See Faust, Frederick (Schiller)

Bolt, Robert (Oxton) 1924-1995 .... **CLC 14**
See also CA 17-20R; 147; CANR 35;
DAM DRAM; DLB 13; MTCW

Bombet, Louis-Alexandre-Cesar
See Stendhal

Bomkauf
See Kaufman, Bob (Garnell)

Bonaventura................... **NCLC 35**
See also DLB 90

Bond, Edward 1934-....... **CLC 4, 6, 13, 23**
See also CA 25-28R; CANR 38;
DAM DRAM; DLB 13; MTCW

Bonham, Frank 1914-1989......... **CLC 12**
See also AAYA 1; CA 9-12R; CANR 4, 36;
JRDA; MAICYA; SAAS 3; SATA 1, 49;
SATA-Obit 62

Bonnefoy, Yves 1923-........ **CLC 9, 15, 58**
See also CA 85-88; CANR 33; DAM MST,
POET; MTCW

Bontemps, Arna(ud Wendell)
1902-1973 .... **CLC 1, 18; BLC**
See also BW 1; CA 1-4R; 41-44R; CANR 4,
35; CLR 6; DAM MULT, NOV, POET;
DLB 48, 51; JRDA; MAICYA; MTCW;
SATA 2, 44; SATA-Obit 24

Booth, Martin 1944-.............. **CLC 13**
See also CA 93-96; CAAS 2

Booth, Philip 1925-............... **CLC 23**
See also CA 5-8R; CANR 5; DLBY 82

Booth, Wayne C(layson) 1921- ..... **CLC 24**
See also CA 1-4R; CAAS 5; CANR 3, 43;
DLB 67

Borchert, Wolfgang 1921-1947 ..... **TCLC 5**
See also CA 104; DLB 69, 124

Borel, Petrus 1809-1859......... **NCLC 41**

Borges, Jorge Luis
1899-1986 ... **CLC 1, 2, 3, 4, 6, 8, 9, 10,**
13, 19, 44, 48, 83; DA; DAB; DAC;
HLC; SSC 4; WLC
See also CA 21-24R; CANR 19, 33;
DAM MST, MULT; DLB 113; DLBY 86;
HW; MTCW

Borowski, Tadeusz 1922-1951 ...... **TCLC 9**
See also CA 106

Borrow, George (Henry)
1803-1881 .... **NCLC 9**
See also DLB 21, 55

Bosman, Herman Charles
1905-1951 .... **TCLC 49**

Bosschere, Jean de 1878(?)-1953... **TCLC 19**
See also CA 115

Boswell, James
   1740-1795 ..... **LC 4; DA; DAB; DAC;**
                                    WLC
   See also CDBLB 1660-1789; DAM MST;
   DLB 104, 142

Bottoms, David 1949-............. **CLC 53**
   See also CA 105; CANR 22; DLB 120;
   DLBY 83

Boucicault, Dion 1820-1890...... **NCLC 41**

Boucolon, Maryse 1937-
   See Conde, Maryse
   See also CA 110; CANR 30

Bourget, Paul (Charles Joseph)
   1852-1935 .... **TCLC 12**
   See also CA 107; DLB 123

Bourjaily, Vance (Nye) 1922- .... **CLC 8, 62**
   See also CA 1-4R; CAAS 1; CANR 2;
   DLB 2, 143

Bourne, Randolph S(illiman)
   1886-1918 .... **TCLC 16**
   See also CA 117; DLB 63

Bova, Ben(jamin William) 1932-.... **CLC 45**
   See also AAYA 16; CA 5-8R; CAAS 18;
   CANR 11; CLR 3; DLBY 81;
   INT CANR-11; MAICYA; MTCW;
   SATA 6, 68

Bowen, Elizabeth (Dorothea Cole)
   1899-1973 ..... **CLC 1, 3, 6, 11, 15, 22;**
                                    SSC 3
   See also CA 17-18; 41-44R; CANR 35;
   CAP 2; CDBLB 1945-1960; DAM NOV;
   DLB 15, 162; MTCW

Bowering, George 1935-........ **CLC 15, 47**
   See also CA 21-24R; CAAS 16; CANR 10;
   DLB 53

Bowering, Marilyn R(uthe) 1949-... **CLC 32**
   See also CA 101; CANR 49

Bowers, Edgar 1924- .... **CLC 9**
   See also CA 5-8R; CANR 24; DLB 5

Bowie, David .... **CLC 17**
   See also Jones, David Robert

Bowles, Jane (Sydney)
   1917-1973 .... **CLC 3, 68**
   See also CA 19-20; 41-44R; CAP 2

Bowles, Paul (Frederick)
   1910- .... **CLC 1, 2, 19, 53; SSC 3**
   See also CA 1-4R; CAAS 1; CANR 1, 19,
   50; DLB 5, 6; MTCW

Box, Edgar
   See Vidal, Gore

Boyd, Nancy
   See Millay, Edna St. Vincent

Boyd, William 1952-........ **CLC 28, 53, 70**
   See also CA 114; 120; CANR 51

Boyle, Kay
   1902-1992 ..... **CLC 1, 5, 19, 58; SSC 5**
   See also CA 13-16R; 140; CAAS 1;
   CANR 29; DLB 4, 9, 48, 86; DLBY 93;
   MTCW

Boyle, Mark
   See Kienzle, William X(avier)

Boyle, Patrick 1905-1982......... **CLC 19**
   See also CA 127

Boyle, T. C. 1948-
   See Boyle, T(homas) Coraghessan

Boyle, T(homas) Coraghessan
   1948- .... **CLC 36, 55, 90; SSC 16**
   See also BEST 90:4; CA 120; CANR 44;
   DAM POP; DLBY 86

Boz
   See Dickens, Charles (John Huffam)

Brackenridge, Hugh Henry
   1748-1816 .... **NCLC 7**
   See also DLB 11, 37

Bradbury, Edward P.
   See Moorcock, Michael (John)

Bradbury, Malcolm (Stanley)
   1932-.................... **CLC 32, 61**
   See also CA 1-4R; CANR 1, 33;
   DAM NOV; DLB 14; MTCW

Bradbury, Ray (Douglas)
   1920- .... **CLC 1, 3, 10, 15, 42; DA;**
                                    DAB; DAC; WLC
   See also AAYA 15; AITN 1, 2; CA 1-4R;
   CANR 2, 30; CDALB 1968-1988;
   DAM MST, NOV, POP; DLB 2, 8;
   INT CANR-30; MTCW; SATA 11, 64

Bradford, Gamaliel 1863-1932..... **TCLC 36**
   See also DLB 17

Bradley, David (Henry, Jr.)
   1950-................... **CLC 23; BLC**
   See also BW 1; CA 104; CANR 26;
   DAM MULT; DLB 33

Bradley, John Ed(mund, Jr.)
   1958-..................... **CLC 55**
   See also CA 139

Bradley, Marion Zimmer 1930-..... **CLC 30**
   See also AAYA 9; CA 57-60; CAAS 10;
   CANR 7, 31, 51; DAM POP; DLB 8;
   MTCW

Bradstreet, Anne
   1612(?)-1672 ...... **LC 4, 30; DA; DAC;**
                                    PC 10
   See also CDALB 1640-1865; DAM MST,
   POET; DLB 24

Brady, Joan 1939- .... **CLC 86**
   See also CA 141

Bragg, Melvyn 1939- .... **CLC 10**
   See also BEST 89:3; CA 57-60; CANR 10,
   48; DLB 14

Braine, John (Gerard)
   1922-1986 .... **CLC 1, 3, 41**
   See also CA 1-4R; 120; CANR 1, 33;
   CDBLB 1945-1960; DLB 15; DLBY 86;
   MTCW

Brammer, William 1930(?)-1978 .... **CLC 31**
   See also CA 77-80

Brancati, Vitaliano 1907-1954..... **TCLC 12**
   See also CA 109

Brancato, Robin F(idler) 1936- ..... **CLC 35**
   See also AAYA 9; CA 69-72; CANR 11,
   45; CLR 32; JRDA; SAAS 9; SATA 23

Brand, Max
   See Faust, Frederick (Schiller)

Brand, Millen 1906-1980.......... **CLC 7**
   See also CA 21-24R; 97-100

Branden, Barbara .... **CLC 44**
   See also CA 148

Brandes, Georg (Morris Cohen)
   1842-1927 .... **TCLC 10**
   See also CA 105

Brandys, Kazimierz 1916-......... **CLC 62**

Branley, Franklyn M(ansfield)
   1915-...................... **CLC 21**
   See also CA 33-36R; CANR 14, 39;
   CLR 13; MAICYA; SAAS 16; SATA 4,
   68

Brathwaite, Edward Kamau 1930-... **CLC 11**
   See also BW 2; CA 25-28R; CANR 11, 26,
   47; DAM POET; DLB 125

Brautigan, Richard (Gary)
   1935-1984 .... **CLC 1, 3, 5, 9, 12, 34, 42**
   See also CA 53-56; 113; CANR 34;
   DAM NOV; DLB 2, 5; DLBY 80, 84;
   MTCW; SATA 56

Brave Bird, Mary 1953-
   See Crow Dog, Mary
   See also NNAL

Braverman, Kate 1950- .... **CLC 67**
   See also CA 89-92

Brecht, Bertolt
   1898-1956 ..... **TCLC 1, 6, 13, 35; DA;**
                                    DAB; DAC; DC 3; WLC
   See also CA 104; 133; DAM DRAM, MST;
   DLB 56, 124; MTCW

Brecht, Eugen Berthold Friedrich
   See Brecht, Bertolt

Bremer, Fredrika 1801-1865 ..... **NCLC 11**

Brennan, Christopher John
   1870-1932 .... **TCLC 17**
   See also CA 117

Brennan, Maeve 1917-............. **CLC 5**
   See also CA 81-84

Brentano, Clemens (Maria)
   1778-1842 .... **NCLC 1**
   See also DLB 90

Brent of Bin Bin
   See Franklin, (Stella Maraia Sarah) Miles

Brenton, Howard 1942-........... **CLC 31**
   See also CA 69-72; CANR 33; DLB 13;
   MTCW

Breslin, James 1930-
   See Breslin, Jimmy
   See also CA 73-76; CANR 31; DAM NOV;
   MTCW

Breslin, Jimmy .... **CLC 4, 43**
   See also Breslin, James
   See also AITN 1

Bresson, Robert 1901-............ **CLC 16**
   See also CA 110; CANR 49

Breton, Andre
   1896-1966 ..... **CLC 2, 9, 15, 54; PC 15**
   See also CA 19-20; 25-28R; CANR 40;
   CAP 2; DLB 65; MTCW

Breytenbach, Breyten 1939(?)- .. **CLC 23, 37**
   See also CA 113; 129; DAM POET

Bridgers, Sue Ellen 1942- .... **CLC 26**
   See also AAYA 8; CA 65-68; CANR 11,
   36; CLR 18; DLB 52; JRDA; MAICYA;
   SAAS 1; SATA 22

Bridges, Robert (Seymour)
   1844-1930 .... **TCLC 1**
   See also CA 104; CDBLB 1890-1914;
   DAM POET; DLB 19, 98

Author Index

Bryusov, Valery Yakovlevich
1873-1924 . . . . **TCLC 10**
See also CA 107

Buchan, John 1875-1940 . . . **TCLC 41; DAB**
See also CA 108; 145; DAM POP; DLB 34,
70, 156; YABC 2

Buchanan, George 1506-1582 . . . . **LC 4**

Buchheim, Lothar-Guenther 1918- . . . **CLC 6**
See also CA 85-88

Buchner, (Karl) Georg
1813-1837 . . . . **NCLC 26**

Buchwald, Art(hur) 1925- . . . . **CLC 33**
See also AITN 1; CA 5-8R; CANR 21;
MTCW; SATA 10

Buck, Pearl S(ydenstricker)
1892-1973 . . . . **CLC 7, 11, 18; DA; DAB;
DAC**
See also AITN 1; CA 1-4R; 41-44R;
CANR 1, 34; DAM MST, NOV; DLB 9,
102; MTCW; SATA 1, 25

Buckler, Ernest 1908-1984 . . . . **CLC 13; DAC**
See also CA 11-12; 114; CAP 1;
DAM MST; DLB 68; SATA 47

Buckley, Vincent (Thomas)
1925-1988 . . . . **CLC 57**
See also CA 101

Buckley, William F(rank), Jr.
1925- . . . . **CLC 7, 18, 37**
See also AITN 1; CA 1-4R; CANR 1, 24;
DAM POP; DLB 137; DLBY 80;
INT CANR-24; MTCW

Buechner, (Carl) Frederick
1926- . . . . **CLC 2, 4, 6, 9**
See also CA 13-16R; CANR 11, 39;
DAM NOV; DLBY 80; INT CANR-11;
MTCW

Buell, John (Edward) 1927- . . . . **CLC 10**
See also CA 1-4R; DLB 53

Buero Vallejo, Antonio 1916- . . . **CLC 15, 46**
See also CA 106; CANR 24, 49; HW;
MTCW

Bufalino, Gesualdo 1920(?)- . . . . **CLC 74**

Bugayev, Boris Nikolayevich 1880-1934
See Bely, Andrey
See also CA 104

Bukowski, Charles
1920-1994 . . . . **CLC 2, 5, 9, 41, 82**
See also CA 17-20R; 144; CANR 40;
DAM NOV, POET; DLB 5, 130; MTCW

Bulgakov, Mikhail (Afanas'evich)
1891-1940 . . . . **TCLC 2, 16; SSC 18**
See also CA 105; DAM DRAM, NOV

Bulgya, Alexander Alexandrovich
1901-1956 . . . . **TCLC 53**
See also Fadeyev, Alexander
See also CA 117

Bullins, Ed 1935- . . **CLC 1, 5, 7; BLC; DC 6**
See also BW 2; CA 49-52; CAAS 16;
CANR 24, 46; DAM DRAM, MULT;
DLB 7, 38; MTCW

Bulwer-Lytton, Edward (George Earle Lytton)
1803-1873 . . . . **NCLC 1, 45**
See also DLB 21

Bunin, Ivan Alexeyevich
1870-1953 . . . . **TCLC 6; SSC 5**
See also CA 104

Bunting, Basil 1900-1985 . . . . **CLC 10, 39, 47**
See also CA 53-56; 115; CANR 7;
DAM POET; DLB 20

Bunuel, Luis 1900-1983 . . **CLC 16, 80; HLC**
See also CA 101; 110; CANR 32;
DAM MULT; HW

Bunyan, John
1628-1688 . . . . . . **LC 4; DA; DAB; DAC;
WLC**
See also CDBLB 1660-1789; DAM MST;
DLB 39

Burckhardt, Jacob (Christoph)
1818-1897 . . . . **NCLC 49**

Burford, Eleanor
See Hibbert, Eleanor Alice Burford

Burgess, Anthony
. **CLC 1, 2, 4, 5, 8, 10, 13, 15, 22, 40, 62,
81, 94; DAB**
See also Wilson, John (Anthony) Burgess
See also AITN 1; CDBLB 1960 to Present;
DLB 14

Burke, Edmund
1729(?)-1797 . . . . **LC 7; DA; DAB; DAC;
WLC**
See also DAM MST; DLB 104

Burke, Kenneth (Duva)
1897-1993 . . . . **CLC 2, 24**
See also CA 5-8R; 143; CANR 39;
63; MTCW

Burke, Leda
See Garnett, David

Burke, Ralph
See Silverberg, Robert

Burke, Thomas 1886-1945 . . . . **TCLC 63**
See also CA 113

Burney, Fanny 1752-1840 . . . . **NCLC 12, 54**
See also DLB 39

Burns, Robert 1759-1796 . . . . **PC 6**
See also CDBLB 1789-1832; DA; DAB;
DAC; DAM MST, POET; DLB 109;
WLC

Burns, Tex
See L'Amour, Louis (Dearborn)

Burnshaw, Stanley 1906- . . . . . **CLC 3, 13, 44**
See also CA 9-12R; DLB 48

Burr, Anne 1937- . . . . **CLC 6**
See also CA 25-28R

Burroughs, Edgar Rice
1875-1950 . . . . **TCLC 2, 32**
See also AAYA 11; CA 104; 132;
DAM NOV; DLB 8; MTCW; SATA 41

Burroughs, William S(eward)
1914- . . . . **CLC 1, 2, 5, 15, 22, 42, 75;
DA; DAB; DAC; WLC**
See also AITN 2; CA 9-12R; CANR 20;
DAM MST, NOV, POP; DLB 2, 8, 16,
152; DLBY 81; MTCW

Burton, Richard F. 1821-1890 . . . . **NCLC 42**
See also DLB 55

Busch, Frederick 1941- . . . **CLC 7, 10, 18, 47**
See also CA 33-36R; CAAS 1; CANR 45;
DLB 6

Bush, Ronald 1946- . . . . **CLC 34**
See also CA 136

Bustos, F(rancisco)
See Borges, Jorge Luis

Bustos Domecq, H(onorio)
See Bioy Casares, Adolfo; Borges, Jorge
Luis

Butler, Octavia E(stelle) 1947- . . . . . **CLC 38**
See also BW 2; CA 73-76; CANR 12, 24,
38; DAM MULT, POP; DLB 33;
MTCW; SATA 84

Butler, Robert Olen (Jr.) 1945- . . . . . **CLC 81**
See also CA 112; DAM POP; INT 112

Butler, Samuel 1612-1680 . . . . **LC 16**
See also DLB 101, 126

Butler, Samuel
1835-1902 . . . . . . **TCLC 1, 33; DA; DAB;
DAC; WLC**
See also CA 143; CDBLB 1890-1914;
DAM MST, NOV; DLB 18, 57

Butler, Walter C.
See Faust, Frederick (Schiller)

Butor, Michel (Marie Francois)
1926- . . . . **CLC 1, 3, 8, 11, 15**
See also CA 9-12R; CANR 33; DLB 83;
MTCW

Buzo, Alexander (John) 1944- . . . . . . **CLC 61**
See also CA 97-100; CANR 17, 39

Buzzati, Dino 1906-1972 . . . . **CLC 36**
See also CA 33-36R

Byars, Betsy (Cromer) 1928- . . . . **CLC 35**
See also CA 33-36R; CANR 18, 36; CLR 1,
16; DLB 52; INT CANR-18; JRDA;
MAICYA; MTCW; SAAS 1; SATA 4,
46, 80

Byatt, A(ntonia) S(usan Drabble)
1936- . . . . **CLC 19, 65**
See also CA 13-16R; CANR 13, 33, 50;
DAM NOV, POP; DLB 14; MTCW

Byrne, David 1952- . . . . **CLC 26**
See also CA 127

Byrne, John Keyes 1926-
See Leonard, Hugh
See also CA 102; INT 102

Byron, George Gordon (Noel)
1788-1824 . . . . . **NCLC 2, 12; DA; DAB;
DAC; WLC**
See also CDBLB 1789-1832; DAM MST,
POET; DLB 96, 110

C. 3. 3.
See Wilde, Oscar (Fingal O'Flahertie Wills)

Caballero, Fernan 1796-1877 . . . . . **NCLC 10**

Cabell, James Branch 1879-1958 . . . **TCLC 6**
See also CA 105; DLB 9, 78

Cable, George Washington
1844-1925 . . . . **TCLC 4; SSC 4**
See also CA 104; DLB 12, 74; DLBD 13

Cabral de Melo Neto, Joao 1920- . . . **CLC 76**
See also DAM MULT

Cabrera Infante, G(uillermo)
1929- . . . . **CLC 5, 25, 45; HLC**
See also CA 85-88; CANR 29;
DAM MULT; DLB 113; HW; MTCW

Cade, Toni
See Bambara, Toni Cade

Cadmus and Harmonia
See Buchan, John

Caedmon fl. 658-680............ **CMLC 7**
See also DLB 146

Caeiro, Alberto
See Pessoa, Fernando (Antonio Nogueira)

Cage, John (Milton, Jr.) 1912-..... **CLC 41**
See also CA 13-16R; CANR 9;
INT CANR-9

Cain, G.
See Cabrera Infante, G(uillermo)

Cain, Guillermo
See Cabrera Infante, G(uillermo)

Cain, James M(allahan)
1892-1977 .... **CLC 3, 11, 28**
See also AITN 1; CA 17-20R; 73-76;
CANR 8, 34; MTCW

Caine, Mark
See Raphael, Frederic (Michael)

Calasso, Roberto 1941- .... **CLC 81**
See also CA 143

Calderon de la Barca, Pedro
1600-1681 .... **LC 23; DC 3**

Caldwell, Erskine (Preston)
1903-1987 .... **CLC 1, 8, 14, 50, 60;**
SSC 19
See also AITN 1; CA 1-4R; 121; CAAS 1;
CANR 2, 33; DAM NOV; DLB 9, 86;
MTCW

Caldwell, (Janet Miriam) Taylor (Holland)
1900-1985 .... **CLC 2, 28, 39**
See also CA 5-8R; 116; CANR 5;
DAM NOV, POP

Calhoun, John Caldwell
1782-1850 .... **NCLC 15**
See also DLB 3

Calisher, Hortense
1911- .... **CLC 2, 4, 8, 38; SSC 15**
See also CA 1-4R; CANR 1, 22;
DAM NOV; DLB 2; INT CANR-22;
MTCW

Callaghan, Morley Edward
1903-1990 ..... **CLC 3, 14, 41, 65; DAC**
See also CA 9-12R; 132; CANR 33;
DAM MST; DLB 68; MTCW

Callimachus
c. 305B.C.-c. 240B.C........ **CMLC 18**

Calvino, Italo
1923-1985 ..... **CLC 5, 8, 11, 22, 33, 39,**
73; SSC 3
See also CA 85-88; 116; CANR 23;
DAM NOV; MTCW

Cameron, Carey 1952-............ **CLC 59**
See also CA 135

Cameron, Peter 1959-............ **CLC 44**
See also CA 125; CANR 50

Campana, Dino 1885-1932....... **TCLC 20**
See also CA 117; DLB 114

Campanella, Tommaso 1568-1639.... **LC 32**

Campbell, John W(ood, Jr.)
1910-1971 .... **CLC 32**
See also CA 21-22; 29-32R; CANR 34;
CAP 2; DLB 8; MTCW

Campbell, Joseph 1904-1987 .... **CLC 69**
See also AAYA 3; BEST 89:2; CA 1-4R;
124; CANR 3, 28; MTCW

Campbell, Maria 1940-...... **CLC 85; DAC**
See also CA 102; NNAL

Campbell, (John) Ramsey
1946- .... **CLC 42; SSC 19**
See also CA 57-60; CANR 7; INT CANR-7

Campbell, (Ignatius) Roy (Dunnachie)
1901-1957 .... **TCLC 5**
See also CA 104; DLB 20

Campbell, Thomas 1777-1844 .... **NCLC 19**
See also DLB 93; 144

Campbell, Wilfred................. TCLC 9
See also Campbell, William

Campbell, William 1858(?)-1918
See Campbell, Wilfred
See also CA 106; DLB 92

Campos, Alvaro de
See Pessoa, Fernando (Antonio Nogueira)

Camus, Albert
1913-1960 .... **CLC 1, 2, 4, 9, 11, 14, 32,**
63, 69; DA; DAB; DAC; DC 2; SSC 9;
WLC
See also CA 89-92; DAM DRAM, MST,
NOV; DLB 72; MTCW

Canby, Vincent 1924-............. **CLC 13**
See also CA 81-84

Cancale
See Desnos, Robert

Canetti, Elias
1905-1994 .... **CLC 3, 14, 25, 75, 86**
See also CA 21-24R; 146; CANR 23;
DLB 85, 124; MTCW

Canin, Ethan 1960-............... **CLC 55**
See also CA 131; 135

Cannon, Curt
See Hunter, Evan

Cape, Judith
See Page, P(atricia) K(athleen)

Capek, Karel
1890-1938 ...... **TCLC 6, 37; DA; DAB;**
DAC; DC 1; WLC
See also CA 104; 140; DAM DRAM, MST,
NOV

Capote, Truman
1924-1984 ...... **CLC 1, 3, 8, 13, 19, 34,**
38, 58; DA; DAB; DAC; SSC 2; WLC
See also CA 5-8R; 113; CANR 18;
CDALB 1941-1968; DAM MST, NOV,
POP; DLB 2; DLBY 80, 84; MTCW

Capra, Frank 1897-1991........... **CLC 16**
See also CA 61-64; 135

Caputo, Philip 1941-.............. **CLC 32**
See also CA 73-76; CANR 40

Card, Orson Scott 1951- .... **CLC 44, 47, 50**
See also AAYA 11; CA 102; CANR 27, 47;
DAM POP; INT CANR-27; MTCW;
SATA 83

Cardenal (Martinez), Ernesto
1925- .... **CLC 31; HLC**
See also CA 49-52; CANR 2, 32;
DAM MULT, POET; HW; MTCW

Carducci, Giosue 1835-1907....... **TCLC 32**

Carew, Thomas 1595(?)-1640........ **LC 13**
See also DLB 126

Carey, Ernestine Gilbreth 1908-.... **CLC 17**
See also CA 5-8R; SATA 2

Carey, Peter 1943-............ **CLC 40, 55**
See also CA 123; 127; INT 127; MTCW

Carleton, William 1794-1869...... **NCLC 3**
See also DLB 159

Carlisle, Henry (Coffin) 1926-...... **CLC 33**
See also CA 13-16R; CANR 15

Carlsen, Chris
See Holdstock, Robert P.

Carlson, Ron(ald F.) 1947-........ **CLC 54**
See also CA 105; CANR 27

Carlyle, Thomas
1795-1881 .. **NCLC 22; DA; DAB; DAC**
See also CDBLB 1789-1832; DAM MST;
DLB 55; 144

Carman, (William) Bliss
1861-1929 .... **TCLC 7; DAC**
See also CA 104; DLB 92

Carnegie, Dale 1888-1955 .... **TCLC 53**

Carossa, Hans 1878-1956........ **TCLC 48**
See also DLB 66

Carpenter, Don(ald Richard)
1931-1995 .... **CLC 41**
See also CA 45-48; 149; CANR 1

Carpentier (y Valmont), Alejo
1904-1980 .... **CLC 8, 11, 38; HLC**
See also CA 65-68; 97-100; CANR 11;
DAM MULT; DLB 113; HW

Carr, Caleb 1955(?)-.............. **CLC 86**
See also CA 147

Carr, Emily 1871-1945.......... **TCLC 32**
See also DLB 68

Carr, John Dickson 1906-1977 ...... **CLC 3**
See also CA 49-52; 69-72; CANR 3, 33;
MTCW

Carr, Philippa
See Hibbert, Eleanor Alice Burford

Carr, Virginia Spencer 1929-....... **CLC 34**
See also CA 61-64; DLB 111

Carrere, Emmanuel 1957- .... **CLC 89**

Carrier, Roch 1937-..... **CLC 13, 78; DAC**
See also CA 130; DAM MST; DLB 53

Carroll, James P. 1943(?)-......... **CLC 38**
See also CA 81-84

Carroll, Jim 1951- .... **CLC 35**
See also AAYA 17; CA 45-48; CANR 42

Carroll, Lewis .... NCLC 2, 53; WLC
See also Dodgson, Charles Lutwidge
See also CDBLB 1832-1890; CLR 2, 18;
DLB 18, 163; JRDA

Carroll, Paul Vincent 1900-1968.... **CLC 10**
See also CA 9-12R; 25-28R; DLB 10

Carruth, Hayden
1921- ...... **CLC 4, 7, 10, 18, 84; PC 10**
See also CA 9-12R; CANR 4, 38; DLB 5,
165; INT CANR-4; MTCW; SATA 47

Carson, Rachel Louise 1907-1964... **CLC 71**
See also CA 77-80; CANR 35; DAM POP;
MTCW; SATA 23

Carter, Angela (Olive)
1940-1992 ...... **CLC 5, 41, 76; SSC 13**
See also CA 53-56; 136; CANR 12, 36;
DLB 14; MTCW; SATA 66;
SATA-Obit 70

Crane, R(onald) S(almon)
1886-1967 . . . . **CLC 27**
See also CA 85-88; DLB 63

Crane, Stephen (Townley)
1871-1900 . . . . . . **TCLC 11, 17, 32; DA;**
DAB; DAC; SSC 7; WLC
See also CA 109; 140; CDALB 1865-1917;
DAM MST, NOV, POET; DLB 12, 54,
78; YABC 2

Crase, Douglas   1944- . . . . **CLC 58**
See also CA 106

Crashaw, Richard   1612(?)-1649 . . . . . . **LC 24**
See also DLB 126

Craven, Margaret
1901-1980 . . . . **CLC 17; DAC**
See also CA 103

Crawford, F(rancis) Marion
1854-1909 . . . . **TCLC 10**
See also CA 107; DLB 71

Crawford, Isabella Valancy
1850-1887 . . . . **NCLC 12**
See also DLB 92

Crayon, Geoffrey
See Irving, Washington

Creasey, John   1908-1973 . . . . **CLC 11**
See also CA 5-8R; 41-44R; CANR 8;
DLB 77; MTCW

Crebillon, Claude Prosper Jolyot de (fils)
1707-1777 . . . . **LC 28**

Credo
See Creasey, John

Creeley, Robert (White)
1926- . . . . . **CLC 1, 2, 4, 8, 11, 15, 36, 78**
See also CA 1-4R; CAAS 10; CANR 23, 43;
DAM POET; DLB 5, 16; MTCW

Crews, Harry (Eugene)
1935- . . . . **CLC 6, 23, 49**
See also AITN 1; CA 25-28R; CANR 20;
DLB 6, 143; MTCW

Crichton, (John) Michael
1942- . . . . **CLC 2, 6, 54, 90**
See also AAYA 10; AITN 2; CA 25-28R;
CANR 13, 40; DAM NOV, POP;
DLBY 81; INT CANR-13; JRDA;
MTCW; SATA 9

Crispin, Edmund . . . . **CLC 22**
See also Montgomery, (Robert) Bruce
See also DLB 87

Cristofer, Michael   1945(?)- . . . . **CLC 28**
See also CA 110; DAM DRAM; DLB 7

Croce, Benedetto   1866-1952 . . . . . . **TCLC 37**
See also CA 120

Crockett, David   1786-1836 . . . . **NCLC 8**
See also DLB 3, 11

Crockett, Davy
See Crockett, David

Crofts, Freeman Wills
1879-1957 . . . . **TCLC 55**
See also CA 115; DLB 77

Croker, John Wilson   1780-1857 . . **NCLC 10**
See also DLB 110

Crommelynck, Fernand   1885-1970 . . **CLC 75**
See also CA 89-92

Cronin, A(rchibald) J(oseph)
1896-1981 . . . . **CLC 32**
See also CA 1-4R; 102; CANR 5; SATA 47;
SATA-Obit 25

Cross, Amanda
See Heilbrun, Carolyn G(old)

Crothers, Rachel   1878(?)-1958 . . . . . **TCLC 19**
See also CA 113; DLB 7

Croves, Hal
See Traven, B.

Crow Dog, Mary . . . . **CLC 93**
See also Brave Bird, Mary

Crowfield, Christopher
See Stowe, Harriet (Elizabeth) Beecher

Crowley, Aleister . . . . **TCLC 7**
See also Crowley, Edward Alexander

Crowley, Edward Alexander   1875-1947
See Crowley, Aleister
See also CA 104

Crowley, John   1942- . . . . **CLC 57**
See also CA 61-64; CANR 43; DLBY 82;
SATA 65

Crud
See Crumb, R(obert)

Crumarums
See Crumb, R(obert)

Crumb, R(obert)   1943- . . . . **CLC 17**
See also CA 106

Crumbum
See Crumb, R(obert)

Crumski
See Crumb, R(obert)

Crum the Bum
See Crumb, R(obert)

Crunk
See Crumb, R(obert)

Crustt
See Crumb, R(obert)

Cryer, Gretchen (Kiger)   1935- . . . . . . **CLC 21**
See also CA 114; 123

Csath, Geza   1887-1919 . . . . **TCLC 13**
See also CA 111

Cudlip, David   1933- . . . . **CLC 34**

Cullen, Countee
1903-1946 . . . . . . **TCLC 4, 37; BLC; DA;**
DAC
See also BW 1; CA 108; 124;
CDALB 1917-1929; DAM MST, MULT,
POET; DLB 4, 48, 51; MTCW; SATA 18

Cum, R.
See Crumb, R(obert)

Cummings, Bruce F(rederick)   1889-1919
See Barbellion, W. N. P.
See also CA 123

Cummings, E(dward) E(stlin)
1894-1962 . . . . . . **CLC 1, 3, 8, 12, 15, 68;**
DA; DAB; DAC; PC 5; WLC 2
See also CA 73-76; CANR 31;
CDALB 1929-1941; DAM MST, POET;
DLB 4, 48; MTCW

Cunha, Euclides (Rodrigues Pimenta) da
1866-1909 . . . . **TCLC 24**
See also CA 123

Cunningham, E. V.
See Fast, Howard (Melvin)

Cunningham, J(ames) V(incent)
1911-1985 . . . . **CLC 3, 31**
See also CA 1-4R; 115; CANR 1; DLB 5

Cunningham, Julia (Woolfolk)
1916- . . . . **CLC 12**
See also CA 9-12R; CANR 4, 19, 36;
JRDA; MAICYA; SAAS 2; SATA 1, 26

Cunningham, Michael   1952- . . . . **CLC 34**
See also CA 136

Cunninghame Graham, R(obert) B(ontine)
1852-1936 . . . . **TCLC 19**
See also Graham, R(obert) B(ontine)
Cunninghame
See also CA 119; DLB 98

Currie, Ellen   19(?)- . . . . **CLC 44**

Curtin, Philip
See Lowndes, Marie Adelaide (Belloc)

Curtis, Price
See Ellison, Harlan (Jay)

Cutrate, Joe
See Spiegelman, Art

Czaczkes, Shmuel Yosef
See Agnon, S(hmuel) Y(osef Halevi)

Dabrowska, Maria (Szumska)
1889-1965 . . . . **CLC 15**
See also CA 106

Dabydeen, David   1955- . . . . **CLC 34**
See also BW 1; CA 125

Dacey, Philip   1939- . . . . **CLC 51**
See also CA 37-40R; CAAS 17; CANR 14,
32; DLB 105

Dagerman, Stig (Halvard)
1923-1954 . . . . **TCLC 17**
See also CA 117

Dahl, Roald
1916-1990 . . . . . . **CLC 1, 6, 18, 79; DAB;**
DAC
See also AAYA 15; CA 1-4R; 133;
CANR 6, 32, 37; CLR 1, 7; DAM MST,
NOV, POP; DLB 139; JRDA; MAICYA;
MTCW; SATA 1, 26, 73; SATA-Obit 65

Dahlberg, Edward   1900-1977 . . . **CLC 1, 7, 14**
See also CA 9-12R; 69-72; CANR 31;
DLB 48; MTCW

Dale, Colin . . . . **TCLC 18**
See also Lawrence, T(homas) E(dward)

Dale, George E.
See Asimov, Isaac

Daly, Elizabeth   1878-1967 . . . . **CLC 52**
See also CA 23-24; 25-28R; CAP 2

Daly, Maureen   1921- . . . . **CLC 17**
See also AAYA 5; CANR 37; JRDA;
MAICYA; SAAS 1; SATA 2

Damas, Leon-Gontran   1912-1978 . . . **CLC 84**
See also BW 1; CA 125; 73-76

Dana, Richard Henry Sr.
1787-1879 . . . . **NCLC 53**

Daniel, Samuel   1562(?)-1619 . . . . **LC 24**
See also DLB 62

Daniels, Brett
See Adler, Renata

Deledda, Grazia (Cosima)
1875(?)-1936 . . . . TCLC 23
See also CA 123

Delibes, Miguel . . . . CLC 8, 18
See also Delibes Setien, Miguel

Delibes Setien, Miguel 1920-
See Delibes, Miguel
See also CA 45-48; CANR 1, 32; HW;
MTCW

DeLillo, Don
1936- . . . . . CLC 8, 10, 13, 27, 39, 54, 76
See also BEST 89:1; CA 81-84; CANR 21;
DAM NOV, POP; DLB 6; MTCW

de Lisser, H. G.
See De Lisser, Herbert George
See also DLB 117

De Lisser, Herbert George
1878-1944 . . . . TCLC 12
See also de Lisser, H. G.
See also BW 2; CA 109

Deloria, Vine (Victor), Jr. 1933- . . . . CLC 21
See also CA 53-56; CANR 5, 20, 48;
DAM MULT; MTCW; NNAL; SATA 21

Del Vecchio, John M(ichael)
1947- . . . . CLC 29
See also CA 110; DLBD 9

de Man, Paul (Adolph Michel)
1919-1983 . . . . CLC 55
See also CA 128; 111; DLB 67; MTCW

De Marinis, Rick 1934- . . . . CLC 54
See also CA 57-60; CANR 9, 25, 50

Dembry, R. Emmet
See Murfree, Mary Noailles

Demby, William 1922- . . . . CLC 53; BLC
See also BW 1; CA 81-84; DAM MULT;
DLB 33

Demijohn, Thom
See Disch, Thomas M(ichael)

de Montherlant, Henry (Milon)
See Montherlant, Henry (Milon) de

Demosthenes 384B.C.-322B.C. . . . . CMLC 13

de Natale, Francine
See Malzberg, Barry N(athaniel)

Denby, Edwin (Orr) 1903-1983 . . . . . CLC 48
See also CA 138; 110

Denis, Julio
See Cortazar, Julio

Denmark, Harrison
See Zelazny, Roger (Joseph)

Dennis, John 1658-1734 . . . . LC 11
See also DLB 101

Dennis, Nigel (Forbes) 1912-1989 . . . . CLC 8
See also CA 25-28R; 129; DLB 13, 15;
MTCW

De Palma, Brian (Russell) 1940- . . . . CLC 20
See also CA 109

De Quincey, Thomas 1785-1859 . . . NCLC 4
See also CDBLB 1789-1832; DLB 110; 144

Deren, Eleanora 1908(?)-1961
See Deren, Maya
See also CA 111

Deren, Maya . . . . CLC 16
See also Deren, Eleanora

Derleth, August (William)
1909-1971 . . . . CLC 31
See also CA 1-4R; 29-32R; CANR 4;
DLB 9; SATA 5

Der Nister 1884-1950 . . . . TCLC 56

de Routisie, Albert
See Aragon, Louis

Derrida, Jacques 1930- . . . . CLC 24, 87
See also CA 124; 127

Derry Down Derry
See Lear, Edward

Dersonnes, Jacques
See Simenon, Georges (Jacques Christian)

Desai, Anita 1937- . . . . . . CLC 19, 37; DAB
See also CA 81-84; CANR 33; DAM NOV;
MTCW; SATA 63

de Saint-Luc, Jean
See Glassco, John

de Saint Roman, Arnaud
See Aragon, Louis

Descartes, Rene 1596-1650 . . . . LC 20

De Sica, Vittorio 1901(?)-1974 . . . . . CLC 20
See also CA 117

Desnos, Robert 1900-1945 . . . . TCLC 22
See also CA 121

Destouches, Louis-Ferdinand
1894-1961 . . . . CLC 9, 15
See also Celine, Louis-Ferdinand
See also CA 85-88; CANR 28; MTCW

Deutsch, Babette 1895-1982 . . . . CLC 18
See also CA 1-4R; 108; CANR 4; DLB 45;
SATA 1; SATA-Obit 33

Devenant, William 1606-1649 . . . . LC 13

Devkota, Laxmiprasad
1909-1959 . . . . TCLC 23
See also CA 123

De Voto, Bernard (Augustine)
1897-1955 . . . . TCLC 29
See also CA 113; DLB 9

De Vries, Peter
1910-1993 . . . . CLC 1, 2, 3, 7, 10, 28, 46
See also CA 17-20R; 142; CANR 41;
DAM NOV; DLB 6; DLBY 82; MTCW

Dexter, Martin
See Faust, Frederick (Schiller)

Dexter, Pete 1943- . . . . CLC 34, 55
See also BEST 89:2; CA 127; 131;
DAM POP; INT 131; MTCW

Diamano, Silmang
See Senghor, Leopold Sedar

Diamond, Neil 1941- . . . . CLC 30
See also CA 108

Diaz del Castillo, Bernal 1496-1584 . . LC 31

di Bassetto, Corno
See Shaw, George Bernard

Dick, Philip K(indred)
1928-1982 . . . . CLC 10, 30, 72
See also CA 49-52; 106; CANR 2, 16;
DAM NOV, POP; DLB 8; MTCW

Dickens, Charles (John Huffam)
1812-1870 . . . . . . NCLC 3, 8, 18, 26, 37,
50; DA; DAB; DAC; SSC 17; WLC
See also CDBLB 1832-1890; DAM MST,
NOV; DLB 21, 55, 70, 159; JRDA;
MAICYA; SATA 15

Dickey, James (Lafayette)
1923- . . . . CLC 1, 2, 4, 7, 10, 15, 47
See also AITN 1, 2; CA 9-12R; CABS 2;
CANR 10, 48; CDALB 1968-1988;
DAM NOV, POET, POP; DLB 5;
DLBD 7; DLBY 82, 93; INT CANR-10;
MTCW

Dickey, William 1928-1994 . . . . . . CLC 3, 28
See also CA 9-12R; 145; CANR 24; DLB 5

Dickinson, Charles 1951- . . . . CLC 49
See also CA 128

Dickinson, Emily (Elizabeth)
1830-1886 . . . . NCLC 21; DA; DAB;
DAC; PC 1; WLC
See also CDALB 1865-1917; DAM MST,
POET; DLB 1; SATA 29

Dickinson, Peter (Malcolm)
1927- . . . . CLC 12, 35
See also AAYA 9; CA 41-44R; CANR 31;
CLR 29; DLB 87, 161; JRDA; MAICYA;
SATA 5, 62

Dickson, Carr
See Carr, John Dickson

Dickson, Carter
See Carr, John Dickson

Diderot, Denis 1713-1784 . . . . LC 26

Didion, Joan 1934- . . . . . CLC 1, 3, 8, 14, 32
See also AITN 1; CA 5-8R; CANR 14;
CDALB 1968-1988; DAM NOV; DLB 2;
DLBY 81, 86; MTCW

Dietrich, Robert
See Hunt, E(verette) Howard, (Jr.)

Dillard, Annie 1945- . . . . CLC 9, 60
See also AAYA 6; CA 49-52; CANR 3, 43;
DAM NOV; DLBY 80; MTCW;
SATA 10

Dillard, R(ichard) H(enry) W(ilde)
1937- . . . . CLC 5
See also CA 21-24R; CAAS 7; CANR 10;
DLB 5

Dillon, Eilis 1920-1994 . . . . CLC 17
See also CA 9-12R; 147; CAAS 3; CANR 4,
38; CLR 26; MAICYA; SATA 2, 74;
SATA-Obit 83

Dimont, Penelope
See Mortimer, Penelope (Ruth)

Dinesen, Isak . . . . CLC 10, 29; SSC 7
See also Blixen, Karen (Christentze
Dinesen)

Ding Ling . . . . CLC 68
See also Chiang Pin-chin

Disch, Thomas M(ichael) 1940- . . . CLC 7, 36
See also AAYA 17; CA 21-24R; CAAS 4;
CANR 17, 36; CLR 18; DLB 8;
MAICYA; MTCW; SAAS 15; SATA 54

Disch, Tom
See Disch, Thomas M(ichael)

d'Isly, Georges
See Simenon, Georges (Jacques Christian)

Drummond de Andrade, Carlos
    1902-1987 . . . . **CLC 18**
    See also Andrade, Carlos Drummond de
    See also CA 132; 123

Drury, Allen (Stuart) 1918- . . . . **CLC 37**
    See also CA 57-60; CANR 18;
    INT CANR-18

Dryden, John
    1631-1700 . . . . **LC 3, 21; DA; DAB;**
                                    DAC; DC 3; WLC
    See also CDBLB 1660-1789; DAM DRAM,
    MST, POET; DLB 80, 101, 131

Duberman, Martin 1930- . . . . **CLC 8**
    See also CA 1-4R; CANR 2

Dubie, Norman (Evans) 1945- . . . . . . **CLC 36**
    See also CA 69-72; CANR 12; DLB 120

Du Bois, W(illiam) E(dward) B(urghardt)
    1868-1963 . . . . . . **CLC 1, 2, 13, 64; BLC;**
                                    DA; DAC; WLC
    See also BW 1; CA 85-88; CANR 34;
    CDALB 1865-1917; DAM MST, MULT,
    NOV; DLB 47, 50, 91; MTCW; SATA 42

Dubus, Andre 1936- . . . **CLC 13, 36; SSC 15**
    See also CA 21-24R; CANR 17; DLB 130;
    INT CANR-17

Duca Minimo
    See D'Annunzio, Gabriele

Ducharme, Rejean 1941- . . . . **CLC 74**
    See also DLB 60

Duclos, Charles Pinot 1704-1772 . . . . . **LC 1**

Dudek, Louis 1918- . . . . **CLC 11, 19**
    See also CA 45-48; CAAS 14; CANR 1;
    DLB 88

Duerrenmatt, Friedrich
    1921-1990 . . . . . . **CLC 1, 4, 8, 11, 15, 43**
    See also CA 17-20R; CANR 33;
    DAM DRAM; DLB 69, 124; MTCW

Duffy, Bruce (?)- . . . . **CLC 50**

Duffy, Maureen 1933- . . . . **CLC 37**
    See also CA 25-28R; CANR 33; DLB 14;
    MTCW

Dugan, Alan 1923- . . . . **CLC 2, 6**
    See also CA 81-84; DLB 5

du Gard, Roger Martin
    See Martin du Gard, Roger

Duhamel, Georges 1884-1966 . . . . **CLC 8**
    See also CA 81-84; 25-28R; CANR 35;
    DLB 65; MTCW

Dujardin, Edouard (Emile Louis)
    1861-1949 . . . . **TCLC 13**
    See also CA 109; DLB 123

Dumas, Alexandre (Davy de la Pailleterie)
    1802-1870 . . . . **NCLC 11; DA; DAB;**
                                    DAC; WLC
    See also DAM MST, NOV; DLB 119;
    SATA 18

Dumas, Alexandre
    1824-1895 . . . . **NCLC 9; DC 1**

Dumas, Claudine
    See Malzberg, Barry N(athaniel)

Dumas, Henry L. 1934-1968 . . . . . **CLC 6, 62**
    See also BW 1; CA 85-88; DLB 41

du Maurier, Daphne
    1907-1989 . . . . **CLC 6, 11, 59; DAB;**
                                    DAC; SSC 18
    See also CA 5-8R; 128; CANR 6;
    DAM MST, POP; MTCW; SATA 27;
    SATA-Obit 60

Dunbar, Paul Laurence
    1872-1906 . . . . . . **TCLC 2, 12; BLC; DA;**
                                    DAC; PC 5; SSC 8; WLC
    See also BW 1; CA 104; 124;
    CDALB 1865-1917; DAM MST, MULT,
    POET; DLB 50, 54, 78; SATA 34

Dunbar, William 1460(?)-1530(?) . . . . **LC 20**
    See also DLB 132, 146

Duncan, Lois 1934- . . . . **CLC 26**
    See also AAYA 4; CA 1-4R; CANR 2, 23,
    36; CLR 29; JRDA; MAICYA; SAAS 2;
    SATA 1, 36, 75

Duncan, Robert (Edward)
    1919-1988 . . . . **CLC 1, 2, 4, 7, 15, 41, 55;**
                                    PC 2
    See also CA 9-12R; 124; CANR 28;
    DAM POET; DLB 5, 16; MTCW

Duncan, Sara Jeannette
    1861-1922 . . . . **TCLC 60**
    See also DLB 92

Dunlap, William 1766-1839 . . . . **NCLC 2**
    See also DLB 30, 37, 59

Dunn, Douglas (Eaglesham)
    1942- . . . . **CLC 6, 40**
    See also CA 45-48; CANR 2, 33; DLB 40;
    MTCW

Dunn, Katherine (Karen) 1945- . . . . . **CLC 71**
    See also CA 33-36R

Dunn, Stephen 1939- . . . . **CLC 36**
    See also CA 33-36R; CANR 12, 48;
    DLB 105

Dunne, Finley Peter 1867-1936 . . . . **TCLC 28**
    See also CA 108; DLB 11, 23

Dunne, John Gregory 1932- . . . . **CLC 28**
    See also CA 25-28R; CANR 14, 50;
    DLBY 80

Dunsany, Edward John Moreton Drax
    Plunkett 1878-1957
    See Dunsany, Lord
    See also CA 104; 148; DLB 10

Dunsany, Lord . . . . **TCLC 2, 59**
    See also Dunsany, Edward John Moreton
    Drax Plunkett
    See also DLB 77, 153, 156

du Perry, Jean
    See Simenon, Georges (Jacques Christian)

Durang, Christopher (Ferdinand)
    1949- . . . . **CLC 27, 38**
    See also CA 105; CANR 50

Duras, Marguerite
    1914-1996 . . **CLC 3, 6, 11, 20, 34, 40, 68**
    See also CA 25-28R; 151; CANR 50;
    DLB 83; MTCW

Durban, (Rosa) Pam 1947- . . . . **CLC 39**
    See also CA 123

Durcan, Paul 1944- . . . . **CLC 43, 70**
    See also CA 134; DAM POET

Durkheim, Emile 1858-1917 . . . . . . **TCLC 55**

Durrell, Lawrence (George)
    1912-1990 . . . . **CLC 1, 4, 6, 8, 13, 27, 41**
    See also CA 9-12R; 132; CANR 40;
    CDBLB 1945-1960; DAM NOV; DLB 15,
    27; DLBY 90; MTCW

Durrenmatt, Friedrich
    See Duerrenmatt, Friedrich

Dutt, Toru 1856-1877 . . . . **NCLC 29**

Dwight, Timothy 1752-1817 . . . . . **NCLC 13**
    See also DLB 37

Dworkin, Andrea 1946- . . . . **CLC 43**
    See also CA 77-80; CAAS 21; CANR 16,
    39; INT CANR-16; MTCW

Dwyer, Deanna
    See Koontz, Dean R(ay)

Dwyer, K. R.
    See Koontz, Dean R(ay)

Dylan, Bob 1941- . . . . . . **CLC 3, 4, 6, 12, 77**
    See also CA 41-44R; DLB 16

Eagleton, Terence (Francis) 1943-
    See Eagleton, Terry
    See also CA 57-60; CANR 7, 23; MTCW

Eagleton, Terry . . . . **CLC 63**
    See also Eagleton, Terence (Francis)

Early, Jack
    See Scoppettone, Sandra

East, Michael
    See West, Morris L(anglo)

Eastaway, Edward
    See Thomas, (Philip) Edward

Eastlake, William (Derry) 1917- . . . . . **CLC 8**
    See also CA 5-8R; CAAS 1; CANR 5;
    DLB 6; INT CANR-5

Eastman, Charles A(lexander)
    1858-1939 . . . . **TCLC 55**
    See also DAM MULT; NNAL; YABC 1

Eberhart, Richard (Ghormley)
    1904- . . . . **CLC 3, 11, 19, 56**
    See also CA 1-4R; CANR 2;
    CDALB 1941-1968; DAM POET;
    DLB 48; MTCW

Eberstadt, Fernanda 1960- . . . . **CLC 39**
    See also CA 136

Echegaray (y Eizaguirre), Jose (Maria Waldo)
    1832-1916 . . . . **TCLC 4**
    See also CA 104; CANR 32; HW; MTCW

Echeverria, (Jose) Esteban (Antonino)
    1805-1851 . . . . **NCLC 18**

Echo
    See Proust, (Valentin-Louis-George-Eugene-)
    Marcel

Eckert, Allan W. 1931- . . . . **CLC 17**
    See also CA 13-16R; CANR 14, 45;
    INT CANR-14; SAAS 21; SATA 29;
    SATA-Brief 27

Eckhart, Meister 1260(?)-1328(?) . . **CMLC 9**
    See also DLB 115

Eckmar, F. R.
    See de Hartog, Jan

Eco, Umberto 1932- . . . . **CLC 28, 60**
    See also BEST 90:1; CA 77-80; CANR 12,
    33; DAM NOV, POP; MTCW

Eddison, E(ric) R(ucker)
1882-1945 .... **TCLC 15**
See also CA 109

Edel, (Joseph) Leon 1907- ...... **CLC 29, 34**
See also CA 1-4R; CANR 1, 22; DLB 103;
INT CANR-22

Eden, Emily 1797-1869 .... **NCLC 10**

Edgar, David 1948-............... **CLC 42**
See also CA 57-60; CANR 12;
DAM DRAM; DLB 13; MTCW

Edgerton, Clyde (Carlyle) 1944- .... **CLC 39**
See also AAYA 17; CA 118; 134; INT 134

Edgeworth, Maria 1768-1849... **NCLC 1, 51**
See also DLB 116, 159, 163; SATA 21

Edmonds, Paul
See Kuttner, Henry

Edmonds, Walter D(umaux) 1903- .. **CLC 35**
See also CA 5-8R; CANR 2; DLB 9;
MAICYA; SAAS 4; SATA 1, 27

Edmondson, Wallace
See Ellison, Harlan (Jay)

Edson, Russell .... **CLC 13**
See also CA 33-36R

Edwards, Bronwen Elizabeth
See Rose, Wendy

Edwards, G(erald) B(asil)
1899-1976 .... **CLC 25**
See also CA 110

Edwards, Gus 1939-.............. **CLC 43**
See also CA 108; INT 108

Edwards, Jonathan
1703-1758 .... **LC 7; DA; DAC**
See also DAM MST; DLB 24

Efron, Marina Ivanovna Tsvetaeva
See Tsvetaeva (Efron), Marina (Ivanovna)

Ehle, John (Marsden, Jr.) 1925-.... **CLC 27**
See also CA 9-12R

Ehrenbourg, Ilya (Grigoryevich)
See Ehrenburg, Ilya (Grigoryevich)

Ehrenburg, Ilya (Grigoryevich)
1891-1967 .... **CLC 18, 34, 62**
See also CA 102; 25-28R

Ehrenburg, Ilyo (Grigoryevich)
See Ehrenburg, Ilya (Grigoryevich)

Eich, Guenter 1907-1972 .... **CLC 15**
See also CA 111; 93-96; DLB 69, 124

Eichendorff, Joseph Freiherr von
1788-1857 .... **NCLC 8**
See also DLB 90

Eigner, Larry .... **CLC 9**
See also Eigner, Laurence (Joel)
See also CAAS 23; DLB 5

Eigner, Laurence (Joel) 1927-1996
See Eigner, Larry
See also CA 9-12R; 151; CANR 6

Eiseley, Loren Corey 1907-1977 ..... **CLC 7**
See also AAYA 5; CA 1-4R; 73-76;
CANR 6

Eisenstadt, Jill 1963- .... **CLC 50**
See also CA 140

Eisenstein, Sergei (Mikhailovich)
1898-1948 .... **TCLC 57**
See also CA 114; 149

Eisner, Simon
See Kornbluth, C(yril) M.

Ekeloef, (Bengt) Gunnar
1907-1968 .... **CLC 27**
See also CA 123; 25-28R; DAM POET

Ekelof, (Bengt) Gunnar
See Ekeloef, (Bengt) Gunnar

Ekwensi, C. O. D.
See Ekwensi, Cyprian (Odiatu Duaka)

Ekwensi, Cyprian (Odiatu Duaka)
1921- .... **CLC 4; BLC**
See also BW 2; CA 29-32R; CANR 18, 42;
DAM MULT; DLB 117; MTCW;
SATA 66

Elaine .... **TCLC 18**
See also Leverson, Ada

El Crummo
See Crumb, R(obert)

Elia
See Lamb, Charles

Eliade, Mircea 1907-1986 .... **CLC 19**
See also CA 65-68; 119; CANR 30; MTCW

Eliot, A. D.
See Jewett, (Theodora) Sarah Orne

Eliot, Alice
See Jewett, (Theodora) Sarah Orne

Eliot, Dan
See Silverberg, Robert

Eliot, George
1819-1880 ..... **NCLC 4, 13, 23, 41, 49;**
DA; DAB; DAC; WLC
See also CDBLB 1832-1890; DAM MST,
NOV; DLB 21, 35, 55

Eliot, John 1604-1690 .... **LC 5**
See also DLB 24

Eliot, T(homas) S(tearns)
1888-1965 ..... **CLC 1, 2, 3, 6, 9, 10, 13,**
15, 24, 34, 41, 55, 57; DA; DAB; DAC;
PC 5; WLC 2
See also CA 5-8R; 25-28R; CANR 41;
CDALB 1929-1941; DAM DRAM, MST,
POET; DLB 7, 10, 45, 63; DLBY 88;
MTCW

Elizabeth 1866-1941............. **TCLC 41**

Elkin, Stanley L(awrence)
1930-1995 ...... **CLC 4, 6, 9, 14, 27, 51,**
91; SSC 12
See also CA 9-12R; 148; CANR 8, 46;
DAM NOV, POP; DLB 2, 28; DLBY 80;
INT CANR-8; MTCW

Elledge, Scott .... **CLC 34**

Elliott, Don
See Silverberg, Robert

Elliott, George P(aul) 1918-1980..... **CLC 2**
See also CA 1-4R; 97-100; CANR 2

Elliott, Janice 1931-.............. **CLC 47**
See also CA 13-16R; CANR 8, 29; DLB 14

Elliott, Sumner Locke 1917-1991 ... **CLC 38**
See also CA 5-8R; 134; CANR 2, 21

Elliott, William
See Bradbury, Ray (Douglas)

Ellis, A. E. .... **CLC 7**

Ellis, Alice Thomas .... **CLC 40**
See also Haycraft, Anna

Ellis, Bret Easton 1964-........ **CLC 39, 71**
See also AAYA 2; CA 118; 123; CANR 51;
DAM POP; INT 123

Ellis, (Henry) Havelock
1859-1939 .... **TCLC 14**
See also CA 109

Ellis, Landon
See Ellison, Harlan (Jay)

Ellis, Trey 1962-................. **CLC 55**
See also CA 146

Ellison, Harlan (Jay)
1934- .... **CLC 1, 13, 42; SSC 14**
See also CA 5-8R; CANR 5, 46;
DAM POP; DLB 8; INT CANR-5;
MTCW

Ellison, Ralph (Waldo)
1914-1994 .... **CLC 1, 3, 11, 54, 86;**
BLC; DA; DAB; DAC; WLC
See also BW 1; CA 9-12R; 145; CANR 24;
CDALB 1941-1968; DAM MST, MULT,
NOV; DLB 2, 76; DLBY 94; MTCW

Ellmann, Lucy (Elizabeth) 1956-.... **CLC 61**
See also CA 128

Ellmann, Richard (David)
1918-1987 .... **CLC 50**
See also BEST 89:2; CA 1-4R; 122;
CANR 2, 28; DLB 103; DLBY 87;
MTCW

Elman, Richard 1934-............. **CLC 19**
See also CA 17-20R; CAAS 3; CANR 47

Elron
See Hubbard, L(afayette) Ron(ald)

Eluard, Paul.................... **TCLC 7, 41**
See also Grindel, Eugene

Elyot, Sir Thomas 1490(?)-1546 ..... **LC 11**

Elytis, Odysseus 1911-......... **CLC 15, 49**
See also CA 102; DAM POET; MTCW

Emecheta, (Florence Onye) Buchi
1944- .... **CLC 14, 48; BLC**
See also BW 2; CA 81-84; CANR 27;
DAM MULT; DLB 117; MTCW;
SATA 66

Emerson, Ralph Waldo
1803-1882 ..... **NCLC 1, 38; DA; DAB;**
DAC; WLC
See also CDALB 1640-1865; DAM MST,
POET; DLB 1, 59, 73

Eminescu, Mihail 1850-1889 ..... **NCLC 33**

Empson, William
1906-1984 .... **CLC 3, 8, 19, 33, 34**
See also CA 17-20R; 112; CANR 31;
DLB 20; MTCW

Enchi Fumiko (Ueda) 1905-1986.... **CLC 31**
See also CA 129; 121

Ende, Michael (Andreas Helmuth)
1929-1995 .... **CLC 31**
See also CA 118; 124; 149; CANR 36;
CLR 14; DLB 75; MAICYA; SATA 61;
SATA-Brief 42; SATA-Obit 86

Endo, Shusaku 1923- ..... **CLC 7, 14, 19, 54**
See also CA 29-32R; CANR 21;
DAM NOV; MTCW

Engel, Marian 1933-1985......... **CLC 36**
See also CA 25-28R; CANR 12; DLB 53;
INT CANR-12

Engelhardt, Frederick
See Hubbard, L(afayette) Ron(ald)

Enright, D(ennis) J(oseph)
1920- .... CLC **4, 8, 31**
See also CA 1-4R; CANR 1, 42; DLB 27;
SATA 25

Enzensberger, Hans Magnus
1929- .... CLC **43**
See also CA 116; 119

Ephron, Nora 1941- .... CLC **17, 31**
See also AITN 2; CA 65-68; CANR 12, 39

Epsilon
See Betjeman, John

Epstein, Daniel Mark 1948- .... CLC **7**
See also CA 49-52; CANR 2

Epstein, Jacob 1956- .... CLC **19**
See also CA 114

Epstein, Joseph 1937- .... CLC **39**
See also CA 112; 119; CANR 50

Epstein, Leslie 1938- .... CLC **27**
See also CA 73-76; CAAS 12; CANR 23

Equiano, Olaudah
1745(?)-1797 .... LC **16; BLC**
See also DAM MULT; DLB 37, 50

Erasmus, Desiderius 1469(?)-1536.... LC **16**

Erdman, Paul E(mil) 1932- .... CLC **25**
See also AITN 1; CA 61-64; CANR 13, 43

Erdrich, Louise 1954-.......... CLC **39, 54**
See also AAYA 10; BEST 89:1; CA 114;
CANR 41; DAM MULT, NOV, POP;
DLB 152; MTCW; NNAL

Erenburg, Ilya (Grigoryevich)
See Ehrenburg, Ilya (Grigoryevich)

Erickson, Stephen Michael 1950-
See Erickson, Steve
See also CA 129

Erickson, Steve .... CLC **64**
See also Erickson, Stephen Michael

Ericson, Walter
See Fast, Howard (Melvin)

Eriksson, Buntel
See Bergman, (Ernst) Ingmar

Ernaux, Annie 1940- .... CLC **88**
See also CA 147

Eschenbach, Wolfram von
See Wolfram von Eschenbach

Eseki, Bruno
See Mphahlele, Ezekiel

Esenin, Sergei (Alexandrovich)
1895-1925 .... TCLC **4**
See also CA 104

Eshleman, Clayton 1935- .... CLC **7**
See also CA 33-36R; CAAS 6; DLB 5

Espriella, Don Manuel Alvarez
See Southey, Robert

Espriu, Salvador 1913-1985......... CLC **9**
See also CA 115; DLB 134

Espronceda, Jose de 1808-1842... NCLC **39**

Esse, James
See Stephens, James

Esterbrook, Tom
See Hubbard, L(afayette) Ron(ald)

Estleman, Loren D. 1952- .... CLC **48**
See also CA 85-88; CANR 27; DAM NOV,
POP; INT CANR-27; MTCW

Eugenides, Jeffrey 1960(?)- .... CLC **81**
See also CA 144

Euripides c. 485B.C.-406B.C. .... DC **4**
See also DA; DAB; DAC; DAM DRAM,
MST

Evan, Evin
See Faust, Frederick (Schiller)

Evans, Evan
See Faust, Frederick (Schiller)

Evans, Marian
See Eliot, George

Evans, Mary Ann
See Eliot, George

Evarts, Esther
See Benson, Sally

Everett, Percival L. 1956- .... CLC **57**
See also BW 2; CA 129

Everson, R(onald) G(ilmour)
1903- .... CLC **27**
See also CA 17-20R; DLB 88

Everson, William (Oliver)
1912-1994 .... CLC **1, 5, 14**
See also CA 9-12R; 145; CANR 20; DLB 5,
16; MTCW

Evtushenko, Evgenii Aleksandrovich
See Yevtushenko, Yevgeny (Alexandrovich)

Ewart, Gavin (Buchanan)
1916-1995 .... CLC **13, 46**
See also CA 89-92; 150; CANR 17, 46;
DLB 40; MTCW

Ewers, Hanns Heinz 1871-1943 ... TCLC **12**
See also CA 109; 149

Ewing, Frederick R.
See Sturgeon, Theodore (Hamilton)

Exley, Frederick (Earl)
1929-1992 .... CLC **6, 11**
See also AITN 2; CA 81-84; 138; DLB 143;
DLBY 81

Eynhardt, Guillermo
See Quiroga, Horacio (Sylvestre)

Ezekiel, Nissim 1924-............. CLC **61**
See also CA 61-64

Ezekiel, Tish O'Dowd 1943- .... CLC **34**
See also CA 129

Fadeyev, A.
See Bulgya, Alexander Alexandrovich

Fadeyev, Alexander............... TCLC **53**
See also Bulgya, Alexander Alexandrovich

Fagen, Donald 1948-............. CLC **26**

Fainzilberg, Ilya Arnoldovich 1897-1937
See Ilf, Ilya
See also CA 120

Fair, Ronald L. 1932-............. CLC **18**
See also BW 1; CA 69-72; CANR 25;
DLB 33

Fairbairns, Zoe (Ann) 1948- .... CLC **32**
See also CA 103; CANR 21

Falco, Gian
See Papini, Giovanni

Falconer, James
See Kirkup, James

Falconer, Kenneth
See Kornbluth, C(yril) M.

Falkland, Samuel
See Heijermans, Herman

Fallaci, Oriana 1930-............. CLC **11**
See also CA 77-80; CANR 15; MTCW

Faludy, George 1913-............. CLC **42**
See also CA 21-24R

Faludy, Gyoergy
See Faludy, George

Fanon, Frantz 1925-1961..... CLC **74; BLC**
See also BW 1; CA 116; 89-92;
DAM MULT

Fanshawe, Ann 1625-1680.......... LC **11**

Fante, John (Thomas) 1911-1983 ... CLC **60**
See also CA 69-72; 109; CANR 23;
DLB 130; DLBY 83

Farah, Nuruddin 1945-....... CLC **53; BLC**
See also BW 2; CA 106; DAM MULT;
DLB 125

Fargue, Leon-Paul 1876(?)-1947 ... TCLC **11**
See also CA 109

Farigoule, Louis
See Romains, Jules

Farina, Richard 1936(?)-1966 .... CLC **9**
See also CA 81-84; 25-28R

Farley, Walter (Lorimer)
1915-1989 .... CLC **17**
See also CA 17-20R; CANR 8, 29; DLB 22;
JRDA; MAICYA; SATA 2, 43

Farmer, Philip Jose 1918-....... CLC **1, 19**
See also CA 1-4R; CANR 4, 35; DLB 8;
MTCW

Farquhar, George 1677-1707........ LC **21**
See also DAM DRAM; DLB 84

Farrell, J(ames) G(ordon)
1935-1979 .... CLC **6**
See also CA 73-76; 89-92; CANR 36;
DLB 14; MTCW

Farrell, James T(homas)
1904-1979 .... CLC **1, 4, 8, 11, 66**
See also CA 5-8R; 89-92; CANR 9; DLB 4,
9, 86; DLBD 2; MTCW

Farren, Richard J.
See Betjeman, John

Farren, Richard M.
See Betjeman, John

Fassbinder, Rainer Werner
1946-1982 .... CLC **20**
See also CA 93-96; 106; CANR 31

Fast, Howard (Melvin) 1914- ...... CLC **23**
See also AAYA 16; CA 1-4R; CAAS 18;
CANR 1, 33; DAM NOV; DLB 9;
INT CANR-33; SATA 7

Faulcon, Robert
See Holdstock, Robert P.

Faulkner, William (Cuthbert)
1897-1962 ..... CLC **1, 3, 6, 8, 9, 11, 14,
18, 28, 52, 68; DA; DAB; DAC; SSC 1;
WLC**
See also AAYA 7; CA 81-84; CANR 33;
CDALB 1929-1941; DAM MST, NOV;
DLB 9, 11, 44, 102; DLBD 2; DLBY 86;
MTCW

Fo, Dario 1926-.................. **CLC 32**
See also CA 116; 128; DAM DRAM;
MTCW

Fogarty, Jonathan Titulescu Esq.
See Farrell, James T(homas)

Folke, Will
See Bloch, Robert (Albert)

Follett, Ken(neth Martin) 1949- .... **CLC 18**
See also AAYA 6; BEST 89:4; CA 81-84;
CANR 13, 33; DAM NOV, POP;
DLB 87; DLBY 81; INT CANR-33;
MTCW

Fontane, Theodor 1819-1898 ..... **NCLC 26**
See also DLB 129

Foote, Horton 1916-.......... **CLC 51, 91**
See also CA 73-76; CANR 34, 51;
DAM DRAM; DLB 26; INT CANR-34

Foote, Shelby 1916- .... **CLC 75**
See also CA 5-8R; CANR 3, 45;
DAM NOV, POP; DLB 2, 17

Forbes, Esther 1891-1967......... **CLC 12**
See also AAYA 17; CA 13-14; 25-28R;
CAP 1; CLR 27; DLB 22; JRDA;
MAICYA; SATA 2

Forche, Carolyn (Louise)
1950- .... **CLC 25, 83, 86; PC 10**
See also CA 109; 117; CANR 50;
DAM POET; DLB 5; INT 117

Ford, Elbur
See Hibbert, Eleanor Alice Burford

Ford, Ford Madox
1873-1939 ...... **TCLC 1, 15, 39, 57**
See also CA 104; 132; CDBLB 1914-1945;
DAM NOV; DLB 162; MTCW

Ford, John 1895-1973............. **CLC 16**
See also CA 45-48

Ford, Richard 1944-.............. **CLC 46**
See also CA 69-72; CANR 11, 47

Ford, Webster
See Masters, Edgar Lee

Foreman, Richard 1937-.......... **CLC 50**
See also CA 65-68; CANR 32

Forester, C(ecil) S(cott)
1899-1966 .... **CLC 35**
See also CA 73-76; 25-28R; SATA 13

Forez
See Mauriac, Francois (Charles)

Forman, James Douglas 1932-...... **CLC 21**
See also AAYA 17; CA 9-12R; CANR 4,
19, 42; JRDA; MAICYA; SATA 8, 70

Fornes, Maria Irene 1930-...... **CLC 39, 61**
See also CA 25-28R; CANR 28; DLB 7;
HW; INT CANR-28; MTCW

Forrest, Leon 1937- .... **CLC 4**
See also BW 2; CA 89-92; CAAS 7;
CANR 25; DLB 33

Forster, E(dward) M(organ)
1879-1970 ..... **CLC 1, 2, 3, 4, 9, 10, 13,
15, 22, 45, 77; DA; DAB; DAC; WLC**
See also AAYA 2; CA 13-14; 25-28R;
CANR 45; CAP 1; CDBLB 1914-1945;
DAM MST, NOV; DLB 34, 98, 162;
DLBD 10; MTCW; SATA 57

Forster, John 1812-1876 .... **NCLC 11**
See also DLB 144

Forsyth, Frederick 1938-...... **CLC 2, 5, 36**
See also BEST 89:4; CA 85-88; CANR 38;
DAM NOV, POP; DLB 87; MTCW

Forten, Charlotte L. .... **TCLC 16; BLC**
See also Grimke, Charlotte L(ottie) Forten
See also DLB 50

Foscolo, Ugo 1778-1827.......... **NCLC 8**

Fosse, Bob .... **CLC 20**
See also Fosse, Robert Louis

Fosse, Robert Louis 1927-1987
See Fosse, Bob
See also CA 110; 123

Foster, Stephen Collins
1826-1864 .... **NCLC 26**

Foucault, Michel
1926-1984 .... **CLC 31, 34, 69**
See also CA 105; 113; CANR 34; MTCW

Fouque, Friedrich (Heinrich Karl) de la Motte
1777-1843 .... **NCLC 2**
See also DLB 90

Fourier, Charles 1772-1837 ...... **NCLC 51**

Fournier, Henri Alban 1886-1914
See Alain-Fournier
See also CA 104

Fournier, Pierre 1916-.......... **CLC 11**
See also Gascar, Pierre
See also CA 89-92; CANR 16, 40

Fowles, John
1926- ...... **CLC 1, 2, 3, 4, 6, 9, 10, 15,
33, 87; DAB; DAC**
See also CA 5-8R; CANR 25; CDBLB 1960
to Present; DAM MST; DLB 14, 139;
MTCW; SATA 22

Fox, Paula 1923-................ **CLC 2, 8**
See also AAYA 3; CA 73-76; CANR 20,
36; CLR 1; DLB 52; JRDA; MAICYA;
MTCW; SATA 17, 60

Fox, William Price (Jr.) 1926- ..... **CLC 22**
See also CA 17-20R; CAAS 19; CANR 11;
DLB 2; DLBY 81

Foxe, John 1516(?)-1587 .... **LC 14**

Frame, Janet .... **CLC 2, 3, 6, 22, 66**
See also Clutha, Janet Paterson Frame

France, Anatole .... **TCLC 9**
See also Thibault, Jacques Anatole Francois
See also DLB 123

Francis, Claude 19(?)- .... **CLC 50**

Francis, Dick 1920- .... **CLC 2, 22, 42**
See also AAYA 5; BEST 89:3; CA 5-8R;
CANR 9, 42; CDBLB 1960 to Present;
DAM POP; DLB 87; INT CANR-9;
MTCW

Francis, Robert (Churchill)
1901-1987 .... **CLC 15**
See also CA 1-4R; 123; CANR 1

Frank, Anne(lies Marie)
1929-1945 .... **TCLC 17; DA; DAB;
DAC; WLC**
See also AAYA 12; CA 113; 133;
DAM MST; MTCW; SATA 87;
SATA-Brief 42

Frank, Elizabeth 1945-........... **CLC 39**
See also CA 121; 126; INT 126

Frankl, Viktor E(mil) 1905-........ **CLC 93**
See also CA 65-68

Franklin, Benjamin
See Hasek, Jaroslav (Matej Frantisek)

Franklin, Benjamin
1706-1790 ..... **LC 25; DA; DAB; DAC**
See also CDALB 1640-1865; DAM MST;
DLB 24, 43, 73

Franklin, (Stella Maraia Sarah) Miles
1879-1954 .... **TCLC 7**
See also CA 104

Fraser, (Lady) Antonia (Pakenham)
1932- .... **CLC 32**
See also CA 85-88; CANR 44; MTCW;
SATA-Brief 32

Fraser, George MacDonald 1925-.... **CLC 7**
See also CA 45-48; CANR 2, 48

Fraser, Sylvia 1935-............. **CLC 64**
See also CA 45-48; CANR 1, 16

Frayn, Michael 1933-...... **CLC 3, 7, 31, 47**
See also CA 5-8R; CANR 30;
DAM DRAM, NOV; DLB 13, 14;
MTCW

Fraze, Candida (Merrill) 1945-..... **CLC 50**
See also CA 126

Frazer, J(ames) G(eorge)
1854-1941 .... **TCLC 32**
See also CA 118

Frazer, Robert Caine
See Creasey, John

Frazer, Sir James George
See Frazer, J(ames) G(eorge)

Frazier, Ian 1951-................ **CLC 46**
See also CA 130

Frederic, Harold 1856-1898...... **NCLC 10**
See also DLB 12, 23; DLBD 13

Frederick, John
See Faust, Frederick (Schiller)

Frederick the Great 1712-1786 ...... **LC 14**

Fredro, Aleksander 1793-1876..... **NCLC 8**

Freeling, Nicolas 1927- .... **CLC 38**
See also CA 49-52; CAAS 12; CANR 1, 17,
50; DLB 87

Freeman, Douglas Southall
1886-1953 .... **TCLC 11**
See also CA 109; DLB 17

Freeman, Judith 1946-............ **CLC 55**
See also CA 148

Freeman, Mary Eleanor Wilkins
1852-1930 .... **TCLC 9; SSC 1**
See also CA 106; DLB 12, 78

Freeman, R(ichard) Austin
1862-1943 .... **TCLC 21**
See also CA 113; DLB 70

French, Albert 1943- .... **CLC 86**

French, Marilyn 1929-...... **CLC 10, 18, 60**
See also CA 69-72; CANR 3, 31;
DAM DRAM, NOV, POP;
INT CANR-31; MTCW

French, Paul
See Asimov, Isaac

Freneau, Philip Morin 1752-1832 .. **NCLC 1**
See also DLB 37, 43

Freud, Sigmund 1856-1939 .... **TCLC 52**
See also CA 115; 133; MTCW

Friedan, Betty (Naomi) 1921- ...... **CLC 74**
See also CA 65-68; CANR 18, 45; MTCW

Friedlaender, Saul 1932- .... **CLC 90**
See also CA 117; 130

Friedman, B(ernard) H(arper)
1926- .... **CLC 7**
See also CA 1-4R; CANR 3, 48

Friedman, Bruce Jay 1930- .... **CLC 3, 5, 56**
See also CA 9-12R; CANR 25; DLB 2, 28;
INT CANR-25

Friel, Brian 1929- .... **CLC 5, 42, 59**
See also CA 21-24R; CANR 33; DLB 13;
MTCW

Friis-Baastad, Babbis Ellinor
1921-1970 .... **CLC 12**
See also CA 17-20R; 134; SATA 7

Frisch, Max (Rudolf)
1911-1991 ..... **CLC 3, 9, 14, 18, 32, 44**
See also CA 85-88; 134; CANR 32;
DAM DRAM, NOV; DLB 69, 124;
MTCW

Fromentin, Eugene (Samuel Auguste)
1820-1876 .... **NCLC 10**
See also DLB 123

Frost, Frederick
See Faust, Frederick (Schiller)

Frost, Robert (Lee)
1874-1963 .... **CLC 1, 3, 4, 9, 10, 13, 15,
26, 34, 44; DA; DAB; DAC; PC 1; WLC**
See also CA 89-92; CANR 33;
CDALB 1917-1929; DAM MST, POET;
DLB 54; DLBD 7; MTCW; SATA 14

Froude, James Anthony
1818-1894 .... **NCLC 43**
See also DLB 18, 57, 144

Froy, Herald
See Waterhouse, Keith (Spencer)

Fry, Christopher 1907- ...... **CLC 2, 10, 14**
See also CA 17-20R; CAAS 23; CANR 9,
30; DAM DRAM; DLB 13; MTCW;
SATA 66

Frye, (Herman) Northrop
1912-1991 .... **CLC 24, 70**
See also CA 5-8R; 133; CANR 8, 37;
DLB 67, 68; MTCW

Fuchs, Daniel 1909-1993 .... **CLC 8, 22**
See also CA 81-84; 142; CAAS 5;
CANR 40; DLB 9, 26, 28; DLBY 93

Fuchs, Daniel 1934- .... **CLC 34**
See also CA 37-40R; CANR 14, 48

Fuentes, Carlos
1928- ...... **CLC 3, 8, 10, 13, 22, 41, 60;
DA; DAB; DAC; HLC; WLC**
See also AAYA 4; AITN 2; CA 69-72;
CANR 10, 32; DAM MST, MULT,
NOV; DLB 113; HW; MTCW

Fuentes, Gregorio Lopez y
See Lopez y Fuentes, Gregorio

Fugard, (Harold) Athol
1932- .... **CLC 5, 9, 14, 25, 40, 80; DC 3**
See also AAYA 17; CA 85-88; CANR 32;
DAM DRAM; MTCW

Fugard, Sheila 1932- .... **CLC 48**
See also CA 125

Fuller, Charles (H., Jr.)
1939- .... **CLC 25; BLC; DC 1**
See also BW 2; CA 108; 112;
DAM DRAM, MULT; DLB 38;
INT 112; MTCW

Fuller, John (Leopold) 1937- .... **CLC 62**
See also CA 21-24R; CANR 9, 44; DLB 40

Fuller, Margaret .... **NCLC 5, 50**
See also Ossoli, Sarah Margaret (Fuller
marchesa d')

Fuller, Roy (Broadbent)
1912-1991 .... **CLC 4, 28**
See also CA 5-8R; 135; CAAS 10; DLB 15,
20; SATA 87

Fulton, Alice 1952- .... **CLC 52**
See also CA 116

Furphy, Joseph 1843-1912 .... **TCLC 25**

Fussell, Paul 1924- .... **CLC 74**
See also BEST 90:1; CA 17-20R; CANR 8,
21, 35; INT CANR-21; MTCW

Futabatei, Shimei 1864-1909 ..... **TCLC 44**

Futrelle, Jacques 1875-1912 ..... **TCLC 19**
See also CA 113

Gaboriau, Emile 1835-1873 ...... **NCLC 14**

Gadda, Carlo Emilio 1893-1973 .... **CLC 11**
See also CA 89-92

Gaddis, William
1922- ..... **CLC 1, 3, 6, 8, 10, 19, 43, 86**
See also CA 17-20R; CANR 21, 48; DLB 2;
MTCW

Gaines, Ernest J(ames)
1933- .... **CLC 3, 11, 18, 86; BLC**
See also AITN 1; BW 2; CA 9-12R;
CANR 6, 24, 42; CDALB 1968-1988;
DAM MULT; DLB 2, 33, 152; DLBY 80;
MTCW; SATA 86

Gaitskill, Mary 1954- .... **CLC 69**
See also CA 128

Galdos, Benito Perez
See Perez Galdos, Benito

Gale, Zona 1874-1938 .... **TCLC 7**
See also CA 105; DAM DRAM; DLB 9, 78

Galeano, Eduardo (Hughes) 1940- ... **CLC 72**
See also CA 29-32R; CANR 13, 32; HW

Galiano, Juan Valera y Alcala
See Valera y Alcala-Galiano, Juan

Gallagher, Tess 1943- .... **CLC 18, 63; PC 9**
See also CA 106; DAM POET; DLB 120

Gallant, Mavis
1922- ...... **CLC 7, 18, 38; DAC; SSC 5**
See also CA 69-72; CANR 29; DAM MST;
DLB 53; MTCW

Gallant, Roy A(rthur) 1924- .... **CLC 17**
See also CA 5-8R; CANR 4, 29; CLR 30;
MAICYA; SATA 4, 68

Gallico, Paul (William) 1897-1976 ... **CLC 2**
See also AITN 1; CA 5-8R; 69-72;
CANR 23; DLB 9; MAICYA; SATA 13

Gallup, Ralph
See Whitemore, Hugh (John)

Galsworthy, John
1867-1933 ...... **TCLC 1, 45; DA; DAB;
DAC; SSC 22; WLC 2**
See also CA 104; 141; CDBLB 1890-1914;
DAM DRAM, MST, NOV; DLB 10, 34,
98, 162

Galt, John 1779-1839 .... **NCLC 1**
See also DLB 99, 116, 159

Galvin, James 1951- .... **CLC 38**
See also CA 108; CANR 26

Gamboa, Federico 1864-1939 ...... **TCLC 36**

Gandhi, M. K.
See Gandhi, Mohandas Karamchand

Gandhi, Mahatma
See Gandhi, Mohandas Karamchand

Gandhi, Mohandas Karamchand
1869-1948 .... **TCLC 59**
See also CA 121; 132; DAM MULT;
MTCW

Gann, Ernest Kellogg 1910-1991 .... **CLC 23**
See also AITN 1; CA 1-4R; 136; CANR 1

Garcia, Cristina 1958- .... **CLC 76**
See also CA 141

Garcia Lorca, Federico
1898-1936 ... **TCLC 1, 7, 49; DA; DAB;
DAC; DC 2; HLC; PC 3; WLC**
See also CA 104; 131; DAM DRAM, MST,
MULT, POET; DLB 108; HW; MTCW

Garcia Marquez, Gabriel (Jose)
1928- .... **CLC 2, 3, 8, 10, 15, 27, 47, 55,
68; DA; DAB; DAC; HLC; SSC 8; WLC**
See also AAYA 3; BEST 89:1, 90:4;
CA 33-36R; CANR 10, 28, 50;
DAM MST, MULT, NOV, POP;
DLB 113; HW; MTCW

Gard, Janice
See Latham, Jean Lee

Gard, Roger Martin du
See Martin du Gard, Roger

Gardam, Jane 1928- .... **CLC 43**
See also CA 49-52; CANR 2, 18, 33;
CLR 12; DLB 14, 161; MAICYA;
MTCW; SAAS 9; SATA 39, 76;
SATA-Brief 28

Gardner, Herb(ert) 1934- .... **CLC 44**
See also CA 149

Gardner, John (Champlin), Jr.
1933-1982 ..... **CLC 2, 3, 5, 7, 8, 10, 18,
28, 34; SSC 7**
See also AITN 1; CA 65-68; 107;
CANR 33; DAM NOV, POP; DLB 2;
DLBY 82; MTCW; SATA 40;
SATA-Obit 31

Gardner, John (Edmund) 1926- ..... **CLC 30**
See also CA 103; CANR 15; DAM POP;
MTCW

Gardner, Noel
See Kuttner, Henry

Gardons, S. S.
See Snodgrass, W(illiam) D(e Witt)

Garfield, Leon 1921- .... **CLC 12**
See also AAYA 8; CA 17-20R; CANR 38,
41; CLR 21; DLB 161; JRDA; MAICYA;
SATA 1, 32, 76

Garland, (Hannibal) Hamlin
  1860-1940 . . . . **TCLC 3; SSC 18**
  See also CA 104; DLB 12, 71, 78

Garneau, (Hector de) Saint-Denys
  1912-1943 . . . .**TCLC 13**
  See also CA 111; DLB 88

Garner, Alan 1934- . . . .**CLC 17; DAB**
  See also CA 73-76; CANR 15; CLR 20;
  DAM POP; DLB 161; MAICYA;
  MTCW; SATA 18, 69

Garner, Hugh 1913-1979 . . . . **CLC 13**
  See also CA 69-72; CANR 31; DLB 68

Garnett, David 1892-1981 . . . . **CLC 3**
  See also CA 5-8R; 103; CANR 17; DLB 34

Garos, Stephanie
  See Katz, Steve

Garrett, George (Palmer)
  1929- . . . .**CLC 3, 11, 51**
  See also CA 1-4R; CAAS 5; CANR 1, 42;
  DLB 2, 5, 130, 152; DLBY 83

Garrick, David 1717-1779 . . . . **LC 15**
  See also DAM DRAM; DLB 84

Garrigue, Jean 1914-1972 . . . . **CLC 2, 8**
  See also CA 5-8R; 37-40R; CANR 20

Garrison, Frederick
  See Sinclair, Upton (Beall)

Garth, Will
  See Hamilton, Edmond; Kuttner, Henry

Garvey, Marcus (Moziah, Jr.)
  1887-1940 . . . .**TCLC 41; BLC**
  See also BW 1; CA 120; 124; DAM MULT

Gary, Romain . . . . **CLC 25**
  See also Kacew, Romain
  See also DLB 83

Gascar, Pierre . . . . **CLC 11**
  See also Fournier, Pierre

Gascoyne, David (Emery) 1916- . . . . **CLC 45**
  See also CA 65-68; CANR 10, 28; DLB 20;
  MTCW

Gaskell, Elizabeth Cleghorn
  1810-1865 . . . .**NCLC 5; DAB**
  See also CDBLB 1832-1890; DAM MST;
  DLB 21, 144, 159

Gass, William H(oward)
  1924- . . . **CLC 1, 2, 8, 11, 15, 39; SSC 12**
  See also CA 17-20R; CANR 30; DLB 2;
  MTCW

Gasset, Jose Ortega y
  See Ortega y Gasset, Jose

Gates, Henry Louis, Jr. 1950- . . . . . . **CLC 65**
  See also BW 2; CA 109; CANR 25;
  DAM MULT; DLB 67

Gautier, Theophile
  1811-1872 . . . . **NCLC 1; SSC 20**
  See also DAM POET; DLB 119

Gawsworth, John
  See Bates, H(erbert) E(rnest)

Gay, Oliver
  See Gogarty, Oliver St. John

Gaye, Marvin (Penze) 1939-1984 . . . **CLC 26**
  See also CA 112

Gebler, Carlo (Ernest) 1954- . . . . **CLC 39**
  See also CA 119; 133

Gee, Maggie (Mary) 1948- . . . . **CLC 57**
  See also CA 130

Gee, Maurice (Gough) 1931- . . . . **CLC 29**
  See also CA 97-100; SATA 46

Gelbart, Larry (Simon) 1923- . . **CLC 21, 61**
  See also CA 73-76; CANR 45

Gelber, Jack 1932- . . . . **CLC 1, 6, 14, 79**
  See also CA 1-4R; CANR 2; DLB 7

Gellhorn, Martha (Ellis) 1908- . . **CLC 14, 60**
  See also CA 77-80; CANR 44; DLBY 82

Genet, Jean
  1910-1986 . . . **CLC 1, 2, 5, 10, 14, 44, 46**
  See also CA 13-16R; CANR 18;
  DAM DRAM; DLB 72; DLBY 86;
  MTCW

Gent, Peter 1942- . . . . **CLC 29**
  See also AITN 1; CA 89-92; DLBY 82

Gentlewoman in New England, A
  See Bradstreet, Anne

Gentlewoman in Those Parts, A
  See Bradstreet, Anne

George, Jean Craighead 1919- . . . . . . **CLC 35**
  See also AAYA 8; CA 5-8R; CANR 25;
  CLR 1; DLB 52; JRDA; MAICYA;
  SATA 2, 68

George, Stefan (Anton)
  1868-1933 . . . .**TCLC 2, 14**
  See also CA 104

Georges, Georges Martin
  See Simenon, Georges (Jacques Christian)

Gerhardi, William Alexander
  See Gerhardie, William Alexander

Gerhardie, William Alexander
  1895-1977 . . . . **CLC 5**
  See also CA 25-28R; 73-76; CANR 18;
  DLB 36

Gerstler, Amy 1956- . . . . **CLC 70**
  See also CA 146

Gertler, T. . . . . **CLC 34**
  See also CA 116; 121; INT 121

Ghalib . . . . **NCLC 39**
  See also Ghalib, Hsadullah Khan

Ghalib, Hsadullah Khan 1797-1869
  See Ghalib
  See also DAM POET

Ghelderode, Michel de
  1898-1962 . . . . **CLC 6, 11**
  See also CA 85-88; CANR 40;
  DAM DRAM

Ghiselin, Brewster 1903- . . . . **CLC 23**
  See also CA 13-16R; CAAS 10; CANR 13

Ghose, Zulfikar 1935- . . . . **CLC 42**
  See also CA 65-68

Ghosh, Amitav 1956- . . . . **CLC 44**
  See also CA 147

Giacosa, Giuseppe 1847-1906 . . . . . . **TCLC 7**
  See also CA 104

Gibb, Lee
  See Waterhouse, Keith (Spencer)

Gibbon, Lewis Grassic . . . . **TCLC 4**
  See also Mitchell, James Leslie

Gibbons, Kaye 1960- . . . . **CLC 50, 88**
  See also DAM POP

Gibran, Kahlil
  1883-1931 . . . . **TCLC 1, 9; PC 9**
  See also CA 104; 150; DAM POET, POP

Gibran, Khalil
  See Gibran, Kahlil

Gibson, William
  1914- . . . . **CLC 23; DA; DAB; DAC**
  See also CA 9-12R; CANR 9, 42;
  DAM DRAM, MST; DLB 7; SATA 66

Gibson, William (Ford) 1948- . . . **CLC 39, 63**
  See also AAYA 12; CA 126; 133;
  DAM POP

Gide, Andre (Paul Guillaume)
  1869-1951 . . . . **TCLC 5, 12, 36; DA;**
               DAB; DAC; SSC 13; WLC
  See also CA 104; 124; DAM MST, NOV;
  DLB 65; MTCW

Gifford, Barry (Colby) 1946- . . . . **CLC 34**
  See also CA 65-68; CANR 9, 30, 40

Gilbert, W(illiam) S(chwenck)
  1836-1911 . . . .**TCLC 3**
  See also CA 104; DAM DRAM, POET;
  SATA 36

Gilbreth, Frank B., Jr. 1911- . . . . **CLC 17**
  See also CA 9-12R; SATA 2

Gilchrist, Ellen 1935- . . **CLC 34, 48; SSC 14**
  See also CA 113; 116; CANR 41;
  DAM POP; DLB 130; MTCW

Giles, Molly 1942- . . . . **CLC 39**
  See also CA 126

Gill, Patrick
  See Creasey, John

Gilliam, Terry (Vance) 1940- . . . . **CLC 21**
  See also Monty Python
  See also CA 108; 113; CANR 35; INT 113

Gillian, Jerry
  See Gilliam, Terry (Vance)

Gilliatt, Penelope (Ann Douglass)
  1932-1993 . . . . **CLC 2, 10, 13, 53**
  See also AITN 2; CA 13-16R; 141;
  CANR 49; DLB 14

Gilman, Charlotte (Anna) Perkins (Stetson)
  1860-1935 . . . . **TCLC 9, 37; SSC 13**
  See also CA 106; 150

Gilmour, David 1949- . . . . **CLC 35**
  See also CA 138, 147

Gilpin, William 1724-1804 . . . . . . **NCLC 30**

Gilray, J. D.
  See Mencken, H(enry) L(ouis)

Gilroy, Frank D(aniel) 1925- . . . . **CLC 2**
  See also CA 81-84; CANR 32; DLB 7

Ginsberg, Allen
  1926- . . . . . . **CLC 1, 2, 3, 4, 6, 13, 36, 69;**
         DA; DAB; DAC; PC 4; WLC 3
  See also AITN 1; CA 1-4R; CANR 2, 41;
  CDALB 1941-1968; DAM MST, POET;
  DLB 5, 16; MTCW

Ginzburg, Natalia
  1916-1991 . . . . **CLC 5, 11, 54, 70**
  See also CA 85-88; 135; CANR 33; MTCW

Giono, Jean 1895-1970 . . . . **CLC 4, 11**
  See also CA 45-48; 29-32R; CANR 2, 35;
  DLB 72; MTCW

Giovanni, Nikki
1943- ...... **CLC 2, 4, 19, 64; BLC; DA;**
DAB; DAC
See also AITN 1; BW 2; CA 29-32R;
CAAS 6; CANR 18, 41; CLR 6;
DAM MST, MULT, POET; DLB 5, 41;
INT CANR-18; MAICYA; MTCW;
SATA 24

Giovene, Andrea 1904-............. **CLC 7**
See also CA 85-88

Gippius, Zinaida (Nikolayevna) 1869-1945
See Hippius, Zinaida
See also CA 106

Giraudoux, (Hippolyte) Jean
1882-1944 .... **TCLC 2, 7**
See also CA 104; DAM DRAM; DLB 65

Gironella, Jose Maria 1917- .... **CLC 11**
See also CA 101

Gissing, George (Robert)
1857-1903 .... **TCLC 3, 24, 47**
See also CA 105; DLB 18, 135

Giurlani, Aldo
See Palazzeschi, Aldo

Gladkov, Fyodor (Vasilyevich)
1883-1958 .... **TCLC 27**

Glanville, Brian (Lester) 1931- ...... **CLC 6**
See also CA 5-8R; CAAS 9; CANR 3;
DLB 15, 139; SATA 42

Glasgow, Ellen (Anderson Gholson)
1873(?)-1945 .... **TCLC 2, 7**
See also CA 104; DLB 9, 12

Glaspell, Susan (Keating)
1882(?)-1948 .... **TCLC 55**
See also CA 110; DLB 7, 9, 78; YABC 2

Glassco, John 1909-1981 .... **CLC 9**
See also CA 13-16R; 102; CANR 15;
DLB 68

Glasscock, Amnesia
See Steinbeck, John (Ernst)

Glasser, Ronald J. 1940(?)- .... **CLC 37**

Glassman, Joyce
See Johnson, Joyce

Glendinning, Victoria 1937-........ **CLC 50**
See also CA 120; 127; DLB 155

Glissant, Edouard 1928-........ **CLC 10, 68**
See also DAM MULT

Gloag, Julian 1930- .... **CLC 40**
See also AITN 1; CA 65-68; CANR 10

Glowacki, Aleksander
See Prus, Boleslaw

Glueck, Louise (Elisabeth)
1943-............... **CLC 7, 22, 44, 81**
See also CA 33-36R; CANR 40;
DAM POET; DLB 5

Gobineau, Joseph Arthur (Comte) de
1816-1882 .... **NCLC 17**
See also DLB 123

Godard, Jean-Luc 1930-........... **CLC 20**
See also CA 93-96

Godden, (Margaret) Rumer 1907-... **CLC 53**
See also AAYA 6; CA 5-8R; CANR 4, 27,
36; CLR 20; DLB 161; MAICYA;
SAAS 12; SATA 3, 36

Godoy Alcayaga, Lucila 1889-1957
See Mistral, Gabriela
See also BW 2; CA 104; 131; DAM MULT;
HW; MTCW

Godwin, Gail (Kathleen)
1937-............ **CLC 5, 8, 22, 31, 69**
See also CA 29-32R; CANR 15, 43;
DAM POP; DLB 6; INT CANR-15;
MTCW

Godwin, William 1756-1836...... **NCLC 14**
See also CDBLB 1789-1832; DLB 39, 104,
142, 158, 163

Goethe, Johann Wolfgang von
1749-1832 .... **NCLC 4, 22, 34; DA;**
DAB; DAC; PC 5; WLC 3
See also DAM DRAM, MST, POET;
DLB 94

Gogarty, Oliver St. John
1878-1957 .... **TCLC 15**
See also CA 109; 150; DLB 15, 19

Gogol, Nikolai (Vasilyevich)
1809-1852 .... **NCLC 5, 15, 31; DA;**
DAB; DAC; DC 1; SSC 4; WLC
See also DAM DRAM, MST

Goines, Donald
1937(?)-1974 .... **CLC 80; BLC**
See also AITN 1; BW 1; CA 124; 114;
DAM MULT, POP; DLB 33

Gold, Herbert 1924-....... **CLC 4, 7, 14, 42**
See also CA 9-12R; CANR 17, 45; DLB 2;
DLBY 81

Goldbarth, Albert 1948-........ **CLC 5, 38**
See also CA 53-56; CANR 6, 40; DLB 120

Goldberg, Anatol 1910-1982 .... **CLC 34**
See also CA 131; 117

Goldemberg, Isaac 1945-.......... **CLC 52**
See also CA 69-72; CAAS 12; CANR 11,
32; HW

Golding, William (Gerald)
1911-1993 .... **CLC 1, 2, 3, 8, 10, 17, 27,**
58, 81; DA; DAB; DAC; WLC
See also AAYA 5; CA 5-8R; 141;
CANR 13, 33; CDBLB 1945-1960;
DAM MST, NOV; DLB 15, 100; MTCW

Goldman, Emma 1869-1940....... **TCLC 13**
See also CA 110; 150

Goldman, Francisco 1955-......... **CLC 76**

Goldman, William (W.) 1931-.... **CLC 1, 48**
See also CA 9-12R; CANR 29; DLB 44

Goldmann, Lucien 1913-1970 ...... **CLC 24**
See also CA 25-28; CAP 2

Goldoni, Carlo 1707-1793 .... **LC 4**
See also DAM DRAM

Goldsberry, Steven 1949-......... **CLC 34**
See also CA 131

Goldsmith, Oliver
1728-1774 ...... **LC 2; DA; DAB; DAC;**
WLC
See also CDBLB 1660-1789; DAM DRAM,
MST, NOV, POET; DLB 39, 89, 104,
109, 142; SATA 26

Goldsmith, Peter
See Priestley, J(ohn) B(oynton)

Gombrowicz, Witold
1904-1969 .... **CLC 4, 7, 11, 49**
See also CA 19-20; 25-28R; CAP 2;
DAM DRAM

Gomez de la Serna, Ramon
1888-1963 .... **CLC 9**
See also CA 116; HW

Goncharov, Ivan Alexandrovich
1812-1891 .... **NCLC 1**

Goncourt, Edmond (Louis Antoine Huot) de
1822-1896 .... **NCLC 7**
See also DLB 123

Goncourt, Jules (Alfred Huot) de
1830-1870 .... **NCLC 7**
See also DLB 123

Gontier, Fernande 19(?)- .... **CLC 50**

Goodman, Paul 1911-1972 .... **CLC 1, 2, 4, 7**
See also CA 19-20; 37-40R; CANR 34;
CAP 2; DLB 130; MTCW

Gordimer, Nadine
1923- .... **CLC 3, 5, 7, 10, 18, 33, 51, 70;**
DA; DAB; DAC; SSC 17
See also CA 5-8R; CANR 3, 28;
DAM MST, NOV; INT CANR-28;
MTCW

Gordon, Adam Lindsay
1833-1870 .... **NCLC 21**

Gordon, Caroline
1895-1981 ... **CLC 6, 13, 29, 83; SSC 15**
See also CA 11-12; 103; CANR 36; CAP 1;
DLB 4, 9, 102; DLBY 81; MTCW

Gordon, Charles William 1860-1937
See Connor, Ralph
See also CA 109

Gordon, Mary (Catherine)
1949-.................... **CLC 13, 22**
See also CA 102; CANR 44; DLB 6;
DLBY 81; INT 102; MTCW

Gordon, Sol 1923-................. **CLC 26**
See also CA 53-56; CANR 4; SATA 11

Gordone, Charles 1925-1995 ...... **CLC 1, 4**
See also BW 1; CA 93-96; 150;
DAM DRAM; DLB 7; INT 93-96;
MTCW

Gorenko, Anna Andreevna
See Akhmatova, Anna

Gorky, Maxim.......... TCLC 8; DAB; WLC
See also Peshkov, Alexei Maximovich

Goryan, Sirak
See Saroyan, William

Gosse, Edmund (William)
1849-1928 .... **TCLC 28**
See also CA 117; DLB 57, 144

Gotlieb, Phyllis Fay (Bloom)
1926-.................... **CLC 18**
See also CA 13-16R; CANR 7; DLB 88

Gottesman, S. D.
See Kornbluth, C(yril) M.; Pohl, Frederik

Gottfried von Strassburg
fl. c. 1210-................. **CMLC 10**
See also DLB 138

Gould, Lois .... **CLC 4, 10**
See also CA 77-80; CANR 29; MTCW

Gourmont, Remy (-Marie-Charles) de
1858-1915 . . . . **TCLC 17**
See also CA 109; 150

Govier, Katherine 1948- . . . . **CLC 51**
See also CA 101; CANR 18, 40

Goyen, (Charles) William
1915-1983 . . . . **CLC 5, 8, 14, 40**
See also AITN 2; CA 5-8R; 110; CANR 6;
DLB 2; DLBY 83; INT CANR-6

Goytisolo, Juan
1931- . . . . **CLC 5, 10, 23; HLC**
See also CA 85-88; CANR 32;
DAM MULT; HW; MTCW

Gozzano, Guido 1883-1916 . . . . **PC 10**
See also DLB 114

Gozzi, (Conte) Carlo 1720-1806 . . **NCLC 23**

Grabbe, Christian Dietrich
1801-1836 . . . . **NCLC 2**
See also DLB 133

Grace, Patricia 1937- . . . . **CLC 56**

Gracian y Morales, Baltasar
1601-1658 . . . . **LC 15**

Gracq, Julien . . . . **CLC 11, 48**
See also Poirier, Louis
See also DLB 83

Grade, Chaim 1910-1982 . . . . **CLC 10**
See also CA 93-96; 107

Graduate of Oxford, A
See Ruskin, John

Graham, John
See Phillips, David Graham

Graham, Jorie 1951- . . . . **CLC 48**
See also CA 111; DLB 120

Graham, R(obert) B(ontine) Cunninghame
See Cunninghame Graham, R(obert)
B(ontine)
See also DLB 98, 135

Graham, Robert
See Haldeman, Joe (William)

Graham, Tom
See Lewis, (Harry) Sinclair

Graham, W(illiam) S(ydney)
1918-1986 . . . . **CLC 29**
See also CA 73-76; 118; DLB 20

Graham, Winston (Mawdsley)
1910- . . . . **CLC 23**
See also CA 49-52; CANR 2, 22, 45;
DLB 77

Grahame, Kenneth
1859-1932 . . . . **TCLC 64; DAB**
See also CA 108; 136; CLR 5; DLB 34, 141;
MAICYA; YABC 1

Grant, Skeeter
See Spiegelman, Art

Granville-Barker, Harley
1877-1946 . . . . **TCLC 2**
See also Barker, Harley Granville
See also CA 104; DAM DRAM

Grass, Guenter (Wilhelm)
1927- . . . . . **CLC 1, 2, 4, 6, 11, 15, 22, 32,
49, 88; DA; DAB; DAC; WLC**
See also CA 13-16R; CANR 20;
DAM MST, NOV; DLB 75, 124; MTCW

Gratton, Thomas
See Hulme, T(homas) E(rnest)

Grau, Shirley Ann
1929- . . . . **CLC 4, 9; SSC 15**
See also CA 89-92; CANR 22; DLB 2;
INT CANR-22; MTCW

Gravel, Fern
See Hall, James Norman

Graver, Elizabeth 1964- . . . . **CLC 70**
See also CA 135

Graves, Richard Perceval 1945- . . . . **CLC 44**
See also CA 65-68; CANR 9, 26, 51

Graves, Robert (von Ranke)
1895-1985 . . . . . . **CLC 1, 2, 6, 11, 39, 44,
45; DAB; DAC; PC 6**
See also CA 5-8R; 117; CANR 5, 36;
CDBLB 1914-1945; DAM MST, POET;
DLB 20, 100; DLBY 85; MTCW;
SATA 45

Gray, Alasdair (James) 1934- . . . . . . **CLC 41**
See also CA 126; CANR 47; INT 126;
MTCW

Gray, Amlin 1946- . . . . **CLC 29**
See also CA 138

Gray, Francine du Plessix 1930- . . . . **CLC 22**
See also BEST 90:3; CA 61-64; CAAS 2;
CANR 11, 33; DAM NOV;
INT CANR-11; MTCW

Gray, John (Henry) 1866-1934 . . . . **TCLC 19**
See also CA 119

Gray, Simon (James Holliday)
1936- . . . . **CLC 9, 14, 36**
See also AITN 1; CA 21-24R; CAAS 3;
CANR 32; DLB 13; MTCW

Gray, Spalding 1941- . . . . **CLC 49**
See also CA 128; DAM POP

Gray, Thomas
1716-1771 . . . . . . **LC 4; DA; DAB; DAC;
PC 2; WLC**
See also CDBLB 1660-1789; DAM MST;
DLB 109

Grayson, David
See Baker, Ray Stannard

Grayson, Richard (A.) 1951- . . . . **CLC 38**
See also CA 85-88; CANR 14, 31

Greeley, Andrew M(oran) 1928- . . . . **CLC 28**
See also CA 5-8R; CAAS 7; CANR 7, 43;
DAM POP; MTCW

Green, Anna Katharine
1846-1935 . . . . **TCLC 63**
See also CA 112

Green, Brian
See Card, Orson Scott

Green, Hannah
See Greenberg, Joanne (Goldenberg)

Green, Hannah . . . . **CLC 3**
See also CA 73-76

Green, Henry . . . . **CLC 2, 13**
See also Yorke, Henry Vincent
See also DLB 15

Green, Julian (Hartridge) 1900-
See Green, Julien
See also CA 21-24R; CANR 33; DLB 4, 72;
MTCW

Green, Julien . . . . **CLC 3, 11, 77**
See also Green, Julian (Hartridge)

Green, Paul (Eliot) 1894-1981 . . . . . . **CLC 25**
See also AITN 1; CA 5-8R; 103; CANR 3;
DAM DRAM; DLB 7, 9; DLBY 81

Greenberg, Ivan 1908-1973
See Rahv, Philip
See also CA 85-88

Greenberg, Joanne (Goldenberg)
1932- . . . . **CLC 7, 30**
See also AAYA 12; CA 5-8R; CANR 14,
32; SATA 25

Greenberg, Richard 1959(?)- . . . . **CLC 57**
See also CA 138

Greene, Bette 1934- . . . . **CLC 30**
See also AAYA 7; CA 53-56; CANR 4;
CLR 2; JRDA; MAICYA; SAAS 16;
SATA 8

Greene, Gael . . . . **CLC 8**
See also CA 13-16R; CANR 10

Greene, Graham
1904-1991 . . . . **CLC 1, 3, 6, 9, 14, 18, 27,
37, 70, 72; DA; DAB; DAC; WLC**
See also AITN 2; CA 13-16R; 133;
CANR 35; CDBLB 1945-1960;
DAM MST, NOV; DLB 13, 15, 77, 100,
162; DLBY 91; MTCW; SATA 20

Greer, Richard
See Silverberg, Robert

Gregor, Arthur 1923- . . . . **CLC 9**
See also CA 25-28R; CAAS 10; CANR 11;
SATA 36

Gregor, Lee
See Pohl, Frederik

Gregory, Isabella Augusta (Persse)
1852-1932 . . . . **TCLC 1**
See also CA 104; DLB 10

Gregory, J. Dennis
See Williams, John A(lfred)

Grendon, Stephen
See Derleth, August (William)

Grenville, Kate 1950- . . . . **CLC 61**
See also CA 118

Grenville, Pelham
See Wodehouse, P(elham) G(renville)

Greve, Felix Paul (Berthold Friedrich)
1879-1948
See Grove, Frederick Philip
See also CA 104; 141; DAC; DAM MST

Grey, Zane 1872-1939 . . . . **TCLC 6**
See also CA 104; 132; DAM POP; DLB 9;
MTCW

Grieg, (Johan) Nordahl (Brun)
1902-1943 . . . . **TCLC 10**
See also CA 107

Grieve, C(hristopher) M(urray)
1892-1978 . . . . **CLC 11, 19**
See also MacDiarmid, Hugh; Pteleon
See also CA 5-8R; 85-88; CANR 33;
DAM POET; MTCW

Griffin, Gerald 1803-1840 . . . . **NCLC 7**
See also DLB 159

Griffin, John Howard 1920-1980 . . . . **CLC 68**
See also AITN 1; CA 1-4R; 101; CANR 2

Griffin, Peter 1942- . . . . **CLC 39**
See also CA 136

Griffiths, Trevor 1935- . . . . **CLC 13, 52**
See also CA 97-100; CANR 45; DLB 13

Grigson, Geoffrey (Edward Harvey)
1905-1985 . . . . **CLC 7, 39**
See also CA 25-28R; 118; CANR 20, 33;
DLB 27; MTCW

Grillparzer, Franz 1791-1872 . . . . . . **NCLC 1**
See also DLB 133

Grimble, Reverend Charles James
See Eliot, T(homas) S(tearns)

Grimke, Charlotte L(ottie) Forten
1837(?)-1914
See Forten, Charlotte L.
See also BW 1; CA 117; 124; DAM MULT,
POET

Grimm, Jacob Ludwig Karl
1785-1863 . . . . **NCLC 3**
See also DLB 90; MAICYA; SATA 22

Grimm, Wilhelm Karl 1786-1859 . . **NCLC 3**
See also DLB 90; MAICYA; SATA 22

Grimmelshausen, Johann Jakob Christoffel
von 1621-1676 . . . . **LC 6**

Grindel, Eugene 1895-1952
See Eluard, Paul
See also CA 104

Grisham, John 1955- . . . . **CLC 84**
See also AAYA 14; CA 138; CANR 47;
DAM POP

Grossman, David 1954- . . . . **CLC 67**
See also CA 138

Grossman, Vasily (Semenovich)
1905-1964 . . . . **CLC 41**
See also CA 124; 130; MTCW

Grove, Frederick Philip . . . . **TCLC 4**
See also Greve, Felix Paul (Berthold
Friedrich)
See also DLB 92

Grubb
See Crumb, R(obert)

Grumbach, Doris (Isaac)
1918- . . . . **CLC 13, 22, 64**
See also CA 5-8R; CAAS 2; CANR 9, 42;
INT CANR-9

Grundtvig, Nicolai Frederik Severin
1783-1872 . . . . **NCLC 1**

Grunge
See Crumb, R(obert)

Grunwald, Lisa 1959- . . . . **CLC 44**
See also CA 120

Guare, John 1938- . . . . **CLC 8, 14, 29, 67**
See also CA 73-76; CANR 21;
DAM DRAM; DLB 7; MTCW

Gudjonsson, Halldor Kiljan 1902-
See Laxness, Halldor
See also CA 103

Guenter, Erich
See Eich, Guenter

Guest, Barbara 1920- . . . . **CLC 34**
See also CA 25-28R; CANR 11, 44; DLB 5

Guest, Judith (Ann) 1936- . . . . **CLC 8, 30**
See also AAYA 7; CA 77-80; CANR 15;
DAM NOV, POP; INT CANR-15;
MTCW

Guevara, Che . . . . **CLC 87; HLC**
See also Guevara (Serna), Ernesto

Guevara (Serna), Ernesto 1928-1967
See Guevara, Che
See also CA 127; 111; DAM MULT; HW

Guild, Nicholas M. 1944- . . . . **CLC 33**
See also CA 93-96

Guillemin, Jacques
See Sartre, Jean-Paul

Guillen, Jorge 1893-1984 . . . . **CLC 11**
See also CA 89-92; 112; DAM MULT,
POET; DLB 108; HW

Guillen (y Batista), Nicolas (Cristobal)
1902-1989 . . . . . **CLC 48, 79; BLC; HLC**
See also BW 2; CA 116; 125; 129;
DAM MST, MULT, POET; HW

Guillevic, (Eugene) 1907- . . . . **CLC 33**
See also CA 93-96

Guillois
See Desnos, Robert

Guiney, Louise Imogen
1861-1920 . . . . **TCLC 41**
See also DLB 54

Guiraldes, Ricardo (Guillermo)
1886-1927 . . . . **TCLC 39**
See also CA 131; HW; MTCW

Gumilev, Nikolai Stephanovich
1886-1921 . . . . **TCLC 60**

Gunesekera, Romesh . . . . **CLC 91**

Gunn, Bill . . . . **CLC 5**
See also Gunn, William Harrison
See also DLB 38

Gunn, Thom(son William)
1929- . . . . **CLC 3, 6, 18, 32, 81**
See also CA 17-20R; CANR 9, 33;
CDBLB 1960 to Present; DAM POET;
DLB 27; INT CANR-33; MTCW

Gunn, William Harrison 1934(?)-1989
See Gunn, Bill
See also AITN 1; BW 1; CA 13-16R; 128;
CANR 12, 25

Gunnars, Kristjana 1948- . . . . **CLC 69**
See also CA 113; DLB 60

Gurganus, Allan 1947- . . . . **CLC 70**
See also BEST 90:1; CA 135; DAM POP

Gurney, A(lbert) R(amsdell), Jr.
1930- . . . . **CLC 32, 50, 54**
See also CA 77-80; CANR 32;
DAM DRAM

Gurney, Ivor (Bertie) 1890-1937 . . . **TCLC 33**

Gurney, Peter
See Gurney, A(lbert) R(amsdell), Jr.

Guro, Elena 1877-1913 . . . . **TCLC 56**

Gustafson, Ralph (Barker) 1909- . . . . **CLC 36**
See also CA 21-24R; CANR 8, 45; DLB 88

Gut, Gom
See Simenon, Georges (Jacques Christian)

Guterson, David 1956- . . . . **CLC 91**
See also CA 132

Guthrie, A(lfred) B(ertram), Jr.
1901-1991 . . . . **CLC 23**
See also CA 57-60; 134; CANR 24; DLB 6;
SATA 62; SATA-Obit 67

Guthrie, Isobel
See Grieve, C(hristopher) M(urray)

Guthrie, Woodrow Wilson 1912-1967
See Guthrie, Woody
See also CA 113; 93-96

Guthrie, Woody . . . . **CLC 35**
See also Guthrie, Woodrow Wilson

Guy, Rosa (Cuthbert) 1928- . . . . **CLC 26**
See also AAYA 4; BW 2; CA 17-20R;
CANR 14, 34; CLR 13; DLB 33; JRDA;
MAICYA; SATA 14, 62

Gwendolyn
See Bennett, (Enoch) Arnold

H. D. . . . . **CLC 3, 8, 14, 31, 34, 73; PC 5**
See also Doolittle, Hilda

H. de V.
See Buchan, John

Haavikko, Paavo Juhani
1931- . . . . **CLC 18, 34**
See also CA 106

Habbema, Koos
See Heijermans, Herman

Hacker, Marilyn
1942- . . . . **CLC 5, 9, 23, 72, 91**
See also CA 77-80; DAM POET; DLB 120

Haggard, H(enry) Rider
1856-1925 . . . . **TCLC 11**
See also CA 108; 148; DLB 70, 156;
SATA 16

Hagiwara Sakutaro 1886-1942 . . . . **TCLC 60**

Haig, Fenil
See Ford, Ford Madox

Haig-Brown, Roderick (Langmere)
1908-1976 . . . . **CLC 21**
See also CA 5-8R; 69-72; CANR 4, 38;
CLR 31; DLB 88; MAICYA; SATA 12

Hailey, Arthur 1920- . . . . **CLC 5**
See also AITN 2; BEST 90:3; CA 1-4R;
CANR 2, 36; DAM NOV, POP; DLB 88;
DLBY 82; MTCW

Hailey, Elizabeth Forsythe 1938- . . . **CLC 40**
See also CA 93-96; CAAS 1; CANR 15, 48;
INT CANR-15

Haines, John (Meade) 1924- . . . . **CLC 58**
See also CA 17-20R; CANR 13, 34; DLB 5

Hakluyt, Richard 1552-1616 . . . . **LC 31**

Haldeman, Joe (William) 1943- . . . . . **CLC 61**
See also CA 53-56; CANR 6; DLB 8;
INT CANR-6

Haley, Alex(ander Murray Palmer)
1921-1992 . . . . **CLC 8, 12, 76; BLC; DA;**
DAB; DAC
See also BW 2; CA 77-80; 136; DAM MST,
MULT, POP; DLB 38; MTCW

Haliburton, Thomas Chandler
1796-1865 . . . . **NCLC 15**
See also DLB 11, 99

Hall, Donald (Andrew, Jr.)
1928- . . . . **CLC 1, 13, 37, 59**
See also CA 5-8R; CAAS 7; CANR 2, 44;
DAM POET; DLB 5; SATA 23

Hall, Frederic Sauser
See Sauser-Hall, Frederic

Hall, James
See Kuttner, Henry

Hall, James Norman 1887-1951 . . . **TCLC 23**
See also CA 123; SATA 21

Hall, (Marguerite) Radclyffe
    1886-1943 . . . . TCLC 12
    See also CA 110; 150

Hall, Rodney 1935- . . . . CLC 51
    See also CA 109

Halleck, Fitz-Greene 1790-1867 . . NCLC 47
    See also DLB 3

Halliday, Michael
    See Creasey, John

Halpern, Daniel 1945- . . . . CLC 14
    See also CA 33-36R

Hamburger, Michael (Peter Leopold)
    1924- . . . . CLC 5, 14
    See also CA 5-8R; CAAS 4; CANR 2, 47;
    DLB 27

Hamill, Pete 1935- . . . . CLC 10
    See also CA 25-28R; CANR 18

Hamilton, Alexander
    1755(?)-1804 . . . . NCLC 49
    See also DLB 37

Hamilton, Clive
    See Lewis, C(live) S(taples)

Hamilton, Edmond 1904-1977 . . . . . . CLC 1
    See also CA 1-4R; CANR 3; DLB 8

Hamilton, Eugene (Jacob) Lee
    See Lee-Hamilton, Eugene (Jacob)

Hamilton, Franklin
    See Silverberg, Robert

Hamilton, Gail
    See Corcoran, Barbara

Hamilton, Mollie
    See Kaye, M(ary) M(argaret)

Hamilton, (Anthony Walter) Patrick
    1904-1962 . . . . CLC 51
    See also CA 113; DLB 10

Hamilton, Virginia 1936- . . . . . . CLC 26
    See also AAYA 2; BW 2; CA 25-28R;
    CANR 20, 37; CLR 1, 11, 40;
    DAM MULT; DLB 33, 52;
    INT CANR-20; JRDA; MAICYA;
    MTCW; SATA 4, 56, 79

Hammett, (Samuel) Dashiell
    1894-1961 . . . . CLC 3, 5, 10, 19, 47;
                                            SSC 17
    See also AITN 1; CA 81-84; CANR 42;
    CDALB 1929-1941; DLBD 6; MTCW

Hammon, Jupiter
    1711(?)-1800(?) . . . . NCLC 5; BLC
    See also DAM MULT, POET; DLB 31, 50

Hammond, Keith
    See Kuttner, Henry

Hamner, Earl (Henry), Jr. 1923- . . . CLC 12
    See also AITN 2; CA 73-76; DLB 6

Hampton, Christopher (James)
    1946- . . . . CLC 4
    See also CA 25-28R; DLB 13; MTCW

Hamsun, Knut . . . . TCLC 2, 14, 49
    See also Pedersen, Knut

Handke, Peter 1942- . . CLC 5, 8, 10, 15, 38
    See also CA 77-80; CANR 33;
    DAM DRAM, NOV; DLB 85, 124;
    MTCW

Hanley, James 1901-1985 . . . CLC 3, 5, 8, 13
    See also CA 73-76; 117; CANR 36; MTCW

Hannah, Barry 1942- . . . . CLC 23, 38, 90
    See also CA 108; 110; CANR 43; DLB 6;
    INT 110; MTCW

Hannon, Ezra
    See Hunter, Evan

Hansberry, Lorraine (Vivian)
    1930-1965 . . . . . . CLC 17, 62; BLC; DA;
                                    DAB; DAC; DC 2
    See also BW 1; CA 109; 25-28R; CABS 3;
    CDALB 1941-1968; DAM DRAM, MST,
    MULT; DLB 7, 38; MTCW

Hansen, Joseph 1923- . . . . CLC 38
    See also CA 29-32R; CAAS 17; CANR 16,
    44; INT CANR-16

Hansen, Martin A. 1909-1955 . . . . . TCLC 32

Hanson, Kenneth O(stlin) 1922- . . . . CLC 13
    See also CA 53-56; CANR 7

Hardwick, Elizabeth 1916- . . . . CLC 13
    See also CA 5-8R; CANR 3, 32;
    DAM NOV; DLB 6; MTCW

Hardy, Thomas
    1840-1928 . . . . . . TCLC 4, 10, 18, 32, 48,
        53; DA; DAB; DAC; PC 8; SSC 2; WLC
    See also CA 104; 123; CDBLB 1890-1914;
    DAM MST, NOV, POET; DLB 18, 19,
    135; MTCW

Hare, David 1947- . . . . CLC 29, 58
    See also CA 97-100; CANR 39; DLB 13;
    MTCW

Harford, Henry
    See Hudson, W(illiam) H(enry)

Hargrave, Leonie
    See Disch, Thomas M(ichael)

Harjo, Joy 1951- . . . . CLC 83
    See also CA 114; CANR 35; DAM MULT;
    DLB 120; NNAL

Harlan, Louis R(udolph) 1922- . . . . . CLC 34
    See also CA 21-24R; CANR 25

Harling, Robert 1951(?)- . . . . CLC 53
    See also CA 147

Harmon, William (Ruth) 1938- . . . . . CLC 38
    See also CA 33-36R; CANR 14, 32, 35;
    SATA 65

Harper, F. E. W.
    See Harper, Frances Ellen Watkins

Harper, Frances E. W.
    See Harper, Frances Ellen Watkins

Harper, Frances E. Watkins
    See Harper, Frances Ellen Watkins

Harper, Frances Ellen
    See Harper, Frances Ellen Watkins

Harper, Frances Ellen Watkins
    1825-1911 . . . . TCLC 14; BLC
    See also BW 1; CA 111; 125; DAM MULT,
    POET; DLB 50

Harper, Michael S(teven) 1938- . . CLC 7, 22
    See also BW 1; CA 33-36R; CANR 24;
    DLB 41

Harper, Mrs. F. E. W.
    See Harper, Frances Ellen Watkins

Harris, Christie (Lucy) Irwin
    1907- . . . . CLC 12
    See also CA 5-8R; CANR 6; DLB 88;
    JRDA; MAICYA; SAAS 10; SATA 6, 74

Harris, Frank 1856-1931 . . . . TCLC 24
    See also CA 109; 150; DLB 156

Harris, George Washington
    1814-1869 . . . . NCLC 23
    See also DLB 3, 11

Harris, Joel Chandler
    1848-1908 . . . . TCLC 2; SSC 19
    See also CA 104; 137; DLB 11, 23, 42, 78,
    91; MAICYA; YABC 1

Harris, John (Wyndham Parkes Lucas)
    Beynon 1903-1969
    See Wyndham, John
    See also CA 102; 89-92

Harris, MacDonald . . . . CLC 9
    See also Heiney, Donald (William)

Harris, Mark 1922- . . . . CLC 19
    See also CA 5-8R; CAAS 3; CANR 2;
    DLB 2; DLBY 80

Harris, (Theodore) Wilson 1921-. . . . CLC 25
    See also BW 2; CA 65-68; CAAS 16;
    CANR 11, 27; DLB 117; MTCW

Harrison, Elizabeth Cavanna 1909-
    See Cavanna, Betty
    See also CA 9-12R; CANR 6, 27

Harrison, Harry (Max) 1925- . . . . . . CLC 42
    See also CA 1-4R; CANR 5, 21; DLB 8;
    SATA 4

Harrison, James (Thomas)
    1937- . . . . CLC 6, 14, 33, 66; SSC 19
    See also CA 13-16R; CANR 8, 51;
    DLBY 82; INT CANR-8

Harrison, Jim
    See Harrison, James (Thomas)

Harrison, Kathryn 1961- . . . . CLC 70
    See also CA 144

Harrison, Tony 1937- . . . . CLC 43
    See also CA 65-68; CANR 44; DLB 40;
    MTCW

Harriss, Will(ard Irvin) 1922- . . . . . . CLC 34
    See also CA 111

Harson, Sley
    See Ellison, Harlan (Jay)

Hart, Ellis
    See Ellison, Harlan (Jay)

Hart, Josephine 1942(?)- . . . . CLC 70
    See also CA 138; DAM POP

Hart, Moss 1904-1961 . . . . CLC 66
    See also CA 109; 89-92; DAM DRAM;
    DLB 7

Harte, (Francis) Bret(t)
    1836(?)-1902 . . . . TCLC 1, 25; DA; DAC;
                                    SSC 8; WLC
    See also CA 104; 140; CDALB 1865-1917;
    DAM MST; DLB 12, 64, 74, 79;
    SATA 26

Hartley, L(eslie) P(oles)
    1895-1972 . . . . CLC 2, 22
    See also CA 45-48; 37-40R; CANR 33;
    DLB 15, 139; MTCW

Hartman, Geoffrey H. 1929- . . . . CLC 27
    See also CA 117; 125; DLB 67

Hartmann von Aue
    c. 1160-c. 1205 . . . . CMLC 15
    See also DLB 138

Hartmann von Aue 1170-1210 . . . . CMLC 15

Henry, Patrick 1736-1799 . . . . **LC 25**

Henryson, Robert 1430(?)-1506(?). . . . **LC 20**
See also DLB 146

Henry VIII 1491-1547 . . . . **LC 10**

Henschke, Alfred
See Klabund

Hentoff, Nat(han Irving) 1925- . . . . . **CLC 26**
See also AAYA 4; CA 1-4R; CAAS 6;
CANR 5, 25; CLR 1; INT CANR-25;
JRDA; MAICYA; SATA 42, 69;
SATA-Brief 27

Heppenstall, (John) Rayner
1911-1981 . . . . **CLC 10**
See also CA 1-4R; 103; CANR 29

Herbert, Frank (Patrick)
1920-1986 . . . . . . **CLC 12, 23, 35, 44, 85**
See also CA 53-56; 118; CANR 5, 43;
DAM POP; DLB 8; INT CANR-5;
MTCW; SATA 9, 37; SATA-Obit 47

Herbert, George
1593-1633 . . . . **LC 24; DAB; PC 4**
See also CDBLB Before 1660; DAM POET;
DLB 126

Herbert, Zbigniew 1924- . . . . **CLC 9, 43**
See also CA 89-92; CANR 36;
DAM POET; MTCW

Herbst, Josephine (Frey)
1897-1969 . . . . **CLC 34**
See also CA 5-8R; 25-28R; DLB 9

Hergesheimer, Joseph
1880-1954 . . . . **TCLC 11**
See also CA 109; DLB 102, 9

Herlihy, James Leo 1927-1993 . . . . . . **CLC 6**
See also CA 1-4R; 143; CANR 2

Hermogenes fl. c. 175- . . . . **CMLC 6**

Hernandez, Jose 1834-1886 . . . . . . **NCLC 17**

Herodotus c. 484B.C.-429B.C. . . . . **CMLC 17**

Herrick, Robert
1591-1674 . . . . . **LC 13; DA; DAB; DAC;
PC 9**
See also DAM MST, POP; DLB 126

Herring, Guilles
See Somerville, Edith

Herriot, James 1916-1995 . . . . **CLC 12**
See also Wight, James Alfred
See also AAYA 1; CA 148; CANR 40;
DAM POP; SATA 86

Herrmann, Dorothy 1941- . . . . **CLC 44**
See also CA 107

Herrmann, Taffy
See Herrmann, Dorothy

Hersey, John (Richard)
1914-1993 . . . . . . **CLC 1, 2, 7, 9, 40, 81**
See also CA 17-20R; 140; CANR 33;
DAM POP; DLB 6; MTCW; SATA 25;
SATA-Obit 76

Herzen, Aleksandr Ivanovich
1812-1870 . . . . **NCLC 10**

Herzl, Theodor 1860-1904 . . . . **TCLC 36**

Herzog, Werner 1942- . . . . **CLC 16**
See also CA 89-92

Hesiod c. 8th cent. B.C.- . . . . **CMLC 5**

Hesse, Hermann
1877-1962 . . . . **CLC 1, 2, 3, 6, 11, 17, 25,
69; DA; DAB; DAC; SSC 9; WLC**
See also CA 17-18; CAP 2; DAM MST,
NOV; DLB 66; MTCW; SATA 50

Hewes, Cady
See De Voto, Bernard (Augustine)

Heyen, William 1940- . . . . **CLC 13, 18**
See also CA 33-36R; CAAS 9; DLB 5

Heyerdahl, Thor 1914- . . . . **CLC 26**
See also CA 5-8R; CANR 5, 22; MTCW;
SATA 2, 52

Heym, Georg (Theodor Franz Arthur)
1887-1912 . . . . **TCLC 9**
See also CA 106

Heym, Stefan 1913- . . . . **CLC 41**
See also CA 9-12R; CANR 4; DLB 69

Heyse, Paul (Johann Ludwig von)
1830-1914 . . . . **TCLC 8**
See also CA 104; DLB 129

Heyward, (Edwin) DuBose
1885-1940 . . . . **TCLC 59**
See also CA 108; DLB 7, 9, 45; SATA 21

Hibbert, Eleanor Alice Burford
1906-1993 . . . . **CLC 7**
See also BEST 90:4; CA 17-20R; 140;
CANR 9, 28; DAM POP; SATA 2;
SATA-Obit 74

Hichens, Robert S. 1864-1950 . . . . . **TCLC 64**
See also DLB 153

Higgins, George V(incent)
1939- . . . . **CLC 4, 7, 10, 18**
See also CA 77-80; CAAS 5; CANR 17, 51;
DLB 2; DLBY 81; INT CANR-17;
MTCW

Higginson, Thomas Wentworth
1823-1911 . . . . **TCLC 36**
See also DLB 1, 64

Highet, Helen
See MacInnes, Helen (Clark)

Highsmith, (Mary) Patricia
1921-1995 . . . . **CLC 2, 4, 14, 42**
See also CA 1-4R; 147; CANR 1, 20, 48;
DAM NOV, POP; MTCW

Highwater, Jamake (Mamake)
1942(?)- . . . . **CLC 12**
See also AAYA 7; CA 65-68; CAAS 7;
CANR 10, 34; CLR 17; DLB 52;
DLBY 85; JRDA; MAICYA; SATA 32,
69; SATA-Brief 30

Highway, Tomson 1951- . . . . . . **CLC 92; DAC**
See also DAM MULT; NNAL

Higuchi, Ichiyo 1872-1896 . . . . **NCLC 49**

Hijuelos, Oscar 1951- . . . . . . **CLC 65; HLC**
See also BEST 90:1; CA 123; CANR 50;
DAM MULT, POP; DLB 145; HW

Hikmet, Nazim 1902(?)-1963 . . . . . . **CLC 40**
See also CA 141; 93-96

Hildesheimer, Wolfgang
1916-1991 . . . . **CLC 49**
See also CA 101; 135; DLB 69, 124

Hill, Geoffrey (William)
1932- . . . . **CLC 5, 8, 18, 45**
See also CA 81-84; CANR 21;
CDBLB 1960 to Present; DAM POET;
DLB 40; MTCW

Hill, George Roy 1921- . . . . **CLC 26**
See also CA 110; 122

Hill, John
See Koontz, Dean R(ay)

Hill, Susan (Elizabeth)
1942- . . . . **CLC 4; DAB**
See also CA 33-36R; CANR 29;
DAM MST, NOV; DLB 14, 139; MTCW

Hillerman, Tony 1925- . . . . **CLC 62**
See also AAYA 6; BEST 89:1; CA 29-32R;
CANR 21, 42; DAM POP; SATA 6

Hillesum, Etty 1914-1943 . . . . **TCLC 49**
See also CA 137

Hilliard, Noel (Harvey) 1929- . . . . . . **CLC 15**
See also CA 9-12R; CANR 7

Hillis, Rick 1956- . . . . **CLC 66**
See also CA 134

Hilton, James 1900-1954 . . . . **TCLC 21**
See also CA 108; DLB 34, 77; SATA 34

Himes, Chester (Bomar)
1909-1984 . . . . **CLC 2, 4, 7, 18, 58; BLC**
See also BW 2; CA 25-28R; 114; CANR 22;
DAM MULT; DLB 2, 76, 143; MTCW

Hinde, Thomas . . . . **CLC 6, 11**
See also Chitty, Thomas Willes

Hindin, Nathan
See Bloch, Robert (Albert)

Hine, (William) Daryl 1936- . . . . **CLC 15**
See also CA 1-4R; CAAS 15; CANR 1, 20;
DLB 60

Hinkson, Katharine Tynan
See Tynan, Katharine

Hinton, S(usan) E(loise)
1950- . . . . **CLC 30; DA; DAB; DAC**
See also AAYA 2; CA 81-84; CANR 32;
CLR 3, 23; DAM MST, NOV; JRDA;
MAICYA; MTCW; SATA 19, 58

Hippius, Zinaida . . . . **TCLC 9**
See also Gippius, Zinaida (Nikolayevna)

Hiraoka, Kimitake 1925-1970
See Mishima, Yukio
See also CA 97-100; 29-32R; DAM DRAM;
MTCW

Hirsch, E(ric) D(onald), Jr. 1928- . . . **CLC 79**
See also CA 25-28R; CANR 27, 51;
DLB 67; INT CANR-27; MTCW

Hirsch, Edward 1950- . . . . **CLC 31, 50**
See also CA 104; CANR 20, 42; DLB 120

Hitchcock, Alfred (Joseph)
1899-1980 . . . . **CLC 16**
See also CA 97-100; SATA 27;
SATA-Obit 24

Hitler, Adolf 1889-1945 . . . . **TCLC 53**
See also CA 117; 147

Hoagland, Edward 1932- . . . . **CLC 28**
See also CA 1-4R; CANR 2, 31; DLB 6;
SATA 51

Hoban, Russell (Conwell) 1925- . . **CLC 7, 25**
See also CA 5-8R; CANR 23, 37; CLR 3;
DAM NOV; DLB 52; MAICYA;
MTCW; SATA 1, 40, 78

Hobbs, Perry
See Blackmur, R(ichard) P(almer)

Howard, Richard 1929- ..... **CLC 7, 10, 47**
See also AITN 1; CA 85-88; CANR 25;
DLB 5; INT CANR-25

Howard, Robert Ervin 1906-1936... **TCLC 8**
See also CA 105

Howard, Warren F.
See Pohl, Frederik

Howe, Fanny 1940- .... **CLC 47**
See also CA 117; SATA-Brief 52

Howe, Irving 1920-1993.......... **CLC 85**
See also CA 9-12R; 141; CANR 21, 50;
DLB 67; MTCW

Howe, Julia Ward 1819-1910 ..... **TCLC 21**
See also CA 117; DLB 1

Howe, Susan 1937-.............. **CLC 72**
See also DLB 120

Howe, Tina 1937-................ **CLC 48**
See also CA 109

Howell, James 1594(?)-1666 .... **LC 13**
See also DLB 151

Howells, W. D.
See Howells, William Dean

Howells, William D.
See Howells, William Dean

Howells, William Dean
1837-1920 .... **TCLC 7, 17, 41**
See also CA 104; 134; CDALB 1865-1917;
DLB 12, 64, 74, 79

Howes, Barbara 1914- .... **CLC 15**
See also CA 9-12R; CAAS 3; SATA 5

Hrabal, Bohumil 1914-........ **CLC 13, 67**
See also CA 106; CAAS 12

Hsun, Lu
See Lu Hsun

Hubbard, L(afayette) Ron(ald)
1911-1986 ....**CLC 43**
See also CA 77-80; 118; CANR 22;
DAM POP

Huch, Ricarda (Octavia)
1864-1947 .... **TCLC 13**
See also CA 111; DLB 66

Huddle, David 1942- .... **CLC 49**
See also CA 57-60; CAAS 20; DLB 130

Hudson, Jeffrey
See Crichton, (John) Michael

Hudson, W(illiam) H(enry)
1841-1922 .... **TCLC 29**
See also CA 115; DLB 98, 153; SATA 35

Hueffer, Ford Madox
See Ford, Ford Madox

Hughart, Barry 1934-............ **CLC 39**
See also CA 137

Hughes, Colin
See Creasey, John

Hughes, David (John) 1930- .... **CLC 48**
See also CA 116; 129; DLB 14

Hughes, Edward James
See Hughes, Ted
See also DAM MST, POET

Hughes, (James) Langston
1902-1967 ..... **CLC 1, 5, 10, 15, 35, 44;**
BLC; DA; DAB; DAC; DC 3; PC 1;
SSC 6; WLC
See also AAYA 12; BW 1; CA 1-4R;
25-28R; CANR 1, 34; CDALB 1929-1941;
CLR 17; DAM DRAM, MST, MULT,
POET; DLB 4, 7, 48, 51, 86; JRDA;
MAICYA; MTCW; SATA 4, 33

Hughes, Richard (Arthur Warren)
1900-1976 .... **CLC 1, 11**
See also CA 5-8R; 65-68; CANR 4;
DAM NOV; DLB 15, 161; MTCW;
SATA 8; SATA-Obit 25

Hughes, Ted
1930- .... **CLC 2, 4, 9, 14, 37; DAB;**
DAC; PC 7
See also Hughes, Edward James
See also CA 1-4R; CANR 1, 33; CLR 3;
DLB 40, 161; MAICYA; MTCW;
SATA 49; SATA-Brief 27

Hugo, Richard F(ranklin)
1923-1982 .... **CLC 6, 18, 32**
See also CA 49-52; 108; CANR 3;
DAM POET; DLB 5

Hugo, Victor (Marie)
1802-1885 .... **NCLC 3, 10, 21; DA;**
DAB; DAC; WLC
See also DAM DRAM, MST, NOV, POET;
DLB 119; SATA 47

Huidobro, Vicente
See Huidobro Fernandez, Vicente Garcia

Huidobro Fernandez, Vicente Garcia
1893-1948 .... **TCLC 31**
See also CA 131; HW

Hulme, Keri 1947- .... **CLC 39**
See also CA 125; INT 125

Hulme, T(homas) E(rnest)
1883-1917 .... **TCLC 21**
See also CA 117; DLB 19

Hume, David 1711-1776............ **LC 7**
See also DLB 104

Humphrey, William 1924-......... **CLC 45**
See also CA 77-80; DLB 6

Humphreys, Emyr Owen 1919-..... **CLC 47**
See also CA 5-8R; CANR 3, 24; DLB 15

Humphreys, Josephine 1945-.... **CLC 34, 57**
See also CA 121; 127; INT 127

Hungerford, Pixie
See Brinsmead, H(esba) F(ay)

Hunt, E(verette) Howard, (Jr.)
1918- .... **CLC 3**
See also AITN 1; CA 45-48; CANR 2, 47

Hunt, Kyle
See Creasey, John

Hunt, (James Henry) Leigh
1784-1859 .... **NCLC 1**
See also DAM POET

Hunt, Marsha 1946-.............. **CLC 70**
See also BW 2; CA 143

Hunt, Violet 1866-1942 .... **TCLC 53**
See also DLB 162

Hunter, E. Waldo
See Sturgeon, Theodore (Hamilton)

Hunter, Evan 1926- .... **CLC 11, 31**
See also CA 5-8R; CANR 5, 38;
DAM POP; DLBY 82; INT CANR-5;
MTCW; SATA 25

Hunter, Kristin (Eggleston) 1931-... **CLC 35**
See also AITN 1; BW 1; CA 13-16R;
CANR 13; CLR 3; DLB 33;
INT CANR-13; MAICYA; SAAS 10;
SATA 12

Hunter, Mollie 1922-............. **CLC 21**
See also McIlwraith, Maureen Mollie
Hunter
See also AAYA 13; CANR 37; CLR 25;
DLB 161; JRDA; MAICYA; SAAS 7;
SATA 54

Hunter, Robert (?)-1734............. **LC 7**

Hurston, Zora Neale
1903-1960 .... **CLC 7, 30, 61; BLC; DA;**
DAC; SSC 4
See also AAYA 15; BW 1; CA 85-88;
DAM MST, MULT, NOV; DLB 51, 86;
MTCW

Huston, John (Marcellus)
1906-1987 .... **CLC 20**
See also CA 73-76; 123; CANR 34; DLB 26

Hustvedt, Siri 1955-.............. **CLC 76**
See also CA 137

Hutten, Ulrich von 1488-1523....... **LC 16**

Huxley, Aldous (Leonard)
1894-1963 ..... **CLC 1, 3, 4, 5, 8, 11, 18,**
35, 79; DA; DAB; DAC; WLC
See also AAYA 11; CA 85-88; CANR 44;
CDBLB 1914-1945; DAM MST, NOV;
DLB 36, 100, 162; MTCW; SATA 63

Huysmans, Charles Marie Georges
1848-1907
See Huysmans, Joris-Karl
See also CA 104

Huysmans, Joris-Karl.............. TCLC 7
See also Huysmans, Charles Marie Georges
See also DLB 123

Hwang, David Henry
1957- .... **CLC 55; DC 4**
See also CA 127; 132; DAM DRAM;
INT 132

Hyde, Anthony 1946-............. **CLC 42**
See also CA 136

Hyde, Margaret O(ldroyd) 1917- ... **CLC 21**
See also CA 1-4R; CANR 1, 36; CLR 23;
JRDA; MAICYA; SAAS 8; SATA 1, 42,
76

Hynes, James 1956(?)-........... **CLC 65**

Ian, Janis 1951- .... **CLC 21**
See also CA 105

Ibanez, Vicente Blasco
See Blasco Ibanez, Vicente

Ibarguengoitia, Jorge 1928-1983.... **CLC 37**
See also CA 124; 113; HW

Ibsen, Henrik (Johan)
1828-1906 .... **TCLC 2, 8, 16, 37, 52;**
DA; DAB; DAC; DC 2; WLC
See also CA 104; 141; DAM DRAM, MST

Ibuse Masuji 1898-1993.......... **CLC 22**
See also CA 127; 141

Ichikawa, Kon 1915-.............. **CLC 20**
See also CA 121

Jeffrey, Francis 1773-1850. . . . . . **NCLC 33**
See also DLB 107

Jelakowitch, Ivan
See Heijermans, Herman

Jellicoe, (Patricia) Ann 1927- . . . . . . **CLC 27**
See also CA 85-88; DLB 13

Jen, Gish . . . . **CLC 70**
See also Jen, Lillian

Jen, Lillian 1956(?)-
See Jen, Gish
See also CA 135

Jenkins, (John) Robin 1912- . . . . **CLC 52**
See also CA 1-4R; CANR 1; DLB 14

Jennings, Elizabeth (Joan)
1926- . . . . **CLC 5, 14**
See also CA 61-64; CAAS 5; CANR 8, 39;
DLB 27; MTCW; SATA 66

Jennings, Waylon 1937- . . . . **CLC 21**

Jensen, Johannes V. 1873-1950. . . . **TCLC 41**

Jensen, Laura (Linnea) 1948- . . . . . . **CLC 37**
See also CA 103

Jerome, Jerome K(lapka)
1859-1927 . . . . **TCLC 23**
See also CA 119; DLB 10, 34, 135

Jerrold, Douglas William
1803-1857 . . . . **NCLC 2**
See also DLB 158, 159

Jewett, (Theodora) Sarah Orne
1849-1909 . . . . **TCLC 1, 22; SSC 6**
See also CA 108; 127; DLB 12, 74;
SATA 15

Jewsbury, Geraldine (Endsor)
1812-1880 . . . . **NCLC 22**
See also DLB 21

Jhabvala, Ruth Prawer
1927- . . . . **CLC 4, 8, 29, 94; DAB**
See also CA 1-4R; CANR 2, 29, 51;
DAM NOV; DLB 139; INT CANR-29;
MTCW

Jibran, Kahlil
See Gibran, Kahlil

Jibran, Khalil
See Gibran, Kahlil

Jiles, Paulette 1943- . . . . **CLC 13, 58**
See also CA 101

Jimenez (Mantecon), Juan Ramon
1881-1958 . . . . **TCLC 4; HLC; PC 7**
See also CA 104; 131; DAM MULT,
POET; DLB 134; HW; MTCW

Jimenez, Ramon
See Jimenez (Mantecon), Juan Ramon

Jimenez Mantecon, Juan
See Jimenez (Mantecon), Juan Ramon

Joel, Billy . . . . **CLC 26**
See also Joel, William Martin

Joel, William Martin 1949-
See Joel, Billy
See also CA 108

John of the Cross, St. 1542-1591 . . . . **LC 18**

Johnson, B(ryan) S(tanley William)
1933-1973 . . . . **CLC 6, 9**
See also CA 9-12R; 53-56; CANR 9;
DLB 14, 40

Johnson, Benj. F. of Boo
See Riley, James Whitcomb

Johnson, Benjamin F. of Boo
See Riley, James Whitcomb

Johnson, Charles (Richard)
1948- . . . . **CLC 7, 51, 65; BLC**
See also BW 2; CA 116; CAAS 18;
CANR 42; DAM MULT; DLB 33

Johnson, Denis 1949- . . . . **CLC 52**
See also CA 117; 121; DLB 120

Johnson, Diane 1934- . . . . **CLC 5, 13, 48**
See also CA 41-44R; CANR 17, 40;
DLBY 80; INT CANR-17; MTCW

Johnson, Eyvind (Olof Verner)
1900-1976 . . . . **CLC 14**
See also CA 73-76; 69-72; CANR 34

Johnson, J. R.
See James, C(yril) L(ionel) R(obert)

Johnson, James Weldon
1871-1938 . . . . **TCLC 3, 19; BLC**
See also BW 1; CA 104; 125;
CDALB 1917-1929; CLR 32;
DAM MULT, POET; DLB 51; MTCW;
SATA 31

Johnson, Joyce 1935- . . . . **CLC 58**
See also CA 125; 129

Johnson, Lionel (Pigot)
1867-1902 . . . . **TCLC 19**
See also CA 117; DLB 19

Johnson, Mel
See Malzberg, Barry N(athaniel)

Johnson, Pamela Hansford
1912-1981 . . . . **CLC 1, 7, 27**
See also CA 1-4R; 104; CANR 2, 28;
DLB 15; MTCW

Johnson, Samuel
1709-1784 . . . . . **LC 15; DA; DAB; DAC;
WLC**
See also CDBLB 1660-1789; DAM MST;
DLB 39, 95, 104, 142

Johnson, Uwe
1934-1984 . . . . **CLC 5, 10, 15, 40**
See also CA 1-4R; 112; CANR 1, 39;
DLB 75; MTCW

Johnston, George (Benson) 1913- . . . **CLC 51**
See also CA 1-4R; CANR 5, 20; DLB 88

Johnston, Jennifer 1930- . . . . **CLC 7**
See also CA 85-88; DLB 14

Jolley, (Monica) Elizabeth
1923- . . . . **CLC 46; SSC 19**
See also CA 127; CAAS 13

Jones, Arthur Llewellyn 1863-1947
See Machen, Arthur
See also CA 104

Jones, D(ouglas) G(ordon) 1929- . . . . **CLC 10**
See also CA 29-32R; CANR 13; DLB 53

Jones, David (Michael)
1895-1974 . . . . **CLC 2, 4, 7, 13, 42**
See also CA 9-12R; 53-56; CANR 28;
CDBLB 1945-1960; DLB 20, 100; MTCW

Jones, David Robert 1947-
See Bowie, David
See also CA 103

Jones, Diana Wynne 1934- . . . . **CLC 26**
See also AAYA 12; CA 49-52; CANR 4,
26; CLR 23; DLB 161; JRDA; MAICYA;
SAAS 7; SATA 9, 70

Jones, Edward P. 1950- . . . . **CLC 76**
See also BW 2; CA 142

Jones, Gayl 1949- . . . . **CLC 6, 9; BLC**
See also BW 2; CA 77-80; CANR 27;
DAM MULT; DLB 33; MTCW

Jones, James 1921-1977. . . . **CLC 1, 3, 10, 39**
See also AITN 1, 2; CA 1-4R; 69-72;
CANR 6; DLB 2, 143; MTCW

Jones, John J.
See Lovecraft, H(oward) P(hillips)

Jones, LeRoi . . . . **CLC 1, 2, 3, 5, 10, 14**
See also Baraka, Amiri

Jones, Louis B. . . . . **CLC 65**
See also CA 141

Jones, Madison (Percy, Jr.) 1925- . . . **CLC 4**
See also CA 13-16R; CAAS 11; CANR 7;
DLB 152

Jones, Mervyn 1922- . . . . **CLC 10, 52**
See also CA 45-48; CAAS 5; CANR 1;
MTCW

Jones, Mick 1956(?)- . . . . **CLC 30**

Jones, Nettie (Pearl) 1941- . . . . **CLC 34**
See also BW 2; CA 137; CAAS 20

Jones, Preston 1936-1979 . . . . **CLC 10**
See also CA 73-76; 89-92; DLB 7

Jones, Robert F(rancis) 1934- . . . . **CLC 7**
See also CA 49-52; CANR 2

Jones, Rod 1953- . . . . **CLC 50**
See also CA 128

Jones, Terence Graham Parry
1942- . . . . **CLC 21**
See also Jones, Terry; Monty Python
See also CA 112; 116; CANR 35; INT 116

Jones, Terry
See Jones, Terence Graham Parry
See also SATA 67; SATA-Brief 51

Jones, Thom 1945(?)- . . . . **CLC 81**

Jong, Erica 1942- . . . . . . **CLC 4, 6, 8, 18, 83**
See also AITN 1; BEST 90:2; CA 73-76;
CANR 26; DAM NOV, POP; DLB 2, 5,
28, 152; INT CANR-26; MTCW

Jonson, Ben(jamin)
1572(?)-1637 . . . . . . **LC 6, 33; DA; DAB;
DAC; DC 4; WLC**
See also CDBLB Before 1660;
DAM DRAM, MST, POET; DLB 62,
121

Jordan, June 1936- . . . . **CLC 5, 11, 23**
See also AAYA 2; BW 2; CA 33-36R;
CANR 25; CLR 10; DAM MULT,
POET; DLB 38; MAICYA; MTCW;
SATA 4

Jordan, Pat(rick M.) 1941- . . . . **CLC 37**
See also CA 33-36R

Jorgensen, Ivar
See Ellison, Harlan (Jay)

Jorgenson, Ivar
See Silverberg, Robert

Josephus, Flavius c. 37-100 . . . . . . **CMLC 13**

Kempe, Margery 1373(?)-1440(?) ..... **LC 6**
See also DLB 146

Kempis, Thomas a 1380-1471 ...... **LC 11**

Kendall, Henry 1839-1882...... **NCLC 12**

Keneally, Thomas (Michael)
1935- ..... **CLC 5, 8, 10, 14, 19, 27, 43**
See also CA 85-88; CANR 10, 50;
DAM NOV; MTCW

Kennedy, Adrienne (Lita)
1931- .... **CLC 66; BLC; DC 5**
See also BW 2; CA 103; CAAS 20; CABS 3;
CANR 26; DAM MULT; DLB 38

Kennedy, John Pendleton
1795-1870 .... **NCLC 2**
See also DLB 3

Kennedy, Joseph Charles 1929-
See Kennedy, X. J.
See also CA 1-4R; CANR 4, 30, 40;
SATA 14, 86

Kennedy, William 1928-... **CLC 6, 28, 34, 53**
See also AAYA 1; CA 85-88; CANR 14,
31; DAM NOV; DLB 143; DLBY 85;
INT CANR-31; MTCW; SATA 57

Kennedy, X. J.................. **CLC 8, 42**
See also Kennedy, Joseph Charles
See also CAAS 9; CLR 27; DLB 5;
SAAS 22

Kenny, Maurice (Francis) 1929- .... **CLC 87**
See also CA 144; CAAS 22; DAM MULT;
NNAL

Kent, Kelvin
See Kuttner, Henry

Kenton, Maxwell
See Southern, Terry

Kenyon, Robert O.
See Kuttner, Henry

Kerouac, Jack ..... **CLC 1, 2, 3, 5, 14, 29, 61**
See also Kerouac, Jean-Louis Lebris de
See also CDALB 1941-1968; DLB 2, 16;
DLBD 3; DLBY 95

Kerouac, Jean-Louis Lebris de 1922-1969
See Kerouac, Jack
See also AITN 1; CA 5-8R; 25-28R;
CANR 26; DA; DAB; DAC; DAM MST,
NOV, POET, POP; MTCW; WLC

Kerr, Jean 1923-................. **CLC 22**
See also CA 5-8R; CANR 7; INT CANR-7

Kerr, M. E.................... **CLC 12, 35**
See also Meaker, Marijane (Agnes)
See also AAYA 2; CLR 29; SAAS 1

Kerr, Robert .... **CLC 55**

Kerrigan, (Thomas) Anthony
1918- .... **CLC 4, 6**
See also CA 49-52; CAAS 11; CANR 4

Kerry, Lois
See Duncan, Lois

Kesey, Ken (Elton)
1935- ...... **CLC 1, 3, 6, 11, 46, 64; DA;
DAB; DAC; WLC**
See also CA 1-4R; CANR 22, 38;
CDALB 1968-1988; DAM MST, NOV,
POP; DLB 2, 16; MTCW; SATA 66

Kesselring, Joseph (Otto)
1902-1967 .... **CLC 45**
See also CA 150; DAM DRAM, MST

Kessler, Jascha (Frederick) 1929-.... **CLC 4**
See also CA 17-20R; CANR 8, 48

Kettelkamp, Larry (Dale) 1933- .... **CLC 12**
See also CA 29-32R; CANR 16; SAAS 3;
SATA 2

Keyber, Conny
See Fielding, Henry

Keyes, Daniel 1927-.... **CLC 80; DA; DAC**
See also CA 17-20R; CANR 10, 26;
DAM MST, NOV; SATA 37

Keynes, John Maynard
1883-1946 .... **TCLC 64**
See also CA 114; DLBD 10

Khanshendel, Chiron
See Rose, Wendy

Khayyam, Omar
1048-1131 .... **CMLC 11; PC 8**
See also DAM POET

Kherdian, David 1931-........... **CLC 6, 9**
See also CA 21-24R; CAAS 2; CANR 39;
CLR 24; JRDA; MAICYA; SATA 16, 74

Khlebnikov, Velimir .... **TCLC 20**
See also Khlebnikov, Viktor Vladimirovich

Khlebnikov, Viktor Vladimirovich 1885-1922
See Khlebnikov, Velimir
See also CA 117

Khodasevich, Vladislav (Felitsianovich)
1886-1939 .... **TCLC 15**
See also CA 115

Kielland, Alexander Lange
1849-1906 .... **TCLC 5**
See also CA 104

Kiely, Benedict 1919-......... **CLC 23, 43**
See also CA 1-4R; CANR 2; DLB 15

Kienzle, William X(avier) 1928- .... **CLC 25**
See also CA 93-96; CAAS 1; CANR 9, 31;
DAM POP; INT CANR-31; MTCW

Kierkegaard, Soren 1813-1855.... **NCLC 34**

Killens, John Oliver 1916-1987..... **CLC 10**
See also BW 2; CA 77-80; 123; CAAS 2;
CANR 26; DLB 33

Killigrew, Anne 1660-1685.......... **LC 4**
See also DLB 131

Kim
See Simenon, Georges (Jacques Christian)

Kincaid, Jamaica 1949- ... **CLC 43, 68; BLC**
See also AAYA 13; BW 2; CA 125;
CANR 47; DAM MULT, NOV;
DLB 157

King, Francis (Henry) 1923- ..... **CLC 8, 53**
See also CA 1-4R; CANR 1, 33;
DAM NOV; DLB 15, 139; MTCW

King, Martin Luther, Jr.
1929-1968 .... **CLC 83; BLC; DA; DAB;
DAC**
See also BW 2; CA 25-28; CANR 27, 44;
CAP 2; DAM MST, MULT; MTCW;
SATA 14

King, Stephen (Edwin)
1947- ...... **CLC 12, 26, 37, 61; SSC 17**
See also AAYA 1, 17; BEST 90:1;
CA 61-64; CANR 1, 30; DAM NOV,
POP; DLB 143; DLBY 80; JRDA;
MTCW; SATA 9, 55

King, Steve
See King, Stephen (Edwin)

King, Thomas 1943-......... **CLC 89; DAC**
See also CA 144; DAM MULT; NNAL

Kingman, Lee..................... **CLC 17**
See also Natti, (Mary) Lee
See also SAAS 3; SATA 1, 67

Kingsley, Charles 1819-1875 ..... **NCLC 35**
See also DLB 21, 32, 163; YABC 2

Kingsley, Sidney 1906-1995........ **CLC 44**
See also CA 85-88; 147; DLB 7

Kingsolver, Barbara 1955-...... **CLC 55, 81**
See also AAYA 15; CA 129; 134;
DAM POP; INT 134

Kingston, Maxine (Ting Ting) Hong
1940- .... **CLC 12, 19, 58**
See also AAYA 8; CA 69-72; CANR 13,
38; DAM MULT, NOV; DLBY 80;
INT CANR-13; MTCW; SATA 53

Kinnell, Galway
1927- .... **CLC 1, 2, 3, 5, 13, 29**
See also CA 9-12R; CANR 10, 34; DLB 5;
DLBY 87; INT CANR-34; MTCW

Kinsella, Thomas 1928- .... **CLC 4, 19**
See also CA 17-20R; CANR 15; DLB 27;
MTCW

Kinsella, W(illiam) P(atrick)
1935- .... **CLC 27, 43; DAC**
See also AAYA 7; CA 97-100; CAAS 7;
CANR 21, 35; DAM NOV, POP;
INT CANR-21; MTCW

Kipling, (Joseph) Rudyard
1865-1936 ...... **TCLC 8, 17; DA; DAB;
DAC; PC 3; SSC 5; WLC**
See also CA 105; 120; CANR 33;
CDBLB 1890-1914; CLR 39; DAM MST,
POET; DLB 19, 34, 141, 156; MAICYA;
MTCW; YABC 2

Kirkup, James 1918- .... **CLC 1**
See also CA 1-4R; CAAS 4; CANR 2;
DLB 27; SATA 12

Kirkwood, James 1930(?)-1989 ...... **CLC 9**
See also AITN 2; CA 1-4R; 128; CANR 6,
40

Kirshner, Sidney
See Kingsley, Sidney

Kis, Danilo 1935-1989 .... **CLC 57**
See also CA 109; 118; 129; MTCW

Kivi, Aleksis 1834-1872 .... **NCLC 30**

Kizer, Carolyn (Ashley)
1925- .... **CLC 15, 39, 80**
See also CA 65-68; CAAS 5; CANR 24;
DAM POET; DLB 5

Klabund 1890-1928............. **TCLC 44**
See also DLB 66

Klappert, Peter 1942-............. **CLC 57**
See also CA 33-36R; DLB 5

Klein, A(braham) M(oses)
1909-1972 .... **CLC 19; DAB; DAC**
See also CA 101; 37-40R; DAM MST;
DLB 68

Klein, Norma 1938-1989 .... **CLC 30**
See also AAYA 2; CA 41-44R; 128;
CANR 15, 37; CLR 2, 19;
INT CANR-15; JRDA; MAICYA;
SAAS 1; SATA 7, 57

Kuprin, Aleksandr Ivanovich
1870-1938 . . . . **TCLC 5**
See also CA 104

Kureishi, Hanif 1954(?)- . . . . **CLC 64**
See also CA 139

Kurosawa, Akira 1910- . . . . **CLC 16**
See also AAYA 11; CA 101; CANR 46;
DAM MULT

Kushner, Tony 1957(?)- . . . . **CLC 81**
See also CA 144; DAM DRAM

Kuttner, Henry 1915-1958 . . . . **TCLC 10**
See also CA 107; DLB 8

Kuzma, Greg 1944- . . . . **CLC 7**
See also CA 33-36R

Kuzmin, Mikhail 1872(?)-1936 . . . . **TCLC 40**

Kyd, Thomas 1558-1594 . . . . . . **LC 22; DC 3**
See also DAM DRAM; DLB 62

Kyprianos, Iossif
See Samarakis, Antonis

La Bruyere, Jean de 1645-1696 . . . . . . **LC 17**

Lacan, Jacques (Marie Emile)
1901-1981 . . . . **CLC 75**
See also CA 121; 104

**Laclos, Pierre Ambroise Francois Choderlos
de** 1741-1803 . . . . **NCLC 4**

Lacolere, Francois
See Aragon, Louis

La Colere, Francois
See Aragon, Louis

La Deshabilleuse
See Simenon, Georges (Jacques Christian)

Lady Gregory
See Gregory, Isabella Augusta (Persse)

Lady of Quality, A
See Bagnold, Enid

**La Fayette, Marie (Madelaine Pioche de la
Vergne Comtes** 1634-1693 . . . . . . **LC 2**

Lafayette, Rene
See Hubbard, L(afayette) Ron(ald)

Laforgue, Jules
1860-1887 . . . . **NCLC 5, 53; PC 14;
SSC 20**

Lagerkvist, Paer (Fabian)
1891-1974 . . . . **CLC 7, 10, 13, 54**
See also Lagerkvist, Par
See also CA 85-88; 49-52; DAM DRAM,
NOV; MTCW

Lagerkvist, Par . . . . **SSC 12**
See also Lagerkvist, Paer (Fabian)

Lagerloef, Selma (Ottiliana Lovisa)
1858-1940 . . . . **TCLC 4, 36**
See also Lagerlof, Selma (Ottiliana Lovisa)
See also CA 108; SATA 15

Lagerlof, Selma (Ottiliana Lovisa)
See Lagerloef, Selma (Ottiliana Lovisa)
See also CLR 7; SATA 15

La Guma, (Justin) Alex(ander)
1925-1985 . . . . **CLC 19**
See also BW 1; CA 49-52; 118; CANR 25;
DAM NOV; DLB 117; MTCW

Laidlaw, A. K.
See Grieve, C(hristopher) M(urray)

Lainez, Manuel Mujica
See Mujica Lainez, Manuel
See also HW

Lamartine, Alphonse (Marie Louis Prat) de
1790-1869 . . . . **NCLC 11**
See also DAM POET

Lamb, Charles
1775-1834 . . . . **NCLC 10; DA; DAB;
DAC; WLC**
See also CDBLB 1789-1832; DAM MST;
DLB 93, 107, 163; SATA 17

Lamb, Lady Caroline 1785-1828 . . **NCLC 38**
See also DLB 116

Lamming, George (William)
1927- . . . . **CLC 2, 4, 66; BLC**
See also BW 2; CA 85-88; CANR 26;
DAM MULT; DLB 125; MTCW

L'Amour, Louis (Dearborn)
1908-1988 . . . . **CLC 25, 55**
See also AAYA 16; AITN 2; BEST 89:2;
CA 1-4R; 125; CANR 3, 25, 40;
DAM NOV, POP; DLBY 80; MTCW

Lampedusa, Giuseppe (Tomasi) di . . . **TCLC 13**
See also Tomasi di Lampedusa, Giuseppe

Lampman, Archibald 1861-1899 . . **NCLC 25**
See also DLB 92

Lancaster, Bruce 1896-1963 . . . . **CLC 36**
See also CA 9-10; CAP 1; SATA 9

Landau, Mark Alexandrovich
See Aldanov, Mark (Alexandrovich)

Landau-Aldanov, Mark Alexandrovich
See Aldanov, Mark (Alexandrovich)

Landis, John 1950- . . . . **CLC 26**
See also CA 112; 122

Landolfi, Tommaso 1908-1979 . . . **CLC 11, 49**
See also CA 127; 117

Landon, Letitia Elizabeth
1802-1838 . . . . **NCLC 15**
See also DLB 96

Landor, Walter Savage
1775-1864 . . . . **NCLC 14**
See also DLB 93, 107

Landwirth, Heinz 1927-
See Lind, Jakov
See also CA 9-12R; CANR 7

Lane, Patrick 1939- . . . . **CLC 25**
See also CA 97-100; DAM POET; DLB 53;
INT 97-100

Lang, Andrew 1844-1912 . . . . **TCLC 16**
See also CA 114; 137; DLB 98, 141;
MAICYA; SATA 16

Lang, Fritz 1890-1976 . . . . **CLC 20**
See also CA 77-80; 69-72; CANR 30

Lange, John
See Crichton, (John) Michael

Langer, Elinor 1939- . . . . **CLC 34**
See also CA 121

Langland, William
1330(?)-1400(?) . . . . . . **LC 19; DA; DAB;
DAC**
See also DAM MST, POET; DLB 146

Langstaff, Launcelot
See Irving, Washington

Lanier, Sidney 1842-1881 . . . . **NCLC 6**
See also DAM POET; DLB 64; DLBD 13;
MAICYA; SATA 18

Lanyer, Aemilia 1569-1645 . . . . . . **LC 10, 30**
See also DLB 121

Lao Tzu . . . . **CMLC 7**

Lapine, James (Elliot) 1949- . . . . **CLC 39**
See also CA 123; 130; INT 130

Larbaud, Valery (Nicolas)
1881-1957 . . . . **TCLC 9**
See also CA 106

Lardner, Ring
See Lardner, Ring(gold) W(ilmer)

Lardner, Ring W., Jr.
See Lardner, Ring(gold) W(ilmer)

Lardner, Ring(gold) W(ilmer)
1885-1933 . . . . **TCLC 2, 14**
See also CA 104; 131; CDALB 1917-1929;
DLB 11, 25, 86; MTCW

Laredo, Betty
See Codrescu, Andrei

Larkin, Maia
See Wojciechowska, Maia (Teresa)

Larkin, Philip (Arthur)
1922-1985 . . . . **CLC 3, 5, 8, 9, 13, 18, 33,
39, 64; DAB**
See also CA 5-8R; 117; CANR 24;
CDBLB 1960 to Present; DAM MST,
POET; DLB 27; MTCW

Larra (y Sanchez de Castro), Mariano Jose de
1809-1837 . . . . **NCLC 17**

Larsen, Eric 1941- . . . . **CLC 55**
See also CA 132

Larsen, Nella 1891-1964 . . . . . **CLC 37; BLC**
See also BW 1; CA 125; DAM MULT;
DLB 51

Larson, Charles R(aymond) 1938- . . . **CLC 31**
See also CA 53-56; CANR 4

Las Casas, Bartolome de 1474-1566 . . **LC 31**

Lasker-Schueler, Else 1869-1945 . . **TCLC 57**
See also DLB 66, 124

Latham, Jean Lee 1902- . . . . **CLC 12**
See also AITN 1; CA 5-8R; CANR 7;
MAICYA; SATA 2, 68

Latham, Mavis
See Clark, Mavis Thorpe

Lathen, Emma . . . . **CLC 2**
See also Hennissart, Martha; Latsis, Mary
J(ane)

Lathrop, Francis
See Leiber, Fritz (Reuter, Jr.)

Latsis, Mary J(ane)
See Lathen, Emma
See also CA 85-88

Lattimore, Richmond (Alexander)
1906-1984 . . . . **CLC 3**
See also CA 1-4R; 112; CANR 1

Laughlin, James 1914- . . . . **CLC 49**
See also CA 21-24R; CAAS 22; CANR 9,
47; DLB 48

Lemann, Nancy 1956- . . . . **CLC 39**
See also CA 118; 136

Lemonnier, (Antoine Louis) Camille
1844-1913 . . . . **TCLC 22**
See also CA 121

Lenau, Nikolaus 1802-1850 . . . . . . **NCLC 16**

L'Engle, Madeleine (Camp Franklin)
1918- . . . . **CLC 12**
See also AAYA 1; AITN 2; CA 1-4R;
CANR 3, 21, 39; CLR 1, 14; DAM POP;
DLB 52; JRDA; MAICYA; MTCW;
SAAS 15; SATA 1, 27, 75

Lengyel, Jozsef 1896-1975 . . . . **CLC 7**
See also CA 85-88; 57-60

Lennon, John (Ono)
1940-1980 . . . . **CLC 12, 35**
See also CA 102

Lennox, Charlotte Ramsay
1729(?)-1804 . . . . **NCLC 23**
See also DLB 39

Lentricchia, Frank (Jr.) 1940- . . . . . . **CLC 34**
See also CA 25-28R; CANR 19

Lenz, Siegfried 1926- . . . . **CLC 27**
See also CA 89-92; DLB 75

Leonard, Elmore (John, Jr.)
1925- . . . . **CLC 28, 34, 71**
See also AITN 1; BEST 89:1, 90:4;
CA 81-84; CANR 12, 28; DAM POP;
INT CANR-28; MTCW

Leonard, Hugh. . . . . **CLC 19**
See also Byrne, John Keyes
See also DLB 13

Leonov, Leonid (Maximovich)
1899-1994 . . . . **CLC 92**
See also CA 129; DAM NOV; MTCW

Leopardi, (Conte) Giacomo
1798-1837 . . . . **NCLC 22**

Le Reveler
See Artaud, Antonin (Marie Joseph)

Lerman, Eleanor 1952- . . . . **CLC 9**
See also CA 85-88

Lerman, Rhoda 1936- . . . . **CLC 56**
See also CA 49-52

Lermontov, Mikhail Yuryevich
1814-1841 . . . . **NCLC 47**

Leroux, Gaston 1868-1927 . . . . **TCLC 25**
See also CA 108; 136; SATA 65

Lesage, Alain-Rene 1668-1747 . . . . . . **LC 28**

Leskov, Nikolai (Semyonovich)
1831-1895 . . . . **NCLC 25**

Lessing, Doris (May)
1919- . . . . . **CLC 1, 2, 3, 6, 10, 15, 22, 40,
94; DA; DAB; DAC; SSC 6**
See also CA 9-12R; CAAS 14; CANR 33;
CDBLB 1960 to Present; DAM MST,
NOV; DLB 15, 139; DLBY 85; MTCW

Lessing, Gotthold Ephraim
1729-1781 . . . . **LC 8**
See also DLB 97

Lester, Richard 1932- . . . . **CLC 20**

Lever, Charles (James)
1806-1872 . . . . **NCLC 23**
See also DLB 21

Leverson, Ada 1865(?)-1936(?) . . . . **TCLC 18**
See also Elaine
See also CA 117; DLB 153

Levertov, Denise
1923- . . . . . . **CLC 1, 2, 3, 5, 8, 15, 28, 66;
PC 11**
See also CA 1-4R; CAAS 19; CANR 3, 29,
50; DAM POET; DLB 5, 165;
INT CANR-29; MTCW

Levi, Jonathan. . . . . **CLC 76**

Levi, Peter (Chad Tigar) 1931- . . . . . **CLC 41**
See also CA 5-8R; CANR 34; DLB 40

Levi, Primo
1919-1987 . . . . **CLC 37, 50; SSC 12**
See also CA 13-16R; 122; CANR 12, 33;
MTCW

Levin, Ira 1929- . . . . **CLC 3, 6**
See also CA 21-24R; CANR 17, 44;
DAM POP; MTCW; SATA 66

Levin, Meyer 1905-1981 . . . . **CLC 7**
See also AITN 1; CA 9-12R; 104;
CANR 15; DAM POP; DLB 9, 28;
DLBY 81; SATA 21; SATA-Obit 27

Levine, Norman 1924- . . . . **CLC 54**
See also CA 73-76; CAAS 23; CANR 14;
DLB 88

Levine, Philip 1928- . . **CLC 2, 4, 5, 9, 14, 33**
See also CA 9-12R; CANR 9, 37;
DAM POET; DLB 5

Levinson, Deirdre 1931- . . . . **CLC 49**
See also CA 73-76

Levi-Strauss, Claude 1908- . . . . **CLC 38**
See also CA 1-4R; CANR 6, 32; MTCW

Levitin, Sonia (Wolff) 1934- . . . . **CLC 17**
See also AAYA 13; CA 29-32R; CANR 14,
32; JRDA; MAICYA; SAAS 2; SATA 4,
68

Levon, O. U.
See Kesey, Ken (Elton)

Lewes, George Henry
1817-1878 . . . . **NCLC 25**
See also DLB 55, 144

Lewis, Alun 1915-1944 . . . . **TCLC 3**
See also CA 104; DLB 20, 162

Lewis, C. Day
See Day Lewis, C(ecil)

Lewis, C(live) S(taples)
1898-1963 . . . . . **CLC 1, 3, 6, 14, 27; DA;
DAB; DAC; WLC**
See also AAYA 3; CA 81-84; CANR 33;
CDBLB 1945-1960; CLR 3, 27;
DAM MST, NOV, POP; DLB 15, 100,
160; JRDA; MAICYA; MTCW;
SATA 13

Lewis, Janet 1899- . . . . **CLC 41**
See also Winters, Janet Lewis
See also CA 9-12R; CANR 29; CAP 1;
DLBY 87

Lewis, Matthew Gregory
1775-1818 . . . . **NCLC 11**
See also DLB 39, 158

Lewis, (Harry) Sinclair
1885-1951 . . . . . **TCLC 4, 13, 23, 39; DA;
DAB; DAC; WLC**
See also CA 104; 133; CDALB 1917-1929;
DAM MST, NOV; DLB 9, 102; DLBD 1;
MTCW

Lewis, (Percy) Wyndham
1884(?)-1957 . . . . **TCLC 2, 9**
See also CA 104; DLB 15

Lewisohn, Ludwig 1883-1955 . . . . . **TCLC 19**
See also CA 107; DLB 4, 9, 28, 102

Leyner, Mark 1956- . . . . **CLC 92**
See also CA 110; CANR 28

Lezama Lima, Jose 1910-1976 . . . **CLC 4, 10**
See also CA 77-80; DAM MULT;
DLB 113; HW

L'Heureux, John (Clarke) 1934- . . . . **CLC 52**
See also CA 13-16R; CANR 23, 45

Liddell, C. H.
See Kuttner, Henry

Lie, Jonas (Lauritz Idemil)
1833-1908(?) . . . . **TCLC 5**
See also CA 115

Lieber, Joel 1937-1971 . . . . **CLC 6**
See also CA 73-76; 29-32R

Lieber, Stanley Martin
See Lee, Stan

Lieberman, Laurence (James)
1935- . . . . **CLC 4, 36**
See also CA 17-20R; CANR 8, 36

Lieksman, Anders
See Haavikko, Paavo Juhani

Li Fei-kan 1904-
See Pa Chin
See also CA 105

Lifton, Robert Jay 1926- . . . . **CLC 67**
See also CA 17-20R; CANR 27;
INT CANR-27; SATA 66

Lightfoot, Gordon 1938- . . . . **CLC 26**
See also CA 109

Lightman, Alan P. 1948- . . . . **CLC 81**
See also CA 141

Ligotti, Thomas (Robert)
1953- . . . . **CLC 44; SSC 16**
See also CA 123; CANR 49

Li Ho 791-817 . . . . **PC 13**

Liliencron, (Friedrich Adolf Axel) Detlev von
1844-1909 . . . . **TCLC 18**
See also CA 117

Lilly, William 1602-1681 . . . . **LC 27**

Lima, Jose Lezama
See Lezama Lima, Jose

Lima Barreto, Afonso Henrique de
1881-1922 . . . . **TCLC 23**
See also CA 117

Limonov, Edward 1944- . . . . **CLC 67**
See also CA 137

Lin, Frank
See Atherton, Gertrude (Franklin Horn)

Lincoln, Abraham 1809-1865 . . . . . **NCLC 18**

Lind, Jakov . . . . **CLC 1, 2, 4, 27, 82**
See also Landwirth, Heinz
See also CAAS 4

Author Index

Markham, Edwin 1852-1940 . . . . . **TCLC 47**
See also DLB 54

Markham, Robert
See Amis, Kingsley (William)

Marks, J
See Highwater, Jamake (Mamake)

Marks-Highwater, J
See Highwater, Jamake (Mamake)

Markson, David M(errill) 1927- . . . . **CLC 67**
See also CA 49-52; CANR 1

Marley, Bob . . . . **CLC 17**
See also Marley, Robert Nesta

Marley, Robert Nesta 1945-1981
See Marley, Bob
See also CA 107; 103

Marlowe, Christopher
1564-1593 . . . . . **LC 22; DA; DAB; DAC;**
DC 1; WLC
See also CDBLB Before 1660;
DAM DRAM, MST; DLB 62

Marmontel, Jean-Francois
1723-1799 . . . . **LC 2**

Marquand, John P(hillips)
1893-1960 . . . . **CLC 2, 10**
See also CA 85-88; DLB 9, 102

Marquez, Gabriel (Jose) Garcia
See Garcia Marquez, Gabriel (Jose)

Marquis, Don(ald Robert Perry)
1878-1937 . . . . **TCLC 7**
See also CA 104; DLB 11, 25

Marric, J. J.
See Creasey, John

Marrow, Bernard
See Moore, Brian

Marryat, Frederick 1792-1848 . . . . **NCLC 3**
See also DLB 21, 163

Marsden, James
See Creasey, John

Marsh, (Edith) Ngaio
1899-1982 . . . . **CLC 7, 53**
See also CA 9-12R; CANR 6; DAM POP;
DLB 77; MTCW

Marshall, Garry 1934- . . . . **CLC 17**
See also AAYA 3; CA 111; SATA 60

Marshall, Paule
1929- . . . . **CLC 27, 72; BLC; SSC 3**
See also BW 2; CA 77-80; CANR 25;
DAM MULT; DLB 157; MTCW

Marsten, Richard
See Hunter, Evan

Marston, John 1576-1634 . . . . **LC 33**
See also DAM DRAM; DLB 58

Martha, Henry
See Harris, Mark

Martial c. 40-c. 104 . . . . **PC 10**

Martin, Ken
See Hubbard, L(afayette) Ron(ald)

Martin, Richard
See Creasey, John

Martin, Steve 1945- . . . . **CLC 30**
See also CA 97-100; CANR 30; MTCW

Martin, Valerie 1948- . . . . **CLC 89**
See also BEST 90:2; CA 85-88; CANR 49

Martin, Violet Florence
1862-1915 . . . . **TCLC 51**

Martin, Webber
See Silverberg, Robert

Martindale, Patrick Victor
See White, Patrick (Victor Martindale)

Martin du Gard, Roger
1881-1958 . . . . **TCLC 24**
See also CA 118; DLB 65

Martineau, Harriet 1802-1876 . . . . **NCLC 26**
See also DLB 21, 55, 159, 163; YABC 2

Martines, Julia
See O'Faolain, Julia

Martinez, Jacinto Benavente y
See Benavente (y Martinez), Jacinto

Martinez Ruiz, Jose 1873-1967
See Azorin; Ruiz, Jose Martinez
See also CA 93-96; HW

Martinez Sierra, Gregorio
1881-1947 . . . . **TCLC 6**
See also CA 115

Martinez Sierra, Maria (de la O'LeJarraga)
1874-1974 . . . . **TCLC 6**
See also CA 115

Martinsen, Martin
See Follett, Ken(neth Martin)

Martinson, Harry (Edmund)
1904-1978 . . . . **CLC 14**
See also CA 77-80; CANR 34

Marut, Ret
See Traven, B.

Marut, Robert
See Traven, B.

Marvell, Andrew
1621-1678 . . . . . . **LC 4; DA; DAB; DAC;**
PC 10; WLC
See also CDBLB 1660-1789; DAM MST,
POET; DLB 131

Marx, Karl (Heinrich)
1818-1883 . . . . **NCLC 17**
See also DLB 129

Masaoka Shiki . . . . **TCLC 18**
See also Masaoka Tsunenori

Masaoka Tsunenori 1867-1902
See Masaoka Shiki
See also CA 117

Masefield, John (Edward)
1878-1967 . . . . **CLC 11, 47**
See also CA 19-20; 25-28R; CANR 33;
CAP 2; CDBLB 1890-1914; DAM POET;
DLB 10, 19, 153, 160; MTCW; SATA 19

Maso, Carole 19(?)- . . . . **CLC 44**

Mason, Bobbie Ann
1940- . . . . **CLC 28, 43, 82; SSC 4**
See also AAYA 5; CA 53-56; CANR 11,
31; DLBY 87; INT CANR-31; MTCW

Mason, Ernst
See Pohl, Frederik

Mason, Lee W.
See Malzberg, Barry N(athaniel)

Mason, Nick 1945- . . . . **CLC 35**

Mason, Tally
See Derleth, August (William)

Mass, William
See Gibson, William

Masters, Edgar Lee
1868-1950 . . . . . **TCLC 2, 25; DA; DAC;**
PC 1
See also CA 104; 133; CDALB 1865-1917;
DAM MST, POET; DLB 54; MTCW

Masters, Hilary 1928- . . . . **CLC 48**
See also CA 25-28R; CANR 13, 47

Mastrosimone, William 19(?)- . . . . . . **CLC 36**

Mathe, Albert
See Camus, Albert

Matheson, Richard Burton 1926- . . . **CLC 37**
See also CA 97-100; DLB 8, 44; INT 97-100

Mathews, Harry 1930- . . . . **CLC 6, 52**
See also CA 21-24R; CAAS 6; CANR 18,
40

Mathews, John Joseph 1894-1979 . . . **CLC 84**
See also CA 19-20; 142; CANR 45; CAP 2;
DAM MULT; NNAL

Mathias, Roland (Glyn) 1915- . . . . . . **CLC 45**
See also CA 97-100; CANR 19, 41; DLB 27

Matsuo Basho 1644-1694 . . . . **PC 3**
See also DAM POET

Mattheson, Rodney
See Creasey, John

Matthews, Greg 1949- . . . . **CLC 45**
See also CA 135

Matthews, William 1942- . . . . **CLC 40**
See also CA 29-32R; CAAS 18; CANR 12;
DLB 5

Matthias, John (Edward) 1941- . . . . . . **CLC 9**
See also CA 33-36R

Matthiessen, Peter
1927- . . . . **CLC 5, 7, 11, 32, 64**
See also AAYA 6; BEST 90:4; CA 9-12R;
CANR 21, 50; DAM NOV; DLB 6;
MTCW; SATA 27

Maturin, Charles Robert
1780(?)-1824 . . . . **NCLC 6**

Matute (Ausejo), Ana Maria
1925- . . . . **CLC 11**
See also CA 89-92; MTCW

Maugham, W. S.
See Maugham, W(illiam) Somerset

Maugham, W(illiam) Somerset
1874-1965 . . . . **CLC 1, 11, 15, 67, 93;**
DA; DAB; DAC; SSC 8; WLC
See also CA 5-8R; 25-28R; CANR 40;
CDBLB 1914-1945; DAM DRAM, MST,
NOV; DLB 10, 36, 77, 100, 162; MTCW;
SATA 54

Maugham, William Somerset
See Maugham, W(illiam) Somerset

Maupassant, (Henri Rene Albert) Guy de
1850-1893 . . . . . **NCLC 1, 42; DA; DAB;**
DAC; SSC 1; WLC
See also DAM MST; DLB 123

Maurhut, Richard
See Traven, B.

Mauriac, Claude 1914- . . . . **CLC 9**
See also CA 89-92; DLB 83

McPherson, William (Alexander)
1933- . . . . **CLC 34**
See also CA 69-72; CANR 28;
INT CANR-28

Mead, Margaret 1901-1978 . . . . **CLC 37**
See also AITN 1; CA 1-4R; 81-84;
CANR 4; MTCW; SATA-Obit 20

Meaker, Marijane (Agnes) 1927-
See Kerr, M. E.
See also CA 107; CANR 37; INT 107;
JRDA; MAICYA; MTCW; SATA 20, 61

Medoff, Mark (Howard) 1940- . . . **CLC 6, 23**
See also AITN 1; CA 53-56; CANR 5;
DAM DRAM; DLB 7; INT CANR-5

Medvedev, P. N.
See Bakhtin, Mikhail Mikhailovich

Meged, Aharon
See Megged, Aharon

Meged, Aron
See Megged, Aharon

Megged, Aharon 1920- . . . . **CLC 9**
See also CA 49-52; CAAS 13; CANR 1

Mehta, Ved (Parkash) 1934- . . . . **CLC 37**
See also CA 1-4R; CANR 2, 23; MTCW

Melanter
See Blackmore, R(ichard) D(oddridge)

Melikow, Loris
See Hofmannsthal, Hugo von

Melmoth, Sebastian
See Wilde, Oscar (Fingal O'Flahertie Wills)

Meltzer, Milton 1915- . . . . **CLC 26**
See also AAYA 8; CA 13-16R; CANR 38;
CLR 13; DLB 61; JRDA; MAICYA;
SAAS 1; SATA 1, 50, 80

Melville, Herman
1819-1891 . . . . . **NCLC 3, 12, 29, 45, 49;
DA; DAB; DAC; SSC 1, 17; WLC**
See also CDALB 1640-1865; DAM MST,
NOV; DLB 3, 74; SATA 59

Menander
c. 342B.C.-c. 292B.C. . . . . **CMLC 9; DC 3**
See also DAM DRAM

Mencken, H(enry) L(ouis)
1880-1956 . . . . **TCLC 13**
See also CA 105; 125; CDALB 1917-1929;
DLB 11, 29, 63, 137; MTCW

Mercer, David 1928-1980 . . . . **CLC 5**
See also CA 9-12R; 102; CANR 23;
DAM DRAM; DLB 13; MTCW

Merchant, Paul
See Ellison, Harlan (Jay)

Meredith, George 1828-1909 . . . **TCLC 17, 43**
See also CA 117; CDBLB 1832-1890;
DAM POET; DLB 18, 35, 57, 159

Meredith, William (Morris)
1919- . . . . **CLC 4, 13, 22, 55**
See also CA 9-12R; CAAS 14; CANR 6, 40;
DAM POET; DLB 5

Merezhkovsky, Dmitry Sergeyevich
1865-1941 . . . . **TCLC 29**

Merimee, Prosper
1803-1870 . . . . **NCLC 6; SSC 7**
See also DLB 119

Merkin, Daphne 1954- . . . . **CLC 44**
See also CA 123

Merlin, Arthur
See Blish, James (Benjamin)

Merrill, James (Ingram)
1926-1995 . . . . **CLC 2, 3, 6, 8, 13, 18, 34,
91**
See also CA 13-16R; 147; CANR 10, 49;
DAM POET; DLB 5, 165; DLBY 85;
INT CANR-10; MTCW

Merriman, Alex
See Silverberg, Robert

Merritt, E. B.
See Waddington, Miriam

Merton, Thomas
1915-1968 . . **CLC 1, 3, 11, 34, 83; PC 10**
See also CA 5-8R; 25-28R; CANR 22;
DLB 48; DLBY 81; MTCW

Merwin, W(illiam) S(tanley)
1927- . . . **CLC 1, 2, 3, 5, 8, 13, 18, 45, 88**
See also CA 13-16R; CANR 15, 51;
DAM POET; DLB 5; INT CANR-15;
MTCW

Metcalf, John 1938- . . . . **CLC 37**
See also CA 113; DLB 60

Metcalf, Suzanne
See Baum, L(yman) Frank

Mew, Charlotte (Mary)
1870-1928 . . . . **TCLC 8**
See also CA 105; DLB 19, 135

Mewshaw, Michael 1943- . . . . **CLC 9**
See also CA 53-56; CANR 7, 47; DLBY 80

Meyer, June
See Jordan, June

Meyer, Lynn
See Slavitt, David R(ytman)

Meyer-Meyrink, Gustav 1868-1932
See Meyrink, Gustav
See also CA 117

Meyers, Jeffrey 1939- . . . . **CLC 39**
See also CA 73-76; DLB 111

Meynell, Alice (Christina Gertrude Thompson)
1847-1922 . . . . **TCLC 6**
See also CA 104; DLB 19, 98

Meyrink, Gustav . . . . **TCLC 21**
See Meyer-Meyrink, Gustav
See also DLB 81

Michaels, Leonard
1933- . . . . **CLC 6, 25; SSC 16**
See also CA 61-64; CANR 21; DLB 130;
MTCW

Michaux, Henri 1899-1984 . . . . . . **CLC 8, 19**
See also CA 85-88; 114

Michelangelo 1475-1564 . . . . **LC 12**

Michelet, Jules 1798-1874 . . . . . . **NCLC 31**

Michener, James A(lbert)
1907(?)- . . . . **CLC 1, 5, 11, 29, 60**
See also AITN 1; BEST 90:1; CA 5-8R;
CANR 21, 45; DAM NOV, POP; DLB 6;
MTCW

Mickiewicz, Adam 1798-1855 . . . . . **NCLC 3**

Middleton, Christopher 1926- . . . . . . **CLC 13**
See also CA 13-16R; CANR 29; DLB 40

Middleton, Richard (Barham)
1882-1911 . . . . **TCLC 56**
See also DLB 156

Middleton, Stanley 1919- . . . . **CLC 7, 38**
See also CA 25-28R; CAAS 23; CANR 21,
46; DLB 14

Middleton, Thomas
1580-1627 . . . . **LC 33; DC 5**
See also DAM DRAM; MST; DLB 58

Migueis, Jose Rodrigues 1901- . . . . . **CLC 10**

Mikszath, Kalman 1847-1910 . . . . . **TCLC 31**

Miles, Josephine
1911-1985 . . . . **CLC 1, 2, 14, 34, 39**
See also CA 1-4R; 116; CANR 2;
DAM POET; DLB 48

Militant
See Sandburg, Carl (August)

Mill, John Stuart 1806-1873 . . . . . **NCLC 11**
See also CDBLB 1832-1890; DLB 55

Millar, Kenneth 1915-1983 . . . . **CLC 14**
See also Macdonald, Ross
See also CA 9-12R; 110; CANR 16;
DAM POP; DLB 2; DLBD 6; DLBY 83;
MTCW

Millay, E. Vincent
See Millay, Edna St. Vincent

Millay, Edna St. Vincent
1892-1950 . . . . . . **TCLC 4, 49; DA; DAB;
DAC; PC 6**
See also CA 104; 130; CDALB 1917-1929;
DAM MST, POET; DLB 45; MTCW

Miller, Arthur
1915- . . . . **CLC 1, 2, 6, 10, 15, 26, 47, 78;
DA; DAB; DAC; DC 1; WLC**
See also AAYA 15; AITN 1; CA 1-4R;
CABS 3; CANR 2, 30;
CDALB 1941-1968; DAM DRAM, MST;
DLB 7; MTCW

Miller, Henry (Valentine)
1891-1980 . . . . **CLC 1, 2, 4, 9, 14, 43, 84;
DA; DAB; DAC; WLC**
See also CA 9-12R; 97-100; CANR 33;
CDALB 1929-1941; DAM MST, NOV;
DLB 4, 9; DLBY 80; MTCW

Miller, Jason 1939(?)- . . . . **CLC 2**
See also AITN 1; CA 73-76; DLB 7

Miller, Sue 1943- . . . . **CLC 44**
See also BEST 90:3; CA 139; DAM POP;
DLB 143

Miller, Walter M(ichael, Jr.)
1923- . . . . **CLC 4, 30**
See also CA 85-88; DLB 8

Millett, Kate 1934- . . . . **CLC 67**
See also AITN 1; CA 73-76; CANR 32;
MTCW

Millhauser, Steven 1943- . . . . **CLC 21, 54**
See also CA 110; 111; DLB 2; INT 111

Millin, Sarah Gertrude 1889-1968 . . **CLC 49**
See also CA 102; 93-96

Milne, A(lan) A(lexander)
1882-1956 . . . . **TCLC 6; DAB; DAC**
See also CA 104; 133; CLR 1, 26;
DAM MST; DLB 10, 77, 100, 160;
MAICYA; MTCW; YABC 1

Milner, Ron(ald) 1938- . . . . **CLC 56; BLC**
See also AITN 1; BW 1; CA 73-76;
CANR 24; DAM MULT; DLB 38;
MTCW

Murry, John Middleton
1889-1957 . . . . TCLC **16**
See also CA 118; DLB 149

Musgrave, Susan 1951- . . . . CLC **13, 54**
See also CA 69-72; CANR 45

Musil, Robert (Edler von)
1880-1942 . . . . TCLC **12**; SSC **18**
See also CA 109; DLB 81, 124

Muske, Carol 1945- . . . . CLC **90**
See also Muske-Dukes, Carol (Anne)

Muske-Dukes, Carol (Anne) 1945-
See Muske, Carol
See also CA 65-68; CANR 32

Musset, (Louis Charles) Alfred de
1810-1857 . . . . NCLC **7**

My Brother's Brother
See Chekhov, Anton (Pavlovich)

Myers, L. H. 1881-1944 . . . . TCLC **59**
See also DLB 15

Myers, Walter Dean 1937- . . . CLC **35**; BLC
See also AAYA 4; BW 2; CA 33-36R;
CANR 20, 42; CLR 4, 16, 35;
DAM MULT, NOV; DLB 33;
INT CANR-20; JRDA; MAICYA;
SAAS 2; SATA 41, 71; SATA-Brief 27

Myers, Walter M.
See Myers, Walter Dean

Myles, Symon
See Follett, Ken(neth Martin)

Nabokov, Vladimir (Vladimirovich)
1899-1977 . . . . . CLC **1, 2, 3, 6, 8, 11, 15,
23, 44, 46, 64; DA; DAB; DAC; SSC 11;
WLC**
See also CA 5-8R; 69-72; CANR 20;
CDALB 1941-1968; DAM MST, NOV;
DLB 2; DLBD 3; DLBY 80, 91; MTCW

Nagai Kafu . . . . TCLC **51**
See also Nagai Sokichi

Nagai Sokichi 1879-1959
See Nagai Kafu
See also CA 117

Nagy, Laszlo 1925-1978 . . . . CLC **7**
See also CA 129; 112

Naipaul, Shiva(dhar Srinivasa)
1945-1985 . . . . CLC **32, 39**
See also CA 110; 112; 116; CANR 33;
DAM NOV; DLB 157; DLBY 85;
MTCW

Naipaul, V(idiadhar) S(urajprasad)
1932- . . . . CLC **4, 7, 9, 13, 18, 37; DAB;
DAC**
See also CA 1-4R; CANR 1, 33, 51;
CDBLB 1960 to Present; DAM MST,
NOV; DLB 125; DLBY 85; MTCW

Nakos, Lilika 1899(?)- . . . . CLC **29**

Narayan, R(asipuram) K(rishnaswami)
1906- . . . . CLC **7, 28, 47**
See also CA 81-84; CANR 33; DAM NOV;
MTCW; SATA 62

Nash, (Frediric) Ogden 1902-1971 . . CLC **23**
See also CA 13-14; 29-32R; CANR 34;
CAP 1; DAM POET; DLB 11;
MAICYA; MTCW; SATA 2, 46

Nathan, Daniel
See Dannay, Frederic

Nathan, George Jean 1882-1958 . . . TCLC **18**
See also Hatteras, Owen
See also CA 114; DLB 137

Natsume, Kinnosuke 1867-1916
See Natsume, Soseki
See also CA 104

Natsume, Soseki . . . . TCLC **2, 10**
See also Natsume, Kinnosuke

Natti, (Mary) Lee 1919-
See Kingman, Lee
See also CA 5-8R; CANR 2

Naylor, Gloria
1950- . . . . . CLC **28, 52; BLC; DA; DAC**
See also AAYA 6; BW 2; CA 107;
CANR 27, 51; DAM MST, MULT,
NOV; POP; MTCW

Neihardt, John Gneisenau
1881-1973 . . . . CLC **32**
See also CA 13-14; CAP 1; DLB 9, 54

Nekrasov, Nikolai Alekseevich
1821-1878 . . . . NCLC **11**

Nelligan, Emile 1879-1941 . . . . TCLC **14**
See also CA 114; DLB 92

Nelson, Willie 1933- . . . . CLC **17**
See also CA 107

Nemerov, Howard (Stanley)
1920-1991 . . . . CLC **2, 6, 9, 36**
See also CA 1-4R; 134; CABS 2; CANR 1,
27; DAM POET; DLB 5, 6; DLBY 83;
INT CANR-27; MTCW

Neruda, Pablo
1904-1973 . . . . . CLC **1, 2, 5, 7, 9, 28, 62;
DA; DAB; DAC; HLC; PC 4; WLC**
See also CA 19-20; 45-48; CAP 2;
DAM MST, MULT, POET; HW; MTCW

Nerval, Gerard de
1808-1855 . . . . . NCLC **1**; PC **13**; SSC **18**

Nervo, (Jose) Amado (Ruiz de)
1870-1919 . . . . TCLC **11**
See also CA 109; 131; HW

Nessi, Pio Baroja y
See Baroja (y Nessi), Pio

Nestroy, Johann 1801-1862 . . . . . . NCLC **42**
See also DLB 133

Neufeld, John (Arthur) 1938- . . . . . . CLC **17**
See also AAYA 11; CA 25-28R; CANR 11,
37; MAICYA; SAAS 3; SATA 6, 81

Neville, Emily Cheney 1919- . . . . CLC **12**
See also CA 5-8R; CANR 3, 37; JRDA;
MAICYA; SAAS 2; SATA 1

Newbound, Bernard Slade 1930-
See Slade, Bernard
See also CA 81-84; CANR 49;
DAM DRAM

Newby, P(ercy) H(oward)
1918- . . . . CLC **2, 13**
See also CA 5-8R; CANR 32; DAM NOV;
DLB 15; MTCW

Newlove, Donald 1928- . . . . CLC **6**
See also CA 29-32R; CANR 25

Newlove, John (Herbert) 1938- . . . . . CLC **14**
See also CA 21-24R; CANR 9, 25

Newman, Charles 1938- . . . . CLC **2, 8**
See also CA 21-24R

Newman, Edwin (Harold) 1919- . . . . CLC **14**
See also AITN 1; CA 69-72; CANR 5

Newman, John Henry
1801-1890 . . . . NCLC **38**
See also DLB 18, 32, 55

Newton, Suzanne 1936- . . . . CLC **35**
See also CA 41-44R; CANR 14; JRDA;
SATA 5, 77

Nexo, Martin Andersen
1869-1954 . . . . TCLC **43**

Nezval, Vitezslav 1900-1958 . . . . . . TCLC **44**
See also CA 123

Ng, Fae Myenne 1957(?)- . . . . CLC **81**
See also CA 146

Ngema, Mbongeni 1955- . . . . CLC **57**
See also BW 2; CA 143

Ngugi, James T(hiong'o) . . . . CLC **3, 7, 13**
See also Ngugi wa Thiong'o

Ngugi wa Thiong'o 1938- . . . . . CLC **36**; BLC
See also Ngugi, James T(hiong'o)
See also BW 2; CA 81-84; CANR 27;
DAM MULT, NOV; DLB 125; MTCW

Nichol, B(arrie) P(hillip)
1944-1988 . . . . CLC **18**
See also CA 53-56; DLB 53; SATA 66

Nichols, John (Treadwell) 1940- . . . . CLC **38**
See also CA 9-12R; CAAS 2; CANR 6;
DLBY 82

Nichols, Leigh
See Koontz, Dean R(ay)

Nichols, Peter (Richard)
1927- . . . . CLC **5, 36, 65**
See also CA 104; CANR 33; DLB 13;
MTCW

Nicolas, F. R. E.
See Freeling, Nicolas

Niedecker, Lorine 1903-1970 . . . . CLC **10, 42**
See also CA 25-28; CAP 2; DAM POET;
DLB 48

Nietzsche, Friedrich (Wilhelm)
1844-1900 . . . . TCLC **10, 18, 55**
See also CA 107; 121; DLB 129

Nievo, Ippolito 1831-1861 . . . . NCLC **22**

Nightingale, Anne Redmon 1943-
See Redmon, Anne
See also CA 103

Nik. T. O.
See Annensky, Innokenty Fyodorovich

Nin, Anais
1903-1977 . . . . . . CLC **1, 4, 8, 11, 14, 60;
SSC 10**
See also AITN 2; CA 13-16R; 69-72;
CANR 22; DAM NOV, POP; DLB 2, 4,
152; MTCW

Nishiwaki, Junzaburo 1894-1982 . . . . PC **15**
See also CA 107

Nissenson, Hugh 1933- . . . . CLC **4, 9**
See also CA 17-20R; CANR 27; DLB 28

Niven, Larry . . . . CLC **8**
See also Niven, Laurence Van Cott
See also DLB 8

Niven, Laurence Van Cott 1938-
See Niven, Larry
See also CA 21-24R; CAAS 12; CANR 14,
44; DAM POP; MTCW

Okigbo, Christopher (Ifenayichukwu)
1932-1967 ..... **CLC 25, 84; BLC; PC 7**
See also BW 1; CA 77-80; DAM MULT,
POET; DLB 125; MTCW

Okri, Ben 1959- .... **CLC 87**
See also BW 2; CA 130; 138; DLB 157;
INT 138

Olds, Sharon 1942-........ **CLC 32, 39, 85**
See also CA 101; CANR 18, 41;
DAM POET; DLB 120

Oldstyle, Jonathan
See Irving, Washington

Olesha, Yuri (Karlovich)
1899-1960 .... **CLC 8**
See also CA 85-88

Oliphant, Laurence
1829(?)-1888 .... **NCLC 47**
See also DLB 18

Oliphant, Margaret (Oliphant Wilson)
1828-1897 .... **NCLC 11**
See also DLB 18, 159

Oliver, Mary 1935-........... **CLC 19, 34**
See also CA 21-24R; CANR 9, 43; DLB 5

Olivier, Laurence (Kerr)
1907-1989 .... **CLC 20**
See also CA 111; 150; 129

Olsen, Tillie
1913- ..... **CLC 4, 13; DA; DAB; DAC;**
SSC 11
See also CA 1-4R; CANR 1, 43;
DAM MST; DLB 28; DLBY 80; MTCW

Olson, Charles (John)
1910-1970 ..... **CLC 1, 2, 5, 6, 9, 11, 29**
See also CA 13-16; 25-28R; CABS 2;
CANR 35; CAP 1; DAM POET; DLB 5,
16; MTCW

Olson, Toby 1937- .... **CLC 28**
See also CA 65-68; CANR 9, 31

Olyesha, Yuri
See Olesha, Yuri (Karlovich)

Ondaatje, (Philip) Michael
1943- ... **CLC 14, 29, 51, 76; DAB; DAC**
See also CA 77-80; CANR 42; DAM MST;
DLB 60

Oneal, Elizabeth 1934-
See Oneal, Zibby
See also CA 106; CANR 28; MAICYA;
SATA 30, 82

Oneal, Zibby .... **CLC 30**
See also Oneal, Elizabeth
See also AAYA 5; CLR 13; JRDA

O'Neill, Eugene (Gladstone)
1888-1953 ...... **TCLC 1, 6, 27, 49; DA;**
DAB; DAC; WLC
See also AITN 1; CA 110; 132;
CDALB 1929-1941; DAM DRAM, MST;
DLB 7; MTCW

Onetti, Juan Carlos
1909-1994 .... **CLC 7, 10; SSC 23**
See also CA 85-88; 145; CANR 32;
DAM MULT, NOV; DLB 113; HW;
MTCW

O Nuallain, Brian 1911-1966
See O'Brien, Flann
See also CA 21-22; 25-28R; CAP 2

Oppen, George 1908-1984 .... **CLC 7, 13, 34**
See also CA 13-16R; 113; CANR 8; DLB 5,
165

Oppenheim, E(dward) Phillips
1866-1946 .... **TCLC 45**
See also CA 111; DLB 70

Orlovitz, Gil 1918-1973 .... **CLC 22**
See also CA 77-80; 45-48; DLB 2, 5

Orris
See Ingelow, Jean

Ortega y Gasset, Jose
1883-1955 .... **TCLC 9; HLC**
See also CA 106; 130; DAM MULT; HW;
MTCW

Ortese, Anna Maria 1914-........ **CLC 89**

Ortiz, Simon J(oseph) 1941-....... **CLC 45**
See also CA 134; DAM MULT, POET;
DLB 120; NNAL

Orton, Joe .... **CLC 4, 13, 43; DC 3**
See also Orton, John Kingsley
See also CDBLB 1960 to Present; DLB 13

Orton, John Kingsley 1933-1967
See Orton, Joe
See also CA 85-88; CANR 35;
DAM DRAM; MTCW

Orwell, George
..... **TCLC 2, 6, 15, 31, 51; DAB; WLC**
See also Blair, Eric (Arthur)
See also CDBLB 1945-1960; DLB 15, 98

Osborne, David
See Silverberg, Robert

Osborne, George
See Silverberg, Robert

Osborne, John (James)
1929-1994 ..... **CLC 1, 2, 5, 11, 45; DA;**
DAB; DAC; WLC
See also CA 13-16R; 147; CANR 21;
CDBLB 1945-1960; DAM DRAM, MST;
DLB 13; MTCW

Osborne, Lawrence 1958- .... **CLC 50**

Oshima, Nagisa 1932- .... **CLC 20**
See also CA 116; 121

Oskison, John Milton
1874-1947 .... **TCLC 35**
See also CA 144; DAM MULT; NNAL

Ossoli, Sarah Margaret (Fuller marchesa d')
1810-1850
See Fuller, Margaret
See also SATA 25

Ostrovsky, Alexander
1823-1886 .... **NCLC 30, 57**

Otero, Blas de 1916-1979......... **CLC 11**
See also CA 89-92; DLB 134

Otto, Whitney 1955-............. **CLC 70**
See also CA 140

Ouida .... **TCLC 43**
See also De La Ramee, (Marie) Louise
See also DLB 18, 156

Ousmane, Sembene 1923- .... **CLC 66; BLC**
See also BW 1; CA 117; 125; MTCW

Ovid 43B.C.-18(?).......... **CMLC 7; PC 2**
See also DAM POET

Owen, Hugh
See Faust, Frederick (Schiller)

Owen, Wilfred (Edward Salter)
1893-1918 ...... **TCLC 5, 27; DA; DAB;**
DAC; WLC
See also CA 104; 141; CDBLB 1914-1945;
DAM MST, POET; DLB 20

Owens, Rochelle 1936-............. **CLC 8**
See also CA 17-20R; CAAS 2; CANR 39

Oz, Amos 1939- ... **CLC 5, 8, 11, 27, 33, 54**
See also CA 53-56; CANR 27, 47;
DAM NOV; MTCW

Ozick, Cynthia
1928- .... **CLC 3, 7, 28, 62; SSC 15**
See also BEST 90:1; CA 17-20R; CANR 23;
DAM NOV, POP; DLB 28, 152;
DLBY 82; INT CANR-23; MTCW

Ozu, Yasujiro 1903-1963 .... **CLC 16**
See also CA 112

Pacheco, C.
See Pessoa, Fernando (Antonio Nogueira)

Pa Chin .... **CLC 18**
See also Li Fei-kan

Pack, Robert 1929-............... **CLC 13**
See also CA 1-4R; CANR 3, 44; DLB 5

Padgett, Lewis
See Kuttner, Henry

Padilla (Lorenzo), Heberto 1932-... **CLC 38**
See also AITN 1; CA 123; 131; HW

Page, Jimmy 1944-............... **CLC 12**

Page, Louise 1955-............... **CLC 40**
See also CA 140

Page, P(atricia) K(athleen)
1916- .... **CLC 7, 18; DAC; PC 12**
See also CA 53-56; CANR 4, 22;
DAM MST; DLB 68; MTCW

Page, Thomas Nelson 1853-1922.... **SSC 23**
See also CA 118; DLB 12, 78; DLBD 13

Paget, Violet 1856-1935
See Lee, Vernon
See also CA 104

Paget-Lowe, Henry
See Lovecraft, H(oward) P(hillips)

Paglia, Camille (Anna) 1947-....... **CLC 68**
See also CA 140

Paige, Richard
See Koontz, Dean R(ay)

Pakenham, Antonia
See Fraser, (Lady) Antonia (Pakenham)

Palamas, Kostes 1859-1943 .... **TCLC 5**
See also CA 105

Palazzeschi, Aldo 1885-1974....... **CLC 11**
See also CA 89-92; 53-56; DLB 114

Paley, Grace 1922-.... **CLC 4, 6, 37; SSC 8**
See also CA 25-28R; CANR 13, 46;
DAM POP; DLB 28; INT CANR-13;
MTCW

Palin, Michael (Edward) 1943-..... **CLC 21**
See also Monty Python
See also CA 107; CANR 35; SATA 67

Palliser, Charles 1947-........... **CLC 65**
See also CA 136

Palma, Ricardo 1833-1919........ **TCLC 29**

Pancake, Breece Dexter 1952-1979
See Pancake, Breece D'J
See also CA 123; 109

Poet of Titchfield Street, The
See Pound, Ezra (Weston Loomis)

Pohl, Frederik   1919- . . . . **CLC 18**
See also CA 61-64; CAAS 1; CANR 11, 37;
DLB 8; INT CANR-11; MTCW;
SATA 24

Poirier, Louis   1910-
See Gracq, Julien
See also CA 122; 126

Poitier, Sidney   1927- . . . . **CLC 26**
See also BW 1; CA 117

Polanski, Roman   1933- . . . . **CLC 16**
See also CA 77-80

Poliakoff, Stephen   1952- . . . . **CLC 38**
See also CA 106; DLB 13

Police, The
See Copeland, Stewart (Armstrong);
Summers, Andrew James; Sumner,
Gordon Matthew

Polidori, John William
1795-1821 . . . . **NCLC 51**
See also DLB 116

Pollitt, Katha   1949- . . . . **CLC 28**
See also CA 120; 122; MTCW

Pollock, (Mary) Sharon
1936- . . . . **CLC 50; DAC**
See also CA 141; DAM DRAM, MST;
DLB 60

Polo, Marco   1254-1324 . . . . **CMLC 15**

Polonsky, Abraham (Lincoln)
1910- . . . . **CLC 92**
See also CA 104; DLB 26; INT 104

Polybius   c. 200B.C.-c. 118B.C. . . . . **CMLC 17**

Pomerance, Bernard   1940- . . . . **CLC 13**
See also CA 101; CANR 49; DAM DRAM

Ponge, Francis (Jean Gaston Alfred)
1899-1988 . . . . **CLC 6, 18**
See also CA 85-88; 126; CANR 40;
DAM POET

Pontoppidan, Henrik   1857-1943 . . . **TCLC 29**

Poole, Josephine . . . . **CLC 17**
See also Helyar, Jane Penelope Josephine
See also SAAS 2; SATA 5

Popa, Vasko   1922-1991 . . . . **CLC 19**
See also CA 112; 148

Pope, Alexander
1688-1744 . . . . . . **LC 3; DA; DAB; DAC;
WLC**
See also CDBLB 1660-1789; DAM MST,
POET; DLB 95, 101

Porter, Connie (Rose)   1959(?)- . . . . . **CLC 70**
See also BW 2; CA 142; SATA 81

Porter, Gene(va Grace) Stratton
1863(?)-1924 . . . . **TCLC 21**
See also CA 112

Porter, Katherine Anne
1890-1980 . . . . . . **CLC 1, 3, 7, 10, 13, 15,
27; DA; DAB; DAC; SSC 4**
See also AITN 2; CA 1-4R; 101; CANR 1;
DAM MST, NOV; DLB 4, 9, 102;
DLBD 12; DLBY 80; MTCW; SATA 39;
SATA-Obit 23

Porter, Peter (Neville Frederick)
1929- . . . . **CLC 5, 13, 33**
See also CA 85-88; DLB 40

Porter, William Sydney   1862-1910
See Henry, O.
See also CA 104; 131; CDALB 1865-1917;
DA; DAB; DAC; DAM MST; DLB 12,
78, 79; MTCW; YABC 2

Portillo (y Pacheco), Jose Lopez
See Lopez Portillo (y Pacheco), Jose

Post, Melville Davisson
1869-1930 . . . . **TCLC 39**
See also CA 110

Potok, Chaim   1929- . . . . . . **CLC 2, 7, 14, 26**
See also AAYA 15; AITN 1, 2; CA 17-20R;
CANR 19, 35; DAM NOV; DLB 28, 152;
INT CANR-19; MTCW; SATA 33

Potter, Beatrice
See Webb, (Martha) Beatrice (Potter)
See also MAICYA

Potter, Dennis (Christopher George)
1935-1994 . . . . **CLC 58, 86**
See also CA 107; 145; CANR 33; MTCW

Pound, Ezra (Weston Loomis)
1885-1972 . . . . . . **CLC 1, 2, 3, 4, 5, 7, 10,
13, 18, 34, 48, 50; DA; DAB; DAC; PC 4;
WLC**
See also CA 5-8R; 37-40R; CANR 40;
CDALB 1917-1929; DAM MST, POET;
DLB 4, 45, 63; MTCW

Povod, Reinaldo   1959-1994 . . . . **CLC 44**
See also CA 136; 146

Powell, Adam Clayton, Jr.
1908-1972 . . . . **CLC 89; BLC**
See also BW 1; CA 102; 33-36R;
DAM MULT

Powell, Anthony (Dymoke)
1905- . . . . **CLC 1, 3, 7, 9, 10, 31**
See also CA 1-4R; CANR 1, 32;
CDBLB 1945-1960; DLB 15; MTCW

Powell, Dawn   1897-1965 . . . . **CLC 66**
See also CA 5-8R

Powell, Padgett   1952- . . . . **CLC 34**
See also CA 126

Power, Susan . . . . **CLC 91**

Powers, J(ames) F(arl)
1917- . . . . **CLC 1, 4, 8, 57; SSC 4**
See also CA 1-4R; CANR 2; DLB 130;
MTCW

Powers, John J(ames)   1945-
See Powers, John R.
See also CA 69-72

Powers, John R. . . . . **CLC 66**
See also Powers, John J(ames)

Powers, Richard (S.)   1957- . . . . **CLC 93**
See also CA 148

Pownall, David   1938- . . . . **CLC 10**
See also CA 89-92; CAAS 18; CANR 49;
DLB 14

Powys, John Cowper
1872-1963 . . . . **CLC 7, 9, 15, 46**
See also CA 85-88; DLB 15; MTCW

Powys, T(heodore) F(rancis)
1875-1953 . . . . **TCLC 9**
See also CA 106; DLB 36, 162

Prager, Emily   1952- . . . . **CLC 56**

Pratt, E(dwin) J(ohn)
1883(?)-1964 . . . . **CLC 19; DAC**
See also CA 141; 93-96; DAM POET;
DLB 92

Premchand . . . . **TCLC 21**
See also Srivastava, Dhanpat Rai

Preussler, Otfried   1923- . . . . **CLC 17**
See also CA 77-80; SATA 24

Prevert, Jacques (Henri Marie)
1900-1977 . . . . **CLC 15**
See also CA 77-80; 69-72; CANR 29;
MTCW; SATA-Obit 30

Prevost, Abbe (Antoine Francois)
1697-1763 . . . . **LC 1**

Price, (Edward) Reynolds
1933- . . **CLC 3, 6, 13, 43, 50, 63; SSC 22**
See also CA 1-4R; CANR 1, 37;
DAM NOV; DLB 2; INT CANR-37

Price, Richard   1949- . . . . **CLC 6, 12**
See also CA 49-52; CANR 3; DLBY 81

Prichard, Katharine Susannah
1883-1969 . . . . **CLC 46**
See also CA 11-12; CANR 33; CAP 1;
MTCW; SATA 66

Priestley, J(ohn) B(oynton)
1894-1984 . . . . **CLC 2, 5, 9, 34**
See also CA 9-12R; 113; CANR 33;
CDBLB 1914-1945; DAM DRAM, NOV;
DLB 10, 34, 77, 100, 139; DLBY 84;
MTCW

Prince   1958(?)- . . . . **CLC 35**

Prince, F(rank) T(empleton)   1912- . . **CLC 22**
See also CA 101; CANR 43; DLB 20

Prince Kropotkin
See Kropotkin, Peter (Aleksieevich)

Prior, Matthew   1664-1721 . . . . **LC 4**
See also DLB 95

Pritchard, William H(arrison)
1932- . . . . **CLC 34**
See also CA 65-68; CANR 23; DLB 111

Pritchett, V(ictor) S(awdon)
1900- . . . . **CLC 5, 13, 15, 41; SSC 14**
See also CA 61-64; CANR 31; DAM NOV;
DLB 15, 139; MTCW

Private 19022
See Manning, Frederic

Probst, Mark   1925- . . . . **CLC 59**
See also CA 130

Prokosch, Frederic   1908-1989 . . . . **CLC 4, 48**
See also CA 73-76; 128; DLB 48

Prophet, The
See Dreiser, Theodore (Herman Albert)

Prose, Francine   1947- . . . . **CLC 45**
See also CA 109; 112; CANR 46

Proudhon
See Cunha, Euclides (Rodrigues Pimenta) da

Proulx, E. Annie   1935- . . . . **CLC 81**

Proust, (Valentin-Louis-George-Eugene-)
Marcel
1871-1922 . . . . **TCLC 7, 13, 33; DA;
DAB; DAC; WLC**
See also CA 104; 120; DAM MST, NOV;
DLB 65; MTCW

Prowler, Harley
See Masters, Edgar Lee

Rawlings, Marjorie Kinnan
    1896-1953 . . . . **TCLC 4**
    See also CA 104; 137; DLB 9, 22, 102;
    JRDA; MAICYA; YABC 1

Ray, Satyajit   1921-1992 . . . . **CLC 16, 76**
    See also CA 114; 137; DAM MULT

Read, Herbert Edward   1893-1968 . . . . **CLC 4**
    See also CA 85-88; 25-28R; DLB 20, 149

Read, Piers Paul   1941- . . . . . **CLC 4, 10, 25**
    See also CA 21-24R; CANR 38; DLB 14;
    SATA 21

Reade, Charles   1814-1884 . . . . **NCLC 2**
    See also DLB 21

Reade, Hamish
    See Gray, Simon (James Holliday)

Reading, Peter   1946- . . . . **CLC 47**
    See also CA 103; CANR 46; DLB 40

Reaney, James   1926- . . . . **CLC 13; DAC**
    See also CA 41-44R; CAAS 15; CANR 42;
    DAM MST; DLB 68; SATA 43

Rebreanu, Liviu   1885-1944 . . . . **TCLC 28**

Rechy, John (Francisco)
    1934- . . . . **CLC 1, 7, 14, 18; HLC**
    See also CA 5-8R; CAAS 4; CANR 6, 32;
    DAM MULT; DLB 122; DLBY 82; HW;
    INT CANR-6

Redcam, Tom   1870-1933 . . . . **TCLC 25**

Reddin, Keith . . . . **CLC 67**

Redgrove, Peter (William)
    1932- . . . . **CLC 6, 41**
    See also CA 1-4R; CANR 3, 39; DLB 40

Redmon, Anne . . . . **CLC 22**
    See also Nightingale, Anne Redmon
    See also DLBY 86

Reed, Eliot
    See Ambler, Eric

Reed, Ishmael
    1938- . . . **CLC 2, 3, 5, 6, 13, 32, 60; BLC**
    See also BW 2; CA 21-24R; CANR 25, 48;
    DAM MULT; DLB 2, 5, 33; DLBD 8;
    MTCW

Reed, John (Silas)   1887-1920 . . . . . . **TCLC 9**
    See also CA 106

Reed, Lou . . . . **CLC 21**
    See also Firbank, Louis

Reeve, Clara   1729-1807 . . . . **NCLC 19**
    See also DLB 39

Reich, Wilhelm   1897-1957 . . . . **TCLC 57**

Reid, Christopher (John)   1949- . . . . . **CLC 33**
    See also CA 140; DLB 40

Reid, Desmond
    See Moorcock, Michael (John)

Reid Banks, Lynne   1929-
    See Banks, Lynne Reid
    See also CA 1-4R; CANR 6, 22, 38;
    CLR 24; JRDA; MAICYA; SATA 22, 75

Reilly, William K.
    See Creasey, John

Reiner, Max
    See Caldwell, (Janet Miriam) Taylor
    (Holland)

Reis, Ricardo
    See Pessoa, Fernando (Antonio Nogueira)

Remarque, Erich Maria
    1898-1970 . . . . **CLC 21; DA; DAB; DAC**
    See also CA 77-80; 29-32R; DAM MST,
    NOV; DLB 56; MTCW

Remizov, A.
    See Remizov, Aleksei (Mikhailovich)

Remizov, A. M.
    See Remizov, Aleksei (Mikhailovich)

Remizov, Aleksei (Mikhailovich)
    1877-1957 . . . . **TCLC 27**
    See also CA 125; 133

Renan, Joseph Ernest
    1823-1892 . . . . **NCLC 26**

Renard, Jules   1864-1910 . . . . **TCLC 17**
    See also CA 117

Renault, Mary . . . . **CLC 3, 11, 17**
    See also Challans, Mary
    See also DLBY 83

Rendell, Ruth (Barbara)   1930- . . **CLC 28, 48**
    See also Vine, Barbara
    See also CA 109; CANR 32; DAM POP;
    DLB 87; INT CANR-32; MTCW

Renoir, Jean   1894-1979 . . . . **CLC 20**
    See also CA 129; 85-88

Resnais, Alain   1922- . . . . **CLC 16**

Reverdy, Pierre   1889-1960 . . . . **CLC 53**
    See also CA 97-100; 89-92

Rexroth, Kenneth
    1905-1982 . . . . . . **CLC 1, 2, 6, 11, 22, 49**
    See also CA 5-8R; 107; CANR 14, 34;
    CDALB 1941-1968; DAM POET;
    DLB 16, 48, 165; DLBY 82;
    INT CANR-14; MTCW

Reyes, Alfonso   1889-1959 . . . . **TCLC 33**
    See also CA 131; HW

Reyes y Basoalto, Ricardo Eliecer Neftali
    See Neruda, Pablo

Reymont, Wladyslaw (Stanislaw)
    1868(?)-1925 . . . . **TCLC 5**
    See also CA 104

Reynolds, Jonathan   1942- . . . . **CLC 6, 38**
    See also CA 65-68; CANR 28

Reynolds, Joshua   1723-1792 . . . . **LC 15**
    See also DLB 104

Reynolds, Michael Shane   1937- . . . . **CLC 44**
    See also CA 65-68; CANR 9

Reznikoff, Charles   1894-1976 . . . . **CLC 9**
    See also CA 33-36; 61-64; CAP 2; DLB 28,
    45

Rezzori (d'Arezzo), Gregor von
    1914- . . . . **CLC 25**
    See also CA 122; 136

Rhine, Richard
    See Silverstein, Alvin

Rhodes, Eugene Manlove
    1869-1934 . . . . **TCLC 53**

R'hoone
    See Balzac, Honore de

Rhys, Jean
    1890(?)-1979 . . . . **CLC 2, 4, 6, 14, 19, 51;
                                                        SSC 21**
    See also CA 25-28R; 85-88; CANR 35;
    CDBLB 1945-1960; DAM NOV; DLB 36,
    117, 162; MTCW

Ribeiro, Darcy   1922- . . . . **CLC 34**
    See also CA 33-36R

Ribeiro, Joao Ubaldo (Osorio Pimentel)
    1941- . . . . **CLC 10, 67**
    See also CA 81-84

Ribman, Ronald (Burt)   1932- . . . . **CLC 7**
    See also CA 21-24R; CANR 46

Ricci, Nino   1959- . . . . **CLC 70**
    See also CA 137

Rice, Anne   1941- . . . . **CLC 41**
    See also AAYA 9; BEST 89:2; CA 65-68;
    CANR 12, 36; DAM POP

Rice, Elmer (Leopold)
    1892-1967 . . . . **CLC 7, 49**
    See also CA 21-22; 25-28R; CAP 2;
    DAM DRAM; DLB 4, 7; MTCW

Rice, Tim(othy Miles Bindon)
    1944- . . . . **CLC 21**
    See also CA 103; CANR 46

Rich, Adrienne (Cecile)
    1929- . . . . **CLC 3, 6, 7, 11, 18, 36, 73, 76;
                                                        PC 5**
    See also CA 9-12R; CANR 20;
    DAM POET; DLB 5, 67; MTCW

Rich, Barbara
    See Graves, Robert (von Ranke)

Rich, Robert
    See Trumbo, Dalton

Richard, Keith . . . . **CLC 17**
    See also Richards, Keith

Richards, David Adams
    1950- . . . . **CLC 59; DAC**
    See also CA 93-96; DLB 53

Richards, I(vor) A(rmstrong)
    1893-1979 . . . . **CLC 14, 24**
    See also CA 41-44R; 89-92; CANR 34;
    DLB 27

Richards, Keith   1943-
    See Richard, Keith
    See also CA 107

Richardson, Anne
    See Roiphe, Anne (Richardson)

Richardson, Dorothy Miller
    1873-1957 . . . . **TCLC 3**
    See also CA 104; DLB 36

Richardson, Ethel Florence (Lindesay)
    1870-1946
    See Richardson, Henry Handel
    See also CA 105

Richardson, Henry Handel . . . . **TCLC 4**
    See also Richardson, Ethel Florence
    (Lindesay)

Richardson, John
    1796-1852 . . . . **NCLC 55; DAC**
    See also CA 140; DLB 99

Richardson, Samuel
    1689-1761 . . . . . . **LC 1; DA; DAB; DAC;
                                                        WLC**
    See also CDBLB 1660-1789; DAM MST,
    NOV; DLB 39

Savan, Glenn 19(?)- .... **CLC 50**

Sayers, Dorothy L(eigh)
1893-1957 .... **TCLC 2, 15**
See also CA 104; 119; CDBLB 1914-1945;
DAM POP; DLB 10, 36, 77, 100; MTCW

Sayers, Valerie 1952- .... **CLC 50**
See also CA 134

Sayles, John (Thomas)
1950- .... **CLC 7, 10, 14**
See also CA 57-60; CANR 41; DLB 44

Scammell, Michael .... **CLC 34**

Scannell, Vernon 1922- .... **CLC 49**
See also CA 5-8R; CANR 8, 24; DLB 27;
SATA 59

Scarlett, Susan
See Streatfeild, (Mary) Noel

Schaeffer, Susan Fromberg
1941- .... **CLC 6, 11, 22**
See also CA 49-52; CANR 18; DLB 28;
MTCW; SATA 22

Schary, Jill
See Robinson, Jill

Schell, Jonathan 1943- .... **CLC 35**
See also CA 73-76; CANR 12

Schelling, Friedrich Wilhelm Joseph von
1775-1854 .... **NCLC 30**
See also DLB 90

Schendel, Arthur van 1874-1946 ... **TCLC 56**

Scherer, Jean-Marie Maurice 1920-
See Rohmer, Eric
See also CA 110

Schevill, James (Erwin) 1920- ...... **CLC 7**
See also CA 5-8R; CAAS 12

Schiller, Friedrich 1759-1805 .... **NCLC 39**
See also DAM DRAM; DLB 94

Schisgal, Murray (Joseph) 1926- ..... **CLC 6**
See also CA 21-24R; CANR 48

Schlee, Ann 1934- .... **CLC 35**
See also CA 101; CANR 29; SATA 44;
SATA-Brief 36

Schlegel, August Wilhelm von
1767-1845 .... **NCLC 15**
See also DLB 94

Schlegel, Friedrich 1772-1829 .... **NCLC 45**
See also DLB 90

Schlegel, Johann Elias (von)
1719(?)-1749 .... **LC 5**

Schlesinger, Arthur M(eier), Jr.
1917- .... **CLC 84**
See also AITN 1; CA 1-4R; CANR 1, 28;
DLB 17; INT CANR-28; MTCW;
SATA 61

Schmidt, Arno (Otto) 1914-1979 .... **CLC 56**
See also CA 128; 109; DLB 69

Schmitz, Aron Hector 1861-1928
See Svevo, Italo
See also CA 104; 122; MTCW

Schnackenberg, Gjertrud 1953- ..... **CLC 40**
See also CA 116; DLB 120

Schneider, Leonard Alfred 1925-1966
See Bruce, Lenny
See also CA 89-92

Schnitzler, Arthur
1862-1931 .... **TCLC 4; SSC 15**
See also CA 104; DLB 81, 118

Schopenhauer, Arthur
1788-1860 .... **NCLC 51**
See also DLB 90

Schor, Sandra (M.) 1932(?)-1990 ... **CLC 65**
See also CA 132

Schorer, Mark 1908-1977 .... **CLC 9**
See also CA 5-8R; 73-76; CANR 7;
DLB 103

Schrader, Paul (Joseph) 1946- ...... **CLC 26**
See also CA 37-40R; CANR 41; DLB 44

Schreiner, Olive (Emilie Albertina)
1855-1920 .... **TCLC 9**
See also CA 105; DLB 18, 156

Schulberg, Budd (Wilson)
1914- .... **CLC 7, 48**
See also CA 25-28R; CANR 19; DLB 6, 26,
28; DLBY 81

Schulz, Bruno
1892-1942 .... **TCLC 5, 51; SSC 13**
See also CA 115; 123

Schulz, Charles M(onroe) 1922- .... **CLC 12**
See also CA 9-12R; CANR 6;
INT CANR-6; SATA 10

Schumacher, E(rnst) F(riedrich)
1911-1977 .... **CLC 80**
See also CA 81-84; 73-76; CANR 34

Schuyler, James Marcus
1923-1991 .... **CLC 5, 23**
See also CA 101; 134; DAM POET; DLB 5;
INT 101

Schwartz, Delmore (David)
1913-1966 ... **CLC 2, 4, 10, 45, 87; PC 8**
See also CA 17-18; 25-28R; CANR 35;
CAP 2; DLB 28, 48; MTCW

Schwartz, Ernst
See Ozu, Yasujiro

Schwartz, John Burnham 1965- .... **CLC 59**
See also CA 132

Schwartz, Lynne Sharon 1939- ..... **CLC 31**
See also CA 103; CANR 44

Schwartz, Muriel A.
See Eliot, T(homas) S(tearns)

Schwarz-Bart, Andre 1928- .... **CLC 2, 4**
See also CA 89-92

Schwarz-Bart, Simone 1938- .... **CLC 7**
See also BW 2; CA 97-100

Schwob, (Mayer Andre) Marcel
1867-1905 .... **TCLC 20**
See also CA 117; DLB 123

Sciascia, Leonardo
1921-1989 .... **CLC 8, 9, 41**
See also CA 85-88; 130; CANR 35; MTCW

Scoppettone, Sandra 1936- .... **CLC 26**
See also AAYA 11; CA 5-8R; CANR 41;
SATA 9

Scorsese, Martin 1942- .... **CLC 20, 89**
See also CA 110; 114; CANR 46

Scotland, Jay
See Jakes, John (William)

Scott, Duncan Campbell
1862-1947 .... **TCLC 6; DAC**
See also CA 104; DLB 92

Scott, Evelyn 1893-1963.......... **CLC 43**
See also CA 104; 112; DLB 9, 48

Scott, F(rancis) R(eginald)
1899-1985 .... **CLC 22**
See also CA 101; 114; DLB 88; INT 101

Scott, Frank
See Scott, F(rancis) R(eginald)

Scott, Joanna 1960- .... **CLC 50**
See also CA 126

Scott, Paul (Mark) 1920-1978.... **CLC 9, 60**
See also CA 81-84; 77-80; CANR 33;
DLB 14; MTCW

Scott, Walter
1771-1832 .... **NCLC 15; DA; DAB;
DAC; PC 13; WLC**
See also CDBLB 1789-1832; DAM MST,
NOV, POET; DLB 93, 107, 116, 144, 159;
YABC 2

Scribe, (Augustin) Eugene
1791-1861 .... **NCLC 16; DC 5**
See also DAM DRAM

Scrum, R.
See Crumb, R(obert)

Scudery, Madeleine de 1607-1701..... **LC 2**

Scum
See Crumb, R(obert)

Scumbag, Little Bobby
See Crumb, R(obert)

Seabrook, John
See Hubbard, L(afayette) Ron(ald)

Sealy, I. Allan 1951- .... **CLC 55**

Search, Alexander
See Pessoa, Fernando (Antonio Nogueira)

Sebastian, Lee
See Silverberg, Robert

Sebastian Owl
See Thompson, Hunter S(tockton)

Sebestyen, Ouida 1924- .... **CLC 30**
See also AAYA 8; CA 107; CANR 40;
CLR 17; JRDA; MAICYA; SAAS 10;
SATA 39

Secundus, H. Scriblerus
See Fielding, Henry

Sedges, John
See Buck, Pearl S(ydenstricker)

Sedgwick, Catharine Maria
1789-1867 .... **NCLC 19**
See also DLB 1, 74

Seelye, John 1931- .... **CLC 7**

Seferiades, Giorgos Stylianou 1900-1971
See Seferis, George
See also CA 5-8R; 33-36R; CANR 5, 36;
MTCW

Seferis, George .... **CLC 5, 11**
See also Seferiades, Giorgos Stylianou

Segal, Erich (Wolf) 1937- .... **CLC 3, 10**
See also BEST 89:1; CA 25-28R; CANR 20,
36; DAM POP; DLBY 86;
INT CANR-20; MTCW

Seger, Bob 1945-................. **CLC 35**

Seghers, Anna .... **CLC 7**
See also Radvanyi, Netty
See also DLB 69

Sherman, Jonathan Marc . . . . CLC 55

Sherman, Martin   1941(?)- . . . . CLC 19
See also CA 116; 123

Sherwin, Judith Johnson   1936- . . . CLC 7, 15
See also CA 25-28R; CANR 34

Sherwood, Frances   1940- . . . . CLC 81
See also CA 146

Sherwood, Robert E(mmet)
1896-1955 . . . . TCLC 3
See also CA 104; DAM DRAM; DLB 7, 26

Shestov, Lev   1866-1938 . . . . TCLC 56

Shevchenko, Taras   1814-1861 . . . . NCLC 54

Shiel, M(atthew) P(hipps)
1865-1947 . . . . TCLC 8
See also CA 106; DLB 153

Shields, Carol   1935- . . . . CLC 91; DAC
See also CA 81-84; CANR 51

Shiga, Naoya   1883-1971 . . . CLC 33; SSC 23
See also CA 101; 33-36R

Shilts, Randy   1951-1994 . . . . CLC 85
See also CA 115; 127; 144; CANR 45;
INT 127

Shimazaki Haruki   1872-1943
See Shimazaki Toson
See also CA 105; 134

Shimazaki Toson . . . . TCLC 5
See also Shimazaki Haruki

Sholokhov, Mikhail (Aleksandrovich)
1905-1984 . . . . CLC 7, 15
See also CA 101; 112; MTCW;
SATA-Obit 36

Shone, Patric
See Hanley, James

Shreve, Susan Richards   1939- . . . . . . CLC 23
See also CA 49-52; CAAS 5; CANR 5, 38;
MAICYA; SATA 46; SATA-Brief 41

Shue, Larry   1946-1985 . . . . CLC 52
See also CA 145; 117; DAM DRAM

Shu-Jen, Chou   1881-1936
See Lu Hsun
See also CA 104

Shulman, Alix Kates   1932- . . . . . . CLC 2, 10
See also CA 29-32R; CANR 43; SATA 7

Shuster, Joe   1914- . . . . CLC 21

Shute, Nevil . . . . CLC 30
See also Norway, Nevil Shute

Shuttle, Penelope (Diane)   1947- . . . . . CLC 7
See also CA 93-96; CANR 39; DLB 14, 40

Sidney, Mary   1561-1621 . . . . LC 19

Sidney, Sir Philip
1554-1586 . . . . . LC 19; DA; DAB; DAC
See also CDBLB Before 1660; DAM MST,
POET

Siegel, Jerome   1914- . . . . CLC 21
See also CA 116

Siegel, Jerry
See Siegel, Jerome

Sienkiewicz, Henryk (Adam Alexander Pius)
1846-1916 . . . . TCLC 3
See also CA 104; 134

Sierra, Gregorio Martinez
See Martinez Sierra, Gregorio

Sierra, Maria (de la O'LeJarraga) Martinez
See Martinez Sierra, Maria (de la
O'LeJarraga)

Sigal, Clancy   1926- . . . . CLC 7
See also CA 1-4R

Sigourney, Lydia Howard (Huntley)
1791-1865 . . . . NCLC 21
See also DLB 1, 42, 73

Siguenza y Gongora, Carlos de
1645-1700 . . . . LC 8

Sigurjonsson, Johann   1880-1919 . . . TCLC 27

Sikelianos, Angelos   1884-1951 . . . . TCLC 39

Silkin, Jon   1930- . . . . CLC 2, 6, 43
See also CA 5-8R; CAAS 5; DLB 27

Silko, Leslie (Marmon)
1948- . . . . CLC 23, 74; DA; DAC
See also AAYA 14; CA 115; 122;
CANR 45; DAM MST, MULT, POP;
DLB 143; NNAL

Sillanpaa, Frans Eemil   1888-1964 . . . CLC 19
See also CA 129; 93-96; MTCW

Sillitoe, Alan
1928- . . . . CLC 1, 3, 6, 10, 19, 57
See also AITN 1; CA 9-12R; CAAS 2;
CANR 8, 26; CDBLB 1960 to Present;
DLB 14, 139; MTCW; SATA 61

Silone, Ignazio   1900-1978 . . . . CLC 4
See also CA 25-28; 81-84; CANR 34;
CAP 2; MTCW

Silver, Joan Micklin   1935- . . . . CLC 20
See also CA 114; 121; INT 121

Silver, Nicholas
See Faust, Frederick (Schiller)

Silverberg, Robert   1935- . . . . CLC 7
See also CA 1-4R; CAAS 3; CANR 1, 20,
36; DAM POP; DLB 8; INT CANR-20;
MAICYA; MTCW; SATA 13

Silverstein, Alvin   1933- . . . . CLC 17
See also CA 49-52; CANR 2; CLR 25;
JRDA; MAICYA; SATA 8, 69

Silverstein, Virginia B(arbara Opshelor)
1937- . . . . CLC 17
See also CA 49-52; CANR 2; CLR 25;
JRDA; MAICYA; SATA 8, 69

Sim, Georges
See Simenon, Georges (Jacques Christian)

Simak, Clifford D(onald)
1904-1988 . . . . CLC 1, 55
See also CA 1-4R; 125; CANR 1, 35;
DLB 8; MTCW; SATA-Obit 56

Simenon, Georges (Jacques Christian)
1903-1989 . . . . CLC 1, 2, 3, 8, 18, 47
See also CA 85-88; 129; CANR 35;
DAM POP; DLB 72; DLBY 89; MTCW

Simic, Charles   1938- . . . CLC 6, 9, 22, 49, 68
See also CA 29-32R; CAAS 4; CANR 12,
33; DAM POET; DLB 105

Simmel, Georg   1858-1918 . . . . TCLC 64

Simmons, Charles (Paul)   1924- . . . . . CLC 57
See also CA 89-92; INT 89-92

Simmons, Dan   1948- . . . . CLC 44
See also AAYA 16; CA 138; DAM POP

Simmons, James (Stewart Alexander)
1933- . . . . CLC 43
See also CA 105; CAAS 21; DLB 40

Simms, William Gilmore
1806-1870 . . . . NCLC 3
See also DLB 3, 30, 59, 73

Simon, Carly   1945- . . . . CLC 26
See also CA 105

Simon, Claude   1913- . . . . . . CLC 4, 9, 15, 39
See also CA 89-92; CANR 33; DAM NOV;
DLB 83; MTCW

Simon, (Marvin) Neil
1927- . . . . CLC 6, 11, 31, 39, 70
See also AITN 1; CA 21-24R; CANR 26;
DAM DRAM; DLB 7; MTCW

Simon, Paul   1942(?)- . . . . CLC 17
See also CA 116

Simonon, Paul   1956(?)- . . . . CLC 30

Simpson, Harriette
See Arnow, Harriette (Louisa) Simpson

Simpson, Louis (Aston Marantz)
1923- . . . . CLC 4, 7, 9, 32
See also CA 1-4R; CAAS 4; CANR 1;
DAM POET; DLB 5; MTCW

Simpson, Mona (Elizabeth)   1957- . . . CLC 44
See also CA 122; 135

Simpson, N(orman) F(rederick)
1919- . . . . CLC 29
See also CA 13-16R; DLB 13

Sinclair, Andrew (Annandale)
1935- . . . . CLC 2, 14
See also CA 9-12R; CAAS 5; CANR 14, 38;
DLB 14; MTCW

Sinclair, Emil
See Hesse, Hermann

Sinclair, Iain   1943- . . . . CLC 76
See also CA 132

Sinclair, Iain MacGregor
See Sinclair, Iain

Sinclair, Mary Amelia St. Clair   1865(?)-1946
See Sinclair, May
See also CA 104

Sinclair, May . . . . TCLC 3, 11
See also Sinclair, Mary Amelia St. Clair
See also DLB 36, 135

Sinclair, Upton (Beall)
1878-1968 . . . . . . CLC 1, 11, 15, 63; DA;
DAB; DAC; WLC
See also CA 5-8R; 25-28R; CANR 7;
CDALB 1929-1941; DAM MST, NOV;
DLB 9; INT CANR-7; MTCW; SATA 9

Singer, Isaac
See Singer, Isaac Bashevis

Singer, Isaac Bashevis
1904-1991 . . . . CLC 1, 3, 6, 9, 11, 15, 23,
38, 69; DA; DAB; DAC; SSC 3; WLC
See also AITN 1, 2; CA 1-4R; 134;
CANR 1, 39; CDALB 1941-1968; CLR 1;
DAM MST, NOV; DLB 6, 28, 52;
DLBY 91; JRDA; MAICYA; MTCW;
SATA 3, 27; SATA-Obit 68

Singer, Israel Joshua   1893-1944 . . . TCLC 33

Singh, Khushwant   1915- . . . . CLC 11
See also CA 9-12R; CAAS 9; CANR 6

Sinjohn, John
See Galsworthy, John

Sorrentino, Gilbert
1929- .... **CLC 3, 7, 14, 22, 40**
See also CA 77-80; CANR 14, 33; DLB 5;
DLBY 80; INT CANR-14

Soto, Gary 1952-........ **CLC 32, 80; HLC**
See also AAYA 10; CA 119; 125;
CANR 50; CLR 38; DAM MULT;
DLB 82; HW; INT 125; JRDA; SATA 80

Soupault, Philippe 1897-1990 ...... **CLC 68**
See also CA 116; 147; 131

Souster, (Holmes) Raymond
1921- .... **CLC 5, 14; DAC**
See also CA 13-16R; CAAS 14; CANR 13,
29; DAM POET; DLB 88; SATA 63

Southern, Terry 1924(?)-1995 ...... **CLC 7**
See also CA 1-4R; 150; CANR 1; DLB 2

Southey, Robert 1774-1843 .... **NCLC 8**
See also DLB 93, 107, 142; SATA 54

Southworth, Emma Dorothy Eliza Nevitte
1819-1899 .... **NCLC 26**

Souza, Ernest
See Scott, Evelyn

Soyinka, Wole
1934- .... **CLC 3, 5, 14, 36, 44; BLC;
DA; DAB; DAC; DC 2; WLC**
See also BW 2; CA 13-16R; CANR 27, 39;
DAM DRAM, MST, MULT; DLB 125;
MTCW

Spackman, W(illiam) M(ode)
1905-1990 .... **CLC 46**
See also CA 81-84; 132

Spacks, Barry 1931-.............. **CLC 14**
See also CA 29-32R; CANR 33; DLB 105

Spanidou, Irini 1946-............. **CLC 44**

Spark, Muriel (Sarah)
1918- ..... **CLC 2, 3, 5, 8, 13, 18, 40, 94;
DAB; DAC; SSC 10**
See also CA 5-8R; CANR 12, 36;
CDBLB 1945-1960; DAM MST, NOV;
DLB 15, 139; INT CANR-12; MTCW

Spaulding, Douglas
See Bradbury, Ray (Douglas)

Spaulding, Leonard
See Bradbury, Ray (Douglas)

Spence, J. A. D.
See Eliot, T(homas) S(tearns)

Spencer, Elizabeth 1921-......... **CLC 22**
See also CA 13-16R; CANR 32; DLB 6;
MTCW; SATA 14

Spencer, Leonard G.
See Silverberg, Robert

Spencer, Scott 1945-.............. **CLC 30**
See also CA 113; CANR 51; DLBY 86

Spender, Stephen (Harold)
1909-1995 ...... **CLC 1, 2, 5, 10, 41, 91**
See also CA 9-12R; 149; CANR 31;
CDBLB 1945-1960; DAM POET;
DLB 20; MTCW

Spengler, Oswald (Arnold Gottfried)
1880-1936 .... **TCLC 25**
See also CA 118

Spenser, Edmund
1552(?)-1599 .... **LC 5; DA; DAB; DAC;
PC 8; WLC**
See also CDBLB Before 1660; DAM MST,
POET

Spicer, Jack 1925-1965 ...... **CLC 8, 18, 72**
See also CA 85-88; DAM POET; DLB 5, 16

Spiegelman, Art 1948-............. **CLC 76**
See also AAYA 10; CA 125; CANR 41

Spielberg, Peter 1929-............. **CLC 6**
See also CA 5-8R; CANR 4, 48; DLBY 81

Spielberg, Steven 1947-........... **CLC 20**
See also AAYA 8; CA 77-80; CANR 32;
SATA 32

Spillane, Frank Morrison 1918-
See Spillane, Mickey
See also CA 25-28R; CANR 28; MTCW;
SATA 66

Spillane, Mickey .... **CLC 3, 13**
See also Spillane, Frank Morrison

Spinoza, Benedictus de 1632-1677 .... **LC 9**

Spinrad, Norman (Richard) 1940-... **CLC 46**
See also CA 37-40R; CAAS 19; CANR 20;
DLB 8; INT CANR-20

Spitteler, Carl (Friedrich Georg)
1845-1924 .... **TCLC 12**
See also CA 109; DLB 129

Spivack, Kathleen (Romola Drucker)
1938- .... **CLC 6**
See also CA 49-52

Spoto, Donald 1941-.............. **CLC 39**
See also CA 65-68; CANR 11

Springsteen, Bruce (F.) 1949- ...... **CLC 17**
See also CA 111

Spurling, Hilary 1940-............. **CLC 34**
See also CA 104; CANR 25

Spyker, John Howland
See Elman, Richard

Squires, (James) Radcliffe
1917-1993 .... **CLC 51**
See also CA 1-4R; 140; CANR 6, 21

Srivastava, Dhanpat Rai 1880(?)-1936
See Premchand
See also CA 118

Stacy, Donald
See Pohl, Frederik

Stael, Germaine de
See Stael-Holstein, Anne Louise Germaine
Necker Baronn
See also DLB 119

**Stael-Holstein, Anne Louise Germaine Necker
Baronn** 1766-1817 .... **NCLC 3**
See also Stael, Germaine de

Stafford, Jean 1915-1979 ... **CLC 4, 7, 19, 68**
See also CA 1-4R; 85-88; CANR 3; DLB 2;
MTCW; SATA-Obit 22

Stafford, William (Edgar)
1914-1993 .... **CLC 4, 7, 29**
See also CA 5-8R; 142; CAAS 3; CANR 5,
22; DAM POET; DLB 5; INT CANR-22

Staines, Trevor
See Brunner, John (Kilian Houston)

Stairs, Gordon
See Austin, Mary (Hunter)

Stannard, Martin 1947-........... **CLC 44**
See also CA 142; DLB 155

Stanton, Maura 1946- .... **CLC 9**
See also CA 89-92; CANR 15; DLB 120

Stanton, Schuyler
See Baum, L(yman) Frank

Stapledon, (William) Olaf
1886-1950 .... **TCLC 22**
See also CA 111; DLB 15

Starbuck, George (Edwin) 1931-.... **CLC 53**
See also CA 21-24R; CANR 23;
DAM POET

Stark, Richard
See Westlake, Donald E(dwin)

Staunton, Schuyler
See Baum, L(yman) Frank

Stead, Christina (Ellen)
1902-1983 .... **CLC 2, 5, 8, 32, 80**
See also CA 13-16R; 109; CANR 33, 40;
MTCW

Stead, William Thomas
1849-1912 .... **TCLC 48**

Steele, Richard 1672-1729 .... **LC 18**
See also CDBLB 1660-1789; DLB 84, 101

Steele, Timothy (Reid) 1948-....... **CLC 45**
See also CA 93-96; CANR 16, 50; DLB 120

Steffens, (Joseph) Lincoln
1866-1936 .... **TCLC 20**
See also CA 117

Stegner, Wallace (Earle)
1909-1993 .... **CLC 9, 49, 81**
See also AITN 1; BEST 90:3; CA 1-4R;
141; CAAS 9; CANR 1, 21, 46;
DAM NOV; DLB 9; DLBY 93; MTCW

Stein, Gertrude
1874-1946 ...... **TCLC 1, 6, 28, 48; DA;
DAB; DAC; WLC**
See also CA 104; 132; CDALB 1917-1929;
DAM MST, NOV, POET; DLB 4, 54, 86;
MTCW

Steinbeck, John (Ernst)
1902-1968 ...... **CLC 1, 5, 9, 13, 21, 34,
45, 75; DA; DAB; DAC; SSC 11; WLC**
See also AAYA 12; CA 1-4R; 25-28R;
CANR 1, 35; CDALB 1929-1941;
DAM DRAM, MST, NOV; DLB 7, 9;
DLBD 2; MTCW; SATA 9

Steinem, Gloria 1934-............. **CLC 63**
See also CA 53-56; CANR 28, 51; MTCW

Steiner, George 1929-............. **CLC 24**
See also CA 73-76; CANR 31; DAM NOV;
DLB 67; MTCW; SATA 62

Steiner, K. Leslie
See Delany, Samuel R(ay, Jr.)

Steiner, Rudolf 1861-1925 .... **TCLC 13**
See also CA 107

Stendhal
1783-1842 .... **NCLC 23, 46; DA; DAB;
DAC; WLC**
See also DAM MST, NOV; DLB 119

Stephen, Leslie 1832-1904 .... **TCLC 23**
See also CA 123; DLB 57, 144

Stephen, Sir Leslie
See Stephen, Leslie

Stephen, Virginia
See Woolf, (Adeline) Virginia

Stephens, James 1882(?)-1950...... **TCLC 4**
See also CA 104; DLB 19, 153, 162

Stephens, Reed
See Donaldson, Stephen R.

Steptoe, Lydia
See Barnes, Djuna

Sterchi, Beat 1949-.............. **CLC 65**

Sterling, Brett
See Bradbury, Ray (Douglas); Hamilton, Edmond

Sterling, Bruce 1954-............. **CLC 72**
See also CA 119; CANR 44

Sterling, George 1869-1926....... **TCLC 20**
See also CA 117; DLB 54

Stern, Gerald 1925-.............. **CLC 40**
See also CA 81-84; CANR 28; DLB 105

Stern, Richard (Gustave) 1928-... **CLC 4, 39**
See also CA 1-4R; CANR 1, 25; DLBY 87;
INT CANR-25

Sternberg, Josef von 1894-1969..... **CLC 20**
See also CA 81-84

Sterne, Laurence
1713-1768...... **LC 2; DA; DAB; DAC;
WLC**
See also CDBLB 1660-1789; DAM MST,
NOV; DLB 39

Sternheim, (William Adolf) Carl
1878-1942.................. **TCLC 8**
See also CA 105; DLB 56, 118

Stevens, Mark 1951- .... **CLC 34**
See also CA 122

Stevens, Wallace
1879-1955........ **TCLC 3, 12, 45; DA;
DAB; DAC; PC 6; WLC**
See also CA 104; 124; CDALB 1929-1941;
DAM MST, POET; DLB 54; MTCW

Stevenson, Anne (Katharine)
1933-.................... **CLC 7, 33**
See also CA 17-20R; CAAS 9; CANR 9, 33;
DLB 40; MTCW

Stevenson, Robert Louis (Balfour)
1850-1894..... **NCLC 5, 14; DA; DAB;
DAC; SSC 11; WLC**
See also CDBLB 1890-1914; CLR 10, 11;
DAM MST, NOV; DLB 18, 57, 141, 156;
DLBD 13; JRDA; MAICYA; YABC 2

Stewart, J(ohn) I(nnes) M(ackintosh)
1906-1994.............. **CLC 7, 14, 32**
See also CA 85-88; 147; CAAS 3;
CANR 47; MTCW

Stewart, Mary (Florence Elinor)
1916-............... **CLC 7, 35; DAB**
See also CA 1-4R; CANR 1; SATA 12

Stewart, Mary Rainbow
See Stewart, Mary (Florence Elinor)

Stifle, June
See Campbell, Maria

Stifter, Adalbert 1805-1868...... **NCLC 41**
See also DLB 133

Still, James 1906-................ **CLC 49**
See also CA 65-68; CAAS 17; CANR 10,
26; DLB 9; SATA 29

Sting
See Sumner, Gordon Matthew

Stirling, Arthur
See Sinclair, Upton (Beall)

Stitt, Milan 1941-................ **CLC 29**
See also CA 69-72

Stockton, Francis Richard 1834-1902
See Stockton, Frank R.
See also CA 108; 137; MAICYA; SATA 44

Stockton, Frank R. .... **TCLC 47**
See also Stockton, Francis Richard
See also DLB 42, 74; DLBD 13;
SATA-Brief 32

Stoddard, Charles
See Kuttner, Henry

Stoker, Abraham 1847-1912
See Stoker, Bram
See also CA 105; DA; DAC; DAM MST,
NOV; SATA 29

Stoker, Bram
1847-1912........ **TCLC 8; DAB; WLC**
See also Stoker, Abraham
See also CA 150; CDBLB 1890-1914;
DLB 36, 70

Stolz, Mary (Slattery) 1920-....... **CLC 12**
See also AAYA 8; AITN 1; CA 5-8R;
CANR 13, 41; JRDA; MAICYA;
SAAS 3; SATA 10, 71

Stone, Irving 1903-1989........... **CLC 7**
See also AITN 1; CA 1-4R; 129; CAAS 3;
CANR 1, 23; DAM POP;
INT CANR-23; MTCW; SATA 3;
SATA-Obit 64

Stone, Oliver 1946-.............. **CLC 73**
See also AAYA 15; CA 110

Stone, Robert (Anthony)
1937-................ **CLC 5, 23, 42**
See also CA 85-88; CANR 23; DLB 152;
INT CANR-23; MTCW

Stone, Zachary
See Follett, Ken(neth Martin)

Stoppard, Tom
1937-...... **CLC 1, 3, 4, 5, 8, 15, 29, 34,
63, 91; DA; DAB; DAC; DC 6; WLC**
See also CA 81-84; CANR 39;
CDBLB 1960 to Present; DAM DRAM,
MST; DLB 13; DLBY 85; MTCW

Storey, David (Malcolm)
1933-................. **CLC 2, 4, 5, 8**
See also CA 81-84; CANR 36;
DAM DRAM; DLB 13, 14; MTCW

Storm, Hyemeyohsts 1935-......... **CLC 3**
See also CA 81-84; CANR 45;
DAM MULT; NNAL

Storm, (Hans) Theodor (Woldsen)
1817-1888.................. **NCLC 1**

Storni, Alfonsina
1892-1938............. **TCLC 5; HLC**
See also CA 104; 131; DAM MULT; HW

Stout, Rex (Todhunter) 1886-1975... **CLC 3**
See also AITN 2; CA 61-64

Stow, (Julian) Randolph 1935-.. **CLC 23, 48**
See also CA 13-16R; CANR 33; MTCW

Stowe, Harriet (Elizabeth) Beecher
1811-1896..... **NCLC 3, 50; DA; DAB;
DAC; WLC**
See also CDALB 1865-1917; DAM MST,
NOV; DLB 1, 12, 42, 74; JRDA;
MAICYA; YABC 1

Strachey, (Giles) Lytton
1880-1932................. **TCLC 12**
See also CA 110; DLB 149; DLBD 10

Strand, Mark 1934-...... **CLC 6, 18, 41, 71**
See also CA 21-24R; CANR 40;
DAM POET; DLB 5; SATA 41

Straub, Peter (Francis) 1943-...... **CLC 28**
See also BEST 89:1; CA 85-88; CANR 28;
DAM POP; DLBY 84; MTCW

Strauss, Botho 1944-.............. **CLC 22**
See also DLB 124

Streatfeild, (Mary) Noel
1895(?)-1986................. **CLC 21**
See also CA 81-84; 120; CANR 31;
CLR 17; DLB 160; MAICYA; SATA 20;
SATA-Obit 48

Stribling, T(homas) S(igismund)
1881-1965.................... **CLC 23**
See also CA 107; DLB 9

Strindberg, (Johan) August
1849-1912...... **TCLC 1, 8, 21, 47; DA;
DAB; DAC; WLC**
See also CA 104; 135; DAM DRAM, MST

Stringer, Arthur 1874-1950....... **TCLC 37**
See also DLB 92

Stringer, David
See Roberts, Keith (John Kingston)

Strugatskii, Arkadii (Natanovich)
1925-1991.................... **CLC 27**
See also CA 106; 135

Strugatskii, Boris (Natanovich)
1933-...................... **CLC 27**
See also CA 106

Strummer, Joe 1953(?)-........... **CLC 30**

Stuart, Don A.
See Campbell, John W(ood, Jr.)

Stuart, Ian
See MacLean, Alistair (Stuart)

Stuart, Jesse (Hilton)
1906-1984........ **CLC 1, 8, 11, 14, 34**
See also CA 5-8R; 112; CANR 31; DLB 9,
48, 102; DLBY 84; SATA 2;
SATA-Obit 36

Sturgeon, Theodore (Hamilton)
1918-1985............... **CLC 22, 39**
See also Queen, Ellery
See also CA 81-84; 116; CANR 32; DLB 8;
DLBY 85; MTCW

Sturges, Preston 1898-1959...... **TCLC 48**
See also CA 114; 149; DLB 26

Styron, William
1925-.......... **CLC 1, 3, 5, 11, 15, 60**
See also BEST 90:4; CA 5-8R; CANR 6, 33;
CDALB 1968-1988; DAM NOV, POP;
DLB 2, 143; DLBY 80; INT CANR-6;
MTCW

Suarez Lynch, B.
See Bioy Casares, Adolfo; Borges, Jorge
Luis

Su Chien 1884-1918
See Su Man-shu
See also CA 123

Suckow, Ruth 1892-1960 . . . . **SSC 18**
See also CA 113; DLB 9, 102

Sudermann, Hermann 1857-1928 . . **TCLC 15**
See also CA 107; DLB 118

Sue, Eugene 1804-1857 . . . . **NCLC 1**
See also DLB 119

Sueskind, Patrick 1949- . . . . **CLC 44**
See also Suskind, Patrick

Sukenick, Ronald 1932- . . . . . **CLC 3, 4, 6, 48**
See also CA 25-28R; CAAS 8; CANR 32;
DLBY 81

Suknaski, Andrew 1942- . . . . **CLC 19**
See also CA 101; DLB 53

Sullivan, Vernon
See Vian, Boris

Sully Prudhomme 1839-1907 . . . . . . **TCLC 31**

Su Man-shu . . . . **TCLC 24**
See also Su Chien

Summerforest, Ivy B.
See Kirkup, James

Summers, Andrew James 1942- . . . . . **CLC 26**

Summers, Andy
See Summers, Andrew James

Summers, Hollis (Spurgeon, Jr.)
1916- . . . . **CLC 10**
See also CA 5-8R; CANR 3; DLB 6

Summers, (Alphonsus Joseph-Mary Augustus)
Montague 1880-1948 . . . . **TCLC 16**
See also CA 118

Sumner, Gordon Matthew 1951- . . . . **CLC 26**

Surtees, Robert Smith
1803-1864 . . . . **NCLC 14**
See also DLB 21

Susann, Jacqueline 1921-1974 . . . . . . **CLC 3**
See also AITN 1; CA 65-68; 53-56; MTCW

Su Shih 1036-1101 . . . . **CMLC 15**

Suskind, Patrick
See Sueskind, Patrick
See also CA 145

Sutcliff, Rosemary
1920-1992 . . . . **CLC 26; DAB; DAC**
See also AAYA 10; CA 5-8R; 139;
CANR 37; CLR 1, 37; DAM MST, POP;
JRDA; MAICYA; SATA 6, 44, 78;
SATA-Obit 73

Sutro, Alfred 1863-1933 . . . . **TCLC 6**
See also CA 105; DLB 10

Sutton, Henry
See Slavitt, David R(ytman)

Svevo, Italo . . . . **TCLC 2, 35**
See also Schmitz, Aron Hector

Swados, Elizabeth (A.) 1951- . . . . **CLC 12**
See also CA 97-100; CANR 49; INT 97-100

Swados, Harvey 1920-1972 . . . . **CLC 5**
See also CA 5-8R; 37-40R; CANR 6;
DLB 2

Swan, Gladys 1934- . . . . **CLC 69**
See also CA 101; CANR 17, 39

Swarthout, Glendon (Fred)
1918-1992 . . . . **CLC 35**
See also CA 1-4R; 139; CANR 1, 47;
SATA 26

Sweet, Sarah C.
See Jewett, (Theodora) Sarah Orne

Swenson, May
1919-1989 . . . . **CLC 4, 14, 61; DA; DAB;
DAC; PC 14**
See also CA 5-8R; 130; CANR 36;
DAM MST, POET; DLB 5; MTCW;
SATA 15

Swift, Augustus
See Lovecraft, H(oward) P(hillips)

Swift, Graham (Colin) 1949- . . . . **CLC 41, 88**
See also CA 117; 122; CANR 46

Swift, Jonathan
1667-1745 . . . . . . **LC 1; DA; DAB; DAC;
PC 9; WLC**
See also CDBLB 1660-1789; DAM MST,
NOV, POET; DLB 39, 95, 101; SATA 19

Swinburne, Algernon Charles
1837-1909 . . . . . . **TCLC 8, 36; DA; DAB;
DAC; WLC**
See also CA 105; 140; CDBLB 1832-1890;
DAM MST, POET; DLB 35, 57

Swinfen, Ann . . . . **CLC 34**

Swinnerton, Frank Arthur
1884-1982 . . . . **CLC 31**
See also CA 108; DLB 34

Swithen, John
See King, Stephen (Edwin)

Sylvia
See Ashton-Warner, Sylvia (Constance)

Symmes, Robert Edward
See Duncan, Robert (Edward)

Symonds, John Addington
1840-1893 . . . . **NCLC 34**
See also DLB 57, 144

Symons, Arthur 1865-1945 . . . . **TCLC 11**
See also CA 107; DLB 19, 57, 149

Symons, Julian (Gustave)
1912-1994 . . . . **CLC 2, 14, 32**
See also CA 49-52; 147; CAAS 3; CANR 3,
33; DLB 87, 155; DLBY 92; MTCW

Synge, (Edmund) J(ohn) M(illington)
1871-1909 . . . . **TCLC 6, 37; DC 2**
See also CA 104; 141; CDBLB 1890-1914;
DAM DRAM; DLB 10, 19

Syruc, J.
See Milosz, Czeslaw

Szirtes, George 1948- . . . . **CLC 46**
See also CA 109; CANR 27

Tabori, George 1914- . . . . **CLC 19**
See also CA 49-52; CANR 4

Tagore, Rabindranath
1861-1941 . . . . **TCLC 3, 53; PC 8**
See also CA 104; 120; DAM DRAM,
POET; MTCW

Taine, Hippolyte Adolphe
1828-1893 . . . . **NCLC 15**

Talese, Gay 1932- . . . . **CLC 37**
See also AITN 1; CA 1-4R; CANR 9;
INT CANR-9; MTCW

Tallent, Elizabeth (Ann) 1954- . . . . . **CLC 45**
See also CA 117; DLB 130

Tally, Ted 1952- . . . . **CLC 42**
See also CA 120; 124; INT 124

Tamayo y Baus, Manuel
1829-1898 . . . . **NCLC 1**

Tammsaare, A(nton) H(ansen)
1878-1940 . . . . **TCLC 27**

Tan, Amy 1952- . . . . **CLC 59**
See also AAYA 9; BEST 89:3; CA 136;
DAM MULT, NOV, POP; SATA 75

Tandem, Felix
See Spitteler, Carl (Friedrich Georg)

Tanizaki, Jun'ichiro
1886-1965 . . . . . . **CLC 8, 14, 28; SSC 21**
See also CA 93-96; 25-28R

Tanner, William
See Amis, Kingsley (William)

Tao Lao
See Storni, Alfonsina

Tarassoff, Lev
See Troyat, Henri

Tarbell, Ida M(inerva)
1857-1944 . . . . **TCLC 40**
See also CA 122; DLB 47

Tarkington, (Newton) Booth
1869-1946 . . . . **TCLC 9**
See also CA 110; 143; DLB 9, 102;
SATA 17

Tarkovsky, Andrei (Arsenyevich)
1932-1986 . . . . **CLC 75**
See also CA 127

Tartt, Donna 1964(?)- . . . . **CLC 76**
See also CA 142

Tasso, Torquato 1544-1595 . . . . **LC 5**

Tate, (John Orley) Allen
1899-1979 . . . . **CLC 2, 4, 6, 9, 11, 14, 24**
See also CA 5-8R; 85-88; CANR 32;
DLB 4, 45, 63; MTCW

Tate, Ellalice
See Hibbert, Eleanor Alice Burford

Tate, James (Vincent) 1943- . . . **CLC 2, 6, 25**
See also CA 21-24R; CANR 29; DLB 5

Tavel, Ronald 1940- . . . . **CLC 6**
See also CA 21-24R; CANR 33

Taylor, C(ecil) P(hilip) 1929-1981 . . . **CLC 27**
See also CA 25-28R; 105; CANR 47

Taylor, Edward
1642(?)-1729 . . . **LC 11; DA; DAB; DAC**
See also DAM MST, POET; DLB 24

Taylor, Eleanor Ross 1920- . . . . **CLC 5**
See also CA 81-84

Taylor, Elizabeth 1912-1975 . . . **CLC 2, 4, 29**
See also CA 13-16R; CANR 9; DLB 139;
MTCW; SATA 13

Taylor, Henry (Splawn) 1942- . . . . . . **CLC 44**
See also CA 33-36R; CAAS 7; CANR 31;
DLB 5

Taylor, Kamala (Purnaiya) 1924-
See Markandaya, Kamala
See also CA 77-80

Tolkien, J(ohn) R(onald) R(euel)
1892-1973 ...... **CLC 1, 2, 3, 8, 12, 38;
DA; DAB; DAC; WLC**
See also AAYA 10; AITN 1; CA 17-18;
45-48; CANR 36; CAP 2;
CDBLB 1914-1945; DAM MST, NOV,
POP; DLB 15, 160; JRDA; MAICYA;
MTCW; SATA 2, 32; SATA-Obit 24

Toller, Ernst 1893-1939 .... **TCLC 10**
See also CA 107; DLB 124

Tolson, M. B.
See Tolson, Melvin B(eaunorus)

Tolson, Melvin B(eaunorus)
1898(?)-1966 .... **CLC 36; BLC**
See also BW 1; CA 124; 89-92;
DAM MULT, POET; DLB 48, 76

Tolstoi, Aleksei Nikolaevich
See Tolstoy, Alexey Nikolaevich

Tolstoy, Alexey Nikolaevich
1882-1945 .... **TCLC 18**
See also CA 107

Tolstoy, Count Leo
See Tolstoy, Leo (Nikolaevich)

Tolstoy, Leo (Nikolaevich)
1828-1910 ...... **TCLC 4, 11, 17, 28, 44;
DA; DAB; DAC; SSC 9; WLC**
See also CA 104; 123; DAM MST, NOV;
SATA 26

Tomasi di Lampedusa, Giuseppe 1896-1957
See Lampedusa, Giuseppe (Tomasi) di
See also CA 111

Tomlin, Lily .... **CLC 17**
See also Tomlin, Mary Jean

Tomlin, Mary Jean 1939(?)-
See Tomlin, Lily
See also CA 117

Tomlinson, (Alfred) Charles
1927- .... **CLC 2, 4, 6, 13, 45**
See also CA 5-8R; CANR 33; DAM POET;
DLB 40

Tonson, Jacob
See Bennett, (Enoch) Arnold

Toole, John Kennedy
1937-1969 .... **CLC 19, 64**
See also CA 104; DLBY 81

Toomer, Jean
1894-1967 ...... **CLC 1, 4, 13, 22; BLC;
PC 7; SSC 1**
See also BW 1; CA 85-88;
CDALB 1917-1929; DAM MULT;
DLB 45, 51; MTCW

Torley, Luke
See Blish, James (Benjamin)

Tornimparte, Alessandra
See Ginzburg, Natalia

Torre, Raoul della
See Mencken, H(enry) L(ouis)

Torrey, E(dwin) Fuller 1937- ...... **CLC 34**
See also CA 119

Torsvan, Ben Traven
See Traven, B.

Torsvan, Benno Traven
See Traven, B.

Torsvan, Berick Traven
See Traven, B.

Torsvan, Berwick Traven
See Traven, B.

Torsvan, Bruno Traven
See Traven, B.

Torsvan, Traven
See Traven, B.

Tournier, Michel (Edouard)
1924- .... **CLC 6, 23, 36**
See also CA 49-52; CANR 3, 36; DLB 83;
MTCW; SATA 23

Tournimparte, Alessandra
See Ginzburg, Natalia

Towers, Ivar
See Kornbluth, C(yril) M.

Towne, Robert (Burton) 1936(?)- .... **CLC 87**
See also CA 108; DLB 44

Townsend, Sue 1946- .. **CLC 61; DAB; DAC**
See also CA 119; 127; INT 127; MTCW;
SATA 55; SATA-Brief 48

Townshend, Peter (Dennis Blandford)
1945- .... **CLC 17, 42**
See also CA 107

Tozzi, Federigo 1883-1920 .... **TCLC 31**

Traill, Catharine Parr
1802-1899 .... **NCLC 31**
See also DLB 99

Trakl, Georg 1887-1914 .... **TCLC 5**
See also CA 104

Transtroemer, Tomas (Goesta)
1931- .... **CLC 52, 65**
See also CA 117; 129; CAAS 17;
DAM POET

Transtromer, Tomas Gosta
See Transtroemer, Tomas (Goesta)

Traven, B. (?)-1969 .... **CLC 8, 11**
See also CA 19-20; 25-28R; CAP 2; DLB 9,
56; MTCW

Treitel, Jonathan 1959- .... **CLC 70**

Tremain, Rose 1943- .... **CLC 42**
See also CA 97-100; CANR 44; DLB 14

Tremblay, Michel 1942- ...... **CLC 29; DAC**
See also CA 116; 128; DAM MST; DLB 60;
MTCW

Trevanian .... **CLC 29**
See also Whitaker, Rod(ney)

Trevor, Glen
See Hilton, James

Trevor, William
1928- ..... **CLC 7, 9, 14, 25, 71; SSC 21**
See also Cox, William Trevor
See also DLB 14, 139

Trifonov, Yuri (Valentinovich)
1925-1981 .... **CLC 45**
See also CA 126; 103; MTCW

Trilling, Lionel 1905-1975 .... **CLC 9, 11, 24**
See also CA 9-12R; 61-64; CANR 10;
DLB 28, 63; INT CANR-10; MTCW

Trimball, W. H.
See Mencken, H(enry) L(ouis)

Tristan
See Gomez de la Serna, Ramon

Tristram
See Housman, A(lfred) E(dward)

Trogdon, William (Lewis) 1939-
See Heat-Moon, William Least
See also CA 115; 119; CANR 47; INT 119

Trollope, Anthony
1815-1882 ..... **NCLC 6, 33; DA; DAB;
DAC; WLC**
See also CDBLB 1832-1890; DAM MST,
NOV; DLB 21, 57, 159; SATA 22

Trollope, Frances 1779-1863 ..... **NCLC 30**
See also DLB 21

Trotsky, Leon 1879-1940 .... **TCLC 22**
See also CA 118

Trotter (Cockburn), Catharine
1679-1749 .... **LC 8**
See also DLB 84

Trout, Kilgore
See Farmer, Philip Jose

Trow, George W. S. 1943- .... **CLC 52**
See also CA 126

Troyat, Henri 1911- .... **CLC 23**
See also CA 45-48; CANR 2, 33; MTCW

Trudeau, G(arretson) B(eekman) 1948-
See Trudeau, Garry B.
See also CA 81-84; CANR 31; SATA 35

Trudeau, Garry B. .... **CLC 12**
See also Trudeau, G(arretson) B(eekman)
See also AAYA 10; AITN 2

Truffaut, Francois 1932-1984 ...... **CLC 20**
See also CA 81-84; 113; CANR 34

Trumbo, Dalton 1905-1976 .... **CLC 19**
See also CA 21-24R; 69-72; CANR 10;
DLB 26

Trumbull, John 1750-1831 .... **NCLC 30**
See also DLB 31

Trundlett, Helen B.
See Eliot, T(homas) S(tearns)

Tryon, Thomas 1926-1991 .... **CLC 3, 11**
See also AITN 1; CA 29-32R; 135;
CANR 32; DAM POP; MTCW

Tryon, Tom
See Tryon, Thomas

Ts'ao Hsueh-ch'in 1715(?)-1763 .... **LC 1**

Tsushima, Shuji 1909-1948
See Dazai, Osamu
See also CA 107

Tsvetaeva (Efron), Marina (Ivanovna)
1892-1941 .... **TCLC 7, 35; PC 14**
See also CA 104; 128; MTCW

Tuck, Lily 1938- .... **CLC 70**
See also CA 139

Tu Fu 712-770 .... **PC 9**
See also DAM MULT

Tunis, John R(oberts) 1889-1975 ... **CLC 12**
See also CA 61-64; DLB 22; JRDA;
MAICYA; SATA 37; SATA-Brief 30

Tuohy, Frank .... **CLC 37**
See also Tuohy, John Francis
See also DLB 14, 139

Tuohy, John Francis 1925-
See Tuohy, Frank
See also CA 5-8R; CANR 3, 47

Turco, Lewis (Putnam) 1934- ... **CLC 11, 63**
See also CA 13-16R; CAAS 22; CANR 24,
51; DLBY 84

Vazov, Ivan (Minchov)
1850-1921 .... TCLC **25**
See also CA 121; DLB 147

Veblen, Thorstein (Bunde)
1857-1929 .... TCLC **31**
See also CA 115

Vega, Lope de 1562-1635 .... LC **23**

Venison, Alfred
See Pound, Ezra (Weston Loomis)

Verdi, Marie de
See Mencken, H(enry) L(ouis)

Verdu, Matilde
See Cela, Camilo Jose

Verga, Giovanni (Carmelo)
1840-1922 .... TCLC **3**; SSC **21**
See also CA 104; 123

Vergil
70B.C.-19B.C. ..... CMLC **9**; DA; DAB;
DAC; PC **12**
See also DAM MST, POET

Verhaeren, Emile (Adolphe Gustave)
1855-1916 .... TCLC **12**
See also CA 109

Verlaine, Paul (Marie)
1844-1896 .... NCLC **2, 51**; PC **2**
See also DAM POET

Verne, Jules (Gabriel)
1828-1905 .... TCLC **6, 52**
See also AAYA 16; CA 110; 131; DLB 123;
JRDA; MAICYA; SATA 21

Very, Jones 1813-1880 .... NCLC **9**
See also DLB 1

Vesaas, Tarjei 1897-1970 .... CLC **48**
See also CA 29-32R

Vialis, Gaston
See Simenon, Georges (Jacques Christian)

Vian, Boris 1920-1959 .... TCLC **9**
See also CA 106; DLB 72

Viaud, (Louis Marie) Julien 1850-1923
See Loti, Pierre
See also CA 107

Vicar, Henry
See Felsen, Henry Gregor

Vicker, Angus
See Felsen, Henry Gregor

Vidal, Gore
1925- ..... CLC **2, 4, 6, 8, 10, 22, 33, 72**
See also AITN 1; BEST 90:2; CA 5-8R;
CANR 13, 45; DAM NOV, POP; DLB 6,
152; INT CANR-13; MTCW

Viereck, Peter (Robert Edwin)
1916- .... CLC **4**
See also CA 1-4R; CANR 1, 47; DLB 5

Vigny, Alfred (Victor) de
1797-1863 .... NCLC **7**
See also DAM POET; DLB 119

Vilakazi, Benedict Wallet
1906-1947 .... TCLC **37**

Villiers de l'Isle Adam, Jean Marie Mathias
Philippe Auguste Comte
1838-1889 .... NCLC **3**; SSC **14**
See also DLB 123

Villon, Francois 1431-1463(?) ...... PC **13**

Vinci, Leonardo da 1452-1519 .... LC **12**

Vine, Barbara .... CLC **50**
See also Rendell, Ruth (Barbara)
See also BEST 90:4

Vinge, Joan D(ennison) 1948- ..... CLC **30**
See also CA 93-96; SATA 36

Violis, G.
See Simenon, Georges (Jacques Christian)

Visconti, Luchino 1906-1976 ...... CLC **16**
See also CA 81-84; 65-68; CANR 39

Vittorini, Elio 1908-1966 ...... CLC **6, 9, 14**
See also CA 133; 25-28R

Vizinczey, Stephen 1933- .... CLC **40**
See also CA 128; INT 128

Vliet, R(ussell) G(ordon)
1929-1984 .... CLC **22**
See also CA 37-40R; 112; CANR 18

Vogau, Boris Andreyevich 1894-1937(?)
See Pilnyak, Boris
See also CA 123

Vogel, Paula A(nne) 1951- .... CLC **76**
See also CA 108

Voight, Ellen Bryant 1943- .... CLC **54**
See also CA 69-72; CANR 11, 29; DLB 120

Voigt, Cynthia 1942- .... CLC **30**
See also AAYA 3; CA 106; CANR 18, 37,
40; CLR 13; INT CANR-18; JRDA;
MAICYA; SATA 48, 79; SATA-Brief 33

Voinovich, Vladimir (Nikolaevich)
1932- .... CLC **10, 49**
See also CA 81-84; CAAS 12; CANR 33;
MTCW

Vollmann, William T. 1959- .... CLC **89**
See also CA 134; DAM NOV, POP

Voloshinov, V. N.
See Bakhtin, Mikhail Mikhailovich

Voltaire
1694-1778 ..... LC **14**; DA; DAB; DAC;
SSC **12**; WLC
See also DAM DRAM, MST

von Daeniken, Erich 1935- .... CLC **30**
See also AITN 1; CA 37-40R; CANR 17,
44

von Daniken, Erich
See von Daeniken, Erich

von Heidenstam, (Carl Gustaf) Verner
See Heidenstam, (Carl Gustaf) Verner von

von Heyse, Paul (Johann Ludwig)
See Heyse, Paul (Johann Ludwig von)

von Hofmannsthal, Hugo
See Hofmannsthal, Hugo von

von Horvath, Odon
See Horvath, Oedoen von

von Horvath, Oedoen
See Horvath, Oedoen von

von Liliencron, (Friedrich Adolf Axel) Detlev
See Liliencron, (Friedrich Adolf Axel)
Detlev von

Vonnegut, Kurt, Jr.
1922- ...... CLC **1, 2, 3, 4, 5, 8, 12, 22,
40, 60**; DA; DAB; DAC; SSC **8**; WLC
See also AAYA 6; AITN 1; BEST 90:4;
CA 1-4R; CANR 1, 25, 49;
CDALB 1968-1988; DAM MST, NOV,
POP; DLB 2, 8, 152; DLBD 3; DLBY 80;
MTCW

Von Rachen, Kurt
See Hubbard, L(afayette) Ron(ald)

von Rezzori (d'Arezzo), Gregor
See Rezzori (d'Arezzo), Gregor von

von Sternberg, Josef
See Sternberg, Josef von

Vorster, Gordon 1924- .... CLC **34**
See also CA 133

Vosce, Trudie
See Ozick, Cynthia

Voznesensky, Andrei (Andreievich)
1933- .... CLC **1, 15, 57**
See also CA 89-92; CANR 37;
DAM POET; MTCW

Waddington, Miriam 1917- .... CLC **28**
See also CA 21-24R; CANR 12, 30;
DLB 68

Wagman, Fredrica 1937- .... CLC **7**
See also CA 97-100; INT 97-100

Wagner, Richard 1813-1883 .... NCLC **9**
See also DLB 129

Wagner-Martin, Linda 1936- .... CLC **50**

Wagoner, David (Russell)
1926- .... CLC **3, 5, 15**
See also CA 1-4R; CAAS 3; CANR 2;
DLB 5; SATA 14

Wah, Fred(erick James) 1939- ..... CLC **44**
See also CA 107; 141; DLB 60

Wahloo, Per 1926-1975 .... CLC **7**
See also CA 61-64

Wahloo, Peter
See Wahloo, Per

Wain, John (Barrington)
1925-1994 .... CLC **2, 11, 15, 46**
See also CA 5-8R; 145; CAAS 4; CANR 23;
CDBLB 1960 to Present; DLB 15, 27,
139, 155; MTCW

Wajda, Andrzej 1926- .... CLC **16**
See also CA 102

Wakefield, Dan 1932- .... CLC **7**
See also CA 21-24R; CAAS 7

Wakoski, Diane
1937- ..... CLC **2, 4, 7, 9, 11, 40**; PC **15**
See also CA 13-16R; CAAS 1; CANR 9;
DAM POET; DLB 5; INT CANR-9

Wakoski-Sherbell, Diane
See Wakoski, Diane

Walcott, Derek (Alton)
1930- .... CLC **2, 4, 9, 14, 25, 42, 67, 76**;
BLC; DAB; DAC
See also BW 2; CA 89-92; CANR 26, 47;
DAM MST, MULT, POET; DLB 117;
DLBY 81; MTCW

Waldman, Anne 1945- .... CLC **7**
See also CA 37-40R; CAAS 17; CANR 34;
DLB 16

Waldo, E. Hunter
See Sturgeon, Theodore (Hamilton)

Waldo, Edward Hamilton
See Sturgeon, Theodore (Hamilton)

Walker, Alice (Malsenior)
1944- . . . . **CLC 5, 6, 9, 19, 27, 46, 58;**
BLC; DA; DAB; DAC; SSC 5
See also AAYA 3; BEST 89:4; BW 2;
CA 37-40R; CANR 9, 27, 49;
CDALB 1968-1988; DAM MST, MULT,
NOV, POET, POP; DLB 6, 33, 143;
INT CANR-27; MTCW; SATA 31

Walker, David Harry 1911-1992. . . . **CLC 14**
See also CA 1-4R; 137; CANR 1; SATA 8;
SATA-Obit 71

Walker, Edward Joseph 1934-
See Walker, Ted
See also CA 21-24R; CANR 12, 28

Walker, George F.
1947- . . . . **CLC 44, 61; DAB; DAC**
See also CA 103; CANR 21, 43;
DAM MST; DLB 60

Walker, Joseph A. 1935- . . . . **CLC 19**
See also BW 1; CA 89-92; CANR 26;
DAM DRAM, MST; DLB 38

Walker, Margaret (Abigail)
1915- . . . . **CLC 1, 6; BLC**
See also BW 2; CA 73-76; CANR 26;
DAM MULT; DLB 76, 152; MTCW

Walker, Ted . . . . **CLC 13**
See also Walker, Edward Joseph
See also DLB 40

Wallace, David Foster 1962- . . . . **CLC 50**
See also CA 132

Wallace, Dexter
See Masters, Edgar Lee

Wallace, (Richard Horatio) Edgar
1875-1932 . . . . **TCLC 57**
See also CA 115; DLB 70

Wallace, Irving 1916-1990 . . . . **CLC 7, 13**
See also AITN 1; CA 1-4R; 132; CAAS 1;
CANR 1, 27; DAM NOV, POP;
INT CANR-27; MTCW

Wallant, Edward Lewis
1926-1962 . . . . **CLC 5, 10**
See also CA 1-4R; CANR 22; DLB 2, 28,
143; MTCW

Walley, Byron
See Card, Orson Scott

Walpole, Horace 1717-1797 . . . . **LC 2**
See also DLB 39, 104

Walpole, Hugh (Seymour)
1884-1941 . . . . **TCLC 5**
See also CA 104; DLB 34

Walser, Martin 1927- . . . . **CLC 27**
See also CA 57-60; CANR 8, 46; DLB 75,
124

Walser, Robert
1878-1956 . . . . **TCLC 18; SSC 20**
See also CA 118; DLB 66

Walsh, Jill Paton . . . . **CLC 35**
See also Paton Walsh, Gillian
See also AAYA 11; CLR 2; DLB 161;
SAAS 3

Walter, Villiam Christian
See Andersen, Hans Christian

Wambaugh, Joseph (Aloysius, Jr.)
1937- . . . . **CLC 3, 18**
See also AITN 1; BEST 89:3; CA 33-36R;
CANR 42; DAM NOV, POP; DLB 6;
DLBY 83; MTCW

Ward, Arthur Henry Sarsfield 1883-1959
See Rohmer, Sax
See also CA 108

Ward, Douglas Turner 1930- . . . . . . **CLC 19**
See also BW 1; CA 81-84; CANR 27;
DLB 7, 38

Ward, Mary Augusta
See Ward, Mrs. Humphry

Ward, Mrs. Humphry
1851-1920 . . . . **TCLC 55**
See also DLB 18

Ward, Peter
See Faust, Frederick (Schiller)

Warhol, Andy 1928(?)-1987 . . . . **CLC 20**
See also AAYA 12; BEST 89:4; CA 89-92;
121; CANR 34

Warner, Francis (Robert le Plastrier)
1937- . . . . **CLC 14**
See also CA 53-56; CANR 11

Warner, Marina 1946- . . . . **CLC 59**
See also CA 65-68; CANR 21

Warner, Rex (Ernest) 1905-1986 . . . . **CLC 45**
See also CA 89-92; 119; DLB 15

Warner, Susan (Bogert)
1819-1885 . . . . **NCLC 31**
See also DLB 3, 42

Warner, Sylvia (Constance) Ashton
See Ashton-Warner, Sylvia (Constance)

Warner, Sylvia Townsend
1893-1978 . . . . **CLC 7, 19; SSC 23**
See also CA 61-64; 77-80; CANR 16;
DLB 34, 139; MTCW

Warren, Mercy Otis 1728-1814 . . . **NCLC 13**
See also DLB 31

Warren, Robert Penn
1905-1989 . . . . **CLC 1, 4, 6, 8, 10, 13, 18,**
39, 53, 59; DA; DAB; DAC; SSC 4; WLC
See also AITN 1; CA 13-16R; 129;
CANR 10, 47; CDALB 1968-1988;
DAM MST, NOV, POET; DLB 2, 48,
152; DLBY 80, 89; INT CANR-10;
MTCW; SATA 46; SATA-Obit 63

Warshofsky, Isaac
See Singer, Isaac Bashevis

Warton, Thomas 1728-1790 . . . . **LC 15**
See also DAM POET; DLB 104, 109

Waruk, Kona
See Harris, (Theodore) Wilson

Warung, Price 1855-1911 . . . . **TCLC 45**

Warwick, Jarvis
See Garner, Hugh

Washington, Alex
See Harris, Mark

Washington, Booker T(aliaferro)
1856-1915 . . . . **TCLC 10; BLC**
See also BW 1; CA 114; 125; DAM MULT;
SATA 28

Washington, George 1732-1799 . . . . . . **LC 25**
See also DLB 31

Wassermann, (Karl) Jakob
1873-1934 . . . . **TCLC 6**
See also CA 104; DLB 66

Wasserstein, Wendy
1950- . . . . **CLC 32, 59, 90; DC 4**
See also CA 121; 129; CABS 3;
DAM DRAM; INT 129

Waterhouse, Keith (Spencer)
1929- . . . . **CLC 47**
See also CA 5-8R; CANR 38; DLB 13, 15;
MTCW

Waters, Frank (Joseph)
1902-1995 . . . . **CLC 88**
See also CA 5-8R; 149; CAAS 13; CANR 3,
18; DLBY 86

Waters, Roger 1944- . . . . **CLC 35**

Watkins, Frances Ellen
See Harper, Frances Ellen Watkins

Watkins, Gerrold
See Malzberg, Barry N(athaniel)

Watkins, Gloria 1955(?)-
See hooks, bell
See also BW 2; CA 143

Watkins, Paul 1964- . . . . **CLC 55**
See also CA 132

Watkins, Vernon Phillips
1906-1967 . . . . **CLC 43**
See also CA 9-10; 25-28R; CAP 1; DLB 20

Watson, Irving S.
See Mencken, H(enry) L(ouis)

Watson, John H.
See Farmer, Philip Jose

Watson, Richard F.
See Silverberg, Robert

Waugh, Auberon (Alexander) 1939- . . **CLC 7**
See also CA 45-48; CANR 6, 22; DLB 14

Waugh, Evelyn (Arthur St. John)
1903-1966 . . . . . . **CLC 1, 3, 8, 13, 19, 27,**
44; DA; DAB; DAC; WLC
See also CA 85-88; 25-28R; CANR 22;
CDBLB 1914-1945; DAM MST, NOV,
POP; DLB 15, 162; MTCW

Waugh, Harriet 1944- . . . . **CLC 6**
See also CA 85-88; CANR 22

Ways, C. R.
See Blount, Roy (Alton), Jr.

Waystaff, Simon
See Swift, Jonathan

Webb, (Martha) Beatrice (Potter)
1858-1943 . . . . **TCLC 22**
See also Potter, Beatrice
See also CA 117

Webb, Charles (Richard) 1939- . . . . . . **CLC 7**
See also CA 25-28R

Webb, James H(enry), Jr. 1946- . . . . **CLC 22**
See also CA 81-84

Webb, Mary (Gladys Meredith)
1881-1927 . . . . **TCLC 24**
See also CA 123; DLB 34

Webb, Mrs. Sidney
See Webb, (Martha) Beatrice (Potter)

Webb, Phyllis 1927- . . . . **CLC 18**
See also CA 104; CANR 23; DLB 53

Webb, Sidney (James)
1859-1947 . . . . **TCLC 22**
See also CA 117

Webber, Andrew Lloyd . . . . **CLC 21**
See also Lloyd Webber, Andrew

Weber, Lenora Mattingly
1895-1971 . . . . **CLC 12**
See also CA 19-20; 29-32R; CAP 1;
SATA 2; SATA-Obit 26

Webster, John
1579(?)-1634(?) . . . . . . **LC 33; DA; DAB;**
DAC; DC 2; WLC
See also CDBLB Before 1660;
DAM DRAM, MST; DLB 58

Webster, Noah 1758-1843 . . . . **NCLC 30**

Wedekind, (Benjamin) Frank(lin)
1864-1918 . . . . **TCLC 7**
See also CA 104; DAM DRAM; DLB 118

Weidman, Jerome 1913- . . . . **CLC 7**
See also AITN 2; CA 1-4R; CANR 1;
DLB 28

Weil, Simone (Adolphine)
1909-1943 . . . . **TCLC 23**
See also CA 117

Weinstein, Nathan
See West, Nathanael

Weinstein, Nathan von Wallenstein
See West, Nathanael

Weir, Peter (Lindsay) 1944- . . . . **CLC 20**
See also CA 113; 123

Weiss, Peter (Ulrich)
1916-1982 . . . . **CLC 3, 15, 51**
See also CA 45-48; 106; CANR 3;
DAM DRAM; DLB 69, 124

Weiss, Theodore (Russell)
1916- . . . . **CLC 3, 8, 14**
See also CA 9-12R; CAAS 2; CANR 46;
DLB 5

Welch, (Maurice) Denton
1915-1948 . . . . **TCLC 22**
See also CA 121; 148

Welch, James 1940- . . . . **CLC 6, 14, 52**
See also CA 85-88; CANR 42;
DAM MULT, POP; NNAL

Weldon, Fay
1933- . . . . **CLC 6, 9, 11, 19, 36, 59**
See also CA 21-24R; CANR 16, 46;
CDBLB 1960 to Present; DAM POP;
DLB 14; INT CANR-16; MTCW

Wellek, Rene 1903-1995 . . . . **CLC 28**
See also CA 5-8R; 150; CAAS 7; CANR 8;
DLB 63; INT CANR-8

Weller, Michael 1942- . . . . **CLC 10, 53**
See also CA 85-88

Weller, Paul 1958- . . . . **CLC 26**

Wellershoff, Dieter 1925- . . . . **CLC 46**
See also CA 89-92; CANR 16, 37

Welles, (George) Orson
1915-1985 . . . . **CLC 20, 80**
See also CA 93-96; 117

Wellman, Mac 1945- . . . . **CLC 65**

Wellman, Manly Wade 1903-1986 . . **CLC 49**
See also CA 1-4R; 118; CANR 6, 16, 44;
SATA 6; SATA-Obit 47

Wells, Carolyn 1869(?)-1942 . . . . . . **TCLC 35**
See also CA 113; DLB 11

Wells, H(erbert) G(eorge)
1866-1946 . . . . **TCLC 6, 12, 19; DA;**
DAB; DAC; SSC 6; WLC
See also CA 110; 121; CDBLB 1914-1945;
DAM MST, NOV; DLB 34, 70, 156;
MTCW; SATA 20

Wells, Rosemary 1943- . . . . **CLC 12**
See also AAYA 13; CA 85-88; CANR 48;
CLR 16; MAICYA; SAAS 1; SATA 18,
69

Welty, Eudora
1909- . . . . . . **CLC 1, 2, 5, 14, 22, 33; DA;**
DAB; DAC; SSC 1; WLC
See also CA 9-12R; CABS 1; CANR 32;
CDALB 1941-1968; DAM MST, NOV;
DLB 2, 102, 143; DLBD 12; DLBY 87;
MTCW

Wen I-to 1899-1946 . . . . **TCLC 28**

Wentworth, Robert
See Hamilton, Edmond

Werfel, Franz (V.) 1890-1945 . . . . . . **TCLC 8**
See also CA 104; DLB 81, 124

Wergeland, Henrik Arnold
1808-1845 . . . . **NCLC 5**

Wersba, Barbara 1932- . . . . **CLC 30**
See also AAYA 2; CA 29-32R; CANR 16,
38; CLR 3; DLB 52; JRDA; MAICYA;
SAAS 2; SATA 1, 58

Wertmueller, Lina 1928- . . . . **CLC 16**
See also CA 97-100; CANR 39

Wescott, Glenway 1901-1987 . . . . **CLC 13**
See also CA 13-16R; 121; CANR 23;
DLB 4, 9, 102

Wesker, Arnold 1932- . . **CLC 3, 5, 42; DAB**
See also CA 1-4R; CAAS 7; CANR 1, 33;
CDBLB 1960 to Present; DAM DRAM;
DLB 13; MTCW

Wesley, Richard (Errol) 1945- . . . . **CLC 7**
See also BW 1; CA 57-60; CANR 27;
DLB 38

Wessel, Johan Herman 1742-1785 . . . . **LC 7**

West, Anthony (Panther)
1914-1987 . . . . **CLC 50**
See also CA 45-48; 124; CANR 3, 19;
DLB 15

West, C. P.
See Wodehouse, P(elham) G(renville)

West, (Mary) Jessamyn
1902-1984 . . . . **CLC 7, 17**
See also CA 9-12R; 112; CANR 27; DLB 6;
DLBY 84; MTCW; SATA-Obit 37

West, Morris L(anglo) 1916- . . . . . **CLC 6, 33**
See also CA 5-8R; CANR 24, 49; MTCW

West, Nathanael
1903-1940 . . . . . **TCLC 1, 14, 44; SSC 16**
See also CA 104; 125; CDALB 1929-1941;
DLB 4, 9, 28; MTCW

West, Owen
See Koontz, Dean R(ay)

West, Paul 1930- . . . . **CLC 7, 14**
See also CA 13-16R; CAAS 7; CANR 22;
DLB 14; INT CANR-22

West, Rebecca 1892-1983 . . **CLC 7, 9, 31, 50**
See also CA 5-8R; 109; CANR 19; DLB 36;
DLBY 83; MTCW

Westall, Robert (Atkinson)
1929-1993 . . . . **CLC 17**
See also AAYA 12; CA 69-72; 141;
CANR 18; CLR 13; JRDA; MAICYA;
SAAS 2; SATA 23, 69; SATA-Obit 75

Westlake, Donald E(dwin)
1933- . . . . **CLC 7, 33**
See also CA 17-20R; CAAS 13; CANR 16,
44; DAM POP; INT CANR-16

Westmacott, Mary
See Christie, Agatha (Mary Clarissa)

Weston, Allen
See Norton, Andre

Wetcheek, J. L.
See Feuchtwanger, Lion

Wetering, Janwillem van de
See van de Wetering, Janwillem

Wetherell, Elizabeth
See Warner, Susan (Bogert)

Whale, James 1889-1957 . . . . **TCLC 63**

Whalen, Philip 1923- . . . . **CLC 6, 29**
See also CA 9-12R; CANR 5, 39; DLB 16

Wharton, Edith (Newbold Jones)
1862-1937 . . . . . . **TCLC 3, 9, 27, 53; DA;**
DAB; DAC; SSC 6; WLC
See also CA 104; 132; CDALB 1865-1917;
DAM MST, NOV; DLB 4, 9, 12, 78;
DLBD 13; MTCW

Wharton, James
See Mencken, H(enry) L(ouis)

Wharton, William (a pseudonym)
. . . . **CLC 18, 37**
See also CA 93-96; DLBY 80; INT 93-96

Wheatley (Peters), Phillis
1754(?)-1784 . . . . **LC 3; BLC; DA; DAC;**
PC 3; WLC
See also CDALB 1640-1865; DAM MST,
MULT, POET; DLB 31, 50

Wheelock, John Hall 1886-1978 . . . . **CLC 14**
See also CA 13-16R; 77-80; CANR 14;
DLB 45

White, E(lwyn) B(rooks)
1899-1985 . . . . **CLC 10, 34, 39**
See also AITN 2; CA 13-16R; 116;
CANR 16, 37; CLR 1, 21; DAM POP;
DLB 11, 22; MAICYA; MTCW;
SATA 2, 29; SATA-Obit 44

White, Edmund (Valentine III)
1940- . . . . **CLC 27**
See also AAYA 7; CA 45-48; CANR 3, 19,
36; DAM POP; MTCW

White, Patrick (Victor Martindale)
1912-1990 . . **CLC 3, 4, 5, 7, 9, 18, 65, 69**
See also CA 81-84; 132; CANR 43; MTCW

White, Phyllis Dorothy James 1920-
See James, P. D.
See also CA 21-24R; CANR 17, 43;
DAM POP; MTCW

White, T(erence) H(anbury)
1906-1964 . . . . **CLC 30**
See also CA 73-76; CANR 37; DLB 160;
JRDA; MAICYA; SATA 12

Wilson, Angus (Frank Johnstone)
1913-1991 . . CLC 2, 3, 5, 25, 34; SSC 21
See also CA 5-8R; 134; CANR 21; DLB 15,
139, 155; MTCW

Wilson, August
1945- . . . . CLC 39, 50, 63; BLC; DA;
DAB; DAC; DC 2
See also AAYA 16; BW 2; CA 115; 122;
CANR 42; DAM DRAM, MST, MULT;
MTCW

Wilson, Brian   1942- . . . . CLC 12

Wilson, Colin   1931- . . . . CLC 3, 14
See also CA 1-4R; CAAS 5; CANR 1, 22,
33; DLB 14; MTCW

Wilson, Dirk
See Pohl, Frederik

Wilson, Edmund
1895-1972 . . . . CLC 1, 2, 3, 8, 24
See also CA 1-4R; 37-40R; CANR 1, 46;
DLB 63; MTCW

Wilson, Ethel Davis (Bryant)
1888(?)-1980 . . . . CLC 13; DAC
See also CA 102; DAM POET; DLB 68;
MTCW

Wilson, John   1785-1854 . . . . NCLC 5

Wilson, John (Anthony) Burgess   1917-1993
See Burgess, Anthony
See also CA 1-4R; 143; CANR 2, 46; DAC;
DAM NOV; MTCW

Wilson, Lanford   1937- . . . . CLC 7, 14, 36
See also CA 17-20R; CABS 3; CANR 45;
DAM DRAM; DLB 7

Wilson, Robert M.   1944- . . . . CLC 7, 9
See also CA 49-52; CANR 2, 41; MTCW

Wilson, Robert McLiam   1964- . . . . . CLC 59
See also CA 132

Wilson, Sloan   1920- . . . . CLC 32
See also CA 1-4R; CANR 1, 44

Wilson, Snoo   1948- . . . . CLC 33
See also CA 69-72

Wilson, William S(mith)   1932- . . . . . CLC 49
See also CA 81-84

Winchilsea, Anne (Kingsmill) Finch Counte
1661-1720 . . . . LC 3

Windham, Basil
See Wodehouse, P(elham) G(renville)

Wingrove, David (John)   1954- . . . . . . CLC 68
See also CA 133

Winters, Janet Lewis . . . . CLC 41
See also Lewis, Janet
See also DLBY 87

Winters, (Arthur) Yvor
1900-1968 . . . . CLC 4, 8, 32
See also CA 11-12; 25-28R; CAP 1;
DLB 48; MTCW

Winterson, Jeanette   1959- . . . . CLC 64
See also CA 136; DAM POP

Winthrop, John   1588-1649 . . . . LC 31
See also DLB 24, 30

Wiseman, Frederick   1930- . . . . CLC 20

Wister, Owen   1860-1938 . . . . TCLC 21
See also CA 108; DLB 9, 78; SATA 62

Witkacy
See Witkiewicz, Stanislaw Ignacy

Witkiewicz, Stanislaw Ignacy
1885-1939 . . . . TCLC 8
See also CA 105

Wittgenstein, Ludwig (Josef Johann)
1889-1951 . . . . TCLC 59
See also CA 113

Wittig, Monique   1935(?)- . . . . CLC 22
See also CA 116; 135; DLB 83

Wittlin, Jozef   1896-1976 . . . . CLC 25
See also CA 49-52; 65-68; CANR 3

Wodehouse, P(elham) G(renville)
1881-1975 . . . CLC 1, 2, 5, 10, 22; DAB;
DAC; SSC 2
See also AITN 2; CA 45-48; 57-60;
CANR 3, 33; CDBLB 1914-1945;
DAM NOV; DLB 34, 162; MTCW;
SATA 22

Woiwode, L.
See Woiwode, Larry (Alfred)

Woiwode, Larry (Alfred)   1941- . . . CLC 6, 10
See also CA 73-76; CANR 16; DLB 6;
INT CANR-16

Wojciechowska, Maia (Teresa)
1927- . . . . CLC 26
See also AAYA 8; CA 9-12R; CANR 4, 41;
CLR 1; JRDA; MAICYA; SAAS 1;
SATA 1, 28, 83

Wolf, Christa   1929- . . . . CLC 14, 29, 58
See also CA 85-88; CANR 45; DLB 75;
MTCW

Wolfe, Gene (Rodman)   1931- . . . . CLC 25
See also CA 57-60; CAAS 9; CANR 6, 32;
DAM POP; DLB 8

Wolfe, George C.   1954- . . . . CLC 49
See also CA 149

Wolfe, Thomas (Clayton)
1900-1938 . . . . . TCLC 4, 13, 29, 61; DA;
DAB; DAC; WLC
See also CA 104; 132; CDALB 1929-1941;
DAM MST, NOV; DLB 9, 102; DLBD 2;
DLBY 85; MTCW

Wolfe, Thomas Kennerly, Jr.   1931-
See Wolfe, Tom
See also CA 13-16R; CANR 9, 33;
DAM POP; INT CANR-9; MTCW

Wolfe, Tom . . . . CLC 1, 2, 9, 15, 35, 51
See also Wolfe, Thomas Kennerly, Jr.
See also AAYA 8; AITN 2; BEST 89:1;
DLB 152

Wolff, Geoffrey (Ansell)   1937- . . . . . CLC 41
See also CA 29-32R; CANR 29, 43

Wolff, Sonia
See Levitin, Sonia (Wolff)

Wolff, Tobias (Jonathan Ansell)
1945- . . . . CLC 39, 64
See also AAYA 16; BEST 90:2; CA 114;
117; CAAS 22; DLB 130; INT 117

Wolfram von Eschenbach
c. 1170-c. 1220 . . . . CMLC 5
See also DLB 138

Wolitzer, Hilma   1930- . . . . CLC 17
See also CA 65-68; CANR 18, 40;
INT CANR-18; SATA 31

Wollstonecraft, Mary   1759-1797 . . . . . . LC 5
See also CDBLB 1789-1832; DLB 39, 104,
158

Wonder, Stevie . . . . CLC 12
See also Morris, Steveland Judkins

Wong, Jade Snow   1922- . . . . CLC 17
See also CA 109

Woodcott, Keith
See Brunner, John (Kilian Houston)

Woodruff, Robert W.
See Mencken, H(enry) L(ouis)

Woolf, (Adeline) Virginia
1882-1941 . . . . TCLC 1, 5, 20, 43, 56;
DA; DAB; DAC; SSC 7; WLC
See also CA 104; 130; CDBLB 1914-1945;
DAM MST, NOV; DLB 36, 100, 162;
DLBD 10; MTCW

Woollcott, Alexander (Humphreys)
1887-1943 . . . . TCLC 5
See also CA 105; DLB 29

Woolrich, Cornell   1903-1968 . . . . CLC 77
See also Hopley-Woolrich, Cornell George

Wordsworth, Dorothy
1771-1855 . . . . NCLC 25
See also DLB 107

Wordsworth, William
1770-1850 . . . . NCLC 12, 38; DA; DAB;
DAC; PC 4; WLC
See also CDBLB 1789-1832; DAM MST,
POET; DLB 93, 107

Wouk, Herman   1915- . . . . CLC 1, 9, 38
See also CA 5-8R; CANR 6, 33;
DAM NOV, POP; DLBY 82;
INT CANR-6; MTCW

Wright, Charles (Penzel, Jr.)
1935- . . . . CLC 6, 13, 28
See also CA 29-32R; CAAS 7; CANR 23,
36; DLB 165; DLBY 82; MTCW

Wright, Charles Stevenson
1932- . . . . CLC 49; BLC 3
See also BW 1; CA 9-12R; CANR 26;
DAM MULT, POET; DLB 33

Wright, Jack R.
See Harris, Mark

Wright, James (Arlington)
1927-1980 . . . . CLC 3, 5, 10, 28
See also AITN 2; CA 49-52; 97-100;
CANR 4, 34; DAM POET; DLB 5;
MTCW

Wright, Judith (Arandell)
1915- . . . . CLC 11, 53; PC 14
See also CA 13-16R; CANR 31; MTCW;
SATA 14

Wright, L(aurali) R.   1939- . . . . CLC 44
See also CA 138

Wright, Richard (Nathaniel)
1908-1960 . . . . CLC 1, 3, 4, 9, 14, 21, 48,
74; BLC; DA; DAB; DAC; SSC 2; WLC
See also AAYA 5; BW 1; CA 108;
CDALB 1929-1941; DAM MST, MULT,
NOV; DLB 76, 102; DLBD 2; MTCW

Wright, Richard B(ruce)   1937- . . . . . . CLC 6
See also CA 85-88; DLB 53

Wright, Rick   1945- . . . . CLC 35

Wright, Rowland
See Wells, Carolyn

Wright, Stephen Caldwell   1946- . . . . CLC 33
See also BW 2

Literary Criticism Series
Cumulative Topic Index

This index lists all topic entries in Gale's *Classical and Medieval Literature Criticism, Contemporary Literary Criticism, Literature Criticism from 1400 to 1800, Nineteenth-Century Literature Criticism,* and *Twentieth-Century Literary Criticism.*

Topic Index

Topic Index

Topic Index

NCLC Cumulative Nationality Index

Arnold, Thomas **18**
Austen, Jane **1, 13, 19, 33, 51**
Bagehot, Walter **10**
Barbauld, Anna Laetitia **50**
Beardsley, Aubrey **6**
Beckford, William **16**
Beddoes, Thomas Lovell **3**
Bentham, Jeremy **38**
Blake, William **13, 37**
Borrow, George (Henry) **9**
Bronte, Anne **4**
Bronte, Charlotte **3, 8, 33**
Bronte, (Jane) Emily **16, 35**
Browning, Elizabeth Barrett **1, 16**
Browning, Robert **19**
Bulwer-Lytton, Edward (George Earle Lytton) **1, 45**
Burney, Fanny **12, 54**
Burton, Richard F. **42**
Byron, George Gordon (Noel) **2, 12**
Carlyle, Thomas **22**
Carroll, Lewis **2, 53**
Clare, John **9**
Clough, Arthur Hugh **27**
Cobbett, William **49**
Coleridge, Samuel Taylor **9, 54**
Coleridge, Sara **31**
Collins, (William) Wilkie **1, 18**
Cowper, William **8**
Crabbe, George **26**
Craik, Dinah Maria (Mulock) **38**
De Quincey, Thomas **4**
Dickens, Charles (John Huffam) **3, 8, 18, 26, 37, 50**
Disraeli, Benjamin **2, 39**
Dobell, Sydney Thompson **43**
Eden, Emily **10**
Eliot, George **4, 13, 23, 41, 49**
FitzGerald, Edward **9**
Forster, John **11**
Froude, James Anthony **43**
Gaskell, Elizabeth Cleghorn **5**
Gilpin, William **30**
Godwin, William **14**
Hazlitt, William **29**
Hemans, Felicia **29**
Hood, Thomas **16**
Hopkins, Gerard Manley **17**
Hunt (James Henry) Leigh **1**
Ingelow, Jean **39**
Jefferies, (John) Richard **47**
Jerrold, Douglas William **2**
Jewsbury, Geraldine (Endsor) **22**
Keats, John **8**
Kemble, Fanny **18**
Kingsley, Charles **35**
Lamb, Charles **10**
Lamb, Lady Caroline **38**
Landon, Letitia Elizabeth **15**
Landor, Walter Savage **14**
Lear, Edward **3**
Lennox, Charlotte Ramsay **23**
Lewes, George Henry **25**
Lewis, Matthew Gregory **11**
Linton, Eliza Lynn **41**
Macaulay, Thomas Babington **42**
Marryat, Frederick **3**
Martineau, Harriet **26**
Mayhew, Henry **31**
Mill, John Stuart **11**
Mitford, Mary Russell **4**
Montagu, Elizabeth **7**
More, Hannah **27**

Morris, William **4**
Newman, John Henry **38**
Norton, Caroline **47**
Oliphant, Laurence **47**
Pater, Walter (Horatio) **7**
Patmore, Coventry **9**
Peacock, Thomas Love **22**
Planche, James Robinson **42**
Polidori, John Willam **51**
Radcliffe, Ann (Ward) **6, 55**
Reade, Charles **2**
Reeve, Clara **19**
Robertson, Thomas William **35**
Robinson, Henry Crabb **15**
Rossetti, Christina (Georgina) **2, 50**
Rossetti, Dante Gabriel **4**
Sala, George Augustus **46**
Shelley, Mary Wollstonecraft (Godwin) **14**
Shelley, Percy Bysshe **18**
Smith, Charlotte (Turner) **23**
Southey, Robert **8**
Surtees, Robert Smith **14**
Symonds, John Addington **34**
Tennyson, Alfred **30**
Thackeray, William Makepeace **5, 14, 22, 43**
Trollope, Anthony **6, 33**
Trollope, Frances **30**
Wordsworth, Dorothy **25**
Wordsworth, William **12, 38**

FILIPINO
Rizal, Jose **27**

FINNISH
Kivi, Aleksis **30**
Lonnrot, Elias **53**
Runeberg, Johan **41**

FRENCH
Augier, Emile **31**
Balzac, Honore de **5, 35, 53**
Banville, Theodore (Faullain) de **9**
Barbey d'Aurevilly, Jules Amedee **1**
Baudelaire, Charles **6, 29, 55**
Becque, Henri **3**
Beranger, Pierre Jean de **34**
Bertrand, Aloysius **31**
Borel, Petrus **41**
Chateaubriand, Francois Rene de **3**
Comte, Auguste **54**
Constant (de Rebecque), (Henri) Benjamin **6**
Corbiere, Tristan **43**
Daudet, (Louis Marie) Alphonse **1**
Dumas, Alexandre **9**
Dumas, Alexandre (Davy de la Pailleterie) **11**
Feuillet, Octave **45**
Flaubert, Gustave **2, 10, 19**
Fourier, Charles **51**
Fromentin, Eugene (Samuel Auguste) **10**
Gaboriau, Emile **14**
Gautier, Theophile **1**
Gobineau, Joseph Arthur (Comte) de **17**
Goncourt, Edmond (Louis Antoine Huot) de **7**
Goncourt, Jules (Alfred Huot) de **7**
Hugo, Victor (Marie) **3, 10, 21**
Joubert, Joseph **9**
Kock, Charles Paul de **16**
Laclos, Pierre Ambroise Francois Choderlos de **4**
Laforgue, Jules **5, 53**
Lamartine, Alphonse (Marie Louis Prat) de **11**
Lautreamont, Comte de **12**
Leconte de Lisle, Charles-Marie-Rene **29**
Maistre, Joseph de **37**

Mallarme, Stephane **4, 41**
Maupassant, (Henri Rene Albert) Guy de **1, 42**
Merimee, Prosper **6**
Michelet, Jules **31**
Musset, (Louis Charles) Alfred de **7**
Nerval, Gerard de **1**
Nodier, (Jean) Charles (Emmanuel) **19**
Pixerecourt, Guilbert de **39**
Renan, Joseph Ernest **26**
Rimbaud, (Jean Nicolas) Arthur **4, 35**
Sade, Donatien Alphonse Francois **3**
Sainte-Beuve, Charles Augustin **5**
Sand, George **2, 42**
Scribe, (Augustin) Eugene **16**
Senancour, Etienne Pivert de **16**
Stael-Holstein, Anne Louise Germaine Necker **3**
Stendhal **23, 46**
Sue, Eugene **1**
Taine, Hippolyte Adolphe **15**
Tocqueville, Alexis (Charles Henri Maurice Clerel) **7**
Verlaine, Paul (Marie) **2, 51**
Vigny, Alfred (Victor) de **7**
Villiers de l'Isle Adam, Jean Marie Mathias Philippe Auguste **3**

GERMAN
Arnim, Achim von (Ludwig Joachim von Arnim) **5**
Arnim, Bettina von **38**
Bonaventura **35**
Buchner, (Karl) Georg **26**
Droste-Hulshoff, Annette Freiin von **3**
Eichendorff, Joseph Freiherr von **8**
Fontane, Theodor **26**
Fouque, Friedrich (Heinrich Karl) de la Motte **2**
Goethe, Johann Wolfgang von **4, 22, 34**
Grabbe, Christian Dietrich **2**
Grimm, Jacob Ludwig Karl **3**
Grimm, Wilhelm Karl **3**
Hebbel, Friedrich **43**
Hegel, Georg Wilhelm Friedrich **46**
Heine, Heinrich **4, 54**
Hoffmann, E(rnst) T(heodor) A(madeus) **2**
Holderlin, (Johann Christian) Friedrich **16**
Immerman, Karl (Lebrecht) **4, 49**
Jean Paul **7**
Kant, Immanuel **27**
Kleist, Heinrich von **2, 37**
Klinger, Friedrich Maximilian von **1**
Klopstock, Friedrich Gottlieb **11**
Kotzebue, August (Friedrich Ferdinand) von **25**
Ludwig, Otto **4**
Marx, Karl (Heinrich) **17**
Morike, Eduard (Friedrich) **10**
Novalis **13**
Schelling, Friedrich Wilhelm Joseph von **30**
Schiller, Friedrich **39**
Schlegel, August Wilhelm von **15**
Schlegel, Friedrich **45**
Schopenhauer, Arthur **51**
Storm, (Hans) Theodor (Woldsen) **1**
Tieck, (Johann) Ludwig **5, 46**
Wagner, Richard **9**
Wieland, Christoph Martin **17**

GREEK
Solomos, Dionysios **15**

HUNGARIAN
Arany, Janos **34**
Madach, Imre **19**
Petofi, Sandor **21**

Nationality Index

Title Index

ISBN 0-8103-7004-2

9 780810 370043